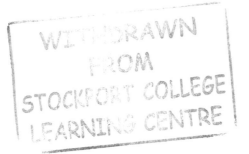

Social Psychology

Social Psychology

8th Edition

SHELLEY E. TAYLOR
University of California, Los Angeles

LETITIA ANNE PEPLAU
University of California, Los Angeles

DAVID O. SEARS
University of California, Los Angeles

PRENTICE HALL
Englewood Cliffs, New Jersey 07632

Library of Congress Cataloging–in–Publication Data

Taylor, Shelley E
   Social psychology / Shelley E. Taylor, Letitia Anne Peplau, Sears, David O. — 8th ed.
     p. cm.
   Sears' name appears first on previous edition.
   Includes bibliographical references and index.
   ISBN 0–13–222630–8
   1. Social psychology. I. Peplau, Letita Anne. II. Sears, David O. III. Title.
HM251.F68 1994

302—dc20 93–5510
CIP

Acquisitions editor: Peter Janzow
Managing editor: Heidi Freund
Production editor: Hilda Tauber
Production coordinator: Herb Klein, Tricia Kenny
Interior design and page layout: Meryl Poweski
Design direction: Paula Martin, Maureen Eide
Photo editor: Lorinda Morris–Nantz
Photo research: Rona Tucillo
Cover design: Patricia Wosczyk
Cover art: Fernand Léger, *Homage to Jacques Louis David* (1948–49)
       Musée National d'Art Moderne. Copyright ARS,
       New York Scala/Art Resource

Printed in the United States of America
10 9 8 7 6 5 4 3 2 1

ISBN 0-13-222630-8

Prentice-Hall International (UK) Limited, *London*
Prentice-Hall of Australia Pty. Limited, *Sydney*
Prentice-Hall Canada Inc, *Toronto*
Prentice-Hall Hispanoamericana, S.A., *Mexico*
Prentice-Hall of India Private Limited, *New Delhi*
Prentice-Hall of Japan, Inc., *Tokyo*
Simon & Schuster Asia Pte. Ltd., *Singapore*
Editora Prentice-Hall do Brasil, Ltda, *Rio de Janeiro*

Contents

V

Preface

Social psychology is more useful today than ever before. Violence in our cities, heroic acts of altruism, teenage conformity, passionate love, our sense of identity, the impact of TV on kids — these and many other aspects of social life are illuminated by social psychological research. Social psychology also helps us to understand the stories behind today's news headlines on such topics as AIDS, sexual harassment, divorce, and religious cults. Not surprisingly, nurses, lawyers, political analysts, teachers, business leaders, and people in many different professions are finding social psychology valuable in their work. In writing this book, we have tried to present the basic theories and findings of social psychology and to show how social psychological principles are relevant to contemporary social issues.

As the 21st century nears, we face the challenge of living in an increasingly multicultural society. Television and jet travel are bringing the citizens of the world closer together, and making it essential that we take a more global perspective on social life. Social psychologists are now trying to incorporate sociocultural and global perspectives into their research, and we have included the best of this new work in our book. To give these issues the emphasis they deserve, we introduce a sociocultural perspective in Chapter 1. Throughout the text, we report the latest cross–cultural studies and present new work on culture and ethnicity.

This book has grown and changed with the times. But certain basic principles and goals have guided us in the development of this edition:

- We believe that social psychology, like any science, is cumulative. As researchers push toward exciting new frontiers, they build on the accumulated knowledge of the field. The new findings of today are best understood as adding to this body of knowledge. A primary goal in this text is to present the "basics" of the field—the core theories and findings that form the shared heritage of our discipline.

- We have also been sensitive to the important changes taking place in contemporary social psychology. Our new emphasis on sociocultural perspectives and cross-cultural research is one illustration. Over time, the core of the field has gradually shifted. There is more emphasis today on social cognition, on the self, and on personal relationships, and less emphasis on attitude change and group dynamics. This changing core is reflected in major revisions made for this edition. We have made every effort to include the most recent new research and the most advanced theories in social psychology.

- Another goal has been to offer an integrated presentation of the field. As we discuss different topics, we try to keep the main theoretical ideas and traditions of social psychology firmly in view, so that students can see the underlying conceptual continuities in the field. For example, we introduce social cognition and attribution theory early in the book and then show how they have been used to understand such topics as attitude change, prejudice, aggression, and bias against women.

- The application of research methods and theories to understanding social issues is a major theme in social psychology. Throughout the text, we highlight ways in which social psychology sheds light on everyday experiences and social problems. We conclude with a section on social psychology in action that explores the most recent social psychological research and theory on health, the environment, and politics.

• The success of any text depends ultimately on its ability to communicate clearly to student readers and to spark interest in the field. Our goal has been to present materials simply, without oversimplifying. The text is comprehensive, but not encyclopedic. We have written a textbook for undergraduate students, not a handbook of social psychology for professionals. We have paid special attention to selecting examples that illustrate basic principles in a lively way and to sharing our own personal enthusiasm for the field.

SPECIAL FEATURES OF THE EIGHTH EDITION

Cultural Perspective

We have made every effort to include new multicultural and global perspectives in social psychology throughout the book. To further emphasize these issues, each chapter contains a new feature, CULTURAL HIGHLIGHT, which presents some of the best available work on culture and human diversity. For example, in the Social Cognition chapter, we compare the art of telling stories in Africa and the United States. In the Self chapter, we contrast conceptions of the self in America and Japan. In the Personal Relationships chapter, we examine the balance of power in Mexican-American, African-American, and Anglo marriages. In the chapter on group behavior, we contrast the spirit of competition in Anglo and Latino cultures.

Research Focus

To help students learn to "think like social psychologists," we have included throughout the text detailed discussions of a few key research studies, describing the research process and the decisions researchers made. In addition, each chapter features a RESEARCH CLOSEUP, focusing

on a topic at the forefront of social psychology today such as memory and the self, mood and persuasion, and date rape.

Organization

The book is organized to provide a systematic presentation of the material. A beginning chapter on theory and methods is followed by five major sections that progress from individual-level topics to dyads and groups, and then to specific applications of social psychology.

Part One on perceiving people and events provides expanded coverage of new work on social cognition. There are separate chapters on person perception, social cognition, attribution, and the self. Part Two discusses attitudes and influence. A single integrated chapter reviews work on attitude formation and change. Our discussion then moves to an analysis of prejudice and then to general processes of social influence. Part Three examines social interaction and relationships. A chapter on interpersonal attraction is followed by a new chapter on personal relationships that surveys recent research in this growing area. We then broaden to study group behavior and the pervasive influence of gender in social life. Part Four focuses on helping and hurting others. Included are chapters on prosocial behavior and on aggression. In Part Five on social psychology in action, three chapters examine more applied topics: social psychological perspectives on health, the environment, and politics.

We think this sequence will fit well with the teaching preferences of many instructors. However, each chapter is self-contained and so the chapters can be used in any order.

Highlights of New Content

The many changes in this edition reflect major trends in social psychology in the 1990s. Some highlights of the new material are:

● An entirely new chapter on the self has been added to reflect the growing importance of this topic in social psychological research.

- A consolidated chapter covers both attitude formation and attitude change.

- A new chapter on personal relationships provides expanded coverage of recent research on close relationships, including dating and marriage.

- The chapter on gender includes the latest meta-analyses of sex differences in social behavior and research on the changing social roles of women and men.

- The latest research on sexual harassment, date rape, and stranger rape is analyzed in the chapter on aggression.

- Three concluding chapters discuss applications of social psychology to health, the environment, and politics.

Classic and Contemporary Approach

Our conviction that social psychology is a cumulative, evolving science leads us to emphasize both the classic studies that have traditionally formed the foundation of the field, and the best new research of today. This approach gives students a solid understanding of the longstanding issues and controversies in the field, and provides exposure to the exciting new developments shaping social psychology in the 1990s and beyond. Throughout, we emphasize continuity. Contemporary research does not merely "reinvent the wheel," but rather represents innovative approaches to longstanding core questions about social life that have aroused the curiosity of social psychologists for decades. This emphasis on the continuity between classic and contemporary research is, we believe, a distinctive and valuable component of our approach.

Helping Students to Learn Social Psychology

To enhance the effectiveness of the text, we have kept the clarity and interest level high and have made a particular effort to avoid technical language. Furthermore, we are confident that the new full-color format and the many color illustrations will reinforce the content and help students to share our enthusiasm for social psychology.

Each chapter opens with an outline of its main topics and concludes with a point-by-point summary of major concepts and findings. Key terms, which are printed in bold type in the text, are listed at the end of each chapter and are defined in the glossary. Each chapter also includes annotated suggestions for further reading. An extensive, up-to-date bibliography appears at the end of the book.

ANCILLARY MATERIALS

For instructors who want to provide students with well-chosen primary source materials, we recommend *Readings in Social Psychology: Classic and Contemporary Contributions*, 2nd edition, edited by Peplau, Sears, Taylor, and Freedman (ISBN 0–13–761081–5). This paperback introduces students to landmark research in the history of social psychology, including papers by Solomon Asch, Leon Festinger, Harold Kelley, Stanley Milgram, Muzafer Sherif, and others. Only articles accessible to the beginning student have been included, and each is prefaced by an analysis to facilitate understanding. An introductory essay on how to read a social psychology article is a helpful adjunct.

Social Psychology, 8th edition, is accompanied by the following set of teaching and learning tools that constitute a support package of computer, video, and print supplements.

Supplements for Instructors

- *Instructor's Resource Manual* prepared by Alan Swinkels. Material from each chapter of the text has been assembled as a guide for planning class lectures and activities. The manual features chapter overviews, learning objectives, lecture suggestions, demonstration activities, discussion topics, and audiovisual resources.

- *Test Item File* prepared by Thomas and Sandra Dunn. A test bank with over 1600 questions, this supplement allows instructors to develop any number and variety of tests covering key terms, concepts, and applications from the textbook. Conceptual, applied, and factual questions are available in multiple choice, short answer, true/false, and essay forms.

- *"800-Number" Telephone Test Preparation Service.* Instructors can call a special toll-free number and select up to 200 questions from the *Test Item File*. The test (with an alternative version, if requested) and answer key are mailed within 48 hours, ready for duplication.

- *Grade Manager* (3.5" MS–DOS, Macintosh Formats). This software enables instructors to track an unlimited number of students and classes and calculate final grades based on their own criteria.

- *Prentice Hall Test Manager 2.0* (3.5" MS–DOS, Macintosh Formats). A computerized testing package featuring full control over printing with print preview, mouse support, on-screen VGA graphics with import capabilities for TIFF and PCX file formats and ability to export your files to WordPerfect, Word, and ASCII.

- *Handout and Transparency Masters* prepared by Alan Swinkels. This is an extensive set of questionnaires, activities, and visual aids for stimulating classroom discussion.

- *ABC News/Prentice Hall Video Library.* This customized supplement presents feature segments from award-winning ABC News programming, providing a contemporary look at topics such as cultural diversity, gender, prejudice, and relationships.

Supplements for Students

- *Study Guide* prepared by Thomas and Sandra Dunn. Coordinated chapter-by-chapter with the textbook, each chapter features learning objectives, a detailed outline, self-test questions, and an acrostic. Exercises ask students to recall facts, then to understand concepts, and finally to apply what they have learned.

- *The New York Times Program.* The New York Times and Prentice Hall are sponsoring a *Themes of the Times* program designed to enhance student access to current information in the classroom.

Through this program, the core subject matter provided in the text is supplemented by a collection of time-sensitive articles from one of the world's most distinguished newspapers, *The New York Times*. These articles demonstrate the vital, ongoing connection between what is learned in the classroom and what is happening in the world around us.

To enjoy the wealth of information of *The York Times* daily, a reduced subscription rate is available in deliverable areas. For information, call toll-free: 1-800-631-1222.

Prentice Hall and The New York Times are proud to co-sponsor *Themes of the Times*. We hope it will make the reading of both textbooks and newspapers a more dynamic, involving process.

Acknowledgments

Special thanks to Garrett Songhawke, Michelle Nieto, Susan Campbell, Khanh Bui, and Judith Lacertossa for their invaluable help in researching and preparing the manuscript. We are grateful to Prentice Hall for continuing support, and especially to our psychology editor, Peter Janzow, and to Hilda Tauber, production editor. We also appreciate the useful feedback we have received from students who have used this book.

This text has benefited greatly from the thoughtful reviews of the manuscript by David Boninger, University of California, Los Angeles; Arnie Cann, University of North Carolina at Charlotte; Bernardo J. Carducci, Indiana University Southeast; Russell Cropanzano, Colorado State University; Alan L. Ellis, University of Kentucky; Sharon Herzberger, Trinity College; Marianne Miserandino, University of Rochester; Vaida Thompson, University of North Carolina at Chapel Hill; Ann L. Weber, University of North Carolina at Asheville; and George I. Whitehead, III, Salisbury State University.

Finally, we express our thanks to Jonathan L. Freedman of the University of Toronto and to the late J. Merrill Carlsmith of Stanford University who, along with David O. Sears, conceived the first edition of this book and published it in 1970.

About the Authors

SHELLEY E. TAYLOR is Professor of Psychology and Chair of the Social Psychology program at the University of California, Los Angeles. Shelley received her A. B. in Psychology from Connecticut College and her Ph.D. in Social Psychology from Yale University. She taught at Harvard University until 1979 when she joined the faculty at UCLA. She has won a number of awards for her work, including the American Psychological Association's Distinguished Scientist Award for an Early Career Contribution, and a Research Scientist Development Award from the National Institute of Mental Health. She is currently a consulting editor for the *Journal of Personality and Social Psychology* and has served on the editorial boards of many other journals. Her other books include *Social Cognition* (with Susan T. Fiske), *Health Psychology*, and *Positive Illusions*. She has published numerous articles and book chapters in social cognition and health psychology.

LETITIA ANNE PEPLAU is Professor of Psychology at the University of California, Los Angeles. Anne received her B. A. in Psychology from Brown University and her Ph.D. in Social Psychology from Harvard University. Since 1973, she has taught at UCLA, where she has served as chair of the Social Psychology program and acting Co-Director of the Center for the Study of Women. Anne has served on the editorial boards of several journals, including the *Journal of Personality and Social Psychology*, the *Journal of Personal and Social Relationships,* and *Psychology of Women Quarterly*. Her other books include *Loneliness: A Sourcebook of Current Theory, Research and Therapy* (edited with Daniel Perlman), *Close Relationships* (with Harold H. Kelley, et al.) and an introductory text, *Psychology* (with Zick Rubin and Peter Salovey). She has published numerous articles and book chapters in social psychology on such topics as loneliness and social support, friendship, heterosexual dating, homosexual relationships, and social power.

DAVID O. SEARS is Professor of Psychology and Political Science at the University of California, Los Angeles, and former Dean of Social Sciences. David received his B.A. in History from Stanford University, and his Ph.D. in Psychology from Yale University in 1962, and has taught at UCLA since then. He has been a visiting professor at Harvard University and the University of California, Berkeley, a Guest Scholar at the Brookings Institution, a Guggenheim Fellow, and a Fellow at the Center for Advanced Study in the Behavioral Sciences. His other books include *Public Opinion* (with Robert E. Lane), *The Politics of Violence: The New Urban Blacks and the Watts Riot* (with John B. McConahay), *Tax Revolt: Something for Nothing in California* (with Jack Citrin), and *Political Cognition: The 19th Annual Carnegie Symposium on Cognition* (edited with Richard R. Lau). He has published articles and book chapters on a wide variety of topics in social and political psychology, including attitude change, mass communications, ghetto riots, political socialization, voting behavior, and racism.

1
Theories and Methods in Social Psychology

FOCUS OF THIS CHAPTER

The Social Psychological
   Approach

Historical Roots of Social
   Psychology

Theories in Social Psychology

The Goals of Social Psychological
   Research

Research Questions: Theoretical
   and Descriptive

Research Participants

Correlational Versus
   Experimental Designs

Field Versus Laboratory Settings

Methods of Data Collection

Bias in Research

Research Ethics

Cultural Highlight
America's Diverse Population

Research Closeup
Meta-analysis in Social Psychology

Social psychology is the scientific study of social behavior. It considers how we perceive other people and social situations, how we respond to others and they to us, and how we are affected by social situations. **Social psychology** studies how the thoughts, feelings, and behaviors of individuals are influenced by other people. To begin, consider two examples of the many topics that social psychologists examine.

While driving to school and listening to music on the car radio, Jason was jolted out of his dreamlike state by a bright red sports car that suddenly cut in front of him. The young woman driver was going considerably faster than the speed limit. She sped around a corner and disappeared. Jason was a little startled, but then reflected on the experience. He immediately categorized the driver as a spoiled rich kid, probably from the wealthy neighborhood near campus. He also came to a quick judgment about the causes of her behavior: She cut in front of him not to avoid a pothole but because she is a reckless driver. Jason's experience is typical. We often form clear impressions of a person based on only the briefest contact. We will delve into this process of impression formation in Chapter 2 on Person Perception.

In 1964, a young woman named Kitty Genovese came home from work late one night. As she neared the front of her apartment building in Kew Gardens, New York, she was viciously attacked and repeatedly stabbed. During a half-hour struggle with the attacker, Kitty repeatedly screamed that she was being stabbed and begged for help. Thirty-eight people living in adjacent houses and apartments later said they had heard her screams. But no one came to her aid or even called the police.

The police were not called until 20 minutes after she died; they arrived 2 minutes later. Even then, none of her neighbors came out into the street until an ambulance arrived to take her body away. Why didn't anyone help Kitty Genovese? At the time, many commentators saw the event as a sign of growing apathy and indifference to human suffering. Social psychologists responded to the tragedy by using scientific methods to study why bystanders sometimes fail to help strangers in distress and also why bystanders sometimes risk their lives to save people trapped by floods or earthquakes. We will discuss research on helping strangers in need in Chapter 13 on prosocial behavior.

As these examples suggest, the scope of social psychology is quite broad. In reading this book, you will learn that some social psychologists study perceptions and attitudes: how people view each other, how they interpret other people's behavior, and how their attitudes form and change. Other social psychologists focus on various types of interactions between people, including friendship and altruism, prejudice and aggression, conformity and power. Social psychologists also study how people act in groups, and how groups affect their members. The ideas and research methods of social psychology have been applied to a variety of important social issues and everyday experiences, including social factors in physical health, the effects of the environment on psychological well-being, and politics. Social psychology tries to answer questions about how people affect one another and how they behave in social situations. Not all these questions have been answered fully. The job of social psychologists is to ask important questions and then to look for answers.

THE SOCIAL PSYCHOLOGICAL APPROACH

Of course, many other fields also study social behavior. What is unique about social psychology is its distinctive approach. The social psychological approach differs from disciplines that study large-scale societal processes and from those that focus on the individual. Let's compare these three approaches using the specific example of violent crime in big cities.

The *societal level* of analysis is used by sociologists, economists, political scientists, and other social scientists. These scholars attempt to understand general patterns of social behavior, such as rates of homocide, voting behavior, or consumer spending. According to this viewpoint, social behavior can be explained by such forces as economic hard times, class conflicts, clashes between competing ethnic groups, a regional crop failure, governmental policies, or technological change. The goal of societal analysis is to identify links between broad social forces and general patterns of social behavior. To study violence in urban areas, social scientists might identify relationships between rates of violent crime and such factors as poverty, immigration, or the industrialization of a society.

The *individual level* of analysis is typically used by clinical and personality psychologists who explain behavior in terms of a person's unique life history and psychological characteristics. According to this viewpoint, personality traits and motives can explain why individuals behave as they do, and why two people may react quite differently to the same situation. Emphasis is given to individual differences in childhood experiences, in ability and motivation, and in personality or psychological adjustment. The individual approach would tend to explain violent crime in terms of the unique histories and characteristics of the criminal. For example, of all the bank tellers in Chicago, why does one individual go berserk and shoot five of his co-workers? To understand such behavior, the individual approach would consider the personality and background of the person. Was the bank teller depressed or suffering from paranoid delusions or using drugs? What kind of life had the bank teller led? For example, was he physically abused as a child?

Social psychologists adopt a different level of analysis—the *interpersonal level.* Social psychologists typically focus on a person's current social situation. That social situation includes the other people in the environment, their attitudes and behaviors, and their relationship to the individual. To understand violent crime, social psychologists might consider what kinds of interpersonal situations create feelings of anger that may increase violent behavior. One important explanation from social psychology is that frustrating situations make people angry, and so increase the tendency to act aggressively. This is called the **frustration–aggression hypothesis.** It predicts that when we are blocked from achiev-

These demonstrators hold strong and opposite views about whether or not abortion should be legal. What individual, interpersonal, or societal factors might explain which viewpoint a person supports?

ing a desired goal, we feel frustrated and angry, and are more likely to lash out. This effect of frustration is one explanation for violent crime.

The frustration–aggression hypothesis can also explain how large-scale economic and societal factors create situations that lead to violence and crime. For instance, people who are poor and crowded into urban slums are frustrated; they cannot get good jobs, cannot find affordable housing, cannot provide a safe environment for their children, and so on. This frustration may produce anger which can be the direct cause of violent crime. The frustration–aggression hypothesis focuses on the immediate social situation, the feelings and thoughts such situations produce in people of many different backgrounds, and the effects of those subjective reactions on behavior.

Each of these three approaches (societal, interpersonal, and individual) is worthwhile and indeed essential if we are to understand complex social behavior fully. And there is, of course, considerable overlap among disciplines in the kinds of studies that are done. A single question—What causes violent crime?—can be answered in many different ways. This book will introduce you to the social psychological perspective on human behavior.

HISTORICAL ROOTS OF SOCIAL PSYCHOLOGY

In attempting to explain behavior, social psychologists draw on a variety of different theories. Before discussing current theories in social psychology, it is useful to consider some of the historical roots of the field. In the early 1900s,

three major theoretical perspectives were developed by pioneering psychologists, all of which have left their mark on contemporary social psychology.

Sigmund Freud, the founder of **psychoanalytic theory,** was fascinated by the rich mental life of the human animal. Freud proposed that behavior is motivated from within by powerful internal drives and impulses such as sexuality and aggression. He also believed that adult behavior is shaped by unresolved psychological conflicts that can be traced to childhood experiences in the family. Psychoanalytic theorists seek to understand the inner forces, both conscious and unconscious, that energize and direct behavior.

A second major theory, **behaviorism,** offered a very different perspective on human experience. As developed by Ivan Pavlov, John B. Watson, B. F. Skinner, and others, behaviorism focused on the observable behavior of humans and other animals. Behaviorists were not particularly interested in subjective thoughts and feelings; they preferred to study what they could directly observe and measure, that is, overt behavior. Behaviorists examined ways that the environment shapes the behavior of animals, and proposed that current behavior is the result of past learning. Behaviorists identified a series of principles to explain the specific processes through which this all-important learning occurs. Although much of their research was conducted with rats and pigeons, behaviorists believed that the same principles applied to humans.

The perspective of **gestalt** psychology was developed by Wolfgang Kohler, Kurt Koffka, Kurt Lewin, and other European psychologists

John B. Watson (1878-1958)   Kurt Lewin (1890-1947)

B. F. Skinner (1904-1990)   Sigmund Freud (1856-1939)

who immigrated to the United States in the 1930s. Their focus was on the way individuals perceive and understand objects, events, and people. In their view, people do not perceive situations or events as made up of many discrete elements, but rather as "dynamic wholes." Think about your best friend. When you last saw her, did you perceive her as a collection of arms, legs, fingers, and other features? Probably not. More likely, you perceived her as a total unit integrating the relationships among her various body parts into the familiar "whole" or person you know and like. This emphasis on perceiving the environment as a whole that is more than the sum of its parts is known as gestalt psychology, from the German word for shape or form.

Each of these three important theories arose from the work of a few charismatic individuals who inspired a fierce sense of loyalty to their ideas and, often, an equally fierce rejection of other viewpoints. These pioneers modeled their theories on those of the physical sciences. Their goal was to explain and predict *all* human behavior, and they wanted theories as detailed, universal, and complete as, for example, atomic theory in physics. Many of these theories were applied to the analysis of social behavior and to research in social psychology. The idea of developing general theories is important, but in the long run the problems studied by social psychologists have turned out to be too complex to be explained by any one of these general theories.

Even so, social psychological approaches to a wide variety of different problems have been guided by a few basic ideas easily traced back to the general theories of yesteryear. In contemporary social psychology, the legacy of psychoanalytic theory can be seen most clearly in the analysis of motivation and emotion in social life. Social psychologists recognize that behavior is influenced by personal motives and by the emotional reactions we have to situations and people. The legacy of behaviorism is a continuing concern with how learning shapes social behavior. Social psychologists are interested, for example, in how we learn to be helpful or to obey authority or to espouse conservative politi-

cal views. In broad terms, how does experience shape our attitudes and behaviors? Finally, the legacy of gestalt psychology is found in the current emphasis on social cognition, the study of how we perceive and understand our social world. Basic gestalt principles have been greatly expanded in recent years, as we will see in the next chapters of this book.

THEORIES IN SOCIAL PSYCHOLOGY

In the following sections, we introduce some of the major contemporary theories in social psychology. At this point, our intention is not to be comprehensive or detailed. Rather, we want to convey their essence and particularly the contrasts among them, so that we can refer to these theories in later chapters. To permit a clear comparison of the theories, we will apply each approach to the specific problem of understanding violent crime.

Consider this situation: At 3 A.M. one morning, a police officer sees a high school dropout, Larry, coming out of the rear door of a liquor store with a bag full of money. The store, like everything else in the neighborhood, has long been closed for the night. The officer shouts at Larry to stop and put his hands up. Larry turns, pulls a pistol from his pocket, and shoots the officer, wounding him in the leg. Larry is later apprehended and ultimately sent to jail. The statistics predict that Larry's stay in jail will not be productive or happy; it will be costly for society, and the chances of his committing further crimes are fairly high. We will refer to Larry in describing major contemporary theories in social psychology.

Motivational Theories

One general approach focuses on the individual's own needs or motives. Both everyday experience and social psychological research provide many examples of the ways in which our needs influence our perceptions, attitudes, and behavior. For example, to enhance our self-esteem and satisfy a need to feel good about ourselves, we may blame others for our failures and take personal credit only for successes. The fear aroused by a major earthquake may lead people to seek out the company of others as a way to reduce personal discomfort and feel less frightened. Television commercials often deliberately attempt to arouse insecurity in order to sell products, suggesting, for example, that bad breath will wreck our social life unless we purchase the brand of mouthwash in the ad.

The Freudian or psychoanalytic view of human motivation emphasized the importance of a few powerful in-born impulses or drives, especially those associated with sexuality and aggression. In contrast, social psychologists consider a much more diverse range of human needs and desires. Social psychologists also emphasize ways in which specific situations and social relationships can create and arouse needs and motives. For example, the experience of moving away from home to go to college often creates feelings of loneliness among young adults. Geographical moves disrupt established social networks and sources of companionship, and arouse unmet needs for intimacy and a sense of "belonging." The desire to create a new group of friends at college may lead new students to join clubs, go to social events, and talk to strangers in the cafeteria. Unmet needs for companionship can also lead some students to seek distractions from this discomfort by throwing themselves into their studies or by abusing alcohol or drugs. The core idea is that situations can create or arouse needs, which, in turn, lead people to engage in behaviors to reduce the need.

To understand Larry's behavior in robbing the liquor store, a motivational approach would try to uncover Larry's psychological needs. Was he motivated by a need for money, perhaps to buy food or to support a drug habit? Or was the robbery a way to gain status in Larry's peer group? Did Larry shoot the police officer out of fear or anger? A social psychological analysis might go further, to try to identify in detail ways in which Larry's social environment fostered the particular needs and motives that led to the robbery and shooting.

Learning Theories

For many years, **learning theory** was the dominant approach in psychology. The central idea is that a person's current behavior is determined by prior learning. In any given situation, a person learns certain behaviors which, over time, may become habits. When presented with the same situation, the person tends to behave in the same habitual way. When a hand is extended to us, we shake it, because that is how we have learned to respond to an extended hand. When someone says something nasty to us, we may say something nasty in return, or we may try to make the other person like us, depending on what we have learned to do in the past. As applied to social behavior by Albert Bandura (1977) and others, this approach has been called **social learning theory.**

There are three general mechanisms by which learning occurs. One is **association** or classical conditioning. Pavlov's dogs learned to salivate at the sound of a bell because they were presented with food every time the bell was rung. After a while they would salivate to the sound of the bell even in the absence of the meat because they associated the bell with meat. We can also learn attitudes by association. For example, the word "Nazi" is generally associated with horrible crimes. We believe that Nazis are bad because we have learned to associate them with atrocities.

A second learning mechanism is **reinforcement,** a principle explored by Clark Hull, B. F. Skinner, and others. People learn to perform a particular behavior because it is followed by something pleasurable and need-satisfying (or they learn to avoid behavior that is followed by unpleasant consequences). A child may learn to help other people because her parents praise her for sharing her toys and smile approvingly when she offers to help with chores. Or a student may learn not to contradict the professor in

One of the most powerful mechanisms of learning is imitation. Like this boy, children often imitate a parent or other adults they admire and respect.

class because each time he does, the professor frowns, looks angry, and snaps back at him.

A third mechanism is **observational learning.** People often learn social attitudes and behaviors simply by observing the attitudes and behaviors of other people, known technically as *models*. Children learn regional and ethnic speech patterns by listening to the speakers around them. Adolescents may acquire their political attitudes simply by listening to their parents' conversations during election campaigns. In observational learning, other people are an important source of information. **Imitation** or **modeling** occurs when a person not only observes but actually copies the behavior of a model. Observational learning can occur without any external reinforcement. However, whether or not people actually perform a behavior learned through observation will be influenced by the consequences the action has for them. A little boy may learn a lot about baby dolls from watching his sisters, but be discouraged from playing with them himself because his traditional parents say, "Dolls aren't for boys."

The learning approach has three distinctive features. First, the causes of behavior are believed to lie mainly in the past learning history of the individual. To return to our example of Larry shooting the police officer, we might find that in his previous encounters with the police, they had been rough, rude, antagonistic, suspi-

cious, and unsympathetic. Perhaps Larry had been reinforced in the past for responding violently to situations involving conflict with authority. Or perhaps his father often acted in violent ways so that Larry learned to imitate a violent model. The learning theorist is especially concerned with past experience and somewhat less with the details of the current situation.

Second, the learning approach tends to locate the causes of behavior mainly in the external environment and not in the individual's subjective interpretation of what is happening. It emphasizes the ways others respond to a person's actions and the models to which the individual has been exposed. All these are external to the individual.

Third, the learning approach usually aims to explain overt behavior instead of psychological or subjective states. It would try to explain Larry's overt act—shooting the police officer—not such subjective states as perceptions of the situation (whether or not Larry expected the police officer to attack him) or emotions (whether Larry was fearful or angry).

Cognitive Theories

The main idea in the cognitive approach is that a person's behavior depends on the way he or she perceives the social situation. People spontaneously organize their perceptions, thoughts, and beliefs about a situation in simple, meaningful ways. No matter how chaotic or arbitrary the situation, people will impose some order on it. And this organization, this perception and interpretation of the world, significantly affects how we behave in social situations.

The cognitive perspective in social psychology derives from the early work of gestalt psychologists. Kurt Lewin applied gestalt ideas to social psychology, emphasizing the importance of the social environment as perceived by the individual—what Lewin called the person's "psychological field." In Lewin's view, behavior is affected both by the individual's characteristics (such as ability, personality, genetic dispositions) and by the social environment as he or she perceives it.

A core idea in the cognitive perspective is

that people tend spontaneously to *group* and *categorize* objects. Put this book down and look around you. Instead of seeing objects individually, you see them as parts of larger groupings. In a library you see a row of books on a shelf as a unit, not as so many individual books. You probably perceive other people in the library in groups, perhaps as students and librarians, or as the line of people at the check-out desk, or as a couple in love. At home, you experience the pile of dirty dishes by the kitchen sink as an oppressive heap, not as individual dishes. We tend to group objects according to some very simple principles, such as similarity (dishes look more like each other than the stove and refrigerator do, so we group the dishes together), proximity (books stacked in a pile go together; the isolated books strewn all over the library table do not), or past experience (Santa Claus and Christmas trees go together, so do doctors and stethoscopes, but Santa Claus and stethoscopes do not).

Second, people readily perceive some things as standing out (*figure*) and some things as just being in the background (*ground*). Usually colorful, moving, noisy, unique, nearby stimuli stand out as figure, whereas bland, drab, stationary, quiet, common, far-away stimuli comprise the background. Our attention is drawn to cheerleaders at a football game not because they are so numerous—there may be only a dozen in a crowd of nearly 100,000 people—but because cheerleaders move a lot, yell, wave their arms, and wear colorful uniforms. In contrast, we experience the crowd as just that—a crowd—not as a collection of thousands of distinctive, fascinating individuals.

These two principles—that we spontaneously group or categorize the things we perceive and that we focus attention particularly on the most prominent (figural) stimuli—are central to our perception of physical objects and of the social world. As social thinkers, we try to arrive at meaningful interpretations of how people feel, what they want, what kinds of people they are, and so forth.

One important direction for research on cognition has been the study of causal **attributions,** the ways in which people use information to determine the causes of social behavior. For example, how do we decide that a salesperson's ingratiating behavior is caused by a genuine liking for us as opposed to the desire to butter us up for a big sale? Why do we think someone turned us down for a date? Why did the audience at our music recital give such a loud and enthusiastic response to our performance? The answers to these questions about causes can have a strong influence on our feelings and behavior. Deciding that the recital audience applauded because we gave a flawless performance may lead us to feel proud and to redouble our efforts to become a professional musician. In contrast, deciding that they applauded because they were friends and family who always overlook our faults may not enhance our self-esteem or professional aspirations.

In recent years, the cognitive perspective in social psychology has been stimulated by new developments in cognitive psychology, the study of how people process information. As applied to social psychology, research on **social cognition** focuses on how we put together social information about people, social situations, and groups to make inferences about them (Fiske & Taylor, 1991). Social cognition researchers examine the flow of information from the environment to the person. Three types of social cognition research are important.

First, research on social perception examines the ways people perceive and encode social information. It considers such questions as why we pay attention to some actions that people perform and ignore others. For example, why do we overlook a person scratching his head, but pay attention if he shouts?

Second, research on social inference examines the ways people integrate or put information together to arrive at impressions and conclusions about the social world. For example, when students visit colleges to decide which one to attend, how do they sort the information they have gathered and put it together to arrive at the conclusion that one school is a warm and friendly place and that another school is much too impersonal?

Third, research on social memory examines how individuals store and retrieve information about people and social events. For example, how does an eyewitness to a murder store information about the crime? How can the prosecutor best help this witness to remember specific details of the event?

Cognitive approaches differ from learning approaches in two major ways. First, cognitive approaches focus on current perceptions rather than on past learning. Second, they emphasize the importance of the individual's perception or interpretation of a situation, not the objective "reality" of the situation as it might be viewed by a neutral observer. To return to Larry's run-in with the law, cognitive approaches would emphasize the importance of the way Larry interpreted his situation. How did Larry perceive his actions in taking the money? When the police officer shouted at Larry to stop, how did Larry interpret the event? He probably perceived this person as an official whose job is to arrest people and who is likely to be prejudiced against people like Larry. He may have seen the officer as threatening, biased, or perhaps even cruel. Ultimately, it was Larry's interpretation of the situation that led him to shoot the police officer.

Decision-making Theories

Decision-making theories assume that people are motivated to obtain rewards and avoid costs. People calculate the costs and benefits of various actions and pick the best alternatives in a fairly logical, reasoned way. They choose the alternative that gives them the greatest benefit at the least cost. Numerous decision-making theories have been developed, each using slightly different terms and concepts. For example, **incentive theory** views decision-making as a process of weighing the pros (positive incentives) and cons (negative incentives) of various possible alternatives and then adopting the best one. The relative strengths of the pros and cons determine the final decision. To return to Larry's situation, let's suppose that he has the choices of fleeing, surrendering, or shooting. He thinks that if he flees, he may be shot, which

adds up to a considerable cost. If he surrenders, he will go to jail, another major cost. However, he may think that by shooting the police officer, he can get away—and with the money, too.

Expectancy-value theory extends the simple notion of considering costs and benefits by adding an assessment of the likelihood of each alternative (Edwards, 1954). This theory holds that decisions are based on the product or combination of two factors: (1) the value of each possible outcome or alternative and (2) the probability or "expectancy" that each outcome will actually result from the decision. Larry may try to flee despite the fact that he might get shot and killed, a major cost indeed. But he may estimate that the officer is not very likely to hit him with a bullet in the dark and in a backyard with many obstacles. So the probability of being shot is low. Going to jail is not as bad as being shot, but surrendering means he is almost certain to go to jail. The probability of surrender leading to prison is very high.

Sometimes the decisions we make actually do follow fairly well the rational procedures suggested by decision-making theories. In deciding which of two colleges to attend, for example, a student might list the pros and cons associated with each, assess the importance of each factor listed, and come up with some kind of score indicating which college is better. However, social psychologists also recognize that in real life, judgments and decisions do not always follow strict rationality. As we will see in Chapter 3, people often use shortcuts that enable them to make decisions, form judgments, or solve problems quickly and efficiently, but not always thoroughly and according to strictly rational standards. In addition, many judgments and decisions are swayed by motivational factors, such as emotional reactions or personal goals. The high school senior trying to decide between two colleges may come up with a formal "decision" based on the pros and cons of each school, but if the answer doesn't "feel right," that is, doesn't fit with his or her emotional leanings, the senior may ignore the score sheet in favor of emotional preferences. In short, rational decision-making models sometimes apply to everyday decision making, problem solving, and judgments. But there are limits on the degree to which people actually use rational principles in their daily lives.

Social Exchange Theories

Social exchange theories shift the focus of analysis from the behavior of one individual to the behavior of two or more individuals who interact with each other. The principles of social exchange build on the work of both learning theorists and decision-making theorists. The core idea in social exchange theory is that as two people interact with each other, they exchange benefits and costs. In some instances, they may do this very deliberately. You may agree to help your roommate learn Spanish in return for help with your advanced calculus course. In the heat of an argument, you and a friend may "trade" insults. But even when we are not aware of it, the process of interaction creates rewards or benefits (information, smiles of approval, money, feelings of being loved, etc.) and costs (boredom, disapproval, feelings of being misunderstood, etc.) for the people involved. **Social exchange theories** analyze interpersonal interaction on the basis of the costs and benefits to each person of possible ways they can interact.

For example, the interactions between Larry and the police officer might turn hostile because of their conflicting interests. Larry would benefit from escaping, while the police officer would benefit from arresting him. In contrast, an exchange theory analysis of the interaction between a nurse and a patient might focus on the benefits to the patient from cooperating with the nurse (the patient gets the right care and is helped toward recovery) and the benefits to the nurse of being friendly (the patient cooperates, and the nurse gets a reputation for doing a good job). In this case, the interests of both parties converge on sharing a cooperative and friendly interaction. Social exchange theory is particularly useful for analyzing bargaining situations in which two parties must come to a common agreement despite their separate interests. It has also been elaborated by Harold Kelley and others to apply to personal relationships among friends and family. We will discuss social exchange theory in detail in Chapter 10.

Sociocultural Perspectives

In recent years, social psychologists have paid more attention to how people's diverse social backgrounds influence their thoughts, feelings, and behavior. Consider the pace of life. In some cultures, punctuality is important and the general speed of life is relatively fast. In other cultures, people have more casual attitudes about time and a slower pace of daily life. Robert Levine has studied cultural differences in the pace of life. In one study, Levine (1988) asked college students in the United States and Brazil when they would consider a friend late for a lunch appointment. Americans said a friend would be late after 19 minutes, but Brazilians gave the friend nearly twice as long, not considering a friend late until 34 minutes after the time of the appointment. In a comparative study of several countries, Levine (1990) used ingenious ways to assess the tempo of a culture, including the average walking speed of pedestrians, the speed

Culture affects all facets of life from our favorite foods to our beliefs about masculinity and femininity. These traditional Moroccan women wear very conservative clothes in public to protect their body from view.

with which postal clerks respond to a standard request for stamps, and the accuracy of public clocks. Levine found significant cross-cultural differences on all three measures. Both Japan and the United States are relatively fast-paced cultures with accurate public clocks. In contrast, Italy and Indonesia are relatively slower and have less accurate public clocks.

Edward Hall (1959) described unspoken cultural rules about the use of time as a "silent language" that we learn through experience in a culture. Lack of familiarity with cultural differences in time can create problems when people travel to other countries. For example, American Peace Corps volunteers reported having more trouble getting used to the relatively slow pace of life and lack of punctuality in other countries than they did in adjusting to unfamiliar foods or different standards of living (Spradley & Phillips, 1972).

In seeking to understand differences such as these, psychologists have come to recognize the importance of **culture**—the shared beliefs, values, traditions, and behavior patterns of particular groups (Berry, Poortinga, Segall, & Dasen, 1992). These groups can be nations, ethnic groups, religious communities, or even teenage gangs and college fraternities. Culture is taught by one generation to the next, through a process known as **socialization.** Children, for instance, may learn about their culture not only from parents and friends, but also from story books and television programs. New fraternity members are expected to learn the traditions, songs, and secrets of their group from senior members of the fraternity.

An important aspect of culture are **social norms**—rules and expectations about how group members should behave. Social rules govern a surprisingly broad range of behaviors, from how close we stand when talking with a friend to what we wear (or don't wear) at the beach. Some norms apply to everyone in a social group, regardless of their position. On campus, everyone is expected to obey traffic signs and to put litter in wastebaskets. But frequently, the norms that apply depend on your position, for instance, whether you are a professor or a student. Professors are supposed to come to class

on time, prepare lectures and lead class discussions, write and grade tests, serve on college committees, and so on. Rather different norms apply to students, who are expected to take notes in class, study for tests, write term papers, pay tuition, and so on.

The term **social role** refers to the set of norms that apply to people in a particular position, such as teacher or student. One perspective on social roles uses imagery borrowed from the theater. The individual acting in society is like an actor in a play. In the theater the script sets the stage, defines the role that each actor will enact, and dictates what actors say and do. Similarly, cultures present us with many preestablished social rules of behavior. For example, when children enter school, they learn many rules of classroom behavior, such as sitting quietly in their seats or raising their hand to speak. In marriage, traditional roles prescribe that the husband should be the breadwinner and the wife should be in charge of childcare and housekeeping.

The sociocultural perspective is useful in understanding behavior *within* a particular social or cultural context. To return to our example of Larry robbing a liquor store and shooting a police officer, we might find that Larry belongs to a teenage gang. Perhaps this group condones stealing money and accords higher status to gang members who carry a gun. His gang may have a shared history of violent encounters with the police, which led Larry to be suspicious and quick to fire his weapon. An analysis of the beliefs, traditions, and norms of Larry's gang might help explain his actions. Another example of a sociocultural analysis behavior within a culture is provided in Chapter 12, where we discuss how the social roles men and women play help to explain many of the male–female differences we notice in everyday life.

The sociocultural perspective also emphasizes comparisons *between* different cultures or social groups. Unless we attend specifically to cultural differences we are likely to overlook their importance. We tend to assume that the behaviors of our own culture are "standard" or typical. One benefit of foreign travel is that it causes us to take a fresh look at taken-for-granted aspects of our own behavior, such as our beliefs about punctuality and the use of time. Similarly, social psychologists are beginning to conduct cross-cultural studies as a way to learn how social behavior is affected by differences in cultural values, norms, and roles.

The behavior of our youthful criminal Larry reflects in part the culture in which he lives. As we will describe in Chapter 14, the United States is one of the most violent societies on earth. American children watch countless acts of murder and mayhem on television, and often engage in fierce competition at school and in sports. Many Americans believe parents are right to use physical punishment to discipline children. Further, life in many urban areas provides easy access to handguns and other weapons that can turn the expression of anger into a deadly act of violence. Larry's attitudes were shaped in part by exposure to cultural messages about violence, and his act of shooting the police officer was made possible by situational opportunities to obtain a gun and ammunition. Other cultures, however, have very different norms and values about violence. For example, in traditional Eskimo culture, where people live in small, closeknit groups and depend on each other for survival, the expression of anger is strongly discouraged and physical violence is uncommon (Briggs, 1970).

One goal of cross-cultural research on social behavior is to identify important ways in which cultures differ from each other. A useful distinction is between cultures that emphasize **individualism** and those that emphasize **collectivism** (Triandis, McCusker, & Hui, 1990). The cultural norms and values of America and European societies emphasize the importance of personal independence and individualism. Western literature from the *Illiad* to *The Adventures of Huckleberry Finn* tells of self-reliant heroes who leave home to seek self-fulfillment (Triandis, 1990). In an individualist culture, a person's behavior is guided largely by individual goals, rather than the goals of collectives such as the family, the work group, or the tribe. If a conflict arises between an individual's personal goals and the goals of the group, it is acceptable to put self-interests first. Further, a person's sense of self is based largely on individual attributes and accomplishments, rather than membership in social groups.

In contrast, collectivist cultures emphasize loyalty to the family, adherence to group norms, and the preservation of harmony in social relations with members of one's own group. The cultural norms and values of many African, Asian, and Latin American societies emphasize collectivism. This can be seen in literature from Asia, which often celebrates a hero who performs his duty to his family or to the emperor, sometimes in the face of strong temptations to pursue more pleasurable pastimes. In a collectivist culture, group goals are expected to take priority over individual preferences, and the self is defined largely in terms of group membership. Collectivist cultures value a person who can fit in comfortably with the group. Thus, a Japanese folk saying warns: "The nail that stands out gets pounded down" (cited by Markus & Kitayama, 1991, p. 224). But individualist cultures applaud individuals who stand out from others; Americans note that "the squeaky wheel gets the grease."

Sometimes what appears to be the same concept has different meanings in individualist and collectivist cultures (Triandis, Bontempo, Villareal, Asai, & Lucca, 1988). In the United States, "self-reliance" typically implies freedom to do one's own thing, freedom from the constraints of the group. In a collectivist culture, "self-reliance" is more likely to mean not being a burden on others, not making excessive demands on one's family or friends.

In large and complex societies such as the United States or Canada, individuals are often exposed to more than one cultural or ethnic group. Several studies indicate that Hispanic Americans tend to be more collectivist than non-Hispanics in the United States (Marin & Triandis, 1985). However, the longer Hispanic Americans are exposed to Anglo-American culture, the more individualist they tend to become. Collectivism also tends to be strong among Asian Americans (Triandis, 1990). Sometimes individuals who live in two cultural worlds have concerns about which cultural pat-

As television and jet travel bring the citizens of the world closer together, many of us are influenced by other cultures. These teenagers in China have adopted a distinctly American style of dress.

terns to follow. One 10th-grade Chinese-born girl who immigrated to the United States at age 12 described her feelings as follows:

> I don't know who I am. Am I the good Chinese daughter? Am I an American teenager? I always feel I am letting my parents down when I am with my friends because I act so American, but I also feel that I will never really be an American. I never feel really comfortable with myself anymore. (Cited in Olsen, 1988, p. 30)

We will return to the topic of identification with ethnic groups in Chapter 5 on the Self.

Sociocultural approaches provide a useful perspective on social behavior, both within our culture and across cultures. Throughout this book, we present research that seeks to understand cultural and ethnic diversity. In addition to materials in the text, each chapter has a special feature called "Cultural Highlights" that illustrates an important aspect of human diversity.

Social Psychological Theories Today

Over the years, social psychologists have found that the topics we study often cannot be fully understood using any single general theory, such as social learning theory. Rather it proves useful to try to combine and integrate ideas from different theoretical traditions. Instead of focusing primarily on overt behavior, thinking, or emotions, newer theorists seek to understand the interrelationships among behavior, thoughts, and feelings. For example, social learning theorists have come to appreciate the importance of subjective expectations in understanding human behavior. As you read about research on specific topics in social psychology, such as aggression or conformity, consider how current social psychological analyses try to encompass all facets of human experience including behavior, cognition, and motivation.

Another trend is for social psychologists to develop theories that can account for a certain limited range of phenomena, such as helping a stranger in distress, forming a positive impression of another person, or feeling crowded. These are called **middle-range theories** because they focus on a specific aspect of social behavior and do not try to encompass all of social life. The frustration–aggression hypothesis is one illustration of a middle-range theory. In this book, you will be introduced to many of these more focused theories. But as you will see, these specific theories and models continue to reflect the influence of our basic theoretical traditions.

THE GOALS OF SOCIAL PSYCHOLOGICAL RESEARCH

One of the exciting aspects of social psychology is that it explores topics that are relevant to our everyday experiences. Social psychology strives to help us understand love and altruism as well as conflict and prejudice. Personal experience is often very important in leading psychologists to study particular topics and in generating initial hypotheses about social life. For example, social psychological research on prejudice was sparked by intense concerns about discrimination against Jews, African Americans, and other ethnic minorities in our society. It is important to understand, however, that although social psychological research often begins with personal experiences and social concerns, it does not stop at armchair speculation. A hallmark of social psychology is its commitment to scientific methodology.

Social psychology is an empirical science. This means that social psychologists use systematic methods of gathering information to learn about social life and to test the usefulness of their theories. Sometimes research confirms their commonsense views about social life, and sometimes it does not. Consider these statements and decide if you think each one is true or false:

- In choosing friends and lovers, a fundamental principle is that opposites attract.
- When people are anxious, they prefer to be with other people.
- TV ads that try to frighten people usually backfire and are less effective than ads that do not arouse fear.
- If you pay a man to give a speech that goes against his own beliefs, he will usually change his mind to agree with the speech. The more money you pay him for the speech, the greater will be the change in his personal attitudes.
- The idea that women are better than men at interpreting other people's "body language" and facial expressions is a myth.

You may not agree with all of these statements, but it is fair to say that they all sound plausible. Yet research, to be described in later chapters in this book, shows that *all* these statements are oversimplifications and several are false.

Why do our informal observations of social life sometimes lead us to wrong conclusions? Often, our own experiences are simply not representative of most people or most social situations. Sometimes we are biased and misinterpret

what happens; we see things as we want them to be, not as they really are. Sometimes we see correctly but remember wrong. In contrast, scientific research collects data in ways that reduce bias. Psychologists strive to observe representative groups of people, and to keep track of the "numbers" so we do not rely on memory or general impressions. Psychologists are not always entirely successful in avoiding limitations and bias in their work. For example, psychology has been criticized for relying too often on white, middle-class college students as research subjects—a group that is hardly representative of society at large. What is unusual about scientific research, however, is the conscious effort to identify and overcome bias—an issue we will discuss more fully later in this chapter.

Social psychologists conduct scientific research on social behavior. Our research has four broad goals.

DESCRIPTION. A major goal is to provide careful and systematic descriptions of social behavior that permit us to make reliable generalizations about how people act in various social settings. Are men more aggressive than women? Do children generally grow up to have the same political attitudes as their parents? Are there typical reactions when a love affair ends? In thinking up solutions to problems, do people work better alone or in a group? A thorough knowledge of how people behave is essential.

CAUSAL ANALYSIS. Much research in psychology seeks to establish relationships between cause and effect. Do expensive ad campaigns actually influence how people vote in elections? Does frustration typically lead to anger and aggression? Does a college education cause students to become more liberal in their social attitudes? Fundamental to all scientific inquiry is the search to identify cause and effect relations.

THEORY BUILDING. Another goal is to develop theories about social behavior that help us to understand why people behave the way they do. As we learn more about general principles and the specifics of particular types of behavior, we gain a better understanding of social life. Theories help us to organize what we know about social behavior, and can lead to new predictions that can be tested in further research.

APPLICATION.   Social psychological knowledge can help to solve everyday social problems. For example, the application of social psychology may help people learn to control their own aggressive impulses or develop more satisfying personal relationships. It may also assist policymakers to design interventions that can help many people, for example, by reducing smoking. Today, researchers are using social psychological principles to find ways to encourage sexually active adults to engage in safer sex practices and to understand prejudice against people with AIDS. The possibilities for applying social psychological research are numerous, but to be successful, they must be based on a firm research foundation.

Throughout this book, we describe specific examples of social psychological research. These include both classic studies that have been influential in the history of social psychology and very recent studies on the forefront of contemporary research. In addition, each chapter has a special feature called "Research Closeup" that profiles research on a particular interesting or timely topic.

RESEARCH QUESTIONS: THEORETICAL AND DESCRIPTIVE

All research begins with a question, and there are two basic kinds of questions in social psychology: those that are directly related to a theory and those that are primarily descriptive.

A *theoretical question* starts with a theory we want to test. A theory can be any abstract generalization that tells us what to expect in more specific, concrete cases. A good example is Darley and Latané's middle-range theory of the diffusion of responsibility in helping situations. Earlier in this chapter, we described the case of Kitty Genovese who was murdered while 38

neighbors listened to the attack. Why didn't anyone help to stop the attack or even call the police?

Darley and Latané (1968) hypothesized that people are *least* likely to help when they think there are other witnesses to the emergency, so that they do not feel directly and personally responsible. As we will see in Chapter 13, there is now considerable empirical support for this prediction. This hypothesis follows from Darley and Latané's more general theory of the **diffusion of responsibility:** Anything that diminishes an individual's sense of responsibility for solving a problem makes that person less likely to take action. This general theory leads to many specific hypotheses:

- People are less likely to help in an emergency when there are other witnesses.
- People work harder on a task or problem if they are alone than if they are in a large group.
- People pay less attention to instructions when co-workers are also listening.

From one theoretical statement about the diffusion of responsibility, we can deduce what to expect in numerous specific situations. Theories can usually generate hypotheses or predictions about how people will behave in a variety of situations.

Diffusion of responsibility is a good example of a middle-range theory. It deals with a moderate range of phenomena—situations in which individuals are trying to solve problems and their responsibility for the solution varies. It does not attempt to deal with all social behavior. In later chapters on helping behavior, group productivity, and aggression, we will discuss research that has tested hypotheses derived from the theory of diffusion of responsibility.

In summary, a theoretical research question begins with a specific prediction derived from a theory. The major goal of theoretical research is to evaluate the theory. If the hypothesis is confirmed, the theory is supported. If the hypothesis is not confirmed, two possibilities are suggested: Either we've conducted a poor test of the theory, or the theory is at least partially wrong. We can then go back and discard the theory or alter it to make it consistent with the new finding. Theoretical research can also be designed to compare two theories or to assess the limits and exceptions to a theory.

Often, however, research is not concerned with theory. Researchers are simply interested in discovering more about a particular behavior or experience. Research motivated by *descriptive questions* is designed to gather information about the specific phenomenon in question. For example, researchers might be interested in how divorced couples differ from those who remain married for many years. The researchers might compare married and divorced couples on many dimensions, such as how similar the husband and wife are in age, social class background, and political and religious values. The researchers might also investigate how divorced versus married couples handle disagreements and conflicts, whether they have children or not, whether both members of the couple have paid jobs, and so on. Many different factors might be explored systematically in an effort to describe differences between couples who stay together and those who break up.

The ultimate goal of psychology, indeed of any science, is to have unifying theories that explain known facts in a particular realm. Theories help us understand, appreciate, and cope with the world. Without a theory, data are often difficult to understand and to fit into the rest of our knowledge. On the other hand, sometimes we need to begin by collecting descriptive data because we do not yet have an adequate theory. A solid understanding of how people behave provides the foundation for developing good theories. So there is great value in both kinds of research—research that focuses on testing hypotheses derived from theories and research that describes basic facts about important aspects of social life.

RESEARCH PARTICIPANTS

How do we decide which people to study? One obvious starting point is that we should study the people about whom we later want to gener-

alize. If we want to generalize about women who work fulltime, we should study employed women. But clearly we will never be able to afford to study all working women. So instead we study some smaller number of women, chosen in such a way that they are representative of the larger group. This is known as a *representative sample.*

The best way to ensure this general representativeness is to study a random sample of the larger population to which we want to generalize. In formal terms, a **random sample** means that each person in the larger population has an equal chance of being included in the study. If we selected a sample of telephone numbers from the phone directory at random (using a table of random numbers, for example), we could be assured that ours was a random sample of all listed phone numbers in the area covered by that telephone book. The laws of probability assure us that a large and truly random sample will almost always be representative of the population within a certain margin of error. It will include approximately the same proportion of women, ethnic minorities, unemployed people, older adults, and so forth as the population from which we have sampled. The CULTURAL HIGHLIGHT describes the current ethnic and social diversity of the American population.

Most of the time, social psychologists want their research results to apply to people in general, not just to college students in Boston or first-grade children in Austin, Texas, or people who use laundromats in Nashville, Tennessee. Yet it is expensive to study random samples of the general population, as you can readily imagine. So social psychologists try to make realistic compromises between the goal of collecting valid data that can be generalized beyond the few people studied, on the one hand, and practicality on the other.

A common compromise is to use college students as subjects. It has often been said that American social psychology is based on college sophomores, because they are the ones who are most readily available. About 75 percent of all published articles in social psychology use undergraduate subjects and about two-thirds use undergraduates in the laboratory (Sears,

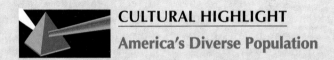

CULTURAL HIGHLIGHT
America's Diverse Population

For the most part, social psychological research has used white college student samples for its studies. Such samples are too narrow. The gap between the experiences of white educated young adults and the experiences of the rest of the population is substantial and is likely to widen as the composition of our society changes in coming years.

According to the 1990 census, roughly 76 percent of Americans are non-Hispanic whites, 12 percent are African Americans, 9 percent are Hispanics (of any race), 3 percent are Asian Americans and Pacific Islanders, and fewer than 1 percent are American Indians (Bureau of the Census, 1992). However, demographers predict that the ethnic mix of the United States will change dramatically in the 21st century. Changing patterns of immigration are a major factor. Of the more than 7 million immigrants who came to the United States in the 1980s, less than 20 percent came from Europe. Instead, four out of five

came from Asia, Latin America, and the Caribbean (Immigration and Naturalization Service, 1989). By the year 2090, it is estimated that non-Hispanic whites will make up less than half of the U. S. population, Hispanics will comprise about 25 percent, and Asian Americans and African Americans will each comprise about 13 percent. The American Indian population is expected to remain less than 1 percent.

The face of American society is changing in other ways as well. The public visibility of lesbians and gay men has increased dramatically. Although no one knows for sure the sexual orientation distribution of the American public, conservative estimates are that at least 7 to 10 million people are gay and lesbian, and an unknown number of others are bisexual.

In addition, the number of older adults is increasing steadily. In 1960, less than 10 percent of Americans were age 65 or older. Today that figure

has increased to 14 percent. It is estimated that by 2080, nearly a third of the population will be 65 or older (Current Population Reports, 1989).

There is also growing awareness of the many people with physical disabilities (Asch, 1988). It is estimated that about 14 percent of Americans have a disabling condition that limits their daily activities, for example, preventing them from going to school, keeping house, or having a job (Kraus & Stoddard, 1989). These disabilities include not only being blind, deaf, or paralyzed, but also other relatively hidden conditions such as arthritis, diabetes, or severe back problems that interfere with daily life.

These examples highlight the enormous social and cultural diversity of the American population. As we move toward the year 2000 and beyond, a challenge for social psychologists will be to broaden our research so that it becomes more truly a psychology of all the people.

1986). How dissatisfied should we be with this reliance on college student samples?

Our need for a representative sample depends on the question we are asking. For descriptive research in which we are trying to describe the characteristics of a given population, a representative sample is very important. Suppose we are commissioned to study how best to introduce computers into business offices where the employees have worked together for years, are almost all women, and never went past high school. It would be entirely unreason-

able to study this question with a sample of college students who had never met each other before the study and who had no experience with any kind of office work. On the other hand, in some basic, theory-testing research, the representativeness of the sample is less crucial. For example, according to Darley and Latané's diffusion of responsibility theory, people should be less responsive to a person in need when other people are present than if they are alone. This should be equally true of college students, shoppers at a suburban mall, or passengers on an urban subway. The assumption is that all people react in about the same way to a stranger in distress.

However, there are areas in which college students may actually be somewhat misleading as a source of data (Sears, 1986). College students are much younger, higher in social class, and better at test taking than is the general population. Their attitudes may be less well developed and more open to change. As a result, using college students in studies where any of these factors make a difference may be unwise. For example, studies of personality should take into account the fact that most college sophomores are still rather young and their personalities have not developed as fully as have those of older adults. The same is likely to be true of their political and social attitudes. Although college students are convenient subjects, they are not always the most appropriate participants for social psychological research.

In addition to a reliance on college student samples, psychological research has also been criticized for an overrepresentation of white males among research participants. Beginning in the 1970s, feminist psychologists documented a common tendency to use male subjects rather than females or samples containing both sexes. Further, research on particular topics such as aggression and achievement motivation was almost entirely based on male subjects. Critics questioned whether theories based on male subjects would be applicable to females. In the past twenty years, heightened awareness of gender bias and the entry of more women into the profession of psychology have improved the gender balance of research samples (Berscheid, 1992; Gannon, Luchetta, Rhodes, Pardie, & Segrist, 1992).

Ethnic minority groups have also been seriously underrepresented in psychological studies, a pattern that continues to this day. For example, Sandra Graham (1992) recently analyzed trends in published research on African Americans in six major psychology journals from 1970 to 1989. She counted the proportion of journal articles in which African Americans were the focus of the study, or in which data from two or more racial groups were compared. Overall, only 3.6 percent of the articles she reviewed met one of these criteria, and the proportion of articles on blacks actually declined from 5.2 percent in the early 1970s to 2.0 percent in the late 1980s. Noting that American society is becoming more ethnically diverse, Graham cautions that "academic psychology cannot maintain its integrity by continuing to allow ethnic minorities to remain so marginalized in mainstream research" (1992, p. 638).

Critics believe that our tendency to build psy-

As these pupils in a public elementary school illustrate, the American population is becoming more and more ethnically diverse. Yet ethnic minority groups are often underrepresented in psychological studies.

chological knowledge on a narrow range of research participants creates several problems. First, we run the risk of developing theories that have limited generalizability (Pepitone & Triandis, 1988). A psychology of college sophomores may not be an adequate psychology of humankind, and may not provide an adequate basis for applying psychological principles to social problems. Second, by not studying the life experiences of ethnic minorities or people from diverse social backgrounds, we may overlook important social behaviors that would enrich our understanding of the human condition. Finally, just as space travel to the moon provided a new and informative perspective on the planet earth, so too cross-cultural comparisons may help us to see our own experiences in new ways.

CORRELATIONAL VERSUS EXPERIMENTAL DESIGNS

After an investigator has decided what research question to ask, another difficult decision still remains: how to conduct the study. There are two basic research designs: correlational and experimental. In correlational studies, the researcher carefully observes and records the relationship between two or more factors. For example, a researcher might ask whether physical attractiveness is related to a student's popularity with other students. In a correlational design, the researcher would not influence the students' behavior in any way, but would merely record information about the attractiveness of each student and how much he or she is liked by other students.

In contrast, the hallmark of an experimental design is intervention: The researcher puts people in a controlled situation and assesses how they react. To study the link between physical attractiveness and popularity, a researcher using an experimental design might enlist the assistance of a paid confederate who is sometimes dressed to look very attractive and sometimes dressed to look very unappealing. The researcher might then bring student volunteers

into the laboratory for a brief interaction with another student (really the paid confederate). After a short meeting, the student's liking for the confederate would be measured. In this experimental design, the researcher controls the student's exposure to an attractive versus unattractive peer, the setting in which they interact, and the way in which liking for the peer is measured. We will take a close look at both correlational and experimental research designs, and highlight the advantages and disadvantages of each.

Correlational Research

Correlational research consists of observing the relationship between two or more factors, known technically as "variables." **Correlational research** asks if there is an association between the variables. More specifically, when variable *A* is high, is variable *B* also high (a positive correlation), or low (a negative correlation), or is *B*'s value unrelated (no correlation)? Height and weight are positively correlated because tall people tend to weigh more than short people. In contrast, the amount of clothing worn and the temperature on a given day tend to be negatively correlated—people usually wear less clothing on hot days. However, height and amount of clothing are probably uncorrelated; in general, tall people and short people probably wear about the same number of pieces of clothing.

A good example of correlational research comes from studies of whether or not watching violence on television is related to aggressive behavior. Correlational studies have examined the association between how much time a child spends watching violent programs on television and the amount of aggressive behavior in which the child engages. Are the children who watch the most violence on television also the most aggressive in their daily behavior? Huesmann (1982) found that elementary school children who watched violent programs the most were also described by their peers as the most aggressive. In this study, viewing violent programs on television was positively correlated with aggressive behavior among those children.

ADVANTAGES. There are several advantages to correlational designs. Correlational techniques enable us to study problems where intervention is impossible. Many important issues are of this type. For example, we cannot randomly assign people to experience passionate love, earthquakes, or cancer, nor can we randomly assign people to live in big cities or to grow up in small families. Such factors are clearly beyond the control of even the most ingenious and dedicated researchers. Both ethical and practical considerations limit the opportunities that researchers have to intervene in the lives of others. In such situations, correlational designs offer the best possible method for understanding the connections among various facets of people's lives.

A second advantage of correlational research is efficiency. Correlational studies allow us to collect more information and test more relationships than we can in most experiments. If we use a correlational approach to explore what causes some children to be more aggressive than others, we could collect information on a great many factors, including television viewing, family history, intelligence, personality, relationships with other children, and so on. Moreover, we could measure aggressive behavior in a number of different ways: in terms of teachers' impressions, our own observations of children in school, their reputations for aggressiveness among other children, parents' reports, and so on. We could then use statistical procedures to uncover associations among this large set of variables. The experimental method is relatively inefficient for collecting large amounts of data on many variables.

DISADVANTAGES. Although correlational research is helpful in describing the interrelationships among variables, it does not provide clear-cut evidence of cause-and-effect relationships. In correlational studies, the cause and effect relationship can be ambiguous in two ways. The **reverse-causality problem** occurs whenever two variables are correlated with each other, and each one can just as plausibly be the cause as the effect. In this case, we know that variables *A* and *B* are related, but we cannot tell whether *A* causes *B,* or whether the reverse is true and so *B* causes *A.* Studies showing a correlation between viewing violent television and levels of aggressive behavior illustrate this problem. Such results could indicate that TV violence causes aggression in everyday life. But the opposite might also be true: Perhaps children who are very aggressive in their daily lives are especially interested in watching people fight and so spend more time watching violent TV programs. In other words, perhaps children's aggressive behavior is the cause of their TV viewing. In short, a correlation between two variables does not, by itself, tell you which variable is the cause and which is the effect.

The other serious ambiguity in correlational research is the possibility that neither variable *A* nor variable *B* directly affects the other. Rather, some other unspecified factor may influence both of them. This is called the **third-variable problem.** For example, the correlation between TV violence and aggressive behavior may be created by a third factor. Perhaps disadvantaged families who live in cramped households and experience a good deal of frustration in their lives tend simultaneously to watch more TV and to be more aggressive. Among such families, TV viewing and aggressive behavior would be correlated, but the correlation might be due to a third variable—poverty and frustration—that caused both. The correlation between watching televised violence and aggressive behavior would be called "spurious" because it was artificially created by a third variable that was not considered. Television would have no causal role itself in producing aggressive behavior.

These two ambiguities are often, but not always, a problem in correlational studies. Sometimes we can rule out the reverse causality problem. For example, many studies have found a correlation between gender and aggressive behavior, with boys being more aggressive than girls. In this case, we can be confident that aggressive behavior is *not* the cause of the child's gender: Children do not begin sexually neutral and then become physiologically male or female depending on whether or not they fight on the playground. Here the direction of causality is clear: Something about being a boy versus being a girl affects a child's aggressiveness.

The third-variable problem is not always a fatal difficulty, because we can sometimes check to see whether the most plausible third variable is really responsible for the correlation we have observed. For example, we could add measures of frustration and anger in the child's family to Huesmann's (1982) correlational study of elementary school children. Then we could check to see whether the correlation of TV viewing with aggressive behavior was in fact due to home life. Does it hold both in angry, aggressive families and in happy, peaceful families? If so, we can conclude that the third variable (home life) was not responsible for the original correlation.

Of course, this procedure does not completely eliminate the third-variable problem. There still could be some other third variable (now actually a fourth) that we still had not measured, such as verbal skills. Perhaps, children with poor verbal skills prefer watching shows with a great deal of physical activity rather than slower-paced shows with more talking. Again, to test this possibility, the solution would be to measure this new third variable, verbal skill, and then see if the original correlation held up for both highly verbal children and those below average in verbal skills.

This sounds as if it could go on and on. But at some point the process ends, because we can no longer think of any more plausible third variables. That does not mean there are none, but that for the moment, we will accept the correlation as reflecting a cause-and-effect relationship until someone thinks of another possible variable to be examined.

Experimental Research

In an **experiment,** the researcher creates two (or more) conditions that differ from each other in well-specified ways. Individuals are randomly assigned to one of these different conditions, and then their reactions are measured. For example, in experiments on media violence, one group of children might be shown a violent film, and another group shown a nonviolent film. All the children might then be placed in a test situation in which their aggressive behavior can be measured. If those shown the violent film behave more aggressively, we can say that filmed violence is a cause of aggressive behavior in this setting.

A good example of this experimental approach to the study of media violence is a study by Hartmann (1969). He had one group of teenage boys watch a 2-minute film showing two boys shooting baskets and then getting into an argument and finally a fistfight. A second group was shown another 2-minute film depicting an active but cooperative basketball game. After watching the film, each boy was asked to help out in what was described as a study of the effects of performance feedback on learning. The subject was supposed to be a "teacher" and to administrator a shock to a "learner" every time that "learner" made a mistake in the learning task. The "teacher" could deliver as strong a shock as he wanted, within certain limits. (In reality, the shocks were fake, and the "learner" was a confederate of the experimenter.) It turned out that the boys who had seen the violent film delivered stronger shocks than those who had seen the nonviolent one. In this situation, at least, observing filmed violence caused an increase in aggressive behavior.

The great strength of the experimental method is that it avoids the ambiguities about causality that plague most correlational studies. In social psychology, experiments consist of randomly assigning people to different conditions and seeing if there is any difference in their responses. If the experiment has been done properly, any difference in responses between the two conditions must be due to the difference in the conditions. In more formal terms, the factor controlled by the researcher (the "cause") is called the **independent variable,** because it is determined by the researcher. In the Hartmann study, the independent variable was the type of film the boys watched. The outcome or "effect" being studied is called the **dependent variable,** because its value is dependent on the independent variable. In the Hartmann study, the dependent variable was the amount of electric

TABLE 1-1
Characteristics of Correlational and
Experimental Research

	Correlational	Experimental
Advantages of Experiments		
Independent variable	Varies naturally	Controlled by researcher
Random assignment	No	Yes
Unambiguous causality	No	Yes
Theory testing	Often	Usually
Advantages of Correlational Studies		
Exploratory	Often	Usually not
Real world problems	Often	Usually not
Tests many relationships	Usually	Usually not

shock the subject administered to another person. Experiments provide clear evidence that differences in the dependent variable are caused by differences in the independent variable.

In experimental research, much attention is given to creating the independent and dependent variables. The psychologist will usually start with an abstract or conceptual definition of the variable in question. For example, the variable "observing violence" might be defined as watching acts that hurt or are intended to hurt another person. The researcher must then go from this fairly general conceptual definition to an operational definition. An **operational definition** is the specific procedure or operation that is used to manipulate or measure the variable in the experiment. For example, the experimenter might create two versions of a film, one violent and another nonviolent. If the experimenter is attempting to manipulate only the amount of violence in a film, then the two films should not differ in other ways, such as length, being in color versus being in black and white, or being a cartoon versus being realistic. The experimenter's control over the independent variable is crucial because it allows us to pinpoint the cause of any differences that emerge between the two groups of people.

The second essential feature of an experiment is that subjects must be randomly assigned to conditions. This can be done by flipping a coin, by cutting a deck of cards, or more commonly and more precisely, by using a table of random numbers. **Random assignment** of subjects to conditions is crucial because it means that differences between subjects in all conditions are due only to chance. If subjects in each group differ in some systematic way beforehand, we cannot interpret any later differences in behavior as being due solely to the experimental conditions. The differences in behavior could be due to those pre-existing factors and not to the independent variable.

The advantages of correlational and experimental research are summarized in Table 1-1. Correlational studies are particularly effective in the collection of large amounts of data; they provide ideas and hypotheses that can be studied in more detail experimentally. Correlational studies have the disadvantage of causal ambiguity, so it is often helpful for experimental research to supplement correlational studies. There are many cases in which both methods are useful and can complement each other.

FIELD VERSUS LABORATORY SETTINGS

Another decision in designing research concerns where the study should be conducted: in a field setting or in a laboratory. Research done in the field examines behavior in its "natural habitat." We might study factory workers' productivity right in the factory, or people's television viewing in their own living rooms, or commuters' responses to an emergency on the subway train they normally ride to work, or college students' relationships with their roommates in a dormitory.

Laboratory research, in contrast, is done in an artificial situation, one the person normally does not inhabit. Some laboratory research is conducted in a specially outfitted room in a psychology building at a college or research institute. The lab room may have all kinds of special equipment, such as video monitors to show films to subjects, audio equipment to record conversations between subjects, one-way mirrors to permit observation of group interactions, physiological recording equipment, or computers. Or the laboratory may simply be a room or lecture hall where people can fill out questionnaires. The point is that the subject comes to a setting selected and controlled by the researcher.

Although much research in social psychology has been conducted in the laboratory, some has always been conducted in the field. Both experimental and correlational research can be done in either the laboratory or the field, and each setting has advantages and disadvantages.

Advantages of the Laboratory

The major advantage of laboratory research is the control it permits over the situation. Researchers can be quite certain about what is happening to each subject. If they are doing experimental work, they can randomly assign the subjects to conditions, expose them to specific experiences, minimize the effects of extraneous factors, and go a long way toward eliminating unwanted variations in the procedure. Laboratory researchers have great control over the dependent variable and can measure more precisely than is often possible in the field. Therefore, the laboratory is the ideal place to study the exact effects of one variable on another. All these advantages fall under the heading of **internal validity.** Internal validity is high when we can be confident that the effects we observe in the dependent variable are actually caused by

the independent variables we manipulated in the experiment (and are not caused by other uncontrolled factors).

In field settings, it is generally difficult to assign subjects to conditions randomly, to be certain they are all experiencing the same thing, to get precise measures of the dependent variable, and so on. In particular, it is difficult to design pure manipulations of the independent variable and to obtain pure measures of the dependent variable. The researcher must find or arrange circumstances that produce specific differences between the conditions.

In an ambitious field study of the effects of TV violence, Feshbach and Singer (1971) studied adolescent boys who lived in seven different boarding schools in California and New York. With the help of the school staff, the researchers were able to assign boys randomly to two different "TV diets." All boys watched selected prime-time TV shows for at least 6 hours a week for 6 weeks. In the violent TV condition, the boys watched shows with aggressive content, including Westerns and crime stories. In the nonviolent condition, boys watched situation comedies and other nonaggressive programs. Staff ratings of the boys' behavior constituted the measure of aggression. Contrary to what you might expect, the researchers found that the boys shown the violent programs were actually somewhat *lower* in aggressiveness than boys shown the nonviolent programs. Watching TV violence seemed to reduce aggressive behavior. Why might this unexpected result have occurred?

The researchers discovered that most of the boys *preferred* the more violent programs. Therefore, those boys assigned to the nonviolent television condition may have been more frustrated than the other group because they were prevented from watching their favorite programs. Consequently, it is not clear whether the results are due to the content of the shows the boys watched or to differences in the level of frustration between boys in the violent versus nonviolent TV conditions. This would not be such a problem in a laboratory study, because the researchers would not have had to interfere with the boys' normal television viewing practices and therefore would not have induced frustration in one group and not in the other.

Another advantage of the laboratory is convenience and cost. It is usually much easier and cheaper for researchers to set up a study in a room down the hall from their office than to go where people are living their daily lives.

Advantages of the Field

The most obvious advantage of field settings is that they are more realistic and therefore allow results to be generalized more readily to real-life situations. This is called **external validity** to reflect the fact that the results are more likely to be valid in situations outside of (external to) the specific research situation itself (Campbell & Stanley, 1963). External validity is high when the results of a study can be generalized to other settings and populations. Consider the differences between two studies described in this chapter: the Hartmann (1969) laboratory experiment on TV violence and the Feshbach and Singer (1971) field experiment on the same topic.

In Hartmann's laboratory study, the independent variable, filmed violence, was artificial. The researcher created a brief film, especially pre-

pared for the study. In Feshbach and Singer's field study, the independent variable was the violence actually shown on prime-time television all over the country. In Hartmann's laboratory study, the dependent variable, aggressive behavior, was artificial: the amount of shock delivered in the teacher–learner situation constructed especially for the study. In the Feshbach and Singer field study, the dependent variable was naturalistic and consisted of observers' ratings of how much physical and verbal aggression the boys engaged in during their normal interactions with peers and teachers. Suppose we want to generalize from these two studies to the effects of prime-time television on teenage boys' aggression in their everyday lives. In the field study, we are already dealing with exactly the kinds of TV violence, everyday aggressive behavior, and real-life situations of interest. So it would be more appropriate to generalize from the field study. The field study, therefore, has greater external validity.

Another advantage of work in the field is that we are sometimes able to deal with extremely powerful variables and situations that could not be studied in the laboratory. We can observe people in extreme situations—when they are waiting for open-heart surgery in a hospital or huddled together under artillery bombardment. Sometimes ingenious researchers are able to

Social psychological research is not confined to the laboratory. Studies have also been conducted at summer camps, in college dormitories, on urban subways, and even at the beach.

take advantage of "natural experiments"—cases in which the independent variable is manipulated by nature rather than by the experimenter. For example, we could not randomly assign homeowners to experience a destructive natural disaster, to see if this changed their perceptions of personal control over their life. But Parker, Brewer, and Spencer (1980) were able to approximate this design by studying a community that had suffered a devastating brush fire. Chance factors such as rapid changes in the wind direction determined which homes were destroyed and which were saved, and so provided a rough equivalent of random assignment to conditions of disaster and non-disaster.

Because research in the field deals with everyday life, it tends to minimize suspicion by the subjects. Their responses are more spontaneous and less susceptible to the kinds of bias suspicion can produce in the laboratory. Whenever college students know they are subjects in an experiment, there is always the possibility that they are not behaving naturally. For instance, they may be try to please the experimenter or present themselves in a socially desirable manner, or they may distrust the experimenter and not believe the experimental manipulation. Any of these effects could produce bias in the results or obscure actual cause-and-effect relationships. The advantages of field and laboratory research are compared and summarized in Table 1-2.

METHODS OF DATA COLLECTION

The next step is to decide on a technique of data collection. Basically, we have three options: (1) We can ask research participants to report on their own behaviors, thoughts, or feelings, (2) we can observe participants directly, or (3) we can go to an archive and use data originally collected for other purposes.

SELF-REPORT.   Perhaps the most common technique of data collection in social psychology uses self-reports. People can be asked their preference between two presidential candidates, as in national polls done before each election. Children can be asked to report on their perception of their classmates' aggressiveness, or on their own actual television viewing behavior, as in Huesmann's study. People can be asked to fill out detailed questionnaires about their romantic relationships. In all these cases, the basic data are the individuals' own reports about their thoughts, feelings, and actions.

The big advantage of self-report questionnaires or interviews is that they allow the investigator to measure subjective states such as perceptions, attitudes, or emotions. These can only be inferred indirectly from observational studies. For example, it would be difficult for observers to tell how lonely another person feels without getting that person's self-report. The principal disadvantage of self-report is that we

TABLE 1-2
Characteristics of Field and Laboratory Research

	Field	Laboratory
Advantages of Laboratory		
Control over variables	Low	High
Random assignment	Rarely	Almost always
Convenience and economy	Low	High
Advantages of Field		
Realism	High	Low
Impact of independent variables	Tends to be higher	Tends to be lower
Minimizes suspicion and bias	Yes	No
External validity	High	Low

must rely on people to give honest descriptions of their own internal feelings. People are often willing to give honest and full answers, especially when their privacy is carefully protected. But researchers also know that people sometimes disguise socially unacceptable feelings (such as racial prejudices) and that people are sometimes not fully aware of their own feelings.

OBSERVATIONAL RESEARCH.   Direct observation is a widely used research technique. In experimental studies, researchers interested in helping behavior have staged fake emergencies in public places to see how many people are willing to come to the aid of a stranger in distress. In studies of group behavior, researchers might make video recordings of a group discussion and systematically count such things as the number of times each person speaks, the number of times each person is interrupted by someone else, the amount of smiling and joking, how frequently group members look at the leader, and so on. Marital researchers have obtained permission to place microphones in homes and to record family interactions so that they can learn about the frequency of conflict, fighting, praising, and other types of interaction.

ARCHIVAL RESEARCH.   In **archival research,** the investigator uses data that were previously collected for another purpose. For example, researchers who wanted to examine whether violence against blacks was associated with frustration based on economic difficulties used historical records to correlate cotton prices and lynching of blacks in the southern United States (Hovland & Sears, 1940). They found that the greatest number of lynchings occurred during the years with the lowest cotton prices. Perhaps the best-known archival data come from the U.S. Census that has been conducted every 10 years for two centuries. But many specialized data banks also exist with the records of polls, surveys, and large-scale studies.

There are many advantages to using archival data. The most obvious is that it is inexpensive. The U.S. Census costs millions of dollars to col-

Every ten years, the U.S. Census Bureau sends trained interviewers to collect vital statistics about the general population. This information then becomes part of a vast archive, spanning 200 years, that is available for use by social scientists.

lect, but the data can be used for next to nothing. Archival data also allow us to test hypotheses at various time points or even trends over time, rather than being limited to one historical moment. We might want to know how many people say they would vote for a woman for president, and the availability of archival data on that question over many years can provide a rich historical context for our findings. On the other hand, archival data almost always were collected with some research question in mind other than the one we wish now to investigate. As a result, the questions are usually not exactly the ones we would ask, or they may be worded the wrong way for our purposes, or the participants in the study may not be exactly the group we would prefer. Nevertheless, data archives can often provide a useful source of data for social psychological research.

BIAS IN RESEARCH

All scientists are concerned about possible bias in their research, and social psychologists are no exception. Two kinds of bias are particularly troublesome in social psychology: the effects of the experimenter's behavior and bias associated with a subject's feelings about being in a study.

Experimenter Bias

One problem that is particularly troublesome in social psychology is **experimenter bias.** Research participants are extremely susceptible to influence by the experimenter. If the experimenter implies, consciously or otherwise, that he or she would like subjects to respond in a certain way, there is a tendency for participants to respond in that way. Subtle cues tend to be picked up by subjects and to influence their behavior. For example, consider the studies of media violence in which subjects give electric shocks to another person after watching either a violent or a nonviolent movie. A well-intentioned but perhaps overly eager experimenter, expecting that subjects in the violent-movie condition may be the most aggressive, might subtly encourage these subjects to give more shocks by smiling, nodding, or making eye contact when the expected behavior occurred. For the subjects who had seen the nonviolent movie, the researcher might frown or act cold when they gave the shock, because they were violating the hypothesis.

There are two solutions to the problem of experimenter bias. One is to keep the people who actually conduct the research (often research assistants) uninformed about the hypotheses or the experimental conditions to which a particular subject was assigned. For example, in research on TV violence, we could have one experimenter show the movies, and a second researcher administer the shock task, and arrange it so that the second experimenter did not know which movie the subject has seen. The second experimenter is said to be "blind" to the condition the subject is in.

A second solution is to standardize the situation in every way possible. If everything is standardized and there are no differences between conditions other than those that are deliberate, there should be no bias. In the extreme case, the subjects might appear for an experiment, find a written instruction on the door telling them to enter and turn on a tape recorder, have all instructions presented on tape, and complete the experiment before they meet a live experimenter. In this way, every factor in the situation would be absolutely standardized, and experimenter bias would be eliminated.

In actual practice, the solution to the problem of bias is usually a combination of the two procedures we have described. As much as possible, the researcher is kept "blind" to the subjects' experimental conditions. Also as much as possible, instructions are standardized by the use of tapes or written materials.

Subject Bias and Demand Characteristics

Another source of bias in social psychology research stems from the subject's motives and goals when serving in the role of a research participant. **Demand characteristics** refer to "features introduced into a research setting by virtue of the fact that it *is* a research study and that the subjects know that they are part of it" (Aronson, Brewer, & Carlsmith, 1985, p. 454). The basic idea is that the mere fact of knowing that you are being studied may alter your behavior. Subjects may try to "figure out" the true purpose of the experiment and alter their responses on the basis of their guesses about the study. They may try to give the "correct" or socially desirable response—to portray themselves as smart or politically liberal or religious or sexually responsible, depending on their interpretation of the situation. If subjects' responses are biased in these ways, it becomes difficult for researchers to draw accurate conclusions.

Weber and Cook (1972) have carefully analyzed the roles subjects adopt in laboratory experiments. They distinguish several different roles: "good subjects," who try to help the researchers by confirming the hypothesis; "negativistic subjects," who try to sabotage the experiment; "faithful subjects," who scrupulously follow the instructions and try to avoid acting on the basis of any suspicions about the nature of the study (either to help or to hurt the research); and "apprehensive subjects," who are mainly anxious about their own performance.

These biases are almost impossible to eliminate entirely, but they can be minimized in a variety of ways. The goal is to produce a situation in which subjects respond spontaneously without worrying about the correctness of their response or trying to figure out what the situation "demands." Several approaches are commonly used. When possible, researchers may use unobtrusive measures, in which the subjects do not know that they are being studied. For instance, pedestrians who encounter a handicapped person who has fallen on a city street may never know that the person is actually a researcher conducting a study of helping behavior. Another approach is to guarantee participants that their responses are anonymous; no one, including the researcher, will know how any individual reacted.

Perhaps the most common approach is to try to keep subjects unaware of the goals and hypotheses of the study. For instance, a researcher interested in sex differences in initiating conversations with strangers might ask subjects to volunteer for a study of political attitudes or taste preferences. While the subjects are waiting for the alleged study to begin, their behavior in the waiting room might be observed, perhaps with the help of a confederate who behaves in a standardized way in the waiting room. In this situation, subjects would expect to participate in one type of study and might not suspect that the time they spend in the waiting room is of any interest to the researcher. All these techniques reduce the possibility that participants' reactions will be distorted or changed by their concerns about social desirability.

Replication

We have reviewed a variety of research issues including the selection of research participants, the choice of correlational versus experimental designs, and the use of lab versus field settings. We have emphasized that each type of research has its own advantages and disadvantages. We also discussed various kinds of bias that can affect social research.

It is important to emphasize that no one study, however beautifully crafted, is ever perfect. Each procedure has its own defects. And we can virtually never test the entire population of interest to us, so there is always some margin of error in our ability to generalize our results. Because any single study is flawed, a hallmark of good research in social psychology is **replication.** In its simplest form, replication means that we are able to reproduce the findings of other researchers if we recreate their methods. So, for example, researchers should be able to recreate the experimental procedures used by Darley and Latané to study the effects of diffusion of responsibility on helping behavior—and should find comparable results. This is a fundamental requirement for all science, that different researchers working in different settings can all produce the same effects. Of course, in social research, it is seldom possible to recreate precisely every aspect of a study, because the subject population may be somewhat different, the social and political climate may have changed over time, and so on. Consequently, when we are able to replicate results, we have much greater confidence in their accuracy.

In addition to conducting exact replications, it is also important to conduct conceptual replications. In a *conceptual replication,* different research procedures are used to explore the same conceptual relationship (Aronson et al., 1985). For example, we have seen that research on the effects of TV violence on aggressive behavior has been conducted in both lab and field settings, using both correlational and experimental designs, and using diverse measures of aggressive behavior and a wide variety of violent films. To the extent that all these different techniques yield the same results, we become increasingly confident that we understand the phenomenon in question. The RESEARCH CLOSEUP for this chapter discusses

As the number of studies on a particular topic increases, researchers are confronted with a new problem: how to read and synthesize research findings to arrive at general conclusions. Consider work on sex differences in helping behavior. Eagly and Crowley (1986) identified no fewer than 172 separate studies that investigated male–female differences in helping behavior! How are researchers to handle this ever-increasing quantity of empirical research?

In recent years, new statistical techniques called **meta-analysis** have been developed to help researchers review and synthesize empirical findings systematically (Miller & Cooper, 1991; Schmidt, 1992). The first step is for the researcher to find as many studies as possible on the same topic. Then, meta-analysis uses statistical methods to pool information from all available studies. The goal is to arrive at an overall estimate of the size of the finding—for instance, the size of a particular sex difference. We might find, for instance, that the average sex difference on skill X is less than a tenth of a standard deviation—quite a small effect that may not be of much practical importance.

In meta-analysis, statistics are also used to test for the consistency (homogeneity) of findings across studies. When results from different studies are found to be highly consistent, we can have much confidence in the finding. When results of studies differ, meta-analysis techniques direct the researcher to look for other factors that may be important. For example, if we find 40 studies showing that men are better at skill X and 40 studies showing that women are better at skill X, we might suspect that some factor other than gender makes a difference. Perhaps men are better at skill X only when tested by a male experimenter, or only in group testing situations, or only if they come from working-class backgrounds. Instead of merely commenting that the findings are inconsistent, the goal is to try to identify the reasons for the inconsistency. So additional analyses would be conducted, taking these new factors into account. As you read this textbook, you will find references to meta-analyses about numerous facets of social behavior.

meta-analysis, a popular new method for interpreting the results of many studies on the same topic.

The basic point is that we should be cautious about taking too seriously the results of a single study on a topic. Rather, we should ask whether any particular finding has been confirmed in other studies. And we should also ask how large and important the finding is in practical terms. For example, of all the possible variation in human aggression, how much can be attributed to TV violence? Are the sex differences we hear about so often really big enough to make a difference in everyday life? As you read magazines and newspapers or watch the news on TV, you will often hear about research on such diverse topics as the health dangers of cholesterol, the latest word on teen sex, the virtue of seatbelts, and the causes of child abuse. Use your knowledge of research methods and the importance of replication to be a sensible and cautious consumer of research reports.

RESEARCH ETHICS

During the late 1950s and early 1960s, many people became concerned about the ethics of research on human subjects. Some of the concern stemmed from the discoveries of Nazi atrocities during World War II, such as the dangerous and often fatal medical experiments carried out by doctors in concentration camps on unwilling prisoners. Ethical issues were also raised by the discovery of medical experimentation of dubious ethicality in the United States, such as the notorious Tuskegee case. In 1932, the U.S. Public Health Service began a 40-year experiment on 399 poor and semiliterate black men in Tuskegee, Alabama, who had syphilis. The goal was to trace the effects of syphilis on untreated males over many years. The men were told they were being treated, but in fact they were never given medication, despite the fact that penicillin became available in the 1940s and was highly effective against the disease. Even by 1972, treatment was still withheld from the survivors as the study continued.

In social psychology, concern was raised about the use of deception. Consider some of the lab studies of the effects of TV violence on aggression. Is it ethical for a researcher to tell a subject to administer what he or she believes are painful electric shocks to another person when, in fact, the shock machine is fake and the other person is a confederate? Might the experiment cause the subject to feel guilty for hurting another person? If at the end of the study the researcher explains that the shock machine was not real, will the subjects feel foolish that they were duped by the experimenter?

Such studies raise a number of issues. When are researchers justified in deceiving subjects about the research they are participating in? When is it legitimate to do harmful things to subjects? Is it justifiable to expose subjects to risks if the potential scientific value of a study is great? These questions led to efforts within many professional associations to define ethical behavior. In 1972, the American Psychological Association developed a set of guidelines, later published as *Ethical Principles in the Conduct of Research with Human Participants,* which is revised from time to time as new issues arise (Blanck, Bellack, Rosnow, Rotheram-Borus, & Schooler, 1992). In addition, the United States government has also established procedures for the review of all research funded by federal monies. The government requires each university and research institution that receives federal funds to establish a committee of researchers to review all proposed research using human subjects. This institutional review board is responsible for ensuring that all research is conducted according to a set of general principles laid down by the federal government. Two important ethical principles in psychological research are informed consent and minimal risk.

Informed Consent and Debriefing

Informed consent means that a subject must voluntarily agree to participate, without any coercion, and must understand what the participation involves. The researcher has an obligation to tell potential subjects as much as possible about the study before asking them to participate. Subjects should be informed about the research procedures, any risks and/or benefits of the research, and their right to refuse to participate or to withdraw anytime during the research without penalty. Any exception to this general guideline must be approved by the institutional review board after careful examination of the planned research.

The requirement of informed consent sounds quite reasonable, but can sometimes create problems for social psychologists. As we have just seen, it may be important not to tell subjects the true purpose of the study, to avoid biasing their responses. Even in the simplest research, subjects are rarely told the specific hypotheses that are being tested. Several of the studies we discussed in this chapter did not provide fully informed consent, and it is hard to see how they could have. Imagine what would happen if researchers first told subjects that the study concerned willingness to help strangers in distress, and then tested to see if the subjects would help in an emergency. It is difficult to believe that this research would be valid.

Some people believe that deception of any kind is unethical in psychological research. They think it demeans the subjects and should never be used. A more moderate position endorsed by most research psychologists is that deception should not be used if at all possible, or used only after considering whether the benefits of the study outweigh any possible harmful effects. Subjects, however, should always be volunteers. Perhaps they need not be told everything that will happen, but they should know that they are in an experiment and should freely give their permission. In other words, only someone who has given informed consent or consent based on trust should be exposed to potentially distressing conditions.

At the end of their participation in a study, subjects should always be debriefed. By **debriefing** we mean that the purposes and procedures of the research are explained in some detail. Participants should be given an opportunity to ask questions and express their feelings. A friendly discussion between the researcher and participants can help subjects to recover from any upset the research may have caused and to learn from their research experience. When research deals with very sensitive topics, it may be important for the researcher to suggest ways in which participants can learn more about the topic by reading or consulting with experts. Sometimes researchers offer to send participants written information about the results of the research, once the research findings have been analyzed.

Minimal Risk

A second ethical guideline for research is to minimize potential risks to the subjects. **Minimal risk** means that the risks anticipated in the research are no greater "than those ordinarily encountered in daily life." What are the kinds of risk social psychological research can pose?

One of the most important is the invasion of privacy. An individual's right to privacy must be respected and valued. Researchers studying especially sensitive topics, such as sex, drug or alcohol use, illegal behavior, or religious beliefs, must protect the subjects' right to withhold such information and/or to have their responses kept in strict confidence. On the other hand, public behavior and events on the public record do not have to be protected as carefully. Anyone can go to the local courthouse and look up information on births, marriages, and deaths. Threats to privacy, like all risks involved in social psychological research, can change over time as the society itself changes. For example, people are much more willing to discuss details of their sexual relationships now than they were a generation ago. Today, there is widespread concern about keeping the results of AIDS testing confidential, because disclosure that a person has been infected can jeopardize his or her health insurance, employment, and standing in the community. Responsible researchers protect subjects' privacy by guaranteeing confidentiality and often by having the person participate in the study anonymously.

The other main category of risk in social psychology research comes from stresses of various kinds. Subjects in some studies may become bored, anxious, or fearful. Some studies may threaten the individual's self-respect. As we will see in Chapter 4, many studies in recent years have investigated the causal explanations that people make for their own successes and failures. To do such studies frequently requires that subjects be exposed to success or failure on an experimental task. A gratuitous failure experience in a psychology experiment is no fun. Being deceived is itself an unpleasant experience for some people. Smith and Richardson (1983) surveyed students who had participated in psychology experiments at the University of Georgia. Twenty percent of students reported experiencing some harmful consequence, such as being deceived, feeling humiliated, experiencing physical discomfort, or being angered. Such reports were almost twice as common among students who had participated in deception experiments as among those who had not. Most students reported no harm, of course, but a substantial minority did.

How much risk should a subject be exposed to? The first and most important principle is once again informed consent. If at all possible, the subjects must be allowed to make that decision for themselves, based on adequate information. The situation is like the decision people face about what surgical procedure to undergo: Ultimately, the decision must be in the hands of the patient, but it must be as informed a decision as possible.

It is not always possible to inform a subject fully about the exact nature of a study. In such cases, the researcher and the institutional review board must decide how much risk to allow. As stated above, the risks faced in the research should be no more severe than those likely to be encountered in normal life. Being threatened with an injection may be frightening, but it is a usual occurrence. Being threatened with isolation for 5 hours is also frightening, but it is not a common occurrence; most people never face this threat. So we would be more hesitant about deceiving a person about isolation than about a harmless injection.

Finally, another general rule many researchers and review boards use in evaluating risk is that the subjects should leave the study in essentially the same state of mind and body in which they entered. That is, participation in the study should have no substantial effect that carries over once the subject has finished the experiment. The study may be pleasant, interesting, and enjoyable, or mildly unpleasant, boring, or tedious, but the subjects' state of mind, knowledge of themselves, and general attitudes should not be altered by the experiences. This guideline, if followed closely, would ensure that subjects would not have been exposed to excessive risk.

At its best, social psychological research offers the joy of new discoveries about human experience. The thoughtful use of scientific methods can do much to advance our understanding of social life and social problems. But psychological research also carries with it the responsibility to treat research participants with sensitivity and high ethical standards and to repay their valuable assistance by sharing our research results with the public. In the chapters that follow, we offer a guided tour of the major findings and theories in social psychology.

KEY TERMS

archival research
association
attribution
behaviorism
collectivism
correlational research
culture
debriefing
decision-making theories
demand characteristics
dependent variable
diffusion of responsibility
expectancy-value theory
experiment
experimenter bias

external validity
frustration–aggression hypothesis
gestalt
imitation
incentive theory
independent variable
individualism
informed consent
internal validity
learning theory
meta-analysis
middle-range theories
minimal risk
modeling
observational learning

operational definition
psychoanalytic theory
random assignment
random sample
reinforcement
replication
reverse-causality problem
social cognition
social exchange theory
socialization
social learning theory
social norm
social psychology
social role
third-variable problem

SUMMARY

1. Social psychology is the scientific study of how the thoughts, feelings, and behaviors of individuals are influenced by other people. Social psychology emphasizes how factors in the immediate social situation affect behavior. It is less concerned with large social forces than are the other social sciences, and it is less concerned with unique personal characteristics and individual differences than are personality and clinical psychology.

2. Major theoretical approaches in social psychology include motivational theories, learning theories, cognitive theories, decision-making theories, and social exchange theories. These are not necessarily contradictory. Rather, each emphasizes one aspect of the causes of behavior without necessarily claiming that the others are unimportant or irrelevant.

3. A sociocultural perspective emphasizes how behavior is affected by cultural values, social norms, and social roles. Cultures differ in the relative emphasis they give to individualism versus collectivism.

4. Today, most social psychologists are working to develop middle-range theories or models to explain specific aspects of human behavior, such as the diffusion of responsibility or the frustration–aggression hypothesis.

5. We all know a great deal about social behavior from our daily observations and experience. Systematic research is necessary to test which of our intuitions are right and which are wrong. Social psychological research has four goals: description, causal analysis, theory building, and application.

6. Descriptive research starts with a general question about human behavior and tries to describe behavior accurately and to discover relationships among variables. Theoretical research is designed to test a theory, to compare two theories, or to assess the limits and exceptions to a theory.

7. Research participants should represent the people about whom we later want to generalize. A random sample is ideal but costly, and so many researchers compromise and use more readily available samples such as college students. Critics warn that an over-reliance on white, middle-class, college students may bias research results and limit their generalizability.

8. Correlational research asks whether two or more variables are related, without trying to manipulate either variable. Correlational research can deal with many variables at once, and can investigate phenomena that cannot usually be manipulated in the laboratory, such as crime, divorce, or rape. But correlational research usually does not allow strong causal conclusions to be drawn.

9. In an experiment, subjects are randomly assigned to conditions that differ only in specific deliberately varied ways (independent variable). If there is any difference in the resulting behavior (dependent variable), it is due to the independent variable controlled by the researcher. Experiments permit unambiguous causal statements.

10. Laboratory research provides more control and greater internal validity, but research in field settings is closer to the real world and often has greater external validity. The most common sources of data in social psychology are self-reports, systematic observations of behavior, and data archives.

11. Great care must be taken to avoid the effects of bias. Unless the experimenter is "blind" to experimental conditions and hypotheses, he or she can unintentionally bias the results. When responding to demand characteristics of the research situation, subjects may try to give "correct" or socially desirable responses, thus biasing results. Because any one study is inevitably flawed, replication is an essential feature of good research.

12. Social psychologists face many ethical issues in doing research. They must be careful to guard the safety of subjects, to respect their privacy, and to ensure that the research does not cause harm. Current guidelines emphasize obtaining informed consent to whatever extent possible and exposing subjects to no more than minimal risk.

SUGGESTED READINGS

Aron, A., & Aron, E. (1989). *The heart of social psychology* (2nd ed.). Lexington, MA: D. C. Heath (paperback). A delightful insider's view of the field, filled with fascinating stories about important people and research in social psychology.

Cook, T. D., & Campbell, D. T. (1979). *Quasi-experimentation: Design and analysis issues for field settings*. Chicago: Rand McNally. The use of nonexperimental techniques in field studies is becoming increasingly important.

Judd, C. M., Smith, E., & Kidder, L. H. (1991). *Research methods in social relations* (6th ed.) An excellent introduction to research design, subject selection, methods of assessment, data analysis, and research ethics.

Lindzey, G., & Aronson, E. (Eds.). (1985). *The handbook of social psychology* (3rd ed., 2 vols.). New York: Random House. A comprehensive survey of the major topics, theories, and methods in social psychology, written by leading experts.

Ross, L., & Nisbett, R. E. (1991). *The person and the situation: Perspectives of social psychology*. New York: McGraw-Hill (paperback). A lively introduction to key issues in the field; includes a chapter on the social psychology of culture.

Sears, D. O. (1986). College sophomores in the laboratory: Influences of a narrow database on social psychology's view of human nature. *Journal of Personality and Social Psychology, 51*, 515–520. An analysis of the possible dangers of relying too heavily on college sophomores in laboratory experiments.

2
Person Perception

FOCUS OF THIS CHAPTER

What Information Do We Use?
Integrating Impressions
The Cognitive Approach
Accuracy of Judgments
Nonverbal Communication
The Problem of Deception

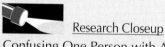
Research Closeup
Confusing One Person with Another

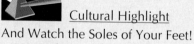
Cultural Highlight
And Watch the Soles of Your Feet!
Nonverbal Communication Across
Cultures

wo freshmen destined to be roommates arrive at college and meet for the first time. Each one's personality—how easily each one is to get along with, how nice each is—will have an important effect on the other's life. In the first few minutes of their meeting, each tries to form an impression of the other, because they know they will be spending a great deal of time together during the year. How late does each one stay up studying at night? What kind of music does the other like? How does each feel about parties in the room? They try to find out as much about each other as they can.

People use whatever information is available to form these impressions of others—to make judgments about their personalities or hypotheses about the kinds of persons they are. In this chapter we deal with this process, which is called **person perception:** how we make impressions, what biases affect them, what kinds of information we use in arriving at them, and how accurate our impressions are.

WHAT INFORMATION DO WE USE?

Our knowledge and expectations about others are determined by the impressions we form of them. A glance at someone's picture or at an individual passing on the street gives us ideas about the kind of person he or she is. Even hearing a name tends to conjure up images of what its owner is like. When two people meet, if only for an instant, they form impressions of each other. With more contact, they form fuller and richer impressions that determine how they behave toward each other, how much they like

each other, whether they will associate often, and so on.

PHYSICAL CUES. As this discussion implies, generally we draw on other people's appearance and behavior to infer qualities about them. Such factors as a person's sex, race, and physical appearance can lead us to form remarkably detailed impressions. The observation that a person is female, for example, may lead to the imputation of a variety of other characteristics, such as being nice or motherly. The observation that someone is black may call up a stereotype held about black people in general (Devine, 1989). We also use behavior to draw inferences about people. We observe a fellow student helping an elderly person across the street and infer that she is kind.

FROM BEHAVIORS TO TRAITS. The central point is that very quickly we move from observable information, such as appearance and behavior, to personality trait inferences about what the person is like (e.g., Albright, Kenny, & Malloy, 1988). Traits are a more economical and general way of describing a person than is referring to behaviors (Allen & Ebbesen, 1981). If someone asked you what your roommate is like and you had to recount each behavior you could remember, it would take you a long time and the person to whom you were describing your roommate might be little better informed by the process. Instead, you would use traits to summarize aspects of your roommate ("He is a good-natured, sloppy, night person with a penchant for loud rock music."). From this, the audience could infer that your roommate is generally easy to get along with, although he stays up late at night, plays his music loud, and doesn't pick up after himself. People use traits to describe others from the moment they first observe them, although the more we know someone, the more likely we are to use traits to describe the person (Park, 1986). In fact, the tendency to infer personality traits from people's appearance and behavior appears to occur rapidly, spontaneously, and automatically, so much so that people may not even be aware that they are doing it (Trope, 1986b, Gilbert, Pelham, & Krull, 1988).

COMPETENCE AND SOCIABILITY. The trait inferences that we make about other people fall out along two important dimensions. We tend to evaluate others in terms of their task-related qualities or intellectual competence, and their interpersonal or social qualities (Rosenberg, Nelson, & Vivekananthan, 1968; Kim & Rosenberg, 1980). But, of course, within these general dimensions, we also make more detailed impressions or judgments about a person, such as how nice he is to his parents versus his friends or how good he is at physics versus music.

THE PERSEVERANCE OF TRAITS. Once we have made personality trait inferences about the

meaning of another person's behavior, those inferences take on a life of their own. For example, you may recall your impression of your friend as kind and helpful long after you have forgotten the specific instance when she helped the elderly person across the street (Wyer, Srull, & Gordon, 1984). Asked if your friend is kind and helpful, you are more likely to refer back to your prior trait judgment than to a specific event (Fiske, Neuberg, Beattie, & Milberg, 1987). Trait inferences, then, are made quickly, virtually spontaneously, on the basis of minimal information about a person, and then often persist long after the information on which they were originally based has been forgotten.

Thus, people tend to form extensive impressions of others on the basis of very limited information. Having talked with a person for only a few minutes, people will tell us how much they like him and how much they think they will like the person if they can get to know him better. They will also make judgments about a large number of that person's specific characteristics. They are generally willing to estimate another's intelligence, age, background, race, religion, educational level, honesty, warmth, and so on. Although ordinarily individuals are not overly confident of opinions formed in this way, they generally are willing to make such judgments.

People form impressions of each other quickly. They use minimal information, such as sex, appearance, or a brief interaction to draw inferences about each other. What information do you think these students are using to form impressions of each other?

INTEGRATING IMPRESSIONS

As we have seen, people move quite quickly from observations of another's appearance and behavior to inferences about their personality. But how are these separate inferences put together into an overall impression? What are the most important aspects of impressions, and how do we put together information that may seemingly be inconsistent, such as the observation that our roommate is nice but self-centered?

Evaluation

The most important and powerful aspect of first impressions is **evaluation.** Do we like or dislike this person? How much do we like or dislike him? Our immediate impression may be composed of other dimensions; he may seem friendly, talkative, and helpful. But all these specific traits are fundamentally tied to the question of whether we like or don't like him (Park & Fink, 1989).

Put more formally, the evaluative dimension is the most important of a small number of basic dimensions that organize these unified impressions of people. This point was shown in a classic study by Osgood, Suci, and Tannenbaum (1957) using a measurement procedure called the semantic differential. In this method, subjects were given a list of trait pairs and asked to indicate which trait particular persons and objects fell closest to. The list consisted of such trait pairs as happy–sad, good–bad, strong–weak, and warm–cold, and the items the subjects had to rate ranged from mothers to boulders. For example, the subject had to rate whether "mothers" were "happy" or "sad," and so on. Osgood and his associates then analyzed the responses for any basic dimensions on which all things had been described.

Three underlying dimensions accounted for most of the ratings: *evaluation* (good–bad), *potency* (strong–weak), and *activity* (active–passive). Once a particular person or object was placed on these three dimensions, little additional information could be gotten from additional ratings. In other words, once we know that someone rates "mother" as very good, moderately strong, and somewhat passive, we learn little more about these perceptions of "mother" by asking for additional ratings. These three dimensions of person perception have a high degree of cross-cultural generalizability, being evident in the perceptions of members of many diverse cultures (Osgood, 1977; Osgood, May, & Miron, 1975).

Of the three, evaluation is the main dimension underlying perceptions, with potency and activity playing lesser roles. Once we place someone on this dimension, many other perceptions of him or her fall into place. Our evaluation of a person pervades our memories of what he or she is like (see Zajonc, Pietromonaco, & Bargh, 1982; Zajonc & Markus, 1984). A favorable or unfavorable impression in one context extends to most other situations and to other seemingly unrelated characteristics. On the whole, negative information seems to be more powerful in this respect than positive information. That is, in impression formation, we tend to pay special attention to negative information (Fiske, 1980; Pratto & John, 1991). And when we come to form an overall impression of the person, that negative information is weighed more heavily (Coovert & Reeder, 1990; Yzerbyt & Leyens, 1991; see Taylor, 1990, for a review).

The Averaging Principle

Suppose you've just met someone, and you notice that she is neat, tall, dark-haired, attractive, flirtatious, and "preppy" in dress. Or you meet someone else who is a premed student, deeply religious, a tennis expert, an extrovert, and engaged to be married. How do we put such separate pieces of information together into simple overall impressions?

Psychologists have two main views on this matter, one emphasizing learning and the other cognitive factors. The learning approach, in its simplest form, suggests that people combine information in a rather mechanical, simple-minded fashion, without thinking about it much. Just as a pigeon or a rat develops a habit rather mechanically, without seeming to interpret or give the experience meaning, so a person forms an impression without reinterpreting or analyzing available information very much. If we receive mainly favorable ideas about a person, we develop a favorable impression of that person. If we hear mainly unfavorable or lukewarm things, we develop that kind of impression instead.

Mixed impressions of others seem to follow an **averaging principle** (Anderson, 1965). Suppose Susan has just met her blind date, John. She quickly perceives that he is witty, intelligent, and courteous—but very short and poorly dressed. She processes this information in terms of how positive or negative she thinks those traits are. Suppose that she were asked to indicate her degree of favorable or unfavorable evaluation of those traits on a scale from +10 (very positive) to –10 (very negative). She might feel that being witty or intelligent are extremely favorable qualities and assign them the maximum value each (+10), that being courteous is quite favorable (+4), that being very short is somewhat unfavorable (–5), and that being poorly dressed is very unfavorable (–9). The averaging model suggests the person would receive an overall evaluation that was approximately an average of the five traits—that is, he would be considered moderately positive (+2). This is shown in Table 2-1.

Others have suggested that inferences are formed on the basis of an **additive principle.** It holds that people integrate separate pieces of information by adding scale values rather than averaging them. The major difference occurs when the person is confronted with two pieces of information on the same side of zero, one more extreme than the other. Suppose Susan had liked John very much (+6) but then she learned something new about him that was only mildly favorable, such as that he is "cautious" (+1). According to the averaging principle, she should like him a little *less* as a result, because the average (+3.5) is lower than the original evaluation (+6). According to the additive principle, however, she should like him more, because adding any additional positive information to an already positive impression should make it even more favorable.

Norman Anderson, in a series of careful experiments (1959, 1965), produced strong evidence in favor of an averaging rather than an additive principle. He found that when a piece of information that is only moderately favorable was combined with a previous very favorable impression, the overall evaluation did not increase and could even decrease. Similarly, two strongly negative traits produced a more negative evaluation than two strongly negative plus two moderately negative traits.

As a result of further research, Anderson proposed a refinement that predicts impression formation even more accurately—the weighted averaging model (1968a). According to this model, people form an overall impression by averaging all traits but giving more weight to those they feel are most important. For example, an administrator interviewing scientists as candidates for a laboratory job would probably weigh "intelligent" more heavily than "attractive," but someone hiring an actor for a television commercial might reverse that priority. An administrator interviewing candidates for a job as a counselor in a rape crisis center might give "warmth" more weight than either intelligence or attractiveness. This research indicates quite convincingly that the best way to account for impression formation is the weighted averaging principle, though it is probably not the only principle at work.

TABLE 2-1
Susan Sizes Up Her Blind Date, John

Individual Traits	Susan's Evaluation
Witty	+10
Intelligent	+10
Courteous	+4
Very short	–5
Poorly dressed	–9
Overall impression	+10/5 = +2.00

Consistency

Evaluation also introduces distortions and inaccuracies into the person perception process in several different ways. One is that people tend to form evaluatively consistent characterizations of others, even when they have only a few pieces of information. We have a tendency to view others in a way that is internally consistent. Since evaluation is the most important dimension in person perception, it is not surprising that we tend to categorize people as good or bad, not as both.

We may then go on to perceive other traits as consistent with this basic evaluation. If a person is likable, she should also be attractive, intelligent, generous, and so on. If she is bad, she should be sneaky, ugly, and inept. Another person is not generally seen as both honest and dishonest, warm and frightening, considerate and sadistic. Even when there is contradictory information about someone, he or she usually will be perceived as consistently good or bad, likable or dislikable. The perceiver distorts or rearranges the information to minimize or eliminate the inconsistency. This may also happen when people perceive objects, but it is particularly strong in person perception.

This tendency toward evaluative consistency is called the **halo effect.** A person is seen as likable or not very likable, and all other qualities are perceived as consistent with this judgment. It is called the halo effect because one who is labeled "good" is surrounded with a positive aura, and other good qualities are attributed to him or her. The converse (what might be called a "negative halo" or a "forked tail" effect) is that someone labeled "bad" is seen as having all bad qualities.

Of course, it isn't always possible to make an impression of a person entirely evaluatively consistent. A man may be very nice to his friends, but treat his dog quite badly. A woman may be very outgoing with her friends, but clam up when she is with strangers. When traits are at least mildly congruent with each other, they are easy to integrate with each other. When they are incongruent and difficult to reconcile with each other, people sometimes just leave them unintegrated and recognize the incongruency (Casselden & Hampson, 1990).

Positivity Bias

Another general evaluative bias in person perception is toward positive evaluations of other persons. They are much more common than negative ones. This tendency for positive evaluations of other people to outnumber negative evaluations has been called the **positivity bias** (Sears, 1983).

For example, in one study students rated 97 percent of their professors in college favorably (that is, above "average" on a rating scale), despite all the mixed experiences students have in their college classes (Sears, 1983). Similarly, public opinion polls show that individual political leaders are consistently approved of more often than they are disapproved of (Sears, 1982). In Gallup polls done in the United States since the mid-1930s, about three-fourths of the specific persons asked about were liked by more people than disliked them. As you might expect, then, when an impression changes, it generally tends to become more favorable rather than more unfavorable, everything else being equal (Sears & Whitney, 1973).

There are some plausible hypotheses about why people are evaluated so leniently. One stems from what Boucher and Osgood (1969) have called the "Pollyanna principle" (see also Matlin & Stang, 1978). They have suggested that people feel better if they are surrounded by good things, pleasant experiences, nice people, good weather, and so on. Even when their houses are falling down, they are sick, neighbors are terrible to them, and the weather is dismal, they will evaluate their situation favorably. The result: Most events are evaluated "above average" most of the time; pleasant events are thought more common than are unpleasant ones; good news is communicated more frequently than is bad news; and pleasant words are recalled more accurately and recognized more quickly than are unpleasant ones. As a result, positive words are more common than negative words, in a wide variety of cultures and contexts.

Sears (1983), on the other hand, contends there is a special positivity bias in our evaluations of other human beings which he describes as the *person-positivity bias*. People feel more similarity to any other person they evaluate than they do to more impersonal objects, and therefore extend them a more generous evaluation. In fact, the person-positivity bias operates most in evaluations of individual people, and it does not show up as strongly when impersonal objects are being evaluated (see also Miller & Felicio, 1990).

Motivated Perception

Sometimes we are motivated to hold particular beliefs about another person. In being so motivated, we selectively search for information that will support the beliefs we want to hold. In one study (Klein & Kunda, 1992), subjects were told that a fellow student would either be their partner or their opponent in a forthcoming game. Those who expected the student to be their partner were motivated to see him as very high in ability, whereas those who expected him to be an opponent were motivated to see him as low in ability. After interacting with the student in a simulated quiz show during which the student got some answers correct and others wrong, the subjects' impressions corresponded to their motivations. Those who expected the student to be their partner thought he was smarter than those who expected him to be their opponent. This occurred even though the fellow student exhibited exactly the same pattern of answers in both conditions.

GOALS.　As we have seen, the impressions that we form of other people are not simply passive reflections of their attributes. One must actively organize information about another person into a more integrated impression. One factor that influences how this organization is achieved is the individual's goals in person per-

ception. For example, goals have been manipulated experimentally by telling subjects either to form a coherent impression of a person (impression formation goal) or to try to remember the separate bits of information they may be exposed to (remembering goal). Generally speaking, under impression goal conditions people form more organized impressions that reflect the underlying structure of the input information than when their goal is simply remembering the information (Lichtenstein & Srull, 1987; Matheson, Holmes, & Kristiansen, 1991).

Anticipating interacting with somebody creates very different social goals than simply trying to learn about them, and research shows that people remember more and organize the information differently when they expect to interact with someone in the future. For example, Devine, Sedikides, and Fuhrman (1989) asked subjects to learn information about five people under various goal conditions. One of the five persons was termed the target, and subjects' goals with respect to the target were manipulated. They anticipated interacting with the target, were told to form an impression of the target, were told to compare themselves with the target, were asked to compare the target with a friend, or were simply asked to recall the target's attributes. As Table 2-2 shows, anticipating interacting with the target in the future produced the greatest recall of the target's behavior. Paradoxically, compared to all the other goal conditions, simply being instructed to remember the target's attributes produced the lowest recall, both compared to other goal conditions and compared to the other four comparison persons.

Sometimes we may have a goal of forming an accurate impression. We may be trying to decide if a certain student should be our lab partner, if we should hire a friend to tutor us in chemistry, or if we should go out with the persistent young man in math class. The need to be accurate usually produces more extensive and less biased information-gathering about a person. In one study (Neuberg, 1989), students were asked to interview a job candidate. Half were led to expect that the candidate would be unpleasant, and the other half were given no

TABLE 2-2
The Impact of Goals on Recalling a Person's Attributes:
Expecting to Interact Led to Greater Recall Than in Any
Other Goal Condition

Recall	Anticipated Interaction	Impression	Self-comparison	Friend Comparison	Memory
Target	4.38	4.00	3.31	3.38	3.00
Average of four other people	1.80	2.33	2.53	2.22	2.23

Source: Devines, Sedikides & Fuhrman (1989), p. 686.

expectation about the interviewee. Crosscutting this expectation, half of the students were encouraged to form accurate impressions about the target, the others were not. Students who did not have a goal to be accurate formed impressions of the person that were relatively negative, consistent with the expectation they had been given. However, subjects who had been encouraged to be accurate formed more positive impressions, actively undermining the expectation they had been given through their more extensive and less biased information-gathering about the target.

One particularly powerful goal is communication. The process of putting information together for another person greatly influences not only what information people communicate to that other person, but also the impressions they finally form themselves. Sedikides (1990) asked subjects to form their own impressions of a target, but then to communicate either positive, negative, or neutral information about the target to a third individual. Communication goals completely determined the information provided to the third individual, overriding the subject's own impressions. In fact, subjects actually reformulated their own impressions in the direction of the positive, negative, or neutral impression thay had been instructed to convey.

AFFECTIVE CUES. Sometimes we use our own internal state as a basis for judging other people, and this can lead to systematic errors. For example, when we are aroused, we tend to perceive other people in a more extreme manner than

when we are not aroused (Clark, Milberg, & Erber, 1984; Stangor, 1990). Thus, for example, if you have just finished playing a brisk tennis game and you meet someone who strikes you as sleazy, your impression of the person as sleazy is likely to be more extreme than if you met the person having just come from reading a book.

Mood is another factor that can influence how another person is perceived (Erber, 1991). When we are in a good mood, we tend to see another person more positively, and when we are in a bad mood, we tend to view that person more negatively. These effects are especially true when the other person is behaving neutrally (Stangor, 1990; see also Isen, 1984, for a review).

To summarize, then, the process of putting together person information often depends heavily on motivational factors. These may include particular goals that we have, an affective state that we are in, or a motivation to hold a particular belief about another person. However, the process of person perception is also heavily cognitive, and it is to this issue that we now turn.

THE COGNITIVE APPROACH

We have described person perception as dominated by two assumptions: (1) that the process of impression formation reflects somewhat mechanically the nature of the stimulus person, and (2) that it is dominated by evaluation rather than cognition. Although there is much value in both these assumptions, they oversimplify the process. We do not just take in a literal copy of the environment. We are active, organizing perceivers. The focus on evaluation, though central to impression formation, is also incomplete. It ignores cognitive processing mechanisms.

The cognitive approach to impression formation emphasizes somewhat different features of the process. First, although human beings clearly have a greater capacity for processing information than other animals, it is not infinite. We can absorb only a limited amount of the stimulation we are bombarded with every minute, and when we need to retrieve it from our memory, we cannot get it all back in a flash. So any analysis of person perception must start out by acknowledging our limited processing abilities. We might be described as lazy perceivers (McGuire, 1969) or somewhat more charitably as **cognitive misers** (Taylor, 1981a). When we perceive other people and events, we try to cut corners and save effort.

Second, while we take in information selectively, we then organize it into a meaningful **gestalt** that makes sense out of the full input. Each piece of information is taken as an aspect of a coherent whole, rather than simply another isolated trait to be averaged into the overall impression. The major implication for impression formation is that processing is not mechanical, but involves an attempt to perceive some coherent *meaning* in the stimulus object.

The cognitive approach, therefore, views people as trying to develop meaningful impressions out of the information they have about another person (or event, or whatever), rather than just averaging in each separate element separately. This is what lies behind the old saying that "the whole is greater than the sum of its parts." The perceiver does not consider each separate piece of information in isolation, but tries to come to an impression about the person as a whole.

This emphasis on cognitive process is one of the main approaches to social psychology (Fiske & Taylor, 1991). At its core is the view that person perception is a cognitive process: People are actively organizing perceivers, not passive receptacles; they are motivated by the need to develop coherent and meaningful

impressions, not just likes and dislikes. And our limited processing capacities lead to the use of a series of cognitive shortcuts. These can produce efficiencies in processing, but they can also produce biases and errors. The cognitive approach is a supplement to the simpler, more mechanical processes described earlier. It asks what else is going on besides the simple judgment of liking or disliking.

Four general ideas have been developed from the cognitive approach:

1. Processing information about people involves perceiving some coherent *meaning* in the stimulus object. We try to understand the context for a person's behavior rather than interpret behavior in isolation.

2. Perceivers tend to pay special attention to the most *salient* features of the perceptual field rather than giving equal attention to everything. That is, figures who stand out, or figural aspects of a particular person, get more attention than does the background. On a rainy day, our attention is drawn to the police officer in the middle of a crowded intersection, because he or she is wearing a bright orange raincoat and all the other colors in the intersection are drab.

3. We organize the perceptual field by *categorizing* or grouping stimuli. Of course, everything we see, hear, smell, or feel is a little different from everything else, but we do not perceive them that way. Rather, we tend to see each separate stimulus as part of a category or group—a Porsche as a car and a person wearing a white lab coat as a doctor—even though each of these may have features that make them quite different from other cars or doctors.

4. We perceive stimuli as part of some kind of *structure.* Each separate stimulus tends to be related to others in time, space, and a causal flow. We see a downhill skier as part of a broader context: she is in a ski race, so she begins skiing when the starter gives the order, she skis between the flags down the hill, and she stops when she crosses the finish line. All we literally see is a young woman in motion, but that is part of a

much more complex cognitive structure that includes our knowledge of the rules of slalom racing and our impression of her grace, agility, and power. In other words, we spontaneously embed the individual in a broader structure of knowledge.

Seeking Meaning

CONTEXT.   The cognitive approach assumes that perceivers are trying to arrive at a meaningful impression of whole persons, rather than just to absorb each new piece of information separately. Their understanding of any new piece of information will depend in part on the context. The meaning of "intelligent" in the context of knowing that a person is a "warm, caring therapist" will probably be quite positive. But the meaning of "intelligent" when the person is otherwise a "cold, ruthless foreign spy" will probably be more negative; it makes the person seem even more dangerous. To predict the impact of new information, we need to know the context, because that influences its meaning.

Considerable research has shown that context does indeed influence the impact new information has on an existing impression. But the effects of context are a matter of some debate. Anderson (1966), consistent with his averaging approach, suggests that the influence of context on the value of a new attribute can be predicted by just averaging in its value along with the value of the new information. In this example, suppose "intelligent" is a + 2 when it is considered by itself. And suppose the value of the "cold, ruthless, foreign spy" context is −4. In this case, the contribution of "intelligent" to the overall impression would be influenced by its context, and so would be an average of its own value and that of its context, or − 1. On the other hand, if the value of "warm, caring" context is + 4, including "intelligent" would produce an overall impression of + 3 in that context. Anderson describes this effect of context as a *generalized halo effect*. As you can see, he does not assume much deliberate thought; the new attribute merely mechanically absorbs some of the good or bad feelings associated with the context.

For Asch (1946), on the other hand, working mainly out of the cognitive approach, the whole is more than an average of its parts. Perceivers create a meaningful whole out of the information given, and the whole will change with different information. So any given attribute will have different meaning if it is placed in a different context. Wearing only a bikini has quite a different meaning in a symphony concert hall than it does on a summer beach and would be evaluated quite differently.

Asch says a new attribute undergoes a **shift of meaning** when placed in a new context. "Intelligence" in a cold, ruthless person could be threatening, potentially hostile, and destructive. In a warm, caring person, "intelligence" might be expected to contribute to empathy, to insight, and to the ability to give to another person.

Considerable research has been done on these two explanations for context effects. One way to approach the controversy is to determine whether in fact a given trait has a different meaning in different contexts. Hamilton and Zanna (1972) and Zanna and Hamilton (1977) found that the connotations of a particular trait changed when placed in different contexts. For example, in a positive context the word "proud" bore the connotation of "confident." In a negative context, it connoted "conceited." Further, Wyer (1974) found that the evaluations of these connotations also reflected the context. To use this example, the connotation ("conceited") of the original trait ("proud") implied by a negative context itself bore a negative evaluation. Such studies show that contextual effects are partly determined by a shift-of-meaning phenomenon.

CENTRAL TRAITS.   A second point on which the evaluative and cognitive approaches potentially differ concerns whether or not certain traits imply more about an individual than others. The averaging approach simply assumes that all traits enter into the impression at whatever value they have; for example, "cold" is always a − 5, "warm" is always a + 7. The cognitive approach, instead, assumes that some traits are inherently more meaningful than others. For example, the pair of traits "warm–cold" appears to be associated with a great number of other characteristics, whereas the pair "polite–blunt" is associated with fewer. Traits that are highly associated with many other characteristics have been called **central traits** (Asch, 1946).

In a classic demonstration of their importance, Kelley (1950) gave students in psychology courses personality trait descriptions of a guest lecturer before he spoke. Half the students received a description containing the word "warm," and the other half were told the speaker was "cold"; in all other respects the lists were identical. The lecturer then came into the class and led a discussion for about 20 minutes, after which the students were asked to give their impressions of him. The results are shown in Table 2-3. There were great differences between the impressions formed by students who were told he was warm and those who were told he was cold. In addition, those students who expected the speaker to be warm tended to interact with him more freely and to initiate more conversations with him. The different descriptions affected not only the students' impressions of the other person, but also their behavior toward him.

The averaging model has been adapted to handle such phenomena. Its weighted averaged version assumes that some traits are more important than others, and therefore are weighted more heavily. Presumably warmth is one of these. Most of the time, it is very important to us whether someone is warm or cold, and perhaps not very important whether they are good jumpers or not. So we weigh very heavily any information about warmth or coldness in coming to an overall impression and give little weight to information about jumping ability. But this example also illustrates Asch's point about how context influences meaning. In the context of a party, "warm–cold" is probably quite a central trait, because it is so important to whether we enjoy the person or not. In the context of a basketball game or Olympic tryouts, "warm–cold" may not be central, and jumping ability may be weighted much more heavily.

Salience

People are sensitive to many cues in others, and use these cues to form impressions. But clearly people do not use all the cues available to them. A major relevant principle of perception is the **figure–ground principle.** According to this, people direct their attention to those aspects of the perceptual field that stand out—the figure—rather than to the background or setting—the ground. In the case of impression formation, the main implication is that the most salient cues will be utilized most heavily. If a student appears in a wheelchair the first day of class, everyone else in the room is likely to form an impression that is most heavily influenced by the fact of the person's physical handicap. Clothing, hair style, and perhaps even age, race, and sex will all be secondary.

What determines the **salience** of one cue as opposed to another? A number of clearly specifiable objective conditions make cues stand out. *Brightness, noisiness, motion,* or *novelty* are the most powerful conditions, according to gestalt principles of object perception (McArthur & Post, 1977). A man in a bright red sweater

TABLE 2-3
Effect of "Warm" and "Cold" Descriptions on Ratings of Other Qualities

Quality	Instructions[2]	
	Warm	Cold
Self-centered	6.3	9.6
Unsociable	5.6	10.4
Unpopular	4.0	7.4
Formal	6.3	9.6
Irritable	9.4	12.0
Humorless	8.3	11.7
Ruthless	8.6	11.0

Source: Adapted from H. H. Kelley (1950). *Journal of Personality, 18,* p. 434. Used with permission of Duke University Press.
  [2]The higher the rating, the more the person was perceived as having the quality.

stands out in a crowded classroom, and the sweater is his most salient feature. The student who gets up shouting in the middle of a lecture and leaves the room draws our attention because she is noisy and moving, and almost everything else in the classroom is quiet and stationary. So, anything that makes a cue objectively *unusual* in its context makes it subjectively more salient and more likely to be noticed.

EFFECTS OF SALIENCE.   Salience has a number of consequences for person perception. Salient behaviors draw more attention than do subtler, less obvious ones (McArthur, 1981). Second, salience influences perceptions of causality in that more salient people are seen as having more influence over their social context. The student who sits in front of the class and asks an occasional question is more likely to be perceived as dominating the discussion than the student who sits at the back and talks just as much.

Third, evaluations of salient people are more extreme than evaluations of less salient people. Taylor, Fiske, Close, Anderson, and Ruderman (1977) ran a series of experiments in which they varied the "solo" status of black group members; some groups had an even mixture of white and black members, other groups had only one black member. The "solo" black was clearly more salient than were the blacks in the evenly divided groups. A pleasant black group member was evaluated more favorably when "solo" than when in an evenly divided group, and an unpleasant one was evaluated more negatively.

Last, salience increases the coherence of an impression (Taylor, 1981b). If the salient person is a member of a stereotyped group, such as "drug addict," he or she will be seen as possessing other stereotyped attributes of that group, such as having criminal tendencies, weak moral character, slovenly manner and dress, and a lack of honesty.

Salient stimuli draw the most attention; they are seen as the most causally powerful, they produce the most extreme evaluative judgments, and they produce more consistency of judgment. These effects of salience have been described as "top of the head" by Taylor and Fiske (1978) because they seem to occur at the relatively superficial level of simply directing our attention. That is, they occur because they focus the perceiver's attention one way or another, not because they involve very deep changes in thinking. As might be expected, therefore, they seem to be strongest when the stimuli are sufficiently interesting and exciting to attract the perceiver's real attention. The

Which person in this group is most salient? Does the solo woman stand out? Salient people attract attention, we remember more about them, and we often interpret their behavior in stereotyped terms.

salience of different stimuli matters more when the perceiver is responding to exciting conversations, such as humorous debates, than when he or she is responding to stiffer, more formal and boring situations (McArthur, 1981). But salience effects appear to be rather general, occurring on important issues as well as unimportant ones (Taylor et al., 1979; Borgida & Howard-Pitney, 1983).

NEGATIVITY.　People weigh negative information more heavily than positive information in arriving at a complete impression (Taylor, 1991a). That is, a negative trait affects an impression more than a positive trait, everything else being equal (Fiske, 1980). This has been called the **negativity effect.** It follows that a positive impression is easier to change than a negative one (Hodges, 1974). People are more confident of evaluations based on negative traits than those based on positive traits (Hamilton & Zanna, 1972). The averaging principle does not hold for negative traits quite as well as it does for positive traits. The difference is particularly noticeable with more extreme negative traits. They seem to have a "blackball" effect: One extremely negative trait produces an extremely negative impression, no matter what other traits the person possesses (Anderson, 1965). For example, Lau (1982) found that voters' evaluations of presidential and congressional candidates in the period from 1968 to 1980 were more strongly shaped by negative information about the candidate than by positive information. When we are told that a prominent public leader is a "crook," our evaluation of him becomes quite negative, regardless of what else we know about him (e.g., Coovert & Reeder, 1990). If we are told he is "patient," we will just average that mildly positive quality in with whatever else we know about him.

The main explanation for this negativity effect is based on the figure–ground principle. As we noted in the discussion of the person-positivity bias, positive evaluations of other people are much more common than negative evaluations. Negative traits, being more unusual, are therefore more distinctive. In a simple percep-

tual sense, then, a negative trait is *figural;* it stands out the way an unusual deformity or bright clothing or something of great size stands out (Fiske, 1980). People may simply pay more attention to those negative qualities and give them more weight. For example, Lau (1985) found that negative information had more impact on evaluations of presidential candidates among those voters who were most trusting of government. That is, the negativity effect was strongest among those who generally respect political leaders, for whom negative information would be most figural.

The negativity effect is probably due mainly to the positivity bias we discussed earlier. The positivity bias suggests that positive evaluations outnumber negative evaluations. The negativity effect suggests that because negative evaluations are therefore more unusual, they then have more impact on impressions when they are present.

Categorization

Perceivers do not respond to salient stimuli in isolation; they immediately and spontaneously perceive stimuli as part of some group or category. We do not see that unshaven, dirty, disheveled man in the park with worn-out shoes and a couple of old shopping bags as just another human being; we immediately categorize him as a derelict. When we go to a basketball game, we usually categorize people right away into members of one or another of five social groups: players on one team or the other, referees, cheerleaders, and spectators. The **categorization** or grouping process is immediate and spontaneous, and does not take any time or thought, any more than you need to think about what category of objects your pencil belongs to.

CATEGORIZING PEOPLE.　At the crudest level, we categorize on the basis of natural similarities in appearance. We tend to assign people to the category of "men" or "women" on the basis of their physical characteristics, usually sex and culturally defined differences in appearance (hair length, makeup, type of clothing). The same is true of assigning people to other social groupings such as racial categories.

How do we go about putting people and objects into categories? Generally speaking, we compare a person or object with the **prototype** of the category. The prototype is an abstract ideal of the category. In our category for football player, for example, we probably have an abstract idea of what the person's body type is like, what he does in his free time, and perhaps even what fraternity he belongs to. Categorizing a new person as a football player, one may compare his attributes with those of the prototype for the category.

For some categories, people pay attention to **exemplars** of the category rather than prototypes (Rothbart & Lewis, 1988). Whereas a prototype is an abstract set of attributes of a category, an exemplar is a real example of the category. Thus, for example, in meeting a new person and trying to figure out if he is a football player, one may compare him to one's friend, Brian, whom one considers to be the exemplar of the category, football player, rather than comparing him to the more abstract prototype for the category, football player. When we learn the abstract attributes of categories, we also learn particular instances of the category that we have actually encountered. In many cases, then, we categorize objects and people by seeing if they resemble the exemplars that we store in that category. For example, if one is sizing up a new partner as a possible long-term boyfriend or girlfriend, usually the person is compared not only with a prototype for the ideal boyfriend or girlfriend, but also with "old flames," particular past boyfriends or girlfriends that made one's heart beat faster for a time (Fiske, 1982; Fiske, Neuberg, Beattie, & Milberg, 1987).

Overall, it is clear that people rely on a complex mix of ways for recognizing and classifying people and their behavior. We use prototypes for categories, groups, and situations about which we have little information, and we use both exemplars and prototypes for categories about which we have more information (Judd & Park, 1988; Linville, Fisher and Salovey, 1989).

What are the consequences of categorization?

Are these people acting in isolation or are they working together? We organize our perceptions by categorizing and grouping people, and in so doing we see them as part of a structured whole.

It speeds information processing time, as the "cognitive miser" idea suggests. For example, Brewer, Dull, and Lui (1981) presented subjects with photos of people in three different categories, "grandmother," "young woman," and "senior citizen," along with verbal labels clearly identifying their category. Then they presented the subjects with additional information about each target person, and measured how long the subjects took to incorporate the information into their impressions. Information consistent with the prototype of the category ("kindly" for "grandmother") was processed faster than information inconsistent with it (such as "aggressive" for grandmother).

Categorization can also lead to predictable sources of error, as the RESEARCH CLOSEUP suggests.

Schemas

A more complex organization of cognition is called a **schema**. This refers to an organized, structured set of cognitions, including some knowledge about the object, some relationships among the various cognitions about it, and some specific examples (Taylor & Crocker,

RESEARCH CLOSEUP
Confusing One Person with Another

How often have you called someone by the wrong first name? Perhaps you were having a conference with your teacher and accidentally called him "Dad." Or maybe you called your new boyfriend by the old one's name. All of us occasionally make these kinds of errors, and some of them get us into serious trouble! Psychologists have recently discovered that these errors can tell us a great deal about how we organize the information we have about people.

In a study conducted by Fiske, Haslam, and Fiske (1991), faculty, staff, and graduate students at a large university were asked to list all the times they could remember that they had been called by someone else's name. After these respondents had provided the incidents, they were coded for the relationships between the respondent and the person who had called them by the wrong name, and the relationship the person who made the error had with the person whose name the respondent was called by. It turns out that we tend to confuse two people when we have similar relationships to both people. So, for example, you may have called your teacher, "Dad," because both of them are male authority figures. And one of the more common errors, calling a boyfriend or girlfriend by the previous boyfriend or girlfriend's name, occurs for similar reasons: A supportive and intimate relationship with one person gets momentarily mixed up with a supportive, warm, and intimate relationship with another.

People rarely make errors involving a very different type of relationship. So, for example, you are very unlikely to call your professor by your ex-boyfriend's name, unless, perhaps, you are involved in a heated intellectual argument with the professor, and heated intellectual arguments were the mainstay of your relationship with your past boyfriend.

What is the significance of these errors? It suggests that the cognitive structure of our social relations and the perceptions we hold of other people are organized in memory not only in terms of those specific individuals, but also in terms of the nature of our social relationships with them. One of the reasons why we confuse people with each other, then, is that when we retrieve information from memory, information about one boyfriend or girlfriend, for example, may be stored close to information about another boyfriend or girlfriend, and we inadvertently retrieve the wrong information—in this case, the wrong name.

1981). We might, for example, have a schema of a "preppie," a WASP college student who wears alligator shirts and khaki pants, buys clothes from L. L. Bean, is partial to pink and kelly green, sports oxford cloth button-down shirts with madras ties, and likes to sail, jog, and play tennis. This "preppie" schema would probably not include going bowling, wearing Caterpillar tractor caps, driving a 1979 Chrysler Imperial, or having a beer belly.

What all schemas have in common is not their content, but their structural characteristics and the effects these have on processing.

Schemas help us to process complex bodies of information by simplifying and organizing them. They can help us to remember and organize details, speed up processing time, fill in gaps in our knowledge, and interpret and evaluate new information. As we will see, such preexisting cognitive structures organize the processing of new information. Our perceptions of new information are biased to make them consistent with what we already know. If we think someone is "warm," for example, we are more likely to talk to him and interpret his behavior as reflecting that warmth.

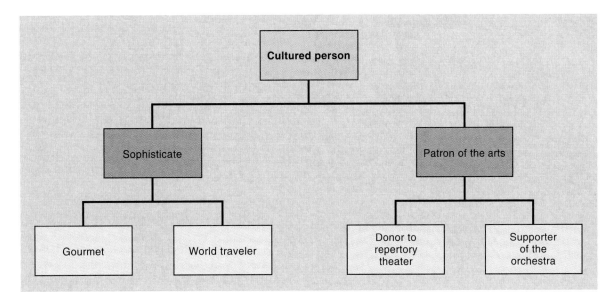

Figure 2-1 A schema for "cultured person." (*Source:* Adapted from Cantor & Mischel, 1979.)

Person schemas are structures about people. They can focus on a particular person—for example, Abraham Lincoln. The schema might include such elements as his being deliberate, honest, serious about his duties, and concerned for oppressed people. This would be a schema if in your view these qualities were all related to one another in President Lincoln, in the sense that you perceive them all as aspects of his basically decent and conscientious personality, not unrelated traits he just happened to display from time to time. Person schemas can also focus on particular types of people. For example, our schema of an "extrovert" might include such elements as "spirited," "outgoing," "enthusiastic," and "self-assured." The reasons we develop schemas for individuals is to help us gather information about them and to guide our subsequent social interactions with them. Figure 2-1 presents a diagrammable representation of a schema for a cultured person.

We also have *role schemas*. These represent the organized, abstract concepts we have of people in a particular role, such as cowboy, professor, receptionist, or devoted lover. Sometimes these schemas are unrealistic. If our schema for "devoted lover" includes elements such as always understanding, always supportive, never angry, never childish, and always concerned first with the other person's happiness, we could be in trouble. Not many people will live up to that schema.

Other schemas focus on groups. The most familiar is the group **stereotype,** which attributes specific traits to a particular group of people. An early study by Katz and Braly (1933) found white college students checking "superstitious," "lazy," and "happy-go-lucky" as the most common traits of blacks, and "scientifically minded," "industrious," and "stolid" as most common for Germans. Such stereotypes would be schematic if each perceived trait was part of a coherent underlying structure about the group. You might expect a student who is in the Beta fraternity to act like other Betas, or a black football player to act like other black football players, or people from Boston or Texas or Iran to resemble one another. All these involve having a particular schema for the personality and behavior of members of a group. We will take up stereotypes in some detail in Chapter 7.

People also have schemas for events, or stan-

People have schemas for particular social and occupational roles. Role schemas tell us what kind of behavior to expect from individuals in these roles, such as the filming being done by this photographer.

dard series of events. Sometimes such schemas are called *scripts* (Abelson, 1976). A script is a standard sequence of behavior over a period of time. One script might be called "ordering for a group in a Chinese restaurant." Everyone sits down, and the waiter brings the menus. Several people talk at once, giving their favorite dishes, while others say they never know what to have and would someone else just please decide. Then people go through the menu section by section, haggling over which soup to have, bargaining away their favorite beef dish (which no

People have scripts for common, organized sequences of behavior, such as ordering food in a restaurant or paying for a purchase in a store. These scripts help us to anticipate what will happen next and to prepare our behavior accordingly.

one else wants) for sweet and sour pork (which at least one ally does) and finally appointing the most self-confident and brash person to communicate the whole negotiated package to the waiter.

We could generate similar scripts for other ritualized series of events, such as having a baby, taking a shower, taking a final exam, or playing a basketball game. The essence of a script is in its boundedness in time, its causal flow (early events cause later ones), and in its being a simple, coherent, perceptual unit.

Organizing Impressions of Persons

Once we have formed impressions of other people, how do we organize them? Conceivably, we could think of important situations that we are in, such as "in the dorm" or "in class," and organize our impressions of people within those situations. But typically we don't. Our impressions of others are organized around them as people, and this is true even when those others are practically strangers. Thus, instead of thinking of Bob in terms of his being a fellow student in class, we think of Bob and his particular attributes, such as friendly, attractive, and serious.

How is this trait information organized? Psychologists have identified several ways in which we think about others. One viewpoint, called the **associationistic view,** maintains that we think of others in terms of trait covariations (e.g., Hamilton, 1981, 1989). According to this view, our expectations about a person's unknown qualities, such as shyness, are derived from beliefs about how traits go together. Thus, for example, on overhearing someone say that Bob is spirited, we might infer that he was probably outgoing and self-confident, even in the absence of other information about him. These inferences come from the web of presumed relationships among traits.

The **dimensional view** maintains that the structure of our thinking about other people relies on a small number of underlying dimensions. That is, we do not think about people at the microscopic level of individual trait covariations. Rather, we think about people in terms of a few global dimensions. As we have already seen, Osgood, Suci, and Tannenbaum (1957) considered those dimensions to be evaluation (good, bad), potency (strong, weak), and activity (active, passive) (see also Rosenberg, 1976). People also draw a major distinction between how a person is socially and how he or she is intellectually, and so these, too, appear to be important dimensions that we use to organize our impressions of people.

The **typological view** argues that people think of others in terms of types. Thus, for example, we might classify one friend as an extrovert, another as mature, and a third as a depressed, lonely type of person. We would see their other qualities as following from the general type of person we think they are (Anderson & Sedikides, 1991). There is evidence that people use all three ways of thinking about others— associationistic, dimensional, and typological.

ACCURACY OF JUDGMENTS

How accurately do people usually perceive others? One implication of these various evaluative and cognitive biases is that person perception must not be very accurate. On the other hand, people must be reasonably accurate for society to function as smoothly as it does. After all, we interact with other people a great many times every day, and these interactions usually require fairly accurate judgments. Since most interactions proceed without serious difficulties or mistakes, person perception must be fairly accurate.

People perceive external, visible attributes fairly accurately. It is generally no more difficult to judge the height of a person than it is to judge the height of a bookcase. The same is true of weight, skin color, or style of clothing. It is also fairly easy to make judgments about somebody's social role, as long as the appropriate cues are provided. The man in the blue suit with the gun strapped to his side is a police officer, and we treat him accordingly. The woman in the business suit with a briefcase rushing down a platform toward a train is obviously a commuter in a hurry to get to work, and we get out of her way to make it easier for her to catch the train. The contexts in which we see people enable us to make accurate assumptions about their roles.

But person perception becomes more difficult when we try to infer *internal states*—traits, feelings, emotions, and personalities. The bookcase obviously has none of these. However, we look at people and perceive them as angry, happy, sad, or frightened. We form an impression of another person and think of her as warm, honest, and sincere. We also make judgments about such internal characteristics as the person's attitudes toward various issues. We guess whether she is a Republican or a Democrat, religious or nonreligious, an environmentalist or not.

Judgments of such internal states as emotions, personality traits, and attitudes are often extremely difficult. The person's internal state cannot be observed directly—it must be inferred from whatever cues are available. Therefore, the question of accuracy focuses primarily on the judgments individuals can make of internal states, and on the cues used to make these judgments.

The Eye of the Beholder

One possibility raised by the tendency toward consistency is that perceivers may impose their own perspectives on the target person, rather than reflecting the real qualities of the target. For example, beauty may truly be in "the eye of the beholder" rather than being in the person being evaluated. This would lead to considerable inaccuracy in person perception, because everyone would have a different perception of the same person.

It does seem to be true that different people organize their perceptions of others along different dimensions. For example, one person might always describe others in terms of their sense of humor, another person in terms of their honesty, and still another in terms of their intelligence. This variety of perspectives was illustrated in a study by Dornbusch, Hastorf, Richardson, Muzzy, and Vreeland (1965). All children at a summer camp were asked to describe, in their own words, every other child. These descriptions were then analyzed in two ways: in terms of the characteristics each child used in making descriptions and in terms of the characteristics used in describing each child. The experimenters could then examine whether the same child was described the same way by most people or whether the same perceiver used the same characteristics to describe all the other children.

Intuitively, we would guess that perceivers would tend to describe a particular child the same way in terms of some outstanding characteristic, such as a sense of humor or aggressiveness. This was not the case. There was no agreement about which dimensions described any given child. Rather, each rater tended to use the same characteristics no matter which child was being described. The children differed among themselves as to which characteristics they used, but they all had their favorites which they used for virtually all their descriptions of others. So perceptions of other children depended more on who was *perceiving* than on who was *being perceived* (see also Beck, McCauley, Segal, & Hershey, 1988). The major implication of this phenomenon is that people do not see the world in the same way; they emphasize different aspects of other people and notice and focus on different qualities. These differences also extend to perceptions of physical characteristics.

Perceivers do arrive at more consensus on the likability of specific target persons than they do on their traits or other attributes, however. When one person talks about another's warmth and sense of humor and someone else talks about his kindness and good-naturedness, the only disagreement may be one of semantics. We generally agree more on how likable other people are than on why they are likable—whether it is their sense of humor, considerateness, intellectual ability, or whatever.

Park (1986) demonstrated this in a study of her seminar students. These seven students, who did not know each other well before the class, agreed to write out impressions of each other each week through the school term. This provided an opportunity to determine whether their impressions were due to the "eye-of-the-beholder" effect: Did each perceiver use his or her own favorite dimensions to describe all the various target persons, but different dimensions from those used by the other perceivers? Or were their impressions due to the real qualities of each target person? Did the perceivers generally agree on which dimensions applied to each target person?

She found a considerably stronger "eye-of-the-beholder" effect on the specific dimensions used to describe other people than on evaluations of those people. That is, two different judges tended to evaluate a given target person in about the same way, but each perceiver tended to use their own particular dimensions to describe the person, such as "yuppie," "the sunny, California beach type," "kind," "aware of her faults," or "loud and boisterous."

Judging Personality

Considerable research has been done judging the accuracy of perceptions of personality traits, such as dominance–submission or need for affiliation. This work is discouraging, for a number of reasons. First, as we have just seen, people's perceptions of others are determined more by their own idiosyncratic preferences for particular personality dimensions than by the objective attributes of the person being evaluated. This and other biases in person perception described earlier in this chapter lead social psychologists to believe that people are not very accurate in judging other people's personality dispositions. Second, it is very difficult to measure personality traits, so there is a problem in identifying the proper criteria for accuracy.

But a more major problem is that, according to some influential psychologists (such as Mischel, 1979), any given personality trait may influence behavior consistently in only a fairly limited range of situations. That is, we may have unique, idiosyncratic dispositions that make us regularly react in our own distinctive way to any given situation, but these may not be constant from one set of situations to another. It may, therefore, be more useful to think of personality traits as holding in some fairly limited set of situations, rather than to think of traits as holding in all situations.

For example, we know a man who frequently cheats at pool, and when he is playing golf, he often seems to replay poor shots without giving himself a penalty. But he is scrupulously honest in his dealings with coworkers and subordinates. Should we describe him generally as a "somewhat dishonest person"? Or are we better off saying that he is honest in professional situations and cheats at competitive games?

The problem this raises for the accuracy of person perception is that if personality traits are limited to certain classes of situations, they become more difficult for observers to judge accurately. The observers would need to perceive both the person's tendencies and the situation accurately. But people tend not to do this. As we will see in Chapter 5, observers have a tendency to ascribe general personality traits to people, ignoring the fact that people may behave quite differently in different situations.

Nonetheless, researchers have persisted in studying how people infer the traits of others. But because of the difficulties that exist in establishing criteria for accuracy, they have shifted their focus away from whether perceptions of others are accurate to whether there is agreement among raters or with judges (Funder, 1987). Some traits have behavioral manifestations that are more observable than others (Kenrick, McCreath, Govern, King, & Bordin, 1990), and so we ought to find greater agreement among judges on those more readily observable traits. This appears to be the case. For example, people show a lot of agreement in rating whether someone is extraverted or not, but they show a lot less agreement if their judgments are related to intelligence, honesty, or conscientiousness, traits that are more difficult to observe and to clearly confirm or disconfirm (Park & Judd, 1989). Ratings of likeability are even less likely to produce agreement among judges. People tend to form idiosyncratic preferences for other people, and so what seems to be an objective judgment, namely whether another person is likeable or not, is actually highly subjective (Park & Flink, 1989).

Another way in which researchers have addressed the accuracy issue, without actually establishing criteria for accuracy, is to measure the degree to which someone's judgments of another person match that person's own self-perceptions. Thus, for example, if you were asked to rate your roommate Suzie's friendliness, your rating of her friendliness might be compared with Suzie's self-rating to see how much you agree. Generally speaking, agreement between peer ratings and target ratings vary directly with how well they are acquainted (Malloy & Albright, 1990). When you know a person better, you are more likely to see that person the way the person sees himself or herself. When you know a person less well, however, agreement is more likely to be found if the particular attribute being evaluated is publicly visible, that is, has qualities that are actually open to observation (Paunonen, 1989).

Accurate perception of another person's attributes can often be improved by information about the situations in which it occurs. Certain situations allow more expression of particular traits, and so those situations may be more useful to perceivers in helping them infer the traits of others and, correspondingly, in being more accurate in their perceptions (Kenrick, McCreath, et al., 1990). In one study (Shoda, Mischel, & Wright, 1989), child counselors were shown videotaped segments of children's behavior and asked to judge the children on their personal qualities, such as how aggressive they were. Impressions among the judges were similar when they were based on the behaviors presented with no situation specified (e.g., "child hits"). However, when the investigators told the counselors what the situations were in which the child's behavior had occurred (e.g., "child hits when provoked"), the judges' impressions even more accurately predicted the children's typical behavior, in this case, the child's actual level of aggression. Similarly, knowledge of another individual's goals influences the degree to which people will make trait inferences from the observation of behavior.

If a particular behavior is strongly suggested by a particular goal, then judges are much more likely to make a trait inference about an individual from that behavior. Thus, for example, if

Linda wants badly to make the cheerleading squad and trips an opponent during practice, one may infer her ruthlessness with greater confidence than if she merely trips an opponent in the absence of a particular goal.

Somewhat surprisingly, even strangers are able to rate others in a manner consistent with those others' self-perceptions after relatively brief exposures to their behaviors. However, stranger–self agreements seem to occur primarily for behaviors that have a lot of observable referents, such as extraversion or warmth (Berry, 1990, 1991; Borkenau & Liebler, 1992; Paunonen, 1991; Watson, 1989), or when the consequences of accurate trait assessment are important (Gangestad, Simpson, DiGeronimo, & Biek, 1992).

Judges are more likely to reach consensus about another person's attributes if their outcomes are dependent on their inferences. Subjects in one study (Flink & Park, 1991) were told that they would observe eight of their peers being interviewed, and then choose one of the interviewees to teach them a game (outcome dependency). The judges then rated each of the targets on a number of attributes. Outcome dependency greatly increased the consensus among the judges and reduced idiosyncratic judgments based on factors irrelevant to the judgment, such as liking. Outcome dependency also seems to make judges more sensitive to the variability in a person's behavior across situations (Wright & Dawson, 1988). That is, they notice when a person is inconsistent and when he is not. Consequently, impression accuracy improves.

Unfortunately, though, when we take our inferences into the area of predicting future behavior, we fare rather badly. That is, for the most part, we are overconfident in predicting the behavior both of other people and even of ourselves (Dunning, Griffin, Milojkovic, & Ross, 1990; Vallone, Griffin, Lin, & Ross, 1990). This seems to be due to two factors. First, when people express high confidence that certain things will happen to themselves or others in the future, this is rarely warranted. As confidence increases, the gap between accuracy and confidence widens. Thus, for example, when California college students were asked to indicate how likely it was that their roommate would take his or her first job in California, many students expressed high confidence in this outcome; many of them were wrong, because finding and accepting a first job depends upon many factors in addition to the geographic locale in which you might want to live. Second, predictions that are statistically unlikely are very rarely accurate. Thus, for example, when asked how likely it was that most of their close friends during college would live outside their dorm, those students who said "highly likely" were usually wrong. They apparently ignored the fact that people usually form friendships on the basis of propinquity, namely who lives close by.

Recognition of Emotions

Much of the work on the accuracy of person perception has focused on the recognition of emotions, on whether a person is happy or afraid, horrified or disgusted. In a typical study, a person is presented with a set of photographs of people portraying different emotions, and asked to judge what those emotions are (Figure 2-2). Research has now shown the virtual universal recognition of several facial expressions of emotion in both literate (Ekman, 1972; Izard, 1971) and preliterate (Ekman & Friesen, 1971; Ekman, Sorensen, & Friesen, 1969) cultures. In a recent confirmation of this now-standard finding, Matsumoto (1992) had American and Japanese college undergraduates view expressions of six universal emotions (anger, disgust, fear, happiness, sadness, and surprise) posed by American and Japanese males and females. Both the Japanese and the American students were able to discriminate among the emotions, and to do so whether the person portraying the emotion was Japanese or American.

Even when they cannot discriminate very well among individual emotions, people can distinguish the major groups of emotions using facial cues. In fact, one study (Nakamura, Buck, & Kenny, 1990) found that people can better

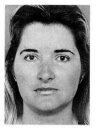
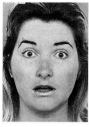

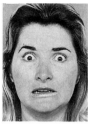

Figure 2-2 Examples of stimuli used in the study of perceptions of emotion. Each picture portrays a different emotion. Try to identify them before looking at the answers. (Top, left to right: neutral, surprise, happiness. Bottom: fear, sadness, anger.)

judge emotions from a person's facial and gestural expressions than they can from knowing the context that gave rise to the emotion.

Woodworth (1938) suggested that emotions can be arranged on a continuum, with the ease of distinguishing between any two emotions being related to the distance between them on this continuum. The continuum of emotions is

1. Happiness, joy
2. Surprise, amazement
3. Fear
4. Sadness
5. Anger
6. Disgust, contempt
7. Interest, attentiveness

People seem to be quite good at distinguishing emotions in categories that are three, four, or five points apart—they rarely confuse happiness with disgust or surprise with contempt. People have a particularly easy time distinguishing pleasant from unpleasant emotions in others' faces (again indicating the importance of the evaluative dimension in person perception). But they find it almost impossible to discriminate emotions in the same category or only one group away. Happiness and surprise are frequently confused, as are anger and disgust, for example.

More recent studies using the same kind of approach find a simpler structure with two basic underlying dimensions: pleasantness and arousal (Russell & Bullock, 1985). Positive emotions such as excitement and happiness were distinguished from negative ones such as fear, anger, and disgust. Among the positive emotions, arousing ones such as excitement can be distinguished from nonarousing ones such as contentment. Similarly, negative arousing emotions such as fear and anger can be distinguished from nonarousing ones such as sadness.

One artificial aspect of these studies has been that they involve static, posed faces, frequently using just one model. Later studies have used videotaped presentations, such as of ordinary people viewing a variety of emotionally evocative situations (Wagner, MacDonald, & Manstead, 1986). Others have used several different actors portraying different emotions in videotaped scenes (for example, Wallbott & Scherer, 1986). Again, the typical finding has been that expressions can be differentiated fairly well into those that express positive emotions (such as happiness) or negative emotions (disgust, sadness, or anger). To some extent high arousal can be distinguished from low arousal. But beyond that, accuracy is not very great.

The accuracy of recognizing emotions in others also depends upon how intense the emotional experience is. In one study in which a woman watched slides that were slightly pleasant or slightly unpleasant, the emotional expressions she registered in response to the slides were quite modest. Student subjects observing her responses were unable to detect whether she was watching positive or negative slides. However, electrodes attached to her face picked up subtle facial movements, suggesting that nonverbal behaviors that are too subtle to be noticed by an observer may nonetheless indicate a person's affective response (Cacioppo, Petty, Losh, & Kim, 1986; Cacioppo, Martzke, Petty, & Tassinary, 1988).

Universal Emotional Expressions

People are at least crudely accurate in judging others' emotions, then. One reason might be that all people use the same facial expression for expressing a given underlying emotion. Perhaps we all smile when we feel happy, grimace when we feel pain, frown when we are worried, and so on. To illustrate this, Craig and Patrick (1985) induced pain by immersing subjects' hands and wrists into icy water just at freezing temperature. They found such consistent responses as raising cheeks with tight eyelids, raising the upper eyelid, parting the lips, and closing eyes or blinking.

In 1871, on the basis of his evolutionary theory, Charles Darwin proposed that facial expressions convey the same emotional states in all cultures. His argument was that universal expressions have evolved because they have great survival value: they allow animals to communicate emotions and thereby control others' behavior. For example, if one animal shows an angry or threatening face, others may behave more submissively, which allows the first animal to win the encounter without risking an actual fight.

In fact, virtually all species of Old World monkeys and apes have been found to use facial gestures to signal dominance or submissiveness. Differing eyebrow positions seem to be crucial: Typically, the brows are lowered on dominant or threatening individuals and raised on submissive or receptive individuals (Keating et al., 1981). The evolutionary argument is that there may be a link between the facial expressions used by subhuman primates to communicate with and control other species members, and those used by humans for the same purpose. If so, presumably the same link between emotion and facial expression would exist among humans across all (or most) cultures.

Are there such universals in humans? Do we have particular facial expressions or body postures for each emotion? Or is it possible that one person's expression of disgust is another person's expression of contentment? The link between lowered-brow expressions and dominance in nonhuman primates suggests a possible similar link in human beings. To test for this, Keating and others (1981) had people from each of a number of countries in Europe, Africa, North and South America, and Asia pose with brows lowered, and again with brows raised. The researchers also tested for a link between perceptions of smiling and dominance/submission because a number of studies had suggested that primates' grins may communicate submissiveness. On the other hand, there is also evidence that among humans, smiling is related to happiness. The subjects were presented with pictures of a person from their own country and asked, in their native language, to judge the pose for dominance and happiness. The only differences in poses were brow position and smiling or not. Keating found that nonsmiling and lowered-brow poses were generally associated with dominance, especially among the most Westernized peoples. Smiles were identified with happiness. It is possible that the analog to the human smile is the primate submissive grin. When an ape grins, it means submission. Perhaps there is an evolutionary link to the human tendency to express sociability and submissiveness in the same manner.

These findings parallel those from other studies in the West in which lowered brows are identified with anger, assertive behavior, working on competitive tasks, and dominance. Raised brows are associated with social deference in a number of ways: with children's fleeing during disputes, with perceptions of fear or surprise, and as a signal inviting social contact. Smiles are generally associated with greeting, approval-seeking behavior, and happiness or joy (Keating et al., 1981).

An even tougher test of the universality of particular emotional expressions was a study conducted with people from a remote part of New Guinea who had never lived in any Western settlement or government towns, had seen no movies, understood neither English nor

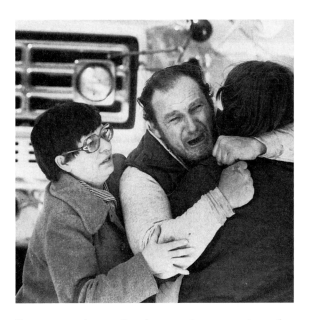

Because certain emotional expressions are universal, most people looking at this picture would assume that the man is deeply unhappy about something. In fact, he has just learned that his family was killed in a fatal fire.

Pidgin, and had never worked for a Caucasian. Presumably these people had had no visual contact with conventional Western facial expression of emotions. Each was given a brief story depicting an emotion, such as for sadness, "His child has died, and he feels very sad." Then the participant was given one photograph Western observers overwhelmingly agreed depicted that emotion and two pictures depicting other emotions. On the average, both children and adults chose the "correct" picture more than 80 percent of the time (Ekman & Friesen, 1971). This does not prove there are no cultural differences in the facial expression of emotion, but it does provide evidence of universals that transcend cultural boundaries. In particular, happiness, sadness, anger, and disgust can be detected with high levels of agreement both within and across cultures. Fear and surprise were often confused with each other (Ekman, 1982).

There are some qualifications, however. Cultures do differ substantially in *amount* of emotional expression that is customary. Swedes tend to be relatively impassive; Italians are quite expressive. Sometimes social norms forbid honest expression: We are supposed to conceal disgusted reactions to someone with a terrible deformity, or anger from being belittled by a superior at work. Still, the level of consensus on the meaning of facial expressions is impressive, given the fact that most of these studies have used photographs and hence provide no information about context.

NONVERBAL COMMUNICATION

If you think about it, you will realize that you make judgments about another person's emotional state on the basis of more than facial expression. What other cues do we use? What are the ways in which people communicate their internal states in general, and what cues do observers use in detecting them?

Generally speaking, people communicate information about themselves through three main channels (Richmond, McCroskey, & Payne, 1991). The most obvious is *verbal communication*, the content of what a person says. The other channels are nonverbal and provide a whole set of much subtler cues. *Nonverbal communication* is the sum of the ways in which we transmit information without using language. The communication comes to us through a visible channel, which includes such expressive behaviors as facial expression, gesture, posture, and appearance. And it comes to us through a paralinguistic channel, namely, what is left in the speech signal when the content has been removed, such as the pitch, amplitude, rate, voice quality, and contour of speech.

The visible and paralinguistic channels have generated a good bit of research and they do prove informative to perceivers. As research has progressed, a wide variety of different nonverbal cues have been identified, and observers seem to get quite different kinds of information from them. However, as helpful as they can be, nonverbal communications provide no magic clues to another person's internal states. Perceivers usually require other information about a person.

The Visible Channel

Some of the main nonverbal cues of the visible channel are expressed through distance, gesture, and eye contact (Feldman & Rimé, 1991).

DISTANCE.   In general, the more friendly and intimate a person feels toward another, the closer he or she will stand. Friends stand closer than strangers (Aiello & Cooper, 1972), people who want to seem friendly choose smaller distances (Patterson & Sechrest, 1970), and people who are sexually attracted to each other stand close (Allgeier & Byrne, 1973). Although most people do not think much about personal space, we are all aware that standing close is usually a sign of friendship or interest. It may be one of the most important and easiest ways of telling someone you have just met that you like him or her. The other person is immediately aware of your interest, and if he or she is not interested, will generally move away to make that clear.

GESTURES.   In recent years many popular books have been published on the subject of **body language.** These books suggest that you can tell exactly what someone is thinking or per-fectly interpret what they say merely by observing their bodily movements and posture. An open palm is an invitation, crossed legs are defensive, and so on. Clearly bodily gestures and posture carry information. There are straightforward, direct gestures and very subtle ones. Many bodily movements are generally accepted and convey specific information or directions—the gestures for "stop" and "come" are examples, as are pointing and gestures for "sit down," "yes," "no," "go away," "goodbye." Various obscene gestures have well-known meanings. In a sense, all these gestures are a sign language.

But gestures have meaning mainly when observers and participants understand the context, and especially when they understand the culture. An open palm is not always an invitation: putting a hand up with palm out means, "stop," not "go"; the reverse gesture, with the palm in and the fingers moving toward the body, means "come" or "enter." No one has constructed a reliable dictionary of gestures. Popular books on body language are usually not based on scientific research and should be read with healthy skepticism. The meaning of gestures depends on the context, on the person

People from different cultures have different customs regarding touching and other non-verbal communication during casual conversation. These American women, for example, are comfortable not touching, whereas the two men on a street in Spain stand close together and touch repeatedly during their conversation.

doing the action, on the culture, and probably on other factors also.

The importance of nonverbal communications and gestures in particular has now made its way into the popular culture. Media experts who "handle" congressional, senatorial, or presidential candidates often work as much on their candidates' gestures and other nonverbal communication as on the content of their presentation. During the 1988 campaign season, Roger Ailes, George Bush's media consultant, was quoted in *Newsweek* (Warner & Fineman, 1988, p. 19) as telling Bush during a rehearsal for one of the debates, "There you go with that f–ing hand again. You look like a f–ing pansy!" (cited in DePaulo, 1990).

EYE CONTACT.   Eye contact is an especially interesting form of nonverbal communication. As with other forms, the meaning of eye contact varies greatly and depends on the context. But in nearly all social interactions, eye contact does communicate information.

At the minimum, eye contact indicates interest or lack of it. Hollywood movies often have a couple staring into each other's eyes to portray love, affection, or great concern. Certainly we are all familiar with eye contact held for a long time as a means of demonstrating attraction for someone. An otherwise casual conversation can become an expression of romantic interest if one of the speakers maintains eye contact. Conversely, avoiding or breaking the contact is usually a sign that the person is not interested. Indeed, when someone does not make eye contact during a conversation, we tend to interpret this as an indication that he or she is not really involved in the interaction.

But there are obvious exceptions to this general principle. Someone who is conveying bad news or saying something painful may avoid eye contact. Lack of eye contact can sometimes mean the person is shy or frightened. When people have feelings they are embarrassed about, they do not like to be the focus of a direct gaze. In a study by Ellsworth, Friedman, Perlick, and Hoyt (1978), female college students were told they would have to discuss questions "about rather intimate personal areas of your life, things that college students usually do not like to talk about." Each student then had to wait with a confederate who stared directly at her 75 percent of the time, or just glanced at her once. By far, most subjects preferred the gaze-averting confederate. This was not true of other subjects who were not expecting an embarrassing conversation. The direct gaze apparently threatened the embarrassed women.

Moreover, eye contact can be used more actively, to threaten. In another experiment, someone stared at a subject who was in a position to act aggressively toward the starer. Subjects who were stared at were less aggressive than when there was no staring (Ellsworth & Carlsmith, 1973). Apparently prolonged eye contact can be interpreted as a threat and causes people to escape or act in a conciliatory manner. We can all probably remember teachers who have used this technique very effectively.

It is perhaps not surprising that eye contact can have two seemingly contradictory meanings—friendship or threat. In both cases, eye contact indicates greater involvement and higher emotional content. Whether the emotion is positive or negative depends on the context; the nonverbal cues themselves have no fixed meaning.

FACIAL EXPRESSIONS.   Facial expressions also can be intended to communicate to others. One interesting case of this is mimicry. It has often been observed that people (and chimpanzees) physically mimic the responses of others. Darwin noted that in particular people mimic distress when others are feeling it. It is possible that this mimicry is an expression of sympathy for the victim; the mimic may want the other person to know that distress about the painful experience is shared.

To test this idea, Bavelas, Black, Lemery, and Mullett (1986) had undergraduate women individually view a person accidentally drop a heavy TV monitor on an already injured finger, one with a heavily taped splint on it. In some cases the victim, a confederate (badly bruised!) then looked directly at the observer; in other cases no eye contact was made. Most of the observers in turn displayed an expression of pain, but it quickly faded in the absence of eye contact. Moreover, the observers were considerably more likely to smile when eye contact was made, probably in an effort to be reassuring. The facial expressions of the observers were in fact rated as more "knowing" and "caring" in the eye contact condition than without, suggesting that they were successfully communicating feelings of empathy and sympathy.

Paralanguage

Variations in speech other than the actual verbal contact, called **paralanguage,** carry a great deal of meaning. Pitch of the voice, loudness, rhythm, inflection, and hesitations convey information. Parents can often tell whether their baby is hungry, angry, or just mildly cranky by how it cries. Dogs bark in different ways, and each means something different to someone familiar with the animal. And, of course, the significance and meaning of adult speech depend in part on these paralinguistic factors.

A simple statement such as "You want to move to Japan" can mean entirely different things depending on emphasis and inflection. Say it aloud as a flat statement with no emphasis, and it sounds like a mere statement of fact. Say it with an inflection (rising voice) at the end, and it questions the wisdom of going to Japan; you are expressing doubt that it is a good place to move to. Say it with added emphasis on the first word, and it turns into a question as to whether or not the person addressed is qualified; you are raising doubts about whether or not the person is capable of getting along in such a foreign country. The short phrase "I like you" may indicate almost anything from mild feelings to intense passion, depending on its paralinguistic characteristics.

These variations are often crucial in conveying emotion. In fact, they are so important that they often must be added to written language. To show that someone thought Japan was an unlikely choice, the sentence might read, " 'You want to move to Japan?' he said with disbelief." To describe the feeling behind a statement of liking, one might write, " 'I like you,' she murmured passionately." Without these paralinguistic clues, the statements are hard to interpret.

One of the difficulties in studying paralanguage (and most other kinds of nonverbal behavior) is that the cues have no fixed meaning. We all agree on the meaning of words. We all know what "Japan" refers to, and with some variations we know that when someone says he "likes" you, he is making a statement of positive feelings. But people differ considerably in the meanings they attach to paralinguistic cues. For some people, a pause may be for emphasis; for others, it may mean uncertainty. Higher pitch may mean excitement or lying; loudness can indicate anger, emphasis, or excitement. The particular meaning depends on the context. It is hard to interpret what is communicated when a speaker talks louder at you. If a person makes a fist, does it show anger? If a person hugs you, does it show affection? Interpretation depends on individual habits and characteristics as well as on ethnic customs, as the CULTURAL HIGHLIGHT suggests.

Multiple Channels

Which of these three channels of communication—verbal, visible, and paralinguistic—provides the most information about a person's real emotions? Many writers in recent years have speculated that observers weigh nonverbal cues most heavily and tend almost to disregard verbal communication. For example, Birdwhistell (1970) says that no more than 30 to 35 percent of the social meaning of conversation is carried by the words. Mehrabian (1972) estimated that only 7 percent of the communication of emotion was accomplished by the verbal channel, 55 percent was accomplished by the visual channel, and 38 percent by the paralinguistic channel. Other writers have gone even further, arguing that the visible channel dominates over verbal content in the communication of emotion; that is, "video"

CULTURAL HIGHLIGHT

And Watch the Soles of Your Feet!
Nonverbal Communication Across Cultures

Over the past decade, many U.S. business people and military personnel have been sent to Saudi Arabia, where they encountered a very different culture from our own. Because the customs are so different between Saudi Arabia and the United States, it is easy for an American to inadvertently offend Saudis. Consequently, manuals have been put together to help these business people and military personnel learn what to do and what not to do when interacting with the Saudi Arabians (Goldstein, 1990).

Arabian men and women, for example, have very different customs regarding touching. Saudi men and women are not supposed to touch each other at all. Americans are told that they should respect this custom,

especially in interactions with Arabian women. Even American couples are urged not to hold hands in public or engage in other forms of touching or romantic behavior, because of its potential to offend their Saudi hosts.

Paradoxically, Arabs sometimes touch more, because they have a closer interpersonal distance than Americans. This may make Americans feel uncomfortable. Speaking to this issue, the manual for American military personnel notes, "An Arab entering [an elevator] may stand right next to you and be touching, even though no one else is in the elevator. The same may happen on a bus, airplane, or park bench."

Even handshakes follow different norms in the two

cultures. Whereas in the United States a firm handshake is a sign of strength and good character, in Arabian culture handshakes between men are expected to be soft and gentle.

And finally, in Arabic cultures it is an insult to allow the sole of one's shoe to face another person. When in conversation with Arabs, one must sit properly and avoid crossing one's legs in order to avoid this type of offense (Kammeyer, Ritzer, & Yetman, 1992).

Nonverbal behavior, then, conveys a great deal of information that is culture-dependent, and failure to respect these cultural differences can result in awkward misunderstandings.

---

information is more important than "audio" (DePaulo, Rosenthal, Eisenstat, Rogers, & Finkelstein, 1978).

The question of which channels are taken most seriously becomes particularly important when the observer is receiving conflicting cues from different channels. How do you interpret your girlfriend's feelings when she says she loves you but moves away from you and won't look at you? The verbal and visible channels of her communication seem to conflict. What if your roommate shouts at you at the top of her lungs that she is really *not* mad at you *at all* for breaking her favorite coffee cup? Shakespeare said, "Methinks she doth protest too much." Conflicts across channels ought to be particularly important in interpreting apparently deceptive

communications. In such cases, is nonverbal, and especially visible, communication truly relied on most heavily as some of these researchers suggest?

Such claims have now been subjected to rigorous tests. In one of the clearest of such studies, Krauss, Apple, Morency, Wenzel, and Winton (1981) presented subjects with videotapes of the 1976 televised debate between the two candidates for vice president, Walter Mondale and Robert Dole. The debate started pleasantly, but turned rather heated and rancorous. The researchers selected 12 passages for each speaker, half of which seemed to display positive emotions and half negative. Then each subject was presented these passages in one of four conditions: (1) audiovisual—the standard videotaped

TABLE 2-4

Importance of Various Channels of Information in Judgments About Vice-Presidential Debates

Dimension of Judgment	Verbal Only	Video Only	Audio Filtered
Evaluation	51.8[a]	2.2	8.8
Potency	3.4	29.6	45.1[a]
Activity	0.1	36.8	5.2

[a]$p < .05$.
Source: Adapted from Krauss et al. (1981), pp. 316–317.
Note: The entry is the percentage of variance in judgment of full audiovisual communication that was accounted for by each individual channel. Rows do not sum to 100 percent because factors other than these three channels account for some of the full-channel judgment process.

version; (2) verbal only—a written transcript as published in *The New York Times*; (3) video only—with the audio channel turned off; and (4) paralinguistic—the audio track only, but with content filtered out so that speech was unintelligible, while nonverbal features such as pitch, loudness, rate, and so on were preserved.

The written transcript turned out to be critical for detecting whether positive or negative emotions were being expressed; that is, verbal information was most important, contrary to speculations about the importance of nonverbal communications. The data from this study are shown in Table 2-4.

The visible channel made little contribution to observers' judgments. Paralinguistic information did contribute to judgments of the potency and activity levels of the speakers' presentations. That is, observers who were given only the unintelligible soundtrack gave the same kinds of judgments about energy levels as did those given full audiovisual information. The implication is that paralinguistic information, like eye contact, can be sufficient to detect energy and involvement, even if it is not sufficient to detect the particular kind of emotion expressed.

A follow-up study by Apple and Hecht (1982) found that paralinguistic information could be particularly useful in detecting sadness. They had speakers deliver sentences that varied in the kind of emotion they presented: happiness, sadness, anger, surprise. No visual cues were provided, and the verbal content of the sentence was screened out from the recording. Listeners were able to identify the sadness sentences quite readily, but they could identify the others at only slightly better than chance levels. The authors speculate that sadness is expressed through distinctive paralinguistic cues (slow, soft, low-pitched speech), whereas the other emotions are expressed with more energetic cues that easily confuse the listener.

In general, then, nonverbal cues—paralinguistic or visible—are not very precise guides, by themselves, to emotional feelings in others (Krauss, Morrel-Samuels, & Colasante, 1991). There is nothing magically or unambiguously communicative about nonverbal cues. Most can communicate a variety of messages depending on the context. A touch on the arm by an attractive acquaintance means something quite different from the same touch made by a homeless person in a subway station. Being tapped on the shoulder by your boss may mean something still different. A smile on the face of a bully as he moves in on helpless prey means something quite different from the smile on a friend's face when he or she sees you walking across the campus. Nonverbal cues can be informative, but only when they are solidly embedded in a familiar context, when we know the role of the other person, have some notion of his or her general goals, know the norms for the situation, and so on. When we do not have a known or familiar context, as in a first visit to a foreign country, we frequently feel lost and can make little sense of nonverbal cues.

THE PROBLEM OF DECEPTION

A particularly important area of conflict between verbal and nonverbal cues is judging when people are lying or otherwise trying to deceive observers. Police, judges, and jurors are constantly trying to learn the truth from people who try to mislead them.

Nonverbal Leakage

As might be expected from our discussion of nonverbal communication, one important theory is that people will give away deception through nonverbal cues even when they are successful in lying verbally. Ekman and Friesen (1974) argue that people attend more to what they are saying than to what they are doing with their bodies. If they are trying to deceive someone, for example, they may lie verbally in a calm way, but reveal their true emotions through nonverbal cues. In Ekman's terms, there is **nonverbal leakage.** True emotions "leak out" even if the person tries to conceal them. A student may say she is not nervous about a test, but will bite her lower lip and blink more than usual, actions that often indicate nervousness. A young man waiting for a job interview may attempt to appear calm and casual, but will cross and uncross his legs continually, straighten his tie, touch his face, play with his hair. As a result, he will in fact come across as a nervous wreck.

Liars often betray themselves through paralinguistic expressions of anxiety, tension, and nervousness. It sometimes is possible to tell when someone is lying by noting the pitch of the voice. Several studies (Ekman, Friesen, & Scherer, 1976; Krauss, Geller, & Olson, 1976) indicate that the average (or more technically, fundamental) pitch of the voice is higher when someone is lying than when he or she is telling the truth. The difference is small, and one cannot tell just by listening. But electronic vocal analysis reveals lying with considerable accuracy. In addition, shorter answers, longer delays in responding, more speech errors, and more nervous, less serious answers all are characteristic of people perceived as liars or instructed to tell lies (Apple, Streeter, & Krauss, 1979; Kraut, 1978; Zuckerman, DePaulo, & Rosenthal, 1981).

The concept of leakage implies that some nonverbal channels leak more than others because they are less controllable. The musculature of a smile, for example, changes when people are being truthful as opposed to when they are lying (Ekman, Friesen, & O'Sullivan, 1988). But several studies (Zuckerman, DePaulo, & Rosenthal, 1981) have found that the body is more likely to reveal deception than the face. Paralinguistic cues can also leak because, like the body, tone of voice is less controllable than facial expression. Liars, for example, may be better able to modify, that is suppress and exaggerate, facial expressions than tone of voice (Zuckerman, Larrance, Spiegel, & Klorman, 1981). But people need not be lying to leak. For example, Babad, Bernieri, and Rosenthal (1989) compared the behavior of biased and unbiased teachers in their instruction of their students. Although there were no differences between the two groups of teachers in their active teaching behaviors, biased teachers demonstrated systematic and substantial leakage of negative affect in their nonverbal behavior when interacting with the students they preferred less.

The leakage hypothesis proposes, then, that when people are trying to conceal something, they may be able to control their verbal content and facial expressions fairly well, but their deception may leak out in bodily gestures and paralinguistic cues.

Nonverbal channels may leak more than verbal channels, because when conveying information verbally, a person both produces and hears exactly what he or she said and consequently can correct statements that may not have been said in a way that conveys quite the right impression. However, in the nonverbal channel, we usually do not see our nonverbal behaviors, and consequently may be less able to regulate them (DePaulo, 1990). Thus, while we may try to regulate our nonverbal behavior, we may not always be successful, because we lack the kind of feedback that we get from our own verbal behavior.

Accuracy of Detection

Perceivers do quite consistently perceive deceptive messages as somewhat less truthful than truthful messages (see DePaulo, 1990, for a review). Across dozens of studies, deception accuracy usually exceeds chance, but rarely by an impressive margin (DePaulo et al., 1982). Not surprisingly, people can detect the fact of lying better than they can figure out the nature of the liar's true feelings.

For one thing, people have trouble distinguishing deception from genuine ambivalence. This was illustrated in a study by DePaulo and coworkers (1982). They had people record messages that (1) truthfully described their positive (or negative) feelings about another person, (2) untruthfully described their positive (or negative) feelings, or (3) truthfully described their genuinely mixed feelings about another person. These messages were presented to observers through different channels. They found that observers were not able to distinguish truthful messages about mixed feelings from deceptive messages about positive or negative feelings. Perhaps people are able to distinguish true expressions of positive or negative feelings from everything else, but are not able to isolate deception itself without any further information—all they know is that the person does not sound wholeheartedly positive or negative.

On the other hand, people usually do have other information about the person's motives. They usually know whether or not the person has a reason to want to lie. It may be that we are better at detecting deception when we know the person has such reasons. To test this, DePaulo, Stone, and Lassiter (1985a) had people (hereafter termed "senders") describe their opinions on four issues to their "partners." They manipulated lying by instructing the senders to agree or disagree honestly on two issues and to pretend to agree or disagree on two others. Then they varied the incentive for senders to lie in several ways. In the high-incentive conditions, the partner was of the opposite sex, the partner was attractive, and the sender was instructed to feign agreement. Presumably all these would give the sender reason to be most ingratiating. In the other conditions, the sender would have less apparent incentive to lie: the partner was unattractive, or of the same sex, or the sender was instructed to feign disagreement. These communications were videotaped and later played back to neutral judges, varying which channels were available. The judges rated the communications on a scale of sincerity–insincerity.

The main finding was that lies were easiest to detect when they were apparently motivated by ingratiation, that is, when the sender had the greatest motivation to lie—communicating agreement to an attractive partner of the opposite sex. Deception was harder to detect without any specific information about reasons to lie— that is, when the sender was communicating disagreement to an unattractive member of one's own sex.

Does it help to be warned explicitly that a target person may be lying? One would think so, because perceivers then should attend more closely to "leaky" channels, such as the face and tone of voice. However, it seems not to help very much. In a study by Toris and DePaulo (1984), subjects participated in simulated job interviews. The applicants were told to be honest in some cases and dishonest in others, while the interviewers were told to expect the applicant to try to convey a false impression in some cases and were given no warning in others. However, this warning of deceptiveness just made the interviewers suspicious about everyone, perceiving all applicants as more deceptive; they were no more accurate in singling out the dishonest ones. Not only that, but they were less confident of their own judgments.

Research investigations may actually overestimate the degree to which people can detect deception in everyday life. As social perceivers, most of the time we are very busy trying to form impressions of others, cull what is useful for oneself from the conversation at hand, and manage the impressions that we are conveying to others. Under such circumstances, we tend to take others' self-presentations at face value, rather than questioning whether they are trying to convey a false impression (Gilbert, Krull, & Pelham, 1988; see also Gilbert & Krull, 1988). In fact, when people are deliberately trying to convey an emotion that they may not really be experiencing, their nonverbal behaviors convey that impression even more clearly than when they are actually experiencing the state. Posed expressions of emotion are easier to read than are spontaneous ones (see DePaulo, 1990, for a review). This combination of the deceiver being easy to read and the perceiver being relatively uncritical means that in most social situations, deceptive self-presentations are likely to be taken at face value (DePaulo, 1990).

The Giveaways

When observers are able to discover deception, what cues do they use? Is the leakage hypothesis correct? Is the body less controllable than the face, and do people catch deception primarily through nonverbal bodily cues? Or is the voice an even leakier channel than the body? It may be that the tone of voice—pitch, loudness, speed, and so forth—is even more difficult to control than the body, even when the person can control the content of verbal communication.

Most of the research shows that all these cues help a little to trap a potentially deceptive communicator. But they are really useful only when the observer also has access to the content of the person's speech. A typical study is one done by Zuckerman, Amidon, Bishop, and Pomerantz (1982). They had "senders" describe either a target person they liked (a "liked target") or someone they disliked (a "disliked target"), and they did so in one of three modes: "truth," in which they conveyed their true feelings; "conceal-

ment," in which they tried to conceal their true feelings; and "deception," in which they tried to communicate feelings opposite to those they really had. The "receivers" did not know the senders' true feelings, or which mode the sender was instructed to use.

Some receivers had full audiovisual (face plus verbal content), others heard only the audio channel (verbal content, no face), others had access to visual plus filtered speech (face, no verbal content), and still others, filtered speech only (no verbal content, no face). The question was how access to the face, to verbal content, and to paralinguistic cues affected observers' ability to detect whether the sender really liked or disliked the target.

The results showed that either face or tone of voice added significantly to ability to detect deception. This can be seen in Table 2-5. The receivers were significantly able to distinguish a liked from a disliked target when given only filtered speech, without being able to see the face or hear any verbal content (as indicated by the fact that they perceived the truly liked target as liked +.31 more, on the average, than the truly disliked target). Second, adding access to the face significantly increased detection of the sender's true feelings, as indicated by the fact that face plus filtered speech is higher (+.74) than filtered speech only (+.31), even when verbal content was not available. Both channels are

TABLE 2-5

Accuracy of Perception of Communicators' True Feelings About Target Person

	Verbal Content	
	Available	Not Available
Face present	+ .85	+ .74
Face absent	+ .84	+ .31

Source: Adapted from Zuckerman et al. (1982), p. 353.
Note: The entry is the perception of communicator's true feeling about the liked target minus the perception of communicator's true feelings about the disliked target, each rated on a nine-point scale.

somewhat leaky, then, in the sense that both communicated significantly to the receiver about a possibly deceptive sender's true feelings, even when the perceiver could not understand the content of the communications.

The main finding, however, is that accuracy is greatest when verbal content is available. The table shows the highest accuracy in the left-hand column, with verbal content available. Moreover, adding visual nonverbal cues helps the perceiver very little when verbal content is available (+ .85 is almost identical to + .84). This seems to be more true if the situation is a familiar one. When a situation is unfamiliar, however, people seem to draw on both verbal and nonverbal cues for detecting deception (Stiff et al., 1989).

A large number of reviews have identified the specific behaviors that reliably distinguish lies from truth. Liars blink more, hesitate more, and make more errors when they are speaking, perhaps because it is arousing to lie. They tend to speak in higher-pitched voices and their pupils are more likely to be dilated. Liars are more likely to feel guilty or anxious, and this may explain why liars fidget more, speak more hesitatingly and less fluidly, and make more negative and distancing statements than do those telling the truth. The voice tone of liars also often sounds negative. Interchannel discrepancies are more likely to occur. Thus, for example, someone attempting to convey an impression of warmth may smile and make eye contact but lean away from the person with whom he is conversing, rather than leaning forward (DePaulo et al., 1985a; for general reviews, see DePaulo et al., 1985b; Zuckerman, DePaulo, & Rosenthal, 1981; DePaulo, 1990).

Paradoxically, one of the best sources of information regarding deception may be the sender's motivation to lie. Intuitively, it seems that people who are the most highly motivated to deceive others will be most successful. However, considerable research suggests that when people are especially motivated to get away with their lies, they actually become more obvious to observers (e.g., DePaulo, LeMay, & Epstein, 1991; DePaulo, Kirkendol, Tang, & O'Brien, 1988). Typically, these lies are revealed not verbally, but nonverbally. Motivated liars seem to work harder to control their nonverbal behavior, sometimes attempting to suppress it altogether in a rigid effort not to give anything away. In other cases, they may deliberately try to control all their verbal and nonverbal behaviors. Both strategies fail because observers can perceive this rigid or controlled behavior through the nonverbal channels and more successfully discern the effort to lie (DePaulo, 1990).

We have discussed a number of studies that have tried to determine what cues help detect lying in another person. For the most part, nonverbal cues do not seem to be sufficient. Rather, people infer lying from other kinds of information they receive about the person: whether the supposed liar seems to have something to gain from lying, or fits the stereotype of a liar, or whether the verbal communication suggests lying. Nonverbal cues add something when this other information is available, but are not sufficient by themselves.

Nonverbal Behavior and Self-presentation

So far, our discussion has implied that nonverbal behavior is either spontaneous and un-self-conscious or it is a potential source of leakage about deception. But nonverbal behavior is also subject to a certain amount of self-regulation (DePaulo, 1992). Whenever people are motivated to convey a particular impression in a social setting, they are very likely to do so, in part, by managing their nonverbal behaviors. The goal of such nonverbal control may sometimes be deception, but it may also be simply to convey an image to another person that represents how we actually feel.

Think about the last time a friend shared a problem with you. If you listened patiently and sympathetically, as most of us do, at least initially, you were probably aware not only of saying the right things, such as "That's too bad" or "That's a terrible way to treat anybody." You may also have been aware of the appropriate nonverbal behaviors, such as making eye contact with your friend while he talked and nodding sympathetically. You knew, for example, not to smile, but to look serious, and not to open your mail and skim it while he was explaining his problem. While not intending to deceive your friend in any way, your nonverbal behaviors were clearly monitored, at least to a degree, so that you conveyed the appropriate sentiments and reactions to your friend's disclosures.

Increasingly, psychologists have been interested in these self-presentational aspects of nonverbal behavior (DePaulo, 1992). Over a lifetime, we learn a great deal about the self-presentation of nonverbal behavior, indeed so much so that it becomes almost automatic in adulthood. For example, by the time we are in college, we may not have to think much about the fact that we should stop fidgeting, make extended eye contact, and look sympathetic when another person is telling us a problem. It may occur virtually spontaneously in response to the friend's distress. But like verbal behavior, nonverbal behavior is learned. Taught to "sit like a lady" in childhood, a behavior that may require uncomfortable amounts of practice, one may do so quite unconsciously in adulthood. Ekman (1972) calls these cultural norms regarding how one conveys emotions to others *display rules*. Display rules govern not only which emotion should be conveyed in a particular situation, but how the emotion should be conveyed.

Generally speaking, people deliberately regulate their nonverbal behavior in ways that enhance the correspondence between their self-presentation and how they truly think about themselves (Swann, 1984; DePaulo, 1992). We wear buttons to convey our political beliefs, choose clothing that represents us as conservative or liberal, and act open and outgoing if we feel we are that way, and more standoffish and shy if we are not.

Nonverbal behavior can also be used to further social goals. Talking with a woman he may

wish to date, a man smiles a lot, makes extended eye contact, stands fairly close, and might rest his hand against the wall in back of his intended partner. Caught in a conversation with someone to whom he is not attracted, he stands farther away, glances from time to time around the room, maintains a more serious expression, and keeps his arms folded in front of him.

People's ability to use nonverbal behavior in self-presentational efforts varies considerably. Often, nonverbal behaviors cannot be regulated successfully. The ability to do so depends on several factors, including our knowledge of the appropriate nonverbal behavior for a particular situation, our ability, practice and experience in conveying that impression, and our confidence in conveying the impression. The ability to convey a particular impression nonverbally also depends on a person's characteristic demeanor, characteristic level of expressiveness, personal style, and the range of expressive experience he or she has (DePaulo, 1992). Several factors, however, may paradoxically work against conveying an appropriate self-presentation through nonverbal behavior. As just noted, being highly motivated to convey a particular impression may actually act as an impediment to successful self-presentation when people try too hard to control their verbal and nonverbal behavior (e.g., Baumeister, 1988; Heckhausen & Strang, 1988; DePaulo & Kirkendol, 1989). Similarly, people who are spontaneously expressive, while perhaps more able than those who are not to convey a variety of emotions, may find that their spontaneous expressions interfere with the self-presentation they are attempting to achieve (Friedman & Miller-Herringer, 1990). Spontaneously expressive people probably convey impressions more successfully than people who are not so spontaneous, unless they are trying to convey an impression that is at odds with what they are really feeling.

There are sex differences in the use of nonverbal behavior. Girls and women are more expressive, more involved in their interpersonal interactions, and more open in the expression of emotion (DePaulo, 1992). They use more nonverbal behavior in interacting with others, such as touching, eye contact, expressive body movements, smiling, and gazing. Women are also more accurate interpreters of nonverbal cues than are men (Hall, 1978).

It is easy to interpret such effects in sex-role terms. Generally, women have been regarded as the experts in the social and emotional areas of life, and nonverbal behavior can clearly help in this regard. However, some studies suggest that these sex differences develop very early in life, as early as three months (Malatesta & Haviland, 1982). Consequently, it is difficult to disentangle the roles of nature and nurture in attempting

to understand these robust sex differences (DePaulo, 1992).

In conclusion, it appears that when people are motivated to convey a particular impression of themselves in a social interaction, they will attempt to do so, in part, by controlling their nonverbal behaviors. Although sometimes such behaviors are undertaken to deceive others, more commonly they may be employed to convey an accurate impression of the self and one's feelings in that situation. Moreover, people seem to be fairly successful at it, as long as they are not trying to convey a false impression.

KEY TERMS

additive principle	evaluation	person perception
associationistic view	exemplar	positivity bias
averaging principle	figure–ground principle	prototype
body language	gestalt	salience
categorization	halo effect	schema
central traits	negativity effect	shift of meaning
cognitive miser	nonverbal leakage	stereotype
dimensional view	paralanguage	typological view

SUMMARY

1. People often decide very quickly what other people are like and base their decisions on minimal information, such as appearance or gender. They infer enduring qualities in others from brief exposure to behavior in limited situations.

2. The evaluative dimension is the most important organizing principle behind first impressions. People seem to decide first how much they like or dislike another person and then ascribe characteristics to that person that fit this pleasant or unpleasant portrait.

3. People tend to form highly consistent impressions of others, even with very little information.

4. Various identifiable perceptual biases distort our judgments of others, such as the halo effect (we tend to think that a person we like

is good in every dimension) and the positivity bias (we tend to like most people, even some who are not so likable).

5. There are two rival points of view about how people process information about others: the learning approach, which has people essentially averaging information in a quite mechanical manner, and the gestalt approach, which has people forming more coherent and meaningful impressions.

6. Our judgments of other people are not always accurate. In particular, we have a hard time judging people's emotions from their facial expressions. We can tell fairly easily if the emotion is a positive or a negative one, but we have difficulty telling which positive or negative emotion is being experienced. Nevertheless, there do seem to be

some universal connections across cultures between certain emotions and certain facial expressions.

7. We use a wide variety of cues in arriving at impressions of people, including physical appearance, verbal behavior, and nonverbal cues. Nonverbal communication includes cues from both the visible channel (such as facial expressions, gestures, and posture) and the paralinguistic channel (cues in speech when the content has been removed, such as the pitch, rate, and delays of speech).

8. Verbal communication is probably the single most important source of information about other people. However, visible and paralinguistic information make an important additional contribution, particularly when the content helps us to interpret their meaning.

9. Deception leaks out in numerous nonverbal ways, such as nervous gestures or high-pitched and rapid speech. Observers can usually detect deception at slightly better than chance levels, but they need all three channels of communication to do so effectively.

SUGGESTED READINGS

Anderson, N. H. (1965). Averaging vs. adding as a stimulus-combination rule in impression formation. *Journal of Experimental Social Psychology, 70,* 394–400. This gives the flavor of averaging research, using trait adjectives about hypothetical stimulus persons.

Asch, S. E. (1946). Forming impressions of personality. *Journal of Abnormal and Social Psychology, 41,* 258–290. This is the classic statement of the gestalt approach to impression formation and, indeed, to social perception in general.

Buck, R. (1984). *The communication of emotions.* New York: Guilford. A general resource on emotion and communication with extensive focus on the nonverbal communication of emotion.

DePaulo, B. M. (1992). Nonverbal behavior and self-presentation. *Psychological Bulletin, 111,* 203–243. A comprehensive, recent review of how nonverbal behavior successfully and unsuccessfully communicates particular impressions.

Fiske, S. T. (1993). Social cognition and perception. In M. R. Rosenzweig & W. L. Porter (Eds.), *Annual Review of Psychology* (Vol. 44). Palo Alto, CA: Annual Reviews, Inc. A state-of-the-art review of the most recent developments in person perception research.

Hall, E. T. (1966). *The hidden dimension.* Garden City, NY: Doubleday. An original statement by one of the pioneers in the study of nonverbal communication.

Schneider, D. J., Hastorf, A. H., & Ellsworth, P. C. (1979). *Person perception* (2nd ed.). Reading, MA: Addison-Wesley. Still one of the best resources in the field, this paperback pursues the material in this chapter in more detail.

3
Social Cognition

FOCUS OF THIS CHAPTER

Social Inference
Schemas
Schematic Processing
Mental Shortcuts: Using
  Cognitive Heuristics
Which Schemas are Used?
Schemas in Action

Research Closeup
Why I Will Never Get Divorced—
  The Construction of Self-Serving
  Theories

Cultural Highlight
The Art of Telling Stories

Imagine that you have completed college and are interviewing at a company for your first job. You have met the personnel director and some prospective coworkers. You also have toured the facilities, seen where your office would be if you were to join the firm, and learned a great deal about the work the company does and your responsibilities to the company. How do you decide if this is indeed the kind of company you want to work for and if you would like the work itself and the people you would work with? Answering these questions involves processes called social cognition.

Social cognition is the study of how people form inferences from social information in the environment (Fiske & Taylor, 1991). It explores how people make social judgments about other individuals or social groups, about social roles, and about their own experiences in social settings. The process of making social judgments is more difficult than we might imagine. Often, the information available to us is incomplete, ambiguous, or downright contradictory. We may be confronted with many complex details. How do we use all this information to arrive at a coherent judgment? This is the core question in research on social cognition.

Much of the early work on social cognition compared the social judgments actually made by people to those we would expect from a **rational model of inference.** By rational model, we mean that there are logical and correct ways to put information together to reach a judgment. Presumably, to make correct decisions and wise judgments, people should try to use social information as logically and carefully as possible (Einhorn & Hogarth, 1981). In the interests of making accurate inferences, people should try hard to avoid logical errors and subjective biases. Consequently, rational models of inference were considered to be appropriate standards against which to evaluate people's everyday processes for forming judgments and making decisions.

Studies comparing actual social judgments to the rational model have taught us much about the processes of social cognition. Contrary to what the rational model predicts, however, people's everyday methods of gathering and combining social information are often illogical. In the next section, we discuss some of the typical errors and biases that affect the social perceiver. Then we turn to newer research that explains some of the reasons why the social perceiver is not completely rational.

SOCIAL INFERENCE

Any social inference is composed of several steps: gathering information, deciding what information to use to reach a judgment, and integrating the information into a judgment. For example, as you are learning about your possible new employer, you are gathering information about the people, products, and general feel of the organization, and you are gathering information from people around you through the questions you ask and the types of facilities or people that you request to see. When you return home and mull over your visit, you must then decide which of the multitude of information you received will be most relevant to your decision, and then integrate that information into an overall impression or judgment concerning whether or not this company is the right one for you. Each of these steps in the social inference process appears to be subject to particular kinds of errors and biases.

Gathering Information

When people gather information that is relevant to some inference they will ultimately form, they might plan to do so in an even-handed and unbiased manner. However, research suggests that actual information gathering is often subject to several sources of bias.

PRIOR EXPECTATIONS.   Suppose you learn that a college acquaintance of yours, an uptight, serious, humorless fellow, works for the company you are considering and finds it very much to his liking. If he likes the company so much, you might suspect that it is because he has found people there who are like he is. Consequently, you might infer that everyone at the company must be stiff and uptight. Accordingly, as you learn about the company with this suspicion in mind, you might selectively gather information consistent with this prior expectation. You might note that prospective coworkers seem a little stiff or formal when you meet them and conclude that indeed your classmate is typical of the people at this firm.

Are these people prospecting for gold, seaching for a lost contact lens, interpreting animals tracks, or collecting insects? Because much behavior is fundamentally ambiguous, social inference processes give social interactions structure and meaning.

But in doing so, you might fail to remember that most people are a little stiff or formal when they are meeting someone for the first time. Their formality might simply be due to the fact that you are a stranger to them. They might actually turn out to be very friendly people. But with your prior expectations in mind, you might dismiss them as stiff and formal people without giving them a chance. This is how prior expectations can bias the process of gathering information.

Of course, prior expectations are very helpful in sifting through a lot of information that may otherwise be uninterpretable. They can provide structure and meaning for information that would otherwise be hard to interpret. However, sometimes prior expectations can cause us to draw inaccurate inferences. Three conditions are especially problematic (Nisbett & Ross, 1980). The first is faulty expectations. For example, your belief that the company is stiff and stodgy merely because it attracted one such individual to its ranks is likely to be incorrect. Therefore, letting this expectation guide your collection of information will probably lead you to incorrect answers. A second condition under which prior expectations can be problematic occurs when the social perceiver fails to recognize how prior expectations bias the collection of information. For example, you may be unaware that your impressions of your stodgy college classmate are actually guiding your judgments of your prospective coworkers. This lack of awareness means that later on you will be unable to correct the biasing effect of your prior impression. Your judgments concerning your prospective coworkers will stray on the stodgy and serious side without your realizing that your own biases contributed to this inference. Third, prior expectations can create problems when they overrule consideration of information altogether. If you decide on the basis of your college classmate's attributes not to meet your potential coworkers at all, you would be guilty of this error.

BIASES IN THE INFORMATION.   Once the social perceiver has decided what information is relevant to an inference, information must actually be collected. The individual must determine which bits of information from the available wealth should be examined. For example, obviously you cannot meet everybody during your job interview visit, and so the people you do meet will help give you an impression of the qualities of your coworkers. But forming judgments on the basis of limited information can be thrown off when there are *biases in the information*. For example, if you are introduced to a particularly outgoing and friendly coworker, your impression of the attributes of the workers in the company may be falsely influenced toward the outgoing and friendly side.

Even when people are warned that information may be biased, they sometimes fail to understand the full implications of that bias. For example, in one study (Hamill, Wilson, & Nisbett, 1980), researchers told subjects that they would be viewing a videotape of an interview with a prison guard. Some subjects were told that this prison guard was typical of most prison guards, whereas others were told that he was very different from most prison guards. In the third condition, subjects were not given information about how typical the guard was. Half the subjects then saw a tape in which the prison guard appeared as a highly compassionate, concerned individual. The other half saw a tape portraying him as an inhumane, macho, cruel person. Subjects were later asked a set of questions about the criminal justice system that included questions about what kind of people become prison guards. The results showed that subjects exposed to the interview of the humane guard were more favorable in their attitudes toward prison guards than were subjects who saw the interview with the inhumane prison guard. More important, subjects' inferences about prison guards were unaffected by whether or not they had been told that the interview with the prison guard was typical or not typical.

Consider an analogous situation in your hypothetical job interview. Suppose you wanted to meet some of your coworkers but were told that they were away at a seminar this week and unable to meet with you. But so that you could form some impressions of the workers of the company, you might be introduced to one or two of the company's employees from a neighboring office but with whom you would not be

working directly. You might find that your judgments about your prospective coworkers would be influenced by the one or two individuals you do meet. You might fail to correct for the fact that these individuals actually have a different job and would not be in your work group at all. Therefore, your impressions of them might have little if anything to do with the attributes of your actual coworkers.

SMALL SAMPLE. Inferences are also problematic when they are based on very little information. People are sometimes unaware that a small sample of information can actually produce a very biased picture. For example, if you are introduced to only two of your prospective coworkers who seem pleasant enough but you will actually be working with 20 individuals, there is the possibility that these two are not typical of the larger group. The other 18 may not be quite as pleasant. But sometimes people forget that they are dealing with very little information and make confident inferences nonetheless (see Nisbett & Kunda, 1986).

STATISTICAL VS. CASE HISTORY INFORMATION. Another distinction that is important in understanding how people use information is between **statistical information** and **case history information.** Statistical information involves information about a large number of individuals, whereas case history information involves information about only a few specific individuals. It turns out that when people are exposed to both statistical information and a contradictory but colorful case history, the case history often has more influence on their judgments (Taylor & Thompson, 1982). This occurs even when the statistical information is objectively better. For example, one type of information you might want to gather during your job interview is knowledge about how quickly people advance in the company. Clearly, the most appropriate information to look at is the statistical information about promotion rates for all the employees and for those in your division particularly. However, suppose you are told about Mark Comet, a particularly dynamic fellow who managed to go from clerk to associate vice president in three short years. It is very likely that the case

Decision making often involves collecting and integrating complex information. People typically think they are more consistent, use more information, and make more complex judgments than is actually the case.

history of Mark Comet's dramatic rise to fame and fortune within the company will bias your impression of how quickly people advance. It may lead you to ignore the more appropriate statistical information that would suggest that most people advance fairly slowly within the company.

Most of us seem to know that we really should use broadly based statistical information in making our judgments. People draw on statistics all the time when they are trying to make a persuasive argument, and a person can often be quite persuasive if he or she has statistical information available. If a case history does not lead us to a strong conclusion, we are more likely to rely on the statistical evidence available (Lynch & Ofir, 1989). However, generally speaking, when more engaging anecdotal case history evidence is present, people often ignore relevant statistical evidence and are instead overly persuaded by the case histories (Bar-Hillel & Fischoff, 1981; see Schwarz, Strack, Hilton, & Naderer, in press).

Impact of Negative Information

Suppose that during the course of gathering information about your prospective company, you learned one or two negative pieces of information. You might, for example, encounter one disgruntled employee about to be let go for poor performance, who questions why you would ever want to work at this place. Chances are,

you would attach some significance to this observation, perhaps more than it was worth. This is a common finding in research on judgments and decisions.

Negative information attracts more attention than positive information (Pratto & John, 1991). Subsequently, negative information is weighted more heavily than positive aspects when judgments are made (Coovert & Reeder, 1990). In studies of all kinds, ranging from forming impressions about other people to evaluating positive and negative information to reach a decision or judgment, the negative information figures more prominently (Taylor, 1991a).

Integrating Information

The next task in the inference process involves bringing information together and combining it into a social judgment. When people's integrative capabilities are compared against rational models, it appears that the human judgment process is rather haphazard and does not closely follow the principles of a rational model.

Consider the example of college admissions. When there are many applicants and only a few openings, one must develop criteria for deciding which people to admit and which to reject. Most college admissions departments have a formula for admitting students that dictates how heavily they weight SAT scores, high school grades, letters of recommendation, the personal essay, and other sources of information. With such clear standards available, one would assume that the college admissions decision makers do a good job of using this formula to determine who will be admitted and who will not. However, it turns out that when there are clear standards for combining information into a judgment, a computer typically outperforms a human decision maker (Meehl, 1954; Dawes, Faust, & Meehl, 1989).

Why is this the case? Human decision makers have great faith in their abilities to make decisions. When asked what procedures they use to make decisions, they typically report being more consistent, using more pieces of information, and making more complex judgments than is actually the case. The reason that computers typically outperform human judges is that the computer consistently uses criteria established by people, weights information in a standard way, combines the information according to the formula, and reaches a judgment. The human decision maker, in contrast, may be swayed by pet theories or stereotypes that influence the information selected. Extensive studies have pitted human judges against the computer or other mechanical aids and have yielded the same conclusion (Meehl, 1954; Dawes et al., 1989): When people can specify the rules of inference they want to use to combine information into an overall decision or judgment, computers and other mechanical aids always do a better job of following these rules than human judges do.

Imagine how this process might work after your job interview. A small group of individuals who had met you during your visit would be assigned the task of deciding whether to hire you. Each person would have only a modest amount of information about you. One person might point out that you seemed nervous under pressure as evidenced by the fact that you dropped your roll on the floor during lunch. Another, however, might argue that you may be a potential Mark Comet, given that you both have competitive tennis in your background. Another might point out that your transcript shows you have high grades in virtually every subject, suggesting great ability. The next person, however, might complain that although you did well in everything, you have not shown any special talents. In short, then, each evaluator may have certain idiosyncratic ways of viewing the information derived from your brief visit which he or she considers relevant to the overall judgment of whether you should be hired. It is indeed unnerving to realize one's fate often depends upon this type of decision-making process.

Judgments of Covariation

In addition to putting information together to form coherent impressions of people and events, we are also concerned with figuring out "what goes with what" in social life. Many of our beliefs involve statements about the relationship between things. For example, the adage "All work and no play makes Jack a dull boy" implies that working too hard and being dull are related and that playing and not being dull go together. Similarly, the statement "Blondes have more fun" implies a relationship between being blonde and having fun and between not being blonde and having less fun. Technically, such ideas about the associations between things are called judgments of **covariation.**

In making judgments about covariation, people are prone to certain errors. Consider the statement, "Blondes have more fun." As Figure 3-1 illustrates, the first step in assessing covariation is deciding what information is relevant. To determine if blondes actually have more fun, one needs to look at both blondes and non-blondes and examine the frequency with which they have fun and do not have fun. However, most people believe that cell A (fun-loving blondes) is the relevant information from which to determine whether blondes have more fun. They fail to recognize that the number of brunettes and redheads who have fun and do not have fun are just as relevant as the number of blondes who have fun or do not. After all, to know if blondes have more fun, one needs to know that there are brunettes and redheads who are having less fun.

The second step in assessing covariation is gathering instances of blonde, brunette, and redheaded men and women to see if they are having fun or not. As we already noted, people are very poor at gathering information. They tend to draw on their own acquaintances, which may represent a biased sample. Most people assessing whether blondes have more fun would think about a few blonde friends and leave the information-gathering task at that.

The third step in the covariation process is classifying instances as to the type of evidence they represent, and again, the social perceiver's expectations can get in the way. Cases that contradict the proposed relationship may be mislabeled as supportive instances if they are ambiguous, or they may be dismissed as due to error or faulty information gathering if they are not ambiguous. Positive instances are more

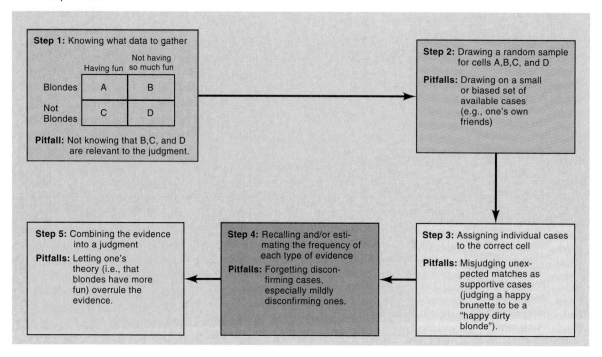

Figure 3-1   The assessment of covariation and its pitfalls. Do blondes have more fun?

quickly or easily identified and incorporated into the inference task (Klayman & Ha, 1987). Thus, for example, happy blondes will quickly be seen as relevant. Happy brunettes may be judged to be happy "dirty blondes" and happy redheads labeled "strawberry blondes." Unhappy blondes might be judged to have dyed their hair blonde, and thus be irrelevant to assessing whether blondes have more fun.

Information must next be put together, which requires recalling the frequency of each type of evidence. Unfortunately, the social perceiver remembers confirming cases well but tends to forget cases that contradict the relationship, especially those that are mildly disconfirming (Crocker, Hannah, & Weber, 1983). For example, the ecstatic raven-haired woman might be remembered, but the contented brown-haired individual might be forgotten.

In short, then, when people are making judgments of covariation, they rarely follow the rational model for so doing. Instead, prior expectations lead them to focus primarily on positive instances (such as fun-loving blondes) and to pay relatively less attention to other evi-

dence (Klayman & Ha, 1987). Thus, when a relationship between two variables is expected (for example, if the perceiver believes that blondes have more fun), a person is likely to overestimate the degree of relationship that exists between the two factors or impose a relationship when none exists. This intriguing phenomenon has been called illusory correlation.

ILLUSORY CORRELATION.   At least two factors can produce an illusory correlation. The first is *associative meaning,* in which two items are seen as belonging together because they "ought" to be, on the basis of prior expectations. Thus, members of minority groups are often seen as having attributes stereotypically associated with their group because of their membership, when in fact, any given individual in the group may not exhibit the stereotypic behavior or may contradict it altogether (Hamilton & Gifford, 1976; Schaller & Maas, 1989). The second basis of illusory correlation is *paired distinctiveness,* in which two items are thought to go together because they share some unusual feature. For example, individuals who are salient by virtue of an irrelevant factor such as appearance or seating position are thought to have a more potent role in the conversation in which they participate (Taylor & Fiske, 1978). Illusory correlations, then, can substitute for real correlations when people have prior expectations or theories about whether or not two factors go together (see also Fiedler, 1991).

MOOD AND INFERENCE. Perhaps you have noticed that when you get a good grade on a test, you're nicer to your roommate, or when you've had a nice time with your girlfriend or boyfriend, you're more likely to help someone who needs it. Or perhaps you have noticed that when you're feeling cheerful, your work goes more smoothly. These examples illustrate some of the effects that mood has on inference and behavior.

How have psychologists uncovered the effects of mood on our beliefs and behavior? Like Peter Pan teaching the Darling children how to fly, psychologists lead people to think happy thoughts by surprising them with an unexpected gift, inducing them to concentrate on happy experiences ("Think of Christmas, think of snow"), asking them to recall a time in the past when they were very happy, or having them read a series of statements that suggest a progressively happier state of mind. Before very long, people exposed to these techniques report that they feel more cheerful, even euphoric. Alternatively, psychologists can make people unhappy by getting them to think about times in the past when they were sad, or having them read a series of statements that suggest a progressively more glum mood. Thus, these techniques can also change mood in a negative direction. But negative moods are harder to induce than positive moods, and once in them, people are more likely to try to escape negative moods.

What is the effect of mood on behavior? When we are in a good mood, we tend to be more sociable and more altruistic in our behavior. We spend more time with others and help others more, for example. What happens when we're in a bad mood? You might think that people in a bad mood would be more withdrawn and help other people less, and sometimes this

How would you regard this scene if you were the girl's father? The boy's ex-girlfriend? The person who had arranged the first date between these two? The interpretations we make and the affect we experience are heavily determined by the motives we bring to social situations.

is true. But often, people who are in a bad mood want to escape that bad mood, and so instead of acting consistent with their bad mood, they try to work themselves out of it by being sociable, by helping others, or by engaging in other positive actions (e.g., Cunningham, Shaffer, Barbee, Wolff, & Kelley, 1990). This means that the effects of positive mood on prosocial behavior are stronger than the effects of negative mood in producing antisocial behavior (see Isen, 1987; J. D. Mayer & Salovey, 1988, for reviews; Schaller & Cialdini, 1988).

Mood also influences memory. Perhaps you've received a piece of good news and then found yourself mentally remembering other past experiences of being happy, feeling good, or feeling competent. Under many circumstances, people remember material whose valence fits their current mood state (Mayer,

Gayle, Meehan, & Haarman, 1990; for reviews, see Blaney, 1986; Isen, 1987). This effect is called **mood congruent memory.** People tend to recall positive material when they're in a positive mood. Does mood congruent memory work for negative moods as well? Sometimes people recall more negative material when they're in a negative mood. This seems to be especially true of people who are depressed (Blaney, 1986). But remember that the effects of negative mood are more variable, so sometimes people in a negative mood think of positive things, in part so they can work themselves out of the bad mood.

Mood also affects judgments. Cheerful people like just about everything better than people who are not in a good mood: themselves, their health, their cars, other people, the future, and even politics (see Fiske & Taylor, 1991, for a

RESEARCH CLOSEUP

Why I Will Never Get Divorced— The Construction of Self-serving Theories

For many years, the study of social cognition looked primarily at cognitive processes, virtually ignoring emotional and motivational factors. Increasingly, however, it has become clear that how we process and put together information can be heavily influenced by our emotions, our personal goals, and our self-serving interests. Ziva Kunda (1987) suggests that people generate and evaluate theories in a self-serving manner, constructing theories that are consistent with the belief that good things will happen to them and bad things will not.

For example, upon learning that the divorce rate for first marriages is 50 percent, most people predict that they will not be in that 50 percent, but rather will remain married to their spouse for their lifetime. They convince themselves that this is the case by highlighting their personal attributes that might be associated with a stable marriage and downplaying the significance of or actively refuting information that might suggest a vulnerability to divorce. Thus, for example, one might point to one's parents' enduring marriage, the close family life that existed in one's early childhood, and the fact that one's high school relationship lasted a full four years as evidence for a likely stable marriage. The fact that one's husband has already been divorced once, a factor that predicts a second divorce, might be interpreted not only as not leading to divorce in one's own case, but as a protective factor. ("He does not want this marriage to fail like the last one, so he's working especially hard to keep our relationship strong.")

To test this point, Kunda (1987) gave college student subjects a description of a target person and a list of the target's attributes. The list included such facts as the target was extroverted, dependent, religious, and conservative. Other information specified whether the target's mother had worked or been in the home while the person was young, and whether the target person had had at least one serious relationship before entering college. A third of the subjects read that the target person was divorced, a third that the person was happily married, and a third were given no information about the outcome of the marriage. Subjects then rated each of the target's attributes on a scale ranging from 1 ("made divorce much more likely") to 9 ("made stable marriage much more likely"). After completing this questionnaire, subjects were asked to indicate their own standing on each of the background attributes and the likelihood that they would end up in a divorce.

The results showed that subjects judged attributes on which they matched the target person as better for marriage than attributes on which they did not match the target person. The ability to draw seemingly rational relationships between our own assets and good events and to argue away associations between our own attributes and negative events helps us to maintain the beliefs that we want to hold.

review). Do unhappy people dislike everything? Again, the evidence is mixed. Sometimes, unhappy people make negative judgments about others, but other times, they do not. Negative mood has a less reliable impact on judgments than positive mood.

Mood influences not only what we remember and how we evaluate our world but also the way in which we make judgments. Happy people are expansive, inclusive, and impulsive in their decision making. That is, they make decisions quickly, they work quickly at simple tasks, they make more unusual connections among the things they are thinking about, they have looser and less organized associations, and they group more varied things together into the same category (Isen, 1987; Murray, Sujan, Hirt, & Sujan, 1990). A negative mood seems to slow down the processing of information. People are more methodical and precise, they make decisions more slowly, they make more complex causal attributions, and they work more slowly (Flett, Pliner, & Blankstein, 1989).

Happy people also do not like to get negative feedback and they are especially "loss-averse" (Esses, 1989). This means that risky decisions that highlight how one might do badly seem worse to people who are feeling happy (Isen, Nygren, & Ashby, 1988). People in a negative mood, on the other hand, do not seem to be as strongly affected by negative feedback and losses may not loom as large for them either.

What, then, might be the effect of your mood on extracting and processing information from your job interview? If you were in a good mood at the time you visited, you would probably pay disproportionate attention to all of the positive features of the job and work environment. If you were in a bad mood, however, you might focus more on the apparent disadvantages of the position. Later, when you had to make a decision about the job, if you were in a good mood, you might make the decision quite impulsively based on the positive features of the experience. On the other hand, if you were in a bad mood, you might survey your impressions more methodically and even get quite bogged down in making the decision.

In short, affective factors such as mood can affect judgment and decision making in impor-

tant ways. Another example of this fact is shown in the RESEARCH CLOSEUP.

Inference: A Summing Up

Overall, how well does the social perceiver fare on tasks of social inference? The evidence we just considered suggests that, when evaluated against rational models, social inference suffers from some predictable errors and biases (Sherman, Judd, & Park, 1989; Fiske & Taylor, 1991). Social inference and its potential pitfalls are shown in Figure 3-2. This evaluation prompts at least two reactions. The first is concern over disconcerting ways in which social perceivers let their prior expectations override and ignore relevant information. The second reaction is puzzlement. How do people manage in their social lives as well as they seem to if their social judgments are biased?

Some researchers are now coming to the opinion that rational models may often be inappropriate bases for evaluating social inference (e.g., McArthur & Baron, 1983; Funder, 1987; Swann, 1984). One reason is that the conditions of the real world are often such as to make use of a rational model nearly impossible. Much of the time social information is unreliable, biased, and incomplete. Even reliable, unbiased, and complete information may not be presented to the average social perceiver in a clear or usable fashion, and sometimes information that is needed is not available.

Consider, again, the use of the rational model in the judgment, Do blondes have more fun? Is it really worth it to you to get a sample of blondes, observe whether they have fun, get a sample of brunettes and redheads, see whether they have fun, and calculate a statistical relationship? How many people would you need to survey? How long should you wait before you decide that any given person is not having fun? The conditions that maximize accuracy seldom occur in real life, and accordingly in many situations, social perceivers could not apply a rational model even if they were so inclined (see Crocker, 1981; Nisbett et al., 1982).

Rational models describe ideal inferential processes under conditions in which time and

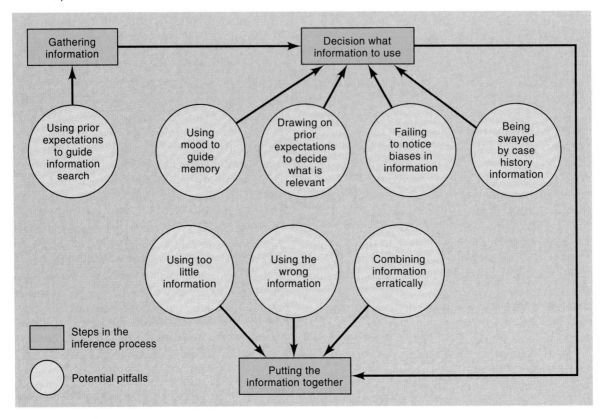

Figure 3-2   Social inference and its pitfalls.

environment are frozen. Yet people make inferences in environments that are constantly changing and that provide feedback. Inferences are made in a world filled with consequences. Once ventured, an inaccurate inference may be corrected by the environment because other people or new information show it to be wrong. One can then change the inference. For example, if you believe a particular acquaintance is overly serious and say so to a friend, the friend may inform you about the acquaintance's silly side, forcing you to change your belief.

Many of the errors produced by faulty inferential procedures do not truly matter. For example, suppose you pick a particular group of friends on the basis of their flashy fun-filled lives rather than their personal qualities. Suppose you then find out that they are into drugs, fast cars, and hard rock, and these are activities you do not want to participate in. You can gradually withdraw from the circle of

friends and make new ones without any long-term repercussions. Spending time with a particular group of people does not force you to spend the rest of your life with them.

Perhaps most important is the fact that the tasks facing the social perceiver may be fundamentally different from the tasks defined by rational models of inference. Rational models of inference place a premium on *accuracy* of inference. For the social perceiver, *efficiency*, that is, processing information quickly, may be at least as important. Consider the sheer volume of information that an individual encounters in a particular day. Even an act as simple as crossing the street requires watching the lights and signs, the flow of the traffic, and the pedestrians on one's own side and the other side of the street. If people truly had to make all their inferences using rational models of inference, they might still be plotting a course to follow across the street when the light changed back to "Don't

Walk." In other words, rational models of inference assume that a person has time to do inferential work, and given the blooming, buzzing confusion of the real world, time is a very expensive commodity.

Consequently, people draw on their preexisting conceptions of people and situations and use inferential shortcuts to make social judgments quickly and efficiently. This is not to say that the errors we have just documented in the social inference process are inconsequential. Indeed, they can often have problematic consequences in that people clearly make what are objectively wrong decisions and inferences. Improving the inference process, therefore, is an important priority for social cognition researchers. But it must be done in the context of understanding the processes people typically use, rather than the rational models of inference developed by statisticians (see Lord, Lepper, & Preston, 1984; Fong, Krantz, & Nisbett, 1986; Nisbett, Fong, Lehman, & Chang, 1987).

To begin to understand how the social perceiver actually forms inferences and why those inferences do not correspond to the assumptions of rational models requires an important observation. The act of bringing information together and solving a problem, as we have noted, can be a time-consuming task involving substantial processing capabilities. When one's attention is absorbed in forming a particular inference, there is relatively little attention that is available to perform other tasks such as monitoring the environment successfully, solving other problems, and the like. However, memory seems to have almost a limitless capacity. Think, for example, of the number of popular songs for which you know all the lyrics. The number may total in the hundreds or even thousands. Or think of all the friends you have and everything that you know about each of them. These simple tasks point out the astonishing amount of information that we are able to carry in our heads and retrieve from memory when we need it. Thus, problem solving is very costly in that it consumes attention and drains resources for other tasks, whereas memory appears to be nearly limitless and does not drain resources for other tasks. For example, knowing a great deal about one friend does not preclude learning a

great deal about another friend. This important difference is fundamental to how people actually make inferences. Rather than engaging in elaborate and often time-consuming problem solving for each individual task that the environment presents, instead people often draw on the knowledge that they have stored in memory to interpret the environment that confronts them, namely, their schemas.

SCHEMAS

What we have so far been referring to as prior expectations goes under the general term *schemas*. As we saw in Chapter 2, a schema is an organized, structured set of cognitions about some concept or stimulus which includes knowledge about the concept or stimulus, some relations among the various cognitions about it, and some specific examples (Fiske & Taylor, 1991). As Chapter 2 made clear, schemas can be about particular people, social roles, the self, attitudes about particular objects, stereotypes about groups, or perceptions of common events.

Schemas are important because people draw on them to interpret the environment. That is, each time we are confronted with a new situation, we don't try to understand it afresh. Instead we draw on our knowledge of past similar situations for making interpretations, and this is the way schemas help us to process information. They help us to recognize what aspects of a situation or stimulus are important. They add structure and organization to information. Schemas enable us to remember information better, to organize details, and to process information relevant to the schema very quickly. Schemas can sometimes fill in gaps and knowledge as well as help people interpret and evaluate new information.

Organization of Schemas

An important feature of schemas is that they often have some hierarchical organization. They have some abstract and general elements, and some more concrete, specific ones. Suppose we had a schema of a "cocktail party." We know that cocktail parties usually are held in the late afternoon or evening, usually in someone's home. They have guests and usually a host and a hostess; they have some food and a lot of alcoholic drinks (all of which are more likely to be prepared and served by the host and hostess rather than by the guests). Normally people interact by standing and talking to each other rather than by watching one common event (like a singer) or sleeping or running in circles. In short, we have a clear, well-developed, somewhat abstract picture in our minds about a "cocktail party." It has a standard sequence, a number of elements, and clear causal interrelationships among them.

At a more specific level, the schema might well have different categories of cocktail parties, all of which would be clearly distinct. For example, a wine-and-cheese party held at the opening of an art gallery would be clearly different from the weekly Saturday night bashes at the country club, where all the local businesspeople and their spouses get together and drink too much, or from a formal diplomatic reception at a foreign embassy. At a still more specific level, our schema might include several specific parties we have attended. All told, we might have a hierarchical schema of a "cocktail party" that would include a general, abstract concept covering all kinds of cocktail parties we have gone to.

As we saw in Chapter 2, many schemas contain exemplars, which are the best examples of a schema. For example, your schema of "bird" probably includes being small, feathered, mottled brown in color, with a long tail, and little clawed feet. But the exemplar or best example of the category may be a robin or a blue jay (E. E. Smith & Medin, 1981). Exemplars need not correspond to all the schema's typical features and may, in fact, be rather different from those typical features, as the robin and blue jay are in the case of birds.

So far, our discussion of schemas makes them sound very orderly. However, often the associations contained within a schema more closely resemble a tangled web than a hierarchy (Cantor & Kihlstrom, 1987). For example, a politician, a con man, and a clown are all examples of extroverts. Being socially skilled is associated with being a politician, a con man, or a

An exemplar is a model example of a category. Florence Griffith-Joiner is an exemplar of the category, track star.

clown, but being self-confident is associated with being a politician or a con man, but not necessarily with being a clown. Thus, the more specific attributes embedded in a schema (socially skilled, self-confident) may overlap with many or few of the upper-level concepts (politician, clown, con man) (Anderson & Klatsky, 1987). Social categories, then, are related in very flexible and complex ways, not always in neat, tidy, hierarchical fashion.

Individual Differences in Schemas

To some extent, we all share the same schemas. Most of us have schemas about teachers, extroverts, and check cashing. However, many schemas are personal and reflect individual interests and values. For example, a person who

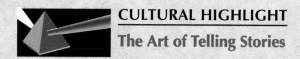

CULTURAL HIGHLIGHT
The Art of Telling Stories

"Maakga was the son of a warlike king. He was to become his father's successor to the throne. From childhood, he was assigned a group of boys his own age, to be his attendants. Maakga was a like-able boy, jovial and full of jokes. He loved hunting and he was very good at it. One day he called on his companions and asked them to go on a hunt with him. Early on the following day, they began their long journey . . ." (Dube, 1982, p. 239)

Schemas involve not only what information people hold about different objects, roles, events, or people, but how that information is put together. Each culture has different ways of training its young people to think about and organize the information it conveys to them through socialization. Whereas students in the United States are generally taught to think about cultural traditions using abstract symbols such as the flag, children in other cultures are often encouraged to understand their society through stories.

Researcher Ernest Dube (1982) illustrated this important point in a cross-cultural study of storytelling. Dube had students from three different groups listen to tape-recorded stories like the one whose beginning appears above. The groups were young African men and women in Botswana who could not read or write, junior high school students in Botswana, and junior high school students in upstate New York. Each group listened to both an African story and an American story and were then asked to retell the stories into a tape recorder. The tape recordings were scored for accuracy, that is, whether the respondent got the gist of the story and the events that occur in it.

On the whole, African subjects remembered the stories much better than did the American students. They remembered not only the African story better, but the American story as well. Even African subjects who could not read and write were able to per-

form this task well, better than the American students.

What accounts for the African subjects' better performance on this memory task? The likely explanation is that Africans are more familiar with telling stories than are Americans. Storytelling is encouraged in many African cultures as a way of transmitting cultural themes. Children hear stories from their elders and in turn tell them to younger brothers and sisters. In America, storytelling is less common.

One can say, then, that the natives of Botswana have a schema for storytelling, a way of thinking that enables them to take in the information in a story, organize it in memory, and retell it easily, because of the practice they have in dealing with organized sequences of related events. While American students may excel at other kinds of information transmission, storytelling is not one of them, because of the culture's lack of emphasis on it (Dube, 1982).

loves the out-of-doors may have schemas for hiking, volleyball, and sailing, whereas the stay-at-home television watcher will not. Having a schema for a particular domain will, in turn, greatly modify how one processes information. For example, a veteran baseball coach will have a richer and more detailed set of baseball schemas and will impute more meaning to an outfielder's play than will a foreigner attending his first baseball game (Lurigio & Carroll, 1985;

Markus, Smith, & Moreland, 1985). A person to whom honesty is important will be more likely to judge other people according to whether they are dishonest or not than will someone who is not as concerned with the trait of honesty (Cantrambone & Markus, 1987). To summarize, then, some schemas may be widely shared within a given culture, whereas others may be quite idiosyncratic. An example of these differences is provided in the CULTURAL HIGHLIGHT.

SCHEMATIC PROCESSING

Advantages

SCHEMAS AID INFORMATION PROCESSING. Schemas are important because they help us process an enormous amount of information swiftly and economically. Indeed, schemas make processing more efficient in several different ways. They help us remember information, interpret new information, draw inferences from it, and evaluate whether or not we agree with it. They help us fill in gaps in our knowledge by suggesting what is likely to be true. And they help us prepare for the future by structuring our expectations about what is likely to happen. These advantages of schematic processing have been demonstrated in a wide variety of studies (see Fiske & Taylor, 1991; Markus & Zajonc, 1986, for reviews).

SCHEMAS AID RECALL. Memory often works best when we can bring back some schematic representation of past events or people, because the schema will bring many details along with it (Hirt, 1990). For example, Cohen (1981) presented subjects with a videotape of a woman and her husband sitting in their home. Half were told that the woman was a librarian, and half that she was a waitress. Some of the features of the woman fit the schema of a librarian (as measured separately), such as wearing glasses, eating salad, drinking wine, and playing the piano. Others fit the schema of a waitress, such as having a bowling ball in the room and no bookshelves and eating a chocolate birthday cake. Later the subjects were asked to recall the details of the videotape. They remembered the schema-consistent details better, no matter whether recall was assessed immediately or a week later.

But schema-inconsistent material is not always recalled poorly. Both schema-consistent and schema-inconsistent material are remembered much better than things that are simply irrelevant to the schema (Hastie & Kumar, 1979; Brewer, Dull, & Lui, 1981); this may be because it is difficult to learn material that is irrelevant to a schema.

Sometimes information that contradicts a schema is better recalled than information that is consistent with a schema. This is especially likely when a person has a very poorly developed or an extremely well-developed schema. People who are unfamiliar with a schema and attempting to learn it show an initial advantage for remembering schema-inconsistent information (Ruble & Stangor, 1986). Similarly, people who are highly familiar with a domain may more easily recognize inconsistencies. People with moderately well-formed schemas may be most attentive to consistent information (Higgins & Bargh, 1987). Consider, for example, the impressions that might be formed of Harry, a policeman who raises kittens and does needlepoint in his spare time. Those just meeting Harry and those who know him very well may be especially attentive to the schema-inconsistent behaviors, whereas those with a moderately well-developed conception of Harry may attend more to his schema-consistent behavior, such as his concern for abiding by the law or helping people in need (Borgida & DeBono, 1989).

SCHEMAS SPEED UP PROCESSING. Markus (1977) identified subjects with self-schemas of being independent, self-schemas of being dependent, and neither self-schema. She read them sentences about certain independent or dependent behaviors. People with self-schemas were able to indicate more quickly than those without self-schemas whether or not the behavior was typical of them. Processing time was much longer for schema-inconsistent than for schema-consistent information. But not all research finds that schemas speed up processing. In some cases, evoking a schema slows things down by introducing a more complex mass of information that must be processed (Fiske & Taylor, 1991). So, for example, if you are strongly ambivalent about your dependency needs, you might take more time to decide if a dependent behavior is typical of you than would someone who is aschematic with respect to dependency.

SCHEMAS AID AUTOMATIC INFERENCE. Another important attribute of schematic processing is that some schema-related inferences appear to occur almost automatically without any conscious effort on an individual's part. For example, if a particular person you meet seems to be especially friendly, you may automatically attribute other attributes associated with friendliness to him, such as kindness and warmth, and be completely unaware that you have done so. These automatic effects are most likely to occur if the information in the environment strongly suggests a particular schema, or if there is some kind of affective or emotional relationship involved (Bargh, 1984; Smith & Lerner, 1986; Fazio, Sanbonmatsu, Powell, & Kardes, 1986).

SCHEMAS ADD INFORMATION. A schema can help us fill in missing information when there are gaps in our knowledge. If we read about a policeman but have no information about his clothing, we imagine him to be wearing a blue uniform. We assume a nurse will be warm and caring, and a queen to be rather aloof and haughty. Missing information is filled in by adding schema-consistent details, even when we must invent them.

Exemplars of schemas are often used to fill in missing information. For example, if "blue jay" is your exemplar, or best example, of the category "birds," then on briefly glimpsing some new bird, you may assume that the bird has a crest, because the blue jay has a crest. However, if the exemplar of your category for birds is "robin," you might be less likely to assume that the new bird you have just seen has a crest (Read, 1987; Rothbart & Lewis, 1988).

SCHEMAS AID INTERPETATION. For example, when a pediatrician diagnoses a child as having mumps, it enables her to make a whole series of other inferences with confidence: how the child got the disease, what symptoms should be present, what the course of the disease will be, what treatment is best, and so on. To a person with no schema for mumps, none of this would be possible. The problem would just seem mysterious. Schemas allow confident inferences about matters that would otherwise not be clear (Read & Cesa, 1991). This effect seems to occur more for strong schemas than weak ones, however. When people use weakly developed categories, such as day people versus night people,

Schemas help us to understand stiuations. Once we learn that this man is packing food at a volunteer foodbank, we understand the meaning of his actions.

the schema itself seems to be weakened by new and potentially irrelevant information (Fiske & Neuberg, 1990).

SCHEMAS PROVIDE EXPECTATIONS. Schemas also contain expectations for what should happen. These expectations in turn can determine how pleasant or unpleasant we find a particular situation. When experience matches expectations, the result may be pleasant, whereas violations of expectations are often experienced as unpleasant. Suppose a black student who had worked to educate himself was nonetheless unable to find a job at his level of expertise. This experience might violate his expectations and would be likely to make him quite angry. A sense of deprivation relative to expectation has been cited as one of the causes of ghetto riots and other forms of social rebellion (Sears & McConahay, 1973).

SCHEMAS CONTAIN AFFECT. Affect is the feelings we have about the domain. Consequently, use of a particular schema can produce an emotional response, termed *schema-driven affect*. For example, most of us have a fairly well-developed schema for "politician." It may include information about what the politician does in his or her job, and what kinds of people are attracted to being a politician. The schema will also include any affective responses we have to the concept of politician. For example, some of us will feel positively about politicians, thinking of them as helpful statesmen, whereas others may feel negatively about politicians, thinking of them as sly, self-serving, power-hungry individuals. When information in the environment fits a particular schema, then it will trigger the affect attached to that schema (Fiske & Neuberg, 1990). The affect that is triggered by a schema is an efficient affective processing device: One can say "I know that type and I know how I feel about him or her" (Westen, 1988; Pavelchak, 1989; Fiske et al., 1987).

Under some circumstances, bringing a schema to bear on an object or an event can actually change the feelings one has toward that object or event. A series of studies by Tesser (see Tesser & Conlee, 1975; Millar & Tesser, 1986) suggests that simply thinking about something with a schema in mind can intensify the affect one feels for that object. If, for example, you feel that a professor belittled the comments you made in class, the longer you think about it, the more upset you are likely to become. Under other circumstances, however, schemas may make affect more complex, not more extreme (Linville & Jones, 1980; Linville, 1982). For example, if a good friend of yours snaps at you one day, this behavior may produce a fairly complex evaluation. You have so much information about your friend and about yourself that coming up with an explanation for this behavior may be difficult (Gilovich, 1987). Your evaluation of the incident may be complex.

Liabilities of Schemas

All these advantages of schematic processing have their accompanying disadvantages, and many of them are precisely the errors and biases that we discussed at the beginning of this chapter. The tendencies to be overly accepting of information that fits a schema or theory, to fill in gaps in thinking by adding elements that do not belong but are schema consistent (Zuroff, 1989), to apply schemas even when they do not fit very well, and to be unwilling to change schemas can all be *liabilities*. We can easily be misled by oversimplifications.

There are so many familiar examples of the dangers of this kind of stereotyping that it hardly seems necessary to belabor the point. Everyone knows that people frequently behave in ways contrary to the stereotype generally held about their groups. Yet schematic processing can lead the perceiver to some dangerously false inferences about individual members of the group. (We will discuss these issues in somewhat more detail in Chapters 11 and 12.)

Implicit personality theories, a type of schema we discussed in Chapter 2, can also lead to errors, since there is a strong tendency for people to infer from the presence of one trait the presence of others. Knowing that someone is intelligent causes most people to expect the person also to be imaginative, clever, active, conscientious, deliberate, and reliable. Knowing that someone is inconsiderate leads most people to expect him or her also to be irritable, boastful, cold, hypercritical, and so on. These inferences are not derived logically from the given trait; they are based on assumptions about personality. Intelligence does not necessarily denote activity, nor does inconsiderateness denote irritability. The tendency to make these assumptions is sometimes called the **logical error,** because people see certain traits as going together and assume that someone who has one of them also has the others.

So schematic processing has the advantage of speed and efficiency and of making events comprehensible and predictable. It has the disadvantage of leading to wrong interpretations, inaccurate expectations, and inflexible modes of response.

Whenever we encounter regularities in research findings, we must ask the question, Are these findings universally true or true only for certain cultures? In other words, do the findings describe all people, or do they describe only the people on whom the research has been conducted, usually Americans and Western Europeans? In the case of schemas, there has been relatively little cross-cultural research. However, two points seem very clear. First, it is virtually essential that people have schema-like constructs in order to interpret their experience. If we did not have abstract conceptions of common situations and

The content of schemas differs across cultures. Americans have two or three different terms for snow, including "slush" and "powder." The Inuktitut, however, have 33 different names for snow, which help them to navigate snow successfully and make effective use of it.

social roles, for example, each new situation and every new person would require us to start from scratch. Clearly, this does not happen in any culture. Consequently, it seems clear that in every culture people hold schemas for situations, social roles, and events.

What seems equally clear, however, is that the content of those schemas will differ substantially across cultures. While most cultures have two or three terms for snow, the Inuktitut (native people of Northern Canada) have words for at least 33 different types of snow, including hard, compressed, frozen snow (*aniugavinirq*), drifting snow (*natiruvaaq*), and a very fine snowfall (*suagutsik*) (*Snow Country*, 1991). The existence of schemas and their processing advantages and disadvantages, then, may well be universal. Their content, however, varies substantially across cultures.

MENTAL SHORTCUTS: USING COGNITIVE HEURISTICS

Because problem-solving activity typically consumes so much time and attention, people often resort to mental shortcuts that reduce seemingly complex problem solving to more simple judgments. These shortcuts help people invoke their schemas to process information in the environment. These shortcuts have been called **heuristics** (Tversky & Kahneman, 1974).

The Representativeness Heuristic

Is John, the new guy in your math class, really the incurable romantic he seems to be, or is he a cad who moves on every woman he meets? Is Linda a dependable person who can be counted on to do her share of a joint project or not? The act of identifying people or events as examples of particular schemas is fundamental to all social inference and behavior. The question, What is it? must be answered before any other cognitive task can be performed. A mental shortcut called the *representativeness heuristic* provides a rapid method for accomplishing this task.

Basically, the representativeness heuristic matches information in the environment against schemas to determine the likelihood that the match is appropriate. Consider the following description: "Steve is very shy and withdrawn, invariably helpful, but with little interest in people or the world of reality. A meek and tidy soul, he has a need for order and structure and a passion for detail" (Tversky & Kahneman, 1974). Suppose you are now asked to guess Steve's occupation. Is he a farmer, a circus clown, a librarian, a con artist, or a pediatrician?

With adequate information about the number and characteristics of the people in these different occupations, one could conceivably estimate the likelihood of a meek clown, a shy con artist, and so on. This task, however, would likely take a long time, and good information on which to form these judgments would undoubtedly be lacking. In such cases, the representativeness heuristic provides a quick solution. One decides whether Steve is representative of (or similar to) the average person in each of the occupational categories and makes one's judgment about his occupation accordingly. Students given this task usually guessed that Steve is a librarian because the description of Steve is *representative* of attributes that are stereotypically associated with librarians (Tversky & Kahneman, 1974).

The representativeness heuristic, then, helps one to decide if a particular person or event is an example of a particular schema. However, this quite rapid method of identifying people and events is occasionally fallible because people sometimes fail to take into account other important qualifying information. For example, if Steve lives in a town with lots of farmers and only one librarian, the likelihood that he is a farmer and not a librarian is very high. The representativeness heuristic would not incorporate this qualifying information. As we noted earlier, people often ignore relevant statistical information that they ought to incorporate into their inferences. Under these kinds of circumstances then, use of the representativeness heuristic would probably produce an incorrect answer.

THE CONJUNCTION ERROR. The representativeness heuristic can also lead us to combine information that does not belong together, simply because the information seems like it ought to go together. In one study, students were told that a fellow student was gregarious and literary. When asked how likely it was that he was an engineering major, they responded that it was very unlikely. However, when asked how likely it was that he would start out as an engineering major but switch to journalism, subjects gave this a much higher rating (Slovic, Fischhoff, & Lichtenstein, 1977). Presumably, they could readily imagine how a gregarious, literary person would decide journalism was for him and not engineering, but they could not imagine how such a person would remain an engineer. But note in this example that the likelihood that any given student is an engineer is much higher than the likelihood of a student beginning as an engineering major and then switching to journalism. Thus, although starting out in engineering and switching to journalism seems more likely because it fits our ideas of what gregarious and literary people do, it is far less probable than the likelihood of staying in engineering. This error is called the **conjunction error.** It is an error, because people believe the combination of two events (majoring in engineering *and* switching to journalism) is more likely than either of the events alone (majoring in engineering *or* majoring in journalism), which is statistically incorrect reasoning (Gavanski & Roskos-Ewoldsen, 1991).

The Availability Heuristic

Sometimes we try to answer such questions as How often does a person break a leg skiing? or How many college students are psychology majors? These are questions about the frequency of events or the likelihood that a particular event will happen. A common way that people answer such questions is to use examples that come to mind. If you can think of lots of college students who are psychology majors among your friends and acquaintances, you may assume that there are many psychology majors on campus. Or if you can think of several people who broke their legs skiing, you may assume that the chances of breaking your leg skiing are rather high. Using the ease of remembering examples or the amount of information you can quickly remember as a guide to making an inference is called using the *availability heuristic* (Tversky & Kahneman, 1973).

As is the case with the representativeness heuristic, little cognitive work need be performed to accomplish this task. If you have no trouble thinking of psychology majors among your acquaintances, you will probably assume that a great many people in college are psychology majors, whereas if you have trouble bringing to mind examples of psychology majors, you may conclude that relatively few individuals are psychology majors.

Under many circumstances, use of the availability heuristic produces correct answers. After all, when examples of something can be easily brought to mind, it is usually because there are lots of them. Therefore, availability is often a good estimate of frequency. However, there are also biasing factors that can increase or decrease the availability of some kinds of phenomena or events without altering their actual overall frequency. For example, if you are a psychology major, many of your friends and acquaintances are likely to be psychology majors as well, and consequently you will have relatively little difficulty bringing examples of psychology majors to mind. Because of this bias among your friends, you are likely to overestimate the frequency of psychology majors. In contrast, another student who is a chemistry major and who spends most of his time hanging out with chemists or physicists would probably underestimate the number of psychology majors on campus, because he cannot bring examples of many psychology majors to mind (Gabrielcik & Fazio, 1984).

The availability heuristic, then, enables you to answer questions like how many are there and how often does something happen on the basis of how quickly or easily examples can be retrieved from memory. The ease with which the process can be accomplished, or the volume of information that can be retrieved quickly, determines the answer (see also Schwarz, Bless, Strack, Klump et al., 1991).

The Simulation Heuristic

Suppose you borrowed your father's car during a college vacation and smashed it up following a party you attended. How would you answer the question, "What is Dad going to think when he finds out I've smashed up the car?" You may think through what you know about your father and his reaction to crises, run through this information in your mind, and generate several possibilities. The ease with which particular endings come to mind is used to judge what is likely to happen. Your father could refuse to pay your college tuition next term, or he could ignore the whole thing, but in your mind it is easiest to imagine that he will strongly suggest that you find a job so that you can help pay for the car. This inferential technique is known as

the *simulation heuristic* (Kahneman & Tversky, 1982).

The simulation heuristic may be used for a wide variety of tasks, including prediction ("What will Dad say?"), causality ("Was I driving badly or was the other guy driving badly?") (Wells & Gavanski, 1989; Wells, Taylor, & Turtle, 1987), and affective responses (Kahneman & Miller, 1986; Landman, 1988). On this latter point, consider the situation of a near miss:

> Mr. Crane and Mr. Tees were scheduled to leave the airport on different flights, at the same time. They traveled from town in the same limousine, were caught in a traffic jam, and arrived at the airport 30 minutes after the scheduled departure time of their flights.
>
> Mr. Crane is told his flight left on time. Mr. Tees is told that his flight was delayed, and just left 5 minutes ago.
>
> Who is more upset: Mr. Crane or Mr. Tees? (Kahneman & Tversky, 1982, p. 203)

Virtually everyone says, "Mr. Tees." Why? Presumably, one can imagine no way that Mr. Crane could have made his plane, whereas, were it not for that one long light or the slow baggage man or the illegally parked car or the error in the posted departure gate, Mr. Tees would have made it. Thus, the simulation heuristic and its ability to generate "if only" conditions can be used to understand the psychology of near misses and the frustration, regret, grief, or indignation they may produce. Abnormal or exceptional events lead people to imagine alternatives that are normal, and consequently dissimilar to the actual outcome (Kahneman & Miller, 1986). The contrast between the exceptional circumstance and the normal situation intensifies the emotional reaction to the unusual situation.

People simulate the future as well as the past, and imagining hypothetical future events makes those events seem more likely (Anderson & Godfrey, 1987). For example, Heath, Acklin, and Wiley (1991) found that physicians who simulated an HIV-exposure experience during the course of their medical practice saw themselves as being at significantly greater risk than those physicians who did not simulate an HIV-exposure experience. Simulation was strongly related to worry about on-the-job exposure to HIV infection. In another study, Gregory, Cialdini, and Carpenter (1982) contacted residents of two middle-class neighborhoods on behalf of a local cable television company. Half the residents were given information about the cable company, whereas the other half was instructed to imagine themselves experiencing the benefits and features of the cable service. Those who imagined themselves using the service were more likely to want the cable service, had more favorable attitudes toward cable, intended to acquire additional information, and reported that they would be more likely to subscribe to the cable service in the future. In addition, more subjects in the imagination condition actually accepted a free week of service and subsequently subscribed to the cable service than did those who simply received information about it. Thus, imagining alternatives via simulation can have a broad impact on expectations, causal attributions, impressions, and the affect experienced in situations (Wells & Gavanski, 1989).

The Anchoring Heuristic

Imagine that someone asks you to guess how many people attended the UCLA–USC football game last night in the Los Angeles Coliseum. You have absolutely no idea, but you do know that last week's game in the Coliseum drew a crowd of 55,000. Assuming that the UCLA–USC contest drew a much bigger crowd, you might guess that 70,000 people attended. In this case, you have no information about the specific event in question, but you use information about a similar event as a reference point or "anchor." You then adjust reference information to reach a final conclusion (Tversky & Kahneman, 1974).

In fact, when people are attempting to form judgments from ambiguous information, they will often reduce ambiguity by starting with the beginning reference point or anchor and then adjusting it. Social judgments are no exception, since information about social situations is often ambiguous, and therefore anchors can be helpful when one is trying to interpret the meaning of ambiguous information and behavior (Plous, 1989; Cervone & Peake, 1986).

TABLE 3-1
Some Heuristic Strategies for Making Judgments Under Uncertainty

Representatives	Probability judgment	Representativeness is a judgment of how relevant A is to B; high relevance yields high estimates that A originates from B	Deciding that George (A) must be an engineer because he looks and acts like your stereotype of engineers (B)
Availability	Frequency of probability judgments	Availability is the estimate of how frequently or likely a given instance or occurence is, based on how easily or quickly an association or examples come to mind	Estimating the divorce rate on the basis of how quickly you can think of examples of divorced friends
Simulation	Expectations, causal attributions, impressions, and affective experience	Simulation is the ease with which a hypothetical scenario can be constructed	Getting angry because of a frustrating event on the basis of how easily you can imagine the situation occuring otherwise
Adjustment and anchoring	Estimates of position on a dimension	Anchoring and adjustment is the process of estimating some value by starting with some initial value and then adjusting it to the new instance	Judging how hard a friend studies based on how hard you study

A common anchor that is used in social perception is the self. For example, suppose someone asks you whether Ellen, a classmate of yours, is smart. It may be easiest for you to answer this question by trying to decide if Ellen is smarter than you or not. If she seems to be smarter than you are, you may decide that she is very smart. But if she seems to be not as quick as you are, you may decide that she is not very bright. Your judgment about Ellen's intelligence, then, is based not on her absolute standing on an I.Q. test or some other objective information, but rather on whether she seems brighter or less bright than yourself (see Markus & Smith, 1981; Markus, Smith, & Moreland, 1985). The anchoring heuristic, then, provides people with a departure point for a judgment task that might otherwise be ambiguous. In social judgment tasks, the self seems to be a common anchor. For a description of the various heuristic strategies, see Table 3-1.

WHICH SCHEMAS ARE USED?

Suppose you observe two people feverishly searching a room. How do you decide what they are doing? In other words, how do you select which schemas to apply to the situation? Sometimes appropriate schemas are suggested by the nature of the information itself. For example, if you know the two people in question are roommates who keep gerbils and you see an empty cage, you may guess that they are trying to find their missing gerbils. Under other circumstances, information in the environment may not immediately suggest what schemas to invoke. Are the two searchers looking for something that they have lost? Are they burglars? Are they undercover policemen conducting a drug bust? In this section, we consider the factors that influence which schemas people use to interpret information.

Natural Contours

The most obvious and probably also the most powerful determinant of which schema is used is the structure of the information itself. That is, schemas follow the *natural contours* of the information we receive. If you are watching a football game, you will employ your schemas for football games, football players, and cheerleaders for interpreting what is going on in the field. The information in the environment makes it obvious which schemas to use, and you would not invoke your schemas for cocktail parties, tennis games, or final examinations to interpret what is going on.

But people cannot absorb everything in their environment at once. They tend to perceive behavior in coherent, meaningful chunks of action that are marked off by **breakpoints** (Newtson, 1976; Newtson, Hairfield, Bloomingdale, & Cutino, 1987). For example, imagine watching an outfielder break into a run at the sound of the bat hitting the ball; he dashes to the outfield wall, leaps up, catches the ball, lands on his feet, sets for a throw, and then throws the ball to the third baseman to stop the baserunner. Newtson argues that we perceive such a flow of activity as a sequence of separate behaviors, not as one continuous act. Breakpoints occur between the separate actions and mark where one ends and another begins.

Breakpoints are inherent in any stream of behavior; they are not imposed on it by the perceiver. In this sense, they follow the natural contours of the information we receive. To identify these breakpoints, Newtson had subjects watch a film and push a button to indicate when they thought one segment had ended and another had begun. This method is quite reliable: perceivers agree on where certain breakpoints occur in films of someone in action, and they perceive the same breakpoints again when shown the film five weeks later. It also seems quite easy and comfortable for subjects to do. All this argues that the breakpoints occur naturally within the flow of behavior in a given scene.

When do breakpoints occur? Some ingenious research has tied them to changes in behavior, specifically to changes in the movement of different parts of the body (Newtson, Engquist, & Bois, 1977). Breakpoints also occur when the state of objects associated with the person

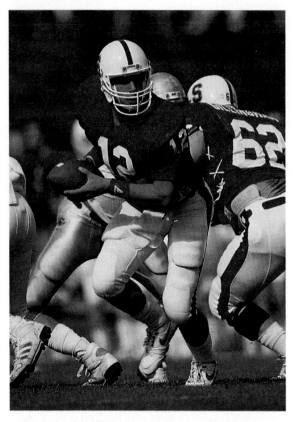

People perceive behavior in coherent, meaningful chunks of action, marked by breakpoints. For example, in a football game, a completed pass would form a natural unit, marked at the beginning by the throw and at the end by the successful reception.

The more general point, then, is that we do not simply take in environmental information whole when forming an inference. Rather, we absorb meaningful, structured chunks of it. The chunking process is partly imposed on the flow of behavior by the perceiver's own experiences and expectations. And partly the chunks reflect the real changes within the behavioral sequence.

Salience

Environmental salience is also a factor that influences which schemas people use to interpret information. As we saw in Chapter 2, sometimes our interpretation of other people's behavior is influenced by what information about them is made salient by the environment. For example, if Linda is the only woman in a group that is otherwise composed of men, her sex will be particularly salient, and therefore her behavior may be interpreted according to a gender schema for women (Taylor, Fiske, Close, Anderson, & Ruderman, 1978). For example, her request for help from a newcomer to the group might be interpreted as a sign of dependence, a trait sometimes associated with women. However, if Linda is in a group composed of several men and several women, her behavior toward the newcomer might not be interpreted in gender-related terms. Instead, a schema for "newcomers" might be invoked, and her gesture might simply be interpreted as an effort to make the newcomer feel at home. Salience, then, can influence the processing of information in the environment by determining which schemas will be invoked to interpret information that may be subject to multiple interpretations.

changes. For example, breakpoints would be perceived when a baseball's trajectory is suddenly interrupted by the outfielder's glove, when it disappears from view, or when it suddenly flies through the air back toward the infield. And people use more breakpoints when they encounter unexpected actions or have little prior information, presumably because they need the breakpoints to try to understand the meaning of the action more fully (Wilder, 1986; Graziano, Moore, & Collins, 1988). Breakpoints convey the most information about a sequence of behavior. When the breakpoint moments of a film are shown to subjects as still photos in order, they convey the story almost as well as the full movie itself. People also seem to remember the breakpoints better than any other moments during the sequence.

The salient physical features that people have, such as their race and sex, appear to be particularly predominant in cueing schemas. Indeed, physical features may take priority over other features, such as social schemas (Deaux & Lewis, 1984). From the earliest moments of perception, people use age, race, sex, attractiveness, and similar qualities to form impressions, and indeed may do so quite automatically. One study, for example (Devine, 1989), found immediate and virtually automatic stereotyped reactions to black-and-white stimulus persons. Surprisingly, both high- and low-prejudice people were equally likely to show these automatic stereotyped reactions. However, when circumstances were provided that allowed for more time to consider the information, low-prejudice people actively rejected the automatic stereotyped responses and replaced them with equality-oriented thoughts. The unnerving conclusion is that schemas, including negatively toned ones, quite automatically guide the processing of information and that tolerance, open-mindedness, and freedom from prejudice come only with enough time to notice that one must adopt such cautions.

Roles

When one seeks ways to organize information about people, role schemas probably take precedence over other kinds of information such as traits. There are many ways to be extraverted (e.g., such as like a comedian, a political leader, or a bully), but there are relatively fewer ways to fulfill a concrete role (such as being a politician). Consequently, role schemas are informative, rich, and well articulated, providing greater information across a wide range of dimensions. They are also more distinctive than traits, leading to more unique associations. Knowing that someone is a cheerleader, for example, says a lot about exactly how she is outgoing and in what situations she is outgoing, whereas just being told that she is an extravert does not convey nearly as much information.

Moreover, role schemas are more useful than traits for recall (Bond & Brockett, 1987; Bond & Sedikides, 1988). To see the advantage of role in memory, think of all the people in a particular seminar that you are taking. How easy was that? Now think of all the self-centered people you know. How easy is that? Chances are, the social groupings lead to the generation of more names more quickly than do traits. People seem to think of others first within a role context, and only then according to personality traits.

Primacy

Often, which schema is used to interpret a person or a situation will be determined very early by information present in the situation. For example, when introduced to a friend with the words, "This is George, he's running for student body president," one is inclined to think of George and his subsequent behavior in terms of whether or not he would be a good student body president, and to consider his behavior as determined at least in part by the fact that he is running for office. One reason why **primacy** is so important is that when people have an organizing structure from the very outset, it influences the interpretation of information as that information is taken in. When this occurs, the effects are more powerful than if the schema is applied afterward (e.g., Wyer, Srull, Gordon, & Hartwick, 1982; see Fiske & Taylor, 1991, for a review).

Priming

When a schema has been recently used, it is likely to be used again to interpret new information. Suppose you have just come from a classroom discussion in which the professor castigated the class for its lack of commitment to intellectual pursuits. Walking across campus, you meet Stan who enthusiastically tells you that he has just been appointed to the cheering squad. How do you interpret the enthusiasm? In the context of the prior lecture, you may regard his behavior as shallow and unintellectual. In contrast, if you had just come from a discussion of the importance of being a well-rounded college student, you might interpret the behavior as a sign of extracurricular interests. This tendency for recently used schemas to be employed in unrelated subsequent situations is called the **priming effect.**

A study that demonstrates this point was conducted by Higgins, Rholes, and Jones (1977). Subjects were first exposed to trait words designed to invoke either the positive schema of adventurousness (such as brave) or the negative schema of recklessness (such as foolish, careless). In a second study ostensibly unrelated to the first task, they read about Donald who shot rapids, drove in a demolition derby, and planned to learn skydiving. People who had previously been exposed to the positive schema of adventurousness evaluated Donald more positively than did people who had been primed with the negative schema of recklessness. This priming effect did not occur when the primed schemas were not applicable to the description of Donald (such as neat or shy).

Essentially, then, activating a schema puts it at the top of the mental heap, making it easily accessible for interpreting new information (Srull & Wyer, 1979; Wyer & Srull, 1980, 1981). However, an important qualification is that previously activated schemas are invoked to explain new information only when the schema can meaningfully be applied to the new information. When new information is irrelevant to the primed schemas, those schemas are not used to interpret it (Higgins & Bargh, 1987; Erdley & D'Agostino, 1988).

Importance

Which schemas are used to interpret information by the environment and how many schemas are called up can also be influenced by the importance of the information being processed. When the circumstances for making inferences are relatively trivial, people may make schematic inferences relatively quickly with little thought. They may, for example, invoke a schema on the basis of which information is most salient. However, in circumstances when the outcome of an inference is important, or a person is accountable for the inference, that person may spend more time studying the situation and invoke more schemas, yielding more complex inferences (Chaiken, 1980; Harkness, DeBono, & Borgida, 1985; Tetlock & Boettger, 1989; Tetlock, Skitka, & Boettger, 1989). For example, if asked your impression of a fellow classmate, you may answer relatively quickly that he or she seems nice, if your judgment of the person has no particular importance to you.

However, if you are trying to decide whether or not to ask this classmate out on a date, you would probably spend more time thinking through what you know about the person to decide whether or not he or she is fun, attractive, nice, and attracted to you. Your inferences might consequently be more complex, based on more than one schema.

Individual Differences

Not everyone interprets the same information the same way. One reason is that different people have different schemas. For example, one person might describe other people primarily in terms of their sense of humor or warmth, whereas someone else might consider these characteristics to be relatively unimportant and instead be concerned with another person's diligence and religiousness.

In the last chapter, we noted that people hold self-schemas—organized knowledge structures about themselves that organize important chunks of their self-concept. Self-schemas affect not only how people perceive themselves but how they perceive others. People use their self-schemas to interpret other people's behaviors. For example, a man whose masculinity is very important to him will be more likely to interpret others' behavior in masculine or nonmasculine terms (Markus, Smith, & Moreland, 1985; Cantrambone & Markus, 1987). People also attach more importance to information about another person if it is relevant to their own self-schema, and when they are forming impressions of others, they recall more such material (Carpenter, 1988). So, for example, if being intelligent is important to you as a student, you are particularly likely to notice whether another person is intelligent or not and to remember that information when you later think about the person.

Groups of people may differ in their schemas. One interesting case concerns the theories people hold about intelligence. College students have schemas for intelligence that relate it closely to academic performance, whereas nonstudents (people interviewed in supermarkets or at a railway station) viewed intelligence as more closely related to everyday problem solving, social competence, and the like (Sternberg et al., 1981).

Goals

Which schemas are brought to bear on information in the environment is also based on the goals a social perceiver has in a particular situation (Wyer & Srull, 1986; Hastie, Park, & Weber, 1984). As we have seen, schemas are not just passive reflections of the information in the environment. The person must actively organize the information into a more abstract, cognitive structure. One way in which this organizing cognitive activity is triggered is through an individual's goals (e.g., Trzebinski & Richards, 1986).

When we have a particular goal in a situation, such as trying to remember what someone says or trying to form an impression of someone, we organize information in a way that fits our particular goals. This point was clearly illustrated in Chapter 2, when we saw how the different goals we might have in interacting with another person heavily determine both the impressions we form and the information we recall about that person.

Do People Always Use Schemas?

Schemas are important because they help people make sense of experience quickly. If we approached every situation as if for the first time, it would be impossible for us to function in our everyday lives. Schemas, then, represent our social learning, the social categories that we use to impute meaning to the people we meet and the situations we encounter.

But as we also noted earlier in the chapter, there are liabilities to schematic processing. Sometimes we make assumptions about people and situations on the basis of our schemas that turn out not to be true. If we had paid more attention to the information at hand instead of jumping to conclusions on the basis of our

schemas, certain mistakes could be avoided. For example, categorizing another person as loudmouthed, opinionated, arrogant, and conservative may not matter much under most circumstances, but if the person happens to be the father of the girl you are hoping to date, you might want to pay closer attention to his qualities and opinions.

OUTCOME DEPENDENCY. Under certain circumstances we pay less attention to our schemas and more attention to the data at hand. What are those circumstances? One condition that leads to less frequent use of schemas and more attention to the information is *outcome dependency*. When your outcomes depend on someone else's actions, you pay more attention to the other person (Bersheid, Graziano, Monson, & Dermer, 1976; Rush & Russell, 1988; Sande, Ellard, & Ross, 1986) and pay more attention to schema-inconsistent information, apparently because it is potentially informative (Erber & Fiske, 1984). When people's outcomes are involved, they probe for more information about others (Darley, Fleming, Hilton, & Swann, 1988). For example, competitors remember more about members of a group with which they are in competition compared with those not in competition with the group (Judd & Park, 1988).

NEED TO BE ACCURATE. The *need to be accurate* is another condition that leads people to pay more attention to data and less attention to their schemas. Asked if the nerdy guy with glasses and books is smart, you may draw on your schema which tells you that nerds usually are smart. However, if it is up to you to decide whether or not to admit him to your debating team, you will probably want more information than your stereotype about nerds will provide. Consequently, you will pay closer attention to his actual behavior, focusing less on the ways in which he matches your schema for nerds.

ACCOUNTABILITY. When people have to justify their decisions to other people and *accountability* is therefore high, they tend to go beyond the schema to look more closely at the data (Tetlock, 1983, 1985; Tetlock & Boettger, 1989).

For example, you will probably pay more attention to information about another person if you must decide whether to admit him to your fraternity than if you are simply asked your impression of him.

IMPRESSION FORMATION AND TIME PRESSURE.
Conversely, other facts favor schema use over careful consideration of the data. For example, when people are *forming impressions* or *making decisions under time pressure,* they tend to use their schemas more. In one study, male and female subjects were asked to judge the suitability of male and female candidates for particular jobs. When the decisions were made under time pressure conditions, male subjects as well as female subjects with conservative attitudes toward women, tended to discriminate against the female job applicants. In the absence of time pressure, however, discrimination toward the female applicants was less strong. Under time pressure conditions, then, the subjects resorted to their attitudes about men and women in jobs for making the judgments, whereas when they had time to consider the evidence and found that the female applicants were at least as well qualified as the male applicants, their degree of discrimination against the female candidates was considerably less (Bechtold, Naccarato, & Zanna, 1986; see also Devine, 1989).

We also fall back on our schemas when all the available information seems to fit the schema well and when we are not particularly motivated to examine the data more thoroughly. However, when we are told that a task is important or when some of the information is incongruent with the schema, we are more likely to engage in systematic processing of the data (Maheswaran & Chaiken, 1991).

To summarize, then, when there are pressures in the situation to be accurate, people tend to look at data more closely, sometimes rejecting easy schematically based conclusions. They may attend to more of the information and particularly pay attention to schema-inconsistent information. Conditions that seem to favor this kind of data-driven processing are outcome dependency, accountability, or other situational cues suggesting a need to be accurate. In contrast, other circumstances favor more schematically based processing. In particular, any pressure to form a judgment quickly or in a coherent way that can be communicated easily to others may favor the use of schemas (Fiske & Taylor, 1991).

SCHEMAS IN ACTION

The use of schemas for processing information is important not only because it helps people to form judgments and make decisions, but because it provides guidelines for interactions with others. One of the factors that influences behavioral guidelines is action identification.

ACTION IDENTIFICATION.
If you are engaged in some behavior such as mowing the lawn, and someone asks you what you are doing, you may look at him in surprise. Isn't it obvious what you're doing? But a theory by Vallacher and Wegner (1986) argues that any action can be identified in any of several different ways. Certainly you are cutting the grass, and that would be the most obvious response to the question. But you could be just cutting the grass because it needs cutting, or you could be cutting the grass to please your father so that he will loan you the car for the evening. Actions can be identified, then, at relatively low levels of behavior or at higher levels in service of some goal (Vallacher & Wegner, 1989).

Action identification theory maintains that the way one thinks about a particular action has implications for behavior. Actions identified at low levels are subject to context effects that might cue higher levels of action identity. So, for example, if a neighbor passes by and calls to you, "I see you're making your yard beautiful," this would suggest to you a higher goal than just cutting the grass. It might lead you into other behaviors consistent with that goal, such as trimming the hedges and washing the bird droppings off the front steps (Wegner, Vallacher, Kiersted, & Dizadji, 1986). In contrast, if you had identified your action at a higher level to begin with (cutting the grass so your father will loan you the car), your neighbor's comment that you are making the yard beautiful

Is this person cutting off dead leaves, making a garden, or beautifying the environment? The way we identify our actions, termed *action identification*, determines how we interpret another person's behavior and what subsequent actions we think the person will undertake. If we think she is merely trimming dead leaves, we might consider her unlikely to plant a tree. But if we think she is beautifying the environment, planting a tree would be consistent with this action identification.

would have less effect on your behavior. You might simply think to yourself, "That's not why I'm doing it."

Actions identified at higher levels are more flexible than actions identified at lower levels. For example, if you have labeled your action as cutting the grass and your lawn mower runs out of gas, the action will come to a stop. However, if you identified the action as doing something to please your father so he would loan you the car, after the lawn mower runs out of gas, you might look for something else you could do that would achieve the same effect, such as washing his car or trimming the bushes.

Actions that are successful tend to be identi-

fied and maintained at relatively high levels, whereas actions that are unsuccessful tend to drop down to lower levels of identification (Vallacher, Wegner, & Frederick, 1987; Vallachar, Wegner, & Somoza, 1989). For example, your identification of your action as "cutting the grass" is likely to drop to a lower level if you run into trouble maneuvering around shrubs and stones. You may change the identification of your behavior to "trying to cut around the shrub without mowing it down" or "trying to get the rocks out of the way" rather than the somewhat higher-action identification of cutting the grass.

What are the implications of action identification theory? Sometimes, the level at which we identify an action can keep us from fully experiencing the meaning of the situation. For example, people who have lost a loved one often get through the funeral and burial service not by thinking about the loved one's departure, but by concentrating on very low-level actions, such as wearing the right clothes and making sure that there will be enough food for people after the service. As another example, Vallacher and Wegner (1986) argue that when people are committing crimes, they tend to focus on low levels of identification, such as "getting up to the second-story window," rather than the higher-level action identification of "stealing from somebody." In both these examples, people are able to avoid the full unpleasant implications of their actions by identifying them at lower levels.

CONFIRMATORY HYPOTHESIS TESTING. We learn about other people in many ways. Sometimes we hear about them before meeting them, or we may have hints about the kind of people they are like on the basis of their initial behavior. Regardless of how we form an impression of another person, we may relatively quickly develop ideas concerning what the person is like. As we are interacting with the person, how do these ideas (or schemas) influence one's behavior?

Considerable research suggests that people behave toward others in ways that tend to confirm the beliefs they hold about those others. Perceivers employ interaction strategies for eliciting information from others that preferentially support these schemas (Snyder & Gangestad, 1981; Harris, Milich, Johnston, & Hoover, 1990).

How does this process work? Suppose you learned that Susan, an attractive young woman in your psychology class, is with the cheering squad for the school, and you quickly form an image of her as an outgoing, athletic, and enthusiastic person. In talking with her, you might ask her about the various sports she has played, the parties she has been to this year, what she thinks of the games she has attended, and so on. All of this information tends to confirm your view of her as an extroverted, athletic, fun-loving person. However, after seeing her for several weeks, you might discover that she is actually rather shy and introverted, she's fairly klutzy at sports, and she is not a cheerleader at all, but rather coordinates uniform purchases and bus transportation to out-of-town games. You might wonder how you came to be so deceived. Looking back on the situation, however, reveals that Susan may have done nothing at all to deceive you. Rather, you deceived yourself by selectively seeking information that supported your beliefs. There aren't many college students who didn't play some kind of sport in high school or attend at least a couple of parties. Because you asked Susan about these kinds of activities, this is the information she gave you, which augmented your image of her as a fun-loving, athletic party girl (Swann, Giuliano, & Wegner, 1982).

This process has been called **confirmatory hypothesis testing,** and it has been demonstrated under a broad range of circumstances (see Higgins & Bargh, 1987, for a review). For example, M. Snyder and Swann (1978) told college student subjects that they would be interviewing another student. Half were told to find out if the other was an extrovert (that is, outgoing and sociable), and half were told to find if the other was an introvert (that is, shy and retiring). All subjects were then given a set of questions assessing introversion and extroversion, and they were told to pick out a set of questions to ask the other student. Students who were told to find out if the person was an extrovert preferentially selected extroversion questions (such as,

"What would you do if you wanted to liven things up at a party?"), and those who were told to find out if the person was an introvert picked introversion questions (such as, "What factors make it really hard for you to open up to people?"). These questions, in turn, made the target students appear especially extroverted or introverted, respectively, simply because they answered the questions they were asked (see also Curtis & Miller, 1986).

Although a number of studies have found evidence for confirmatory hypothesis testing, there are conditions under which we are less likely to selectively confirm a hypothesis through leading questions. Holding an opposite hypothesis or having a need for valid information reduces the degree to which people selectively confirm hypotheses (Devine, Hirt, & Gehrke, 1990; Kruglanski & Mayseless, 1988; Skov & Sherman, 1986; Trope & Mackie, 1987). For example, when we expect to have to work with a target in the future, we ask better questions and are less likely to engage in question-asking techniques that selectively confirm their prior expectations (Darley, Fleming, Hilton, & Swann, 1988). And when we have more than one hypothesis in mind, we will test for these alternative hypotheses as well (McDonald, 1990).

SELF-FULFILLING PROPHECIES. Sometimes a prior schema we have about an individual will influence not only the kind of information we ask or seek from the person and the subsequent inferences we draw, but will also affect the other person's actual behaviors and self-impressions. When a perceiver's false expectations about another person lead that person to adopt those expected attributes and behavior, this is called a **self-fulfilling prophecy** (see Figure 3-3).

For example, Snyder, Tanke, and Berscheid (1977) gave college student men a folder of information about a woman on campus that included a picture representing the woman as either highly attractive or as unattractive. In actuality, the photos were fake and were randomly assigned to women regardless of their true looks. Each student was then asked to phone the woman whose folder he had read and

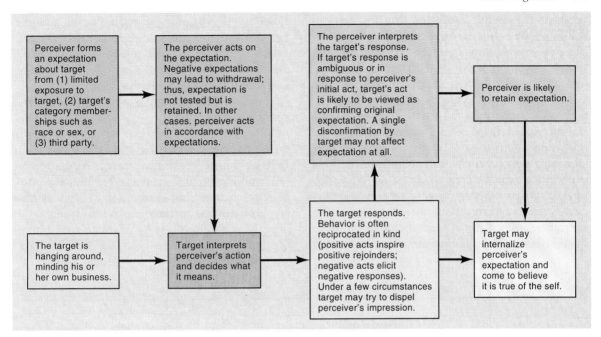

Figure 3-3 The development of a self-fulfilling prophecy. (*Source:* Adapted from Darley & Fazio, 1980.)

chat for 10 minutes. Tape recordings were made of the conversations. The men who believed they were talking to attractive women behaved more warmly on the phone than did the men with unattractive women. Even more remarkable, the women who had been miscast as highly attractive were perceived by other students judging the tapes to be more friendly, likable, and sociable in their interactions with the men than those miscast as unattractive. These kinds of self-fulfilling prophecies have been widely demonstrated (see Darley & Fazio, 1980; Jussin, 1989, for reviews).

WHEN EXPECTATIONS CHALLENGE SELF-CONCEPTIONS. This implication of the discussion thus far is that schemas are so powerful that they not only influence how information in the environment is interpreted, but also help push the environment to become consistent with the schema. Obviously, this is not always the case. For example, sometimes people hold beliefs about others that those others feel are untrue about themselves. Consequently, those others may be motivated to disconfirm what they feel is an incorrect belief. For example, if a professor whose opinion you value saw you commit a foolish prank with some of your friends, you might be highly motivated to correct the professor's low opinion of you.

Under these circumstances, whose viewpoint will triumph? The perceiver's misconceptions or the target's beliefs about the self? Research by Swann and Ely (1984) attempted to address this question by considering the certainty of perceiver's expectations and target's self-conceptions. Perceivers first formed relatively certain or uncertain expectations about targets that were inconsistent with the target's self-conceptions. Thus, for example, some perceivers were led to believe that the target was extroverted (when the target perceived herself to be introverted), whereas other perceivers were led to believe the target was introverted (when the target considered herself extroverted). The perceivers then interacted with targets who either possessed relatively certain or uncertain self-conceptions about their introversion or extroversion. The results indicated that the target's self-concept was a stronger determinant than the perceiver's expectancy of the perceiver's ultimate opinion of the target. That is, after they had interacted together, the perceivers' impressions of the targets were more in line with the targets' self-concepts than with the perceivers' initial expectations. Only when targets were uncertain about their introversion or extroversion and perceivers were certain about their expectations did behavioral confirmation occur. That is, when perceivers were certain and targets were uncertain about their attributes, the perceivers' expectations tended to win out. The general point, then, is that perceivers' expecta-tions may have some effect on a target's behavior. But they do not lead targets to act in ways that are counter to their self-concepts (Miller & Turnbull, 1986; Higgins & Bargh, 1987; Major, Cozzarelli, Testa, & McFarlin, 1988).

Overall, then, schemas and schematic processing are important for several reasons. They help people to organize their past experiences in ways that can be useful in new situations. They help in the processing of new information by determining what is relevant, by filling in gaps, by influencing what is recalled, and by making some inferences automatic. And they can act as effective guidelines for behavior in social inter-actions.

KEY TERMS

breakpoints	heuristics	priming effect
case history information	illusory correlation	rational model of inference
confirmatory hypothesis testing	logical error	self-fulfilling prophecy
conjunction error	mood congruent memory	social cognition
covariation	primacy	statistical information

SUMMARY

1. Social cognition is the branch of social psychology that examines how people form inferences from social information in the environment.

2. When we examine how people make impressions and form inferences and compare those processes against rational methods for accomplishing these tasks, we find that social perceivers are prone to certain errors and biases in their judgments. In particular, prior expectations and theories weigh heavily into the judgment process.

3. These predictable errors and biases appear to stem from the fact that people need to make judgments relatively quickly and efficiently to process the multitude of information they encounter.

4. Cognitive structures called schemas help us organize information about the world. Schemas make information processing more efficient and speedy, aid recall, fill in missing information, and provide expectations. However, they sometimes lead to erroneous inferences or may lead us to reject good but inconsistent evidence.

5. Heuristics are shortcuts that help relate information in the environment to schemas. Heuristics reduce complex or ambiguous problems to more simple, judgmental operations.

6. The schemas that are most likely to be used to interpret information are those that match the natural contours of that information. In addition, which schemas a social perceiver uses is influenced by salience, social roles, goals, primacy, priming, the importance of the judgment context, and individual differences.

7. People sometimes attend more to the evidence than to their schemas, especially if

they need to be very accurate, they will be held accountable for their judgments, or their future outcomes depend on their judgments.

8. Schemas not only help people form judgments and make decisions but provide guidelines for interactions with others. In some cases, schemas may be so powerful that they bring about self-fulfilling prophecies.

SUGGESTED READINGS

Fiske, S. T., & Taylor, S. E. (1991). *Social cognition* (2nd ed.). New York: McGraw-Hill. A readable introduction to the field of social cognition for college students; available in paperback.

Hastorf, A., & Isen, A. M. (1982). *Cognitive social psychology.* New York: Elsevier-North Holland. An edited collection that emphasizes applications of social cognition to such areas as emotion, stereotyping, legal psychology, organizational psychology, and health psychology.

Higgins, E. T., Ruble, D. N., & Hartup, W. W. (1983). *Social cognition and social development.* Cambridge, UK: Cambridge University Press. An edited collection that examines how social cognition research elucidates social development and close relationships in children and adults.

Kahneman, D., Slovic, P., & Tversky, A. (1982). *Judgment under uncertainty: Heuristics and biases.* Cambridge, UK: Cambridge University Press. An edited collection of research on shortcuts, errors, and biases in social inference processes.

Markus, H., & Zajonc, R. B. (1985). The cognitive perspective in social psychology. In G. Lindzey & E. Aronson (Eds.). *Handbook of social psychology.* New York: Random House. A thoughtful analysis of the historical development of social cognition with an emphasis on current work in the field.

4
Attribution

FOCUS OF THIS CHAPTER

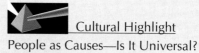

Cultural Highlight
People as Causes—Is It Universal?

Research Closeup
Do Attributions Matter?—Attributions and Disease

Travelers in the Los Angeles Airport were recently treated to an unusual scene. A well-dressed man with an attaché case, obviously waiting for his plane, was approached by two men in gray suits who showed identification and asked to see his. Upon looking over his identification, they put handcuffs on him, confiscated his briefcase, and led him away. Those also waiting for the plane began to talk furiously among themselves, unusual behavior for strangers in a waiting room. Who were the two men in the gray suits? Had the passenger been arrested? Had anyone overheard the conversation? What was in the attaché case? Could it have been a bomb? Was it drugs? Who was the man? The waiting passengers shared information and speculated about the causes of the unusual event long after the plane had arrived and they were all airborne.

Often we ask ourselves why when we encounter some event. The process of finding a causal explanation reveals the complexity of the task. Usually we do not have direct information about people's internal states. We have access only to limited cues, such as their facial expressions or gestures, what the person says about his or her internal state, what, if anything, we know about the person's past behavior, and so on. So we must make inferences on the basis of the indirect information provided by external cues. Thus, our causal explanation for behavior must be inferred from these cues. The process of so doing is called attribution theory.

When Are Attributions Made?

When do people engage in this process of asking why? Although human beings are supposedly a curious species, they do not go around asking why about everything that happens. They do not ask why the sun comes up in the morning, why a boxer on TV is wearing boxing gloves, or why the bus they are riding has started moving as the red light has changed to green. Most natural events and human actions do not inspire much cognitive effort to search out correct causal explanations. What, then, are the conditions under which we do undertake the search for a cause?

As the opening example implies, people tend to ask why questions when something unexpected or unusual happens (Hastie, 1984; Wong & Weiner, 1981). Unexpected events create a need for greater predictability, both to prevent nasty surprises and because a simple, predictable world permits inferences to be made virtually automatically. As a result, people tend not to ask why questions about expected events, such as the sun's rise in the morning or the moon's rise at night. Newspaper readers, government officials, and social scientists want answers when there is a sudden, unexpected outburst of racial violence or student unrest, but not when things are humming along as usual.

Bad, painful, and unpleasant events also inspire a search for causal attributions (Bohner, Bless, Schwarz, & Strack, 1988). To illustrate this point, researchers talked with distressed couples who had come to a clinic for marital therapy. All were asked to list a variety of positive or negative events that happened in their marriage and how frequently those events occurred. They were then asked for their thoughts about these events, which were coded for the presence of causal attributions. The authors found that the most attributional thoughts were made about the most distressing events: their partner's frequent negative behaviors or infrequent positive behaviors (Holtzworth-Munroe & Jacobson, 1985). For example, the frequent event, "he's always late for dinner," might elicit the additional thought, "because he's just not a punctual person," which would attribute his lateness to his personality.

Not surprisingly, the most extremely distressing events in life stimulate the greatest search for causal explanation. Taylor, Lichtman, and Wood (1984) found that 95 percent of a sample of cancer victims made attributions about the cause for their disease. Among family members for whom the disease was presumably less painful, only 70 percent did so. Bulman and Wortman (1977) poignantly document the

efforts of paraplegics crippled by spinal cord injuries to analyze why it happened to them. Most of the injuries were the results of accidents, but still the victims wanted more definitive explanations.

And finally, it is important to explain why when people are uncertain about something that is important to them. These conditions were clearly identified in a field study exploring workers' reactions to the layoffs of some of their coworkers. The surviving workers who had received very clear explanations from their managers regarding the bases of the prior layoffs were more committed to the work organization, put in more effort relative to the pre-layoff period, and felt better about the reasons behind the layoffs. These effects were especially pronounced for those who had felt very uncertain about the layoffs initially and for whom understanding the layoffs was very important (Brockner, DeWitt, Grover, & Reed, 1990).

Why Are Attributions Important?

Causal **attributions** are important for several reasons. First, attributions help people to predict and control the environment. The reason unexpected and negative events give rise to more causal explanation than expected or positive events is that people need to be able to avoid, offset, or at least anticipate these kinds of events in the future. Causal attributions, then, fit in with broader needs to predict and control the environment (Kelley, 1972; Pyszczynski & Greenberg, 1981; Bohner et al., 1988; Anderson, 1991).

Causal attributions are also important because they determine our feelings, attitudes, and behavior. According to Weiner (1986), for example, anger usually results when something negative happens to us and we perceive it as being under someone else's control. For example, if you are standing on a curb and a car whips past, splashing dirty water all over you, you might feel angry if you felt the driver could have avoided splashing you. You might feel less angry if there was only one lane and the driver had no choice. Pity arises when a negative event happens to

Unexpected or negative events that leave people uncertain are most likely to lead them to ask why the event occurred. Workers who are laid off may be in great need of an adequate causal explanation.

Causal attributions help us predict and control the environment. They determine our feelings and reactions to others, and they help influence our future behavior. If you encountered these two people, you would want to know what was wrong.

someone else and no one could have controlled it. You feel sorry for a person with multiple sclerosis; no one could have prevented the disease. Other emotions follow directly from attributions, as we will see.

Our expectations about the future are also influenced by attributions for past events. When we attribute our past successes to ability, we are likely to expect future successes (Weiner, 1986). If we attribute our A's in high school English to a natural talent for literary analysis, we will be more optimistic about similar successes in our college career. But, if we attribute those past A's to teachers who were easy graders, we are not likely to expect such high grades later on.

Attributions have a clear impact not only on expectations and emotions but also on future performance. Dweck (1975), for example, showed that training children to make internal attributions for their behavior—training them, for example, to explain successes and failures as resulting from the amount of effort they put into the task—can make them work harder in the future, increasing the likelihood of success.

In these and numerous other ways, our understanding of the causes of behavior are crucial mediators of our reactions to the social world. Our reactions to other people—liking, aggression, helping, conformity, and so on—frequently depend on how we interpret the world and the causal attributions we make for the events around us.

BASIC PRINCIPLES OF CAUSAL ATTRIBUTION

Although there are different approaches to the attribution process, they rest on a common set of basic principles called **attribution theory.**

Heider's Naive Psychology

Theorizing about attributions began with Fritz Heider (1958). He was interested in how people in everyday life figure out what causes what. Like most in the cognitive tradition in social psychology, he proposed two strong motives in all human beings: the need to form a coherent understanding of the world and the need to control the environment.

One of the essentials for satisfying these motives is the ability to predict how people are going to behave. If we cannot predict how others will behave, we will view the world as random, surprising, and incoherent. We would not know whether to expect reward or punishment for our work performance, a kiss or a punch in the jaw from a friend.

Similarly, to have a satisfactory level of control of our environment, we must be able to predict others' behavior. To avoid an accident, we need to be able to predict that the big truck will not suddenly make a U-turn into our front bumper. To control our diet, we need to be able to count on getting a club sandwich when we order it in a restaurant rather than suddenly being presented with an entire roast pig.

To be able to predict how others are going to behave, we need some elementary theory of human behavior. Heider proposed that everyone, not just psychologists, searches for explanations in other people's behavior. He called the result a **naive psychology**—that is, a general theory of human behavior held by each ordinary person.

Dimensions of Causality

LOCUS OF CAUSALITY. The central issue in most perceptions of causality is whether to attribute a given act to *internal* states or to *external* forces. That is, what is the "locus of causality"? You have asked the young woman who sits next to you in lecture to go out to a movie this weekend, but she has said she is busy. What is the "real" cause of her refusal? It could be due to some internal state, such as her lack of attraction to you. Or it could be due to some external factor, such as that she really does have some other obligation. **Internal attributions** include all causes internal to the person, such as moods, attitudes, personality traits, abilities, health, preferences, or wishes. **External attributions** would include all causes external to the person, such as pressure from others, money, the nature of the social situation, the weather, and so on. Is this young woman really busy (an external attribution), or has she just decided that she is not interested in dating you (an internal attribution)?

STABILITY OR INSTABILITY. A second dimension of causality is whether the cause is stable or unstable. That is, we need to know whether the cause is a relatively permanent feature of that external environment or of the internal dispositions of the person. Some external causes are quite stable, such as rules and laws (the prohibition against running a red light, or against breaking the throwing arm of an overly successful quarterback), or occupational roles (professors are called upon to give lectures year in and year out).

Other external causes are quite unstable. The weather has a lot of influence over whether we spend Saturday out shopping or at home reading, but the weather varies a lot. Sometimes Oral Hershiser gets every pitch where he wants it, and sometimes his control is not so good and his pitches go where they are easier to hit. So his success is controlled by an unstable, external cause. Certain jobs vary in the external demands they place on the jobholder. Being a general places quite different external forces on a person in wartime than in peacetime.

Internal causes can also be stable or unstable. Woody Allen has a genius for making funny remarks: his talent for humor is quite stable. On the other hand, Hamlet is famous for his lack of stable resolve about what to do with his stepfather. Some baseball players are legendary for going on hot streaks and then becoming mired in terrible slumps; on the average they are quite talented, but the talent seems quite unstable. Similarly, in the achievement domain, a student's success or failure at a particular task could be attributed to ability (which is internal and relatively stable), effort (which is internal and usually fairly unstable), luck (which is external and unstable), or task difficulty (which is external and stable).

CONTROLLABILITY. A third general dimension of attributions is *controllability*, according to Weiner (1982, 1986). We perceive some causes as within control and others as beyond control. Perceived controllability or uncontrollability can coexist with any combination of locus and stability, as Table 4-1 indicates. For example, an internal unstable cause like temporary effort is generally seen as controllable; a student can try to work hard, or can decide not to. A stable internal cause like ability, however, is usually seen as uncontrollable. A "born genius" is someone born with that ability. Similarly, luck, which is an external unstable factor, is also typically seen as uncontrollable, whereas unusual help from others, though external and unstable, is presumably under those others' control.

Some researchers have questioned whether these are the best dimensions for understanding causal attribution and, indeed, whether they are causal dimensions at all. There is, for example,

TABLE 4-1
Possible Causes of Achievement Outcomes According to Locus, Stability, and Controllability

Controllability	Internal		External	
	Stable	Unstable	Stable	Unstable
Controllable	Typical effort exerted	Temporary effort exerted (for this particular task)	Some forms of teacher bias	Unusual help from others
Uncontrollable	Ability	Mood	Task difficulty	Luck

Source: Adapted from Rosenbaum (1972), p. 21; Weiner (1979).

only weak evidence that people think in terms of these standard attribution dimensions (Anderson, 1991), and researchers have especially criticized the internal–external dimension, arguing that the two may not be opposites, but actually co-occur (White, 1991; Bassili & Racine, 1990; Taylor & Koivumaki, 1976). Nonetheless, these dimensions have been helpful in accounting for how people understand a broad array of situations, including helping requests (Schmidt & Weiner, 1988), the perception of people who have stigmas such as AIDS (Weiner, Perry, & Magnusson, 1988), and the interpretation of sporting events (Tenenbaum & Furst, 1986). Moreover, these dimensions show some degree of cross-cultural generalizability, emerging in cultures as diverse as the United States, Britain, China, Belgium, West Germany, India, and South Korea (Schuster, Forsterling, & Weiner, 1989; Hau & Salili, 1991).

HOW ATTRIBUTIONS ARE MADE

The Naive Scientist

Harold Kelley has generated the most formal and comprehensive analysis of attribution, which he calls the *covariation model*. The principle of **covariation** means that we tend to look

for an association between a particular effect and a particular cause across a number of different conditions. If a given cause is always associated with a particular effect in many different situations, *and* if the effect does not occur in the absence of that cause, we attribute the effect to that cause. The cause always covaries with the effect; whenever the cause is present, so is the effect, and whenever the cause is absent, so is the effect.

Suppose your roommate gets grouchy and complains about everything right before exams, but is quite pleasant the rest of the time. Do you conclude that she is a grouch in general, that is, that she has a generally grouchy personality? Probably not. Instead, you would attribute her complaints to the tensions associated with exams, rather than to her being generally a short-tempered person. Her grouchiness is almost always associated with exams and does not occur in the absence of exams, so you attribute it to exams, not to her personality. This principle of covariation is, of course, exactly the same as the scientific method scientists use. A scientist also arrives at a judgment of causality by seeing that a particular factor is associated with a particular effect across a number of different conditions. This is why Kelley's model is called the naive scientist model. Although most people are not scientists, we are able to use certain scientific principles such as covariation to infer causality (Forsterling, 1989).

Kelley suggests that people use three specific types of information to arrive at causal attribution. They check to see whether or not the same effect occurs across (1) *stimulus objects,* (2) *actors* (persons), and (3) *contexts.* This is perhaps easiest to grasp with a simple example. Suppose our friend Mary shows up at work one day and tells us that she went to a local nightclub the night before. She tells us the show featured a comedian. She laughed hysterically at his jokes and, in fact, thought he was the funniest comic she had heard in years. We should definitely go see him.

We want a causal attribution for her hysterical laughter. If the cause was that the comedian really is very funny, we should follow her advice. But if it was just something unusual about Mary, or about the situation that night, we would not be so likely to go. That is, we try to decide whether her behavior is caused by something specific to the stimulus object (the comedian), to the actor (Mary), or to the context (the people she was with, the drinks, etc.).

Kelley suggests that we would search for an attribution by checking each dimension in turn.

Consensus is one of the sources of information people use to make causal attributions. If everyone laughs at a comedian, we infer that he is funny, but if only a few people laugh, we infer that he is not funny.

This involves answering three questions for ourselves: (1) Is the behavior specific to a particular stimulus object? Does Mary always laugh at *any* comedian, or did she really laugh unusually hard only at this one? (2) Is the behavior specific to a particular actor? Have we heard the same report from others, or is Mary the only one who laughed at this comedian? (3) Is the behavior specific to a particular context or occasion? Did she laugh each night she went to see this comedian, or did she only laugh the night there was a packed house and she was with her best friend and had one more drink than usual?

Kelley's theory suggests that people use all three of these kinds of information in trying to arrive at a causal attribution:

1. *Distinctiveness information.* Does the person act in this manner only in regard to this stimulus object, and not in regard to other objects? Is Mary's reaction distinctive to this particular object?

2. *Consensus information.* Do other people act in the same way in this situation? Did other people like this comedian as well?

3. *Consistency information.* Does this person consistently react the same way at other times or in other situations? Did Mary react this way to this comedian on only this one occasion?

Kelley hypothesizes this process occurs when we attribute a given effect to a given cause. We quickly review our store of information along these three dimensions. The review may be implicit and rapid rather than deliberate and conscious, but still we review what we know.

For an external attribution to be made—that is, for the comedian's comic ability to be the true cause of Mary's laughter—all three tests have to be passed in the appropriate manner: high distinctiveness, high consensus, and high consistency. Her reaction has to be distinctive to this comedian and not to others, other people have to like the comedian, and she has to like the comedian consistently in this and other situations.

For an internal attribution to be made—that is, for her laughter to be attributed to her general disposition to laugh at anything—low dis-

TABLE 4-2
Why Did Mary Laugh at the Comedian?

Condition	Available Information			Most Common Attribution
	Distinctiveness	Consensus	Consistency	
1	High—she didn't laugh at anyone else.	High—everyone else laughed too.	High—she always laughs at him.	Stimulus object: The comedian (61%)
2	Low—she always laughs at comedians.	Low—hardly anyone else laughed.	High—she always laughs at him.	Person: Mary (86%)
3	High—she didn't laugh at anyone else.	Low—hardly anyone else laughed.	Low—she has almost never laughed at him.	Context: (72%)

Source: Adapted from McArthur (1972).

tinctiveness, low consensus, and high consistency must hold. She laughs at all comedians, no one else does, and she laughs in all places and at all times.

In a classic study, McArthur (1972) tested Kelley's predictions. She gave subjects a simple hypothetical event, varied the kind of consensus, distinctiveness, and consistency information available to them, and then measured their attributions. The three main predictions and the results are shown in Table 4-2, using the same example. The first condition is the same as the example just described and promotes an attribution to the object itself, since it passes all three tests. Everyone else was also laughing, Mary didn't laugh at any of the other performers, but she always laughed at this one. So he must be a funny comedian. Mostly, the subjects saw it that way too; given this pattern of information, 61 percent attributed her reaction to the comedian (the other 39 percent made other attributions).

The second condition leads the observer to make a person attribution: Mary laughs at any comedian and always laughed at this one, but hardly anyone else did. Mary must be a laugher (86 percent). The third condition leads us to think there is something special about the context: she didn't laugh at anyone else, she had almost never laughed at him before, and hardly anyone else had laughed. Something unique must have happened. And 72 percent did attribute her laughter to the particular circumstances.

Does this indicate that people do in fact behave like "naive scientists"? The people participating in this and in many other studies of causal attributions do, in fact, use consistency, distinctive, and consensus information. Of the three, however, use of consensus information is typically the weakest (McArthur, 1972; Wright, Luus, & Christie, 1990). That is, we seem to be more attentive to what a target did or did not do (distinctiveness) and whether or not the target was consistent, than to other people's responses to that target (consensus). Despite this qualification, many studies have found that people usually arrive at the attributions that we would expect from Kelley's rational decision-making model. At the same time it is obvious that not everyone did so. When the situation genuinely matters, people are even more likely to process information in a systematic manner. Harkness, DeBono, and Borgida (1985) presented a similar task to college women, this time having to do with "Tom's" decisions about dating women with various characteristics. In a high-involvement condition, they were told they themselves would date Tom later on in the month, while in a low-involvement condition, no mention of dating was made. Their attributions fit the covariation model more accurately when they expected to date him, that is, when the situation had some real stakes for them.

Sometimes there may be several possible causal explanations for a particular behavior, and we need guidelines to determine which attribution is correct. This dilemma raises a second major principle used to make causal attributions, termed the **discounting principle:** "the role of a given cause in producing a given effect is discounted if other plausible causes are also present" (Kelley, 1972, p. 8). That is, we are less likely to attribute the effect to any particular cause, and make less confident attributions, if more than one cause is likely. An insurance salesperson is very nice to us and offers us coffee, but we may not be able to make a confident attribution about why he or she is so friendly. We could attribute the behavior to a real liking for us. More likely, we may discount that possible cause and attribute the behavior partly to the salesperson's wanting our business. On the other hand, if the person knows we have no money to buy insurance, we may not do any such discounting, because the desire for business is no longer a plausible cause. By and large, research findings do seem to follow the pattern described by the covariation and discounting principles (e.g., Olson, 1992; Cheng & Novick, 1990).

ATTRIBUTIONS ABOUT OTHERS

One of the most important and common tasks of causal attribution is understanding why other people do what they do. The most basic question is this: When do we infer that others' actions reflect real dispositions, such as traits, attitudes, or other internal states? When do we assume that others are simply responding to the external situation? Or, using the terms we will use through most of this chapter, when do we make a **dispositional** as opposed to a **situational attribution?**

We know that people do not always say or do what they really believe. A prisoner of war may say things contrary to his real attitudes. Or a boy may try to act cheerful and happy in school the morning after his girlfriend has jilted him. On the other hand, sometimes a POW expresses real, heartfelt criticism of his own nation's war effort. This certainly happened in Vietnam with some American soldiers and airmen. And the boy may have some genuine sense of relief if the relationship had been depressing him for a long time. So how can we tell when a person's actions are a true reflection of his or her internal attitudes or other dispositions?

According to psychologists E. E. Jones and Keith Davis, there are several cues that we can use to determine whether a person's behavior reflects an underlying disposition. One is the *social desirability* of the behavior. Socially undesirable behavior leads people to infer underlying dispositions, whereas with socially desirable behavior, the inference is not so clear. For example, suppose a person is applying for the summer job of social director of a summer camp and knows that being extroverted and having people skills are important requirements of the job. If she behaved in an extroverted, socially skilled manner, it might be difficult for the job interviewer to determine if she was really extroverted and socially skilled or if she was simply appearing so for the purpose of creating a positive impression in the job interview. However, if the job called for extroversion and she behaved in an introverted fashion, the job interviewer could infer with some confidence that the candidate was actually introverted. Otherwise, why would she behave in that way when the situation so clearly called for different behavior? (Jones, Davis, & Gergen, 1961; see Jones & McGillis, 1976).

Another basis for inferring dispositions is whether the behavior of an actor is situationally constrained or whether it occurs from the actor's *choice*. Suppose you are asked to take part in a classroom debate and the teacher assigns you a position of arguing in favor of capital punishment. Knowing that you had been assigned this side of the debate, it would be unwise of your audience to infer that your statements reflected your true beliefs. However, if you had chosen to argue in favor of capital punishment, the audience might appropriately conclude that your statements do reflect your underlying beliefs. Choice enables you to discount the possibility of external pressure.

A number of studies have examined the discounting principle when perceivers are asked to determine another person's true attitude. Jones and Harris (1967) presented subjects with essays written by other students in four conditions: the essays supported Fidel Castro or opposed him and were supposedly written on an assigned topic or with free choice of position. With the free-choice conditions, observers readily inferred that the writer's expressed opinion was the same as his or her underlying attitude. The pro-Castro and the anti-Castro speeches were seen as reflecting underlying pro- and anti-Castro attitudes, respectively. The subjects discounted the possibility of external causality, given the presence of free choice. On the other hand, when the writer was described as having no choice of position (strong external forces), observers still generally felt that the written position reflected the underlying attitude, but they were less sure that this was so. Data from their two very similar experiments are shown in Table 4-3.

A third condition that can help determine whether an action is produced by a person's dispositional qualities is whether the behavior is part of a *social role*. Behavior that is constrained by a role is not necessarily informative about a person's underlying beliefs or behaviors. For example, if a firefighter helps to put out a fire, we do not infer that he is helpful; he is simply doing his job. But when people in well-defined social roles display out-of-role behaviors, those actions can be used to infer underlying dispositions, since an explanation related to role is effectively ruled out. For example, if a priest argues in favor of a woman's right to an abortion, you may infer confidently that his behavior reflects his true beliefs, since it so clearly contradicts the abortion attitudes one expects in a priest.

Another factor that influences whether we will make a dispositional attribution about another's behavior is our *expectancy* about the individual's true dispositions (Jones & McGillis,

When a firefighter puts out a fire, we do not infer that he or she is being helpful. But when private citizens help to put out a fire, we infer helpfulness, because such behavior is not part of their social role.

1976). Usually we know more about the person than just one behavior. Expectations based on past information can help to rule out certain causal explanations for a particular behavior. We know our friend has long been a supporter of black liberation movements in South Africa. So when we have dinner with her parents and see her nodding agreeably at her parents' conservative statements, we nevertheless infer that she is a strong supporter of the movement and make an external attribution for her nodding. We have past information about her attitudes on this issue that gives us an expectancy about what she really believes. We use that information, along with our perception of her current overt behavior (which seems to be somewhat antimovement) and the external forces (she does not want to get into an argument with her parents), to give us a confident attribution (Fleming

TABLE 4-3
Attitude Attributed to Writer

Condition	Pro-Castro	Anti-Castro
Experiment 1		
Choice	59.6[a]	17.4
No choice	44.1	22.9
Experiment 2		
Choice	55.7	22.9
No choice	41.3	23.7

Source: Jones & Harris (1967), pp. 6, 10.
[a] A high score indicates a pro-Castro position attributed to the writer.

& Darley, 1989). If people act in a way consistent with our prior expectations about them, we believe the behavior is dispositionally caused. If they behave in a new and different way, we believe it is situationally caused.

Finally, when we learn that there are other potential explanations for someone's behavior, we are less likely to make dispositional attributions. For example, in a pair of studies (Fein, Hilton, & Miller, 1990), students read an essay ostensibly written by a fellow student. Some of the students believed that the essay writer was trying to ingratiate himself, other students learned that he was trying to avoid an unwanted job, and other students were told that he was instructed to write the essay he did. Those who believed that the essay writer's behavior might have been motivated by a desire to ingratiate himself or to avoid an unwanted job resisted making dispositional attributions, whereas those informed that the student had been assigned the essay position nonetheless made dispositional attributions for his behavior (Fein et al., 1990). Of course, the students should have inferred from the fact that the essay writer was assigned his position that a dispositional explanation for the behavior was inappropriate. However, recall that people are very attuned to dispositional explanations for behavior (such as alternative motives), but not very sensitive to context information (such as learning that the essay writer had no choice).

To summarize, often we are in the position of wanting to know why a person committed a particular action. The goal of our attributional search is a dispositional attribution, that is, trying to find some stable internal quality of the person that explains the action. To arrive at an explanation for behavior, we use cues about the person and the behavior as well as our past knowledge which includes whether or not the behavior is part of a social role, whether it was undertaken out of choice or not, whether the behavior fits with our past knowledge and expectations about the person, and whether the action is socially desirable or not. As the discounting principle suggests, we use these and other cues to consider whether or not any plausible external forces might have led the person to behave in the particular way, and if so, we should be less likely to make a dispositional attribution for that behavior.

ATTRIBUTIONS ABOUT THE SELF

One of the most interesting hypotheses in attribution theory is that we arrive at perceptions of our own internal states in much the same way as we arrive at perceptions of others' states. We have to infer them from our own overt behavior and from our perceptions of the environmental forces surrounding us. This idea derives from the general assumption that our own emotions, attitudes, traits, and abilities are often unclear and ambiguous to us. We may have quite limited access to our internal processes, being only somewhat aware of the factors that influence our behavior (Nisbett & Wilson, 1977).

Thus, in self-perception, just as in the perception of others, we search for invariant associations of causes and effects and use the discounting principle to divide up responsibility among various plausible causes. If we perceive strong external forces pushing us in the direction of our own behavior, we are more likely to come to a situational attribution. In the absence of clear external forces, we assume that a dispositional attribution is more correct. This approach has generated a good deal of research on the self-perception of attitudes, motivation, and emotion.

Attitudes

Psychologists have long assumed that people figure out their own attitudes by *introspection,* by reviewing the various cognitions and feelings in their consciousness. Bem (1967) argued instead that we receive only minimal and ambiguous internal cues to our attitudes. If so, we must infer our own attitudes by observing our own overt behavior. When we observe our own behavior in a situation with no strong external forces, we assume we are simply expressing our own true attitudes and make an internal attribution. In contrast, when there are strong external pressures on us to do something (such as having been assigned a particular position in a debate), we perceive our statements to be externally caused.

In other words, we learn about our own attitudes by observing how we behave in environments with different external pressures in them, not by introspecting to see how we feel. Bem does not hold that people never use internal evidence, just that, to a surprising degree, people rely on the external evidence of their overt behavior, and the conditions under which it occurs, to infer their own true attitudes (Bem, 1972; Lassiter, 1986).

To test Bem's self-perception theory, we would need to manipulate an individual's perception of his behavior while holding other factors constant (such as the actual behavior and the pressure of the environment). Then we could determine whether the person's perception of his own behavior determined his perception of his own attitudes. To test this, Salancik and Conway (1975) cleverly manipulated subjects' descriptions of their own religious behavior: Some were asked if they "occasionally" read a religious newspaper or magazine, attended a church or synagogue, or consulted a minister about personal problems. Many students had engaged in at least these minimal religious acts, so students in this condition reported lots of religious behavior. Others were asked if they "frequently" did each of these things. Since most college students do not do them frequently, students in this condition reported very little religious behavior.

Since the two groups were randomly selected, they were presumably in fact almost exactly the same in actual behavior. But because of these differences in the wording of the questions, the first group of subjects described themselves as engaging in quite a variety of religious behaviors, while the second group described few religious acts. And sure enough, when later asked about their own overall religious attitudes in the form of the question "How religious are you?" the first group, which had been subtly induced to describe themselves as engaging in more religious behaviors, said they were more religious in general.

Attributions and Motivation

A similar idea has been applied to the self-perception of motivation. The idea is that performing a task for high rewards will lead to an external attribution—"I did it because I was paid so well for it." Performing the same task for minimal reward will lead to an internal attribution—"I couldn't have done it for that small amount of money, so I must have done it because I really enjoyed it." This leads to the paradoxical prediction that minimal rewards will lead to the greatest intrinsic interest in a task because the person attributes performance to intrinsic interest, not to extrinsic reward. Put another way, **overjustification** (receiving extrinsic rewards for something one would do anyway out of intrinsic interest) undermines intrinsic interest in the activity.

The earliest demonstration of overjustification varied whether or not nursery school children were given awards for engaging in a task (playing with felt-tip pens) which they enjoyed doing anyway (Lepper, Greene, & Nisbett, 1973). Some children were told they would get a "Good Player Award" with a gold star and ribbon if they would draw pictures with a felt-tip pen for a few minutes. Other children were not told about any award. All the children then did the drawing, and the first group was given their awards. A few days later, all the children were observed in a free-play situation with felt-tip pens provided. The children who had been given the awards spent half as much time drawing as the no-award children did. Their intrinsic interest in drawing had been undermined by the extrinsic reward. This finding has been reported in many contexts since then (see Deci & Ryan, 1985).

An interesting consequence of overjustification is that it can even undermine not just the productivity of people's work on a task, but their creativity as well. Amabile, Hennessey, and Grossman (1986) found that the creativity of children's storytelling was significantly reduced when they were offered an explicit reward for telling the story.

If extrinsic rewards for engaging in pleasurable tasks reduce intrinsic interest, then external threats that prevent engaging in specific behaviors ought to increase interest. For example, the stricter the penalty for using an illegal drug, the more attractive the drug should seem to be. Here people attribute their avoidance of the activity to the threat, not the unpleasantness of the activity itself. Wilson and Lassiter (1982) found some evidence for this hypothesis, when they varied threatened punishment for cheating.

The same reasoning would also suggest that the overjustification effect would be increased when external rewards are made more salient (Ross, 1975) and decreased when the initial interest in the activity is made more salient. In an experiment to test this latter point, Fazio (1981) had children play with Magic Markers, and then later varied whether or not they were shown photos of themselves engaged in this highly pleasurable task on the earlier occasion. Otherwise, the experiment closely resembled the study by Lepper and others (1973) described earlier. For the children shown photos of their earlier play, intrinsic interest in playing with the Magic Markers was highly salient, so extrinsic rewards had little undermining effect. They knew they had really enjoyed the Magic Markers, so they attributed their later play to their own pleasure, not to the reward.

Any cues in an achievement situation that suggest external constraints or control on a person's behavior should also produce the overjustification effect, undermining intrinsic interest. Sansone, Sachau, and Weir (1989) found that instruction from a teacher undermined intrinsic motivation, unless the students had received prior feedback on the task or had been alerted that this was a skill-based task. When the students had received no prior feedback on their performance or no information that the task was skill-based, the instructions seemed to be coming out of the blue, and therefore looked like an effort to control their behavior, consequently undermining their intrinsic interest. These authors also found that when a task was represented as involving fantasy and creativity, instruction likewise undermined intrinsic motivation, presumably because the students felt the instructions were encroaching on their personal

When an intrinsically motivated activity, such as artistic creativity, comes to be seen as under external control, intrinsic interest may be undermined, leading to poorer performance. Unwanted feedback from others can be interpreted as external control.

freedom to pursue the task as they wanted to. Performance impairment and decrements in intrinsic motivation also occur when students are exposed to teachers who are pressured to maximize students' performance and who use controlling strategies to do so (Flink, Boggiano, & Barrett, 1990). All of these findings are consistent with the idea that any cue in a situation that suggests external control of otherwise intrinsically motivated behavior can undermine that intrinsic motivation and lead to poorer performance.

The implications of this research are important. Rewards can sometimes backfire: Instead of encouraging us, they can turn us away from activities we would otherwise enjoy (Kassin &

Lepper, 1984). And punishments may sometimes make a forbidden activity seem all the more attractive.

The Attribution of Emotions

Traditional theories of emotion propose that we recognize what we feel by considering our physiological state, our mental state, and the external stimulus causing these states. But recent evidence indicates that many emotional reactions are biochemically similar. We can distinguish high arousal from low arousal, but not various types of emotion. For example, it is hard to tell the difference between intense jealousy and intense love. We need other information to identify our own emotions.

Stanley Schachter (1964) suggested that perceptions of our emotions depend on (1) the degree of physiological arousal we experience and (2) the cognitive label we apply, such as "angry" or "happy." To arrive at a cognitive label, we review our own behavior and the situation. If we feel physiologically aroused and are laughing at a comedy show on television, we might infer that we are happy. If we are snarling at someone for shoving us on a crowded street, we might infer that we are angry. In each case, our behavior and our interpretation of the situation provide us with the cognitive label that allows us to interpret our internal experience of emotional arousal. Like Bem's theory of self-perception, this point of view emphasizes the ambiguity of internal states and proposes that self-perception is therefore highly dependent on perceptions of overt behavior and of the external environment.

LABELING AROUSAL.   High degrees of physiological arousal give rise to a search for an appropriate attribution. If a plausible attribution exists for the arousal, it will be accepted. If no such attribution exists, the person will search the environment for something that could have caused the arousal. Whatever the environment provides as an explanation will also provide the label for the emotion.

To illustrate this point, Schachter and Singer (1962) conducted a now classic experiment. One group of undergraduate students was injected with epinephrine; half were told its true side effects (e.g., rapid breathing, flushing, increased heart rate), and half were told to expect effects that are not, in fact, produced by epinephrine (e.g., dizziness, slight headache). A control group of subjects was given no drug. Subjects were then placed in a room with a confederate of the experimenter and were instructed to fill out some papers. After a brief time (during which the epinephrine took effect in those who had received it), the confederate began to act in either a euphoric manner (engaging in silly antics and making paper airplanes) or in an angry manner (ripping up the papers and stomping around the room).

Schachter and Singer reasoned that if physiological experience is indeed subject to various interpretations, then those subjects who had been misinformed about the side effects of epinephrine and who later found themselves in a state of arousal would be searching for an explanation for their state. For these subjects, the behavior of the confederate could act as a salient cue for explaining their arousal, suggesting to those subjects in the euphoric condition that they were also euphoric and to those in the angry condition that they were angry. Subjects who had been informed about the side effects of epinephrine, in contrast, already had an adequate explanation for their arousal state and could remain amused or annoyed by the confederate without acquiring his mood. Subjects in the control condition would have no arousal state to explain and also should not catch the mood of the confederate. Generally speaking, this is what Schachter and Singer found. The procedure and results of this experiment are shown in Table 4-4.

What was important for the experience of emotion was, first, the *arousal* and, second, the *cognitive label* or the attribution made for the arousal. When the experimenter provided a label attributing the arousal to the drug, the subjects acted as if they experienced no particular emotion. When they did not know the drug was

TABLE 4-4
The Schachter-Singer Experiment

Condition	Sequence				
	Step 1	Step 2	Step 3	Step 4	Step 5
	Given Arousing Drug	Told It Would Be Arousing	Confederate's Behavior	Presumed Attribution for Own Arousal (Unmeasured)	Own Behavior (Measured)
No explanation	Yes	No	⎧ Euphoric or angry ⎫	Situational	Euphoric or angry
Informed	Yes	Yes	⎨ in all cases ⎬	Drug	Calm
No arousal	No	No	⎩ ⎭	None	Calm

Source: Adapted from Schachter & Singer (1962).

responsible for their arousal, they took their cues about the emotions from the external environment.

False Feedback Studies

One implication of Schachter's reasoning is that internal arousal states are so ambiguous that they can be attributed to any plausible stimulus. Which emotion is experienced therefore may depend more on available plausible causes than it does on the nature of the actual internal sensations. Even fake internal sensations should be sufficient, given an external cause that can supply a plausible label.

Valins (1966) tested this idea by giving random false feedback to subjects about their own arousal. He presented heterosexual male subjects with slides of nude females. After each slide he provided them with faked feedback through earphones about their heart rates. After some slides, subjects heard increased heartbeats, which they thought were their own; after others, they heard decreased heartbeats; and after still others, they heard what they thought were irrelevant sounds. Valins found that subjects rated the nudes accompanied by the supposedly changed heartbeat as the most attractive.

After the experiment was over, subjects were allowed to take some slides home. Most chose slides that had been associated with the fake feedback about changed heartbeat. Presumably they had searched the environment for a plausible cause for the change in their heartbeats, found the slides of the nude females to be a reasonable cause, and therefore labeled their arousal as sexual. This study suggests that people infer their own emotions from the perception of arousal (in this case, faked changes in heartbeat) and a plausible external cause (in this case, pictures of nudes).

Misattribution

Schachter and Singer demonstrated that states of arousal are malleable and can be labeled in any of several ways depending on the situational cues that make a particular emotional explanation salient. The false-feedback studies conducted by Valins and his associates extended this idea to suggest that when people get false feedback that they are aroused when in fact they are not, they come to attribute affect to those stimuli that they believe aroused them. Nisbett and Schachter (1966) took these ideas a step further and proposed that people may be able to misattribute real arousal to a neutral stimulus. If this is true, they reasoned, it can have major clinical and therapeutic impacts. By leading people to attribute anxiety to neutral external forces, one may cure them of the debilitating effects of anxiety on their own performance.

To demonstrate this point, Nisbett and Schachter (1966) conducted a study to see if people could be induced to attribute their arousal to a neutral source. They gave a group of subjects an ordinary sugar pill. Experimental subjects were told the pill would produce physiological symptoms, such as hand tremors and palpitations; control subjects were told it would produce only nonphysiological symptoms. All subjects were then administered painful electric shock. The hypothesis was that the experimental subjects would attribute their physiological reactions after the shock to the pill rather than to the shock itself, and so would perceive the shock as hurting less. The control subjects, having no basis for an attribution to the pill, would blame their reactions on the shock itself. And indeed it was found that these control subjects found the shock more painful than did the experimental subjects. A number of these **misattribution** studies have been done, and they generally share the same basic idea: if people can be persuaded to misattribute their negative emotional states from the real external causes to some other, more neutral cause, the level of emotional distress associated with the real external cause will diminish (Olson, 1988).

SOME LIMITATIONS. Can it really be the case that we get almost no information about our own attitudes and emotions by introspection? Do outside observers know as much about our own internal feelings as we do? This is surely too extreme.

First, this self-perception process works mainly when there is ambiguity or uncertainty about our internal states. People do have attitudes that endure and are not based entirely on current behavior. We do not decide about whether we like steak on the basis of whether we have recently eaten steak. We have real feelings toward steak and it is those feelings that determine our responses. Israelis have certain attitudes about Nazis, and bigots have certain attitudes about minorities, which they are quite

clear about regardless of their most recent behavior. When we are slapped in the face, we do not have to wait to see if we strike back to know if we are angry. When our boyfriend says he no longer loves us, we know we feel hurt no matter whether tears come or not.

The misattribution of arousal to a neutral source is most likely when the actual source of arousal is unclear or ambiguous (Olson & Ross, 1988). For example, a person is unlikely to misattribute arousal caused by the presence of a coiled snake, but might well misattribute residual arousal caused by bumping into a fellow student in the lunch line. Arousal is more likely to be misattributed if the neutral source to which arousal is to be transferred is highly salient and credible (Olson & Ross, 1988). For example, if a male subject is shown a series of beautiful nudes, it may be easy to alter his preferences among them based on false feedback, but it is unlikely that the same subject, shown a nude Miss July and a nude hippopotamus and given false feedback that his heartbeat has accelerated more for the hippo, will seriously think he desires the hippo and want to take the slide home. Another limitation is that the self-perception process seems to work best when people do not care very much about what response they make. When it really matters, people seem to monitor their own attitudes and emotions more carefully and are less influenced by external cues (Taylor, 1975).

When these misattribution or reattribution studies were first done, they gave some promise of providing a new therapeutic tool for dealing with disruptive anxieties, fears, depressions, low self-esteem, and other seemingly neurotic emotions. A variety of studies have tried to apply reattribution therapies to public speaking anxiety, test anxiety, depression, and other unwanted emotions (Forsterling, 1986). The general technique has been to try to get the person to reattribute anxieties to less threatening sources. However, the effects have been short-lived, unreliable, limited to weak anxieties, or very slight (see Slivken & Buss, 1984; Olson & Ross, 1988; Parkinson, 1985). So the technique is probably not powerful enough for therapeutic purposes.

Attribution and Affect

Some attributions generate specific emotions. Weiner's (1986) theory, shown in Figure 4-1, is that success produces very general positive feelings (like happiness) and failure produces generally negative feelings (like sadness). Under some conditions, such as when the outcome is different from what was expected or when the outcome is extremely important, people try to figure out why they succeeded or failed. The attribution they make stimulates specific kinds of emotions. For example, you may feel bad if you get a D on the midterm, but *which* bad emotion you feel will depend on how you explain the low grade. If you think the test was unfair and you blame the teacher, you will feel angry; if you think you did poorly because you are not smart enough to do better, you may feel depressed, but if you feel you didn't study hard enough, you may feel guilty.

Weiner (1982, 1986) has shown that which emotion people experience depends on their attribution. Different attributions produce different emotions. Consider the situation of academic achievement. When a person is successful, internal attributions (ability, effort) produce pride, while external attributions (easy test, a helpful roommate) may produce gratitude. Failures explained by internal causes (lack of effort, low ability) breed feelings of shame, while failures explained externally (test harder than expected or unfair) may produce surprise or anger (Weiner, Russell & Lerman, 1979; Weiner, 1986).

The controllability of perceived causes is also important. Internal attributions for negative outcomes, such as a poor grade on a midterm, can produce quite different emotions, depending on the controllability of the cause. Guilt comes from controllable internal causes, such as effort ("I could have studied and I just wasted the whole evening"), while depression comes from causes that cannot be controlled very well, such as lack of ability ("I'm just not smart enough to do this") or personality characteristics ("I'm not

Figure 4-1 Attributional analysis of emotion. (*Source:* Adapted from B. Weiner, 1986, p. 122.)

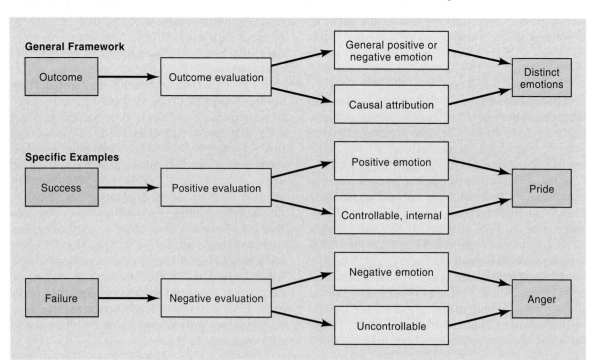

Our causal attributions influence our emotions. When a person is successful, an internal attribution for success, such as to ability or effort, produces pride, while external attributions, for example, to an easy test, do not. Failure attributed to internal causes, such as lack of effort or low ability, breeds shame, while failure explained externally, such as an unfair test, may produce surprise or anger.

self-disciplined enough to be in college") (Weiner et al., 1979; Weiner, 1986). Anger is associated with controllable causes. One example Weiner gives is: "My roommate brought her dog into our no-pets apartment without asking me first. When I got home she wasn't there, but the barking dog was. . . . As well, the dog had relieved itself in the entry" (1986, p. 137). The person was angry at the roommate, because she could have controlled whether the dog was there or not. A chronically lying boyfriend or husband, a woman who is on welfare for years but who could be working, a foreign country that deliberately shoots down one of our domestic airliners—all attract anger, because these actions are interpreted as controllable.

Pity or sympathy, on the other hand, is aroused by behavior interpreted as uncontrollable. A handicapped child who accidentally knocks over a vase may elicit sympathy (she couldn't help it); a drunk who does it elicits anger (he should not have been drunk; he could have controlled himself). To show this, Weiner (1980) described to college students either a person who apparently was drunk and fell down in a subway, "He is carrying a liquor bottle wrapped in a brown paper bag and smells of liquor," or a person who was ill and fell down. The college students said that they would have negative affects such as anger toward the drunk, but not toward the ill person.

But how culture-bound are these attribution–emotion links? Do members of other cultures make them in the same way that Americans do? In one study (Stipek, Weiner, & Li, 1989), many of these attribution–emotion links were demonstrated in the People's Republic of China. This finding is important because many regard China as quite different from the United States, not only in terms of emotions that are typically experienced, but also in the value placed on achievement, the context in which the attribution–emotion linkages were examined. Thus, these attribution–emotion linkages appear to hold up across different cultures. Attributions are important, then, not only because they enable us to make sense of situations and to determine future behavior, but also because they help determine the emotional reactions we experience (Graham & Weiner, 1991).

Attributions and Culture

Theories and research on causal attributions have identified a number of valuable generalizations concerning when we ask why questions and how we go about answering them. But to what extent are attribution theory and research culturally bounded? It is important to realize that most of the studies conducted on causal attributions have been done in Western societies, chiefly the United States and Western European nations. To what extent would these theoretical and empirical generalizations apply to other cultures?

This question is more complex than may be apparent. A first important question is, Do people in other cultures ask why questions? Considerable research shows that, when asked to provide causal explanations, members of cultures as diverse as Nigeria, Holland, Hong Kong, India, Britain, Japan, Germany, and the United States can do so. Whether all do so spontaneously, however, has yet to be addressed (Bond, 1983).

Can our theories in fact generalize about how people make causal attributions? As we have seen, there appear to be some cross-cultural similarities among attributional dimensions and cross-cultural consistencies concerning the links between attributions and emotions, as uncovered by Weiner and his research group. However, some have suggested that the covariation model developed by Kelley (1967) may have little relevance in understanding the attributions of non-Western cultures (Semin, 1980). For the most part, however, whether theories of how people form causal attributions apply across cultures has yet to be demonstrated.

CULTURAL HIGHLIGHT
People as Causes—Is It Universal?

Suppose you saw someone shouting angrily and waving his arms at another person. What would you conclude about him? If you are an American or a Western European, chances are you would regard him as a hostile and aggressive person. But how universal is this tendency to explain events in terms of dispositional attributions? How fundamental is the fundamental attribution error?

Amassing cross-cultural research suggests that the tendency to explain events in terms of people's enduring qualities is not as universal as we once thought. One important study to demonstrate these cross-cultural limitations was conducted by psychologist Joan Miller (1984). She asked Americans and Hindus from India of different ages to explain some common events. She found that American adults were more likely to use

internal, dispositional attributions, while Hindu adults were more likely to invoke the external context. For example, an American who was asked to explain her neighbor's cheating on her taxes said, "That's just the type of person she is. She's very competitive." Or a colleague who stole someone else's idea and presented it as his own was described by an American as "just a very self-absorbed person. He was interested only in himself." In both cases, dispositions were invoked to explain the behavior.

What about someone who was cheated of 1500 rupees by a man who was supposed to do some construction work and didn't, and kept the advance? A Hindu said, "The man is unemployed. He is not in a position to give that money [back]." Another, explaining why someone put his name as first author on a paper from his student's

thesis, said, "She was his student. She would not have the power to . . . publish it by herself" (Miller, 1984, pp. 967–968). The situation explains behavior, according to these Hindu respondents. Further evidence for the cultural explanation of these findings is that differences between the two cultures are not present among young children; they show up only with age, as would be the case if they needed to be learned over time.

The well-documented tendency to explain behavior in terms of enduring dispositions is a cultural phenomenon found largely in the United States and much of Western Europe. In other countries, such as the Indian society described by Miller, the important role of context and situational factors is acknowledged when people offer causal explanations for events.

At a still more specific level of analysis, do different societies demonstrate the same basic principles of causal attribution? As we shall see, one of the most consistent findings in attribution research is that we make attributions to other people, especially to their stable dispositions. This phenomenon, however, appears to be a very Western one. As the CULTURAL HIGHLIGHT illustrates, adults in non-Western cultures generally place less emphasis on dispositional aspects of an agent and, rather, make more contextual or situational explanations for behavior than American or Western European adults (Shweder & Bourne, 1982; Markus & Kitayama, 1991).

When we turn to the specific content of attributions, we find even less agreement. The content of attributions appears to be heavily dependent on people's knowledge and belief systems (Agar, 1981; Taylor, 1982). For example, Levy-Bruhl (1925) reports how the natives of a New Guinea tribe ascribed a pleurisy epidemic to the presence of a missionary, his sheep, two goats, and finally, a picture of Queen Victoria. Many non-Western societies invoke what would seem to Westerners to be magical explanations as causal accounts (Fauconnet, 1928; see Hewstone, 1989).

In summary, then, the degree to which principles and empirical findings of attribution theory generalize across cultures is a complex issue. While we know that members of a diverse array of cultures *can* answer why questions, it is not yet known whether they spontaneously do so. The generalizability of most attribution theories has yet to be empirically tested. What once seemed like basic principles of attribution, such as the tendency to attribute people's behavior to their dispositions, now appear to have a heavily cultural component (Mizokawa & Ryckman, 1990). And finally, the specific content of attributions shows the least amount of cross-cultural uniformity.

BIASES IN THE ATTRIBUTION PROCESS

Attribution theory, as described up to this point, tends to suggest a rational, logical process. It assumes that people process information in a quite orderly way and that they are fairly objective in assessing the usefulness of information and combining it to produce a conclusion. However, as we saw in the last chapter, people tend to be miserly in their expenditure of cognitive effort. Moreover, we know that people do not spend most of their waking moments diligently trying to ferret out the causes of events. Furthermore, people are far from logical and rational in all their thoughts and behaviors. In that context, we now turn to several biases that have been identified in attributional processes. We begin with a consideration of biases that derive from the tendency to respond more to salient or figural stimuli than to background stimuli and to simplify perception by developing meaningful, structured impressions.

Salience

One way we simplify cognitive processing is by overreacting to salient stimuli. This bias leads us to perceive the most salient stimulus as the most influential. If something is in motion or colorful or loud or novel, we are likely to see it as a cause of whatever else is changing in the environment. The person who is running down the street is seen as having caused the bank alarm to go off. A loud thunderclap is perceived as causing people to scurry for cover.

Sometimes, the most salient stimuli are, in fact, the strongest causes of people's behavior, so such attributions would then be accurate. But biases arise because the most perceptually salient stimuli sometimes dominate causal explanations, even when they are not actually the most powerful causes.

Taylor and Fiske (1975) tested this idea, that whatever is perceptually salient will be seen as the dominant cause. Two confederates served as "actors." They engaged in conversation, facing each other. The subjects were "observers" sitting behind the confederates or next to them. Each actor thus had observers sitting behind him and facing him. Clearly, the actor and his behavior would be more salient for those who faced him than for those who sat behind him. But both actors were equally salient for the observers sitting to the side, equidistant from the two actors.

This arrangement is illustrated in Figure 4-2.

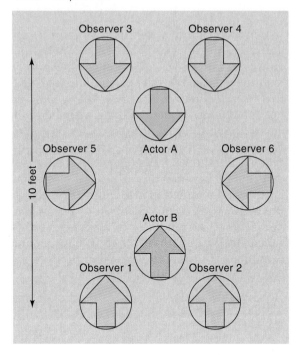

Figure 4-2 Seating arrangements for actors and observers, with arrows indicating visual orientation. (*Source:* Adapted from Taylor & Fiske, 1975, p. 441.)

The confederates held a standardized 5-minute conversation, chatting as if they had just met. They exchanged information about majors, common job plans, hometowns, family, extracurricular activities, and the like. The conversation was carefully set up to make sure that roughly the same conversation occurred in all experimental groups.

Then the subjects were asked for their causal perceptions: How much had each confederate set the tone of the conversation, determined the kind of information exchanged, and caused the other actor to behave as he did? The results are shown in Table 4-5. It shows that the more perceptually salient actor (the confederate the subject faced) was seen as dominant and that the less salient actor (the confederate the subject sat behind) was seen as less influential. Subjects sitting equidistant from both confederates saw both as about equally potent. Thus, actor A was seen as most powerful by those facing him

(observers 1 and 2), while actor B was seen as most powerful by those facing *him* (observers 3 and 4)—even though all subjects in reality were observing exactly the same interaction (and one in which both actors contributed about equally, according to unbiased observers 5 and 6 in the center).

But what makes people salient? You are salient if you are the only one of your kind in a roomful of other people. For example, if you are the only student in a crowd of professors, the only homosexual in a group of heterosexuals, or the only black in a group of whites, you feel conspicuous. All eyes have a single target. When your solo status is known or obvious, as in the case of salient physical attributes, this is indeed the case. Research on salience supports the idea that it is an uncomfortable experience being the solo and being the center of attention (Taylor, 1981c).

The finding that perceptual salience induces exaggeration of a person's causal role turns out to be quite general (Taylor, Crocker, Fiske, Sprinzen, & Winkler, 1979; Frank & Gilovich, 1989; Robinson & McArthur, 1982). In fact, people seem to make causal attributions to salient stimuli so readily that some have argued that the causality ascribed to perceptually salient

TABLE 4-5

Mean Ratings of Causal Role Attributed by Observers to Each Actor as a Function of the Observer's Seating Position

Observer's Position	Actor	
	A	B
Facing actor A (observers 1 and 2)	20.25	15.54
Center (observers 5 and 6)	17.51	16.75
Facing actor B (observers 3 and 4)	12.00	20.75

Source: Taylor & Fiske (1975), p. 441.

stimuli is a virtually automatic consequence of the perceptual experience and does not involve any deliberate causal inference on the part of the perceiver (McArthur & Baron, 1983).

Overattributing Actions to Dispositions

Another bias in the causal attribution process is that we are too likely to explain others' behavior as resulting from such dispositions as their general personality traits or their attitudes, while we tend to overlook the importance of the situations they are in. When we ask for information from a clerk at a window in the college administration building and he seems impersonal, brusque, and unhelpful, we think he is a cold, unfriendly person. We tend to ignore the fact that he must have scores of such brief encounters with anonymous complaining students each day. It probably is his particular job situation, rather than his personality, that makes him act brusquely. Overattribution to dispositions, and underestimation to situations, is so common that Ross (1977) has called it the **fundamental attribution error.**

As one example of this fundamental error, recall the Jones and Harris (1967) study of attributions about the attitudes of people writing essays on Fidel Castro. Essay writers who freely chose to take a pro-Castro position were regarded as truly much more pro-Castro than were writers taking an anti-Castro position. But internal attributions were made even when the writer had no choice about which position to take in the essay. Even when the writer had been assigned his essay position, observers overestimated the role of internal dispositions (the writer's true position on Castro) and underestimated the strength of the external situation (that is, the lack of choice about what position to take) in trying to explain the position taken in the essay. This can be seen in Table 4-3.

The finding that observers make internal attributions even when actors have no choice is

an important one. It illustrates the principle that causal attributions for the behavior of others are biased in the direction of overemphasizing dispositions and underemphasizing the environment. Many subsequent studies have found substantially the same thing. The phenomenon seems to hold up even when the subjects have themselves actually and knowingly induced the speaker's behavior (Gilbert & Jones, 1986). And the phenomenon holds up even when observers themselves have been through the same procedure and know that no choice is involved (Miller, Jones, & Hinkle, 1981).

All in all, it appears that the tendency to take speakers' positions as reflective of their true attitudes seems amazingly resilient, even in conditions when it should be easy to make an external attribution: when speakers have no choice, are unenthusiastic, give weak arguments, and are simply reading someone else's speech. Only under the most extreme situational constraints, and with very weak arguments delivered in drab, written form, does the phenomenon disappear and do observers begin to see the full causal role of external forces (see Reeder, Fletcher, & Furman, 1989; Fleming & Darley, 1989; Miller, 1976; Watson, 1982).

Why do we do this? Why do we resist information about external constraints? Salience is one likely explanation for this attributional bias. According to Heider, "Behavior . . . has such salient properties that it tends to engulf the field"; that is, we pay so much attention to the person's behavior that we tend to ignore the situation in which it occurs. The behavior becomes figural and stands out against the surrounding ground of the situation. And as we have seen in the previous section, such salience leads to the perception of causality. Thus, the essay writer, rather than the situation, is seen as the primary causal factor. But salience cannot fully explain the fundamental attribution error. It is also strong when paper-and-pencil descriptions of other people's behaviors are used, settings that preclude the dominance of the perceptual field by the actor's behavior (Winter & Uleman, 1984; Winter, Uleman, & Cunniff, 1985).

As we saw in Chapter 3, research now suggests that attributions of dispositional qualities to other people on the basis of their behavior may be made spontaneously without awareness, perhaps even automatically, upon simply learning that another person has committed a particular behavior (Trope, 1986b; Gilbert, Pelham, & Krull, 1988).

The ability to qualify dispositional inferences with relevant situational information about the context seems to be part of a second, less spontaneous, more thoughtful process that involves correcting the initial dispositional inference (Gilbert, McNulty, Giuliano, & Benson, 1992). In many cases, the social perceiver never gets to that second stage of correction. This is particularly true if the behavior being explained is ambiguous or difficult to comprehend (Gilbert et al., 1992). People also fail to get to that correction phase when they are cognitively "busy," that is, thinking about their future activities, trying to make a good impression, or engaging in other tasks that consume attention (e.g., Gilbert, Pelham, & Krull, 1988; Osbourne & Gilbert, 1992). Presumably, this is because the busy perceiver pays even less attention to nonsalient situational factors than the unbusy perceiver who can take in at least some qualifying contextual information and use it to correct his or her dispositional inferences. Most of us are cognitively busy most of the time. Thus, if anything, research may underestimate the strength of the fundamental attribution error.

A lot of recent attention has focused on whether interpreting others' behaviors as stemming from their dispositions is really a bias or not. In some respects, it may be quite functional. When we are required to communicate to others or about them, we need to simplify a rich and detailed store of information about them into brief and meaningful form (Hoffman, Mischel, & Baer, 1984). Traits (or other dispositions) are convenient summaries for all of that information. It is easier to say, "She's a little immature" than to list all the behaviors that lead us to say that.

On the other hand, it is clear that Americans and Western Europeans offer disposition explanations for behavior far more than do members of other cultures (e.g., Miller, 1984; Shweder & Bourne, 1982). As the Cultural Highlight shows, people from many other countries are far more likely to use situational and contextual information to qualify inferences about others. Thus, the dispositional attribution bias appears to be not only a bias, but one that is especially prevalent in our own culture.

Actors Versus Observers

One of the most interesting aspects of the fundamental attribution error is that it holds for observers, but not for actors. Actors instead seem to overemphasize the role of external factors in explaining their own behavior. For example, some parents set fairly restrictive rules for their adolescent children, such as that they can go out on dates during weekends only, they have to be home at a certain hour, they can watch television only during certain hours, and so on. How is this rule making interpreted? The "observers," namely, the adolescents, frequently perceive their rules as dispositionally caused: The parents are mean, authoritarian, arbitrary, and old-fashioned. The "actors" themselves, the parents, are often more likely to explain their behavior in terms of the situation: They are just doing what is best for their children, living up to the role of the parent, or responding to the rebelliousness and irresponsibility of the children themselves.

How do both sides interpret it if the adolescents repeatedly violate the rules? The "observers," this time the parents, interpret it dispositionally: The adolescents are rebellious, irresponsible, and so on. The "actors," this time the adolescents, interpret their own behavior as situationally caused: The party was fun so they didn't want to leave, the parents' rules are unreasonably strict, the parents misunderstand them, and so on. In short, observers infer dispositional causes, actors infer situational ones. Both groups are explaining the same behavior, but with quite different attributions.

This **actor–observer bias** (Jones & Nisbett, 1972) has proved to be one of the most widely researched of the various attributional biases. In one of its earliest demonstrations, Nisbett, Caputo, Legant, and Marachek (1973) asked male students to write a paragraph on what they most liked about the woman they dated and why they had chosen their major. Then they were asked to answer the same questions as if they were their best friend. Responses were scored for the extent to which the behavior was attributed to the actor's disposition (such as, "I need someone I can relax with" or "I want to make a lot of money") or externally, to aspects of the woman or major (such as, "she's smart and fun," or "chemistry is a high-paying field"). The subjects gave more situational reasons for their own behavior and more dispositional reasons for a friend's behavior.

A related tendency is that actors not only see their own behavior as less dispositionally based than observers do; they also see their behavior as less stable (Baxter & Goldberg, 1988; Sande, Goethals, & Radloff, 1988). When behavior is thought to result from a disposition, that disposition remains stable across situations, but when behavior is credited to situational factors, it should change as the situation changes. One may regard one's own periods of gloominess as temporary reactions to bad circumstances, but regard another's bouts of gloominess as stable indicators of an inherently gloomy personality.

Jones and Nisbett offered two explanations for this difference in actors' and observers' attributions. One was that the participants have access to *different information* and therefore naturally come to different conclusions. Actors have access to much more historical information about their own behavior in different situations than the usual observer. They know how their own behavior has varied across situations, and therefore attribute it to the characteristics of each particular situation, rather than perceiving themselves as behaving uniformly due to some general predisposition. This explanation comes from the covariation principle described earlier.

The other explanation, and the one pursued by most researchers, is that the difference is due mainly to *different perspectives,* with the key factor again being differences in salience. The observer is naturally focused on the actor. This special salience of the actor leads the observer to overattribute the actor's behavior to dispositions, as we have already seen. This is the fundamental attribution error. But the actor is not looking at her own behavior. She is looking at the situation—the place, the other people, their expectations, and so on. The actor's own behavior is not as salient to herself as it is to an observer who is watching her. For this reason, the actor will see the situation as more salient and therefore more causally potent. In short, for the observer, the actor's behavior engulfs the field, and so it becomes perceived as the major causal force. For the actor, the environment is more salient than behavior, and engulfs the field and becomes the major causal explanation. There is evidence for both the perceptual explanation (Storms, 1973) and the informational explanation (Eisen, 1979), and it is likely that both types of factors contribute to this effect (see also Van Heck & Dijkstra, 1985).

Differences in actors' and observers' attributions are weakened under certain conditions. People are more likely to attribute positive outcomes to dispositional factors and negatively valenced outcomes to situational factors, regardless of whether they are committed by actors or observers (e.g., Tillman & Carver, 1980; Taylor & Koivumaki, 1976). For example, we are more likely to see a person's friendliness as part of her nature, but her impatience as due to frustrating circumstances. The actor–observer effect can also be reversed when people feel empathy for the person whose behavior they are observing. Regan and Totten (1975) found that if the observer adopted an empathetic attitude and tried to think of and see things the way the actor did, the observer would come to see the world the way the actor does, namely, in terms of situational factors. The surrounding situation became more prominent, presumably as it would for the actor himself or herself. Personal involvement in an actor's plight yields similar effects (Chen, Yates, & McGinnies, 1988). People tend to see the world as the actor does if they believe they will be involved in similar circumstances in the future.

False Consensus

People tend to imagine that everyone responds the way they do. They tend to see their own behavior as typical. This tendency to exaggerate how common one's own opinions and behavior are is called the **false consensus** effect. In an early demonstration of this effect, students were asked if they would walk around their college campus for 30 minutes wearing a large sandwich board with the message "Eat at Joe's." Some students agreed; others refused. But both groups estimated that about two-thirds of the other students on the campus would make the same choice they did. Both groups clearly could not be right (Ross, Greene, & House, 1977).

This false consensus effect has been shown to occur in a broad array of different situations (Mullen et al., 1985; Mullen & Hu, 1988). For example, smokers in junior high and high school are likely to estimate much higher levels of smoking, both among youths in school and in the general population, than are nonsmokers (Sherman, Presson, Chassin, Corty, & Olshavsky, 1983). It begins early: Even school-age children demonstrate the effect (Wetzel & Walton, 1985). There are several possible explanations for the false consensus effect. One possibility stems from the fact that people seek out the company of others who are similar to them and who behave as they do (selective exposure). Consequently, estimates of others' beliefs about behavior may simply reflect the biased sample of people one has available for social inference. If our friends think as we do, this provides a certain degree of consensus. Another possibility is that our own opinions are especially salient and that when we focus on a particular opinion, consensus is increased because our own position is the only one in consciousness (Marks & Miller, 1987). Were we to consider the validity of other positions, the estimate of consensus might not be so high.

A third possibility is that in trying to predict how we might respond in a situation, we resolve ambiguous details in our mind in a way that favors a preferred course of action. We fail to recognize that our own choices are a result not simply of the objective situation, but of our subjective construal of the situation as well (Gilovich, 1990). For example, the person who imagines that others will point and laugh if she appears in a sandwich board will probably decline to wear one and assume that others, anticipating the same harassment, would do the same.

A fourth possibility is that people have a need to see their own beliefs and behaviors as good, appropriate, and typical, and so they attribute them to others to maintain high self-esteem. Research investigations suggest that all these explanations have some value in explaining the false consensus effect (Marks & Miller, 1987).

On certain person attributes, people show a **false uniqueness** effect (Marks, 1984; Snyder & Fromkin, 1980; Tesser & Paulhus, 1983). For example, when people are asked to list their best abilities and estimate how others stand on these abilities, they underestimate their peers' abilities. To value an ability and consider it special, people seem to need to feel distinctive and uniquely good at the ability (Tesser, 1988). On attitude issues, in contrast, people overestimate the frequency with which others agree with them, providing false consensus. Attitudes and opinions, then, show false consensus effects, whereas one's own highly valued skills and abilities tend to show false uniqueness effects (Kernis, 1984).

The false consensus effect has important implications for how people interpret social reality. It may be one vehicle by which people maintain that their beliefs and opinions are right. It may, for example, lead people to assume that there are lots of others out there who agree with them, when that may not be the case (Granberg, 1987; Judd & Johnson, 1981). Consequently, under certain conditions, the false consensus effect may function as a justification for the imposition of political or religious beliefs on others.

The Self-serving Attributional Bias

After your football team has soundly beaten an opponent, how often do you hear from the opponent a gratifying, "Gee, you're better than we are, aren't you?" Usually you hear that it was luck, the field conditions were poor, and they'll beat you next year. On the other hand, when you have just been badly beaten, the smug look and condescending "Bad luck" from the opponent are particularly grating, because you know that they do not believe it was bad luck for a moment; they think they are better. This tendency to take credit for success and deny responsibility for failure is known as the **self-serving attributional bias** (D. T. Miller & Ross, 1975; Mullen & Riordan, 1988; Fletcher & Ward, 1988).

Overall, there is more evidence that people take credit for success than that they deny responsibility for failure. People are sometimes willing to accept responsibility for failure if they can attribute it to some factor over which they have future control, such as effort. For example, if your team loses the game and blames it on the condition of the field, that will not do much to help them improve next time. But, if they realize that they failed to complete almost every pass, they have something to work on for next week's game.

Much work on self-serving biases has assumed that the biases stem from a need to protect the ego from assault. Presumably, one feels better when one causes good things to happen and not bad things. But cognitive factors appear to be involved, too (Taylor & Riess, 1989). People expect to succeed and may accept responsibility for success because it fits their expectations. People try to succeed, and when they do, their apparent self-enhancing explanation for success may reflect little more than the perceived covariation between their effort and the outcome. When people estimate the amount of control they have in a situation, they utilize instances in which they have been successful more than instances in which they have been unsuccessful, and hence overestimate the amount of control they have. All these factors can contribute to the self-enhancing bias (Miller & Ross, 1975). Indeed, efforts to try to determine if the self-serving bias is cognitively or motivationally based have generally failed, and researchers have assumed that both kinds of factors are involved (Bradley, 1978).

As the football example implies, self-serving biases include not only explanations for one's own behavior, but explanations for one's intimates, close friends, and other groups with which one is allied (e.g., Lau & Russell, 1980; Winkler & Taylor, 1979). At the group level, this bias has been termed the ethnocentric or group-serving bias, and it refers to the tendency of ingroup members to attribute internal causes to positive ingroup behavior and negative outgroup behavior and to attribute negative ingroup behavior and positive outgroup behavior to external causes (Hewstone & Jaspars, 1982; Mullen & Riordan, 1988).

The self-serving attributional bias shows up across cultures. Members of many cultures regard their own culture in a more favorable light than they regard other cultures (Smith, Whitehead, & Sussman, 1990). Also, men may be more likely to offer self-serving attributions for their actions than women. In a study conducted in Italy (Maass & Volpato, 1988), men blamed their partners more for unsatisfying sexual experiences than did women. Women, in contrast, made self-derogatory attributions for unsatisfying sex, attributing it to themselves rather than to their partners. Other research similarly suggests that the self-serving attributional bias may be more characteristic of men than women (Deaux, 1976).

Self-serving attributional biases may actually be quite adaptive, despite their apparent tendency to play fast and loose with the facts. Attributing success to one's own effort, particularly one's enduring characteristics, creates expectations that may make people more likely to attempt related tasks in the future (see Taylor & Brown, 1988). In one study, unemployed workers who attributed their firings to external factors, made greater efforts to become reemployed and actually were more likely to find jobs (Schaufeli, 1988).

Self-centered Bias

People consistently exaggerate their own contributions to shared activities, a bias called the **self-centered bias.** How does this bias differ from the self-serving bias just described? Whereas the self-serving bias involves taking credit for success but not failure, the self-centered bias consists of taking more than one's share of responsibility for a jointly produced outcome, regardless of whether the outcome is successful or unsuccessful. Ross and Sicoly (1979) did several studies of married couples' estimates of relative contributions to joint activities, college basketball players' estimates of their own roles in recent games, and recent college graduates' estimates of their own contribution to their bachelors' theses. In each case, people exaggerated their own contributions.

Thompson and Kelley (1981) found the same thing: Each member of a couple consistently claimed that he or she took more than half the responsibility for such joint activities as carrying the conversation when the two of them were alone, waiting for the other person, resolving conflicts, or being sensitive to the other's needs.

What accounts for the self-centered bias? First, it is easier to notice one's own contributions than those of another person. One may be distracted from another's contributions or not even be physically present when the other person is doing his or her share of the joint task. It may also be easier to recall one's own contributions than those of another person, since they are more personally salient. There may be motivational factors involved as well. Thinking about how much you have contributed may increase your self-esteem, particularly for positive tasks. Which of these explanations is correct? As in the previous biases discussed, there appears to be no one factor that accounts for the bias, but several contributing factors.

Biases: *Where Do They Come From?*

We have now considered several biases that enter into the process of making causal attributions. Why do they occur? Some represent cognitive shortcuts, ways of cutting through masses of available information efficiently to reach a good explanation. As we saw in the last chapter, people tend to be stingy with their cognitive resources, and were they to spend most of their waking moments diligently trying to ferret out the causes of events, there would be little time and cognitive energy left over for other tasks. Consequently, certain of the biases in causal attributions, such as the tendency to attend to salient stimuli, may simply make the process of forming causal attributions more rapid and efficient. Biases due to cognitive factors, then, represent the need to have a coherent, clear understanding of the environment, and to produce such an understanding with as much efficiency as possible.

Other biases arise from people's efforts to satisfy their own needs and motives. In addition to the need for a coherent understanding of the world, people have other needs—for love, revenge, self-esteem, prestige, material goods, and so on. These factors, too, play a substantial role in biasing causal attributions. Many of these motivational factors fall into two categories: self-serving biases that enhance self-esteem and biases that enhance the sense that people can control their lives.

Finally, biases also stem from the desire to impress others. People typically want to create a favorable impression in the minds of other people and therefore adopt certain of their behaviors as strategic means of enhancing their self-presentation. Most biases seem to stem from a combination of factors: cognitive factors, motivational needs, and self-presentational concerns.

THE ILLUSION OF CONTROL

We have seen how people tend to distort the social world perceptually into a more orderly, organized, predictable, and sensible thing than it really is. They do it in many ingenious ways, using first impressions, schemas, scripts, attributional biases, and a wide variety of other cognitive mechanisms. But people not only perceive the world as more orderly than it really is. They distort it in more *controllable* directions as well. They systematically overestimate their own control over events and underestimate the role of chance or uncontrollable factors (Taylor & Brown, 1988). Langer (1975) has called this the **illusion of control.**

The typical experiment of illusion of control has led subjects to exaggerate their control over chance outcomes. For example, Wortman (1975) put two different marbles in a can and told subjects that each marble stood for a different prize. Some subjects were told which marble stood for the prize they wanted, and some were not. Then subjects either chose a marble or were given one, without being allowed to see which marble was which. There was no conceivable way they could actually control the outcome. Nevertheless, when they knew in advance which marble stood for the prize they wanted and were allowed to choose a marble, they thought they were more responsible for the outcome than when they were just given a marble. They had the illusion of control.

How common is the illusion of control? It appears to be quite common. Psychologists have demonstrated it in a wide array of circumstances and with many different groups of people. Most of us seem to believe that we have more control over events in our lives than may actually be the case (Taylor & Brown, 1988). There are, however, circumstances that can undermine this illusion of control, or at least undermine the perception that one can exert control over events that are actually determined by chance: When the stakes are high, the effect is lessened (Dunn & Wilson, 1990).

A Just World

The illusion of control implies that people have more control over their fates than they actually do. One consequence of this illusion is the tendency to blame victims of misfortune for their adverse circumstances. A person who is involved in a traffic accident must have been driving carelessly. Victims of theft are perceived as having brought it on themselves by not taking adequate security precautions (Tyler &

Devintz, 1981). A woman who is raped must have been acting in a provocative manner and brought it on herself. Even victims blame themselves. For example, many rape victims see themselves as having behaved in the wrong way, such as hitchhiking or leaving their apartment window unlocked (Janoff-Bulman, 1979). Women's characters seem particularly to be blamed for such attacks as robbery or rape: they are too passive, or careless, or trusting (Howard, 1984). Minorities who are discriminated against are often seen as being too pushy, unmotivated, or passive and are believed to alienate people with their demands; they therefore are seen as deserving their fates.

To explain such observations, Lerner (1965) has offered the notion that we believe in a **just world:** Good people get good outcomes, and bad things happen to bad people. The key idea is that observers attribute chance events to the victims' moral dispositions. That is, instead of making the seemingly obvious attribution to luck, fate, or some other aspect of the situation, people make an attribution to the victim's moral character. Thus, I blame you for being a lousy driver because someone ran a red light and hit you at an intersection on the way to campus. To test this notion, Lerner ran several laboratory experiments in which victims were picked at random to be given electric shock (Lerner, 1970). Even so, the other subjects tended to denigrate them, as if the victims were responsible for their chance misfortunes.

Lerner interprets these indications of a belief in a just world as reflecting a need to believe that we can control events, much like the illusion of control. To protect this sense of control, we blame people for the bad things that happen to them. If people in general are responsible for any disaster that befalls them, presumably we ourselves can avoid personal disaster by acting properly. One unfortunate consequence of the tendency to see the world as a just place, as Lerner (1980), Ryan (1971), and others have pointed out, is that it provides a justification for the oppression of society's victims. If people themselves are responsible for the fact that they are sick, poor, or disabled, there is no need for the rest of us to help them.

Control: An Adaptive Illusion?

What happens when this sense of control is threatened? Suppose a woman student is followed by a strange man one night on the way home back to her dormitory from the library. She has always felt safe in this well-lighted part of campus, but suddenly she feels alone and very vulnerable. He finally comes close to her and grabs her arm and tries to pull her off the path. She breaks away and runs to the dormitory, panic-stricken. She arrives there safely. But after this episode, she no longer feels safe walking at night alone on that path. She has lost her sense of control; something bad can happen to her at any moment, no matter what she does. How do people who have lost the illusion of control respond?

Reactions vary all the way from seeking information (Swann & Stephenson, 1981), to experiencing pain and stress more intensely, to declines in performance (Glass & Singer, 1972), and to emotional reactions such as anger or hostility (Brehm & Brehm, 1981) or hopelessness and apathy (Abramson, Seligman, & Teasdale, 1978). But a major response is the attempt to restore control. Even when people get cancer, a disease that is among the most difficult to control and whose causes are very poorly understood, they try to regain a sense of mastery in a variety of ways. Taylor (1983, p. 1164) reports these efforts to restore control among women afflicted with breast cancer:

> [Where the cancer came from] was an important question to me at first. The doctor's answer was that it was a multifaceted illness. I looked over the known causes of cancer, like viruses, radiation, genetic mutation, environmental carcinogens, and the one I focused on very strongly was diet. I know now why I focused on it. It was the only one that was simple enough for me to understand and change. You eat something that's bad for you, you get sick.

And one spouse described his wife:

> She got books, she got pamphlets, she studied, she talked to cancer patients, she found out everything that was happening to her, and she

fought it. She went to war with it. She calls it taking in her covered wagons and surrounding it.

Indeed, a number of psychologists feel that a strong sense of control over oneself and one's life is extremely adaptive, even if it is based in part on illusion: "Far from impeding adjustment, illusion may be essential for adequate coping" (Taylor, 1983, p. 29; see also Taylor & Brown, 1988).

INDIVIDUAL DIFFERENCES IN ATTRIBUTIONS

Locus of Control

Some people's sense of personal control is so great that they almost seem to believe that they make the sun come up in the morning and set at night, whereas other people seem never to see a connection between their behavior and what happens to them. The propensity to explain events in terms of oneself versus the environment is termed **locus of control**. Developed by Rotter (1966), the theory argues that people differ in the expectations they hold about the sources of good and bad things that happen to them. Internals credit themselves with the ability to control the occurrence of reinforcing events, both positive and negative. Other people, termed externals, perceive reinforcing events as under the control of luck, chance, or powerful other individuals—factors external to themselves.

Locus of control influences both how people perceive the events that befall them and how they interpret the experiences of others. For example, in one study (Phares, Wilson, & Klyver, 1971), college student subjects were made to fail on an intellectual task that they had performed under either distracting or nondistracting conditions. Under the distracting conditions, both internals and externals blamed the distraction for their failure. However, when there was no distraction and accordingly no obvious existing attribution for failure, internals blamed themselves for the poor performance,

TABLE 4-6
Assessment of Locus of Control

(Choose one option for each question.)

1. a. Promotions are earned through hard work and persistence.
   b. Making a lot of money is largely a matter of getting the right breaks.
2. a. In my experience, I have noticed that there is usually a direct connection between how hard I study and the grades I get.
   b. Many times the reactions of teachers seem haphazard to me.
3. a. When I am right I can convince others.
   b. It is silly to think that one can really change another person's basic attitudes.
4. a. In our society, a man's future earning power is dependent upon his ability.
   b. Getting promoted is really a matter of being a little luckier than the next guy.
5. a. If one knows how to deal with people, they are really quite easily led.
   b. I have little influence over the way other people behave.

Source: Reprinted with permission from *Psychology Today* Magazine. Copyright © 1971 (Sussex Publishers, Inc.).

whereas externals were more likely to blame external factors. Thus, locus of control represents a chronic way of explaining one's own successes, failures, or other experiences when environmental conditions do not provide an obvious explanation.

Locus of control is assessed through a scale that includes items like those in Table 4-6. If you answer option a for all or most of the items, then you would be a high internal locus of control person, whereas more option b answers would push you toward the external extreme.

Attributional Style

Recently, research has examined the pessimistic attributional style, characterized by a tendency to regard negative events as caused by internal, stable, and pervasive factors (Abramson et al., 1978). When a person expects that desirable outcomes are unlikely, when he or she expects undesirable outcomes to occur, and when the person sees no way to change this situation, helplessness, depression, and adverse health consequences can occur, according to the theory. How severe these consequences are and how much of the toll they take on a person's self-esteem depends on attributions. Global, stable, and internal attributions for negative events produce the most far-reaching, adverse consequences. This **pessimistic explanatory style**, as it is called, has been associated with depression in the United States and in other countries (Abramson, Seligman, & Teasdale, 1978; Crittenden & Lamug, 1988).

Suppose Denise is a college student who wants to go to medical school but does poorly on the MCATs (medical entrance exams). Depression may occur if she believes no amount of effort on her part can change the outcome. If Denise blames the failure on herself, her self-esteem will also decline, and if she blames it on a global factor such as her own incompetence, these adverse responses will generalize, perhaps preventing her from applying to law school, psychology graduate school, or any other training program. If her attribution is stable, such as blaming her lack of ability, it will persist. Taking a year off from school, for example, would not make the situation better. To the extent that Denise is convinced that nothing can change the situation, her ability or motivation to do anything will be worse, and if the outcome is important—she has wanted to be a doctor all her life like her mother before and her grandmother before that—her depression and low self-esteem will worsen. In addition to its association with depression, pessimistic explanatory style has now been related to problems of living, such as loneliness (Anderson & Riger, 1991), as well as to poor health outcomes, as the RESEARCH CLOSEUP shows.

Whether the so-called pessimistic explanatory style actually causes depression remains debatable. Attributions certainly affect one's expectations regarding success or failure, which may, in turn, be related to depression (Hull & Mendolia, 1991). Pessimistic explanatory style is clearly associated with and may help maintain depression and keep people from being able to shake off the negative effects of their self-

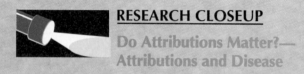

RESEARCH CLOSEUP

Do Attributions Matter?— Attributions and Disease

Think about the last time something bad occurred in your life. You may have gotten sick, done poorly on an exam, had an argument with your parents or your best friend. How did you explain to yourself what happened? Did you decide that your behavior might have been at fault and that you could change it the next time? Or did you decide that this problem would occur over and over again, that it was just out of your hands? Do such explanations merely satisfy our curiosity, or do they have an impact on our lives? Increasingly, research suggests that the way you explain events in your life can actually affect your physical and mental health.

The pessimistic explanatory style is the tendency to perceive negative events as caused by internal, stable, and pervasive factors. People who explain events in their life via the pessimistic attributional style typically credit life's unpleasant events to their own internal, stable, pervasive failings. For some time, psychologists have suspected that this attributional style is implicated in depression (e.g., Peterson & Seligman, 1984). More recently, researchers have investigated whether pessimistic attributional style is also a risk factor for disease.

In a study by Christopher Peterson, Martin Seligman, and George Valliant (1988), interviews were conducted with graduates of the Harvard University classes of 1942 to 1944, to see how the graduates habitually interpreted the negative events in their lives. At the time of the interview the subjects were 25 years old. The men were asked about difficult experiences they had encountered in World War II, such as combat or relations with superiors, and they were asked whether they had dealt successfully or unsuccessfully with those situations. Their answers were coded as reflecting either an optimistic or pessimistic attributional style.

An example of explaining a negative event in terms of pessimistic explanatory style was provided by one man: "I cannot seem to decide firmly on a career. . . . This may be my unwillingness to face reality." In contrast, another man referred to his army career in the following way: "My career in the army has been checkered, but on the whole, characteristic of the army." The difference between these responses is that the first man referred to negative events in terms of his own stable qualities, with no apparent hope for escape. Although the second man also described negative experiences, he attributed them to external factors ("That's the army").

The study found that those men who explained negative events by referring to their own internal, stable, pervasive negative qualities had significantly poorer health between ages 45 through 60, some 25 to 30 years later. This was true even when their physical and mental health at age 25 was taken into account. Thus, the pessimistic explanatory style in early adulthood seems to be a risk factor for poor health in middle and late adulthood.

destructive attributions (e.g., Anderson, 1990; Barnett & Gotlib, 1988; Cochran & Hammen, 1985; Anderson, Jennings, & Arnoult, 1988; Sweeney et al., 1986). Its causal role in depression has yet to be clearly established.

Valuing Internal Control: A Cultural Phenomenon?

A number of phenomena described in this chapter have been seen to reveal a pervasive bias toward perceiving internal or dispositional control of behavior. The fundamental attribution error overestimates internal control. Work on the illusion of control, the just world, and the pessimistic explanatory style all document how people prefer to believe in internal control, and are often disrupted psychologically when they are forced to face their own helplessness and the randomness of much that affects their lives. Why does this pervasive sense of control exist?

One possibility has been considered in the preceding discussions. Perhaps, at a simple perceptual level, actors and observers alike tend to see an act as so thoroughly connected to the actor (in what Heider called a "unit relation") that they cannot easily attribute it to some external cause (Jones, 1979). Another possibility is that all human beings share a strong emotional commitment to the feeling of free will, and to feeling that they are free to act any way they choose. The illusion of choice or control may be crucial to our motivational systems and feelings of well-being, for some adaptive reasons deriving from natural selection (Brehm, 1966; Monson & Snyder, 1977). Perhaps it is only the belief in internal control that keeps us actively trying to manipulate our environment, which in turn is crucial for survival (Taylor & Brown, 1988).

There seems to be little question about the fact that we value a strong sense of internal control. We like other people who believe in internal control more than we like those who believe in external control. When we try to make a positive impression on others, we are more likely to indicate a belief in internal control than a belief in external control, and when other people fail, they are liked better if they make an internal attribution for the failure than if they make an external attribution for it (Jellison & Green, 1981; Carlston & Shovar, 1982; Weary, Jordan, & Hill, 1985). In short, there seems to be a general tendency to emphasize internal causative factors, and people who display that tendency most are the most liked and approved of. Belief in internal control seems therefore to be a strong and persuasive cultural norm.

But a third possibility is that this bias toward internal attribution is a cultural norm particularly characteristic of Americans. Many observers have noted how dedicated Americans are to individualistic values, to the beliefs that individual people can control their own destinies, are responsible for their outcomes, and so on. The Horatio Alger myth is one of our hardiest: Poverty is due to the laziness and stupidity of the poor, while wealth is due to the genius and hard work of the successful. Inkeles (1983), for example, reports that when Americans were asked to explain why one person has succeeded and another failed, despite having the same skill and training, 1 percent invoke fate or God's will. But in six developing countries he found luck or fate was the explanation of about 30 percent.

Individualism has been traced back to America's Protestant heritage (see, for example, McClelland, 1976; Sears & McConahay, 1973; Sniderman & Brody, 1977). More interdependent cultures emphasize the collective and interpersonal causes of events, and not so much the free acts of individuals (Sampson, 1977). The tradition in the United States, on the other hand, is that individuals stand on their own two feet. Most Americans do not think of themselves as part of a larger social whole, such as an extended family or church or community. For example, in the United States, the decision to marry is supposed to be the free choice of the persons involved and is based on romantic love. In many other cultures, such decisions are made collectively by family or kinship groups because marriages are thought to affect the whole community.

Some Eastern countries, such as Japan, are not concerned with exerting control over the environment and making sure that their desires and goals are met. Rather, they are more concerned with fitting in, adjusting their behavior to meet the needs of others and the demands of situational norms. Thus, whereas Americans and other Westerners tend to regard the environment and other people, in part, as means to the fulfillment of their own goals, members of Eastern or interdependent cultures are much more likely to modify personal goals to the needs and demands of others (Rothbaum, Weisz, & Snyder, 1982). On the whole, then, the value placed on internal control and its role in attribution processes seems to be due heavily to cultural factors and not so much to factors intrinsic to the cognitive or perceptual system.

KEY TERMS

actor–observer bias	false consensus	misattribution
attribution	false uniqueness	naive psychology
attribution theory	fundamental attribution error	overjustification
covariation	illusion of control	pessimistic explanatory style
discounting principle	internal attributions	self-centered bias
dispositional attribution	just world	self-serving attributional bias
external attributions	locus of control	situational attribution

SUMMARY

1. Attribution theory is concerned with how people infer the causes of social events. Although causal attributions can be made by most people for most events, people are most likely to ask why questions when something unexpected, unusual, or unpleasant happens.

2. People make causal attributions to help them predict and control the environment. Attributions also influence feelings, attitudes, and behavior.

3. People explain behavior as internal or external to the person, stable or unstable, and controllable or uncontrollable.

4. To infer the causes of behavior, people employ a covariation principle, meaning that they look for an association between a particular effect and a particular cause across a number of different conditions. A second important principle is that people discount the role of one cause in producing a given effect if other plausible causes are also present.

5. Kelley's theory suggests that people base their attributions on three kinds of covariation information: distinctiveness (Is this the only situation in which the person does this?), consensus (Would other people do the same thing in that situation?), and consistency (Does the person always do this in this situation?).

6. Other people's personality traits and attitudes are normally inferred from their overt behaviors by considering the external forces operating on them at the time. If these forces are strong, attributions are shared between external and internal causes. If these forces are weak, internal attributions are made.

7. Attribution theory can be applied to self-perception as well as to the perception of others. That is, the same principles may account for how we infer the causes for our own acts and how we infer the causes of others' acts.

8. To some extent, we infer our own attitudes from our own behavior, particularly when we are not especially involved in our attitudes and when they have little consequence for our future lives.

9. The internal cues we receive from our own emotional arousal state are more ambiguous and undifferentiated than has commonly been assumed in the past. Consequently, we

infer both the nature and degree of our own emotional arousal by an attributional process that relies on evidence about our own behavior, indications of our arousal states, and environmental conditions that provide labels for what might have produced the arousal.

10. In its purest form, attribution theory describes a logical, rationalistic mechanism for arriving at causal explanations. But several systematic biases have been discovered.

11. In general, people ascribe more causality to salient stimuli. When inferring the causes of other people's behavior, their explanations rely overly on internal dispositions and less on external forces. This has been called the fundamental attribution error. It is particularly true for observations of other people's behavior. Self-perceptions tend in the opposite direction. We overattribute causality for our own behavior to external forces. Together, these form the actor–observer bias.

12. People are heavily influenced by the need to give explanations that support or protect their own self-esteem. This leads to self-serving biases, self-centered biases, self-handicapping, egocentric biases, and false consensus.

13. People seem to need an illusion of control over their environments. Their perceptions exaggerate their own level of control, and they become emotionally distressed when they feel they have no control. They believe in a just world in which people get what they deserve, seemingly based on the assumption that people can control their own outcomes.

14. People differ reliably in their perceived locus of control for events. Some people are more likely to explain outcomes in terms of internal (personal) causes, whereas others are more likely to explain outcomes in terms of external (situational) causes.

SUGGESTED READINGS

Kelley, H. H. (1967). Attribution theory in social psychology. In David Levine (Ed.), *Nebraska symposium on motivation.* Lincoln: University of Nebraska Press. Still the best and most coherent basic statement of attribution theory.

Jones, E. E., Kanouse, D. E., Kelley, H. H., Nisbett, R. E., Valins, S., & Weiner, B. (1972). *Attribution: Perceiving the causes of behavior.* Morristown, NJ: General Learning Press. An influential early collection of theoretical statements on attribution theory. Includes excellent chapters on the actor–observer effect, self-perception, and negativity, among others.

Hewstone, M. (1989). *Causal attribution.* Cambridge, MA: Basil Blackwell, Inc. A good contemporary collection of work on attribution.

Ross, M., & Fletcher, G. J. O. (1985). Attribution and social perception. In G. Lindzey & E. Aronson (Eds.), *Handbook of social psychology.* New York: Random House. A thorough presentation of attribution research and its relationships to research on social perception.

Weiner, B. (1986). *An attributional theory of motivation and emotion.* New York: Springer. A comprehensive account of Weiner's attributional theory, emphasizing achievement and affect.

5
The Self

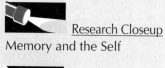
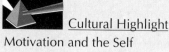

I was all of 11 when I first "knew" what I was, in a tentative, semiconscious sort of way, hoping to be proved wrong, but knowing for certain, down deep, that it was snake eyes for keeps. . . . I was watching *Superman* in the den. My father passed through with one of his guests. He was saying something like: "I've read that, too; but 10 percent just couldn't be right. There couldn't be that many people with homosexual tendencies.". . . That is all there was to it. They passed by; I sat there with my head aimed at the TV—but my face on fire with recognition. I *knew,* I'm not sure how, but I *knew* I was in that 10 percent." (Reid, 1973, pp. 30–31).

In *The Best Little Boy in the World* (Reid, 1973), "John Reid" recounts in moving and often humorous detail his emerging sense of himself as gay and how he reconciled it with others' views of what he should be. How one experiences one's self, what one considers to be one's most distinguishing qualities, and how they may be similar to or different from the ways others think of one's self are important aspects of identity. In this chapter, we will consider the nature of the self, how we know our own characteristics, and how we use our self-conceptions to guide our selection of activities, the development of our personal beliefs, and our interactions with other people.

WHAT IS THE SELF?

The self is first and foremost the collection of beliefs that we hold about ourselves. What are our important characteristics? What are we good at? What do we do poorly at? What kinds of situations do we prefer or avoid? The collection of beliefs we hold about who we are is called the **self-concept.** One person may think of herself as a black woman who plans to become a sociology professor. Another might think of himself as a boy who is not very academically inclined but good at most sports. A third person may think of himself primarily in terms of a future goal, such as the desire to become the biggest real estate mogul in the Midwest. The self-concept, then, is the content of our beliefs about ourselves.

Self-esteem is the evaluation we make of ourselves. That is, we are concerned not only with what we are like, but how we value those qualities. Table 5-1 shows some of the items from a commonly used measure of self-esteem (Rosenberg, 1965). As you can see, the items measure the general value that people place on themselves, whether they are fundamentally good or bad people, talented or not. People with

---

TABLE 5-1
Self-esteem Scale

Indicate whether each item is true (T) or false (F) for you.

_____ 1. I feel that I have a number of good qualities.
_____ 2. I feel I do not have much to be proud of.
_____ 3. At times I think I am no good at all.
_____ 4. I feel I am a person of worth, at least on an equal basis with others.
_____ 5. All in all, I feel that I am a failure.
_____ 6. On the whole, I am satisfied with myself.

If you answered "true" on items 1, 4, and 6, you would be scoring high on self-esteem. If you answered "true" to items 2, 3, and 5, you would score low on self-esteem. The entire scale is 10 items long.

Source: Adapted from Rosenberg, M., Society and the adolescent self-image. Copyright © 1965 by Princeton University Press. © renewed. Used by permission.

high self-esteem have a clear sense of what their personal qualities are, think well of themselves, set appropriate goals, use feedback in a self-enhancing manner, and cope successfully with difficult situations. People with low self-esteem, on the other hand, have less clear self-conceptions (Campbell, 1990), think poorly of themselves, often select unrealistic goals or shy away from goals altogether, tend to be pessimistic about the future, and have more adverse emotional and behavioral reactions to criticism or other kinds of negative feedback (Kernis, Brockner, & Frankel, 1989).

In addition to our overall sense of self-esteem, we hold specific evaluations about our abilities in particular areas. Joan may think well of herself generally, but know that she is not very diplomatic and not very good at artistic undertakings. David may generally think poorly of himself, but know that he is an ace pitcher on the softball team.

How does a sense of self develop? One of the most influential theories of how the self develops was put forth by Erik Erikson (1963), who argued for a stage theory of ego development. He maintained that identity formation is the critical task an adolescent or young adult must accomplish. In so doing, identity comes together, marking the transition between childhood and adulthood. Erikson believed that the goal of this process is "the ability to experience one's self as something that has continuity and sameness, and to act accordingly" (Erikson, 1963, p. 38). Once having acquired a firm sense of identity, the young adult has a basis for making job or career plans and for establishing intimate relationships.

While Erikson was no doubt correct in his assessment of adolescence and young adulthood as pivotal times for developing a sense of self, it would be false to claim that the sense of self develops and is maintained only or primarily during this time. The sense of self begins in infancy, with the recognition that one is a separate individual (Butterworth, 1992; Pervin, 1992a, 1992b). Very young children have fairly clear conceptions of their personal qualities and what they are good or bad at. Moreover, many changes occur in middle and late adulthood that

may influence the self-conceptions that people hold. Thus, while psychologists continue to believe that Erikson was essentially right in arguing that issues of identity are especially important in adolescence and young adulthood, it is also clearly the case that the development of a personal sense of self is a lifelong process, beginning in childhood and never truly ending (Waterman & Archer, 1990).

WHERE DOES SELF-KNOWLEDGE COME FROM?

Knowledge of the self comes from many sources. Some of it may seem to be spontaneous, much as the opening example suggests, a realization that something is true of one's self without any certainty of where that knowledge comes from. More commonly, however, we can identify the origins of our beliefs about ourselves in specific experiences.

Socialization

Much of our self-knowledge comes from **socialization.** During childhood, we are treated in particular ways by parents, teachers, and friends, and we participate in religious, ethnic, or cultural activities that later come to be significant aspects of ourselves. From attending synagogue at an early age, taking Hebrew lessons, and eventually participating in a bar mitzvah or bas mitzvah, the Jewish child comes to regard being Jewish as an important part of his or her identity. A child who spends her weekend being taken to art exhibits and concerts by her parents may come to think of herself as a cultured person. Socialization, then, forms the core of our early experience, and the regularities in those experiences may eventually come to be internalized as important aspects of the self-concept.

Reflected Appraisal

We also learn about ourselves through the reactions that other people have to us. C. H. Cooley (1902) developed the concept of "looking-glass

Much self-knowledge comes from socialization. By participating in activities that are important to our families, we come to regard these activities as important to ourselves as well.

self," maintaining that people perceive themselves as others perceive and respond to them. Our perceptions of how other people react to us are called **reflected appraisals.**

In a humorous example of the importance of reflected appraisal, Baldwin, Carrell, and Lopez (1990) recruited Catholic students for a study during which the students encountered a picture of the scowling face of either the Pope or an unfamiliar other person. Later, the students were asked to evaluate some of their personal qualities. Practicing Catholics exposed to the scowling picture of the Pope evaluated themselves more harshly than non-practicing Catholics exposed to the picture of the Pope, or Catholics exposed to the picture of the unfamiliar other person. Apparently, just the picture of the scowling Pope was enough to shake these students' self-images!

Feedback from Others

Sometimes people give us explicit feedback about our qualities. This process often begins in socialization, when our parents tell us not to be so shy, how good we are at the piano, how math is not our strong point, or what a good reader we are. Generally speaking, there is a strong relationship between how parents think about their children's abilities and children's own self-conceptions on these same dimensions (Felson & Reed, 1986).

In later childhood and early adolescence, feedback from peers may be more important. All of us can remember whether we were picked early or late when team captains were choosing members for athletic teams, and we got some sense of our popularity from whether we were picked quickly or not to be in someone's carpool for a field trip. Adolescence brings with it additional sources of direct feedback, such as whether one is asked out on a date by many people or few, or whether the people one asks out accept or decline. And we get direct feedback from teachers on our academic abilities in the form of comments and grades.

Research has suggested that, on the whole, people prefer objective feedback about their personal attributes (Festinger, 1954). Objective feedback is regarded as less biased and more fair than personal opinion. But the opinions of others also count. In particular, when those opinions are shared by a large number of people, we may come to believe that they are true.

Self-perception

As we saw in Chapter 4, people also infer their personal qualities from observing their own behavior. That is, in the process of observing ourselves, we see ourselves consistently preferring certain activities over others, certain foods over others, or certain people over others. From observing these regularities, we may gain self-knowledge.

However, as Bem's (1967, 1972) **self-perception** theory also suggests, this source of self-knowledge may be useful primarily for aspects of the self that are not particularly central or important. We do not need to observe ourselves avoiding anchovies on our pizza to know that we do not like anchovies. We do not need to observe ourselves ordering flowers for our mother on Mother's Day to know that we love our mother. Many important aspects of the self have clear internal referents in the form of enduring beliefs, attitudes, and affective preferences. And so it is likely that self-perception as a source of self-knowledge applies primarily to more incidental than to important aspects of the self.

Environmental Distinctiveness

The self-concept is also heavily influenced by factors that make you distinctive. For example, McGuire and his associates (McGuire & McGuire, 1982; McGuire & Padawer-Singer, 1976) asked students to "tell us about yourself," and found that students often mentioned aspects of themselves that make them distinctive. For example, a boy is more likely to mention that fact if he is the only boy in his family. If he has three sisters, none of them is as likely to mention the fact that she is a girl. We also mention things about ourselves that make us distinctive in the particular situation. So, for example, an African-American woman is more likely to mention that she is African-American if there are relatively few African-Americans in a group, whereas she is more likely to mention the fact that she is a woman if she is in a group with predominantly men.

Social Comparisons

Some of the time when we want to evaluate ourselves on a particular dimension or quality, information is not readily available. For example, if you want to know if you are a graceful dancer, there is no test you can take to find that out. You could conceivably consult an expert, but perhaps an expert isn't available. You could ask other people if you are a graceful dancer, but you might be shy about doing so.

Consequently, sometimes we assess our personal qualities by comparing ourselves to other people. You know if you are a good dancer or not by observing those around you and noting whether you seem to be dancing more gracefully than those other people. This process is termed **social comparison.** Generally speaking, people prefer similar others for self-evaluation (Festinger, 1954). For example, if you want to know if you are a good tennis player, comparing yourself to someone of roughly equal ability gives you a good sense of where you stand. Someone whose abilities are far discrepant from your own is less informative. We will return to social comparison processes shortly.

Social Identity

Social identity is the "part of an individual's self-concept which derives from [his or her] membership in a social group (or groups) together with the value and emotional significance attached to that membership" (Tajfel, 1981, p. 248). These groups include one's family, one's community, one's religious or ethnic group, and other groups that highlight or reinforce important aspects of the self. In childhood, the groups in which one participates often occur as a part of socialization. We are born into a particular family, a particular ethnic group, and sometimes a particular religious group. As we get older, the attributes we value in ourselves lead us to pick social groups that reflect and reinforce those values. And so, self-concept and social identity mutually determine and shape each other.

Much of the research on social identity has focused specifically on **ethnic identity.** Ethnic identity is the part of an individual's self-knowledge that concerns his or her membership in a particular ethnic group. Developing a sense of self can raise particular issues for minority group members. During the adolescent and young adult years when people are forming their sense of themselves, reconciling ethnic background with mainstream culture can be difficult for African-Americans, Asian-Americans, Native Americans, those from Hispanic back-

TABLE 5-2

Four Identity Orientations Based on Degree of Identification with One's Ethnic Group and the Majority Group

Identification with Majority Group	Identification with Ethnic Group	
	Strong	Weak
Strong	Integrated Acculturated Bicultural	Assimilated
Weak	Separated Ethnically identified Ethnically embedded Dissociated	Marginal

Source: Phinney (1990).

grounds, and other ethnic minorities (Spencer & Markstrom-Adams, 1990). As Table 5-2 suggests, some adolescents may identify with both mainstream culture and their ethnic group, creating what is called a bicultural or *integrated* identity (Phinney, 1990). Others may maintain a strong ethnic identity but have few ties to the majority culture, maintaining a *separated* identity. Individuals who give up their ethnic heritage in favor of mainstream culture are said to be *assimilated.* Finally, some adolescents and young adults develop only weak ties to both their ethnic culture and the mainstream culture, and feel *marginal,* like outsiders in both cultures (Phinney, 1990, 1991).

Research shows that these distinctions are important, because they predict the amount of contact that individuals have with their ethnic group and with the larger society. For example, Dona (1991) found that Central American refugees in Canada who were assimilated spent less time with fellow Central Americans than did those who were integrated or those who maintained a separatist ethnic identification. In turn, individuals who were integrated had more contact with Canadian society than individuals who maintained a separated identity (Dona, 1991). In a review of research on ethnic identity, Phinney (1991) found that a strong ethnic iden-

tity is typically related to high self-esteem, but only when accompanied by a positive mainstream orientation. Among individuals who hold a strong ethnic identity without some adaptation to the mainstream culture, self-esteem can be more problematic.

What leads people to become highly identified with their ethnic or racial group? In a study of African-American college students, those whose parents were members of predominantly black organizations, who had taken black studies courses, and who had experienced racism or racial prejudice were more likely to have their African-American background as a strong feature of their self-concept (Baldwin, Brown, & Rackley, 1990; Thompson, 1990, 1991). Thus, participation in ethnically related activities and being treated in particular ways because of one's ethnic or racial background foster a sense of ethnic identity.

Some researchers have argued that when ethnic identity is enhanced by experiences of prejudice or discrimination, individuals who are ethnically identified will have poor self-concepts or low self-esteem. This, however, does not appear to be the case (Spencer & Markstrom-Adams, 1990; Phinney, 1990). There is no consistent evidence that ethnically identified adolescents or young adults see themselves negatively or have low self-esteem (Phinney, 1991). In fact, there is some research evidence to suggest that, when individuals perceive negative feedback to be directed at them because of

Ethnic identity is an important part of self-knowledge that comes from membership in a particular ethnic group and participation in the group's valued activities.

their racial or ethnic identity, they actually preserve their self-esteem by making an attribution to the prejudice held by the evaluator rather than to their own character or behavior (Crocker et al., 1991; Chavira & Phinney, 1991).

In summary, then, self-knowledge comes from many sources: early socialization, the reflected appraisals of others, explicit feedback from others, self-perception of our own behavior, environmental distinctiveness, social comparison of our personal attributes with those of other people, and memberships in social groups. And sometimes, as in the opening example, we simply know who we are, without knowing where that knowledge came from.

ASPECTS OF SELF-KNOWLEDGE

What form does our self-knowledge take? That is, how are the beliefs that we hold about ourselves represented cognitively?

Self-schemas

In Chapter 3, we considered the concept of schema. A schema is an organized, structured set of cognitions about some concept or stimulus. Just as people hold schemas about what other people and events are like, they also hold schemas about themselves. **Self-schemas** describe the dimensions along which you think about yourself. You may, for example, be very concerned about maintaining and displaying your independence. You might refuse to take money from your parents for college, do your own laundry, not ask your roommate for help with your math, and the like. Or you might consider yourself more dependent, and think a lot about ensuring security for yourself by surrounding yourself with people you can depend on, like your brother, girlfriend, doctor, minister, and so on. In either case, you would have a strong self-schema concerning the independence–dependence dimension. On the other hand, you may not think of yourself very much in connection with that dimension, in which

case you would not be thinking schematically in those terms. You would be described as aschematic on the dimension of independence–dependence.

People are schematic on dimensions that are important to them, on which they think of themselves as extreme, and on which they are certain that the opposite is not true. If independence is important to you and you think of yourself as extremely independent and not at all dependent, it implies that you have accumulated considerable knowledge about yourself on that domain. For example, you should be certain that you would never ask anyone for help setting up your stereo, even at the potential cost of damage to it or yourself. When you hold a schema for yourself on a particular dimension, it helps you to identify situations as relevant to that dimension. For example, if you think of yourself as independent, you would be quick to see that the purchase of a new stereo system with complex instructions for installation requires independent behavior. Moreover, the recognition that situations are schema relevant sets guidelines for your own behavior. Thus, you would recognize not only that the situation calls for independent behavior, but that you will be the one to wade through the instructions and set up the stereo.

Hazel Markus (1977) conducted an experiment to test some of these points. First, she had a group of college students rate themselves in terms of their independence and dependence. From these ratings, she selected those who considered themselves independent (independent schematics), those who considered themselves dependent (dependent schematics), and those who did not consider themselves particularly independent or dependent (those who were aschematic on the dimension). She then showed the students computer slides of trait adjectives associated with dependence (such as obliging) and independence (such as assertive). Students were told to press a button to indicate "me" if the word was self-descriptive, and "not me" if the word was not self-descriptive. The prediction was that the subjects would be able to decide faster that the word was self-descriptive if they had a schema relevant to the trait word.

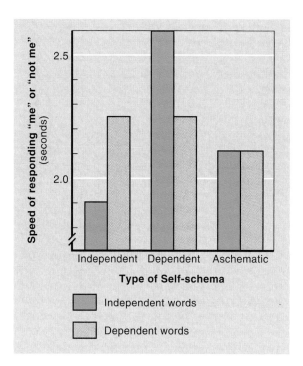

Figure 5-1 How self-schemas speed up the processing of self-relevant information. (*Source:* Based on Markus, 1977.)

As predicted and as seen in Figure 5-1, independent schematics judged independent words to be self-descriptive much faster than they judged dependent words to be, and dependent schematics judged dependent trait adjectives to be much more self-descriptive much faster than they judged trait words related to independence. Aschematics did not differ between the two.

Not all self-schemas are positive. People also hold well-articulated beliefs about themselves on negative qualities. For example, someone who thinks of herself as overweight will quickly notice that eating situations are relevant to her; she might plan in advance what she will eat and may count the calories that she consumes. Being weight schematic also means that she is likely to notice weight-relevant behaviors in others (Carpenter, 1988; Dodge & Tomlin, 1987; Hill, Smith, & Hoffman, 1988; Park & Hahn, 1988). Thus, for example, she may more quickly notice and infer that someone who has only cottage cheese and peaches for lunch is on a diet than

would someone who is not so concerned with weight (Wurf & Markus, 1983).

People not only hold self-conceptions about their current qualities, they also hold conceptions of themselves that may become self-descriptive at some time in the future (Markus & Nurius, 1986). These are called **possible selves.** Some of these involve goals or roles to which people aspire, such as the five-year-old's desire to be a firefighter or the student's expectation of becoming a doctor. Most possible selves seem to be positive. That is, people think of themselves in the future primarily in good terms (Markus & Nurius, 1986). However, some possible selves represent fears concerning what one may become in the future, such as the suspicion that one's enthusiastic consumption of alcohol on certain occasions may eventually lead to full-blown alcoholism.

Possible selves function in much the same way as self-schemas. They help people to articulate their goals and develop behaviors that will enable them to fulfill those goals. In a study by Ruvolo and Markus (1992), subjects were told to imagine themselves either being successful at work, lucky at work, failing at work despite clear effort, or failing because of bad luck.

Possible selves are goals or roles to which people aspire that are currently not self-descriptive but may become so.

RESEARCH CLOSEUP
Memory and the Self

You're trying to remember your best friend's clothing size, so you can buy her a birthday gift when you go out to do your errands. It's hectic, and you're afraid you might forget. You think, "Size 10 is half her age," and try to remember it that way. Then you recall that she is exactly one size bigger than you are. Now you will not forget it.

Memory for other people's characteristics is improved when they are linked to the self. For example, a shy person is more likely to remember her roommate saying that Jeff has overcome his terrible shyness than that he is an excellent auto mechanic. A number of experiments have tested for this **self-referencing effect,** that is, improved memory for others' characteristics when they are linked to the self. For example, Kuiper and Rogers (1979) presented trait adjectives such as "shy" or "outgoing" to subjects in several different conditions. In the "self-reference" condition, subjects were asked "whether the word describes you." In the "other-reference" condition, the subjects were asked "whether the word describes the experimenter." The other conditions asked subjects to rate the word in simple mechanical terms,

such as whether it was short or long or whether it was specific or general. Later the subjects were asked to recall all the adjectives with which they had been presented. Those words presented in the self-reference context were much better recalled than were those placed in more neutral contexts, and the person found the task less difficult and had more confidence in his or her ratings. These findings are shown in Table 5-3.

Later experiments obtained similar findings (Lord, 1980; Brown, Keenan, & Potts, 1986; Reeder, McCormick, & Esselman, 1987). However, self-reference does not always improve memory relative to the other-person context (Klein, Loftus, & Burton, 1989). When the other people are personally well known to the subject, such as a lab instructor who has been teaching the person all term, the self-reference effect disappears (Kuiper & Rogers, 1979; Bower & Gilligan, 1979).

Why does the self-reference effect occur? The explanation most favored by researchers is that self-referencing produces a "deeper processing" (Craik & Tulving, 1975), because self-referencing gets the person to consider a wider and deeper range

of associations to the stimulus object (Rogers, Kuiper, & Kirker, 1977). Consistent with this view, the self-reference effect seems to be dependent on getting people to think about traits in connection with their own personal experiences, not just the self. To illustrate this, Bellezza (1984) presented subjects with traits and had them relate the trait either to some real incident from their lives or to some personal body part. For example, the subject might have related the term "hostile" to an experience of getting into an argument with someone else, or alternatively, to the body part "fist." Thinking about the trait in connection with the personal experience made it more memorable than did thinking about it in connection with the body part (Keenan, Golding, & Brown, 1992).

The extra meaningfulness provided by reference to the self seems, then, to stem from the rich array of experiences it brings to mind from our past. Self-referencing calls up an organized self-schema to which we can relate information about the stimulus to be recalled and helps to create an elaborated memory of that stimulus (Klein & Loftus, 1988; see also Greenwald & Banaji, 1989).

TABLE 5-3
Self-reference Produces Better Recall, Less Difficulty, More Confidence

Experimental Condition	Question	Recall	Mean Difficulty Rating	Mean Confidence Rating
Stuctural	Rate whether you feel the word is long or short.	.18	3.08	3.83
Semantic	Rate whether you feel the word has a specific meaning or relates to a specific situation.	.15	4.25	3.83
Other-reference	Rate whether you feel the word describes the experimenter.	.18	5.00	2.75
Self-reference	Rate whether you feel the word describes you.	.31	2.00	6.00

Source: Adapted from Kruper & Rogers (1979).
Note: Recall values can range from 0 to 1.00, where 1.00 indicates that all were recalled. Difficulty and confidence ratings were made on a 7-point scale, with 7 as extremely difficult or extremely confident.

Subsequently, subjects worked on a task that measured persistence. Those subjects asked to envision themselves as successful because of their own efforts worked longer on the task than did subjects who envisioned themselves as failing or as succeeding due to luck, presumably because they had a vision of the successful possible self firmly in mind. Thus, possible selves provide focus and organization for the pursuit of goals. They help people to recruit appropriate self-knowledge and develop plans that enable them to rehearse the actions they need to undertake in pursuit of their goals (Markus & Ruvolo, 1989).

Self-schemas, including possible selves, then, have many important functions regarding self-knowledge and the self in action. Knowing about our personal qualities enables us to identify quickly whether situations are relevant to us or not. Self-schemas help us to remember schema-relevant information. They help us to make inferences about the meaning of our past behavior and to make decisions and judgments that guide our future behavior. Research also suggests that relating other material to ourselves—people or situations—makes that material more memorable, as the RESEARCH CLOSEUP suggests.

Self-discrepancies

Other aspects of the self that influence our thoughts and behavior concern discrepancies between how we actually are and how we ideally want to be or think we ought to be. Psychologist Tory Higgins (1987, 1989) suggests that these **self-discrepancies** produce strong emotions. When we perceive a discrepancy between our personal qualities and what we would ideally like to be (**ideal self**), we experience disappointment, dissatisfaction, or sadness, what are called dejection-related emotions, as well as a reduction in self-esteem (Moretti & Higgins, 1990). Discrepancies between our actual self and what we think we ought to be (**ought self**) produce agitation-related emotions such as fear or anxiety.

To test these points, Higgins, Klein, and Strauman (1985) asked college students to fill out a questionnaire that asked them about their self-perceptions, including how they would ideally like to be and how they felt they ought to be. The first time, the subjects filled the questionnaire out for themselves. At a later time, they filled it out from the standpoint of their father, mother, and closest friend. They also rated the extent to which each of the personal attributes they rated was relevant or meaningful to them.

Discrepancies between their actual self and the ideal self did indeed produce dejection-related emotions (Higgins et al., 1987) and loss of self-esteem (Moretti & Higgins, 1990). For example, wanting to be center forward on the basketball team but failing to become so produced disappointment and sadness. Perceived discrepancies between one's actual self and a friend's or parent's ideal self produced anxiety. For example, perceiving that one was not going to be the successful businessman of one's father's dream produced anxiety but not sadness. The more important the personal attribute was to the respondent, the greater the emotion experienced.

SELF-REGULATION

Self-regulation refers to the ways in which people control and direct their own actions (Markus & Wurf, 1987). As we have seen, people have enormous quantities of information stored about themselves, including their personal characteristics, their goals and desires, and their conceptions of themselves in the future. But how do these relate to ongoing feeling and action? In this section, we turn explicitly to the issues of how conceptions of the self regulate thought, emotion, and action in social situations. To understand self-regulation, we must understand what is meant by the working self-concept.

The Working Self-concept

Which aspect of the self influences our thoughts and ongoing behavior depends in large part on what aspect of the self-concept is relevant for a particular situation. The aspect of the self-concept that is accessed for a particular situation is called the **working self-concept.** In a classroom situation, the academic self is likely to be the dominant determinant of our thoughts and feelings, whereas if we are reminded about a party coming up on Friday, the social self may be accessed. Thus, the working self-concept is important because it draws on our overall self-concept but guides social behavior in specific situations and is, in turn, modified by what goes on in the situation.

The working self-concept can sometimes be at odds with the stable self-concept. Think about a time that you had an argument with a friend and snapped at her. Afterward, you probably didn't feel very good about yourself, and she probably didn't think much of you either. Yet you probably have a stable sense of yourself as a nice person who is easy to get along with. After that particular incident, you may not have thought well of yourself for at least several hours or perhaps even a few days. Over time, however, your stable self-concept won out and you again thought of yourself as pleasant and easy to get along with, despite the fact that there may be occasional times when you are not this way at all.

Changes in the working self-concept produce changes in the permanent self-concept only when the working self-concept is stable over time. For example, while in college, you may not think of yourself as particularly authoritative. Yet upon graduation, if you get a job supervising several other people in a bank and you do this day in and day out for months or even years, you may come to think of yourself as authoritative, and that may become an important part of your stable self-concept. It was not so before, but became so because you are now consistently in a situation that evokes this kind of authoritative manner. The working self-concept, in this case, became part of the stable self-concept.

Self-complexity

Another aspect of the self that is important for self-regulation involves **self-complexity.** Some people think of themselves in one or two predominant ways, whereas others think of themselves in terms of a variety of qualities. One college student may think of herself primarily as a student, focusing her attention and beliefs about herself on how well she does in her courses. Another may think of herself in more complex ways, as a student, a daughter, a girlfriend, a member of the track team, and a part-time employee.

In analyzing the differences between people who hold simple versus complex perceptions of the self, Patricia Linville (1985) suggests that people with simple self-conceptions will be buoyed by success in their particular area of importance but will be very vulnerable to failure. So, for example, the student who is focused primarily on her grades and who gets a bad grade may feel very upset and depressed because of it. People who are more complex, however, may be buoyed by success but have other aspects of themselves that buffer them in the case of failures or setbacks. The student who has an academic setback but has a complex self may temporarily turn her attention away from her schoolwork to prepare for a track meet, and thus cope somewhat more successfully with the academic setback. Self-complexity, then, can act as a buffer against stressful life events. In particular, it may help prevent people from becoming depressed or ill in response to setbacks. A setback in one area of life is less devastating when other aspects of our lives are rewarding and satisfying than when we derive most of our identity from one aspect of the self.

Self-efficacy and Personal Control

Other aspects of the self that influence self-regulation include **self-efficacy** beliefs, that is, the expectations that we hold about our abilities to accomplish certain tasks (Bandura, 1986b). Whether or not we will undertake a particular activity, attempt to do a particular task, or strive to meet a particular goal depends on whether or

not we believe we will be efficacious in performing those actions (e.g., Wood & Bandura, 1989). The smoker will not stop smoking unless she believes she can do it, however much she may want to stop. Faced with a challenging paper, the student who believes he has the capabilities to do the paper effectively will be more likely to start it and persist at it than the student who has doubts about his ability to complete it successfully. Psychologists believe that early experiences with success and failure lead people to develop fairly stable conceptions of their self-efficacy in different life domains (Bandura, 1986b; Dweck & Licht, 1980).

It is important to realize that self-efficacy beliefs are highly specific control-related perceptions of one's perceived ability to perform a particular outcome. They are not general feelings of control. So, for example, if you want to know if someone will work hard to try out for the tennis team, you need to know his self-efficacy beliefs related to making the tennis team, not his general feelings of himself as an effective person.

Self-awareness

Self-regulation is also influenced by our direction of attention, specifically, whether attention is directed inward toward the self or outward toward the environment (Duval & Wicklund, 1972). Usually our attention is focused outward toward the environment, but sometimes our attention is focused inward on ourselves. Certain experiences in the world automatically focus attention inward, such as catching sight of ourselves in the mirror, having our picture taken, or more subtly, being evaluated by others, or even just being in a minority in a group situation. We begin to think of ourselves not as a moving actor in the environment, but as the object of our own and others' attention. This state is called **self-awareness** (Duval & Wicklund, 1972; Wicklund & Frey, 1980).

In general, self-awareness leads people to evaluate their behavior against a standard and to set an adjustment process in motion for meeting the standard. Suppose, for example, that you go out to an elegant restaurant and you are seated facing your date but also, to your irrita-

Certain experiences, such as being filmed, put us in a state of self-awareness. Self-awareness causes people to compare and evaluate themselves according to available standards.

tion, you are looking directly into a mirror on the wall behind you. Try as you might, each time you look up, you catch sight of your own face. You notice your windblown hair, the awkward way you smile, and the unattractive way you chew. Feeling utterly foolish by the time the main course arrives, you flee to the bathroom to comb your hair, vowing that if you still look as bad when you return, you will change tables.

Self-attention causes people to compare themselves to standards, such as physical appearance, intellectual performance, athletic prowess, or moral integrity. We attempt to conform to the standard, evaluate our behavior against that standard, decide that it either matches the standard or does not, and continue adjusting and comparing until we meet the standard or give up. This process is called feedback, and the theory is called the **cybernetic theory of self-regulation.**

To understand why focus of attention is important in self-regulation, consider the role that self-focus may play in the maintenance of depression. Psychologists have argued that anxiety or depression may focus attention on the self chronically, and thereby interfere with the ability to monitor one's performance effectively on specific tasks or in a social setting (Baumeister, 1990; Strack, Blaney, and Gschneidinger, 1985; Salovey, 1992; Wood, Saltzberg, & Goldsamt, 1990). The argument is that depression leads people into a pessimistic self-focus. In response to failure, a depressed person persists in attending inwardly longer than does a nondepressed person (Greenberg & Pyszczynski, 1986; Wood, Saltzberg, Neale, Stone, & Rachmiel, 1990). The individual chronically attends to the self, focusing on the discrepancy between his or her actual behavior and the desired state. Because no behavior can be found to reduce the discrepancy, these factors eventually promote a negative self-image. The depressive self-focusing style, then, is thought to be a factor that both maintains and exacerbates already-existing depression (see also Pyszczynski, Hamilton, Herring, & Greenberg, 1989).

People also differ in whether they attend primarily to public or to private aspects of themselves. This distinction has been called public versus private self-consciousness (Fenigstein, Scheier, & Buss, 1975). People high in **public self-consciousness** are concerned with autonomy and issues of identity (Schlenker & Weigold, 1990). They are concerned with what other people think about them, the way they look, and how they appear to others. Those high in **private self-consciousness** try to figure themselves out, think about themselves a lot, and are more attentive to their inner feelings. When the publicly self-conscious person becomes self-aware, he or she may try hard to adjust behavior to conform to external standards, such as others' values or attitudes, especially if he or she is also low in private self-consciousness (Doherty & Schlenker, 1991). In contrast, when the privately self-conscious person becomes self-aware, he or she may be more attentive to internal goals and beliefs, and thus try harder to meet personal standards (Froming & Carver, 1981; Scheier & Carver, 1980; Nasby, 1989). Which are you? Or are you high on both? Answer the questions in Table 5-4.

TABLE 5-4
Self-consciousness Scale

Indicate whether you generally agree (A) or disagree (D) with each of the following items.

_____ 1. I'm always trying to figure myself out.
_____ 2. I'm concerned about my style of doing things.
_____ 3. Generally, I'm not very aware of myself.
_____ 4. I reflect about myself a lot.
_____ 5. I'm concerned about the way I present myself.
_____ 6. I'm self-conscious about the way I look.
_____ 7. I never scrutinize myself.
_____ 8. I'm generally attentive to my inner feelings.
_____ 9. I usually worry about making a good impression.

If you answered "agree" on items 1, 4, and 8, and "disagree" on items 3 and 7, you would be scoring high on the private self-conciousness scale. If you answered "agree" to items 2, 5, 6, and 9, your score would be high on the public self-conciousness scale. Note that the entire scale is considerably longer than the excerpt above.

Source: Adapted from Fenigstein, Scheier, & Buss (1975).

MOTIVATION AND THE SELF

So far, we have considered the working self-concept, self-efficacy expectations, and focus of attention as determinants of how people regulate their activities in the environment. It is also important to know the motivations that drive self-regulation. Generally speaking, people seek an accurate, stable, and positive self-conception, and will seek out situations or behave in ways that further those aspects of the self.

The Need for an Accurate Self-concept

To make our future outcomes predictable and controllable, we need to have a fairly accurate assessment of our abilities. Psychologist Yaacov Trope has argued that, in the absence of factors that might induce people to save face or strive to succeed, people usually pick tasks that will be most informative about their abilities, tasks that he termed diagnostic (Trope, 1975, 1979, 1980, 1983). If you, a college student, want to know if

you are a good dancer, you are unlikely to go to a children's dancing class or to a ballroom competition. You will do extremely well in the first setting and incredibly poorly in the second (unless you have been trained in competitive ballroom dancing). The situation most diagnostic for your dancing ability would be a college dance or party.

Overall, Trope's work suggests that having an accurate sense of self is an important determinant of our selection of a task, especially when our knowledge of a particular ability is uncertain (Sorrentino & Roney, 1986). Accurate self-assessment enables us to anticipate and control our future performance (Trope & Bassok, 1982). Research suggests that we are most likely to seek accurate self-relevant information when we anticipate that the news will be good, but we also show a desire for self-assessment when we anticipate that the news may be bad (Brown, 1990).

The Need for a Consistent Self-concept

Related to the need for accuracy is the need to have a sense of self that is consistent. We do not want to think of ourselves as changing dramatically from situation to situation, but rather need to believe that we have certain intrinsic qualities that remain relatively stable over time (Swann, 1983). People, then, seek out and interpret situations that confirm their already-existing self-conceptions, and they avoid or resist situations and feedback that are at odds with their existing self-conceptions. This process is termed **self-verification.** Imagine, for example, that a seminar has just ended, and a fellow classmate comes up to you and says, "Boy, you don't talk much in class, do you?" Perhaps you didn't talk in class that particular day, but you may think of yourself as someone who usually does. You may find that, at the very next class, you talk even more than you usually do, by way of convincing your fellow student, as well as yourself, that your conception of yourself as an active class participant is a correct one.

A series of studies by Swann and Read (1981b) suggests that this need to see ourselves as consistent is quite pervasive. In one study, college students were led to believe that fellow college students' evaluations of them would be either consistent or inconsistent with their own self-image. When given a chance to see those evaluations, the students spent more time perusing consistent than inconsistent feedback. This was true even if the consistent attributes were ones on which people perceived themselves negatively.

In their second study, Swann and Read found that, when interacting with others, people use behavioral strategies that confirm their self-conceptions. That is, they deliberately act in ways that confirm the existing self-image. This tendency is especially strong when you believe that others have incorrect beliefs about you. Thus, the earlier example of volunteering more in class to counteract a fellow student's false impression illustrates this point, and similar effects have been found in several experiments as well (Swann & Read, 1981a).

This need to see the self in a consistent manner extends to several other strategies of self-regulation. We selectively interact with others who see themselves as we see them (Swann & Pelham, 1990; Swann, Stein-Seroussi, & Giesler, 1992). People choose signs and symbols in their clothing and appearance that say things about who they are (Swann & Read, 1981a; Swann, 1983). Thus, for example, if you want people to think of you as an athlete, you may be sure to wear your athletic jersey instead of a T-shirt to class. When we feel certain of our self-attributes, we feel good about ourselves (Baumgardner, 1990).

So insistent can the need for a consistent self-concept be that it can even affect one's health. We know that when people experience a lot of negative events in their lives, they can become ill. One argument for why this effect may occur is that these negative experiences are inconsistent with one's positive view of self. Brown & McGill (1989) reasoned that, if this explanation of the adverse effects of stress is correct, then people who hold negative self-views should become ill in response to positive life events. That is, happy events should cause these people

People choose signs and symbols in their clothing and appearance to make statements about who they are. This process is called self-verification.

stress and make them ill, because positive events are inconsistent with their self-views. Brown and McGill conducted a study in which self-esteem was measured, as well as the frequency of positive life events the students had recently experienced, such as good grades, happy family occasions, and successful personal encounters. They then related the life events and self-esteem to illness rates four months later. The results indicated that desirable life events were associated with more illness, but only among the subjects low in self-esteem. Among subjects with high self-esteem, positive life events were linked with better health.

The previous discussion implies that people spend much of their time seeking out situations and ways of behaving in accordance with their existing self-concept. In fact, this picture is probably not accurate. Most of the time, people are able to maintain their views of themselves without any active or conscious effort. Maintaining a consistent sense of self is part of the process of interacting with family, friends, and coworkers in familiar settings, performing familiar tasks. However, when people receive discrepant feedback from others, they may then be motivated to focus active attention on the threat to a consistent self-conception, and thus, enact efforts to dispel the incorrect view (Swann & Hill, 1982).

Self-improvement

In addition to wanting an accurate sense of self, people are also motivated by the desire to improve. The educational process, for example, assumes that people will strive to get better at fundamental learning tasks. Most sports and many leisure activities are things we want to get better at, rather than simply staying the same. Once employed, we want to get better at our jobs, so we can maintain or enhance our standing in our work organization. Thus, many of the self-regulatory activities that we have discussed are in service of this need to improve.

What kinds of information and situations do we seek when our goal is self-improvement? Earlier, we discussed Hazel Markus' concept of possible selves, the visions that people have of themselves in the future. Markus argues that, by clearly articulating visions of ourselves in desired activities, we are able to set appropriate goals, make progress toward achieving those goals, and chart how well we are doing with respect to those goals. The would-be college professor can chart and plan her personal progress better if she has a clear view of what she will be like in this future role. Thus, possible selves give explicit vision to the goals that we set for ourselves in the future, helping us to attain them.

As we will shortly see, social comparison theorists (Taylor & Lobel, 1989; Wood, 1989) have argued that self-improvement may also be facilitated by social contact with other people. Specifically, these theorists argue that comparison of the self against someone who is doing better on a desired skill or attribute, so-called *upward comparisons,* are helpful for enabling people to improve. The college football player may keep pictures of his favorite pro players on his wall to inspire him and remind him of the steps he needs to take to reach the same level of success. Thus, people who embody the attributes or skills we wish to attain can be motivating and

can also be a source of specific information that is helpful for improvement.

While social psychologists have not yet exhaustively pursued the question of self-improvement—namely the conditions under which we seek to improve ourselves, the attributes on which we wish to improve, and the sources of information and inspiration we turn to—they have begun to understand the issue.

Self-enhancement

Clearly, we need to have accurate information about our abilities and opinions. Without some degree of accuracy and consistency in our self-image, we would be vulnerable to a host of faulty judgments and decisions. We also need to set goals, acquire new skills and information, and generally improve on the abilities and skills that are important to us. Yet our self-regulatory activities are also heavily determined by the need to feel good about ourselves and to maintain self-esteem. These **self-enhancement** needs appear to be quite stable, but they become especially important following situations of threat, failure, or blows to self-esteem (Wills, 1981; Brown & Gallagher, 1992).

One way in which people seem to satisfy their self-enhancement needs is by holding self-perceptions that are falsely positive and somewhat exaggerated with respect to their actual abilities, talents, and social skills (Greenwald, 1980; Taylor & Brown, 1988). Taylor and Brown have called these **positive illusions.** For example, when students are asked to describe how accurately positive and negative personality adjectives describe them, most regard positive traits as considerably more characteristic of themselves than negative ones (e.g., Brown, 1986). We remember positive information about ourselves well, but negative information often slips conveniently from mind (Kuiper & Derry, 1982; Kuiper & McDonald, 1982; Kuiper et al., 1985). If pressed, most of us would have more difficulty reconstructing circumstances when we have failed than reconstructing circumstances when we have succeeded (Silverman, 1964). And often we remember our performance as more positive than it actually was (Crary, 1966).

As we saw in the chapter on causal attributions, people are more likely to attribute positive than negative outcomes to themselves (Miller & Ross, 1975). We credit the volleyball win to our own spectacular plays, but the loss to "a bad day" or "poor team coordination." When we do acknowledge our negative qualities, we often regard them as less important or consequential than our positive qualities (e.g., Campbell, 1986; Haraciewicz, Sansone, & Manderlink, 1985). While dimly recognizing that we have no talent in some areas of our lives (such as athletics), we keep those negative self-perceptions from mind by avoiding thinking about them and avoiding situations that would bring them to the fore (Showers, 1992).

Our self-perceptions are more positive than judgments made about us by observers. In a study that illustrates this point, Lewinsohn et al. (1980) had observers watch college students complete a task. The observers then rated the subjects on a number of personality dimensions, such as friendliness, warmth, or assertiveness. The students also rated themselves on these attributes. The results showed that self-ratings were significantly more positive than observer ratings. In other words, the students saw themselves in more flattering terms than they were seen by others.

Are there conditions when people are more accurate or balanced in their self-appraisals? Evidence suggests that people who are low in self-esteem or moderately depressed are more even-handed in their self-perceptions. They tend to recall both positive and negative information, their self-perceptions are more congruent with the evaluations of others, and they are less likely to show the self-serving attributional bias of taking credit for good but not bad outcomes. In short, then, the person who experiences subjective distress is more likely to process self-relevant information in an unbiased and balanced manner than the person high in self-esteem, who tends to be self-enhancing.

Why are most people so apparently self-enhancing in their self-perceptions and, moreover, why do these self-enhancing perceptions exist if they do not conform to reality? Taylor and Brown (1988) argued that self-enhancing

Sometimes just feeling good about ourselves (self-enhancement) is important.

positive illusions are adaptive. When we feel good about ourselves, we are happy, our social interactions go more smoothly, and we are more likely to help others. Feeling good about ourselves keeps us motivated and engaged in productive and creative work. Who, for example, would continue to work on a major project if he or she anticipated that it would be unsuccessful or that it would fail? Believing that we are talented and that our efforts will be successful keeps us going. In short, then, our self-enhancing self-perceptions foster many of the tasks that are regarded as evidence for successful life adjustment: a sense of personal well-being, pleasant social interactions, and the ability to engage in creative, productive work.

Of the motives that guide self-regulation,

self-enhancement has received the most attention, and below we detail several specific theories that address important aspects of self-enhancement.

SELF-AFFIRMATION. As already noted, psychologists believe that self-enhancement needs become especially important under conditions of threat. When people have received some blow to their self-worth brought about by a failure at some important task, they may try to emphasize or otherwise recruit positive features of themselves, by way of compensating for the blow to self-esteem. The attractive student who fails an exam may seek out members of the opposite sex who will flatter the ego. Or the college student who is not making friends easily may proudly display high school sports trophies. **Self-affirmation** theory, developed by Claude Steele, explicitly predicts that people will cope with specific threats to their self-worth by affirming unrelated aspects of themselves (see also Wicklund & Gollwitzer, 1982).

In an experiment that tests some of these points, Brown and Smart (1991) gave students who were either high in self-esteem or low in self-esteem either a success or a failure experience through an alleged test of their intellectual ability. Subsequently, the students were asked to rate themselves on a series of trait adjectives. Half of the items referred to social traits and attributes, whereas the other half referred to traits and attributes related to the task on which they had gotten the feedback, namely achievement-related traits and attributes. High self-esteem subjects who failed exaggerated the positivity of their social qualities, consistent with the predictions of self-affirmation theory. However, low self-esteem subjects actually did the reverse. For them, the failure experience seemed to generalize, so that not only did their self-ratings on intellectual attributes suffer, but so did their self-perceptions on social activities. Thus, while the predictions of self-affirmation theory appear generally to be true, they may be more true of high self-esteem than low self-esteem individuals (Steele, 1988; Wicklund & Gollwitzer, 1982).

TESSER'S SELF-EVALUATION MAINTENANCE MODEL. Tesser and his associates (see Tesser,

1988, for a review) have suggested another social mechanism whereby people facilitate and maintain their positive impressions of themselves, namely how they deal with the performances of other people around them who threaten or enhance their own sense of self. John's best friend Mark recently won a prestigious prize for writing a fictional short story. How will John react? Will he be overjoyed and eager to tell others about his friend's success? Or might he instead feel envious of Mark's success and unhappy to be reminded that he is a less talented writer? More generally, when does the successful performance of another individual enhance our personal self-evaluation, and when does it threaten our sense of self-worth? Abe Tesser (1988) has developed a model for **self-evaluation maintenance** designed to answer this question.

Tesser's model focuses on the motive for self-enhancement. The performance of other people in our social environment can affect our self-evaluation, especially when we are psychologically close to them. In the model, perceived closeness can come from having a relationship with another person, such as being a friend or relative. But closeness can also be based on shared characteristics, such as race, gender, religion, or physical proximity. In general, the behavior of people who are close has greater impact on us than the behavior of people who are psychologically distant. In addition, Tesser focuses on situations in which the other person performs relatively better than we do. The performance of others is less important to our self-evaluation when it is mediocre or poor. According to Tesser, the critical situation arises when a person we are close to performs well.

In such situations, what determines whether our reaction is to take pride in their accomplishments or to suffer by comparison? A key factor is whether the performance is relevant to our self-definition. If John aspires to be an award-winning creative writer, then knowledge that a close friend has outperformed him is likely to threaten his self-evaluation and lead to feelings of envy and discomfort. On the other hand, if John has no particular concern about his writing ability and sees creative writing as irrelevant to his sense of self, then he should take pleasure in the success of a close friend since it poses no threat to his self-evaluation.

In more technical terms, the main ideas of the Self-Evaluation Maintenance Model can be summarized as follows:

1. *The comparison effect.* When another person outperforms us on a behavior that is *relevant* to our self-definition, the better his or her performance and the closer our relationship, the greater is the threat to our self-evaluation. We feel envious, frustrated, or even angry.

2. *The reflection effect.* When another person outperforms us on a behavior that is *irrelevant* to our self-definition, the better his or her performance and the closer our relationship, the more we can gain in self-evaluation. A process of reflection leads us to feel positive and to take pride in the other person's success.

It is important to note the crucial role of the personal relevance of the behavior in question. The very same factors—closeness and high performance—can lead to opposite effects, depending on whether the behavior is relevant or irrelevant to our self-definition.

Emotional arousal also appears to be critical to self-evaluation maintenance. That is, when another person outperforms us on a behavior important to our self-definition, we attempt to maintain high self-evaluation only if we actually experience strong emotions in response to the other person's success. If emotional arousal does not occur or if it is misattributed to some neutral source, then the dynamics of self-evaluation maintenance take place to a far lesser degree (Tesser, Pilkington, & McIntosh, 1989; see also Tesser & Collins, 1988).

The self-evaluation maintenance model leads to many testable predictions about social interaction, and, in general, research findings have been supportive (Tesser, 1988; Tesser & Collins, 1988). For example, an individual whose self-evaluation has been diminished by the successful performance of a close friend can try to repair the situation in several ways. One

approach is to reduce the degree of closeness with the high-performing friend. John, for instance, might spend less time with Mark or come to value his friendship less. Another approach is to change one's self-definition. John might decide that creative writing is not really his ambition after all and that he should focus on literary criticism or art history. A third approach is to change the performance difference. John might put greater effort into improving his own writing skills, or try to convince himself that Mark's prize was based on luck rather than high ability.

In short, the successes of people close to us can be a mixed blessing. They sometimes bring us pleasure, but sometimes they cause us to suffer by comparison.

SOCIAL COMPARISON THEORY

Earlier, we noted that social comparisons can be an important source of self-knowledge. When we want to know how we stand on a particular quality and objective information is not available, we may compare ourselves with others to get a clear sense of our ability or our standing on the attribute in question. This idea is the central core of one of social psychology's most important theories, social comparison theory, and we consider it here in more detail.

In 1954, Leon Festinger, a pioneer in modern social psychology, developed **social comparison theory.** Festinger believed that people are motivated to make accurate assessments of their level of ability and the correctness of their attitudes. To do this, they assess their own standing in comparison to others like themselves. As an illustration of the choice of similar others for comparison, Festinger suggested that beginning chess players would prefer to compare themselves to other beginners rather than to master players. Festinger's theory of social comparison can be summarized in three statements:

1. People have a drive to evaluate their opinions and abilities accurately.

2. In the absence of direct physical standards,

people evaluate themselves through comparisons with other people.

3. In general, people prefer to compare themselves to similar others.

Today, our understanding of social comparison processes is considerably more complex than Festinger's original model (Goethals & Darley, 1987; Taylor & Lobel, 1989; Wood, 1989). The scope of social comparison theory has been broadened. We now know that people make comparative judgments not only about their abilities and opinions, but also about their emotions, their personality, and their outcomes on such dimensions as salary or prestige. As we will see in later chapters, the process of social comparison affects many aspects of social life. For example, the belief that our current dating partner is more wonderful than anyone we have ever dated before or could be dating now has important implications for our satisfaction and commitment to the relationship. The belief that our social or ethnic group is economically or socially disadvantaged compared to other groups in society can increase discontent and intergroup conflict (see Chapter 13).

The Goals of Social Comparison

Festinger's assertion that accuracy is the only goal of social comparison has been challenged. It now appears that social comparisons can be made in the service of a variety of personal goals and motives. These motives, not surprisingly, are the same ones that drive self-regulation more generally.

ACCURATE SELF-EVALUATION. As Festinger suggested, people sometimes desire truthful knowledge about themselves, even if the outcome is not favorable. Learning that we are the worst player on the volleyball team may spur us to greater effort or encourage us to change sports.

SELF-ENHANCEMENT. Rather than seeking truthful self-evaluation, people may seek comparisons that show themselves in a favorable light. A student who is struggling to learn calcu-

lus may prefer to emphasize that he's doing better than other students who are flunking the course. A desire for self-enhancement can lead people to make **downward social comparisons** with others who are less fortunate, less successful, or less happy than they are (Wills, 1981).

SELF-IMPROVEMENT. As we noted earlier, people sometimes compare themselves with others who can serve as models of success. Contrary to what Festinger assumed, an aspiring chess player may deliberately compare his opening strategies to those of great masters, in order to assess his stage of learning accurately, to learn from the insights of the masters, or to be inspired by their model (Taylor & Lobel, 1989; Wood, 1989). That is, a desire for self-improvement can lead to **upward social comparisons** with people who are more successful. The danger, of course, is that comparisons with much better performers can be discouraging and lead to feelings of incompetence, but as we have seen, such comparisons can also be motivating and inspiring (Taylor & Lobel, 1989; Buunk, Collins, Taylor, Van Yperen, & Dakof, 1990).

The Comparison Process

Festinger focused on situations in which a person deliberately chooses to make a social comparison. Illustrations of such situations are easy to find. For example, after surviving a frightening earthquake, a person may actively seek to compare his reactions with others' and spend hours talking with neighbors and friends about their experiences. At other times, however, social comparisons are not intentionally sought, but are rather forced upon us by the situation (Wood, 1989). For example, when elementary school children play baseball, it is very clear who is good at the sport and who is not. Children may not want to undergo this social comparison experience, but find it an unavoidable part of their life at school.

Unsolicited comparisons can have important effects on the individual. This point was demonstrated in a classic experiment by Stanley Morse and Kenneth Gergen (1970). Subjects in their study were undergraduate men who responded

These competing athletes illustrate the theory of self-evaluation maintenance. The success of people close to us can bring pleasure, but at times it can make us feel envious.

to an ad in the school newspaper offering two part-time jobs in "personality research." When the student arrived for his job interview, he was asked to fill out some questionnaires which included a measure of self-esteem. He was then exposed to another job applicant, who was brought into the same room to fill out the application materials. The experimental manipulation varied the appearance of the other job candidate (actually a confederate of the researchers).

Half the subjects were confronted with "Mr. Dirty," a young man wearing ripped trousers, a smelly sweatshirt, and no socks. He seemed very disorganized and glanced around the room frequently while filling out the forms. In contrast, half the subjects were randomly assigned to encounter "Mr. Clean," a well-groomed and confident young man who wore a dark suit and carried an attaché case. Later in the study, the subject's self-esteem was reassessed to see what impact exposure to Mr. Clean or Mr. Dirty might have had. As predicted, subjects who had an opportunity for downward comparison with Mr. Dirty increased their self-esteem; based on the comparison, they felt better about themselves. Subjects who had an opportunity for upward comparison with Mr. Clean suffered a drop in self-esteem; based on the comparison, they felt less good about themselves. The point is that unsolicited opportunities for social comparison can have important effects on our self-evaluation.

Festinger emphasized that people prefer to compare themselves to similar others. But just what dimensions of similarity are most important? Consider the case of a college student enrolled in a large history class who wants to evaluate how well she is doing. She might decide to compare herself with all the other students in the class. She could do this by finding out where she ranks in the class based on her grades. However, she might decide that this is not the best comparison because students taking the course differ widely in how many history courses they had in high school.

Instead, she might decide to compare herself only to other nonhistory majors who, like herself, have a limited background in the subject. In technical terms, this would be a comparison based on **related attributes similarity.** The basis of similarity is not her performance, but rather her background or preparation for the course, an attribute that should be related to performance (Goethals & Darley, 1987).

On the other hand, the student might want to know how she compares to other women in the class. In this case, she is selecting comparison targets who are similar in gender, a dimension of similarity that is presumably unrelated to performance in the course. There is evidence that people often make comparisons based on similarity in gender, race, or ethnicity, even when these attributes are not directly relevant to task performance.

Finally, the student might want information about the range of performance in this course, and so be interested in comparing herself to the best and to the worst students in the group. People are especially likely to seek information about the best and the worst cases when the meaning of the underlying dimension is unclear to them. If you were told you were moderately good at "integrative orientation," not knowing what integrative orientation means, you might seek out information about people who had done especially well or especially poorly to find out what someone who is really good at this skill or really bad at this skill is like. In this case, comparisons with others who are very different from the self in performance might prove instructive in learning what the dimension is. In summary, each type of comparison provides different information (Wood, 1989). All may be useful, depending on the individual's goals.

The section on social comparison processes as a source of self-knowledge has been quite lengthy. This would seem to imply that social comparison may be the most important way in which we know ourselves. This is unlikely to be the case, however. Although social psychologists have been particularly interested in social comparison as a source of self-knowledge, it is likely that other sources of self-knowledge, such as objective information, one's personal storehouse of memories, and direct feedback from others, provide more regular and more useful sources of self-knowledge. When we want to know what we are like, we get an evaluation of ourselves on that dimension either through objective information or by asking someone what we are like. Social comparison processes are an indirect way of gaining this information, and how useful the information is depends on whether we have chosen the comparison target well. Consequently, it seems likely that social comparison is a source of self-knowledge and self-evaluation, but it may not be a major one.

SELF-PRESENTATION

John is carefully preparing for an important job interview. He rehearses what he'll say about his past work experience. He gets his hair trimmed and ponders which suit to wear and whether a vest would look too formal. He buys a new briefcase to carry his papers and makes a point of arriving early for his appointment. When he meets the interviewer, John remembers to give a strong handshake, and smiles pleasantly. During the interview, John tries to look attentive and to answer questions thoroughly. In short, he makes every effort to present himself as an energetic, competent person who would be successful in the job.

A pervasive aspect of social interaction is the desire to manage the impression we make on others. The term **self-presentation** refers to our efforts to control the impression we convey. The fundamental goal of self-presentation is to structure the interaction so that we obtain a desired outcome. In John's case, the goal is to obtain a job offer.

We often want people to view us positively—as an interesting, friendly, intelligent, and caring person. But sometimes we strive to convey other images instead (Kowalski & Leary, 1990). For example, the schoolyard bully might want to present himself as tough and intimidating. At other times, our goal may be to minimize a bad impression, for instance, by finding a plausible excuse for showing up late for an exam.

Self-presentation is often a deliberate activity. In his job interview, John is quite conscious of his desire to present himself as hard-working and talented. However, in familiar situations, self-presentational activities can become automatic (Baumeister, Hutton, & Tice, 1989). With his friends, John may habitually present himself as a fun-loving guy who doesn't take work too seriously. When self-presentation in a particular setting becomes routine, people don't have to think about impression management much and so can focus their attention on other aspects of the situation.

Sociologist Erving Goffman has compared self-presentation to acting in a play (1959). Like dramatic actors, we often pay special attention to appearances—to the way we look and dress and also to our mannerisms and habits. When we "dress up" for a date or remember not to chew gum on the job, we are controlling appearances in order to convey a desired image. We sometimes rely on props to assist in our self-presentation. Serving the right wine, driving a classy car, and flashing a new engagement ring are ways people use physical objects to convey a particular impression. Setting the stage can also be important. This might involve turning down the lights and playing soft music as a prelude to romance, or taking a friend on a wilderness hike to convey our interest in nature. Another feature of self-presentation is rehearsal. Before a social event, we may think about what we'll say and do, mentally trying out various approaches.

Goffman observed that people often distinguish between front-stage and back-stage regions in their social interactions. Back regions are where people prepare for a performance; front regions are where the action takes place. When preparing for a dinner party, the nervous amateur chef may spend the entire day in the kitchen, frantically trying to follow complicated recipes and using every pot in the house. However, the chef's front-stage behavior may be quite different. When the guests are seated at the dining table and praise the delectable meal, the chef may appear calm and experienced, saying, "Oh, it's just a little something I whipped up this afternoon."

An important aspect of self-presentation is knowing one's audience. For a fashion-conscious teenager, the trendy clothes and hair styles that are popular among peers may be considered tasteless and outlandish by older relatives. The ability to "take the role of the other," to anticipate how others will perceive and react to our actions, is essential for successful impression management. Thus, one of the challenges of social interaction is being able to change our behavior from situation to situation, depending on our self-presentational goals and on the nature of the audience.

Making a Good Impression

Perhaps the most common motive in self-presentation is to make a good impression (Schlenker, 1980). How do people accomplish this objective? Several tactics of successful impression management have been identified (Fiske & Taylor, 1991).

One strategy is to conform to the norms of the social situation. To look good at a party, a person might tell interesting stories and jokes. In contrast, at a funeral, expressions of sadness and sympathy for the family would be more appropriate. Another strategy is to match the behavior of other people. If your new acquaintance boasts about her tennis prowess, you might do well to boast about your own accomplishments. But if she behaves modestly and downplays her expertise, a similar degree of modesty might create the most positive impression.

A useful distinction can be made between two additional strategies for creating a positive impression: self-promotion and ingratiation. **Self-promotion** refers to conveying positive information about the self, either through one's actions or by saying positive things about the self. In contrast, **ingratiation** or flattery refers to

saying positive things about the listener. Jones and Pittman (1982) have suggested that these two tactics reflect different goals: Whereas the self-promoter wants to be seen as competent, the flatterer wants to be liked. In some situations, such as a job interview, the person may try to accomplish both goals simultaneously, coming across as both likeable and talented.

Self-promotion can be tricky. Telling about one's accomplishments can enhance self-presentation, but it can also backfire and create the impression of being conceited or insecure (Cialdini & De Nicholas, 1989; Jones & Pittman, 1982). This happens because observers often evaluate a person on more than one dimension at the same time. The blatant self-promoter may indeed convince others that he or she is competent, but may also display conspicuous egotism.

An important factor in self-promotion is the context in which people talk about themselves. One study compared impressions of people who made positive statements about their intellectual ability under several different conditions (Holtgraves & Srull, 1989). People who mentioned their intellectual accomplishments were seen more favorably if these statements were made in response to specific questions. For instance, if a person was asked how he had done on his midterm, his answer that he got 93 percent correct made a favorable impression. Similarly, positive statements about the self enhanced one's image if they were made in a context of mutual disclosures by both partners. So Andy's statement that he did very well in the chess club tournament was seen positively if it was part of a conversation in which Bob also indicated that he had done very well in bridge. In contrast, if people seemed to go out of their way to say good things about their own ability without being asked and without others providing similar information, they were perceived as less likeable, less considerate, and more egotistical. In short, the context of the conversation makes an important difference in how observers interpret self-promoting statements.

Another tactic of positive impression management is the careful use of modesty (Cialdini & De Nicholas, 1989). For example, the female basketball star whose brilliant plays have just saved her team from losing the championship might describe her performance as "pretty good" but emphasize that she couldn't have done it without the work of the entire team. By understating her accomplishments, she will probably be seen as both likeable and competent. The trick, of course, is to know when modesty will be effective. There are two rules of thumb. First, modesty boosts a person's public image only when the performance has actually been successful. Modesty about a poor performance is not image-enhancing. Second, modesty works to boost one's public image only when the audience already knows the full extent of the person's success. The champion athlete can afford to be modest because her fame precedes her.

Self-presentation involves both verbal and nonverbal behavior. In Chapter 2, we described ways in which nonverbal behavior contributes to self-presentation. In general, self-presentations are most convincing when verbal and nonverbal messages are the same. A person who says he's "very happy" but uses a glum and depressed tone of voice will not be very credible. In contrast, a person who says she would like to get to know us better, smiles, makes frequent eye contact, and sits close by is much more believable. And sometimes, our self-presentations are so convincing that we actually come to believe them ourselves. Specifically, when the presentation we have made to others is both convincing and compatible with our own self-views, then we may come to believe it, just as we hope members of our audience do (Schlenker & Trudeau, 1990).

We engage in impression management not only by the things we ourselves do, but also by associating ourselves with people who are successful, powerful, or famous. Robert Cialdini and his coworkers have used the term BIRGing to refer to the tendency to *bask in the reflected glory* of others (Cialdini et al., 1976; Cialdini & De Nicholas, 1989). Cialdini believes that people enhance their individual self-presentation by highlighting their associations with successful others, even when these connections are quite trivial. If a person tells us he comes from the same hometown as President Bush, or that he once met Barbra Streisand, or that his friend won a million dollars in the lottery, he is trying to impress us by his mere association with the rich and famous.

Ineffective Self-presentation

Self-presentation is not always effective. Sometimes our actions do not show us in a positive light. We may forget our mother's birthday or spill a bowl of soup in our lap at a restaurant. In such case, the best we can do is to minimize our losses.

Embarrassment is a common and unpleasant emotion experienced when there is a disruption in our self-presentation (Parrott, Sabini, & Silver, 1988; Schlenker, 1980). These can be minor lapses in impression management, for instance, when a waiter drops a tray of food or when we inadvertently call someone by the wrong name. Flaws in self-presentation can also involve more serious failures in performance, such as when a professional actor forgets his lines or a famous scientist is shown to have misinterpreted her data. The embarrassed person usually responds with efforts to resume the interrupted pattern of interaction. The person may apologize or give an excuse, and then attempt to pick up where he or she left off. An embarrassing situation is uncomfortable for everyone present, and so others are also motivated to help the embarrassed person save face.

Excuses can play an important role in impression management. A poor performance on a test or in a sports competition calls into question our abilities. One way to handle a less than stellar performance is to give excuses (Snyder & Higgins, 1988; Kernis & Grannemann, 1990). Consistent with attribution theory (Chapter 4), people often try to excuse their failures as due to external and uncontrollable causes. It is more gratifying to say you failed the test because it was unfair and all the other students also flunked (external, uncontrollable cause) than to admit that the test was easy and you were not able to master the material (low ability).

The importance of excuses is not limited to achievement settings. Failure to meet a social obligation, such as being late for an appointment, can also create impression management problems. Again, you will probably make a better impression—and avoid arousing anger in the other person—if you blame your late arrival on a flat tire, rather than saying you forgot to set the alarm clock (Weiner, Amirkhan, Folkes, & Verette, 1987).

Self-handicapping

A related but more desperate strategy for dealing with failure has been called **self-handicapping** (Berglas & Jones, 1978; Baumeister & Scher, 1988). People sometimes engage in actions that produce insurmountable obstacles to success so that later, when they experience the resulting inevitable failure, they can attribute it to the obstacle, not to their own lack of ability. The student who stays up all night before the calculus exam can attribute his low grade to fatigue, not to his complete lack of ability to comprehend math; the golfer who rarely practices can attribute her afternoon in the woods and sandtraps to lack of practice, not lack of ability; the alcoholic can attribute the loss of his job to his drinking, not to poor performance. In Kelley's attribution framework, the ability attribution is discounted because another plausible cause is present: the handicap.

In an experiment testing the self-handicapping phenomenon, Shepperd and Arkin (1989) informed college student subjects that they would be taking a test described as either a

valid or an invalid predictor of academic success. In addition, half the subjects were led to believe that during the course of the test they would hear a high-pitched ringing that might interfere with their test performance, whereas others were not led to believe that there was a distractor in their environment. Subjects were then asked if they wished to listen to music while they performed the test and were given a choice between music that might facilitate their performance on the task or music that might worsen it. The results indicated that subjects self-handicapped, that is, chose music that was expected to interfere with their task performance, when they anticipated an important task (the test measuring academic success). However, this occurred only when there was no preexisting handicap in the environment. Subjects taking the test but expecting to do so in the presence of the adverse ringing sound apparently had no need for additional self-handicapping, and thus were less likely to choose music that interfered with their performance. The results of this experiment are presented in Figure 5-2.

People also protect their images of their own competence by claiming to have handicaps that prevent success, even when those handicaps do not necessarily exist. Snyder and others have shown that in evaluative situations threatening failure, people may claim such symptoms as test anxiety, social anxiety, shyness, depression, or a

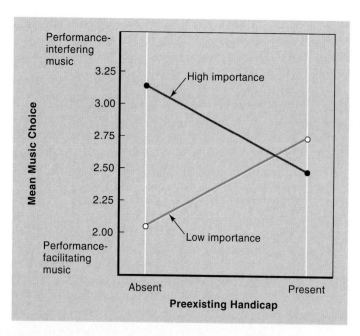

Figure 5-2 Subjects who expected to take an important test chose distracting music, apparently to have an advance explanation for their failure on the test. However, this effect occurred only when there was no pre-existing handicap in the environment. (*Source:* Adapted from Shepperd, J. A., & Arkin, R. M. Determinants of self-handicapping: Task importance and the effects of pre-existing handicaps on self-generated handicaps. *Personality and Social Psychology Bulletin, 15,* 101–112, copyright 1989, by Sage Publications, Inc. Reprinted by permission of Sage Publications, Inc.)

history of traumatic incidents (Snyder & Higgins, 1988). Reporting such symptoms can also protect people from having to make ability attributions for their own failures: The cool response you get from that beautiful girl that just moved onto your dorm floor is because you are shy, not because you are ugly. As you might expect, when people claim such excuses, it tends to reduce their negative affect about failure, at least as long as no one else knows the real truth about the situation (Mehlman & Snyder, 1985).

There are two versions of the self-handicapping strategy, then: *behavioral* self-handicapping, in which people actively construct genuine handicaps, such as fatigue, alcohol, drugs, lack of punctuality, inattention, and so on, and *self-reported* handicaps, in which people claim to be ill, anxious, shy, or the victim of traumatic incidents, when such states might excuse poor performance (Leary & Shepperd, 1986; Arkin & Baumgardner, 1985). In both cases, as with self-serving attributional biases in general, the key motives are self-enhancement, or the need to boost one's ego, and self-protection, or the ego-defensive motive of avoiding a stable, uncontrollable, internal attribution for failure, such as an inherent lack of ability (Rhodewalt, Morf, Hazlett, & Fairchild, 1991; Tice, 1991).

An unfortunate implication of this analysis is that self-presentational pressures may sometimes cause people to lie—to others and to themselves—about the true reasons for their actions. At times, the desire to impress others favorably may conflict with a desire to be honest.

Self-monitoring

All of us are social actors who consider the impressions we make on others. But for some people, a concern with self-presentation is ever-present. **Self-monitoring** is the tendency to emphasize impression management to a great extent. Mark Snyder and his colleagues have developed a paper-and-pencil test to assess this personality disposition (Briggs & Cheek, 1988; Snyder, 1987; Snyder & Gangestad, 1986). Individuals high in self-monitoring are especially sensitive to situational cues about appropriate behavior. On the Self-Monitoring Scale, they would agree with such statements as:

Staying up all night before an exam may help you learn overlooked material, but it can also be a self-handicapping strategy: When you fail, you can attribute your low grade to fatigue and not have to question your ability.

"I would probably make a good actor."
"I may deceive people by being friendly when I really dislike them."
"In different situations and with different people, I often act like very different persons."

In contrast, individuals low in self-monitoring are less attuned to situational demands; their self-presentation is controlled to a larger extent by their inner attitudes and values. They would agree with such statements as:

"I can only argue for ideas that I already believe."
"I have trouble changing my behavior to suit different people and different situations."
"I have never been good at games like charades or improvisational acting."

High and low self-monitoring individuals differ in several ways (Snyder, 1987). In comparison to low self-monitors, high self-monitors make a greater effort to learn about other people and to size up social situations (e.g., Fiske & Von Hendy, 1992). They pay more attention to information about people they are going to meet and interact with. And they are also more likely to tailor their behavior to fit the demands of the situation. For instance, high self-monitors are

161

more skilled at using their faces and voices to pose particular emotions. Self-monitoring may affect interaction in a wide variety of settings. In dating situations, for example, high self-monitors seem to place great importance on the physical attractiveness of a partner, whereas low self-monitors seem to give greater weight to personality (Glick et al., 1988; Snyder, Berscheid, & Glick, 1985). Because high self-monitors are attuned to situational demands, their behavior may vary more from one situation to another.

In reading about self-monitoring, you may have tried to figure out where you or your friends fall on this continuum. You may also have wondered which orientation is best or most useful. In fact, there are pros and cons to both high and low self-monitoring. High self-monitors may think of themselves as practical-minded people who try to make the best of social situations. Their perceptiveness and social sensitivity enable them to interact effectively in diverse settings. But carried to an extreme, high self-monitors can be criticized as self-interested opportunists who change themselves and their opinions to suit the situation. A similar dilemma exists for low self-monitors. On the one hand, they may think of themselves as principled people who stick up for what they believe in and remain firm in their goals despite social influences. But carried to an extreme, low self-monitors can be criticized as insensitive, inflexible, and uncompromising. Fortunately, most people fall in between these two extremes.

CULTURE AND THE SELF

The conception of self that has guided this chapter is based largely on research by Western psychologists, namely researchers in the United States, Canada, and Western Europe. Consequently, the portrait of the self they paint is heavily influenced by Western culture. Those who conduct research on the self often draw their conclusions as if they applied universally. But is this true? Does the view of self that characterizes Western cultures apply to other cultures?

Research that compares independent, or Western, cultures, such as the United States and Western Europe, with collectivist cultures, including Asian, Hispanic, Southern European, and Native American cultures, suggests that conceptions of the self vary greatly (Triandis, McCusker, & Hui, 1990; Rotenberg & Cranwell, 1989). In a thoughtful investigation of this point, Markus and Kitayama (1991) explicitly contrasted American culture with Japanese culture to illustrate the substantial differences in self-conceptions that may exist between Western, independent cultures and Eastern, collectivist cultures.

In America, there is a strong emphasis on individuality and how one can best distinguish oneself from others by discovering and making use of one's unique talents. This **independent self** is "a bounded, unique, more or less integrated motivational and cognitive universe, a dynamic center of awareness, emotion, judgment, action, organized into a distinctive whole and set contrastively, both against other such wholes and against a social and natural background" (Geertz, 1975, p. 48). In our culture, "the squeaky wheel gets the grease." Not only do we construe the self as an independent functioning unit, we actually define it as a fundamental task of socialization. Westerners teach their children how to be independent and alone (Kitayama, 1992).

In Japan, "the nail that stands out gets pounded down" (Markus & Kitayama, 1991, p. 224). Japanese mothers teach their children to fear loneliness. The **interdependent self** of Japanese culture consists of seeing oneself as part of an encompassing social relationship and realizing that one's behavior is determined and dependent on what one perceives to be the thoughts, feelings, and actions of others in the relationship (Markus & Kitayama, 1991). The self becomes meaningful and complete largely within the context of a social relationship, rather than through independent, autonomous action. Although the interdependent self is regarded as possessing a set of internal qualities, such as abilities or opinions, these attributes are thought to be situation-specific and unstable, rather than as defining characteristics of the self (Cousins, 1989). Thus, the interdependent self is not a bounded whole, but rather changes its structure with the nature of the social context. In interdependent cultures, so fundamental is the emphasis on blending in, that those attributes that uniquely differentiate one person from another are not regarded as particularly representative of the self. So, for example, while Americans would regard a particularly talented musical child as a distinctive quality of that child, the Japanese might not.

The Western viewpoint regards the self as composed of individual attributes, such as ambition, good humor, or extravertedness (Trafimow, Triandis, & Goto, 1991). These attributes are considered distinctively one's own, even when they are shared with others. A student, for example, may regard herself as creative, but this judgment is independent of judgments she might make about her roommate's creativity. Even if she regards both herself and her roommate as creative, her creativity is independent of her roommate's, not shared. In contrast, the Japanese view of the interdependent self does not regard the individual in terms of distinctive qualities, but rather those that are shared. Because people are regarded as fundamentally connected to each other, they are thought to have attributes in common, rather than attributes that they uniquely possess (Trafimow, Triandis, & Goto, 1991). Thus, two students might be creative together interdependently and not independently. These different views of the self are illustrated in Figure 5-3.

Markus and Kitayama suggest that this conception of self as independent versus interdependent is a fundamentally important aspect of an individual's self-system. It influences how one thinks about one's personal characteristics, how one relates to others, what emotions are experienced in different situations, and what motivates people to engage in action.

While research comparing those with an interdependent versus independent sense of self is just beginning, it is easy to see how this distinction would have profound implications for the self-relevant phenomena covered in this chapter. For example, recall that self-enhancement has been regarded as a ubiquitous and important self-relevant need. Americans take pride in their unique and special accomplishments. Clearly, this is less likely to be the case in a culture that is interdependently focused. For example, a Japanese worker may be happiest when his contributions aid the collective good, and may not need or wish to have his unique

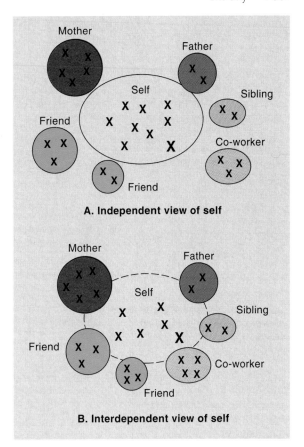

Figure 5-3 Conceptual representations of the self: (a) Independent construal; (b) interdependent construal. (*Source:* Markus & Kitayama, 1991.)

contributions acknowledged (see the CULTURAL HIGHLIGHT). While Americans may take pleasure in contributing to a collective product, the recognition of their own contribution would no doubt be an important source of pride.

There are potentially important cognitive consequences of different construals of the self. For example, those with an independent sense of self see themselves as distinctive. While they may regard other people as like them, they do not regard themselves as similar to other people. In contrast, among those with interdependent selves, the self and others should be considered part of a specific social context in which both are embedded. Thus, both self and others should be construed as quite similar.

To test this point, Kitayama, Markus, Tummala, Kurokawa, & Kato (1990) asked American and Indian subjects to make judg-

What motivates you to strive and succeed? In the United States, we usually consider motivation to reside internally, rooted in the individual need to achieve and even in the need to surpass others. In interdependent cultures, however, motivation is experienced in receptivity to others, in the desire to adjust to their needs and demands, and in the ability to restrain one's own inner needs or desires. While there is striving to excel and accomplish tasks, it is not in the service of self-promotion, but in the service of demonstrating and furthering one's interdependence with others.

Consider what happened in an American plant located in Japan when Japanese women, hired to wire electronic products, were paid on a piece-rate system that rewarded those who produced more over those who produced less:

About two months after opening, the head foreladies approached the plant manager. "Honorable plant manager," they said humbly as they bowed, "we are embarrassed to be so forward, but we must speak to you, because all of the girls have threatened to quit work this Friday." "Why," they wanted to know, "can't our plant have the same compensation system as other Japanese companies? When you hire a new girl, her starting wage should be fixed by her age. An 18-year-old should be paid more than a 16-year-old. Every year on her birthday, she should receive an automatic increase in pay. The idea that any one of us can be more productive than another must be wrong, because none of us in final assembly could make a thing unless all of the other people in the plant had done their jobs right first. To single one person out as being more productive is wrong and is also personally humiliating to us." The company changed its compensation system to the Japanese model. (Ouchi, 1981, p. 41)

Clearly, then, we cannot make assumptions about what motivates people to work hard and do well using the assumptions of our own culture. We must understand what motivates members of other cultures and, in so doing, may discover that those others' hard work and striving are in service of very different goals.

---

ments of similarity between themselves and others. (India, like Japan, is a collectivist culture with an interdependent sense of self.) Typically, research in America finds that the self is judged to be quite dissimilar to others, whereas others are judged to be similar to the self (e.g., Holyoak & Gordon, 1983). Kitayama and his colleagues replicated this study in both the United States and India, and the results are illustrated in Figure 5-4. In the United States, students saw themselves as quite dissimilar to others, but saw others as very similar to themselves. Thus, they perceived themselves to be more distinctive than they perceived others to be. Exactly the reverse was found in India. The self was seen as very similar to other people, that is, as not especially distinctive, but others were seen as relatively different from the self.

There are other cognitive consequences of different views of the self. Recall from Chapter 4 the study by Miller comparing Americans and Indians in terms of their attributions for the events that go on around them. Americans' attributions for events are marked by the fundamental attribution error, namely the tendency to see individuals as the causes of their own behavior. Indian respondents, in contrast, gave situational explanations for behavior. This finding can be expected to generalize to other cultures with an interdependent sense of self and a corresponding perception of the self as embedded in the social situation.

Markus and Kitayama also argued that people with independent versus interdependent selves will experience fundamentally different kinds of emotions. Those with independent senses of self, such as is found in our own culture, should frequently experience ego-focused emotions, such as the experience of pride ("I did well") or frustration ("I was treated unfairly"). In contrast, cultures with interdependent conceptions of self may experience other-focused

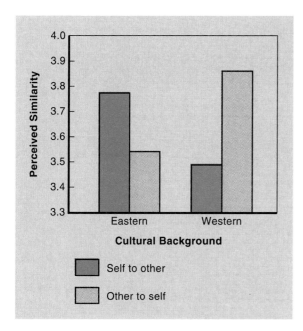

Figure 5-4 Mean perceived similarity of self to other and other to self by subjects with Eastern and Western cultural backgrounds. (*Source:* Markus & Kitayama, 1991.)

emotions. As an example, Markus and Kitayama describe the experience of *amae*, the Japanese word for the sense of being lovingly cared for and dependent upon another's indulgence. *Amae* is the formation and maintenance of a mutually reciprocal interdependent relationship with another person. There is no equivalent for *amae* in English.

What other phenomena that we have studied with reference to the self might be influenced by independent versus interdependent construals of the self? The self-serving bias is likely to be one such phenomenon. Recall from Chapter 4 that people tend to see themselves as the origins of actions that have good but not bad consequences. Such attributions are thought to have self-enhancing qualities. We would expect to find that the self-serving bias is greatly lessened or even nonexistent in cultures like Japan that have an interdependent sense of self. Indeed, some recent research suggests that this is the case. Takata (1987) found no self-enhancing bias among Japanese students, but rather the opposite, a bias in a self-effacing direction. When Japanese students outperformed another person, they tended to regard their success as situa-

tionally caused, whereas when they were outperformed by another, they were more likely to see that other person's personal qualities as responsible for the other's success (see Shikanai, 1978). The more modest self-attributions and self-perceptions of the Japanese and others with an interdependent sense of self appears to be a robust and general finding (Markus & Kitayama, 1991).

Similarly, self-esteem is likely to vary substantially, depending on the sense of self that a person holds. Recall from Table 5-1 the kinds of items that assess self-esteem, such as "I am a person of worth." Members of cultures with an independent sense of self should be more likely to endorse such items than members of cultures where the self is viewed interdependently. Consistent with this point, Kagan and Knight (1979) compared Mexican-American and Anglo-American children on self-esteem and its determinants. Among Mexican-Americans, high self-esteem was significantly related to cooperative behavior. In contrast, among Anglo-American children, self-esteem was related to competitive behavior. The authors concluded that self-esteem is, to an important degree, dependent on fulfilling cultural norms.

The differences between independent and interdependent self-conceptions are summarized in Table 5-5. It seems reasonable to assume that many of the other processes we have studied in this chapter—self-affirmation (Steele, 1988), self-verification (Swann, 1983), self-consciousness (Fenigstein, Scheier, & Buss, 1975), self-control (Carver & Scheier, 1981), and self-handicapping (Jones & Berglas, 1978)—would also take somewhat different shape in a culture that construes the self in interdependent terms.

Clearly, then, we are only beginning to understand the self and the cultural differences in the ways in which the self is experienced. Many of the phenomena we have identified in this chapter properly describe Western behavior, but may not extend, at least in the same form, to Eastern cultures or other collectivist societies. On the other hand, other phenomena may generalize across all cultures. Research on the self, then, while having assumed a clearer shape and focus over recent decades, nonetheless leaves many important issues to be explored.

TABLE 5-5
Summary of Key Differences Between an Independent and an Interdependent Construal of Self

Feature Compared	Independent	Interdependent
Definition	Separate from social context	Connected with social context
Stucture	Bounded, unitary, stable	Flexible, variable
Important features	Internal, private (abilities, thoughts, feelings)	External, public (statuses, roles, relationships)
Tasks	Be unique	Belong, fit-in
	Express self	Occupy one's proper place
	Realize internal attributes	Engage in appropriate action
	Promote own goals	Promote others' goals
	Be direct: say what's on your mind	Be indirect: read other's mind
Role of others	*Self-evaluation:* others important for social comparison, reflected appraisal	*Self-definition:* relationships with others in specific contexts define the self
Basis of self-esteem[a]	Ability to express self, validate internal attributes	Ability to adjust, restrain self, maintain harmony with social context

[a] Esteeming the self may be primarily a Western phenomenon, and the concept of self-esteem should perhaps be replaced by self-satisfaction, or by a term that reflects the realization that one is fulfilling the culturally mandated task.
Source: Markus & Kitayama (1991).

KEY TERMS

cybernetic theory of self-regulation
downward social comparison
ethnic identity
ideal self
independent self
ingratiation
interdependent self
ought self
positive illusions
possible selves
private self-consciousness
public self-consciousness
reflected appraisals

related attributes similarity
self-affirmation
self-awareness
self-complexity
self-concept
self-discrepancies
self-efficacy
self-enhancement
self-esteem
self-evaluation maintenance model
self-handicapping
self-monitoring
self-perception

self-presentation
self-promotion
self-referencing effect
self-regulation
self-schema
self-verification
social comparison
social comparison theory
social identity
socialization
upward social comparison
working self-concept

SUMMARY

1. The self is the collection of beliefs that we hold about ourselves. The contents of these beliefs is called the self-concept. The evaluation we make of them is called self-esteem.
2. Self-knowledge comes from early socialization, reflected appraisals of others, direct feedback from others, self-perception, envi-

ronmental distinctiveness, social comparison processes, and social identity.
3. Beliefs about ourselves may be represented as self-schemas, which serve for the self the same functions that schemas serve more generally, and possible selves, images of ourselves in the future that represent what

we may become. Discrepancies between our self-conceptions and our ideals or sense of what we ought to be produce strong emotions.

4. Self-regulation refers to how we control and direct our actions. Self-regulation is influenced by the working self-concept, beliefs in our self-efficacy, our degree of self-complexity, and our focus of attention, termed self-awareness.

5. Several motivations drive self-regulation. People seek to have an accurate self-concept, a consistent self-concept, and a positive self-concept. They also seek information and situations that help them improve.

6. Self-affirmation refers to efforts to bolster our self-conceptions in one area following threat to self-conceptions in another aspect of self. Self-evaluation maintenance refers to the processes we engage in when someone close to or distant from us outperforms us on a personally relevant or irrelevant task.

7. Often, we compare our own attributes, opinions, and emotions with those of other people, a process called social comparison. Typically, we prefer comparisons with someone similar, but sometimes we make upward comparisons to people better than ourselves, or downward comparisons to people doing more poorly than the self.

Social comparison can aid in accurate or self-enhancing evaluations, and can also foster self-improvement.

8. Self-presentation concerns the efforts we make to control the impression we convey. As in theater, we construct our behavior in situations in order to make a desired impression, usually a positive one. Appropriate self-promotion and modesty are two strategies that often lead to good impressions.

9. Poor impressions on others can be managed or controlled by making excuses or by self-handicapping, that is, engaging in actions or claiming to have problems that produce insurmountable obstacles to success.

10. Self-monitoring is the degree to which we monitor our own behavior with respect to the environment. High self-monitors are sensitive to situational cues and change their behavior in response to them, whereas the behavior and impressions of low self-monitors are controlled to a greater extent by their inner attitudes and values.

11. Cultural analyses suggest that Westerners construe the self as independent, unique, important, and free-standing, whereas collectivist cultures construe the self as interdependent, part of an encompassing social relationship. This distinction is thought to influence profoundly self-relevant phenomena.

SUGGESTED READINGS

Baumeister, R. S. (1986). *Identity: Cultural change and the struggle for self.* New York: Oxford University Press. A provocative historical and cultural perspective on the self.

Berkowitz, L. (Ed.). (1988). *Advances in experimental social psychology: Social psychological studies of the self: Perspectives and programs* (Vol. 21). New York: Academic Press. A detailed review of current research topics on the self.

Goffman, E. (1959). *The presentation of self in everyday life.* Garden City, NY: Doubleday. An engaging and entertaining analysis of self-presentation that is classic but still filled with wit and insight.

Markus, H. R., & Kitayama, S. (1991). Culture and the self: Implications for cognition, emotion, and motivation. *Psychological Review, 98,* 224–253. A thoughtful essay on differences in conceptions of the self held by independent and collectivist cultures.

Pervin, L. A. (Ed.). (1992). *Psychological Inquiry, 3*(1). Recent theoretical contributions on views of the self.

Rosenberg, M. (1979). *Conceiving the self.* New York: Basic Books. A classic, still valuable overview of important issues concerning the origins and nature of the self.

6
Attitudes
and Attitude Change

FOCUS OF THIS CHAPTER

Theories of Attitudes
Persuasion
Attitude Change Over Time
Attitudes and Behavior

Cultural Highlight
American Views of Equality
and Achievement

Research Closeup
Mood and Persuasion

What makes someone a conservative or a liberal, a Republican or a Democrat, pro-diversity or anti-diversity? Why are some people prejudiced and others not? Why do you like one person in your class and staunchly avoid another? All of these are examples of **attitudes,** which have been the central core of social psychology for many years. This chapter will consider what attitudes are, how they are formed, and how they can be changed.

Defining Attitudes

Although most of us have a sense of what an attitude is, defining it in objective terms has been surprisingly difficult. One common definition was developed by G. W. Allport (1935), who proposed that "an attitude is a mental and neural state of readiness, organized through experience, exerting a directive or dynamic influence upon the individual's response to all objects and situations with which it is related" (p. 810).

Despite the apparent usefulness of this definition, it actually embodies a number of assumptions about attitudes, not all of which are accurate. One assumption is that attitudes are enduring. Yet we know that people can often come up with a new attitude on the spur of the moment to a previously unencountered person or object. Another assumption is that attitudes exert a direct or dynamic influence on behavior. Yet as we shall see, the relationship between attitudes and behavior can sometimes be weak.

So that the concept of attitudes will fit all that we know about how they operate, psychologists have converged on a bare-bones definition. An emerging consensus is that attitudes involve the categorization of a stimulus along an evaluative dimension based on cognitive, affective, and behavioral information. The **cognitive component** consists of the thoughts the person has about that particular attitude object, including facts, knowledge, and beliefs. The affective (or evaluative) component consists of all the person's emotions and affects toward the object, especially positive or negative evaluations. The **behavioral component** consists of the person's tendency to act regarding the object.

Consider our friend Evan's attitude toward safe sex, shown diagramatically in Figure 6-1. The focus of the attitude is on the attitude object, which in this case is condom use. Surrounding the object are the various factors perceived as relevant to condom attitudes. Some of these are impersonal factors, such as qualities of condoms. Others are people, such as one's parents, roommates, or friends, and their beliefs about safe sex and condom use. Others are personal states, such as one's own feelings about condoms, and others are simply attributes of the object itself, such as its availability or cost. These clusters of cognitions and their links to the main attitude object constitute the cognitive component of an attitude.

The affective component consists of the positive or negative feelings associated with the cognitive elements and the central attitude object itself. In Figure 6-1, positive and negative evaluations of the elements and central object are indicated by plus and minus signs, respectively. Evan's negative feelings about condoms may come from the awkwardness that exists in purchasing them and later using them, and the concern that they may reduce sexual enjoyment.

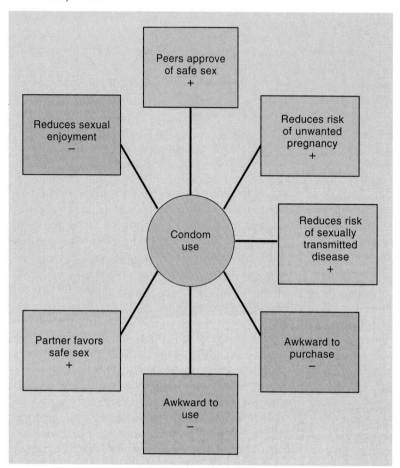

Figure 6-1 Evan's attitude toward condom use. The core object is related to several other cognitions. The signs refer to the affective component of his overall attitude toward condom use and his affects toward the separate cognitions he associates with condom use. A positive sign (+) refers to a favorable affect and a negative sign (−) to an unfavorable affect.

But there are also many positive links to condom use, such as the safety it provides, peer approval regarding the importance of safe sex, and the belief that one is doing the right thing. Finally, there is a behavioral component. An attitude contains some tendency to behave in connection with the attitude object—in this case, whether or not Evan is willing to buy and use condoms.

This three-component definition of attitudes is the one that most social psychologists share at present. Additional facts about attitudes to keep in mind include their *cognitive complexity.* For many attitude objects, we have a great many complex thoughts and beliefs. They may not all be factually correct, and they may contradict each other. In Figure 6-1, for example, we have shown only a few of the cognitions an individual could have regarding safe sex and condom

use. Some of these beliefs will be more or less important, and others of them will be more or less amenable to persuasion by others. Thus, complexity is an essential feature of attitudes.

Even though attitudes tend to be cognitively complex, they are often evaluatively quite simple. As we noted in Chapter 2 impressions of other people quickly tend to become evaluatively consistent, and the same is true of attitudes. Despite some of his negative evaluations of condoms, Evan's attitude toward condom use is fundamentally positive.

Among the implications of cognitive complexity coupled with evaluative simplicity is the fact that overall evaluations toward attitude objects are often difficult to change, whereas one may alter the cognitions that go into the makeup of an attitude relatively easily. A final important aspect of attitudes is their links to decisions and behavior. Attitudes make it possible to quickly access relevant information and related attitudes, because they provide important linkages among information held in memory (Judd, Drake, Downing, and Krosnick, 1991). They can enable people to make decisions very quickly, because they provide information for making choices (Sanbonmatsu & Fazio, 1990). The links to behavior are somewhat more tenuous. Sometimes behavior is controlled by attitudes and sometimes it is not. Evan may be in favor of condom use generally, but if there is a troop of 11-year-old Girl Scouts at the drug store when he goes in to make his purchase, he may not actually purchase condoms, despite his generally positive attitude toward safe sex.

Behavior can change attitudes, too. Suppose Evan's attitude toward safe sex was not positive, but more ambivalent. If he encountered a partner who insisted upon safe sex, his attitudes might begin to shift in the direction of being more pro-safe sex. So relations between attitudes and behavior can go either way. Attitudes may control behavior, but behavior sometimes controls attitudes.

THEORIES OF ATTITUDES

Several theories, initially outlined in Chapter 1, are helpful for understanding where attitudes come from and how they might be changed. The learning approach regards attitudes as habits, like anything else that is learned. Principles that apply to other forms of learning also determine the formation of attitudes. The cognitive consistency approach asserts that we seek consistency among our attitudes, and between attitudes and behavior. It emphasizes the acceptance of attitudes that fit into our overall cognitive structure. Motivational approaches to attitudes maintain that we adopt attitudes that maximize our gains. Each side of an issue has costs and benefits, and motivational approaches maintain that an individual will adopt the side on which the net gains are greater. Finally, the elaboration likelihood model considers the conditions that lead us to argue against or passively accept a persuasive communication designed to change

our attitudes. These approaches are not necessarily contradictory or inconsistent with each other. Instead, they represent different theoretical orientations and emphasize different factors in explaining attitudes and attitude change.

Learning Theory

The **learning** approach began at Yale University with the work of Carl Hovland and associates (Hovland, Janis, & Kelley, 1953) during the 1950s. The assumption behind this approach is that attitudes are acquired in much the same way as other habits. People learn information and facts about different attitude objects, and they also learn the feelings and values associated with those facts. A child learns that an animal is a dog, that dogs are friendly, and that they are good. Finally, the child learns to like dogs. As can be seen, the child acquires both the cognitions and affects associated with the attitude object. Moreover, she or he learns them through the same processes and mechanisms that control other kinds of learning.

This means that basic learning processes should apply to the formation of attitudes. We acquire information and feelings by the process of **association.** If a history teacher shows us a picture of a mean-looking military man in a Stormtrooper uniform and says the word "Nazi" in a hostile voice, we form an association between negative feelings and the word "Nazi." The process of association leads to attitudes toward things as well as people, including the flag, political parties, or a bill pending in Congress.

Learning can also occur through **reinforcement** and **punishment.** If you take a class in psychology and get an A in it and enjoy it, the act of taking psychology classes is reinforced, and you are likely to take more such courses in the future. If you take a course and get an F, you are more likely to stay away from similar courses in the future.

Attitudes can also be learned through **imitation.** People imitate others, especially if those others are strong, important people. Consequently, a major source of basic political and social attitudes

Many important attitudes are acquired in early childhood. We associate our country with the patriotic activities we experienced as children. In particular, we may imitate the attitudes of others who are strong, important people in our lives.

in early life is the family. Children are likely to imitate their parents' attitudes. In adolescence, they are more likely to imitate peers' attitudes on many matters.

The learning approach to attitudes is relatively simple. It views people as primarily passive. They are exposed to stimuli, they learn through association, reinforcement, or imitation, and this learning process determines the person's attitude. The final attitude contains all of the associations, values, and other bits of information the individual has accumulated.

Learning theory accounts of attitude change and persuasion emphasize two main methods whereby attitudes may be acquired or changed: message learning and transfer of affect.

MESSAGE LEARNING. **Message learning** is regarded as crucial to attitude change. If a person learns a message, change should follow. This obvious point is nonetheless quite controversial. Learning a persuasive message is actually much less important to attitude change than we might expect. Most studies show only weak relationships between learning the content of a

persuasive communication, as assessed by memory for the information in it, and attitude change (Greenwald, 1968; McGuire, 1985; Chaiken & Stangor, 1987; Moser, 1992).

To be sure, it is vital that a listener know what position is being advocated. If the President is advocating military aid to a Central American nation, the listener must learn that, and not think that the President wants to send toys to Norway. But beyond this basic need to know what the communication is about, remembering the details of a message is not strongly related to how persuasive the message is.

TRANSFER OF AFFECT. Learning theory also suggests that people are persuaded when they transfer an affect from one object to another that is associated with it. To understand **transfer of affect,** imagine a television commercial for an automobile. To persuade you to have a positive attitude toward the car, it is associated with many other positive objects. We are not simply told how powerful, quiet, and comfortable the car is, we are shown beautiful women, handsome men, lovely children, or cute dogs in the background. Presumably, all these attractive features become associated with the car, thus increasing our positive feelings toward the car. In other words, people simply transfer the affect about one object (happy family life) to another (the car).

A test of the transfer of affect idea was conducted by Lorge (1936). He presented American students with the following message: "I hold that a little rebellion, now and then, is a good thing, and as necessary in the political world as storms are in the physical." He found that students agreed with the message when it was attributed to Thomas Jefferson, but disagreed with it when it was attributed to Lenin. Lorge argued that the positive affect associated with Jefferson transferred to the message and made it more positive, whereas the negative affect associated with Lenin transferred to the message when he was described as author, with the opposite effect. Later research has supported this transfer of affect idea in a wide variety of contexts, although it appears to work better for material with which people are relatively unfamiliar and less well when people are already familiar with the attitude objects (Cacioppo, Marshall-Goodell, Tassinary, & Petty, 1992).

Cognitive Consistency

The second major theoretical framework for studying attitudes and persuasion is **cognitive consistency.** The cognitive consistency tradition depicts people as striving for coherence and meaning in their cognitions. It argues that people who have several beliefs or values that are inconsistent with one another strive to make them consistent. Similarly, if their cognitions are already consistent and they are faced with a new cognition that would produce inconsistency, they strive to minimize the inconsistency. Trying to maintain or restore cognitive consistency is the primary motive underlying this perspective. There are several relevant theories, all of which emphasize the importance of cognitive consistency.

Balance Theory

The earliest consistency theory was **balance theory.** Balance theory considers the consistency among the affects within a simple cognitive system held by a person (Heider, 1958). Balance theory is usually described in terms of a person, another person, and an attitude object. There are three relevant evaluations: (1) the first person's evaluation of the other person, (2) the first person's evaluation of the attitude object, and (3) the other person's evaluation of the attitude object. For example, consider Michelle's attitudes toward her teacher and toward legalized abortion. If we consider only simple positive–negative feelings, there is a limited number of combinations of these elements. They are diagrammed in Figure 6-2, with the symbol *P* standing for Michelle (person), *O* for the teacher (other person), and *X* for legalized abortion (attitude object). The arrows indicate the targets of the feelings. A plus sign means a positive affect, and a minus sign means a negative one. The upper left triad shows that Michelle likes her teacher and that they both support legalized abortion.

The first assumption of balance theory is that some of these simple cognitive systems are cognitively balanced and others are not. The notion of balance comes originally from gestalt theories of perceptual organization. People try to achieve "good form" in their perceptions of others, just as they try to achieve "good form" or "good figures" in their perceptions of inanimate objects. Balanced relations between people fit; they go together; they make a sensible, coherent, meaningful picture. The main motive pushing people toward balance is trying to achieve a harmonious, simple, coherent, and meaningful view of social relationships. A balanced system is one in which you agree with a liked person or disagree with a disliked person. Imbalance exists when you disagree with a liked person or agree with a disliked person.

On the left side of Figure 6-2 are the four balanced situations—situations in which the relations among the elements are consistent with each other. When Michelle likes her teacher and both support abortion, the system is balanced. If Michelle likes her teacher and both oppose abortion, balance also exists: Neither supports abortion, and they are united in opposition to it. Nor is there a conflict if Michelle and her teacher disagree about abortion, but Michelle dislikes the teacher. The imbalanced systems occur when Michelle and her teacher like each other but disagree about abortion, or dislike each other and agree about it. The inconsistency lies in the fact

We acquire attitudes in part by association. A car paired with a beautiful woman, for example, leads us to feel that the car is a good one and that owning it will bring social rewards.

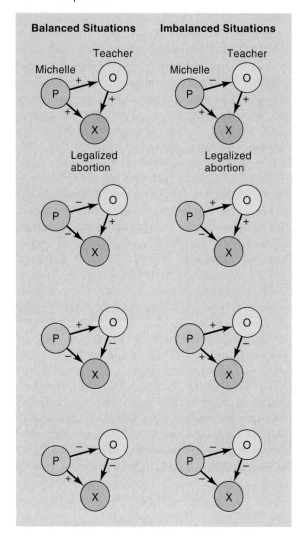

Balanced Situations **Imbalanced Situations**

Figure 6-2 The balance model. There are eight possible configurations of two people and one object. According to the model, the imbalanced structures tend to become balanced by a change in one or more elements.

that we expect those we like to have attitudes similar to ours, and we expect those we dislike to have different attitudes. In general, imbalance is present when the system has an odd number of negative relations.

The second assumption of the balance model is that imbalanced configurations tend to change toward balanced ones. This assumption gives the model its importance. Imbalanced systems produce pressures toward attitude change and continue this pressure until they are balanced. That is, the systems on the right side of

the figure will change toward becoming those on the left.

The change can occur in many ways. Balance theory uses a *least effort principle* to predict the direction of change. People will change as few affective relations as they can to produce a balanced system. Any of the relations may be altered to produce balance. For example, if Michelle supports abortion but the teacher does not, and Michelle likes the teacher, balance could be produced in several ways. Michelle could decide that she really does dislike the teacher or that she actually opposes abortion. Alternatively, she might distort reality by misperceiving that the teacher really supports abortion. Which mechanism is chosen depends on the ease of using it and on the individual doing the changing. The important point is that various possibilities exist.

Research on balance theory has generally supported these predictions: People do adjust imbalanced systems toward balance, and in ways that minimize the number of changes that must be made (Abelson et al., 1968). But balance pressures seem to be weaker when we dislike the other person than when we like him or her. Newcomb (1968) calls such situations "nonbalanced" rather than "imbalanced." He points out that we simply do not care very much whether we agree or disagree with someone we dislike; we just cut off the relationship and forget about the whole thing.

Aside from this, balance theory describes the notion of cognitive consistency in extremely simple terms and provides a convenient way of conceptualizing attitudes. It makes it clear that in a given situation there are various ways to resolve an inconsistency. It focuses our attention on one of the most important aspects of attitude change—the factors that determine which of various **modes of resolution** is adopted (Hummert, Crockett, & Kemper, 1990).

Cognitive Dissonance Theory

The most influential of the cognitive consistency theories has been **cognitive dissonance theory**, proposed by Leon Festinger (1957). Like other cognitive consistency theories, cognitive disso-

Balanced relations occur when people achieve good form in their perceptions of each other. Mary likes Sara, Sara likes Elaine, and Elaine likes Mary. They go together, making a sensible, coherent, and meaningful picture.

nance theory assumes that there is a pressure toward consistency. Dissonance theory deals especially with inconsistencies between one's attitudes and one's behavior. **Dissonance** is defined as an aversive motivational state that results when some behavior we engage in is inconsistent with our attitudes. Dissonance creates psychological tension, and people feel pressure to reduce or remove it. Reducing it means restoring consistency, or consonance. The main way of reducing dissonance, if the behavior cannot be revoked or changed in some way, is to

change our attitude. Dissonance theory has been explored in several specific situations.

DISSONANCE FOLLOWING A DECISION. One situation that almost always arouses dissonance is making a decision. When we must decide between two or more alternatives, the final choice is virtually always inconsistent with at least some of our beliefs. After we make the decision, all the good aspects of the unchosen alternative and all the bad aspects of the chosen alternative are inconsistent with the decision.

Dissonance can be reduced by improving our evaluation of the chosen alternative or by lowering our evaluation of the unchosen alternative. After making decisions, there is a tendency for us to increase our liking for what we chose and to decrease our liking for what we did not choose. A study by Brehm (1956) demonstrated this empirically. College women were shown eight products, such as a toaster, a stopwatch, and a radio, and were asked to indicate how much they would like to have each of them. They were then shown two of the eight products and told they would be given whichever they chose. After the objects were chosen and the subjects received the one they had selected, they were asked to rate all the objects again. As shown in Table 6-1, on the second rating there was a strong tendency for the women in the high-dissonance condition to increase their eval-

TABLE 6-1
Dissonance Reduction Following a Decision

Condition	Rating of Chosen Object	Rating of Unchosen Object	Total Dissonance Reduction
High dissonance (objects initially rated close)	+.32	−.53	+.85
Low dissonance (objects initially rated far apart)	+.25	−.12	+.37
No dissonance (gift with no choice)	.00	None	.00

Note: The entries in the first two columns are the mean changes in evaluation of the chosen and unchosen objects from before to after the decision. The difference between the two is the total amount of dissonance reduction, shown in the third column.
Source: Brehm (1956).

uation of the item they had picked and to decrease their evaluation of the rejected item.

In a no-dissonance control group (shown on the bottom line in the table), instead of choosing between two items and receiving their preference, the women were simply given one of the products they had rated favorably. When they rerated all the products, they showed no tendency to improve the evaluation of the object they owned. This condition demonstrates that the reevaluation in the high-dissonance condition was not simply due to pride of ownership; making the decision was the critical factor.

The tendency toward reevaluation is particularly strong when the two alternatives are initially rated close in attractiveness. Brehm tested this notion also. In the high-dissonance condition he gave the women a choice between a product they had ranked high and one they had ranked next best. In the low-dissonance condition the women were given a choice between a high-ranked product and one they ranked as much inferior. As shown in Table 6-1, the high-dissonance condition generated considerably more dissonance reduction.

In the Brehm study, dissonance was created by choosing between two alternatives. But postdecisional dissonance can also be produced when we commit ourselves to a single course of action. This point was dramatically illustrated in a classic study of a doomsday group that predicted the world was going to end on a particular day, and believed that they would be saved by a ship from outer space. In the book describing this unusual group, *When Prophecy Fails* (Festinger, Riecken, & Schachter, 1956), the authors observed the group members' reactions to their own prophecy and, more importantly, to its ultimate failure (that is, the world did not end as they expected). In the days and weeks after making their original prediction, group members sold many of their belongings and prepared for the end of the world. When the fateful day arrived and passed without the world being destroyed, they were initially greatly shaken. Their response, however, was not to give up their beliefs and return to normal life. They could not have reduced dissonance by knowing that nothing had come of all the effort they had put into their plans. Instead, they

decided that the day had been put off, and that the end of the world was still coming soon. Moreover, they began to argue that their efforts had actually postponed the end of the world, and they became very active in trying to get new supporters to their cause. Presumably this helped reduce their dissonance by justifying their original behavior.

Part of the appeal of cognitive dissonance theory is that it often makes counterintuitive predictions. In this case, common sense might have suggested that the group would give up after its prediction had failed so miserably. But dissonance theory predicts that this disproof would lead them not to abandon the theory, but rather to argue it even more forcefully. And that is just what happened.

COUNTERATTITUDINAL BEHAVIOR. Cognitive dissonance theory has also been applied to the effects of counterattitudinal behavior, also called **attitude-discrepant behavior.** When a person holds a belief and performs an act inconsistent with it, dissonance is produced. Because it is difficult to take back the action itself, the dissonance typically must be relieved by changing the attitude.

For example, many people enter law school because they believe they can help the poor and needy, and improve society. Yet when they later go into legal practice, most of them find that it involves repetitive and routine work that has more to do with business contracts and tax advantages than helping the poor and needy. These once idealistic individuals then find themselves justifying and even enjoying what they do. They may come to believe that nothing much can be done to help the poor, and even that they do not deserve much help. Why the change?

Dissonance theory would argue that they began engaging in attitude-discrepant behavior when they first got a job, because that was the condition of the job. To get paid, they had to work long hours on relatively uninspiring drudgery. But this created dissonance: Their behavior was inconsistent with their attitudes. So with time, they adjusted their attitudes to become more consistent with their behavior.

But dissonance, and consequent attitude

These Vietnam veterans did not support the war in which they fought. What prevented military service from producing dissonance-reducing pro-war attitude change?

change, is not always generated by engaging in attitude-discrepant behavior. Many young American men who were drafted to fight in Vietnam did not believe in the value of the war. And many of them continued to be quite opposed to it throughout their service, despite engaging in various attitude-discrepant behaviors required of soldiers on active duty. Thus, much of the research on this topic has tried to distinguish the conditions under which attitude-discrepant behavior produces dissonance-reducing attitude change from conditions in which it does not.

The most interesting prediction of dissonance theory concerns the level of incentive required to produce attitude change. On the one hand,

there has to be enough incentive to make a person commit a counterattitudinal act. But if there is too much pressure on the individual, or too much incentive to perform the discrepant act, there is no inconsistency, and very little dissonance is produced. Paradoxically, then, after a certain point, the more incentive for performing a counterattitudinal behavior, the less we will change our attitude to justify having done it.

Suppose you are offered a menial summer job but the pay is extremely good, such as day labor on a construction site. You would experience no dissonance, and so you should feel no pressure to reevaluate your job. It is a crummy job, but at least you earn good money. But suppose you were working at a menial job in the local hospital. In that case dissonance would be created, because the job is crummy and you aren't getting paid much either. You might reduce your dissonance by reevaluating the job. Perhaps you start to think that it is an educational experience, that you are doing good things for people who need your help, or that you have met some very interesting people.

An early study to demonstrate the effect of insufficient justification on attitude change was conducted by Festinger and Carlsmith (1959). Students participating in an experiment worked on an exceedingly dull task. After they had completed it, the experimenter explained that he was studying the effect of preconceptions on performance. He explained that some people were told ahead of time that the task was interesting, others were told the task was boring, and yet a third group was told nothing at all. The experimenter then asked the subject to help him out by giving the next subject favorable information about the task before performing it.

At this point, the key experimental manipulation was introduced. Some subjects were told the experimenter would pay them $1 for helping and others were told they would be paid $20. Virtually all the subjects agreed to describe the task to the next subject as very enjoyable. There was also a control group, the members of which were not asked to lie. Soon afterward, the experimenter had all the subjects indicate how much they had actually enjoyed the task.

Those who were paid $1 rated the task more positively than did those who were paid $20

TABLE 6-2
Positive Attitudes Resulting from
Attitude-Discrepant Behavior

		Dependent Variable
Condition	Enjoyment of Task	Willingness to Participate in Similar Experiments
$1 reward	+1.35	+1.20
$20 reward	−.05	−.25

Note: A positive number indicates greater enjoyment of the task or greater willingness to participate in similar experiments.
Source: Adapted from Festinger & Carlsmith (1959).

(Table 6-2). They found the task more enjoyable and were more willing to participate in other similar experiments, despite being paid less money to do it. This is what dissonance theory would predict. The larger amount of money served as a sufficient reason for performing the task; therefore, little dissonance was experienced. However, the subjects receiving only a dollar for misrepresenting the task to the next subject had insufficient justification for what they were doing; they experienced dissonance, and they resolved their dissonance by changing their attitude toward the task. Many similar experiments have been conducted, obtaining similar results. There is some debate over exactly why the insufficient justification effect occurs (Freedman, Cunningham, & Krismer, 1992), but the effect of insufficient justification on dissonance reduction is well supported.

THREATS. In principle, negative incentives ought to work exactly the same way as positive incentives. One way to try to get people to perform disliked tasks is to threaten them with punishment. If we do not wear a tie to work or pay our income taxes or do our homework, we are penalized. Threats are also used to prevent people from doing things they may want to do. For stealing cookies from the cookie jar, playing with a forbidden toy, driving too fast, or selling cocaine, we may be punished. The severity of possible punishments varies enormously. We may get a mild reprimand, miss dessert, be fined $100, spend five years in jail, or even face execution.

But greater threat should produce less dissonance and so less attitude change. In an experiment designed to test this idea, children were shown a group of toys and then forbidden to play with a particularly desirable toy (Aronson & Carlsmith, 1963). They were threatened with either mild or severe punishment if they played with the forbidden toy. The children were then left alone in the room with the toys, and the amount of time they spent playing with the forbidden toy was assessed. After playing with the toys, they were asked how much they liked them, including the forbidden toy. What would dissonance theory predict? Children who were severely threatened would not be expected to play with the toy, but also should not devalue the toy either. After all, they know why they are not playing with it: They have been threatened with punishment. However, children who received a mild threat do not have a sufficient justification for avoiding the toy, and consequently, when asked to rerate the toys, might reevaluate the toy, deciding that it wasn't all that attractive anyway. This is, in fact, what the experimenters found. The children reduced their evaluation of the forbidden toy more under mild threat than under severe threat.

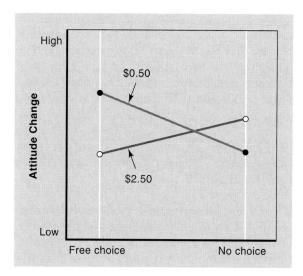

Figure 6-3 The effects of incentive and choice on attitude change. (*Source:* Linder, Cooper, & Jones, 1967.)

CHOICE. Another major contributor to dissonance is the feeling of *choice* about the behavior. Attitude-discrepant behavior creates dissonance only when the behavior is freely chosen (or at least the person feels it is freely chosen). This is shown quite clearly in a study by Linder, Cooper, and Jones (1967). Students wrote an essay that disagreed with their opinions. Some subjects were made to feel they had a choice about whether or not they wrote the essay; others were given no choice. Half the subjects in each condition were paid $2.50, and half were paid $0.50. The amount of attitude change in the four conditions is shown in Figure 6-3.

With free choice, the typical dissonance effect appeared. There was more change with less incentive. With no choice, the dissonance effect did not obtain. There was more change with greater incentive. So the feeling of choice about one's behavior is a critical precondition for the occurrence of attitude change produced by one's dissonant behavior.

IRREVOCABLE COMMITMENT. Another key to attitude change as a dissonance-reducing mechanism is the person's **commitment** to the decision or behavior. As long as we feel irreversibly committed to a course of action, dissonance pro-

motes attitude change. But if we feel that we can get out of the decision if it works out badly, or that we can do it half-heartedly, or that we may not have to go through with it at all, dissonance will not be present, and no attitude change may occur.

FORESEEABLE CONSEQUENCES. For dissonance to occur, people need to believe that they could have foreseen the negative consequences of their decisions. If a classmate decides to walk to class on the left side of the street rather than the right side, and as she walks along a brick suddenly falls off a roof and hits her on the head, this is a terrible misfortune. But she should not experience dissonance. "I chose to walk on the left side of the street" is not dissonant with "a brick hit me on the head." The two cognitions are not relevant to each other. On the other hand, if she knew that there was some chance that she would get hit on the head, perhaps because there was high-rise construction on that side of the street, dissonance would probably be aroused.

In a test of this point, Goethals, Cooper, and Naficy (1979) asked students at Princeton to record speeches favoring the doubling of the size of the freshman class. (This was a disagreeable possibility to the subjects, given Princeton's reputation as a relatively small, elite college.) Some students were told the speech might be given to the board of admissions, which was considering such an increase (foreseen consequences); others were told that it would be given to some groups, but the groups were not named (foreseeable consequences). Still others were not told of any further use of the speech (unforeseen consequences). After the speech was recorded, all were told that their counterattitudinal speech would be given to the board of admissions.

Under what circumstances did the subjects change their attitudes in the dissonance-reducing direction of their speech? Either foreseen or foreseeable consequences promoted attitude change in the direction of the subject's speech. Only unforeseeable consequences did not.

RESPONSIBILITY FOR CONSEQUENCES. The importance of perceived choice is that it brings with it perceived responsibility for all consequences, whether or not it is "logical" to feel responsible for them. If decision makers feel responsible for the consequences, then dissonance occurs whether the consequences could reasonably have been foreseen or not. If they feel no responsibility for the outcome, there is no dissonance, regardless of how disastrous the results.

In one study (Pallak, Sogin, & Van Zante, 1974), a boring task was reevaluated in a more favorable direction, consistent with dissonance reduction, even when the negative consequences (learning that the task was just wasted time) were not known until after the task was completed—as long as the subject completed it under high perceived choice. This effect seems to occur because people make internal attributions for their behavior, and consequently see themselves as responsible for any outcomes associated with it (Sogin & Pallak, 1976).

So the critical question regarding unforeseen negative consequences is whether or not people feel their prior behavior was responsible for bringing those consequences about. That is why perceived choice is so important. When we choose something that works out badly, we feel responsible for the outcome, and it creates dissonance. Indeed, some psychologists now argue that perceived personal responsibility for aversive consequences is so important in producing attitude change that it does not even matter whether the behavior is counterattitudinal or not. Even acts that are consistent with our attitudes should produce attitude change (strengthening our prior attitudes), if they produce bad outcomes and we feel responsible for the acts (Scher & Cooper, 1989).

EFFORT. The more effort one takes in executing behavioral acts that have aversive consequences, the more dissonance should be aroused. If you volunteer for the Marine Corps and basic training is exhausting, painful, and stressful, then dissonance should be created: You should think more and more that you made the right choice and love the Marine Corps. The attitude change helps to justify the effort you have expended (or even expect to expend; see Wicklund, Cooper, & Linder, 1967).

These, then, are the main preconditions for cognitive dissonance, and for the attitude change that results from taking decisive action: minimum incentives, perceived choice, irrevocable commitment, foreseeable consequences, personal responsibility for those consequences, and great effort.

Self-Perception Theory: A Challenge to Dissonance

Cognitive dissonance theory originally inspired research on the effects of behavior on attitude change, and for a number of years provided the only theoretical interpretation of these findings. Bem (1967) then offered another interpretation: **self-perception theory.** As we saw in the last chapter, he argued that often we do not really know what our attitudes are and simply infer them from our own behavior and the circumstances in which this behavior occurs. If we choose to eat oranges from a basket of seven kinds of fruit and somebody asks us how we feel about oranges, we say to ourselves, "I just chose oranges; nobody forced me to; therefore, I must really like oranges." Accordingly, we tell the person we like oranges.

It is easy to see how this might apply to attitude-discrepant behavior. A subject is paid $1 to tell someone that a particular task was very enjoyable. When the subject is subsequently asked how enjoyable he himself thought the task was, he says to himself: "I said that the task was enjoyable and I was paid only one dollar. One dollar is not enough to make me lie, so I must really think that the task is enjoyable." On the other hand, $20 is perhaps a sufficient amount to tell a small lie. So the subject then might say to himself, "The reason I said it was enjoyable was just to get the $20; I didn't really believe it." Thus, self-perception theory makes the same predictions as dissonance theory; the more people are paid to make a discrepant statement, the less they will believe it.

Note that cognitive dissonance theory and self-perception theory make the same prediction, but for entirely different reasons. The two theories offer radically different views of attitudes and of the way in which behavior influences attitudes. The traditional view of attitudes reflected in dissonance theory is that they are strong, enduring predispositions. When people engage in counterattitudinal behavior, they suffer from unpleasant tensions that can be relieved only by giving up these cherished attitudes. Bem's self-perception theory suggests that our expressions of attitudes are, instead, rather casual verbal statements. We have no great stake in our attitudes; rather, we seem simply to be trying to cooperate with a curious questioner by giving a plausible answer, without strong conviction or feelings. So we readily change our superficial answers.

Dissonance theorists at first reacted with horror to Bem's reinterpretation. Their initial response was to try to design experiments that would disprove Bem's interpretations. This proved to be surprisingly difficult. Today, social psychologists assume that both processes occur on some occasions. The question is, when is one more likely to occur than the other?

The self-perception process should be most likely to occur when our attitudes are vague and ambiguous. It would not be surprising if we should arrive at an attitude about a new and unfamiliar laboratory task on the basis of our perceptions of our behavior in the experimental situation. It would be more surprising if we were to use self-perception to figure out our attitude about our favorite foods, like broiled lobster, sushi, or pizza with anchovies. We do not need to feel ourselves salivate or watch ourselves devour every last morsel to know that we love those things.

Self-perception theory works, then, when people do not possess well-defined prior attitudes (Taylor, 1975). To test this, Chaiken and Baldwin (1981) separated subjects with strong, consistent attitudes toward the environment (concerning nuclear power, solar energy, outlawing nonreturnable soft drink bottles, aerosol cans, and so on) from those with weak, inconsistent attitudes. Then they varied whether the subjects perceived their own usual behavior as pro- or anti-environment. They did this by manipulating subjects' perceptions of their own behavior. For example, a person asked "Have you ever recycled a soft drink can?" is likely to say, "Yes," and perceive herself as pro-environ-

mental. Someone asked "Do you always recycle your soft drink cans?" is likely to answer, "No," and may feel that she is not very supportive of the environment.

The hypothesis that the self-perception process would work only for those without strong and well-defined prior attitudes was quite strongly supported. Among the subjects whose prior attitudes were strong and highly consistent, the manipulation of self-reported environmentalist behaviors had no significant effect on attitudes, as shown in Figure 6-4. However, among those with initially weak and inconsistent attitudes, the manipulation had the effect predicted by Bem's self-perception theory: People who had been induced to perceive their behavior as pro-environment perceived themselves as being more pro-environmental in their attitudes than did those induced to describe their behavior as more anti-environment.

The conclusion is that self-perception theory holds primarily for individuals who do not possess well-defined prior attitudes. People who have had few prior experiences with respect to the attitude issue (Wood, 1982) or little prior experience with the attitude objects (Tybout & Scott, 1983) tend to infer their attitudes from the observation of their behavior. On the other

Figure 6-4 Attitudes toward environmentalism as a function of induced reports of own behavior and prior attitude strength.

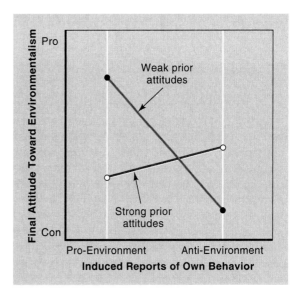

hand, when people do have well-defined prior attitudes, we might expect the dissonance process rather than the self-perception process to operate.

Another aspect of this controversy concerns whether dissonance actually produces an uncomfortable drive state. Whereas cognitive dissonance theory argues that it does, Bem's analysis maintains that attitude-discrepant behavior should not arouse any particular discomfort or drive. Fortunately, this question is testable. If dissonance is a drive, then it should result in physiological arousal. To test this point, Elkin and Leippe (1986) had students write counterattitudinal essays, varying choice and effort. The high-choice, high-effort condition should have produced the most dissonance. These authors found that both choice and effort produced greater physiological arousal, in terms of galvanic skin response.

Recall from our discussion of misattribution in the last chapter that subjective arousal states can sometimes be reduced if we can be induced to attribute them to other stimuli. If dissonance is an arousal state, it should also be amenable to misattribution. Specifically, no attitude change should occur if dissonance-based arousal can be attributed to some other cause. To test this, Zanna and Cooper (1974) gave subjects a pill; in one condition they were told the pill would make them feel tense, and in the other, that it would make them feel relaxed. Subjects were then induced to write counterattitudinal essays under either high- or low-choice conditions.

Subjects who were told they would feel tense because of the pill showed no dissonance effect; that is, high choice produced no more attitude change than low choice. Presumably the subject could attribute arousal to the pill, and therefore there was no dissonance and no dissonance-produced attitude change. However, when subjects were told the pill would make them feel relaxed, the high-choice condition produced more attitude change in the direction of the essay than did the low-choice condition, in line with the usual dissonance effect. Presumably the subject could not attribute arousal to the pill, because it was supposedly a relaxation pill. This study provides additional evidence that dissonance

effects do depend on some kind of aversive arousal mechanism, which can be eliminated or reduced if the subject can attribute arousal to some extraneous stimulus (see also Losch & Cacioppo, 1990).

In short, both cognitive dissonance theory and self-perception theory explain attitude change under particular circumstances: dissonance theory with more controversial, involving issues, and self-perception theory with more vague, uninvolving, minor, or novel issues.

Other Consistency Principles

COGNITION AND AFFECT. People not only try to make their cognitions consistent with their behavior, they also try to make their cognitions consistent with their affects. That is, our beliefs are determined in part by our affective preferences, and vice versa. Suppose a voter doesn't really know anything about the new governor but develops a strong negative affect toward him because he can't stand his voice. Consistency theory suggests the voter will then acquire the cognitions necessary to support that negative evaluation. He may begin to believe the governor is incompetent, has misguided policies, and is surrounded by dishonest cronies. In other words, people will alter their beliefs and sense of the facts to fit their evaluative preferences, even if they do not have any good, new information that would justify doing so.

Rosenberg (1960) provided a striking demonstration of the cognitive changes created by a change in affect toward an attitude object. He obtained from white subjects a comprehensive description of their attitudes toward blacks, racial integration, and the whole question of relations between blacks and whites. He then hypnotized the subjects and told them that their attitude toward blacks moving into their community was the opposite of what it had previously been. For example, subjects who had previously been strongly against integrated housing were told they now favored it. The subjects were then awakened from their hypnotic trance and questioned about their current attitudes about blacks and integration.

Rosenberg found that the change in this one affect he had produced under hypnosis was followed by many dramatic reversals in the subjects' cognitions relevant to integration. For example, the subjects who had originally been opposed to integrated housing came to believe integration was necessary to remove racial inequality, that it was the only fair thing to do, and so on. These ramifying changes tended to reduce the inconsistency that had resulted from the induced affective change. The important point is that he changed their affects without supplying any new cognitions or changing any old ones, since he did it by hypnotic induction. As the theories of cognitive consistency would predict, the pressures toward reducing inconsistency resulted in a variety of cognitive changes once affect had been changed.

This process is important because many attitudes are acquired as strong affects without many supporting cognitions. For example, many children grow up liking the Democratic Party because their parents are Democrats, loving the country because they were born in it, and so on. As they grow older, they come up with supporting cognitions to justify these attitudes that originally were based solely on affective preferences.

CONSISTENCY: A CULTURAL CAVEAT. As can be seen, consistency has been an important principle in theories of attitudes, and as we will see, it is also important to research on persuasion. Recently, however, cautions have emerged to suggest that consistency among attitudes, between cognitions and affect, and between attitudes and behavior, may not be as important as theorists and researchers have assumed.

In particular, a concern with being consistent may be characteristic of Western attitudes, that is, the attitudes of Americans and Western Europeans, but not nearly as characteristic of Easterners. For example, in Japan, where concern is less focused on individual attitudes than on interdependency and responsiveness to social situations, the need for consistency and expressions of consistency can be quite low (Markus & Kitayama, 1991). In their social interactions, Japanese may express quite different attitudes, depending on the situation they are in, because they feel that those with whom they are interacting will appreciate those particular attitudes. Americans, on the other hand, are more likely to express consistent attitudes across situations (Ouchi, 1981). To Americans, the Japanese behavior can appear shifty and unprincipled, whereas to the Japanese, the American stubborn adherence to a particular position may appear rude and insensitive to social norms. Other so-called interdependent cultures may similarly place a lower value on consistency than is true in Western societies.

Generally speaking, then, the perception that consistency is an important principle of attitudes is beginning to wane. In addition to the substantial cross-cultural differences, there is evidence that even Westerners are able to tolerate substantial degrees of inconsistency among their attitudes, which does not appear to have the adverse effects that dissonance theory and other consistency theories have described. Consistency, then, may be more of a value than a fundamental cognitive principle, and thus its importance concerning attitudinal phenomena will vary directly with the value placed on consistency. Another example of the importance of values and attitudes appears in the CULTURAL HIGHLIGHT.

Expectancy-Value Theory

People often respond to persuasive communications in terms of incentives, that is, the costs or benefits associated with particular attitude positions. According to this theory, attitude formation and change is a process of weighing the pros and cons of various possible attitudes on a topic and then adopting the best alternative. This approach is best embodied in **expectancy-value theory** (Edwards, 1954).

Expectancy-value theory assumes that people adopt a position based on their thoughtful assessment of its pros and cons, that is, on the basis of the values of its possible effects. But it adds the notion that people take into consideration not only the value but also the likelihood of its possible effects. People adopt positions that

CULTURAL HIGHLIGHT

American Views of Equality and Achievement

Do you believe that America is the land of equality? Do you believe that anyone can get ahead by taking advantage of opportunities and working hard enough? Surveys show that the overwhelming majority of Americans—rich and poor, male and female, black and white—answer yes to both of these questions (Kluegel & Smith, 1986; Kluegel, 1990). The questions represent two of the most cherished values we hold, equality and achievement.

Equality and achievement have historically provided the foundation of American institutions (Lipset, 1963). On the one hand, the value of equality has made the American dream theoretically within the reach of everyone. On the other hand, the value placed on achievement virtually ensures that some people will be more successful than others. How do we resolve the apparent contradiction between these two values and the attitudes that derive from them?

We learn from an early age that America is the land of opportunity, a place where everyone is equal. As we grow up and learn that everyone is not equal, rather than change our values, we change the attitudes that bolster those values, explaining away threats to these

deeply cherished views. For example, most Americans acknowledge that the poor, African-Americans, and women are substantially disadvantaged relative to white men (Kluegel & Smith, 1986). How are these perceptions reconciled with views of equality and achievement?

The poor, women, and African-Americans are often regarded as not having taken advantage of the opportunities available to everyone else. When asked what the chances are for different groups getting ahead, 66 percent of Americans say that people who grew up in poor families have at least an average or better-than-average chance of getting ahead; 92 percent of Americans believe that growing up in a working-class family gives you an average or better-than-average chance of getting ahead; 73 percent of Americans say that African-Americans have an average or better-than-average chance of getting ahead; and 60 percent believe that women have an average or better-than-average chance of getting ahead. There is, apparently, blatant unawareness or disregard for the barriers that keep the poor, blacks, and women from having the same opportunities that the average American white male has.

Americans believe that if the poor, blacks, and women only tried harder, they would do better. For example, in a survey when Americans were asked to choose between two response options, "black people may not have the same opportunities as whites" or "blacks haven't prepared themselves enough to make use of the opportunities that come their way," 90 percent of respondents chose the latter alternative (Kluegel & Smith, 1986). Even when racism and sexism are acknowledged as barriers to the achievement of African-Americans and women, they tend to be perceived as rooted in the behavior of specific racist or sexist individuals, and not intrinsic to the American economic system. Blacks and women themselves endorse similar positions, although to a somewhat lesser extent than white males (Kluegel & Smith, 1986).

These observations illustrate the very important point that attitudes are formed and remain stable because they serve psychological functions for an individual. When attitudes are in service of important values, even blatantly contradictory evidence may be distorted or explained away, so that the fundamental values themselves need not be questioned.

would most likely lead to good effects, and reject positions that would most likely lead to bad effects. Stated more formally, the theory assumes that in adopting attitudes, people try to maximize the subjective utility of the various expected outcomes, which is the product of (1) the *value* of a particular outcome and (2) the *expectancy* that this position will produce that outcome.

Suppose you are trying to decide whether to go to your friend's party tonight. The expectancy-value analysis is presented in Table 6-3. You would try to think of the various possible outcomes of going to the party (dance, drink beer, not study for tomorrow's midterm, meet someone new), the values of those outcomes (enjoy the dancing, drinking beer, and meeting someone new, get a hangover, and do badly on the midterm), and the expectancy of those outcomes (certain to dance and to get a terrible grade, but unlikely to meet anyone new at a small party). Taking both expectancy and value into consideration, it's time to start studying: An inevitable terrible grade is not balanced by a little fun dancing and drinking.

The expectancy-value approach is similar to the learning approach in that the attitude is determined more or less by a sum of the positive and negative elements. One difference is that expectancy-value theories ignore the individual's past history and consider only the current balance of incentives. Another difference is that expectancy-value theories emphasize what people have to gain or lose by taking a particular position. Whether or not their friends would like them, how enjoyable the experience is, and so forth are the critical considerations. When there are conflicting goals, people adopt the position that maximizes their gains. A third difference is that the expectancy-value approach treats people as calculating, active, rational decision makers. In contrast, the learning approach treats people as more emotional and possibly controlled by the environment.

Cognitive Response Theory

Cognitive response theory (Greenwald, 1968; Petty, Ostrom, & Brock, 1981) seeks to understand attitudes and attitude change processes by understanding the thoughts that people generate in response to persuasive communications. The theory assumes that people react to various aspects of a particular position with positive or negative thoughts (or cognitive responses).

TABLE 6-3
Go to the Party or Study? An Expectancy–Value Analysis

	Value	×	Expectancy	=	Subjective Utility
Choice 1—Go to party					
Dance	+2	×	3	=	+6
Meet someone new	+3	×	1	=	+3
Drink beer	+1	×	3	=	+3
Get hangover	−3	×	2	=	−6
Do poorly on midterm	−3	×	3	=	−9
Total attitude					−3
Choice 2—Study					
Improve midterm grade	+3	×	3	=	+9
Be bored	−1	×	1	=	−1
No hangover	+2	×	3	=	+6
Total attitude					+14

Note: Value is on a +3 (very good) to −3 (very bad) scale; expectancy, on a 3 (certain to happen) to 0 (certain not to happen) scale; subjective utility is the product of value and expectancy.

These thoughts, in turn, determine whether or not the individual will support the position.

Suppose you listen to a televised speech by a senator who advocates cutting government Medicare payments to the elderly, and you might say to yourself, "But what about retired people on small pensions, or people who can't support themselves, like the handicapped or the poor? Somebody has to support these people, and government programs are about the only way to do it." These negative cognitive responses would mean that you are unlikely to adopt the senator's position. But if you said to yourself, "That's right. Taxes are too high, and those programs are probably just paying for extravagant hospital costs for people who should pay their own medical bills anyway," you are likely to support the speaker's position. The key assumption of the cognitive response viewpoint is that people are active processors of information who generate cognitive responses to messages, rather than passive recipients of the messages they happen to be exposed to.

Cognitive response theory predicts that attitude change will depend on how much and what kind of **counterarguing** a message triggers. If the message stimulates strong and effective counterarguing, resistance to change will follow. Conversely, persuasion can be produced by interfering with the counterarguing process. If we cannot think of any good counterarguments or can be distracted from thinking about them while listening to a message, the communication is more likely to be accepted.

Sometimes we are quite lazy and not motivated to analyze the pros and cons of complex arguments. Other times, however, we are motivated to learn arguments, sift through them for the points that meet our needs, and counterargue if we disagree with them. To take account of this contrast, Petty and Cacioppo (1986) developed the **elaboration likelihood model** of persuasion, which analyzes cognitive responses to persuasive communications. They argue that people can respond to a communication in either a thoughtful, deliberate way or in a more automatic, emotional way. They propose that, under some circumstances, people are motivated to engage in thoughtful consideration of the pros and cons of an argument, whereas

under other conditions, they are not. Under other conditions, people are likely to draw their conclusions from peripheral cues associated with the communication but irrelevant to the merits of the arguments. These include the attractiveness and prestige of the source or the pleasantness of the context (e.g., a beautiful woman or a handsome man smoking the advertised brand of cigarette).

Petty and Cacioppo draw a distinction between central routes to persuasion and peripheral routes to persuasion. Detailed information processing and reviewing and evaluation of arguments characterize the central route to persuasion. When people draw on more superficial peripheral cues without thoughtful consideration of the real arguments, this is termed the peripheral route to persuasion. In a similar vein, Chaiken (1980, 1987) has described **systematic processing,** which involves careful scanning and consideration of arguments from heuristic processing, which involves using simple decision rules, such as the idea that longer arguments are stronger or that consensus implies that a position is correct.

The distinction between central and peripheral processing has become a major one in attitude change research. It is of particular importance because it bears directly on the question of how rationally we respond to persuasion attempts. Does the perceiver care about the quality and price of a product, or just about the "hype" that advertising specialists surround it with? Does the voter respond to real issues and real qualities of the candidates, or just to superficial images presented on television? The answer is that we do both under different circumstances. These circumstances are covered in Table 6-4 and will be elucidated in the sections on persuasion that follow.

PERSUASION

With this theoretical background in mind, we now turn directly to the important topic of persuasion. While our attitudes on a given topic are intrinsically interesting, attitudes become even more important in the context of persuasion. Persuasion is ubiquitous in our society.

TABLE 6-4
**When Does Systematic Processing Take Place
and When are Peripheral Cues Used?**

Category of Independent Variable	Conditions Promoting	
	Systematic Processing	Use of Peripheral Cues
Source	Number of independent sources	Likability Physical attractiveness Expertise
Message	Repetition Rhetorical questions/arguments Written message High discrepancy	Length of message Number of arguments Video message
Target	Issue involvement Need for cognition Prior information	Response involvement
Situation	Forewarning Distraction Intent to persuade	Audience response Pleasant mood music Attractive models/actors

Advertisers attempt to convince us that their product is better than others. Politicians try to convince us that they deserve our votes. Citizens groups attempt to influence our attitudes toward the environment, abortion, busing, and other heated topics of the day. When do people adhere to their original attitudes in the face of a persuasive communication, and when do they respond to a persuasive communication and change their attitudes? Figure 6-5 presents a model of the persuasion process, which will guide our discussion of the variables involved in successful persuasion.

The Communicator

The first thing we notice in a communication situation is the communicator, or the source. Some communicators are authoritative, like a high school teacher or a scientist. Others may be humorous, like the football players at a crowded bar, urging us to buy a particular beer. One of the most straightforward and reliable findings in attitude research is that the more favorably people evaluate the communicator, the more likely they are to evaluate the communication favorably and to modify their attitudes in the

direction of the communication. This follows directly from the transfer of affect idea in learning approaches to attitudes. Evaluations of communicators, whether positive or negative, transfer to the positions they advocate. Several aspects of a communicator influence whether or not the communicator is evaluated favorably.

CREDIBILITY. People are more persuaded by highly credible communicators than by those low in credibility. The first study of **credibility** to demonstrate this effect was a classic paper by Hovland and Weiss (1952). Subjects heard communications on issues such as the advisability of selling antihistamines without a prescription or whether the steel industry was to blame for the steel shortage. Each communication came from either a high- or a low-credibility source. For example, the communication on antihistamines was said to come either from *The New England Journal of Medicine* or from a monthly mass-circulation pictorial magazine. The results indicated that communications attributed to high-credibility sources produced more attitude change than those from low-credibility sources.

The importance of high credibility in a source has been demonstrated many times and is no longer controversial. Subsequent research has

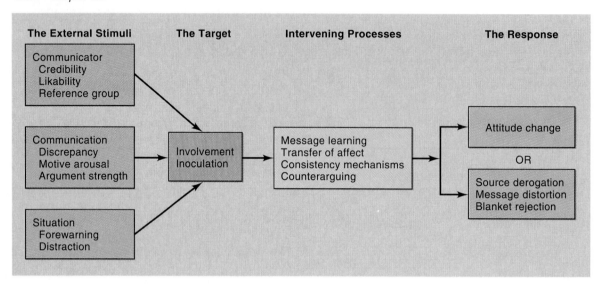

Figure 6-5 Model of the persuasion process.

suggested, however, that there are two separate components of credibility, namely expertise and trustworthiness (Hovland & Weiss, 1952).

EXPERTISE. Expert sources are typically more persuasive than nonexpert sources. In a typical study of this point, subjects were told they were participating in a study on aesthetics, and were asked to evaluate nine stanzas from obscure modern poems. They then read someone else's evaluation of the stanzas they had not liked very much. The communicator argued that the poem was better than the subject had indicated. The crucial variable was the source of the communication. For some subjects it was represented as the poet T. S. Eliot, whereas for others it was represented as a student at Mississippi State Teachers College. After reading the communication, the subjects reevaluated the poems. There was more change in response to the high-credibility communicator, namely T. S. Eliot, than with the low-credibility communication (Aronson, Turner, & Carlsmith, 1963).

The question of expertise raises additional interesting questions not yet fully answered. First, how far can experts in one field transfer the influence of their expertise to other fields? Are great scientists or athletes or rock musicians persuasive on issues such as international poli-

tics or which brand of panty hose to purchase? The transfer of affect notion might suggest that they would be. But the question of how far expertise transfers has not yet been fully addressed.

A second question concerns the process by which expertise works. Does it motivate the listener to pay closer attention to the arguments and be more persuaded by their merits? Or is expertise just a simple cue that allows one to change one's attitude without expending any energy in processing the details of the argument? We will return to this question shortly.

TRUSTWORTHINESS. Regardless of expertise, it is important that a communicator be perceived as unbiased and trustworthy. One way that communicators can bring this about is to argue for positions that would seem to be contrary to their self-interest. Consider a situation in which a district attorney and a criminal are each making statements about whether or not law enforcement agencies should be strengthened. Normally, a district attorney should be seen as better informed and more prestigious than a criminal, and therefore more persuasive. In a study by Walster, Aronson, Abrahams, and Rottman (1966), this is exactly what happened— as long as the speaker was advocating less power for law enforcement agencies. With that position, the district attorney was much more persuasive than the convicted criminal, as shown in Figure 6-6. But what if the criminal takes a position against his own self-interest and argues in favor of strengthened law enforcement? In this case, the criminal becomes quite persuasive and, indeed, even matches the persuasive power of the district attorney.

How do we decide whether a communicator is trustworthy? The audience's judgments are based on attributions of the speaker's statement. As we saw in Chapter 4, we are especially likely to make dispositional attributions when another person's statement is consistent with expectations derived from his or her past behavior. When a criminal says he is against strengthening law enforcement agencies, we assume that he makes this statement because he is a criminal, and it is to his personal advancement to have weak law enforcement agencies. When a communicator says something contrary to expectations, however, we are more likely to make an attribution to the entity, namely the issue itself. If the criminal argues in favor of strengthened law enforcement agencies, we are likely to assume that he knows the weaknesses

Figure 6-6 Effectiveness of communicators when advocating positions for and against their own self–interest. (*Source:* Walster, Aronson, Abrahams, & Rottman, 1966, p. 333.)

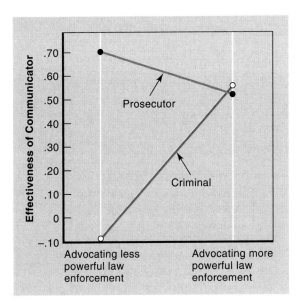

Communicators who are perceived to be trustworthy and credible produce more attitude change in their audiences. Eleanor Roosevelt is exemplary.

of law enforcement agencies, and really believes that they should be remedied, since it would so clearly work against any future plans he might have to remain a criminal. In short, communicators are seen as especially trustworthy when they have little to gain from the particular stance they adopt, but somewhat less trustworthy when they have incentives for making the statements they have or stand to gain personally from persuading others of their position.

Another factor that seems to enhance perceptions of trustworthiness is multiple sources. If several people say the same thing, they are more persuasive than if a single person makes the same argument, presumably because several individuals would be less subject to a personal idiosyncratic bias (Harkins & Petty, 1981). But multiple sources have this advantage only if their judgments are regarded as really independent of each other. Three independent sources are more persuasive than one, but only if those three are not seen as members of the same group. Multiple sources, then, produce more attitude change only when they are clearly putting forward three independent judgments.

LIKING. Since we try to make our cognitions consistent with our affect, it follows that we should also change our attitudes to agree with those of the people we like. In general, this has been shown to be true (e.g., Roskos-Ewoldsen & Fazio, 1992). Chaiken (1979), for example, showed that students rated by other students as physically attractive were also more persuasive communicators. We tend to be influenced more by those who are similar to us than by those who are different (Brock, 1965). In a test of this point, Wood and Kallgren (1988) manipulated the likeability of a graduate student delivering a talk in the following way. He was described as having recently transferred to the subject's university, and then he either praised their faculty and student body in comparison to those at his old university or said his previous school was better. Not surprisingly, he was liked better in the former case, and when he later gave a speech against environmental preservation, he produced more attitude change in his audience.

REFERENCE GROUPS. We are also persuaded when a position is adopted by a group of people we like or identify with. Such groups are called **reference groups.** Mackie (1987) told some subjects that a majority (82 percent) of the students at their university supported the proposition that the United States should act to ensure a military balance in the Western Hemisphere. Others were told that 82 percent opposed the proposition. She then presented subjects with speeches of equal strengths on both sides, so they all received the same arguments. In four experiments, she found that subjects moved toward the side that their peers supported, whichever side that was.

Two reasons why reference groups are so effective in producing attitude change are liking and similarity (Holtz & Miller, 1985). If people admire a group, they want to be like the group's members. When the other members express a particular opinion, each member wants to hold a similar opinion. And, consequently, people lean in the direction of changing their opinions to make them agree with those of their reference groups.

Messages from ingroups are also more persuasive because they seem to change how messages are processed. Mackie, Worth, and Asuncion (1990) found that communications from nonreference groups were processed at a very peripheral level and subjects were unpersuaded by either a strong or weak message. Subjects were, however, more persuaded by a strong message from the ingroup than by a weak one, suggesting more content-focused processing of the reference group's message. This effect was especially true when the issue was relevant to one's reference group.

In short, *where* a communication comes from—that is, the nature of the communicator—is clearly important in terms of how a message is evaluated. Attractive, likeable, credible, expert, trustworthy individuals are more persuasive than those who lack these attributes. Interestingly, however, it appears that communicator characteristics may be more important in audiovisual messages than in written messages. In audiovisual messages such as television, a great deal more information is available about the communicator, such as nonverbal information, appearance, and so on. In written communications, information about the communicator is less salient, and so message content should be relatively more important. In a study by Chaiken and Eagly (1983), evidence for these conjectures was found. They found that a communicator's likeability contributed to opinion change only in a video or audio message. In written messages, it was the quality of the arguments that made a difference (Chaiken & Eagly, 1983). The general principle is that source characteristics have their clearest effects when people cannot or will not scrutinize the arguments. When the source's characteristics themselves are especially salient, as in audiovisual messages, they have more impact on attitude change.

DEROGATING THE SOURCE. Just as communicator characteristics can enhance the persuasiveness of a communication, they can also be used to discredit a communication. When faced with a communication that is inconsistent with our attitudes, we can reduce inconsistency by deciding that the source of the communication is unreliable or negative in some other way. This is called **source derogation.** Such an attack on the source of a communication is common in politics, informal debates, courtroom trials, and practically every kind of disagreement. The defense attorney in a trial tries to discredit the witness whose testimony is damaging. The politician calls his opponent a Communist or a liar or some other name when he finds it difficult to argue on the issues themselves.

Attacking the source of the communication is an effective way of reducing the pressure produced by a discrepant communication. It has the additional benefit of making all future arguments from the opponent much less powerful. When an opponent has been discredited, anything he or she says carries less weight.

THE COMMUNICATOR AS A PERIPHERAL CUE.

As we have seen, characteristics of a communicator, such as whether he or she is trustworthy, expert, or likeable, are important determinants of whether we accept a persuasive communication. People who dislike or do not trust a communicator often reject the message by attacking the source. But sometimes a communicator's conclusion is accepted simply because it comes from an expert or from an otherwise favorably evaluated source, regardless of the arguments put forth. How can the communicator have these different effects?

The prediction from the elaboration likelihood model is that communicator characteristics are used as simple **peripheral cues** to persuasion when we cannot or are not motivated to process arguments carefully. Under circumstances when we are motivated to engage in little cognitive effort, we know we can rely on a trusted communicator's viewpoint, so we can avoid thinking the argument through ourselves. What are the conditions that lead us to use the communicator as a peripheral cue? If we cannot remember any of the arguments presented very well, we tend to rely on the source to determine

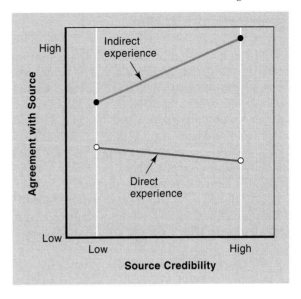

Figure 6-7 Effects of communicator characteristics depend on prior experience. (*Source:* Wood & Kallgren, 1988; Wu & Shaffer, 1987.)

our attitude in response to the communication (Wood & Kallgren, 1988).

Having direct experience with an attitude object diminishes the need for relying on a peripheral cue like communicator expertness. In one study (Wu & Shaffer, 1987), the experimenters gave subjects ostensibly different brands of peanut butter and labeled them as different, but, in fact, they were identical. Some subjects tasted them (direct experience) while other subjects simply looked at the two jars and were given information about others' reactions (indirect experience). Both then rated the peanut butters on a series of attributes. The experimenter then gave the subjects a computed summary score that informed each subject which brand he or she preferred. The subjects were then given a typed message either from a high-credibility professional product evaluator who had tested the products or from a low-credibility evaluator who had not. As shown in Figure 6-7, the high-credibility source was more persuasive only when the subjects had indirect experience with the products. Direct experience with the peanut butter nullified the advantage of source credibility, and subjects instead relied on their personal experience.

The Communication

In addition to the communicator, the communication itself is clearly important. The actual content of the message clearly influences whether people will accept it or not. Of course, it is easier to sell something good. Crest became the best-selling toothpaste, in part, because it really did offer protection against cavities, and the automobile became popular because it was a useful product. Given a particular product or opinion to sell, however, a number of variables in the communication itself have important effects on the degree to which people are persuaded by it.

DISCREPANCY.   A major factor that influences how much we will be persuaded by a communication is how discrepant that communication is from our own position. The greater the **discrepancy,** the greater the potential pressure to change. If the typical person needs eight hours of sleep a night, but hears a distinguished health scientist say that only six hours are necessary, that attitude is under some pressure. If the communication argues that only four hours of sleep are really necessary, there is even more pressure. As might be expected, there tends to be more attitude change the greater the discrepancy between our initial position and the position advocated by the communicator (Hovland & Pritzker, 1957). However, there are at least two complicating factors. First, as the discrepancy between our position and the advocated position becomes great, we may find it increasingly difficult to change our attitude to eliminate the discrepancy. Extremely discrepant statements, for example, make us doubt the credibility of the source rather than change our attitudes. To take the previous example, if we hear a scientist say that two hours of sleep are adequate, this is likely to be highly discrepant from our own position. We are likely to be less influenced and to begin to doubt the communicator's credibility (e.g., Freedman, 1964; Eagly & Telaak, 1972). Taken together, these effects predict that there will be a U-shaped relationship between discrepancy and attitude change, namely that relatively little attitude change will occur with low-discrepant and high-discrepant

communications, and that maximum attitude change will occur with moderately discrepant communications.

It follows that greater credibility should allow communicators to advocate more discrepant opinions successfully, because these opinions will not be rejected easily. In contrast, a low-credibility source makes rejection relatively easy, and so the maximum amount of attitude change should occur at lower levels of discrepancy. These predictions were confirmed in a study by Bochner and Insko (1966). They had a Nobel Prize winner (high credibility) and a YMCA instructor (low credibility) give messages regarding the number of hours of sleep the average person required per night. As predicted, there was more change in opinion regarding the necessary amount of sleep at moderate levels of discrepancy than at higher levels. In addition, as expected, the optimal level of discrepancy was greater for the high-credibility source. The YMCA instructor produced the most attitude change when he advocated three hours of sleep, but the high-credibility source got the maximum attitude change when he argued that only one hour was really necessary. These effects are illustrated in Figure 6-8.

Discrepancy affects how a message is perceived. When a discrepant position is quite close to that of an audience, they perceive it as closer than it really is. This process is called *assimilation.* Exaggerating the closeness of a discrepant position makes it easy to reduce the small discrepancy or may eliminate the need for change by making the two positions essentially identical. On the other hand, when the source's position is very discrepant from that of the audience, it is perceived to be farther away. This process is called **contrast.** When the position is perceived to be extreme, it may be perceived as so extreme as to be ridiculous, making it easy to discredit the communicator (Hovland, Harvey, & Sherif, 1957).

STRONG VERSUS WEAK ARGUMENTS.   Sometimes the arguments in a communication are strong and compelling, and sometimes they are weak and specious. The evidence for the role of unsafe sex practices in spreading AIDS, for

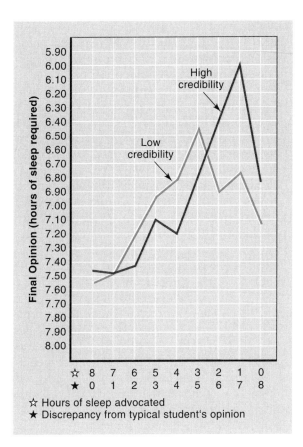

☆ Hours of sleep advocated
★ Discrepancy from typical student's opinion

Figure 6-8 Opinion change produced by high- and low-credibility communicators at various levels of discrepancy. (*Source:* Bochner & Insko, 1966.)

audiences into thinking about their topic ("Do you want the best education possible?"). Other times, would-be persuaders simply state their arguments ("Curtis College will give you the best education possible"). The asking of rhetorical questions should stimulate thought. Consequently, it should lead people to scrutinize arguments more closely, thus enhancing the advantage of strong arguments. In fact, research has generally supported this finding. For example, in one study, Burnkrant and Howard (1984) found that introducing an unpopular proposal, such as raising college tuition, with a rhetorical question stimulated more thinking about the communication, enhancing the advantage of strong arguments. Rhetorical questions often motivate more thinking, especially favorable thoughts about strong arguments, and consequently give an advantage to those arguments (see also Petty & Cacioppo, 1986; Petty, Rennier, & Cacioppo, 1987; Howard, 1990). This finding is illustrated in Figure 6-9.

REPETITION. Does repetition increase the persuasiveness of a message? Consider your reaction to seeing the same athlete in the same

example, is very compelling. The evidence that Elvis is still alive is very weak.

One would think that strong arguments would always produce more attitude change than weak ones, but that is not always the case. People respond more favorably to strong arguments in a persuasive communication primarily when they are motivated to pay close attention and are able to think carefully about the arguments. Under many circumstances, however, people do not give a message very detailed or careful thought. Thus, the strength of arguments is not necessarily a crucial factor in terms of how persuasive they are (Petty & Cacioppo, 1986).

RHETORICAL QUESTIONS. Sometimes would-be persuaders ask questions to provoke their

Figure 6-9 Effects on attitude of grammatical form and argument quality. (*Source:* Burnkrant & Howard, 1984.)

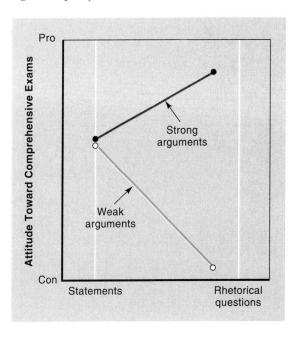

television commercial downing the same brand of beer at the same bar week after week. Does the repetition reinforce your association between that brand and the athlete, or do you just get sick of the commercial and tune it out?

Much research by Zajonc and others shows that familiarity based on repetition increases liking, as we will see in Chapter 9. This general finding implies that repetition generally should increase attitude change. With persuasive communications, however, repetition appears to increase attitude change only up to a point. Cacioppo and Petty (1979) presented students with communications containing eight different arguments on increasing university expenditures. Each communication was presented either once, three times, or five times. The authors found that agreement increased with more exposure up to a point, but then fell off. This inverted-U function occurred whether the communication advocated a position that was desirable to the target and therefore very low in discrepancy from their existing position, or whether it was an undesirable, high-discrepancy position (see also Gorn & Goldberg, 1980).

Why is repetition good for persuasion only up to a point? It is easy to imagine that repetition might have two separate effects: It may increase the opportunity to consider the content of a persuasive communication, and therefore enhance the processing of the message, but it may also increase the chances of tedium, and therefore produce a negative reaction. For example, when the beer commercial comes on, one's reaction might be, "Oh, not again!"

The implication of this argument is that repetition will help strong arguments, because people will process them more completely. But it may hurt weak arguments, because it exposes their flaws or simply makes them tedious (Cacioppo & Petty, 1985).

How can tedium be dealt with? Presumably, one can vary the content a little. Consistent with this argument, repetition of commercials for a particular product seem to increase in effectiveness if the commercials are varied somewhat, but not if exactly the same commercial is used each time (Cacioppo & Petty, 1985).

PERIPHERAL CUES AND MESSAGE CHARACTERISTICS. As we have seen, under some circumstances, peripheral cues can be very important in determining attitude change. When we have little motivation to think about the arguments in a message (for example, when the issue has little importance to us), or when we are unable to process the arguments well (such as when we are uninformed or distracted), then peripheral cues become very important in determining attitude change.

The number of arguments in a message and the length of those arguments are two such peripheral cues (Cacioppo & Petty, 1985). Presenting more arguments in a message increases attitude change when the issue is not very relevant to the person, and therefore provides little motivation to think about it. Presenting more arguments increases attitude change for strong and weak arguments alike, indicating that little processing is going on. Similarly, longer messages have a more persuasive impact than short messages, but only among those who are uninformed, who presumably give those messages little thought. Among the better informed, strength of arguments is a more important factor, presumably because the better informed are more motivated to pay attention to the nature of the arguments themselves (Wood, Kallgren, & Priesler, 1985).

A variety of factors, then, determine whether any given message will be persuasive. When people have the time and interest to pay attention to a message, strong arguments have a decided advantage. In the absence of strong arguments, peripheral cues, such as source characteristics or the sheer number of arguments, have more impact.

DISTORTING THE MESSAGE. Message factors may also be important in rejecting a persuasive communication. Specifically, cognitive consistency theories maintain that inconsistency between our own position and that advocated in a message may be resolved by distorting or misperceiving the communication to reduce the discrepancy between it and our own position. The Surgeon General writes an article recommending that sexually active young adults should practice safer sex because they may be at risk for AIDS. Young adults who do not want to practice safer sex may read this message and decide that the Surgeon General says not to worry too much about AIDS because the evidence about heterosexual transmission is not yet conclusive. They can do this by misperceiving the article when reading it, by distorting the article in memory, or perhaps by reading only part of the article and reconstructing the rest of it mentally. However accomplished, the result is the same: The message becomes considerably less discrepant. Sadly, in the case of AIDS, the price of distorting a health warning can be high indeed.

BLANKET REJECTION. The most primitive (and perhaps most common) mode of inconsistency resolution is simply to reject the communication altogether. Rather than refuting the arguments on logical grounds or weakening them by attacking their source, individuals simply reject arguments for no apparent reason.

A typical response by a smoker to a well-reasoned, logical attack on cigarette smoking is to say that the arguments are not good enough to make her stop. She does not answer them; she just does not accept them. It often takes more than a good argument to convince people of something.

The Target

Target individuals, namely the persons to be persuaded, vary in a number of respects that affect persuasion as well. Targets may be predisposed to agree with a message or predisposed to disagree with it. They may be familiar or unfamiliar with the arguments. They may already know arguments against the communicator's position or they may not know any arguments against the communicator's position. And, finally, they may have personal motives that affect how willing they are to change in response to a persuasive message. We begin this section with a consideration of motive arousal.

The arousal of motives is among the most

common propagandistic techniques. For example, attempts are often made to arouse hostility. National enemies are decried in times of war. Hatred is aroused against people who produce child pornography or make racist statements. Similarly, fear is often used to try to convince people to change their opinions. Various surgeon generals have tried to get people to stop smoking or adopt safer sex practices by publicizing the health consequences of doing otherwise.

AGGRESSION AROUSAL. The learning approach to attitude change suggests that motive arousal would lead to attitude change only when accepting the message will reduce arousal. Aggression arousal, then, should produce attitude change only when the communication urges an aggressive position. In a study by Weiss and Fine (1956), some subjects were put through an annoying, frustrating experience designed to make them feel aggressive. Other subjects had the opposite experience, a pleasant, satisfying one. Then both groups were exposed to a persuasive communication that took a lenient attitude toward juvenile deliquency or one that took a punitive stance. The experimenters hypothesized that subjects who had been made to feel aggressive would accept the punitive communication, because it would provide them with a way of expressing their aggression. The lenient message would be more likely to satisfy the relatively nonaggressive needs of the subjects who had had the pleasant experience. The results were generally in line with these expectations. Personal frustrations, then, might make a person more vulnerable to persuasive communications advocating military action, attacks on minorities, or harsh treatment of dissidents, but probably they would not increase susceptibility to such nonaggressive appeals as charity campaigns.

FEAR AROUSAL. The case of fear is more complex. The learning theory approach would suggest that fear-arousing messages would be accepted if the communication offered fear-reducing recommendations. But the empirical evidence suggests that the level of fear must also be considered.

The original study of fear and attitude change was conducted by Janis and Feshbach (1953). They showed high school students a film that emphasized the importance of brushing one's teeth three times a day. The film described the dangers of not doing so, and explained the advantages of good dental care. High fear was aroused by showing hideous pictures of badly decayed teeth and gums. In the mild-fear condition, subjects saw less dramatic and less frightening pictures, and in the no-fear or control condition, subjects saw no pictures of diseased teeth.

The subjects in the high-fear condition were more impressed by the presentation and agreed with it more. However, a week later, subjects in the no-fear condition had actually changed their behavior more than had subjects in either of the fear conditions. The authors concluded that the persuasive arguments alone had succeeded without the fear-arousing slides. Too much fear, they felt, may have turned the subjects off, so they paid little attention to the communication.

Other experiments, however, have produced the opposite result, showing that the arousal of fear tends to facilitate both attitude and behavior change. In one study (Dabbs & Leventhal, 1966), college students were urged to get inoculations for tetanus. The disease was described in detail. It was pointed out how serious it was, that it was often fatal, and that it was easy to catch. In the high-fear condition, the symptoms of the disease were made very explicit and everything was done to make the situation as frightening as possible. In a second condition, a moderate amount of fear was aroused, and in the third condition, very little fear was aroused. In addition, the students were told that the inoculation was extremely effective and that it gave almost complete protection against the disease. Students were then asked how important they thought it was to be inoculated and whether they intended to do it. The university health service cooperated by recording how many of the students went for inoculations during the next month.

The findings (Table 6-5) are straightforward

TABLE 6-5
Effects of Fear Arousal on Attitudes and Behavior

Condition	Intention to Take Shots[a]	Percentage Taking Shots
High fear	5.17	22
Low fear	4.73	13
Control	4.12	6

[a] The figures are ratings on a scale from 1 (lowest) to 7 (highest).
Source: Adapted from Dabbs & Levanthal (1986).

and impressive. The greater the fear aroused, the more the subjects intended to get shots. Perhaps more important, higher fear induced more students to go to the health service and receive inoculations. Thus, fear arousal both produced attitude change and affected the relevant behavior. Generally speaking, the research on the effectiveness of fear appeals has shown this effect. Fear arousal seems to increase the effectiveness of a persuasive communication (Higbee, 1969; Leventhal, 1970).

Whether persuasion is enhanced by fear appeals, however, may depend in part on whether the message provides expectations of reassurance. A recent study (Gleicher & Petty, 1992) exposed college students to either a low-fear or a moderately fearful message about crime on the college campus. In addition, subjects were exposed to both strong and weak arguments and were given a message that either was reassuring or not. With a low-fear message, subjects differentiated between strong and weak arguments, being more persuaded by the strong ones. However, under moderate fear conditions, the effect of fear on argument processing depended on whether the subjects believed that reassurance would be provided by the message. When subjects believed that the solution presented in the message would be effective, they evaluated the arguments favorably, regardless of whether they were strong or weak. When expectations regarding the solution were unclear, however, subjects evaluated the quality of the arguments more closely. These results suggest that fear may shift people into peripheral processing if they expect a persuasive message to alleviate their fear.

There are now two general theories about the effects of fear, both of which go beyond the original needs satisfaction idea derived from learning theory. Janis (1967) argued that fear produces more attitude change up to a point. However, after a certain point, fear may become so intense that it arouses defensive mechanisms, thereby producing less attitude change. Thus, Janis argues that fear appeals show a curvilinear relationship to attitude change, being most effective at moderate levels.

Others have approached the problem from an expectancy-value approach, viewing the individual as more cognitive and rational than does the Janis model (Leventhal, 1970; Rogers & Mewborn, 1976). These theories take into account the nature of the feared event, the person's perceived vulnerability, and the perceived effectiveness of the recommended measures. This perspective argues that fear should increase attitude change when a person feels vulnerable to the feared event and if highly effective measures are recommended, but not if the person feels invulnerable or there is little or no remedy. As we will see in Chapter 16, the expectancy-value account of the relation between fear and attitude change is often used in health communications to get people to change their behaviors, such as stopping smoking, using condoms, or adopting a low-cholesterol diet.

To sum up, the evidence indicates that increasing fear usually increases the effectiveness of a persuasive communication. But when too much fear is aroused, the effects may be disruptive, causing people to be too frightened to act, or leading them to ignore or reject the communication. At moderate levels, however, fear-arousing arguments are more effective in producing attitude change than are arguments that cause little or no fear.

Other affective states also influence persuasion and how a persuasive message is processed. The RESEARCH CLOSEUP shows that mood can heavily determine how we respond to a persuasive message.

Persuasive communications designed to arouse fear usually are effective. However, if the message arouses too much fear, the effects may be disruptive, leading people to ignore or reject the communication.

EGO INVOLVEMENT. Another factor related to the target and whether he or she will be persuaded by a communication relates to **ego involvement.** According to Sherif and Cantril (1947), attitudes that become highly entwined with the ego are highly resistant to change. Sherif and Cantril believed that ego involvement was more likely to occur when attitudes were linked to important reference groups, such as one's nation, religion, ethnicity, or social class. Later work has distinguished between several different kinds of ego involvement,

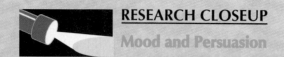

Did you know that your mood can actually affect how you respond to a persuasive message, such as an advertisement or a political appeal (Schwarz, Bless, & Bohner, 1991)? When we are in a neutral or a bad mood, we tend to pay attention to a message. We're likely to notice whether the arguments are good ones or not, we scrutinize the message closely, and we remember it well later on. But when we are in a good mood, we tend to accept a persuasive appeal. We don't engage in much systematic processing of the message (Worth & Mackie, 1987), and we fail to differentiate between strong and weak arguments (Petty & Cacioppo, 1981). If we are asked about our reactions to the message, we are likely to have little elaboration of it and little recall of the message itself (Chaiken, 1980). So a positive mood really does make us agreeable!

However, in an ingenious study, Mackie and Worth (1989) found that people in a positive mood are not always quite so accepting of persuasive messages. In their study, half the students participating were unexpectedly told that they had won two dollars, and they received an envelope with the two dollars enclosed. This was the positive mood manipulation. The other students were told nothing about winning, nor did they receive any money, and conse-

quently, they were in a neutral mood. Following these manipulations, subjects read a speech about saving the environment. Half the subjects read a message that contained strong valid arguments, and the other half read a message containing very weak arguments. The message appeared briefly, and then subjects were asked to list the thoughts they had had while reading the speech and their reactions to the arguments. As previous research had found, subjects in the positive mood did not recall the arguments very well, nor did they discriminate between strong and weak arguments, compared to subjects in the neutral mood, as Figure 6-10 indicates.

However, in a second condition, subjects were permitted to look over the message for as long as they liked before going on to list their thoughts and respond to the message. Under these conditions, subjects in a positive mood appeared to engage in systematic processing. Compared to subjects in a neutral mood, those in a positive mood remembered more details of the message and differentiated between strong and weak arguments more than subjects who were in the neutral mood.

Why do people in a positive mood show enhanced processing of a persuasive message with unlimited exposure time,

but reduced systematic processing when exposure is limited? Mackie and Worth (1989) reasoned that the effects could be either motivational or cognitive in origin. The motivational explanation would suggest that people in a positive mood want to hold onto that mood and not interrupt it by processing a persuasive message. However, the manipulation of viewing time enabled subjects to control the length of time that they reviewed the message, and since those in a positive mood looked at the message longer, the motivational explanation clearly does not hold.

Mackie and Worth (1989) concluded that a good mood takes up cognitive processing. It gives us things to think about and occupies our time. Therefore, when in a good mood, we have less cognitive capacity left over to process a persuasive message when exposed to it only briefly. However, under unlimited exposure conditions, people in a positive mood have the opportunity to overcome the limits that a positive mood puts on processing capacity, and can use the extended time to process a persuasive message.

Mood clearly influences how we process persuasive messages (Schwarz, Bless, & Bohner, 1991), then, but it also depends on how much time we have.

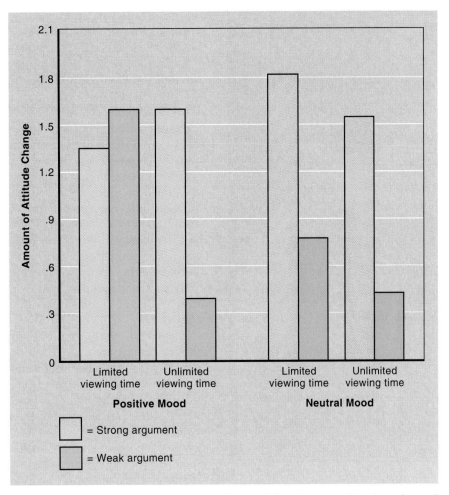

Figure 6-10 Attitude change in the advocated direction as a function of mood, exposure time, and argument quality. (*Source:* Mackie & Worth, 1989.)

however, with somewhat different dynamics. These include commitment, issue involvement, and response involvement.

Commitment. An important aspect of involvement is our **commitment** to our own initial attitude on an issue (e.g., Chaiken & Stangor, 1987). Resistance to a persuasive message depends in great part on the strength of this commitment. Commitment may come from several sources. First, commitment increases when we engage in behavior on the basis of an attitude. A person who has just bought a new car, for example, is

more committed to the belief that it is a fine car than he was before he bought it.

Second, commitment is increased when we take a public stance to an attitude position (Hovland, Campbell, & Brock, 1957). Someone who has just told all her friends that she thinks smoking is an evil, dirty habit is more committed to this attitude than if she had kept her thoughts to herself. Expressing an attitude publicly makes it difficult to change, because change would involve a public admission that she was wrong.

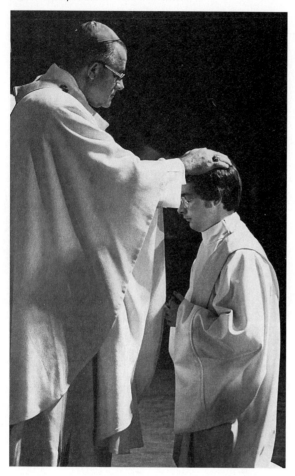

Committing one's self to a course of action maintains attitudes in favor of that course of action. The consequences of commitment are even stronger if the commitment is public.

Third, freely choosing an attitude position produces a greater feeling of commitment than being forced or nudged into a position. In one study (Freedman & Steinbrunner, 1964), subjects were given information about a candidate for graduate school and were asked to rate him under circumstances of either high or low choice. The subjects were either made to feel that they had made up their own minds and freely made their particular rating, or that they had little to do with the decision and had been virtually forced to make the rating they did. Subjects were then exposed to information that strongly contradicted their initial rating, and were allowed to change the rating if they

desired. Those who had made the first rating with a feeling of free choice changed less than those in the low-choice condition.

A fourth source of commitment is direct experience with an attitude object. For example, as we saw earlier, Wu and Shaffer (1987) showed that subjects directly exposed to brands of peanut butter were less vulnerable to countercommunications than were those who were indirectly exposed.

Commitment to an initial attitude position shifts the amount of discrepancy at which maximum attitude change occurs. The greater the commitment to one's initial attitude, the lower is the discrepancy at which rejection of the source starts to substitute for attitude change. Therefore, the greater the commitment, the lower is the discrepancy at which maximum attitude change occurs (Freedman, 1964; Rhine & Severance, 1970).

In general, then, commitment reduces the amount of attitude change produced by a discrepant, persuasive communication. If changing an attitude would cause us to give up more, suffer more, or change more of our other attitudes or behaviors, commitment to the initial attitude position increases and makes it more difficult to change. We become more likely to use other modes of resolution instead.

Issue Involvement. A second type of ego involvement occurs when an issue has important consequences for the individual. This has been called issue involvement (or personal relevance), because we are involved in the issue, rather than detached from it. Issue involvement is a key variable in elaboration likelihood theory (Petty & Cacioppo, 1986, 1990). Issue involvement motivates people to attend closely to the issue and to the relevant arguments. Consequently, when we are involved in an issue, strong arguments are more persuasive than weak ones (Petty & Cacioppo, 1990). For example, if you were told your tuition might double next year, you would probably pay very close attention to the validity of the arguments for the increase. In contrast, if you heard that tuition was being increased at a college in Bulgaria, you might not scrutinize the arguments very carefully. An issue that is not personally relevant tends not to produce the motivation to process the information. Under such conditions, people pay more attention to such peripheral cues as communicator expertise or the length of the arguments.

Response Involvement. Even when we are not very committed to our prior attitude or the issue is not personally relevant, our attitudinal response may nonetheless be very important, because it will receive public scrutiny and bring social approval or disapproval. This kind of involvement is called response involvement (Zimbardo, 1960). The response-involved person is concerned primarily with whether others will approve, while the issue-involved person is more concerned with the quality of arguments, because the issue is what matters.

These contrasting effects of issue and response involvement were compared by Leippe and Elkin (1987). They manipulated issue involvement by telling subjects that their university was considering instituting comprehensive examinations. Some students were told that the exams would be put into effect the next year, thereby affecting them, whereas others were told that the exams would not be put into effect until some years later. Response involvement was manipulated by telling some subjects they would discuss the issue with another student and a professor, while others were not told of any such discussions.

Only the subjects who were both highly issue-involved and weakly response-involved—those who expected to be personally affected by the issue but did not have to worry about what image they would present to others—gave real scrutiny to the arguments, as reflected in greater attitude change in response to strong than to weak arguments. With high response involvement, that is, when subjects were preoccupied with their self-presentation, the strength of arguments was virtually ignored. When the issue had no personal relevance, strengths of argument likewise had no effect.

To summarize, the original concept of ego involvement has been broken down into three separate types of commitment, each with somewhat different psychological dynamics. Commitment (or position involvement) repre-

sents involvement in the individual's specific position and produces pressure to defend that position. Exposure to a discrepant communication often produces responses other than attitude change, such as source derogation, misperception, or blanket rejection of the message. Issue involvement refers to the perception that the issue is personally relevant. It promotes more open and diligent information processing, spurred by an effort to get at the best position. Response involvement refers to concern about how our overt expressions of attitude will be received by others. It breeds concern about self-presentation and the social acceptability of our attitude, rather than concern about the quality of arguments or merits of the case.

The Situation

So far, we have considered the communicator, the message, and the target as factors that influence attitudes and responses to persuasive communications. But a persuasive communication is usually delivered within a broader situational context in which other things are happening that also affect how successful persuasion attempts may be.

FOREWARNING OF POSITION. If you are highly committed to a position and are told that you are about to be exposed to a discrepant communication, you will probably be better able to resist persuasion by that message. In a study by Freedman and Sears (1965), teenagers were told 10 minutes beforehand that they were going to hear a talk entitled, "Why Teenagers Should Not Be Allowed to Drive." Other teenagers were not told about the talk until just before the speaker began. Those who had been warned ahead of time were less influenced by the talk than those who had not. **Forewarning** had enabled them to resist the message.

Why does this occur? Most likely, our defenses and counterarguments are in some way exercised and therefore strengthened. When we hear that someone is going to try to change our mind on an attitude position about which we care deeply, we may begin to counterargue the message, anticipating what the speaker is likely to say. Petty and Cacioppo (1977) showed that the delay period between forewarning and exposure to a communication allows people to generate more counterarguments. Given time, a forewarned person can convince herself that the communicator is unreliable, prejudiced, or misinformed, for example.

What happens, however, if the attitude position espoused is not one about which you care a great deal? When the listener is not very committed to a position, forewarning turns out to have the opposite effect. It actually facilitates attitude change. The warning seems to operate as a cue for getting the person to begin thinking about reasons why the position about to be advocated would be a good one (Apsler & Sears, 1968).

Being forewarned about a person's intent to persuade usually makes people more skeptical about the message. Do you think a prospective customer will successfully resist the persuasive efforts of this salesman?

FOREWARNING OF INTENT. Another kind of forewarning involves signaling the intent to persuade. We may not know the exact position a communicator is going to take, but we know that the communicator is going to try to persuade us of a position. When an issue is relevant and important to us, and we are forewarned that someone intends to change our mind, we are likely to counterargue what we expect the arguments to be, and thus show heightened resistance to attitude change. To show this, Petty and Cacioppo (1979) told subjects that a message was "designed specifically to try to persuade you and other college students" or that it was prepared as part of a class project. The message then argued for comprehensive exams for all seniors. In the high-relevance condition, the exam was to be instituted at college the coming year, whereas in the low-relevance condition, it would be instituted far in the future or at another university. The most counterarguing against this unpopular proposal and the least attitude change occurred with forewarning and high personal relevance.

DISTRACTION. So far, we have considered attitude change primarily in circumstances where people were actually considering a persuasive message. People whose opinions are attacked usually try to resist changing their attitudes, particularly when they are committed to them. They counterargue, derogate the communicator, and generally marshal their forces to defend their positions. An important implication of this is that the ability to resist persuasion is weakened by anything that makes it harder to counterargue the discrepant communication. In particular, distracting attention may enable a persuasive message to get through.

A study by Festinger and Maccoby (1964) demonstrated this effect of **distraction.** Subjects listened to a speech against fraternities while watching a film. For some of the subjects, the film showed the person making the speech. For others, the film was a funny satire on modern art. Presumably, those watching the irrelevant film were more distracted from the anti-fraternity speech than those watching the person speak. Subjects who initially disagreed with the speech (that is, who were in favor of fraternities) were more influenced in the distraction than in the nondistraction condition. Taking the subjects' minds off the speech increased its effectiveness.

Mild amounts of distraction do seem to enhance persuasion (Petty & Brock, 1981). Cognitive response analysis suggests why. Distraction should increase persuasion only when it interferes with an otherwise effective counterarguing process. Thus, distraction should lead to more persuasion concerning a familiar issue about which we know our arguments than on an issue about which we do not have ready arguments. If we do not have arguments against an issue, then distraction does not keep us from counterarguing. Distraction appears to work best when communications are very discrepant from our own attitude position and when we are very involved with the topic, presumably because these are the conditions that inspire the most vigorous counterarguing (Petty & Brock, 1981).

But there are clear limits on the effects of distraction. Obviously, too much distraction prevents a persuasive message from being heard at all and reduces its effectiveness to zero. Advertisements in which the content of the message is very funny may have this paradoxical effect, inasmuch as subjects are laughing so hard at the events in the ads, they may forget what the product is.

INOCULATION. In the aftermath of the Korean War, psychologists became interested in reports of "brain-washing" of American prisoners of war by the Chinese Communists. A number of POWs had given public speeches denouncing the American government, and several said publicly that they wished to remain in China when the war was over, rather than return to the United States. Psychologist William McGuire speculated that some soldiers might have been vulnerable to influence because they were attacked on matters with which they were inexperienced and ignorant. Many soldiers, especially less-educated ones, had never had to defend the United States against the sophisticated Marxist arguments used by the Chinese.

McGuire hypothesized that an important source of resistance to change comes from past experience with an issue. He pictured the target faced with a persuasive communication as being like someone attacked by a virus or a disease. The stronger the persuasive message (virus), the more damage it would do; but the stronger the person's defenses, the better able he or she would be to resist persuasion (disease).

There are two ways to strengthen people's defenses against a disease. We can strengthen their bodies generally by giving them vitamins or exercise and the like, or we can strengthen their defenses against a particular disease by building up antibodies. If people are given mild cases of smallpox that they are able to fight off, for example, their bodies produce antibodies which in the future provide an effective and strong defense against more powerful attacks. McGuire argued that these two approaches are also applicable to persuasion attempts.

The first procedure to strenghten resistance by building up the person's opinion directly involves providing additional arguments to support the original position. McGuire termed this a **supportive defense.** The second approach is the **inoculation defense.** McGuire argued that the more effective way of increasing resistance is to build up defenses. Someone whose opinion has been attacked and successfully defended should later be able to resist attacks because a strong defense has been built up. The inoculation defense involves two things. It begins with a weak attack. (The attack must be weak or it would change the attitude and the battle would be lost.) Then the target is helped to defend against the mild attack by being given an argument directed specifically against the attack, or by being told that the attack is not very good and should be easy to refute.

A study by McGuire and Papageorgis (1961) used both supportive and inoculation methods to build up defenses. There were three groups of subjects: One group received support for their position, one group had their position attacked weakly and the attack refuted, and the third group received neither procedure. Afterward, all groups were subjected to a strong attack on their initial position. The supportive method helped subjects resist persuasion a little, but the inoculation method helped a great deal. Subjects receiving this preparation changed their attitudes much less than did subjects in the other two groups.

One implication is that supportive defenses should work best when a target simply needs to be taught specific arguments. The inoculation defense should work better when targets must be stimulated to think up their own defensive arguments. Consistent with this view, subsequent research has shown that supportive defenses are effective when a subsequent attack contains arguments similar to the content of the supporting arguments. But supportive defenses are relatively ineffective if new arguments are used. In contrast, inoculation is effective even when an attack includes new arguments (McGuire, 1964).

Cognitive response theory provides a good explanation for inoculation effects. It suggests that, in refuting a mild attack, people exercise all their defenses. They prepare arguments supporting their own position, construct counterarguments against the opposite position, derogate the source of the opposing view, and so on, which provides the individual with a stronger and better-defended position.

ATTITUDE CHANGE OVER TIME

So far we have focused on immediate responses to communications; that is, under what conditions does a televised speech, radio ad, or conversation with a friend *immediately* produce attitude change? In many cases, however, we want to know how attitudes change over time. We especially want to know the effects of repeated exposure to a message and what effects are likely to last when the exposure ends.

Spontaneous Attitude Change

Thinking about an attitude object tends to make the attitude more extreme (Tesser, 1978). According to Tesser, we review and rehearse our cognitions, and consistency pressures move them toward more evaluatively consistent clusters. So if you spend more than the usual amount of time thinking about your best friend, you will probably like her better. You might remember additional qualities or enjoyable experiences you shared. And you might reinterpret some of your less pleasant memories to excuse your friend's behavior. However, if you think about your enemy more often, you will probably dislike her even more. You would lengthen your list of offenses and find seamy motives for her apparently good and generous acts.

Basically, Tesser's hypothesis is that thinking about an issue produces more polarized attitudes because thinking allows people to generate more consistent attitudes. But all this cognitive activity requires that the individual already have a knowledge structure, or schema, about the issue. Without some schematic understanding of the issue, it would be difficult to generate new beliefs, or know how to reinterpret old ones, and so on.

The implication is that thought will polarize attitudes only if we already have a schema about the issue, and if the thought is specifically focused on that issue rather than on some other irrelevant or competing issue (Liberman & Chaiken, 1991). To test this, Chaiken and Yates (1985) tested two groups of people, some who already had a highly consistent knowledge structure about the issue (capital punishment), and others who did not. Then every person wrote an essay either about this issue or about a different, irrelevant issue (censorship). Only the highly consistent subjects who wrote an essay on capital punishment developed more extreme attitudes on that topic. No significant polarization occurred in any of the other conditions. To polarize attitudes, then, the thought must be relevant to the issue, we must have sufficient cognitive resources, and there must be no alternative issues competing for attention (Liberman & Chaiken, 1991).

Persistence of Attitude Change

Another question concerns the persistence of attitude change over time, once it has been induced by a communication. It seems clear that, in general, memory for the details of an argument decays with time in a way resembling an Ebbinghaus forgetting curve; that is, decreases are rapid at first, then diminish later on. In general, though, the persistence of attitude change is not necessarily dependent on retention of the details of arguments. As indicated earlier, memory for arguments is of only secondary importance in the persistence of attitude change. Other events that occur after the communication are of much greater significance.

One important factor may be whether or not the recipient is later reminded of important cues other than the arguments themselves, such as the credibility of the source. Kelman and Hovland (1953), for example, manipulated source credibility and found the usual difference on an immediate posttest: The high-credibility source had produced more attitude change. Three weeks afterward, the credibility difference was gone. The low-credibility source's message was, by then, just as effective. This rebound in the persuasiveness of the low-credibility source's message was called the **sleeper effect.** The original credibility difference could be reinstated, however, if the subject was reminded of the original source of the message.

A *dissociation* interpretation was offered for the increased effectiveness of the low-credibility source (Hovland, Janis, & Kelley, 1953). The recipient was originally presented with two pieces of information: the message and its endorsement by the low-credibility source. Immediately afterward, the recipient remembers both. But the low-credibility source acts as a discounting cue that enables the recipient to discount or ignore the message. So there was little immediate attitude change. As time goes on, the credibility of the source becomes increasingly dissociated from the message; that is, the recipient remembers the message but forgets who said it. The message therefore becomes more persuasive with time, as it is increasingly relieved of the stigma of being associated with a low-credibility source.

An alternative interpretation is the *differential decay* hypothesis (Pratkanis et al., 1988), which assumes that the impact of a discounting cue (such as a low-credibility source) on persuasion

dissipates more quickly than does the impact of the message itself. The reason is that it is more difficult to remember the combination of message and source than it is simply to remember your own new position on the issue. Immediately after hearing the message, both the discounting cue and the message are accessible in memory, so there is little immediate apparent attitude change. But a few days later, the impact of the discounting cue may be lost, while that of the message is retained, producing the surge in attitude change described as the sleeper effect. This process is shown in Figure 6-11.

The implication is that such sleeper effects should occur primarily when the discounting cue originally followed the message. If you find out that the source has low credibility *after* you have heard the message, you will have already listened to the arguments and taken them seriously. But if you learn that the source has low credibility before you even hear the message, you probably will not even pay attention to the

Figure 6-11 The differential decay explanation of the sleeper effect. At short delays, message and discounting cue are hypothesized (dotted lines) to have near equal impact. However, the impact of the cue dissipates rapidly to yield an observable (solid line) sleeper effect. (*Source:* Pratkanis et al., 1988.)

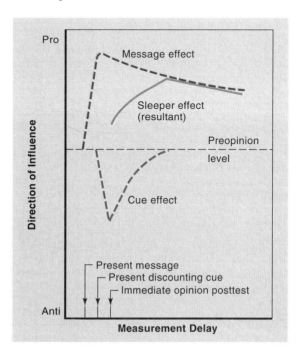

message, so there will be no original persuasive impact of the arguments to shine through once the suppressing impact of the low-credibility source has dissipated (Pratkanis et al., 1988).

Low credibility is not the only discounting cue. Attitude change may also be artificially suppressed by forewarning the recipient about the communicator's intent, as we have seen. People tend to become stubborn when they feel the source is trying to persuade them. But over time, such people seem to show increased attitude change, presumably as the discounting cue (persuasive intent) is forgotten (Watts & Holt, 1979).

If there is a lesson in all this, it may be that there is no such thing as a free lunch in the day of a persuader. A low-credibility source may get a message through, but the message is always vulnerable to its weak auspices becoming salient again. Or, we may momentarily trick a person into changing by failing to warn her, but with time the persuasive impact may be lost.

Pratkanis and colleagues (Pratkanis, Greenwald, Leippe, & Baumgardner, 1988) report a study demonstrating this effect. When the discounting cue was given before the message, it prevented substantial message impact right off the bat, so little attitude change occurred, either immediate or delayed. But when the cue was given immediately afterward, the sleeper effect occurred. The discounting cue substantially reduced the initial impact of the message, but attitude change surged forward when measured again six weeks later. Presumably, by that time the discounting cue no longer had any effect, whereas the impact of the message persisted.

ATTITUDES AND BEHAVIOR

Originally it was simply assumed that people's attitudes determined their behavior. Devout Christians should behave honestly, frugally, and compassionately, and people who are prejudiced against Hispanics should be unlikely to send their child to a school with mostly Hispanic students. Much of the interest in attitudes comes from the assumption that they do affect behavior.

And yet we know of many instances in which behavior does not follow from attitudes. Television evangelists involved in public scandals seem not to have behaved in accordance with conventional religious beliefs. How many times have you seen people smile and say how pleased they are to meet someone when you know they are bored stiff or hate them? So to what extent do attitudes in fact control behavior?

The degree of influence of attitudes over behavior has become one of the most important controversies in attitude research. In a classic study, La Piere (1934), a white professor, toured the United States with a young Chinese student and his wife. They stopped at 66 hotels and motels and ate at 184 restaurants. Although at the time there was rather strong prejudice against Asians in the United States, all but one

Sometimes attitudes influence people's behavior, but other times they may not. In this picture, the demonstrators are clearly acting on behalf of their attitudes. Yet while many of the bystanders no doubt hold similar attitudes, they are not participating in the protest for other reasons.

of the hotels and motels gave them space, and they were never refused service at a restaurant. Sometime later, a letter was sent to the same establishments asking whether they would accept Chinese as guests. Of the 128 replying, 92 percent said they would not. That is, the Chinese couple received nearly perfect service in person, but nearly universal discrimination in the subsequent letters. La Piere, and many after him, interpreted these findings as reflecting a major inconsistency between behavior and attitudes (Wicker, 1969).

Yet this conclusion has been widely criticized as underestimating attitude–behavior consistency. Indeed, later studies show much higher degrees of consistency than Wicker reported (see Schuman & Johnson, 1976). An example is voting behavior. Kelley and Mirer (1974) analyzed large-scale surveys conducted during four presidential election campaigns. Voters' partisan attitudes, as revealed in preelection interviews, were highly related to actual voting behavior: 85 percent of the respondents showed a correspondence between attitude and behavior, despite the fact that the interviews took place one month before election day, on the average. Moreover, almost all the inconsistent voters had only weak attitudes.

But everyone acknowledges there is substantial variation across different situations in just how consistent attitudes and behavior are. In recent years, the major research effort has gone into trying to determine the conditions that yield greater or lesser degrees of consistency between attitudes and behavior.

Strength of the Attitude

One important condition for high attitude–behavior consistency is that the attitude be a strong and clear one. Inconsistencies most often involve weak or ambivalent attitudes. As mentioned, Kelley and Mirer (1974) found that most attitude–vote inconsistencies came from voters with conflicted or weak attitudinal preferences to start with. Similarly, behavior consistent with attitudes may not follow when the affective and cognitive components of the attitude conflict (Norman, 1975; Millar & Tesser, 1989).

Anything that contributes to a strong attitude should increase attitude–behavior consistency. One factor is the amount of information we have about the attitude object. For example, Kallgren and Wood (1986) found that students' environmental behaviors (agreeing to a home visit to hear about a recycling project, or signing petitions to protect the environment) and attitudes were more consistent among those who knew the most about preservation of the environment.

Another factor that strengthens attitudes is rehearsing and practicing them. Fazio, Chen, McDonel, and Sherman (1982) showed that attitude–behavior consistency is greater when people think about and express their attitudes, presumably because this helps to strengthen the attitude.

Having direct personal experience with an issue gets us to think and talk about it more than if it is remote to us. So attitude–behavior consistency will be greater when we have direct experience with the attitude object than when we only hear about it from someone else or read about it (Fazio & Zanna, 1981). Regan and Fazio (1977) showed this with students at Cornell University during a severe housing shortage. Many freshmen had to spend the first few weeks of the fall semester in temporary housing—usually a cot in a dormitory lounge. Unlike students assigned immediately to permanent housing, they experienced the shortage personally. While all this was going on, the researchers measured students' attitudes toward the crisis and their interest in possible behavioral actions, such as signing and distributing petitions, or joining committees to study the crisis. Attitudes and behavior were closely related for the students with direct personal experience with the crisis. In contrast, behavior was not at all related to attitudes among students with only second-hand experience, such as those who only talked to friends or read about the crisis in the student paper.

Another source of attitude strength comes from having some vested or selfish interest in the issue. Sivacek and Crano (1982) found support for this notion using the issue of the minimum drinking age. A ballot proposal in Michigan in 1978 would have raised the legal drinking age from 18 to 21. Presumably, students under age 21 had more of a selfish interest in the issue than did older students. Indeed, attitudes toward the proposal were considerably more tightly correlated with behavior (volunteering to call voters) among those with a vested interest than among the disinterested.

There are, of course, other reasons why attitudes are strong. But these examples illustrate the general point: The attitude–behavior relationship is stronger when the attitude is a strong one.

Stability of the Attitude

Attitudes may change over time. The attitude held by a person some months or years ago will certainly not affect behavior as much as the person's current attitude. One would not expect to find a close relationship between a college girl's attraction to a boy and her dating behavior with him if her attraction is measured when she is a freshman and her behavior is measured when she is a senior. Therefore, consistency between attitudes and behavior ought to be maximum when they are measured at about the same time.

Longer time intervals diminish the attitude–behavior correlation because attitudes change. But the person and the situation change in other ways as well. We might find that a woman's attitude about having children at age 25 does not predict her behavior at age 30. The woman might continue not to want to have a child, or her husband may have threatened her with divorce if she did not agree to have children. The longer the interval between measuring the attitude and measuring the behavior, the more such unforeseen contingencies can arise. So, when assessing whether or not people "do what they say," make sure you don't try to hold them to something they said two years ago. Things may have changed!

Relevance of Attitudes to Behavior

Another obvious, but often ignored, point is that the more relevant attitudes are to behavior, the more they will be related. Attitudes vary quite a bit in how relevant they are to the act in ques-

TABLE 6-6
Effects of Attitude Relevance on the Correlation Between Attitude and Behavior (Use of Birth Control Pills During the Following 2 Years)

Attitude Measure	Correlation with Behavior
Least relevant	
Attitude toward birth control in general	.08
Attitude toward birth control pills	.32
Attitude toward using birth control pills	.52
Most relevant	
Attitude toward using birth control pills during the next 2 years	.57

Source: Davidson & Jaccard (1979).

tion. La Piere's asking proprietors about their feelings toward Chinese people in general is plainly not as relevant as asking about their attitudes toward this particular couple. In general, behavior tends to be more consistent with attitudes specifically relevant to it than with very general attitudes that apply to a much larger class of potential behaviors.

This point is clear in a study of the predictors of oral contraceptive use (Davidson & Jaccard, 1979). Attitudes toward using birth control pills in the next two years correlated strongly with actual behavior, but attitudes toward birth control in *general* correlated only slightly with the use of oral contraceptives in the next two years (see Table 6-6).

Salience of Attitude

In most situations, several different attitudes may be relevant to behavior. Cheating on college examinations might be determined by lax attitudes about honesty or by a strong desire to get into law school. A school superintendent's decision to prevent a gay rights sympathizer from addressing a high school assembly might be dictated by his dislike for controversy within the school or by his distaste for gays. So one important determinant of the consistency of behavior with a particular attitude should be the salience of the attitude in question.

When a particular attitude is made salient, it is more likely to be related to behavior. To show this, Snyder and Swann (1976) assigned subjects to a mock jury situation and gave them a sex discrimination case. In the "attitude salient" condition, subjects' attitudes about affirmative action were made salient by instructing them to take a few minutes before the case to organize their thoughts on affirmative action. In the "attitude not salient" condition, subjects were not given any warning that affirmative action was involved. When attitudes were made salient, they were highly related to jurors' verdicts in the case. But attitudes about affirmative action were not closely related to verdicts when they had not been made salient.

As you might expect, salience is particularly crucial when the attitude is not a very strong one. When the attitude is very strong, presumably it does not have to be brought very forcefully to the person's attention to be strongly related to behavior. Borgida and Campbell (1982) studied students during a campus parking shortage at the University of Minnesota. Students who usually drove to campus were more directly affected by the shortage than were others, because they either spent a long time looking for a parking place or got a lot of parking tickets. Presumably the daily drivers had stronger attitudes, since they had direct experience with the shortages. The researchers exposed some students in each group to a conversation that included complaints about the parking situation, to make attitudes about parking more salient. Others heard a conversation on summer job plans and the merits of racquetball. It turned out that the conversation making the parking issue salient enhanced the consistency of attitude and behavior (willingness to sign a full-page ad in the campus newspaper) only for the students with little experience with the issue, who presumably had the weakest attitudes.

To take this point one step farther, making the affective component of the attitude more salient increases its power over behavior, whereas making the cognitive component more salient makes *it* more powerful (Millar & Tesser, 1986). However, when the cognitive and affective components of an attitude are consistent

with each other, it does not matter which is made more salient: Both will be highly correlated with the behavior when either is made salient (Millar & Tesser, 1989).

Situational Pressures

Whenever people engage in overt behavior, they can be influenced both by their attitudes and by the situation. When situational pressures are strong, attitudes will not determine behavior as strongly as when such pressures are relatively weak. This is easy to see in the La Piere study. Well-dressed, respectable-looking people asking for rooms are hard to refuse, despite feelings of prejudice against their ethnic group. The external pressures are even stronger when the law requires giving a room to anyone who wants one and can pay for it.

Overall, then, sometimes attitudes are strongly related to behavior and sometimes they are not. Some factors that are important are shown in Table 6-7.

The Reasoned Action Model

Perhaps the most influential effort to generate and test a general theory of attitude–behavior links is Fishbein and Ajzen's *theory of reasoned action* (1975; Ajzen & Fishbein, 1980). This theory is an attempt to specify the factors that determine attitude–behavior consistency. It begins with the assumption that we behave in

---

TABLE 6-7
Conditions that Contribute to High Attitude–Behavior Consistency

Attitude is strong
   Unconflicted attitude
   Affective and cognitive components are consistent
   Information about attitude object
   Direct personal experience with attitude object
Attitude is stable over time
Attitude is relevant to the behavior
Attitude is salient
No conflicting situational pressures

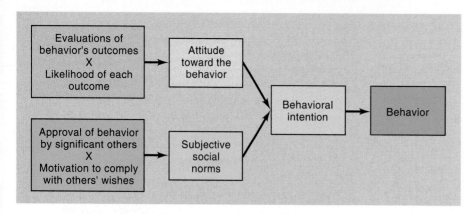

Figure 6-12 The reasoned action model of factors determining a person's behavior.

accord with our conscious intentions, which are based in turn on our rational calculations about the potential effects of our behavior and about how other people will feel about it. The **reasoned action model** is diagrammed in Figure 6-12.

The central point of the theory of reasoned actions is that a person's behavior can be predicted from **behavioral intentions.** If a woman says that she intends to use the pill to avoid getting pregnant, she is more likely to do so than is someone who does not intend to. Behavioral intentions can themselves be predicted from two main variables: the person's attitude toward the behavior (does she think taking the pill is a good step for her?) and subjective **social norms** (her perception of what others think she should do; does her husband want her to? what about her church, and her mother?). The person's attitude toward the behavior is predicted using the expectancy value framework: The desirability of each possible outcome is weighted by the likelihood of that outcome (for example, avoiding pregnancy is extremely important to this woman, and the pill is almost certain to prevent pregnancy; the pill has mildly unpleasant side effects, but they do not affect everyone who takes it). Subjective social norms are predicted by the perceived expectations of significant others weighted by the motivation to conform to those expectations (for example, her husband may strongly want her to take the pill, and she wants to please him; her church strongly opposes it, but she thinks its views are outdated and no longer cares about them).

The reasoned action model appeals to many social psychologists both because it makes people seem reasonable and because it places attitudes in a central place in determining behavior. It also has the value of great simplicity: It purports to explain any behavior on the basis of a small number of variables. Consequently the model has been widely used. A simple example is a study by Manstead and colleagues (Manstead, Proffitt, & Smart, 1983) predicting whether pregnant women would wind up breast-feeding or bottle-feeding their babies. For prenatal questionnaires, the researchers measured behavioral intentions (did the woman intend to breast-feed?), attitudes toward the behavior (for example, did she believe that breast-feeding establishes a closer mother–baby bond, and how important is that bond?), and subjective social norms (what did the woman's husband, mother, closest female friend, and doctor prefer, and how motivated was the woman to follow their wishes?). The researchers found the model was very successful in predicting later behavior. The correlation of these various attitudes with actual postbirth breast-feeding was .77, which is quite high. The model has also been used successfully to predict a variety of other behaviors.

Of course, no model is perfect. What are some of the difficulties with this one? The notion that our intentions determine our behavior gives the model much of its appeal and distinctiveness. But the role of behavioral intention is a principal source of problems as well. For one thing, as everyone knows, good intentions are not always enough. Sometimes we do not have the ability or resources to do something we intend to do. As a result, it has been suggested that an additional variable—perceived control over outcomes—be added to the model (Ajzen & Madden, 1986; Madden, Ellen, & Ajzen, 1992). As in the case of attributional analyses of perceived control discussed in the previous chapter, both internal and external control are

210

relevant. Illustrating the importance of a sense of internal control, Schifter and Ajzen (1985) found that female students' intentions to lose weight were more likely to result in genuine weight loss among those who felt they could control their weight and could successfully lose weight if they tried. Attitudes about the desirability of weight loss had little effect on behavior for those who felt helpless about their ability to lose weight. A recent review (Madden et al., 1992) confirms that adding control to the theory improves its ability to predict intentions and behavior, and that this is especially true when the behaviors present potential problems with respect to control (such as losing weight or stopping smoking).

However, factors not included in the model, such as external constraints and opportunities, as well as perceived susceptibility and fear, may also be important. Boyd and Wandersman (1991) interviewed 190 college undergraduates about their intentions to use condoms during sexual intercourse. Three months after completing the initial questionnaire, subjects were recontacted by phone to record the frequency of condom use during the intervening period. Although behavioral intention was a strong predictor of reported condom use, perceived susceptibility to and fear of AIDS significantly predicted condom use as well. It is likely, too, that access to condoms and a willingness to purchase them also contributes to this behavior. So, we can intend to use condoms, yet not have access to them when we need them, or we can intend not to, yet wind up using them if they are available and our partner insists upon them.

As we have seen earlier in this chapter, attitudes about the desirability of a behavior do not always control our actions. Prior behavior influences future behavior above and beyond attitudes. To some extent people are simply creatures of habit. How a woman fed her first child influences how she will feed her second, no matter what she or all her friends and family members think is right (Manstead et al., 1983). In a study many readers may relate to, Ajzen and Madden (1986) found previous class attendance to be the single strongest predictor of college students' future class attendance,

irrespective of any of their attitudes about attending class.

Finally, it is sometimes difficult to get measures of behavioral intention that are truly independent of attitudes toward the behavior, on the one hand, and actual behavior, on the other. Sometimes behavioral intention is not, as measured, very different from attitude toward the behavior. Asking a pregnant woman whether she intends to breast-feed her baby may be almost the same thing as asking her whether she thinks it is a good idea or not. Under such circumstances attitudes are more successful in predicting behavioral intentions than in predicting actual behavior (e.g., Ajzen & Madden, 1986). But it may not add very much to our understanding to bring behavioral intention in as a separate factor.

This is a particular danger when researchers use self-reported behavior rather than observe it directly. Then it may be artificially correlated with attitudes toward the behavior, especially if the behavior has strong moral implications. Hessing, Elffers, and Weigel (1988), for example, interviewed individuals who had been identified by Dutch tax officials as having knowingly evaded taxes in two separate tax years (and who had paid the resulting bills without protest) as well as individuals identified as having submitted honest tax returns. They found that self-reported tax evasion was scarcely related at all to objective tax evasion: 69 percent of the evaders reported that they had *not* evaded taxes and 25 percent of the nonevaders reported that they *had* evaded taxes!. Not surprisingly, both attitudes toward tax evasion and subjective social norms predicted self-reported behavior much better than they did actual behavior. Apparently, people reported their behavior more in terms of what they thought they *should* have done than in terms of what they actually *had* done.

With these reservations, this theory helps to understand the role attitudes play in determining behavior. In general, we believe a great deal of evidence now supports the idea that attitudes affect behavior. But there are numerous other factors that play a major role in determining the degree of attitude–behavior consistency.

KEY TERMS

association
attitude-discrepant behavior
attitudes
balance theory
behavioral component
behavioral intention
cognitive component
cognitive consistency
cognitive dissonance
    theory
cognitive response
    theory
commitment
contrast

counterarguing
credibility
discrepancy
dissonance
distraction
ego involvement
elaboration-likelihood model
expectancy-value theory
forewarning
imitation
incentive theory
inoculation defense
learning
message learning

modes of resolution
peripheral cues
punishment
reasoned action model
reference group
reinforcement
self-perception theory
sleeper effect
social norms
source derogation
supportive defense
systematic processing
transfer of affect

SUMMARY

1. Attitudes have a cognitive (thought) component, an affective (feeling) component, and a behavioral component. Attitudes are usually cognitively complex but evaluatively simple.

2. The learning approach views attitudes as learned by association, reinforcement, and imitation. Cognitive consistency theories view people as attempting to maintain consistency among their attitudes, and among the affective, cognitive, and behavioral components of a particular attitude. The expectancy-value approach views attitudes as cost–benefit calculations by the individual based on the pros and cons of the arguments.

3. Dissonance theory focuses on how behavior affects attitudes. Dissonance arises following decisions and following behavioral acts contrary to the individual's attitudes. Dissonance is typically resolved by changing attitudes.

4. Postdecisional dissonance is greatest when people have free choice, remain committed to their decisions, and feel responsible for foreseeable consequences.

5. Dissonance following attitude-discrepant behavior depends on barely sufficient incentives to commit the behavior, such as threats or promised rewards. The maximum dissonance occurs with minimum incentive and clear personal responsibility for negative consequences of the act.

6. Alternative explanations for these dissonance effects have been generated by self-perception theory. When we have rather vague, undefined attitudes, behavioral acts may lead to new perceptions of our own attitudes, thus leading to attitude–behavior consistency through self-perception rather than dissonance reduction.

7. Cognitive response theory and the elaboration-likelihood model distinguish between systematic processing, which involves close scrutiny of the arguments, and the use of peripheral cues irrelevant to message content.

8. A useful model of the attitude change situation classifies possible influences on the target in terms of communicator (or source), communication, and situational and target variables.

9. Credible, trustworthy, and liked sources are the most potent communicators, as are reference groups with which the target identifies.

Source characteristics are often processed as peripheral cues. To avoid changing attitudes, people sometimes derogate the source.

10. An important aspect of a communication is its discrepancy from the target's initial attitude. Attitude change tends to increase with more discrepancy up to a point, when it starts to fall off again. With high source credibility and/or low commitment, this falloff point occurs at higher levels of discrepancy.

11. Communications can arouse emotional needs such as anger or fear and tend to be accepted if the position advocated reduces the need it has aroused. Very high levels of fear seem to arouse defensive reactions, however, and reduce the likelihood of attitude change.

12. The degree of commitment to an attitude (position involvement) is a critical determinant of persuasion. With high commitment, there is less persuasion.

13. Strong arguments are more effective than weak ones when the target can be induced to think about them, such as when the issue is personally relevant (high issue involvement).

14. Repetition of a message is important if attitude change is to be maintained. But too much repetition leads to boredom and lessened support for it.

15. A person can become inoculated against persuasion by being exposed to weak versions of the forthcoming persuasive arguments, and learning to combat them.

16. Forewarning of the position to be advocated increases resistance to change when the listener is highly committed to a very discrepant position.

17. Distraction can facilitate persuasion by reducing the listener's defenses against very discrepant messages.

18. Sometimes behavior arises from attitudes, but sometimes it does not. Attitude–behavior consistency is high when attitudes are strong, stable, salient, and clearly relevant to the behavior, and when there are few conflicting situational pressures.

19. The reasoned action model holds that behavior is controlled by behavioral intentions, which in turn are determined by attitudes toward the behavior and by subjective social norms.

SUGGESTED READINGS

Abelson, R. P., Aronson, E., McGuire, W. J., Newcomb, T. M., Rosenberg, M. J., & Tannenbaum, P. E. (1968). *Theories of cognitive consistency: A sourcebook.* Chicago: Rand McNally. An extensive compilation of papers on almost every version of consistency theory. Its nickname is TOCCAS.

Chaiken, S., & Stangor, C. (1987). Attitudes and attitude change. In M. R. Rosenzweig & L. W. Porter (Eds.), *Annual Review of Psychology, 38,* 575–630. A thoughtful review of recent research on attitudes. The best recent statement of social psychologists' thinking about attitudes. It is especially detailed on the question of systematic versus heuristic processing.

Cooper, J., & Fazio, R. H. (1984). A new look at dissonance theory. In L. Berkowitz (Ed.), *Advances in experimental social psychology* (Vol. 17). New York: Academic Press. An update of research on cognitive dissonance theory.

Festinger, L. (1957). *A theory of cognitive dissonance.* Stanford, CA: Stanford University Press. The original statement of cognitive dissonance theory. It is elegant in its simplicity and offers plausible speculations about a broad range of psychological phenomena.

Hovland, C. I., Janis, I. L., & Kelley, H. H. (1953). *Communication and persuasion.* New Haven, CT: Yale University Press. The original presentation of the pioneering program in experimental studies of attitude change. Much of the work we describe in Chapter 6 springs from work originally presented here.

Petty, R. E., & Cacioppo, J. T. (1981). *Attitudes and persuasion: Classic and contemporary approaches.* This book provides a nice overview and gives good coverage of the cognitive response application.

Petty, R. E., & Cacioppo, J. T. (1986). *Communication and persuasion: Central and peripheral routes to attitude change.* New York: Springer. A complete presentation of the elaboration-likelihood model of attitude change.

Zanna, M. P., & Fazio, R. H. (1982). The attitude–behavior relation: Moving toward a third generation of research. In M. P. Zanna, E. T. Higgins, & C. P. Herman (Eds.), *Consistency in social behavior: The Ontario symposium* (Vol. 2). Hillsdale, NJ: Erlbaum. A review of research on attitudes and behavior that is sensitive to the complexities of their relationship.

7
Prejudice

FOCUS OF THIS CHAPTER

Components of Group Antagonism
Learning Prejudice
Motives for Prejudice
Cognitive Bases of Prejudice
The Changing Face of Prejudice
Reducing Prejudice

 Research Closeup
On Being a "Typical" Member of a Category

 Cultural Highlight
Collectivist Versus Individualistic Outlook—Implications for Prejudice

People's prejudices concern their perceptions of other individuals and groups, and their attitudes and behavior toward them. Prejudice can be one of the most destructive aspects of human social behavior, often producing chilling acts of violence. Over 6 million European Jews were murdered by the Nazis in the 1940s under the guise of "purifying" the European racial stock. Today only a fraction of that number of Jews remain in Europe. The number of North American Indians dropped from an estimated 3 million in the seventeenth century to 600,000 today. The Spanish genocide of Indians in Latin America is even more appalling.

But racial prejudice against blacks by whites has been perhaps the most severe and tenacious social problem faced by the United States. It dates back at least as far as the earliest contact between English travelers and Africans in the sixteenth century. The English were especially struck by the Africans' blackness, a color with overwhelmingly bad connotations for the English of the day. They perceived the Africans as looking like apes, as engaging in savage and uncivilized behavior, and as having "heathen" religions (Jordan, 1968). These earliest white impressions contain most of the antiblack stereotypes still common in the twentieth century.

When Africans were imported into America as slaves, they were treated as property, and often as subhuman beings. Although the slave trade was abolished in 1808, almost 90 percent of all blacks in the United States were still slaves in 1860, just before the outbreak of the Civil War. And emancipation did not noticeably improve their lot. For example, in the half-century before World War II, thousands of individual blacks were lynched by mobs of whites. And at the beginning of World War II, most blacks lived in the South, where they still were largely segregated by law. Restaurants, movie houses, and buses had separate sections for blacks and whites.

After World War II, racial lynchings came to a nearly complete halt. Most kinds of formal segregation were finally outlawed in 1964. The civil rights movement resulted in many other improvements as well. But in recent years, life has again gotten worse for many blacks. More live below the poverty line, housing and public schools continue to deteriorate in inner-city areas, and crime has taken a major toll.

But African Americans are not the only minority group subjected to prejudice. Many of the nearly 20 million Latinos living in the United States are relatively disadvantaged, with low educational achievement, low-paying jobs, and high poverty rates. They too are subject to considerable prejudice. Japanese Americans have fared relatively well economically in recent years. But in 1942 the federal government sent over 120,000 Japanese Americans to internment camps for the duration of World War II, generally without benefit of individual review or due process, and forced them to abandon most of their possessions. Only in 1988 did the government pay $20,000 to each surviving internee, as a gesture to redress the injustice. Gay men and lesbians have also historically been subject to much prejudice from the heterosexual majority. This prejudice has been so intense that most stayed "in the closet" until recently, keeping their sexual preferences secret to protect themselves.

In fact, virtually every social group has been the victim of prejudice at one time or another. One indication is the wide variety of derogatory labels that have been applied to every imaginable group in America, whether Irish (micks),

Under the system of slavery, African-Americans were the only peoples in the United States ever to be systematically bought and sold as property. Slave auctions, like livestock auctions, were routine parts of life in the South before the Civil War.

Germans (krauts), French (frogs), Italians (wops, dagos), Poles (polacks), Jews (kikes, hebes, hymies), blacks (niggers, coons, jigaboos, jungle bunnies), Hispanics (spics, greasers, wetbacks, beaners), or Asians (slants, slopes, Chinks, Japs, flips), or gays and lesbians (faggots, fairies, dykes). Even white Anglo-Saxon Protestants are called "WASPS" on occasion, not always fondly.

However, in the United States the "peculiar institution" of slavery, and the legalized system of segregation that followed it, were unique to Americans of African descent. Achieving equality has been more difficult for them than for any other minority group, in the United States and indeed throughout the world, and racial prejudice has been a central reason. Because this problem has been so difficult and important in the United States, most of the research on prejudice has focused on it, as will much of our discussion, though examples concerning other racial and ethnic groups will be introduced. We will deal with prejudice concerning gender in Chapter 12.

COMPONENTS OF GROUP ANTAGONISM

Prejudice is exhibited when members of one group (called the **ingroup**) display negative attitudes and behavior toward members of another group (called the **outgroup**). Such group antagonisms have three interrelated but distinguishable elements. **Stereotypes** are beliefs about the typical characteristics of group members, such as beliefs that Asian Americans are timid, nonathletic, good only at math, and clannish, or that Polish Americans are strong, clumsy, and stupid. **Prejudice** refers to negative evaluations toward the outgroup, such as feeling disgusted by or angry at lesbians, or evaluating them negatively in general. **Discrimination** refers to overt behavior, such as barring gays from military service.

Stereotypes

Stereotypes, the cognitive component of group antagonism, are beliefs about the personal attributes shared by people in a particular group or social category. For example, nineteenth-century Native Americans were most commonly stereotyped in novels, textbooks, and films as dirty, cruel, and warring savages, wearing feathers or war bonnets, riding horses, and using nonverbal signals to communicate with each other. Twentieth-century Native Americans are more often depicted as silent, passive, drunken, lazy, and immoral (Trimble, 1988).

Stereotypes often influence perceptions about individual members of the outgroup. For example, Sagar and Schofield (1980) presented sixth graders with brief verbal descriptions and artist's drawings of interactions between two children, such as one asking another for cake or bumping the other in the hallway. The races of the two children were systematically varied in the drawings. The sixth graders were then asked to tell a story about what had happened. Both black and white children described the behavior as more mean and threatening when blacks were involved than when whites were. Presumably this is due to the stereotype that such interactions are likely to be more hostile than friendly if blacks are involved.

Prejudice

Prejudice is the evaluation of a group or of a single individual based mainly on the person's group membership. For example, a study of Canadians found sharply different evaluations of different ethnic groups: English, Scottish, Dutch, and French Canadians were favorably evaluated, whereas Chinese, Greek, African, Indian, and East Indian Canadians were viewed negatively (Berry, Kain, & Taylor, 1977). As a result, prejudice has the same like–dislike quality of the evaluative or affective dimensions discussed earlier regarding impressions (Chapter 2) and attitudes (Chapter 6). But prejudice has the additional quality of prejudgment. The perceiver evaluates other people on the basis of their social or racial category rather than on the basis of information about them as individuals.

Unflattering stereotypes often go together with unfavorable prejudices. For example, people who are prejudiced against gays may describe people with AIDS as immoral, disgusting, and dirty (Pryor et al., 1989). But stereotypes and prejudice are not identical. For example, for many years Americans had high levels of prejudice against both blacks and Jews, but with quite different stereotypes about the two groups: blacks were regarded as lazy, not very smart, and good at athletics, while Jews were supposed to be shrewd, mercenary, and ambitious.

The effects of prejudice are destructive and wide ranging. For one thing, our judgments about individual group members are influenced by our prejudices about their group. In one typi-

cal study, people with negative attitudes toward gay men were more resistant than others to interacting with someone with AIDS, even though his infection was described as coming from a blood transfusion rather than from sexual activities (Pryor, Reeder, & McManus, 1991).

In another study, white college students read a description of an alleged rape of a 19-year-old woman by a 21-year-old man on the campus. The races of both victim and defendant were varied. Results showed that the black defendant was more often judged guilty than was the white, especially when the victim was white. The bias against the black defendant was also greatest when the evidence was marginal (Ugwuegbu, 1979). This is typical: Prejudice influences perceptions of individual group members most strongly when there is some ambiguity about the real situation.

Prejudice also influences people's political responses. For example, when a black candidate is on the ballot, a white voter's prejudice is often the best predictor of which candidate the voter will support. In 1984, when Jesse Jackson first ran for the presidency, the most prejudiced whites were the most likely to vote against him (Sears, Citrin, & Kosterman, 1987). Whites' prejudice against blacks also contributes to greater opposition to affirmative action or busing (Jessor, 1988; Kluegel & Smith, 1983). Prejudice against Latinos contributes to opposition to bilingual education, and prejudice against Asian Americans, to opposition to affirmative action for them (Citrin, Reingold, & Green, 1989; Sears & Huddy, 1993). Similarly, anti-gay prejudices contribute to support for highly restrictive policies regarding HIV-positive individuals, such as requiring them to carry identification, quarantining them, or tattooing them (Price & Hsu, 1992). In all these areas, other influences are important as well. For example, conservatives' opposition to excessive government regulation also contributes to opposition to affirmative action programs. But in each case prejudice has a significant effect.

Prejudice refers mainly to negative attitudes toward the outgroup. **Ethnocentrism** refers to the belief that the ingroup is the center of everything and is superior to all outgroups. Thus the ingroup is perceived as most virtuous and hold-

Following a new surge of immigration to the United States beginning in the 1960s, and the rise of "multiculturalism" as a set of beliefs supporting persistence of foreign cultures after immigration, "Americanism" has again become a potent political force.

ing the best values; the outgroup is contemptible, immoral, inferior, weak, untrustworthy, and criminal (Brewer, 1986).

These positive attitudes toward the ingroup can have some of the same effects as prejudice against the outgroup. Among Anglo adults in California, "traditional Americanism" (based on beliefs about what makes someone a "true American," such as speaking and writing English or defending America when it is criticized) increased opposition to policies that would benefit Latinos and Asians, such as voting rights for non-English speakers (Citrin et al., 1990).

Prejudice also influences attributions about a group's performance. **Group-serving biases** lead people to make internal attributions for the outgroup's failures (blacks do not work hard) and external attributions for their successes (black medical students are only admitted through special breaks). In analogous fashion, people make internal attributions for the ingroup's success (such as crediting the Allied victory in the Persian Gulf war to their superior fighting force) and external attributions for its failures (the Nazis blamed Germany's economic difficulties in the 1920s on a Jewish conspiracy). This is a variant of the *self-serving attribution* discussed in Chapter 5 (Hewstone & Islam, 1992; Schaller, 1992).

Perceivers do generally make more favorable attributions for ingroup members than they do for outgroup members (Hamilton & Trolier, 1986). A good example concerns whites' explanations for blacks' socioeconomic disadvantages, such as low income or educational level. Whites' traditional attribution for this was stable and internal: Blacks were seen as innately inferior. Today whites are more likely to use unstable internal attributions, such as lack of effort or low aspirations. Blacks, on the other hand, are more likely to focus on external causes such as discrimination (Bobo, 1989).

Another good example concerns blacks' and whites' attributions for the widespread ghetto

TABLE 7-1
What Do You Think Caused the Watts Riots?

	Blacks		Whites
Perceived Causes	Arrestees	Community Sample	Community Sample
Stable external (grievances about society, pent-up hostility)	85%	64%	34%
Unstable external (weather, accident, chance happening)	8	11	28
Stable internal (Communists, criminals, agitators)	2	9	29
Don't know, no answer	6	17	10
Total	101%[a]	101%[a]	101%[a]

[a] Rounding error.
Source: Adapted from Sears and McConahay (1973), p. 160.

rioting during the 1960s. As Table 7-1 shows, blacks tended to attribute the rioting to the miserable situation blacks found themselves in and to the justifiable hostility those conditions produced. Whites, on the other hand, were more likely to blame chance external factors or bad individual rioters.

These differences in attributions for minorities' disadvantages have great political significance. If the real causes lie in bad conditions, as the minorities themselves tend to believe, then those conditions should be changed, through improved housing and health care, jobs, education programs, income redistribution, and so on. If the true causes lie in minorities' internal characteristics, such as lack of effort or ability, or criminality, or in the case of the rioting, in unstable external factors such as hot weather, nothing need be done. If criminals were responsible, a harsh "law and order" policy might be appropriate.

Discrimination

Discrimination is the behavioral component of group antagonism. This consists of negative behaviors toward individuals based on their group membership. For example, in the criminal justice system blacks are more likely than whites to be excluded from juries (especially in cases involving black defendants), to get harsher sentences, to serve longer in prison, and to be sentenced to death (especially for raping a white woman). These racial differences hold up even when such factors as severity and frequency of offense are held constant (Nickerson, Mayo, & Smith, 1986). The use of quotas in college admissions to limit the number of Jewish students, as many private universities did before 1960, or of Asian-American students, as is sometimes charged today, is another example of discrimination. The use of quotas to aid minorities has been described as "reverse discrimination" because it favors a minority group at the expense of the majority.

Discrimination, as the behavioral component of group antagonism, is not always consistent with prejudiced attitudes. This was illustrated in Chapter 6 by the study showing that restaurant

Until 1964, Southern cities such as Dallas required blacks to sit in the back of the bus, while whites sat in the front.

and hotel owners verbally refused to accept Asian customers, but behaviorally did accept the Chinese couple who appeared on their doorsteps (La Piere, 1934). Conversely, a great deal of prejudice can coexist with relatively little discrimination, particularly if there are firm legal prohibitions against it. No matter how prejudiced a restaurant owner might be, it is illegal to refuse to serve someone based on his or her race. Anti-discrimination laws have made such discriminatory behavior less common.

LEARNING PREJUDICE

There are a number of theories about the origins of prejudice, most of which derive from the general theories introduced in Chapter 1 and applied to attitudes in Chapter 6. Perhaps the simplest, *social learning theory*, views prejudice as being learned the same way people learn other attitudes and values.

Socialization

Children are not born with stereotypes and prejudiced attitudes. They must learn them—from their family, their peers, the media, and the society around them. *Socialization* refers to the process by which children and adolescents learn those attitudes. This can take place through each of the social learning mechanisms described earlier. For example, children may simply imitate the prejudices of adults and friends, they may be reinforced for using derogatory ethnic humor, or they may simply learn to associate particular minority groups with poverty, crime, dirtiness, and other bad things.

Much of the learning of prejudice occurs outside the home. Prejudice is a **social norm** of the group in which the individual lives, or even of the society at large. Such norms are learned as part of the process of socialization. It is easy to document the existence of norms of ethnic and racial prejudice all over the world. For example, white North Americans have historically tended to be prejudiced against those who originally came from Africa, Asia, and Latin America and to favor those who came from Western Europe (Lambert & Klineberg, 1967). Russians have historically been prejudiced against Jews, the English against Africans, the Chinese against Japanese, the Japanese against Koreans, and so on.

These social norms of prejudice are often acquired very early in life. By age 4 or 5, most American children are aware of the differences between blacks and whites in our society and of the prevailing norms about race, at least in some form. Anglo children's recognition of other ethnic groups (e.g., Latinos or Asian Americans) tends to be delayed a few years. Prejudice is also learned very early. In one typical study, most urban white children displayed some signs of racial prejudice by the age of 5. By age 7, most also showed signs of prejudice against Asians or native Americans (Aboud, 1988).

Parents play a particularly important role in the child's acquisition of prejudice. There are consistent correlations between parents' and children's racial and ethnic attitudes (Ashmore & Del Boca, 1976). Parents often transmit these attitudes without directly instructing their children, since attitudes can be learned by association or by imitation as well as by direct reinforcement. Children observe their parents' attitudes and behavior and pick up many nonverbal cues in their reactions to people from other groups.

The experiences children have during these early years are crucial, because by early adolescence racial prejudice has crystallized and is much more difficult to break down. And as children grow older, their peer groups become increasingly important. Normally peer groups mostly reinforce parents' views, because of the similarities in social background and values of people sharing a common community environment. But occasionally the parents' attitudes conflict with peers' attitudes, and the older the child gets, the more influential peers will be (Tedin, 1974).

The Media

The media represent another potential source of social learning, especially for children. Minorities have historically been given relatively little attention in the media. For example, a study of *New Yorker* cartoons from 1946 to 1987 revealed that blacks were vastly underrepresented, appearing in only 0.4 percent of the cartoons in that period, despite comprising over 10 percent of the U.S. population (Thibodeau, 1989). As shown in Table 7-2, blacks have regularly been portrayed in passive roles. The major change that has occurred in recent years is that they are now rarely presented in such traditionally stereotyped roles as maid or entertainer. Instead they tend to be presented as "tokens," appearing in the background as part of a racially integrated crowd or group.

On prime-time television, as well, blacks appear much more often than they used to, and are no longer shown only in subordinate roles. One study showed that over 70 percent of the cross-racial interactions presented at least some of the black characters in positions of authority or technical sophistication (Weigel, Loomis, & Soja, 1980). But such cross-racial interactions tended to be infrequent, distant, formal, and centered on the workplace. So if children were to take their cue from television today, they would assume that relations between the races were somewhat rare, distant, formal, and occurring primarily at work. Of course, this is not necessarily to blame television; this may simply reflect society at large. And we should remem-

TABLE 7-2
American Blacks in New Yorker Cartoons

Time Period	Cartoons with Blacks	Blacks in Passive Roles	Blacks in Stereotyped Roles	Blacks in Token Roles
1946–1955	0.2%	71%	100%	0%
1956–1965	0.1	67	44	11
1966–1975	0.7	77	18	40
1976–1987	0.4	94	22	74

Source: Adapted from Thibodeau (1989), pp. 486–487.

ber that all this is still a great improvement over either ignoring minorities or presenting them only in stereotyped roles, as was most common a generation ago.

In other cases the media may actually contribute to reducing prejudice. Most of the public's information about the AIDS epidemic has come from the media (Singer et al., 1987). The best recent research suggests that support for restrictive policies against HIV-positive individuals is greatest among those least informed about AIDS. And misinformation about the epidemic has clearly been reduced by exposure to it in the media (Price & Hsu, 1992). Interestingly, several studies also show that anti-gay prejudice interferes with accurate reception of media information about AIDS (Stipp & Kerr, 1989; Pryor et al., 1991). So the media probably have helped reduce prejudice against people with AIDS. But even when the media try to present information that will correct inaccurate stereotypes, prejudice may interfere.

MOTIVES FOR PREJUDICE

Other theories of prejudice focus on the needs of the individual and how prejudice can help satisfy them. Such theories are examples of motivational or decision-making theories because they focus on individuals' motives and on the incentives provided to individuals for adopting prejudiced attitudes. There are several distinct versions of such theories.

Psychodynamic Approaches

Theories of prejudice that analyze it as an outgrowth of motivational tensions within the individual are sometimes called **psychodynamic theories** because they emphasize the particular dynamics of the specific individual's personality. One such theory treats prejudice as *displaced aggression* (see Chapter 14). Displacement occurs when a source of frustration or annoyance cannot be attacked because of fear or simple unavailability. If there is an economic depression and a man loses his job, he feels angry and aggressive, but there is no obvious person at fault. Under these circumstances, people look for a scapegoat—someone whom they can blame for their difficulties and whom they can attack. One example is a study showing that lynchings of blacks in the South before World War II increased as economic conditions deteriorated (Hovland & Sears, 1940). Poor whites could not aggress against the real sources of their frustration—large economic forces—so they aggressed against a more convenient and probably safer target—local blacks.

Another psychodynamic theory treats prejudice as a personality disorder. The best known example of this theory is found in work on the *authoritarian personality* (Adorno et al., 1950), an effort to understand the origins of anti-Semitism. The study concluded that prejudice develops from the authoritarian personality syndrome, characterized by exaggerated submission to authority, hostility, and mysticism, as shown in Table 7-3.

This policeman is checking a Jewish cemetery in Germany where neo-Nazis have spray painted swastikas on the gravestones. As with many longstanding group antagonisms, European anti-Semitism returns to public view over and over.

Research on authoritarianism quickly got caught up in technical methodological disputes (see Christie & Jahoda, 1954; Kirscht & Dillehay, 1967). As a result, the concept of authoritarianism lay dormant for many years. Recently, Bob Altemeyer (1988) has given new life, and a new

understanding, to the concept. To be sure, he also defines the authoritarian syndrome in terms of exaggerated submission to authority, extreme levels of conformity to conventional standards of behavior, self-righteous hostility, and punitiveness toward deviants and minorities. This, too, is shown in Table 7-3. He also limits this syndrome to right-wing authoritarianism; he finds that authoritarians tend to support established authority rather than challenge it as those on the political left do.

Where Altemeyer departs most dramatically from the original theory is in placing the origins of prejudice not in personality conflicts, but in (1) direct learning from parents and peers and (2) personal experiences, such that people with extensive experience with unconventional people and with minorities are not likely to become authoritarians. In a sense his view is hopeful. Authoritarianism is not linked irreversibly to our personalities, changeable only through lengthy psychotheoarpy (if then), but is responsive to new learning experiences and direct contact with new kinds of people.

TABLE 7-3
Two Concepts of Authoritarianism

	The Authoritarian Personality (Adorno et al., 1950)	*Enemies of Freedom* (Altemeyer, 1988)
Content	Exaggerated need to submit to strong authority	Authoritarian submission to the established, legitimate authorities
	Rigid adherence to conventional patterns of behavior; harsh punishment for deviant behavior	Conventionalism—high degree of adherence to standard social conventions
	Generalized hostility	Authoritarian aggression against various persons, as sanctioned by established authorities
Origins	Mystical, superstitious cast of mind	Social learning from parents and peers
	Personality conflicts	Lack of personal experiences with nonconventional people or minorities

Realistic Group Conflict

The theory of **realistic group conflict** argues that when two groups are in competition for scarce resources, they threaten each other. This creates hostility between them and thus produces mutually negative evaluations. So prejudice is an inevitable consequence of a real conflict over resources both groups want. This is a motivational analysis; prejudice arises when one group frustrates the other group's needs. Perhaps it can be minimized if both groups get more of their needs satisfied, but it cannot be eliminated altogether because real conflicts of interest cannot be eliminated completely (Bobo, 1988a; LeVine & Campbell, 1972).

For example, the theory would lead us to expect antagonism toward Asian Americans from other minority groups. In recent years, increasing numbers of Asian Americans have been excelling in academic work. When they are admitted to prestigious universities, correspondingly fewer students from other groups are admitted, so it would not be surprising if prejudice against Asian Americans began to rise. Indeed, historical analyses suggest that Chinese and Japanese immigrants to the United States were well received as long as they did menial work no one else wanted to do. Only later, when they began to compete with Caucasians for jobs, did prejudice mount. Similarly, opposition to the civil rights movement among whites was greatest when the movement was scoring its greatest successes, in the 1960s. In recent years, as blacks have become less demanding, whites have been less opposed to the movement (Bobo, 1988a).

Relative Deprivation

Realistic group conflict theory describes prejudice as a response to the real frustrations of life. But sometimes people *perceive* themselves to be deprived relative to others, even though in reality they may be doing very well indeed. These perceptions of **relative deprivation** can also create intergroup hostility. For example, in a fast-growing economy, most people's economic situations may be improving. But feelings of relative deprivation may be created among those whose situations are improving more slowly, as they see others increasingly able to afford things they cannot. This in turn might lead to antagonism against the favored group. This was one factor in the riots in black ghettoes in the 1960s. Although both whites and blacks were improving economically, blacks felt that their situations were not improving as much as those of whites, contributing to antiwhite violence (Sears & McConahay, 1973).

There are two kinds of relative deprivation. *Egoistic deprivation* is the feeling that I am deprived relative to other people. *Fraternal deprivation* is the feeling that my ingroup is deprived relative to other groups, regardless of whether or not I am personally. The deprivation is among "us," and not necessarily of "me." It can lead to individual whites being upset by affirmative action even if they are not personally affected by it. They may have secure jobs themselves, and their children may be finished with college, but they may be upset because affirmative action signals a displacement of whites by blacks (Bobo, 1988a; Sears & Kinder, 1985).

Fraternal deprivation proves to be stronger than egoistic deprivation in fomenting group antagonism, nationalism, and social protest. For example, it activated social protest among unemployed youths in Australia, among gay men and lesbians in Toronto, and among whites who felt that they were not gaining as fast as blacks (Birt & Dion, 1987; Bobo, 1988b; Vanneman & Pettigrew, 1972; Walker & Mann, 1987). In all these cases, egoistic deprivation had little effect.

COGNITIVE BASES OF PREJUDICE

Earlier we analyzed extensively the cognitive processes that produce the impressions one person has of another (Chapters 2 and 3). Extending such cognitive theories from impressions of individual persons to impressions of groups and of group members has been one of the most active research areas on prejudice in recent years. The central idea is that certain systematic cognitive biases naturally accompany the perception of other people. These seemingly harmless cognitive biases can, all by themselves, produce stereotyping and prejudice even in the absence of prejudiced socialization, neurotic motives, or real competition between groups for resources.

Categorization

Perceivers naturally categorize other people into groups, the most common being gender, racial, and age groups. We immediately identify a stranger as a man or woman, black or white, child, grownup, or old person. Beyond that, many dimensions can be used to categorize people further. The social context determines which categories are most important. In Northern Ireland, the categories of Catholic and Protestant are especially salient. The distinction between English-speaking and French-speaking citizens is very important in Canada, though elsewhere both are often seen as just Canadians.

This **categorization** process has a number of important consequences. Processing information about individuals is markedly simplified and more efficient if they can readily be placed in categories. In *category-based processing,* the perceiver categorizes the stimulus person, then attends to additional information only to determine if it is consistent with the category. The tedious alternative is to process information about the individual on a piecemeal basis, attribute by attribute, which is called *attribute-based processing* (Brewer, 1988; Fiske & Neuberg, 1990).

Category-based processing comes into play when information about people is stored in terms of social categories rather than in terms of specific individuals. One illustration is a study in which people observed group discussions including equal numbers of blacks and whites. The observers were more likely to confuse the contributions of people within a race than across races. They remembered that something was said by a black person or a white person, but not which specific person said it (Taylor et al., 1978).

There is good news and bad news about category-based processing. Its big advantage is that it allows the perceiver to process a great deal of information quickly and effortlessly. The perceiver does not have to consider all the individual attributes of the other person. The problem is that it can lead to oversimplified stereotypes that simply feed prejudices. Such social categories as "jock" or "feminist" immediately provide rich associations and connotations (Anderson & Klatsky, 1987), but they gloss over the important individual characteristics of those in each category.

On what basis do people categorize others into groups? The perceptual *salience* of various cues is most important. Skin color differentiates blacks and whites; body type, clothing, and voice differentiate men and women; accent differentiates foreigners from natives, and so on. As indicated in Chapter 2, we pay more attention to salient stimuli, so we tend to focus on these differences when we encounter members of these groups, especially when they stand out in the environment.

And these group differences tend to be especially salient when the individual is unusual in his or her social context. Some of the most salient people in our society are the "solos"—the one female astronaut in a news conference, the only black on the Supreme Court, the one white player starting in a professional basketball game, and so on. One of the consequences of being a solo is that that person will attract an unusual amount of attention. For example, solo blacks in otherwise all-white groups have been shown to be perceived as talking more and being more influential than they were either in groups that were racially evenly divided or in racially homogeneous groups. The solo's contributions were also remembered better than those of the minorities in the more evenly integrated group (Taylor et al., 1977).

Race or gender or age are particularly salient attributes, but they produce such large and inclusive categories that they do not simplify person perception very much. So we also use subtler cues that allow us to make finer distinctions within such general categories. This is called **subcategorization** or "subtyping." For example, the global racial category "blacks" is

The sole status of the only black on the U.S. Supreme Court makes his group category especially salient.

frequently broken down into such subtypes as "black athlete," "black businessman," and "black on welfare" (Devine & Baker, 1991).

The problem with subtyping is that it can prevent stereotypes from changing. When we encounter a person who contradicts a stereotype, like a successful black businessman, we can avoid change by subtyping, saying, in essence, such people are not typical and "the exception proves the rule" (Johnston & Hewstone, 1992). The **typicality effect** is described in the RESEARCH CLOSEUP.

Stereotypes are usually described as irrational and unfair because they over-generalize, usually ascribing the same negative attributes to all members of the group whether or not they fit each individual. But if categorization into groups (and the ensuing stereotyping) is based on real cues that happen to be quite salient, is it therefore more based in reality than this would suggest? If so, stereotyping would be less irrational and unfair than usually charged.

To some extent reality does play a part; people of different races really do look different. But it must be remembered that salience depends not just on what receives our attention, but also on where we direct our attention. And that in turn depends to a large degree on the norms we have learned. In the United States, for example, race is extremely salient, primarily because of our history of having placed African

American slaves in a lower caste. But even this seemingly simple categorization is controlled not just by skin color, but by arbitrary social norms as well. The arbitrariness of separation into black and white is perhaps illustrated most vividly by the famous "separate-but-equal" Supreme Court decision in 1896, *Plessy v. Ferguson*. It defined a Louisiana pupil with one black great-grandparent and seven white great-grandparents as colored, and assigned the pupil to an all-Negro segregated school. One can just as easily imagine using a criterion of having more than half of one's great-grandparents of African descent, or calling someone colored only if they had no white ancestors at all. This rule in fact was quite arbitrary, dictated by the stigma of having African blood.

In other cultures, other dimensions are more important in categorization, such as religion in the former Yugoslavia, Lebanon, Israel, or Northern Ireland; people are either Muslim, Christian, Jew, Catholic, or Protestant, and not much else matters. In every society, lots of categories are potentially salient, but we tend to rely heavily on only a few, and that selection is based on the conventional norms of our society. So we must not think that categorizing on the basis of salient attributes is necessarily rational or accurate.

Finally, the label that is attached to a category is critical to category-based processing. That

RESEARCH CLOSEUP
On Being a "Typical" Member of a Category

One of the crucial consequences of prejudice is that it influences our behavior toward individual members of the outgroup. When is our behavior toward a member of an outgroup consistent with our attitudes toward an outgroup as a whole? This is one of the oldest questions in social psychology, as we indicated in the last chapter. Recent research has focused on whether or not the individual group member is perceived as typical of the group. If such people are perceived as exceptions or otherwise atypical, we may not apply our prejudices to them. For example, we may react quite stereotypically to a young, feminine nurse, because she seems typically female. But we may not apply our gender prejudices to a tough mathematical economist, because she is not typical.

The main hypothesis is that attitude–behavior consistency should be greatest when the group member fits the prototype of the group as a whole. Lord,

Lepper, and Mackie (1984) tested this hypothesis using male Princeton students' orientations toward homosexuals. First the students' prototypes of gay men were measured in terms of specific traits. Then the students were presented with the description of a specific individual, "John B.," who was thinking of transferring to Princeton. He was described either as fitting that prototype closely or as being somewhat uncharacteristic of it. The researchers then tested for the students' behavioral orientation toward John B.: Would the students be willing to show him around campus, introduce him to their friends, or host a weekend visit? The students' willingness to help John B. was much more consistent with their general attitudes toward homosexuals when he fit their prototype of gay men than when he did not.

This has been described as the "typicality effect": Behavior toward a specific outgroup member is more consistent with general prejudices about the

group when the individual is perceived as typical of the group. Are there some kinds of people who are more susceptible to the typicality effect than others? In a later study, the same research team hypothesized that the typicality effect would be more common among people who were quite familiar with the group. Such "experts" at using the group category should be more practiced at lumping all group members together and treating them as if they were all the same. So their judgments would not be dependent on the individual's being typical. They might respond to a gay football player with their anti-gay prejudices, because they would know that a gay person is a gay person, whether or not he seemed typically gay. Indeed, that is what the experiment found: The typicality effect limiting attitude–behavior consistency to typical members of the outgroup occurred primarily among those relatively unfamiliar with the group in question (Lord et al., 1991).

label is what evokes evaluations of the category. To use an extreme example, the evaluation linked to a category is quite different if the label for Americans with origins in Mexico is "Chicano" (or "Latino") as opposed to "beaner." Because category labels are so emotionally charged, they are often the focal points of intense controversy. Americans of Mexican descent obviously would much prefer to be called Chicanos or Latinos than beaners or wetbacks.

Labels may change quite dramatically over time. For example, the dominant label for the descendants of African slaves was "Negro" in the 1950s. But with the successes of the civil rights movement in the 1960s, many activists advocated replacing it with "black," to make a symbolic break with the past. Both individual blacks and predominantly black organizations then shifted quite swiftly in their own usage. Today, "African American" is rapidly becoming the preferred usage to symbolize equality with other immigrant groups whose label reflects their geographical origins (Smith, 1992).

Ingroups Versus Outgroups

Numerous studies show that the mere act of categorization can produce discrimination when it involves categorizing people into "us" (an ingroup) and "them" (an outgroup). Being in the ingroup places one in a unique perspective. Americans are likely to perceive Japanese very differently than a Japanese person would. And the Japanese in turn will perceive Americans quite differently. Being in an ingroup has three important consequences.

Ingroup members perceive other ingroup members as more similar to them than outgroup members are. This is the so-called **assumed similarity effect.** This greater assumed similarity occurs with real groups that do in fact have distinctive opinions. For example, fraternity members perceive themselves as more similar to each other than to commuter students, and vice versa (Holtz & Miller, 1985). But even when group members have been arbitrarily or randomly assigned to the group, observers perceive members of the group as being similar to each other, and dissimilar to members of other groups. Allen and Wilder (1979) assigned students to groups ostensibly on the basis of artistic preferences and found that they assumed other ingroup members were especially similar to them on matters wholly unrelated to art. Making group membership more salient by discussing possible conflicts with other groups further enhances this assumed similarity (Miller & Brewer, 1986) and leads to viewing outgroup members more in terms of conventional stereotypes (Wilder & Shapiro, 1991).

A second consequence of categorization into ingroup and outgroup is that we tend to see the outgroup as more homogeneous than the ingroup in terms of traits, personality, and even number of subtypes: *They* are all alike, whereas *we* are quite diverse!" So we tend to perceive a member of an outgroup as just another anonymous group member rather than perceiving him or her as an individual. We see the person as "an Asian" rather than as Stanley Wong.

This is called the **outgroup homogeneity effect.** For example, members of one sorority rated the members of their own sorority as more dissimilar from each other than they did the members of each of several other sororities (Jones, Wood, & Quattrone, 1981; Park & Rothbart, 1982).

In like fashion, people also perceive any individual member of the ingroup as more complex than they do individual members of the outgroup. Their personalities are seen as more multidimensional and as having more variety and richness. For example, white subjects see whites as more complex than blacks, and young subjects see the young as more complex than the elderly (and vice versa!) (see Linville & Jones, 1980).

Another indication of our perceiving "us" as diverse is that we are more likely to see subcategories within our ingroup than in other groups (Park & Judd, 1990). We can distinguish several different groups of friends within our sorority, and the new pledges seem quite different from the seniors. But we are not nearly as aware of the various subgroups in other sororities. Similarly, the elderly are more likely than the young to distinguish between such subcategories of old people as grandmothers, elder statesmen, and senior citizens (Brewer, Dull, & Lui, 1981).

One implication of the outgroup homogeneity effect is that eyewitnesses should be more

Early in World War II, Japanese-Americans were taken from their homes and sent to isolated concentration camps far from their means of livelihood. They had not been accused of any wrong-doing. Here a group is being marched under army escort to an evacuation point, for transport to the camps.

accurate in distinguishing among members of the ingroup than among members of the outgroup. Studies testing this hypothesis typically have shown black and white subjects a series of slides with faces of members of both races, then a much larger set of slides from which they are asked to identify the faces they saw earlier. In all studies, white subjects made more errors in identifying black than white faces, and in most cases the reverse held for black subjects as well (Anthony, Copper, & Mullen, 1992). Indeed, there is a tendency for all of "them" to look alike and all of "us" to look uniquely different.

Finally, this categorization of individuals into ingroup and outgroup leads to more favorable attitudes and behavior toward members of the ingroup, and less favorable attitudes and behavior toward members of the outgroup. This is the **ingroup favoritism effect** (Tajfel et al., 1971). Once people feel they belong to a group, they tend to favor fellow group members at the expense of members of other groups, by giving them more favorable evaluations or more favorable allocations of rewards.

The simplest demonstrations of such effects use the **minimal intergroup situation** designed by Henri Tajfel (1969). In these studies, students were brought into a laboratory and arbitrarily divided into two groups. In one typical study, they were divided into two groups supposedly on the basis of their preference between the two modern painters Klee and Kandinsky (though in fact they were assigned randomly to the two groups). They had no actual interaction with fellow group members (the ingroup) or members of the other group (the outgroup), but they were asked to evaluate all individuals in the experiment and distribute some rewards to them.

The general finding has been that the participants evaluate ingroup members more positively, and reward them more, than they do outgroup members (Brewer, 1979). Ingroup favoritism also has shown up in more favorable descriptions of other ingroup members' traits, expecting more favorable treatment from the ingroup, making more favorable attributions about fellow ingroup members' behavior than about outgroup members' behavior, and finding ingroup communicators more persuasive than outgroup communicators (Allen & Wilder, 1975; Hamilton & Trolier, 1986; Howard & Rothbart, 1980; Mackie, Worth, & Asuncion, 1990; Wilder, 1990).

A second important finding is that subjects generally try to maximize the ingroup's *advantage* over the outgroup regardless of whether that maximizes the absolute reward for the ingroup (Brewer, 1979; Tajfel & Turner, 1986). That is, they are usually more interested in beating the outgroup than they are in getting as much as possible for their own group. This finding is inconsistent with the realistic group conflict model, in which people are supposed to be maximizing the gains of the ingroup. And it occurs despite the fact that the ingroup–outgroup distinction in these experiments is in reality almost completely meaningless, since these subjects could not reward themselves, could not be rewarded by other group members, and had no interaction with members from either group. So the purely cognitive act of categorization, on whatever basis, seems to trigger ingroup favoritism and discrimination against the outgroup, even when there are no selfish gains to be made or any especially pleasurable interaction with the ingroup or unpleasant interaction with the outgroup.

Social Identity

Why does the mere act of categorizing individuals into an ingroup and an outgroup exaggerate perceived differences between the groups (the outgroup homogeneity effect) and lead to more favorable treatment of ingroup members (the ingroup favoritism effect)? There are two main explanations.

The most obvious is that we generally have more direct experience with the ingroup. Indeed, it is easy to show that the outgroup homogeneity effect is a distortion based partly on ignorance. The outgroup is perceived more stereotypically by ingroup than outgroup members, indicating an inaccurate overgeneralization (Judd, Ryan, & Park, 1991). In general, greater familiarity with a social group leads us to perceive greater individuality of the members and variability of their attributes (Linville, Fischer, & Salovey, 1989). This is partly because we are likely to remember things about individuals in the ingroup because we are more familiar with them (Park & Rothbart, 1982; Judd & Park, 1988). However, this greater familiarity with ingroup members would not explain homogeneity or favoritism effects in groups where experience with individual group members is nonexistent, such as in the minimal intergroup situation. Nor would it explain such effects in studies that hold constant real experience with members of both groups (Judd & Park, 1988; Linville et al., 1986).

So the more common explanation for the ingroup favoritism effect comes from **social identity theory,** as developed by Henri Tajfel (1982). As discussed in Chapter 5, our sense of self is intimately linked to our identification with social groups. When asked to answer the question "Who am I?" people typically refer to social groups. One person might explain that she is a woman, a Catholic, a Canadian, and a school teacher. Another person might say that he is a conservative Jew, a New Yorker, and a member of the Republican party. Groups provide individuals with a sense of meaning and identity.

Today, social identity theory is one of the most active research areas in social psychology (Hogg & Abrams, 1990; Turner, 1985). It involves three basic assumptions. First, people categorize the social world into ingroups and outgroups, as we have seen. Second, people strive for a positive self-concept and derive a sense of self-esteem from their social identity as a member of an ingroup. Third, self-concept is partly dependent on how people evaluate their ingroup relative to other groups. If they evaluate the ingroup better, they should have higher self-esteem. If they evaluate it worse, they should have lower self-esteem. This process produces a kind of social competition between the groups, in which people try to boost the status of their own group as a way of boosting their own self-esteem.

This presumed role of self-esteem yields several predictions. First, if our social identity is based on self-categorization into an ingroup,

self-categorization in a successful group should bolster our self-esteem. Second, if our self-esteem is partially based on feeling the ingroup is superior, ingroup favoritism should also boost our self-esteem by boosting the status and power of the ingroup. It is comforting to bask in the reflected glory of belonging to a group that is more powerful, important, or successful than other groups. This was illustrated in a study of college football fans (Cialdini et al., 1976). The day after their team was victorious, students were more likely to show their pride in the college by wearing school sweaters and scarves than on a day following defeat.

Third, if ingroup favoritism is motivated by the need to enhance self-esteem, it should be greater when our self-esteem is low or threatened. Prejudice against outgroups should also be greatest under the same circumstances. So far the evidence on this last point is not very strong. People with low self-esteem are usually the most prejudiced against outgroups, but also are most negative about the ingroup as well (Wills, 1981). They seem to be more negative about everything. And mixed results have come from experiments designed to test the assumption that ego-threatened people are more hostile than others to outgroups (e.g., Crocker et al., 1987).

The value of social identity in enhancing individual self-esteem remains the weakest link in social identity theory. An important possible solution is to recognize that people have needs for both personal and social identity; that is, people have both a "private self" and a "collective self" (Tajfel & Turner, 1986; Trafimow, Triandis, & Goto, 1991). Private self-esteem may not have much to do with one's social identity, but group members who are high in *collective* self-esteem should be especially likely to care deeply about their ingroup and how well it does. So they might be especially threatened by competition with outgroups. For example, there is some evidence that ethnic minorities may be especially sensitive to being placed in experimental outgroups in which they are again a minority. One study tested for the amount of cooperation or competition between groups of Hispanics and of Anglos. Hispanics competed

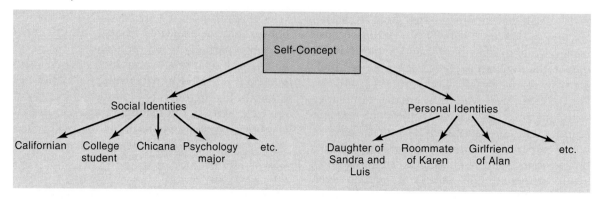

Figure 7-1   The self-concept is made up of social identities based on group affiliations and personal identities based on our unique individual characteristics.

more than Anglos, and cooperated less, when outnumbered by them. But when the two ethnic groups were equal in numbers, Hispanics behaved very much like Anglos (Garza & Santas, 1991). This suggests that the sense of collective self-esteem experienced by ethnic minorities can be threatened when they are reminded of their minority status.

Only recently have both private and collective self-identity been measured separately (Luhtanen & Crocker, 1992). In a study using the minimal intergroup situation, subjects high in collective self-esteem displayed the most ingroup-enhancing behavior. Personal self-esteem had no such effect, consistent with the notion that personal self-esteem is less at stake than collective self-esteem in intergroup conflict situations (see Figure 7-1) (Crocker & Luhtanen, 1990).

If our private and collective selves need to be distinguished, what is the relationship between them? Recently Marilynn Brewer (1991) has argued that individuals need a certain level of both similarity to and differentiation from others, so she has proposed an "optimal distinctiveness model" of social identity. It suggests that people seek self-categorizations that "simultaneously provide for a sense of belonging and a sense of distinctiveness" (p. 475). Perhaps we need to have *some* sense of group membership, but it is not enough to be merely an anonymous member of a large impersonal entity. To satisfy these two needs at once may require seeking some intermediate identity. Being a student at a large state university may be too impersonal

and therefore not enough, while having lunch regularly with a best friend might not feel like being in a group at all. Perhaps being a member of a skiing club or an intramural basketball team or a group that gives volunteer tutorial help to poor children would give us a sense of "optimal distinctiveness."

In short, threats to collective self-esteem, rather than to private self-esteem, may be responsible for prejudice against outgroups. But collective self-esteem may have its maximum power when it gives us some sense of optimal distinctiveness.

Schemas

If stereotypes are cognitive structures regarding a social group, they can be thought of as **schemas,** with the same consequences we have already discussed in Chapter 3 on social cognition. New information inconsistent with schemas tends to be rejected, and ambiguous information becomes interpreted as consistent with the group stereotype. This was illustrated in the Sagar and Schofield (1980) study cited earlier, in which children interpreted a black child's behavior in a drawing as more mean and threatening than a white child's. Like any schema, stereotypes distort reality to achieve order. In that sense, they are not necessarily bizarre, deviant, or pathological. They become destructive when they ignore the evidence of reality and are generalized to all group members.

Priming a schema should make it salient and increase its influence over the individual's thinking, as we saw in Chapter 3 on social cognition. Indeed, imagining stereotypes seems to prime them and increase their believability. Subjects who were asked to imagine a situation involving a stereotype about an occupational group (such as "an aggressive lawyer") subsequently believed those stereotypes more than did subjects not asked to imagine them or asked to imagine a scene with a nonstereotyped trait (Slusher & Anderson, 1987).

Priming can occur quickly, nonconsciously, and involuntarily. For example, Devine (1989) suggests that virtually all Americans learn a common set of negative stereotypes about blacks. Those stereotypes are automatically activated in the presence of a member (or some symbolic equivalent) of the group. Similarly, Perdue and Gurtmann (1990) suggest that negative stereotypes associated with the aged are automatically activated when presented with questions about "old" persons. Automatic priming happens so quickly that people are scarcely even aware of it, so their racial prejudice or ageism is evoked before they even know it. Automatic processing also tends to be more affective than cognitive; it consists more of emotional responses toward the group than of factual beliefs about it (Stangor, Sullivan, & Ford, 1991). As a consequence, group stereotypes operate quite efficiently; people respond quickly and can remember them well (Andersen, Klatzky, & Murray, 1990).

Priming our own *self-categorization* as a member of an ingroup has much the same effects as priming any other schema. We are then more likely to perceive ourselves as possessing the stereotyped attributes of the ingroup. For example, Hogg and Turner (1987) made gender salient in small discussion groups, priming the subjects' gender self-schemas. The subjects then aligned their self-descriptions more closely to their own gender stereotypes. The men perceived themselves as more competitive, assertive, and forceful, while the women perceived themselves as more helpful, compassionate, and sympathetic.

A study on the elderly makes the same point. In it, older adults tended to bias their memories of their own physical and psychological attributes when they were younger to fit the schemas they had about the aging process; e.g., a subject very sensitive to temperature changes would think that he must have been less sensitive to temperature changes when he was younger (McFarland, Ross, & Giltrow, 1992).

Priming schemas about an outgroup can lead to one of the most destructive effects discussed here. The stereotype can be a **self-fulfilling prophecy,** producing stereotype-confirming behavior on the part of the outgroup members. Members of the victimized group begin to live up to the stereotype, to exhibit the very characteristics the stereotype says they have. If we think all Poles are bumblers, we are likely to interact with them as if we expected them to bumble at any opportunity. And this will increase the likelihood that they will behave in a stereotype-confirming way and become real bumblers.

The chain of self-fulfilling prophecy involves five steps, as shown at the top of Figure 7-2: (1) The stereotype about how the other person will behave (2) influences the stereotype holder's own behavior, which (3) influences the target person's behavior, and that in turn contributes to (4) the perception of the target person's behavior as confirming the stereotype rather than as a response to the holder's own behavior. This then leads to (5) the target person's coming to accept that stereotype as an accurate self-description.

Snyder and Swann (1978) demonstrated this in an ingenious way, as shown at the bottom of Figure 7-2. They told each subject (the "perceiver") that he was going to interact with another subject (the "target") who was described either as hostile, liking contact sports, cruel, and insensitive, or as nonhostile, liking poetry and sailing, kind, and cooperative. The description given set up the perceiver's stereotype of the target (step 1).

Then the perceiver and target (who was also a naive subject) engaged in a series of reaction time tests that allowed both to behave in a hostile way (by administering loud, painful, distracting noises to each other). Not surprisingly, it turned out that expecting a hostile partner led perceivers to administer more high-intensity

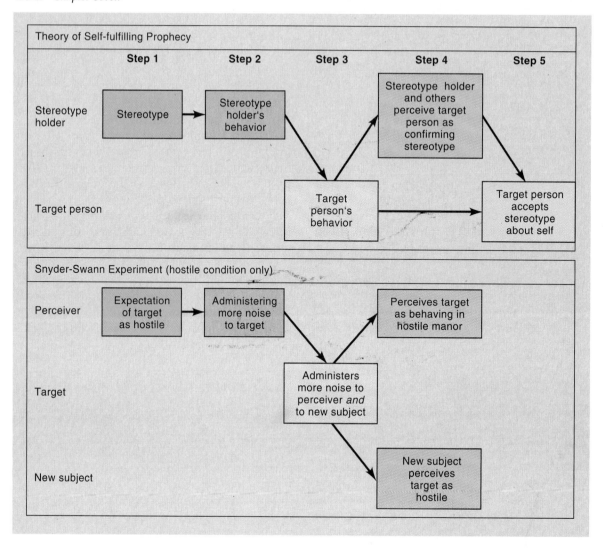

Figure 7-2 Stereotypes as self-fulfilling prophecies: Theory and experiment. (*Source:* Adapted from Snyder & Swann, 1978.)

noises (step 2). But the targets, completely ignorant of how they had been described to the other person, also administered more noise if they had been described as hostile (step 3). Remember, the targets had been described as hostile or nonhostile at random, so the higher level of hostile behavior had to be caused by the perceiver's expectations. And the perceivers, reasonably enough, saw the "hostile" target as more hostile than the "nonhostile" target, confirming their stereotypical expectations, given the target's actual hostile behavior (step 4).

The most interesting aspect of this experi-

ment then followed. The target was put through the same task with a new, completely naive subject. Neither knew about the "hostile" or "nonhostile" description randomly assigned earlier to the target. Nevertheless, the target continued to live up to expectations. He gave more noise (step 3, again) and was regarded as more hostile in this new interaction (step 4, again). This experiment demonstrated that expectations affect the stereotyper's own behavior toward a victim, then the victim's behavior in return confirms the stereotype, and the victim later behaves in a stereotype-confirming manner in new situations, even toward people who are completely ignorant of the stereotype.

Perhaps the most destructive result comes from the fifth step in this process: The target person actually comes to believe that the stereotype accurately applies to him or her. In a similar study by Fazio and his colleagues (1981), the subjects exhibited behavior in the experiment itself that confirmed the expectations of their partners. This repeated the Snyder-Swann findings. But when the subject was placed in a completely different social situation, interacting with a new person, the subject's behavior still lived up to the original expectations, and the subject's own self-ratings also conformed to the original partner's expectations. In short, not only was the stereotype holder's behavior influenced by these arbitrary expectations, but the victim's own behavior and self-perceptions also came to reflect the stereotype.

Comparison of Theories

We have now considered three main theories of prejudice: social learning, psychodynamic, and cognitive. Each of these broad theoretical approaches points to different factors as causes of prejudice. There is some truth in all of them. For example, normal cognitive processes of categorization and of special attention to salient stimuli can increase stereotypes and discriminatory behavior. It is doubtful that such cognitive processes are sufficient to produce a consistent pattern of bias all by themselves, however. They require prior learning that produces prejudice against particular groups, and specific stereotypical content. Blacks are stereotypically thought to be lazy and musical, and Asians hard-working, though both are perceptually different from whites. The perceptual distinctiveness of these minority groups may help to get a pattern of group discrimination started, and certainly helps to maintain it.

In general, social learning plays a major role in defining what "appropriate" prejudice is, what the "correct" stereotypes are, and what is acceptable behavior toward other groups and what is not. The wide variations in the treatment of any given group around the globe and across history testify to that, as do the major differences in the treatment of different groups within a society. In 1850, blacks could be bought and sold like cattle; today elaborate legal machinery protects their right to be treated like other people. Slavery hardly existed for other groups in this country, nor for blacks in many other societies. In most Muslim countries women must wear veils, may not engage in premarital or extramarital sexual relations, and do not compete with men for jobs. American women are not so restricted today, though in the nineteenth century they were much less free. Personality tensions and cognitive biases therefore operate within a cultural framework that determines how much prejudice exists, when it can be expressed, and toward whom. This cultural framework is transmitted through learning.

THE CHANGING FACE OF PREJUDICE

Much has changed since the earliest sociopsychological studies of prejudice in the 1930s. Hitler has come and gone, discrediting anti-Semitism with his slaughter of European Jewry. The civil rights movement helped end the institution of racial segregation. The women's movement and activism on behalf of people with AIDS and many other disadvantaged groups have filled the news and occasionally the streets as well. What has changed, and what has not? Again we will focus primarily on racial prejudice, because it has been most researched, but similar findings hold for prejudice against Hispanics, women, gay men and lesbians, the disabled, and other groups.

Declining Old-fashioned Racism

Racial and ethnic prejudice has generally declined, at least in the United States, in the years since World War II. The virulent anti-Semitism in Europe and America in the nineteenth and early twentieth centuries was of great concern. But surveys done in the United

Interracial contact is least common when it involves such intimate relationships as marriage.

States since the early 1960s have found it is substantially reduced, despite the persistence of a few negative stereotypes (Quinley & Glock, 1979; Smith, 1990). Similarly, despite centuries of intense anti-Semitism in Russia and Eastern Europe, a recent survey showed a surprisingly low level of anti-Semitism among residents of Moscow (Gibson & Duch, 1992). However, anti-Semitism was greater among those whose financial situations were deteriorating, an ominous note for a nation whose economy is so troubled.

The traditional forms of racism against blacks in America involved such stereotypes as laziness and lack of intelligence, along with support for racial segregation in such areas as housing, schools, and jobs. This has been called **old-fashioned racism** (McConahay, 1986), and it, too, has declined. In years gone by, most whites felt that white and black children should go to separate schools, that whites and blacks should be forbidden to marry, and that whites should get preference for available jobs. As late as 1964, 25 percent of whites favored racial segregation. But today, many fewer whites hold these attitudes (Hochschild & Herk, 1989; Schuman et al., 1985).

A number of such examples are shown in Table 7-4. Old-fashioned racism is likely to continue to decline in the future. Whites who still hold onto such beliefs tend to come from such dwindling groups as those raised before World War II and/or without a high school degree (Bobo & Kluegel, 1991).

Nevertheless, racial prejudice continues to exist in the United States. We can cite four indicators:

1. Many whites continue to wish to maintain distance from blacks. As of 1983, 60 percent did not approve of interracial marriages, the highest level of disapproval in 13 Western nations (Pettigrew, 1988; Schuman et al., 1985). About one-third do not want black neighbors, and about 20 percent continue not to want integrated schools (Dovidio & Gaertner, 1986).

2. Negative stereotypes of minorities persist as well. In a 1990 national survey, 62 percent of whites thought blacks were lazier than whites, and 53 percent thought blacks were less intelligent (Smith, 1991). Only 6 percent had more negative images of whites than blacks on those items. Hispanics bore the brunt of very similar stereotypes from whites. It should be noted, though, that these persisting stereotypes take a more moderate, qualified form than they did in the past. Most whites see only small overall racial and ethnic differences in these traits, with much overlap between groups. Very few hold to the total, categorical belief in the superiority of the white race common a century ago.

3. Support for government policies designed to promote racial equality has not kept pace with the decline in old-fashioned racism. Whites do not give much support to affirmative action, open housing laws, busing for integration, or government spending for other programs benefiting minorities (Schuman et al., 1985). Some of those data are also shown in Table 7-4.

4. Blacks continue to be much less convinced than are whites that prejudice and discrim-

234

TABLE 7-4
Changes Over Time in Whites' Racial Attitudes: General Principles of Racial Equality and Implementing Policies

	Historical Era		
	Early	Late	Change
General Principles			
Oppose *segregation*	75% (1964)	95% (1978)	+20%
Oppose laws against *intermarriage*	39 (1964)	66 (1982)	+27
White and black students should go to same *schools*	32 (1942)	90 (1982)	+58
Negroes should have as good a chance as whites to get any kind of *job*	45 (1944)	97 (1972)	+52
Vote for well-qualified black for president if nominated by own party	37 (1958)	81 (1983)	+44
Implementing Policies			
Federal government should ensure that white and black children go to same *schools*	42 (1964)	25 (1978)	–17
Favor *busing*	13 (1972)	21 (1983)	+8
Government provide *special aid to minorities*	22 (1970)	18 (1982)	–4
Support increased *government spending on blacks*	27 (1973)	26 (1983)	–1

Source: Adapted from Schuman, Steeh, & Bobo (1985), Tables 3–1 and 3–2. The years involved in the comparison are shown in parentheses.

ination are things of the past. In 1981, over 60 percent felt that they were discriminated against in getting jobs, while only 25 percent of whites did (Bobo, 1989). In 1988, 69 percent of blacks, as against 37 percent of whites, believed that blacks do not have the same opportunities as whites have (Hochschild & Herk, 1989).

New Forms of Prejudice

A lively set of controversies has arisen about the possible interpretation of this contrast between the seeming disappearance of old-fashioned racism and evidence of continued resistance to change. There are four discernibly different points of view, displayed in Figure 7-3.

ILLUSORY CHANGE. Some have argued that declining old-fashioned racism merely represents *illusory change*: Old-fashioned racism is on the wane only because it has become socially unacceptable to voice it. Behind their polite facade of opposition to old-line segregationism, people retain the same old racism. According to this view, whites' opposition to affirmative action occurs because it poses issues of racial equality less directly, and so people can express their true racism without fear of being found out and denounced for it. Experiments testing this view show that whites express less old-fashioned racism to black interviewers than they do to white interviewers, as if they were deliberately holding it back from the former. But they express just as much indirect racism to black as to white interviewers, as if they thought the blacks would not be offended by it (McConahay et al., 1981).

REALISTIC GROUP CONFLICT. The *realistic group conflict* interpretation, in contrast, assumes that the decline in old-fashioned racism is genuine, but agrees that it is superficial. It is easy to support equality in the abstract, but supporting actual implementation has real and costly implications. For example, whites may lose jobs to blacks if affirmative action programs really

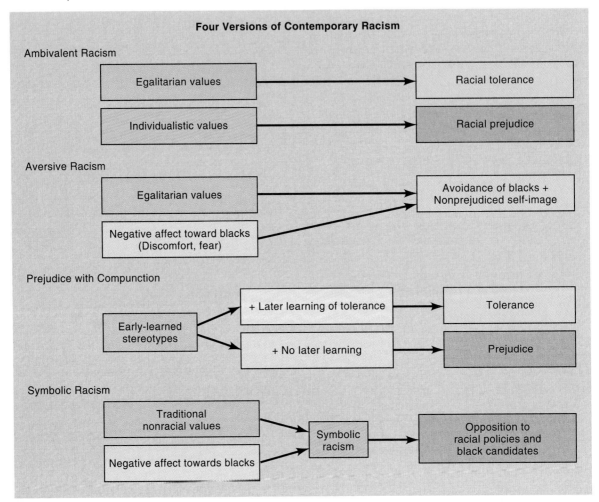

Figure 7-3 Four versions of contemporary racism.

work, so whites resist (Jackman, 1978). In essence whites try to buy off blacks with vague promises of equality, but when it comes to real change, with real resource consequences, whites resist any real change (Bobo, 1988a; Jackman & Muha, 1984).

There is some evidence for this view. As indicated earlier, whites were most negative toward black activism when it was at its strongest, in the 1960s. Second, whites' rejection of black activism may be influenced by a sense of fraternal deprivation, a feeling that blacks are getting too much at the expense of whites (Bobo, 1988a, b).

But realistic group conflict theory seems to be only half right. It fares well when dealing with

people's concerns about their group's well-being, as just indicated. But, like social identity theory, it does more poorly when dealing with people's fears about their own personal situations. The theory should predict that threats by an outgroup to an ingroup member's well-being would stimulate prejudice against that outgroup. So whites who most perceive their neighborhoods as being threatened by minorities, such as through crimes committed by ethnic gangs or influxes of minority children into the schools, ought to be the most prejudiced (Rothbart, 1976).

However, a number of studies have shown that threats posed by blacks to whites' own lives have surprisingly little impact on whites' levels of prejudice or on their preferences regarding government racial policies (Sears & Funk, 1991). For example, the impact of affirmative action programs on a white individual's personal well-being has little effect on his or her attitudes toward the programs. So realistic group conflict seems to create prejudice through threatening the group's well-being, not by directly affecting the personal lives of ingroup members.

SYMBOLIC RACISM. Others suggest that old-fashioned racism is not very widespread, and instead, has been replaced by a more modern, potent form of prejudice called **symbolic racism** (Kinder & Sears, 1981; McConahay & Hough, 1976; Sears & McConahay, 1973). According to this view, the most powerful version of racial prejudice today focuses on racial symbols such as "quotas," "gang violence," "reverse discrimination," or "welfare." The opposition of whites to racial progress is at an abstract, symbolic level, both because of their unfavorable emotional reaction to blacks and because it violates their other values. So symbolic racism is a combination of two attitudes acquired in early socialization: antiblack affect (such as disgust or anger) and traditional American values that have nothing to do with race (such as the value of hard work and the belief that no group should get special favors). Symbolic racism, therefore, is reflected in such attitudes as that blacks are making unfair demands for special treatment and that they therefore are getting undeserved gains in areas such as jobs or college admissions.

Research on symbolic racism has focused on four points:

1. Symbolic racism is a stronger predictor than old-fashioned racism of white opposition to policies intended to help minorities, such as busing, affirmative action, bilingual education, and welfare. It also predicts opposition to black political leaders such as former Mayor Tom Bradley of Los Angeles and Jesse Jackson. Old-fashioned racism is not a strong predictor of these attitudes anymore.

2. Attitudes toward these racial policies and leaders are not as well predicted by variables central to other theories, such as realistic group conflict theory. As we have seen, real personal threats that blacks pose to whites' personal lives, such as of criminal violence, busing, or loss of jobs due to affirmative action, do not have the same force.

3. Symbolic racism itself does seem to be a joint product of antiblack attitudes and of nonracial traditional values (see Jessor, 1988; Sears, 1988). This is important because even if somehow whites became more favorable to blacks, some symbolic racism might remain insofar as blacks were perceived as continuing to violate those traditional values.

4. Finally, the symbolic racism thesis has been extended to other areas as well. The combination of traditional values and anti-outgroup prejudices has also been shown to explain opposition to bilingual education (Sears & Huddy, 1993), support for English as an official language (Citrin et al., 1990), and support for restrictive attitudes toward persons with AIDS (Price & Hsu, 1992).

There have been three general critiques of the symbolic racism thesis. Some feel that opposition to pro-black policies like affirmative action can be explained by nonracial conservatism alone without having to assume that prejudice is involved (e.g., Roth, 1990). Presumably, people can be opposed to affirmative action because they think it is an ineffective policy, or because they feel government should not be regulating hiring in private companies, not just because they are racially prejudiced. And clearly there is some truth to that, although anti-black affect does make a significant contribution for many people even with those other factors taken into consideration (Sears & Citrin, 1985; Sears & Kosterman, 1991).

A second critique suggests that the symbolic racism thesis ignores the role of *group* interest; whites may not oppose pro-black policies like affirmative action because it might hurt them personally, but because they see it as disadvantaging whites in general (e.g., Bobo, 1988a). Research on this question, however, suggests that such opposition focuses more intensely on the unfairness of special treatment given to minorities than on the unfair deprivation of whites (Jessor, 1988; Kinder & Sanders, 1990).

Third, the original theory emphasized individualism as the key nonracial traditional value, but much evidence shows that inegalitarian values are more important (see Sears & Kosterman, 1991). It is less that blacks are seen as insufficiently self-reliant, with a poor work ethic, and more that many whites are not fully committed to promoting social equality. This suggests a more deep-seated resistance to racial equality than originally expected.

AMBIVALENCE. In 1944, the great Swedish social scientist Gunnar Myrdal wrote that "the American dilemma" lay in white Americans' contradictory beliefs: On the one hand, they believed in freedom and equality for all, while on the other hand they were strongly racially prejudiced. Some contemporary social psychologists see the same **ambivalent racism** operating in white Americans today. Most, it is said, do feel some special sympathy for minorities, out of a recognition that they have been handicapped by special disadvantages. But they also perceive minorities as contributing to their own plight, particularly through lack of ambition, criminal behavior, drug and alcohol abuse, promiscuity, and so on. This leaves the white person with "conflicting sentiments, consisting of friendliness and sympathy on one side and disdain and aversion on the other" (Katz et al., 1986, p. 42).

Three versions of this ambivalence can be distinguished. One is **aversive racism** (Kovel, 1970; Gaertner & Dovidio, 1986). In this view, whites are conflicted between their genuinely egalitarian value systems and their negative feelings toward blacks. But whites are ashamed of their negative feelings, so they avoid blacks. Then they are not confronted with their true prejudices, and can protect their self-images as unprejudiced persons. So instead of the hostility of old-fashioned racism, they feel discomfort and uneasiness around blacks. Evidence of aversive racism comes from studies of whites' nonverbal behavior in interactions with blacks. Whites tend to sit farther away, use less friendly voice tones, make less eye contact and more speech errors, and terminate an interview more quickly when talking to blacks than when talking to other whites (Pettigrew, 1985).

A second kind of ambivalence has been proposed by Patricia Devine (1989; Devine et al., 1991). As indicated earlier, she suggests that virtually all Americans learn the conventional stereotypes about blacks early in life, and that these are automatically evoked in adulthood. Some whites, but not all, also acquire norms of racial tolerance as they are growing up. These too can get evoked later on, but through more deliberate, voluntary, controlled processing. Such people then wind up being relatively low in prejudice. Such people can to some extent consciously inhibit the automatically evoked stereotypes, but probably cannot eliminate them altogether. Rather, they will slip on occasion, and react with some guilt and self-criticism—in Devine's terms, with "prejudice with compunction." On the other hand, people who have not learned these tolerant norms as strongly will not try as hard to inhibit their automatic stereotyping, and will display "prejudice without compunction." Her research illustrates this contrast using both blacks and gay men as the target outgroups (Devine et al., 1991).

A third kind of ambivalence suggests that most whites have two conflicting racial schemas: one composed of egalitarian values that focuses on concerns for social justice, and another composed of individualistic values that focuses on self-reliance (Katz & Hass, 1988). In one study based on this theory, subjects became more racially tolerant when their egalitarian schema was primed. But when their individualistic schema was primed, they began to think about welfare dependency, high school dropouts, and other aspects of the stereotypically poor work ethic among minorities, and their racial prejudice went up.

ATTRIBUTIONS FOR MINORITIES' DISADVANTAGES. Egalitarian values hold that all groups should be treated equally, whereas individualistic values hold that people should be rewarded

TABLE 7-5
Whites' Explanations for the Black–White Economic Gap

External Attribution	Internal Attribution			
	Yes—Weak Motivation	Yes—Inadequate Ability	No—Neither	Total
Yes—Discrimination and/or lack of educational opportunity	23%	11%	30%	64%
No—Neither	20	10	6	36
Total	43	21	36 =	100%

Note: Entry is the percentage of whites in the 1988-1989 national General Social Surveys who explained blacks' economic disadvantage with the combination of external and/or internal attributions shown.
Source: Adapted from Kluegel (1990), pp. 515 and 517.

according to their own ability and effort. A parallel contrast can be made in attributions for minorities' socioeconomic disadvantages (in education, income, and so on). If whites perceive the disadvantages as the minorities' own fault, that is, as due to internal and controllable causes such as unwillingness to work hard, whites will be more prejudiced and will not support special government aid to minorities. If, however, the disadvantage is seen as caused by external circumstances that minorities cannot control, such as racial discrimination or poor educational opportunities, special help might be supported.

And, indeed, people who make purely external attributions do support increasing government spending for blacks much more than do those who make purely internal attributions (Bobo, 1991; Kluegel, 1990; Kluegel & Bobo, 1991). As a result, the question turns to how many people have each of these attributions, and where do they come from? Whites are divided among three major explanations of blacks' disadvantages (Kluegel, 1990). As shown in Table 7-5, 30 percent focus solely on blacks' internal inadequacies (whether lack of ability or lack of motivation), 30 percent focus solely on blacks' external disadvantages (whether discrimination or lack of educational opportunity), 34 percent give some credence to both, and the remaining 6 percent pick none of these. Clearly, white Americans are divided about how to explain blacks' economic disadvantages.

It is likely that these internal attributions are in part the product of whites' racial prejudices. Internal attributions are made most often by the most prejudiced whites, while less prejudiced whites are more likely to make external attributions, such as to discrimination and lack of educational opportunity (Apostle et al., 1983; Bobo, 1989). For example, about 55 percent of those who believe that blacks have inferior ability support laws against racial intermarriage, whereas only about 10 percent do so among those who attribute blacks' disadvantage solely to external circumstances (Kluegel, 1990). Not surprisingly, such internal attributions are fairly closely linked to the other variables that predict old-fashioned prejudice: Older, less-educated, more conservative, and more religious people are much more likely to attribute blacks' disadvantages to inferior ability (Kluegel, 1990). In a similar vein, heterosexuals who attribute homosexuality to internal, controllable causes have more negative attitudes toward gays than those who perceive homosexuality as beyond the gay person's control (Whitley, 1990). For example, people are more likely to be anti-gay if they believe that homosexuality reflects a deliberately chosen life-style than if they believe it is just an accident of the person's own genetic endowment.

Much research is currently underway to test these theories. They are all different, but share some similar elements. They all assume that most whites have some genuine sympathy for

CULTURAL HIGHLIGHT

Collectivist vs. Individualistic Outlook— Implications for Prejudice

At several junctures in this book we have discussed the broad distinction between individualistic and collectivist cultures. Harry Triandis (1989) has argued that the private self is especially emphasized in individualistic cultures such as North America or Europe, while in collectivistic cultures such as those of East Asia, Africa, or Latin America there is more emphasis on the needs of the ingroup than on one's own needs, more on duty to the ingroup than on pleasure for the self, more on shared beliefs than on distinctive beliefs, and more on intense emotional attachment to the ingroup.

Triandis' research finds that people from collectivistic cultures perceive their ingroups to be more homogeneous. Ingroup members are perceived as behaving more intimately and subordinately toward other ingroup members, and tend to emphasize values that promote the welfare of their group (Triandis, McCusker, & Hui, 1990). Similarly, students in Hong Kong had longer but fewer interactions with fewer people than did students from the United States, more group

interaction, and greater self-disclosure (Wheeler et al., 1989).

What might be the implication of this distinction for prejudice? Several lines of research have suggested that in North America, individualism is associated with higher levels of prejudice. "Ambivalent racism" can be stimulated when individualistic values are made more salient (Katz & Hass, 1988). Making internal, individualistic attributions for blacks' socioeconomic disadvantages is associated both with higher levels of prejudice and opposition to policies intended to remedy those disadvantages (Kluegel, 1990). And a more collectivist orientation is associated with less prejudice and more racial tolerance. Egalitarian values, in the research on symbolic racism, contribute to more support for policies intended to eliminate racial inequality and for minority political candidates (Sears & Kosterman, 1991), and making egalitarianism salient reduces prejudice (Katz & Hass, 1988).

The individualistic–collectivist distinction has not been explicitly extended to the

case of prejudice to date, but we might speculate as follows. Collectivist cultures place more emphasis on the "collective self" than on the "private self" (Triandis, 1989). The implication is that prejudice against other ingroup members might be lessened in cultures that emphasize more collectivist orientations, with perceptions of the self as interdependent with other group members (Chapter 5), and with more of a tendency to attribute behavior to the society, the group, and the environment rather than to the self (Chapter 4). A fellow group member might not be stigmatized to the same degree for physical deformities or a lack of certain skills. On the other hand, prejudice against outgroups might be intensified in a culture with a dominant "collective self," because it would lead to a stronger sense of social identity. This in turn might intensify outgroup homogeneity effects (seeing all of "them" as being indistinguishable foreigners) and ingroup favoritism effects (biasing the giving of rewards toward fellow ingroup members). What do you think?

general egalitarian principles and that most do reject the old ideas of white superiority and segregation. But they all acknowledge that prejudice has not disappeared; whites have continuing antagonism toward blacks, whether it is based on early socialization or on real conflicts of interest.

We have been focusing on whites' prejudice against blacks because it has been historically painful for America, and as a result has drawn by far the most research. Most of these same theories could be used to analyze other groups' prejudices as well. For example, blacks' antagonisms against Koreans could be due to realistic group conflict (Korean merchants own a disproportionate number of retail stores in the ghetto, and often do not hire black workers), Asian Americans' disparagement of Mexican American farm workers could be due to a form of symbolic racism (aversion to their life styles mixed with feeling they do not work hard enough), and so on. The CULTURAL HIGHLIGHT raises interesting questions about how prejudice might be addressed by cultures with a collectivist orientation as opposed to individualistic societies.

REDUCING PREJUDICE

Studies of attitude change, as summarized in Chapter 6, would make it appear that our attitudes are quite susceptible to change. Similarly, as will be seen in Chapter 8, studies of conformity and obedience suggest that our behavior can be influenced rather readily. So it might seem that prejudice and discrimination might be easily controlled as well.

But things turn out not to be so easy. As Hovland (1959) pointed out, it is generally easy to change attitudes in the controlled environment of a laboratory. Even a simple written essay can produce changes in attitudes toward foreign aid or brushing teeth. But attempts to change attitudes and behavior in the world outside the laboratory tend to be much less successful. Indeed, survey studies show that racial and ethnic attitudes are normally extremely stable through adulthood (Sears, 1983). It is likely that unusually powerful techniques are required if prejudice is to be reduced.

The main theoretical approach to prejudice reduction has emphasized direct intergroup contact. The pervasiveness of racial segregation in America in housing, schools, jobs, and most other areas of life led many social scientists after World War II to conclude that sheer ignorance of blacks and their lives helped to create whites' erroneous and oversimplified racial stereotypes. Greater interracial contact was expected to inform whites, break down their stereotypes, and ultimately reduce their prejudice (Myrdal, 1944).

Cognitive consistency theories argue that "similarity breeds liking." We like new people or groups partly on the basis of the similarity of their attitudes and values with our own. For example, a study of multiculturalism in Canada found that evaluations of groups such as English Canadians, immigrants in general, or Italian Canadians were closely related to how "similar to me" the group was perceived as being (Berry et al., 1977). The groups that people judged as most similar to themselves were liked the best. Therefore, many social scientists felt that lack of interracial contact, due to segregation, led white Americans to assume greater dissimilarity in values between the races than existed in fact. If so, more contact between the races would increase awareness of the true value similarities, increase liking, and decrease prejudice.

But does contact really reduce prejudice? The classic early studies took advantage of the fact that America's major institutions gradually became less segregated in the decades following World War II, giving social scientists opportunities to test the effects of contact. The first studies examined desegregation of the Army. At the start of World War II, military policy was constructed to avoid racially mixed units. However, as time went by and white infantry replacements came to be in short supply, the Army allowed black volunteers to join previously all-white units. Surveys before this desegregation showed that most white soldiers opposed it, but afterward there was much less opposition (Stouffer et al., 1949). The greatest change came from those white soldiers who were most closely associated with the blacks. Unrealistic stereotypes decreased markedly because of the greater knowledge gained by familiarity. And no realistic conflicts arose between the groups, because instead of competing, they were fighting a common enemy. Similar findings were obtained in early studies of the desegregation of housing (Deutsch and Collins, 1951) and work situations, such as in department stores, police departments, and government offices.

Today, there is still evidence of much racial separation: A national survey of friendship patterns found only 9 percent of white adults could name a "good friend" who was black, and only

21 percent could name at least one black acquaintance (Jackman & Crane, 1986). Those whites who did have a black friend or acquaintance were the least prejudiced. All this would suggest that contact is successful in reducing prejudice, at least under some conditions.

On the other hand, school desegregation does not invariably reduce prejudice. The "separate-but-equal" doctrine permitted Southern states to maintain separate school systems for white and black children until the 1960s. And in Northern metropolitan areas, housing segregation has resulted in extensive de facto school segregation. To try to desegregate the schools, court-ordered busing plans were adopted in many areas, but often they did not have the effects hoped for (see Aronson & Gonzalez, 1988; Gerard, 1988). As a result, most experts have concluded that the specific *type* of interracial contact, rather than mere contact itself, is the crucial factor.

Contact Theory

The pivotal *Brown v. Board of Education* Supreme Court decision abolishing separate schools for blacks and whites was advised in part by a brief prepared by several distinguished social psychologists, using Gordon Allport's (1954) **contact theory**. They predicted that desegregation would help reduce prejudice if it were carried out in a way that ensured four key conditions: interracial contact, an

Team sports provide one arena for cooperative and sustained close contact between different ethnic groups.

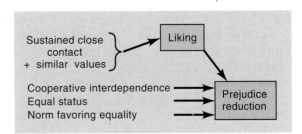

Figure 7-4 The contact theory of prejudice reduction.

absence of interracial competition for scarce resources, equal status for members of both races, and firm support from the relevant authorities (see Figure 7-4) (Brewer & Miller, 1984; Cook, 1988).

Sustained close contact is important—It is not enough for people to coexist occasionally in the same geographical space. Sustained close contact is required if prevailing stereotypes about outgroup characteristics are to be disconfirmed. We have seen numerous examples of the difficulties people have in overcoming their own schemas, stereotypes, and expectations. As a result, a great deal of new evidence is often required to produce change, especially when these beliefs have been in place for many years, and are constantly reinforced by others. A single integrated experience or contact with a "token" member of a minority group is usually not enough to disconfirm stereotypes. One "exception to the rule" does not do the job (Weber & Crocker, 1983).

Cooperative interdependence is also necessary. Members of the two groups need to be working together for common goals and to depend on each others' efforts, as in World War II, rather than competing with each other for scarce resources. The classic study demonstrating the destructive effects of competition on intergroup relations is the Robbers' Cave experiment conducted by Sherif and coworkers (1961). They initially encouraged competition between two groups of boys at a summer camp. But so much anger and hostility between the groups was created that it emerged even at noncompetitive events, such as watching a movie. The researchers later successfully reduced this hostility by getting the boys to work cooperatively to solve a common problem.

The contact must also be of *equal status.* Resentments build up if the traditional status imbalance is maintained, and stereotypes cannot easily be broken down. Contact occurs, for example, when a Hispanic cleaning woman works for a wealthy white woman, but contact of this kind perpetuates traditional stereotypes.

Social norms favoring equality must be the consensus among the relevant authorities and the community at large. When intergroup contact is forced on a situation in which everyone in the ingroup opposes the contact (as, for instance, in a school district in which a court orders busing and the white school board, superintendent, teachers, and parents all want continued racial segregation), it will be hard for the contact between children to have beneficial effects.

Much research has been done to test the hypotheses of contact theory. For example, Clore and coworkers (1978) ran an interracial summer camp in which campers, administrative staff, and counselors were all evenly divided between blacks and whites. The researchers tried to maximize (1) close contact, by mixing the living arrangements by race; (2) cooperative interdependence, by creating primitive conditions that demanded cooperation, such as fire building, cooking, and planning activities; and (3) equal status, by selecting campers from similar backgrounds. The one-week experience was successful in increasing the percentage of interracial choices campers made for partners in playing games. Similar findings have emerged from Stuart Cook's (1984) program of research involving long-term interaction in either school or work situations.

Social psychologists have been active in trying to introduce such procedures into desegregated schools, with the idea that desegregation can reduce prejudice only if these conditions prevail. Standard educational procedures have been compared with new procedures introducing interdependent "teams" that cooperate to complete classroom assignments. For example, Eliot Aronson and his colleagues have used what they call a *jigsaw technique.* Children are placed in small learning groups, usually consisting of six participants. They meet in the group for about an hour a day to focus on one particular lesson. Each person is assigned one portion of the day's lesson and is responsible for teaching that material to the rest of the group. For example, in one exercise the students are given the biography of Joseph Pulitzer, the newspaper publisher. Paragraph 1 is about his ancestors, paragraph 2 about his pre-adult life, and so forth. Since no one can put together the whole biography without the information contributed by others, the students are interdependent. Furthermore, since each student is put into the role of being an expert, they all have equal status. Ultimately, each student's learning is evaluated separately, but unless all cooperate in contributing their unique pieces of knowledge, none can do very well. As a result, the subjects should learn to cooperate and learn from each other.

Aronson and his coworkers report good success with this technique in increasing peer liking across ethnic and racial groups, and in increasing the self-esteem of minority children (Aronson et al., 1978; Aronson & Gonzalez, 1988). The most extensive review found that 63 percent of the cooperative classrooms showed improved academic performance, against 4 percent of the traditional competitive classrooms (Slavin, 1983).

Prospects for Tolerance

What are the prospects for prejudice reduction in our society? First, what kinds of situations would be likely to reduce prejudice, and what kinds would not? By the principles discussed in this section, being teammates on a professional football team would. Being fellow conspirators in a prison break would. Having a Latino janitor in an office building or Filipino maid in a middle-class household would not. Having students of different groups in a lecture class probably would not. Pitting an all-black football team

For many years, a focal point of racial conflict in the United States has been the treatment of black males by white police officers. The beating of Rodney King, shown in this videotape segment, was viewed by many blacks as simply the latest in a long line of such mistreatment. Many police, on the other hand, pointed to the unusually high crime rate among urban black males to explain such tensions.

against an all-white team would not. But having interracial teams solve homework problems in a statistics class would. Placing white and black students in different "tracks" in a high school, attending different classes, would not; nor would a firm in which the executives are all white and the clerical workers are Asian, and in which the two groups have little close interaction.

Are the most helpful kinds of intergroup situations common in our society? Unfortunately, through most of our history they have not been. Prior to the 1950s, American society was organized in a way that afforded almost no opportunities for equal status and cooperative, interdependent contact between members of different races. Almost all American institutions (colleges, professional sports, military units, etc.) were segregated. Most blacks lived in the South, where Jim Crow segregation was the law in public accommodations, schools, transportation, and politics.

Today, contact of this type occurs much more frequently, at least in work situations, where real integration has beneficial effects. One recent study found that black graduate students in relatively well-integrated programs were better adjusted, had higher grades, and were less likely to consider dropping out of school (DeFour & Hirsch, 1990).

But in many other areas of life, whites and blacks have relatively little contact with each other. One survey showed that only 21 percent of whites named even one black as an acquaintance (Jackman & Crane, 1986). Even when interracial contact is intended, as in school desegregation plans, the phenomenon of "white flight" (white children leaving public schools as soon as they are desegregated) illustrates how hard it is to ensure interracial contact. Even if substantial numbers of children from both races are in the school, they show a strong tendency to associate more with their own race than with any other (Schofield, 1978).

Cooperative interdependence is important and works, but mainly if it also leads to success in the task at hand. If people are cooperating in wars, games, or classroom jobs and things go badly and they fail, it is too easy to blame the minority member. For this reason, Cook (1984) reports that the competence of the group member is the critical factor in gaining respect and attraction from others.

Another complication is with equal status (Brewer & Miller, 1984). Integration frequently occurs by bringing minorities in at the bottom of the ladder, whether as students or apprentices, or in the least desirable jobs. They then have to interact with whites who outrank them. The new immigrant child who can barely speak

The acquittal of Los Angeles Police Department officers involved in the beating of Rodney King triggered violent disruptions in Los Angeles in May 1992. Korean merchants were especially targeted by blacks, and expressed great hostility in return.

English and who has only one dress to wear to school will not be equal in status to a wealthy doctor's daughter, whatever the teacher's efforts.

As a result, many efforts at intergroup contact do not meet the conditions that would make them work. Relatively few desegregation plans, as implemented, resemble the favorable conditions specified by the social psychologists' contact theory. These plans tend to yield positive effects (Cook, 1988; Taylor & Katz, 1988), but they are the exceptions.

Today, intergroup conflicts may be more important than ever. Countries such as France, Germany, the Netherlands, and England, as well as Canada and the United States, are facing the problems posed by increasing ethnic diversity. Violent ethnic conflicts are in the headlines from all over the world—in the former Soviet Union, the former Yugoslavia, throughout Africa, in Sri Lanka and India, and in mideast nations such as Iraq. In the United States, large ethnic groups pose new challenges, whether it is the entry of Latinos into labor markets where they displace blacks and other minorities, or the black political successes in local governments that lead to charges of discrimination against other minorities, the Korean family merchants under fire from other minorities in cities like Los

Angeles and New York, the Asian-American students whose great academic successes have led to resentments from others, or the school districts in our large cities which struggle with children speaking as many as 70 different native languages within a single elementary school.

As a result, there are demands for the restriction of immigration and for English to be an "official language," counterposed by ethnic groups' demands for inclusion and recognition at all levels of the society. On the college campuses, "hate speech," "diversity," and affirmative action in admissions and faculty appointments are daily issues. "Hate acts" occur even in seemingly serene settings populated by highly educated individuals in close contact with each other. In Canada, "multiculturalism" became a major issue in the 1970s (Berry et al., 1977), but it has now hit with full force in the United States as well.

These practical difficulties do not mean that the effort to reduce prejudice should be abandoned, because there are important moral and legal reasons for it. Indeed, reducing prejudice may be more important than ever, as our nation once again becomes more ethnically diverse and as groups such as gays and the disabled increasingly demand equality. But we must remember that no one approach is going to solve the problem. Intergroup antagonism seems to be a fundamental aspect of the human condition. Every society in the world takes group membership into consideration when determining how it will treat any individual.

In a sense, modern nations such as France, Canada, or the United States have embarked on a particularly ambitious program of group equality, set up by such idealistic guidelines as the American Bill of Rights and later constitutional amendments (especially the Fourteenth). At the same time, these nations have tried to accommodate a bewildering variety of groups from all parts of the world, such as, in the United States, large numbers of Africans, Vietnamese, Hungarians, Latinos, Russian Jews, and British Puritans. It is not surprising, therefore, that group equality should have failed to some degree. We cannot be complacent, because all too much suffering in our society is caused by prejudice. But it is also well to acknowledge the considerable measure of harmony and group tolerance that has allowed such a Noah's ark of humanity to coexist and to cooperate for so many years.

KEY TERMS

ambivalent racism

assumed similarity effect

aversive racism

categorization

cognitive consistency

contact theory

discrimination

ethnocentrism

group-serving biases

ingroup

ingroup favoritism effect

minimal intergroup
   situation

old-fashioned racism

outgroup

outgroup homogeneity
   effect

prejudice

psychodynamic theories

realistic group conflict

relative deprivation

schema

self-fulfilling prophecy

social identity theory

social norm

stereotype

subcategorization

symbolic racism

typicality effect

SUMMARY

1. Prejudice, stereotypes, and discrimination correspond to the affective, cognitive, and behavioral components of intergroup antagonism.

2. Stereotypes and prejudice strongly influence the individual's attitudes and behavior in a variety of areas.

3. Social learning is probably the strongest determinant of stereotypes and prejudices against minority groups. Prejudices frequently develop in childhood and adolescence and are difficult to change thereafter.

4. Group conflict theories view prejudice as stemming from the realities of intergroup competition; psychodynamic theories see prejudice as stemming from the individual's particular personality dynamics.

5. Cognitive approaches view stereotyping and prejudices as arising from such normal cognitive processes as categorization, especially into ingroup and outgroup, and schematic processing, as well as a means of getting self-esteem from one's own social identity.

6. The various theories tend to focus on different phenomena rather than providing competing explanations for the same events.

7. Although some forms of racial prejudice have diminished in recent years, others have

emerged to take their place, notably ambivalence between affect-based racial prejudices and more cognitive beliefs in equal rights, and the blend of anti-minority affect and race-free traditional values called "symbolic racism."

8. Interracial contact is probably the most effective technique for reducing prejudice, but by itself it is not effective. It is more likely to be successful if it involves sustained close contact, cooperative interdependence, and equal status, and is supported by local norms.

9. Our society is not organized to provide the kinds of interracial contact that best break down racial prejudices. For that reason, special efforts need to be made if prejudice is to be reduced substantially.

SUGGESTED READINGS

Brewer, M. B. (1991). The social self: On being the same and different at the same time. *Personality and Social Psychology Bulletin, 17,* 475–482. A provocative new theory about the links between personal and social identity.

Devine, P. (1989). Stereotypes and prejudice: Their automatic and controlled components. *Journal of Personality and Social Psychology, 56,* 5–18. A fresh explanation for the paradox of declining racial prejudice without the disappearance of conventional racial stereotypes.

Dovidio, I. F., & Gaertner, S. L. (Eds.). (1986). *Prejudice, discrimination, and racism.* New York: Academic Press. An excellent collection of essays on race relations, summarizing the most interesting recent research.

Katz, P., & Taylor, D. (Eds.). (1988). *Towards the elimination of racism: Profiles in controversy.* New York: Plenum. A stimulating collection of essays on the major controversies in race relations research, presenting one pro and one con on each controversy.

Kluegel, J. R. (1990). Trends in whites' explanations of the black-white gap in socioeconomic status, 1977–1989. *American Sociological Review, 55,* 512–525. Documents a shift toward motivational rather than ability attributions, and the sharp divisions among whites both in how blacks' disadvantages are to be explained and how they are to be remedied.

Miller, N., & Brewer, M. B. (Eds.). (1984). *Groups in contact: The psychology of desegregation.* New York: Academic Press. A comprehensive collection of research articles on the contact hypothesis.

Price, V., & Hsu, M. (1992). Public opinion about AIDS policies: The role of misinformation and attitudes toward homosexuals. *Public Opinion Quarterly, 56,* 29–52. The best recent account of prejudice against AIDS victims.

Schuman, H., Steeh, C., & Bobo, L. (1985). *Racial attitudes in America: Trends and interpretations.* Cambridge, MA: Harvard University Press. The most comprehensive description of postwar changes in Americans' racial attitudes.

Stephan, W. G. (1985). Intergroup relations. In G. Lindzey and E. Aronson (Eds.), *Handbook of social psychology* (3rd ed., Vol. 2, pp. 599–658). New York: Random House. A thorough review of research, from the cognitive perspective.

Tajfel, H., & Turner, J. C. (1986). The social identity theory of intergroup behavior. In Worchel, S. & Austin, W. G. (Eds.). *Psychology of intergroup relations* (2nd ed.). Chicago: Nelson-Hall. An authoritative account of social identity theory.

Trafimow, D., Triandis, H. C., & Goto, S. G. (1991). Some tests of the distinction between the private self and the collective self. *Journal of Personality and Social Psychology, 60,* 649–655. Research on how private and collective self-cognitions relate to each other, and to East–West cultural differences.

8
Social Influence

FOCUS OF THIS CHAPTER

Conformity
Compliance
Obedience to Authority

Cultural Highlight
Culture and Conformity

Research Closeup
Power in the Classroom

Consider these examples of social influence:

- In the 1950s, American college men were virtually all clean-shaven, with short hair. Only farmers wore blue jeans as everyday clothing. College women almost invariably had short hair and dressed in blouses and skirts, with hemlines well below the knee. By the late 1960s, college students of both sexes grew their hair long and wore blue jeans regularly. How would you describe fashion trends at your college today? Why do so many students tend to dress so similarly?

- As you approach the local supermarket, a young woman stops you and asks you to sign a petition urging the city to build a new shelter for homeless families. You somewhat reluctantly read and sign the petition. Next the woman asks you to donate $5 to help the homeless. You give her a dollar and duck into the market. Why did you comply, at least partially, with her requests?

- In Nazi Germany during World War II, Adolf Hitler ordered his troops into battle—a common practice for heads of state during wartime. But he also ordered the construction of concentration camps where millions of civilians were put to death. Why did so many people obey Hitler's extraordinary orders to kill children and unarmed civilians?

Social psychologists have long been interested in how our behavior is influenced by other people and groups. We have already explored some aspects of social influence in our analysis of the processes of attitude change (Chapter 6). In this chapter, we will examine three important types of social influence: conformity, compliance, and obedience to authority.

Conformity is the tendency to change one's beliefs or behaviors in ways that are consistent with group standards. College students are presumably free to pick their own clothes and hairstyles. But students often prefer to dress like others in their social group, thus conforming to current campus fashions. What factors affect conformity to group pressures?

When people do what they are asked to do, even though they might prefer not to, we call it **compliance.** The distinguishing feature of compliance is that we are responding to a request from another individual or group. Compliance can occur in many settings—when a friend asks us for a ride to the airport, or a group of Halloween trick-or-treaters ask for candy, or a Red Cross volunteer asks for donations.

In some social situations, we perceive one person or group as having the **legitimate authority** to influence our behavior. The government has a right to ask citizens to pay taxes; parents have a right to ask their children to wash the dinner dishes; and medical personnel have the right to ask us to take off our clothes for a physical exam. In these cases, social norms permit those in authority to make requests and dictate that subordinates should obey. Although authorities often make reasonable and appropriate requests, they sometimes abuse their power. The Nazi military leaders who ordered the mass murder of millions of civilians during World War II are a case in point.

CONFORMITY

Americans are ambivalent about conformity. On the one hand, we know that sometimes a person has to "go along to get along." Conforming to group norms is often the price of acceptance and social harmony. On the other hand, we value individualism and worry that people can easily be pressured to go against their personal beliefs "because everyone is doing it."

The question of when conformity is a social good and when it is harmful can be a matter of heated controversy, as a recent U.S. Supreme Court decision illustrates. In 1992, the high court ruled in a 5–4 decision that public schools may not include prayers or invoke the name of God during a grade school or high school ceremony. Justice Anthony M. Kennedy explained that school children are a captive audience and acutely sensitive to peer pressure. Consequently, he reasoned, a school-sponsored prayer poses a special "risk of compelling conformity" in religious beliefs. "What to most believers may seem nothing more than a reasonable request that the nonbeliever respect their religious practices, in a school context may appear to the nonbeliever or dissenter to be an attempt . . . to enforce a religious orthodoxy" (cited in Savage, 1992, p. A1). Kennedy concluded that the court must protect childrens' freedom of conscience from subtle coercive pressures in school. Critics immediately denounced the decision as censoring the religious expression of the majority of school children.

Some of the earliest research in social psychology investigated conformity, and we will begin by describing two classic studies.

A Guess in the Dark: The Sherif Study

The task in a pioneering study by Muzafer Sherif (1935) seemed straightforward: A male college student sat in a darkened room and watched a single point of light. He was told that the light would move and that his job was to estimate how far it moved. Most subjects found it extremely difficult to estimate how far the light moved, since it often appeared to move at varying speeds and in different directions. Actually, the study used a perceptual illusion known as the *autokinetic effect:* A single point of light seen in the dark appears to move, even though it is really stationary.

Given the ambiguity of this situation, subjects could not be sure of their own judgments, and their initial estimates varied enormously. Several people thought the light moved only 1 or 2 inches, whereas one person thought it moved as much as 800 feet! Apparently, this person thought he was in a gymnasium, although actually he was in a small room.

After each subject had made several estimates, a second person was brought into the room, also supposedly a subject but in fact a confederate of the researcher. The confederate had been trained to make his estimates consistently lower or higher than those of the real subject. The judgment procedure was repeated for a number of trials. Under these conditions, the subject soon began to make his estimates more and more similar to those of the confederate. For instance, if the subject began by estimating that the light moved between 10 and 14 inches and the confederate said it moved only 2 inches, on the next trial the subject tended to lower his estimate, and on the following trial he would lower it even more. By the end of the series, the subject's estimates were very similar to those of the confederate.

As Plain as Day: The Asch Study

Solomon Asch wondered if conformity occurs only in ambiguous situations such as the Sherif study where people are quite uncertain about the correct answer. If the stimulus situation were clear, would people conform? Asch reasoned that when people face an unambiguous situation, they will trust their own perceptions and give their independent judgment, even when every member of a group disagrees with them. Asch (1955) designed an experiment to test this hypothesis.

Five male college students arrived to take part in a study on perception. They sat around a

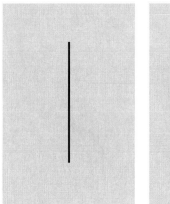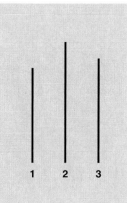

Figure 8-1 A stimulus like the ones in the Asch conformity study. Subjects were shown two cards. One contained the "standard." The second contained three comparison lines, one of which was the same length as the standard. Subjects were asked which comparison line was the same as the standard.

table and were told they would be judging the lengths of lines. They were shown a card on which three black lines of varying lengths had been drawn and a second card containing only one line. Their task was to choose the line on the first card that was most similar in length to the line on the second card. As shown in Figure 8-1, it was an easy task. One of the lines was exactly the same length as the standard, whereas the other two were quite different from it.

When the lines were shown, the five subjects answered aloud in the order in which they were seated. The first subject gave his choice and then each of the others responded in turn. Since the judgment was so easy, there were no disagreements. When all had responded, a second set of lines was shown, responses were given, and a third set of lines was presented.

At this point the experiment seems dull and pointless. On the third trial, however, the first subject looked carefully at the lines as before and then gave what was obviously the wrong answer. In the example in Figure 8-1, he might have said line 1 rather than line 2. The next subject gave the same wrong answer, as did the third and fourth subjects. When it was time for the fifth subject to respond, he was quite disturbed. It was clear to him that the others were giving wrong answers. He knew that line 2 was

most similar to the standard. Yet everyone else said it was line 1.

Under these circumstances, people sitting in the fifth position sometimes gave the wrong answer—they agreed with the others even though they knew the answer was incorrect. In fact, among these college students with good eyesight and presumably sharp minds, the wrong answer was given about 35 percent of the time. Some subjects never gave the wrong answer, some did all the time, but overall they averaged about one wrong response in three. Of course, in this classic study the situation was staged. The first four "subjects" were confederates of the experimenter and were responding according to a prearranged script. But the real subject did not know this, and he gave the wrong answer rather than disagree with the others.

It is important to keep the clarity of this judgment task in mind if we are to understand the phenomenon. There is a tendency to think that the conforming subjects were uncertain of the correct choice and therefore were swayed by the majority. This was not the case. The subjects were quite sure of the correct choice and, in control groups with no group pressure, subjects chose correctly 100 percent of the time. When subjects conformed, they conformed despite the fact that they knew the correct answer.

Later studies have demonstrated similar conformity effects using other physical stimuli, as well as opinion statements, statements of fact, and logical syllogisms. Subjects have agreed that there is no population problem in the United States because 6000 miles of continent separates San Francisco from New York, that men are 8 to 9 inches taller than women on the average, and that male babies have a life expectancy of only 25 years. In other words, regardless of the type of stimulus and of how clear the correct choice is, when individuals are faced with a unanimous group opinion, the pressure exerted by the majority is often strong enough to produce conformity.

People often conform, even when doing so means contradicting their own perceptions of the world. In many cases, individuals continue to believe that their private judgments are correct and that the group is wrong. Nevertheless, when asked to respond publicly, they give the same wrong answers that the others give. This is what we mean by conformity.

Why Do People Conform?

People conform for two major reasons: to be right and to be liked (Campbell & Fairey, 1989). This is consistent with the analysis of attitude change presented earlier in Chapter 6. There, we saw that people are more likely to be influenced by a persuasive communication from a person (communicator) who is knowledgeable, trustworthy and likeable. Similarly, people are more apt to conform to group behaviors when they think the group members are right and when they want to be liked by the group.

INFORMATIONAL INFLUENCE: THE DESIRE TO BE RIGHT.   One reason for conformity is that the behavior of other people often provides useful information. A thirsty traveler at an oasis in the Sahara Desert who sees Arabs drinking from one well and avoiding another well would be smart to copy their behavior. By drinking from the popular well, the traveler may avoid drinking contaminated water. The tendency to conform based on informational influence depends on two aspects of the situation: how well-informed we believe the group is and how confident we are in our own independent judgment.

The more we trust the group's information and value their opinions, the more likely we are to go along with the group. If our thirsty traveler in the desert sees that the Arabs drinking at the oasis are city dwellers on their first tourist trip to the desert, he or she might be inclined to wonder how much they know about wells and so may not conform to their example. If the Arabs are clearly desert nomads traveling on their usual route, the person would be far more likely to trust them and follow their example. Anything that increases confidence in the correctness of the group should increase conformity. Conversely, anything that leads us to doubt the group's knowledge or trustworthiness should decrease conformity.

Balanced against the individual's confidence

in the group is the individual's confidence in his or her own views. Early studies found that the more ambiguous or difficult the task, the more likely people were to conform to group judgments (Coleman, Blake, & Mouton, 1958), presumably because they were less certain of their own judgment. For example, the Sherif task was more difficult than the Asch task, and so produced more conformity. Other research has found that the less competent and knowledgeable we feel about a topic, the more likely we are to conform (Wiesenthal et al., 1976). For example, Campbell, Tesser, and Fairey (1986) experimentally manipulated subjects' level of self-confidence versus doubt in their ability to solve a hidden figures test. Later, when asked to solve problems in a group setting, individuals high in self-doubt conformed significantly more than those with low self-doubt.

A useful distinction can be made between change in a person's public actions (going along with the group) and change in a person's private beliefs (actually agreeing with the group). When conformity is based on informational influence—on the belief that group members are right—we usually change our minds as well as our behavior.

NORMATIVE INFLUENCE: THE DESIRE TO BE LIKED.   A second major reason for conformity is to gain the approval, or avoid the disapproval, of other people. We often want others to accept us, like us, and treat us well. Normative influence occurs when we alter our behavior to conform to group norms or standards. For example, in deciding how to dress for the senior prom, we may try to wear the "right" clothes so that we will fit in, give a good impression, and avoid embarrassment. We may not really like wearing formal clothes, but do it anyway because it is socially appropriate for the occasion. Similarly, when we're with our health-conscious friends, we may eat salads and fresh fish, even though we don't especially like them; when we're alone, we're more likely to follow our personal preferences, which may be for hamburgers and fries. In such situations, conformity leads to an outward change in public behavior, but not necessarily to a change in private opinions.

We all want to be liked by our friends, but sometimes the price of acceptance is conforming to group norms. Normative influence occurs when we change our behavior to conform to group standards.

In summary, the motivation to conform can stem from a desire to be right or a desire to be liked by the group. Informational influence occurs when a person is uncertain of the correct response and so uses group behavior as a guide to action. This is illustrated by Sherif's study using an ambiguous moving point of light. Normative influence occurs when a person goes along with group norms to gain acceptance or approval. This is illustrated in Asch's study where subjects sometimes denied the clear evidence of their own senses to give public judgments that agreed with the group.

When Do People Conform?

We are more apt to conform in some situations rather than in others. Several important features of the group situation can affect conformity. These include group size, unanimity, and commitment. In addition, there are individual differences in the desire for individuation or uniqueness that can also affect conformity.

GROUP SIZE. Suppose there are two men in a room and one of them says it is very warm. If the room is in fact quite cold, the second man would probably disagree with the first. He would feel cold and would assume that the other person was mistaken or feverish. If forced to make a public statement on the temperature of the room, he would probably say he thought it was rather cold.

If the room contained five people and four of them said it was warm, the situation would change. Even if one man felt cold, he would be

likely to doubt his own perceptions. After all, it is unlikely that all four of the others were feverish or mistaken. If the person were asked how he felt, he might be uncertain enough to agree with the rest. He might say the room was warm and then wonder what was wrong with him. Four people tend to be more trustworthy than one, in terms of both honesty and the reliability of their opinions; it is harder to mistrust a group than one person (Insko et al., 1985).

Many experiments have demonstrated that conformity usually increases as the size of the unanimous majority increases, at least up to a point (Tanford & Penrod, 1984). In some of his early experiments, Asch (1955) varied the size of the majority from 2 to 15. As shown in Figure 8-2, he found that two people produced more conformity pressure than one, three a lot more than two, and four about the same as three. Somewhat surprisingly, Asch found that increasing the size of the group past four did not increase the amount of conformity for his line judgment task.

Later studies have found that the optimal group size for conformity depends on the situation. Stanley Milgram and his associates (1969) used a crowded street in New York City as their laboratory. These researchers played the old game of looking up to see whether anyone else would look up also. This time it was done as a deliberate experiment, and careful observations were made of pedestrians who walked by. Research assistants dressed in ordinary street clothes stood and looked up at the sixth-floor window of an office building across the street. Milgram varied whether 1, 2, 3, 5, 10, or 15 assistants stood around looking up at the window. The chief measure was the percentage of

253

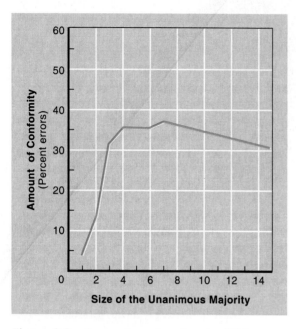

Figure 8-2 Group size and conformity. With one other group member, subjects made few errors (less than 4 percent). As the size of the group increased, the percentage of errors increased, peaking at 37 percent wrong responses with a 7-person unanimous majority. (*Source:* Adapted from "Opinions and Social Pressure," by Solomon Asch. Copyright © 1955 by Scientific American, Inc. All rights reserved.)

passers-by who actually stopped and looked up at the window. When 1 assistant was looking up, only 4 percent of the passers-by also looked up; with 5 assistants, it went up to 16 percent; with 10, it was 22 percent; and with 15, it increased to 40 percent. In this study, the more people who looked up, the greater the tendency for passers-by to conform.

GROUP UNANIMITY. An important factor in producing conformity is the unanimity of the group opinion. A person faced with a unanimous majority is under great pressure to conform. If, however, a group is not united, there is a striking decrease in the amount of conformity. When even one other person does not go along with the rest of the group, conformity drops to about one-fourth the usual level. One of the most impressive aspects of this phenomenon is that it does not seem to matter who the nonconforming person is. Regardless of whether this dissenter is a highly prestigious expert or some-

one of low prestige and uncertain expertise, conformity tends to drop to low levels (Asch, 1955; Morris & Miller, 1975). Furthermore, a sole dissenter can reduce conformity even if he or she gives wrong answers. If the correct answer is A, the majority says B, and another person says C, the real subject is less likely to conform than if everyone agrees on one incorrect answer. Simply having some disagreement within the group makes it easier for an individual to remain independent (Allen & Levine, 1971).

The dramatic decrease in conformity when unanimity is broken seems to be due to several of the factors we have already discussed. First, the amount of trust or confidence in the correctness of the majority decreases whenever there is disagreement, even if the dissenter is less knowledgeable or less reliable than those who make up the majority. The mere fact that someone else also disagrees with the group indicates that there is room for doubt, that the issue is not perfectly clear, and that the majority might be wrong. This reduces the individual's reliance on the majority opinion as a source of information and accordingly reduces conformity.

Second, if another group member endorses the position the individual favors, it serves to strengthen the individual's self-confidence about that judgment. As we have seen, greater confidence reduces conformity. A third consideration involves reluctance to appear deviant. The lone dissenter stands out. When someone else also disagrees, neither person is quite as deviant as he or she would be alone.

This suggests that even one deviant voice can have an important effect as long as there are other people who inwardly disagree with the majority but are afraid to speak up. It may also explain why totalitarian governments allow no dissent. Even one small dissenting voice could encourage others to do likewise, and the regime might be endangered.

COMMITMENT TO THE GROUP. Conformity is affected by the strength of the bonds between individuals and the group (Forsyth, 1990). **Commitment** refers to all the forces, positive and negative, that act to keep an individual in a relationship or group.

The first American women who demonstrated for the right to vote were a small minority. Over time, this resourceful and determined minority successfully changed public opinions, obtaining to right to vote for women in 1920.

Positive forces attracting an individual to a group can include liking other group members, believing the group accomplishes important goals, feeling that group members work well together, and expecting to gain from belonging to the group. Another important factor is the individual's sense of identification with the group and group values (Hogg & Turner, 1987). Groups with high morale, where members enjoy working together and believe they function well as a team, are more vulnerable to conformity pressures than are less cohesive groups. We'll examine this issue further in Chapter 11 when we discuss the dangers of "groupthink."

Negative forces keeping an individual from leaving a group also increase commitment. These include such barriers as having few alternatives or having made large investments in the group that would be costly to give up. For example, some people stay in a work group only because they need the money, not because they like or respect their coworkers. In general, the more committed a person is to a group, the greater the pressures for conformity to group standards.

THE DESIRE FOR INDIVIDUATION. People differ in their willingness to do things that publicly differentiate them from others. Whereas some people are more comfortable blending in with a group and going along with group opinions, others prefer to stand out. Christina Maslach and her colleagues have developed a paper-and-pencil test to measure people's willingness to engage in public behavior that sets them apart from others (Maslach et al., 1985, 1987).

A person scores high on individuation by indicating that he or she would be willing to do such things as "present a personal opinion, on a controversial topic, to a group of strangers" or "speak up about your own ideas even if you are uncertain whether you are correct." In contrast, a person scoring low on individuation would hesitate to do such behaviors. Research indicates that high-individuation people are more likely to say that they have distinctive ways of dressing, use a distinctive nickname, and own unique possessions. In a laboratory study of conformity, high-individuation subjects were less likely to go along with the majority view and more likely to engage in what the researchers called "creative dissent." This research emphasizes the importance of individual differences in susceptibility to group influence. Cultural differences in conformity are the topic of the CULTURAL HIGHLIGHT for this chapter.

CULTURAL HIGHLIGHT
Culture and Conformity

An important difference among cultures is the extent to which they emphasize individualism versus collective interests (Triandis, 1989). In individualist societies such as the United States and Western Europe, childrearing stresses self-reliance and assertion; children are given a good deal of independence, and creativity is encouraged. In contrast, collectivist societies, such as those in Africa and Latin America, emphasize the importance of ties to the social group. Parents are concerned with compliance, proper behavior, and a respect for group traditions (Berry, Poortinga, Segall, & Dasen, 1992). As a result, we might expect conformity to group norms to be more important in collectivist cultures than in individualist cultures (Schwartz, 1990).

Cross-cultural research provides some support for this hypothesis. In an early study, Berry (1967) used an Asch-type line judgment task to compare conformity in three cultural groups. Individuals from Scotland were selected to represent a Western, individualistic culture. To represent a collectivist culture, Berry sampled from the Temne culture of Sierra Leone, a farming people described by anthropologists as emphasizing tradition and conformity. To represent a non-

Western individualistic culture, Berry selected the Eskimo of Baffin Island, a group that relies on hunting and fishing and has been characterized by anthropologists as valuing self-reliance and ingenuity. All participants had normal vision. As predicted, clear cultural differences emerged. The Eskimo respondents showed the least conformity (mean of less than 3 out of 15), followed by the Scots (mean of about 4). The greatest conformity was shown by the Temne respondents (mean of almost 9 on the 15-point scale).

A similar pattern emerged in a study comparing Chinese adults in Taiwan and Americans in New Mexico (Huang & Harris, 1973). Chinese culture has been described as valuing adherence to tradition and respect for authority. Consequently, it was predicted that Chinese adults would show greater conformity than their American counterparts. In this field study, pedestrians were asked to participate in an opinion survey about using flowers and plants to beautify the environment. To introduce conformity, another pedestrian (actually a confederate of the researchers) was tested at the same time, and always answered first. There were no "right" answers to the opinion

questions used in this field study. The measure of conformity was the degree to which naive subjects imitated the responses of the confederate. As predicted, more conformity was observed in the Chinese sample than in the American sample. Another study using an Asch-type line judgment procedure also found higher levels of conformity among Japanese college students than those reported in earlier studies of American students (Matsuda, 1985).

These and other studies suggest that there are systematic differences between cultures in the value placed on conformity versus independence, and that these cultural values can affect actual behavior. In interpreting these results, it is essential to keep our own value biases in mind. Since Americans tend to value independence and sometimes consider "conformity" a dirty word, we may see these cross-cultural results as showing the superiority of our own culture. Yet as Triandis (1989) and others are quick to point out, greater reliance on tradition and adherence to group norms may be beneficial in other cultures. Further, we should not forget that even in a highly individualistic society such as ours, conformity to social norms is a common element of social life.

Minority Influence: Innovation in Groups

Conformity to majority patterns is a basic aspect of social life. But our emphasis on the power of the majority should not blind us to the importance of **minority influence.** Sometimes a forceful minority with a new idea or unique perspective can effectively change the position of the majority.

Early studies showing that dissent reduces conformity began to raise questions about the existence of an "all-powerful" majority. In the past 20 years, the major new developments in conformity research have been attempts to understand the influence of minorities (Maass & Clark, 1984; Trost, Maass, & Kenrick, 1992). Pioneering work by the French psychologist Serge Moscovici (1985) has been especially important. In an early experiment, Moscovici, Lage, and Naffrechoux (1969) used an Asch-type conformity paradigm but with a majority of naive subjects and a minority of confederates. Subjects were shown an unambiguous physical stimulus, namely slides of colors. In this study, members of 6-person groups were asked to rate the color of the slides. In actuality, all slides were blue but varied in their luminance. In control groups of 6 naive subjects, virtually all slides were described as blue. In the experimental group, however, two confederates consistently labeled the blue slides as "green." Subjects had previously been told that all group members had normal vision, so these "green" responses could not be attributed to color blindness. With this minority pressure, about a third of the subjects reported seeing at least one "green" slide, and 8 percent of all judgments was that slides were "green." Clearly, the minority view had a noticeable effect on the naive majority.

The *behavioral style* of a minority is important. To be effective, a minority must be consistent and forceful. This behavioral style is interpreted by the majority as a sign of the minority's confidence and certainty in its position (Maass & Clark, 1984). Although members of a consistent minority may be liked less than members of the majority, they tend to be seen as more competent and honest (Bassili & Provencal, 1988). As a minority persists in its position over time, the majority may start to question the correctness of its views. Ultimately, some majority members may "convert" by changing their own position in the direction of the minority. If enough members change their views, the minority may be transformed into a new majority.

Research has identified other factors that also determine the influence of minorities (Maass & Clark, 1984; Moscovici, Mugny, & van Avermaet, 1985). First, minorities are more influential when they are able to refute the majority viewpoint effectively, for instance, by logical arguments (Clark, 1990). Second, minorities are most effective when their behavioral style is logically consistent but not "rigid," that is, when they are seen as having a well-defined position but a flexible style of presentation. Third, the general social climate of the society can also make a difference. A minority will be more effective if it argues for a position in line with current social trends outside of the group. For example, in an era of increasing sexual conservatism, a minority arguing for sexual permissiveness will be less effective than a minority arguing for sexual restraint.

Minorities are also more likely to succeed when they are similar to the majority group in most respects except for the particular behavior or attitude in question (Volpato, Maass, Mucchi-Faina, & Vitti, 1990). A member of the Republican party trying to convince other Republicans to change their views on foreign aid would be a *single minority* (also called an "ingroup minority"), similar to the majority group in party membership and differing only in beliefs about foreign aid. In contrast, a member of the Democratic party trying to get Republicans to change their policies on foreign aid would be a double minority (or "outgroup minority"), differing in both political party and views about foreign aid. Research suggests that the Republican will generally be more influential than the Democrat in swaying a group of Republicans.

A study by Maass and Clark, for example, (1984) found that an ostensibly gay minority arguing for gay rights had less influence on heterosexuals than did a heterosexual minority arguing for gay rights, in part because the gay minority was seen as having more self-interest in the issue. Another study showed that conservative male subjects were more strongly influenced by a man arguing for a liberal position on abortion than by a woman taking the same liberal stance (Maass et al., 1982). When a minority group is perceived as having a personal stake in its position, its views can more easily be discounted as reflecting self-interest. More generally, minorities have more influence when their position is taken seriously and seen as reflecting certainty and competence. Minorities are less influential when they can be discounted as bizarre, dogmatic, or self-serving.

A current controversy is whether the processes of majority influence (conformity) and minority influence (innovation) are fundamentally the same or different. There is evidence on both sides of this debate, and it is too soon to decide definitively between the single-process versus dual-process perspectives. A brief look at each will highlight the issues in question.

Several theorists (Latané & Wolf, 1981; Tanford & Penrod, 1984) have made the case that the effects of majorities and minorities both reflect a single underlying influence process. Majority and minority influence differ in quantity, not quality; majorities usually have more influence because they have more members. Results from several studies are consistent with this single-process view (e.g., Wolf, 1987).

On the other hand, Moscovici and other researchers (Maass & Clark, 1984; Nemeth, 1986) believe that there may be important qualitative differences between minority and majority influence. For example, they believe that majority influence most often leads to changes in overt behavior but not necessarily to changes in private attitudes. In contrast, the influence of minorities is more likely to result in changed attitudes, to produce a "conversion" in people's opinions.

Although a dissenting minority can challenge the harmony of group interaction, disagreement may have important benefits for the group (Nemeth, 1992). In a series of studies, Nemeth and her associates have shown that minorities can cause other group members to think more carefully about an issue and to consider a wider variety of possible explanations or novel solutions (Nemeth & Kwan, 1987). In other words, the expression of minority viewpoints can sometimes improve group functioning and can have a beneficial effect out of proportion to the minority's small numbers. This positive effect of minority viewpoints is most likely to occur for tasks that are enhanced by creative thinking and the introduction of multiple perspectives (Nemeth, Mosier, & Chiles, 1992).

Nemeth and Chiles (1988) have also demonstrated the potential carryover effects of exposure to a dissenting minority. Subjects first participated in a group color perception task with a confederate who dissented consistently, dissented inconsistently, or never dissented. Later, subjects participated in a new color perception task with a different group. Their experience in the new group was much like that of the Asch subjects: They were exposed to an incorrect and unanimous majority. The results were clear. Subjects who had first been exposed to a consistent dissenting minority were substantially more likely to maintain their independence and provide correct answers than subjects with no prior experience with dissent.

COMPLIANCE

One of the basic ways we influence other people is to ask them to do (or not to do) something. Think of some of the direct requests you might make of your friends: to drive you to the airport, to lend you money, to refrain from smoking in your car, to tell you what they really think of your new haircut, to join the volunteer group you're organizing, and so on. How should you present these requests in order to increase the chances that your friends will comply? Research on compliance has attempted to understand some of the processes that lead people to comply (or refuse to comply) with requests.

Sometimes we seem to comply with requests for no reason at all. In one study researchers approached people waiting to use a photocopying machine and asked to go first in line because

"I have to make copies" (Langer, Blank, & Chanowitz, 1978). This so-called explanation actually gave no real justification for going out of turn. Yet many subjects went along with the request, apparently not paying much attention to the content of the explanation. Ellen Langer refers to this behavior as *mindlessness*, because the response is made almost without thinking. Perhaps out of habit, we have learned that when someone asks for something, especially something trivial, and gives a reason (even a meaningless reason), we should go along. We spare ourselves the mental effort of thinking about the situation and simply comply with the request. Mindlessness may not explain most instances of compliance, but it is a fascinating aspect of human behavior.

Six Bases of Social Power

People can use a wide variety of ways to try to influence each other. When David Kipnis (1984, p. 186) asked managers in business organizations how they try to influence their coworkers to do something, they said things like:

> "I simply order him to do what I ask."
>
> "I act very humble while making my request."
>
> "I explain the reasons for my request."

In contrast, when Kipnis asked dating couples how they influence their partners, they said things like:

> "I get angry and demand he give in."
>
> "I act so nice that she cannot refuse when I ask."
>
> "We talk about why we don't agree."

The many ways people use to get others to comply with their wishes are an important facet of social influence.

A useful way to classify social influence is provided in a model developed by Bertram Raven and his colleagues (French & Raven, 1959; Raven, 1992). They identify six major bases of power, each reflecting a different type of resource a person might use to influence someone. As summarized in Table 8-1, these are:

1. *Rewards.* One basis for power is the ability to provide positive outcomes for another person—to help that person accomplish a desired goal or to offer a valued reward. Some rewards are highly personal, such as a smile of approval from a special friend. Other rewards, such as money, are impersonal. Sometimes people use reward power by making explicit bargains: A father might promise to take his daughter to the park if she cleans up her room. At other times, the possibility of rewards may be more subtle. An employee may hope that his hard work and

TABLE 8-1
The Six Bases of Power

	Definition	Example
Reward	Power based on providing or promising a positive outcome	If you brush your teeth every night this week, I'll take you to the movies on Saturday.
Coercion	Power based on providing or promising a negative outcome	If you don't brush your teeth, you can't play Nintendo.
Expertise	Power based on special knowledge or ability	The dentist told you to brush twice a day, and he knows best.
Information	Power based on the persuasive content of the message	If you don't brush your teeth, you'll get cavities that will hurt. And the dentist will have to drill holes in your teeth to fill the cavities.
Referent power	Power based on identifying with or wanting to be like another person or group	Your big brother Stan always brushes twice a day.
Legitimate authority	Power based on the influencer's right or authority to make a request	I'm your mother and I'm telling you to brush your teeth—now!

Note: Our examples consider how a parent might use each approach to persuade a child to brush her teeth.
Source: Adapted from Raven & Rubin (1983).

attention to his boss's wishes will lead to a raise in pay, even though no formal agreement has been discussed.

2. *Coercion.* Coercion can range from actual physical force to threats of punishment or subtle signs of disapproval. For example, after trying unsuccessfully to convince a young child to take a nap, a parent may simply place the struggling child in the crib, walk out, and close the door. Or a supervisor may threaten disciplinary action if an employee continues to arrive late for work.

3. *Expertise.* Special knowledge, training, and skill are sources of power. We defer to experts and follow their advice because we believe their knowledge will help us to achieve our personal goals. If a trusted physician advises us to take three little green pills daily for an allergy, we are likely to comply whether or not we know precisely what the pills contain or understand how the medicine works. Likewise, a group of mountain climbers will follow the hazardous route suggested by their experienced guide for scaling the summit.

4. *Information.* We often try to influence people by giving them information or logical arguments that we think will suggest the right course of action to them. A friend might influence us to go to a concert by informing us that our favorite rock group is performing. In this case, the influencer is not an expert. Rather, it is the content of the message that produces the desired effect. The importance of information as a factor in social influence is pervasive. We saw earlier in this chapter that the need for information can motivate conformity. In Chapter 6 on attitude change, we investigated another type of informational influence—the use of persuasion.

5. *Referent power.* A basis of influence with special relevance to personal relationships and groups is referent power. This exists when we admire or identify with a person or group and want to be like them. In such cases, we may voluntarily copy their behavior or do what they ask, because we want to become similar to them. In everyday life we may not think of identification as a type of influence, but it can be very effective. A young child who looks up to an older brother, tries to imitate his mannerisms, and adopts his interests is one illustration. A young man who drinks a particular brand of beer because he identifies with the "macho" image of the sportsmen promoting the product in TV commercials is also being influenced by referent power. Raven (1992) has also discussed the possibility of "negative referent power," which occurs when we want to separate ourself from a disliked or unappealing person or group. To avoid being identified with the unattractive other, we may deliberately avoid copying their behavior.

6. *Legitimate authority.* Sometimes one person has the right or authority to ask another person to act a certain way. The manager who orders a subordinate to do what she wants or the general

A three-year-old copies the gestures of his brother and friends. In Raven's model, social influence based on identification is called "referent power."

who orders his troops into battle is likely to be exercising legitimate authority. Similarly, in most families, parents feel they have the right to tell young children when to go to bed, and children usually feel obligated to comply. Children may try to renegotiate bedtime rules or ask to make an exception for a special occasion, but they usually accept their parents' authority to make rules.

Social roles such as parent–child, police officer–citizen, or supervisor–employee often dictate the legitimate rights and responsibilities of people in a relationship. Even very young children seem to sense that the requests of doctors and dentists should be obeyed. A prerequisite for effective legitimate authority is that all parties agree about the norms in their relationship. When someone deviates from agreed-upon rules, we feel we have the right to remind them of their obligations.

A field experiment at the Bronx Zoo illustrates the potential importance of uniforms in indicating that an individual has legitimate authority (Sedikides & Jackson, 1990). As visitors entered the Tropical Lagoon, they were approached by a person who told them not to touch the handrail of the bird exhibit. Visitors were significantly more likely to comply with this request when it came from someone dressed as a zoo keeper rather than from a person in casual clothes. Apparently the legitimate authority conveyed by the uniform increased the person's influence. Although the request not to touch the handrail was somewhat unusual (why put handrails there in the first place?), not one of the visitors questioned the reason for the request.

A special case of legitimate power is what Raven has called the "power of helplessness." Consider these requests: A small child asks his mother for help in taking off his snow boots; a well-dressed foreign tourist asks in broken English for directions to the bus stop; a partially blind grocery shopper asks for help in reading the price marked on a can of soup. In each case, the person asking for help is in a powerless or helpless condition. And, in each case, others are likely to comply with the request. Our culture has a clear **norm of social responsibility.** We

When children ask for help, their parents usually comply. We feel a sense of social responsibility to help those who cannot help themselves. Here a father teaches his son to ride a bike. In Raven's model, this is called the "power of helplessness."

expect people to help those who are less fortunate, and this social obligation makes it legitimate for those in need to ask for help. However, Raven cautions that the legitimate power of helplessness can sometimes be costly for those who use it. People who constantly rely on helplessness may come to see themselves as incompetent. We will examine this issue further in Chapter 13 on prosocial behavior.

The RESEARCH CLOSEUP examines the uses of power in American classrooms.

In recent years, Raven (1992) has supplemented the six major bases of power with an analysis of other means of influence. For example, "environmental manipulation" occurs when the influencer changes the situation so that the target of influence must comply. An exasperated homeowner, tired of yelling at neighborhood children to stay off her property, may finally erect a sturdy fence to prevent their trespassing. By changing the physical environment, she has changed the children's behavior. Another approach is to invoke the power of third parties. In the heat of an argument, a child may say to his sister, "If you don't stop, I'm going to tell Daddy about what you did." The idea here is to change the sister's behavior by threatening to call on the greater power of a parent.

261

RESEARCH CLOSEUP
Power in the Classroom

Think back to your high school days and the different ways your teachers led a class. One may have been a "dictator" who insisted on strict obedience to orders. Another may have been a "nice guy" who tried to build rapport with students and create a friendly classroom atmosphere. All teachers have the challenge of influencing students—getting students to pay attention, to complete assignments, to study, and to learn. But American teachers differ dramatically in the influence strategies they use in the classroom.

In a recent book, *Power in the Classroom,* Virginia Richmond and James McCroskey (1992) review a growing body of research on social influence at school. Much of this research has used the analysis of six bases of power developed by Bert Raven. Several general conclusions emerge.

Two forms of influence—expert and referent power—appear particularly useful in American classrooms. A teacher using expert power emphasizes his or her experience and knowledge, so that students

comply with requests out of respect for the teacher's expertise. A teacher using expert power might say, "Trust me. I've done this a hundred times and it really works." A teacher using referent power seeks to build a positive relationship with students, so that students want to follow requests in order to please the teacher. The use of expert and referent power tend to set a positive tone in a classroom. Research suggests that these influence approaches can enhance students' motivation to learn and improve their mastery of course materials.

In contrast, two other forms of influence—coercion and legitimate authority—appear to be less effective. A teacher using coercion might say, "Stop talking or I'll send you to the principal's office." A teacher appealing to legitimate authority might say, "Do it because I told you to, and I'm your teacher." Both approaches can produce an immediate change in students' behavior. They can get a student to stop talking or to open a book. But American students tend to find these approaches oppressive. In the long run, coercion and appeals to authority

may not motivate students to want to learn and may not foster an interest in course materials.

The use of rewards in the classroom is common. For example, elementary school teachers offer gold stars, free time, and special treats as inducements for good behavior. In the short run, rewards can motivate students to do homework or read a book chapter. But rewards can also create problems. As Richmond and Roach (1992) observe, when a teacher offers a student a reward, the student may focus on the reward rather than on the learning activity. Ultimately students need to find personal gratification in the act of learning so they can be self-motivated, rather than dependent on external rewards. Further, as we noted in Chapter 4 when we introduced the concept of overjustification, if people are inherently interested in a topic, offering external rewards can actually undermine their intrinsic motivation. In short, the use of rewards is probably most effective when the rewards are small and when rewards are used in conjunction with expert and referent power.

Specific Compliance Techniques

One line of research has investigated the specific techniques people use to gain compliance. Robert Cialdini (1988) has studied car salesmen, con artists, and other professionals who earn a living by getting people to buy their products or go

along with their schemes. He and other social psychology researchers have identified several important compliance techniques.

THE FOOT-IN-THE-DOOR TECHNIQUE. One way of increasing compliance is to induce a person to agree first to a small request. Once someone has agreed to the small action, he or she is more likely to agree to a larger request. This is the so-called **foot-in-the-door technique.** It is used explicitly or implicitly in many advertising campaigns. Advertisers often concentrate on getting consumers to do something connected with the product—even sending back a card saying that they do not want it. The advertisers apparently think that any act connected with the product increases the likelihood that the consumer will buy it in the future.

A classic study by Freedman and Fraser (1966) demonstrated this effect. Experimenters went from door to door and told homemakers they were working for the Committee for Safe Driving. They said they wanted the women's support for this campaign and asked them to sign a petition that was to be sent to the state's senators. The petition requested the senators to work for legislation to encourage safe driving. Almost all the women agreed to sign. Several weeks later, different experimenters contacted the same women and also other women who had not been approached before. At this time, all the women were asked to put in their front yards a large, unattractive sign that read "Drive Carefully."

The results were striking. Over 55 percent of the women who had previously endorsed the petition (a small request) also agreed to post the sign (a relatively large request). In contrast, less than 17 percent of the other women agreed to post the sign. Getting the women to agree to the initial small request tripled the amount of compliance to the large request. This effect has been replicated in several studies (e.g., Seligman, Bush, & Kirsch, 1975).

Why this technique works is not entirely clear. One explanation is that people who agree to a small request get involved and committed to the issue itself, to the behavior they perform, or perhaps simply to the idea of taking some kind of action. Another explanation is based on **self-perception theory,** which was introduced in Chapter 6 on attitudes. The idea here is that in some ways the individual's self-image changes as a result of the initial act of compliance. In the safe-driving experiment, for example, a woman may have thought of herself as the kind of person who does not take social action,

who does not sign petitions, who does not post signs, or, perhaps, who does not agree to things that are asked of her by someone at the door. Once she has agreed to the small request, which was actually difficult to refuse, she may have changed her perception of herself slightly. Once she has agreed to sign a petition, she may come to think of herself as the kind of person who does this sort of thing. Then, when the second request was made, she was more likely to comply than she would have been otherwise.

THE DOOR-IN-THE-FACE TECHNIQUE. Sometimes a technique opposite to the foot-in-the-door also works. First asking for a very large request and then making a smaller request can increase compliance to the small request. This is sometimes called the **door-in-the-face technique,** since the first request is typically so outrageously large that people might be tempted to slam the door in the requester's face. In one study, subjects were asked to volunteer time for a good cause (Cialdini et al., 1975). Some were asked first to give a huge amount of time. When they refused, as almost all did, the experimenter immediately said then perhaps they might agree to a much smaller commitment of time. Other subjects were asked only the smaller request, while a third group was given a choice between the two. The results were striking. In the small-request only condition, 17 percent of subjects agreed. In the choice condition, 25 percent of subjects complied with the smaller request. But in the condition where subjects had first turned down a big request, 50 percent agreed to the smaller request.

This effect is familiar to anyone who has ever bargained about the price of a used car or been involved in negotiations between a labor union and management. The tactic is to ask for the moon and then settle for less. The more you ask for at first, the more you expect to end up with eventually. The idea is that when you reduce your demands, the other person thinks you are compromising and the amount seems smaller. In a compliance situation, such as asking for money for charity, the same might apply. Five dollars doesn't seem like so much when the organization initially asked for a hundred dollars.

These members of the Hare Khrisna religion are using a common influence technique—offering a small present (free refreshments) in hopes that passers-by will read their materials or make a financial donation. This strategy is based on the norm of reciprocity, the idea that when someone gives us something, we feel obligated to return the favor.

Clearly, both the foot-in-the-door and the reverse tactic work at times, but we do not yet know when each of them will operate (Dillard, Hunter, & Burgoon, 1984). Both seem to work best when the behavior involved is prosocial, that is, when the request is to give money or help a worthwhile cause. One difference seems to be that the door-in-the-face technique works when the smaller request follows the larger request immediately and is obviously connected. The foot-in-the-door technique works even when the two requests are seemingly unconnected.

THE LOW-BALL TECHNIQUE. Consider how likely you would be to agree to the following requests. In one case, a researcher calls you on the phone and asks you to participate in an experiment scheduled for 7:00 in the morning. In a second case, a researcher calls and asks you to participate in a study. Only after you initially agree to participate does the researcher inform you that the study will be scheduled at 7:00 A.M. When Robert Cialdini and his associates (1978) compared these two procedures, they found that the second approach was much more effective. When students were told from the outset that an experiment would be conducted early in the morning, only 25 percent agreed to participate and showed up on time. In contrast, using the second approach of initially concealing the time of the study, 55 percent of students agreed to the request and almost all of them actually showed up for the early morning appointment. Once having agreed to participate, few people backed out of their agreement when they were informed about the time of day.

This tactic, in which a person is asked to agree to something on the basis of incomplete information and is later told the full story, is called the **low-ball technique.** Essentially, the person is tricked into agreeing to a relatively attractive proposition, only to discover later that the terms are actually different from those expected. This technique appears to work because once an individual has made an initial commitment to a course of action, he or she is reluctant to withdraw, even when the ground rules are changed. Although this technique can be effective (Burger & Petty, 1981), it is clearly deceptive. To protect consumers from unscrupulous salespersons, laws have been enacted to make low-balling illegal for several industries, such as automobile dealerships.

Our discussion of the foot-in-the-door, door-in-the-face, and low-ball techniques by no means exhausts the possible tactics people use to gain compliance. Research by Jerry Burger (1986) has begun to explore another strategy that he calls the **that's-not-all technique.** Consider this situation: A salesperson describes a new microwave oven to a potential customer and quotes a price. Then, while the customer is mulling over the decision, the salesperson adds, "But that's not all. Today only, we're having a special deal. If you buy the microwave now, we'll give you a five-piece set of microwave dishes at no additional cost." In actuality, the dishes always come with the oven, but by presenting the dishes as a "special deal" or something "just for you," the salesperson hopes to make the purchase even more attractive. The essence of this technique is to present a product at a high price, allow the customer to think about the price, and then improve the deal either by adding an additional product or by lowering the price.

In a series of seven experiments, Burger (1986) has demonstrated the potential effectiveness of the "that's-not-all" approach. In one illustrative study, experimenters held a psychol-

TABLE 8-2	
Compliance Techniques	
Technique	Description
Foot-in-the-door	First, make a small request. When the person complies make another, larger request.
Low-ball	First, make a reasonable request. Then, reveal details that increase the costs involved.
Door-in-the-face	First, make an unreasonably large request. Then immediately make a more modest request.
That's-not-all	First, make a fairly large request. Then immediately offer a discount or bonus that makes the request more reasonable.

ogy club bake sale on campus. At random, half the people who stopped at the table and asked about the cupcakes were told that they could buy a prepackaged set including one cupcake and two cookies for 75 cents. In this control condition, 40 percent of those who inquired actually purchased a cupcake. In the "that's-not-all condition," people who inquired were first told that the cupcakes were 75 cents each. A moment later, they were told that actually, they would get not only the cupcake but also 2 cookies for the 75 cent price. In this "that's-not-all" condition, 73 percent of people bought a cupcake, a substantially higher proportion than in the control condition. Table 8-2 summarizes the four compliance techniques we have discussed

Limits to External Pressure

We have seen that external pressure often increases compliance. But we should also be aware of the limits of these approaches. Many consumers resist the efforts of high-pressured sales clerks, perhaps in part because knowledge of sales techniques enables consumers to resist such practices. Heroic soldiers refuse to divulge secret information even though cruelly tortured, putting commitment to principle above their personal safety. Influence attempts do not always produce the desired effects.

Sometimes too much pressure may actually cause a person to do the opposite of what the influencer desires. Brehm (1966) called this phe-nomenon **reactance.** The basic idea is that people attempt to maintain their personal freedom of action. When this freedom is threatened, they do whatever they can to reinstate it. If an individual perceives an influence attempt as a threat to freedom of action, the person protects it by refusing to comply or by doing the opposite of what is requested. We are all familiar with the child who, when asked to do something, says, "I won't." But when her parents say, "All right, then, don't," the child goes ahead and does what was initially requested. Psychological reactance may be one reason why well-intentioned campaigns to get drivers to buckle seat belts or motor cyclists to wear a protective helmet sometimes backfire. Forcefully telling a biker that he "must" wear a helmet threatens his sense of freedom and so leads him to reassert his independence rather than to comply.

This point is illustrated in recent research on reactance and alcohol consumption by Lillian Bensley and Rui Wu (1991). They reasoned that a very strongly worded antidrinking message might be perceived as a threat to personal freedom and so be less effective than a more moderate antidrinking message. This might be especially true for heavy drinkers who consume alcohol on a regular basis. The researchers compared the impact of two messages. A very strongly worded message emphasized that there is "conclusive evidence" of the harm of drinking and that "any reasonable person must acknowledge these conclusions." A more moderate message said there is "good evidence" of the harm

When told not to touch a hot pot on the stove, a child may assert its independence by doing just the opposite. Psychologists call this phenomenon "reactance."

of alcohol and said that "you may wish to carefully consider" these findings. In a first study, students read one of the two messages and then indicated how much alcohol they intended to drink during the next few days. As predicted, students who read the strong message intended to drink *more* than students who read the moderate message. In a second study, college men who were fairly heavy alcohol drinkers actually consumed more beer after exposure to a strong antidrinking message than to a moderate message. It appears that when Americans are told they "must" do something, they sometimes assert their independence by refusing to comply.

OBEDIENCE TO AUTHORITY

In this final section we take a closer look at one of the six bases of power identified by Raven: obedience to legitimate authority. In any social group, organization, or society, it is important that people obey orders from those who have

legitimate authority. In wartime, generals expect soldiers to obey orders, and severely punish disobedience. We expect drivers to follow the orders of police officers directing traffic. Most people believe that public health officials have the right to require that school children be vaccinated against polio and other communicable diseases. Obedience is based on the belief that the authorities have the right to make requests. In many cases, we agree with the policies of those in charge, and obey orders willingly.

But what about situations in which the demands of the authorities conflict with our own beliefs and values? How do parents respond if they believe that a new vaccination required by public schools is potentially hazardous to their children? How do soldiers and citizens react if they believe their government is pursuing a misguided or immoral policy?

Herbert Kelman and Lee Hamilton (1989) have used the term "crimes of obedience" to describe immoral or illegal acts that are committed in response to orders from an authority. Kelman and Hamilton reject the idea that crimes of obedience are things of the past, committed only in Nazi Germany or by fanatical cults. Rather, they suggest that crimes of obedience continue to occur in our society, for instance when employees carry out orders of corporate executives that violate the law or harm public welfare, when political leaders order their subordinates to engage in shady campaign practices, or when soldiers and guerrilla fighters obey orders to torture or kill unarmed civilians.

The Eichmann Defense: Just Obeying Orders

For many people, the mass murder of European Jews by the Nazis has become a tragic and compelling case study in obedience to authority. Before World War II, nearly 9 million Jews lived in Europe. The European Jewish community had a long tradition of culture, artistic and intellectual achievement, and religious devotion. When Adolf Hitler and the Nazi party came to power in Germany in 1933, they contended that the Aryan race was superior to such "mongrel

to group norms in making both ambiguous and clear-cut perceptual judgments. People conform for two main reasons: to be right (informational influence) and to be liked (normative influence).

3. People are most likely to conform when the majority view is unanimous and when they feel strong commitment to a group. The size of the group also affects conformity.

4. A forceful minority can sometimes change the position of the majority in a group. Minorities are most effective when they are persistent, when their behavior is logically consistent but not "rigid," and when they are able to refute the views of the majority. Single minorities (who differ from the group in only one important way) may be more effective than double minorities (who differ in two ways), because single minorities are less likely to be seen as acting out of self-interest.

5. We may comply with a request for many different reasons. Raven has identified six bases of power that can produce compliance: rewards, coercion, expertise, information, referent power, and legitimate authority. A special case of legitimate power is the "power of helplessness": A strong cultural norm of social responsibility dictates that we should help those who are less fortunate and less powerful than we are.

6. Researchers have identified several specific compliance strategies, including the foot-in-the-door technique, the door-in-the-face technique, the low-ball technique, and the that's-not-all technique.

7. In everyday life, obedience to legitimate authority is often adaptive and contributes to smooth social functioning. But sometimes, people obey orders that are harmful to others and that violate their own personal beliefs and values. In one of the most famous research programs in social psychology, Milgram investigated this phenomenon. He found that a majority of "normal" adults would administer severe electric shocks to a helpless victim if ordered to do so by a researcher.

8. Obedience to legitimate authority is lessened when individuals are made aware of the suffering they cause, feel personally responsible for their actions, observe others who disobey the authority, and are encouraged to question the motives and judgment of the authority.

SUGGESTED READINGS

Cialdini, R. B. (1988). *Influence: Science and practice.* Glenview, IL: Scott, Foresman/Little, Brown. A very readable discussion of the many ways we try to influence other people. The book is based both on empirical research and on the author's experiences with salespeople, public relations agents, fund raisers, and others whose livelihood depends on successfully influencing people.

Kelman, H. C., & Hamilton, V. L. (1989). *Crimes of obedience: Toward a social psychology of authority and responsibility.* New Haven, CT: Yale University Press. An analysis of obedience that gives special attention to the massacre of civilians in Vietnam by U.S. soldiers, the Watergate scandal of President Nixon, and the Iran–Contra affair. The book offers suggestions for teaching people to be less accepting of authority.

Milgram, S. (1974). *Obedience to authority: An experimental view.* New York: Harper & Row. A complete description of Milgram's research program and the many variations he conducted, plus Milgram's own theoretical analysis of his findings.

Miller, A. G. (1986). *The obedience experiments: A case study of controversy in social science.* New York: Praeger. A thoughtful review of Milgram's original studies and later replication studies by other researchers. The book discusses both ethical and methodological critiques of Milgram's work and considers the applicability of these laboratory studies to understanding the Holocaust and other cases of genocide.

Moscovici, S. (1985). Social influence and conformity. In G. Lindzey & E. Aronson (Eds.), *Handbook of social psychology* (3rd ed., Vol. 2, pp. 347–412). New York: Random House. A comprehensive and somewhat technical review of conformity research and theory, with special attention to the influence of minorities.

Staub, E. (1989). *Roots of evil: The psychological and cultural sources of genocide.* New York: Cambridge University Press. A thoughtful analysis of torture and mass murder in such diverse settings as Greece, Cambodia, Argentina, and Russia.

9
Interpersonal Attraction

FOCUS OF THIS CHAPTER

Affiliation
Basic Principles of Attraction
Personal Characteristics
Similarity
Familiarity
Proximity
Love
Loneliness

Cultural Highlight
Arranged Marriages and Love Matches

Research Closeup
The Babyface Effect

You are attending the first meeting of a seminar on American literature, listening to the discussion with one ear and sizing up your new classmates. You've taken an instant dislike to one rather pompous man who seems determined to dominate the conversation. Whenever he opens his mouth, you and the woman sitting across the table exchange knowing glances. She seems to be friendly, and you decide to talk to her during the coffee break. As your eyes travel around the seminar table, you think about each student, making mental notes about those you like and those you don't like.

In recent decades, social psychologists have probed the mysteries of interpersonal attraction, seeking to understand the basic processes that determine whom we like and why we like them. This chapter examines the growing body of scientific research on attraction. We begin with affiliation—the desire to be with other people. Next we review general principles of interpersonal attraction and investigate the importance of such factors as physical attractiveness, attitude similarity, and proximity. Then we consider one very special form of interpersonal attraction, romantic love. We conclude with an analysis of loneliness, the painful experience we have when our social relationships are inadequate.

AFFILIATION

For most of us, the desire for **affiliation,** the basic human tendency to seek the company of other people, is quite strong. Humans are social animals who spend most of their time in the presence of other people. In a carefully controlled study, Reed Larson and his colleagues (1982) asked a sample of adults and a sample of teenagers to carry electronic pagers for a week. At random times from early morning to late evening, the researchers activated the pagers, sounding a beep that signaled participants to fill out a short questionnaire describing what they were doing and whether they were alone or with others. As shown in Table 9-1, these individuals spent almost three quarters of their waking hours with others. People were most likely to be alone when they were doing household tasks, taking a bath, listening to music, or studying at home. In contrast, people were most likely to be with others when they were at school or work.

The earliest roots of human affiliation are found in childhood, when infants form strong attachments to one or more adults. This attachment relationship has been described as the child's first love affair. As we grow up, our social needs become more complex and diverse. We affiliate to have fun, to obtain help, to share sexual intimacies, to feel powerful, to seek approval.

Attachment in Childhood

Infants become attached to the people with whom they interact most often and most lovingly. This usually includes the mother and father, although it can be anyone with whom the infant has regular contact (Bowlby, 1988; Cox et al., 1992). By **attachment** we mean that an infant responds positively to specific people, feels better when they are close, and seeks them out when frightened.

Attachment serves two major functions for children (Shaver & Klinnert, 1982). First, children derive a sense of security from being with the attachment person. When children are

TABLE 9-1
How People Spend Their Time

Activity	Adolescents		Adults	
	Alone	With Others	Alone	With Others
At Home				
Housework	6.7%	5.6%	5.4%	8.6%
Self-care (bathing, etc.)	2.1	0.5	2.2	1.2
Studying (adolescents only)	3.5	1.4	—	—
Eating	0.6	3.1	0.7	2.4
Socializing (includes by phone)	2.6	5.4	—	3.8
Watching television	2.0	3.9	2.2	5.1
Personal reading	2.0	1.4	1.5	1.4
Doing hobbies and art	0.7	0.5	0.3	0.2
Idling, listening to music	1.8	2.5	2.4	3.3
All at home activities	20.0	24.3	14.7	26.0
At Work or School				
Working at work	1.6	2.2	5.9	20.9
In class (adolescents only)	—	15.6	—	—
Other activities at work or school	1.2	13.5	3.6	11.5
All at work or school activities	2.8	31.3	9.5	32.4
In Public				
In transit (on bus, etc.)	1.3	3.3	2.9	3.6
Other practical activities	1.2	6.2	0.8	1.1
Leisure	0.6	9.0	1.2	7.9
All public activities	3.1	18.6	4.9	12.6
TOTAL TIME (Alone + With Others = 100 percent)	25.9	74.1	29.1	70.9

Note: The table shows what percentage of the time people reported that they were alone or with others doing each specific type of activity. For instance, adolescents reported spending 6.7 percent of their time doing housework alone.

Source: Adapted from R. Larson, M. Csikszentmihalyi, & R. Graef, Time alone in daily experience: Loneliness or renewal? In L. A. Peplau & D. Perlman (Eds.) *Loneliness,* p. 43. Copyright 1982 by John Wiley & Sons.

frightened or confronted with unfamiliar situations, they turn to this person for comfort and reassurance. For example, infants show less distress when a stranger approaches if they are being held by their mother than if they are several feet away from her.

A second function of attachment is to provide information about the environment. When children are uncertain about how to respond to a novel situation, they look to their attachment person for guidance. In one study, infants 12 to 18 months old were put in a playroom with their mothers and presented with such novel stimuli as a large remote-controlled spider, a remote-controlled dinosaur, and a life-size model of the incredible Hulk's head (Klinnert, 1981). When one of these strange objects first appeared, most children looked questioningly at

their mother. If the mother (following instructions from the researcher) showed fear, the child usually moved toward the mother. If the mother showed pleasure and smiled, the child moved toward the new toy. Nonverbal cues from the mother guided the child's response.

All children develop an attachment to their primary caretaker. However, the nature of this attachment between infant and parent can vary. Mary Ainsworth and her associates (1978) have identified three major styles of attachment between infants and parents:

- *Secure attachment* occurs when the parent is generally available and responsive to the child's needs.

- *Avoidant attachment* occurs when the parent is generally unresponsive or even rejecting. Infants may initially "protest"

During infancy, babies form strong attachments to their parents.

this lack of attention, but ultimately become "detached" from the caretaker.

- *Anxious/ambivalent attachment* occurs when the primary caretaker is anxious and does not respond consistently to the infant's needs. The caretaker may sometimes be available and responsive, but at other times be unavailable or intrusive.

We can think of a child's style of attachment as an answer to the question, "Can I count on my parent to respond to my needs?" The securely attached child has learned that the answer is "yes," the avoidant child that the answer is "no," and the ambivalent child that the answer is "maybe."

Children's attachment has been explained both by innate biological factors and by learning. The biological view (Bowlby, 1969) emphasizes the survival value of attachment for the child. Human infants are helpless creatures who need to be taken care of, protected, fed, and kept warm. When children are old enough to move around, it is important that they not wander too far from their parents because they might get into danger or get lost. Attachment was adaptive in human evolution because it ensured that children got the attention they needed to survive. The biological explanation of attachment holds that certain behaviors and responses of the infant and parent are "programmed" genetically, and that these cause the attachment to form.

A second explanation is that attachment is learned. The child becomes attached to the parent because the parent feeds and comforts the child; the parent becomes attached to the child because the child rewards the parent. For example, when the child cries, the parent comes because crying usually means the child needs something. The parent arrives and gives the child food or changes a diaper. The child stops crying. Both have been reinforced by the interaction: The child feels better because it is no longer hungry or uncomfortable; the parent feels good because the child has stopped crying. Similarly, the parent is reinforced by the child's smile. Having a baby smile at us is very rewarding, especially if the baby favors us with more smiles than it gives to others. So, the child learns to love its parent if the parent provides the attention and care it needs. And the parent learns to love the child if the child responds to this care with positive reinforcements in the form of smiles, hugs, lack of crying, and so on.

Both the biological and learning approaches probably contain much truth. Clearly, many innate behaviors of the child contribute to the formation of attachment. The child does not have to learn to cry, to smile, or to feel good when comforted; all these inborn responses are important for producing an attachment bond between parent and child. On the other hand, there is no question that seeing a child smile or hearing it stop crying in response to our presence is reinforcing, and that without this reinforcement we might not develop a strong attachment to a child. So one could say that certain innate behavior patterns help produce attachment, and that the mechanism by which they operate is through mutual reinforcement of parent and child.

Work on attachment raises the possibility that the tendency to affiliate is, at least in part, biologically based. As a species, humans may be disposed to form emotional attachments to those with whom they interact regularly and to feel more comfortable and secure in the presence of these people. The capacity for emotional attachment that first appears in infancy continues throughout life, as we form bonds with close friends, lovers, and our own children. We will discuss adult attachment later in this chapter.

Laboratory Studies of Affiliation

Useful insights about adult affiliative tendencies have come from carefully controlled laboratory studies. In the 1950s, Stanley Schachter began an important series of experiments to explore situational factors that increase our desire to be with other people. Schachter (1959) started with the plausible hypothesis that people affiliate to reduce fear. Thus, if we randomly assign adults to a condition where they will experience either high or low fear, we should observe significant differences in their desire for human company.

To test this idea, Schachter recruited women undergraduates. When subjects arrived for the study, they were greeted by an experimenter in a white laboratory coat, surrounded by electrical equipment of various sorts. The experimenter introduced himself as Dr. Gregor Zilstein of the Department of Neurology and Psychiatry, and he explained that the experiment concerned the effects of electric shocks. To make some subjects more afraid than others, the experimenter used two different descriptions of the electric shock.

In the *high-fear condition*, Dr. Zilstein described the shocks in ominous tones. Subjects were told: "These shocks will hurt. . . . In research of this sort, if we're to learn anything at all that will really help humanity, it is necessary that our shocks be intense. . . . These shocks will

be quite painful but, of course, they will do no permanent damage." By continuing at some length in this vein, Dr. Zilstein clearly suggested that the subject was in for a very frightening and painful experience.

In the *low-fear condition*, the instructions tried to make subjects feel relaxed and to minimize the severity of the shocks. Dr. Zilstein described the electric shocks this way: "I assure you that what you will feel will not in any way be painful. It will resemble a tickle or a tingle more than anything unpleasant." Thus, although both groups of subjects were told that the experiment concerned electric shock, one group expected a painful and frightening experience, whereas the other group expected a mild and unthreatening experience. When questioned, women in the high-fear condition were indeed much more afraid.

Following the arousal and measurement of fear, Dr. Zilstein told the subjects there would be a 10-minute delay while he prepared the equipment. He explained that there were a number of rooms in which subjects might wait—comfortable rooms with armchairs and magazines. The experimenter then said it had occurred to him that perhaps some people might prefer to wait alone; others might prefer to wait with other subjects in the experiment. Each subject was asked to indicate whether she preferred to wait alone, with others, or had no preference. She was also asked to indicate the strength of her choice. In this and most subsequent experiments on the topic, the choice and rating of intensity of subjects' desire to affiliate were the basic measures of affiliation.

The results of Schachter's study are shown in Table 9-2. The answer to the question of whether highly fearful subjects want to affiliate more than subjects with low fear is yes. The greater the fear, the greater the tendency to affiliate. Many subsequent studies have confirmed this general finding in a wide range of situations. For example, one recent study compared women who were unhappy and uncertain about how things were going in their marriage with women who felt confident and happy about their marriage. As predicted, the uncertain women were significantly more eager to affili-

When disaster strikes, people often turn to neighbors and friends for comfort and advice. In more technical terms, fear and uncertainty increase the tendency to affiliate.

TABLE 9-2
Effect of Fear on Affiliation

Condition	Waiting Preference			Mean Strength of Affiliation Tendency
	Together	Don't Care	Alone	(Scale from −2 to +2)
High fear	62.5%	28.1%	9.4%	.88
Low fear	33.0	60.0	7.0	.35

Source: Adapted from *The Psychology of Affiliation* by Stanley Schachter with the permission of the publishers, Stanford University Press. Copyright 1959 by Stanley Schachter.

ate, as measured by talking to someone about their marriage (Buunk et al., 1991).

Research has also shown that fear must be distinguished from other stressful situations that may actually *decrease* affiliative tendencies. For instance, if we are confronted with a situation that is not only stressful but also embarrassing, we may prefer to avoid other people. This point was demonstrated by Sarnoff and Zimbardo (1961). Their study included high-fear and low-fear conditions plus a new condition designed to arouse "oral anxiety." In the high-oral-anxiety condition, men were asked to perform a series of embarrassing tasks, such as sucking on baby bottles and rubber nipples. The results were that men in the high-fear condition were eager to affiliate, but men in the embarrassing high-oral-anxiety condition preferred to wait alone. In summary, fear and uncertainty usually increase the desire to affiliate, but there are exceptions to this general tendency.

Given that fearful people usually want company, just what is it that they expect to get from being with others? What is the psychological process involved? Two possibilities have been investigated. The first is the *distraction hypothesis:* Fearful people affiliate to take their minds off their problems. In this case, it should not matter very much whom they affiliate with—almost anyone will do. A second hypothesis is suggested by **social comparison theory.** As we discussed in Chapter 5, this theory states that people want to compare their own feelings and reactions with those of others in the same situation. When we are in a new or unusual situation

and are uncertain about how to react, we turn to others as a source of information. Thus, the social comparison hypothesis is that fearful people should want to affiliate, but *only* with others who are confronted with the same situation.

Several studies have tested these two possibilities, and results generally support the social comparison hypothesis. In one study, for example, some subjects were given a choice of waiting alone or waiting with people taking part in the same study (Schachter, 1959). Other subjects were given a choice of waiting alone or with students who were waiting to see their faculty advisors. As social comparison theory would predict, the fearful subjects preferred to wait with others in the same situation, but not with others in a different situation. As Schachter concluded: "Misery doesn't love just any kind of company, it loves only miserable company" (1959, p. 24).

You may have noticed that in these laboratory studies, subjects were not given the choice of waiting with someone who had already gone through the experiment and who would therefore know just how painful the electric shocks really were. A more recent naturalistic study provided precisely that comparison (Kulik & Mahler, 1989). The subjects were patients about to undergo coronary bypass surgery. The choice they were given was whether to have as their roommate another patient who was awaiting bypass surgery, or a patient who had already had the bypass operation. Given these options, the majority of patients preferred to room with someone who had already had the surgery.

Patients explained their choices with such comments as, "You'd rather talk to a guy that's been through it" or "I think talking to someone who's already been through it would give you more confidence" (p. 188).

The results of research on childhood attachment and affiliation among adults lead to similar conclusions: People affiliate to reduce fear and uncertainty. At any age, affiliation is likely to be most beneficial if we can associate with someone who is both knowledgeable and sympathetic.

The Benefits of Social Relations

The reduction of fear and uncertainty are not the only reasons we seek human company. Many theorists have attempted to classify the major types of benefits people receive in relationships. One illustrative analysis of affiliative needs was proposed by Robert Weiss (1974). He identified what he called six basic "provisions of social relations"—important things that relationships provide for individuals:

- *Attachment* is the sense of security and comfort provided by our closest relationships. As children we are usually strongly attached to our parents; as adults we may experience this intimacy with dating partners, spouses, or close friends.
- *Social integration* is the sense of having shared interests and attitudes. It is often

provided by relationships with friends, coworkers, teammates, fellow churchgoers, neighbors, and so on. Such relationships offer companionship and give a sense of belonging to a community.

- *Reassurance of worth* is provided when others support our sense of being a competent and valued person.
- *A sense of reliable alliance* involves knowing that there are people who will assist us in times of need. When emergencies arise, we often turn to our families for help.
- *Guidance* is provided by counselors, teachers, doctors, friends, and others to whom we turn for advice and information.
- The *opportunity for nurturance* occurs when we are responsible for the well-being of another person. Taking care of someone provides us with a sense of being needed and important.

Many other typologies of the benefits of social relations have also been developed, and they emphasize somewhat different functions served by personal relationships. Most noteworthy are analyses by researchers interested in how social relations contribute to a person's mental and physical health. They use the term **social support** to refer to interpersonal exchanges in which one person give help or assistance to another (Wills, 1991). Researchers have identified several important types of social support. For instance, instrumental support refers to providing financial assistance or other types of goods and services. Informational support refers to providing advice, guidance, or useful information. We will present a fuller discussion of social support in Chapter 15 on health.

The analysis of the specific benefits provided by social relationships highlights two major points about human affiliation. First, the rewards of companionship are numerous and diverse. We could undoubtedly add many other social needs to the lists proposed by Weiss and others. Second, this approach emphasizes that no single relationship can fulfill all our affiliative needs. A love relationship may provide a sense of attachment, but not a sense of belonging to a community. A teacher can provide guidance about academic and career issues, but

Social relations provide many diverse benefits. In scouting, boys can enjoy the fun of companionship, learn new skills, and gain experience working cooperatively with a group.

is not likely to lend us money or drive us to the airport. Consequently, a rich and healthy social life requires a network of social relations capable of satisfying a variety of human needs.

BASIC PRINCIPLES OF ATTRACTION

We saw in Chapter 2 that the major dimension of first impressions is evaluation. Why is it that we like some people and not others? What determines whom we select as our friends? Perhaps the most general answer is that we like people who reward us and who help us to satisfy our needs. Learning and social exchange theories explain the specific mechanisms through which this occurs.

ASSOCIATION. A useful principle from learning theory is **association.** As applied to interpersonal attraction, the core idea is that we come to like people who are associated with good experiences and dislike people who are associated with bad experiences. A study by May and Hamilton (1980) illustrates the association principle. These researchers were interested in the impact of pleasant versus unpleasant background music on interpersonal attraction. They first determined which type of music college women generally liked most (rock music) and least (avant-garde classical music). They then had other women students rate photographs of male strangers. While the women made their ratings, they heard rock music, avant-garde classical music, or no music. The results were clear-cut. Women rated the men most favorably when they were associated with enjoyable music and least favorably when their photos were associated with disliked music. The idea is that liking for someone can be influenced by a conditioned emotional response to events such as music that are arbitrarily paired with that person.

This association notion is important. Yet, its very truth and simplicity should not blind us to other processes that may reverse it on occasion. Someone with whom you spend a very painful or stressful time may wind up a close friend, even though by association the person should

make you think of pure misery. For example, in one study, pairs of unacquainted college women were exposed either to very noxious, unpredictable bursts of loud noise or to a low level of noise (Kenrick & Johnson, 1979). Although subjects in the high-noise condition hated the experience, they liked their partner significantly more than subjects in the low-noise condition. Sometimes shared misery creates a sense of solidarity that forms the basis for friendship.

REINFORCEMENT. A second principle from learning theory is **reinforcement.** We like people who reward us in one way or another. One important type of reward is social approval, and many studies have shown that we tend to like people who evaluate us positively. In one experiment, subjects went through a series of brief interactions with another person who was secretly a confederate of the researchers (Aronson & Linder, 1965). After each interaction, the subject overheard an interview between the confederate and the experimenter in which the confederate gave his impressions of the subject.

In one condition, the confederate was quite flattering. He said at the beginning that he liked the subject, and continued to make positive statements about the subject after each interaction. In another condition, the confederate was critical. He said he was not sure that he liked the subject much and gave fairly negative descriptions of him. He continued being negative throughout the interviews. Afterward, the subjects were asked how much they liked the confederate. As expected, subjects liked the confederate significantly more if he said positive things about them than if he was negative in his evaluation.

SOCIAL EXCHANGE. This perspective, introduced in Chapter 1, proposes that our liking for another person is based on our assessment of the costs and benefits the person provides us. According to **social exchange theory,** we like people when we perceive our interactions with them to be profitable, that is, when the rewards we get from the relationship outweigh the costs. Thus, we may like Stan because he is smart, funny, and a good athlete, and because these good qualities outweigh his annoying tendency to be late. Social exchange theory also emphasizes that we make comparative judgments, assessing the profits we get from one person against the profits we get from another. We will consider this social exchange perspective in more detail in Chapter 10.

With these general principles in mind, we now turn to research on more specific factors that influence interpersonal attraction. Four powerful determinants of liking are personal qualities of the other individual, similarity, familiarity, and proximity. As we discuss each of these important factors, we will also note occasional exceptions that differ from the general pattern.

PERSONAL CHARACTERISTICS

Just what is it that makes us like one person more than another? There is no single answer to this question. Some people find red hair and freckles irresistible; others dislike them

intensely. Some of us prize compassion in our friends; others value intelligence. Individuals vary in the things they find most rewarding in other people. There are also large cultural differences in those personal qualities considered socially desirable. Many Americans equate feminine beauty with being thin, but other societies consider plump women the most attractive. Researchers have sought to identify some of the general characteristics associated with liking in our society.

Some years ago, Norman Anderson (1968b) compiled a list of 555 personality traits that are used to describe people. He then asked college students to indicate how much they would like a person who had each of these characteristics. A sample from the list appears in Table 9-3.

There seemed to be general agreement among the students on which characteristics were desirable and which undesirable. At the top of the list, six traits related to trust in one way or another: *trustworthy, sincere, honest, loyal, truthful,* and *dependable*. The traits rated lowest included

TABLE 9-3
Likableness of Personality Traits

Highly Likable	Slightly Positive to Slightly Negative	Highly Unlikable
Sincere	Persistent	Ill-mannered
Honest	Conventional	Unfriendly
Understanding	Bold	Hostile
Loyal	Cautious	Loud-mouthed
Truthful	Perfectionist	Selfish
Trustworthy	Excitable	Narrow-minded
Intelligent	Quiet	Rude
Dependable	Impulsive	Conceited
Thoughtful	Aggressive	Greedy
Considerate	Shy	Insincere
Reliable	Unpredictable	Unkind
Warm	Emotional	Untrustworthy
Kind	Bashful	Malicious
Friendly	Naive	Obnoxious
Happy	Restless	Untruthful
Unselfish	Daydreamer	Dishonest
Humorous	Materialistic	Cruel
Responsible	Rebellious	Mean
Cheerful	Lonely	Phony
Trustful	Dependent	Liar

Source: Adapted from Anderson (1968b), pp. 273–77.

liar and *phony*. Two other themes that emerged in the list of highly likable traits were personal warmth and competence. We feel affection for people who show interpersonal warmth, and we respect people we view as competent (Lydon, Jamieson, & Zanna, 1988; Rubin, 1973). Let's take a closer look at warmth and competence.

Warmth

What makes one person seem warm and friendly, while another comes across as cold and aloof? We don't yet have a complete answer to this question, but one important ingredient is having a positive outlook (Folkes & Sears, 1977). People appear warm when they like things, praise them, and approve of them, in other words, when they have a positive attitude toward people and things. In contrast, people seem cold when they dislike things, disparage them, say they are awful, and are generally critical.

To test this idea, researchers had subjects read or listen to interviews in which the interviewee was asked to evaluate a long list of things such as political leaders, cities, movies, and college courses (Folkes & Sears, 1977). Sometimes the interviewees expressed predominantly positive attitudes—they liked most of the politicians, cities, movies, and courses. In other cases, the interviewees expressed mainly negative attitudes. As predicted, subjects liked the interviewees more if they were positive rather than negative in their attitudes. Folkes and Sears concluded that the explanation lay in the greater warmth communicated by the positive attitude. Other analyses showed that the liking effect was not due to any greater perceived intelligence, knowledge, or similarity of attitudes on the part of the positive interviewees. Other research shows that in addition to saying positive things, people can also communicate warmth by such nonverbal behaviors as smiling, watching attentively, and expressing emotions (Friedman, Riggio, & Casella, 1988).

Recent studies of the so-called "babyface effect" have shown that infantile facial features can also affect our social perceptions and interactions (see RESEARCH CLOSEUP).

Competence

In general, we like people who are socially skilled, intelligent, and competent. The particular type of competence that matters most depends on the nature of our relationship with the person: We are attracted to friends who are good conversationalists, to mechanics who are good at fixing cars, to professors who are knowledgeable lecturers, and so on. Competent people are usually more rewarding to be with than inept people.

Research has investigated one aspect of interpersonal competence—the ability to be an interesting rather than boring conversationalist (Leary, Rogers, Canfield, & Coe, 1986). In one study, college students reported being bored by speakers who talked too much about themselves or about trivial, banal topics. Students also reported being bored with people who were overly passive, tedious, and serious in their interactions. In a second study, students listened to taped conversations designed so that the target speaker was either boring or interesting. Students evaluated the boring speakers quite negatively. Boring speakers were liked less, and rated as less friendly, enthusiastic, popular, and more impersonal. In contrast, being an interesting conversationalist enhanced a person's likability (Leary et al., 1986).

An interesting exception to the competence-leads-to-liking principle is the case of someone who is a little "too perfect" for comfort. In one study, participants listened to a tape recording of a student who was trying out for a College Quiz Bowl team (Aronson, Willerman, & Floyd, 1966). In one condition, the candidate gave an outstanding performance and answered nearly every question correctly. In a second condition, the candidate gave a mediocre performance. As an added twist to the experiment, after the tryout was over, the candidate was sometimes heard to spill coffee on his suit.

The results showed the usual competence-leads-to-liking effect: The outstanding candidate was liked better than the mediocre one. However, the outstanding candidate was liked even better when he made a minor blunder or *pratfall* than when his performance was flawless. Apparently, spilling coffee served to "human-

RESEARCH CLOSEUP
The Babyface Effect

When artists and cartoonists want to create a particularly cute and appealing character, such as Bambi, they often use a set of features characteristic of infants: large round eyes, a short nose, a large forehead, thin eyebrows, and a small chin. Leslie Zebrowitz (1990) has investigated the impact of these "babyface" features on our reactions to humans. Her basic hypothesis is that we tend to perceive people with babyface features as more childlike in their personalities than people with mature facial features.

There is now considerable evidence to support this assertion (Friedman & Zebrowitz, 1992; Zebrowitz & Montepare, 1992). Babyfaced adults are seen as warmer, kinder, more affectionate and more honest than their mature-faced age mates. Babyfaced adults are also seen as physically weaker, more naive, more easily fooled, and more submissive. Careful research has shown that the babyface effect is unrelated to physical attractiveness (Zebrowitz & Montepare, 1992).

In an illustrative study, Diane Berry and Leslie Zebrowitz (1988a) investigated the impact of babyfaced features on judgments about a defendant in a mock trial. Subjects read descriptions of individuals on trial for crimes that resulted either from negligence (e.g., keeping poor income tax records) or from intentional deceit (e.g., deliberately falsifying income tax records). Participants were more likely to believe that negligence had occurred if the defendant was babyfaced rather than mature-faced. In contrast, subjects were more likely to believe that there had been deliberate deceit if the defendant had a mature face rather than a babyface. In other words, people tended to associate facial immaturity with incompetence rather than dishonesty.

In another study, researchers found that, compared to mature-faced individuals, baby-faced job applicants were seen as more qualified for a job requiring warmth and nurturance (day care teacher) and less qualified for a job involving finances (loan officer) (Zebrowitz, Tenenbaum, & Goldstein, 1991). Other research suggests that the producers of television commercials tend to select facially mature actors to present expert messages and babyfaced individuals to convey a sense of trust and honesty (Brownlow & Zebrowitz, 1990).

There is also evidence that babyfaced features can affect our perception of children. Adults may hold higher expectations for facially mature children than for babyfaced children of the same age (Berry & Zebrowitz, 1988b). For instance, they might assign more difficult mental tasks to facially mature children than to babyfaced kids. One unfortunate consequence of having unreasonable expectations for facially mature children is that it may increase their risk for child abuse (McCabe, 1988). Adults may be more lenient toward babyfaced children, perceiving them as less competent, less able to follow orders, and less likely to lie.

Taken together, these findings suggest that physical features associated with facial maturity may have surprisingly pervasive effects on social judgments and interactions.

ize" the brainy student and so made him more likable. In contrast, the blunder only detracted from the evaluations of the mediocre applicant. He was liked less when he spilled coffee than when he didn't.

Physical Attractiveness

One of the first things we notice about a person is physical appearance. Other things being equal, we tend to like attractive people more than those considered unattractive (Hatfield & Sprecher, 1986). One reason is the stereotype that a person who is physically attractive has other good qualities as well (see recent meta-analyses by Eagly et al., 1991 and by Feingold, 1992). There is much evidence that attractive people are thought to be more socially skilled and friendly (but also more vain) than less attractive people.

More surprising, attractive people are also perceived to possess qualities that seem irrelevant to physical beauty, such as intelligence, dominance, and mental health. Here are just a few of the research findings: Teachers evaluate cute children as being smarter and more popular than unattractive kids with identical academic records (Clifford & Walster, 1973). Students rate a lecture by a female teacher as being more interesting and judge the woman to be a better teacher if she is made up to look attractive rather than plain (Chaikin et al., 1978). Even in the courtroom, attractive defendants sometimes receive more lenient sentences (Wuensch, Castellow, & Moore, 1991).

People with physical disabilities often suffer from stereotypes about physical attractiveness (Asch, 1988). In one study, college students associated the general category "woman" with such terms as soft, lovable, married, and intelligent, but they associated "disabled woman" with such terms as ugly, lifeless, crippled,

Beauty is often an advantage in social relations. Other things being equal, attractive people tend to be liked more than people considered less physically attractive.

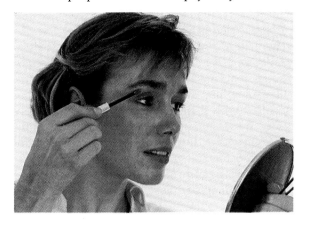

lonely, and someone to feel sorry for (Hanna & Rogovsky, 1986). In another study, high school students rated a student with a hearing aid as more introverted, afraid, depressed, and insecure than a nondisabled student (Silverman & Klees, 1989).

In addition to the stereotype that good-looking people have other good qualities, a second reason for liking attractive people is the so-called *radiating effect of beauty*. People may find it rewarding to be seen with a particularly attractive person because they think it will enhance their own public image. Michael Kernis and Ladd Wheeler (1981) hypothesized that this radiating effect of beauty occurs if a person is seen with an attractive friend, but does not occur if the attractive other is a stranger. To test this idea, they designed a laboratory experiment.

Subjects saw two people, a target person of average attractiveness and a same-sex person of either above-average or below-average looks. As a further variation, these people were sometimes presented as being friends and sometimes as strangers. As predicted, the friends and strangers conditions produced opposite results. When the two people were believed to be friends, a radiating effect occurred. The target person was rated as more attractive when seen with a very attractive friend, and less attractive when seen with a very unattractive friend. However, when the two people were thought to be strangers, a contrast effect occurred. The average-looking target person was rated less favorably when paired with a very attractive stranger. Gender did not affect these patterns: The same results were found regardless of whether the people being evaluated were male or female. Other studies have also shown that both men and women are rated more favorably when they are accompanied by an attractive romantic partner or friend than when they have an unattractive companion (Geiselman, Haight, & Kimata, 1984).

One area in which physical attractiveness is especially important is in heterosexual dating. In a classic study, Elaine Walster and her colleagues (1966) held a "computer dance" in which college students were randomly assigned to each other as dates for the evening. The researchers secretly made ratings of the physical attractiveness of each participant. At the end of the evening, students were asked to rate how much they liked their assigned partner. People who were rated as more attractive were liked more. In more recent studies, researchers have investigated interpersonal attraction at commercial dating services where people see photographs or videotapes of potential dates (Green, Buchanan, & Heuer, 1984; Walsh, et al., 1992). Again, physical attractiveness was a major factor in partner selection. Although clients had information about potential partners' hobbies, interests, backgrounds, and personal goals, both women and men chose better looking people and rejected less attractive people. Finally, many studies show that although both sexes view a dating partner's physical attractiveness as an asset, men place greater value on attractiveness than women do (Feingold, 1990; Jackson, 1992).

Although the effects of physical attractiveness are widespread, we should be careful not to overstate their importance. Like most stereotypes, they affect our judgments less as we acquire more specific individuating information about a particular person (Eagly et al., 1991).

SIMILARITY

Another basic factor in interpersonal attraction is similarity. We tend to like people who are similar to us in attitudes, interests, values, background, and personality (Brehm, 1992). This similarity effect applies to friendship, dating, and marriage. There is much truth in the old adage that "birds of a feather flock together."

Research Findings

Theodore Newcomb (1961) provided one of the first demonstrations that similarity leads to friendship. He rented a large house near the University of Michigan and offered male undergraduates free housing in return for taking part in his research. Before the students arrived, they filled out questionnaires about their attitudes and values. Newcomb controlled the assignment of rooms so that some roommates had very similar attitudes and other roommates had very different attitudes. By the end of the semester, roommates with similar preacquaintance attitudes generally liked each other and ended up as friends; dissimilar roommates tended to dislike each other and did not become friends.

Attraction through similarity has been the focus of much research. In a series of experiments, Donn Byrne (1971) and his associates carefully examined attitude similarity. To rule out other factors that might influence liking, such as appearance or personality, Byrne developed the **phantom-other technique.** In a typical study, participants fill out questionnaires describing their own attitudes. They then read questionnaires allegedly filled out by a stranger. In actuality, there is no other person (hence, the term "phantom other"). Experimenters deliberately write answers to be either very similar, moderately similar, or dissimilar to the subject's own answers. Subjects are then asked how much they think they would like the other person. The results of studies using this method have shown that attitude similarity strongly determines liking. The more similar the attitudes, the greater the anticipated liking. This effect has been demonstrated with very diverse groups including children, college students, medical patients, job trainees, and alcoholics.

The importance of similarity extends well beyond attitudes. Similarity in ethnic background, religion, politics, social class, education, and age all influence attraction. For example, studies of elementary and high school students find that friends tend to be of the same race and gender. Friends are also similar in age, year in school, grades, and extracurricular interests (e.g. Hallinan, 1992; Kandel, 1978). A recent study found that randomly assigned college roommates who had similar personalities were more satisfied with their relationship and more likely to room together again the next year than roommates with differing personalities (Carli, Ganley, & Pierce-Otay, 1991).

In dating and marriage, the tendency to choose similar partners is called the **matching principle.** It is unusual for an ardent feminist to date a sex-role traditionalist, or for an orthodox Jew to date a fundamentalist Christian. Dating

Shared interests are an important factor in interpersonal attraction.

partners and spouses tend to be relatively matched not only in their attitudes, but also in their physical appearance, social background, and personality (Schoen & Wooldredge, 1989; Stevens, Owens, & Schaefer, 1990). For example, one study of dating couples found that partners tended to resemble each other in age, intelligence, educational plans, religion, physical attractiveness, and even height (Hill, Rubin, & Peplau, 1976). They were also matched in their attitudes about sexual behavior and sex roles. Furthermore, couples who were most similar in background at the beginning of the study were most likely to be together one year and 15 years later.

Of course, to say that friends and spouses tend to be matched does not mean that they are necessarily identical in every way. When people of different races, religions, and social groups have a chance to interact and to discover shared interests and values, friendship and love often transcend differences in background. The increasing frequency of interracial marriages in the United States is one illustration. According to recent census data, about 1.8 percent of all married couples are interracial, up from 1.3 percent in 1980 and less than 1 percent in 1970 (U.S.

Bureau of the Census, 1990). Individuals from some numerically small groups, such as Japanese Americans and American Indians, are as likely to marry outside their race as within it (John, 1988; Kitano, 1988). Interfaith marriages are also common, with roughly 20 percent of Protestants, 40 percent of Catholics, and 50 percent of Jews in the United States marrying someone of another religion (Stover & Hope, 1993).

Explaining the Effects of Similarity

Why is similarity so important for interpersonal attraction? There are several explanations (Rubin, 1973). First, similarity is usually rewarding. People similar to us will tend to agree with our ideas and bolster our confidence in the rightness of our views. In contrast, it is unpleasant to have someone disagree with us, criticize our beliefs, and challenge our taste and judgment. Similar values and interests provide the basis for sharing activities with another person, whether picketing a nuclear power plant or going to a prayer meeting. Conversely, differences in values and interests can lead to dislike and avoidance (Byrne, Clore, & Smeaton, 1986; Rosenbaum, 1986).

A second explanation for the similarity–liking connection comes from the **cognitive dissonance theory,** described in Chapter 6. According to this theory, people strive to maintain harmony or consistency among their attitudes, to organize their likes and dislikes in a balanced, consistent way. To like someone and at the same time to disagree with that person about fundamental issues is psychologically uncomfortable. We maximize cognitive consistency by liking those who support our views and disliking those who disagree with us. A desire for cognitive consistency can encourage us to select friends who actually share our views, but it can also lead us to exaggerate the degree to which our friends agree with us. We can maintain cognitive consistency by *perceiving* that our friends have similar views, even if our perceptions are wrong.

A third explanation for the similarity effect is that people deliberately select partners who are similar to themselves in attitudes and social desirability. We might all like to date someone who is beautiful, rich, and famous, but most of us wind up with partners who resemble ourselves. Our abstract ideals are brought down to reality by the constraints of social life. This is consistent with the **expectancy-value theory** of decision making discussed in Chapter 1. The theory proposes that people consider not only the reward value of a particular choice (for instance, a potential date's attractiveness), but also the expectancy of being successful with this choice (actually going out with the person). In real life the most socially desirable people are usually most in demand, and so the chance of rejection is usually high. Expectancy-value theory argues that people will go for the most desirable person they can realistically expect to get. People therefore tend to select someone roughly similar to themselves in social desirability.

Research on physical attractiveness illustrates this process. We saw earlier that people usually like handsome men and beautiful women more than less attractive persons. But actual dating partners tend to be matched in physical appeal, with beautiful women dating handsome men, and average-looking men dating average-looking women (Feingold, 1988). For instance, Folkes (1982) studied members of a video-dating service. As part of the service, members watch videotaped interviews of potential dates, and then decide about asking the other person out. Folkes rated members on physical attractiveness and interviewed them about whom they had contacted for a date. She found that both men and women were most likely to pursue a relationship with someone similar to themselves in physical attractiveness. Only the most attractive people sought dates with the most attractive partners.

Although research has amply demonstrated the similarity effect, there remains controversy about the specific mechanisms that cause people in close relationships to have similar attitudes (e.g., Aron, 1988; Jussim & Osgood, 1989; Kalick & Hamilton, 1988). To understand three possible mechanisms, consider why a boyfriend and girlfriend might have similar beliefs about religion.

- *Selective attraction.* One possibility is that each person has strong religious views and uses these to screen potential dates. Only

similar partners are acceptable; dissimilar others are rejected. This selection effect could occur very early in the initial choice of friends and dating partners, or later on as partners get to know each other better and decide whether or not to continue the relationship.

- *Social influence.* Another possibility is that partners are initially different in their attitudes but gradually persuade each other to change their views. As a result, they may become more similar over time. The mechanism here is one of social influence, in which partners' attitudes change in the direction of greater similarity.

- *Environmental factors.* A third possibility is that their relationship was strongly affected by shared environmental factors that led people with similar attitudes to meet each other. For instance, students attending a religious college may all have fairly similar views about religion. In this case, their apparent "matching" is actually an effect of a social environment that limits the pool of potential partners.

In everyday life, the causes of similarity and matching are complex, and several different mechanisms may work together to produce the often observed association of similarity and liking.

Limits to the Similarity Effect

Although similarity usually leads to liking, there are exceptions to this general pattern. Sometimes similarity is threatening. If someone similar to us has a heart attack or suffers from some other unfortunate fate, we may worry that we are also vulnerable and so we may prefer to avoid that person. This point was demonstrated by Novak and Lerner (1968). In a variation of the phantom-other technique, subjects read a questionnaire supposedly completed by another student whose attitudes were either very similar or dissimilar to their own. The researchers also led students to believe that this other person was either emotionally disturbed or normal.

In the "disturbed" condition, the other person had written at the end of the questionnaire,

"I don't know if this is relevant or not, but last fall I had a kind of a nervous breakdown and I had to be hospitalized for a while. I've been seeing a psychiatrist ever since. As you probably noticed, I'm pretty shaky right now." In the "normal" condition, no such information was added. For subjects confronted with a normal person, attitude similarity increased liking as usual. However, for subjects confronted with an emotionally disturbed person, attitude similarity *decreased* liking; people were more eager to avoid the other person if he was similar than if he was different.

Another point is that differences between people are sometimes very rewarding. Few of us want to associate with clones, people who are identical to us in virtually every respect. The joys of friendship include stimulation and novelty—learning about new ideas and coming to appreciate the rich variety of human experiences. We are most open to the rewards of difference when we feel that the other person accepts us. In one study, Walster and Walster (1963) hypothesized that college students would be more willing to associate with dissimilar strangers if they knew in advance that the strangers would like them. Subjects chose to participate in a discussion group with people who were very similar to themselves (other college students) or with people who were very dissimilar (psychologists, factory workers). Before making their choice, some students were told that people in all groups were disposed to like them; others were told that group members were disposed to dislike them. When students were assured of being liked, they greatly preferred to be with dissimilar people. When students thought they might be disliked, they wanted to talk to similar others. A feeling of acceptance may be a prerequisite for disregarding differences.

A further advantage of having friends with different interests and skills is that it enables us pool our shared knowledge in mutually beneficial ways. For example, in planning a group camping trip, it is convenient to have one person who knows about tents and equipment, someone else who can plan meals, and a third person who knows the area and can pick a good campsite. In a traditional marriage, where the wife is the "homemaking expert" and the husband is the "breadwinning expert," the spouses' roles are different but complementary. When we say that "opposites attract," we are often referring to complementary role relationships such as these, where people with different skills and knowledge contribute to a shared enterprise. However, most cases of complementarity require that partners have similar values and goals, such as a desire to spend a weekend camping in the wilderness or shared beliefs about how to organize married life.

FAMILIARITY

A third factor in liking is familiarity. Consider Parisians' reactions to the Eiffel Tower. When it was first constructed, they were outraged and thought it was hideous, a blot on the landscape of their beautiful city. Today it is a beloved monument, and has even come to symbolize Paris. Familiarity can produce liking not only for objects but for people as well.

The Mere Exposure Effect

Familiarity is an important factor in interpersonal attraction. Simply being exposed frequently to a person can increase our liking for that person. This **mere exposure effect** has been demonstrated by Robert Zajonc (1968) and his associates.

In one study, Zajonc showed college students pictures of faces. Some of the faces were shown as many as 25 times, others only once or twice. Afterward, subjects indicated how much they liked each face and how much they thought they would like the person pictured. The results are presented in Figure 9-1. The more often the subjects had seen a face, the more they said they liked it and thought they would like the person. The same result has been found for repeated exposure to actual people. In a recent study, Moreland and Beach (1992) enlisted the aid of four college women who served as confederates in a field experiment. A pretest showed that all women were rated as equally attractive. In the main study, each woman attended a large lecture class in social psychology, posing as a stu-

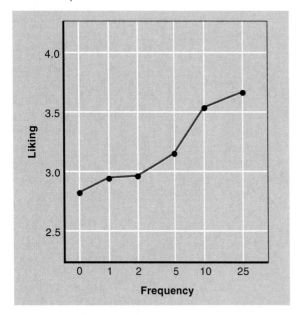

Figure 9-1 The relationship between frequency of exposure and liking. Subjects were shown photographs of different faces and the number of times each face was shown was varied. The more often the subjects saw a particular face, the more they said they liked the person pictured. (*Source:* Adapted from Zajonc, 1968.)

dent in the course. Each woman attended a different number of class sessions—once, 5 times, 10 times, or 15 times during the term. At the end of the term, students in the class were asked to rate each woman, based on a casual photo shown as a slide. The more often students had seen a woman, the more they thought they would like her.

Another ingenious demonstration of the familiarity effect involves people's reaction to their own faces. Faces are not perfectly symmetrical; the left eye may be a little higher than the right, a smile a little crooked, hair parted on the right instead of the left, and so on. Our friends see our face as it looks to an outside observer. But we see a different face—the mirror image of the one our friends see. For us, the right eye is higher, the part is on the left, and so on.

According to the mere exposure hypothesis, our friends should prefer our face from the perspective they are used to, and we should prefer our mirror image. Research has supported this prediction (Mita, Dermer, & Knight, 1977). Researchers photographed college women and

showed these pictures to the women and to their friends. Some pictures were true prints and others were made from reverse negatives (what we would see in the mirror). The women themselves preferred the mirror image (by 68 to 32 percent). Their friends, however, preferred the true prints (by 61 to 39 percent). Each liked best the face that they had seen the most.

Explaining the Effects of Familiarity

Why does familiarity increase liking? First, repeated exposure often improves our recognition of someone, and this may be a helpful step in coming to like them. But mere exposure effects have also been demonstrated when subjects are unable to recognize the person or object in question (Bornstein, 1989). Second, as people become more familiar, they also become more predictable. The more we see the new neighbor in our apartment building, the more we learn about her and the better we can predict how she will behave in the elevator and the laundry room. As a result, we feel more comfortable in her presence.

A third consequence of mere exposure is that we tend to assume that people are similar to ourselves. The Moreland and Beach (1992) study described earlier, where women attended a social psychology class from 0 to 15 times, addressed this issue. Students rated women who attended frequently as more similar in personality, background, and plans for the future.

Limits to Mere Exposure

As you might expect, there are limits to the mere exposure effect. Exposure is most effective in enhancing liking for a person or object that is initially perceived as pleasant or at least neutral, but not for one that is initially perceived as negative. To make this point, Zajonc uses the example of repeatedly seeing a particular man in handcuffs. After a while, we become convinced he really is a criminal. Researchers tested this idea by showing subjects pictures of people presented positively (as scientists), neutrally (dressed in a sports shirt), or negatively (in a

Because the human face is not perfectly symmetrical, the way we see our own face in the mirror differs subtly from the way other people see us during interaction. The left photo shows a woman as her friends view her. The right photo is a "reverse image" that shows the woman as she appears to herself in the mirror. Research finds that people like best the face they have seen the most.

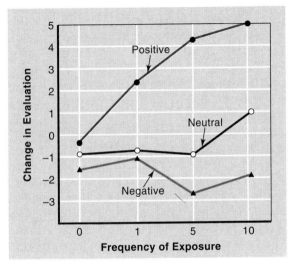

Figure 9-2 Mean change in evaluation of stimulus persons, as a function of frequency of exposure and picture content (positive, neutral, or negative). Positive scores indicate a positive shift in evaluations. (*Source:* Adapted from Perlman & Oskamp, 1971.)

police lineup). As shown in Figure 9-2, repeated exposure to positive and neutral pictures increased liking, but had no effect on negative pictures (Perlman & Oskamp, 1971).

Another exception to the familiarity–liking connection occurs when two people have conflicting interests, needs, or personalities. As long as they see little of each other, the conflicts are minimized. They may not particularly like each other, but they have little reason to dislike each other. When contact is increased, however, the conflicts are aggravated. They come to dislike each other even more as a result of frequent contact. A third limitation is that a lot of repetition can cause boredom and satiation (Bornstein, Kale & Cornell, 1990). There is probably an optimal level of exposure to maximize liking, depending on the people and the situation.

PROXIMITY

Probably the single best predictor of whether two people are friends is how far apart they live. If one person lives in Brazil and the other in China, it is almost certain they are not friends. If one lives in Chicago and the other in Phoenix, or even if they live on opposite sides of the same city, it is unlikely they are friends. In fact, if two people live only 10 blocks apart, it is much less likely that they are friends than if they live next door to each other. Proximity is a powerful force in interpersonal attraction.

Research Findings

In the 1950s, W. H. Whyte (1956) studied friendship patterns in Park Forest, a newly built suburban town. Almost everyone moved to this community at about the same time. Because all the houses were similar, residents had chosen their homes and neighborhoods pretty much by chance. There were no "better" areas, and no cheap houses. It was almost as though a large group of families had been randomly assigned to houses.

Whyte tracked the social activities of residents by reading the social column in the local newspaper. Almost everyone at a baby shower lived within a few blocks of one another, and almost everyone who lived in the area was there. The same was true on the other side of town at a weekend barbecue. In the whole town, there were practically no friends who did not live near one another. Most people who lived close together became friends.

The same proximity effect occurs on a smaller scale in apartment buildings and dormitories. A study by Leon Festinger, Stanley Schachter, and Kurt Back (1950) investigated friendship patterns in Westgate West, a large apartment complex. Westgate West had 17 separate two-story buildings, each containing 10 apartments (5 on a floor). The layout is shown in Figure 9-3. The apartments were almost identical. More important, residents did not choose where they lived; they were given apartments as the apartments became vacant. In other words, like Park Forest, Westgate West came close to being a field experiment with residents randomly assigned to a condition.

All residents were asked, "Which three people in Westgate West do you see socially most often?" Results clearly showed that residents were most friendly with those who lived near them. People on the same floor mentioned their next-door neighbor more often than their neighbor two doors away, and their neighbor two doors away more often than their neighbor at the other end of the hall. Of next-door neighbors, 41 percent were chosen, whereas only 22 percent of those two doors away and 10 percent

of those at the end of the hall were chosen. In actuality, the physical distances involved were very small. People who lived next door were 19 feet apart (in the case of the two middle apartments, 32 feet apart), and the maximum distance between two apartments on one floor was only 88 feet. But these distances, only a few extra seconds in walking time, were important factors in determining social interaction.

In addition, people who lived on different floors became friends much less often than those on the same floors even when the physical distance between them was roughly the same. This was probably because it takes more effort to go up or down stairs than to walk down a hall. Thus, people on different floors were in a sense farther away psychologically than were those on the same floor. The investigators referred to this as *functional distance,* meaning that the probability people would socialize was determined by the design of the apartment house as well as by actual distance. The closer people lived, as measured by either physical or functional distance, the more likely they were to be friends.

Another demonstration of the proximity effect comes from a study done at the Training Academy of the Maryland State Police (Segal, 1974). Trainees were assigned to dormitory rooms and to seats in classrooms by their last name in alphabetical order. Thus, the closer their last names were alphabetically, the more likely trainees were to spend time in close proximity, both in and out of the classrooms. After six months, each trainee was asked to name his closest three friends on the force. To an astonishing degree, the trainees' friends turned out to be those with names near theirs in the alphabet. On the average, each person chose as a friend

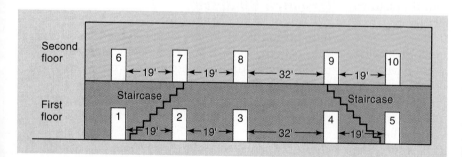

Figure 9-3 Floor plan of Westgate West. All the buildings in the housing development had the same layout. In the study, functional distance was defined as the number of doors apart two people lived. (*Source:* Adapted from Festinger, Schachter, & Back, 1950, with the permission of the publishers, Stanford University Press.)

someone whose last name was only 4.5 letters away from his in the alphabet. Despite an intensive training period in which all trainees became well acquainted, the mere fact of being assigned to a dorm room and sitting close together in class dictated friendship.

Explaining the Effects of Proximity

The proximity effect incorporates many of the factors that we have already seen are important for interpersonal attraction. First, proximity usually increases familiarity. We see our next-door neighbor more often than the person down the street. This repeated exposure, in and of itself, can enhance liking. Second, proximity is often linked to similarity. Although the citizens of Park Forest did not select their neighbors, people who decided to live in that community tended to start out with common characteristics. They all had enough money to afford nice homes, they wanted to live in suburbia, most had children, and so on. Over time, Park Forest neighbors developed other points of shared interest, as they gossiped about the noisy teenagers down the block or complained about the pothole in their street. In other words, we often choose to live and work with people who resemble us, and our geographic closeness further enhances our similarities.

A third factor is that people who are physically close are more easily available than those who are distant. Obviously, we cannot like or be friends with someone we have never met! We choose our friends from people we know. The ready availability of people close by also affects the balance of rewards and costs of interacting, a point emphasized by social exchange theory. It takes little effort to chat with a neighbor or to ask her about bus service to the airport. Even if a neighbor's company is only moderately pleasant, we come by it "cheaply" and so we may find it profitable. In contrast, long-distance relationships require time, planning, and money. When good friends move apart, they often vow to keep in touch regularly. But many find that their contacts dwindle to an occasional birthday card or phone call.

A fourth explanation of the proximity effect is based on cognitive consistency. It is psychologically distressing to live or work side by side with someone we dislike, and so we experience cognitive pressure to like those with whom we must associate. One formulation of this theory was proposed by Fritz Heider (1958). He distinguished between *unit relations* and *sentiment relations*. People or objects that "belong together" comprise a unit. For instance, most people would perceive Sam as having a unit relationship with his parents or coworkers. Proximity is a common basis for unit relationships. Sam has a unit relationship with his roommate or next door neighbor. Sentiment relations involve feelings—liking or disliking—between the person and the other. Does Sam like his roommate? The basic idea of Heider's **balance theory** is that we strive to maintain balance between our sentiment and unit relations. More specifically, we are motivated to like those we are connected to, and to seek proximity with those we like.

When does this desire to balance unit relations with sentiment relations affect liking? The most obvious case is when we are in a unit relation with someone we dislike. Then our unit relation is unbalanced by our negative sentiment relation. Suppose you arrive at college to meet your assigned roommate and instantly dislike him or her. To try to balance your unit relation with your sentiment relation, you have two options. You can avoid the roommate as much as possible and try to move to another room. Or you can reevaluate the roommate, trying to see some good qualities, to avoid conflicts, to make the best of the situation. The issue comes down to which of these relations, unit or sentiment, you are able to change. Often it is nearly impossible to break off the unit relation. Your dorm counselor may insist that you cannot change roommates until the term ends. Therefore, you experience pressure to increase your liking for your roommate.

This effect has been demonstrated experimentally (Tyler & Sears, 1977). Women participants in this study first met a person who was quite obnoxious. This person (actually a confederate of the experimenter) forgot the subject's name, snapped gum, blew smoke in her face, claimed the subject was saying silly things, and did not look at the subject when she talked. This was done to establish a negative sentiment relation. Next, the experimenter told the subject either that she would spend another 40 minutes talking to the obnoxious person (creating a unit relation with the unpleasant person), or that she would spend 40 minutes talking to someone else. Finally, the subject was taken into a separate room to fill out a questionnaire which, among other things, asked how much she liked the confederate. As predicted, liking for the obnoxious person was significantly higher if the subject anticipated continued interaction than if she did not.

Other studies have also shown that the anticipation of interaction increases liking. In one study, college students agreed to let the researchers organize their dating life for a period of five weeks (Berscheid et al., 1976). The subjects were shown videotapes of various people, separated at random into those described as future dates and those described as people they would not date. The prospective dates were liked significantly more. In general, if we know we are going to interact with someone in the future, we tend to play up the person's positive traits and to ignore or minimize the negative ones. A desire for cognitive balance motivates us to like our neighbors, roommates, and others in close proximity.

There are, of course, exceptions to the proximity–liking connection. Sometimes no amount of cognitive reevaluation will convince us that the rude secretary in our office is really nice or that our bratty kid sister is really a little angel. Proximity is most likely to foster attraction when the people involved have similar attitudes and goals. Indeed, when there are initial antagonisms or conflicts between people, increased proximity and contact may actually intensify negative feelings.

In summary, research has shown that similarity, familiarity, and proximity are powerful forces in interpersonal attraction. To give a complete account of the processes of interpersonal attraction, we have also noted various exceptions to these patterns. But these minor exceptions should not obscure the importance of the general principles involved.

These factors are not only causes of liking,

but consequences as well. Proximity causes liking, but once we like someone, we often take steps to ensure that we will be close to them in the future. First-year roommates may be thrown together by chance. But if their proximity leads to friendship, they will probably try to live together the following year. Similarity can work in the same way. Similarity may bring two people together in the first place, but as their friendship continues and they share ideas and experiences, they tend to become even more similar because of their association. Similarity is both a cause and a consequence of liking.

LOVE

Long a favored subject for poets and songwriters, love is now a popular topic for scientific research as well (Hendrick & Hendrick, 1992). Most Americans consider love to be essential to a successful marriage. In the 1960s, Kephart asked young adults about the love–marriage connection. The question he posed to over 1000 college students was: "If a boy (girl) had all the qualities you desired, would you marry this person if you were not in love with him (her)?" The results are shown in Table 9-4.

Thirty years ago, most men said no, they wouldn't marry a woman they didn't love. However, most women said they were undecided; only one woman in four clearly answered no. In the intervening years, both sexes—but especially women—have become more romantic in their approach to marriage. In 1976 and again in 1984, researchers asked new generations of American college students the same question (Simpson, Campbell, & Berscheid, 1986). In 1976, 86 percent of men and 80 percent of women said they would not marry without love; in 1984, the proportion of men who said no was the same, but women had increased to 85 percent.

A recent study asked this same question of university students from the United States, Russia, and Japan (Sprecher et al., 1992). Students could answer only yes or no; there was no "undecided" category. As in previous research, the vast majority of American young

TABLE 9-4
Would You Marry Without Love?

How college students answered the question "If a man (woman) had all the other qualities you desired, would you marry this person if you were not in love with him (her)? (Numbers are percentages.)

	1967		1976		1984	
	Men	Women	Men	Women	Men	Women
Yes	11.7	4.0	1.7	4.6	1.7	3.6
Undecided	23.7	71.7	12.1	15.4	12.7	11.5
No	64.6	24.3	86.2	80.0	85.6	84.9

Note: In all years, data are questionnaire responses from college men and women. The earliest data were collected by Kephart (1967); his question was worded identically to that above except that he used "boy (girl)" instead of "man (woman)".

Source: Adapted from Simpson, Campbell & Berscheid, *Personality and Social Psychology Bulletin,* Vol. 12, No. 3, September 1986, pp. 364–368. Copyright by The Society for Personality and Social Psychology, Inc. Reprinted by permission of Sage Publications, Inc.

Loving and being loved in return are vital to human happiness. Stereotypes sometimes suggest that people with mental and physical handicaps lead loveless lives, but this in not necessarily true. The partners in this couple both have a form of mental retardation known as Downs Syndrome.

people endorsed love as a basis of marriage: 91 percent of men and 87 percent of women said they would not marry without love, as did 80 percent of Japanese men and 81 percent of Japanese women. Russians were more variable, with 70 percent of men but only 59 percent of women insisting on love. Russian women tended to show the same kind of pragmatism found among American women earlier in the century: They were willing to marry without love if other conditions were right. For a look at societies where free choice of a mate is atypical, see the CULTURAL HIGHLIGHT on arranged marriages.

Love Versus Liking

One of the first researchers to study romantic love scientifically was Zick Rubin (1970, 1973). He was interested in the connection between love and liking. One view is that love is merely an intense form of liking. According to this unidimensional view, our positive feelings of attraction range along a continuum from mild liking to strong liking to mild love to strong love. A contrasting view, and the one Rubin favored, is that liking and love are qualitatively

CULTURAL HIGHLIGHT

Arranged Marriages and Love Matches

Most Americans find it hard to imagine marriage without love. The individualistic orientation of our culture places a high premium on personal choice in matters of the heart. In contrast, many traditional societies throughout the world reject individual choice and romance as a basis for marriage. In parts of India, for example, marriages are arranged by parents. Giri Raj Gupta (1992) explains that love is not viewed as an important basis for marriage. When parents select a bride, they emphasize her good character, obedience, domestic skills, religiousness, and appearance. In selecting a groom, the social and economic standing of the family, and the young man's education and earning potential are paramount.

Teenagers who grow up in traditional societies often welcome their parents' help in selecting a mate. When David and Vera Mace (1960) explained American marriage customs to girls in India, they expressed serious concerns about the hazards of free choice. One girl asked if an American girl who is shy and does not call attention to herself might not get married. Another girl said it would be humiliating to have to attract a boy. "It makes getting married a sort of competition in which the girls are fighting each other for the boys. And it encourages a girl to pretend she's better than she really is" (pp. 144–145). Other girls praised their parents' judgment about a potential husband. "It's so important that the man I marry should be the right one. I could so easily make a mistake if I had to find him for myself" (p. 145).

Anthropologist Francis Hsu (1981) has painted a similar portrait of marriage in traditional Chinese culture. For centuries, it was common for Chinese marriages to be arranged by parents and hired go-betweens; the partners might not even meet until their wedding (Xiaghe & Whyte, 1990). Proponents of arranged marriage emphasize that parents are better judges of character than children, that passion is an unrealistic basis for marriage, and that well-matched partners from compatible families gradually learn to find love and satisfaction with each other.

In recent times, some people in collectivist cultures have begun to question traditional marriage patterns. After the Chinese Communists came to power, for instance, they promoted freedom of choice in marriage. Supporters of the old system worried that this new freedom would lead to unhappy marriages.

A recent study of a representative sample of wives from the city of Chengdu in the People's Republic of China investigated this issue (Xiaghe & Whyte, 1990). The survey found that there has been an increase in personal decision-making about marriage. Yet the influence of parents remains strong. Unlike the United States, China does not have a cultural tradition of dating in which young people can "try out" prospective partners. As a result, many young people rely on introductions from relatives, and going out with several prospective partners is uncommon. Contrary to the dire predictions of traditionalists, the researchers found that the Chinese women who had greater choice in the selection of a mate reported higher levels of marital satisfaction and were less likely to divorce than other women.

distinct and represent two different dimensions. This view seems consistent with folk wisdom that we can like someone a great deal, but not be in love with him or her, and that we can feel passionate love for someone we do not totally like or respect.

To study this issue, Rubin first compiled many statements that people thought reflected liking and other statements that people thought reflected love. These included such things as idealization, trust, sharing emotions, believing someone is intelligent, and tolerating the other's faults. Next Rubin asked several hundred college students to rate how characteristic each of these statements was of their feelings toward their boyfriend or girlfriend and also toward a nonromantic friend of the other sex. Rubin believed that if love and liking are distinct, some statements would characterize a romantic partner but not a friend. The results of this first study supported the idea that love and liking are distinct.

Based on these findings, Rubin constructed two separate paper and pencil tests, a Love Scale and a Liking Scale. Each scale consists of nine statements. A sample liking statement is: "I have great confidence in _____'s good judgment." Respondents rate each statement on a nine-point scale from strongly disagree to strongly agree.

To collect further evidence that these scales were measuring somewhat different attitudes, Rubin recruited 182 dating couples at the University of Michigan. Both members of each couple filled out detailed questionnaires about their relationship which included the Love and Liking Scales. They also participated in lab experiments. Rubin's results supported the distinction between love and liking. For example, he found that although students rated their dating partner and best friend equally high on the Liking Scale, they rated their boyfriend or girlfriend much higher on the Love Scale. In an experimental session, Rubin found that couples who scored high on the Love Scale spent more time making eye contact than did low scorers, confirming the idea that lovers often gaze into each other's eyes. Those with high love scores were more likely to say that they and their partner were in love, and gave a higher estimate of

the probability of eventually marrying the partner.

In a follow-up study six months later, Rubin examined whether love scores were related to staying together versus breaking up. Partners with high love scores were more likely to stay together, but only if they were also high in "romanticism," the belief that true love conquers all. Taken together, these and more recent data suggest that there are important qualitative differences between liking and love.

The Experience of Romantic Love

Before turning to research findings on romantic love, let's set the stage by considering this newspaper story of young love:

> On Monday, Cpl. Floyd Johnson, 23, and the then Ellen Skinner, 19, total strangers, boarded a train at San Francisco and sat down across the aisle from each other. Johnson didn't cross the aisle until Wednesday, but his bride said, "I'd already made up my mind to say yes if he asked me to marry him." "We did most of the talking with our eyes," Johnson explained. Thursday the couple got off the train in Omaha with plans to be married. Because they would need to have the consent of the bride's parents if they were married in Nebraska, they crossed the river to Council Bluffs, Iowa, where they were married Friday.

This account may remind you of such starstruck lovers from literature as Romeo and Juliet. But have you personally ever experienced this rather magical love at first sight?

When university students were asked how closely their own most intense love experience corresponded to this romantic model, only 40 percent said that there was a strong resemblance (Averill & Boothroyd, 1977). Another 40 percent said that they had never experienced anything at all like this story. The rest thought their most intense love relationship bore only a partial similarity to this one. This range of answers highlights one of the dilemmas of love researchers: how to capture the essential features of love, and at the same time depict the diverse experiences of people in love. Some common ways

TABLE 9-5
Definitions of Love

When people say "I love you," they can mean very different things. Researchers have identified six different ways in which people commonly define love (Lasswell & Lobsenz, 1980; Lee, 1973). These love styles are idealized types; each individual may define love in a way that combines more than one style. The statements quoted below are from a love questionnaire developed by Clyde and Susan Hendrick (1989).

- *Romantic love:*   Love is an all-consuming emotional experience. Love at first sight is typical, and physical attraction is essential. A romantic lover might agree with the statement that "My lover and I have the right physical 'chemistry' between us."

- *Possessive love:*   The possessive lover is emotionally intense, jealous, obsessed with the beloved. The possessive lover is highly dependent on the beloved, and therefore fears rejection. He or she might agree that "When my lover doesn't pay attention to me, I feel sick all over."

- *Best friends love:*   Love is a comfortable intimacy that slowly grows out of companionship, mutual sharing, and self-disclosure. A best friends lover is thoughtful, warm, and companionate. He or she might agree that "My most satisfying love relationships have developed from good friendships."

- *Pragmatic love:*   This is the "love that goes shopping for a suitable mate, and all it asks is that the relationship work well, that the two partners be compatible and satisfy each other's basic needs" (Lee, 1973, p. 124). The practical lover seeks contentment rather than excitement. He or she might agree that "One consideration in choosing a partner is how he/she will reflect on my career."

- *Altruistic love:*   This style of love is unconditionally caring, giving, and forgiving. Love means a duty to give to the loved one with no strings attached. An altruistic lover might agree "I cannot be happy unless I place my lover's happiness before my own."

- *Game playing love:*   This person plays at love as others play tennis or chess: to enjoy the "love game" and to win it. No relationship lasts for long, usually ending when the partner becomes boring or too serious. A game player might agree that "I enjoy playing the 'game of love' with a number of different partners."

people conceptualize love are presented in Table 9-5.

Undaunted by this challenge, researchers have begun to identify the various thoughts, feelings, and behaviors that are associated with romantic love (Kelley, 1983). Most of the information we have about love comes from studies of young middle class white adults in our society. Yet the experience of love is quite different in other cultures and at other historical times (Hunt, 1959). We therefore need to be cautious about generalizing from current findings to all lovers.

THOUGHTS OF LOVE.   Rubin's Love Scale conceptualizes love as an attitude toward another person, as a distinctive cluster of thoughts about the loved person. Rubin identified three main themes reflected in his scale items. One theme, which Rubin called attachment, is a sense of needing the partner. A sample statement is "It would be hard for me to get along without _____." These statements reflect a person's awareness of their dependence on the other to provide valued rewards. A second theme concerns caring for the other person, as illustrated in this item: "I would do almost anything for _____." The desire to promote the other person's welfare and to be responsive to his or her needs is a central idea. The third theme emphasizes trust and self-disclosure. These ideas of love contrast with the Liking Scale, which concerns beliefs that the other person is likable, intelligent, well-adjusted, and has good judgment. According to Rubin, liking combines feelings of affection and of respect.

BEHAVIORS OF LOVE.   In assessing whether someone loves us, we usually depend not only on words, but also on actions. If someone professes love but forgets our birthday, goes out with other people, criticizes our appearance, and never confides in us, we may doubt his or her sincerity. Swensen (1972) asked people of different ages what behaviors they thought were most closely associated with love for a romantic partner or spouse. The answers fell into seven categories or types of love behaviors:

1. Saying "I love you" and other verbal statements of affection.
2. Physical expressions of love, such as hugging or kissing.
3. Verbal self-disclosure.
4. Communicating nonverbally such feelings as happiness and relaxation when the other is present.
5. Material signs of love, such as giving presents or doing tasks to help the other person.
6. Nonmaterial signs of love, such as showing interest in the person's activities, respecting his or her opinions, or giving encouragement.
7. Showing a willingness to tolerate the other and to make sacrifices to maintain the relationship.

Swensen found that many of these romantic love behaviors were also seen as signs of love for parents, siblings, and same-sex friends.

King and Christensen (1983) identified specific events that indicate how far a heterosexual dating couple has progressed toward marriage. In most cases, the college couples in this research went through a predictable sequence of events moving toward greater commitment. Events that usually occurred early in the development of a relationship included spending a whole day together and calling the partner by an affectionate name. At a later stage, partners started referring to each other as "boyfriend" and "girlfriend," and received invitations to do things together as a couple. A further development was to say "I love you" and to date each other exclusively. A common next step was to discuss living together or marriage, and to take a vacation together. Events indicating greatest progress included living together or becoming engaged. Although couples varied in how far their relationship had developed and in the speed with which they moved toward permanence, most couples followed a similar sequence of key events.

FEELINGS OF LOVE. One feature that often distinguishes romantic love from friendship is the experience of physical symptoms. According to popular songs, a lover's heart skips a beat now and then, and a lover loses sleep and has trouble concentrating. To investigate this matter, researchers asked 679 university students to rate the intensity of various feelings they had had during their current or most recent love experience (Kanin, Davidson, & Scheck, 1970).

The most common reactions were a strong feeling of well-being (reported by 79 percent of students) and great difficulty concentrating (reported by 37 percent of students). Other reactions included "floating on a cloud" (29 percent), "wanted to run, jump, and scream" (22 percent), feeling "nervous before dates" (22 percent), and feeling "giddy and carefree" (20 percent). Strong physical sensations such as cold hands, butterflies in the stomach, or a tingling spine were reported by 20 percent and insomnia by 12 percent of students.

Researchers also found differences between the love experiences of women and men, with women being more likely to report strong emotional reactions (Dion & Dion, 1973). Whether these results reflect actual sex differences in the experience of love or women's greater willingness to disclose such feelings is not known.

In summary, research has identified some of the thoughts, feelings, and behaviors that Americans commonly associate with love. But studies also find that individuals differ in their specific love experiences. This suggests that there are distinct types of love. In the next section, we contrast passionate and companionate love.

Passionate Love and Companionate Love

Passionate love has been described as "a wildly emotional state: tender and sexual feelings, elation and pain, anxiety and relief, altruism and jealousy coexist in a confusion of feelings" (Berscheid & Walster, 1978, p. 177). Emotions play a central role in passionate love. People are swept off their feet by uncontrollable passions that draw them irresistibly toward the loved person. Elaine Hatfield and her colleagues have developed a Passionate Love Scale to assess the intensity of people's experiences with this type of love (Hatfield & Rapson, 1987; Hatfield & Sprecher, 1986). Sample statements on the scale include "Sometimes I feel I can't control my thoughts; they are obsessively on _____" and "I feel a powerful attraction for _____." Hatfield believes that the capacity to experience passionate love is universal, although sociocultural factors can shape the way in which passionate love is expressed.

The physiological arousal that fuels passionate love can have many sources. Sexual desire, the fear of possible rejection, the excitement of getting to know someone, the frustration of outside interference, the anger of a lover's quarrel—all may contribute to the strong emotions experienced in passionate love. For example, Hatfield and her associates (1989) reasoned that anxiety might contribute to passionate love, just as Schachter had found that anxiety increased the desire to affiliate. In two studies, they found that young adolescents who scored higher on measures of anxiety were more likely to report feelings of passionate love. Whatever its diverse sources, the experience of passionate love seems to have an uncontrollable quality. This can provide a convenient justification for lovers to engage in behaviors they might otherwise consider unacceptable, such as an extramarital affair (Berscheid, 1983). The lovers' defense is that they "couldn't stop" themselves.

Another element of passionate love is preoccupation with the other person. The lover is obsessed with thoughts of the new love. There is a tendency to idealize the loved person, to see the person as wonderful and perfect in every way. Passionate love is often said to strike suddenly and fade quickly. This type of love is intense, but fragile and often short-lived.

Companionate love has been defined as "the affection we feel for those with whom our lives are deeply intertwined" (Berscheid & Walster, 1978, p. 177). This is a more practical type of love that emphasizes trust, caring, and tolerance of the partner's flaws and idiosyncrasies. The emotional tone of companionate love is more moderate; warmth and affection are more common than extreme passions. Companionate love develops slowly as two people build a satisfying relationship (Kelley, 1983). Individuals differ sharply in their beliefs about whether passionate or companionate love is the better or truer form. However, many family researchers believe that companionate love provides the most enduring basis for long-term relationships.

The contrast between passionate and companionate love raises interesting questions about the experience of emotions in close relationships. For example, the early stages of a romantic relationship are often characterized by extreme emotions, whereas the later stages are marked by emotional tranquility and moderation. Why might this be? Ellen Berscheid (1983) has suggested that over time, the novelty and surprise of the relationship wear off. Idealization of the partner confronts the reality of human imperfection. The couple develops routine ways of interacting, and life together becomes more settled.

However, Berscheid also suggests that as a relationship continues over time and interdependence grows, the *potential* for strong emotion actually increases. The greater our dependence on another person, the greater the possible influence of the partner in our lives. But, paradoxically, because long-term couples learn to coordinate their activities smoothly, the actual frequency of strong emotions tends to be fairly low. The latent potential for strong emotion may emerge occasionally, however. When partners are separated because of travel or illness, they often have intense feelings of loneliness and desire. Another situation that can arouse strong emotions in a long-term relationship is the threat posed by a partner's involvement with another person.

Jealousy occurs when a person perceives a real or potential attraction between the partner and a rival (Brehm, 1992). **Jealousy** is a reaction to a perceived threat by a rival to the continuity or quality of a valued relationship. A husband's discovery that his wife is secretly dating another man would be an example. Jealousy involves two types of threats: threats to the relationship from the possible loss of the partner and threats to the person's self-esteem from being rejected by the partner or losing to the rival (Mathes, Adams & Davies, 1985). Feelings of anger, anxiety, and depression are common.

Several factors contribute to jealousy (Salovey, 1991). A person who is highly dependent on a relationship, who cares deeply about the relationship and has few alternatives, is more susceptible to jealousy (White & Mullen, 1989). For example, married people who believe they would have few alternatives if their current spouse left them are more vulnerable to jealousy (Hansen, 1985). There is also evidence linking jealousy to insecurity. People who feel inadequate in a relationship or think that their performance falls short of their own expectations are more likely to feel jealous (Salovey & Rodin, 1991).

As you might imagine, there are also cross-cultural differences in the situations that give rise to jealousy (White & Mullen, 1989). In our culture, for instance, it would not be unusual for a wife to feel jealous if her husband had a sexual affair with another woman. In contrast, in societies where cultural rules dictate that a man may have several wives, jealousy among the co-wives is unusual. Instead, co-wives typically have cordial relations unless the husband shows favoritism to one wife or to her children in ways that violate cultural dictates. Similarly, when cultures permit one woman to have multiple husbands, jealousy among the men is unusual.

Adult Romantic Attachment

In 1987, Cindy Hazan and Phillip Shaver proposed that we can understand adult romantic love from the perspective of attachment theory. Their approach has been influential in shaping recent research on romantic relationships, and it offers new insights into the nature of adult love (Shaver & Hazan, forthcoming).

Earlier in this chapter, we saw that infants develop strong emotional ties to their caretakers—bonds that provide an important sense of security. Although all children become attached to their primary caretaker, this attachment can take three forms: secure attachment, avoidant attachment, and anxious/ambivalent attachment. Hazan and Shaver believe that adult love relationships are similar to infant attachments in several ways.

Infant attachment and adult romantic love share common features. Both infants and adult lovers typically show intense fascination with

the other, distress at separation, and efforts to maintain proximity and to spend time together. Like infant attachments, adult romantic bonds are believed to have a biological origin. "Romantic love is a biological process designed by evolution to facilitate attachment between adult sexual partners who, at the time love evolved, were likely to become parents of an infant who would need reliable care" (Hazan & Shaver, 1987, p. 423).

Adult romantic attachments are also similar in form to the three types of infant attachment. Several studies have found that adult romantic experiences can be categorized as secure, avoidant, or anxious/ambivalent. The proportion of adults classified into each of the three attachment types is fairly similarly across studies, and is roughly comparable to the proportion of infants typically found in each group. Here are findings from one illustrative study (Hazan & Shaver, 1987):

> *Secure adults.* Adults were said to have "secure" romantic attachments if they described themselves as finding it relatively easy to get close to others and said they seldom worry about being abandoned. About 56 percent of the adults tested were in the secure group. Secure adults tended to describe their most important love relationship as especially happy, friendly, and trusting. Secure adults were also more likely than others to describe their parents in positive terms—as caring, fair, affectionate, and having a good marriage.

> *Avoidant adults.* "Avoidant" adults (roughly 24 percent of those tested) reported being somewhat uncomfortable getting close to others or trusting a romantic partner completely. In describing their most important love relationship, avoidant lovers reported emotional highs and lows, jealousy, and fear of intimacy. Compared to secure adults, avoidant adults tended to describe their parents as more demanding, critical, and uncaring.

> *Anxious/ambivalent adults.* Finally, those adults (20 percent) who seek intimacy, but worry that others won't reciprocate their love and won't stay with them were called

As a couple builds a life together, the emotional highs and lows of passionate love are often transformed into the more stable affectionate bonds of companionate love.

"anxious/ambivalent." The anxious/ambivalent respondents described their most important love relationship as involving obsession, desire for reciprocation and union, emotional highs and lows, and extreme sexual attraction and jealousy. Compared to secure adults, anxious/ambivalent respondents tended to describe their parents as more intrusive and demanding, and their parents' marriage as unhappy.

Of course, there are also differences between the attachment of infants and adults. Adult attachments are typically reciprocal: Each partner not only receives care but gives care in return. The relationship between infant and adult is not reciprocal in this sense. Another difference is that adult attachments are usually formed between peers. Finally, adult attachments often involve sexual attraction.

Another important idea is that a child's earli-

est love relationships with parents may influence the way he or she approaches romantic involvements in adulthood (Collins & Read, 1990). For example, a securely attached child may come to expect that people are generally trustworthy, responsive, and caring. Hazan and Shaver (forthcoming) call these beliefs a person's "working model" of relationships. As an adult, this person may also show a secure style of attachment to romantic partners, and form satisfying and long-lasting relationships. In contrast, an anxious/ambivalent child might become an adult who seeks love but fears rejection. An avoidant child might become an avoidant adult who fears intimacy and distrusts other people. Of course, attachment styles can change as a person has new life experiences. For example, a rewarding relationship during adolescence or adulthood may enable a person who was insecurely attached as a child to develop a more trusting working model of relationships, and learn to form secure attachments with peers.

There is growing evidence that attachment styles affect the quality of adult romantic relationships. Several studies suggest that securely attached people tend to have more satisfying, committed, close, and well-adjusted relationships, compared to avoidant and anxious people (Shaver & Hazan, forthcoming). For example, a three-year study of dating couples found that secure men and women were more likely to have stable and satisfying relationships than individuals with other attachment styles (Davis & Kirkpatrick, in press). Other studies have also found that the attachment style of college students affects such aspects of their dating relationships as satisfaction, closeness, and commitment (Collins & Read, 1990; Simpson, 1990).

Two recent studies have examined the actual behavior of individuals and couples in controlled settings. One project investigated attachment styles and self-disclosure among a sample of Israeli college students who interacted with an unfamiliar student in a laboratory situation (Mikulincer & Nachshon, 1991). Compared to avoidant individuals, both secure and anxious/ambivalent individuals disclosed more personal information to others. In addition, both secure and anxious/ambivalent individuals liked a high-disclosing partner better than a low-disclosing partner.

Another study examined how dating couples react when the woman is confronted with a stressful situation (Simpson, Rholes & Nelligan, 1992). Dating couples were brought into the laboratory, and a questionnaire measure of attachment style was obtained. Next, each woman was told that she would be "exposed to a situation and set of experimental procedures that arouse considerable anxiety and distress in most people. Due to the nature of these procedures, I cannot tell you any more at the moment" (p. 437). The woman was then shown a darkened, windowless room used for psychophysiological research where the "procedures" were to take place. However, the researcher explained, the equipment was not ready yet, and so the woman was asked to wait for a few minutes with her boyfriend. During the next five minutes, the interaction between the woman and her boyfriend was recorded. Analyses of these videotapes revealed that as their anxiety about the experiment increased, securely attached women turned to their partners as a source of comfort and reassurance, but avoidant women withdrew from their partners both emotionally and physically. In response to their girlfriends' growing anxiety, secure men tended to offer more support, whereas avoidant men offered less.

These and other research findings suggest that an attachment perspective may provide valuable insights about adult romantic relationships. At present, the study of adult attachment is one the most active areas of research in the social psychology of romantic relationships.

LONELINESS

When our social relationships are inadequate and unsatisfying, we become lonely. **Loneliness** refers to the subjective discomfort we feel when our social relations lack some important feature. This deficit may be quantitative: We may have no friends, or fewer friends than we want. Or the deficit may be qualitative: We may feel that our relationships are superficial, or less satisfy-

ing than we would like. Loneliness and aloneness are not the same. Loneliness goes on inside a person and cannot be detected simply by looking at someone. In contrast, aloneness is the objective state of being apart from other people.

There is no inevitable link between aloneness and loneliness: We can be happy alone or lonely in a crowd. Nonetheless, people are somewhat more likely to feel lonely when they are alone. Earlier in this chapter we described a study of how people spend their time (Larsen et al., 1982). This research found that people felt lonelier when they were alone than when they were with others. For teenagers, this pattern resulted primarily from being alone on Friday or Saturday night. Adolescents did not feel particularly lonely if they were alone during the week while studying or shopping. But being alone on a weekend evening when personal preference and social norms suggest you should be out with friends often led to loneliness.

The Experience of Loneliness

In national surveys, roughly one American in four says he or she has felt "very lonely or remote from other people" in the past two weeks (e.g., Bradburn, 1969). Loneliness can range from fleeting twinges of discomfort to severe and persistent feelings of intense misery (Peplau & Perlman, 1982).

Sometimes loneliness is caused by a life change that takes us away from friends and intimate relationships. Situations that commonly cause loneliness include moving to a new town, going away to school, starting a new job, being separated from friends and loved ones, and ending an important relationship. Loneliness can also result when physical illness or a serious accident interferes with social relationships by confining a person to a hospital or reducing physical abilities (Lyons, 1991). Most people eventually recover from situational loneliness and reestablish a satisfying social life, although this is obviously more difficult in some situations than in others.

Some people suffer from loneliness for many years, more or less independent of changes in their lives. They are experiencing chronic loneli-

The misery of time spent alone is seen in this young man's expression of loneliness and rejection. The pleasures of time spent alone are seen in this young woman's romp at the beach.

ness. Such individuals might describe themselves as a "lonely person," rather than someone who is in a lonely period of life. Perhaps 10 percent of American adults suffer from severe and persistent loneliness.

Robert Weiss (1973) has distinguished two types of loneliness, based on the specific social provisions that a person lacks. *Emotional loneliness* results from the absence of an intimate attachment figure, such as might be provided for children by their parents or for adults by a spouse or intimate friend. *Social loneliness* occurs when a person lacks the sense of social integration or community involvement that might be provided by a network of friends or coworkers. It is possible to experience one type of loneliness without the other. Young newlyweds who move to Alaska to seek adventure might not feel emotional loneliness—they have each other. But they are likely to experience social loneliness until they make friends and develop a sense of belonging to their new community. A widow might feel intense emotional loneliness after the death of her husband, but continue to have many social ties to relatives and friends at church.

Who Is at Risk for Loneliness?

No segment of society is immune to loneliness, but some people are at greater risk than others (Peplau & Perlman, 1982). Certain childhood experiences may predispose individuals to loneliness. For instance, there is some evidence that children of divorced parents may be at greater risk for loneliness as adults than children from intact families. In a large survey of Americans, Carin Rubenstein and Phillip Shaver (1982) found that adults whose parents had divorced were more likely than other adults to feel lonely, especially if the divorce occurred before the person was 6 years old. Perhaps surprisingly, the death of a parent during childhood was not related to adult loneliness. To explain these findings, Shaver and Rubenstein (1980) turned to the work on parent–child attachment discussed in this chapter. They suggested that the loss of a parental attachment relationship through divorce affects children in two major ways.

First, children often blame themselves for the divorce. Although it is an irrational belief, many children think that they have in some way caused their parents' marriage to end. This tendency seems especially strong among preschool children, whose cognitive development is immature and self-focused (Wallerstein & Kelly, 1975). If children are older at the time of the divorce, they are usually better able to understand that the divorce was not their fault. The legacy of this self-blame can be persistent low self-esteem—an enduring belief that one is unlovable and unworthy of affection. Studies of adults show a clear link between low self-esteem and loneliness (Olmstead et al., 1991).

The person who lacks self-confidence may be less willing to take risks in social situations and may subtly communicate a sense of worthlessness to others. This, in turn, may set the stage for poor social relationships and for loneliness.

Second, Rubenstein and Shaver speculate that children of divorced parents may come to see other people as rejecting and unreliable. If a child perceives a parent as unresponsive or frustrating, the child may develop a more generalized view of people as untrustworthy and of relationships as undependable. Such a "working model" of relationships established in childhood may persist into adulthood, making it harder for the individual to form rewarding relationships. Consistent with this idea are data showing that children of divorced parents have more negative and less trusting views of other people (Shaver & Rubenstein, 1980).

A recent study has extended this line of reasoning by testing directly whether there is a link between an person's attachment style and loneliness (Hazan & Hutt, 1991). The researchers assessed the attachment styles and loneliness of young adults during the summer before they began college. Then they followed the students throughout their freshman year. The securely attached students showed a predictable pattern of responding to a new social situation. Before college began, they were not particularly lonely. During the fall semester, as they made their way in a new social world, they reported relatively high loneliness. By the end of the year, however, they had found friends and their loneliness scores returned to low summer levels. The anxious/ambivalent students were lonelier than the securely attached students during the summer. During the fall semester, their loneliness actually decreased. Other measures suggested that they were hopeful of finding new relationships at school. By spring, the anxious/ambivalent group had typically found a romantic partner, but their loneliness scores were back to their summer high. Finally, the loneliness of avoidant students was unaffected by going to college. These students reported few friends and little social contact both before and during college.

Other factors also affect the risk of loneliness

(Peplau & Perlman, 1982). Married people are less likely to feel lonely than others. It is interesting to note, however, that some married people—18 percent in one study—do feel lonely. Married people might be lonely because their marriage is not personally satisfying or because they lack friends and associates outside the marriage. Loneliness is more common among the poor than the affluent. Good relationships are easier to maintain when people have the time and money for leisure activities.

Loneliness is also related to age. Stereotypes depict old age as a time of great loneliness. But research shows that loneliness is highest among teenagers and young adults, and lowest among older people (Perlman, 1990). In one large survey, 79 percent of people under age 18 said they were sometimes or often lonely, compared to only 53 percent of those ages 45 to 54, and 37 percent of those 55 years old and over (Parlee, 1979). Researchers have not yet determined the reason for this age pattern. In part, there may be a "generation gap," with young people being more willing to talk about their feelings and acknowledge loneliness than are older adults. It is also true, however, that young people face a great many social transitions, such as leaving home, living on their own, going to college, or taking a first full-time job—all of which can cause loneliness. As people get older, their social lives may become more stable. Age may also bring greater social skills and more realistic expectations about social relations.

During the journey from birth to death, few people escape the misery of loneliness. But rather than being a sign of weakness, loneliness reflects our human needs for social relationships, needs that all people share. That's why the only real cure for loneliness is to establish relationships that meet our basic psychological needs for connectedness.

In this chapter, we have examined human needs for companionship and discussed why we like some people and not others. We also reviewed psychological studies of romantic love and loneliness. In the next chapter, we turn to research about interaction in personal relationships.

KEY TERMS

affiliation
association
attachment
balance theory
cognitive dissonance theory
companionate love

expectancy-value theory
jealousy
loneliness
matching principle
mere exposure effect
passionate love

phantom-other technique
reinforcement
social comparison theory
social exchange theory
social support

SUMMARY

1. The tendency to affiliate begins in childhood, when infants form strong attachments to the significant adults in their lives. Research distinguishes three styles of attachment: secure, avoidant, and anxious/ambivalent.

2. Laboratory experiments have shown that affiliative tendencies are increased when people are afraid or uncertain. Weiss and others have attempted to classify the specific benefits of adult social relations, such as attachment, social integration, and guidance.

3. Three principles affecting interpersonal attraction are association, reinforcement, and social exchange. In general, we like people who reward us and who help us to satisfy our needs.

4. The personal characteristics that tend to increase attraction include sincerity, warmth, competence, and physical attractiveness. Being seen with a beautiful date or friend may have a "radiating effect," causing others to evaluate us more favorably.

5. We tend to perceive people with babyfaced features as more childlike (dependent, honest, weak) in their personalities than people with mature facial features. This is called the babyface effect.

6. We tend to like people who are similar to us in attitudes, values, interests, background, and personality. In dating and marriage, the tendency to select similar partners is called the "matching principle." The effects of similarity can be explained in terms of rewards, cognitive consistency, and the expectancy-value theory of decision making. The processes that lead to similarity among friends include selective attraction, social influence, and environmental factors.

7. Familiarity generally enhances liking. If a person or object is initially evaluated as neutral or mildly positive, repeated exposure usually increases liking. This is called the mere exposure effect.

8. Another factor in interpersonal attraction is proximity. People who are physically close to us tend to be more familiar and are often, coincidentally, similar to us in background or interests. Social exchange theory suggests that people close by are more easily available for interaction, and so the costs of a relationship are usually less. According to cognitive balance theory, we may experience psychological pressure to like those with whom we must interact.

9. Most Americans consider love an essential prerequisite for marriage. Yet in many traditional societies, marriages are arranged by parents or other adults.

10. Rubin has shown that liking and love are qualitatively distinct. Although the two often go together, it is possible to like someone a lot without loving them, and to love a person without fully liking them.

11. Theorists have distinguished between passionate love (the exciting and emotionally charged experience some people have early in a love relationship) and companionate love (the deep affection, trust, and caring a person feels for a long-term partner). Jealousy is a reaction to a perceived threat to a valued relationship by a rival.

12. Shaver and Hazan have extended attachment theory to adult romantic relationships. Adults can be categorized as having a secure, avoidant, or anxious/ambivalent attachment style. Attachment styles may affect the quality of romantic relationships and also a person's risk for loneliness.

13. Loneliness is the subjective discomfort we feel when our social relations are lacking in some important way. Loneliness ranges from a temporary state resulting from a change in our social life to a chronic and enduring condition. Emotional loneliness is caused by the lack of an attachment relationship; social loneliness is caused by the lack of social integration.

SUGGESTED READINGS _____

Brehm, S. S. (1992). *Intimate relationships* (2nd ed.). New York: Random House. A well-written paperback textbook that provides an excellent introduction to the field.

Hatfield, E., & Rapson, R. L. (1993). Historical and cross-cultural perspectives on passionate love. In K. T. Strongman (Ed.), *International Review of Emotion* (Vol. 3). New York: Wiley. An up-to-date review of cross-cultural research on love.

Hatfield, E., & Sprecher, S. (1986). *Mirror, mirror . . . The importance of looks in everyday life.* Albany: State University of New York Press. A lively exploration of the many ways in which physical attractiveness influences us from childhood through old age.

Hendrick, S. S., & Hendrick, C. (1992). *Romantic love.* Newbury Park, CA: Sage. A comprehensive description of research and theory on love, written for a general audience.

Peplau, L. A., & Perlman, D. (Eds.). (1982). *Loneliness: A sourcebook of current theory, research, and therapy.* New York: Wiley Interscience. A survey of research findings and theories.

Shaver, P. R., & Hazan, C. (1993). Adult romantic attachment: Theory and evidence. In D. Perlman & W. Jones (Eds.), *Advances in personal relationships* (Vol. 4). London: Jessica Kingsley Publishers. A review of the latest research applying attachment theory to adult relationships.

10
Personal Relationships

Focus of This Chapter

From Casual Interactions to Close
   Relationships
A Social Exchange Perspective
Self-disclosure and Intimacy
The Balance of Power
Conflict
Satisfaction and Commitment

Cultural Highlight
Power in Mexican American and
African American Marriages

Research Closeup
Turning the Other Cheek

Human relationships are enormously varied. The tender bonds of parents and infants, the good-humored rivalry of tennis partners, and the steadfast love of a couple celebrating their golden wedding anniversary provide just a sampling of the many kinds of personal relationships. Some relationships are freely chosen: We usually pick our friends and lovers. Other relationships are thrust upon us, when we are assigned to a particular first-grade teacher, a college roommate, or a therapist at the counseling center. But from birth to death, relationships are the core of human experience.

Social psychologists try to see beneath the great variation in human relationships to discover general principles. This chapter examines the importance of interdependence in relationships, presents a social exchange perspective on relationships, and explores such relationship issues as self-disclosure, intimacy, power, conflict, satisfaction, and commitment.

FROM CASUAL INTERACTIONS TO CLOSE RELATIONSHIPS

Social interaction occurs when two or more people influence each other—verbally, physically, or emotionally. Talking to a therapist, debating an idea in class, and bumping into a person in a crowded elevator are all examples of social interaction. When two people interact, what each one does affects the other person. The specific ways people can influence each other are diverse. Another person can make us feel happy or sad, tell us the latest gossip or criticize our opinions, help us to get something done or get in our way, give us advice or tell us off. As these examples illustrate, influence in social interaction involves feelings, beliefs, and behavior. The basic theme is that two people have

mutual influence on each other or, in more technical terms, that they are interdependent (Kelley et al., 1983).

Some interactions are very brief. On an airplane, you may strike up a friendly conversation with the person sitting next to you, knowing that you will probably never see this person again. At the other extreme are relationships that endure for years and that involve countless interactions. A useful way to think about the progress from casual interactions to close relationships is in terms of the increasing **interdependence** of the partners. A model of pair interdependence developed by Levinger and Snoek (1972) is presented in Figure 10-1. The model shows two people, P and O, at increasing stages of interdependence.

Initially, the two people are completely unaware of each other. They are at a point of *zero contact* when no interaction has occurred. The stage of *awareness* exists when one person notices or learns something about the other, but no direct contact has taken place. For example, we may take an instant dislike to a student who seems to "know it all" in class, even without ever speaking to her directly. Sometimes we learn about another person from a third party; for example, a friend may encourage us to take a particular class because he thought the professor was unusually good.

Awareness can be unilateral (as shown in Figure 10-1 by the one-way arrow from P to O). Or it can be bilateral, as when two strangers glance at each other across a room. The awareness stage can be quite important. If we form a favorable impression of another person, we may take the initiative to interact with that person. Indeed, people sometimes have intense experiences in the awareness stage, as when fans idolize rock singers and movie stars they have never met.

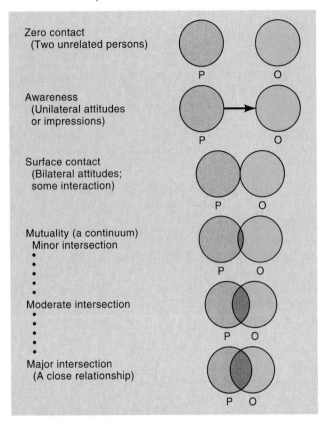

Zero contact
(Two unrelated persons)

Awareness
(Unilateral attitudes
or impressions)

Surface contact
(Bilateral attitudes;
some interaction)

Mutuality (a continuum)
Minor intersection
•
•
•
•

Moderate intersection
•
•
•
•
•

Major intersection
(A close relationship)

Figure 10-1   A model of pair interdependence.
(*Source:* Adapted from Levinger & Snoek, 1972, p. 5.)

The next level, *surface contact,* begins when two people first interact, perhaps by talking or exchanging letters. Surface contact is the beginning of interdependence. When we exchange small talk with a friendly supermarket checker, we are engaging in surface contact. These interactions are usually brief; the topics of conversation are superficial; the impact people have on each other is limited; and the contact is often defined by specific social roles. Many interactions end at this stage of minimal interdependence.

When interaction continues over time, a relationship begins to develop. As the degree of interdependence increases, the pair moves to the stage of *mutuality.* Levinger and Snoek conceptualize mutuality as a continuum ranging from slight interdependence (shown by little overlap in the circles in Figure 10-1) to extensive interdependence (shown by much overlap). For example, during their first year at college, the interdependence of roommates may grow from

a rather limited and emotionally distant mutuality into a close relationship in which their lives are significantly intertwined.

Social psychologists use the term **close relationship** to refer to relationships that involve much interdependence (Berscheid, Snyder & Omoto, 1989; Kelley et al., 1983). These can be relationships with a parent, a best friend, a teacher, a spouse, a coworker, or even an important rival or competitor. All close relationships share three basic characteristics. First, they usually involve frequent interaction that continues over a relatively long period of time. Second, close relationships include many different kinds of activities or events. In a friendship, for example, people discuss many different topics and generally share a wide range of activities and interests. This contrasts with superficial relationships focused around a single activity or topic, such as the occasional exchanges between a homeowner and the local mail carrier.

Third, in close relationships, the influence between people is strong. We may quickly forget a snide remark from a salesclerk, but agonize for weeks about a comment made by our best friend. We may be momentarily grateful for the help offered by a bus driver, but benefit daily from the cooperativeness of our roommate. Further, when two people are highly interdependent, they have the potential for arousing strong emotions in each other. We like to think of our close relationships as a source of positive feelings of love, caring, and concern. But it is also true that our strongest emotions of anger, jealousy, and despair are likely to occur in our closest relationships.

Psychologists are beginning to identify some of the ways in which cultural values and norms affect patterns of social interaction. For example, Harry Reis and Ladd Wheeler (1991) asked college students in Hong Kong, Jordan, and the United States to keep daily diaries of their interactions. An interaction was defined as any encounter with another person or persons that lasted at least 10 minutes and in which the individuals adjusted their behavior in response to one another. Sitting silently next to another student in a lecture would not count as an interaction, but talking to a group of friends at lunch

From childhood to old age, close relationships with loved ones, friends, and colleagues are at the core of human experience.

would qualify. Based on the distinction between individualistic and group-oriented cultures that we introduced in Chapter 1, Reis and Wheeler predicted that students from an individualistic culture such as the United States would have more interactions per day, but would interact less often in groups than students from collectivist cultures such as Hong Kong and Jordan.

The results confirmed these predicted differ-

ences. Americans averaged 6.9 interactions lasting about 346 minutes per day. In contrast, the Chinese had only 3.7 interactions lasting 214 minutes per day, and the Jordanians had 4.7 interactions lasting 216 minutes. Also as predicted, the percentage of interactions that occurred in groups was 29 percent in Hong Kong, 26 percent in Jordan, but only 17 percent in the United States. This study illustrates the basic point that cultural traditions and values shape social relations.

In this chapter, we examine some of the most important features of social relationships. We first present a social exchange perspective on social interaction. Then we discuss the dynamics of self-disclosure, and how the revelation of personal information can create intimacy in a relationship. We conclude with an exploration of power, conflict, and commitment in personal relationships.

A SOCIAL EXCHANGE PERSPECTIVE

The most influential perspective on social relationships is provided by social exchange theories (Blau, 1964; Burgess & Huston, 1979; Kelley & Thibaut, 1978). We should acknowledge at the outset that no single theory can account for all relationship phenomena. Yet exchange theory provides a useful perspective on many aspects of social life. An exchange perspective analyzes the rewards and costs partners give and receive. The theory proposes that we are attracted to those partners we think are best able to reward us, a point we discussed in Chapter 9. The theory also states that we try to arrange our interactions to maximize our own rewards and minimize our costs.

To receive rewards, however, we must also give them. As children we learn a general rule or **norm of reciprocity:** We are expected to reward those who reward us. If people help us, we feel obligated to help them (Gouldner, 1960). If we invite someone to dinner, we expect that person to return the invitation in the future. Social interaction can thus be viewed as a process of exchange between partners.

Rewards and Costs

A reward is anything a person gains from an interaction, such as feeling loved or getting financial assistance. What is rewarding for one person may be of little value for someone else. A useful analysis of the rewards of social interaction was proposed by Foa and Foa (1974), and is

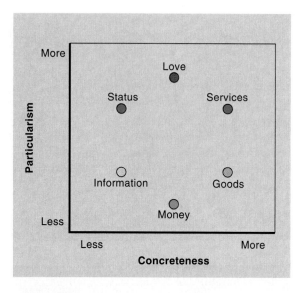

Figure 10-2 Rewards people exchange. (*Source:* Adapted from U. G. Foa, Interpersonal and economic resources, *Science, 171,* 1971, p. 347. Copyright 1971 by the American Association for the Advancement of Science.)

shown in Figure 10-2. They identify six basic types of rewards: love, money, status, information, goods, and services. These can be classified along two dimensions. The dimension of particularism concerns how much the value of a reward depends on who provides it. The value of love, or more specifically the value of such things as hugs and tender words, depends very much on who provides them. Thus, love is a particularistic reward. In contrast, money is useful regardless of who it comes from; money is a nonparticularistic or universal reward. When we say that a relationship is very special to us, we often mean that it provides unique or particularistic rewards that we cannot get elsewhere. The second dimension, concreteness, captures the distinction between tangible rewards—things you can see, smell, and touch—and nonconcrete or symbolic rewards, such as advice or social approval.

Costs are the negative consequences that occur in an interaction or relationship. An interaction might be costly because it requires a great deal of time and energy, because it entails much conflict, because other people disapprove of the relationship and criticize us for it, and so on. A further cost of an interaction is that it may deprive us of the opportunity to do other rewarding activities: If you spend the weekend skiing with a friend, you do not have the time to study for an exam or to visit your parents.

Evaluating Outcomes

Social exchange theory assumes that people keep track of the rewards and costs of a particular interaction or relationship. But people seldom do this very explicitly; we do not usually make lists of the good and bad things about a relationship. Nonetheless, we are aware of the costs and rewards involved. In particular, we focus on the overall outcome we get in a relationship—that is, whether on balance the relationship is profitable for us (rewards outweigh costs) or whether we are experiencing an overall loss (costs outweigh rewards). People do not necessarily evaluate relationship outcomes very consciously or systematically, but the basic process is reflected in such statements as "I'm really getting a lot out of this relationship" or "I don't think our relationship is worth it anymore."

People use several standards for evaluating relationship outcomes. For example, at a party, we may avoid talking to John, whom we find totally obnoxious. Instead, we gravitate to Mike, a rather friendly sort who tells good stories. We continue to chat with Mike until we notice that our best friend Seth has just arrived. At this point, we excuse ourself and go talk to Seth. As this example highlights, we evaluate individuals differently as interaction partners—finding John unacceptable, Mike reasonably positive, and Seth best of all.

The simplest standard for evaluating a relationship is whether it is profitable or costly. A conversation with John is a negative, unpleasant experience, whereas conversing with both Mike and Seth is worthwhile. Also important are comparisons we make between relationships, assessing how one relationship compares to others we have been in or that we know about. Thibaut and Kelley (1959) have emphasized two main comparison standards.

The **comparison level** reflects the quality of outcomes a person believes he or she deserves. This baseline standard differs from one type of interaction to another: Our standard for interacting with a salesclerk differs from our standard for interacting with a romantic partner. Our comparison level reflects our past experiences in relationships. For example, we may consider whether a current dating relationship is as good as those we have had in the past. Or we may compare our new boss at work to our past experiences with other supervisors. We may also compare a current relationship to those we have seen in movies, heard about from friends, or read about in popular psychology books. The comparison level is our personal belief about what constitutes an acceptable relationship. Our comparison level for a particular type of relationship may change as we have new experiences.

A second major standard is the **comparison level for alternatives.** This involves assessing how one relationship stacks up against other relationships that are currently available to us. Is our current dating partner better or worse than the other people we could be going out with right now? Is our current boss better or worse than other people we might realistically work for at this point in our lives? If our relationship is the best we think possible, we may stay in it, even if the gains are small. In contrast, even if a relationship is profitable in absolute terms, we may leave it if a more profitable alternative becomes available.

Coordinating Outcomes

A key fact about interaction is that one person's outcomes are interlinked with the outcomes of the partner. Consider some of the coordination problems that might be encountered by two strangers who sit next to each other on a long airplane trip. Carl arrives first, completely fills the overhead compartment with his carry-on luggage, and claims the middle armrest for his use. A rather gregarious type, Carl hopes to spend the trip talking to the person sitting next to him. Kathy, on the other hand, has brought along work to do and plans to spend the trip reading. She's somewhat annoyed to find the

When friends enjoy many of the same activities, they have an easy time coordinating their interaction. In technical terms, they have correspondent outcomes—what is rewarding for one is rewarding for the other.

overhead compartment full, but manages to find another place for her belongings. After a few pleasantries, Kathy makes it clear that she does not want to begin a long conversation, and Carl thumbs idly through a magazine. Some time later, Carl pulls down the window shade and tries to take a nap. This further annoys Kathy, who was hoping for a glimpse of the landscape below. As Carl nods off, he begins to snore. In frustration, Kathy finally gets up to see if there is another vacant seat. In this example, a failure in coordination prompts one person to try to avoid any further interaction with the other person.

How easy or difficult it is for two people to coordinate their outcomes depends on how much they share common interests and goals. When partners like to do many of the same things and value the same activities, they will have relatively few coordination problems (Surra & Longstreth, 1990). In such cases, they are said to have *correspondent outcomes*, because their outcomes correspond—what is good for one is good for the other, and what is bad for one is bad for both (Thibaut & Kelley, 1959).

When partners have different preferences and values, they have *noncorrespondent outcomes* and, as a result, are more prone to conflicts of interest and coordination problems. In general, partners with similar backgrounds and attitudes tend to have fewer problems of coordination, and so may find it easier to develop a mutually rewarding relationship.

Of course, even well-matched partners experience conflicts of interest from time to time. When this occurs, the partners must negotiate a settlement. Consider a young married couple deciding how to spend the income tax refund they just received. The wife would like to buy a new sofa; the husband would like to buy a video recorder. Since the couple has a limited amount of money available and cannot afford both the sofa and the VCR, they must coordinate their use of the funds and resolve their conflicting interests.

One common solution is to select a less preferred alternative that is acceptable to both partners. The young couple might decide to spend the money on a trip—neither person's first choice, but an alternative that is attractive to both. Another possibility is to take turns, buying the sofa this year and the VCR next year. Coordinating outcomes is a basic issue in relationships (Thibaut & Kelley, 1959).

Settling conflicts of interest by negotiation is at best a time-consuming activity and at worst a source of arguments and bad feelings. Over time, partners often develop rules or **social norms** about coordinating their behavior. Neither spouse may like to take out the garbage or pay the bills, but they may agree that he will do one if she will do the other. Shared norms reduce the need for continual negotiation to arrive at coordinated behavior patterns.

In Chapter 1, we defined **social roles** as clusters of rules about how people should behave in a particular type of interaction or relationship. Roles provide solutions for some of the problems of coordination that participants are likely to encounter. In many types of relationships, cultural rules prescribe certain coordinated patterns. At work, there are usually fairly clear understandings about what the employer and employee will do, and how they will interact. Lawyers and their secretaries do not negotiate about who will draft legal briefs and who will type them, or who will answer the phone and who will make court appearances. Traditional marriage provides another example of a relationship in which roles are at least partly predetermined. The traditional pattern is for wives to do the housekeeping tasks and for husbands to have paying jobs.

When individuals act on the basis of pre-existing cultural rules, they are engaging in the process of *role-taking.* As we grow up, we learn many social roles that guide our interactions with other people. We can contrast this process of role-taking, in which people adopt or conform to cultural roles, with the process of *role-making,* in which people develop their own shared norms for social interaction (Turner, 1962). In many social settings, people improvise and create their own solutions to problems of interdependence. When two friends decide to share an apartment, for example, they need to negotiate who will do what, when, and how: Who will be in charge of paying bills? How will housekeeping be arranged? What are the rules about overnight guests? Many social interactions involve a mix of role-taking and role-making. For instance, even though tradition offers general guidelines for marital roles, each couple must arrive at their own unique agreements about organizing their life together.

According to traditional dating roles, the boyfriend should plan the couple's activities and pay the bills. Today, many young couples are redefining dating roles by sharing both decision making and expenses.

When social guidelines are vague or in the process of change, individuals have greater freedom of action, but they also must put more effort into coordinating interaction successfully. For example, many people today are questioning traditional sex roles. As a result, dating and married couples may be uncertain about who should do what. A couple out on a first date may hesitate as they approach a doorway, trying to decide if the man should open the door for the woman or not. They may pause uncomfortably after a dinner out, waiting to decide whether to split the bill or have the man pay for both. Over time through the process of interacting, couples arrive at understandings about the rules in their relationship that permit smoother, less effortful interaction.

Fair Exchange

People are most content when they perceive their social relations to be fair. We don't like to feel exploited by others, nor do we usually like to take advantage of others. Equity theory, an offshoot of social exchange theory, focuses on fairness in relationships (Greenberg & Cohen, 1982; Walster, Walster, & Berscheid, 1978).

People use various rules for determining whether or not a relationship is fair. Consider the case of two teenage boys trying to decide how to divide a pizza. They might decide to "share and share alike," using the equality rule that everyone should receive equal outcomes. Research suggests that people are more likely to use the *equality* principle when they are interacting with friends rather than strangers (Austin, 1980). Children are more likely than adults to use the equality rule, perhaps because it is the simplest principle (Hook & Cook, 1979).

In dividing the pizza, the boys might instead use the principle of "to each according to need," the idea that the *relative needs* of the people should be taken into account. By this rule, one boy might get a larger piece of pizza if he was especially hungry, or if he hadn't had pizza in a long time. This principle is illustrated by parents who spend much more money on a child who needs dental braces than on another child who has perfect teeth. Parents gear their med-

Learning to share with friends is an important step in understanding principles of fairness in social relations.

ical and dental expenditures to the needs of each child.

A third fairness rule is *equity* or distributive justice. The key idea is that a person's profits should be proportional to his or her contributions (Deutsch, 1985). Here, the boy who contributed more to the cost of buying the pizza, or who had exerted greater effort by making the pizza himself, should be entitled to a larger portion. In this view, equity exists when two or more people receive the same ratio of outcomes to contributions. In more technical terms:

$$\frac{\text{Outcomes of person P}}{\text{Contributions of person P}} = \frac{\text{Outcomes of person O}}{\text{Contributions of person O}}$$

This is the fairness rule that has been the focus of equity research.

Equity theory has three basic assumptions:

1. People in relationships try to maximize their outcomes.
2. Dyads and groups can maximize their collective rewards by evolving rules or norms about how to divide rewards fairly among everyone concerned.
3. When individuals perceive that a relationship is inequitable, they feel distressed and take steps to restore equity.

Research has supported several specific predictions from equity theory (Greenberg & Cohen, 1982). It has been shown, for example, that when relationships are not equitable, both partners feel distressed. It makes sense that the underbenefited (exploited) person feels distress. But research shows that the overbenefited person may also feel distress, perhaps because he or she feels guilty or uncomfortable about the imbalance.

There is also evidence that people will try to restore equity when they perceive a relationship to be unfair. A person can do this in two ways. First, he or she can restore actual equity. For example, a roommate might agree that he hasn't been doing his share of the housework and therefore do extra work to compensate. Second, individuals sometimes use cognitive strategies to alter their perception of the imbalance, thus restoring psychological equity. The roommate might distort reality and argue that he really has done a fair share of the work, thus avoiding the need to change his behavior. Whether people restore actual or psychological equity depends on the costs and benefits associated with each particular strategy. Finally, if it is not possible to restore equity in either of these ways, a person may try to end the relationship.

Much of the research on equity has come from laboratory studies of strangers interacting for short periods of time. More recently, however, studies have begun to show that equity considerations can sometimes influence close relationships (Sprecher, 1992). Satisfaction in dating and marriage is affected by perceptions of equity, with underbenefitted partners generally reporting lower satisfaction. For instance, a study of married and cohabiting couples found that individuals who reported less equity were less happy with their relationship, and the negative effects of inequity on satisfaction persisted one year later (Van Yperen & Buunk, 1990). A concern with fairness may be most important at the beginning of a relationship. A longitudinal study found that equity was a factor in satisfaction early in premarital relationships but not a few months later (Cate, Lloyd, & Long, 1988). Over time, individuals may develop trust in their partner's good intentions and may monitor exchange patterns less closely. The importance of equity for long-term relationships has not been firmly demonstrated.

There also appear to be individual differences in the effects of equity on relationship satisfaction. Individuals who score high on a measure of general concern about fairness in relationships may be more negatively affected by inequity than other people (Sprecher, 1992). Further, women with feminist or nontraditional attitudes about sex roles may be especially sensitive to equity concerns, and so experience greater dissatisfaction than other women or men do if they believe their relationship is unfair (Van Yperen & Buunk, 1991).

Finally, research has generally found that equity is less important to happiness than the absolute level of rewards a person receives in a relationship. Satisfaction is highest when people believe they are getting many rewards, regardless of whether or not they perceive the distribution of rewards to be entirely fair (Surra, 1990). If we believe we are getting a lot from a relationship, we tend to be happy, even if we think we may be getting a bit less than we deserve.

Beyond Exchange

Social exchange principles help us understand many different kinds of relationships. Most people recognize that exchange influences casual relationship, but may resist the idea that exchange factors also govern our most intimate relationships. It is certainly unromantic to suggest, as did sociologist Erving Goffman, that "A proposal of marriage in our society tends to be a way in which a man sums up his social attributes and suggests that hers are not so much bet-ter as to preclude a merger or a partnership in these matters" (1952, p. 456).

Social psychologist Zick Rubin voiced a common concern about exchange theory:

> The notions that people are "commodities" and social relationships are "transactions" will surely make many readers squirm. Exchange theory postulates that human relationships are based first and foremost on self-interest. As such, it often seems to portray friendship as motivated only by what one person can get from another and to redefine love as a devious power game. . . . But although we might prefer to believe otherwise, we must face up to the fact that our attitudes toward other people are determined to a large extent by our assessments of the rewards they hold for us. (1973, p. 82).

It may be helpful to remember that although exchange theory borrows terminology from economics, the rewards and costs involved are often personal and unique: An adorable smile and shared secrets are as much a part of exchange theory as fancy cars and expensive presents.

You may have noticed that in some of your relationships, exchange issues seem to be much more important than in others. For example, you may be willing to trade work shifts with a coworker this week, but clearly expect that he'll do the same for you next week. In contrast, you and your best friend may do many favors for each other and help each other in times of need without consciously keeping mental records of what you give and receive.

Clark and Mills (1979) have distinguished between what they call *exchange relationships* and *communal relationships*. In both types of relationships, exchange processes operate, but the rules governing the giving and receiving of benefits differ significantly. In exchange relationships, people give benefits with the expectation of receiving comparable benefits in return soon afterward. Exchange relationships occur most often with strangers or casual acquaintances and in business relations. In exchange relationships, people feel no special responsibility for the welfare of the other person. In contrast, in communal relationships, people do feel a personal responsibility for the needs of the other.

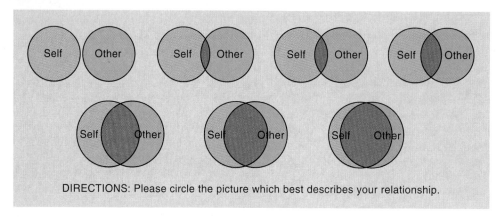

DIRECTIONS: Please circle the picture which best describes your relationship.

Figure 10-3 The Inclusion of Other in the Self (IOS) Scale. (*Source:* Adapted from A. Aron, E. N. Aron, & D. Smollan. Inclusion of other in the self scale and the structure of interpersonal closeness. *Journal of Personality and Social Psychology, 63,* p. 597. Copyright 1992 by the American Psychological Association.)

Communal relationships usually occur with family, friends, and romantic partners. In these relationships, people provide benefits to the partner in order to show concern and to respond to the other's needs, with no expectation of receiving similar benefits in the near future.

Mills and Clark (1982) have conducted a program of research to identify differences between these two relationship orientations. For example, one study found that people pay more attention to the needs of a partner in a communal relationship than in an exchange relationship (Clark, Mills, & Powell, 1986). Another study found that people in a communal relationship would prefer to talk about emotional topics such as things that make them happy or sad; people in an exchange relationship preferred such unemotional topics as their favorite restaurant or knowledge of gardening (Clark & Taraban, 1991). Another recent study showed that a person is perceived as more altruistic if he or she offers to help a casual acquaintance (weak communal relationship where assistance is not necessarily expected) rather than a close friend (strong communal relationship where assistance is typically offered). Similarly, a person is seen as more selfish if he or she does not offer help to a close friend than if he or she fails to assist an acquaintance (Mills, Clark, & Mehta, 1992).

In long-term relationships, patterns of reciprocity and rules of exchange become complex. In our most intimate relationships, we may develop a sense of unity or "we-ness" so that we perceive benefiting a loved one as a way of benefiting ourselves. In recent research, Arthur Aron, Elaine Aron, and Danny Smollan (1992) have investigated the idea that in a close relationship, we come to see the other person as part of ourself. They have shown research participants the pictures presented in Figure 10-3 and asked them to indicate which picture best describes their relationship with a particular person, such as a dating partner or parent. Preliminary findings suggest that people find this an intuitively sensible way to characterize a relationship. As the overlap between self and other increases, people tend to report greater feelings of closeness and more interconnected behaviors such as spending time together. Such a tendency suggests one way in which close relationships may move beyond simple principles of social exchange.

SELF-DISCLOSURE AND INTIMACY

Conversation is an essential aspect of human interaction. When a friend reveals that his childhood fear of lawn sprinklers forced him to walk blocks out of his way to get to elementary school, we feel closer to him emotionally. When a coworker takes us aside to explain that her absence from work was not due to the flu as most people believed, but rather to a miscarriage, we sense a bond of trust and openness. **Self-disclosure** is a special type of conversation in which we share intimate information and feelings with another person. Self-disclosure can be an important pathway to intimacy.

Sometimes we reveal facts about ourselves that might otherwise be unavailable to a listener—the kind of work we do, where we live, or how we voted in the recent election. This is known as *descriptive disclosure,* because our revelations describe things about ourselves (Morton, 1978). A different type of self-disclosure occurs when we reveal our personal opinions and feelings—our affection for another person, our guilt about being overweight, how much we hate our current job. This is called *evaluative disclosure,* because emphasis is given to our personal assessment of people and situations.

There are many reasons why we disclose information to another person (Derlega & Grzelak, 1979). For example, we might tell someone a secret as a way to create greater intimacy in a relationship. Five of the main reasons for self-disclosure are summarized below:

1. *Expression.* Sometimes we talk about our feelings to "get them off our chest." After a hard day at work, we may eagerly tell a friend just how angry we are at our boss and how unappreciated we feel. Simply being able to express our feelings is one reason for disclosure.

2. *Self-clarification.* In the process of sharing our feelings or experiences with others, we may gain greater understanding and self-awareness. Talking to a friend about a problem can help us to clarify our thoughts about the situation.

3. *Social validation.* By seeing how a listener reacts to our self-disclosures, we get information about the correctness and appropriateness of our views. Other people may reassure us that our reactions are "perfectly normal" or suggest that we're "blowing things out of proportion." In

Self-disclosure is a special type of conversation in which we share intimate information and feelings with another person.

either case, listeners provides useful information about social reality.

4. *Social control.* We may reveal or conceal information about ourselves as a means of social control. For instance, we may deliberately refrain from telling things about ourselves to protect our privacy. We may emphasize things we think will make a favorable impression on our listener. In extreme cases, people may deliberately lie to exploit others, as when an imposter claims to be a lawyer but actually has no legal training.

5. *Relationship development.* The sharing of personal information and confidences is an important way to begin a relationship and to move toward increasing levels of intimacy.

In the next section, we will consider how self-disclosure contributes to the growth of personal relationships.

Self-disclosure and Relationship Development

Self-disclosure is one important way to get to know another person and develop a closer relationship. Altman and Taylor (1973) proposed a model to describe how self-disclosure affects the development of a relationship. In their view, the process of forming an intimate relationship

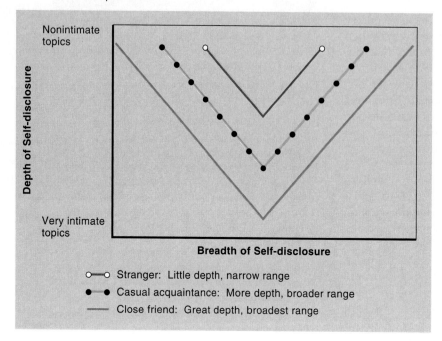

Breadth of Self-disclosure

Figure 10-4 The breadth and depth of self-disclosure are represented as "wedges" into the personality and experience of the person. For strangers, the wedge is narrow and superficial. For a close friend, the wedge is deeper (more intimate) and broader in the range of topics disclosed. (*Source:* Adapted from Altman & Haythorn, 1965, p. 422.)

involves "penetrating" beyond the surface of another person to gain greater and greater knowledge about the person's inner self. Altman and Taylor use the term **social penetration** to describe this process. As shown in Figure 10-4, social penetration occurs along two major dimensions of depth and breadth.

As relationships develop from superficial to intimate, people disclose increasingly more personal things about themselves. This is the depth dimension of social penetration. We might willingly talk with a casual acquaintance about our preferences in food and music, but reserve for close friends discussions of our anxieties and personal ambitions. Only after many years of friendship did one woman reveal to her childhood friend the pain she had suffered in high school because her wealthy mother forced her to wear torn underwear beneath her fashionable clothes since "no one would see."

Relationships also develop from narrow to broad self-disclosure as, over time, people discuss a wider range of topics and share diverse activities. These phases of relationship development are shown in Figure 10-4 as "wedges" that one person makes into the personality and life experiences of another.

The process of getting to know another person is more complex than Figure 10-4 suggests. We don't simply disclose more and more each day. Rather, we may experience cycles of seeking intimacy and avoiding it (Altman et al., 1981). Sometimes we are open, confiding, and candid with a friend, and at other times we are more restrained and distant (Vanlear, 1991). Nonetheless, the development of intimacy results from the cumulative history of self-disclosure in a relationship (Altman & Taylor, 1973).

Reciprocity, Liking, and Self-disclosure

Self-disclosure tends to be reciprocated (Ludwig, Franco, & Malloy, 1986; Miller & Kenny, 1986). If we share intimate information with another person, he or she is likely to respond with equally personal information. If we talk in superficialities, so will the other person. One explanation for this effect is the norm of reciprocity: If someone tells us something personal, we are expected to respond with a comparable revelation.

Liking is an important cause of self-disclosure. We reveal much more to people we like and trust than to those we dislike or barely know. The more interesting question is how the act of self-disclosing affects liking. One view might be that self-disclosure is inherently rewarding, and "the more the better," so the more a person reveals, the more we will like him or her. Research generally supports a different view, however, that we like people most whose self-disclosure is carefully paced and reciprocal (Altman & Taylor, 1973).

For self-disclosure to enhance liking, it must be appropriate to the situation (Derlega & Chaikin, 1975). The disclosure must be slow enough that it does not become threatening to either person. If it races ahead prematurely into areas of great personal intimacy, it will arouse anxiety and defensiveness. Someone who "comes on too strong, too fast" will be disliked (Kaplan et al., 1974). A gradual process of mutual self-disclosure, paced over time, spurs the growth of a relationship. Altman and Taylor proposed that we like best people who disclose at about the same level of intimacy as we do. Someone who discloses more personal details than we do threatens us with a premature acceleration into intimate territory, and we may want to put on the brakes. If we are disclosing at a more intimate level than the other person, we may feel vulnerable or foolish.

There is much evidence that disclosure reciprocity is a key factor in liking. In an early study, Chaikin and Derlega (1974) used a procedure that enabled them to manipulate experimentally the intimacy level of self-disclosures in a pair. Their method was to videotape two actresses improvising a first-acquaintance encounter in a school cafeteria. Each actress did this in two ways: at a high and a low level of self-disclosure. Then the experimenters presented the videotaped conversations to subjects in each of the four combinations of self-disclosure: both women high in self-disclosure, both low, high–low, or low–high.

In the high self-disclosure case, one woman immediately confided about her relationship with her boyfriend, who was her first sexual partner, and about her parents' reactions to their relationship. The other woman's high-intimacy disclosures concerned her mother's nervous breakdown and hospitalization, her fighting with her mother, and the possible divorce of her parents. In the low self-disclosure cases, the women talked about the problems of commuting to school, where they went to high school, and the courses they were taking. After watching one of the videotapes, subjects indicated how much they liked each of the women. The main finding was that liking for both women was higher when they disclosed at the *same* level of intimacy than when they were at different levels. Breaking the reciprocity norm led to less liking, but for different reasons. The woman who disclosed relatively little was perceived as cold, whereas the more intimate norm breaker was seen as maladjusted.

The link between self-disclosure and liking depends on the meaning we attach to a person's revelations and to our own goals in the relationship (Miller, 1990). If Suzanne wants to get closer to her roommate Barbara, she may view Barbara's disclosure that her father has life-threatening cancer as a positive sign of growing trust in their relationship. Eager to help her friend, Suzanne may welcome Barbara's tearful revelation as an opportunity to show understanding and sympathy. In contrast, if the stranger sitting next to Suzanne in the lecture hall strikes up a conversation and begins to talk about her father's struggles with alcoholism, Suzanne may feel embarrassed, wonder about the person's judgment, and try to change the topic. The impact of self-disclosure on liking depends on the nature of the relationship between the individuals.

The Hazards of Self-disclosure

Self-disclosure is an important type of interaction that can enhance liking and the development of a relationship. We often want to share our feelings and experiences with others. But it is also true that we sometimes want to conceal our feelings, to keep our thoughts to ourselves, and to protect our private inner life from scrutiny. In short, our goal is often to control the information others have about us—sharing what we want when we want. The term *informational privacy* refers to our ability to control who knows what about us (Burgoon et al., 1989).

The desire to limit and control the sharing of information highlights the point that self-disclosure can be risky. Revealing personal information makes us vulnerable. One college student hesitated for many months about telling her mother that she is a lesbian, fearing a rift in her close-knit family. When she did reveal her sexual orientation, her mother not only expressed shock and displeasure, but insisted that the daughter seek psychotherapy and told her employer at a summer camp that the daughter was "unfit" to work with children. Many lesbians and gay men would like to be open about their sexual orientation with relatives, friends, and coworkers, but fear that disclosure may lead to hostility, rejection, or discrimination (Franke & Leary, 1991).

Valerian Derlega (1984) has suggested some of the many possible risks individuals may incur when they self-disclose:

1. *Indifference.* We may share information with another person in a bid to begin a new relationship. Sometimes, our disclosure is reciprocated by the other person and a relationship develops. At other times, however, we may find that the other person is indifferent to our disclosures and not at all interested in getting to know us.

2. *Rejection.* Information we reveal about ourselves may lead to social rejection. For example, a college student may not tell her roommate that she has epilepsy, out of a concern that misinformation and fear will lead the roommate to reject her.

3. *Loss of control.* There is some truth to the old adage that "knowledge is power." Sometimes, others use information we share with them to hurt us or to control our behavior. Derlega suggests, for instance, that a teenage boy may tell a friend some little-known but potentially embarrassing information about his fear of women. In an angry moment, the friend may try to intimidate the young man by reminding him of his weakness.

4. *Betrayal.* When we reveal personal information to someone we often assume, or even explicitly request, that the knowledge be treated confidentially. Unfortunately, such confidences are sometimes betrayed.

Not surprisingly, people are most likely to disclose personal information to trusted confidants such as a spouse, close friend, therapist, or religious advisor, or occasionally to people they will never meet again such as a stranger on a bus.

Culture and Self-disclosure

In American society, the sharing of personal feelings is often considered the hallmark of a good friendship or marriage. This is consistent with our cultural emphasis on the importance of the individual and the expression of each person's unique feelings and experiences. However, other cultures have different norms and values about self-disclosure.

Consider, for example, comparisons of our own individualistic culture and the more collectively oriented culture of Japan (Barnlund, 1989). In general, social relations in Japan are more formal and restrained. The Japanese are generally less revealing than their American peers. When an American meets a new person, it is common to ask if the person is married and has children, what type of work the person does, where they went to school, and so on. Americans view this as a routine way of getting to know another person. In contrast, two Japanese meeting for the first time would not ask such personal questions. In Japan, such inquiries would be considered forward and impertinent.

In a cross-cultural study of self-disclosure, Barnlund (1989) asked several hundred Japanese and Americans college students how much they had disclosed to a number of friends and companions on various topics. Disclosure was rated on a 7-point scale from no disclosure to disclosure in "great detail." As shown in Figure 10-5, everyone revealed more to close friends than to distant companions. Cultural differences also emerged, with the Japanese revealing significantly less. Another study (Ting-Toomey, 1991) investigated self-disclosure to an opposite-sex close friend among college students in Japan and the United States. Again, the Americans reported significantly higher levels of self-disclosure than did the Japanese.

If culture influences the general amount and

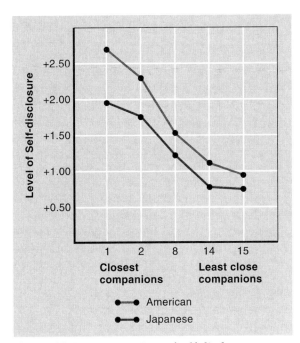

Figure 10-5 A comparison of self-disclosure to closest and least close companions by college students in the United States and Japan. Everyone discloses more to close than to distant companions. But at each level of closeness, Japanese students report revealing less than their American peers. (*Source:* Adapted from Barnlund, 1989, p. 111).

Gender and Self-disclosure

Stereotypes depict men as "silent types" who keep their feelings to themselves, and women as "talkers" who freely share confidences. As one wife complained about her husband, "He doesn't ever think there's anything to talk about. I'm the one who has to nag him to talk" (cited in L. Rubin, 1976, p. 124). How accurate is this stereotype about gender differences in self-disclosure? A recent meta-analysis of 205 studies of self-disclosure found a small but statistically significant sex difference (Dindia & Allen, 1992). Women tend to reveal more than men, and this sex difference is greater in same-sex than in opposite-sex relationships (Reis, 1992).

In same-sex relationships, women do indeed disclose more to women than men disclose to men (Dolgin, Meyer, & Schwartz, 1991; Reis, Senchak, & Solomon, 1985). Throughout adult life, women are more likely than men to have an intimate, same-sex confidant and to emphasize the sharing of personal information. In a study of college students, for example, women were more likely than men to say that they enjoy "just talking" to their best female friend and to indicate that talking helped form the basis of their relationship. In contrast, college men empha-

content of verbal disclosure, it may also affect the connections between personal revelations and satisfaction with a relationship. For instance, whereas many Americans might view low levels of self-disclosure as a sign of marital problems, couples from other cultures might not consider verbal disclosure indicative of the quality of a marriage. Evidence for such cultural differences comes from a study comparing the correlates of marital satisfaction among American couples and couples from India, some who had arranged marriages and some who had chosen their spouse in a "love match" (Yelsma & Athappilly, 1988). For Americans, higher satisfaction was associated with greater verbal disclosure. Couples who talked more about personal matters were happier. The same was also true for Indian women and men in love-based marriages. But for Indian couples in arranged marriages, marital satisfaction was not related to patterns of verbal communication.

In same-sex relationships, women tend to disclose more personal information to women than men disclose to men.

sized sharing activities with their best male friend (Caldwell & Peplau, 1982).

In opposite-sex relationships, gender differences in self-disclosure are less clear-cut. The norm of reciprocity encourages male and female partners to disclose at comparable levels, with some couples disclosing a lot and others revealing relatively little personal information. In general, people disclose more to their romantic partner or spouse than to anyone else, and today's young people expect more self-disclosure in their intimate relationships than did earlier generations (Rands & Levinger, 1979). College dating couples usually disclose at quite high and equal levels (see Rubin, Hill, Peplau, & Dunkel-Schetter, 1980). It should be noted, however, that when exceptions to this equal-disclosure pattern occur in male–female couples, it is usually the man who discloses less.

The fact that men and women often disclose at equal levels does not mean that they necessarily reveal the same kinds of personal information. One study of college students found that in male–female relationships, women were more likely to reveal their weaknesses and to conceal their strengths; men showed a reverse pattern of disclosing their strengths and concealing their weaknesses (Hacker, 1981). Another study found that men disclosed more on "masculine" topics such as when they had been aggressive or had taken risks. Women disclosed more on "feminine" topics such as when they felt childlike or were sensitive about their appearance (Derlega, Durham, Gockel, & Sholis, 1981).

In summary, research does not support the stereotype that all men are inexpressive all the time. There is a tendency for women to reveal more than men, but this effect is small and varies from situation to situation. In heterosexual dating and marriage, men and women often disclose at similar levels. Sex differences may be most pronounced in same-sex relationships, with women friends showing a preference for talking, and men friends showing a greater interest in shared activities.

How are we to explain these sex differences? There is much evidence that cultural norms affect patterns of self-disclosure. In American culture, emotional expression is generally acceptable for women. In contrast, American men are taught to conceal tender emotions and personal concerns, especially from other men (Doyle, 1989). Men are encouraged to channel their emotional revelations exclusively to women, especially to a girlfriend or wife. In other cultures, however, norms about self-disclosure are quite different. As a result, individuals from non-Western cultures do not necessarily show the same patterns of self-disclosure and intimacy found in the United States.

Harry Reis and Ladd Wheeler (1991) compared the self-disclosure patterns of college students in the United States, Hong Kong, and Jordan. Cultural traditions in both Hong Kong and Jordan downplay opposite-sex intimacy for unmarried students and encourage same-sex bonds, especially for men. Consequently, the researchers predicted that whereas American men would disclose relatively little to each other, men in Hong Kong and in Jordan would show higher levels of male–male disclosure. As predicted, the mean level of disclosure in male–male pairs was 6.6 in the United States, 8.2 in Hong Kong, and 8.4 in Jordan. It appears that male socialization in the United States suppresses intimacy among men, in contrast to cultural norms that permit higher levels of male–male intimacy in Hong Kong and Jordan.

Intimacy as an Interpersonal Process

Self-disclosure is one component of intimacy in a relationship. But the mere revelation of personal information is not sufficient to create the psychological experience of closeness. Harry Reis and Phillip Shaver (1988) proposed a model of the way intimacy is created in the interaction of two people. Their model is illustrated in Figure 10-6, which provides an example of an interaction between Anne and Betty. The model involves three major steps.

Step 1. The intimacy process begins when one individual reveals personal feelings or information to another. This sharing of information can be done verbally through self-disclosure, or nonverbally by "body

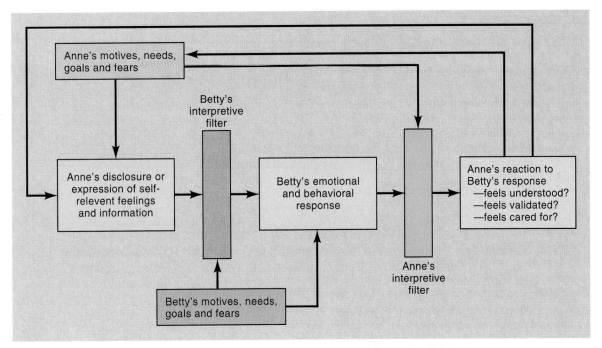

Figure 10-6 Intimacy as an interpersonal process. (*Source:* Adapted from H. T. Reis & P. Shaver, Intimacy as an interpersonal process. In S. W. Duck (Ed.), *Handbook of Personal Relationships,* p. 375. Copyright 1988 by John Wiley & Sons.)

language." In this example, Anne is upset about a problem she is having at work and decides to share her feelings with her friend, Betty. Anne's revelation is triggered by her private mental state—her motives, needs, goals, or fears.

Step 2. As the interaction continues, Betty responds to Anne's disclosure with sympathy and warmth. She moves her chair closer to Anne and asks relevant questions. Betty's behavior reflects her own motives (for example, to be a good friend) and her personal interpretation of Anne's story (technically called her "interpretive filter"). Betty believes that her friend has been treated unfairly at work and tells her so.

Step 3. Anne appreciates Betty's concern. She interprets Betty's questions as a sign of interest and a desire to be helpful (this is shown as Anne's interpretive filter). As a result, Anne feels that Betty has understood her and has agreed with her views. She feels that Betty cares for her well-being.

According to Reis and Shaver, intimacy results from interactions of this sort, in which one person's actions evoke a response from another that makes the person feel understood, validated, and cared for. Self-disclosure by itself does not create intimacy. Rather, the discloser must feel that the listener accepts and understands the discloser's views (Lin, 1992). Reis and Shaver believe that intimate interactions like these promote feelings of trust and emotional closeness that are fundamental to the development of personal relationships.

THE BALANCE OF POWER

In any interaction, people often have different preferences for their activities and try to influence each other in order to accomplish their own goals. **Social power** refers to a person's ability to influence deliberately the behavior, thoughts, or feelings of another person (Huston, 1983; Molm, 1988). In some relationships, both individuals are equally influential. In other relationships,

CULTURAL HIGHLIGHT

Power in Mexican American and African American Marriages

Stereotypes often depict striking ethnic differences among married couples in the United States. Arlene Skolnick (1987) described ethnic stereotypes about marital power in these terms: "While the black family was seen as pathological because of its presumed female dominance, the Mexican American family was viewed as unhealthy because of its patriarchy. In contrast, the ideal middle-class Anglo family was seen as egalitarian and democratic" (p. 179). However, the results of several careful studies of the balance of power in Mexican American and African American marriages strongly refute these stereotypes.

Mexican American Marriages. Are Chicano families typically dominated by an all-powerful husband? To find out, Hawkes and Taylor (1975) interviewed Mexican American farm labor families in California. The interviewers were women who themselves lived in the migrant worker family camps and had been trained to assist in the research. Power was measured by responses to two different kinds of questions: questions about decision making and questions about who actually acts on the decisions. Decision-making questions assessed who decides how to spend the money, how many children the family should have, how to raise the children, and so on. Action-taking questions asked who pays the bills, who takes steps to

control how many children they have, who disciplines the children, and so on. Based on answers to these questions, 62 percent of the families were classified as egalitarian, that is, as having marriages in which both the husband and the wife made decisions and carried them out. The remaining marriages were fairly evenly divided between ones in which the husband or the wife had more influence.

Other studies with both middle-class and working-class families have replicated this finding: a majority of Mexican American marriages are egalitarian (Peplau & Campbell, 1989). Staples and Mirande (1980) conclude that "virtually every systematic study of conjugal roles in the Chicano family has found egalitarianism to be the predominant pattern across socioeconomic groups, educational levels, urban–rural residence, and region of the country" (p. 894).

African American Marriages. Black families in the United States have often been depicted as matriarchial or female-dominated. Some have used the term matriarchy to refer to the greater frequency of female-headed households among African Americans as compared to other ethnic groups. We are interested in a different question: whether the wife is typically the dominant spouse in African-American marriages.

In an illustrative study, Dolores

Mack (1971) recruited 80 couples, evenly divided among black working class, black middle class, white working class, and white middle class families. Mack used three separate measures of power. She assessed spouses' perceptions of the power balance in their marriage. She observed how couples behaved in power-relevant situations, such as coming to a joint decision about a matter on which they initially disagreed. She also observed couples in a bargaining situation. In general, couples tended to show fairly equal power in these situations. No racial differences were found on any of Mack's measures. Black wives were no more—or less—powerful than their white counterparts in any of the research activities. Other studies have also found that equal power is the most common pattern among black couples (DeJarnett & Raven, 1981; Peplau & Campbell, 1989).

In summary, research on Mexican American, African American, and Anglo marriages in the United States finds few overall differences in the frequency of egalitarian, male-dominant, and female-dominant relationships. There is considerable diversity within each ethnic group, and much commonality across groups. Stereotypes that black marriages are matriarchal and Chicano marriages are patriarchal are not supported by empirical research.

there is an imbalance of power with one person making more of the decisions, controlling more of the joint activities, winning more of the arguments, and generally being in a position of dominance. Most research on the balance of power has investigated heterosexual couples.

Assessing the Balance of Power

Today there is much variation among marriages, ranging from couples in which one spouse (usually the husband) makes virtually all decisions to couples in which the spouses share equally in power and decision making. A majority of contemporary American couples describe their marriages as relatively equal in power. But other couples report male dominance or, less frequently, female dominance.

In a recent survey of over 3000 married couples, 64 percent said that the balance of power in their marriage was equal (Blumstein & Schwartz, 1983). Most of the remaining couples said the husband was more powerful, and less than 9 percent said the wife was dominant. Studies of dating couples have generally found similar patterns. For example, in one study, 49 percent of college women and 42 percent of college men reported equal power in their current dating relationship (Peplau, 1984). When the relationship was unequal, it was usually the man who had more say. In the CULTURAL HIGHLIGHT for this chapter, we examine the balance of power in Mexican American and African American marriages.

Partners can achieve equal power in different ways. Some couples strive to share all decisions completely—they shop together, discuss vacation plans, and so on. Other couples adopt a pattern in which each partner has "separate but equal" areas of responsibility. Diane explained that she and her boyfriend had equal power overall but that "in almost every situation, one of us is more influential. There are very few decisions that are fifty–fifty" (Peplau, 1984, p. 129). For instance, she picked their new apartment but Alan decided about moving the furniture. Diane said, "I make the aesthetic decisions and Alan makes the practical ones." Dividing

Most American couples share in decision making about family issues. This American Indian couple is working together to prepare their taxes.

areas of responsibility, sharing decisions totally, or some mixture of the two are all possible avenues to equal power in relationships.

In general, relationship satisfaction is equally high in male-dominant and egalitarian relationships. Consensus between a man and a woman may be more important for couple happiness than the particular pattern a couple follows. The exception occurs in female-dominant relationships. Such relationships are uncommon, and tend to be less satisfying for both partners (Peplau, 1984). It is apparently easier to follow a traditional pattern of male dominance or a newer pattern of equality than to experience a female-dominant relationship.

Tipping the Balance of Power

What factors determine whether or not a relationship is equal in power? Three important factors that affect the balance of power are social norms, relative resources, and the principle of least interest.

SOCIAL NORMS. Patterns of influence in relationships are often dictated by social norms. When teenagers accept a part-time job at a fast-food restaurant, they expect to take orders from the boss and to follow company regulations. It is generally understood that subordinates follow instructions from their superiors, at least in job-related matters. In heterosexual dating and marriage, social convention has traditionally conferred greater authority on men. Until recently, for example, state laws gave husbands legal control over all family property and permitted husbands, as the "head of the household," to decide where the family should live. More informally, women were taught to "look up to" the man they married and to defer to his wishes (Bernard, 1972). Individuals who endorse traditional beliefs about sex roles consider it appropriate for boyfriends and husbands to be the major decision-makers in heterosexual relationships.

RELATIVE RESOURCES. Norms are not the only determinant of the balance of power. Social exchange theory (Blau, 1964) proposes that the relative resources of the two partners also affect their relative power. A resource is anything that "can be used to satisfy or frustrate needs or move persons further from or closer to their goals" (Huston, 1983, p. 206). The prediction from exchange theory is that when partners are imbalanced in their resources, the person who has more resources will have more power. When two students work together on a biology lab assignment, the person who is more knowledgeable or who owns a better microscope is likely to be more influential. In dating or marriage, the partner who earns more money, has more education, has a more prestigious job, is more physically attractive, and so on usually has a power advantage (Scanzoni & Scanzoni, 1981).

THE PRINCIPLE OF LEAST INTEREST. Exchange theory proposes that another determinant of power is the relative dependency of the two partners on the relationship, based on their comparison level for alternatives. In some relationships, both partners are equally attracted and committed, and this tends to build power equality. In other relationships, one partner is more dependent on the relationship (Molm, 1985) or cares more about continuing the relationship. This sets the stage for an imbalance of power.

Sociologist Willard Waller (1938) called this the **principle of least interest:** The less interested partner in a relationship has greater power. An implicit bargain is struck in which the more interested and dependent person

defers to the other's wishes in order to ensure that the relationship will continue. An illustration of this principle is provided by Margaret, an unpopular young woman who had an affair with an older man:

> I accepted his structuring of our relationship. When he chose to deal in wit rather than in real information, I followed suit. When he acted casual about sex, so did I. I wanted something real from him. . . . Even when I knew this was impossible on my terms, I went ahead with it in his way. . . . I didn't back off, because I thought the potential was there, and a dateless summer had taught me that opportunities didn't come up all that often. (Cited in Goethals & Klos, 1970, p. 283)

Ultimately, relationships based on lopsided dependencies usually prove unsatisfactory to both partners. Over time, we would expect these relationships to change toward more equal involvement or to end.

We have discussed three major factors affecting the balance of power: social norms, relative resources, and the principle of least interest. These principles are likely to apply in a wide variety of relationships, not only in dating and marriage but also in relations among friends, coworkers, and family members.

CONFLICT

Conflict is the process that occurs when the actions of one person interfere with the actions of another (Fincham & Bradbury, 1991; Peterson, 1983). The potential for conflict increases as two people become more interdependent. As interactions become more frequent and cover a more diverse range of activities and issues, there are more opportunities for disagreement.

Much of the research on interpersonal conflict has studied heterosexual couples. Conflict is usually quite low during casual dating, but increases significantly in serious dating relationships (Braiker & Kelley, 1979). Among married couples, conflict is fairly common. In a recent survey, nearly all the married people polled reported having "unpleasant disagreements" with their spouse at least occasionally (McGonagle, Kessler & Schilling, 1992). On average, the married couples had one or two disagreements per month. Couples can apparently fight about almost anything, from politics and religion to work and money, from how to spend their time to how to divide household chores. John Gottman (1979) found 85 different kinds of conflict among young married couples! Of course, conflict is not limited to married couples. It also occurs in relationships with coworkers and supervisors, family and neighbors, friends and roommates.

Conflict problems can be grouped into three general categories (Braiker & Kelley, 1979):

1. *Specific behaviors.* Some conflicts focus on specific behaviors of a partner, such as getting drunk at a party or forgetting to pick up milk at the grocery store. A partner's actions may be costly to the other, such as one roommate playing loud music that interferes with another's studying. Or a partner may fail to provide desired rewards, perhaps by refusing to do something that the other wants.

2. *Norms and roles.* Some conflicts focus on more general issues about the rights and responsibilities of partners in a relationship. Conflicts of this sort might concern a failure to live up to promises, a lack of reciprocity, or the neglect of some agreed-upon task. Thus, one roommate might complain that the partner is not doing a fair share of the cleaning. Or a worker and supervisor might disagree about the worker's job responsibilities.

3. *Personal dispositions.* Some conflicts focus on a partner's motives and personality. People frequently go beyond specific behaviors to make attributions about the intentions and attitudes of a partner. One person might complain that the partner is lazy, inconsiderate, or lacks self-discipline.

These three types of conflict reflect the fact that people are interdependent at three levels (Braiker & Kelley, 1979). At the behavioral level, partners have problems coordinating specific activities. At the normative level, they have problems negotiating rules and roles for their relationship. At the dispositional level, they may disagree about each other's personality and intentions. One partner may fail to support or validate the other's self-concept. For example, conflicts can easily arise if Gloria thinks of herself as kind and considerate, but has a boyfriend who insists that she is really selfish and insensitive.

Conflicts can escalate as partners use specific problem behaviors to make more general attributions about each other's character. Dan may initially complain that his roommate left the sink full of dirty dishes. As the discussion continues, Dan may add that the roommate seldom lives up to their agreements about housekeeping. Dan may finally conclude that the roommate is hopelessly sloppy and self-centered.

Another source of conflict in social interactions is that partners may have different interpretations of relationship events (Kelley, 1979). Consider a husband who does not give his wife a present on their wedding anniversary. The wife may interpret this an insult and complain about it to her husband. The husband may see his actions differently and try to justify them to his wife. In such situations, people tend to explain their own and their partner's behaviors differently, consistent with the actor–observer attributional bias discussed in Chapter 4 (Kelley, 1979; Orvis, Kelley, & Butler, 1976).

The complaining person tends to attribute the event to the partner's negative characteristics. The wife might insist, "You forgot our anniversary because you don't really love me anymore." Her motivation may be to punish the husband's perceived misconduct or to challenge him to show he really does care. In contrast, the person who performed the act tends to excuse the behavior ("I meant to buy you something, but I was preoccupied with a big deadline at work") or to justify the action ("I thought we agreed not to spend money on each other"). The husband's explanations are an attempt to avoid blame and to keep the event from disrupting the relationship.

Recent research has examined more closely the role of attributions in marriage (Bradbury & Fincham, 1990). One important finding is that

Conflict and arguments are common in many close relationships. As two people become more interdependent, the potential for conflict increases.

there are systematic differences in the ways that happy and distressed couples explain their partner's actions (Bradbury & Fincham, 1992). More often than not, happy couples tend to make *relationship-enhancing attributions*—to interpret a partner's behaviors in a positive light (Holzworth-Munroe & Jacobson, 1985). For example, a happily married wife might attribute her husband's recent lack of interest in sex to the stress he is under at work. She attributes a negative event to factors that are temporary and outside her husband's control. The same wife might attribute her husband's unexpectedly bringing her flowers to his desire to do something special to show his love. She attributes a positive event to factors that are intentional and enduring. In both cases, the wife's interpretation views the husband's actions in a relationship-enhancing way.

In contrast, a wife in an unhappy marriage might make *distress-maintaining attributions* for her husband's actions. She might interpret his recent disinterest in sex as a sign that he no longer loves her, thus attributing a negative event to an intentional and long-lasting cause. The same distressed wife might view her hus-

band's gift of flowers as an attempt to justify spending money on himself—to a selfish and short-lived cause. Such attributions cast the husband in a negative light, and serve to maintain the wife's discontent.

Differences in the typical attributional styles of happy and distressed couples are summarized in Table 10-1. In the terminology introduced in Chapter 4, happy couples tend to attribute negative partner behaviors to external, unstable, and unintentional causes. They give the partner the benefit of the doubt, and attribute a problem to something that is outside the person's control, temporary, and unintended. Such attributions minimize the partner's responsibility for negative events. Happy couples attribute positive partner behaviors to internal, stable, and intentional causes. A partner's kind act is seen as motivated by enduring, positive qualities of the partner. Such attributions give a partner credit for good events in the relationship. Distressed couples show an opposite pattern, attributing rewarding behaviors to unstable, external or unintentional causes, and negative behaviors to internal, stable, and intentional causes.

Happy and distressed couples also differ on the attributional dimension of *globality* (Bradbury & Fincham, 1990). This dimension concerns whether the causes of the partner's behavior are seen as specific to a particular situation ("he hates washing dishes") or something more global that affects many situations ("he refuses to do anything around the house"). A global attribution for a negative event might be, "You're such a jerk," implying that a wide range of bad things are caused by your personality. A more specific attribution for a negative event would be, "There are times when you can be real annoying," implying that your personality occasionally affects a specific set of outcomes.

Taken together, these differences in attributional style lead partners in distressed relationships to view each other as more selfish and blameworthy, and partners in happy relationships to see each other as relatively caring and responsible. Research is beginning to show that attributions such as these can have important

Table 10-1
A Comparison of Relationship-Enhancing and Distress-Maintaining Attributional Styles

	Relationship-enhancing Attributions	Distress-maintaining Attributions
POSITIVE EVENT *My husband takes me out for an expensive dinner.*	Internal, stable, global *He's always such a sweet and thoughtful person. He loves me.*	External, unstable, specific *He took me out because it's the end of the year, and he can write it off on his expense account.*
NEGATIVE EVENT *My husband forgot my birthday.*	External, unstable, specific *Something unexpected must have come up at work. This isn't like him.*	Internal, stable, global *He's always so thoughtless. He never remembers anything or cares about my feelings.*

consequences in close relationships (Bradbury & Fincham, 1992). In unhappy couples, issues of responsibility and blame are often salient. Interpreting a partner's behaviors as based on selfish and malevolent intentions can magnify feelings of distress, and lead to anger and emotional withdrawal. Over time, such attributions may decrease overall marital satisfaction (Fincham & Bradbury, in press). In contrast, attributions that cast the partner's actions in the best light possible serve to preserve feelings of goodwill and may facilitate more productive problem-solving.

Conflict can help or harm a relationship, depending on how it is resolved. Conflict can provide an opportunity for clarifying disagreements and changing expectations about the relationship. Lovers' quarrels allow lovers to test their own and their partner's dependence on the relationship, to discover the depth of their feelings for each other, and to renew their efforts to create a satisfying relationship. On the other hand, because conflicts arouse strong emotions, they may not provide the best setting for constructive problem solving. The escalation of conflict and the trading of personal insults are unlikely to benefit a relationship. Conflict may be especially harmful when it leads to defensiveness, stubbornness, and withdrawal from interaction (Gottman & Krokoff, 1989).

SATISFACTION AND COMMITMENT

People generally desire relationships that are happy and long-lasting. When a couple falls in love, the partners often wonder how to make their relationship good and how to make it last. At work, employers also want to know how to keep workers happy and how to increase workers' sense of loyalty to the company. For their part, employees are usually concerned with pleasing their boss and keeping their jobs. In more technical terms, two fundamental aspects of relationships are personal satisfaction and commitment to continuing the relationship.

Contrasting Satisfaction and Commitment

There are important differences between satisfaction and commitment (Berscheid & Walster, 1978; Kelley, 1983). In business, for example, a worker may continue in an unhappy job because there are no better alternatives. Or a worker may leave a very satisfying job if a better opportunity comes along. In an "empty-shell marriage," spouses feel little love for each other but stay together because of concern for the welfare of their children, fear of loneliness, or a sense of moral obligation. They are committed, despite low satisfaction. Or consider the case of a woman who loves a man intensely, but recognizes that he does not return her passion. Despite her high satisfaction, she may realize that continuing her commitment is not in her own best interest, and so she may end the relationship to seek a more compatible mate. These examples illustrate the important point that satisfaction and commitment are not the same.

Satisfaction refers to an individual's subjective evaluation of the quality of a relationship. According to a social exchange perspective, satisfaction depends on two factors: the outcomes we receive from the relationship and our general comparison level (Rusbult, 1980, 1983). We are satisfied if a relationship is profitable, that is, if the rewards of the relationship exceed the costs incurred. We are also satisfied if a relationship compares favorably to our hopes and expectations. Perceptions of fairness also affect satisfaction: Even if a relationship provides many benefits, we may not be fully satisfied if we believe that we are being treated unfairly. In business, partners are usually dissatisfied if they perceive the relationship to be inequitable. Similarly, in friendship and love, lopsided relationships in which one person gives much more—or gets much more—than the other are

Some married couples succeed in creating committed relationships that withstand the test of time. In technical terms, commitment refers to both the positive and negative forces acting to keep a person in a relationship.

usually not as satisfying as balanced exchanges (Cate & Lloyd, 1992).

One approach to understanding satisfaction in romantic relationships has been to contrast the experiences of happy and distressed couples (see review by Weiss & Heynman, 1990). Researchers can define couples as "distressed" based on paper-and-pencil tests of relationship functioning or clinical interviews, or because couples have sought marital counseling. Compared to happy couples, distressed couples tend to spend less time in joint activities, to use less humor, and to engage in less affectionate touching. The interactions of distressed couples tend to be more negative: They express more criticism and hostility toward each other and have more frequent arguments. Other comparisons of distressed and happy couples are presented in the Research Closeup.

Commitment refers to all the forces, positive and negative, acting to keep an individual in a relationship. People who are strongly committed to a relationship are likely to stay together "through thick and thin" and "for better or for worse." Positive forces of attraction are one determinant of commitment. If we like another person, enjoy that person's company, and find it easy to get along, we will be positively motivated to continue the relationship. This aspect of commitment has been called *personal dedication* because it refers to an individual's desire to maintain or improve a relationship (Stanley & Markman, 1992). Social exchange theory emphasizes, however, that commitment is also based on negative forces or barriers that make it costly for a person to leave a relationship. This has been called *constraint commitment*, because it focuses on forces that constrain individuals to maintain a relationship regardless of their personal dedication. Factors that can constrain us from leaving a relationship include the lack of attractive alternatives and the investments we have made in the relationship.

AVAILABILITY OF ALTERNATIVES. Our comparison level for alternatives affects commitment. We may dislike our boss and regret having to interact daily, but continue the relationship because we need the salary and can't

RESEARCH CLOSEUP
Turning the Other Cheek

From time to time, most of us act badly toward our friends and lovers—we say or do thoughtless and angry things (Rusbult et al., 1991). Consider a man who returns home from a hard day at work. When his wife tries to start a conversation, he rebuffs her, saying in annoyance, "Just be quiet for a while." How will the wife react? Will she respond to his hurtful comments with a negative remark of her own, or will she "turn the other cheek" and respond in a more conciliatory way? Research on close relationships suggests that the way couples handle this type of situation may be vital to the quality of their relationship.

In general, partners in distressed relationships tend to reciprocate negative comments and behaviors (Gottman, Markman & Notarius, 1977; Weiss & Heyman, 1990). In contrast, partners in happy rela-

tionships are more likely to avoid this sort of vicious cycle. For example, a wife in a distressed relationship might react to her husband's "Just be quiet for a while" by muttering, "You're a real joy!" By responding in an equally negative way, she has set in motion a cycle of negativity. In contrast, a wife in a nondistressed relationship might shrug off her husband's rude remarks, giving him a little time to himself or expressing sympathy that he's probably had a rough day. By responding to a potentially destructive comment in a positive, constructive way, the wife can prevent the situation from escalating from a minor incident into a larger argument.

Research suggests that the ability to avoid trading insults and criticisms is an important factor in the quality of a close relationship. As one researcher noted, "It is less important to

exchange positive behaviors than it is *not* to exchange negative behaviors" (Montgomery, 1988, p. 345).

In recent research, Caryl Rusbult and her colleagues (1991) have shown that a social exchange perspective can help us to understand a partner's willingness to turn the other cheek. In general, people are more likely to react constructively when they feel satisfied with a relationship, view the relationship as central to their lives, have invested in their relationship, believe their alternatives are relatively poor, and feel greater commitment to the relationship. In other words, we are better able to put aside our own feelings and to react constructively when a relationship is usually rewarding and when we believe we have a good deal at stake in keeping the relationship alive.

find another job. We may date someone who falls below our comparison level because he or she is the only eligible person we know. If we are dependent on a relationship to provide things we value and cannot obtain elsewhere, we are unlikely to leave (Attridge et al., 1992). The lack of better alternatives increases commitment.

The link between availability of alternatives and commitment can also work in reverse. That is, people who are highly committed to a relationship may actually reject and devalue alternatives, as a way of resisting temptation. For example, convincing ourselves that our current

dating partner is more wonderful than all others makes it easier to sustain commitment (Simpson, Gangestad, & Lerma, 1990).

The availability of attractive alternatives can lessen commitment to a romantic relationship in two distinct ways (Drigotas & Rusbult, 1992). A first process involves leaving one relationship to pursue a new relationship with a specific other partner. The middle-aged man who leaves his wife to find fulfillment with a younger woman is one illustration. This has been called a single-best-alternative breakup, because an existing relationship is actively defeated by a more attractive alternative partner. In this case, one partner is traded for another. A second process occurs when a person comes to believe that a current relationship is less desirable than a variety of other social alternatives. A woman's commitment to her husband may decline as she notices that she laughs more with a colleague at work, receives more emotional support from her best friend, and finds other men more sexually attractive than her husband. In this case, a person realizes that the current partner offers less than the broader social world.

INVESTMENTS.   Commitment is also affected by the investments we have made in a relationship (Rusbult, 1980, 1983). Investments include time, energy, money, emotional involvement, shared experiences, sacrifices for a partner, and so on. To invest much in a relationship and then find it unrewarding can arouse cognitive dissonance, and so we may feel psychological pressures to see the relationship in a positive light and to downplay its drawbacks (Rubin, 1973). The more we have put into a relationship, the more costly it would be for us to leave it.

Empirical research has demonstrated the importance of exchange considerations for satisfaction and commitment in a variety of types of relationships including both heterosexual couples (Surra, 1990) and gay and lesbian couples (Kurdek, 1992). For example, in a study of dating relationships, Caryl Rusbult (1980) explicitly tested an exchange model. College students completed detailed questionnaires assessing the rewards they got from their dating relationship (such as the partner's attractiveness and intelligence, the couple's ability to coordinate activities) and the costs (such as conflict or the partner's embarrassing behaviors). Participants also indicated how much they had invested or "put things into" the relationship and described the quality of the best available alternative to their current partner.

Finally, they completed several measures of satisfaction and commitment. Consistent with exchange theory, the strongest predictors of satisfaction were rewards and costs; investments and alternatives did not affect satisfaction. The most satisfied people reported many rewards and few costs. In contrast, commitment was

affected by satisfaction, investments, and alternatives. People felt most committed when they were satisfied with the relationship, had invested a lot, and had relatively less desirable alternatives.

In many relationships, satisfaction and commitment go hand in hand. As a new couple discover the special rewards of their developing relationship, they take steps to build commitment. They may stop dating other people and forgo other activities to be with each other. As their affection blossoms into love, they may take public actions to demonstrate their feelings and to build a future together. A wedding ceremony, buying a home together, having children—these investments in the relationship are usually based on love, and further serve to build commitment. If the couple encounters difficult times of conflict and disagreement, their investments may provide the motivation to work to improve the relationship and to rekindle their flagging affection.

Yet satisfaction and commitment do not invariably go hand in hand. Although some unhappy couples are able to improve their relationships and others terminate unrewarding relationships, some couples stay together despite low satisfaction. We referred to these earlier as "empty-shell relationships." A recent national survey found that about 7 percent of married Americans were relatively unhappy in their marriages, but expected to stay together nonetheless (Heaton & Albrecht, 1991). To understand the sources of commitment in unrewarding relationships, the researchers compared the experiences of those in unhappy marriages who expected to stay together and those who considered divorce a possibility. In general, the more highly committed couples had invested more in their relationships; they had been together for a longer time and had more children. The lack of alternatives to marriage also made a difference. For both sexes, the belief that life would be worse if they separated contributed to commitment. For women, the threat of economic loss from divorce was especially important. For men, the fear that their sex life would worsen was especially important. Attitudes about marriage also made a difference. Individuals who believed that marriage is a lifetime commitment and that couples should stay together for the sake of the children were more likely to stay together despite dissatisfaction with the marriage. Finally, people who believed they have greater personal control over their lives reported less commitment to an unhappy marriage. As these data suggest, we sometimes find ourselves stuck in unsatisfying relationships.

Reactions to Dissatisfaction

Caryl Rusbult (1987) and her colleagues have investigated the diverse ways people react when they are dissatisfied with a relationship. Rusbult's model is quite general and has been applied to job dissatisfaction (Rusbult et al., 1988) as well as to dissatisfaction with romantic relationships. Rusbult has identified four common reactions to dissatisfaction, which she calls voice, loyalty, neglect, and exit.

VOICE. This occurs when a person voices the problems, tries to compromise, seeks help, tries to change the self, the partner, or the situation, or more generally works to improve the relationship. Fundamentally, voice is an effort to rescue a relationship in trouble. In a job situation, a worker might give voice to his or her dissatisfaction by discussing problems with a supervisor, suggesting solutions, consulting with a union official, or blowing the whistle on corporate wrongdoing. In a romantic relationship, voice might take the form of trying to talk with the partner, suggesting improvements in the relationship, offering to enter counseling, and so on. Voice is most often used when the person has previously been satisfied with the relationship and has invested fairly heavily in it. In romantic relationships, women are somewhat more likely than men to show this response.

LOYALTY. This means passively but optimistically waiting for things to improve. Loyalty is a conservative response that attempts to maintain the status quo. In a job situation, a

worker might publicly support the organization and perform his or her job well, while hoping that conditions will change. In a personal relationship, a dissatisfied but loyal partner would respond by waiting, hoping, or praying that things will improve with time. This reaction is most likely when the person views the relationship problems as relatively minor, has poor alternatives, has invested a good deal in the relationship, or is not seriously dissatisfied overall.

NEGLECT. This refers to passively allowing a relationship to deteriorate. In a job situation, this might mean letting conditions at work worsen through lack of effort, frequent lateness or absences, or using company time for personal business. In a personal relationship, neglect might be displayed by spending less time with the partner, ignoring the partner, refusing to discuss problems, treating the partner badly, or "just letting things fall apart." This response is most common when the person has not been very satisfied in the past and has made low investments in the relationship.

EXIT. This refers to actively ending a relationship. In a work situation, exit occurs when a person searches for a different job, transfers, or quits. In a romantic relationship, exit might take the form of moving out of a joint residence, physically abusing the partner, or ending the relationship by leaving or getting a divorce. In personal relationships, people are most likely to leave a relationship when they believe they have little to lose. This occurs when the relationship is unhappy, the person has invested relatively little, or the person has reasonable alternatives.

Rusbult has shown that social exchange factors influence the type of problem solving used in personal relationships. For example, in one study, college students were more likely to use relationship-promoting responses of voice and loyalty when they had been satisfied with the relationship before problems arose, when they had made substantial investments in the relationship, and when they had poor alternatives (Rusbult, Zembrodt, & Gunn, 1982). In contrast, students were more likely to use exit strategies when their preproblem satisfaction was relatively low, their investments were low, and they had good alternatives.

From the perspective of continuing the relationship, loyalty and voice are constructive, relationship-promoting responses; neglect and exit are destructive to the relationship. Of course, for the individuals involved, ending a relationship or quitting a job may be a personally helpful and appropriate action.

KEY TERMS

close relationship	equity theory	social interaction
commitment	interdependence	social norms
comparison level	norm of reciprocity	social penetration
comparison level for alternatives	principle of least interest	social power
	self-disclosure	social roles

SUMMARY

1. When two people interact, they influence each other. Interdependence refers to mutual influence between two or more people. As interaction continues over time, a relationship begins to develop. We call a relationship close if there is frequent interaction involving many different kinds of activities and strong mutual influence.

2. The most influential analysis of social interaction comes from social exchange theories. In this view, people are concerned with the outcomes (rewards minus costs) they receive in a relationship. People use several standards to evaluate their relationship outcomes, including a general comparison level and a comparison level for alternatives. When two people are interdependent, they try to coordinate their activities to maximize their joint profits.

3. In a relationship, coordination problems arise because one person's outcomes are dependent on the partner's actions and vice versa. Coordination is easier when partners have correspondent outcomes (similar interests) than when they have noncorrespondent outcomes. Social norms and roles provide solutions to coordination problems.

4. People care whether or not their relationships are fair. Three major rules of fairness are equality, relative needs, and equity. Equity exists when each person's outcomes are proportional to his or her contributions to the relationship. According to equity theory, when individuals perceive inequity in a relationship, they feel distress and take steps to restore actual equity or psychological equity.

5. Close relationships may move beyond simple tit-for-tat patterns of social exchange. Clark and Mills have distinguished between exchange relationships and communal relationships.

6. Self-disclosure is the sharing of personal feelings and information with another individual. There is a norm of reciprocity for self-disclosure so partners tend to disclose at similar levels. Social penetration theory describes how self-disclosure contributes to the development of intimate relationships.

7. Patterns of self-disclosure reflect cultural norms. In the United States, disclosure tends to be lower in male–male relationships than in female–female or opposite-sex relationships.

8. According to Reis and Shaver, intimacy is created when a person's self-disclosure evokes a response in the listener that leads the person to feel cared for and understood.

9. Social power refers to a person's ability to influence deliberately the behavior, thoughts, or feelings of another person. The

balance of power describes whether partners have equal power or whether one person is dominant. In general, most African American, Mexican American, and Anglo couples describe their marriages as fairly equal in power. Three determinants of the balance of power are social norms, the relative resources of the partners, and the "principle of least interest."

10. Conflict occurs when the actions of one person interfere with the actions of another. Conflicts can be about specific behaviors, norms and roles, or personal dispositions. Compared to distressed couples, happily married couples are more likely to make relationship-enhancing attributions and to avoid distress-maintaining attributions.

11. Satisfaction refers to an individual's subjective evaluation of the quality of a relationship. Commitment refers to all the forces, positive and negative, that keep a person in a relationship. Positive factors (satisfaction, liking, love, etc.) increase our sense of personal dedication. Negative factors are barriers that constrain us to continue in a relationship regardless of how satisfying it is. Two important barriers are the lack of alternatives and the investments a person has already made in a relationship.

12. Rusbult has identified four common reactions to dissatisfaction in relationships: voice, loyalty, neglect, and exit.

SUGGESTED READINGS

Brehm, S. S. (1992). *Intimate relationships* (2nd ed.). New York: Random House. A well-written paperback textbook that provides an excellent introduction to the field.

Burgess, R. L., & Huston, T. L. (Eds.) (1979). *Social exchange in developing relationships*. New York: Academic Press. Leading experts use exchange theory to discuss such topics as the initiation of relationships, conflict, and breakups.

Derlega, V., & Berg, J. H. (Eds.). (1987). *Self-disclosure: Theory, research, and therapy*. New York: Plenum. A review of work on self-disclosure, written by professionals.

Fletcher, G. J. O., & Fincham, F. D. (Eds.) (1991). *Cognition in close relationships*. Hillsdale, NJ: Erlbaum. Experts describe new applications of social cognition to understanding interaction in close relationships.

Kurdek, L. A. (Forthcoming) Lesbian and gay couples. In A. R. D'Augelli & C. J. Patterson (Eds.), *Lesbian and gay identities over the lifespan: Psychological perspectives on personal, relational, and community processes*. New York: Oxford University Press. A comprehensive review of research on homosexual relationships.

Noller, P., & Fitzpatrick, M. A. (Eds.) (1988). *Perspectives on marital interaction*. Philadelphia, PA: Multilingual Matters Ltd. An excellent set of papers on conflict, power, communication, and other facets of interaction in marriage.

11
Behavior in Groups

FOCUS OF THIS CHAPTER

Behavior in the Presence of
  Others
Basic Features of Groups
Task Performance in Groups
Competition Versus Cooperation
Leadership

Research Closeup
Social Compensation

Cultural Highlight
The Spirit of Competition

We are all members of groups that have enormous influence on our lives. Most of us are born into a family group and spend much of our childhood interacting with parents and siblings. As we venture into the larger social world, we encounter new groups—perhaps a neighborhood play group, a kindergarten class, or a group at a church or synagogue. As we grow up, we begin to join clubs, sports teams, work groups, political parties, and other organizations.

In this chapter, we begin our exploration of group processes by considering how the mere presence of other people affects our behavior. Then, we examine situations in which people apparently lose their identity in a group—a phenomenon called deindividuation. Next, we define the nature of groups and explore some of the basic processes of group interaction, including communication, decision making, and competition versus cooperation. We conclude by investigating the topic of leadership in groups.

BEHAVIOR IN THE PRESENCE OF OTHERS

How does the presence of other people influence an individual's performance on a task? Consider two examples. Jessica is an outstanding high school runner who hopes one day to try out for the Olympics. She trains very hard, and notices that she runs better with a training partner than by herself. Her best performances have been during actual track meets where she ran against tough competition. Jake is taking his first class in acting. At home in the privacy of his bedroom, he delivers his lines with accuracy and self-confidence. But in front of his classmates, he stumbles over his part. As these contrasting examples suggest, the presence of others sometimes enhances and sometimes impairs an individual's performance.

Social Facilitation

People sometimes perform better in the presence of others than when they are alone. This is called **social facilitation.** Social psychologists have long been fascinated by this phenomenon. Indeed, experimentation in social psychology is often traced to a study of social facilitation conducted by Norman Triplett in 1898. Triplett observed that cyclists seem to race faster when they are in competition than when they are alone. To test this observation, he devised an experiment to see whether children would work harder pulling in a fishing line in a group setting than alone. As predicted, the children worked harder in the presence of others.

Many studies have demonstrated this effect (see review by Guerin, 1986). In the 1920s, for example, Allport (1920, 1924) had subjects work on such tasks as crossing out all the vowels in a newspaper column, doing easy multiplication problems, or writing refutations of a logical argument. Even though participants always worked individually on the task, they were more productive when there were five other people in the room than when they were alone. Social facilitation has been found when the others who are present are actually performing the same task (are "co-actors") and when the other person is an observer or experimenter. Social facilitation is not limited to humans. It has also been demonstrated in rats, cockroaches, and parakeets. For instance, individual ants dig three times more sand when they are in groups than when they are alone (Chen, 1937).

On the other hand, the presence of others sometimes inhibits individual performance, as suggested by the example of Jake who could recite his lines flawlessly alone, but stumbled over his words in public. This is called the **social inhibition** of performance. In Allport's early studies (1924), people in a group setting wrote more refutations of a logical argument, but the quality of the work was lower than when they worked alone. Another study found that the presence of a spectator reduced individual performance on a memory task (Pessin, 1933). Why does the presence of others sometimes improve performance and at other times diminish the quality of performance?

An answer was offered by Robert Zajonc (1965). He suggested that being in the presence of others increases an individual's drive or motivation (see Figure 11-1). Whether this increased drive facilitates or interferes with performance depends on the task. When a task requires a response that is well-learned or innate, called a *dominant response,* increased motivation is helpful. Therefore, the presence of others facilitates performance on relatively simple tasks, such as crossing out vowels or doing easy arithmetic. Similarly, for a highly trained athlete, the presence of others is likely to improve performance. But when a task requires behavior that is complex or poorly learned, then the increased motivation from having others present impairs performance. Examples would be solving difficult arithmetic problems, memorizing new

material, or writing complex logical deductions. For Jake, struggling to remember his lines, an audience may simply increase stage fright and inhibit a good performance. If Jake were more experienced and had performed the part every night for months, the audience might improve his performance. In summary, when a dominant or well-learned response is involved, heightened motivation improves performance, and this is more likely to occur for simple rather than complex tasks.

An interesting illustration comes from an observational study of the behavior of people playing pool in a college student union building (Michaels et al., 1982). The researchers identified pairs of players who were either above or below average in their play, and secretly recorded their scores. Then, teams of four confederates approached the players and watched them closely during several more rounds of play. Zajonc's theory predicts that good players will benefit from an audience, but poor players will not. The results provide clear support for this prediction. When good players were being watched by four others, their accuracy rose from 71 to 80 percent. When poor players were being watched, their accuracy dropped from 36 to 25 percent.

There are currently several views of why the presence of others motivates us (Geen, 1991). A first explanation is the one offered by Zajonc, that there is a fairly simple, innate tendency to become aroused by the mere presence of others. A second view is that others motivate us

Figure 11-1   How the presence of others affects performance: Social facilitation versus inhibition.

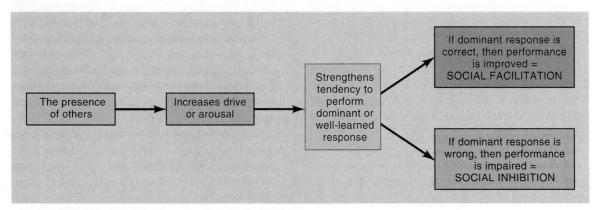

because we have learned to be concerned about looking good in public, an effect known as **evaluation apprehension.** It is not the mere presence of other people that matters, but rather our knowledge that others are evaluating the quality of our performance and our desire to make a good impression. On simple tasks, an awareness that we are being evaluated can spur us to greater effort. But on complex tasks, the pressure of being evaluated may be detrimental.

A third view is that the presence of others is distracting. On easy tasks that do not require full attention, we may compensate for the distraction by concentrating and trying harder, and thus may actually perform better. But the distraction created by other people is harmful to performance on complex tasks. An extension of this idea is the *distraction-conflict model* (Baron, 1986), which suggests that the presence of others creates a conflict between two basic tendencies: (1) to pay attention to the audience and (2) to pay attention to the task. This conflict can increase arousal, which then either helps or hinders task performance, depending on whether the task calls for a dominant response or not. Further, conflict can also create cognitive overload, if the effort required to pay attention simultaneously to a difficult task and to other people exceeds the individual's mental capacities. The various explanations of social facilitation are not necessarily contradictory: It is possible that all these processes can affect human performance, depending on the situation (Geen, 1991).

Social Loafing

Social facilitation highlights the point that the presence of others can sometimes motivate individuals and spur them to greater efforts. But the opposite pattern can also be found: Sometimes individuals work less hard in the presence of others than they would alone. This effect, known as **social loafing,** was first studied in the late 1880s by a French agricultural engineer named Max Ringelmann (see Kravitz & Martin, 1986).

As part of a study of work efficiency in horses, oxen, and men, Ringelmann asked stu-

All eyes are on this golf pro as he putts the ball. Do you think the audience will facilitate or inhibit his performance?

dent volunteers to pull as hard as they could on a rope. He measured their effort in kilograms of pressure using a strain gauge. Sometimes the participants worked alone and sometimes in groups of 7 or 14 people. Common sense and research on social facilitation might predict that the men would work harder when they were part of a team than when they were alone. Just the opposite happened. When pulling alone, individuals averaged about 85 kg per person. In groups of seven, the total group force was only 65 kg per person, and in the largest group, each individual's contribution fell to 61 kg.

More recent studies by Latané and his colleagues (Latané, Williams, & Harkins, 1979) have provided further evidence for social loafing. In one study, undergraduate men were asked to make as much noise as they could by cheering or by clapping. Each person performed alone, in pairs, in groups of four, and in groups of six. The results, presented in Figure 11-2, clearly show that the noise produced by each individual decreased as the size of the group increased. This is the same pattern Ringelmann found. More recent studies show that social loafing can occur not only on physical tasks, such as clapping or shouting, but also on intellectual tasks (Weldon & Gargano, 1988).

Why does social loafing occur? Social evaluation appears to be a key factor (Geen, 1991). Working in a group leads to a relaxation of effort when individuals believe that their own work will be "lost in the crowd"—that no one will know how well they performed and that

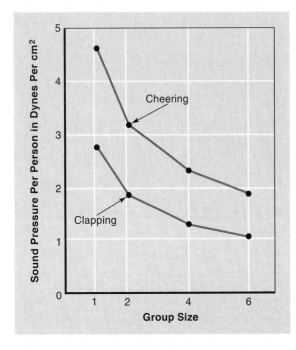

Figure 11-2 A comparison of the intensity of noise an individual makes alone and in groups. (*Source:* Adapted from Latané, Williams, & Harkins, 1979, p. 825.)

they cannot be held responsible for their individual actions (Harkins & Szymanski, 1989). Apparently, people tend to slack off when working in a group provides anonymity. The antidote to social loafing is to make each individual's contribution identifiable. If people believe that their contribution can be evaluated by others, social loafing can be eliminated.

Other factors also influence social loafing. For instance, social loafing is less likely to occur on complex tasks than on simple ones. When the task is difficult or challenging, individuals are less likely to slack off (Jackson & Williams, 1985). Providing rewards for high group productivity can also reduce social loafing. In one study, some students were told they could leave an experiment early if their group generated many solutions to a problem; other students were given the same problem-solving task but were not offered the incentive of leaving early (Shepperd & Wright, 1989). In this case, the anticipation of a reward for high effort counteracted the social loafing effect.

Research has also begun to investigate the cross-cultural generality of the social loafing effect. Several studies using the sound production task (making noise by clapping) have found evidence of social loafing in India, Thailand, Japan, and China (Gabrenya, Wang, & Latané, 1985). These studies suggest the possible univer-

As the number of workers in a group increases, so does the tendency toward loafing on the job.

sality of the social loafing tendency. However, an important limitation of this research is that the clapping task may not be seen by research participants as particularly meaningful or important. Gabrenya, Wang, and Latané (1985) argued that cross-cultural differences should not necessarily be expected on trivial tasks of this sort, but should be found on tasks that people see as reflecting their level of skill or ability.

To test this idea, the researchers created a new sound-tracking test, which was described to participants as a measure of their auditory ability. The researchers predicted that American students from an individualistic culture would show the typical social loafing pattern on this task when working in a group. In contrast, they predicted that Chinese students would show an opposite pattern. Because China is a more group-oriented culture where individuals are taught to work toward group goals and to put the welfare of the group ahead of individual interests, Chinese students were expected to perform better in groups than alone. As predicted, significant differences were found in the behavior of ninth-grade students in Florida and in Taiwan. In a group setting, Americans performed only 88 percent as well as they did alone. In contrast, Chinese students in groups performed at 108 percent of their individual level. A puzzling and unexpected finding was that the Chinese versus American differences in social loafing were found only for boys; girls performed equally well when working alone or in a group. These findings provide some preliminary support for the existence of cultural differences in tendencies toward social loafing, at least on some types of tasks and for males. But more research will be needed for us to reach definite conclusions about the impact of culture on social loafing.

In this section, we have seen that the presence of others sometimes leads to social facilitation and sometimes causes social loafing (Harkins, 1987). Working in the presence of others can spur us to greater effort or lull us into complacency about our individual efforts. Which effect occurs depends on the complexity of the task at hand. It also depends on whether the group context increases our concerns about social evaluation (because others are judging our performance) or reduces social evaluation concerns (because our individual effort is hidden by working in a group). The RESEARCH CLOSEUP for this chapter examines another fascinating aspect of performance in groups known as **social compensation.**

Social Impact Theory

Our discussion so far has concerned the question of when the presence of others has positive or negative effects on individual performance. **Social impact theory** addresses the issue of how strong an influence (either positive or negative) these others have. As developed by Latané (1981), this theory suggests that the total impact of other people on an individual depends on three characteristics of the observers (source of influence): their number, strength, and immediacy. This is shown schematically in Figure 11-3 for a situation in which a group of people (sources) are influencing a single individual (target).

As the *number* of observers increases, so does their impact. To return to the earlier example of our fledgling actor Jake learning lines for a play, the impact of the audience should increase with the number of people present. Jake should experience more stage fright performing in front of 50 people than in front of five people.

Another factor is the *strength* of the social forces, that is, the importance or power of the observers. Strength is determined by such things as the status and age of the observers and their relationship to the individual. Jake might feel significantly worse about performing in front of his teacher or a casting director than in front of his friends.

The third factor is the *immediacy* of the audience, their closeness to the individual in time or space. Jake's reactions should be stronger if he has a live audience than if he is being watched on a video monitor located in another room (Borden, 1980). Latané suggests that social impact can be compared to light falling on a surface: The total amount of light depends on the

RESEARCH CLOSEUP

Social Compensation

Ken is a highly motivated college student, eager to earn top grades so he can get into law school. When the teacher divides Ken's history class into study groups and assigns each team a topic for a jointly graded oral presentation, Ken has a dilemma. He wants to get an A on the project, but he's sure that other students won't work as hard as he usually does. Should he go along with the group and risk getting a C grade, or should he compensate for their low effort by doing most of the work himself? What would you do in this situation?

Research on social loafing might suggest that Ken, like his coworkers, will slack off in the study group. Yet common sense and recent research by Kipling Williams and Steven Karau (1991) suggest that sometimes an individual will expend great effort in a collective setting to compensate for others in the group. Williams and Karau call this effect "social compensation." They believe that two conditions are necessary for an individual to show social compensation: (1) The person must believe that

coworkers are performing inadequately and (2) the person must consider the quality of the group product to be important. In Ken's case, he doesn't trust his teammates to work hard, but he is very concerned about the shared grade they will receive for their report.

Williams and Karau conducted three experiments to test their ideas. In a first study, they assessed the link between trusting one's coworkers and personal effort. They found that students who scored high on a measure of interpersonal trust—and so might expect coworkers to carry their own weight—showed the usual pattern of social loafing in a group. In contrast, students low in trust—who might expect others to loaf—showed a compensatory pattern of working harder in the group.

In a second study, the researchers directly manipulated the subject's expectations about a coworker's effort. Sometimes the coworker (actually a confederate) said that he was going to work hard on the experiment, and sometimes he

said he didn't think he would work very hard. As predicted, subjects with a hardworking teammate performed less well than subjects with a low-effort teammate.

A third study focused on the personal importance of the task. Some subjects were told that the task was important and related to intelligence; others were told that the task was relatively trivial. The researchers also varied whether subjects believed that their partner was high or low in ability. They predicted that the social compensation effect would be seen only when the subject believed that the task was important and that the partner was low in ability. In other conditions, a pattern of social loafing (lower effort) was anticipated. The results provided strong support for these predictions.

In short, when people care about their group's performance, and when they believe that their coworkers are either untrustworthy, unwilling to work hard, or unable to perform well, they work hard to compensate.

number of light bulbs, the wattage of the bulbs, and their closeness to the surface.

Latané believes that social impact theory can help explain why the presence of others sometimes leads to social facilitation and sometimes causes social loafing. In facilitation situations, the person is the sole target of influence from an audience or from coworkers (as shown in Figure 11-3). The social impact of the others is all

directed at the single individual; as the number of people present increases, their social impact on the individual also increases. In contrast, social loafing situations occur when several group members work together on a task assigned by an outsider. As shown in Figure 11-4, each individual is only one of several targets of forces coming from outside the group. Consequently, the social impact of the outsider

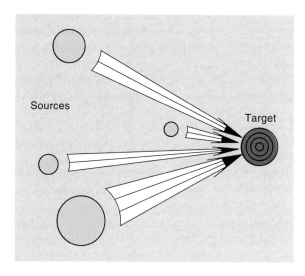

Figure 11-3 The impact of an audience on a target depends on the number of people present (number of circles or "sources"), the immediacy of the people (nearness of the circles to the target), and the strength or importance of the people (size of the circles). (*Source:* Adapted from Latané, 1981, p. 344.)

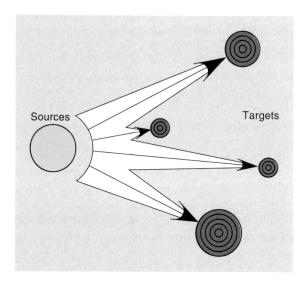

Figure 11-4 When each individual is only one of several targets of social influence, the impact of the audience on the target is lessened. (*Source:* Adapted from Latané, 1981, p. 349.)

is divided among group members. As the size of the group increases, the pressure felt by each individual decreases.

Social impact theory is still relatively new

(Jackson, 1987; Mullen, 1985). There is good empirical support for predictions about the impact of group size. The larger the group or audience, the more impact it has on an individual's performance. Evidence about the importance of strength and immediacy is currently more limited (Sedikides & Jackson, 1990). Put in broader context, social impact theory illustrates a major goal of social psychology: to create theories that can explain diverse social phenomena within a single set of unified principles (Nowak, Szamrej, & Latané, 1990).

Deindividuation

Sometimes people seem to lose themselves in a crowd and find that the anonymity of being in a group can weaken their sense of individual identity. In 1931, a young black man, accused of raping a white woman, was being held in a southern jail. There was no evidence against him except that he was in the general vicinity of the crime. A crowd gathered outside the jail and became more and more excited and enraged. Members of the crowd talked of lynching, and before long the crowd had turned into an angry mob. It rushed the jail, broke down the doors, and dragged the prisoner from his cell. He was tortured and killed in a sadistic orgy of violence.

How can we explain such seemingly irrational and destructive crowd behavior? In 1896 Le Bon suggested that in a mob, the emotions of one person spread through the group. When one person does something, even if it would ordinarily be unacceptable to most of the others, everyone else tends to do it also. Le Bon (1896) called this *social contagion:* Mob behavior is infectious, like a cold spreading through members of a school classroom. Le Bon explained social contagion in terms of a breakdown of normal control mechanisms. Our actions are usually controlled by our values and ethics, and the social rules we have learned. In groups, we sometimes lose a sense of responsibility for our own actions; we feel that the group is responsible. Our own control system is weakened, and so aggressive and sexual impulses are free to be expressed. This can result in violent, immoral acts.

Social psychologists have translated these

ideas into more modern terms (Festinger, Pepitone, & Newcomb, 1952; Zimbardo, 1970). They propose that people in groups sometimes experience **deindividuation.** Personal identity is replaced by an identification with the goals and actions of the group. The individual becomes less aware of his or her own personal values and behavior, and instead focuses on the group and the situation (Diener, 1980; Prentice-Dunn & Spivey, 1986). Deindividuation involves a loss of personal responsibility that reduces members' concern about the consequences of their actions. Deindividuation also involves a diminished self-awareness and a heightened sensitivity to what the group is doing. In a sense, each person in the group thinks of his or her own actions as being part of the group's behavior. This can set the stage for antisocial acts, if the group favors such actions.

A key factor in deindividuation is *anonymity* (Forsyth, 1990). Anything that makes members of a group less personally identifiable should increase the effect. The more anonymous the group members are, the less likely they are to be held accountable for their acts. Consequently, anonymity encourages irresponsible behavior. In a mob, most of the people do not stand out as individuals. They blend together and, in a sense, do not have an identity of their own. Conversely, to the extent that people in a group know they are identifiable, they retain their feelings of individuality and are less likely to act irresponsibly.

An experiment by Zimbardo (1970) illustrates

Halloween costumes often mask personal identity. This and other forms of anonymity increase the tendency toward deindividuation.

the deindividuation effect. Groups of four young women were recruited to take part in a study supposedly involving empathic responses to strangers. In one condition, participants were greeted by name, wore name tags, and were easily identifiable. In another condition, subjects wore oversized white lab coats and hoods, were never called by name, and were difficult to identify. All the groups were given an opportunity to deliver electric shocks to a person not in the group. (In fact, the shocks were fake and the "victim" was a confederate.) The subjects who were not identifiable gave almost twice as many shocks as the others. Apparently, being less identifiable produced a marked increase in aggression, supporting the idea that loss of individuality is one cause of the violence and antisocial behavior sometimes exhibited by groups.

A naturalistic demonstration of the deindividuation effect involved children who were trick-or-treating on Halloween. In this study (Diener et al., 1976), the researchers stationed themselves in homes in the neighborhood. When children arrived at the door, some were asked their names by the adults in the homes, and others were not. Then the children were all given an opportunity to steal extra candy when the adult was not present. Those children who had been asked their names were less likely to steal, even though the chances of being caught were virtually zero in all cases.

Perhaps in these studies it was not the anonymity that increased the violation of norms, but the kind of disguise being worn. Johnson and Downing (1979) have pointed out that in almost all the research, subjects have worn disguises or masks that have negative implications: Zimbardo used Ku Klux Klan outfits, and most Halloween masks are of monsters or ghosts. To test this hypothesis, Johnson and Downing produced anonymity by having people wear either Ku Klux Klan outfits or nurses' outfits, consisting of white hats and coats. Those wearing outfits were compared to others wearing normal clothing. It was found that the Ku Klux Klan outfit had only a slight effect on the level of shock subjects gave (thus not replicating Zimbardo's results). Perhaps more important, the nurses' uniforms actually *reduced* the number of shocks given. Although anonymity sometimes produces increased aggression, these results indicate that people are influenced by the social context, in this case by the type of uniforms they wore. If the uniform implies positive, prosocial behavior, the wearer may behave accordingly.

In summary, the critical factor in deindividuation is not membership in a group, but rather anonymity and reduced self-awareness. The behavioral consequences of deindividuation depend on the norms of the group, which can be either antisocial or prosocial. We will return to the discussion of deindividuation in Chapter 14, which focuses on aggression.

BASIC FEATURES OF GROUPS

So far we have been discussing ways in which the mere presence of others affects an individual's behavior. We now turn our attention to the dynamics of interaction in groups, beginning with a description of the defining features of social groups.

Defining a Group

We spend time in many different kinds of social units, not all of which qualify as groups. Table 11-1 provides some common examples, including being part of an audience or crowd. In everyday language we often speak of all social units as "groups." But social scientists typically use the term group in a narrower, more technical way. In a **group,** people are *interdependent* and have at least the potential for *mutual interaction.* In most groups, members have regular face-to-face contact. This definition of a group is an extension of the basic definition of an interpersonal relationship given in Chapter 10. The definition emphasizes that the essential feature of a group is that members influence one another in some way.

Based on this definition, a social category such as all professional football players does not comprise a group, since the people in this category do not know one another, have face-to-face contact, or influence one another directly. However, the members of the Dallas Cowboys football team are a group because they interact regularly and their actions affect one another. Similarly, all the children who watch "Sesame Street" on television are part of a common audience, but they are not a group. However, all the children in Mrs. Asawa's second-grade class are part of a group.

Groups vary in four important ways. A first dimension is *size*. The smallest group is the

---

TABLE 11-1
Types of Social Units

There are a variety of social groupings or categories, not all of which meet the criteria for being a "group."

Social categories: We often group people together on the basis of a shared attribute. Examples are teenage boys, unemployed heads of household, lesbians, Sunday school teachers, and truck drivers. All members of a social category have some common characteristic, although they are not likely to know each other or to interact.

Audience: All the people watching the 6 o'clock news on Channel 4 are part of the same audience, even though they are not necessarily aware of each other and do not interact.

Crowd: When people are in physical proximity to a common situation or stimulus, we call them a crowd. Examples are fans gathered outside a rock star's dressing room, people waiting outside for a bank to open, or people gathering to watch a street brawl.

Team: A set of people who interact regularly for some particular purpose or activity, such as a work group, sports team, or bridge club, make up a team.

Family: Although there are many types, families usually consist of a set of people who are related by birth or legal arrangements and who may share a common residence.

Formal organization: Larger aggregates of people often work together in some clearly structured way to accomplish a joint goal. Examples are a school system, the American Cancer Society, or the National Rifle Association.

In climbing a dangerous stretch of ice, the lives of these men are interlinked. Interdependence is a basic feature of all groups.

dyad or couple. Most group research has focused on small groups ranging from about 3 to 20 people. As social aggregates get much larger, they tend to become formal organizations and may no longer involve personal knowledge and interaction among all members. To emphasize the distinctions, some researchers prefer the term "small group" for social units in which members have face-to-face interaction.

Second, groups differ widely in values and *goals.* Consider for a moment the differences between a chess club, an intramural volleyball team, the Gay and Lesbian Student Association, and a religious education class. Which, if any, of these groups you might consider joining depends a great deal on your own personal values, interests, and goals.

Third, groups also vary in *duration.* Families may continue to exist for many generations, with new members joining the group through birth or marriage and others leaving through death or divorce. In contrast, members of a jury might work together for a few days on a particular case and then be disbanded at the end of the trial.

Fourth, the breadth or *scope of activities* performed also varies from group to group. Some groups focus on a single issue. For instance, in response to a threatened tuition increase, a group of college students might form a task force to formulate alternatives and present them to the school administration. Here, a group is created for one specific purpose. In contrast, groups such as families engage in a great many different activities.

Research on small groups has sometimes studied naturally occurring groups such as families, teammates, or work groups. But there is also a long tradition of studying "concocted groups" (McGrath, 1984), groups deliberately created by a researcher. In a typical study, groups of strangers are brought together in a lab to spend a few hours working on a group decision-making task. We'll discuss the results of experimental studies on groups later in this chapter. For the moment, it is useful to note that whereas naturally occurring groups are often relatively enduring and broad in scope, most experimental groups are short-lived and relatively narrow in focus.

Group Structure

When people are brought together in a group, they do not remain entirely undifferentiated. They develop patterns of behavior, divide tasks, and adopt different roles (Brown, 1988). We refer to these patterns as the social structure of the group.

An important element of group structure is **social norms,** rules and expectations for behavior in the group. For example, Merei (1949) observed that after only three or more meetings, groups of young children established many informal norms: They decided where each child would sit in the room, who could play with each toy, what sequence of activities should be followed, and so on.

A more recent study by Simon, Eder, and Evans (1992) traced the development of norms about romantic love among groups of teenage girls in sixth through eighth grades in a midwestern community. The researchers conducted in-depth interviews and observations at school over a three-year period. One norm that emerged in these friendship groups was that romantic relationships should be important, but not everything in life. Group members who deviated from this rule were criticized. Girls who made boys their central concern were teased and called "boy-crazy." Girls who showed too little interest in boys risked being labeled as deviant, for instance as "queer" or lesbian.

In sixth grade, relatively little dating actually occurred and it was common for several girls to express interest in the same boy, much as female friends might like the same rock musician or movie star. During seventh grade, however, as group members began to pursue boys more actively, the norms changed. A new rule of exclusivity gradually developed dictating that a girl should not have romantic feelings for a boy who is already attached. Now it was considered inappropriate for a girl to express romantic feelings for a boy who was going with someone else, or who was being pursued by another girl in the group. Through the creation of these and other norms, the groups set guidelines for appropriate attitudes and behavior. A girl who failed to follow group norms was often pressured to conform through criticism expressed in jokes and gossip.

Among friends, social norms are typically informal and are created through face-to-face interaction. In other settings, however, the basic structure of a group is predetermined. The new recruit joining the army, the worker starting a job, and the woman joining a sorority are all confronted with a pre-existing social structure. For example, in a computer software business, there may be four distinct positions: the owner who created the business, the programmers who develop new software packages, sales representatives, and secretaries. Associated with each position is a particular set of rules and understandings about what the person in that position is expected to do, what the responsibilities are, and so on.

The cluster of norms that apply to people in a particular position, such as the programmer or

secretary, constitute their **social role** (Levine & Moreland, 1990). Roles define the division of labor in the group. In some groups, such as the software company, positions, roles, and status are explicit and may even be described in a formal organizational chart, in written job descriptions, or in a contract. Individuals must adapt to the requirements of their position in the group, although they may try to redefine or renegotiate existing patterns. The many social roles that we occupy in school, at work, and in our families and communities structure many of our daily activities.

Another important feature of group structure concerns differences in the **social status** of group members. As we saw in our earlier discussion of social roles (Chapter 1), the positions in most social systems differ in prestige and authority. In a formal organization such as the software company, the owner probably has the highest status, the largest salary, and the most authority to make decisions for the company; the secretary probably has the lowest status, lowest salary, and least influence in directing company policies and group activities. Even in groups whose members are supposedly equal in status, such as groups of friends or members of a jury, some individuals may emerge as more influential than others.

Expectation states theory, developed by Joseph Berger and his colleagues (1986), provides a useful explanation of the creation of status differences in groups. According to this perspective, group members want to achieve certain goals and are willing to confer high status on members who can help the group succeed. When group members first meet, they try to assess each person's ability to contribute to the achievement of group goals, and these assessments in turn form the basis for each person's status in the group.

Consider, for example, how the 12 middle-class members of a newly formed jury might select someone as group leader (Forsyth, 1990, pp. 120–121). Imagine that the group includes these three individuals:

> Susan Able, a 40-year-old white woman college professor who has written several books on management;

John Black, a 35-year-old African American business executive with many years of leadership experience;

Fred White, a 58-year-old white male physician who has an active general practice.

In deciding on a jury foreman, jurors might consider specific task-relevant information, such as Mr. Black's leadership experience in industry or Professor Able's experience in leading classroom discussions. However, jurors might also use what Berger calls *diffuse status characteristics*, general attributes of the person, such as age, sex, ethnicity, or wealth, that we tend to associate (sometimes wrongly) with ability. For instance, the jurors might discount Professor Able's task-relevant qualifications because she is a woman, and women are generally given less status and authority than men in American society. Jurors might also give special weight to Dr. White's high-prestige job (physician) and to his seniority in age, even though these attributes may have little relevance to his abilities as group leader. Research indicates that a person's status in a group is affected both by task-relevant characteristics and also by potentially irrelevant diffuse-status characteristics such as age, ethnic background, or occupational prestige. Both gender and race can serve as diffuse status characteristics in groups, often working to the disadvantage of women and members of ethnic minority groups (Forsyth, 1990).

Group Communication

Communication is essential to group activities, whether it be the endless talking at a committee meeting or the shared intimacies of a late-night conversation among friends.

A feature of most groups is that some people talk a great deal and others say very little. In a seminar, for example, there usually seem to be one or two people who monopolize the discussion, regardless of the topic. They do most of the talking, and the rest say only a few words.

Perhaps the most striking aspect of this phenomenon is that it occurs no matter what the size of the group. Regardless of how many members there are, communication follows a

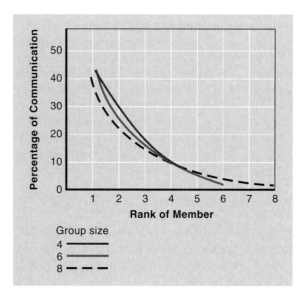

Figure 11-5　The amount of communication by members of a group follows a logarithmic or exponential curve. Regardless of the size of the group, the most talkative person does about 40 percent of the talking, and other group members talk much less. (*Source:* Adapted from Stephen & Mishler, 1952, p. 603.)

fairly regular pattern that can be represented by a logarithmic function. Figure 11-5 illustrates this pattern for groups of four, six, and eight. Note that in all cases, one person does a great deal of talking, the next most talkative person talks considerably less, and so on. In an eight-member group, two people contribute 60 percent of the conversation, one contributes 14 percent, and the other five contribute only 26 percent among them. The exact percentage contributed by each person will vary from group to group. There are even some groups in which all members make equal contributions. But by and large, a pattern roughly similar to the one illustrated appears in most groups.

We have been discussing groups as though every member were free to communicate with every other member. This is true in a discussion group, but there are many groups in which communication is limited. Several studies have investigated the effects of a variety of so-called **communication networks.**

The typical study in this area consists of forming a group to work on some problem and imposing limits on the communication permitted among the members. This is done by putting the subjects in separate rooms or booths and allowing them to communicate only by written messages or by an intercom system. The researchers are then able to control who can talk with whom, and a large number of different communication patterns can be imposed.

Some of these patterns are represented for groups of five people in Figure 11-6. You can see that the structures determine freedom of communication. In the circle, all members are equal—each can talk to two neighbors and to no one else. In the chain, two of the members can each talk to only one person. Obviously, in terms of communication it is worse to be at the end of a chain. The three other members are equal in terms of the number of people they can talk to, but the person in the middle is more central. The two intermediate people are somewhat isolated from the opposite ends. This progression is carried a step further in the Y-shaped structure. With three end members, only one of the others is able to talk to two people, and the fifth member is able to talk to three. In the wheel, one member can talk to everyone else, but all the other members can talk only to the central one.

Research shows that communication patterns such as these affect many aspects of group life

(Ridgeway, 1983; Shaw, 1981). Communication networks influence group morale. In general, the more freedom group members have to talk to each other, the more satisfied they are. So people are often happier in decentralized groups. Commun-

In this football huddle, the quarterback gives teammates instructions for the next play. This illustrates a wheel communication network in which messages are channeled through one person.

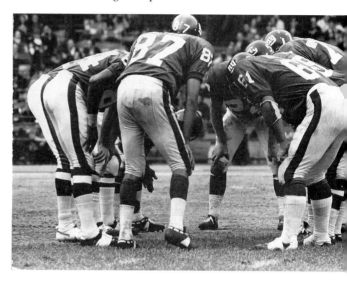

Figure 11-6 Examples of different types of communication networks.

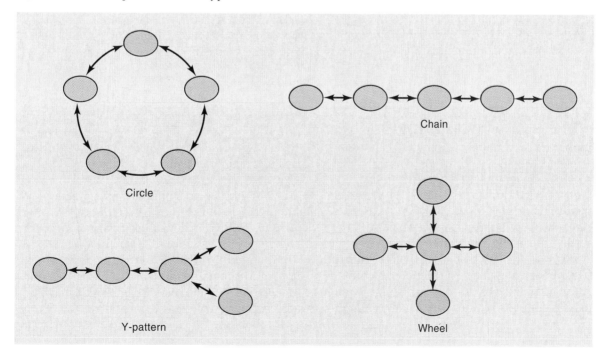

ication networks can also affect the efficiency of group problem solving. In general, centralized groups are more effective when they work on simple problems, but decentralized groups are more effective with complex problems.

Imagine, for example, that each member of a group is given a card with a different symbol on it and that the group task is to make a list of all the symbols. This kind of simple task is ideal for groups with highly centralized communication networks: The leader can easily collect the information from each individual and compile the final list. But complex problems are usually solved more effectively by groups with decentralized communication patterns, where freer interaction among members is possible.

Cohesiveness

In some groups, the bonds among members are strong and enduring, morale is high, and there is a general sense of community. In other groups, members are loosely linked, lack a sense of "groupness," and tend to drift apart over time. **Cohesiveness** refers to the forces, both positive and negative, that cause members to remain in a group (Festinger, 1950). Cohesiveness is a characteristic of a group as a whole, based on the combined commitment of each individual to the group.

A key positive force increasing cohesiveness is the interpersonal attraction that exists among group members (Ridgeway, 1983). When group members like each other and are connected by bonds of friendship, cohesiveness is high. Indeed, researchers have often measured cohesiveness by assessing the amount of liking among group members.

Second, people's motivation to remain in a group is also influenced by the instrumental goals of the group. We often participate in groups as a means to an end—a way to earn a salary, to play a sport we enjoy, or to work for a worthy cause. So, our attraction to a group depends on the match between our goals and those of the group, and on how successfully the group accomplishes its objectives. This point was illustrated in a study by Synder, Lassgard,

and Ford (1986). They investigated how individuals react when they belong to a group (even one artificially constructed by researchers) that fails in performing a group task. Compared to people in successful groups, members of unsuccessful groups did more to "distance" themselves from the group, for example, by not wearing their team badge. Individuals apparently wanted to avoid identification with an unsuccessful group, a finding consistent with social identity theory which we introduced in Chapter 5.

A third positive factor affecting cohesiveness is the extent to which a group interacts effectively and harmoniously. We would undoubtedly prefer to be on a team that works efficiently, rather than on one that wastes our time and misuses our skills. More generally, anything that increases group satisfaction and morale should enhance cohesiveness.

Group cohesiveness is also affected by negative forces that discourage members from leaving, even if they are dissatisfied. Sometimes people stay in groups because the costs of leaving are high or because they have no available alternatives. We may despise our coworkers, but stay at the job because there are no other job openings in town. We may dislike our teachers, but stay in their classes because we have no choice in the matter.

High levels of cohesiveness are usually beneficial to group functioning. When group members enjoy working together, both morale and motivation tend to be high. Further, members of highly cohesive groups are more likely to be influenced by the group and to conform to group norms than members of less cohesive groups (McGrath, 1984). This explains why cohesiveness can sometimes enhance productivity and sometimes hamper it. If the norms of the group are to work hard, put in long hours, and do your best, then cohesiveness will increase productivity. In contrast, if group standards are to slack off and spend more time talking than completing tasks, high cohesiveness will decrease productivity. We will soon consider two other potential drawbacks of high group cohesiveness when we discuss brainstorming and "groupthink."

TASK PERFORMANCE IN GROUPS

Are two heads better than one? Are groups usually more successful in getting a task done than individuals alone would be? Social psychologists have studied these issues in depth.

Problem Solving

To understand when a group is better at problem solving than an individual, we first need to consider the variety of tasks that groups can perform (Steiner, 1972).

An *additive task* is one in which group productivity is the sum of effort from each group member. When several friends work together to push a pickup truck with a dead battery out of a busy intersection, the group effort is the sum of how hard each person works. A crucial factor in additive tasks is whether group members are able to coordinate their efforts effectively. In the truck example, it would be important for everyone to push at the same time and in the same direction. The rope pulling task used by Ringelmann was also an additive task—the total effort exerted was the sum of the effort of each individual. Although social loafing may diminish the contribution of each individual to an additive task, the total contribution still usually exceeds what any one person could do alone. (Try pushing a stalled truck by yourself if you doubt this generalization.) On additive tasks, group productivity is generally superior to the efforts of any one person, and larger groups tend to be more productive than smaller groups (Littlepage, 1991).

A *conjunctive task* is one in which all group members must succeed for the group to succeed. For a spy team to slip successfully across enemy lines, it is essential that every member remain undetected. A false move by any one person endangers the whole mission. For conjunctive tasks, group productivity is only as good as the *least* competent group member, the "weakest link."

In a *disjunctive task*, only one person needs to solve a problem for the entire group to succeed. If a research group is trying to solve a complex mathematical equation, any one person with the right answer can ensure the group's effectiveness. Group performance on disjunctive tasks depends on the skills of the *most* competent member.

An even more complex situation occurs when a group has a task that can be subdivided among group members. In a football game, for example, teammates specialize in particular types of activities. Group productivity depends not only on the effort and skill of the best or worst player, but also on the group's ability to coordinate individual activities, often under time pressure (Kelly & McGrath, 1985) or other situational constraints.

BRAINSTORMING. If an advertising executive must develop catchy slogans for a campaign to encourage drivers to use seat belts, should she have her staff members work on the problem individually, or should she bring them together as a group to work jointly on the task? In the 1950s, advertising executive Alex Osborn (1957) proposed that groups are better at generating creative new ideas and solutions. The particular technique that he advocated is called **brainstorming,** and it is still used today in advertising and industry.

A brainstorming group is given a specific problem to discuss, such as writing advertising slogans for a new brand of toothpaste. Members are instructed to think of as many different suggestions as they can in a short time period. The

Neighbors struggle together to free a car trapped in a snowdrift. In an additive task, the success of the group depends on the combined efforts of all individuals.

rules of brainstorming, as outlined by Osborn, included these:

1. Criticism is ruled out. Negative evaluations of ideas must be withheld until later.
2. Freewheeling suggestions are welcomed. The wilder the idea, the better. It is easier to tame down an idea than to perk it up.
3. Quantity is wanted. The greater the number of ideas, the greater the likelihood of winners.
4. Combinations and improvements are sought. In addition to contributing ideas of your own, you should suggest how the ideas of others can be turned into better ideas or how two or more ideas can be joined into still another one.

In an early study on brainstorming, participants were assigned at random to five-person groups or to an individual condition (Taylor, Berry, & Block, 1958). The people in both conditions were then given five problems and 12 minutes to work on each one. One problem was stated as follows: "Each year a great many American tourists visit Europe, but now suppose that our country wished to get many more European tourists to visit America during their vacations. What steps can you suggest that would get more European tourists to come to this country?" The subjects were told that their task was to consider the problem and to offer as many and as creative solutions as they could. There were obviously no "correct" solutions.

Subjects in the alone condition were divided at random into five-person aggregates. That is, although each person worked alone, for purposes of analysis they were considered a unit, and their total production was compared to the production of the actual groups. The researchers compared 5 hours of work done by a five-person interacting group with 5 hours done by five individuals working alone.

The results, presented in Figure 11-7, can be considered in terms of the quantity of ideas produced and also in terms of their originality. Quantity consisted of the number of different ideas produced by the real groups and the aggregates. If two people in an aggregate produced the same idea, it was counted only once. As the figure shows, individuals working alone

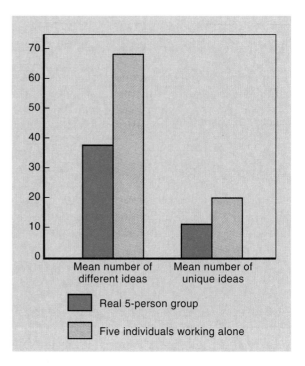

Figure 11-7 Comparing the brainstorming productivity of groups and individuals. (*Source:* Adapted from Taylor, D. W., Berry, P. C., and Block, C. H. (1958). Does group participation when using brainstorming facilitate or inhibit creative thinking? Published in *Administrative Science Quarterly, 2*, pp. 34–35. Reprinted by permission of Administrative Science Quarterly.)

(the aggregates) scored higher than the actual groups. Five individuals working alone produced almost twice as many solutions and unique ideas as five people working together. Subsequent research has replicated this finding: In general, individuals produce more ideas (and often better ideas) when working alone than in brainstorming groups (Mullen, Johnson, & Salas, 1991).

Why isn't brainstorming more effective? In a series of studies, Michael Diehl and Wolfgang Stroebe (1991) have investigated many possible explanations. In general, they believe that whatever benefits a brainstorming group may provide are more than offset by the interfering effects of other people. A major problem is the norm that only one person should speak at a time in a group. As a result, a group member who thinks of a new idea cannot immediately share the idea, but must instead wait a turn to speak. During this waiting time, the person may "rehearse" the idea, but can't simultaneously be thinking up additional new ideas. Further, a person who is trying to think of creative slogans or ideas may find it distracting to have to listen to other people, rather than being able to give full attention to pursuing his or her own ideas.

In summary, brainstorming is not a more effective technique than having individuals work alone. So why do people continue to use these problem-solving groups? First, people may mistakenly believe that groups really are more productive than individuals (Paulus, Dzindolet, Poletes, & Camacho, 1993). After a brainstorming session, group members may be impressed with all the many ideas generated by the discussion. Individuals may recognize that the group produced more solutions than one person would have, but forget the correct comparison which is to the productivity of many individuals simultaneously working alone. In other words, people readily agree that "two heads are better than one" but don't ask the relevant question of whether two heads together are better than two heads alone. A second reason for the popularity of group discussions is that people enjoy being in groups and prefer group discussions to working alone. Group discussions contribute to morale and motivation, even though they take more time.

Group Decision Making

After weeks of hearing testimony, the jurors meet to discuss a controversial case and reach a verdict. A woman has stabbed her husband to death. The prosecutor argued that this was a vicious act of premeditated murder, worthy of the death sentence. The defense attorney argued that the woman had been the victim of years of physical beatings and psychological abuse and that the stabbing was actually an act of self-defense. How will the jury arrive at a joint decision?

Psychologists have identified a set of **decision rules** that groups use in arriving at decisions (Miller, 1989). When a group of friends decide where to go out for dinner, they often try to reach a consensus decision. In contrast, when the president of a company considers relocating

his business to a new city, he may discuss the move with staff members, but will ultimately make an individual decision.

Research has sought to identify factors affecting the decision rules used by groups. The type of decision makes a difference. For example, in situations where a group is discussing a matter of opinion—whether the new yearbook cover should be green or blue, for instance—there is no objectively correct opinion. In such cases, where the topic is familiar, the alternatives are limited, and there is no correct answer, a *majority-wins rule* often prevails. In a majority-wins decision, the group ultimately decides to go along with the position that has the most supporters, even if the majority wins by the slimmest of margins. Research suggests that juries often seem to operate on a *two-thirds majority rule.* In American courts, a defendant is presumed innocent until proven guilty, and unless a strong majority of jurors agree about the defendant's guilt, the jury is likely to find the defendant innocent (Davis, 1989). When groups are discussing matters of fact rather than opinion, where one solution is correct and another is wrong, groups tend to adopt a *truth-wins rule* (Laughlin & Adamopoulos, 1980). As a result of the presentation of information and arguments, group members are persuaded by the truth of a particular position, even if it was initially held by only a minority of group members. Research on these and other decision rules suggests that by knowing the initial opinions of group members and the type of issue being discussed, we can often predict the group's decision in advance.

Group decision rules have consequences for the functioning of the group (Miller, 1989). Strict rules, such as the requirement that a group reach a unanimous decision, usually require more discussion than less stringent rules. Unanimous decisions are harder to reach, often involve compromises, and sometimes result in a failure to reach a decision. However, when groups are able to reach a unanimous decision, they tend to be more satisfied with the outcome than when a minority of members disagree with a group decision.

Unfortunately, groups do not necessarily make wise decisions. Social psychological research indicates that groups are vulnerable to special social forces that can bias decision making. We will discuss two of these phenomena: group polarization and groupthink.

GROUP POLARIZATION. In 1961 James Stoner observed that group decisions are often riskier than the individual views held by the members before discussion. This finding, called the **risky shift,** sparked considerable interest, in part because it seemed to contradict popular belief that groups are relatively conservative and stodgy about decision making.

In a typical risky-shift study, subjects read about a number of complex situations, such as the one described in Table 11-2. In each situation, several choices, ranging from very high risk to very low risk, were available. Subjects were asked to consider each situation carefully and to decide what recommendation they would make or which choice they would prefer. Subjects made their decisions individually and did not know they were going to discuss them later. Then subjects were brought into a group and asked to discuss each problem and to reach a unanimous group decision. Under these conditions, there was a strong tendency for the group decision to involve greater risk than the average of the decisions made by the individuals.

Many studies conducted in the United States, Canada, and Europe replicated this basic finding of a group shift toward greater risk, but some studies began to find exceptions. Some groups actually made more conservative decisions (Fraser, Gouge, & Billig, 1971). Today, research has shown that when the initial opinions of group members are conservative, group discussion results in a shift toward more extreme conservatism. In contrast, when the initial opinions tend toward risk, group discussion results in a shift toward greater risk. The basic finding is that group discussion leads to more extreme decisions, a phenomenon called **group polarization.** Several explanations for group polarization have been offered.

The *persuasive arguments* perspective emphasizes that people gain new information as a result of listening to pro and con arguments in the group discussion (Burnstein & Vinokur, 1975). The more numerous and persuasive the arguments in favor of a position, the more likely

TABLE 11-2
An Example of the Situations Used to Study Group Polarization

Mr. E is president of a light metals corporation in the United Sates. The corporation is quite prosperous, and has strongly considered the possibilities of expansion by building an additional plant in a new location. The choice is between building another plant in the United States where there would be a moderate return on the initial investment, or building a plant in a foreign country. Lower labor costs and easy access to raw materials in that country would mean a much higher return on the initial investment. On the other hand, there is a history of political instability and revolution in the foreign country under consideration. In fact, the leader of a small minority party is committed to nationalizing, that is, taking over, all foreign investments.

Imagine that you are advising Mr. E. Listed below are several probabilities or odds of continued political stability in the foreign country under consideration. Please check the LOWEST probability that you would consider acceptable for Mr. E's corporation to build in that country.

_____ The chances are 1 in 10 that the foreign country will remain politically stable.

_____ The chances are 3 in 10 that the foreign country will remain politically stable.

_____ The chances are 5 in 10 that the foreign country will remain politically stable.

_____ The chances are 7 in 10 that the foreign country will remain politically stable.

_____ The chances are 9 in 10 that the foreign country will remain politically stable.

_____ Place a check here if you think Mr. E's corporation should *not* build a plant in the foreign country, no matter what the probabilities.

Source: Kogan, N. & Wallach, M. A. (1967). Risk taking as a function of the situation, the person, and the group. In *New Directions in Psychology*, Vol. III, pp. 234–235. Copyright 1967 by Holt, Rinehart & Winston.

group members are to adopt that position. However, group discussions do not usually examine all conceivable pro and con arguments, nor do they present all positions with equal conviction (Stasser & Titus, 1985). Often, the majority of arguments tend to support each member's initial position, so that people usually hear more reasons in favor of their own opinion than against it. Group discussion may also encourage members to think about various arguments and to commit themselves more actively to a particular position. The information presented during the discussion may thus convince people of the correctness of their original views, and so lead to more extreme opinions.

A second explanation of group polarization emphasizes *social comparison* and self-presentational processes (Goethals & Darley, 1987). The idea is that group members are concerned with how their own opinions compare to those of others in the group. During discussion, individuals may learn that others have similar attitudes and indeed that some people even have stronger (more extreme) views than they do. A desire to be seen positively, as confident or bold, may lead individuals to shift toward even more extreme positions than those of their fellow group members. This is essentially a form of one-upmanship, in which individuals try to be "better" than average. As Brown explained, "To be virtuous . . . is to be different from the mean—in the right direction and to the right degree" (1974, p. 469). Current research provides support for both persuasive arguments and social comparison processes, and suggests that both occur simultaneously (Isenberg, 1986).

A third possibility is that *social identity processes* are at work (Abrams, Wetherell, Cochrane, Hogg, & Turner, 1990; Mackie, 1986). The idea is that discussion causes individuals to focus on their group membership and to identify with the group. This in turn leads individuals to feel pressure to shift their own views to conform with the perceived norm of their group. However, rather than perceiving the "true" average opinion of the group (as assessed by prediscussion scores), members perceive the group norm as more stereotyped or extreme. Consequently, they conform to what they believe is the group's position by shifting their own attitudes toward greater extremity. Whatever its possible causes, group polarization is an important facet of group decision making.

GROUPTHINK. Sometimes a seemingly reasonable and intelligent group of people make a decision that in retrospect was obviously a disaster. Irving Janis (1982) proposed that this may result from a process he calls **groupthink.** As outlined in Figure 11-8, the process begins with the group feeling invulnerable and excessively

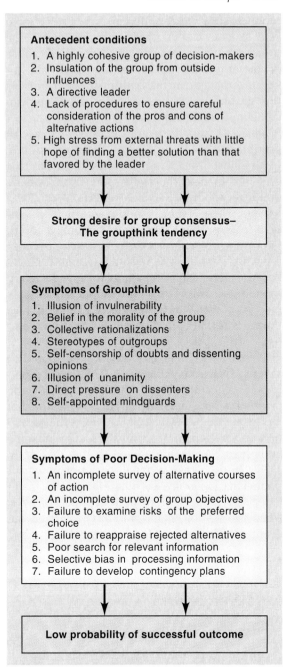

Figure 11-8 An analysis of groupthink. (*Source:* Adapted from Janis, 1982, p. 244.)

optimistic. The group comes to a decision without allowing members to express doubts about it. Members shield themselves from any outside information that might undermine this decision. Finally, the group believes its decision is unanimous, even when considerable unexpressed dissent exists. Under these circumstances, the group maintains extremely high morale because of the mutual support for the decision. But because disagreements both inside and outside the group are prevented, the decisions can sometimes be disastrous.

Janis identified several possible causes of groupthink. He suggested that groupthink occurs most often in highly cohesive groups that are able to seal themselves off from outside opinions and that have very strong, dynamic leaders. These leaders propose a particular solution to a problem and argue strongly for it. Group members do not disagree, partly because they are afraid of being rejected and partly because they do not want to lower group morale. According to Janis, skeptical members may go along with the group or even convince themselves that their own doubts are trivial and not worth expressing.

Janis claimed that groupthink contributed to several disastrous episodes in U.S. foreign policy. He cites the lack of preparation for the Japanese attack on Pearl Harbor in 1941, the Bay of Pigs invasion of Cuba in the 1960s, the escalation of the Vietnam War, and President Nixon's attempted Watergate cover-up in the early 1970s. In each case, a small group of powerful politicians, generally led by the president, made a decision in isolation from dissenting voices or from information that would have changed the eventual decision. Other researchers have applied the groupthink model to more recent disasters, such as the explosion of the space shuttle *Challenger*.

On January 28, 1986, the *Challenger* was launched from the Kennedy Space Center. Seventy-two seconds later, the spacecraft exploded, killing everyone on board as a horrified nation watched the tragedy on television. Expert engineers had warned against the launch, arguing that the air temperature was too cold for safety. But top decision makers disregarded this advice. According to a recent analysis, many elements of groupthink were present in the decisions leading up to the launch (Moorhead, Ference, & Neck, 1991). For example, the people who made the decision to launch the shuttle had worked together for years, had a strong sense of camaraderie, and were led by two top managers who strongly supported the launch even in the face of opposition. The decision makers dismissed the warnings of expert engineers, and pressured the manufacturer of the shuttle to recommend the launch. At the time, the decision makers seemed confident in the correctness of their position. The fact that NASA had had a series of 55 successful missions added to a sense of invulnerability. Ultimately, failure to heed the warnings of experts led to the fateful launch.

Janis offered various suggestions for combatting groupthink and enhancing the effectiveness of group decision making. These include:

1. The leader should encourage each group member to air objections and doubts about proposed decisions. For this to be effective, the leader must be willing to accept criticism of his or her ideas.

2. The leader should initially remain impartial in discussions, stating preferences and expectations only *after* group members have expressed their own views.

3. The group should divide into subcommittees to discuss issues independently and then come together to hammer out differences.

4. Outside experts should be invited to participate occasionally in group discussions and should be encouraged to challenge the views of the group members.

President Bill Clinton meets with his top advisors. How might group processes affect the decision making in this important group?

5. At each meeting, at least one person should be assigned to play devil's advocate to challenge group ideas.

These suggestions are designed to force the group to consider many alternatives, to avoid a false illusion of consensus, and to consider all relevant information.

Despite the intuitive appeal of groupthink, empirical support for Janis's ideas is limited (t'Hart, 1991). Since Janis proposed groupthink, there have been a few experimental tests of specific predictions (e.g., Flowers, 1977) and several other case studies that use the model to analyze a wide variety of decision-making errors (t'Hart, 1990). Recently, Philip Tetlock and his colleagues (1992) conducted a sophisticated analysis of records of 12 different political decisions, such as President Carter's unsuccessful attempt to rescue American hostages in Iran. Tetlock concluded that it was possible to distinguish reliably between groups whose decisions reflected groupthink and groups whose decision making showed good judgment and "vigilance." These results provide support for the existence of the groupthink process. However, the researchers had mixed success in testing factors that Janis proposed as causes of groupthink. Their results confirmed the important role of the leader in determining the quality of decision making. However, they found no support for Janis' prediction that groupthink is caused by high group cohesiveness.

In summary, there is reason to believe that the phenomenon of groupthink exists and has contributed to some disastrous political decisions in the recent past. At the same time, we have learned that the processes causing groupthink are more complex than Janis believed. For instance, many cohesive groups with strong leaders make excellent decisions. Indeed, the various groups involved in the disasters studied by Janis often made reasonable decisions on other occasions. Both the Roosevelt and Kennedy administrations were extremely effective in dealing with other crises. Furthermore, as politicians and generals can readily attest, thoughtful decision making is no guarantee of ultimate success. Sometimes groups engage in careful decision making, take reasonable action, and then, through bad luck or unforeseeable circumstances, fail miserably. Nevertheless, Janis'

analysis of groupthink and the research it has sparked provide a useful reminder of some of the potential pitfalls of group decision making.

COMPETITION VERSUS COOPERATION

In some groups, people interact cooperatively: They help each other, share information, and work together for mutual benefit. In other groups, people compete: They put their own individual goals first and strive to outperform the rest. Social psychologists have long been interested in understanding these human tendencies. In a series of classic studies, early researchers developed ingenious ways to study competition and cooperation systematically in the laboratory.

Classic Laboratory Studies

Much of the research on competition and cooperation has used laboratory games that simulate key features of everyday interaction. We will discuss research using two of the most popular games: the trucking game and the prisoner's dilemma. A common finding from these studies is that subjects—usually middle-class, white American college students—tend to compete, even when cooperation would be a more rewarding strategy.

THE TRUCKING GAME. In a pioneering experiment on competition, Deutsch and Krauss (1960) used a simple two-person game called the *trucking game*. Subjects were each asked to imagine that they were running a trucking company (either the Acme Company or the Bolt Company) and had to get a truck from one point to another as quickly as possible. The two trucks were not in competition; they had different starting points and different destinations. There was, however, one hitch: The faster route for both converged at one point to a one-lane road, and the two trucks had to go in opposite directions. This is shown in Figure 11-9. The only way both could use the road would be for one of them to wait until the other had passed through. If either truck entered the road, the

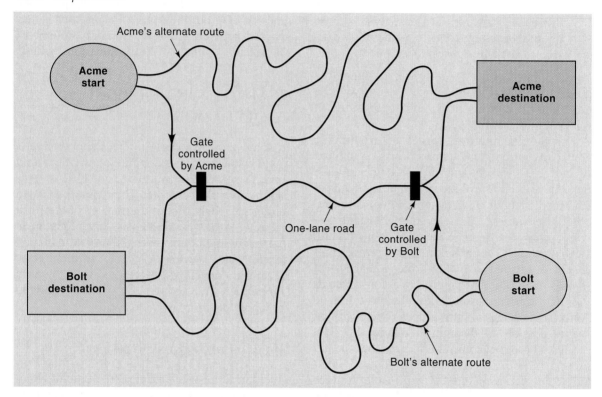

Figure 11-9 Road map of the trucking game. The players must get their truck to its destination as quickly as possible. Although they can do this efficiently only by cooperating and sharing the one-lane road, they often compete, particularly when gates are provided. (*Source:* Adapted from Deutsch & Krauss, 1960, p. 183.)

other could not use it; and if they both entered the road, neither of them could move until one had backed up. In addition, each player had a gate across the direct route that could be raised by pressing a button. If the gate was raised, it prevented the road from being used.

Each truck was provided with an alternative route that did not conflict with the other's, but was much longer. In fact, the game was set up so that taking the alternative route was guaranteed to lose points, whereas taking the direct route would gain points for both sides, even if they alternated at the one-lane section of the road. The players were told that their goal was to earn as many points as possible for themselves. Nothing was said about earning *more* points than the other player. Once the instructions were fully explained, each participant played the trucking game with the same partner for a series of trials.

The results of this experiment were striking. It was clear to the participants that the optimal strategy was to cooperate by alternating in using the one-lane road. In this way, they could both use the direct route, and one would be delayed only a few seconds while the other was getting through. Despite this, there was little cooperation between the players. Instead of allowing each other to use the one-lane road, they fought for its use, they raised their gates, and both players ended up losing points.

In a typical trial, both sides would try to use the road and would meet in the middle, head on. They would stubbornly stay there for a while, each refusing to retreat. The players might laugh nervously or make nasty comments. Finally, one of them would back up, erect the barrier, and use the alternate route. On the next trial, they would do the same thing, and so it went. An occasional cooperative trial might occur, but most trials were competitive.

THE PRISONER'S DILEMMA. The tendency to compete is not due to unique characteristics of the trucking game. It also occurs in many other games, such as the **prisoner's dilemma,** so-called because it is based on a problem faced by two suspects at a police station. The district attorney thinks the suspects have committed a major crime together but has no proof against either one. The prisoners are put into separate rooms, and each is told that he has two alternatives—to confess or not to confess. If neither suspect confesses, they cannot be convicted of a major crime. But the district attorney tells them they can still be convicted of minor crimes so that both will receive minor punishments. Of course, if they both confess, they will both definitely be convicted of the major crime. But the district attorney tells each suspect that he will ask for leniency if the suspect confesses. So if one of them confesses and the other does not, the confessor will be freed for helping the state, and the other suspect will get the maximum penalty. The situation is shown in Figure 11-10.

Obviously, there is a conflict. If one suspect thinks his partner is going to confess, it is best for him to confess also; on the other hand, the best joint outcome is for neither to confess and then

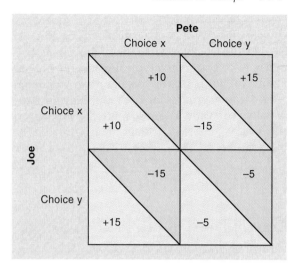

Figure 11-11 Typical prisoner's dilemma game matrix. Pete's payoff is shown in blue; Joe's payoff is shown in yellow. Choice X is cooperative because it allows both players to win. Choice Y is competitive because only the player who chooses it has a chance of winning and both players may lose. With this matrix there is a great deal of competition.

for both to take the minor sentences. Thus, if the suspects trust each other, they should not confess. However, if one suspect is convinced that his partner will not confess, he would do even better to confess and in that way be freed.

We do not know what real prisoners would do under these circumstances. In research on the problem, much of the drama is removed, but the game is basically similar. Instead of playing for their freedom, subjects play for points or money. They play in pairs but usually are not allowed to talk to each other. Each player has a choice of two strategies, and each player's payoff depends on the actions of both the player and the partner.

The exact pattern of payoffs varies; a typical one is shown in Figure 11-11 for two players, Pete and Joe. If both choose option X, each gets 10 points. If Pete chooses X and Joe chooses Y, Pete loses 15 and Joe wins 15. If both choose Y, they both lose 5 points. In other words, they can cooperate (choose X) and both win 10 points, or they can compete (one or both choosing Y) and try to win even more (15 points) but risk losing.

The players are told that the goal is to score as many points as they can. It is clear to virtually all of them that the way to have the highest

Figure 11-10 Example of the prisoner's dilemma game. Two prisoners have the choice of confessing or not confessing. If they trust and support each other by not confessing, each receives a light sentence; if they both confess they received relatively heavy sentences; and if one confesses and the other does not, the former is released while the latter gets a very heavy sentence. The dilemma is that if either one has complete trust in the other, he would do best by being untrustworthy himself and confessing.

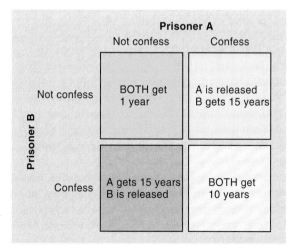

score is for both to select X (the cooperative choice) on every trial in a series of trials. But just as with the trucking game, there is a strong tendency to compete. In a typical game, only about a third of the choices are cooperative. Moreover, as the game progresses (and the players have usually won only a few points), the number of cooperative choices actually goes down. The players choose the competitive strategy more and more often, despite the fact that they know they can win more by cooperating.

Determinants of Competition Versus Cooperation

Many factors determine whether people interact cooperatively or competitively. These include the reward structure of the situation, cultural values about competition, individual differences in competitiveness, communication patterns, and the effects of reciprocity. We will consider each of these determinants of competition.

One important factor is the reward structure of the situation—the way in which rewards and desired outcomes are allocated. A *competitive reward structure* exists when one person's gain is another's loss. If you win a pot in poker, the other players must lose. In an Olympic swimming match, only one person can get the gold medal. If a college course is graded on a curve, only a few students can get A grades. In these situations, the outcomes of group members are negatively linked: An individual does best when

others do poorly. In such situations, a person who wants the available rewards will do best to compete.

In other situations, there is a *cooperative reward structure*. For a soccer team to win games, teammates must work together. People's rewards are positively linked, so what happens to one affects all the others. The better each player does, the more likely it is that the entire team will be victorious. In families and friendship groups, there are usually norms of cooperating. It has been found, for instance, that children are generally more cooperative and less competitive toward friends and siblings than toward strangers (Knight & Chao, 1991). In a cooperative reward situation, an individual who desires rewards will do best to cooperate.

An *individualistic reward structure* exists when the outcomes of individuals are independent of each other. Here, what happens to one person has no impact on the others. If a teacher gives an A to everyone who gets 90 percent correct on a test, it is possible for all students to get an A, or for none to get an A. Each person's grade is independent of how other classmates perform. In this type of situation, there is no extrinsic reason compete.

Often, however, the reward structure in a situation is mixed or unclear. People have choices about whether to cooperate or to compete. This was the case in the trucking game and the prisoners' dilemma game. As we saw, experimental game studies show that when there is a *mixed reward structure,* many middle class U.S. college students adopt a competitive strategy that actually prevents them from maximizing their rewards. How can we explain these findings?

One explanation is that American culture generally values competition and teaches children that it is often appropriate and even desirable to compete with others. The competitive tendencies of middle-class white American students may reflect their adherence to cultural values. Indeed, cross-cultural studies suggest that the United States may be one of the most competitive societies, a point we examine in the CULTURAL HIGHLIGHT.

There also appear to be individual differences within American society in people's personal values about competition. Research suggests that individuals tend to have one of three value

Team sports foster fierce competition when one side can win only at the expense of the other team.

CULTURAL HIGHLIGHT
The Spirit of Competition

It has been suggested that Americans are some of the most competitive people on earth, and cross-cultural studies of children support this view. This point is strikingly illustrated in research comparing Anglo American and Mexican children (Kagan, 1977). In one study, for example, 8-year-old children played a game of marbles with another same-sex child from their own culture (Madsen, 1971). Children had the option of cooperating or competing, but the game was set up so that children could get marbles only by cooperating. Mexican children cooperated on roughly 7 of 10 trials. In contrast, Anglo American children cooperated on fewer than 1 trial in 10. Another study compared Mexican children, Mexican American children, and Anglo American children (Kagan & Madsen, 1971). Among 7- to 9-year-olds, Mexican children cooperated 63 percent of the time, Mexican Americans 29 percent, and Anglo Americans only 10 percent of the time.

How can we explain these clear-cut group differences? Spencer Kagan (1984) has systematically examined possible explanations. In general, people living in cities are more competitive than those who live in rural areas, and people from higher economic classes are more com-petitive than those from poorer backgrounds. But neither of these factors explains the Mexican versus Anglo American differences. When researchers compare children from similar residential and economic back-grounds, the cultural differences still emerge. Nor are the differences in competitiveness due to differences in family size or patterns of parental discipline.

It appears that the cross-cultural patterns reflect broad cultural values about cooperation and competition that are taught not only at home but also in schools, through the media, and through sports and games (Kagan, 1984). The more exposure Mexican children have to U.S. culture, the more competitive they become. We noted earlier that Mexican American children show a pattern of competitiveness in between that of Anglos and Mexicans. Other research suggests that third-generation Mexican American children whose parents were born in the United States are more competi-tive than second-generation chil-dren whose parents were born in Mexico (Knight & Kagan, 1977). Similarly, Mexican American children who speak only Spanish (and so, presumably, are less influenced by Anglo culture) are less competitive than bilingual children (cited in Kagan, 1984). Taken together, these findings suggest that as the influence of American culture and values increases, children tend to become more competitive.

Is there any relationship between competitive tendencies and a child's self-esteem? Spencer Kagan and George Knight (1979) hypothesized that children feel better about them-selves when they live up to cul-tural norms. If this is so, then children from a competitive Anglo culture should show higher self-esteem if they are rel-atively more competitive. In con-trast, for children from a cooperative Mexican culture, high self-esteem should be asso-ciated with greater cooperation. Data from a study of Anglo and second-generation Mexican American children provided sup-port for this hypothesis. On aver-age, the Anglos were more competitive than the Mexican Americans but the groups did not differ in self-esteem. For Anglos, high self-esteem was related to making competitive choices, but for second-genera-tion Mexican Americans high self-esteem was related to mak-ing cooperative choices. In short, children tend to feel good about themselves when their actions conform to cultural standards.

orientations or strategies for interacting with other people (Kuhlman & Wimberley, 1976; McClintock & Liebrand, 1988):

- *Cooperators* are concerned with maximizing the joint rewards received by both self and the partner.
- *Competitors* are oriented toward maximizing their own gains relative to those of the partner. They want to do better than the partner.
- *Individualists* are oriented toward maximizing their own gains, with no concern for the gains or losses of the partner.

When people are confronted with a situation such as the trucking game or prisoner's dilemma, their value orientation has a strong impact on their initial behavior. Cooperators usually initiate cooperative interactions; competitors begin in a more competitive mode. Over time, however, individuals will change their own behavior if the partner does not reciprocate. Confronted with a highly competitive partner, even the most dedicated cooperator may begin to behave competitively.

Communication among partners also influences cooperation. In general, more communication leads to more cooperation (Orbell, van de Kragt, & Dawes, 1988). For example, in the Deutsch and Krauss trucking game study, three different communication conditions were included. Some subjects were required to communicate; others were given the opportunity to talk if they wanted to; a third group was not allowed to communicate. Cooperation was greatest when communication was required, and least when communication was impossible.

Similar results have been found using the prisoner's dilemma game. Wichman (1970) showed that competition was greatest when no communication was possible, somewhat less when partners could talk but not see each other, and least when partners could see and talk to each other. Wichman found that when there was no communication, about 40 percent of responses were cooperative; when verbal communication was permitted, cooperation increased to more than 70 percent of trials. Communication enables partners to urge each

other to cooperate, to discuss their plans, to make promises, to convince each other that they are trustworthy, to learn about each other, and so on.

A final factor is reciprocity. We have seen throughout this book that there is a general norm of reciprocity: People often feel obligated to return both favors and insults. There is some evidence that in the course of interaction, initial competition provokes more competition, and cooperation sometimes (but not always) encourages further cooperation. One strategy that seems especially successful in fostering cooperation is reciprocal concessions. The parties take turns giving up a little. This is the traditional compromise solution to most conflicts: Each side starts with an extreme position and then retreats gradually until a common meeting ground is found.

If one party makes a small concession and then waits for the other to do the same, there is usually greater cooperation eventually (Esser & Komorita, 1975). However, a crucial element of this strategy is timing. A person who gives in too much at once may appear weak and the other will not reciprocate. The concessions must be gradual and sequential. In fact, according to Wall (1977), the most effective technique is to make reciprocal concessions slightly larger than those made by the other person. This reinforces the other's cooperation and results in even larger concessions and quick agreement. Obviously, this does not work unless both sides are willing to cooperate to some extent. If one is totally competitive, the one who tries cooperating will only be exploited and end up with a weaker position than before.

Social Dilemmas

As you hike along a beautiful mountain trail, you stop for a snack. You are tempted to throw away your empty water containers and granola bar wrappers, knowing that your backpack will be lighter if you don't have to carry your trash to the top of the mountain and back. But you hesitate, knowing that if all hikers litter the trail, it will soon be unpleasant for all who use it.

Outdoor enthusiasts hike in Yosemite National Park to enjoy the beauty of nature. Increasingly, these nature lovers confront a troublesome social dilemma: When too many people crowd into the park, no one can enjoy a wilderness experience.

In the Southwest, many communities have suffered severe droughts for years, and water conservation is essential. Individuals living in drought-stricken areas face personal decisions. For instance, should I forego the pleasure of a long shower today so that there will be more water for all in the future?

Each of these examples represents a **social dilemma**—a situation in which the most rewarding short-term choice for an individual will ultimately lead to negative outcomes for all concerned. As Brewer and Kramer describe it, "Social dilemmas exist whenever the cumulative result of reasonable individual choices is collective disaster" (1986, p. 543).

Social dilemmas pit the short-term interests of the individual against the long-term interests of the group (which includes the individual). Today, as we are becoming more aware of the dangers of pollution and the wanton use of natural resources, an understanding of social dilemmas is especially timely. Social dilemma research is currently an active field in social psychology (Kameda et al., 1992; Liebrand, Wilke, & Messick, 1992). Research on social dilemmas extends earlier studies of the trucking game and prisoner's dilemma to more complicated situations. Much of this research has been done in the laboratory, in game-playing situations that replicate essential features of real-life social dilemmas (e.g., Komorita, Parks, & Hulbert,

1992). Central questions are how to resolve social dilemmas and how to encourage individuals to cooperate, in ways that will have long-range benefits for the group.

One approach to solving social dilemmas is to change the reward structure in the situation. For example, an effective way to encourage people to use less water is to change the billing system so that customers are charged higher rates if they use more of this valued resource (Messick & Brewer, 1983). Similarly, we can encourage people to insulate their homes (and use less energy) by offering tax incentives for energy-saving home improvements. Another step is to set up committees or public agencies to make decisions about the use of a valuable resource, rather than leaving such decisions in the hands of individuals. The United States Environmental Protection Agency is one such effort.

Other factors are also important in solving social dilemmas. Not surprisingly, some of the same factors we identified earlier as affecting competition and cooperation are also relevant to social dilemmas. A person's value orientation—whether cooperative, competitive, or individualist—can make a difference in how he or she approaches a social dilemma (Liebrand & van Run, 1985). Communication among the individuals involved may also be important, because it provides an opportunity for individuals to make public promises to cooperate. Fostering a sense of group identity can also increase the tendency to show restraint and to use resources wisely, especially in small groups (Brewer & Kramer, 1986).

LEADERSHIP

Some form of leadership exists in all groups (Hollander, 1985). The central attribute of leadership is social influence. The leader is the person who has the most impact on group behavior and beliefs. He or she is the one who initiates action, gives orders, makes decisions, settles disputes among group members, offers encouragement, serves as a model, and is in the forefront of group activity.

Leadership Structure

Social scientists refer to a group's unique pattern of leadership as the leadership structure of the group. In some groups, this is relatively simple. The committee responsible for planning a New Year's party at the office may consist of one enthusiastic leader and several followers. In other groups, the pattern of leadership is more complex. Who are the leaders in a professional football team? Possible leaders might include the owners, the general manager, the head coach, the captains of the various team units, the quarterback who calls the plays, or individual team members who serve as informal spokesmen for the team. In this case, various individuals are in charge of different aspects of team functioning. So, whereas some groups have only one leader, other groups have two or more. In general, groups that face diverse and complex tasks requiring many types of skills tend to have several leaders, each a specialist in some aspect of the group's activities (Ridgeway, 1983).

FORMAL AND INFORMAL LEADERS. Groups differ in the extent to which their leadership structure is formal or informal. Large organizations such as a business or school have formal organization charts indicating the official chain of command and giving guidelines about patterns of decision making and supervision. Even in smaller groups, such as clubs and fraternities, there may be elected officers with specified responsibilities. At the other extreme, some groups have no formal leaders at all. Friendship groups are one example.

What is important to recognize, however, is that groups without formal leaders still have patterns of informal leadership. One person may be more articulate and persuasive than others in group discussions, and so has more influence on decisions. Someone else may emerge as the person who smoothes over conflicts within the group. All groups, even those that say they are leaderless, have some leadership structure. And even in groups with formal leaders, there is often a pattern of informal leadership that can be very different from the official structure. The president of the student council may be the official head of the group, but unofficially it may be another officer who actually has the greatest influence in decision making.

PATHS TO LEADERSHIP. Individuals can become group leaders in several ways. Some leaders are appointed. An army lieutenant is appointed by people higher up in the military organization to run his or her unit. Because of this position, the lieutenant can give orders to everyone else in the company, but none of them can give the lieutenant orders. In other situations, such as clubs or student government, a leader is elected.

In a third process, a group member gradually emerges as a leader over time. When people interact repeatedly, as in a group of friends or classmates, some individuals typically emerge as informal leaders. These leaders do not have official titles, but most group members would generally agree that a particular person or set of people are the leaders. Outside observers can also spot emergent leaders by watching such things as who talks the most in group discussions and whose opinions are most likely to prevail in group decision making. Many studies have found a strong tendency for the person who talks the most to be perceived as the leader both by other members of the group and by outside observers (Mullen, 1991). Specific leadership activities also make a difference. For instance, in a recent study groups of grade school children were asked to decide which of eight pictures was most suitable for displaying in children's hospital rooms (French & Stright, 1991). Those children who frequently asked others their opinions, who kept the group focused on the task, and who made records of group decisions were perceived as leaders by group members, by teachers, and by other observers.

TASK AND SOCIAL LEADERSHIP. In general, leaders must perform two types of activities. **Task leadership** concerns accomplishing the goals of the group—getting the work of the group done successfully. The task leader gives suggestions, offers opinions, and provides information to the group. He or she controls, shapes, directs, and organizes the group in carrying out a specific task. In contrast, **social leadership** focuses on the emotional and interpersonal aspects of group interaction. The social leader concentrates on keeping the group running smoothly and harmoniously, is concerned about people's feelings, uses humor to relieve tension, and tries to encourage group cohesiveness.

Extensive research has shown that both task and social leadership are important to successful group functioning (Bales, 1970). The qualities necessary for the two types of leadership are somewhat different. A task leader must be efficient, directive, and knowledgeable about the particular task at hand. A social leader must be friendly, agreeable, conciliatory, concerned with feelings, and socially oriented. In some groups, one person is the task leader, and a different person is the social leader. There is some evidence, for instance, that in informal discussion groups, men are more likely to emerge as task leaders and women as social leaders (Eagly & Karau, 1991). But often, a single person combines both functions. In formal settings where a specific individual is designated as the teacher or supervisor, that person may be expected to perform both task and social functions.

Cross-cultural research confirms the importance of these two types of leadership activities (Hui, 1990). In Japan, for instance, Jyuji Misumi (1985) has conducted a series of studies of leadership in education, government, and industry.

He has found that four types of leaders can be distinguished: those who are high on task orientation and low on social orientation; those who are high on social orientation and low on task orientation; those who are high on both, and those who are low on both. In general, "hybrid" leaders who emphasized both group productivity and group morale were more effective than other types of leaders in a variety of settings ranging from teaching school to running a successful engineering project.

Who Becomes a Leader?

The search for factors that cause some people and not others to become leaders is an old one. Two contrasting views have emerged: One emphasizes the unique personal characteristics of the leader, and the other emphasizes the situational forces acting on the group.

The "great person" theory of leadership suggests that some people, because of personality or other unique characteristics, are destined to lead. To test this hypothesis, many empirical studies have compared the characteristics of leaders and followers (Forsyth, 1990). Surprisingly few qualities have been found that consistently separate leaders from followers. In a general way, however, three factors are associated with leadership (Ridgeway, 1983).

First, leaders tend to excel in those abilities that help the group to accomplish its goals. In some situations, intelligence correlates with leadership. In other situations, leadership might be linked to political expertise, physical strength, or skills relevant to the activities and goals of the group. The star of a basketball team (Michael Jordan, for example) almost automatically becomes a task leader of the team.

Second, leaders tend to have interpersonal skills that contribute to successful group interaction. In general, it is an asset to be cooperative, organized, articulate, and interpersonally sensitive. The ability to perceive group needs and to respond to them is important (Ellis, 1988). Such characteristics enhance a person's functioning as a social leader. A third factor is motivation. Leaders usually desire recognition and promi-

Despite very different family backgrounds and personalities, both Malcolm X and John F. Kennedy rose to national prominence in the United States. What complex paths led each man to become a leader?

nence (e.g., Whitney, Sagrestano, & Maslach, 1992). Leaders are more ambitious, achievement-oriented, and willing to assume responsibility. We emphasize, however, that although these qualities enhance a person's leadership potential, none is a sure guarantee of actually becoming a leader.

Another approach to leadership emphasizes situational factors. During World War II, U.S. Admiral Halsey was quoted as saying, "There are no great men. There are only great challenges which ordinary men are forced by circumstance to meet" (quoted in Boal & Bryson, 1988, p. 11). A striking demonstration of situational forces comes from the research on communication networks described earlier in this chapter (Leavitt, 1951). The basic idea is that communication is essential for leadership, so the person who can communicate most freely tends to become the leader. In situations such as a wheel network, where all communications are channeled through one person, that individual typically becomes the leader.

Today, most researchers believe that becoming a leader depends in large part on the *match* between the characteristics of the person and the needs of the situation confronting the group. It should be obvious that different situations require different qualities in a leader. Being a star pitcher may be a real asset in becoming captain of the intramural softball team, but it would not contribute much to heading the debate team.

Styles of Leadership

Leaders vary enormously in their style and effectiveness. Fred Fiedler (1978, 1981) has investigated ways in which a leader's style and the nature of the situation interact to determine the leader's effectiveness. Fiedler calls his analysis a **contingency model of leadership effectiveness.** The model identifies two styles of leadership, corresponding roughly to the distinction between task and social leadership that we made earlier. Those leaders who give higher priority to getting the work of the group done successfully and who deemphasize relations among group members are called *task-oriented leaders*. The coach who says that "winning is the only thing" and ignores the feelings of team members is an example. In Fiedler's model, those leaders who reverse these priorities by putting group relations first and task accomplishment second are called *relationship-oriented leaders*. This sort of coach would say that it doesn't matter whether you win or lose, so long as you enjoy playing your teammates.

Fiedler also classifies group situations along a continuum. At one extreme are high-control situations in which a leader has high legitimate power and is well liked and respected by the group, and in which the group's task is structured and clear-cut. An example would be a popular Scout leader showing a group of children how to set up a tent. At the other extreme are low-control situations in which the leader has little legitimate authority, has poor relations with group members, and is confronted with a task that may require creative or complex solutions. An example would be an inexperienced and unpopular student teacher who is asked to lead a group discussion with high school seniors about ways to improve school spirit.

A main goal of Fiedler's research has been to determine which types of leaders are most effective in which situations. His results, replicated in a number of different studies, are shown in Figure 11-12. Task-oriented leaders are more effective in increasing group productivity in *both* extremely high and extremely low control situations. In other words, both the Scout leader and the student teacher would be advised to focus on the task at hand. Relationship-oriented leaders are most effective in situations where the leader has moderate control: when the leader gets along well with group members but has a complex task, or when the leader is disliked but the task is clear.

One conclusion we can draw from Fiedler's model is that the effectiveness of either type of leader will change if there is a change in control. For example, one study of army infantry squads found that a squad leader's situational control increased from moderate to high as he gained experience and on-the-job training (Bons &

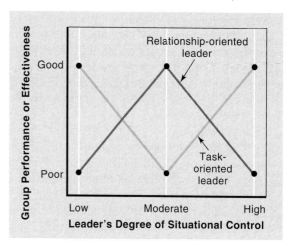

Figure 11-12 Fiedler's model of how group performance is determined by the leader's style and situational control. When control is either very low or very high, task-oriented leaders are more effective in encouraging productivity. When situational control is moderate, relationship-oriented leaders are more effective. (*Source:* Adapted from Fiedler, *American Behavioral Scientist*, Vol. 24, No. 5, 1981, p. 625. Reprinted by permission of Sage Publications, Inc.)

Fiedler, 1976). In accord with Fiedler's theory, task-oriented squad leaders were at first less effective than were relationship-oriented leaders. But as the leaders gained more situational control, the task-oriented leaders became more effective and the relationship-oriented leaders decreased in effectiveness. The key point is that no one style of leadership is effective in all situations. Ultimately, the most effective leader may be the person who can adapt his or her leadership style to match the situation.

The models of leadership that we have considered so far have paid little attention to the role of followers in determining who becomes a leader. The *transactional approach* serves to remedy this gap (Hollander, 1985). The central point of this approach is that the influence between the leader and followers works both ways. The perceptions and attitudes of followers partly determine who becomes leader. Leaders, in turn, usually pay close attention to the views of followers and may modify their leadership behavior in response to the actions of their followers. In small groups, the willingness of group members to accept the leader's influence depends on the processes of social exchange discussed in Chapter 10. Leaders who fail to provide rewards or to move the group toward its goal, who are perceived as unfair, and who are unresponsive to group needs will be disliked, and may jeopardize their leadership position. For example, elected officials who ignore the wishes of their constituents may not win re-election.

Some leaders go beyond meeting the present needs of their followers and, instead, inspire hope in new possibilities. The Reverend Martin Luther King, Jr., motivated many Americans to dream and work for a changed society of racial justice and harmony. Similarly, in his bid for the U.S. Presidency, Robert Kennedy said, "Some men see things as they are and say, why? I dream things that never were and say, why not?" (*New York Times*, 1968, p. 53). Leaders who provide a vision of a better future and inspire followers to take on new challenges are called charismatic or *transformational leaders*. Such leaders can be found not only in politics but in business, the military, and religion, and they range across the liberal–conservative spectrum.

In a program of research, Bernard Bass (1985) and his colleagues have identified several characteristics of transformational leaders. Their inspirational leadership creates trust and a sense of purpose. They treat followers as individuals, not merely as members of a group. They show their followers how to think about problems in new and creative ways. Transformational leaders are often seen by their followers or subordinates as outstanding and unusually effective leaders. For example, a recent study of men in the U.S. Navy found that subordinates reported working harder and feeling greater satisfaction when their superior officer had a transformational style (Yammarino & Bass, 1990).

KEY TERMS

brainstorming	group	social impact theory
cohesiveness	group polarization	social inhibition
communication networks	groupthink	social leadership
contingency model of leadership effectiveness	prisoner's dilemma	social loafing
decision rules	risky shift	social norm
deindividuation	social compensation	social role
evaluation apprehension	social dilemma	social status
expectation states theory	social facilitation	task leadership

SUMMARY

1. Working in the presence of others sometimes leads to social facilitation and sometimes causes social loafing. Which effect occurs depends on the complexity of the task. It also depends on whether the group context increases the individual's concerns about social evaluation (because others are judging the person's performance) or reduces social evaluation concerns (because the individual's own effort is hidden by working in a group).

2. Social impact theory proposes that the influence of an audience on an individual depends on the number of observers, the strength (importance) of the audience, and the immediacy of the audience.

3. People in groups sometimes behave in much more unusual or antisocial ways than individuals alone would. This deindividuation occurs because anonymity reduces the individual's feelings of personal responsibility and because the person's attention is focused on the group rather than on the self.

4. A group is a social unit in which people are interdependent: What happens to one person affects the outcomes of other group members. Social norms are rules and expectations about how people should behave;

social roles define the rights and responsibilities of individuals in particular positions in the group.

5. Communication is essential to group activities. In most groups, some people talk more than others. Limits imposed on communication create various communication networks. Centralized networks (one person is allowed to talk to everyone, but the other people can talk only to the central person) are efficient for solving simple problems. Decentralized networks produce higher morale and are probably superior for solving complex problems.

6. Cohesiveness refers to the positive forces that cause members to want to stay in a group and also to the negative forces that discourage members from leaving a group.

7. Whether individuals or groups are better at solving problems depends on the nature of the task to be performed. Brainstorming is popular as a method for generating creative ideas in a group setting, but it may not be as efficient as having several individuals work alone.

8. Decision-making groups can adopt a variety of decision rules, such as majority-wins or truth-wins rules. Groups tend to make more extreme decisions than individuals would alone. This group polarization effect sometimes leads to riskier decisions, and sometimes to more conservative decisions. Explanations for group polarization emphasize the importance of persuasive arguments, social comparison processes, and social identity.

9. Decision-making groups with a directive leader may be vulnerable to groupthink. This is a decision-making process that discourages criticism and can lead to poor decisions.

10. Much research on competition and cooperation has used laboratory games such as the trucking game and prisoner's dilemma. More recently, researchers have investigated social dilemmas.

11. Americans often tend to compete, even when they would obtain greater external rewards from cooperation. Situational factors affecting competition include the reward structure of the situation and the amount of communication among people. There are also both individual and cultural differences in the tendency to compete. One strategy for reducing competition is reciprocal concessions.

12. Group leaders are those who have the most impact on group behavior and beliefs. A task leader focuses on accomplishing group goals successfully. A social leader strives to maintain harmony and high morale. People who become leaders tend to be socially skilled, to excel in abilities that help the group achieve its goals, and/or to be ambitious. According to Fiedler's contingency model, the success of a leader depends on the match between the leader's style (task-oriented versus relationship-oriented) and the nature of the situation.

SUGGESTED READINGS _____

Baron, R. S., Kerr, N., & Miller, N. (1992). *Group process, group decision, group action.* Buckingham: Open University Press. Provides up-to-date information on core topics in the study of groups including social facilitation, individual versus group performance, and group decision-making.

Fiedler, F. E., & Garcia, J. E. (1987). *New approaches to effective leadership: Cognitive resources and organizational performance.* New York: Wiley. A comprehensive review of Fiedler's theory and research with attention to the impact of intelligence and other "cognitive resources" on leadership.

Janis, I. L. (1982). *Groupthink: Psychological studies of policy decisions and fiascoes* (2nd ed.). Boston: Houghton Mifflin. Presents Janis's theory and reviews research testing hypotheses about groupthink.

Mullen, B., & Goethals, G. R. (Eds.) (1987). *Theories of group behavior.* New York: Springer-Verlag. Presents eight social psychological theories about group behavior.

Worchel, S., Wood, W., & Simpson, J. A. (Eds.) (1992). *Group process and productivity.* Newbury Park, CA: Sage Publications. Presents the latest empirical research on groups.

12
Gender

FOCUS OF THIS CHAPTER

Gender in the Eye of the Beholder
Gender and the Self
Theoretical Perspectives on Gender
Comparing the Social Behavior
  of Women and Men
Changing Roles for Women
  and Men

Research Closeup
Detecting Sexism

Cultural Highlight
Too Many Women—Sex Ratios
  and Social Life

On a radio talk show, the host is discussing teenage sexuality with a medical expert. When they take their first telephone call, a person named Chris asks about the safety of birth control pills. The researcher begins his answer by asking Chris if she herself is considering using the pill. After a pause, Chris blurts out, "I'm a boy." Everyone seems embarrassed, the researcher apologizes, and the host rephrases the question. I, like other listeners, think about Chris's high-pitched voice and gentle manner. Would I have made the same mistake?

A noted psychologist begins a study of the behavior of young children. Concerned that knowledge of a child's gender might influence the way observers interpret the child's activities, the researcher asks parents to bring their children to the study dressed in overalls and T-shirts. To the researcher's surprise, her effort to conceal the toddlers' gender backfires. Although all children arrive in denims, most little girls wear overalls with ruffles or bows.

You glance casually at the driver of the sports car stopped at a traffic light. Noticing a gray sweatshirt and a prominent chin, you assume the person is a man. But something about the face makes you look again. You quickly study the person's physique. The smooth cheeks give no hint of stubble. The shoulders are a bit broad for a woman, but perhaps she's a swimmer. The arm resting on the car door conceals the person's chest, but reveals slender, delicate fingers. Neither rings nor earrings are visible. Then the light changes and the car drives off, leaving you puzzling about the driver's sex.

As these examples indicate, gender is one of the basic categories in social life. In meeting new people, we inevitably try to identify them as male or female. The process of categorizing people and things as masculine or feminine is called **gender typing** (or sex typing). This process usually occurs automatically, without our giving it much thought. Most of the time, cues about gender are readily available from physical characteristics such as facial hair or breasts and from style of dress. People usually display their gender as a prominent part of their self-presentation.

Parents typically dress their children in ways that readily communicate the child's sex. An observational study conducted in surburban shopping malls found that 90 percent of infants were dressed in clothes that were gender-typed in color or style. For instance, whereas 75 percent of the girls wore or carried something pink, none of the boys did. In contrast, 79 percent of the boys wore or carried something blue, while only 8 percent of girls did (Shakin, Shakin, & Sternglanz, 1985). Situations where we cannot identify a person's gender are rare. They call attention to the categorization process and typically lead us to seek information about whether the person is male or female.

The tendency to divide the world into masculine and feminine categories is not limited to person perception; many objects and activities are also defined as masculine and feminine. At an early age, children learn that dolls and cooking utensils are for girls and that toy trucks and guns are for boys (Robinson & Morris, 1986). Most 4-year-olds believe that doctor, police officer, and construction worker are male jobs and that secretary, teacher, and librarian are female jobs (Gettys & Cann, 1981).

The process of gender typing continues in adulthood. College students identify barbells,

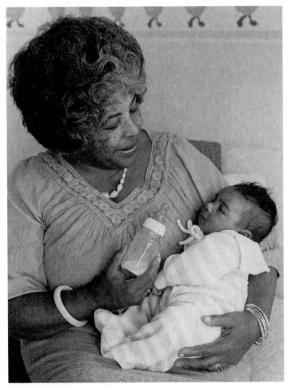

These women represent quite different images of femininity—young beauty queens, a kindly grandmother, and a woman executive. We combine information about gender and other characteristics to form stereotypes about distinct types of males and females. What might you infer about the personality and life aspirations of each of these women?

wrenches, and chest strengtheners as masculine objects, and thimbles, rolling pins, and laundry baskets as feminine. Some objects, such as headphones and electric outlets, are seen as gender neutral (Reis & Jackson, 1981). Married couples often distinguish between "men's work," such as mowing the lawn, taking out the garbage, or barbecuing, and "women's work," such as housecleaning or childcare. Although a few occupations such as psychologist and personnel officer are seen by adults as gender neutral, most jobs are perceived as gender typed (Shinar, 1975). You should have no trouble guessing how most people categorize the following jobs: receptionist, brain surgeon, day care provider, truck driver, nurse, and judge.

The distinction between male and female is a universal organizing principle in social life. As children, boys and girls are expected to learn different skills and to develop different personalities. As adults, men and women typically assume distinctive gender-linked roles as husband or wife, mother or father. Cultures vary in exactly what is defined as masculine or feminine and in the degree to which they accentuate gender differences or similarities. But the use of gender to structure at least some elements of social life has been basic.

In the sections that follow, we will explore the importance of gender in social life. We begin with stereotypes about males and females, and then consider how gender influences a person's self-concept. We review theoretical perspectives on gender, and present the latest research comparing the social behavior of women and men. We conclude with a discussion of changing roles for women and men in American society.

A word about terminology is useful at this

point. Some psychologists believe we should distinguish between the terms "sex" and "gender." Rhoda Unger and Mary Crawford (1992) define *sex* as biological differences in genetics, anatomy, and physical functioning. They define *gender* as "what culture makes out of the 'raw material' of biological sex," that is, the meaning we attach to being male and female (p. 18). At present, however, most psychological researchers do not systematically distinguish between sex and gender in this way. For simplicity, we will use these terms interchangeably in this chapter.

GENDER IN THE EYE OF THE BEHOLDER

We begin with a seemingly simple question: How does a person's sex influence our perception and evaluation of the person and his or her behavior? The emphasis here is on gender as a characteristic of the *target* of impression formation. Research shows that our beliefs about what typical men and women are like can color our perception of individuals and bias our evaluations of their performance.

Gender Stereotypes

How do you think men and women differ? Do you believe that one sex is usually more aggressive or more nurturant than the other? How do the sexes typically compare on such qualities as being courageous, neat, logical, gentle, squeamish, dominant, or gullible? Beliefs about the personal attributes of females and males are **gender stereotypes.** As we saw in Chapter 2, all stereotypes, whether based on gender, race, ethnicity, or other groupings, refer to an image of what the typical member of a particular social category is like. Depictions of the sexes in the mass media illustrate the nature of gender stereotypes in our society.

MEDIA IMAGES OF THE SEXES. Television, movies, pop music, and other mass media convey messages about the nature of masculinity and femininity. You probably know these stereotypes quite well, although you may not have thought about them very much.

On TV, for example, we can see anxious housewives desperately trying to avoid tell-tale spots on the family's clothes or pondering the best food for a finicky cat. Young women appear obsessed with staying thin or competing for a man's attention by wearing the right pantyhose or jeans. Off camera, the voices of male experts solemnly offer advice. On screen, men in impressive offices extol the virtues of electric shavers or copying machines. During weekend sports events, ads for alcoholic beverages show groups of men in rugged outdoor activities.

Systematic research has found that the most common TV commercial depicts a male expert instructing a female consumer about a product. In a study conducted in the 1970s, for example, 70 percent of men were shown as experts, whereas 86 percent of women were product users (McArthur & Resko, 1975). Female experts and male consumers were the exception. In recent years, sex differences in commercials may be lessening (Bretl & Cantor, 1988). Somewhat more men are being shown as parents and consumers. But when commercials have an expert narrator or "voice of authority," this is still almost always a man (Craig, 1992).

These studies and other analyses of newspaper articles, award-winning children's books, college textbooks, modern art, and other diverse elements of culture have found several general themes in the portrayal of the sexes:

- Whereas men are shown in a wide variety of social roles and activities, women are more often restricted to domestic and family roles.
- Men are commonly portrayed as experts and leaders, women as subordinates.
- Men are usually depicted as more active, assertive, and influential than women.
- Although females are slightly more than half the population, they are often underrepresented in the media.

In recent years there have been efforts to change

these media images so they portray men and women in less rigidly gender-typed ways. On TV, for example, we are slowly beginning to see a few women in the business world and a few men in the kitchen.

Do these media portraits of the sexes actually have an effect on people's daily lives? As we have seen elsewhere in this book, it is surprisingly difficult to show that the mass media influence peoples' behavior (Durkin, 1987). Several studies have found that children who watch more television tend to have more stereotyped views about men and women, and also about the types of jobs that are best suited for each sex. In a recent study, for example, the amount of television children watched correlated with their attitudes about the sex-typing of household chores. Further, children who watched more television believed more strongly that *only* girls should wash dishes and help with cooking and *only* boys should mow the lawn and take out the garbage (Signorelli & Lears, 1992). But in correlational studies such as these, the direction of causality is not clear. Does TV encourage traditional attitudes in viewers? Or do sex-role traditionalists watch more television because they find media portrayals of women and men consistent with their pre-existing personal beliefs?

Experimental studies provide more clear-cut evidence about the potential impact of the media. Experiments demonstrate that television can affect viewers' beliefs about gender. In a field experiment, Kimball (1986) studied a Canadian community before and after television became available. After the introduction of television, children's beliefs became more sex-typed, and more similar to those of children in other communities with access to television.

An experimental study of women college students also demonstrated the potential influence of TV (Jennings, Geis, & Brown, 1980). Participants were randomly assigned to one of two conditions. Half the participants saw four commercials depicting the sexes in traditional roles. Men were portrayed as the authorities and were the center of attention; women were shown as sex objects or in domestic roles. The experimental commercials were closely mod-

eled after real ones. In one, for example, a tiny woman serves her large, hungry husband a frozen dinner. The implicit message was that the wife's role is to cater to and please her husband. In another, an attractive man authoritatively extols the virtues of an alcoholic beverage. At the end of the commercial, a seductive woman slithers up to the man and coyly says that she would also choose the same drink. Here the woman is presented as a sex object who follows the man's advice. In the second experimental condition, participants saw reversed-role versions of the same commercials in which the females were the central figures and the males were shown in the homemaking and seductive roles.

Results indicated that exposure to TV commercials had a significant effect on subsequent behavior. After watching the films, participants from both conditions engaged in one of two tasks. Some performed a test designed to measure their conformity, while others were rated on self-confidence as they gave a short, extemporaneous speech. Women who had watched traditional commercials conformed more and showed less self-confidence than women who had watched the nontraditional commercials. The researchers concluded that regardless of whether people buy the product advertised in commercials, they may buy the implicit images of femininity and masculinity conveyed. How well the results of laboratory experiments such as this generalize to everyday life has not yet been determined.

UNDERSTANDING STEREOTYPES. A useful distinction can be made between cultural and personal stereotypes (Ashmore, Del Boca, & Wohlers, 1986). **Cultural stereotypes** are beliefs about the sexes communicated by the mass media, religious teachings, art, and literature. As individuals, we are familiar with cultural stereotypes, but we may or may not agree with them. We may know, for instance, that the culture portrays women as less competent than men, but reject this idea as untrue. **Personal stereotypes** are our own unique beliefs about the attributes of groups of people such as women and men.

The content of stereotypes can be conceptual-

TABLE 12-1
Common Gender Stereotypes

Typical Man	Typical Woman
Aggressive	Gentle
Unemotional	Cries easily
Likes math and science	Enjoys art and literature
Worldly	Does not use harsh language
Ambitious	Tactful
Objective	Religious
Dominant	Interested in own appearance
Competitive	Aware of feelings of others
Self-confident	Strong need for security
Logical	Talkative
Acts as leader	Neat in habits
Independent	Dependent

ized in two major ways. One way we think about gender is in terms of general personality *traits* that characterize each sex. Most of us have beliefs about the global features that distinguish males and females. To get some idea of your own views on this, read the traits listed in Table 12-1, and decide whether you personally think each trait is more characteristic of men or of women, or equally true of both sexes. You will probably find this a fairly easy task. People usually develop broad generalizations about the traits shared by men and women and about the traits that distinguish the sexes.

Research finds that men are commonly rated higher than women on traits associated with competence, such as leadership, objectivity, and independence (Rosenkrantz et al., 1968). In contrast, women are usually rated higher on traits associated with warmth and expressiveness, such as gentleness and awareness of the feelings of others. During the past 20 years, there have been many changes in the roles of American women, including a dramatic increase in the proportion of women employed outside the home. However, despite these changes, stereotypes about the personal attributes of men and women have remained remarkably stable over time (Bergen & Williams, 1991).

Cross-cultural research finds that core elements of gender stereotypes are quite similar in many countries. John Williams and Deborah Best (1990a) studied gender stereotypes among college students in 25 countries around the globe including Nigeria, Spain, New Zealand, India, Japan, Canada, and Brazil. Respondents in every single country identified being adventurous, independent, dominant, and strong as masculine qualities, and being sentimental, submissive, and superstitious as feminine qualities.

In addition to thinking about the sexes in terms of traits, there is a second way in which people think about gender. We often construct images of different types of males and females (Ashmore et al., 1986; Six & Eckes, 1991). Instead of thinking about females "in general," we may think of more specific categories of women, such as mothers, career women, beauty queens, tomboys, or spinsters. Similarly, instead of having a single, uniform image of males, our beliefs about men may distinguish such types as fathers, businessmen, hardhats, sissies, jocks, chauvinists, or nerds (Holland & Skinner, 1987). In other words, we may form **schemas** about specific types of males and females who embody distinctive clusters of traits. Thus, one person might believe that mothers are nurturant and self-sacrificing, that beauty queens are gorgeous but emptyheaded, or that tomboys are youthful, athletic, and adventurous. An important point is that these stereotypes often incorporate some attributes typically associated with the other sex: a career woman may be seen as assertive and independent (masculine traits) as well as attractive and tactful (feminine traits).

Activating Stereotypes

What determines whether we relate to a person largely on the basis of stereotypes or as a unique individual? In other words, what situations increase the influence of stereotypes? Two important factors are the amount of information we have about the person and the salience of the person's group membership.

AMOUNT OF INFORMATION.   The less information available about a person, the more likely we are to perceive and react to him or her on the basis of stereotypes. For example, when people know nothing about a baby except its gender, they sometimes react to the child in stereotyped ways. In one study, adults watched a videotape of a baby (Condry & Condry, 1976). Although everyone watched the same videotape, half were told they were watching a boy and half were told they were watching a girl. People who thought the child was a boy rated the child as significantly more active and forceful than people who thought the child was a girl. The child's ambiguous response to a jack-in-the-box toy was rated as showing more "fear" if the child was a girl and more "anger" if the child was a boy. In a more recent study, children (ages 5, 9, and 15), college students, and mothers watched videotapes of infants labeled as male or female (Vogel et al., 1991). Both the children and the college students rated the "female" infants as smaller, nicer, softer and more beautiful than the "male" infants. Mothers' evaluations of the infants were *not* affected by gender labels, perhaps because their personal experience with

If you saw this woman in a supermarket, you might assume that she is a suburban homemaker or school teacher. In reality, Patty Murray is a newly elected U.S. senator from the state of Washington.

babies made it less important to rely on gender stereotypes.

When we have more information about the unique attributes of a particular person, we rely less on stereotypes (Locksley et al., 1980). For instance, we may believe that most males are highly assertive, and so assume when we meet a new man that he too will be assertive. But we may also have learned from past experience that our friend Leon is shy and unassuming. The effect of gender stereotypes can usually be reduced or eliminated when we have relevant information about a specific person (Biernat, 1991a).

SALIENCE OF GROUP MEMBERSHIP.   A second factor that can activate the use of stereotypes is the salience of the person's group membership, in this case gender. By salient we mean that the person's gender stands out and is a prominent characteristic. For example, a woman's gender is more salient if we can see her in person than if we talk to her by phone or read an article she has written. Another factor affecting gender salience is the proportion of women to men in a group. A person's gender is more salient when he or she is in a numerical minority, such as being the only woman in an all-male work group. "Token integration" often creates groups with just one minority person. Token or "solo" status calls attention to the person's distinctive social category and makes solos especially vulnerable to stereotyping.

A study by Shelley Taylor (1981b) illustrates this point. Students evaluated the members of a six-person tape-recorded discussion group. Some groups had a solo man or a solo woman; others were evenly divided between men and women. After listening to the tape recording, subjects rated the group members. In actuality, the solo's contribution to the discussion was *identical* to that of one of the members of the gender-balanced group. But Taylor found that the solos were perceived as talking more and making a stronger impression than members of the more gender-balanced groups. In addition, solos tended to be perceived as playing gender-stereotyped roles. Solo women were seen as "motherly, nurturant types, bitches, or as the group secretary." Solo men were perceived as "father figures, leaders, or macho types." Group composition accentuated the solo's gender and fostered stereotyped perceptions of the solo's behavior.

The Dangers of Stereotypes

As we saw in Chapter 3 on social cognition, it is quite natural to try to simplify complex life experiences by categorizing and generalizing. Personal stereotypes, like other social schemas, are one way we try to make sense of life. But like other mental crutches, stereotypes have certain inherent problems.

One problem is that stereotypes always over-simplify and sometimes are dead wrong, as we will see later in the chapter. For example, the belief that men are more intelligent than women has been disproved by scientific research. Unfortunately, people seldom examine the accuracy of their stereotypes. If we encounter some-one who does not fit a stereotype, we often simply decide the person is "the exception that proves the rule." We do nothing to change our stereotype. Further, stereotypes are often used to justify prejudice and discrimination against members of certain groups. Historically, the false beliefs that women were not a smart as men and that women lacked ambition was used to deny women an education and to keep them at home.

A second problem is that stereotypes exaggerate differences *between* groups and minimize differences *within* groups (Martin, 1987). Gender stereotypes can make it seem that all men are alike, when in fact there are enormous individual differences among men. The same is true about differences among women. Gender stereotypes can also make it seem that men and women are utterly different, when in fact similarities are usually much greater than differences. For example, men tend to be faster runners than women. But there is enormous variation among men and women in running speed: Individuals of both sexes range from highly trained sprinters and long-distance runners to slow-paced couch potatoes who haven't run anywhere in years. Average differences between males and females in running speed, while real, are much smaller than within-group variation.

A third problem is that we sometimes act in ways that turn stereotypes into self-fulfilling prophecies. If we expect a woman to be pleasant and unassertive, we may act toward her in ways that lead her to act just as we believe she will. This point was cleverly demonstrated in a study by Berna Skrypnek and Mark Snyder (1982). A male college student was led to believe that his partner for an experiment was either a stereo-typic man (independent, assertive, ambitious, and masculine) or a stereotypic woman (shy, gullible, soft-spoken, and feminine). In reality, the partner was always a woman, a naive sub-ject who had been randomly assigned the label of "man" or "woman." The two partners com-municate from separate rooms by a system of lights, so that the partner's true sex was never revealed. The woman was told nothing about her partner, how she has been described to him, or the goals of the study. In this way the researchers systematically manipulated the gen-der expectations of the male subject.

In the first phase of the study, the partners negotiated how to divide work on 12 hypotheti-cal tasks. Some tasks were traditionally mascu-line (fixing a light switch or baiting a fish hook), some were feminine (icing a birthday cake or ironing a shirt), and some were neutral (coding test results, washing windows). The rules set by the experimenter gave the man greater initiative in the bargaining process. As predicted, the man's expectations about his partner shaped his own actions significantly. If he thought his part-ner was a conventional woman, the male subject was more likely to select masculine tasks for himself and to refuse to switch tasks than if he thought his partner was a man. As a result, the female subject wound up being assigned more of the feminine tasks if she was arbitrarily labeled a "female" than if she was believed to be a "male."

In the second phase, the researchers investi-gated whether this initial behavior pattern would continue over time. Accordingly, they changed the rules of the interaction so that the woman now had greater control over the bargaining. Nonetheless, a woman who had been labeled as "female" continued to select more feminine tasks than did a woman labeled as a "male." The woman actually came to initiate behaviors consistent with the gender to which she has been randomly assigned!

This study provides a powerful demonstration that in dyadic interaction, one person's beliefs and stereotypes about another can channel their interaction so that the other person engages in stereotype-confirming behavior. Our actions are shaped not only by our own interests and preferences, but also by the expectations of those with whom we interact. When others expect us to act in gender-typed ways and communicate these expectations through their behaviors, we sometimes put aside personal preferences and instead act out the other's expectations.

Evaluating Performance

Do we typically give women and men equal credit for equal work? Or do gender stereotypes distort judgments of performance? One of the first demonstrations of gender bias in evaluation was provided by Philip Goldberg in 1968. He investigated whether women were biased in evaluations of other women. Goldberg selected six professional journal articles from such fields as law, elementary education, and art history. The articles were edited to about 1500 words each and combined into test booklets. The experimental manipulation concerned the gender of the authors. The same article bore a male name (such as John T. McKay) in one booklet and a female name (such as Joan T. McKay) in another. Each booklet contained three articles by "men" and three by "women." College women read the six articles and then rated each on persuasiveness, style, and competence.

Results indicated that the same article was judged more favorably when it had a male author than when it had a female author. Goldberg's results appeared to show that women are indeed prejudiced against women. But before leaping to a hasty conclusion, it is important to know that Goldberg's findings sparked a flurry of research. The results of over a hundred studies suggest that evaluation bias is considerably more complex than was first imagined (Top, 1991). And evaluation bias can cut both ways, sometimes favoring men and occasionally favoring women. The challenge today is to understand when and how gender bias occurs. Many factors seem to be important.

First, the gender-typing of the task or job makes a difference. In general, men have an advantage in traditionally masculine jobs and women have an advantage in feminine jobs (Glick et al., 1988). In one study, professional personnel consultants rated applicants' résumés for traditionally masculine jobs such as automobile salesperson, feminine jobs such as office receptionist, and gender neutral jobs such as motel desk clerk (Cash, Gillen, & Burns, 1977). For masculine jobs, men were perceived as better qualified, were expected to be more successful, and were given stronger recommendations. For feminine jobs, women were rated more favorably. For gender-neutral jobs, men and women were given similar ratings.

Another study investigated how employers react to male versus female job applicants (Levinson, 1975). College students working on the research team responded by phone to actual job ads that had appeared in the local newspaper. Some of the jobs were traditionally masculine (bus driver, management trainee, security guard) and some were feminine (receptionist, housekeeper, dental assistant). None required advanced training. A male and female applicant with equivalent qualifications called about each job. How would the employers respond to the male and female applicants?

Gender bias was said to occur when the "sex-appropriate" caller was encouraged to apply, but the "sex-inappropriate" caller was not. In one case, for example, a female caller for a restaurant management training program was told that she was disqualified because she had only two years of college and no prior management experience. But a male with the identical background was scheduled for an interview. In all, 28 percent of the women asking about masculine jobs were discouraged, as were 44 percent of the men asking about feminine jobs. This suggests considerable gender bias linked to the gender typing of occupations. In this case, the bias was actually stronger against men than against women.

A second factor influencing evaluation bias is the amount of relevant information available about the person (Pazy, 1992). Gender bias in evaluations is least likely when much information is provided about the individual's ability. One study gave extensive information about a male or female manager, including copies of letters, memos, and other materials allegedly written by the person (Frank & Drucker, 1977). Subjects used this material as a basis for evaluating the manager's sensitivity, organizing and decision-making ability, and communication effectiveness. The experimental manipulation was whether the materials were written by "John Griffin" or "Joan Griffin." Given all this information about the specific individuals, John and Joan were rated identically. No evaluation bias occurred.

Third, there is some evidence that stereotype-breaking behavior can occasionally win a person "extra" credit. In particular, when a woman excels in a traditionally masculine job, she may be perceived more favorably than an equally successful man. One study found that a highly successful female attorney was rated more vocationally competent than was an identically successful male attorney (Abramson et al., 1977). Similarly, another study presented students with descriptions of a person whose quick thinking in an armed robbery helped the police capture a criminal (Taynor & Deaux, 1973). When the person was a woman, she received more positive evaluations than a man in the identical situation. The unusualness of a woman's successful performance in masculine situations appears to win her a more favorable evaluation than her male counterpart. Whether something comparable occurs for men who excel in traditionally feminine activities is an interesting but unanswered question.

Finally, it is important to add that the size of the sex bias in evaluations can be very small. In laboratory studies, it is rare for Joan McKay to be seen as totally incompetent and John McKay to be rated as a stellar performer. When gender effects are found, they usually reflect small mean differences in ratings, perhaps a difference of one point on a 10-point rating scale. In a

How effective is this man as a teacher at a daycare center for preschool children? Research shows that gender bias can color our evaluations of the performance of individuals who work in nontraditional jobs—men in traditionally "feminine" fields as well as women in "masculine" fields.

review of 106 studies, Janet Swim and her associates (1989) found that gender bias typically accounted for less than 1 percent of all the variation in evaluations of performance. Nevertheless, the authors speculate that sex bias may be greater in the real world than in laboratory experiments where subjects are often on their "best behavior."

There is ample evidence that sex bias does exist in actual job settings, although it is difficult to gauge the pervasiveness of this tendency (Nieva & Gutek, 1981). In one national survey, for example, male managers generally perceived women workers as lower than men in skill, motivation, and work habits (Rosen & Jerdee, 1978). Women were believed to be less employable and promotable, and to have less ability to make decisions and to cope with stress. There is also evidence that women managers and leaders are sometimes evaluated less favorably than their male counterparts (Eagly, Makhijani, & Klonsky, 1992). Women managers tend to receive more negative ratings when they adopt a task-oriented and directive (or "masculine") leadership style, when they work in a traditionally masculine field (such as business executive), and when they are evaluated by men.

Consider the true story of Ann Hopkins, one of a handful of female accountants employed by the large firm of Price Waterhouse (Fiske et al., 1991). In 1982, Hopkins had established herself as an outstanding worker; she had brought in

$25 million worth of business, was praised by her clients, and had more billable hours than any of her 87 male peers. Yet when candidates were considered for partnership in the firm, Hopkins was turned down. Critics said she was too "macho," had poor interpersonal skills, and needed a "course at charm school." Instead of changing her clothes and hairstyle, Hopkins filed a law suit against Price Waterhouse, alleging sex bias in promotion procedures. In 1990, after a lengthy trial, the U.S. Supreme Court ruled in her favor, noting that "gender-based stereotyping played a role" in the promotion decision.

During the trial, expert testimony was presented by social psychologist Susan Fiske who reviewed the extensive research literature on sex stereotyping. Fiske argued that Hopkins was vulnerable to stereotyping because she was a token woman in a predominantly male environment, and because she was a woman in a traditionally masculine field. Rather than basing the promotion decision on her actual performance, Hopkins was stereotyped as a "lady partner candidate." Further, unsubstantiated rumors about her social skills were weighed equally with the opinions of people who knew her work well and the objective facts of her performance record. Behaviors that her supporters saw as determined go-getting were interpreted by her critics as abrasive and difficult. In short, processes of gender stereotyping biased the evaluation of her job performance.

So far, we have considered evaluations of the quality of women's and men's performance. Another way in which gender bias can occur is in the **attributions** people make to explain success or failure. Research has found that men's success is more often seen as resulting from ability. In contrast, women's success is more often attributed to the ease of the task (Feather & Simon, 1975), to extreme effort (Taynor & Deaux, 1975), or to luck (Deaux & Emswiller, 1974). We usually evaluate a successful performance more favorably if we attribute it to skill, not luck. Differences in attributions for men's and women's performance may create a subtle bias that diminishes recognition of women's ability

and instead explains female success as due to situational or chance factors.

Attributional bias is not limited to work settings. Consider two school children who both do well in math. When Lisa shows her mom the A grade in math on her report card, her mother proudly credits Lisa with "really working hard" in that course. In contrast, when Tom shows his A to his mom, she proudly credits Tom with being "a little math genius." The girl's success is attributed to high effort and the boy's success to high ability.

A study of junior high school students and their parents indicates that gender-based attributional differences such as these are common (Yee & Eccles, 1988). The researchers investigated how parents perceived their child's math performance. In general, parents were fairly accurate in their assessment of the level of their children's math achievement. But parents gave significantly different explanations for the performance of sons versus daughters. For example, mothers credited a son's success more to talent than a daughter's; mothers attributed a daughter's success more to effort than a son's. Well-meaning parents may unintentionally discourage their talented daughters from pursuing the study of math by subtly communicating that the girl is hardworking rather than gifted.

In summary, a person's gender can influence the way we evaluate that person and the way we explain his or her performance. Evaluation bias sometimes favors men, especially in masculine situations. However, women may have an advantage in feminine situations and when they excel in masculine activities. When substantial information is available about a person, gender bias in evaluation often disappears. Finally, it appears that female and male evaluators are equally prone to engage in evaluative bias based on the performer's gender. The RESEARCH CLOSEUP for this chapter describes new research on bias in evaluations, specifically the detection of sexism. Having seen how the perceptions of other people are affected by whether they are female or male, we turn our attention now to the question of how gender influences our self-perception.

Sexism refers to prejudice (negative attitudes) and discrimination (biased behavior) based on gender. If we are to eliminate sexism, we must first notice when it occurs. A recent study by Robert Baron, Mary Burgess, and Chuan Kao (1991) investigated what happens when sexism against women is expressed by an unexpected source—women. We know that women are sometimes the targets of sexism by men but, of course, women can also engage in sexist acts. Are people equally likely to detect sexism committed by women and by men?

Baron, Burgess, and Kao reasoned that we are less apt to notice bias against women when it is committed by other women. One explanation is based on processes of ingroup/outgroup bias discussed in Chapter 7 on prejudice. The idea is that people are unlikely to discriminate against other ingroup members, but may discriminate against outgroup members. Applied to gender, this would suggest that women are not biased against other women, but might show bias toward men. Similarly, men might show bias toward women, but not toward other men. A second reason we might fail to detect sexism by women against women is that gender stereotypes often associate sexism with men, not with women.

In a preliminary study, the researchers investigated perceptions of ingroup/outgroup bias based on gender. They asked college students to read a series of stories in which the protagonist derogated either women or men. Students were then asked to guess the likely gender, education, and geographical origin of the person. The results were very clear. When the protagonist put down women, 88 percent of subjects (both males and females) believed that the person was male. Only 2 percent thought a woman was likely to derogate another woman, and 9 percent were undecided. In contrast, when the protagonist showed prejudice against males, most subjects (93 percent) believed the person was a female.

In the main study, a new sample of college students read a series of 19 stories, each describing in some detail the interaction between two people. Some of the stories contained no sexist bias, but in others the protagonist acted toward a women on the basis of traditional stereotypes. The target of the sexism was always a woman. Some actions were blatant: In one vignette, a female student was counseled to drop her premedical courses and transfer to nursing. Other actions were more subtle: A woman was expected to prepare food or she was ignored as a decision maker. Half the time, each vignette was written with a male perpetrator, and half the time it had a female perpetrator. After reading each story, subjects were asked to describe in their own words the three "strongest qualities or traits exhibited by the actor/actress in this episode." To avoid influencing subjects' perceptions of the stories, no mention was made of sexism or bias. A story was classified as sexist if subjects used such terms as *prejudiced, sexist,* or *bigot.*

The results provided strong support for the hypothesis that subjects would be more likely to label men's behavior as sexist than women's. Subjects were 8 times more likely to label a particular story as sexist when the actor was male rather than female. For example, 78 percent of students who read the first story with a male actor classified it as sexist compared to only 1 percent of subjects who read the identical story with a female actor. Male and female subjects did not differ significantly in their ratings.

In summary, the same actions directed at women were evaluated quite differently when performed by men versus women. When there is uncertainty about whether an action is biased or not, we may be relatively quick to label men as sexist and much slower to apply the same label to women.

GENDER AND THE SELF

Gender is a basic element in one's self-concept. Knowing that "I am a woman" or "I am a man" is a core part of our personal identity. Further, many people perceive themselves as having gender-typed interests and personalities.

Gender Identity

Knowledge that we are male or female, our sense of **gender identity,** is acquired early in life. By age 2 or 3, children are aware of their own gender and can tell us whether they are a girl or a boy. By age 4 or 5, children can correctly label other people by gender. However, this understanding of gender differs from that of adults. Research by Lawrence Kohlberg (1966) and other developmental psychologists has documented the surprising fact that young children think they can change gender if they want to (Stagnor & Ruble, 1987).

In one study, Kohlberg showed children a picture of a girl and asked whether she could be a boy if she wanted to, or if she played boys' games, or if she wore a boy's haircut and clothes. Most of the 4-year-olds said that she *could* become a boy. By age 6 or 7, however, children insisted that such a gender transformation would be impossible. Kohlberg believed that this shift in children's conception of gender is part of a more general pattern of cognitive development. The same 4-year-old who says she could change gender might also say the family cat could become a dog by cutting off its whiskers.

Young children do not see the physical world as constant (a girl remains a girl, and a cat remains a cat). As children grow older, a combination of experience and maturation enables them to reach a more advanced stage of mental development in which they understand that sex and other physical properties remain the same despite changes in external appearance. An important developmental milestone occurs when children understand that gender is fixed and unchanging: Once a boy, always a boy, and once a girl, always a girl.

For most of us, the acquisition of gender identity is a smooth and trouble-free process. We are classified as male or female at birth, treated as a boy or girl by our parents, and easily learn our own gender as we grow up. For a few people, however, developing gender identity is a problem. **Transsexuals** are a case in point. Such individuals are biologically members of one sex, but develop the belief that they are really members of the other sex. In the most common case, a person is to all outward appearances a male, but the person's psychological reality is being a woman trapped in a male body.

The causes of transsexualism are still a mys-

The much publicized transsexual Christine Jorgenson, as she appeared after undergoing sex-change surgery, and how she looked as the former George W. Jorgenson.

tery (Blanchard & Steiner, 1990). Most often, transsexuals show no signs of biological abnormality. Genetically, hormonally, and physiologically, they are "normal" members of their sex. Yet at a very early age they develop a self-concept at odds with their physical characteristics. This puzzling situation is profoundly disturbing to the individuals involved. Efforts to help transsexuals by psychotherapy have had very little success; it is not easy to change a deeply rooted sense of gender identity. As a result, some have advocated sex-change surgery as one way to reconcile this mind–body problem by altering the body to fit the person's mental identity (Green & Fleming, 1990).

Psychological Masculinity, Femininity, and Androgyny

Gender identity is an either–or matter; people believe they are either a male or a female. However, individuals differ markedly in the degree to which they perceive themselves as having all the different masculine or feminine characteristics that make up conventional gender stereotypes. In terms of their **gender self-concept,** highly "masculine" individuals believe they possess many attributes, interests, preferences, and skills that society typically associates with maleness. Highly "feminine" individuals believe they possess many attributes, interests, preferences, and skills associated with femaleness.

Early tests to measure psychological masculinity and femininity used a forced-choice format. A typical test might ask such questions as whether a person prefers showers (masculine) or tub baths (feminine), whether the person would rather work as a building contractor (masculine) or librarian (feminine), whether the person is active (masculine) or passive (feminine). An important feature of these tests was that they viewed masculinity and femininity as mutually exclusive polar opposites. People got a single score on the test: high scores indicate masculinity (many masculine choices), and low scores indicate femininity (few masculine choices).

In more recent times, some psychologists have challenged this one-dimensional view of psychological masculinity and femininity (Spence, 1991; Spence & Helmreich, 1978). Sandra Bem (1974, 1985), for example, proposed that some people might see themselves as having both masculine and feminine characteristics. Such a person might enjoy both carpentry and cooking, might be very assertive (a masculine trait) at work but very nurturant (a feminine trait) at home, and so on. Bem called these people psychologically androgynous, borrowing from the Greek terms for male (*andro*) and female (*gyne*). Bem emphasized that the androgynous person is not a moderate who falls halfway between extreme masculinity and femininity. Rather, the androgynous person views himself or herself as combining strong masculine and strong feminine attributes. This two-dimensional model is shown in Figure 12-1.

To investigate **androgyny,** Bem (1974) constructed a new test with separate dimensions for masculinity and for femininity, making it possible for a person to score high on both. In the Bem Sex-Role Inventory, people rate their personal qualities using 60 adjectives: 20 masculine (assertive, independent), 20 feminine (affectionate, understanding), and 20 gender neutral (sincere, friendly). When Bem administered her test to samples of college students, she found some traditionally gender-typed individuals, both masculine men (who scored high on M and low on F) and feminine women (who scored high on F and low on M). More interesting, however, was the fact that some people rated themselves high on both masculine and feminine characteristics, showing the androgynous pattern Bem predicted.

The exact percentages of gender-typed and androgynous people vary from study to study. Typical are results from a study of California college students (Bernard, 1980). Roughly 40 percent of students perceived themselves as traditionally gender-typed, and 25 percent were androgynous. An "undifferentiated" subgroup included 29 percent of men and 21 percent of women who scored low on both masculine and feminine traits. Finally, a few people showed a pattern of reverse gender typing—specifically,

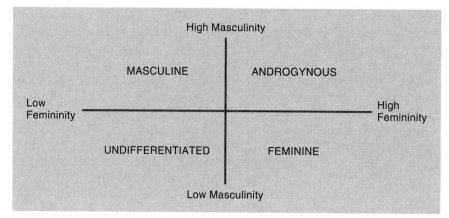

Figure 12-1 A two-dimensional model of psychological masculinity and femininity.

feminine men (5 percent) and masculine women (12 percent). The important point is that although traditional gender typing is the most common pattern, a sizable minority of people perceive themselves as combining both masculine and feminine qualities.

Research on androgyny has raised basic questions about how psychological masculinity and femininity affect well-being. One long-standing view has been that to ensure mental health, boys and men should be masculine in their interests and attributes, whereas girls and women should be feminine. This *congruence model* (Whitley, 1983) proposes that adjustment is enhanced when there is an "appropriate" match between gender and self-concept. In contrast, the newer *androgyny model* of well-being argues that it is better for people to combine both masculine and feminine traits. In particular, it has been proposed that androgynous individuals surpass traditionally sex-typed individuals in having greater behavioral flexibility and higher self-esteem.

BEHAVIORAL FLEXIBILITY. Bem hypothesized that masculine people will perform well in situations calling for task competence or assertiveness; feminine people will do well in situations requiring nurturance or emotional expressivity; and androgynous people will do well in *both* types of situations. Some empirical support for this prediction has been found (Jose &

McCarthy, 1988), although results have not been entirely consistent.

Some research has focused on situations in which psychological masculinity should enhance performance. For example, in a study by Bem (1975), masculine and androgynous individuals did better than feminine individuals on a test of ability to resist group pressure for conformity. In a more recent study of Israeli soldiers, both masculine and androgynous individuals viewed themselves as more likely to succeed in the army and received more positive evaluations from fellow soldiers than did feminine individuals (Dimitrovsky, Singer, & Yinon, 1989). Other studies demonstrate situations in which femininity and androgyny are advantageous. In one study, feminine and androgynous individuals did better on tasks requiring nurturance, including playing with a baby and talking to a transfer student who was having problems adjusting to a new college (Bem, Martyna, & Watson, 1976). Higher femininity has also been linked to greater marital satisfaction for both husbands and wives (Bradbury & Fincham, 1988).

SELF-ESTEEM. Feeling good about oneself is a key ingredient in mental health. The congruence model predicts that self-esteem and psychological adjustment should be highest for masculine men and feminine women—people with "appropriate" gender self-concepts. In contrast, the androgyny model asserts that androgynous individuals who perceive themselves as having both positive masculine and positive feminine attributes should have higher self-esteem than gender-typed individuals. A large number of studies have investigated this topic (Allgood-Merten & Stockard, 1991; Markstrom-Adams, 1989; Whitley, 1988), and they suggest an unexpected conclusion.

Basically, research once again provides no support for the congruence model. But results offer only weak support for the androgyny model. Instead, the biggest factor influencing self-esteem seems to be how a person scores on the dimension of psychological masculinity. Both masculine and androgynous individuals usually have higher self-esteem. This finding holds for both adolescents and adults, and has been found among Hispanic Americans, African Americans, and Asian Americans as well as among white Americans (Stein, Newcomb, & Bentler, 1992). The added benefit for androgynous people of being feminine as well as masculine is statistically significant, but very small in size.

Researchers are still puzzling about why masculinity appears to be so central to self-esteem. One possibility is that in an individualistic culture such as ours, self-esteem is closely linked to traits traditionally labeled as masculine, such as independence, assertiveness, and competence. Another possibility is that self-esteem tests are biased and do not adequately assess elements of self-esteem that are associated with femininity; in other words, the pattern of results may be due to a methodological weakness in the tests being used (Whitley, 1988).

SOME CAUTIONS. Research on the behavioral flexibility and self-esteem of gender-typed and androgynous individuals challenges the model that "appropriate" gender typing is essential to mental health. Masculine men and feminine women do not seem to have an advantage over androgynous individuals. Although the concept of androgyny has provided a useful correction to earlier work on masculinity and femininity, we should be cautious about accepting it uncritically (Morawski, 1987).

First, current androgyny measures are very limited in scope. Most measures of "femininity" focus on self-perceptions of emotional expressiveness and measures of "masculinity" assess self-perceptions of instrumentality or task competence (Spence, 1991). In actuality, most people view masculinity and femininity much more broadly as including appearance, sexual behavior, and social roles as well as personality (Myers & Gonda, 1982). Further, these different components of masculinity and femininity are probably not part of a single, consistent dimension (Biernat, 1991b; Spence, 1991). One woman might, for instance, think of herself as masculine in personality (assertive, ambitious, and independent), feminine in appearance (short and voluptuous), and androgynous in social roles (both a mother and a career woman). Existing androgyny instruments do not capture this complexity.

Second, androgyny is possible only in some domains of life. When it comes to personality, an individual could perceive himself or herself as warmly nurturant in some situations and coldly competitive in others. But in different domains, masculinity and femininity actually are mutually exclusive. In reproduction, for example, insemination and childbearing are each exclusive to one sex.

Third, current work on androgyny tells us little about how salient masculinity and femininity actually are in people's thinking about themselves. The Bem Sex Role Inventory and other tests ask people to rate themselves on traits society labels as masculine or feminine (Biernat, 1991b). But responses to these tests do not tell us whether people spontaneously label their own actions this way. If gender typing is really important, a person might think: "Gee, it makes me feel feminine to prepare such a fine meal for my family," or "I feel more masculine for having stood up to my boss today." But if gender typing is not so vital, people might recognize their own nurturance or assertiveness, but identify these as human traits unrelated to gender. We do not yet know how prominent masculine and feminine labels actually are in people's self-concepts.

Finally, discussions of masculinity and femininity often touch on personal values and ideals. For those who endorse more traditional views about the sexes, the preservation of clear-cut distinctions between masculinity and femininity is an important goal. For those who want to expand the options available to both sexes, the blurring of distinctions is seen as desirable. Indeed, some feminists have rejected androgyny as an ideal because it preserves the notion that there are distinct masculine and feminine qualities even though it gives permission to people to have both types of attributes. Instead, some have argued that we should move toward "sex-role transcendence" (Garnets & Pleck, 1979). Personal attributes and preferences should no longer be associated with gender. Psychological research can clarify how gender affects our self-concept and can identify the consequences of various patterns, but it cannot tell people what to adopt for their own lives.

So far, our discussion of gender has focused on perception—impressions of others and of ourselves. Now we turn to the topic of actual differences in the behavior of women and men.

THEORETICAL PERSPECTIVES ON GENDER

Debates about the nature of sex differences raged long before the existence of social psychology. For centuries, personal experience and intuition were the basis for such discussions. Today, scientific theories and research are providing a more balanced and comprehensive understanding of gender differences in behavior.

Early discussions often asked whether gender differences are caused by "nature or nurture," by biology or learning. We now know that such simple dichotomies are misleading. A full explanation of gender differences must consider *both* the biological capacities of the sexes and the social environment in which males and females live. It has also become clear that there is no single, general explanation for all differences between males and females. Rather, the causes of gender differences in math ability may be quite distinct from the causes of gender differ-

ences in helping behavior, and so on. Four broad perspectives on the origins of gender patterns emphasize the influence of biology, childhood socialization, social roles, and social situations.

Biology

Gender differences are affected by diverse biological factors. Physical differences in height and muscular development, in the ability to bear children and to breast-feed, and so on, are obvious. The impact of sex hormones, both on the unborn fetus and on adults, is a lively topic of investigation, as are possible sex differences in the brain. Sociobiologists propose that genetic evolution also contributes to gender differences in human behavior (Symons, 1979).

Social psychologists do not deny possible biological contributions to human behavior, although most of us leave biological research to experts in other disciplines. The point social psychologists emphasize, however, is that the importance of basic biological differences can be greatly modified by social forces. Childbirth provides an illustration.

Women are physically capable of having a dozen or more babies during a lifetime, but the implications of this biological ability can vary dramatically. Before advances in medical technology, childbirth was hazardous and many women died at relatively young ages. As a result, men tended to live longer than women. Today, women's biological capacity remains the same, but childbirth is safer. Now, women tend to live longer and typically outlive men by several years. In our society, changes have also occurred in the average number of children a woman has. In the past, women had many children and spent most of their adult life in the role of mothers. Today, because of contemporary social attitudes and contraceptive methods, the typical American woman has only two or three children. As a result, mothering activities occupy a much smaller part of women's lives. In short, the impact of biological gender differences can vary markedly depending on the social environment.

Childhood Socialization

This perspective emphasizes the many ways in which people learn about gender and acquire "sex-appropriate" behavior during childhood (Losh-Hesselbart, 1987). An important idea is that society has different expectations and standards for the behavior of males and females. As children grow up, they learn these gender lessons through the processes of reinforcement and modeling described in Chapter 1. Imagine a father whose young daughter enters the living room dressed in Mommy's earrings, silk robe, and high heels, and climbs on Daddy's knee. The father is likely to smile at his daughter, give her a big hug, and compliment her on being such a pretty little girl. Now imagine a 4-year-old boy doing exactly the same thing. Although a modern Daddy might not punish his son, it is likely he would communicate firmly that feminine clothes are not appropriate for boys. A recent meta-analysis found consistent evidence that both mothers and fathers encourage sex-typed activities in their children (Lytton & Romney, 1991).

Another major influence on children are peers—friends, classmates, and siblings (Carter, 1987). One of the most striking features of childhood is the tendency for children to segregate themselves into all-boy and all-girl groups and, often, to avoid persons of the other sex. On a preschool playground, Jake and Danny are on the big swing together. When Laura excitedly asks if she can join them on the swing, the boys emphatically say "No!" Jake adds, "We don't want you on here. We only want boys on here" (Rubin, 1980, p. 102). This pattern of same-sex play first appears in preschool and continues through early adolescence.

One reason why American children may prefer same-sex groups is that children develop sex-typed interests in toys and games (Etaugh & Liss, 1992). Girls like to play with dolls and makeup kits, and boys favor soccer or video games. Another reason is that boys and girls tend to develop distinctive styles of interaction that make same-sex playmates more enjoyable (Maccoby, 1990a). Research shows that boys usually enjoy a rough-and-tumble style of play

Children's toys and games teach lessons about what males and females can and should do in our society. Adults tend to give baby dolls to girls but not to boys—subtly teaching that childcare is fundamentally "women's work."

that emphasizes physical contact, competition, and dominance. Girls, in contrast, engage in less physical contact, try to minimize conflict, and so may find the boys' play style aversive. Eleanor Maccoby explains that "on wheeled vehicles boys (3 to 5) play ramming games while girls ride around and try *not* to bump into each other" (1990b, p. 5). Consequently, the preferred play styles of boys and girls are not compatible. In this case, initially small sex differences in activity level or rough and tumble play lead children to segregate themselves by sex. This in turn leads to the creation of same-sex "cultures" with different play activities and norms about interacting (Maccoby, 1991).

Family and friends are not the only agents of socialization. As we saw earlier, television and other popular media also present many stereotypes about the sexes. Even children's toys convey cultural messages, which can differ from one country to another (Watanabe, 1992). In the United States, the most popular fashion doll is Barbie, a sexy blonde who has a boyfriend, enjoys shopping, and goes to parties dressed in black vinyl. In contrast, Japan's best selling fashion doll for the past 25 years has been Licca, a demure, wide-eyed, rather flat-chested girl who suggests the innocence of a school girl. In each country, manufacturers are selling not only a toy, but also an idealized image of femininity, which emphasizes cuteness in Japan and sexiness in the United States. Recently, a controversy arose when the American makers of Barbie introduced a new talking Barbie whose repertoire included, "Math class is tough." Critics argued that this message might discourage girls from taking math classes, and perpetuate the cultural belief that boys are better suited for math. Ultimately, the manufacturer agreed to remove the statement about math (Smith, 1992).

According to the socialization perspective, the many different social experiences of boys and girls lead to relatively enduring sex differences in attitudes, interests, skills, and personality that continue into adulthood.

Social Roles

A third perspective emphasizes that people's behavior is strongly influenced by their social roles (Eagly, 1987; Eagly & Wood, 1991). The lives of adults are structured by their various roles as family members, workers, and community members. A key idea is that many important social roles are defined differently for the two sexes. Within the family, people usually have quite different expectations for mothers and fathers, for husbands and wives, for sons and daughters. In the world of work, occupational roles are often sex-typed: nursing, clerical work, and elementary education are traditionally female occupations; medicine, construction, and college teaching are traditionally male occupations. In business organizations, women's work roles are often lower in social status, prestige, and power than those of men: He's the boss and she's the secretary.

Traditional social roles affect the behavior of women and men in several ways. They perpetuate a division of labor by gender, with women as homemakers and child care providers, and men as breadwinners. Roles influence the skills and interests people first develop in childhood and later refine as adults. Little girls often play with cooking sets and baby dolls in preparation for adult roles as wives and mothers. In addition, the effects of gender-linked roles may "spill over" into new situations. We may learn from experiences in the family, at church or synagogue, or at work that men have higher status and are more authoritative than women. When we meet a new person, we may use their sex as a cue, inferring, for example, that a man is likely to be a confident leader and that a woman is likely to be a supportive follower (Eagly, 1987). As we saw earlier in this chapter, such expectations can become self-fulfilling prophecies. So,

When researchers compare men and women who work at the same job, they find that their attitudes and behavior tend to be quite similar.

differences in the behavior of women and men often reflect differences in the social roles they occupy in daily life.

In contrast, when men and women actually occupy the same roles, their attitudes and behavior are often remarkably similar. Kay Deaux and Joseph Ullman (1983) studied both women and men who held the same blue collar jobs in the steel industry. They found very few sex differences: Men and women were similar in their self-evaluations, aspirations, and likes and dislikes about their work. Studies of managers in organizations also show great similarity among the managerial styles of women and men in similar job positions (Eagly & Johnson, 1990). It may be that similar sorts of people, regardless of their sex, tend to choose particular occupational roles. It is also likely, however, that the role itself shapes the person who occupies it.

Social Situations

Another major influence on behavior is the social setting. A man might talk about football and cars with his male buddies, peppering his speech with four-letter words, but "clean up his act" and change the topic of conversation with a new girlfriend. The basic assumption in situational models is that "men and women are relatively equal in their potentialities for most social behaviors and [their] behaviors may differ widely as a function of personal choice, the behavior of others, and the situational context" (Deaux & Major, 1987, p. 371). Research is beginning to uncover important situational factors that contribute to sex differences in behavior.

For example, in situations where we want other people to like us, we often try to conform to their expectations about how males and females should behave, regardless of our personal beliefs. In one experiment, college women participated in a simulated job interview (von Baeyer, Sherk, & Zanna, 1981). By random assignment, half the women were informed that the male interviewer was a traditional person, who believed that the ideal woman should be gentle, sensitive, attractive, and passive, and

should be assigned to easier jobs such as making coffee. Other women were informed that the interviewer preferred nontraditional women, who were independent, assertive, and could assume equal job responsibilities with men. Not surprisingly, the women's knowledge about the interviewer influenced how they prepared for the interview. Women expecting a traditional interviewer "dressed up" by wearing more makeup and jewelry than did women expecting to meet a nontraditional interviewer. Women with traditional interviewers also talked less during the interview, and tended to make more traditional statements about themselves. The desire to be liked and accepted by others can lead us to act in more or less gender-typed ways, depending on the situation.

The gender of the person we are with can be a powerful situational determinant of behavior. An empirical demonstration of this idea comes from a study of who interrupts whom in casual conversations. The researchers unobtrusively tape-recorded the conversations of male–male, female–female, and male–female pairs as they chatted spontaneously in coffee shops, drugstores, and other public places (Zimmerman & West, 1975). Interruptions were ten times more frequent in the male–female conversations than in the same-sex ones. More striking, in same-sex pairs, men and women were equally likely to interrupt; but in mixed sex dyads, men initiated 96 percent of all interruption.

A laboratory study of conversations in mixed-sex groups found similar but less extreme results (McMillan, Clifton, McGrath, & Gale, 1977). As shown in Table 12-2, men and women were equally likely to interrupt another person of the same sex. But when cross-sex interruptions occurred, it was five times more likely for a man to interrupt a woman as vice versa.

Cross-cultural research provides further evidence of the ways in which situational forces can influence behavior. Among the Luo people of Kenya, boys and girls are typically assigned to different sorts of household tasks, such as heavy work for boys and childcare for girls (Ember, 1973). When there is no older girl in the family to take care of the "female" tasks, how-

CULTURAL HIGHLIGHT
Too Many Women—Sex Ratios and Social Life

In their book, *Too Many Women: The Sex Ratio Question,* Marcia Guttentag and Paul Secord (1983) investigate the social effects of the ratio of males to females in society. Although approximately equal numbers of males and females are born each year, the ratio of male-to-female adults of marriageable age is quite variable cross-culturally. It is affected by wars, migration, infanticide of girl children, and so on. Among the early European settlers who came to America, for example, men outnumbered women, often by substantial proportions. By contrast, in the United States today, women outnumber men. Ethnic differences in sex ratios have also been noted. For example, among African Americans, there are, on average, only 89.6 males per 100 females (Tucker, 1986). One recent study estimated that for every three unmarried black women in their 20s, there is only roughly one unmarried black man with earnings above the poverty level (Lichter, McLaughlin, Kephart, & Landry, 1992). What are the social and personal consequences of imbalanced sex ratios?

Guttentag and Secord (1983) argue that when there is an undersupply of women, as in America before World War II,

young women are highly valued and protected. Men are eager to form a committed relationship through marriage. Women gain status through marriage and are able to achieve economic mobility by "marrying up." Husbands and wives have very different roles in the family. Both sexes stress sexual monogamy, although a double standard may permit greater sexual freedom for men. In contrast, Guttentag and Secord propose that when women are in oversupply, as in America from 1970 to the present, the relations between the sexes are quite different. Marriage and commitment are deemphasized, and feminist movements are likely to arise.

Research supports this general line of reasoning. One study investigated college students' perceptions of the availability of eligible dating partners on campus (Jemmott, Ashby, & Lindenfeld, 1989). As predicted, students who believed there was an unfavorable sex ratio—who thought that eligible dating partners were relatively scarce—rated their current relationship as more attractive and felt more committed to it than did students who believed they had more dating options.

Research using census data shows that as the availability of

eligible men decreases, greater proportions of women remain unmarried, and single-parent families headed by women increase (Fossett & Kiecolt, 1991). For example, the 1980 census for Los Angeles, California, documented an imbalanced sex ratio for women ages 25–34 (Tucker, 1986). As predicted, white women in this group showed an unusually high rate of never marrying (24 percent). African American women in the same age group were confronted with a more severe shortage of black men, and nearly a third (31 percent) of black women had never married.

The idea that sex ratios in society have profound effects on male–female relationships is thought-provoking and controversial. Guttentag and Secord supported their argument with examples of societies ranging from ancient Greece to medieval Europe to contemporary Africa. Current research is investigating the effects of sex ratios among African Americans and other groups within the United States (e.g., South & Lloyd, 1992). This research provides a fascinating illustration of a way in which sociocultural factors can influence the daily lives of women and men.

TABLE 12-2
Mean Number of Interruptions per Half-Hour in Mixed-Sex Discussion Groups

Sex of Person Who Is Interrupted	Sex of Interrupter	
	Male	Female
Male	2.36	0.93
Female	5.24	2.50

Source: Adapted from McMillan, Clifton, McGrath, & Gale (1977), p. 553.

ever, a boy will be assigned to do this work. Boys who were assigned to do female work tended to be less aggressive, less dominant, and more dependent than other boys. These boys were of course no different from other boys biologically. Rather, the fact that they were assigned to perform traditionally feminine activities affected their temperament and behavior. Research in the United States has found that fathers who have sole responsibility for care of their children (through widowhood or divorce) are very similar to mothers in their nurturance and parenting skills, but differ from married fathers who do little childcare (Risman, 1987). In both examples, caretaking responsibilities shaped males' behavior. The CULTURAL HIGHLIGHT provides another illustration of situational influences on behavior.

In summary, the causes of sex differences in behavior are complex. The goal of contemporary research is to understand the many factors that affect specific behaviors.

COMPARING THE SOCIAL BEHAVIOR OF WOMEN AND MEN

In recent years, a great deal of research has compared the abilities and behavior of males and females, especially that of American children and college students. But the results of these studies are often contradictory and sometimes downright confusing. It turns out to be considerably more difficult to pin down gender differences than might be imagined. We will examine sex differences in social behaviors including aggression, helping, conformity, and nonverbal communication. Before beginning our discussion, however, we will review some basic ideas about meta-analysis, a statistical method first discussed in Chapter 1.

Meta-analyses of Sex Differences

As the number of studies of sex differences has increased, it has become more difficult for investigators to summarize research findings to arrive at general conclusions. Traditionally, reviews of research literature have relied heavily on the judgment of the reviewers to select a balanced sample of studies and to eliminate methodologically flawed research. A persistent problem for reviewers has been inconsistency across studies. What can we conclude if 20 studies find boys are better at some activity, but 10 studies find girls are better at the same activity, and 10 studies find no differences? Often, researchers have used a "vote-counting" approach to resolve these discrepancies, assuming that a sex difference "exists" if it occurs in the majority of studies.

In an effort to develop more systematic ways to review and synthesize empirical findings, researchers have begun to use new techniques called **meta-analysis** (Eagly, 1987; Hyde & Linn, 1986). This approach uses statistical methods to pool information from many studies in order to arrive at an overall estimate of the size of sex differences. We might find, for instance, that the average sex difference on a particular measure is less than one-tenth of a standard deviation—quite a small effect. Meta-analyses also encourage reviewers to consider very carefully how they select a sample of studies to review. It has been suggested, for instance, that reviewers should include not only published studies, but also unpublished doctoral dissertations. The reasoning here is that studies that find no sex differences may be less likely to be accepted for publication, thus biasing published research toward overestimating sex differences. In the following sections, we present some of the findings of recent analyses of sex differences.

Aggression

Around the world, males tend to be more aggressive than females in both childhood and adulthood. Boys are more likely than girls to fight, to taunt and insult others, and to fantasize about aggressive themes (Perry et al., 1989). In adulthood, men are the warriors who defend their tribe or nation. Men are also the sex most likely to use physical force to achieve their goals, a fact reflected in statistics on rape, spouse abuse, and violent crime. According to statistics from the U.S. Federal Bureau of Investigation, 90 percent of those arrested for murder in 1991 were men. (See Table 12-3 for other statistics.) Whether we consider socially approved aggression in wartime, illegal violence, or children's play, males take the lead in aggressive behavior.

Two meta-analyses reviewed more than a hundred studies of aggression (Eagly & Steffen, 1986; Hyde, 1986). They found that males are more aggressive than females in both verbal and physical aggression, although the gender gap is bigger for physical aggression. Larger sex differences are found in naturalistic settings (e.g., hitting and kicking on a playground) than in more controlled laboratory settings (e.g., hitting a plastic bobo doll in a research room). Hyde (1986) suggests that males may be more likely than females to engage in spontaneous aggression, but that males and females respond more similarly in controlled laboratory conditions.

One factor affecting sex differences in aggression is that our society is more tolerant of aggression in males than in females. In childhood, boys are much more likely to be given toy guns and swords, and to be taught about fighting and self-defense. A recent study investigated children's expectations about the consequences of various aggressive acts, such as hitting a child who takes a ball (Perry, Perry, & Weiss, 1989). Compared to boys, girls anticipated more parental disapproval for aggression and thought that they would feel greater guilt. There is also evidence that females are more concerned about the harm their aggression may cause the victim and about the danger of retaliation (Eagly & Steffen, 1986). As a result, females may feel more guilt, anxiety, and fear about aggressive acts, and so inhibit their aggressive impulses (Eagly & Steffen, 1986).

TABLE 12-3
FBI Statistics Comparing Arrests for Violent Crimes by Men and Women

Type of Offense	Total Number	Committed by Men (%)	Committed by Women (%)
Murder and nonnegligent manslaughter	17,397	90	10
Robbery	130,323	91	9
Aggravated assault	333,427	87	13
All violent crime	509,147	89	11

Source: From *Uniform Crime Reports for the United States, 1991,* Federal Bureau of Investigation, U.S. Department of Justice, p. 222.

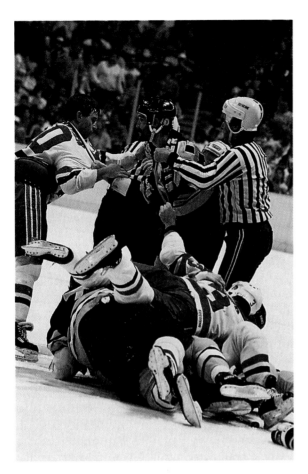

Hockey provides a socially approved context for male aggression. But theorists disagree about whether aggressive sports provide a wholesome outlet for innate male aggressive drives, or rather teach men to become even more aggressive.

Helping

Is one sex more helpful than the other? A meta-analytic review of 172 studies of prosocial behavior (Eagly & Crowley, 1986) found a significant sex difference: Men were more likely than women to offer assistance. However, the researchers noted several important qualifications to this general conclusion. First and foremost, they emphasized that most social psychological studies of helping have investigated bystander intervention, that is, offering aid to a stranger in distress. Studies of prosocial behavior, including those we review in Chapter 13, have not typically investigated other impor-

tant kinds of prosocial behavior such as caring for children, comforting a friend, or taking an elderly relative to a clinic.

Using a social roles perspective, Eagly and Crowley (1986) propose that whereas female roles foster helping that is nurturant and caring, male roles foster helping that is heroic and chivalrous. Bystander intervention research documents men's greater chivalry. Men are more likely than women to help strangers in distress, and the average size of the sex difference is about one-third of a standard deviation. Men are especially likely to help when the victim or requester is female, when there is an audience, and in situations that women perceive as dangerous.

We know less about helping that occurs in private relations among friends and relatives. Eagly and Crowley identified five studies showing that women were more likely than men to do personal favors for friends and to provide advice about personal problems. Studies have also investigated social support—providing assistance, advice, and emotional encouragement to friends and relations. In general, women are more likely than men to provide social support to others (Shumaker & Hill, 1991). Women are also more likely than men to be the primary caregivers for the family, taking major responsibility for care of children and also for aging parents (Unger & Crawford, 1992). Clearly, which sex is more helpful depends on the type of assistance being given.

Conformity

Stereotypes portray women as more yielding, gullible, and conforming than men. According to Eagly (1987), traditional social roles dictate that men should be less easily influenced than women. Social psychological studies have typically investigated conformity and compliance in laboratory settings where an individual interacts with strangers.

Careful reviews of the empirical research on social influence lead to two conclusions. First, when meta-analysis is used to pool findings from a large number of studies, there is a small but statistically significant tendency for women to be more easily influenced than men (Eagly, 1987). Second and equally important is the finding that results are often very inconsistent from study to study. Alice Eagly (1978, 1983) found 62 studies that had investigated sex differences in persuasion—that is, the extent to which a person is influenced by hearing arguments in favor of or against an issue. Only 16 percent of these studies found that women were significantly more easily persuaded; the vast majority found no differences. Similarly, Eagly found 61 studies of responses to group pressures for conformity, as in the Asch experiment described in Chapter 8. Here again, only 34 percent of the studies found that women conformed significantly more; in most cases, the sexes did not differ significantly. Whether sex differences occur or not appears to depend on specific details of the testing situation, such as the nature of the social influence task or the testing materials.

One interesting idea is that sex differences in influenceability may have more to do with the gender typing of the task than with a general disposition for women to conform. People are generally more likely to conform if they lack information about a topic or consider it unimportant. Thus, women are more likely to conform on tasks traditionally viewed as masculine, and men are more likely to conform when confronted with feminine tasks. This point was demonstrated by Sistrunk and McDavid (1971). They asked college women and men to answer a questionnaire about matters of fact and opinion, some concerning masculine topics such as sports cars, politics, and mathematics, and others concerning feminine areas such cosmetics, sewing, or cooking. To introduce conformity pressure, the questionnaire indicated next to each question how a majority of college students had supposedly responded. Results clearly showed the effect of gender typing. Men conformed more than women on feminine items; women conformed more than men on masculine items. Overall, there were no significant differences between the level of conformity of men and of women. Although this interpretation seems quite plausible, more research will be needed to establish its general applicability (Eagly, 1987).

If empirical studies find that sex differences in influenceability are somewhat elusive and small in magnitude, why does the stereotype persist that women are much more yielding? The answer may be found in the roles that men and women typically play in society (Eagly & Wood, 1985). In real life, an important determinant of social influence is a person's prestige or power relative to others in a group. In a business, for example, subordinates are expected to go along with the boss; a nurse usually follows a physician's order. Since men typically have higher occupational status than women, it is more common to observe a woman yielding to a man than vice versa.

Although this behavior pattern is actually based on job status, people may mistakenly infer that women have a general tendency to go along with others. To test this idea, Eagly and Wood (1982) had students read a description of a man influencing a female coworker or a woman influencing a male coworker. Subjects then answered questions about the people described. When subjects had no information about the job titles of these persons, they assumed that women held lower-status jobs and that women were more likely to comply behaviorally with men than vice versa. When explicit job titles were provided, subjects believed that compliance would be based on status rather than gender. Such results support the idea that stereotypes about women's greater influenceability are based in part on knowledge that men often have more prestigious and powerful positions in society.

Nonverbal Communication

Stereotypes about female "intuition" suggest that women may be better than men at decoding or "reading" nonverbal behavior. Thus, it might be speculated that mothers are more expert than fathers at telling whether a crying baby is hungry, wet, or suffering gas pains. Similarly, the stereotype would suggest that women may be better able to sense whether another person is feeling depressed or embarrassed or tired. Many studies have addressed this question by comparing men's and women's accuracy at decoding another person's emotions from facial cues, body language, or tone of voice.

In a typical study, subjects watch a videotape of a person expressing a series of emotions. After viewing each segment of the film, subjects indicate which of several emotions (such as happiness, disgust, or fear) they think is being expressed. In other studies, subjects listen to recordings of voices that have been "content filtered"—altered so that the words are garbled and only the tone is distinct. Judith Hall (1978) reviewed 75 studies that permitted gender comparisons. In 68 percent, women were better decoders than men; in 13 percent, men were better than women; and in 19 percent, no gender differences occurred.

More recent meta-analyses have confirmed and expanded these results (Hall, 1984). On average, women are more skilled at decoding nonverbal cues. The female advantage is greatest for "reading" facial expressions, next largest for body cues, and smallest for decoding voice tone. Women are also better at recognizing faces. This gender difference has been found in school children, teenagers, and adults. Although the size of the sex difference in decoding nonverbal cues varies from study to study, women's greater skill in this domain has consistently been documented by research.

Several possible explanations have been offered for women's greater nonverbal skill. One is that females have a genetically "programmed" sensitivity to nonverbal cues because of their role in caring for preverbal infants. Another suggestion is that women are trained to be experts in emotional matters, and so learn to be more skillful in nonverbal communication. A third explanation emphasizes men's greater dominance in many social settings. Perhaps those in positions of lesser power (who tend to be women) pay more attention to the feelings of those in charge. Consistent with this interpretation is research showing that, regardless of sex, subordinates are more sensitive to the feelings of leaders than leaders are to the feelings of subordinates (Snodgrass, 1992).

Personal Entitlement

What would you consider a good starting salary for a new job? Beth Ann Martin (1989) asked this question of college seniors majoring in business. First she provided students with detailed information about the salaries that previous graduates had earned in recent years. The sex of the previous graduates was not mentioned. Then Martin asked students what they personally would expect to earn at their first job after graduation. On average, men expected to earn $18,203, and women expected to earn $16,607—a substantial difference. In another study, Faye Crosby (1992) carefully matched a sample of full-time male and female workers on occupational prestige, seniority, and other job-related dimensions. In her sample, women workers were consistently paid less than men. Surprisingly, however, women were not unhappy with their own pay or treatment on the job. Although these women workers recognized that *other* women often suffer pay discrimination, they did not believe that they personally were being paid unfairly.

These and other findings suggest that women and men may differ in their sense of **personal entitlement**—what they believe they deserve from their jobs or relationships (Major, 1987). For instance, in laboratory studies women work longer, do more work, and work more accurately and efficiently than do men for the same amount of pay (Major et al., 1984). When subjects are asked to determine fair payment for work on a laboratory task, women pay themselves less than men do. These differences reflect men's and women's sense of the worth of their work.

Two major explanations for this sex difference in personal entitlement have been supported by research (Bylsma & Major, 1992; Major et al., 1984). A *social comparison explanation* suggests that when people evaluate their outcomes (the pay or other rewards that they receive) they tend to make same-sex comparisons. Thus, women usually compare themselves to other underpaid women, and men compare themselves to other more highly compensated men. Consistent with this idea, when men and women are provided with the same explicit information about pay in a given situation, sex differences in personal entitlement are reduced. A second *performance evaluation explanation* is that women and men tend to make different evaluations of what they put into a job, that is, the quality of their work. There is evidence, for instance, that when people do not receive external feedback on the quality of their performance, women have less confidence in their skill and performance than men do (Lenney, 1977). Consistent with this hypothesis, when subjects are given direct feedback about the quality of their work, sex differences in personal entitlement are reduced.

Brenda Major (1989) has proposed that sex differences in personal entitlement on the job stem from societal inequalities. In our culture, men and women tend to work in different types of jobs, and the types of work that women usually perform (e.g. being a secretary, childcare worker, or waitress) are usually paid less than men's. As a result, men and women tend to use different standards to evaluate their own performance, including a tendency to compare one's own rewards to those of others of the same sex. Consequently, women and men differ in their sense of personal entitlement. Major (1989) speculates that this pattern serves to maintain the status quo: "because women do not feel as entitled to high pay for their work as men do, objectively underpaid women may not perceive their job situation as unjust" (p. 108).

Sex Differences in Perspective

Having reviewed research on gender comparisons, a few general points are worth remembering. First, *average* differences between the sexes in behaviors such as reading emotions from nonverbal cues do not mean that all males are socially insensitive and all females are nonverbal experts. There is much individual variation, so some males excel and some females do poorly. Second, demonstrating differences between the sexes does not necessarily mean

that an individual's skills and behaviors are unchangeable. Both men and women could learn to be more (or less) helpful, conforming, attuned to nonverbal cues, or aggressive.

In discussions of gender issues, a frequently asked question is this: Aside from the biological facts of life, just how different are males and females? Psychological research offers no simple answer. At the level of basic abilities and personal dispositions, gender differences are often small in magnitude, no more than a few points on a standardized test. Men and women appear to be remarkably similar in many of their basic human talents. Yet consistent sex differences do seem to exist (for whatever complex reasons) in a few domains such as aggressive behavior and nonverbal decoding skills. At the same time, the daily activities and roles of men and women are often very different indeed. We are much more likely to find women changing baby diapers and men changing flat tires than vice versa. Whether we conclude that the sexes are "fundamentally different" or "basically the same" is a question of perspective. There is probably some truth and some exaggeration in both positions (Hare-Mustin & Marecek, 1988).

CHANGING ROLES FOR WOMEN AND MEN

Newspapers today are filled with stories about the changing roles of men and women. Whether a writer heralds these changes as a "stride toward equality" or laments the collapse of "traditional values," few would deny that the lives of men and women are not what they used to be. One way to assess these changes is to compare contemporary gender roles with older, traditional patterns. Traditional gender roles were organized around two basic principles. One idea was that men and women should perform distinctive activities, that there should be a division of labor by gender. The second idea was that men should be the dominant sex, both at home and in society at large. Let us look at these social roles and how they are changing.

Division of Labor

There is much evidence that rigid distinctions between what men should do and what women should do are breaking down. Studies assessing public attitudes toward gender roles have charted these changes. For example, in 1936, only 18 percent of Americans approved of a married woman working for pay if her husband could support her. By 1976, a majority of men (65 percent) and women (70 percent) approved of wives working outside the home (Boer, 1977). These shifts away from traditional views of gender roles are continuing. Cross-cultural research indicates that traditional attitudes about gender roles are strongest in rural and nonindustrialized societies (Williams & Best, 1990b). Around the world, women tend to have less traditional attitudes than men.

There have also been major changes in women's behavior. As one example, women are now more equal participants in higher education. In 1978, for the first time in history, more women than men entered college in the United States. Women have also begun to train for high-status fields that were once dominated by men. Today, women earn about 40 percent of the professional degrees in law, 33 percent in medicine, and 26 percent in dentistry (*Statistical Abstract of the United States,* 1991). In the field of psychology, women now receive about 54 percent of doctoral degrees.

Perhaps the most dramatic change in this century has been women's increased participation in paid work. In 1940, only 15 percent of married women worked for pay. Today, more than half of all married women (57 percent) have paying jobs, as do a majority of mothers with school age children. Yet women are far from equal partners in the world of work. Women continue to be concentrated in lower-status "female" jobs such as secretary, nurse, and teacher. Partly as a result, the average woman worker earns only about 70 cents for every dollar earned by a man, with African American, Asian American, and Hispanic women faring worse than white women. Even in occupations traditionally dominated by women, men tend to earn more. For example, recent California census data found that full-time male nurses earned roughly $42,880 per year compared to only $35,580 for female nurses. Male teachers and librarians earned $38,700 to women's $28,500 (Hubler & Silverstein, 1992).

Are men today doing more things formerly

Traditional rules about what males and females should do are breaking down. Here, a father gives his daughter a bath.

considered "for women only"? Everyday examples of such changes are easy to find. It is not unusual to see a man shopping for groceries or taking a toddler to the park. Research shows that American men are spending more time with their children now than in the past (Douthitt, 1989). However, men's participation in housework and childcare—*family work* as some call it—is still relatively small compared to women's. In a recent study of a representative sample of married couples with children in the United States, wives performed roughly 80 percent of the housework (Coltrane & Ishii-Kuntz, 1992). Another large-scale survey of married couples found that wives were also responsible for about 80 percent of the childcare (Peterson & Gerson, 1992).

A surprising finding is that the amount of time a husband spends on housework and childcare is often *not* related to whether his wife has a paid job (Douthitt, 1989). On average, a husband whose wife has a 40-hour-a-week job spends no more time on household chores than does a husband whose wife is home full time! Women perform most homemaking and childcare activities, regardless of whether they have a paid job or not. The major difference is that employed wives spend less time on family work (about 28 hours per week) than do full-time homemakers (about 53 hours per week). Whether or not men are currently increasing their contributions to family work is a matter of debate (Godwin, 1991). Some researchers believe that husbands are gradually doing more housework and childcare, and so are moving toward a more balanced division of labor at home. Others see little evidence of change by men. The undisputed fact, however, is that homemaking and childcare continue to be largely "women's work."

What is the psychological impact for women of juggling responsibilities at work and at home? In a recent review of research on this question, Faye Crosby (1991) found that the demands of multiple roles can be difficult and stressful. Working mothers often complain about lack of time and lack of sleep. Despite these and other very real problems, women also benefit from having many roles. One woman explained, "It keeps life interesting. I think it

makes you feel so much more whole to be able to do all these things," (Crosby, p. 88). Research documents the psychological benefits of multiple roles for women (Barnett, Marshall, & Singer, 1992). On average, women who have several roles are happier, higher in self-esteem, and physically healthier than women with few major adult roles. Apparently, the stresses of juggling jobs and family are often outweighed by the benefits, which include variety and social contact, as well as money. The emotional support women receive in one role can also help to allay the stresses of another role. As one woman explained, "Sometimes I have a really rough day at work and then I come home and these two little kids run to the door. . . . Then, I forget the day at work and put all that bad stuff in its pocket. If I didn't have these kids, if I weren't juggling, I'd probably sit there and think about the rotten day for five hours" (Crosby, p. 148).

Male Dominance

The second basic idea in traditional gender roles is that men should be the leaders both at home and in society at large. Changes are clearly occurring in both arenas. In the public sector, laws denying women the vote, forbidding women to own property, and in general defining women as second-class citizens are largely a thing of the past. We have seen the first woman elected governor and the first woman appointed to the U.S. Supreme Court. In recent elections, women have run for public office in unprecedented numbers.

Nonetheless, the numbers of women in the power circles of society are still small. In 1993, women comprised only 6 percent of members of the U.S. Senate and 11 percent of the House of Representatives. For an example closer to home, consider the college you attend. Chances are that there are many women secretaries and a few women professors, but that the chairperson of most departments, most of the deans and top-level administrators, and the president are male. Women are still very far from being equal partners in public affairs.

In personal relationships, the extent of male dominance is harder to assess. At the level of personal dispositions, men and women do not differ in their interest in power or their power motivation (Winter, 1988). However, social convention has traditionally conferred greater authority on men in dating and marriage. Until recently, for example, state laws gave husbands legal control over all family property and permitted husbands, as the "head of the household," to decide where the family should live. As we saw in Chapter 10, many married couples today describe their relationships as equal in power, as do a majority of dating couples. However, when relationships are not equal, it is most often the man who has greater influence.

Even young couples who strongly endorse egalitarian norms sometimes find it hard to achieve these ideals. Individuals who reject the abstract principle of male dominance may nonetheless continue to follow social scripts that encourage male leadership. A study of dating illustrates this idea (Rose & Frieze, 1989). Researchers asked college students to list separately the actions that a man and a woman would do as each prepared for a first date, met the date, and spent time together. The typical dating script is presented in Table 12-4. Note that it is generally assumed that the man will take the leadership role on a date, asking the woman out, deciding where to go, paying for the date, initiating physical contact, and being the one to ask for a second date. In other words, contemporary dating rules continue to cast the man as the person "in charge."

In addition, culturally based patterns of dat-

TABLE 12-4
Typical Script for a First Date

The Woman's Role	The Man's Role
Tell friends and family	*Ask for a date
	*Decide what to do
Groom and dress	Groom and dress
Be nervous	Be nervous
Worry about or change appearance	Worry about or change appearance
Wait for date	Prepare car, apartment
	*Check money
Welcome date to home	Go to date's house
Introduce parents or roommates	Meet parents or roommates
Leave	Leave
	*Open car door for date
Confirm plans	Confirm plans
Get to know date	Get to know date
Compliment date	Compliment date
Joke, laugh, and talk	Joke, laugh, and talk
Try to impress date	Try to impress date
Go to movies, show, or party	Go to movies, show, or party
Eat	Eat
	*Pay
	*Initiate Physical contact
	Take date home
Tell date she had a good time	Tell date he had a good time
	*Ask for another date
	*Tell date will be in touch
Kiss goodnight	Kiss goodnight
	Go home

Note: The man's script has more elements than the woman's. The man typically takes the leadership role (see actions with asterisk).
Source: Adapted from S. Rose & I. H. Frieze (1989, June), *Gender and Society,* (Vol. 3, No. 2). Copyright 1989 by Sociologists for Women in Society. Reprinted by permission of Sage Publications.

ing and marriage continue to create situations in which women have fewer personal resources than their romantic partners. To the extent that women marry men who are older, have more education, earn more money, and have more prestigious jobs, women may be at a relative power disadvantage in heterosexual relationships. Young adults often have somewhat ambivalent attitudes toward power in dating and marriage. On the one hand, they endorse abstract democratic principles of shared deci-

sion making for male–female relationships. On the other hand, they follow traditional patterns of male–female interaction that can have the unintended consequence of giving men greater control.

In contemporary society, multiple definitions of gender roles coexist. The options available to people today, both at work and in personal relationships, are much less limited by gender than in the past.

KEY TERMS

androgyny	gender stereotype	schema
attribution	gender typing	sexism
cultural stereotype	meta-analysis	transsexual
gender identity	personal entitlement	
gender self-concept	personal stereotype	

SUMMARY

1. Gender is one of the most basic categories in social life. The process of labeling people, things, and activities as "masculine" and "feminine" is called gender typing.

2. Gender stereotypes are beliefs about the typical personal attributes of males and females. Cultural stereotypes are societal-level images of the sexes found in the media, art, and literature. Personal stereotypes are the beliefs held by an individual about the typical attributes of men and women.

3. Stereotypes are most likely to influence our perception of other people when we have little information available and when a person's gender is especially salient. One problem with gender stereotypes is that they can bias evaluation of the performance of individual men and women.

4. Gender identity, the knowledge that we are female or male, is acquired early in childhood. An important developmental milestone occurs when children come to understand that gender is constant and

unchanging. Transsexuals have a severe gender identity conflict: They believe their true psychological gender is different from their biological gender.

5. Beliefs about masculinity and femininity are important elements in our self-concept. Androgynous people rate themselves high in both masculine (instrumental) and feminine (expressive) qualities. Research challenges the congruence model assertion that psychological well-being is greatest among traditionally "masculine" men and "feminine" women.

6. There are four major theoretical perspectives on the causes of sex differences. A biological approach emphasizes the impact of physical differences, sex hormones, and genetics. A childhood socialization approach emphasizes ways in which we acquire relatively stable gender-typed characteristics through modeling and reinforcement. A social roles perspective emphasizes that people tend to conform to the expectations of gender-linked

social roles, such as husband or nurse. A final approach emphasizes that people's behavior varies from situation to situation, depending on such factors as the sex composition of the group, the nature of the task or activity, and the social expectations of others.

7. Much research has compared the social behavior of women and men. A new technique called meta-analysis provides a quantitative way to integrate findings from many different studies. Research finds that, on average, males are more aggressive and, in some situations, men may be less vulnerable to social influence. Men are more likely to help a stranger (especially a female) in dis-

tress; women are more likely to provide social support and care for friends and relatives. Females tend to be better at decoding nonverbal communication. Males and females appear to differ in their sense of personal entitlement.

8. In daily life, women and men often use their basic talents and motivation in distinctive, gender-linked ways. Traditional gender roles prescribed a division of labor by sex and conferred great power on men. Despite social change, both these traditional patterns continue. In general, however, people today are less constrained by gender than in the past.

SUGGESTED READINGS

Bohan, J. S. (Ed.) (1992). *Seldom seen, rarely heard: Women's place in psychology.* San Francisco: Westview Press. This anthology considers such issues as the history of women in psychology, sexist bias in psychology, and new directions in gender research.

Eagly, A. H. (1987). *Sex differences in social behavior: A social-role interpretation.* Hillsdale, NJ: Erlbaum. A social role perspective on gender plus an excellent summary of research using meta-analysis.

Pleck, J. H. (1981). *The myth of masculinity.* Cambridge, MA: MIT Press. A detailed analysis of research and theories of

masculinity; somewhat technical, but well worth the effort.

Tavris, C. (1992). *The mismeasure of woman.* New York: Simon & Schuster (paperback). A critical review of gender research on a variety of topics (love, sexuality, morality, menstruation) written for a nonprofessional audience.

Unger, R. & Crawford, M. (1992). *Women and gender: A feminist psychology.* New York: McGraw-Hill. A basic college text on the psychology of gender. Available in paperback.

13
Prosocial Behavior

FOCUS OF THIS CHAPTER

Defining Altruism and Prosocial
  Behavior

Theoretical Perspectives on Helping

Situational Factors: When Do People
  Help?

The Helper: Who Is Most Likely to
  Help?

The Person in Need: Who Is Most Likely
  to Receive Help?

The Experience of Receiving Help

Research Closeup

Volunteer Work—Helping Others and
Helping Ourselves

Cultural Highlight

Helping a Stranger in Distress—Does
Ethnicity Make a Difference?

Wilson Ross, 54, was driving his bread delivery van when he was hit from behind by a truck. The van went out of control and overturned, leaving Ross unconscious. As flames began to appear, Ross dangled helplessly, suspended upside down in the van by his seatbelt. Although several passersby saw the accident and stopped, they were deterred from aiding the victim by the flames. But Jackson E. Stallcup, a Vietnam War veteran who drives a hazardous materials truck for a living, stopped his massive 18-wheeler on the freeway to offer help.

Quickly sizing up the situation, Stallcup crawled through the shattered windshield of the van. He tried unsuccessfully to free Ross by cutting the nylon seat belt with a knife. At this point, Ross regained consciousness and asked Stallcup not to leave him. "I told him I wouldn't leave," Stallcup remembers. Finally, as flames set Ross's clothes on fire, Stallcup located the belt buckle and released Ross, who fell on top of his rescuer. With difficulty, Stallcup pulled the semiconscious man through the windshield. "I crawled out with him on top. As soon as we got out, I heard an explosion. I was lucky. It was a good day for him, a good day for me." The explosion engulfed the van in flames. For his act of heroism, Stallcup was awarded a $2500 prize and a medal from the Carnegie Hero Fund Commission. Since 1904, the Commission has given awards to 7367 individuals who risked their lives to help others in need.

Stallcup's story hints at the complex factors that affect helping. According to newspaper accounts, the crash scene reminded Stallcup of his earlier experiences in the Vietnam War (Connelly, 1989). "I remembered Vietnam and people crying for help when they were hurt or dying. I knew I couldn't handle it if it would happen again. I wouldn't be able to live with

The bravery of firefighters risking their lives to save others contrasts vividly with scenes of people ignoring the plight of those in need of help.

myself if I left this guy and heard him screaming while the truck burned." Stallcup's desire to help was facilitated by his strength and expertise. He carried a knife, which he used to try to free the injured man. Both his war experience and his current job driving hazardous materials may have increased Stallcup's confidence in his ability to handle the crisis. Whereas others were deterred by the dangerous situation, Stallcup was willing to risk his life.

Acts of altruism such as this stand in stark contrast to stories of public apathy to the plight of victims. In Chapter 1 we recounted the tragic story of Kitty Genovese, a young woman stabbed to death on a city street while at least 38 people watched and did nothing. There are countless stories of this sort. People are beaten, raped, robbed, and killed while those who could give assistance stand by. Why do people sometimes help others? And why, sometimes, do they fail to give badly needed assistance?

DEFINING ALTRUISM AND PROSOCIAL BEHAVIOR

Before trying to answer these questions, we should be clear about the meaning of two key concepts: altruism and prosocial behavior. **Altruism** refers to an act performed voluntarily to help someone else when there is no expectation of receiving a reward in any form (except perhaps a feeling of having done a good deed). By this definition, whether or not an act is altruistic depends on the *intentions* of the helper. The stranger who risks his or her own life to pull a victim from a burning car and then vanishes anonymously into the night has performed an altruistic act. Much of the research we will present in this chapter has focused on altruistic acts in which help is given to a stranger in distress.

Prosocial behavior is a much broader category. It includes any act that helps or is designed to help others, regardless of the helper's motives. Many prosocial acts are not altruistic. For example, if you volunteer to work for a charity to impress your friends or to build up your résumé for future job hunting, you are not acting altruistically in the pure sense. Prosocial behavior ranges over a continuum

from the most selfless acts of altruism to helpful acts motivated entirely by self-interest.

Our everyday experiences provide many examples of prosocial behavior. Even young children show the capacity to be helpful to others (Zahn-Waxler, Radke-Yarrow, Wagner, & Chapman, 1992). For example, one study observed children ages 3 to 5 at play in a preschool (Strayer, Wareing, & Rushton, 1979). On average, each child engaged in 15 helpful acts per hour, ranging from giving a toy to another child to comforting an upset friend or helping a teacher.

Prosocial behavior is affected by the type of relationship between people. Whether because of liking, social obligation, self-interest, or empathy, we are more helpful to those we know and care about than to those we don't know. Paul Amato (1990) asked young adults to describe recent examples of situations in which they had helped another person. Most of the time, help was given to friends and relatives. Only 10 percent of the helping episodes concerned a total stranger. Assistance rendered to strangers was usually spontaneous—giving someone directions, helping a person pick up dropped packages, or offering a seat to someone on a bus. In contrast, much of the help offered to acquaintances was planned in advance, such as visiting a sick friend or helping someone move into a new apartment.

Although help offered to strangers is less common than help offered to friends, it is by no means a rare occurrence. Many studies have documented people's willingness to help a stranger in need. Research conducted in a midwestern American city found that over half of women shoppers were willing to give money for bus fare to a university student who explained that his wallet had "disappeared" (Berkowitz, 1972). In New York City, most pedestrians responded positively to requests for help from a passerby. Eighty-five percent of New Yorkers gave the time of day, 85 percent gave directions, and 73 percent gave change for a quarter (Latané & Darley, 1970). In another study on the streets of New York, 50 percent of people who found a wallet that had been "lost" (intentionally by researchers) mailed it back to its owner (Hornstein, Fisch, & Holmes, 1968). Prosocial behavior even occurs on city subways. When a passenger (actually a researcher)

Throughout life, family and friends help each other in many ways both small and large. Here a teenager helps her grandmother with groceries.

fell down with an apparent knee injury, 83 percent of those in the subway offered assistance (Latané & Darley, 1970). In another subway study, a researcher pretending to be physically disabled repeatedly fell down and always received help (Piliavin, Rodin, & Piliavin, 1969).

THEORETICAL PERSPECTIVES ON HELPING

Our understanding of prosocial behavior has benefited from several broad theoretical perspectives that were presented in Chapter 1. First, the decision-making perspective focuses on the processes that influence judgments about when help is needed. It also emphasizes the weighing of costs and benefits in the decision to give help. Second, a learning approach proposes that people learn to be helpful, following basic principles of reinforcement and modeling. Third, sociobiologists have proposed that a predisposition to help is part of our genetic, evolutionary heritage. Finally, others have emphasized

the importance of social rules that dictate when we should help people in need. We will discuss each of these four theories of helping.

The Decision-making Perspective

Helping occurs when an individual decides to offer assistance and then takes action. In any particular situation, the decision to help involves complex processes of social cognition and rational decision making (Borgida, Conner & Manteufel, 1992; Latané & Darley, 1970). There are several steps in the decision to help, as shown in Figure 13-1. A person must first notice that something is happening and decide whether or not help is required. If help is needed, the person considers the extent of his or her own personal responsibility to act. Third, the person evaluates the rewards and costs of helping or not helping. Finally, the person must decide what type of help is needed and just how to provide it. Let's consider each step in detail.

PERCEIVING A NEED. It's 2 A.M. and a piercing scream fills the night air. Some people sleep on, oblivious to all but their private dreams. You wake up with a start. A woman shouts, "Stop it! Leave me alone!" You hear an angry male voice, but you can't quite make out what he's saying. Quickly you ask yourself what is going on—Is it merely a noisy lovers' quarrel or a serious physical attack? Is this an emergency requiring outside intervention?

The crucial first step in any prosocial act is noticing that something is happening and deciding that help is required. In some situations, the need is clear: Flood waters are rising in the river in your town and all able-bodied people are needed to fill sandbags to hold back the water. Or a child has gashed her head playing soccer and needs medical attention. But in many situations, such as hearing screams in the night, it can be difficult to decide. *Uncertainty* is a major reason why people sometimes fail to offer assistance. One study found that when students heard an unmistakable emergency—a maintenance man falling off a ladder and crying out in agony—all of them went to the man's aid. In another condition, where students heard an

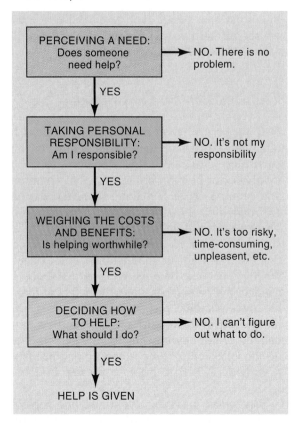

Figure 13-1 The decision-making perspective identifies four crucial steps in the process leading to giving help to a person in distress. At each point, different decisions may lead the person not to offer assistance.

ambiguous emergency—the sounds of an identical fall but without verbal cues that the victim was injured—help was offered only about 30 percent of the time (Clark & Word, 1972).

What cues do people use in deciding whether there is an emergency requiring intervention? Research by Shotland and Huston (1979) identified five important characteristics that lead us to perceive that an event is an emergency:

1. Something happens suddenly and unexpectedly.
2. There is a clear threat of harm to a victim.
3. The harm to the victim is likely to increase over time unless someone intervenes.
4. The victim is helpless and needs outside assistance.
5. Some sort of effective intervention is possible.

For example, most people consider the following events to be emergencies: a drug overdose, a heart attack, a rape in progress, and a car accident with the driver motionless on the ground. People are less certain that an emergency exists if there is a power blackout, if a friend says he is miserable and depressed, or if there is a disabled car on the side of a road.

Our interpretation or definition of a situation is a vital factor in whether or not we offer aid. Shotland and Straw (1976) found that people respond quite differently to an identical fight scene, depending on whether they perceive it as a lovers' quarrel or a fight between strangers. In this study, students came to the psychology department individually in the evening to fill out an attitude questionnaire. While working alone on the task, the student heard a loud fight break out in the corridor (actually staged by drama students). A woman screamed and pleaded with a man to "get away from me." In a "marriage" condition, where the victim yelled "I don't know why I ever married you," only 19 percent of students intervened. But in a "stranger" condition, where the woman yelled, "I don't know you," 65 percent of subjects intervened either directly or by calling the police. Even though the fights were identical in all respects, subjects perceived the situation as more serious and the woman as more eager for help in the "stranger" condition.

In a real-life fight where the relationship between the participants is unclear, onlookers may assume it to be a lovers' quarrel and so decide not to intrude. Perhaps this is unfortunate, but it means that the lack of help is due to a misunderstanding of the situation, not to an unwillingness to help.

TAKING PERSONAL RESPONSIBILITY. The second step in deciding to help is taking personal responsibility. Consider this situation. You're at the beach, lying in the sun. A woman spreads her blanket near yours and tunes her portable radio to a local rock station. After a few minutes she goes for a swim, leaving her radio on the blanket. A bit later a man comes along, notices the radio, snatches it up quickly, and walks off. What do you do? Chances are that you do not try to stop the thief, reminding yourself, perhaps, that it's not your responsibility.

In an experiment recreating the scene just described, only 20 percent of people intervened by going up to the thief and demanding an explanation (Moriarity, 1975). In a second condition, however, the owner of the radio first approached the person next to her on the beach and asked if they would "watch my things" while she went swimming. Among those who said yes, 95 percent later intervened to stop the thief. When individuals feel personal responsibility, they are significantly more likely to help.

Another demonstration of the importance of taking personal responsibility comes from a clever field study (Maruyama, Fraser, & Miller, 1982). On Halloween, groups of children who came to a certain house while trick-or-treating were asked to donate candies for hospitalized children. There were three experimental conditions, designed to manipulate the children's perceptions of responsibility. In one condition, the woman who greeted the kids made each child personally responsible for donating candies by putting the child's name on a bag for the candies. In another condition, she made one child

responsible for the entire group. In the third condition, no one was given responsibility.

The variations in responsibility had clear effects on the number of candies donated by the children, as shown in Figure 13-2. When each child was individually responsible, the average donation was 5 candies; when one child was responsible for the group, average donations dropped to 3; when no one was responsible, an average of only 2 candies per child was given.

Another factor influencing perceived responsibility is competence. We feel a greater sense of obligation to intervene if we have the skills to help effectively. In one study, for instance, participants witnessed a person (actually a confederate) pass out from an electrical shock caused by malfunctioning equipment (Clark & Word, 1974). Of participants who had formal training or experience in working with electrical equipment, 90 percent intervened to help; among those with no electrical skills, only 58 percent intervened.

WEIGHING THE COSTS AND BENEFITS. The decision-making perspective suggests that people consider the potential gains and losses that will result from a particular action, including helping another person (Dovidio, Piliavin, Gaertner, Schroeder, & Clark, 1991). A person will act prosocially if the perceived profits (rewards minus costs) for helping outweigh the profits from not helping.

Sometimes it is relatively easy to help. At other times, helping may involve considerable costs in time, energy, and complications. Telling a passerby the time of day requires little effort; pulling off the freeway to help a stranded motorist would be more time-consuming. In both situations, the cost will depend in part on whether you perceive any inconvenience or possible threat to your own safety. Does the person needing help look respectable, or is there some chance you will be robbed? The greater the perceived costs, the less likely you are to help.

There may also be costs to *not* giving assistance. You may feel guilty about not helping. Other people may see that you have not been helpful, and think badly of you. You may have a general moral value that says you should help when you can, so that not helping means you have failed to live up to your own ethical stan-

Figure 13-2 Increased personal responsibility increases helping. In this study, researchers varied the instructions given to Halloween trick-or-treaters about their responsibility for giving candy to needy children. (*Source:* Adapted from Maruyama, Fraser, & Miller, 1982.)

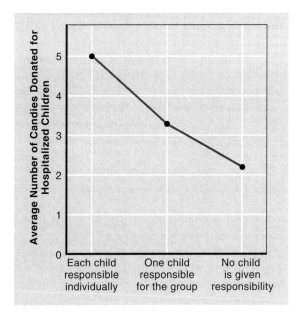

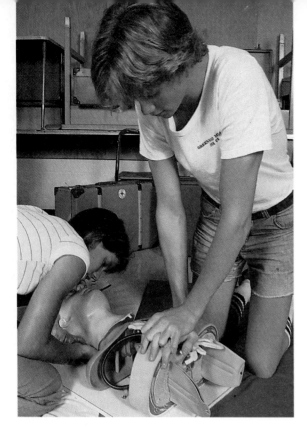

We are more likely to intervene in an emergency if we know how to help effectively. By taking a course in cardio-pulmonary resuscitation (CPR), these people will have the knowledge to help heart attack victims.

dards. Thoughts such as these influence whether or not you offer help.

The benefits of giving help also affect our decision making. The greater the good you believe you will do, the more likely you are to help. The more the person deserves to be helped and the more help you are able to give, the better you may feel about offering assistance. For example, Gruder, Romer, and Korth (1978) had a female confederate telephone people and request aid. The woman's story was that her car had broken down and she needed to reach a service station. She had gotten a wrong number, and asked the person to call the service station for her. In some cases, she was in great need; in others, less. In some cases, she said that the problem was largely her own fault because she had forgotten to take the car in for servicing even though she knew it needed repairs; in others, it was not her fault because the car had broken down with no warning. People helped more when her need was greater and when she was not at fault (and so presumably more deserving of help).

Several researchers have tested this model of helping and have found generally supportive results (see review by Dovidio et al., 1991). It seems likely that cost–benefit considerations do influence helping, at least in some situations. On the other hand, they do not fully explain all helping decisions. Some altruistic acts occur quickly and perhaps even impulsively. The person who instantly jumps into an icy lake to save a drowning child is unlikely to have weighed carefully the expected profits of the action. Rather, such acts may be motivated by basic emotions and values having to do with human life and personal courage.

DECIDING HOW TO HELP AND TAKING ACTION. A final step in the decision-making process is figuring out what type of assistance to offer and then taking action. Should you intervene directly in the fight outside your door or act indirectly by calling the police? Should you try to help the unconscious accident victim or call the paramedics? Whether a person takes direct action or seeks further assistance from someone else depends on many factors, such as the type of aid needed and the expertise of the potential helper. In emergencies, decisions are often made under great stress, urgency, and sometimes even personal danger. Well-intentioned helpers are not always able to give assistance or may even mistakenly do the wrong thing.

Our analysis of different steps in the decision to help highlights the many reasons why people fail to give needed assistance. They may not notice that a problem exists, or may perceive the problem as trivial. They may recognize a need, but not feel personally responsible for helping. They may believe the costs of helping are too great. They may want to help, but be unable to do so. Or they may hesitate, caught in a state of indecision.

The Learning Perspective

A second perspective on prosocial behavior emphasizes the importance of learning. In growing up, children are taught to share and to help. You can probably remember times when you were praised for being helpful or chided for forgetting to help when you should have. Two general learning principles discussed in Chapter 1 are again important here. People learn to help through reinforcement—the effects of rewards and punishment for helping. People also learn through modeling—by observing others who help (Piliavin & Charng, 1990).

Studies show clearly that children will help and share more when they are rewarded for their prosocial behavior. For example, one study found that 4-year-olds were more likely to share marbles with another child when they were rewarded with bubble gum for their generosity (Fischer, 1963). In everyday life, parents and teachers are more likely to reward helpfulness with praise than with bubble gum. Research suggests that some forms of praise may be more effective than others.

In one study, 8- and 9-year old children played a game to win chips that could be traded for toys (Mills & Grusec, 1989). In an initial phase of the study, the researcher urged children to share their chips with poor children who didn't have any toys. With prompting, all children gave away some of their chips. Children were then given one of two types of praise for their helpfulness. In a *dispositional praise* condition, the experimenter emphasized the child's personality by saying, "I guess you're the kind of person who likes to help others whenever you can. Yes, you're a very nice and helpful person." In a *general praise* condition, the researcher emphasized the child's actions rather than personality, saying, "It was good that you gave some of your chips to the poor children. Yes, that was a nice and helpful thing to do." The children were then left alone to play the game again and were told that they could share "with the poor children if you want to, but you really don't have to." Children who had received the dispositional praise, emphasizing that they were a helpful person, were significantly more likely to share than children who received the general praise or no praise at all. Dispositional praise appears to be more effective than global praise.

A study of sixth-grade girls showed the impact of seeing a helpful model (Midlarsky, Bryan, & Brickman, 1973). Girls played a special pinball machine to win chips that could be exchanged for candy and toys. Before her own turn came, each girl watched an adult model

Foster grandparent Linwood Blunt helps his two "grandsons" practice reading. When adults assist children, they provide an important model of helpfulness. The boys, who are partially hearing impaired, are teaching Linwood sign language.

play the game. In one condition, a selfish model put all the chips she won into a jar labeled "my money." In another condition, a charitable model put some of her chips into a jar labeled "money for poor children." Regardless of the condition, the model then urged the girl to think about the poor children who would "love to receive the prizes these chips can buy." Results showed a clear effect of modeling. Girls who had seen a charitable model donated an average of 19 tokens to the poor compared to only 10 tokens given by the girls who saw the selfish model.

Children's television programs can also enhance helpfulness by showing prosocial models. For example, one study exposed first-graders to different episodes from the then-popular children's TV show about a dog named "Lassie" (Sprafkin, Liebert, & Poulos, 1975). Half the children watched an episode that focused on Lassie's efforts to keep her puppy from being given away. At the story's climax, the puppy falls into a mining shaft. Unable to rescue the puppy herself, Lassie brings her owner Jeff and his grandfather to the scene. Jeff risks his life by hanging over the edge of the shaft to save the puppy. In the neutral condition, children watched an episode of Lassie that dramatized Jeff's attempt to avoid taking violin lessons. It contained no examples of humans helping a dog, although Lassie was obviously featured in a positive light.

Children watched the Lassie episode individually and then were given an opportunity to help some puppies, but only at the cost of forgoing personal benefits. Children who had watched the prosocial TV show were significantly more helpful than children who had watched the neutral show. This and other studies (Ahammer & Murray, 1979) show that watching helpful models on TV can increase children's prosocial behavior.

Other research has examined the combined effects of both modeling and reinforcement. In one study, a helpful adult model was used to get boys to behave altruistically by giving some of the tokens they won at bowling to an orphan named Bobby (Rushton & Teachman, 1978). Then the model either rewarded the child for his generosity ("Good for you." "That's really nice of you.") or punished him ("That's kind of silly for you to give to Bobby."). There was also a no-reinforcement condition in which the adult said nothing. As Figure 13-3 shows, children who were rewarded gave more to Bobby on later trials than did children who were punished. Two weeks later, when children again played the same game and were reminded about Bobby, the effects of the earlier reward or punishment still influenced how much they gave to Bobby.

Adults can also be affected by observing helpful models, as a study of blood donors clearly showed. In this clever experiment, female college students first talked to a friendly woman (actually a confederate of the researchers) as part of a study of social interaction (Rushton & Campbell, 1977). The researchers arranged things so that as the two women left the interaction study, they passed a table set up in the corridor, staffed by people asking for blood donations. Half the time, the confederate immediately volunteered, modeling prosocial behavior. In the no-model condition, the confederate stepped aside to talk to someone else and did not volunteer to give blood.

The effects of the model's behavior were striking. A helpful model led 67 percent of sub-

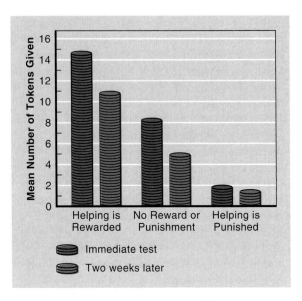

Figure 13-3 Rewards and punishments have clear effects on children's willingness to help. In this study, children were praised, criticized, or given no reinforcement for donating tokens to an orphan named Bobby. Children were then given other opportunities to help Bobby, both immediately and then two weeks later. Children who were rewarded gave the most tokens; children who were punished gave the fewest. (*Source:* Adapted from Rushton & Teachman, *Personality and Social Psychology Bulletin,* Vol. 4, No. 2, 1978, p. 324. Copyright by the Society for Personality and Social Psychology, Inc. Reprinted by permission of Sage Publications, Inc.)

jects to pledge to donate blood, compared to only 25 percent of subjects who saw no model. More impressive were data on whether the women actually followed through on their pledges to give blood. None of the women in the no-model condition actually gave blood, but 33 percent of those who saw the altruistic model did. Similar evidence of modeling effects has been found in a variety of situations, such as donating money to a Salvation Army kettle at Christmas or helping a stranded motorist fix a flat tire (Bryan & Test, 1967).

Adult helping is also influenced by reinforcement. In one study, individuals walking along the main street in Dayton, Ohio, were approached by an attractive woman who asked how to get to a local department store (Moss & Page, 1972). After getting instructions, she either rewarded the helper (by saying, "Thank you very much, I really appreciate this") or punished the helper ("I can't understand what you're saying; never mind, I'll ask someone else"). When the naive subject continued walking down the street, he or she encountered another woman who accidentally dropped a small bag and continued walking as if she didn't know she had lost it. The question of interest was whether the subject would help the woman by returning the bag to her. In the reward condition, 90 percent of people helped; in the punishment condition, only 40 percent helped.

Taken together, these and other studies provide convincing evidence of the power of reinforcement and modeling to shape prosocial behavior. Over time people develop habits of helping and learn rules about who they should help when. For young children, prosocial behavior may depend largely on external rewards and social approval. But as we grow older, helping can become an internalized value, independent of external incentives. It can be enough to know that you've lived up to your own standards and to feel the warm glow of having done a good deed.

Sociobiology

Scientists have long observed prosocial behavior among animal species. Charles Darwin (1871) noted that rabbits will make noise with their hind feet to warn other rabbits of predators. In termite hives, the soldier termites will defend a nest against an intruder by putting themselves in front of the other termites and exposing themselves to great danger (Wilson, 1971). Many soldier termites die so that others may live and the nest survive. Some varieties of baboons have a characteristic pattern of responding to threats (Hall, 1960). The dominant males take the most exposed positions to protect the group and may even rush at an intruder. As the tribe moves away from the threat, the males risk their own safety by remaining behind to protect the rest of the group.

Similarly, dolphins show a fascinating pattern of rescuing injured peers. Since dolphins are mammals, they must breathe air to survive. If an injured dolphin sinks below the surface, it will die. Several observers have reported that dolphins will aid an injured companion. In one case, a dolphin was stunned by an explosion in the water (Siebenaler & Caldwell, 1956). Two other adults came to its aid by holding the animal afloat until it recovered and was able to care for itself.

Among many animals, parents will sacrifice themselves when their young are threatened. An impressive example is the female nighthawk, which responds to a potential attack on her young by flying from the nest as if she had a broken wing, fluttering around at a low level, and finally landing on the ground right in front of the intruder but away from the nest (Armstrong, 1965).

This portrait of animals helping and sacrificing for each other runs counter to the dog-eat-dog, survival of the fittest image that some humans have of the animal kingdom. The existence of altruism has posed a problem for evolutionary theorists: If the most helpful members of an animal species sacrifice themselves for others, they will be less likely to survive and pass along their genes to the next generation by having offspring. How then does a biological predisposition to act altruistically persist among animals or humans (Hoffman, 1981)?

Sociobiology, a theoretical perspective introduced in Chapter 1, has tried to resolve this paradox (Krebs & Miller, 1985; Wilson, 1975). According to sociobiology, any genetically determined trait that has a high survival value (that helps the individual survive) will tend to be passed on to the next generation. In the case of altruism, the tendency to help others may have high survival value for the individual's genes, but not necessarily for the individual. Imagine a bird that has fathered six chicks. Half the genes in each chick come from the father. Together, the six chicks have three times as many of the father's genes as he does himself. If the father sacrifices himself to save the chicks, his particular gene pool is still ahead of the game. Similar analyses can be done for other relatives who have varying percentages of the individual's genes. From the sociobiological

Animals other than humans also help each other. Grooming behavior is common among monkeys and other primates.

ate their genes without investing much in any one infant. Females can produce only a relatively small number of offspring, and so must help each offspring to thrive to ensure the survival of the mother's genes.

The idea that altruism is a genetically determined part of "human nature" is quite controversial. Just how well the theory applies to people is still an open question (Caporael & Brewer, 1991; Fisher, 1991). Nonetheless, the theory raises the intriguing possibility that self-preservation is not always the overwhelming motive that we sometimes think. Biological dispositions for selfishness and aggression may coexist with biological dispositions for altruism.

viewpoint, helping close relatives contributes to the survival of an individual's genes in future generations, and so can be understood by the basic principles of evolutionary biology.

Sociobiologist Robert Trivers (1971) has argued that only mutual or *reciprocal altruism* is biologically based. In his view, the potential costs of altruism to the individual are offset by the possibility of receiving help from others. But such a system of mutual help giving is threatened by potential "cheaters" who accept help but offer none in return. To minimize cheating, natural selection may have favored a disposition to feel guilt and a tendency to enforce mutual helping through social means such as punishing those who do not follow group rules.

The sociobiological approach leads to several specific predictions. For example, animals should be most altruistic to those who are genetically most closely linked to themselves. They should be more helpful to immediate family than to distant relatives or strangers. The theory also predicts that parents will behave more altruistically to healthy offspring than to unhealthy ones who are less likely to survive. Studies of humans support these predictions, although sociobiology is not the only possible interpretation for such findings (Dovidio et al., 1991).

A further prediction is that mothers will usually be more altruistic to their offspring than will fathers. The reasoning here is that in many species males have the biological potential to sire a great many offspring and so can perpetu-

Social Norms: Responsibility, Reciprocity, and Justice

Critics of sociobiology argue that social factors are much more important than biology in determining prosocial behavior among humans. Donald Campbell (1975) suggests that genetic evolution may help explain a few basic prosocial behaviors such as parents' caring for their young, but that it does not apply to more extreme instances of helping a stranger in distress. Such cases are better explained by what Campbell calls "social evolution"—the historical development of human culture or civilization. In this view, human societies have gradually and selectively evolved skills and beliefs that promote the welfare of the group. Because prosocial behavior generally benefits society, it has become part of the social rules or norms. Three norms are especially relevant to helping behavior: social responsibility, reciprocity, and social justice.

First, a **norm of social responsibility** prescribes that we should help others who depend on us. Parents are expected to care for their children, and social agencies may intervene if parents fail to live up to this obligation. Teachers are supposed to help their students, coaches to look after team members, and coworkers to assist each other. The religious and moral codes of many societies emphasize the duty to help others. Sometimes this obligation is even written

These volunteers are serving a free Thanksgiving dinner to people who might otherwise go hungry. Volunteer service is often motivated by beliefs about social responsibility and social justice.

into the law. For example, the state of Minnesota has enacted a statute requiring that "Any person at the scene of an emergency who knows that another person is exposed to or suffered grave physical harm shall, to the extent that he can do so without danger or peril to himself or others, give reasonable assistance to the exposed person." Laws are one way of emphasizing to people that they have a responsibility to help. As we saw earlier in this chapter, an increased sense of personal responsibility does indeed increase the likelihood that a person will provide assistance.

Although all societies have norms of social responsibility, the specifics of whom we are expected to help and when vary from culture to culture. Joan Miller and her associates have compared the beliefs about social responsibility of Hindus in India and of Americans. Hindu culture emphasizes the interconnectedness of people and the obligation of the individual to the social group. In contrast, American culture values individualism and self-reliance. As a result, Miller believes that Americans tend to view the decision to help others as a matter of personal choice, but Hindus view the same decision to help in terms of moral obligations (Miller & Luthar, 1989).

In an illustrative study, 180 American and 180 Hindu subjects evaluated stories about a person in need (Miller, Bersoff, & Harwood,

1990). Sometimes the person's problem was relatively minor (needing an aspirin for a headache) and sometimes the problem was extreme (needing a ride to the hospital because of severe bleeding). The stories also varied the relationship of the helper and person in need (strangers, friends, or a parent/young child). The results are presented in Table 13-1. Both cross-cultural similarities and differences were found. When the person's need was life-threatening, both Hindus and Americans believed there was an obligation to help, even if the person in need was a stranger. In contrast, when the need was minor, Hindus were much more likely than Americans to view assistance as a moral obligation. For example, 88 percent of Hindus believed a person was obligated to help a stranger with a minor problem, compared to only 41 percent of Americans. It appears that Hindus have a broader definition of social responsibilities that often extends beyond family and friends to include strangers in need. In contrast, Americans tend to have a more narrow view of social responsibilities and so are likely to interpret more helping situations as optional matters of personal choice.

Further insights into the differences between individualistic cultures and collectivist cultures are provided by a recent study comparing the United States and Brazil (Bontempo, Lobel, & Triandis, 1990). In this research, college students

TABLE 13-1
Percentage of Subjects Saying the Person Has an Obligation to Help

	Hindus			Americans		
	Parent	Friend	Stranger	Parent	Friend	Stranger
Extreme need	99	99	100	100	98	96
Moderate need	98	100	99	95	78	55
Minor need	96	97	88	61	59	41

Source: Adapted from Miller, Bersoff, & Harwood (1990), p. 38.

in Illinois and Rio de Janeiro were asked questions about helpful behaviors, such as lending money to someone or spending time caring for a serious ill person. Students in both cultures recognized the existence of social obligations to help in such cases. However, whereas the Brazilians said they would actually enjoy doing what was expected of them, the Americans reported little enthusiasm for performing these required prosocial acts.

Second, a **norm of reciprocity** says that we should help those who help us. Several studies have shown that people are more likely to help someone from whom they have already received aid. A study by Regan (1968) illustrated this idea that favors are reciprocated. College students were tested in pairs, one partner secretly being a confederate of the experimenter. The study was described as dealing with perceptual and esthetic judgment. The participants were put in separate rooms and asked individually to rate a series of pictures. They were then given a short break.

In one experimental condition, the confederate did a favor for the subject. During the break, the confederate left the building and returned carrying two bottles of Coca Cola. He handed one to the subject, saying, "I asked him [the experimenter] if I could get myself a Coke and he said it was okay, so I brought one for you, too." All subjects took the Coke. In a second experimental condition, the researcher gave the subject and the confederate drinks, saying, "I brought you guys a Coke." In a third condition, no drinks were provided. After the break, the experimenter gave all subjects a second series of pictures to rate.

After the new pictures were rated, there was another short break, during which the confederate asked the experimenter (loud enough for the subject to hear) whether he could send a note to the subject. The experimenter said that he could as long as it did not concern the experiment. The confederate then wrote the following note (Regan, 1968, p. 19):

> Would you do me a favor? I'm selling raffle tickets for my high school back home to build a new gym. The tickets cost 25 cents each and the prize is a new Corvette. The thing is, if I sell the most tickets I get 50 bucks and I could use it. If you'd buy any, would you just write the number on this note and give it back to me right away so I can make out the tickets? Any would help, the more the better. Thanks.

The measure of helping was how many tickets the subject would agree to buy. The results are shown in Figure 13-4. When the confederate gave the subject a drink and then asked him to do a favor, there was considerably more helping than when the experimenter gave the subject a drink or when no drink was given.

The reciprocity norm seems to be quite strong and has been shown to operate in many cultures (Gergen et al., 1975). The strength of feelings of obligation is influenced by several factors in the situation. For example, a larger favor is reciprocated more often than a smaller favor (Greenberg & Frisch, 1972). People's attributions about the motives of the helper also matter. We

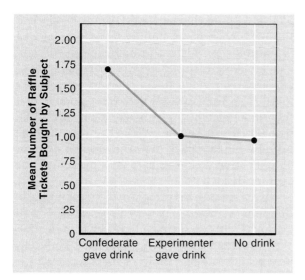

Figure 13-4 According to the norm of reciprocity, we should help someone who has helped us. In this study subjects who had been given a Coke by another subject (actually a confederate) were more likely to help him by purchasing raffle tickets. Subjects who were given a Coke by the experimenter or who received no Coke purchased fewer tickets. In everyday life, favors are often reciprocated. (*Source:* Adapted from Regan, 1968.)

are more likely to return a favor when the original help is perceived to be given intentionally and voluntarily. Goranson and Berkowitz (1966) found that subjects who had been helped by someone tended to repay that specific person, but they were not especially likely to offer aid to someone else.

Third, human groups also develop **norms of social justice,** rules about fairness and the just distribution of resources. As we discussed in Chapter 10, one common fairness principle is **equity.** According to this principle, two people who make equal contributions to a task should receive equal rewards. If one receives more than the other, the people will feel pressure to try to restore equity by redistributing the rewards. The short-changed or underbenefited person obviously feels distressed. The more interesting finding is that even the person who receives more than a fair share (the overbenefited person) may give some to the person who got too little. And a third person, observing the unfair situation, might also be tempted to give to the one who suffered. Everyday acts of "helping the

less fortunate" such as donating to a charity seem to be motivated by a desire to create a more equitable situation.

Numerous studies have demonstrated that overbenefited people will act to restore equity when they can (Walster, Walster, & Berscheid, 1978). In several experiments, subjects played a game in which one person, through no fault of her own, lost a lot of money or trading stamps while the partner won a good deal (Berscheid & Walster, 1967). At the end of the game, the winner (the real subject) was given an opportunity to give some of her winnings to the partner who lost. There was strong tendency to give some of the money to the loser, even though the winner had won legitimately. In contrast, in a condition where both partners had equal winnings, there was little tendency for the subject to give any winnings to the other player.

In another study, one member of a team was given more money than his partner. This overbenefited person tended to give some of the money to the partner in order to make their rewards more equitable (Schmitt & Marwell, 1972). In addition, the overrewarded partner often chose to play a different game when assured that this would result in a more equal division of the rewards. In other words, not only did he give away some of his own money to produce an equitable division, but he also changed the situation to avoid producing more inequity in the future.

These three norms—social responsibility, reciprocity, and social justice—are common in human societies. They provide a cultural basis for prosocial behavior. Through the process of socialization, individuals learn these rules and come to behave in accord with these guidelines for prosocial behavior. Research showing that people are more likely to help relatives and friends than other people can be explained in terms of social norms: We feel greater responsibility for those we are close to and we assume that they will help us if a need arises (Dovidio et al., 1991).

Having reviewed the major theoretical perspectives on helping, we now take a closer look at three specific factors that influence our willingness to give help: characteristics of the situation, characteristics of the potential helper, and characteristics of the person in need.

SITUATIONAL FACTORS: WHEN DO PEOPLE HELP?

Even the most dedicated altruist is less likely to offer aid in some situations than in others. Research has documented the importance of several situational factors, including the presence of other people, the nature of the physical environment, and the pressures of limited time.

The Presence of Others

One of the shocking things about the Kitty Genovese murder is that so many people heard the young woman's screams and yet did not even call the police. Many social commentators interpreted this as a sign of widespread moral decay and alienation in society. A very different hypothesis was offered by social psychologists Bibb Latané and John Darley (1970). They proposed that the very presence of so many onlookers may have caused the lack of helping. Those who witnessed the murder may have assumed that others had already called the police, and so may have felt little personal responsibility to intervene. Darley and Latané called this the **bystander effect.**

To test the idea that the number of witnesses

affects helping, Darley and Latané designed a series of experiments, both in the laboratory and in naturalistic settings. In one experiment, college students taking part in a study overheard an "emergency" next door. They were much more likely to respond if they were alone than if they thought others also knew about the situation (Darley & Latané, 1968). The more people present, the less likely it was that any one individual actually offered help, and the longer the average delay before help was given.

Many studies have replicated this finding in different settings. For example, Latané and Darley (1970) conducted a field study in the Nu-Way Beverage Center in Suffern, New York. The researchers staged a series of robberies with the help of the salesclerk and two pretend criminals. The robberies were staged when either one or two customers were in the store. When the salesclerk went to the back of the store to check on something, two husky young men entered, muttering "They'll never miss this," and walked off with a case of beer. As expected, people who witnessed the crime alone were significantly more likely to report the theft to the clerk than people who were in the store with another customer.

Why does the presence of others inhibit helpfulness? A decision-making analysis of prosocial behavior suggests several explanations. One is the **diffusion of responsibility** created by the presence of other people. If only one person witnesses a victim in distress, then he or she is totally responsible for responding to the situation and will bear all the guilt or blame for nonintervention. But if several people are present, help can come from several people. The obligation to help and the possible costs of failing to help are shared. Further, if a person knows that others are present but cannot actually talk to them or see their behavior, as in the Kitty Genovese case, the person may assume that others have already done something to help, such as calling the police.

Experiments support this idea that it is not simply the number of people present that is crucial, but rather the lessened feelings of personal responsibility that result from being in a group (Korte, 1971; Ross, 1971). Research also shows that

We are more likely to help in an emergency if we are alone than if others are present. This is called the bystander effect. Here, the single witness to a bike accident rushes to help the victim.

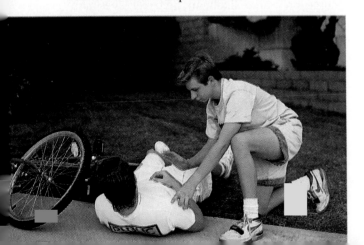

a group leader—presumably the person most responsible for group activities—is much more likely than other group members to help a victim in distress (Baumeister et al., 1988). It appears that group leaders are less susceptible to the diffusion of responsibility than are other group members.

A second explanation for the bystander effect concerns *ambiguity* in the interpretation of the situation. Potential helpers are sometimes uncertain whether a particular situation is actually an emergency. The behavior of other bystanders can influence how we define a situation and react to it. If others ignore a situation or act as if nothing is happening, we too may assume that no emergency exists. The impact of bystanders on interpreting a situation was demonstrated by Latané and Darley (1970).

In this experiment, college men sat filling out a questionnaire. After a few minutes, smoke began to enter the room through an air vent. Soon the smoke was so thick that it was difficult to see and to breathe normally. When subjects were alone, they usually walked around the room to investigate the smoke, and 75 percent reported the smoke to the researcher within four minutes. In a condition where the real subject was in a room with two confederates who deliberately ignored the smoke, only 10 percent of subjects reported the noxious smoke.

A third factor in the bystander effect is **evaluation apprehension.** If we know that other people are watching our behavior, we may get "stage fright." We may worry that we will do something wrong or that others will evaluate our reaction negatively (Baumeister, 1982). Subjects in the smoke-filled room may have feared they would look foolish or cowardly by showing concern about the smoke when others were apparently so calm. The desire to avoid the cost of social disapproval can inhibit action. Of course, there are also situations in which evaluation apprehension can make us more likely to help. If we see someone fall down a flight of stairs or have a heart attack, the socially appropriate response is to offer assistance. In such situations, the knowledge that others are watching may actually increase our tendency to help (Schwartz & Gottlieb, 1980).

Environmental Conditions

The physical setting also influences helpfulness. Think for a moment about whether you are more likely to stop to help a stranded motorist on a pleasant, sunny day or on a cold, rainy one? On a dark street or a well-lighted one? On a country lane or in a big city? Much research has documented the impact on helping of environmental conditions such as weather, city size, and noise level.

The effects of weather were investigated in two field studies by Cunningham (1979). In one study, pedestrians were approached outdoors and were asked to help the researcher by completing a questionnaire. People were significantly more likely to help when the day was sunny and when the temperature was comfortable (relatively warm in winter and relatively cool in summer). In a second study conducted in a climate-controlled restaurant, Cunningham found that customers left more generous tips when the sun was shining. Other research suggests that people are more likely to help a stranded motorist in sunny rather than rainy weather (Ahmed, 1979) and during the day rather than at night (Skolnick, 1977). In short, weather makes a difference in helping.

A common stereotype is that city dwellers are unfriendly and unhelpful, whereas small-town residents are cooperative and helpful. Research finds that when it comes to helping strangers in distress, city size is important (Steblay, 1987). Strangers are more likely to be assisted in small towns than in large cities. There is apparently something about being in a small town that encourages helping and, conversely, something about the urban context that reduces the tendency to help. Incidentally, studies show that the size of the hometown in which a person grew up is *not* related to helping; it's the current environmental setting in which the need for help occurs that matters.

Amato (1983) investigated helping in 55 Australian communities ranging from small villages to major cities. To ensure a diverse sample of prosocial behaviors, five different types of helping were studied. These included a student asking pedestrians to write down their favorite

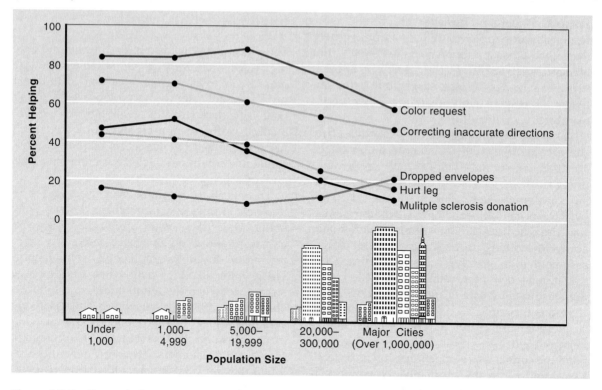

Figure 13-5   Research shows that strangers are more likely to receive help in small towns than in large cities. This figure shows the percentage of times that a stranger received five different kinds of help in cities of varying sizes. (*Source:* Adapted from Amato, 1983, p. 579.)

color as part of a school project, a pedestrian inadvertently dropping an envelope on the sidewalk, a request to donate money to the Multiple Sclerosis Society, overhearing a salesclerk give obviously wrong directions to someone, and witnessing a man with a bandaged leg fall to the ground and cry out in pain.

The results of this study are presented in Figure 13-5. On four of the five helping measures, the percentage of people who helped was significantly greater in small towns than in larger cities. The one exception to this pattern was the lost envelope. It generally brought little helping, and it seemed to elicit more help in the largest cities. What also should be kept in mind, of course, is that these studies dealt only with help offered to strangers: There is no reason to believe that city dwellers are any less helpful than small-town people when it comes to aiding friends and relatives.

Many explanations for the lesser helpfulness of city dwellers to strangers have been offered.

These include the anonymity of urban life, the overload experienced by city dwellers who are constantly bombarded by stimuli including other people, and possible feelings of helplessness from dealing with unresponsive urban bureaucracies. We don't yet know which explanation is most important.

Another environmental factor that can affect prosocial behavior is noise. Starting with the general idea that noise can reduce people's responsiveness to events in the environment, several researchers have investigated whether noisy conditions reduce the likelihood of helping a stranger in distress (Sherrod & Downs, 1974). In one lab study, for example, it was found that noise decreased the likelihood that students would help a person who had dropped some papers on the floor (Mathews & Canon, 1975). When only regular room noise was present, 72 percent of subjects helped, compared to only 37 percent when very loud noise was present. In a field study, the same investigators arranged to have a man wearing a cast on his arm drop some of the books he was carrying. When only typical street noises were present, 80 percent of passersby helped; when a noisy lawn mower was going, only 15 percent helped. The researchers suggested that loud noise causes people to ignore others in their environment and motivates them to leave the situation quickly, thus creating less helpful bystanders.

Time Pressures

Sometimes people feel that they are too hurried to help. A clear demonstration of this effect comes from an experiment by Darley and Batson (1973). As part of this study, individual male students were asked to walk to another building where they were to give a short talk. Some were told to take their time, that the talk would not begin for several minutes. Others were told to hurry because they were already late and the researcher was waiting. As the subject went from one building to the other building, he encountered a shabbily dressed man slumped in a doorway, coughing and groaning. The question of interest was whether or not the subject would offer assistance.

A further twist to the study was that all participants were theology students studying religion. For some, the assigned topic for their talk was the Bible story of the Good Samaritan, about a person who came to the aid of a man who lay injured on the roadside, the victim of robbers. Other students were to talk about a topic not relevant to helping, namely, the sorts of jobs theology students might pursue after graduation. The results of the study showed that time pressure had a strong impact on helping. In a post-experiment interview, all students recalled seeing the victim. But only 10 percent of those in a hurry helped, compared to 63 percent of those who were not in a hurry.

Surprisingly, the speech topic made no difference. Students about to talk on the Good Samaritan were no more likely to offer assistance than those preparing to talk on jobs. The researchers suggested that time pressure caused some students to overlook the needs of the victim. Another factor may have been a conflict about whom to help—the experimenter or the victim.

The possibility that conflict rather than callousness was at work is supported by a second study using a somewhat similar design (Batson et al., 1978). When students arrived for this study, they were sent individually to another building to interact with a computer. Some were told to hurry, and others were not. In addition, some were led to believe that their participation was of vital importance to the researcher, whereas others were told that their data were not essential. As the student walked to the new building, he encountered a male undergraduate slumped on the stairs, coughing and groaning.

Would the subject help this victim? Results presented in Figure 13-6 show that students in a hurry were less likely to help (40 percent) than were those with no pressures (65 percent). But

Figure 13-6 Sometimes time pressures create conflicts: Should we help a stranger in distress or keep an important appointment? In this study, researchers varied both time pressure, and the importance of being on time. This figure shows the percentage of subjects in each condition who offered to help a person in distress. Students in a hurry were less likely to help, especially when it was important to the experimenter that they be on time. (*Source:* Adapted from Batson, Cochran, Biederman, Blosser, Ryan & Vogt, *Personality and Social Psychology Bulletin*, Vol. 4, No. 1, 1978, p. 99. Copyright by the Society for Personality and Social Psychology, Inc. Reprinted by permission of Sage Publications, Inc.)

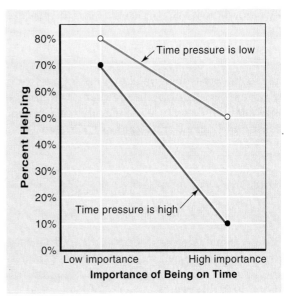

this was primarily true for subjects who thought their research participation was essential. When subjects thought the researcher was not counting on them, those in a hurry were nearly as likely to help (70 percent) as were those not in a hurry (80 percent). These results are consistent with the cost–benefit model discussed earlier. Apparently subjects weighed the costs and benefits to both experimenter and victim before arriving at a final course of action.

In a recent study of helping in England and in the Sudan, Alan Hedge and Yousif Yousif (1992) varied several situational factors simultaneously. To assess helping, the researchers dropped letters that were in stamped envelopes ready to be mailed, but had apparently been "lost." They compared the number of lost letters returned in each of several conditions. Half the letters were lost in big cities (Birmingham, England and Khartoum, Sudan) and half in small towns (Lichfield and Al-gaily). Some letters were marked "urgent" and others were not. Some letters were dropped near a mailbox so that the cost of helping was low; others were dropped in locations away from a mailbox. All three situational variations had a significant effect. More letters were returned in small towns, when they were marked "urgent," and when a mailbox was close at hand. The effect of each factor was independent and additive. In the most extreme comparison, 92 percent of urgent letters lost near a mailbox in a small town were returned, compared to only 41 percent of the nonurgent letters lost away from a mailbox in a big city. Other combinations of situational factors fell in between. For example, 60 percent of urgent letters lost away from a mailbox in a big city were returned. Finally, despite the many differences between Islamic culture in the Sudan and British culture in England, no significant differences in helping were found between the two countries.

THE HELPER: WHO IS MOST LIKELY TO HELP?

Some people offer aid even when situational forces discourage helping, and others fail to help even under the most favorable conditions. Individual differences do exist. In an effort to understand why some people are more likely to help than others, researchers have investigated both relatively fleeting moods and emotions as well as more enduring personality characteristics.

Temporary Mood

There is considerable evidence that people are more willing to help a stranger when they are in a good mood. For example, people are more likely to help if they have found a dime in a phone booth (Isen & Simmonds, 1978), been given a free cookie at the college library (Isen & Levin, 1972), succeeded on some experimental tasks (Isen, 1970), or listened to soothing music (Fried & Berkowitz, 1979) than if these mood-enhancing events have not occurred. Salespeople who rated themselves as being in a positive mood were evaluated by their supervisors as more helpful toward their coworkers and clients (George, 1991). Apparently a warm glow of positive feeling increases the willingness to act prosocially. Although the link between positive moods and helping is well established, the specific reasons for this pattern are currently under investigation (Carlson, Charlin & Miller, 1988; Salovey, Mayer & Rosenhan, 1991).

There are important limitations to the "feel good" effect, however. First, the effects of positive moods can be quite short-lived—only 20 minutes in one study (Isen, Clark, & Schwartz, 1976). Second, a good mood may actually *decrease* helpfulness when giving assistance would detract from the person's good mood (Isen & Simmonds, 1978). People in a good mood apparently want to maintain their positive feelings.

The effects of bad moods such as sadness or depression are more complicated, and research results have not been entirely consistent (Carlson & Miller, 1987). If a bad mood causes us to focus on ourself and our own needs, it may lessen the likelihood of our helping someone else (Thompson, Cowan, & Rosenhan, 1980). On the other hand, if we think helping someone else might make us feel better and so relieve our bad mood, we may be more likely to offer assistance (Cialdini et al., 1987).

Does providing assistance actually make

helpers feel better? Research suggests that it can (Williamson & Clark, 1992). In one study, for example, college students who were able to provide help reported feeling more cheerful and less nervous than students who were not given an opportunity to help (Williamson & Clark, 1989). Helpful students also reported feeling better about themselves (e.g., more generous and considerate, and less selfish or unreliable). In short, helping can improve the helper's mood and self-evaluations.

Motives for Helping: Empathy and Personal Distress

We noted earlier that true altruism is defined by the person's intentions: We act altruistically only when we help with no expectation of receiving personal benefit. This reasoning has led researchers to study the motives that lead people to help, and to contrast helping based on personal distress versus empathy.

To understand this distinction, picture for a moment the sight of people in serious trouble: the mangled bodies of victims in a train crash, a starving child in ragged clothes, or an anguished father whose child has disappeared. Witnessing people in need often evokes powerful emotions. **Personal distress** refers to our own emotional reactions to the plight of others—our feelings of shock, horror, alarm, concern, or helplessness. Personal distress is prominent when people who witness an event are preoccupied with their own emotional reactions. In contrast, **empathy** refers to feelings of sympathy and caring for others, in particular to sharing vicariously or indirectly in the suffering of others. Empathy is prominent when the observer focuses on the needs and emotions of the victim. Personal distress leads us to feel anxious and apprehensive; empathy leads us to feel sympathetic and compassionate. Recent research suggests that the distinctive emotions generated by personal distress and empathy may actually be accompanied by distinctive physiological reactions, including heart rate patterns and facial expressions (e.g., Eisenberg & Fabes, 1990).

In general, personal distress motivates us to reduce our own discomfort. We might do this by helping a person in need, but we can also feel better by escaping from the situation or ignoring the suffering around us. Helping motivated by a desire to reduce our own discomfort is egoistic and not altruistic. In contrast, empathic concern motivates us to help the person in need. Since the goal of empathic concern is to enhance the welfare of someone else, it would clearly be an altruistic motive for helping.

Several studies have shown that empathy increases prosocial behavior (Eisenberg & Miller, 1987; Eisenberg, 1991). For example, in one study, college students learned of the plight of Carol, a student who had broken both legs in a car accident and was seriously behind in her schoolwork (Toi & Batson, 1982). After listening to a tape-recorded interview with Carol, each subject was asked if she would be willing to help Carol. Empathy was manipulated by varying the instructions given to subjects. In a high-empathy condition, subjects were told: "Try to take the perspective of the person interviewed, imagining how she feels about what has happened and how it has affected her life." In a low-empathy condition, subjects were told: "Try to be as objective as possible, paying careful attention to all the information presented. . . . Try not to concern yourself with how the person interviewed feels about what happened."

As expected, subjects in the high-empathy condition experienced significantly greater empathy, as reflected in self-ratings of feeling sympathetic, compassionate, and "moved" by Carol's story. Also as predicted, subjects in the high-empathy condition were significantly more likely to volunteer to help Carol than those in the low-empathy condition, even when it would have been easy to avoid helping. Help was offered by 71 percent of subjects in the high-empathy condition compared to only 33 percent in the low-empathy condition. Taking the perspective of someone in distress can increase helpfulness.

A controversy currently exists, however, about how to interpret studies showing this empathy–helping link (Batson & Oleson, 1991). One view is that instructions emphasizing empathy increase altruistic motivation to help (Batson et al., 1988). In contrast, it has been suggested that when experimenters give instructions designed to enhance empathy, they may actually increase not only the subject's concern for the victim, but also increase the subject's own personal feelings of sadness, depression, or distress (Schaller & Cialdini, 1988). According to the second interpretation, helping based on empathy would not be entirely altruistic because the helper's goal may be to improve his or her own mood.

As this continuing controversy suggests, it is often difficult to sort out the motives that lead one person to help another. Our behavior often has multiple causes. However, these theoretical debates should not diminish our admiration for individuals who risk their own safety in courageous acts of helping. The earthquake victims rescued from a collapsed building care little about the motives of the volunteers who bring them to safety and consider the rescuers heroes regardless of whether their help was motivated by empathy or personal distress.

Personality Characteristics

Efforts to identify a single personality profile of the "helpful person" have not been very successful. Rather, it appears that particular personality traits dispose people to help in specific types of situations (Carlo et al., 1991). For instance, one study found that adults with a high need for approval were more likely to donate money to charity than were those low in need for social approval, but *only* when other people were watching them (Satow, 1975). Presumably, people high in need for approval are motivated by a desire to win praise from others and so act more prosocially only when their good deeds would be noticed (Deutsch & Lamberti, 1986). Three case studies illustrate the complex ways in which personality affects helping: the case of Good Samaritans, the rescuers of Jews in Nazi Europe, and committed blood donors.

GOOD SAMARITANS.   What personal qualities lead a person to intervene in a potentially dangerous emergency? Consider this true story: As

a young man drove by a dance hall, he noticed a man assaulting a young woman. This is how he described the event and his intervention:

> I went over there and I grabbed the dude and shoved him over and I said lay off the chick. So me and him started going at it. I told him to get out of here, man, look at her, man, the girl's mouth's all bleeding, she got her teeth knocked out, she got a handful of hair pulled out. Everybody was just standing around. (Quoted in Huston, Ruggiero, Conner, & Geis, 1981, p. 17)

Before the police arrived, the men exchanged more blows, one of which broke the intervener's jaw. What motivated this man and other "Good Samaritans" to endanger their own welfare to help a stranger?

To find out, Huston, Ruggiero, Conner, and Geis (1981) conducted in-depth interviews with 32 people who had intervened in dangerous crime episodes such as bank holdups, armed robberies, and street muggings. The responses of these Good Samaritans were compared with a group of noninterveners matched for age, sex, education, and ethnic background. Given the dangerous situations involved, it is perhaps not surprising that the Good Samaritans were significantly taller, heavier, and better trained to cope with emergencies than were the noninterveners. All but one of the interveners were men, the exception being a woman who rescued her 83-year-old neighbor from a knife-wielding attacker. The Good Samaritans were more likely than the noninterveners to describe themselves as strong, aggressive, and principled. And they had more life-saving, medical, or police training.

Often these interveners were not primarily motivated by humanitarian concern for the victim, but rather acted from a sense of their own competence and responsibility, based on their training and physical strength. Of course, the personal qualities that lead someone to stop a crime or mugging may be quite different from those that lead someone to donate money to charity or to help a stranger who collapses from a heart attack. Whether a potential helper intervenes depends on the *match* between the person's abilities, values, and motives, and the requirements of the particular situation.

RESCUERS OF JEWS IN NAZI EUROPE. During World War II, Hitler's government systematically killed millions of Jews—a tragedy now known as the Holocaust. For many, the Holocaust symbolizes the very worst aspects of human nature, not only in the brutal acts of murder and genocide committed by the Nazis, but also in the complacency and inaction of the general public. Yet the Holocaust also provides examples of great altruism, in the stories of individuals who risked their lives to shelter Jews from death.

In the summer of 1942, 12-year old Samuel Oliner and his family were forced to live in the squalid, walled-in Bobowa ghetto in Poland. One day, Samuel's entire family was rounded up and shoved into trucks. Samuel's stepmother, hoping that the boy might escape from certain death, urged him to run and hide. Once outside the ghetto, he made his way to the home of a nearby peasant woman named Balwina, a casual acquaintance of his father. Despite grave danger to herself and her family, Balwina sheltered the Jewish boy, taught him ways to pass for Christian, and later arranged for him to work as a hired hand on a farm some miles away. Samuel's family was murdered, but the boy survived because of the brave and altruistic actions of a Christian woman he barely knew.

Samuel ultimately moved to the United States, became a professor of sociology, and undertook a detailed study of "rescuers" who saved the lives of Jews in Nazi Europe. The research team conducted in-depth interviews with 406 rescuers from various European countries and a matched sample of 126 nonrescuers who were similar in sex, education, and geographic area during the war (Oliner & Oliner, 1988). The experiences of these rescuers illustrate several general concepts discussed in this chapter. Many rescuers emphasized the importance of social norms they had learned from their family, community, or religious group, such as the responsibility to help those in need and the religious injunction to "love thy neighbor." Others were motivated by empathy and compassion. In describing how she cared for a ragged and starving Jewish man who had escaped from a concentration camp, one woman

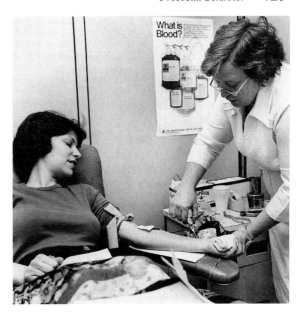

Many adults never donate blood. But some committed donors give blood regularly. Repeat donors overcome their initial fear of giving blood and come to see the act as a statement about their personal identity.

said: "How could one not have helped such a man? . . . He was shivering, poor soul, and I was shivering too, with emotion. I am very sensitive and emotional" (p. 189). The capacity to respond to the suffering of others and the adherence to moral principles of justice and concern enabled rescuers to overcome fear and to overlook serious risks to their own safety.

BLOOD DONORS. Further insights about personality and helpfulness come from studies of individuals who regularly donate their services. Consider the case of blood donors, studied in depth by Jane Piliavin and Peter Callero (1991). Many people have never given blood or have done so only rarely. But a helpful minority donate blood frequently, perhaps every two or three months. How can we explain their persistent helpfulness?

Often, blood donors have the model of a family member or friend who donates blood. This helps donors to overcome the reluctance many people feel to give blood for the first time. Over time, committed blood donors gradually

RESEARCH CLOSEUP

Volunteer Work—Helping Others and Helping Ourselves

Every Tuesday, Carla goes to a local hospital to assist nurses in the children's unit care for "crack babies" suffering painful withdrawal symptoms from drugs used by their mothers during pregnancy. John spent last summer working with a church group to renovate run-down homes in his community. As a trained volunteer at the zoo, Georganne spends one day each week showing school children the wonders of animal life. What these and more than 80 million other Americans have in common is that they volunteer their services to charitable causes (Clary & Snyder, 1991). There are thousands of volunteer groups in America today, helping to clean up beaches after oil spills, provide food and shelter for the homeless, teach English to new immigrants, support museums, and so on (Ellis & Noyes, 1990).

Unlike the spontaneous acts of helping strangers in distress discussed in this chapter, volunteer activities are planned, sustained, and time-consuming.

What motivates these helpful volunteers? Research shows that there is no single answer. Recently, Mark Snyder and Allen Omoto (1992a) studied people doing volunteer work related to AIDS. They identified five different types of motives. Most volunteers emphasized their *personal values:* "because of my humanitarian obligation to help others." About half emphasized *community concern:* "to help members of the gay community." Other motives included a desire for greater *understanding:* "to learn how people cope with AIDS," and a desire for *personal development:* "to gain experience dealing with emotionally difficult topics." A fifth category concerned *esteem enhancement:* "to feel better about myself." So, although all volunteers had a common purpose in wanting to help people with AIDS, they differed in their specific reasons for volunteering.

In a one-year followup, Snyder and Omoto (1992b) investigated why some people quit and others continued to volunteer. Quitters and stayers did not differ in the personal rewards and satisfaction they experienced as volunteers. However, quitters and stayers did differ in the costs they experienced. Quitters were more likely to say that volunteering took up too much time or that they felt embarrassed to do work related to AIDS. People's initial reasons for volunteering also affected how long they continued to serve. Those individuals who gave esteem enhancement or personal development reasons for volunteering were more likely to continue over a one-year period. The researchers believe that these somewhat "selfish" desires to feel good about oneself and to learn about AIDS may help to sustain commitment over time.

These and other studies suggest that the reasons for volunteering are complex and often combine both altruism and self-interest (Clary & Orenstein, 1991). Helping other people and expressing deeply held values are important reasons to volunteer. But so, too, is the opportunity to gain new skills, to meet new people, and to feel good about ourselves.

develop an internal motivation to give blood: They donate because they think they should, not because they have been asked to give blood. Repeat blood donors come to view giving blood as a meaningful activity that enhances their self-concept. So, for example, repeat donors are more likely than others to agree that "blood donation is an important part of who I am" and that "for me, being a blood donor means more than just donating blood." In other words, for repeat donors, the act of giving blood becomes a personal statement about the kind of person they are—a part of their personal identity. In addition, committed donors overcome or "neutralize" the fear of giving blood. For many committed donors, giving blood regularly becomes a habit or routine.

These three examples highlight the diverse

factors that can lead individuals to act in especially helpful ways. Performing volunteer work is another way that people help others. For a discussion of why some people volunteer their time and talents, see the RESEARCH CLOSEUP.

THE PERSON IN NEED: WHO IS MOST LIKELY TO RECEIVE HELP?

As you near the Student Union, someone approaches you and asks for money to make a phone call. Are you more likely to help if the person is clean-cut and neatly dressed than if the person looks rather disheveled? Would it matter if the person explained that his wallet was just stolen, or said that he had forgotten to bring any change to school? Although the true altruist may be blind to everything but the needs of a person in distress, everyday helpfulness is influenced by characteristics of the person in need.

For example, people on a college campus were more likely to give money to the March of Dimes if they were asked for a donation by a paraplegic woman in a wheelchair than if asked by a nondisabled woman (Slochower et al., 1980). In another study, subway riders in New York saw a man carrying a cane stumble and fall to the floor (Piliavin, Piliavin, & Rodin, 1975). Sometimes the victim had a large red birthmark on his face; sometimes he did not. In this situation, the victim was more likely to receive aid if his face was unblemished (86 percent) than if he had an unattractive birthmark (61 percent). In understanding these and other research findings, two themes are important: We are more willing to help people we like and people we think deserve assistance.

Helping Those We Like

In Chapter 9 we saw that our initial liking for another person is affected by such factors as physical attractiveness and similarity. Research on prosocial behavior finds that these same characteristics also influence helping. In at least some situations, those who are physically attractive are more likely to receive aid. For example,

in a field study, researchers placed a completed application to graduate school in a telephone booth at the airport (Benson, Karabenick, & Lerner, 1976). The application was ready to be mailed, but had apparently been "lost." To manipulate appearance, the photo attached to the application was sometimes that of a very good-looking person and sometimes that of a less attractive person. The measure of helping was whether the individual who found the envelope actually mailed it or not. Results showed that people were more likely to send in the application if the person in the photo, whether male or female, was physically attractive. On average, 47 percent of the applications of attractive people were returned, compared to 35 percent of the applications by unattractive people.

The degree of similarity between the potential helper and the person in need is also important (Dovidio, 1984). For example, people are more likely to help a stranger who is from the same country rather than a foreigner (Feldman, 1968). Some years ago, researchers had confederates, who were dressed either as a "hippie" or as a "straight" person, approach students and ask to borrow a dime (Emswiller, Deaux, & Willits, 1971). The researchers also used appearance to categorize the potential helpers as "hippie" or "straight." Results clearly showed that people were most likely to help those similar to themselves. For example, hippie men helped a fellow hippie about 77 percent of the time, but helped a straight person only 32 percent of the time. In a more recent study, shoppers on a busy street in Scotland were more likely to help a person wearing a plain T-shirt than a person wearing a T-shirt emblazoned with the pro-homosexual slogan "GAY still means HAPPY" (Gray, Russell, & Blockley, 1991). It appears that many shoppers perceived themselves to be different from the pro-gay person, and so were less likely to offer assistance when requested. The impact of racial similarity on helping is the topic of the CULTURAL HIGHLIGHT.

Helping Those Who Deserve Help

Whether a person receives help depends in part on the "merits" of the case. For example, people

CULTURAL HIGHLIGHT

Helping a Stranger in Distress—Does Ethnicity Make a Difference?

The finding that similarity affects helping might suggest that people will be more likely to help individuals from their own ethnic or cultural group. For example, Anglos might be most helpful to other Anglos, and Latinos to Latinos. Researchers have investigated help-giving between whites and African Americans. The results turn out to be more complex than we might imagine.

Sometimes, the race of the person in need has no effect on helping (Bickman & Kamzan, 1973). In one study, for example, a young woman confederate, either African American or white, dropped a bag full of groceries as she left a supermarket (Wispé & Freshley, 1971). Would black and white shoppers who encountered this woman in distress show a preference for helping someone of their own race? Contrary to what the researchers had expected, race had no impact on helping. The researchers speculated that in this public situation, social rules of courtesy may have been strong and therefore masked any tendency to help people of one's own race. In public settings, potential helpers may have mixed motives, perhaps preferring to help others who are similar in background but also wanting to avoid appearing inconsiderate or prejudiced in the eyes of others who are present.

In situations where the potential helper is anonymous, a tendency to be more helpful to people from the same racial or ethnic group may emerge. Earlier in this chapter, we described a study in which researchers planted "lost" applications to graduate school at an airport, and studied how frequently people who found the application helped by putting it in the mail (Benson et al., 1976). In this study, all of the potential helpers were white, but half the applications were from an African American student and half were from a white student. Would whites show a preference for helping a person of their own race? In this setting, they did: Significantly more of the applications from whites were returned than those from blacks. The physical attractiveness of the person in the application photo also made a significant difference. The likelihood that a white person gave help was greatest when the person in need was a physically attractive white applicant (52 percent) and least for a physically unattractive black applicant (32 percent). In this anonymous situation, willingness to help was affected by the person's race and physical appearance.

The impact of race on helping may also depend on the racial mixture of the social setting. For instance, in one study, black and white college students served as confederates who "accidentally" dropped a stack of 500 computer cards while walking on a university campus (Wegner & Crano, 1975). In this situation, black students who walked by were more likely to aid a black person in distress than to help a white person. In contrast, white passersby helped both blacks and whites equally often. The researchers speculated that the racial mix of the university, which was predominantly white, may have made a difference. Since black students were a small minority on campus, they may have felt a special sense of solidarity and helpfulness toward other black students. In contrast, whites, being in the numerical majority, may have been less conscious of their own race and so may have felt equally inclined to help other students regardless of race. This study highlights the way in which situational factors, such as the minority status of blacks and the majority status of whites on a campus, can influence whom we define as similar and whom we are most willing to assist.

These studies suggest some of the ways that race and ethnicity can affect prosocial behavior.

in a supermarket were more likely to give someone money so they could buy milk rather than
cookie dough (Bickman & Kamzan, 1973), presumably because milk is more essential for
health than cookies. Passengers on a New York
subway were more likely to help a man who fell
to the ground if he appeared to be sick rather
than drunk (Piliavin, Rodin, & Piliavin, 1969). In
both cases, beliefs about the legitimacy or appropriateness of the problem made a difference.

In addition to evaluating the deservingness of
the need itself, potential helpers may also make
inferences about the causes of the person's need,
following the principles of **attribution theory**
outlined in Chapter 4. A teacher might spend
more time helping a student who missed classes
because of a death in the family rather than
because of a trip to a beach resort. Several studies indicate that the key causal factor is personal
control: We are more likely to help someone if
we believe the cause of the problem was outside
the person's control. For instance, in one study
(Meyer & Mulherin, 1980), college students said
they would be more willing to lend rent money
to an acquaintance if the need arose due to illness (an uncontrollable cause) rather than laziness (a controllable cause). In another study,
students said they would be more likely to lend
their lecture notes to a classmate who needed
them because of something uncontrollable, such
as the professor's being a poor lecturer, rather
than something controllable, such as the classmate's not trying to take good notes (Weiner,
1980). If a person is responsible for his or her
predicament, we are less likely to help.

Attributions also affect our emotional reaction to the person in need (Weiner, 1990). For
example, Darren George (1992) recently studied
actual incidents of help-giving among college
friends. He found that students felt more sympathy and less anger toward a friend who had
an academic problem that was outside his or her
control than toward a friend who was personally responsible for the problem.

In summary, we feel sympathy and concern
for those who suffer through no fault of their
own; we feel anger and disgust toward those
who are responsible for their own problems.
Attributing a person's need for help to a controllable cause may give rise to anger and avoid-

The desperate plight of starving people in Somalia
led to private relief efforts and ultimately to U.S.
intervention. Here, a U.S. Marine gives first aid to a
child.

ance or neglect; in contrast, attributing the person's plight to uncontrollable causes may elicit
sympathy and lead to help-giving (Schmidt &
Weiner, 1988). Figure 13-7 summarizes the
impact of attributions on helping.

THE EXPERIENCE OF RECEIVING HELP

Sometimes we react to getting help with happiness and gratitude. The novice swimmer saved
from drowning by an alert lifeguard is thankful
to be alive and grateful for the help. A soldier
may come to like and respect a particularly
helpful platoon buddy (Cook & Pelfrey, 1985).
But there are also instances when people react
negatively to receiving aid. When Dad offers to
help his five-year-old get dressed, the child may
indignantly insist she would rather do it herself.
Welfare recipients may react toward social
workers with veiled hostility rather than
warmth. Developing nations receiving millions
in U.S. foreign aid complain about American
policies and "exploitation" of their countries.
What these examples point out is that receiving

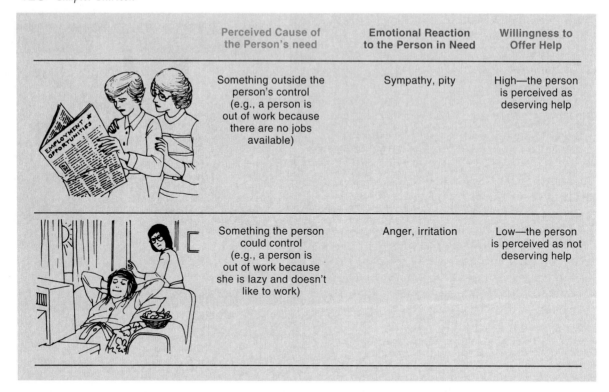

	Perceived Cause of the Person's need	Emotional Reaction to the Person in Need	Willingness to Offer Help
	Something outside the person's control (e.g., a person is out of work because there are no jobs available)	Sympathy, pity	High—the person is perceived as deserving help
	Something the person could control (e.g., a person is out of work because she is lazy and doesn't like to work)	Anger, irritation	Low—the person is perceived as not deserving help

Figure 13-7 An attribution-theory analysis of help-giving. When we encounter a person in distress, we first try to understand the causes of their need. Attributing need to causes under the person's control leads to reactions of anger and contempt, and diminishes the likelihood of offering help. In contrast, attributing the person's need to uncontrollable causes leads to sympathy and increases the probability of offering assistance. (*Source:* Adapted from Schmidt & Weiner, *Personality and Social Psychology Bulletin,* Vol. 14, No. 3, September 1988 Copyright by the Society for Personality and Social Psychology, Inc. Reprinted by permission of Sage Publications, Inc.)

help can be a mixed blessing. Several social psychological theories help to explain these reactions.

Attribution Theory: Threats to Self-esteem

According to attribution theory, people are motivated to understand why they need help and why others are offering to help them. If people can attribute their need to external or uncontrollable forces rather than to personal inadequacies, they will be able to maintain positive self-esteem. Several studies have found that people are more likely to seek help when they can attribute their problem to a difficult situation, rather than to a personal deficiency (Fisher, Nadler, & Whitcher-Alagna, 1982; Tessler & Schwartz, 1972).

Attributions about the motives of those providing help are also important. If we perceive that people are helping us because they genuinely care about us and our welfare, we may get an ego boost. On the other hand, if accepting aid implies that we are incompetent, unsuccessful, or dependent, it may threaten our self-esteem (Fisher et al., 1982). This possibility was demonstrated by Graham and Barker (1990) in a study of attributions for help-giving in the classroom. Children ages 5 to 12 were shown videos of classroom interactions between an elementary school teacher and a group of students working on math problems. In the film, the teacher circulated around the room. She stopped to gaze at one boy's paper, and then moved on without comment. Later, she looked at the work of another boy and leaned down to offer him unsolicited advice, "Let me give you a hint. Don't forget to carry your tens." Later, subjects rated the ability of the two boys. At all age levels, children perceived the student who was offered help as lower in ability than the student who did not receive help. As the researchers noted, a teacher's well-intentioned efforts to be helpful may be perceived by the recipient and by observers as a sign of the recipient's incompetence.

Threats to self-esteem may deter people from seeking help, even when it is badly needed. For instance, people are sometimes reluctant to seek aid from social agencies because they fear humiliation and embarrassment (Williamson, 1974). Even among adult brothers and sisters, who commonly turn to each other for advice and assistance, there are times when people are defensive about seeking help from a sibling (Searcy & Eisenberg, 1992).

Social Exchange Theory: The Costs of Indebtedness

Providing help involves an exchange of resources from one person to another. According to **social exchange theory,** our reactions to receiving help reflect both the benefits we receive from the assistance and the costs we incur from accepting aid. When the exchange of help in a relationship is largely one way, it leads to indebtedness and can create an imbalance of power in the relationship (Nadler, 1991; Worchel, 1984). For example, young adults who receive financial support from their parents may appreciate the assistance, but may also feel that accepting help gives their parents greater rights to influence their lives. In contrast, help is often most appreciated when it can be reciprocated, hence maintaining a balance of equity and power in the relationship.

In short, lopsided help-giving can threaten equity in a relationship, create power imbalances, and lower the recipient's self-esteem. People are more likely to ask for help when they think they will be able to repay the aid in some form (Fisher et al., 1982). People like a benefactor more if they are able to give something in return for the aid they receive (Gross & Latané, 1974). In our personal relationships with friends and relatives, mutual assistance is typical. Friends offer each other advice, exchange gifts, and volunteer to help each other on a continuing basis. Knowing that we've helped a friend in the past and will have a chance to reciprocate help in the future reduces the costs of asking for help (Wills, 1992).

Reactance Theory: Loss of Freedom

Further insights into the experience of receiving help are provided by reactance theory (Brehm, 1966). According to this theory, people want to maximize their personal freedom of choice. If we perceive that our freedom is threatened, we often react negatively with annoyance and hostility. The prospect of losing freedom may also lead us to take steps to reassert our independence. So when foreign aid recipients criticize U.S. policies, they may be symbolically proving their independence and thereby reducing feelings of psychological **reactance.**

Evidence that those who receive aid perceive a substantial loss of freedom comes from a study of welfare recipients (Briar, 1966). Nearly 70 percent of the welfare families surveyed believed they should not complain if a social worker made a surprise visit in the middle of the night, even though they knew this was probably not legal. Most families (67 percent) also said they would feel obligated to get marriage counseling if asked to do so, whether or not they thought it necessary. Intrusions on privacy and personal freedom can easily lead to feelings of hostility toward those providing aid (Gross, Wallston, & Piliavin, 1979).

New Ways to Obtain Help: Self-Help Groups and Computers

We have seen that the experience of receiving help is not always positive. There are times when accepting aid can limit our freedom, diminish our power, and lower our self-esteem. An understanding of these processes helps to explain why people sometimes react negatively or ambivalently toward help givers, and why people may prefer not to ask for help even when they badly need it. Social psychological factors also explain the popularity of two contemporary sources of help: self-help groups and computers.

In self-help groups, people with a common problem work together to help one another (Medvene, 1992). Examples would be groups for pregnant teenagers, for victims of child abuse, for widowed men and women, or for older returning college students. It is estimated that more than 7 million Americans are currently in self-help groups. Self-help groups minimize the costs of receiving help because they are run by the people in need, offer opportunities for reciprocal helping, and foster the knowledge that others have the same problem.

Computers offer a unique opportunity to receive help from a machine rather than a human being. Computers are now being used to teach a variety of subjects from spelling to chess. These teaching computer programs offer users help and advice without the embarrassment of acknowledging one's errors to another person. The appeal of computer assistance was dramatically illustrated in a study by Karabenick and Knapp (1988). College students performed a complex and difficult task on a computer. Half were told they could receive help from a research assistant and half were told that they could get help from the computer. The results were clear-cut. In the personal help condition, students were reluctant to request assistance; only 36 percent of subjects asked the research assistant for help. In contrast, in the computer-help condition, 86 percent of students requested help at least once, and most people asked for help more than once. By offering private assistance with no expectation of reciprocity, computers can reduce the psychological costs of receiving help.

We will continue our analysis of the experience of receiving aid in Chapter 15, when we present research about the health benefits of receiving social support.

In reading this chapter, you have learned a good deal about helping behavior. You now understand many factors that inhibit people from helping, such as the diffusion of responsibility that comes from being with others. You also know that we can teach people to become more altruistic, for instance by showing children helpful models on TV or by giving adults training in life-saving techniques such as CPR that make it possible for them to help people in need.

Research shows that people who are taught about the factors that influence helping are more likely to overcome these obstacles. In one study, college students either heard a lecture or saw a film about prosocial behavior and how the bystander effect can inhibit helping (Beaman et al., 1978). Two weeks later, in a seemingly unrelated context, students encountered a person in need of help, specifically a student sprawled on the floor in a hallway. Some students were alone when they encountered the victim; others were with an unresponsive confederate who ignored the victim. In all conditions, students who had learned about prosocial behavior were significantly more likely to intervene. What effect has learning about prosocial behavior had on you? Will knowledge increase your willingness to help people in distress?

KEY TERMS

altruism	equity	personal distress
attribution theory	evaluation apprehension	prosocial behavior
bystander effect	norm of reciprocity	reactance
diffusion of responsibility	norm of social justice	social exchange theory
empathy	norm of social responsibility	sociobiology

SUMMARY

1. Altruism is helping someone with no expectation of reward or personal benefit. Prosocial behavior includes any act that helps or is designed to help, regardless of the helper's motives.

2. A decision-making perspective emphasizes the complex cognitive processes leading to prosocial behavior. The potential helper must perceive that help is needed, take personal responsibility, weigh the costs and benefits, and decide how to intervene.

3. A learning perspective emphasizes that people learn prosocial behaviors and norms by reinforcement and modeling.

4. Sociobiologists believe that a tendency to help is part of our human evolutionary heritage. In contrast, others emphasize that societies create rules about helping which include social norms of responsibility, reciprocity, and justice.

5. Situational factors affect helping. People are less likely to intervene when others are present. This so-called bystander effect may result from several causes including a diffusion of responsibility, other people influencing how an individual interprets the situation, and evaluation apprehension. Other situational factors that influence helping are weather, city size, noise, and time pressures.

6. Characteristics of the helper are also important. People are more likely to help when they are in a good mood and feel empathy for the plight of the victim. Efforts to identify a single personality profile of the "helpful person" have not been very successful.

7. People are also more helpful to those they like and to those they believe deserve help.

8. People sometimes react to receiving help with a mixture of gratitude and discomfort. Receiving help can lower our self-esteem, make us feel indebted to others, and threaten our sense of freedom.

9. Knowledge about factors that inhibit helping may enable people to overcome these barriers and act in more prosocial ways.

SUGGESTED READINGS

Clark, M. S. (Ed.) (1991). *Prosocial behavior*. Newbury Park, CA: Sage. An excellent collection of theoretical and research reviews.

Latané, B., & Darley, J. M. (1970). *The unresponsive bystander: Why doesn't he help?* New York: Appleton-Century-Crofts. Reviews the classic studies of bystander intervention conducted by these authors.

Oliner, S. P., & Oliner, P. M. (1988). *The altruistic personality: Rescuers of Jews in Nazi Europe*. New York: Free Press. A well-written account of Christians who risked their lives to help Jews escape from Nazi persecution, based on a large-scale study of several hundred rescuers.

Piliavin, J. A., & Callero, P. L. (1991). *Giving blood: The development of an altruistic identity*. Baltimore, MD: The Johns Hopkins University Press. An in-depth analysis of regular blood donors.

Spacapan, S., & Oskamp, S. (Eds.) (1992). *Helping and being helped: Naturalistic studies*. Newbury Park, CA: Sage. Leading experts describe their most recent findings.

14
Aggression

FOCUS OF THIS CHAPTER

Defining Aggression
Sources of Anger
Aggressive Behavior
Reducing Aggressive Behavior
Media Violence
Sexual Violence

Cultural Highlight
Is the United States the Murdering Society?

Research Closeup
Date Rape

When we think of aggression and violence, most of us probably think first of crimes committed by one individual against another. The United States experiences over 20,000 murders per year, over 75,000 rapes, and over 600,000 assaults—in reported crimes alone. Unreported crimes increase these numbers even more. For example, the actual number of annual rapes is estimated at 683,000. The murder rate in the United States far exceeds that in most other civilized countries, as the CULTURAL HIGHLIGHT indicates.

We probably also think of war. In recent years, there have been about 50 wars each decade, almost all in Third World countries—those most oppressed by poverty, disease, and all manner of other problems. And the greatest threat of all comes from the potential for nuclear war. By the 1980s, the United States had over 1000 intercontinental ballistic missiles (ICBMs), each with the explosive power of 700 atomic bombs. Although the breakup of the Soviet Union has diminished the threat of a nuclear war with the United States, other developing countries, including India, Pakistan, China, Iraq, and Libya have or may soon have access to nuclear technology, keeping this a prominent source of anxiety and threat.

This is violence and aggression on a global scale, but in fact most violence is committed against people closest to us—against those in our own families, our spouses, children, and lovers. According to one national survey (Straus & Gelles, 1986), each year 16 percent of all married persons engage in some act of physical violence against their mate. Each year about 1.6 million American husbands engage in severe violence (hitting with fist, using gun or knife) against their wives. Similarly, parents commit a surprising number of violent acts against their own children. The same study showed that 10 percent of the parents had hit their child with an object in the previous year, while 55 percent had slapped or spanked their child. Among college students, the phenomenon of "date rape" has drawn increasing attention. Studies report that up to 45 percent of female college students have experienced forced or unwanted sexual intercourse, which is the legal standard for rape (McCaul, Veltum, Boyechko, & Crawford, 1990).

Not surprisingly, then, aggression has been an important topic for social psychological research. In this chapter we consider the origins of aggressive behavior and ways to reduce violence. We also take a look at the possible effects of violence shown on TV and in films, and we examine the nature of sexual violence.

DEFINING AGGRESSION

Although it might seem that everybody understands what aggression is, there is considerable disagreement about how to define it precisely. The simplest definition of *aggression*, and the one favored by those with a learning or behaviorist approach, is that aggression is any behavior that hurts others. The advantage of this definition is that the behavior itself determines whether or not an act is aggressive.

Unfortunately, this definition ignores the *intention* of the person who does the act, and this factor is critical. If we ignored intent, some actions intended to hurt others would not be labeled aggressive because they turned out to be harmless. Suppose an enraged man fires a gun at a business rival, but the gun turns out to be unloaded. The act is harmless because firing an unloaded gun is not dangerous. Yet we would still want to consider the act aggressive, because

CULTURAL HIGHLIGHT
Is the United States the Murdering Society?

The United States has the dubious distinction of leading the world in murder rate. A recent study (Gartner, 1990) found that men were murdered in the United States at a rate 3.5 times greater than in the second-highest country for male murders, namely Finland. Women in the United States were murdered at a rate 2.6 times that of the second-ranked country, which was Canada. But in comparison to most countries, our rate is even higher. For example, the murder rate for men in the United States is nearly 16 times that of England and Wales, and for women the rate is nearly five times greater than that of England and Wales.

Why is this the case? Several explanations have been offered (Kammeyer, Ritzer, & Yetman, 1992). Compared to other countries, the United States has

a more uneven distribution of economic resources. When there are many poor people in a country or substantial economic differences among groups within a country, the murder rate is higher. A second explanation argues that the United States has a low level of social integration. That is, we have many different ethnic and language groups, and our social instability is further compounded by one of the highest divorce rates in the world. Such instability and lack of integration breeds violence.

A third explanation has to do with the age distribution of the population. Any country that has a high percentage of its population in the 15- to 29-year-old age group will have a higher murder rate. The United States is such a country. People in this age group are often not in traditional family house-

holds, which may act as a brake on violent behavior. A fourth factor is that exposure to officially sanctioned violence increases the murder rate. If the government of a country engages in "legitimate" violence, such as using the death penalty or engaging in war, then the murder rate is higher. Both of these conditions are true in the United States. And finally, the availability of firearms in our country should not be ignored as a potential explanation. Because our Constitution protects the right to bear arms, relatively more people in the United States have guns available to them than do people in virtually any other nation in the world, and sometimes they use them for murdering.

How would *you* go about bringing down our murder rate?

the man was enraged and was trying to kill someone.

Ignoring intention can also produce the opposite error—calling some acts aggressive that are not, by the usual meaning of the term. If a golfer's ball accidentally hits a spectator, has the golfer committed an aggressive act? She has in fact caused somebody a great deal of pain, but surely no one would believe the golfer was being aggressive. Similarly, many acts that are painful are intended to help the victim, such as surgery performed by physicians.

Thus, we need to distinguish hurtful behavior from hurtful intentions. We will define **aggression** as any action that is *intended* to hurt others. This conception is more difficult to

apply, because it does not depend solely on observable behavior. Often it is difficult to know someone's intention. But we will accept this limitation because we can define aggression meaningfully only by including intent.

A second major distinction is needed, between **antisocial** and **prosocial aggression.** Normally we think of aggression as bad, but some aggressive acts are good. We applaud the police officer who shoots a terrorist who has killed innocent victims and is holding others hostage. The question is whether the aggressive act violates commonly accepted social norms or supports them. Unprovoked criminal acts that hurt people, such as assault and battery, murder, and gang beatings clearly violate social norms, so they are described as antisocial. But many aggressive acts are actually dictated by social norms, and therefore are described as prosocial. Acts of law enforcement, appropriate parental discipline, or obeying the orders of commanders in wartime are regarded as necessary.

Some aggressive acts fall somewhere between prosocial and antisocial, and we might label them **sanctioned aggression.** This includes aggressive acts that are not required by social norms, but that are well within their bounds. They do not violate accepted moral standards. A coach who disciplines a disobedient player by benching him or her is usually thought to be well within his rights. So is a shopkeeper who in self-defense hits someone who is criminally assaulting him, or a woman who strikes back at a rapist. None of these acts is required of the person, but they fall within the bounds of what is permitted by social norms.

A third useful distinction is between aggressive behavior and aggressive feelings such as **anger.** Our overt behavior does not always reflect our internal feelings. Someone may be quite angry inside, but make no overt effort to hurt another person. Society discourages and condemns most forms of aggressive behavior, and indeed can exist only if people control their aggressive feelings most of the time. We cannot have people hitting other people, breaking windows, or acting violently whenever they feel like it. Society places strong restraints on such expression, and most people, even those who feel angry much of the time, rarely act aggressively.

We need to consider both the factors that increase anger and the restraints that may prevent it from being translated into aggressive action. We thus have two separate questions: What produces angry feelings and what produces aggressive behavior?

SOURCES OF ANGER

An aggressive feeling is an internal state that cannot be observed directly. We all experience anger, and virtually everyone at one time or another would like to hurt someone else. Indeed, most people report they feel at least mildly or moderately angry anywhere from several times a day to several times a week (Averill, 1983). What causes anger? We will discuss two main factors: attacks by others and frustration. As will be seen, the victim's perceptions of the aggressor's motives also play a major role in generating anger.

Attack

One of the most common sources of anger is being attacked or bothered by another person. Imagine that you are waiting at a red light, and the driver of the car behind you blows the horn just as the light turns green. Or suppose that you are reading a newspaper and someone unexpectedly pours a glass of water down your neck. Or, finally, imagine a student's reaction when he expresses an opinion in class and someone else disagrees with him and says he is stupid to hold such an opinion. In all these cases, someone has done something unpleasant to someone else. Depending on how the injured person takes it, he or she has been annoyed or attacked. It is likely that the person will become angry and feel aggressive toward the source of the attack. A wide variety of aversive stimulation produces aggression. For example, people exposed to foul odors, irritating cigarette smoke, and disgusting scenes show increased aggressive feelings (Berkowitz, 1983).

People often respond to attack with retaliation, in an "eye for an eye" fashion (Baron, 1977). This can produce an escalation of aggression. Gang warfare often starts out with a few insults and ends up in murder, as depicted so clearly in Shakespeare's *Romeo and Juliet.* Similarly, domestic violence often breeds more domestic violence. Cases of family violence sometimes involve not one aggressor and one victim, but a pattern of mutual violence within a married couple or between parents and children (Straus et al., 1981). Attack provokes retaliation, and the violence simply escalates.

Frustration

A second major source of anger is **frustration.** Frustration is the interference with or blocking of the attainment of a goal. If someone wants to

One of the main causes of anger is frustration. Frustration produces anger, which often leads to retaliation.

go somewhere, perform some act, or obtain something and is prevented from doing so we say that person is frustrated.

One of the basic tenets in psychology is that frustration tends to arouse aggressive feelings, as indicated in Chapter 1. Dollard, Doob, and others at Yale began the work on this problem. They asserted that *"aggression is always a consequence of frustration. . . . the occurrence of aggressive behavior always presupposes the existence of frustration and, contrariwise, . . . the existence of frustration always leads to some form of aggression"* (Dollard et al., 1939, p. 1).

The behavioral effects of frustration were demonstrated in a classic study by Barker, Dembo, and Lewin (1941). Children were shown a room filled with attractive toys but were not allowed to enter it. They stood outside looking at the toys, wanting to play with them, but were unable to reach them. After they had waited for some time, they were allowed to play with them. Other children were given the toys without first being prevented from playing with them. The children who had been frustrated smashed the toys on the floor, threw them against the wall, and generally behaved very destructively. The children who had not been frustrated were much quieter and less destructive.

Family life is one major source of frustration. Surprisingly, the most commonly reported source of conflict in American families concerns housekeeping. Families argue and fight endlessly about what and how much to clean, about the quality of food served, about taking the trash out, mowing the lawn, and fixing things. One-third of all American couples say that they *always* disagree about housekeeping. Close behind are conflicts about sex, social activities, money, and children, in that order (Straus et al., 1981).

Economic problems produce especially high levels of frustration within families. There is more family conflict and more domestic violence in working-class than in middle-class families, and more in families with unemployed breadwinners or with especially large numbers of children (Straus et al., 1981). Of course, many working-class families with large numbers of children and marginal economic situations are loving, relatively conflict-free, and free of domestic violence. But on the average, these life stresses lead to greater frustration, and ultimately to more violent incidents.

This effect of frustration may also be seen in broader perspective in society at large. Economic depressions produce frustration that affects almost everyone. The consequence is that various forms of aggression become more common. For example, before World War II, the economy in the southern United States was heavily dependent on cotton. Hovland and Sears (1940) found that lower cotton prices were associated with more lynchings of blacks in the South during the years 1882 to 1930. A drop in the price of cotton signified a depressed period economically, producing frustration and in turn heightened aggressive behavior in terms of lynchings (see also Hepworth & West, 1988).

Job-related problems are also among the greatest sources of frustration and anger. In one study of employed women, problems such as conflicts between supervisors' and coworkers' expectations, job dissatisfaction, and perceived underutilization of skills were all among the strongest predictors of their general hostility levels (Houston & Kelly, 1989).

These examples illustrate the typical effect of frustration. But the original theory suggested that aggression always stemmed from frustration, and frustration always produced aggression (Dollard et al., 1939). It appears now that neither *always* in these assumptions is correct. Although frustration usually arouses anger, there are circumstances when it does not; and

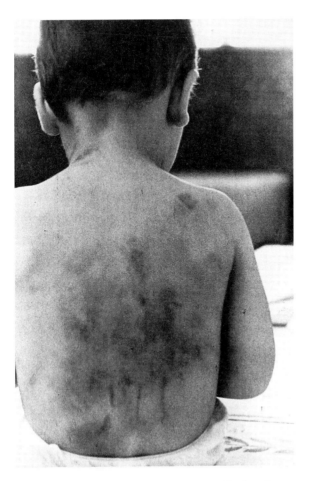

Much violence occurs in families, especially families encountering economic problems. Wives and children especially are victims.

increased anger may not always lead to more aggressive behavior. As we will see in this chapter, factors other than frustration can also produce aggressive behavior.

Attributions

In most cases, for an attack or frustration to produce anger and aggressive behavior, it must be perceived as intended to harm. Our tendency to aggress often depends more on the apparent motives or intentions behind another person's actions—especially when these are potentially provocative—than on the nature of these actions. In terms of causal attributions, anger is most likely when the attack or frustration is perceived as intended by the other person, that is, as being under that person's internal control (Weiner, 1982). However, if the victim attributes the attack or frustration to mitigating circumstances—that is, to conditions beyond the frustrator's control—it should not create so much anger. For example, we would expect more anger among unemployed workers if they were fired by a boss who said she did not like them than if they were laid off because an economic recession forced the entire plant to shut down. Indeed, a survey of occasions on which people felt angry showed that anger was a response to an act perceived as voluntary and unjustified in 59 percent of the episodes, to a potentially avoidable accident or event 28 percent of the time, and to an unavoidable accident or event only 2 percent of the time (Averill, 1983).

The role of perceived internal control in generating anger was shown clearly in an experiment by Greenwell and Dengerink (1973). Male college students were placed in a competitive task with a fictitious opponent. Each was allowed to shock the other. They received information, supposedly from the opponent, indicating either that (1) he was intentionally raising the level of his shock settings over trials or that (2) he was deliberately maintaining those shocks at a constant, moderate level. For half the subjects within each of these groups, the strength of the shocks received actually *did* increase; for the others, it remained constant. The results indicated that the opponent's intentions were more important in determining the subjects' own shock settings than was the strength of the actual shocks they received from this person.

But the timing of information about intention or mitigation is also important. If people already understand the mitigating reasons before they are frustrated, they are less likely to get angry and become aggressive. Explaining all the good reasons afterward, while the person is already steaming, is not so likely to reduce the anger!

To show this, Johnson and Rule (1986) had a confederate anger male undergraduates by giving them bursts of loud noise while insultingly evaluating an essay they had written, describing them as uncreative, poor students. Then the subject could administer loud noise in return to the confederate, under the guise of evaluating the confederate's essay. Mitigating information about the confederate that would explain his behavior was provided to the subject: The confederate had just gotten a poor grade in an important midterm, which would prevent him from entering medical school. This mitigating information was effective in reducing physiological arousal and aggression only when it was given prior to the insults.

However, even prior information about mitigating circumstances or the other person's intentions may have little effect if the attack or other provocation to anger is very great (Zillmann, 1988). Family violence often occurs because intense arguing escalates without any consideration for the reasons for the other person's actions. So mitigating information may come too late or be ineffective in the heat of passion. People really do kill "in the heat of anger," no matter what information they are given.

Apologizing can also undercut aggressive behavior. Generally speaking, we judge others less harshly if they apologize for the behavior that might otherwise instigate aggression (Schwartz, Kane, Joseph, & Tedeschi, 1978). A study conducted in Japan, in which undergraduates were harmed by a fellow student but then received an apology (or not), revealed that victims were more likely to refrain from aggression when the perpetrator had apologized. However, when the harm was severe, the effects of the apology were reduced (Ohbuchi, Kameda, & Agarie, 1989).

ATTRIBUTIONS AND CHRONIC AGGRESSION. Aggression in childhood is quite stable over time (Olweus, 1979). Children who begin school as aggressive tend to remain so throughout their early years of schooling. Aggression in children is important because it predicts such serious outcomes as low academic achievement, dropping out of school in adolescence, juvenile delinquency, and even criminality and psychopathology (Hudley & Graham, 1992).

Attributions play a role in chronic aggressive behavior just as in aggressive incidents. Chronically aggressive children have a strong attributional bias to perceive others as acting against them with hostile intent, particularly in ambiguous situations (Dodge, 1986; Dodge & Coie, 1987). For example, if a child is asked to

imagine that a ball thrown by a peer hit him in the head, and no other information is given, an aggressive child is more likely to believe that the peer did this on purpose than is a child not prone to chronic aggression.

Biased attributions of intention, in turn, evoke retaliatory behavior. Aggressive children, then, typically make inappropriate attributions of intention, and thus feel justified when they retaliate in an aggressive manner. For example, Graham, Hudley, and Williams (1992) found that aggressive minority youth made more attributions of biased intent, reported more anger, and were more likely to endorse aggressive retaliatory behavior than was a comparable group of nonaggressive minority youngsters. Moreover, this causal attribution occurred before both the anger and the aggressive action, suggesting that the attributions caused the subsequent aggression.

Graham and her colleague reasoned that, if biased attributions instigate this kind of aggression, then changing attributions would be a good way to intervene with chronically aggressive children. They developed a 12-session intervention designed to train aggressive African-American male youngsters to infer non-hostile intent following ambiguous peer provocation. The intervention taught these students to understand the meaning of intention, to discriminate between intentional and unintentional provocation, and to make attributions to non-hostile intent following ambiguous negative social outcomes. For example, they might be asked to consider how easy it is for a ball thrown by a peer to accidentally hit someone in the head.

Following the 12-session program, the researchers found marked reductions in these children's perceptions of hostile intention and less endorsement of aggressive behavior. Moreover, the teachers regarded the boys who had been through the attribution training program as significantly less aggressive than they had before the intervention began. What is important about this finding is that the teachers were not even aware that the boys had been through the intervention! Even more convincing, when the children were actually put into the position of experiencing frustration at the hands of a partner, those who had gone through the program were less likely to attribute hostile intention to the pattern and to aggress against the peer than those chronically aggressive children who had not gone through the program. The study suggests, then, that changing attributions for unintentional negative outcomes can reduce what would otherwise have been seen as justifiable retaliatory aggression (Hudley & Graham, 1992).

AGGRESSIVE BEHAVIOR

What is the relationship between anger and aggression? Attack and frustration tend to make people feel angry. But angry people do not always behave aggressively. In the survey mentioned earlier, people reported engaging in overt physical aggression on only 10 percent of the occasions when they felt angry, expressed verbal aggression 49 percent of the time, and engaged in various kinds of nonaggressive calming activities 60 percent of the time (Averill, 1983). Indeed, people typically did *not* behave aggressively when they felt angry, though they usually felt some urge to do so.

It is also possible for people to act aggressively without *feeling* angry. A foot soldier is ordinarily not angry at the anonymous, often unseen, and usually equally frightened enemy soldier he has been ordered to kill. Feelings control behavior to some extent, but other factors play a role as well. We will consider the learning of aggressive behavior, social norms that control when and how aggressive behavior occurs, and aggression designed to achieve goals. Before so doing, however, it is useful to consider some of the different ways in which psychologists have studied aggressive behavior.

Experimenting with Aggression

Aggressive behavior, by its nature, is hurtful. How then can we do experimental research on it? Three techniques have been widely used and will be referred to often throughout this chapter. The first involves exposing subjects to aggression and then observing its impact on their sub-

sequent behavior. This technique is often used with children, as we will shortly see. For example, a child may observe an adult treating a toy aggressively or not, and then the child's behavior toward the same or similar toys is measured.

The **shock-learning technique,** designed by Arnold Buss (1961), involves both a naive subject and a confederate. Both are informed that the experiment concerns the effects of punishment on learning. The confederate is to be the learner and the subject is to be the teacher. When the confederate–learner makes an error, the subject–teacher is to deliver punishment to the learner in the form of electric shock (or sometimes a loud noise). No shock or noise is actually delivered to the confederate–learner, but the subject thinks he or she really is hurting the person. The confederate–learner makes errors on a standard, prearranged schedule, and the subject–teacher can punish for as long and as intensely as he or she wants. The measure of aggression is the duration and intensity of punishment.

The **shock-competition technique** was developed by Stuart Taylor (1967). Two naive subjects are informed that they will compete against each other in a reaction-time task. On each trial, they are allowed to set the level of electric shock (or loud noise) their opponent will receive if the opponent loses. In reality, the experimenter sets both the outcome of the competition (who wins or loses) and the level of shock either one receives.

All three techniques have been widely used. The latter two pose ethical problems, of course. They both rely on deceiving the subjects, so fully informed consent is impossible. It also can be argued that either being shocked or shocking another person is harmful. On the other hand, there is plainly great value to society in understanding aggression and how to control it. If the costs of the research are high, so perhaps are its potential benefits.

Learning to Be Aggressive

The main mechanism determining human aggressive behavior is *past learning*. A newborn infant expresses aggressive feelings quite impulsively. Whenever it is the least bit frustrated, whenever it is denied anything it wants, it cries in outrage, flails its arms, and strikes out at anything within range. In the earliest days of life, an infant does not realize that other people exist and therefore cannot think that others are deliberately trying to harm it. When the infant does discover the existence of others, it continues to vent its rage and probably directs much of it toward these people.

But by the time the individual is an adult, this little savage has his or her anger under firm control and aggresses only under certain circumstances, if at all. This development is primarily due to learning. We learn habits of behaving aggressively in some situations and suppressing anger in others, to aggress against some kinds of people (like siblings) and not others (like police), and in response to some kinds of frustration and not others. These habits are crucial to our control of our own aggressive behavior.

IMITATION. **Imitation** is one important mechanism that shapes a child's behavior. All people, and children, in particular, have a strong tendency to imitate others. A child watches people eat with a fork and tries to do the same. After a while, the child also uses a fork. This imitation extends to virtually every kind of behavior, including aggression. A child observes other people being aggressive or controlling their aggression and copies them. Thus, the child's own aggressive behavior is shaped and determined by what he or she observes others doing.

An experiment by Albert Bandura and his coworkers (Bandura, Ross, & Ross, 1961) illustrated imitative learning of aggressive behaviors. Children watched an adult play with tinker toys and a Bobo doll (a 5-foot, inflated plastic doll). In one condition, the adult began by assembling the tinker toys for about a minute and then turned his attention to the doll. He approached the doll, punched it, sat on it, hit it with a mallet, tossed it in the air, and kicked it about the room, all the while shouting such things as "Sock him in the nose," "Hit him down," "Pow." He continued in this way for 9 minutes, with the child watching. In the other

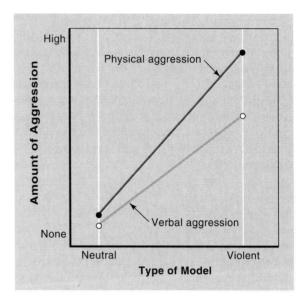

Figure 14-1 Aggression by children witnessing violent or neutral model. *Note:* The entry is the mean amount of physical or verbal aggression children administered to the Bobo doll after watching the type of model indicated. (*Source:* Adapted from Bandura, Ross, & Ross, 1961.)

condition, the adult worked quietly with the tinker toys and ignored the doll.

Some time later, each child was frustrated mildly and then left alone for 20 minutes with a number of toys, including a 3-foot Bobo doll. The children's behavior was rated as shown in Figure 14-1. They tended to imitate many of the actions of the adult. Those who had seen the adult act aggressively were much more aggressive toward the doll than those who had witnessed the adult working quietly on the tinker toys. The first group punched, kicked, and hammered the doll and uttered aggressive comments similar to those expressed by the aggressive adult.

The key theoretical notion in these experiments is that children learn specific aggressive responses by observing others perform them. It follows that such vicarious learning should be increased when the adult's behavior is reinforced and when the situation promotes identification with the adult model. So in the Bandura experiments, more imitative aggression occurred when (1) the model was rewarded, (2) the model was of the same sex as the child, and (3) the model had had a previous nurturant relationship with the child, such as being a friend or teacher of the child (Bandura et al., 1963).

The children in this situation learned to attack a certain type of doll. They might also attack the same kind of doll in a different situation, and perhaps a different kind of doll, as well. Just how far this would extend—Would they also punch their siblings?—is not clear, but it is clear that they would be somewhat more likely to attack some things than they were before. Through the process of imitation, these children showed more aggressive behavior.

REINFORCEMENT. A second mechanism by which aggression is learned is **reinforcement.** When a particular behavior is rewarded, we are more likely to repeat that behavior in the future; when it is punished, we are less likely to repeat it. A boy may come home in tears after being knocked down by another boy at school. His father chastises him for not hitting the boy back. The next time it happens, he does fight back, and even though he comes home a complete mess from his bloody nose, his father praises him effusively. This is one way that children learn the use of retaliatory aggression.

In one study subjects were verbally reinforced ("that's good," "you're doing fine") for shocking a confederate (Geen & Pigg, 1970). Other subjects in a control group shocked the confederate but were not rewarded. The reinforced subjects gave considerably more intense shocks than did nonreinforced subjects. We could give many other examples making the same point: Aggressive acts are, to a major extent, learned responses, and reinforcement is a major facilitator of aggression.

Children do not imitate indiscriminately; they imitate some people more than others. The more important, powerful, successful, and liked the other people are, the more children will imitate them. Also, the people they see most often are the ones they imitate most. Parents usually fit all these criteria, and they are the primary models for a child during the early years. Since parents are both the major source of reinforcement and the chief object of imitation, a child's

future aggressive behavior depends greatly on how parents treat the child and on how they themselves behave.

This joint dependence on the parents for reinforcement and imitation produces an interesting consequence. Punishing a child for acting aggressively might be considered an effective method of teaching the child not to be aggressive, but it often produces the opposite effect. A child who is punished for fighting does tend to be less aggressive—at home. Home is where the risk of punishment is greatest and therefore where the threat of punishment has the strongest inhibiting effect. Unfortunately, the situation is quite different when this child is out of the home. A child who is punished severely for being aggressive at home tends to be more aggressive outside (Sears, Whiting, Nowlis, & Sears, 1953).

The explanation for this effect is that the child imitates the parents' aggressive behavior. When he is in a situation in which he has the upper hand, he acts the way his parents do toward him. They are aggressive and so is he. The punishment teaches him not to be aggressive at home, but it also teaches him that aggression is acceptable if he can get away with it. Regardless of what parents hope, children will continue to do what their parents do as well as what they say.

Social Norms

Through imitation and reinforcement we learn when and how and against whom it is appropriate to aggress. People learn whether or not to aggress in response to certain cues. Which cues are associated with expressing aggression and which are associated with suppressing it is regulated in a very fine-tuned manner by the **social norms** we are all taught for specific situations.

If you are a boy, it is all right to fight back at another boy who hits you on the playground, but it is usually not okay to fight back if your attacker is a girl or a crippled child. And girls are not supposed to hit at all! It is not all right to yell at a teacher who marks your spelling as incorrect or at your grandmother who serves

Social norms dictate that aggression may be tolerated in certain situations. War and sports are two of those circumstances.

you boring meatloaf every time she sees you. It is all right to honk at someone stopped at a green light but not at a red light. Of course, some aggressive behavior is impulsive, and some is inappropriate to the situation. But the most impressive thing is how much aggressive behavior is controlled by the complex, and often subtle, social norms developed by every human culture or subculture.

These social norms specify what kind of aggression is antisocial, what kind is sanctioned, and what is actually prosocial. Slapping or spanking a disobedient 12-year-old is generally regarded as prosocial aggression; in one national survey, 70 percent regarded it as "necessary" (Straus et al., 1981). We also share norms about sanctioned aggression; 60 percent "strongly agreed" that "a man has a right to kill another man in a case of self-defense" (Blumenthal et al., 1972). And most of the time we also agree on what is antisocial aggression. There is broad agreement about what is meant by such terms as "murder" or "assault," reflecting consensus about when violence is antisocial.

Sometimes these norms apply to the whole society; for example, we all generally share the view that it is wrong to kill another person, except under such extreme conditions as self-defense or executions. But occasionally we do not agree. In the 1960s, many blacks felt they were justified in rioting to protest racial discrimination, whereas most whites felt that the blacks were not justified in rioting (Sears & McConahay, 1973). Members of youth gangs may feel that retaliatory killings are justified, whereas most other people would disagree.

Sometimes social norms change, and with them, the frequency of certain types of aggressive behavior. The most obvious cases occur when wars begin and end, and the killing of enemy soldiers changes abruptly from being antisocial to being prosocial aggression and back again. Another example comes from comparing national surveys done in 1975 and in 1985 on the frequency of child abuse (Straus & Gelles, 1986). During this decade, the problem of child abuse had received a great deal of publicity, and considerable resources were put into law enforcement and treatment programs to try to reduce it. The norms about allowable physical punishment of children changed correspondingly. And so the frequency of very severe vio-

442

lence reported by parents against their children (kicked, bit, hit with fist, used gun or knife) dropped by 47 percent in that period.

But such dramatic instances of disagreement and change should not obscure the consensus almost all humans share about the vast majority of aggressive acts. Understanding the differences among antisocial, sanctioned, and prosocial aggression depends on knowing what the relevant social norms are. The distinctions are sometimes quite subtle. But individuals must learn them to function effectively in society. Almost everyone can tell us when aggression is all right and when it is not. The few who cannot make at least the broad distinction are thought insane and are not held responsible for their actions.

Instrumental Aggression

Instrumental aggression occurs when a person uses aggression to attain some practical goal by hurting others, even when he or she is not angry. Boxers are paid to injure their opponents, but may scarcely know them. Paid killers and paid assassins kill for money, not because of anger. Sometimes young thugs mug people in big cities not because they are angry, but to steal money. Slave-trading Europeans committed many acts of violence against seventeenth- and eighteenth-century Africans not out of anger, but for commercial motives.

One particularly important form of instrumental aggression stems from what Le Vine and Campbell (1972) have called **realistic group conflict.** Sometimes two groups are in a situation in which they are competing for the same scarce resources. The two groups may aggress against each other as a way of trying to get those resources. They may or may not be angry at each other. For example, national leaders often take their countries to war with their neighbors not out of anger, but because they want to acquire territory, raw materials, or a better defensive position. In all these cases, aggressive behavior is committed simply as a way to attain other valued goods, and not necessarily because of angry feelings (Struch & Schwartz, 1989). We

discussed this form of aggression in more detail in Chapter 7 on prejudice.

Contagious Violence and Deindividuation

One form of imitative aggression that is important in crime and in crowd behavior is *contagious violence*. The French sociologist Tarde introduced the idea of contagious violence when he noted that news of a spectacular crime in one community produced imitative crimes. (Tarde, 1903). Mob behavior is another example of contagious violence. More recently, Zimbardo (1970) described this phenomenon as *deindividuation* (as we indicated in the chapter on groups), and suggested a number of factors that would produce it: anonymity, diffused responsibility, size, activity, a novel unstructured situation, arousal due to noise, and fatigue. So, for example, the most extreme violence in warfare by primitive peoples is carried out by those who use such deindividuating devices as masks, face and body paint, and special garments (Watson, 1973). Similarly, early twentieth-century white lynch mobs in the United States engaged in more atrocities such as burning, lacerating, or dismembering the black victim when the crowds were especially large (Mullen, 1986).

To test experimentally whether deindividuating factors lead to more aggressive behavior, Prentice-Dunn and Rogers (1983) used the shock-learning technique. In a "deindividuating cues" condition, subjects were not addressed by name and they were told that the experimenter would not know what shock intensities they chose and that they would not meet or see the victim. The experimenter took full responsibility for the victim's well-being, and the room was dimly lit. In an "individuating cues" condition, the subjects wore name tags, were addressed by their first names, and the experimenter took keen interest in the shock intensities selected. Subjects were told that they would meet the victim after the experiment and that the victim's well-being was the subjects' responsibility. The room was well lit. As expected, deindividuation led to significantly greater shock being administered, a lack of feeling of inhibition, and a lack of concern for the victim's, experimenter's, and other group members' reactions.

The companion process to deindividuation is *dehumanization*. When people are motivated to aggress against an individual for whatever reason, they may dehumanize the victim, making the victim seem not to be human, by attributing different beliefs and values to the target of their aggression. One study of Israeli adults (Struch & Schwartz, 1989) studied aggression against ultraorthodox Jewish groups. Aggression was assessed as opposing institutions that served the needs of these groups, supporting acts that would be harmful to them, and opposing personal interaction with them. The strongest predictor of aggression was the degree to which the respondents perceived intergroup conflict of interests, that is, the extent to which they and the ultraorthodox groups were working at cross purposes. A secondary predictor of aggression, however, was the degree to which members of these groups were perceived as "inhuman" and the degree to which dissimilar values were attributed to them.

REDUCING AGGRESSIVE BEHAVIOR

Aggressive behavior is a major problem for human societies. Individual crimes and large-scale social violence are harmful both to individual well-being and to the general social fabric. All societies expend much energy to control this tendency toward violence. So it is vital to understand how to reduce aggressiveness. But every solution proves to have its own risks and unintended consequences. Let us look systematically at the possible techniques for reducing aggressive behavior.

Punishment and Retaliation

It seems obvious that the fear of punishment or retaliation should reduce aggressive behavior. We would expect people to consider future consequences in their calculations about aggression and avoid behaving aggressively if punishment seemed likely. Indeed, when "teachers" in shock-learning experiments were told that the

roles would later be reversed, thereby making them "learners" and vulnerable to being shocked themselves, they reduced their own aggression (Wilson & Rogers, 1975). Consistent with these findings, younger children are consistently more likely to be victims of domestic violence than older children because they are weaker and less likely to retaliate (Straus et al., 1981).

But the threat of punishment or retaliation turns out not to be such a simple way of reducing aggression. As suggested earlier, children who are frequently punished for being aggressive turn out themselves to be more aggressive than normal (Sears, Maccoby, & Levin, 1957). They are also especially likely to abuse their spouses. Perhaps it is because they model themselves on an aggressive parent. Perhaps it is because frequent punishment, like any attack, generates a lot of anger. In any case, punishment of children's aggressiveness does not result in a reduction of their aggressive behavior.

A second problem is that fear of punishment or retaliation seems to spark *counteraggression*. People who are attacked have a tendency to retaliate against their attackers, even when retaliation is sure to provoke more attacks (Dengerink, Schnedler, & Covey, 1978). Many lives have been lost on battlefields (and in presidential and royal palaces) because national leaders have felt that "national honor" demanded counteraggression, even though it almost guaranteed further retaliation and bloodshed.

The effects of anticipated punishment or retaliation are not simple, then. Sometimes they suppress aggression, since the person rationally wants to avoid future pain. But sometimes the threats are interpreted as attacks and inspire even more direct or indirect aggression. A rebellious adolescent boy may interpret even the routine and uniform application of rules in a family or a school as a personal attack, and may become belligerent and uncooperative.

Even if punishment or threat of retaliation were usually temporarily effective in suppressing direct aggression, it is too expensive to be a general solution to the problem. There are too many people in too many places for all to be monitored constantly. As it is, many people who commit serious crimes, such as murder, are never caught and punished. It is impossible to

Children who are frequently punished often turn out to be aggressive as adults.

depend on external controls to minimize violence, and we would not want a society with such repressive control of individual behavior. So the threat of punishment or retaliation is not a general solution to the problem.

Reducing Frustration and Attack

Since frustration and attack are major sources of anger, a better technique might be to reduce the potential for them. All societies, to one degree or another, try to ensure some minimal access to the necessities of life, such as food, clothing, shelter, and family life. A major reason is to avoid large-scale violent disruptions of daily life from especially frustrated groups. Large-scale hostile political demonstrations resulting from collective frustration are usually met by government attempts to relieve that frustration. Sometimes governmental response is somewhat successful, as in the New Deal's response to the Depression of the 1930s; sometimes it is not, as in France in 1789 and Russia in 1917.

Some societies, particularly those organized around socialist philosophies, make a particular effort to minimize the frustration of their citizens. Capitalist societies, on the other hand, tend to accept some frustration as part of the price of freedom. The evidence is that socialist societies generally provide more economic equality, sometimes at the expense of overall productivity, individual freedom, and other costs.

Similarly, most societies make some provision for collective police protection so that ordinary people are not continually subject to attack from bandits or otherwise violent persons. This helps to reduce the chances for widespread violence in two ways: People are protected, and they are not themselves goaded into retaliation. In the nineteenth century, life on the frontier in the United States was often lived without benefit of such tight community control over attack. The result was that people were quite vulnerable to attack and sometimes responded with retaliatory vigilantism.

But even nations conscientiously dedicated to the public's well-being cannot eliminate all individual frustration, attack, and instrumental aggression. None of us ever will have exactly what and as much as we want to eat when we want it. That is the nature of life. So while forward-looking societies are wise to try to minimize as much large-scale frustration as they can, they can never completely eliminate it, or probably even come close. So other techniques for reducing aggression are necessary.

Learned Inhibitions

One technique is for people to learn to control their own aggressive behavior, whether or not they are in danger of being punished. Just as people learn when aggression is desirable or permissible, so too must they learn when aggressive behavior should be suppressed. That is, they must learn inhibitions against expressing aggression. Many factors appear to affect the inhibitions of aggression. We will consider generalized learned inhibitions, cues that bring those inhibitions into play, and substances that cause those inhibitions to be overridden.

AGGRESSION ANXIETY. To some extent, people learn to suppress aggressive responses in general. General learned inhibition is called **aggression anxiety.** This is the anxiety people feel when they are about to commit an aggressive act. They may feel varying degrees of anxiety, depending on the inhibitions they have learned about aggression in general and this aggressive act in particular. Not everyone has equal amounts of aggression anxiety, of course. Women have more than men do. Children reared in middle-class homes tend to have more than children raised in lower-class homes. Parents who use reasoning and withdrawal of affection as disciplinary techniques produce children with more aggression anxiety than do parents who use high degrees of physical punishment (Feshbach, 1970). Presumably reasoning produces more strongly internalized inhibitions about aggression, which is more effective than a simple fear of punishment by others.

We also learn anxiety about expressing aggression in specific situations. All through our lives we are learning and relearning "the ropes," the norms of our social environments. Students learn not to curse their professors to their faces, and professors learn not to throw things at their students. It is legal to kill animals for sport or food, but not to kill each other or someone's pet animal. We all possess a great many finely graded distinctions about what is and what is not permissible aggression. These learned inhibitions represent the most potent controls of human violent behavior we have.

PAIN CUES. These learned inhibitions are triggered by cues that tell us what kind of a situation we are in—one that calls for expression of aggression, or one that calls for inhibition of it. One particularly important set of cues concerns a potential victim's reactions. What effect will it have if the victim shows signs of pain? Will the aggressor have empathy for the victim's suffer-

ing and inhibit further attack? Or will the aggressor feel he is successfully hurting the victim, as intended, and strengthen the tendency to aggress?

To test between these possibilities, Baron conducted a number of studies varying whether or not the aggressor got cues about the pain experienced by his victim. First, using the shock-learning technique, he transmitted the supposed physiological reactions of the shock victim to the subject in the form of a "pain meter." Such pain cues reduced further aggression, whether the subject had been angered or not. Even when the victim was quite dissimilar from the subject, and therefore might be difficult to empathize with, pain cues proved to reduce aggression. Indeed, pain cues reduced aggressive behavior in all conditions except when the aggressor was extremely angry to begin with. Then the victim's pain cues promoted more aggression (Baron, 1971a; 1971b; 1974). In general, then, signs of a victim's suffering seem to inhibit further aggression, except in cases of extreme anger, when they are taken as signs of successful hurting.

For such reasons, *dehumanization* is thought to increase aggression against victims who are far away or anonymous to their attackers. For example, antiwar protestors during the Vietnam war felt that it was easier to bomb North Vietnamese from the great heights of a B-52 or to order troops into battle from the distance of Washington, DC, than to attack at closer, more personal range. Having the victim distant or anonymous should make aggression easier, because the pain cues are absent. Conversely, making the victim more human, so that the attacker empathizes with the person's suffering, should reduce aggression.

ALCOHOL AND DRUGS. Inhibitions can be released as well as implemented, as all of us know. Such **disinhibition** can then result in outbursts of anger and aggression. For example, it is sometimes said that "the conscience is soluble in alcohol." Learned inhibitions against expressing aggression would seem to be among the more common aspects of conscience that are ignored when drinking. Barroom brawls and murders by drunken husbands are legendary, and not just in Hollywood movies. Intoxicated offenders commit as much as 60 percent of the murders in the United States and comparably high proportions of other violent crimes such as rape (including date rape), robbery, assault, domestic violence, and child abuse (Lisak & Roth, 1988; Steele & Southwick, 1985).

Such anecdotes and statistics do not isolate the particular effects of alcohol in these complex situations, however. Nor do they prove that alcohol reduces inhibitions against aggression. Belligerent men may be attracted to bars and to arguments, or alcohol may stimulate sexual desire, and so on. To test more specifically the effects of alcohol on aggressive behavior, Taylor and Gammon (1975) gave subjects either a high dose of alcohol (about three or four stiff drinks for the average subject) or a low dose (about one drink). Then they were given the opportunity to aggress using the shock competition technique. The subject delivered significantly more shock if he had drunk more alcohol. This is a typical finding: Most laboratory studies show that consumption of alcohol generally does increase aggression (see the meta-analysis by Hull & Bond, 1986).

Why does alcohol usually produce more violence? When sober people are provoked to aggression, they are responsive to such inhibiting cues as the instigator's intent and potential retaliation, whereas intoxicated subjects are less attentive to the potential consequences of their behavior (Zeichner & Pihl, 1979). In another shock-competition study, intoxicated subjects who expected their opponent to behave aggressively plunged ahead with retaliatory aggression even if the opponent actually gave the lowest level of shock possible. They seemed to be oblivious to the low level of shock actually given by the opponent. Nonintoxicated subjects noted the discrepancy between their expectation and the opponent's actual behavior and reduced their own aggressive behavior (Leonard, 1989). In short, alcohol seems to produce a loss of inhibitory control, in part because of a loss of perceptiveness about one's self and others.

As well as disinhibiting the individual, alcohol may also heighten attention and reactions to conditions that typically instigate aggression (Taylor & Sears, 1988). In particular, alcohol tends to increase a person's aggressive responses to such provocations as threat, frustration, and malicious intents. For example, in a shock-competition experiment, intoxicated sub-

jects initiated more attacks than did nonintoxicated subjects only when the opponent was more threatening. They did not differ when competing against a nonaggressive opponent (Taylor et al., 1979; also see Lindman et al., 1987).

A further implication of this theory is that alcohol should increase aggression in response even to instigators that do not involve threat, attack, or frustration. For one thing, it should make people more responsive to social pressure to aggress. To test this, Taylor and Sears (1988) repeated the earlier shock-competition experiment using only an opponent who behaved nonaggressively. The subject was not threatened or attacked at all. They also varied how strongly two peer observers attempted to persuade the subject to deliver shock to the opponent; on some trials they tried hard, and on others they tried a little or not at all. As can be seen in Figure 14-2, alcohol (relative to a placebo ginger ale drink with a disguising taste of vodka) increased aggression in response to peer pressure even though the victim was totally inno-

Figure 14-2 Shock administered to nonaggressive opponent as a function of alcohol consumption and social pressure to give shock. *Note:* Entry is the proportion of trials on which the subject administered the strongest possible shock to his opponent. (*Source:* Adapted from Taylor & Sears, 1988, p. 241.)

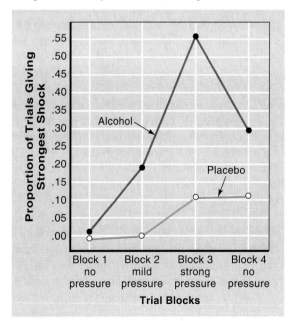

cent and harmless. So alcohol seems both to disinhibit the effect of aggression generally and to heighten people's response to provocation.

Another disinhibiting drug, marijuana, has been shown in experimental studies to reduce aggression (see Taylor et al., 1976). Similarly, a careful review of the extensive clinical and field research on marijuana use concludes that marijuana does not precipitate violence in the majority of those people who use it chronically or periodically. It is possible that some people might have such weak inhibitions against aggression that marijuana would trigger their aggressiveness, but the research evidence on this point is too skimpy to draw a firm conclusion now (Abel, 1977). Other drugs such as PCP ("angel dust") or crack cocaine do seem to trigger violent reactions, but systematic behavioral research on their effects is still in its infancy.

Displaced Aggression

What happens to aggressive feelings when, for one reason or another, they cannot be expressed against the cause of the anger? We are often frustrated or annoyed by someone but unable to retaliate against that person. The person may be too powerful or not available, or we may be too anxious and inhibited to retaliate. In such a situation, we are likely to express aggression in some other way, one of which is called **displaced aggression**—that is, expressing aggression against a substitute target. The child frustrated by her parents may deliberately pour her milk on the dog, or a man whose firm will not promote him may become increasingly angry at ethnic minorities. Either way, the individual expresses anger toward a safer target than the source of the frustration. When people do displace their aggression to an alternate target, what determines who will be selected as the target, and how much aggression will be expressed?

The basic principle of displacement is that the more similar a target is to the original source of frustration, the stronger will be the individual's aggressive impulses toward that target. But anxiety operates in much the same way as anger. Just as the impulse to hurt the source of frustra-

Sometimes frustration leads to displaced aggression, that is, aggressing against a substitute target. This child may have a grievance against her parents or a more powerful sibling, but she is spanking her doll because it can't retaliate.

tion generalizes to other people, so does the anxiety about attacking the source. The more similar the person is to this source, the stronger the anxiety felt toward him or her. In general, therefore, displaced aggression is most likely to be directed toward targets who are perceived as weaker and less dangerous.

Catharsis

Another idea is that pent-up angry feelings might be reduced by expressing aggression. With less anger, the chance of further aggression would be reduced. Freud called this process

catharsis. In simple language, catharsis involves "letting off steam" or "getting it out of your system." If someone annoys us by honking a horn at us, we feel angry. If, at the next traffic light, we find ourselves behind that car and honk at it, this should reduce the anger.

Freud's version of the catharsis theory presupposed that we always have a reservoir of instinctual aggressive energy within us. No matter what the situation is, we have a certain amount of aggressiveness that we need to "get off our chest." The frustration–aggression hypothesis, on the other hand, assumed that anger comes from frustrations and attacks, and so expressing anger would reduce aggressiveness only for those people in whom it had been built up through frustration or attack.

Research on catharsis has considered the effects of both *direct* and *indirect aggression.* Direct aggression is retaliation directly against the person who has made you angry by frustrating or attacking you. Catharsis can be successful in reducing aggression when an angry person expresses that anger directly against his or her frustrator. In one experiment, a confederate insulted subjects, criticized them for being so slow on an experimental task, and expressed doubts about their intellectual ability. Some of the subjects were then given the opportunity to aggress against the confederate, while others were not. The results showed that delivering blasts of noise at the confederate reduced a subsequent tendency to do so (Konecni & Ebbesen, 1976). That is, catharsis resulted from delivering loud noise to the confederate.

However, relying on this kind of direct retaliatory catharsis as a way of reducing aggression is risky because it may have a number of undesirable side effects. There is the possibility of disinhibition. We all control our anger fairly tightly most of the time. But if it is once released, we may relax our inhibitions about further hostilities. Geen and Quanty (1977) cite the reaction of a man who killed four people: "He said . . . he had a funny feeling in his stomach but after the first [killing] . . . it was easy" (p. 29). Another risk is that within any given sequence of behavior, aggression seems to escalate rather than to decline. For catharsis to reduce aggression rather than escalate it, the sequence of

behavior needs to be interrupted: There must be a break in the action, a change in the victim, or a change in the way in which aggression is expressed (Goldstein, Davis, & Herman, 1975).

The catharsis hypothesis also predicts that expressing aggression indirectly should provide catharsis and thus reduce further aggression. Aristotle felt that watching tragic dramas could produce catharsis, because the audience could vicariously experience the actors' emotions. Freud developed the same idea by hypothesizing that people could reduce their aggressive impulses through aggressive fantasy, such as in violent daydreams, cruel jokes, or writing stories. If such indirectly expressed aggression truly did bring about catharsis of aggressive energy, then aggressive behavior might be reduced without all the negative side effects we have enumerated.

By this theory, then, subsequent aggression should be reduced by modes of expressing aggression other than direct physical acts against a frustrator, such as *displaced aggression,* *vicarious aggression* (that is, aggression against your tormentor actually committed by someone else), or *verbal aggression.* There are some studies that find cathartic effects from indirect aggression (e.g., Feshbach, 1955; Konecni & Doob, 1972) but more that do not (see Geen & Quanty, 1977). In fact, indirect aggression turns out to be relatively highly correlated with direct aggression. For example, 56 percent of the married couples in the highest quarter of the population in verbal aggression had engaged in at least one violent episode within the past year, while only 0.5 percent of the couples in the lowest quarter on verbal aggression had had a violent incident (Straus et al., 1981; also see Carlson et al., 1989). So in married couples, verbally "getting it off your chest" is not associated with peace and harmony, but with later outbreaks of even more serious violence.

At the moment, then, social psychologists are skeptical that expressing anger produces cathartic reduction in aggressive behavior. It does seem to reduce the expression of aggression when the person is angry and is able to express aggression in a fairly direct manner against the person whom he or she perceives as responsible for the anger. But even then, sometimes aggression escalates. These are fairly stringent limitations on the catharsis effect.

MEDIA VIOLENCE

It is an understatement to say that in recent years movies have begun to portray a great deal of violence. Content analyses show a long-term trend of increasing violence in films shown in theaters dating from the early 1930s (Comstock, 1982). More recent movies have escalated the amount of carnage as well as its vividness. People do not just die at a distance or clutch their stomachs and fall slowly to the ground. They bleed and suffer, the bullet wounds gape and blood pumps rhythmically from victims' bodies rather than slowly staining their clothes. Whether it is Rambo taking on the communists, gangs of thugs taking over Manhattan, or slashers materializing out of the night, the violence has become extraordinarily vivid.

Television also uses a lot of violence in its programming. Police, gangster, and spy shows, and most television movies include a full complement of fighting, shooting, and killing. Saturday morning cartoons feature more of the same. Although the violence on television is much less explicit and vivid than that in the movies, it is remarkably pervasive.

It is widely assumed that such media violence stimulates people to aggressive behavior.

In 1983 the chief of the California state prisons adopted a policy of preventing "any movie that glorifies sick violence" after he discovered that the movie *The Texas Chainsaw Massacre* had been shown at the men's prison in Chino. But as we have seen, aggression is a complex behavior. Mere exposure to films may or may not have much effect on aggression one way or the other. This question has become one of the more controversial areas in the application of social psychological research to everyday life.

The Surgeon General's Report

Both the public and politicians are concerned about media violence. The U.S. Congress first held public hearings on TV violence in 1952. Later, the U.S. Surgeon General commissioned a report on the topic which was published in 1972 (Surgeon General's Scientific Advisory Committee on Television and Social Behavior). After reviewing available research, the report concluded, rather cautiously, that

> [There is] a preliminary and tentative indication of a causal relation between viewing violence on television and aggressive behavior; an indication that any such causal relation operates only on some children (who are predisposed to be aggressive); and an indication that it operates only in some environmental contexts. (Surgeon General's Scientific Advisory Committee on Television and Social Behavior, 1972, p. 11).

Do the media cause aggression and violence? Research suggests that media portrayals of aggression and violence may have a modest role in increasing aggressive behavior in some people under some circumstances.

This report immediately came under harsh attack, partly because some of the members of the committee that prepared it had worked for the television networks. It was felt, therefore, that they could not be disinterested scientific observers (Cater & Strickland, 1975). Most critics argued that the commission had underestimated the effects of media violence.

Ten years later, the National Institute of Mental Health asked a panel of behavioral scientists to evaluate the effects of televised violence once again. This time the reviewing committee concluded that "the consensus among most of the research community is that violence on television does lead to aggressive behavior by children and teenagers who watch the programs. . . . A causal link between televised violence and aggressive behavior now seems obvious" (National Institute of Mental Health, 1982, p. 6). A similar report was issued in seven volumes by the Canadian Royal Commission.

These reports were supported by many researchers in the field who had long since become persuaded of this conclusion (e.g., Friedrich-Cofer & Huston, 1986; Huesmann, 1982). Other social scientists were more skeptical, feeling that the available evidence did not support a firm conclusion one way or the other (Freedman, 1984).

There are many theories of how and why media violence affects behavior. Most suggest that watching violence should increase the likelihood of aggressive behavior among viewers. For example, learning theory would emphasize that observing aggressive models teaches viewers to behave violently through *imitation*. A related idea is that children learn entire *scripts* about aggression from the media. Then events in their later lives prime those memories and generate aggressive behavior (Berkowitz, 1984; Huesmann, 1988). For example, one common television script is that the bad guy provokes the good guy, who retaliates. The child who has learned this script from television might in later life be too quick to retaliate to minor insults (see also Viemero & Paajanen, 1992).

Much violence in the media is rewarded rather than punished, as in the case of the retaliating good guy. Viewing such rewarded violence *disinhibits* the person: It sends the message that learned inhibitions against aggression should be set aside, freeing the individual to act more aggressively. Only the *catharsis* theory proposes that watching media violence should actually reduce aggression among viewers.

What does research actually find about the effects of media violence? The answer depends in part on the method used to study media effects. We will review three types of research: laboratory experiments, correlational surveys, and field experiments.

Laboratory Experiments on Media Violence

An excellent example of a laboratory experiment on media violence is the work done by Albert Bandura and his colleagues discussed earlier in this chapter. Pre-school-age children were mildly frustrated, and then they observed an adult batting a Bobo doll around. When the children themselves were placed in the room with the doll, they repeated many of the aggressive behaviors performed by the adult. Remember that the point of these experiments was to demonstrate that young children can learn aggressive behavior by imitating the aggressive behavior of adults.

Leonard Berkowitz and his colleagues subsequently conducted another series of laboratory experiments, typically showing a brief film with violent physical aggression to some college students who had been angered and to some who had not been angered. One of the films often used was a 7-minute clip from *The Champion*, a boxing film starring Kirk Douglas. After viewing the film, subjects were given the opportunity to administer shock to a confederate in the standard shock-learning situation. Viewing the violent film generally increased the shocks delivered to the confederate.

Most of these studies were tests of the theory that the cue properties of the situation stimulate learned aggressive responses (Berkowitz, 1974). Anything that associated the subject with the film aggressor, or the confederate with the film victim, should tend to increase aggression. In many respects this theory was supported (see Berkowitz, 1984, for a review). For example, subjects displayed more aggression when told to identify with the winner of the boxing match than with the judge; the confederate received more shock when described as a boxer than as a speech major; and a confederate named "Kirk" got more shocks than one named "Bob" after seeing the actor Kirk Douglas play the boxer who got beaten up in the film. When the film presented justified aggression, by presenting the loser of the boxing match in an unfavorable light, more aggression was displayed. Some studies found that subjects had to be frustrated or angered for the violent film to increase their aggression (though other studies did not find that prior angering had any effect; see Freedman, 1986).

The catharsis hypothesis would make a very different prediction for these studies. It would suggest that subjects who have been angered would experience catharsis through the indirect aggression viewed in the film. While occasional studies have found such a result (Feshbach, 1961), most laboratory experiments have shown that observing aggression provokes more aggression, not less (e.g., Bushman & Geen, 1990). The catharsis effect rarely occurs. Whether one explains the media effect as resulting from imitation, priming, activating, or disinhibition, the result is the same: In these laboratory experiments, observing aggression usually increases aggressive behavior.

What Do Experiments on Media Violence Tell Us?

As clear as the implications of these findings may be, it is a long step from such laboratory studies to the real-life situations to which we might want to generalize. Are these laboratory findings likely to hold up in real life? The laboratory experiments must be judged, therefore, in terms of their **external validity,** as discussed in Chapter 1.

Laboratory situations differ in some important and obvious ways from watching TV at home. First, the laboratory film segments are normally brief and almost entirely composed of a single violent episode, like a few rounds from a boxing match, or an adult beating up a Bobo doll. In contrast, the normal child in real life watches a variety of different television programs. And each program contains quite a mixture of human acts having nothing to do with violence. Even the most violent programs often have humor, romantic entanglements, colorful scenery, and other nonviolent matters. Such diversity presents children with a wide variety of possible behaviors to imitate.

Second, in the laboratory the viewing situation is controlled and socially isolated, providing few distractions from the violence. In real life, people usually watch television with other people and simultaneously engage in other activities, such as eating, doing homework, conversing, playing games, or dancing (Comstock et al., 1978).

Third, the dependent variable in virtually all laboratory experiments is fully sanctioned, and often even prosocial, aggression. Children know it is perfectly all right to hit the Bobo doll. A 5-year-old playing with what is obviously a toy is a far cry from a gang of teenagers holding up a gas station and shooting the manager. Indeed, when the film model was punished for hitting Bobo, imitative aggression was markedly reduced. The shock-learning technique also involves prosocial aggression; the subject is supposedly in a learning experiment and is instructed to punish the victim for errors in order to improve learning. The concern about aggression in real life, in contrast, focuses primarily on such antisocial aggressive acts as unprovoked assaults, armed robbery, assault and battery, rape, and murder.

Fourth, in the laboratory there is usually little possibility of retaliation for being aggressive. And, as we have seen, when the victim can retaliate, the aggressor typically reduces his or her aggression. Finally, in these experiments the aggression measure is usually taken immediately after exposure to the film. Any delay would obviously reduce the effect of the film, and, in fact, several studies have shown that the film's effect typically wears off within a matter of minutes. In real life, the boy does not rush out of his living room with a knife and attack the first person he sees. Most crime is committed long after the person has watched television.

So the external validity of these experiments

is open to some question, particularly since the special conditions of laboratory experiments have themselves been shown to increase aggression. Thus, they may exaggerate the aggression produced by violent films. The experiments do show that media violence *can* produce increased aggressive behavior, but to learn whether it does so we need to turn to studies done under conditions that more nearly resemble real life.

Surveys of Television Watching and Aggression

One solution to the problem of external validity is to conduct **correlational research** to determine whether the children who watch the most violent television are also the ones who are the most aggressive. Since one interesting question is whether viewing violence in childhood produces more aggression in adulthood, a particularly important type of correlational survey is the *longitudinal study* whereby children's television viewing is measured at one time and their aggressive behavior is assessed some years later. Several such studies have been done (Eron et al., 1972; Huesmann et al., 1984; Milavsky et al., 1982). Overall, the correlations between early viewing of violence and later aggressive behavior usually tend to be positive, though statistically significant in only a minority of cases (Friedrich-Cofer & Huston, 1986; Freedman, 1984). However, these correlations can be stable over a 22-year period. In one study, for example, viewing of TV violence at age 8 predicted a variety of aggressive behaviors at age 30. Moreover, the more frequently youngsters watched TV at age 8, the more serious were the crimes for which they were convicted by age 30 (Eron, 1987).

If children who view violence the most are the most aggressive, then the effects of their heavier viewing should cumulate over the years, so the correlation between viewing violence and aggressive behavior should increase with age. Yet in longitudinal studies this has generally not been the case: The correlation between viewing violence and aggressive behavior has been about the same at each age level (Freedman, 1984). It is possible to argue

that consistently positive, even if very weak, correlations reflect socially significant effects (Rosenthal, 1986; Eron, 1987). But the fact is that the relationship is not a very strong one. It is especially weak for girls, and somewhat stronger and more consistent for boys (Viemero & Paajanen, 1992; Huesmann, Eron, Lefkowitz, & Walder, 1984).

Even if we take these relatively weak correlations as reflecting a real relationship, they lend themselves to other causal interpretations. Both of the standard problems with correlational designs pose dangers here. The "reverse causality" problem is that being especially aggressive may generate interest in watching violence rather than vice versa (Friedrich-Cofer & Huston, 1986). The "third-variable" problem also emerges. The viewing of violent programs is highly correlated with the amount of total television viewing, and when that has been taken into account, the effect of violent viewing often disappears (Friedrich Cofer & Huston, 1986). This suggests that viewing unusual amounts of television in general, rather than of violence in particular, may be more characteristic of children who are especially aggressive. And there may be important personality characteristics, not considered in these studies, that produce both aggressive behavior and a special interest in watching violent films (Freedman, 1986). So the correlational studies are equivocal concerning the causal role of media violence in producing aggressive behavior in real life.

Field Experiments

Field experiments would seem to be the answer to these criticisms. Because they are done in real-life situations, field experiments do not present the artificialities and biases present in laboratory studies. And by using experimental designs, they are not vulnerable to alternative causal interpretations. Field studies have typically presented the standard movie and television fare of the day, experimentally varying exposure to violent (as opposed to neutral or nonviolent) films. The subjects have usually been male adolescents living in their normal life situations (though most of them have been in boarding schools, rather than living at home with their parents). Researchers have measured genuine interpersonal aggression in a free, unconstrained atmosphere.

Only a few major field experiments have been conducted. In the first (Feshbach & Singer, 1971), boys in private boarding or state residential schools were randomly assigned to two groups. One group watched largely aggressive television programs such as "Gunsmoke" and "The FBI," while the other group was limited to nonaggressive programs such as the "Ed Sullivan Variety Show" and "Bachelor Father." The boys watched only shows on the designated lists and could watch as much as they wanted as long as they spent at least 6 hours a week watching television. Various measures of aggressiveness were given before and after the six-week viewing period, and both peers and adult supervisors also rated the boys' aggressiveness.

The results showed that boys in the state schools who watched aggressive programs actually became less aggressive. They engaged in fewer fights and argued less with their peers. The effect was the same but somewhat weaker for the boys in the private schools. The conclusion, then, is that observing television violence in real-life situations can actually decrease aggressive behavior, at least under some circumstances.

Three other studies were done in minimum-security penal institutions for juvenile offenders in the United States and Belgium (Leyens et al., 1975; Parke et al., 1977). The boys in some living cottages were shown up to five full-length violent movies, while boys in other cottage were shown neutral films. The Belgian study found an increase in aggression for one cottage shown the violent films but not the other. American studies have also found mixed results.

Friedrich and Stein (1973) put nursery school children on a diet of 12 violent cartoons ("Batman," "Superman"), or prosocial entertainment ("Mister Rogers") or neutral films (e.g., about nature). On most of their several measures of aggression, the groups did not differ significantly. Other similar studies show no effects (Wells, 1973; Milgram & Shotland, 1973).

Some "natural experiments" have occurred when television has been newly introduced into areas where there had been no television. Hennigan and her colleagues (1982) studied the relationship between the introduction of television to various areas of the United States and changes in the crime rate. They found no increase in violent crimes, burglary, or auto theft—the crimes usually portrayed on television. The only change was an increase in larceny—a crime rarely shown on television.

Each of these studies has its flaws. In the Feshbach-Singer study, the adolescent boys in the nonviolent conditions were deprived of their normal favorite programs. This frustration could by itself have increased their aggressiveness, thus eliminating any possible differences between the violent and nonviolent conditions. The Leyens, Parke and associates studies used group-viewing situations in dormitories where boys in prison had been living together for some time. This was perhaps a little like watching movies in a fraternity (except with juvenile delinquents instead of college boys), and it evidently stimulated a good bit of rowdiness during and right after the movies. This rowdy-group context is not the usual one for TV viewing in the home.

Overall, the results of these violent versus nonviolent TV field experiments are not dramatic. Observed violence in movies or television seems not to have affected aggressive behavior much in these real-life situations, one way or the other.

Conclusions

The effects of media violence have become one of the most passionate and most political of research topics in social psychology. We have discussed three different types of evidence regarding the effects of media violence. Laboratory studies seem to show that observed violence increases aggressive behavior. But do laboratory studies generalize to crime in the streets? Most correlational surveys find a modest positive association between children's liking for violent television programs and their behavioral aggression. However, these relationships are not strong, and in some of the best

Horror films have become especially popular in recent years. What effects do you think they have on viewers? Do they inspire imitation, fear, repulsion?

studies are not even statistically significant. And they are vulnerable to alternative interpretations. The field experiments we have described come close to being realistic replicas of real life, with the methodological protection of an experimental design. However, these studies have generally shown that media violence has little systematic effect on interpersonal aggression. In considering the effects of media violence on behavior, one must consider not only its potential to instigate aggression, but also the likelihood that it will instill fearfulness in some children (Ridley-Johnson, Surdy, & O'Laughlin, 1991).

It seems fair to conclude that media violence is not a sufficient condition to produce aggressive behavior, nor is it a necessary one. Aggressive behavior is multiply determined, and media violence in and of itself is unlikely to provoke such behavior. However, from the evidence, we conclude that media violence can be a contributing factor to some aggressive acts in some individuals. Moreover, the relation between media violence and aggressive behavior, though weak, nonetheless shows considerable cross-cultural generalizability. In a number of countries—Israel, Australia, Finland, Poland, South Africa, The Netherlands, and the United States—aggressive children watch more media violence, and exposure to more media violence enhances aggressive behavior (Huesmann, 1986; Huesmann & Miller, in press).

But what are the policy implications of this conclusion? From a policy point of view, the question is whether this evidence is strong enough to urge the suppression of certain kinds of entertainment programs. There are social conditions we all know are important in producing violence, such as unemployment, racial prejudice, poor housing, poor medical care (especially for people with mental health problems), the widespread availability of guns and alcohol and illegal drugs, a highly mobile population that does not settle into tight little self-policing communities, parental indifference to the welfare of their children, among many other things. Given the evidence accumulated to date, television and the movies contribute only a small amount to crime and violence beyond these large social factors.

And we must be careful about censorship of any kind. Today the government might decide that it is illegal to depict a knifing on television, and tomorrow, that it is illegal to depict protest demonstrations, because people might imitate that. Once the principle of censorship is accepted, it becomes harder and harder to draw the line. No matter how passionately we feel about the issue, we must be cautious about taking a stand before we have sufficient evidence. Many psychologists today believe that media violence does generally increase aggressiveness. But the implications of these findings for public policy, if any, are not yet clear.

SEXUAL VIOLENCE

Rape

Rape is one of the most common major crimes in the United States. But what is rape? **Rape** is forced sexual activity without one's partner's consent. Though a sexual crime, rape is, in fact,

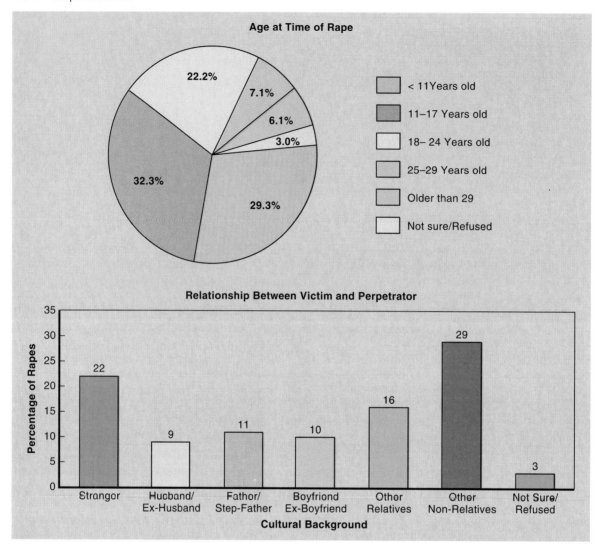

Figure 14-3   Rape as related to the rape victim's age and her relationship to the rapist. (*Source:* National Victim Center, 1992.)

thought to be largely a crime of aggression and power, involving male need for control and domination of women (Brownmiller, 1975; Donat & D'Emilio, 1992). According to a recent Federal survey published by the National Victim Center in 1992, 683,000 adult women were forceably raped in the United States in 1990. By surveying a cross section of 4000 women, the survey authors estimated that more than 12 million American women have been raped at least once in their life. Perhaps most startling is the fact that 61 percent of rape vic-

tims are younger than 18 at the time of their attack, and three out of 10 have not even reached age 11. Yet only 16 percent of these assaults were reported, perhaps because in most cases, the victim knew the rapist, as Figure 14-3 reveals (National Victim Center, 1992).

These recent statistics have shocked the American public, largely because they conflict so strongly with the stereotypes and myths that have traditionally been held about rape. The stereotypic conception of rape involves a woman, outdoors, assaulted by a mentally deranged or socially deviant stranger. Yet over 80 percent of rape victims know the rapist, and in over half the cases, the rapist is a relative or spouse, boyfriend or ex-boyfriend. Statistics on date rape are also startlingly high. Depending on the particular survey, between 28 and 50 percent of college women report that they have been forced into sexual activity against their will (e.g., Koss & Oros, 1982; McCaul, Veltum, Boyechko, & Crawford, 1990). Much rape also occurs within marriage, especially in already-violent marital relationships (Frieze, 1983). Until recently, rape that goes on in families, including marital rape, has been virtually ignored (Sorensen & White, 1992). Some states still do not consider marital rape a form of rape, arguing that only forced sexual activity outside of marriage constitutes rape.

Rape myths abound, and include the idea that "only bad girls get raped," "any healthy woman can resist a rape if she wants to," "women ask for it," and "women cry `rape' when they've been jilted" (Burt, 1980). The fact that at least 30 percent of all rapes involve children clearly contradicts these myths. As the patterns of rape, such as who gets raped by whom, become better known, **date rape** is also coming to be recognized as a serious problem (see RESEARCH CLOSEUP).

Among the most prevalent rape myths is the idea that only disturbed men rape. Many men make a distinction between forcing sexual activity on a woman and rape. Psychologist Neal Malamuth (1981) found that when college student men were asked if they would force a woman to have sex against her will if they could get away with it, about half said they would. But when asked if they would rape a woman if they knew they could get away with it, only about 15 percent of the men said they would. The men did not seem to realize that there is no difference between rape and forcing a woman to have sex against her will. Thus, it seems apparent that many men who have raped women are, on some level, unaware of the fact. Even men who have been convicted of rape typically argue away the seriousness of the crime by maintaining that their behavior was out of their own control or that the woman did something to ask for it (Scully & Marolla, 1984). Indeed, as the

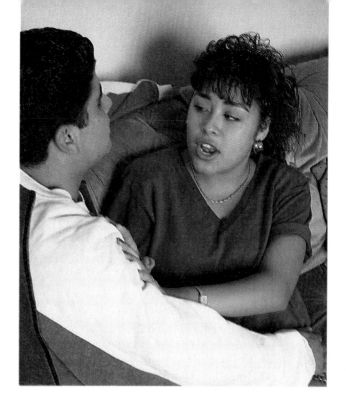

Date rape or acquaintance rape is on the rise. It appears to occur, in part, because men interpret ambiguous cues as a sexual invitation, when women mean only to be friendly.

Research Closeup indicates, men may interpret signs of friendliness in a woman as an interest in sexual activity, and thus be inclined to force sexual activity despite the woman's protests.

The different perceptions that men and women hold of circumstances surrounding rape were nicely illustrated in a study by Muehlenhard (1988). She gave male and female undergraduates 11 scenarios describing dates in which who initiated the date, who paid the expenses of the date, and what was done on the date were varied. Each respondent was then asked to indicate the degree to which the woman was interested in sex and how justified the man would be in having sex with her against her wishes. Muehlenhard found that ratings of willingness to have sex and justifications for use of force were highest when the woman initiated the date, when the couple went to the man's apartment, and when the man paid the dating expenses. Men perceived the woman in the scenario as significantly more interested in sex than women did, suggesting that men may overestimate women's interest in sex. Men also rated force as more justifiable than women did,

RESEARCH CLOSEUP

Date Rape

The following letter appeared recently in the college newspaper of a prominent Western university:

I am writing this letter to a well-respected young man [at my college] who belongs to a prestigious fraternity. You are good-looking, outgoing, and have many friends. I met you for the first and last time at a party last April, and it is a night I will never forget.

I met you early on in the evening. . . . We were standing with a group of people when you introduced yourself and flashed me that winning smile. I was hooked. You asked me to dance and I quickly obliged. You were a great dancer and we were having a terrific time together.

I had a couple of drinks, but you didn't seem to think that I was very relaxed. I believed you, so I took the drinks you kept offering me. . . .

Well, it worked. The punch did relax me for a while, and during that time, you catered to my every whim. . . . Even when I started feeling sick, you were there for me. . . . I asked you to please walk me home. . . . You, however, didn't think that walking home was such a good idea in my condition and you told me just to lie down until I felt better. . . . You were such a nice guy.

[Then] the nice guy disappeared. You used force to hold me down, words to terrify and stun me, and your plan worked. Premeditated rape. You blamed me, though. You told me it was my fault

because I was pretty and you couldn't help yourself.

For you, it was a night of fun, something you can look back at and laugh, while I still look back, and I'm not laughing. You put me through hell. You didn't just rape me, you robbed me, you stole my life from me. Through the feelings of guilt, shame, and fear that you instilled in me, you isolated me from my world . . .

I don't have enough evidence to take you to court and [the college] won't kick you out of school because the party wasn't a university-condoned event. So don't worry, my hands are still tied. The system is stacked in your favor. Congratulations. You win! (Anonymous, 1990)

One of the problems in getting people to understand that date rape *is* rape concerns the stereotypic scripts that people hold for rape versus seduction. When asked to describe a typical rape, most college students picture a woman outdoors attacked by a mentally or socially deranged stranger. When asked to describe a typical seduction, however, most subjects describe acquaintances having sex indoors, after both have imbibed alcohol (Ryan, 1988). Since date rape more frequently follows the seduction script than the stereotypic script for rape, this may interfere with the realization on the part of both men and women that date rape is, in fact, rape. Some studies show that if the woman behaves in any way that might be construed as suggestive, neither men nor women are likely

to regard the incident as rape at all (Muehlenhard & MacNaughton, 1988). Indeed, following a date rape, the woman may feel like a victim but the man may be astonished to discover that she feels that way.

This appears to be true because men and women interpret women's actions on a date very differently. One study (Shotland & Craig, 1988) found that acts such as speaking in a low voice or smiling were interpreted by men as indicating that the woman was interested in sex. Women, in contrast, tended to see the same behaviors as simply friendly (see also Saal, Johnson, & Weber, 1989). Drinking with a man, going to the man's apartment, or wearing sexy clothes were all seen by men as indicating a desire for sex, whereas women regarded these behaviors as normatively appropriate or fashionable (Muehlenhard, 1988).

Clearly, both men and women need better ways to avoid these misunderstandings. Women should know that men may interpret sexy clothes or a flirtatious manner as a desire for sex, and may construe acts such as going to a man's room alone as sexual interest. Women should not hesitate to make their intentions explicit by setting limits on intimacy firmly and by being assertive with someone who is pressing for sex. Men, in turn, need to understand that a woman's clothes and friendly behavior do not necessarily indicate an interest in sex. Men need to get the message that forceable sexual behavior is not acceptable under *any* circumstances, and that "no" should always be interpreted as meaning "no."

suggesting that they may regard some circumstances as appropriate for forcing a partner to have sex (see also Goodchilds et al., 1988; Jenkins & Dambrot, 1987).

Studies consistently find that women have more favorable attitudes toward rape victims than men, a finding that holds up cross-culturally (Lee, 1991; Levett & Kuhn, 1991). There also appear to be fairly reliable sex differences in the degree of fault attributed to the rapist. For example, a study in India found that female students recommended longer imprisonment for a rapist, attributed less fault to the victim, and perceived a greater likelihood of rape overall than men (Kanekar, Shaherwalla, Franco, Kunju, & Pinto, 1991; see also Schult & Schneider, 1991).

There is no other crime in which the victim is so routinely blamed (White & Sorensen, 1992). Myths die hard and are even accepted by many women. Unhappily, rape victims often also blame themselves for a rape. Is it maladaptive to blame oneself for a rape if one is the victim? Janoff-Bulman (1979) made a distinction between two types of self-blame. She argued that a rape victim may assign responsibility for her rape to her own modifiable behaviors, such as not having an adequate lock on her door, which she termed **behavioral self-blame.** Or, she may blame her character for the rape, concluding that she is a bad person or is too trusting (**characterological self-blame**). Janoff-Bulman predicted that women who attributed behavioral blame to themselves would adjust well, inasmuch as they could change their behavior, and thus reduce their risk of being raped again. Women who blamed their own character should be more maladjusted, according to the theory. However, studies with rape victims (Meyer & Taylor, 1986; Frazier, 1990) and studies of perceptions of rape victims by rape counselors (Thornton et al., 1988) have found that both behavioral and characterological self-blame are associated with poor adjustment to rape. (Indeed, self-blame of any kind is associated with poorer adjustment for victims of incest (Gold, 1986) and sexual harassment (Jensen & Gutek, 1982).) Those who blame society for the rape were somewhat better off than those who blamed themselves, but societal blame did not

actually facilitate good adjustment (Meyer & Taylor, 1986).

In fact, adjustment to rape can be difficult. Being raped has negative and often long-lasting psychological consequences. More than a year after a rape, victims experience rape-related fear and anxiety (Kilpatrick, Resnick, & Vernonen, 1981), sexual dissatisfaction (Feldman, Summers, Gordon, & Meagher, 1979), depression (Atkinson, Calhoun, Resnick, & Ellis, 1982) and family-related problems (Ellis, Atkinson, & Calhoun, 1981), compared with age-matched women who have not been raped.

Unfortunately, the legal system often perpetuates the misunderstandings and ambiguities surrounding rape. Studies of policemen suggest that they often hold some myths and stereotypes about rape and rape victims (Krahe, 1991). The Supreme Judicial Courts' Gender Bias Study Committee issued a report in 1989 (Zeprun, 1990) indicating several sources of bias in the trial of rape cases. Jurors apparently expect more corroborating evidence in sexual assault cases than in the case of other serious felonies. There is more of a tendency to call into question a victim's character and stability in sexual assault cases, whereas such evidence is unusual in other comparable felony cases, such as nonsexual assault. Consequently, victims are often discouraged from reporting rape, and may justifiably anticipate that the criminal justice system will put them, rather than the rapist, on trial.

Why do men rape? Originally, rapists were thought to be characterized by a distinctive type of psychopathology. However, it is now clear that convicted rapists are heterogeneous and that sexual aggression is determined by many factors (Prentky & Knight, 1991). A study of college men who admitted having aggressed against women either sexually or nonsexually found that hostile childhood experiences were characteristic of both the sexual and nonsexual aggressors (Malamuth, Sockloskie, Koss, & Tanaka, 1991; see also Barbaree & Marshall, 1991). Attitudes condoning coercive sex are correlated with delivering shock to a woman in a shock learning experiment (Malamuth & Ceniti, 1986) and to unsympathetic responses to a rape victim (Linz, Donnerstein, & Penrod, 1988).

Rapists also endorse rape myths more than do ordinary male citizens (Malamuth & Briere, 1986). Anger toward women and the need for dominance over them are strong characteristics of convicted rapists and of college men who have engaged in sexual aggression (Lisak & Roth, 1988).

Peer influence may also be a powerful factor in producing sexual aggression. Ageton (1983) and Alder (1985) found that, in two separate samples of adolescent boys and adult males, the strongest predictors of sexual aggression were, in the first case, involvement with delinquent peers, and second, having sexually aggressive friends. These findings underscore the fact that rape shares more in common with other crimes of aggression than it does with other forms of sexual activity.

Attitudes toward rape victims may be changing. In a recent study by Harbridge and Furnham (1991), 130 subjects ranging in age from 18 to 60 completed questionnaires regarding attitudes toward rape and its causes. The results indicated that the respondents believed that rape victims are moral, nonprovocative, and not responsible for the rape. The rapist, in turn, was perceived as suffering from a cruel upbringing. Hopefully, in the future, we will see increasing recognition of the faulty perceptions and social dynamics that produce the appallingly high rape rate we currently see.

Sexual Harrassment

Sexual harrassment is an umbrella term for many behaviors. It includes unwelcome sexual advances, requests for sexual activity, and other verbal and physical conduct of a sexual nature that either creates an intimidating, hostile, or offensive work environment or becomes a condition for new or ongoing employment. Sexual harrassment has been gaining increased attention as a problem women and occasionally men suffer in the workplace, because of the attention focused on the issue by the Clarence Thomas Supreme Court confirmation hearings following allegations by Anita Hill of sexual harrassment. Sexual harrassment may take the blatant form of repeated requests for sexual favors, or it may be

Anita Hill's accusations of sexual harassment against Supreme Court nominee Clarence Thomas brought the issue into the public eye and onto psychologists' research agenda.

more subtle, such as patting a woman on the behind, telling lewd stories, or placing pornography around the workplace.

Sexual harrassment appears to be a widespread problem in the workplace. A survey of 23,000 U.S. government workers found that 42 percent of women and 15 percent of men said they had experienced some form of sexual harrassment during the previous two years (U.S. Merit Systems Protection Board, 1981). Studies of college students find that half of women and 20 percent of men report some experience of harrassment at school from faculty, fellow students, or staff (McKinney & Maroules, 1991). Sexual harrassment can occur in any work situation and to anyone, but it is most common when women enter traditionally all-male environments, and it is most typically directed by a male supervisor toward a single woman under 35.

As yet, psychologists have not studied the dynamics of sexual harrassment to the degree that they have focused on rape. It is generally

TABLE 14-1
Typology of Films Used in Research on Sexual Violence

	Sexual	Nonsexual
Violent	Some R-rated films (*Blue Velvet, Straw Dogs*) Some X-rated films (*Story of O*)	Horror films (*Friday the 13th, Texas Chainsaw Massacre*) War films (*Rambo*)
Nonviolent	Teen sex comedies (*Spring Break*) Nonviolent R-rated films (*Body Heat*) Most X-rated films (*Emmanuelle*)	Situation comedies (*Rainman, On Golden Pond*) Family films (*101 Dalmatians, E.T.*)

Source: Adapted from Miller, Bersoff, & Harwood (1990), p. 38.

agreed that, like rape, sexual harrassment involves the abuse of power and the desire to enhance or maintain control and domination over women. We can expect to see social psychological attention focusing on this important issue in the future.

Sexual Violence and the Media

What is the role of sexually explicit films, books, and magazines in promoting sexual violence? Many argue that such pornography degrades women and encourages sexual coercion and violence. For example, a few years ago, a television drama, *Born Innocent*, portrayed an artificial rape scene. A few days later, some adolescent boys carried out a similar artificial rape which some blamed on the movie. Does pornography, and perhaps especially violent erotica, generally contribute to such sex crimes?

In the late 1960s, the liberal President Lyndon Johnson appointed a Commission on Obscenity and Pornography. After a careful review of the research evidence, the committee reported (1970) that it could document no antisocial effects of pornography. Laboratory studies of the effects of pornography had not detected harmful effects. Rather, early socialization and peer influence were the key factors in sexual violence. The early background of sex offenders was generally sexually repressive and restrictive, not permissive. Antisocial aggression among young men was more heavily influenced by peers than by the media. This conclusion was

attacked by political conservatives, religious groups, and feminists, so the conservative President Ronald Reagan's administration appointed another commission. It concluded that sexually explicit depictions of violence are likely to increase sexual violence and coercion, and recommended stricter antiobscenity legislation and prosecution (Attorney General's Commission on Pornography, 1986).

What can social psychology contribute to this debate? Much research has been done in recent years. Most of it has been guided by the theories we have just discussed, hypothesizing that violent sex in the media increases sexual violence through imitation, association of sexual pleasure with violence, and disinhibition. The best studies have used films and some variant of the shock-learning procedure. Most of these studies have used either full-length feature films or short stag films. They have typically manipulated exposure to erotic and violent material independently. Table 14-1 shows some examples of feature films that represent each possible combination of these two dimensions.

VIOLENT EROTICA. One basic question is whether or not there is something special about the *mixture* of violence and sexual themes that triggers unusual levels of aggression against women. We have seen that violent films produce more such aggression in laboratory experiments than do nonviolent films. However, what are the effects of witnessing uniquely *sexual* violence? The most relevant comparison, then, is between witnessing a violent erotic film and witnessing a violent nonerotic film.

To test this, Donnerstein (1983) presented some subjects with a violent–erotic stag film. This depicted a young woman who comes into view, apparently to study with two men. They have been drinking, and she is forced to sit between them and drink. They then tie her up, strip her clothes off, slap her around, and rape her (Donnerstein & Berkowitz, 1981). Other subjects were presented with a similar violent but nonerotic film in which the woman is tied up and slapped around without any nudity or sexual activity. Male subjects angered by a female and then given the violent–erotic film gave more intense shocks to a confederate than in any other condition. Whether this latter finding is replicable or not remains an open question, but at least it does provide some concrete evidence for a harmful effect of violent erotica.

A second important finding is that the female film victim's emotional reaction to being sexually coerced is crucial in determining the viewer's later aggression. In the Donnerstein and Berkowitz (1981) study, the subjects were either angered or not by a female confederate, against whom they could later retaliate. Then they were shown the film in which the victim was raped by two men. But the ending was varied: In one, she is smiling and not resisting, and even becomes a willing participant. In the other, she seems to find the experience humiliating and disgusting. As shown in Figure 14-4, the male viewers delivered more intense shocks to the female confederate when angered, consistent with earlier research. But when they were not angry, they did so only when the film depicted the woman as enjoying the experience.

Even if violent erotica does not directly contribute to violence, it might contribute to the **desensitization** of men to violence against women. It might lead to demeaning or callous attitudes toward women and therefore make violent or coercive sexual behavior more acceptable.

Numerous studies have indeed shown that viewing violent sexuality produces more accepting attitudes about violence against women, and contributes to the acceptance of such myths as

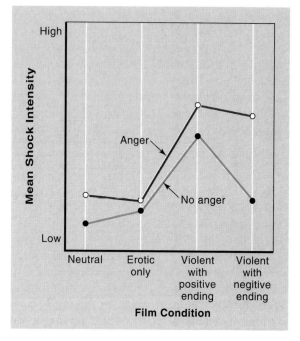

Figure 14-4 Shock intensity as a function of prior angering and type of erotic film. *Note:* Erotic film had little or no aggression; positive ending depicted coercive sex with a woman who was a willing participant, and the negative ending, with a woman who was not. (*Source:* Adapted from Donnerstein & Berkowitz, 1981, p. 150.)

that women often enjoy being forced to perform various sexual acts or even being raped.

An example of desensitization comes from a study by Malamuth and Check (1981). They compared the effects of viewing the films *Swept Away* and *The Getaway* showing women as victims of both erotic an nonerotic aggression, with the effects of viewing more neutral films. This study was particularly useful because the films were viewed in regular theaters, while the viewers' attitudes were measured in regular class sessions, so they were not aware of being subjects in an experiment. The more aggressive films increased males', but not females', acceptance of violence against women. Subsequent studies have found that repeated exposure over a period of days or weeks to stag films depicting sexual violence against women produces desensitization in terms of reducing perceptions that the material was violent and degrading to women, reducing support for sexual equality, and lessening sympathy for victims of rape (e.g., Linz, Donnerstein, & Penrod, 1984; Zillmann & Bryant, 1982; see Malamuth & Briere, 1986, for a review).

As with laboratory experiments on media violence, however, these studies raise problems of external validity. One problem is that most of these studies present single, brief stag films depicting little other than a wide variety of sexual activities, rather than the full-length films to which most men are usually exposed. Later studies, which presented anywhere from two to six full-length, commercially released films, including a wide variety of other normal daily activities, found no effect on the male subjects' aggressive behavior, attitudes toward women, or sympathy for the victim in a rape trial (Malamuth & Ceniti, 1986).

A second problem is that such studies may create experimental **demand characteristics** because the purpose of the experiment may seem obvious. The danger is that the subjects will then try to do the expected thing, to try to seem normal, and thus will inadvertently comply with the researcher's hypothesis. Watching a brief clip of women being sexually abused in a film, and then being asked to shock another woman or express attitudes about sexual violence may be so obviously connected to each other that they yield a biased test of the hypothesis. One solution is to collect the dependent variable under different auspices and in a wholly different context from the films, thus disguising the connection between the two. This is called a *separated post-test*. For example, after the film exposure, Linz and colleagues (1988) had another researcher phone subjects at home to ask them to participate in a study in the law school evaluating a trial. When they arrived, they were asked to be jurors in a rape case. Prior exposure to the films had no effect on evaluations of the rape victim. Similarly, Malamuth and Ceniti (1986) used the shock-learning technique as a separated post-test, and the films had no effect.

In short, the original one-shot laboratory studies, or longer-term studies using short, concentrated clips of sexual violence, did report

increased acceptance of violence on attitude measures taken immediately following exposure. But responses to full-length films and/or on separated post-tests yielded only weak effects.

What are the policy implications of these findings? Whether or not to control the portrayal of sexual violence in the mass media is a difficult question. Because the existing research leaves so many questions unresolved, it is probably premature to advocate legal restrictions. Labeling products as dangerous, akin to food or cigarette labels, is not a viable scheme, inasmuch as it is difficult to establish what may be harmful to viewers. It seems likely that, at present, only educational interventions stressing the kind of information contained in the Research Closeup can mitigate the effects of exposure to sexual violence (Linz, Wilson, & Donnerstein, 1992).

NONVIOLENT EROTICA. To what extent, if any, do the media fuel the high rate of rape we have in this country? The use of force is not a common theme in most men's sexual fantasies or in the erotic materials they most often see. For men fantasies involving the use of force are less common than purely heterosexual or voyeuristic fantasies (Arndt et al., 1985). *Playboy*, which has the largest circulation of the erotic men's magazines, rarely displays violence; only 0.3 percent of all its pictorials and cartoons have contained violence (and even that is declining; see Scott & Cuvelier, 1987). Similarly, many popular R-rated movies display at least some female nudity and nonexplicit sexual acts, and many depict violence against women as well as men, but relatively few portray sexual violence against women. Indeed, the written stories most sexually arousing to men are those that are sexually explicit and nonaggressive (Malamuth et al., 1986, p. 332). Nevertheless, some theorists contend that even nonviolent erotica induces sexual coercion and aggression. Such erotica may promote the dehumanization of women by treating them as sexual objects, as subordinate to men, as existing solely for male sexual satisfaction, as promiscuous and insatiable, and even as desiring coercive sex. Consequently, such erotica may encourage men to pursue women, even when those women do not want sexual activity.

In general, nonviolent erotica seems not to increase aggression beyond the levels of no-film or neutral-film control groups. For example, nonviolent erotic scenes from the films *Body Heat* and *Crimes of Passion,* displaying couples in mutually consenting but nonexplicit sexual activity, had no more effect on male subjects' attitudes toward sexual violence than did watching a couple have a nonsexual, nonviolent conversation (Smeaton & Byrne, 1987). Similarly, a sexually graphic but nonviolent X-rated film (depicting a young female singer's efforts to establish herself in the music industry), shown to a large audience in a largely residential college, produced no increased violence by male viewers against their female companions as recorded in questionnaires completed by the women several days before and after the film (Smith & Hand, 1987).

Exposure to nonviolent erotica may turn out to increase violent behavior under one set of limited conditions: when subjects are angry to start with, when the erotic materials are extremely explicit "hard core" pornography, and when the predominant affect experienced by the subject is negative (disgust or distaste). For example, Donnerstein and Barrett (1978) angered male subjects by having male or female confederates shock them. They then showed them some hard-core black-and-white stag films depicting oral and anal intercourse and female homosexuality. These subjects then delivered more shock to the offending confederate, whether male or female, than did nonangered subjects or subjects shown no film or a neutral wildlife documentary.

Why did this nonviolent erotica increase aggressive behavior? Probably for two reasons. Angering the subjects beforehand provided aggressive cues. And negative affective experiences contribute to aggression. Most hardcore material is inherently not very pleasant to most people (White, 1979). So presumably erotic materials that depict sex in an ugly, disgusting way would be more likely to inspire aggression. However, the most common nonviolent erotic materials are considerably more pleasant, depicting nudity and conventional lovemaking. So it would appear that nonviolent erotica does contribute to aggression only under some limited conditions, even in laboratory situations.

To summarize, it appears that most acts of sexual violence involve a wide variety of converging factors. While the media may be one of these, attitudes, personality, disinhibition due to alcohol, and social influence also clearly play a role (Malamuth & Briere, 1986; Lisak & Roth, 1988).

KEY TERMS

aggression

aggression anxiety

anger

antisocial aggression

behavioral self-blame

catharsis

characterological self-blame

correlational research

date rape

dehumanization

demand characteristics

desensitization

disinhibition

displaced aggression

external validity

field experiment

frustration

imitation

prosocial aggression

punishment

rape

realistic group conflict

reinforcement

sanctioned aggression

sexual harassment

shock-competition technique

shock-learning technique

social norms

SUMMARY

1. Aggression is defined as any action that is intended to hurt another person.

2. Aggressive acts can be antisocial, prosocial, or sanctioned, depending on whether they violate or conform with social norms.

3. Aggressive feelings, or anger, need to be distinguished from aggressive behavior.

4. The major determinants of anger seem to be attack and frustration, particularly if attributed to intent to injure.

5. Major determinants of aggressive behavior are angry feelings and the learning of aggressive responses. Learning can take place through imitation or reinforcement of aggressive responses.

6. Social norms are crucial in determining what aggressive habits are learned.

7. Fear of punishment or retaliation can reduce aggressive behavior. However, it may sometimes result in covert aggression, or actually increase aggression over the longer run.

8. Learned inhibitions of aggression are the most important control over it. Such inhibitions can also result in the displacement of aggression to other innocent parties.

9. Observed aggression generally increases aggression in laboratory studies, especially when the model is rewarded or when the observed victim is similar to the target of the subject's own aggression. However, these results may not generalize to real-life situations.

10. Viewing televised or movie violence, on the other hand, has not been shown to increase aggressive behavior in real-life settings (field experiments). The evidence that media violence contributes to violence and crime in our society is still indirect.

11. Rape is one of the most common forms of aggression. Due to prevailing stereotypes, myths, and misperceptions, men and women often regard sexual coercion in different ways, with many men condoning it under a range of circumstances.

12. The main determinants of sexual violence seem to lie in inegalitarian and coercive attitudes toward women, peer group norms, and abuse of substances such as alcohol. Written and filmed erotica seem to play a relatively minor role.

SUGGESTED READINGS

Bandura, A. (1973). *Aggression: A social learning analysis.* Englewood Cliffs, NJ: Prentice-Hall. The definitive statement by the most influential spokesman for the social learning and imitation approach to aggression.

Berkowitz, L. (1984). Some effects of thoughts on anti- and prosocial influences of media events: A cognitive-neoassociation analysis. *Psychological Bulletin, 95,* 410–427. A recent statement from one of the most important researchers in the field on the effects of aggression, reflecting the influence of social cognition.

Dollard, J., Doob, L., Miller, N. E., Mowrer, O. H., & Sears, R. R. (1939). *Frustration and aggression.* New Haven, CT: Yale University Press. The original statement of the theory that frustration breeds aggression. As well as discussing their laboratory experiments, it ranges far into the larger social manifestations of aggression, such as criminality, war, and fascism.

Malamuth, N. M., & Donnerstein, E. (Eds.) (1984). *Pornography and sexual aggression.* New York: Academic Press. A useful collection of writings on the role of erotica in producing sexual aggression.

National Institute of Mental Health. (1982). *Television and behavior: Ten years of scientific progress and implications for the eighties.* Rockville, MD: NIH. This is the follow-up report on the effects of television, following all the research done in the ten years since the Surgeon General's original report. It is a useful summary, though influenced by the authors' own perspectives.

15
Health

FOCUS OF THIS CHAPTER

Health Behaviors
Stress and Illness
Coping with Stressful Events
Symptoms, Illness, and Treatment
Social Psychological Perspectives
  on Chronic Illness

Research Closeup
Safe Sex

Cultural Highlight
Changing Health Behaviors Using the
  Social Environment

Most of us think about our health in physical terms. We are either sick or healthy, and we know which state we are in on the basis of the cues we get from our body. However, as the following anecdotes suggest, health is a psychological issue as well as a physical one.

- Bob, a 22-year-old member of the tennis team, has been told to stop smoking because it is sapping his energy during matches. He wants to stop, but so far, he has been unable to do so.
- Lisa broke up with her boyfriend last week, and she faces a major test in her chemistry course next week. She has just come down with the flu.
- Ellen recently went to see a physician about her headaches. The doctor was cold and aloof, and seemed to dismiss her complaints as trivial. She has decided not to follow her doctor's advice, but instead to go to a relaxation training course to see if it can help her.
- Mark, who is currently 19, has suffered from diabetes since he was 12 years old. Although he knows he should inject himself with insulin twice a day, he sometimes "forgets" and has ended up in the hospital as an emergency case four times in the last six months.

The realization that health is a psychological as well as a physical issue has given rise to an exciting new field, health psychology. The psychological study of health considers four main areas: (1) promoting and maintaining health; (2) preventing and treating illness; (3) identifying the causes and correlates of health, illness, or other dysfunctions; and (4) improving the

health care system and the formation of health policy (Matarazzo, 1980; Taylor, 1991).

An important lesson of health psychology is that health is not a purely physical matter, but rather a biopsychosocial state. According to the **biopsychosocial model,** a person's state of health is a complex interaction of several factors: biological factors, such as a genetic predisposition to a particular disease or exposure to a flu virus; psychological factors, such as the experience of stress; and social factors, such as the amount of social support one receives from one's friends and family. Once we recognize that psychological and social factors as well as biological ones are involved in health and illness, it is clear that good health is something that everyone achieves by engaging in a healthy life-style, rather than something merely to be taken for granted.

HEALTH BEHAVIORS

At one time, our major health problems involved infectious diseases such as influenza, pneumonia, and tuberculosis. Now, however, these problems have been largely brought under control. Currently, the major health problems faced by citizens of industrialized nations are "preventable" disorders such as heart disease, cancer, and diabetes. These problems are called preventable because they result at least in part from health behaviors that people can control. For example, annual cancer deaths in the United States could be reduced by 25 to 30 percent if everyone stopped smoking (American Cancer Society, 1989). Deaths due to heart disease would decline substantially if people lowered the cholesterol in their diet, stopped smoking, and reacted more effectively to stress (American

TABLE 15-1
Fifteen Specific Ways to Improve Health for Americans

In the 1970s the U.S. Department of Health and Human Services, under Patricia Harris, developed a set of goals to improve the health of the American populace. These goals served as targets for intervening in local health services. Note how many of them involve life-style changes and behavior modification.

A. *Preventive Health Services*
   1. Teaching people how to control high blood pressure
   2. Implementing programs of effective family planning
   3. Establishing programs to improve health care for pregnant women and infants
   4. Establishing effective immunization programs for children and at-risk adults
   5. Educating adolescents and adults regarding the control of sexually transmitted diseases

B. *Health Protection*
   6. Managing toxic chemicals and wastes
   7. Developing and implementing effective occupational safety and health standards
   8. Developing procedures to reduce accidents (especially vehicular accidents) and injuries
   9. Fluoridating water and improving preventive dental health care
   10. Surveillance and control of infectious diseases

C. *Health Promotion*
   11. Reducing smoking
   12. Reducing the misuse of alcohol and drugs
   13. Developing programs for effective nutrition
   14. Improving physical fitness and increasing exercise
   15. Developing effective techniques for the control of stress and violent behavior

Source: Adapted from Harris (1980); Matarazzo (1983).

Heart Association, 1984). Deaths due to vehicular accidents could be reduced by 50 percent if drunk driving were eliminated (DHHS, 1981). An examination of the nation's health goals (see Table 15-1), developed by the Department of Health and Human Services, clearly shows that the majority of these goals are related to life-style factors.

What Is a Health Behavior?

Health behaviors are actions undertaken by people who are healthy to enhance or maintain their good health. The importance of basic health habits was illustrated in a classic study conducted by Belloc and Breslow (1972). These scientists began by defining seven important health habits: sleeping 7 to 8 hours a night, not smoking, eating breakfast each day, having no more than one or two alcoholic drinks each day, getting regular exercise, not eating between meals, and being no more than 10 percent overweight. They then interviewed 6000 residents of Alameda County, California, and asked them to indicate which of these behaviors they regularly practiced. The residents were also asked to indicate how many illnesses they had had, how much energy they had, and how disabled they had been (for example, how many days of work they had missed) over the previous 6 to 12 months. The more health behaviors people practiced, the fewer illnesses of all kinds they reported having, and the more energy they said they had.

Unfortunately, few people follow all these good health behaviors. Although most of us practice some, such as not smoking or keeping our weight down, most of us violate at least a few others, such as not getting enough sleep or not exercising as much as we should (Steele, Gotmann, Leventhal, & Easterling, 1983). Some of the worst offenders are college students. Why is this the case? Most of the country's major health problems strike older people and are uncommon among college students. Therefore, these diseases often seem remote to a student. It may seem almost impossible that the health habits developed in adolescence and young adulthood could possibly influence health so many years away. Yet this is clearly the case.

Health Attitudes and Health Behaviors

Since health behaviors are essential to good health, it is important to understand the attitudes that lead people to practice good health behaviors or to continue to practice faulty ones. The practice of health behaviors centers on five sets of beliefs (Hochbaum, 1958; Rosenstock, 1966; Bandura, 1986b; Rogers, 1984):

1. *General health values,* including interest in health and concern about health

Poor health habits, such as smoking, are the major causes of disease and death in this country. Unfortunately, these behaviors often begin early in life, before people realize the damage their actions will produce.

2. The perception that the *threat to health* posed by a disorder is severe

3. A belief in *personal vulnerability* to a disorder

4. A belief that one is able to perform the response necessary to reduce the threat (*self-efficacy*)

5. A belief that the response will be effective in overcoming the threat (*response efficacy*)

To understand these points, consider the experience of one of our students a few years ago. Bob was the only person in the class who smoked, and he was the object of some pressure from the instructor and the students to quit. Although he acknowledged that smoking is linked to both lung cancer and heart disease, he believed the links to be fairly weak. Moreover, because he was in good health and played a number of sports, he felt relatively invulnerable to these diseases. However, over Thanksgiving vacation, Bob went home to a large family gathering and discovered to his shock that his favorite uncle, a chain smoker all his adult life, had lung cancer and was not expected to live more than a few months. Suddenly his general health became a more salient value for Bob. Bob's feelings of vulnerability to lung cancer changed dramatically because now a member of his own family had been affected. He came to realize in graphic fashion how severe the outcome of smoking can be. Bob's perceptions of the need to stop smoking changed as well. He concluded that stopping might be sufficient to ward off the threat of disease (response effi-

cacy). Moreover, he developed a belief in his own self-efficacy, that he would be able to stop. When Bob returned from Thanksgiving vacation, he had stopped smoking altogether. These relations are diagrammed in Figure 15-1.

Generally, understanding these **health beliefs** has done a good job of predicting health behaviors as varied as flu immunizations (Cummings, Jette, & Rosenstock, 1978), smoking reduction/cessation (Kaufert, Rabkin, Syrotuik, Boyko, & Shane, 1986), exercise (Wurtele & Maddux, 1987), skin cancer prevention activities (such as sunscreen use) (Cody & Lee, 1990), brushing and flossing teeth regularly (Tedesco, Keffer, & Fleck-Kandath, 1991), breast self-examination (Champion, 1990), AIDS-related sexual behavior (Aspinwall, Kemeny, Taylor, Schneider, & Dudley, 1991), condom use (Van der Velde & Van der Pligt, 1991), and dieting to control obesity (Uzark, Becker, Dielman, & Rocchini, 1987).

A final attitudinal component that predicts health behavior has been added by Fishbein and Ajzen, whose reasoned action model we considered in Chapter 6 (Ajzen, 1985; Ajzen & Fishbein, 1977; 1980; Ajzen & Madden, 1986; Fishbein, 1980). The theory of reasoned action maintains that a behavior is a direct result of a behavioral intention. Take the specific case of dieting to reduce cholesterol. Suppose that your father believes cholesterol is a threat to his health and that the outcome (a potential heart attack) is serious. Suppose he also believes he could change his diet in a healthier direction and

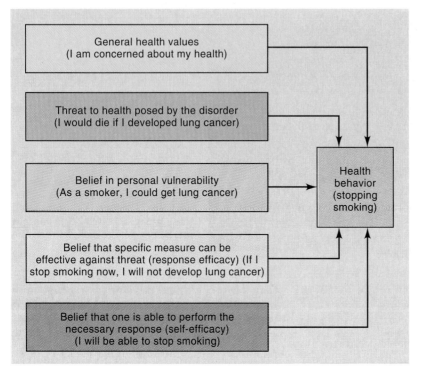

Figure 15-1   The relation of health attitudes to health behaviors.

believes that if he were to do so, it would reduce his risk. He still may not be inclined to undertake the behavior. Knowing if he *intends* to change his diet, then, improves our ability to predict whether he will actually go on the diet or not (e.g., Gielen, Eriksen, Daltroy, & Rost, 1984; Valois, Desharnis, & Godin, 1988).

Through understanding the determinants of health behaviors, it may be easier to see why so few people actually practice good health behaviors overall. The smoker may decide that it is too hard to change (low self-efficacy). The nonexerciser may believe that exercise alone would not reduce the risk of a particular disease (low-response efficacy). The obese individual may not perceive that being overweight is actually a threat to her health (low perceptions of threat). Some of the problems encountered in inducing people to practice safe sex are illustrated in the RESEARCH CLOSEUP. For a health behavior to occur, all these beliefs must fall into place, and there are any number of beliefs or rationalizations a given person may have for not undertaking a particular health behavior.

The finding that health beliefs are important

determinants of preventive health behaviors must be qualified by the fact that much of this research is conducted on relatively affluent middle-class individuals with access to health care. When we look at poverty-level families and at low-income black and Hispanic families, we find instead that the cost of preventive health care, such as whether or not a mammogram is free (Stein, Fox, & Murata, 1991), and access to health care are far more important determinants of health behavior than health beliefs. For example, many lower-class blacks have no regular source of health care and consequently either utilize hospital emergency facilities or remain untreated. Many lower-class Hispanics do not seek help (Lewin-Epstein, 1991). These facts are especially problematic, because low-income blacks and Hispanics typically have poorer health than more affluent whites (Mutchler & Burr, 1991). This appears to be true because people lower in income, education, occupational status, and ethnic status are more vulnerable to a wide range of highly stressful, undesirable life events (McCleod & Kessler, 1990). Far from waning, these social class and ethnic differences

In a recent television program, a man and woman are fondling each other, removing each other's clothes, and making steady progress toward the man's bed. As they approach it, she whispers, "Have you had a blood test?" He responds, "Last month. Negative. You?" She responds, "Negative, too. Do you have protection?" His response: "I'm covered." They fall to the bed and . . . (fade out).

This is Hollywood's idea of a safe-sex encounter. But where did the magic condom come from? Did he put it on in the taxi on the way back to his apartment? Did he put it on in the kitchen while he was pouring them each a glass of wine?

Hollywood's safe sex encounters may be seamless, but in real life, safe sex is not. A first important step is getting people to recognize that safe sex is important, that is, that they are at risk for AIDS and other sexually transmitted diseases. AIDS is beginning to spread into the sexually active young adult population and is spreading fastest among African Americans and Hispanics. Yet levels of knowledge about sexuality generally and AIDS specifically is problematic, especially among less acculturated Hispanic Americans (Marin & Marin, 1990).

Inducing young people to take steps to practice safe sex is also problematic. Sexual counselors advocate asking prospective partners about their sexual histories, yet many young adults indicate that they would lie to a partner to minimize their HIV risk history (Cochran & Mays, 1990). But young adults who utilize partner questioning in the hopes of reducing their HIV risk are less likely to use condoms (Mays & Cochran, in press).

Getting people to use condoms is also problematic. One study found that many adolescents who reported risky behaviors, such as promiscuity, were the least likely to use condoms consistently (Biglan et al., 1990). A study of 442 African American inner city adolescents revealed that 92 percent of the females but only 33 percent of the males thought that at least one member of a couple should be responsible for using birth control (Reis & Herz, 1989).

Adolescents and young adults typically regard condom use as not cool (Collins & Aspinwall, 1989). The very factors that the Hollywood encounter overlooked, namely the interpersonal awkwardness and logistics of actually using condoms, act as barriers to their use.

Clearly, then, safe sex takes more than a couple of hurried questions and a claim of protection. Interventions to increase the practice of safe sex need to address knowledge about sex and sexually transmitted diseases such as AIDS, attitudes toward sexual protection, cultural differences that may bear upon these attitudes, and intervention techniques that directly address how condoms are perceived by the young adult population.

are actually growing (Navarro, 1990; Okie, 1991; Rosenthal, 1990).

Changing Health Attitudes

Research on health attitudes is useful not only because it helps us predict who will practice a particular health behavior, it also explains the conditions under which people might change their health behaviors. In theory, persuasive messages that increase feelings of vulnerability while simultaneously increasing feelings of self-efficacy and response efficacy could induce people to modify their behaviors in a healthy direction. But how would people get this information? One of the goals of preventive health education is to reach as many people as possible, as through the mass media. We have all been exposed to televised or radio messages urging us to increase the

The cost of health care and access to it are the most important determinants of health behavior among the poor. When health programs are accessible and free, they are more likely to be used.

fiber in our diet, reduce our cholesterol, or stop smoking. How successful are these messages?

Unfortunately, evaluation of these efforts suggests somewhat limited success (Atkin, 1979; Lau, Kane, Berry, Ware, & Roy, 1980). Mass media communications seem to bring about changes in health attitudes but only modest changes in behavior. A classic study conducted by the Stanford Heart Disease Prevention Program (Meyer, Nash, McAlister, Maccoby, & Farquhar, 1980) illustrates this point. These researchers developed a mass media intervention designed to get people to change their health habits and reduce their risk of heart disease. Three communities of similar size and social composition were identified and evaluated concerning risk factors associated with heart disease both before and after the study. The risk factors examined included smoking, diet, and exercise.

One town served as a control group and received no campaign. The second and third towns were exposed to a mass media campaign concerning smoking, diet, and exercise over a 2-year period. In the third town, the media campaign was supplemented by face-to-face instruction in the modification of risk factors directed at those people at highest risk for heart disease.

The results indicated modest attitude change and behavior change in the community exposed only to the mass media campaign. The residents were more knowledgeable about risk factors, and they reported that they had reduced their consumption of dietary cholesterol and fats somewhat. There was also some evidence that blood pressure and blood cholesterol levels had been reduced. However, much more dramatic and lasting effects were found when the media campaign was coupled with behavioral instruction for individuals at highest risk (Leventhal, Nerenz, & Strauss, 1980).

This study illustrates two important points. The media may be quite effective in informing people about risks and in gradually changing public opinion about health practices over time (Lau et al., 1980; Leventhal & Cleary, 1980; Mogielnicki et al., 1986). However, the media are not necessarily effective in modifying behavior. Second, what is often needed to modify health behavior successfully is intensive training directly targeted to those at risk for a particular health problem.

Cognitive Behavioral Approaches to Health Behavior Modification

But how do we modify behavior? Increasingly, those who want to alter stubborn health behaviors have focused on the specifics of each individual's habits, health cognitions, and environment that may promote a faulty health behavior or undermine the practice of a desirable new one. This approach, which comes out of social learning theory (Chapter 1), is called cognitive-behavior therapy (Lazarus, 1971; Thoresen & Mahoney, 1974).

SELF-MONITORING. Consider, for example, the case of a woman who is 40 pounds overweight and at risk for heart disease. To get her to reduce her weight, first one needs to understand her eating, the factors that give rise to it, and the stimuli that are associated with it. To address these issues, a psychologist might begin an intervention for weight reduction by having her systematically observe her eating, a proce-

Putting On A Condom Is Just As Simple.

Condoms are one of the simplest and best forms of protection against AIDS. But they're only effective if they are used properly every time you have sex. Why risk not using them? For more information about condoms, AIDS and AIDS prevention, call:

NATIONAL AIDS HOTLINE:	1-800-342-AIDS
Servicio en Espanol:	1-800-344-7432
TTY-Deaf Access:	1-800-243-7889

AMERICA RESPONDS TO AIDS

Mass-media messages designed to change health behaviors can be effective in inducing the motivation to change, but by themselves, they may bring about little behavior change.

dure termed **self-monitoring** (Abel, Rouleau, & Coyne, 1987; Thoresen & Mahoney, 1974). She would be trained to take notes about her eating and the circumstances under which it occurred.

STIMULUS CONTROL. The psychologist might then attempt to alter the stimuli that are associated with eating, a process known as stimulus control. For example, if this woman eats while she is watching television, she might be retrained to eat only at the kitchen table with the television off. By removing the association of television with food, one of the enjoyable factors associated with overeating would thereby be removed. Similarly, the presence of desirable and fattening foods like cookies and ice cream might also act as stimuli for eating, and so this woman might be urged to clear her refrigerator and shelves of these foods.

BEHAVIOR CONTROL. Next she might be taught to reward herself for changing her eating patterns. For example, she might be encouraged to set up a schedule of projected weight goals and then be told to reinforce herself with some pleasurable activity such as going to a movie each time she met a particular weight-loss goal. She might also be encouraged to use techniques of self-punishment. For example, if she failed to bring her eating under control and ate forbidden foods, she might punish herself by unplugging her television for a day or two.

HEALTH-RELEVANT COGNITIONS. The thoughts people have about their health habits also influence the practice of those health habits. Cognitions about one's sense of self-efficacy or self-control are especially important (Abel et al., 1987; Bandura, 1986b; Thoresen & Mahoney, 1974). For example, this woman might inadvertently undermine her diet by thinking, "I'll never be able to do this" or "I've tried to diet many times before and always been unsuccessful." Teaching her to think positively ("I'm going to be successful at this") can help promote health habit change. To increase the sense of personal control, a person may be given behavioral assignments to complete at home that will help further the goals of the health behavior change program. For example, our obese woman might be encouraged to keep a log of her eating each day (Cox, Tisdelle, & Culbert, 1988; Shelton & Levy, 1981).

SOCIAL FACTORS. Psychologists recognize that many health behaviors are related to social factors (Chaney, O'Leary, & Marlatt, 1978). For example, smoking or overeating may occur primarily in social settings to control anxiety. Accordingly, psychologists may encourage smokers or over-eaters to join social-skills training programs or assertiveness training programs so that they can develop new social skills to substitute for their old faulty health behaviors. Our overweight woman might be taught effective social skills to prevent overeating at parties.

BROAD-SPECTRUM APPROACH. The kind of cognitive behavioral change program described here is called **broad-spectrum cognitive-behavioral therapy** because it draws on a wide variety of behavior change techniques (Lazarus, 1971). Such programs have shown at least modest effectiveness in modifying problems of alcohol abuse (DHHS, 1981), smoking (Leventhal & Cleary, 1980), and obesity (Brownell, 1982; Lovibond, Birrell, & Langeluddecke, 1986). Some of these programs are undertaken individually with private therapists. Others are implemented through self-help groups, such as Overeaters Anonymous or Alcoholics Anonymous. Schools may be the target for an intervention, such as

Many people who try to change bad health habits eventually relapse. For example, when people return to settings in which they previously engaged in a problematic behavior (such as drinking), they are strongly tempted to drink again. Relapse prevention techniques need to be integrated into treatment programs.

programs designed to prevent children from beginning to smoke, and worksite interventions have increasingly been used to help people change their health habits (e.g., Cataldo, Green, Herd, Parkinson, & Goldbeck, 1986).

RELAPSE PREVENTION. It is fairly easy to get people to agree to stop smoking, to lose weight, and/or to change their diet for short periods of time. Unfortunately, the problem is long-term maintenance. Most people exposed to most health behavior modification programs return to their unhealthy behavior, a problem termed relapse. Consequently, **relapse prevention** techniques need to be integrated into treatment programs from the outset (Brownell, Marlatt, Lichtenstein, & Wilson, 1986). One useful method of relapse prevention is getting people to identify high-risk situations for relapse. For example, an ex-smoker might identify having a cup of coffee after dinner or playing poker with friends as likely trigger situations for resuming smoking. The person would then be encouraged to think of ways to avoid those situations or to substitute better responses that would make relapse less likely. The ex-smoker, for example, might play poker only with friends who do not smoke (e.g., Baum, Clark, & Sandler, 1991).

Another aspect of relapse prevention is called life-style rebalancing (Marlatt & George, 1988; Marlatt & Gordon, 1985). By getting exercise, changing diet in a healthy direction, trying to reduce stress, and drawing on the social support of others, people alter their life-style generally in a healthy direction, and this change may help them to increase adherence to any particular health habit change as well. While there is currently no foolproof method of relapse prevention, researchers have identified relapse prevention as the most important target for additional work, given the high rate of relapse that does occur (Taylor & Aspinwall, 1990).

Health habits alone are not sufficient to ward off the threat of illness, although they help substantially. Stressful life experiences and the ways people cope with those stressful events also have an impact on health and illness. We examine these issues in the next section.

STRESS AND ILLNESS

Most of us have more experience with stress than we care to remember. Stress is discovering that your alarm clock did not go off the morning of a major test or finding out that your car won't start when you need to drive to a job interview. The experience is fundamentally a physiological one. Your body moves into a state of heightened arousal, your mouth goes dry, your heart beats faster, your hands may shake a little, and you may perspire more heavily.

Most of us think of these experiences as unnerving but temporary, not producing any lasting damage. However, researchers now believe that over time, stress can wear down the body, making it more vulnerable to illness. Repeated exposure to stressful events and repeated engagement of the physiological engagement of the physiological changes that accompany stress (increased blood pressure, blood sugar level, respiration, and the like) exert wear and tear on the physiological system. This, in turn, may lay the groundwork for a variety of disorders, including heart disease, hypertension,

and even cancer (e.g., Jemmott & Locke, 1984; Friedman & Rosenman, 1974; Selye, 1956, 1976).

But what is stress? **Stress** is a negative emotional experience accompanied by predictable physiological, biochemical, and behavioral changes that are designed to reduce or adapt to the stressor either by manipulating the situation to alter the stressor or by accommodating to its effects (Baum, 1990). Most of us think of stress as intrinsic to particular events such as being stuck in traffic, getting a poor grade on a test, being late for an appointment, or losing a notebook. Yet despite some commonalities in the experience of stress, not everyone perceives the same events as stressful. For example, one person may experience a job interview as threatening, while another may welcome it as a challenge. The fact that stress is, to some degree, in the eye of the beholder makes it clearly a psychological process. That is, events are stressful when they are regarded as stressful and not otherwise (Lazarus, 1966; Lazarus & Folkman, 1984).

What Makes Events Stressful?

Some types of events are more likely to be appraised as stressful than others. Any event that requires a person to adjust, make changes, or expend resources has the potential to be stressful. For example, although Christmas is usually viewed as a positive event, it may also be highly stressful, since it can involve last-minute shopping, extensive travel, social occasions with relatives, excessive consumption of alcohol and rich food, and little sleep.

Negative or unpleasant events are more likely to be perceived as stressful than positive ones. For example, a $20 parking ticket typically causes a person more distress than does spending $20 to go to a noisy, crowded rock concert, even though the latter experience may actually be more physiologically arousing. Unpleasant events cause people more psychological distress and produce more physical symptoms than do more positive stressful events (e.g., McFarlane, Norman, Streiner, Roy, & Scott, 1980; Myers, Lindenthal, & Pepper, 1972; Sarason, Johnson, & Siegel, 1978).

Negative, uncontrollable, and unpredictable events are very stressful, and continued exposure to them can compromise health and emotional well-being.

Uncontrollable or unpredictable events are more stressful than controllable or predictable ones (Bandura, Cioffi, Taylor, & Brouillard, 1988; McFarlane et al., 1980; Suls & Mullen, 1981). This is because an event that is uncontrollable or unpredictable does not enable the person going through the stress to make a plan or develop ways of coping with the problem. For example, the sound of static on your own radio may be less distressing than static from a neighbor's radio, because you can always turn off your own radio, whereas you may not have the same degree of control over your neighbor's radio.

Ambiguous events are often perceived as more stressful than clear-cut events. For example, if you have been attracted to a fellow student in a class, and one day this person treats you in a cold, aloof manner, you may ruminate over why this is the case. Did you do something to offend this person? Is he or she simply having a bad day? Presumably, if you knew what was wrong you could correct it quickly, but not knowing means you are stuck trying to figure out what has gone wrong. Clear stressors let people get on with finding solutions and do not leave them stuck at the problem-solving stage (Billings & Moos, 1984; Gal & Lazarus, 1975).

How Stress Can Cause Illness

The experience of stress is a problem for people not only because it produces emotional distress and physiological arousal, but because over time it may lay the groundwork for illness.

MAJOR STRESSFUL LIFE EVENTS. The earliest research to demonstrate this point examined the role of major **stressful life events** in the onset of illness. Newspapers and magazines often highlight colorful cases in which individuals who have experienced a major stressful event suddenly develop a serious illness or even die.

> A dramatic example is the death of the 27-year-old army captain who had commanded the ceremonial troops at the funeral of President Kennedy. He died 10 days after the president of a "cardiac irregularity and acute congestion," according to the newspaper report of medical findings. (Engel, 1971, p. 774)

Much of the research designed to show the importance of major life events in the onset of illness has used a questionnaire called the Social Readjustment Rating Scale. As can be seen in Table 15-2, the Social Readjustment Rating Scale lists a variety of potentially stressful events that require people to make changes in their lives. Through extensive testing, the events selected for the scale were determined to be the ones that, on the average, force people to make the greatest change. The points reflect the relative amount of change that must be made. Thus, for example, if a person's spouse dies, virtually every aspect of life is disrupted, and so this event has the highest number of life change units assigned to it. On the other hand, getting a traffic ticket may be annoying but it is unlikely to produce much change in a person's life.

To obtain a score on the Social Readjustment Rating Scale, one simply checks the events that have occurred within the past year and totals up the point values associated with those events. Although everyone will have experienced at least a few stressful events during the year, some will have experienced a lot, and it is this group, according to Holmes and Rahe, that is most vulnerable to illness.

In one study, Rahe, Mahan, and Arthur (1970) obtained scores on the SRRS from sailors who were about to depart on a six-month cruise. They selected this group because during the six months that the men would be on board ship, they would be subjected to the same rather dull

TABLE 15-2
Social Readjustment Rating Scale

Rank	Life Event	Mean Value
1.	Death of spouse	100
2.	Divorce	73
3.	Marital separation from mate	65
4.	Detention in jail or other institution	63
5.	Death of a close family member	63
6.	Major personal injury or illness	53
7.	Marriage	50
8.	Being fired from work	47
9.	Marital reconciliation with mate	45
10.	Retirement from work	45
11.	Major change in the health or behavior of a family member	44
12.	Pregnancy	40
13.	Sexual difficulties	39
14.	Gaining a new family member (e.g., through birth, adoption, oldster moving in)	39
15.	Major business readjustment (e.g., merger, reorganization, bankruptcy)	39
16.	Major change in financial state (e.g., a lot worse off or a lot better off than usual)	38
17.	Death of close friend	37
18.	Changing to a different line of work	36
19.	Major change in the number of arguments with spouse (either a lot more or a lot less than usual regarding childrearing, personal habits)	35
20.	Taking out a mortage or loan for a major purchase (e.g., for a home, business)	31
21.	Foreclosure on a mortage or loan	30
22.	Major change in responsibilities at work (e.g., promotion, demotion, lateral transfer)	29
23.	Son or daughter leaving home (e.g., marriage, attending college)	29
24.	Trouble with in-laws	29
25.	Outstanding personal achievement	28
26.	Wife beginning or ceasing work outside the home	26
27.	Beginning or ceasing formal schooling	26
28.	Major change in living conditions (e.g., building a new home, remodeling, deterioration of home or neighborhood)	25
29.	Revision of personal habits (dress, manners, associations, etc.)	24
30.	Trouble with the boss	23
31.	Major change in working hours or conditions	20
32.	Change in residence	20
33.	Changing to a new school	20
34.	Major change in usual type and/or amount of recreation	19
35.	Major change in church activities (e.g., a lot more or a lot less than usual)	19
36.	Major change in social activities (e.g., clubs, dancing, movies, visiting)	18
37.	Taking out a mortage or loan for a lesser purchase (e.g., for a car, TV, freezer)	17
38.	Major change in sleeping habits (a lot more or a lot less sleep, or change in part of day when asleep)	16
39.	Major change in number of family get-togethers (e.g., a lot more or a lot less than usual)	15
40.	Major change in eating habits (a lot more or a lot less food intake, or very different meal hours or surroundings)	15
41.	Vacation	13
42.	Christmas	12
43.	Minor violations of the law (e.g., traffic tickets, jaywalking, disturbing the peace)	11

Source: Holmes & Rahe (1967).

and unchanging environment. Therefore, if life events have an impact on the likelihood of illness, one should be able to see differences in the rates of illness of the sailors who had highly stressful lives just before departure, relative to those with less stressful lives just before departure. In fact, the predictions were borne out. Sailors who had experienced more major stressful life events were most likely to get sick and to be sick longer than were those who had experienced few stressful life events.

DAILY HASSLES.   More recently, psychologists have begun to suspect that the more minor stressful events or the daily hassles of life may also have a cumulative and negative impact on health. Such hassles include being stuck in a traffic jam, waiting in line, doing household chores, or having difficulty making a small decision. Interpersonal conflicts are by far the most distressing daily hassles (Bolger, DeLongis, Kessler, & Schilling, 1989). Although research is not yet conclusive, it may emerge that the wear and tear of daily life predicts illness and psychological stress as well or better than the more major but relatively rare stressful events (Kanner, Coyne, Schaeffer, & Lazarus, 1981; Kohn, Lafreniere, & Gurevich, 1992). In short, research suggests that both major stressful events and minor stressors are problematic, not only because they produce psychological distress but because they can also increase the likelihood of physical illness.

COPING WITH STRESSFUL EVENTS

Once we experience an event as stressful, we usually begin to make efforts to cope with that event. **Coping** is the process of attempting to manage demands that are viewed as taxing or exceeding our resources (Lazarus & Folkman, 1984; Lazarus & Launier, 1978). It is the process of trying to manage and master stressful events.

Coping with a stressful event is a dynamic process. For example, the impending breakup of a romantic relationship can produce a variety of responses, including efforts at reconciliation or attempts to find activities that will distract us

from emotions such as sadness or indignation. Generally, researchers distinguish between two types of coping efforts: problem-solving efforts and efforts at emotional regulation (Lazarus & Folkman, 1984; Leventhal & Nerenz, 1982; Pearlin & Schooler, 1978). *Problem-solving efforts* are attempts to do something constructive to change the stressful circumstances. *Emotion-focused coping* involves efforts to regulate the emotional reactions to the stressful event. Both types of coping can occur simultaneously. For example, when romantic partners break up, each person may try to cope with the loss by mulling over the past events and taking steps to meet new people. Table 15-3 presents examples of some coping strategies used by men with AIDS.

Psychologists also study more specific coping strategies (Carver, Scheier, & Weintraub, 1989; Folkman & Lazarus, 1980; Stone, Greenberg, Kennedy-Moore, & Newman, 1991; Amirkhan, 1990). Some of these represent active coping methods, such as seeking information, planning, or attempting to get help from others. Other strategies, involving emotion-focused coping, include positive reinterpretation, acceptance, or turning to religion (Park, Cohen, & Herb, 1990). Psychologists study avoidant coping methods, which involve disengaging behaviorally or mentally from a stressful event, as through substance abuse or distancing. Generally speaking, active coping is used more and is more adaptive in situations that are changeable, whereas emotion-focused coping may be more appropriate for situations that cannot be changed (e.g., Vitaliano, DeWolfe, Maiuro, Russo, & Katon, 1990). Generally speaking, active coping is more effective than avoidant coping, which actually seems to make stressful situations worse (e.g., Holahan & Moos, 1987; Felton, Revenson, & Hinrichsen, 1984).

What Is Successful Coping?

What constitutes successful coping? This is not an easy question to answer, and researchers differ in the criteria they use to measure successful coping. Some emphasize the effects of coping on measures of physiological and biochemical functioning. Coping efforts are generally considered to be more successful if they reduce physiological

TABLE 15-3
Strategies for Coping with AIDS

AIDS has killed many thousands of people, and thousands more live, sometimes for years, with the knowledge that they have the disease. Such a threat requires and elicits many forms of coping, some of which are illustrated in the following exerpts from interviews with gay men living with AIDS. (Reed, 1989.)

● **Social Support or Seeking Information**

A key point in my program is that I have a really good support network of people who are willing to take the time, who will go the extra mile for me. I have spent years cultivating these friendships.

My family has been extremely supportive, and my lover has been extremely supportive, but it really wasn't quite enough. They weren't helping me in the right ways. That's when I went and got a therapist. Basically, she is the one who has helped me cope with [AIDS] and understand it.

● **Direct Action**

My main concern is making it through another day without getting any disorder. I would really like to completely beat it.

My first concern was that, as promiscuous as I have been, I could not accept giving this to anyone. So I have been changing my life-style completely, putting everything else on the back burner.

● **Distraction, Escape, or Avoidance**

It was important to me to focus on something besides AIDS, and my job is the most logical thing, I'm very good at what I do. I have a supervisory position, so I deal with other people's problems, which is good for me, because I take their job problems and solve them and I forget about mine. I think that's a real constructive distraction for me.

I drive. I feel so much more at peace when I am driving down the road in a car, listening to music, having my dog next to me. It is wonderful.

● **Emotional Regularity/Ventilation**

When you're sad, you cry. That's what I've done a lot lately, over silly, well, not silly things, but over small things, and over reminders of a life that's probably cut short, the expectations of things that you were going to do and planned on doing and don't seem possible now.

Sometimes I will allow myself to have darker feelings, and then I grab myself by the bootstraps and say, okay, that is fine, you are allowed to have these feelings but they are not going to run your life.

● **Personal Growth**

In the beginning, AIDS made me feel like a poisoned dart, like I was a diseased person and I had no self-esteem and no self-confidence. That's what I have been working on, is to get the self-confidence and the self-esteem back. I don't know if I will ever be there, but I feel very close to being there, to feeling like my old self.

When something like this happens to you, you can either melt and disappear or you can come out stronger than you did before. I literally feel like I can cope with anything. Nothing scares me, nothing. If I was on a 747 and they said we were going down, I would probably reach for a magazine.

● **Positive Thinking and Restructuring**

Everyone dies sooner or later. I have been appreciating how beautiful the Earth is, flowers, and the things I like. I used to go around ignoring all those things. Now I stop to try and smell the roses more often, and just do pleasurable things.

I have been spending a lot of time lately on having a more positive attitude. I force myself to become aware every time I say something negative during the day, and I go, "Oops," and I change it and I rephrase it. So I say, "Wonderful," about 42,000 times a day. Sometimes I don't mean it, but I am convincing myself that I do.

The last chapter has not been written. The fat lady has not sung. I'm still here.

---

arousal and its indicators such as heart rate, pulse, and skin conductivity. A second criterion of successful coping is whether and how quickly people can return to their previous life activities. Many stressful events disrupt ongoing daily life activities, interfering with work or leisure. To the extent that coping efforts enable a person to resume such activities, coping may be judged to be successful. Finally, and most commonly, researchers judge coping according to its effectiveness in reducing psychological distress. If negative emotions such as anxiety and depression are reduced by a coping effort, the coping effort is judged to be successful (Lazarus & Folkman, 1984).

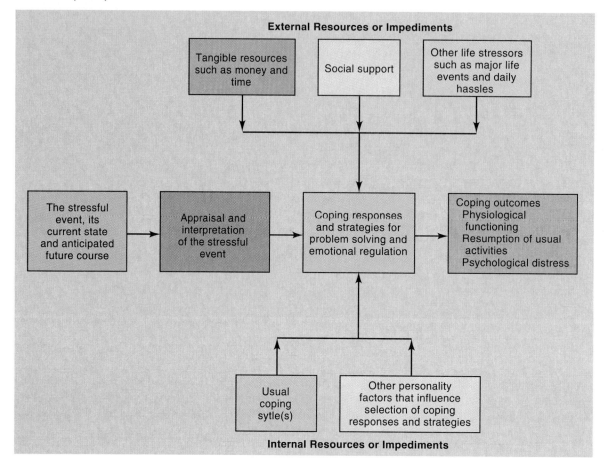

External Resources or Impediments

Tangible resources such as money and time

Social support

Other life stressors such as major life events and daily hassles

The stressful event, its current state and anticipated future course

Appraisal and interpretation of the stressful event

Coping responses and strategies for problem solving and emotional regulation

Coping outcomes
Physiological functioning
Resumption of usual activities
Psychological distress

Usual coping sytle(s)

Other personality factors that influence selection of coping responses and strategies

Internal Resources or Impediments

Figure 15-2   The coping process.

Successful coping depends on a variety of coping resources. Internal resources consist of coping styles and personality attributes. External resources include money, time, social support, and other life events that may be occurring at the same time. All these factors interact with each other to determine coping processes (e.g., Wiebe & McCallum, 1986). A model of the coping process is presented in Figure 15-2. In the next section, we consider a few of these coping resources in detail.

Coping Style

Coping style is one internal coping resource. It consists of a general tendency for a person to deal with a stressful event in a particular way.

AVOIDANCE VERSUS CONFRONTATION.   Some people meet stressful events head on and seem to tackle problems directly, whereas other people avoid stressful events by minimizing their significance or withdrawing from them through alcohol, drugs, or television.

In fact, neither coping style is necessarily more effective than the other in managing stress. Each seems to have its own advantages and liabilities. People who cope by minimizing or avoiding stress appear to cope effectively with short-term threats. However, if the threat is repeated or persists over time, avoidance may not be so successful. Avoiders may be unable to deal with the possibility of future threat and may not make enough efforts to anticipate and manage subsequent problems (Suls & Fletcher, 1985; Taylor & Clark, 1986).

In contrast, individuals who cope with threatening events through confrontation may deal effectively with long-term threats. But in the short run, they may be more anxious as they deal with the stressor directly (e.g. Miller & Mangan, 1983). For example, the avoider may cope well with a trip to the dentist because he puts the event out of his mind until just before it happens. However, the avoider may cope poorly with constant job stress because this is not an event that can easily be put out of mind; the stress recurs daily despite efforts to avoid it. In contrast, the vigilant coper may fret over a visit to the dentist and create internal distress. However, he or she may make constructive efforts to reduce stress on the job, and thereby ameliorate the situation.

TYPE A BEHAVIOR. Some coping styles may succeed in dealing with the psychological discomfort of stressful events but may nonetheless have an adverse effect on health. Perhaps the best example is the **type A behavior** syndrome that has been associated with heart disease. The type A person has a behavioral and emotional style marked by an aggressive, unceasing struggle to achieve more and more in less time, often in competition with other individuals or forces. Type A behavior has three components: easily aroused hostility, a sense of time urgency, and competitive achievement striving (Rosenman, 1978). So-called type B's, with whom type A's are usually compared, are less driven individuals who do not show these behavior patterns in response to stressful events. There are several measures of type A behavior; items from one scale/test are given in Table 15-4.

Type A individuals lead fast-paced lives. They work longer hours and put in more overtime than do type B's. They are impatient with what they perceive as people's slow behavior and may complete people's sentences for them. They often concentrate on several activities simultaneously. Despite the fact that type A's often achieve substantial accomplishments, they may evaluate their achievements in terms of quantity instead of quality and be dissatisfied with their output. They are likely to challenge and compete with others, especially in moderately competitive situations (Rosenman, 1978).

Type A behavior is important because it has

TABLE 15-4
The Jenkins Activity Survey: A Measure of Type A Behavior

The Jenkins Activity Survey measures type A behavior by asking people about their typical responses to frustrating, difficult, and competitive situations. The following are a few examples of items that appear on that survey:

1. When you listen to someone talking and this person takes too long to come to the point, how often do you feel like hurrying along?
   Frequently
   Occasionally
   Never

2. Do you ever set deadlines or quotas for yourself at work or at home?
   No
   Yes, but only occasionally
   Yes, once a week or more

3. Would people you know well agree that you tend to get irritated easily?
   Definitely yes
   Probably yes
   Definitely no
   Probably no

4. Would people who know you well agree that you tend to do most things in a hurry?
   Definitely yes
   Probably yes
   Definitely no
   Probably no

Note: If you answered these questions by giving the high-frequency answers, you show at least some characteristics of the type A individual.

Source: Adapted from Jenkins, Zyzanski, & Rosenman (1979). Jenkins Activity Survey. Copyright © 1965, 1966, 1969, and 1979 by The Psychological Corporation. Reproduced by permission. All rights reserved.

been reliably related to the development of coronary artery disease (Haynes, Feinleib, & Kannell, 1980; Matthews, 1988). Type A's experience excessive arousal in response to stressful events, followed by dramatic decreases in arousal. This pattern may be the mechanism that produces damage to the arteries, although this issue is still under debate (Glass, 1977). Recently, investigators have found that the hostility aspect of type A is the most important in the development of heart disease, more so than time urgency or competitiveness (Dembroski & Costa, 1987; Friedman & Booth-Kewley, 1987; Smith & Brown, 1991).

INTERNAL COPING RESOURCES. Psychologists have identified several personality resources that people may bring to bear on a stressful event to improve psychological adjustment. **Dispositional optimism** is a general belief that good outcomes will occur in life. Such optimism seems to mobilize people to take direct action in response to a stressor, and thus is generally associated with good adjustment to stressful events such as illnesses (Scheier & Carver, 1983; Taylor, Kemeny et al., in press; Scheier et al., 1989). **Hardiness** has been identified as a set of attitudes that makes people stress-resistant. These attitudes include a sense of commitment, a positive response to challenge, and an internal sense of control. These beliefs are believed to buffer hardy people from the negative effects of coping with stress or change (Kobasa, 1979; see also Rhodewalt & Zone, 1989; Allred & Smith, 1989). Pennebaker and his colleagues (e.g., Pennebaker & Beall, 1986; Pennebaker, Kiecolt-Glazer, & Glazer, 1988; Pennebaker, Colder, & Sharp, 1990) have suggested that catharsis, the process of disclosing emotional traumas, may have psychological benefits.

Social Support

In Chapters 7 and 9, we saw how important social relationships are to people for satisfying their social needs. Recent work by health psychologists indicates that socially supportive relationships may also mute the effects of stress, help people cope with stress, and enhance health.

Social support can help keep people well and help them to recover quickly from illness.

Social support is an interpersonal exchange in which one person gives help to another. Social support may be provided in any of several ways. First, *emotional concern* expressed through liking, love, or empathy can be supportive. For example, if you are going through an awkward breakup with a romantic partner, expressions of caring from friends can be very welcome. Second, *instrumental aid,* such as the provision of goods or services during stressful times, can be an act of social support. For example, if you are having difficulty getting to your classes on time because your car is unreliable, a friend's offer to fix your car or to drive you to class would be supportive. Third, *providing information* about a stressful situation can be helpful. For example, if you feel poorly prepared for an exam and someone who took the course last year gives you information about types of questions on the midterm and final, this may be useful in helping you study. Finally, information may be supportive when it is relevant to *self-appraisal,* that is, self-evaluation. For example, if you are uncertain whether you have made the right decision in breaking up with your boyfriend or girlfriend, information from your friends telling you that you did the right thing for the right reasons can be very comforting. Social support can come from a spouse or partner (Sherbourne & Hays, 1990), family members, friends, or social and community contacts, such as clubs and churches or temples.

Research demonstrates that social support effectively reduces psychological distress during stressful times (Cohen & Wills, 1985; Kessler & McLeod, 1985; Littlefield, Rodin, Murray, & Craven, 1990). For example, it helps both men and women cope with stress on the job (Loscocco & Spitze, 1990). Social support also appears to lower the likelihood of illness and to speed recovery from illness (House, Landis, & Umberson, 1988). Some impressive evidence for the importance of social support in combating the threat of illness comes from a survey of adults in Alameda County, California (Berkman & Syme, 1979). Almost 7000 people were interviewed regarding their personal, social, and community ties. Then their death rate was tracked over a nine-year period. The results showed that people who had few social and community ties were more likely to die during this period than were people who had more such ties.

Social support has also been tied to better immune functioning (Baron, Cutrona, Hicklin, Russell, & Lubaroff, 1990) and to more effective functioning in response to a variety of chronic diseases, including cancer, heart disease, diabetes (see Taylor & Aspinwall, 1990, for a review), and rheumatoid arthritis (Manne & Zautra, 1989; Goodenow, Reisine, & Grady,

1990). Social support also influences health habits and health behaviors, as the CULTURAL HIGHLIGHT illustrates.

Research has tried to identify exactly how social support affects stress, and two possibilities have been extensively explored. One hypothesis, called the *direct effects hypothesis*, maintains that social support is always beneficial, during nonstressful as well as during stressful times. The other hypothesis, termed the *buffering hypothesis*, maintains that the physical

CULTURAL HIGHLIGHT

Changing Health Behaviors Using the Social Environment

Many of the interventions designed to change people's faulty health behaviors are targeted to the individual. For example, although they reach large audiences, media messages are designed to help each individual smoker reduce his or her smoking. While such an approach may have some degree of success in a culture that is heavily independent, an approach that focuses more on the social network and the individual's social environment may be more successful in collectively oriented cultures.

This approach seems to be especially valuable in appealing to Hispanic Americans. In many Hispanic cultures, anticipated social support or its absence is a stronger predictor of health habits than health attitudes. Among Hispanic smokers, for example, beliefs about how others respond to one's smoking are important, not only in understanding smoking atti-

tudes and behavior, but also in designing interventions to reduce smoking (Marin, Marin, Otero-Sabogal, Sabogal, & Perez-Stable, 1989). Specifically, messages arguing that quitting smoking provides children with a good example, improves the health of one's family, eliminates bad breath, and saves money appeal to the social interconnectedness of this group much more than the individualistic orientation we typically see in antismoking messages that emphasize personal health risks (Marin, Marin, Perez-Stable, Otero-Sabogal, & Sabogal, 1990).

Increasingly, researchers are recognizing that social support is important for changing health habits among non-Hispanics as well. Researchers find, for example, that weight loss and reductions in smoking are more successfully brought about in a work group situation than through individual intervention

(Brownell, Stunkard, & McKeon, 1985). Physicians find that patients are more likely to adhere to their advice when the spouse and even children are involved in understanding the treatment regimen (Wallston, Alagna, DeVellis, & DeVellis, 1983). People are more likely to practice certain health behaviors, such as safe sex, if they feel they have support from their family and friends (Catania et al., 1991).

We have learned an important lesson from collective cultures, then, about how to appeal to people to change faulty health practices. Understanding how the social environment influences these habits, embedding interventions in the social context, enlisting the cooperation of people who are important in the target individual's life, and appealing to a person's social responsibilities all help to promote successful health behavior change.

and mental health benefits of social support chiefly occur during periods of high stress and not during periods of low stress. Extensive research suggests that social support can have both direct effects and buffering effects (Cohen & Hoberman, 1983; Pilisuk, Boylan, & Acredolo, 1987; Wills, 1984).

Stress Management

Some individuals have difficulty coping with stressful events on their own. Stress management programs have developed to help people deal with these events more effectively (e.g., Chesney, Eagleston, & Rosenman, 1981; Roskies, 1980; Smith, 1989). Such programs train people in techniques that can be used to cope with a wide variety of stressful events, or the focus may be on coping with a particular stressful event (e.g., Meichenbaum & Jaremko, 1983).

As an example, consider the stress of college. College can be a trying experience for many students. For some, it is the first time they are away from home, and they must cope with the problems of living in a dormitory surrounded by strangers. They may have to share a room with a person of very different background and habits. High noise levels, communal bathrooms, institutional food, and difficult academic schedules may all be very trying. In addition, the fledgling college student may discover that academic life is more rigorous than he or she had expected. Whereas each student may have been a star in high school, there is more competition in college. Consequently, course loads are heavier and grades are typically lower. Coping with the first C, D, or F can be a deflating and anxiety-arousing experience.

Some colleges and universities have instituted programs to help students cope with these stressful events by learning stress management techniques. Commonly, in the first phase of such programs, the students learn what stress is and how it creates wear and tear on the system. Students learn that stress is in the eye of the beholder, that college life is not inherently

stressful but can become stressful depending on how a student perceives it. Through these messages, students begin to see that if they acquire appropriate stress management techniques, they may come to experience currently stressful events as less stressful. In sharing their experiences of stress, many students find reassurance in the fact that other students have experiences similar to their own.

In the next phase, students are trained to observe their own behavior closely and to record the circumstances they find most stressful. They also typically record their physiological, emotional, and behavioral reactions to the stressful events. They may write down any efforts they make to cope with the stressful events, such as sleeping, eating, watching television, or taking drugs.

Once they learn to chart stressful responses, students are encouraged to examine what causes those experiences. For example, one student may feel overwhelmed with academic life only when she must deal with speaking out in class, whereas another student may experience stress primarily when he thinks about having to use the computer in a particularly demanding course. By pinpointing the circumstances that initiate a student's feelings of stress, that student can more clearly identify his or her own trouble spots.

Students are next trained to recognize the negative self-talk they may go through when they face stressful events. For example, the student who fears speaking out in class may come to recognize how her self-statements contribute to the stress she feels ("I hate asking questions" and "I always get tongue-tied"). Such negative self-talk undermines feelings of self-efficacy and will become a target for modification later in the intervention.

Typically, students will next set specific goals that they want to meet to reduce the experience of college stress. One student's goal may be to learn to speak in class without suffering overwhelming anxiety. For another, the goal may be to go see a particular professor about a problem. Once the goals have been set, the student identifies some behaviors that can help meet those goals. For example, the student who fears speaking out in class may decide that she will begin to raise her hand whenever she knows the answer to factual questions that will require only a one- or two-word response. By beginning with relatively little speaking out in class, she may then be able to train herself to give longer answers that can ultimately enable her to speak more effectively.

Once the student has set some realistic goals and identified some target behaviors, he or she will learn how to engage in positive self-talk. For example, the student desiring to overcome a fear of oral presentations might remind herself of the occasions when she has spoken successfully in public. Once some success in speaking publicly has been achieved, the same student might encourage herself by highlighting the positive aspects of the experience (for example, holding the attention of the audience or making some good points). As she becomes more effective, she might try to create opportunities to speak publicly and reward herself each time she does so by engaging in some desirable activity such as going to a movie.

Typically, students also learn some ways of modifying the physiological reactions associated with stress. Usually, these methods involve relaxation-training techniques and may include deep breathing, muscle relaxation, guided imagery, or meditation (English & Baker, 1983; Benson, Greenwood, & Klemchuck, 1975). Such methods can help reduce heart rate, muscle tension, and blood pressure. Then, if a student finds that the stress of college life is becoming overwhelming, he or she can take a 5- or 10-minute break, breathe deeply and relax completely, and then return to tasks freer of previous tensions.

Most stress management programs include a wide array of cognitive behavioral techniques that an individual can use to combat stress. Some will work better for some students, and others will work better for other students. By presenting a broad array of coping techniques, students have a broad set of skills from which to choose the ones that work best for them.

SYMPTOMS, ILLNESS, AND TREATMENT

When and how a person decides that he or she is sick is a heavily social and psychological process.

The Recognition and Interpretation of Symptoms

To label yourself as sick, you first have to notice that you are. Noticing symptoms is, in part, a psychological process that depends on focus of attention. People whose attention is chronically focused on themselves, who are socially isolated or live alone, or who have relatively inactive lives are more likely to notice symptoms in themselves. Conversely, people who are externally focused on their environment and activities, who have active social lives and work outside the home, or who live with others are less likely to notice symptoms (Pennebaker, 1983).

Situational factors influence whether or not a person will recognize a particular situation by directing attention inward or outward. Boring situations make people more attentive to their symptoms, whereas interesting situations distract them from attending to bodily states. Joggers, for example, are more likely to experience fatigue and to be aware of their running-related symptoms if they are running on a boring course than if they are running on one that is more interesting (Pennebaker & Lightner, 1980; see also Fillingim & Fine, 1986).

People's expectations can guide the interpretation of information, and so it is with symptom information as well (Leventhal et al., 1980). For example, women who believe that menstruation produces psychological distress and physical symptoms are more likely to report experiencing them. In fact, women who expected to have symptoms and distress exaggerated the degree to which they had experienced them, when their retrospective reports of distress and symptoms were compared against actual diary reports they had kept during their menstrual cycles (McFarland, Ross, & DeCourville, 1989).

Even mood influences symptom experiences. People who are in a poor mood report more aches and pains and greater discomfort than happy individuals (Salovey & Birnbaum, 1989). And a chronically bad mood, such as that found among neurotics or other people with chronic negative affect (such as anxiety or depression), is associated with higher levels of self-reported symptoms and physical illnesses (McCrae & Costa, 1987; Watson & Pennebaker, 1989; Larsen, 1992).

Satisfaction with important areas of one's life, including work and home, is typically associated with low levels of symptoms. But work overload and/or the responsibility for providing support to many other people increases symptoms and compromises physical health (Barnett, Davidson, & Marshall, 1991; Shumaker & Hill, 1991). Women, in particular, experience more symptoms and have more physical illnesses (Kaplan, Anderson, & Wingard, 1991).

Prior experience also shapes reactions to symptoms (Safer, Tharps, Jackson, & Leventhal, 1979; Jemmott, Croyle, & Ditto, 1988). If you have a long history of sore throats, you are more likely to ignore any particular one than if it is an unusual symptom for you.

As we saw in Chapter 3, cognitive theories or schemas about events often strongly affect how those events are perceived and interpreted. Beginning research suggests that such beliefs can be important in symptom interpretation and the management of illness as well. Researchers have suggested that patients form organized, cognitive pictures of their symptoms that influence their illness-related activities (e.g., Bishop, 1990; Nerenz & Leventhal, 1983; Lau, Bernard, & Hartman, 1989; Turk, Rudy, & Salovey, 1986). In essence, these are illness schemas. They include such factors as the name of the illness and its symptoms (i.e., its identity), its cause, duration, and consequences.

People have at least three models of illness (Nerenz & Leventhal, 1983). *Acute* illness is short in duration with no long-term consequences and is believed to be caused by specific viral or bacterial agents. An example is flu. *Chronic* illness is caused by many factors, including faulty health habits, and is long in duration with often severe consequences. Cancer is an example. *Cyclic* illness is marked by alternating periods when there may be no symptoms and others when there are many. Recurrent episodes of herpes is an example.

Sometimes patients adopt an inappropriate model for their disorder. For example, patients suffering from hypertension (high blood pressure) may believe the disease is acute, when in fact, it is chronic. Consequently, they may think that if they feel well, their blood pressure must be under control, and therefore they need no longer take their medication (Meyer, Leventhal, & Gutmann, 1985). In fact, hypertension is called the silent killer precisely because patients often experience no symptoms and conclude erroneously that they no longer need treatment. It is important for practitioners and others involved in health care to explore patients' schemas for their illnesses to see if they are using an appropriate illness model in understanding their disorder and its treatment (Hampson, Glasgow, & Toobert, 1990; Lacroix, Martin, Avendano, & Goldstein, 1991).

Social interaction also affects how people interpret symptoms. Sometimes when we are ill we consult our friends to find out if they have had similar symptoms or to get their opinions on what the symptoms might mean. Warned that a minor sore throat is the first symptom of a serious flu that is going around, you might take better care of yourself than if you learned that others were experiencing a similar symptom and attributing it to pollution in the air. Often, then, people exchange information with family and friends about the interpretation of symptoms before they seek any treatment (Freidson, 1960).

Finally, pain is an important determinant of whether people recognize symptoms and interpret them as serious. Yet pain has a surprisingly heavily cultural component. There are substantial cultural differences in whether a particular stimulus is perceived as painful (e.g., Zborowski, 1952; Morse & Morse, 1988). Even more important, there are large cultural differences in how pain cues are interpreted. In some cultures, for example, individual members respond primarily to the magnitude of the pain they experience, whereas in other cultures, members respond primarily to what they think the pain means; in these latter cultures, severe pain that is perceived as trivial may be ignored, whereas minor pains regarded as indicative of a serious underlying disorder may act as cues for treatment.

In this section, we have stressed the psychological factors that influence when people experience and notice symptoms and interpret them as signs of illness. It is important to realize, though, that the experience of symptoms and the decision whether or not to seek treatment is heavily influenced by quality of life. For example, women get sick more than men, a factor that has been attributed to less paid work, lower wages, more hours spent in household labor, childcare, and helping others, and fewer hours of leisure and sleep than is true for men. Men hold more highly rewarding social roles than women typically do, and, in fact, when gender differences in social roles are equated, males have poorer health than females (Bird & Fremont, 1992). Thus, if gender roles were more equal, particularly in the stress they induce, women would experience health at least equivalent to that of men, perhaps better. Similar inferences apply to other populations that are disadvantaged and suffer disproportionate stress in our society. For example, the vulnerability of African Americans to hypertension and stroke has been interpreted as arising at least in part from a combination of highly stressful living conditions, low income, and racial prejudice (Harburg et al., 1973). Thus, an emphasis on psychological factors must not obscure the very important role that socioeconomic factors play in the experience of symptoms and illness rates.

Patient–Practitioner Interaction

Sometimes symptoms lead us to the medical practitioner's door. Interacting with a physician or nurse regarding medical treatment is a complex social process involving interpersonal communication, person perception, social judgments, and social influence. One of the earliest judgments that most patients make is whether they think the practitioner is technically competent.

But most of us know little about medicine and standards of practice, and so we evaluate medical care using the only information we have: whether we like the practitioner and whether he or she is warm and friendly or cool and uncommunicative. When people are asked what is important to them in their medical care, they rate the manner in which the care is delivered at least as high as the technical quality of care (Feletti, Firman, & Sanson-Fisher, 1986; Scarpaci, 1988).

One of the problems that arises in interactions with practitioners, even when patients and practitioners have some basic confidence in each other, is faulty communication. Practitioners often use jargon and technical language that patients do not understand, and they may inadvertently depersonalize the patient by referring to the patient's symptoms rather than the patient as a person (Chafetz, 1970; Kaufman, 1970).

> Recently, when I was being given emergency treatment for an eye laceration, the resident surgeon abruptly terminated his conversation with me as soon as I lay down on the operating table. Although I had had no sedative or anesthesia, he acted as if I were no longer conscious, directing all his questions to a friend of mine—questions such as, "What's his name?" "What occupation is he in?" "Is he a real doctor?" etc. As I lay there, these two men were speaking about me as if I were not there at all. The moment I got off the table and was no longer a cut to be stitched, the surgeon resumed his conversation with me, and existence was conferred upon me once again (Zimbardo, 1970, p. 298).

Communication between patient and practitioner can be improved by training physicians in effective communication techniques.

Patients, too, contribute to faulty communication by failing to pay attention to what they are being told, and by responding to the wrong cues in the situation and reading too much into a physician's comment (DiMatteo & DiNicola, 1982; Golden & Johnston, 1970; Greer, 1974). For example, a patient may be so distressed by swollen glands that he fails to listen to a physician's instructions about taking penicillin.

The treatment setting contributes to undermining effective communication (see Taylor, 1979). For example, a physician may have a backlog of patients in the waiting room, and accordingly is under pressure to see each patient for as little time as possible. The patient is asked to describe symptoms efficiently and effectively to a physician when the patient may be in a poor state to do so. It is difficult to be coherent when one is in pain, running a fever, or simply anxious about the meaning of a particular problem. In summary, a variety of factors can inadvertently impede communication.

Faulty communication between patient and practitioner is problematic for several reasons. First, it may undermine the use of health services in the future. Patients whose emotional needs are not met in their interactions with physicians are less likely to return to that physician in the future (Ware, Davies-Avery, & Stewart, 1978). Even more important, patients may not adopt the behaviors and treatments recommended by their practitioners.

Adherence to Medical Treatment

The seventeenth-century French playwright Molière aptly described the relationship that physicians and patients often have with respect to treatment recommendations:

> The King: You have a physician. What does he do?
>
> Molière: Sire, we converse. He gives me advice which I do not follow, and I get better.
>
> (Treue, 1958, p. 41, cited in Koltun & Stone, 1986)

Depending on the disorder and recommendation, nonadherence to treatment ranges from a low of 15 percent for such recommendations as tablets or ointments to a staggering high of 93 percent for life-style advice such as to stop smoking or lose weight (Davis, 1968; Turk & Meichenbaum, 1989).

Failure to follow medical advice can be traced to several factors. First, patients who are dissatisfied with the quality of their care may decide deliberately not to follow advice. Second, to follow through on a treatment, a patient must understand it, and often understanding is not achieved. Adherence is high when a patient receives a clear, jargon-free explanation of the origin, diagnosis, and treatment recommendations associated with the disorder (Hauenstein, Schiller, & Hurley, 1987). Adherence is also increased if the instructions are written down, if the patient has repeated back the instructions, if any unclear sections are clarified, and if the instructions are repeated more than once (DiNicola & DiMatteo, 1984). Unfortunately, these seemingly simple steps are often not followed.

The nature of the treatment also influences the patient's behavior. Complex treatments involving several medications are less likely to be taken as directed than treatments involving one medication (Blumenthal & Emery, 1988; Siegel, Grady, Browner, & Hulley, 1988). Patients are less likely to follow treatments that must be continued over several months than treatments that continue for just a few days; over time, adherence falls off. Treatments that interfere with regular life activities produce lower rates of adherence than those that can be implemented relatively easily (Kirscht & Rosenstock, 1979). For example, a patient who has been advised to rest in the middle of a busy working day might find it nearly impossible to do so (Turk & Meichenbaum, 1989).

Adherence is higher with treatments that seem "medical." For example, a patient is more likely to take a foul-tasting pill every three hours for three days than to rest, avoid stressful experiences, stop smoking, or lose weight. The reason is that patients may not see life-style recommendations as truly medical, and therefore may not follow through. They may believe that their social activities, the stressful nature of their work life, and whether or not they smoke are their own business and that the physician's job is restricted to providing "medical" treatments for diagnosable conditions.

Another reason why physicians' recommendations to alter life-style behaviors often show low rates of compliance is because these aspects of life are difficult to modify. As we noted earlier in the chapter, such stubborn health habits as overeating, smoking, or drinking to excess may have become habitual and may be tied to certain cues and stimuli in the social environment. These cues alone can maintain a behavior, even when the motivation to change the behavior is there.

Sometimes people experience *reactance,* a psychological state that results when people feel their freedoms have been arbitrarily restricted (Brehm, 1966; Brehm & Brehm, 1981). The withdrawal of freedom can be very threatening, especially when valued activities are involved. Many illnesses and treatments have precisely these effects. For example, being put on bed rest by a physician may seem like an arbitrary and useless step to you. It may also cause you to miss a midterm and several weekend parties. Under such circumstances, adherence is low, both because the treatment recommendations threaten freedoms and because personal frustration can result when one is unable to do what one wishes (Leigh & Reiser, 1986; Rhodewalt & Strube, 1985; Rhodewalt & Marcroft, 1988).

Improving Patient–Practitioner Communication

How can we improve patient–practitioner communication? Training practitioners to communicate effectively is a good way to begin. For example, in medical school, physicians may be trained how to provide information to patients in a manner that is comprehensible and jargon-free without being simpleminded. Training programs also stress the importance of communicating information clearly and asking the patient to repeat the information to be certain that the patient has understood it. Methods of communicating warmth and friendliness to a patient through such simple nonverbal behaviors as smiling, leaning forward, or shaking hands can also help improve the communication process (DiMatteo, Friedman, & Taranta, 1979; DiMatteo, Hays, & Prince, 1986).

Training physicians in the effective use of techniques of social influence identified in Chapter 8 can also improve the communication process and ultimately increase adherence to treatment (Rodin & Janis, 1979). Physicians are high-status people and have a high degree of authority by virtue of their medical expertise. This type of power is termed *legitimate* power. But doctors can also draw on their *referent power* by becoming significant individuals in their patients' lives. If the patient feels that the physician's approval and acceptance are rewarding, then the practitioner has an additional mode of influence. When the practitioner is able to use both referent power and legitimate power, adherence is increased (Janis, 1983; Raven, 1988; Rodin & Janis, 1979).

Physicians are also in a unique position to influence a patient's behavior because they interact on a one-to-one basis with the patient (Raven, 1988). Health recommendations can be tailored to the individual needs and vulnerabilities of that particular patient. These conditions maximize attitude and behavior change. For example, patients who are told by their physicians that they are particularly vulnerable to lung cancer by virtue of their smoking are more likely to stop than in response to other health communications about smoking such as mass media campaigns (Pederson, 1982). The face-to-face interaction provides an effective setting for holding the patient's attention, repeating and clarifying instructions, extracting commitments from the patient to adhere to the treatment, and assessing any possible sources of resistance to compliance. Thus, for example, the patient for whom bed rest was recommended can explain to the physician about the importance of midterms and not missing social activities, and the patient and physician together may be able to work out a compromise. Finally, because of the face-to-face situation and the likelihood of additional visits, the physician has the patient under surveillance at least to some degree and can monitor progress during subsequent visits.

In summary, then, the processes of diagnosis, treatment recommendations, and following through on treatment are clearly social-psychological ones. Information must be effectively communicated for a patient to adhere to treatment, and effective techniques of social influence can help instill the desire to follow through on treatments.

Psychological Control and Adjustment to Treatment

As has already been noted, feelings of control over one's health and treatment regimen appear to be important for health behaviors and adherence to treatment. So important is control that many psychologists have used it to design interventions with medical patients. The idea is that if patients are given a sense of control during an unpleasant medical procedure, it will enable them to adjust to that procedure more successfully than if they do not have such feelings of control. A substantial amount of research now indicates that when medical patients anticipating noxious procedures are informed about steps they can take either to control the unpleasantness of the procedure or to control their own reactions to it, they show fewer signs of distress and adjust more successfully to the procedures (Averill, 1983; Fiske & Taylor, 1984; Miller, 1979; Thompson, 1981).

Feelings of *psychological control* appear to affect not only adjustment to specific unpleasant medical procedures, but also health more generally. This point was dramatically illustrated in a study of nursing home residents by Langer and Rodin (1976). The purpose of the study was to see if the introduction of an element of control into a nursing home environment could improve the morale and health of these institutionalized elderly people.

Patients on one floor were given small plants to care for (behavior control); they were also asked to choose when they wished to participate in some of the nursing home activities (decision control). Patients on a comparison floor were also given plants, but they were told that the

When people are given control over certain aspects of their daily activities, even simply caring for a small plant, their morale and health may be improved. This is especially important in institutional environments, such as nursing homes, where loss of personal control may be substantial.

staff would care for them. They participated in the same activities as the first group of patients, but they were assigned to times rather than being able to choose those times.

Several weeks later, nurses rated the mood and activity level of the patients, patients reported their own mood, and behavioral measures of patients' activity levels were collected. The results revealed that the patients who had been given some control were more active and had a greater sense of well-being than were those on the comparison floor. A year later, those patients were psychologically and physically healthier than were the patients who had not received the interventions designed to enhance feelings of control (Rodin & Langer, 1977).

The importance of feelings of control is well illustrated by this study, because the control-enhancing manipulations were actually quite modest. The study illustrates how powerful and helpful the variable of psychological control can be, and how it can have a long-term effect on major health outcomes.

SOCIAL PSYCHOLOGICAL PERSPECTIVES ON CHRONIC ILLNESS

At any given time, 50 percent of the population has some chronic condition that requires medical management (Cole, 1974). This includes major conditions such as cancer or heart disease, as well as more minor ones such as a partial hearing loss or recurrent episodes of herpes. Perhaps a more startling statistic is that most of us will eventually develop at least one chronic disability or disease that may alter our daily lives for many years and ultimately be the cause of our death. As we noted at the beginning of this chapter, chronic illness now accounts for the major health problems in this country, and these are conditions with which people often live for many years. Precisely because chronic diseases are chronic, they often have a major impact on the social and psychological lives of these patients. The impact of chronic illness is a relatively new area of investigation for social psychologists, and consequently there is much work to be done in understanding exactly what the psychosocial effects of the various chronic diseases are. A beginning effort toward such understanding has been made in several specific areas.

Illness Cognitions

Researchers have noted that most people suffering from chronic illness develop theories about where their illnesses came from (e.g., Meyerowitz, 1980; Schain, 1976). Such theories about the origins of chronic illness include stress, physical injury, disease-causing bacteria, and God's will. Of perhaps greater interest is where patients ultimately place the blame for ill-

ness. Do they blame themselves, another person, the environment, or a quirk of fate?

Self-blame for illness is widespread. Patients frequently perceive themselves as having brought on their own illnesses by engaging in bad health practices such as smoking or even just by exposing themselves to stress. What are the consequences of self-blame? Unfortunately, a definitive answer to this question is not yet available. Some researchers have suggested that self-blaming patients may adjust poorly to their illness because they focus on things they could have done or should have done to prevent it (see Krantz & Deckel, 1983). Other researchers have suggested that self-blame may sometimes be adaptive, because it leads people to believe they have control over the illness in the future (Bulman & Wortman, 1977). It may be that self-blame is adaptive for some disorders and not others (Taylor, Lichtman, & Wood, 1984).

It does appear, however, that individuals who blame other people for their disorders often adjust more poorly (Taylor et al., 1984; Bulman & Wortman, 1977). Perhaps poorly adjusted people single out others to blame for their illness, or it may be that by blaming other people, these patients adjust less well to their illness because of the unresolved anger and hostility they experience toward those whom they believe to be responsible for their illness (see Downey, Silver, & Wortman, 1990).

Researchers have also examined whether patients who believe they can control their illnesses are better adjusted than are those who do not see their illnesses as under personal control. Patients develop a number of control-related beliefs with respect to chronic illness. They may believe, as do many cancer patients, that they can prevent a recurrence of the disease through good habits or even sheer force of will (Taylor, Helgeson, Reed, & Skokan, 1991). Heart patients or patients suffering from multiple sclerosis may believe that by avoiding stressful situations, they will avoid exacerbating their disorder. We have already noted that feelings of personal control appear to be adaptive in the practice of preventive health behavior, illness-related behaviors, and adjustment to medical procedures. Self-generated feelings of control also appear to be adaptive for chronically ill patients. For example, breast cancer patients who believe that they had some control over their illness were better adjusted to their cancer than were patients without such beliefs (Taylor et al., 1984; Taylor et al., 1991).

Chronic Disease and Patients' Changing Lives

A chronic disease like cancer or diabetes can affect all aspects of a patient's life. Work may be threatened or terminated by the need for extensive treatments or by the debilitating side effects of the disorder. The patient's psychological state is almost certainly affected. The diagnosis of a chronic illness can produce extreme fear and anxiety or depression, as the patient realizes that his or her life activities may be permanently curtailed by the disorder (Burish & Bradley, 1983; Taylor & Aspinwall, 1990). In addition, many patients need to learn a complex variety of self-care activities to aid in the management of their disorders (e.g., Toobert & Glasgow, 1991).

Because of physical changes that occur, loss of income due to job restriction, or the need for help from others, the entire family and even friends are often affected by one individual's experience of chronic illness (Turk & Kerns, 1985). A patient's spouse may suddenly have to take on additional responsibilities that once fell to the partner who is now ill. Young children are sometimes forced into taking on more responsibilities than would normally be expected for their age group. Often, then, it is not just the patient who may experience psychosocial difficulties, but also the spouse, children, and others who must adjust to these changes (Coyne & Smith, 1991).

Problems in social communication and social support can also arise. For example, Wortman and Dunkel-Schetter (1979) have suggested that cancer patients are sometimes inadvertently treated badly by their family members and friends. Cancer can create conflicting reactions in family and friends. Feelings of fear and aver-

sion to cancer develop because the disease is so frightening to most people. But most people also believe appropriate behavior toward cancer patients requires a cheerful, optimistic front, so the patient will feel better. The conflict between these reactions may produce ambivalence toward the patient and anxiety about interacting with him or her. Consequently, family and friends may physically avoid the cancer patient or may avoid open communication about the disease (Dakof & Taylor, 1990). These discrepancies in behavior (i.e., positive verbal but negative nonverbal behavior) can create confusion and upset, as we saw in Chapter 2, and can lead the patient to feel rejected or abandoned by loved ones. Sometimes family members develop their own opinions about how a patient should behave and criticize the patient if he or she does not cope in this way. Such spousal criticism can interfere with coping and psychological adjustment (Manne & Zautra, 1989).

So far, we have focused primarily on the problems and stressors created by chronic disease. This focus obscures an important point, namely, that chronic disease can confer positive as well as negative outcomes. In one study (Collins, Taylor, & Skokan, 1990), over 90 percent of cancer patients reported at least some beneficial changes in their lives as a result of the cancer. These patients reported an increased ability to appreciate each day and the inspiration to do things now instead of postponing them. In terms of relationships, these patients reported that they were putting more effort into their relationships and deriving more pleasure from them. They believed that they had acquired more awareness of others' feelings and more sympathy and compassion for others. They reported feeling stronger, more self-assured, and more compassionate toward the unfortunate. Similar results have been reported for patients who have had heart attacks (Laerum, Johnsen, Smith, & Larsen, 1987; Waltz, 1986), AIDS (Reed, 1989) and physical disabilities (Elliott, Witty, Herrick, & Hoffman, 1991). What seems evident, then, is that sometimes people are able to derive value and benefits from a chronic illness experience while simultaneously accommodating their lives to the

A chronic illness affects not only the patient's life, but the lives of family and often friends as well.

adverse changes posed by disease. Thus, while chronic disease can be a trying and unpleasant experience, it can also be an enobling one, allowing people to derive meaning from their lives (Taylor, 1983).

To summarize, because people often live with chronic illnesses for long periods of time, thes illnesses may pervade all aspects of their lives. Until relatively recently, the health care community largely ignored the changes in self-concept, personal relationships, and work that can result from chronic disease. However, health psychologists are now beginning to examine not only the social and psychological factors that give rise to these chronic conditions, but also those that follow from them. Through such efforts, there is hope that health can be improved by keeping those who are currently healthy in good health and by ameliorating the life circumstances of those who have developed illnesses.

KEY TERMS

biopsychosocial model
broad-spectrum cognitive-
  behavioral therapy
coping
dispositional optimism
hardiness

health behavior
health belief
psychological control
reasoned action model
relapse prevention
self-monitoring

social support
stress
stressful life event
type A behavior

SUMMARY _____

1. Health psychology examines the role of psychological factors in the promotion and maintenance of health; the prevention and treatment of illness; the identification of causes and correlates of health, illness, or dysfunction; and the improvement of the health care system and health policy formation.

2. The major health problems of our country involve life-style disorders, including cancer, diabetes, heart disease, drug and alcohol abuse, and vehicular accidents. Life-style disorders are preventable and can potentially be influenced by psychological interventions.

3. Attitude-change techniques have been applied to understanding the practice of health behaviors. Whether or not a person practices a health behavior depends on general health values, the perceived threat of the particular health hazard, the perceived severity of that hazard, the perceived effectiveness of the particular health practice, and a sense of self-efficacy that one can undertake the recommended health practice. Overall, however, attitudinal approaches to the modification of health behaviors have had fairly modest effects.

4. Increasingly, psychologists have drawn upon cognitive-behavioral analyses of health habits to understand the specific stimuli in an environment and the health cognitions that control health habits. Modification of these stimuli and cognitions may encourage the development of more healthy behaviors.

5. Stress is a major health issue, because it causes psychological distress and because it can have an adverse effect on health. Stress, however, is not intrinsic to situations, but is rather the consequence of a person's appraisal processes. Negative, uncontrollable, and ambiguous events are most likely to be perceived as stressful.

6. Coping consists of problem-solving efforts and efforts at emotional regulation that attempt to reduce the stress of stressful events. Coping resources and liabilities include coping style, social support, time, money, and the presence of other stressful events in one's life. Stress management programs help people to make more effective use of their coping resources in dealing with stressful events.

7. The recognition and interpretation of symptoms are influenced by social-psychological factors. When attention is directed outward, people are less likely to notice symptoms than when attention is directed inward. The interpretation of symptoms is influenced by prior expectations, experience, and illness schemas. Communications with others are influential in whether or not people seek treatment for symptoms.

8. Adherence to treatment is often very low, in part because of communication difficulties between patient and practitioner. Practitioners often provide jargon-filled and simplistic explanations, whereas patients are guilty of not learning or following through on treatment recommendations. Interventions that draw on principles of social influence can help improve this situation.

9. Interventions that utilize the principle of psychological control with patients awaiting noxious medical procedures have been very successful in helping patients adjust to these procedures.

10. Adjustment to chronic illness depends in part on the cognitions people have about their illness, such as its cause and whether they feel they can control it.

11. Communication problems between chronically ill patients and their family members often occur. Friends and family members may not understand or may be unable to meet the communication needs of chronically ill patients who have to work through the impact that the illness is having on their lives.

12. Chronic illness can provide meaning and value to patients even as it also produces adverse changes and poses problems of adjustment.

SUGGESTED READINGS _____

Burish, T. G., & Bradley, L. A. (Eds.) (1983). *Coping with chronic disease: Research and applications.* New York: Academic Press. This edited collection describes the difficulties and issues confronted by patients facing a variety of specific chronic diseases.

Rodin, J., & Salovey, P. (1989). Health psychology. *Annual Review of Psychology, 40,* 533–579. A scholarly review of recent trends in the field of health psychology.

Taylor, S. E. (1991). *Health psychology* (2nd ed.). New York: Random House. A readable and comprehensive introduction to the field of health psychology.

16
The Environment

FOCUS OF THIS CHAPTER

Human Spatial Behavior
Crowding
Environmental Stress: Noise
Architectural Design

Cultural Highlight
Too Close for Comfort

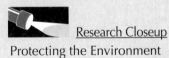
Research Closeup
Protecting the Environment

People are becoming more and more concerned about the environment. In 1992, world leaders met in Brazil for the first global "Earth Summit" to discuss ways to protect the natural environment and use it wisely. The environmental movement has focused attention on the quality of the air we breathe and the water we drink. The nightly news raises questions about the possible destruction of the ozone layer, or the impact of the destruction of the South American rain forest on weather around the globe. Citizens are beginning to realize that virtually all aspects of the world around us can have profound and potentially negative effects on our health and well-being.

Psychologists are also concerned about how the environment affects people. Just as toxic chemicals in the air and the ground can damage physical health, so other characteristics of the environment can damage mental and social health. Noise pollution, urban crowding, and poorly designed buildings all influence the quality of our lives and our day-to-day functioning.

Environmental psychology is the branch of psychology that focuses on the relationship between the physical environment and human behavior and well-being (Saegert & Winkel, 1990; Stokols & Altman, 1987). In this chapter, we review some of the major findings of environmental psychology. We begin with a consideration of the ways in which people use the space around them to control their interactions with other people. Research on spatial behavior helps to explain such everyday events as the home field advantage in sports. Next we turn to two potentially harmful aspects of the environment—crowding and noise pollution. Then we examine how the physical design of classrooms, dormitories, and apartment buildings affects the people who use them.

HUMAN SPATIAL BEHAVIOR

How do people use the space around them to regulate their social interactions? This is one of the questions asked by environmental researchers, who use the term **proxemics** to refer to the study of human spatial behavior (Hall, 1959). A key idea is that individuals try to achieve an optimal degree of involvement and physical closeness with other people, depending on the specific situation. In other words, our use of space is one way of influencing our interaction with other people (Richmond, McCroskey, & Payne, 1991a). We will consider two issues in more detail: personal space and territoriality.

Personal Space

Suppose you are standing by yourself in a physician's waiting room, and the nurse walks up to you. How close does the nurse actually come? Three inches? Ten inches? Two feet? Suppose you are sitting on a park bench, and a well-dressed man sits down immediately next to you. How does that make you feel? Would you feel differently if he sat five feet away? How close to other people do you usually stand? Does it make any difference if they are friends, strangers, or members of your family? Does it make any difference if you are standing at a party, on a bus, or in line at the post office?

As these examples suggest, people have various preferred distances for social interaction, depending on who they are with and the activity. People treat the physical space immediately around them as though it were a part of themselves; this zone has been called their **personal space.** According to Sommer (1969), "Personal space refers to an area with an invisible boundary surrounding the person's body into which intruders may not come. Like [porcupines], people like to be close enough to obtain warmth and comradeship but far enough away to avoid pricking one another" (p. 26). In social interactions, people try to maintain an acceptable balance between being too close for comfort and being awkwardly distant.

Personal space is often measured by the physical distance a person maintains from others. But personal space involves much more than physical distance. At very close distances, we can touch and smell another person, talk in hushed whispers, and see their features very clearly. At far distances, we may need to talk loudly, and we have quite different possibilities for social contact.

Anthropologist Edward Hall (1966) proposed that there are four basic zones for interpersonal interaction, shown in Figure 16-1. These range from the very close "intimate distance" of a lovers' embrace to the "public distance" between a speaker and the audience in a large auditorium. According to Hall, the social situation determines which of these zones people prefer. Intimate and personal distance are typically used for informal interactions with friends, family, or close associates. Social and public distances are used for more formal interactions among casual acquaintances or strangers.

Research has generally supported Hall's basic idea (Aiello, 1987; Burgoon, 1991). For instance, friends prefer to stand closer together than do strangers (Ashton, Shaw, & Worsham, 1980), and people who want to seem friendly choose smaller distances (Patterson & Sechrest, 1970). People who are sexually attracted to each other also stand close (Allgeier & Byrne, 1973). Although people do not usually think much about personal space, we are nonetheless aware of the unwritten rules about space use in our culture. Research on cultural differences in the use of space is discussed in the CULTURAL HIGHLIGHT.

A recent application of personal space research occurred in a controversial court case in Boulder, Colorado (Hern, 1991). In Boulder, anti-abortion activists had been protesting daily at abortion clinics. Their activities included

Figure 16-1 Basic zones of interpersonal interaction. (*Source:* Adapted from *The Hidden Dimension* by Edward T. Hall, copyright © 1966, 1982 by Edward T. Hall. Used by permission of Doubleday, a division of Bantam Doubleday Dell Publishing Group, Inc.)

walking within a few inches of patients entering the clinic, offering them literature, and saying such things as "Don't murder your baby." Supporters of the clinic argued that these activities were intimidating, in part because they violated the patients' personal space. Clinic staff reported that patients were often shaken with fear and anger from these face-to-face encounters

According to Edward Hall, there are distinct zones for interpersonal distance. Lovers maintain "intimate distance" of less than 18 inches. A friendly conversation takes place at a "personal distance" of 18 inches to 4 feet. We use "social distance" of 4 to 7 feet for a formal business meeting.

with strangers. Because of the stress created by these invasions of personal space, they asked the City Council to pass an ordinance guaranteeing patients an 8-foot "buffer zone" for entry to clinics. At court hearings, Edward Hall was called as an expert witness on personal space. Drawing on research findings, he testified that violations of personal space by strangers do break social conventions, would normally be interpreted as a threat, and would be highly distressing. Based on this and other expert testimony, the court ruled that the city could establish a buffer zone to protect the personal space of clinic patients.

Territorial Behavior

People often lay claim to a particular place as "theirs." Have you ever arrived at the library to study for a test only to find that every seat is taken? Some seats are physically occupied, and the rest are "staked out" with coats, books, briefcases, and other markers. In such a situa-

tion, you might consider whether or not to move someone's belongings and take the chair, but probably think better of it, not wanting to face an argument.

A **territory** is an area controlled by a specific individual or group. Psychologist Irwin Altman (1975) has distinguished three main types of human territories: primary, secondary, and public. Territories differ in the degree of control and ownership exerted by particular individuals. As described in Table 16-1, a primary territory such as a home or private office is clearly under personal control. A secondary territory such as a dormitory lounge, sorority house, or school cafeteria may be used regularly by members of a group. In contrast, a public territory such as a seat in an airport waiting room or on a city bus is available to all interested parties on a first-come basis.

Territorial behaviors are actions designed to stake out or mark a territory and to claim ownership. Whereas personal space is physically connected to a person—a distance from the per-

CULTURAL HIGHLIGHT
Too Close for Comfort

If you have traveled much outside the United States, you have no doubt noticed that people in other countries differ in how close they like to be while talking. People in some cultures stand and sit closer together than you are accustomed to, whereas people in other cultures maintain a greater distance (Richmond, McCroskey, & Payne, 1991c). Cultural norms determine typical personal space preferences. For example, one study found that when college students talked to a stranger from their own culture, Japanese students sat about 40 inches apart, Americans sat 35 inches apart, and Venezuelans sat the closest at 32 inches (Sussman & Rosenfeld, 1982). In general, white North Americans, the English, and Scandinavians prefer the greatest conversational distances; southern Europeans prefer closer distances; and Latin Americans and Arabs prefer the closest conversational distance (Little, 1968; Sommer, 1969). Although much observation remains to be done around

the world, clear cultural patterns have been found.

These cultural differences might be considered a piece of interesting but trivial information if it were not for the fact that preferences in personal distance can sometimes have important consequences. People from cultures with different preferences may misinterpret one another's actions. Consider, for example, the possible miscommunication between a white American businessman and a Pakistani businessman when they stand next to each other to talk. The American likes to stand about three or four feet away, whereas the Pakistani would ordinarily stand much closer. Obviously, they cannot both have their way. If they are unaware of the cultural difference, they may execute a little dance around the room. The Pakistani feels uncomfortably far away and moves closer. The American feels uncomfortably close and retreats, which in turn causes the Pakistani to move closer again. Moreover, as this is going on,

the Pakistani may feel that the American is being cold and unfriendly, while the American thinks the Pakistani is being overly intimate and pushy.

The use of personal space can vary not only across cultures, but also within a culture. In the United States, Anglo Americans tend to maintain greater distances than Latino Americans. In one study, for example, pairs of grade school children were observed on a school playground (Aiello & Jones, 1971). Puerto Rican children stood closer than did Anglo kids. As you may have guessed, men and women also tend to use personal space somewhat differently. Pairs of women stand closer together than do pairs of men, and women often tend to stand closer to whomever they are with (Aiello, 1987).

Norms about the use of personal space are part of the unwritten rules of every social group. Rules such as these are one element of our cultural heritage.

son's body to that of other people—territories do not necessarily require physical presence. As the library example suggests, people often try to guard their territory from intrusion while they are absent.

TERRITORIAL MARKERS. One interesting research topic has been the way people mark and personalize their territories (Brown, 1987). **Territorial markers** often serve a protective function. They let others know that a particular

area is claimed. In a study of behavior in the library, Becker (1973) found that people were least likely to select a table that was physically occupied by another person. Not surprisingly, physical presence is a strong marker. But people were also discouraged by the presence of books and personal belongings on a table; the more markers present, the greater the avoidance. Another illustration of territorial markers is the graffiti used by urban gangs to identify their "turf" (Ley & Cybriwski, 1974).

TABLE 16-1
Three Major Types of Human Territories

Type	Characteristics
Primary	A space that is owned and used exclusively by an individual or group, often on a long-term basis. For example, a house or apartment is clearly owned by a person or family, controlled on a relatively permanent basis, and important in their daily lives. Unwelcome intrusions into a primary territory are a serious matter.
Secondary	A space that is used regularly, but shared with others. For example, you may always take the same seat in your chemistry lab and get annoyed if someone else sits in it before you arrive, but you know that the space is not exclusively yours. Secondary territories are semi-public, and so there is more ambiguity of ownership and control.
Public	Places such as a park or airport waiting lounge where everyone presumably has an equal right of access. For example, we may stake out a spot on the beach with a blanket and umbrella, but we know our claim is temporary; getting a choice spot depends on getting there ahead of the other beachgoers. Public territories provide little if any personal control or privacy.

A study in a game arcade found that body gestures can serve as territorial markers (Werner, Brown, & Damron, 1981). A confederate stood by an electronic game called Space Invaders. The researchers varied how far the confederate stood from the machine, and whether or not the confederate placed a hand on the edge of the machine. The confederate never touched the actual controls. New players were significantly less likely to approach the machine when the confederate stood close and when he touched the machine. In public settings where it is not possible to use permanent markers, touch and physical proximity may be subtle signs of temporary "ownership."

THE FUNCTIONS OF TERRITORIAL BEHAVIOR. Territorial behaviors help us to regulate social interaction and can serve many specific functions (Brown, 1987). Territorial rules can simplify and bring order to daily interactions. For instance, when family members share bedrooms, they usually designate some areas for personal use. Each person has his or her own part of the closet, dresser, or side of the bed (Altman, Nelson, & Lett, 1972). Family members tend to have fixed places at the dinner table, places that are changed only when individuals eat alone or when guests are present.

Territoriality also contributes to the maintenance of privacy, that is, our control over the information others have about us and the extent to which social contact occurs. The teenager who plasters his bedroom door with signs saying "Off Limits" and "Keep Out" is guarding his privacy. So, too, are business executives who hold confidential meetings behind closed doors. The goal of territorial behavior is not necessarily to be alone, but rather to *control* access to oneself and one's property.

Finally, territorial behaviors communicate information about ourselves to other people. The rose-covered white picket fence surrounding a suburban house marks the property line, but it also conveys an image of the owners. Territorial markers often reflect an individual's personality or interests. In one study, photographs were taken of the wall decorations in dorm rooms of newly entering first-year university students (Vinsel, Brown, Altman, & Foss, 1980). Virtually all students hung at least one object, such as a poster or photograph, on the wall by the bed. Women were more likely than men to use relationship items, such as personal photos; men were more likely to use impersonal items, such as a sports poster. Differences were also found between the markers of students who later dropped out of the university and those who remained in school. The decorations of continuing students showed more identification with the new school and community, such as school posters and maps of the local area. The

We use territorial markers to claim a particular space and also to personalize an area. The two sisters who share this bedroom have each marked their own half of the room.

displays of dropouts suggested a greater commitment to past life and families.

THE HOME FIELD ADVANTAGE. In competitive sports, teams usually do better when playing at home than on the road. This "home field advantage" has been documented both in the United States and in Europe, and for a variety of team sports (Glamser, 1990). For example, a study of professional basketball, baseball, and football teams found that all teams won a greater percentage of their home games than games played elsewhere (Hirt & Kimble, 1981). The home field advantage was most striking for basketball, where professional teams won about 65 percent of home games but only 35 percent of away games. An analysis of the 1976–77 National Basketball Association season found that even teams that finished last in their division won nearly 60 percent of their home games (Watkin, 1978). And even the most powerful division champions performed relatively poorly on the road. Schwartz and Barsky (1977) have concluded that playing at home is as strong a factor in a team's performance as the quality of the players.

Why is it better to play on your home territory? Greater familiarity with the home field and the fatigue of travel may contribute, but they are not the whole answer (Schwartz & Barsky, 1977). Psychological factors are also involved. Territorial dominance may be one explanation: Home teams may do better because they are on their own turf. An even more important factor concerns the spectators. Teams usually have more fans on hand for home games than for away games. So a team playing at home can usually expect approval and support from the spectators (Sanna & Shotland, 1990). In contrast, visitors may feel wary and inhibited, and expect the audience to be unsupportive or even hostile. According to Schwartz and Barsky (1977), encouragement from an audience is most effective when it is sustained for some time and when the audience is most compact or close together. This may explain why the home team advantage is most pronounced for indoor sports such as basketball, where spectators are in a small enclosed space, rather than for outdoor games such as football, which are played in large arenas.

An interesting reversal of the home field advantage has been documented by Baumeister and Steinhilber (1984). They proposed that when a team is on the brink of winning a championship, playing before a supportive audience may lead to increased self-attention that can impair performance. In a final, decisive game, playing at home may cause players to "choke." To support their claim, the researchers examined records for baseball World Series games and for national basketball championships. Consistent with previous research, they found that playing at home was an advantage for games early in the season. But at the end of the season, teams did worse when they played at home. For example, home baseball teams won 60 percent of the first two games in the World Series, but won only 41 percent of the final games. Although playing at home is often an advantage, it may become a disadvantage when the pressure to win is greatest.

DEFENDING AND SHARING SPACE. Both personal space and territorial behaviors are used to control social interaction. On the one hand, we want to defend ourselves and our territory from unwanted "invasions." But equally important, we often want to share ourselves and our space with friends and loved ones. Thus, our reaction to someone who enters our space can vary greatly, depending on the way we define the situation.

Our attributions about the other person's

motives—whether we interpret the actions as friendly, rude, or possibly even dangerous—are important. When we perceive a person's presence as an intrusion, we can either leave the situation or defend our turf. A study by Koneci and his associates (1975) illustrates the reaction of flight. They had a confederate stand very close to a person who was waiting on a corner to cross the street. In this situation, people apparently interpreted the stranger's behavior as an unwelcome invasion and crossed the street much faster than usual to escape from the stranger's presence.

At other times, however, people defend their territory and resist encroachments by others. For example, one study observed the reactions of people using public telephones (Ruback, Pape, & Doriot, 1989). People talked significantly *longer* if another person approached and stood waiting to use the phone, than if no "intruder" was present. A similar effect was found for people browsing in the open stacks of a university library. Individuals who were looking at books in a particular aisle stayed longer if another person appeared than if they were alone—a reaction consistent with the idea of defending one's space (Ruback, 1987).

Another experiment investigated the effect of having a stranger ask permission to sit next to a person (Sundstrom & Sundstrom, 1977). Confederates approached a same-sex stranger sitting on a public bench. Before sitting down, half the confederates asked permission—they asked whether it was okay if they sat down on the bench. The other half of the time, the confederates sat down without asking permission. It appears that women and men interpreted this situation quite differently. Women seem to have interpreted the request for permission as the beginning of an unwanted social contact. They left sooner when the confederate asked permission than when the confederate did not. In contrast, men seemed to have interpreted the request for permission as a sign of politeness. Men who were asked permission stayed on the bench longer than men who were not asked. The point is that our reaction to others who enter our space depends on how we interpret the situation and the person's motives.

When physical space is limited and we are forced to share it with others, we may feel crowded. The experience of crowding has been an important research topic in environmental psychology.

CROWDING

Rush-hour commuters crammed into a bus are likely to feel crowded. So, too, are holiday shoppers swarming down the escalators of a department store and competing for the attention of a sales clerk. Feeling crowded can occur regardless of the amount of space we actually have available. It is more likely to be aroused when we are physically cramped, but we sometimes feel crowded even when we have plenty of space around us. There are times when three is a crowd, no matter how much space is available. If you like to swim at deserted beaches, the presence of a few other people may make you feel that the beach is overcrowded, whereas you might not feel crowded at a party even if there are fifty other people in a fairly small room. **Crowding** refers to the psychological state of discomfort and stress associated with wanting more space than is available.

Researchers who study crowding find it essential to distinguish between subjective feelings of being crowded and objective measures of population density. **Social density** refers to the objective number of people in a given space. Density might be measured in terms of the number of people per square foot. In contrast, crowding is the subjective experience of feeling cramped and not having enough space. High social density may or may not be unpleasant,

When we must share limited space with others, we often feel unpleasantly crowded. Here, opera enthusiasts jam the lobby and staircases to leave the Metropolitan Opera House at the end of a performance.

but crowding is always unpleasant and negative, by definition. When we say we feel "crowded," we are usually complaining.

Psychological Factors in Crowding

When do people experience the presence of others as crowding? A number of theories emphasize cognitive processes, that is, the way people perceive, interpret, and react to their social environment.

SENSORY OVERLOAD. Stanley Milgram (1970) proposed that whenever people are exposed to too much stimulation, they experience sensory overload. Social density is one source of stimulation that can sometimes produce overstimulation and feelings of being crowded. Milgram believed that sensory overload is always unpleasant and interferes with a person's ability to function properly. People deal with overload by screening out some of the stimulation and attending only to what is most important to them.

Individual differences in reactions to social density may reflect differences in preferred level of stimulation. Some people may like high levels of stimulation—they like the radio blaring all the time, prefer to study in busy rooms, and watch television while carrying on a conversation or doing a crossword puzzle. Others like low levels of stimulation. When they work, it has to be quiet; if they watch television, they do not want any distraction. For high-stimulation people, high social density may be the right level of stimulation and so be perceived as pleasant and exciting. In contrast, for low-stimulation people, high social density may be disruptive and so be perceived as crowding. Research provides support for the importance of sensory overload, but suggests that other factors are also important (Baum & Paulus, 1987).

LOSS OF CONTROL. High social density can make people feel they have lost control over their actions (Baron & Rodin, 1978). The idea is that with so many people in a confined space, each individual is less able to control the situation, to move around freely, or to avoid undesired contact. This results in feeling crowded.

This loss of control can have several negative features. In our culture, people often want to feel in control of their lives, so simply being unable to control the environment may, in itself, be negative. Further, high social density may prevent people from maintaining a desired degree of privacy (Altman, 1975). High density may also lead to problems in the coordination of activities. When three people share a small dorm room, they may literally bump into each other, and have trouble studying or sleeping without interruption. Under high-density conditions, people are more likely to interfere with each other's activities, leading to feelings of frustration and anger (Schopler & Stockdale, 1977).

Research has begun to provide evidence that a lack of perceived control produces the feeling of being crowded. For example, Sherrod (1974) had students work under high-density conditions and provided some with a button that, if pushed, would signal the experimenter to remove them from the situation. Although no one actually used the button, students who were given this sense of control over their environment were less negatively affected by the high-density environment.

ATTRIBUTIONS. A third explanation for crowding emphasizes causal attributions, a concept we first discussed in Chapter 4. According to Stephen Worchel and his colleagues, we feel crowded when we experience physiological arousal and attribute it to the excessive closeness of other people (Worchel & Teddie, 1976). In this view, the subjective experience of crowding requires two elements: A physiological state of arousal and a cognitive label attributing the arousal to the presence of too many people.

According to the attribution perspective, if people in a high-density situation can be induced to attribute their arousal to something other than the people present, they should feel less crowded. This point was demonstrated in a study by Worchel and Yohai (1979). All subjects were exposed to the same level of social density. Some were falsely told that they were being exposed to stressful "inaudible noise," and oth-

These winter campers are sharing a very small living space. What factors will determine whether or not the campers perceive their high-density environment as "crowded"?

ers were given no such information. Consistent with an attributional analysis, subjects who could blame their discomfort on "inaudible noise" reported feeling significantly less crowded than did subjects in the identical density situation who were given no alternative explanation for the source of their arousal.

In general, Worchel and his colleagues argue, when people can be distracted from focusing on the people present in a situation, they should feel less crowded (Webb, Worchel, Riechers, & Wayne, 1986). For example, when subjects in high-density conditions were exposed to arousing (humorous, sexual, or violent) television shows, they experienced significantly less crowding than did people watching a nonarousing program under the same conditions. Indeed, people in cramped quarters rated the humorous movie as funnier and the violent movie as more violent, and tended to enjoy the movies more.

It is likely that sensory overload, loss of control, and causal attributions can all play a part in producing the psychological experience of crowding.

Residential Density

In everyday life, there are many situations that can create feelings of crowding. The impact of living in very cramped spaces has been one important topic of inquiry in environmental psychology.

High residential density can sometimes have negative effects. Studies of cramped conditions in college dormitories and in prisons have found harmful effects of high-density living (Karlin, Epstein, & Aiello, 1978). For example, research at Rutgers University compared students living two to a room versus three to a room, all in rooms designed to hold two students. Tripled students reported significantly more stress and disappointment than doubled students. These effects were more severe for women, who attempted to make their cramped quarters into a homelike environment, than for men, who spent more time away from their rooms. Tripled students of both sexes got significantly lower grades. However, in later years when students were no longer living in high-density rooms, their grades improved. In another study, students in triple rooms reported feeling less control over their environment (Baron, Mandel, Adams, & Griffen, 1976), suggesting that this may be one reason for the negative effects of high-density dorms. Studies of prison inmates also show that higher density living is associated with more frequent health complaints and lower morale (McCain, Cox, & Paulus, 1980; Ruback & Innes, 1988).

On the other hand, there is abundant evidence that high residential density does not always lead to psychological distress. A dramatic demonstration of people's ability to cope successfully with high-density living comes from a case study of Peace Corps volunteers (MacDonald & Oden, 1973). In this study, five married couples agreed voluntarily to share an unpartitioned 30-by-30-foot room during the 12-week training program. The volunteers agreed to this experience in order to gain some insight into the hardships they might encounter once overseas. They were compared to other Peace Corps couples living in more spacious hotel rooms. Despite their very dense living conditions, the couples living communally showed no adverse effects and saw their experience as a positive challenge. They apparently developed high morale and a spirit of cooperation. Clearly, those who volunteered for the communal living arrangement may have had personalities different from those of the nonvolunteers, and they knew that the situation was only temporary. The point of the example, however, is that high-density living can be a positive experience under certain circumstances.

An impressive study of residential density was conducted by Mitchell (1971), who went into a vast number of homes in Hong Kong, one of the most crowded cities in the world. He measured the exact size of each family's living space, computed the density of people in the home, and took measures of anxiety, nervousness, and other symptoms of mental strain. In this study, a typical person shared a space of about 400 square feet with 10 or more people. Yet despite these cramped conditions, Mitchell found no appreciable relationship between density and pathology. Similar results were found in a study in Toronto, Canada (Booth, 1976). In more recent research, the effects of household density was investigated in both rural and urban India. No association was found between residential density and the quality of physical health, mental health, or social relationships. However, regardless of household density, individuals who experienced a greater sense of personal control over their environment reported better psychological adjustment (Ruback & Pandey, 1991).

In summary, the effects of cramped living quarters can be quite variable. High-density living conditions are often stressful and upsetting. These effects are minimized, however, when the crowding lasts for only a short time, when residents have a cooperative attitude, or when individuals perceive some degree of control over the environment (Baum & Paulus, 1987). At least some of the time, people are remarkably successful in adapting to high-density situations.

ENVIRONMENTAL STRESS: NOISE

The physical environment can be a major source of stress (Evans & Cohen, 1987). Some environmental stressors, such as earthquakes or floods, are sudden and powerful; they dramatically alter people's lives. Also important, however, are the daily hassles created by environments that expose us to noise, heat, air pollution, and other irritants. Much research on stress in the physical environment has studied the effects of noise, and we will focus our discussion on this topic.

Unless you are in a specially constructed soundproof chamber, you are always exposed to noise. For those with normal hearing, sound is one of the most important means of knowing about and experiencing the world. A silent world is virtually impossible to imagine. Psychologists are especially concerned about the effects of noise because so much of modern industrial life involves the production of noise, and because the amount of noise to which people are exposed in cities is often extremely high. Not only do traffic, construction, machinery of all kinds, and powerful stereo equipment produce noise of great intensity, but millions of people in a relatively small area can create high noise levels. Just what effect does noise have on us?

Adaptation to Short-term Noise

Sometimes we are exposed to short bursts of very loud noise—sounds of a car alarm going off or the shrill barking of a neighbor's dog. Our

Cities are noisy places. Today, the sound of music blaring from portable stereos often accompanies noise from cars, construction, and people.

initial reaction to a burst of very loud noise is strong. Everyone is familiar with one typical response, the so-called startle reflex. An unexpected loud noise causes us to jump, flex our stomach muscles, blink, and generally react physically (Jones & Broadbent, 1987). Even if we are expecting the noise, we respond physiologically with increased blood pressure, sweating, and other signs of arousal. In addition, loud noise interferes with our ability to perform tasks. We do less well on both simple and complex tasks. Loud noise is upsetting, causes physiological arousal, and prevents us from functioning at our usual level.

However, these disruptive effects generally last only a short while. The most important finding from studies of short-term noise is that people adapt very quickly. It takes only a few minutes for physiological reactions to disappear and for performance to return to normal. After 10 minutes or less, people who are subjected to short bursts of extremely loud noise behave very much like people who hear moderate or low noise. This is true even for noise levels over 100 decibels, which is roughly equivalent to a big jet coming in low over your head or a huge truck rumbling by right next to you. As long as the noise is not so loud that it actually produces pain or physical damage, people adapt to it very quickly.

You can see this effect in a study by Glass and Singer (1972) in which people worked on mental tasks in one of two conditions: Some subjects were exposed to background noise ("no noise" condition) and other subjects were exposed to a meaningless jumble of noise at 108 decibels in short bursts. As shown in Figure 16-2, the loud noise did cause physiological arousal, but the arousal lasted only a few minutes. Moreover, after four minutes, all subjects did equally well on a variety of mental tasks, including simple arithmetic, matching sets of numbers (deciding whether 68134 and 68243 are identical), scrambled words, and higher-level mathematics. Once they have adapted to the noise, people perform almost any task as well with loud noise as they do in quieter environments.

There are, however, a few important exceptions to this finding (Jones & Broadbent, 1987).

Figure 16-2 Physiological response to loud noise. After a strong initial response, subjects adapt quickly. (*Source:* Adapted from Glass & Singer, 1972.)

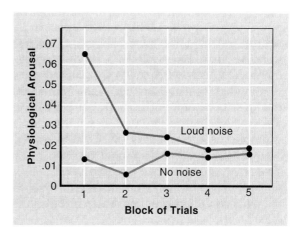

In particular, noise does seem to impair performance on some kinds of tasks, especially complex ones. Donald Broadbent (1957) and others have shown that certain kinds of monitoring tasks are more difficult to do with loud noise. For example, if someone is required to watch three dials to be sure none of them goes over a certain point, high levels of noise interfere with performance. Similarly, it is harder to do two tasks at the same time in a noisy environment. In one study, subjects had to repeat digits they heard over headphones while at the same time turning a steering wheel to track a moving line (Finkelman & Glass, 1970). Noise level did not affect the primary task, which was the tracking, but it made the subjects less accurate at repeating the digits. Presumably, noise is distracting and interferes with the performance of complex tasks that already strain our capacity to concentrate.

When we are only doing one thing at a time, the effects of noise are usually harmless. On the other hand, it is well to remember that some sensitive jobs do involve exactly the kinds of complex monitoring tasks that seem to be affected by loud noise. The pilot of a plane must watch many different dials while operating a variety of instruments; flight controllers have similar problems; and even the typical driver of a car has many things to attend to at once. It is a little frightening to realize that these critical jobs are often performed under conditions of considerable noise.

Finally, we have seen throughout this book that our reactions to situations are influenced by our ability to predict what will happen and to control it. This appears to be true of our reactions to noise. For example, a series of experiments by Glass and Singer (1972) demonstrated that loud noise may have negative aftereffects if the noise is not under the control of the individual. In particular, if the noise is predictable (for example, occurring every 60 seconds or only when there is a warning) or if the person can turn off the noise, no bad effects occur. But if the noise seems to be totally out of the control of the person, certain kinds of performance may suffer once the noise ceases.

HOW NOISE AFFECTS SOCIAL BEHAVIOR. In recent years, researchers have begun to investigate the impact of noise on social behaviors (Cohen & Weinstein, 1981). Noise appears to reduce attention to social cues. In one study, students watched slides while learning lists of nonsense syllables in a noisy or a quiet room (Cohen & Lezak, 1977). The slides showed people in common daily activities and in dangerous situations. For example, one slide showed two men shaking hands in front of a house; another slide showed one man threatening another with a knife in front of a house. After seeing the slides, students were unexpectedly asked questions about them. Those exposed to noise remembered significantly fewer slides than did those in the quiet condition. Similarly, in a field study pedestrians on noisy streets were less likely to notice unusual objects on the sidewalk (such as a woman holding a large teddy bear) than were pedestrians on a quiet street (Korte & Grant, 1980). In other words, loud noise may cause people to narrow the focus of their attention, and so they miss social cues in the environment.

In Chapter 13 on prosocial behavior, we describe several studies showing that people are less helpful in noisy situations than in quiet ones. There is also some evidence that noise can increase aggressiveness (Geen & O'Neal, 1969). In one study students were either angered or treated in a neutral manner, and then were given an opportunity to give electric "shocks" to another person as part of a learning experiment (Donnerstein & Wilson, 1976). Angered students in a noisy room gave significantly more shocks than did nonangered students or angered students in a quiet room.

A second experiment demonstrated that perceived control can alter the noise–aggression link (Donnerstein & Wilson, 1976). In this study, students first worked on math problems in a high-noise or no-noise condition. Later, students were able to give electric "shocks" to another person as part of a learning experiment. Some students had been angered by a confederate of the researcher; some had not. Students who had been exposed to loud noise and were angered gave more shocks than did those who had not been angered or who had not been exposed to the noise. However, angered students who had been able to control the loud noise (to turn it off if they wanted to) were no more aggressive than those not exposed to the noise, even when they did not actually use their control. These and other studies suggest that noise can sometimes increase aggressive behavior, but that this may occur only when people perceive no control over the noise and when they have an independent reason to be angry. In other words, noise may not be a direct cause of aggression, but rather may intensify preexisting aggressive tendencies or increase the tendency to express angry feelings.

Long-term Exposure to Noise

We are all exposed to brief bursts of loud noise from time to time, as a motorcycle zooms down the street or a dog barks nearby. But some people spend prolonged periods of time in very noisy environments, for instance, working in coal mines with loud machinery or under the flight path of jet planes. It has been estimated that roughly 10 million Americans have suffered permanent hearing loss as a result of exposure to loud noise (Leary, 1990). Industrial noise can be a major health hazard. Perhaps more surprising is evidence that young people can unknowingly injure their hearing by listening to music played at very loud levels (Lipscomb, 1982).

In addition to the physical harm created by long-term exposure to noise, research also finds detrimental psychological effects, and these may be especially harmful to children (Evans, Kliewer, & Martin, 1991). A large apartment house in New York City is built over a highway, and because of the design of the building, the noise levels inside are quite high. Lower floors are almost always noisier than higher ones, and this situation provides an ideal setting for a natural experiment on the effects of long-term noise. Cohen, Glass, and Singer (1973) measured reading achievement and ability to make auditory discriminations of children who had lived

in the building for at least four years. Those who lived on lower floors did worse on both measures. The louder the noise on their floor, the less well they read and the poorer their auditory discriminations. Other studies have also found that noisy environments can impair children's intellectual performance (Cohen, Evans, Krantz, Stokols, & Kelly, 1981).

Studies further suggest that although people are able to adapt to short-term noise, they may not adapt to long-term noise, such as that experienced by those who live near a busy airport (Cohen & Weinstein, 1981). Workers in noisy jobs are more prone to accidents, more likely to suffer from headaches, nausea, anxiety, and other symptoms of distress, and more likely to experience reduced productivity toward the end of their work day (Jones & Broadbent, 1987). Noise experts recommend that we take steps to limit the noise level in our environment. This can be done by reducing noise where it is produced, for instance by enclosing noisy equipment or using rubber pads on train tracks near homes. We can also protect ourselves from noise with earplugs, soundproofing in our homes and workplaces, and the use of other noise barriers. Other ways we can protect the environment are discussed in the RESEARCH CLOSEUP.

ARCHITECTURAL DESIGN

One of the most fascinating questions facing environmental psychologists is how the design of buildings, roads, and even shopping centers affects us. Certainly the structures we produce, known technically as the **built environment,** are an important part of our world. And some of them seem to "work" better than others (Richmond, McCroskey, & Payne, 1991b). Some homes are pleasant to be in and function smoothly, while others are drab and inconvenient. Some stores minimize congestion and generally make the shopping experience pleasant; others are cramped and uninviting.

Architects are concerned with making their designs work well, but by and large they have to rely entirely on their own intuition and expe-

Environmentalists urge us all to "reduce, reuse, and recycle" as a way to conserve natural resources. These teens are part of a recycling program for soft drink and other beverage containers.

rience. Until very recently there was no systematic research on how architectural designs affect people, and even now psychologists and sociologists are only beginning to study the problem seriously. But at least they are beginning to understand some of the ways in which designs influence people. For the moment, most of the research done by psychologists has been on the structure of college classrooms and dormitories (obviously of interest to many people at universities) and the design of high-rise versus low-rise housing.

Classroom Design

College classrooms are often drab and dreary places. Walls are painted a variation of "institutional gray," furniture is easy to clean, but uncomfortable and unattractive. Chairs are lined up in straight rows facing the teacher's desk or lectern. In one study, over 80 percent of university students rated their classrooms negatively, describing them as ugly, cramped, stuffy, and uncomfortable (Farrenkopf, 1974). Research by environmental psychologists is beginning to show that unattractive classrooms are not only unappealing; they may also adversely affect academic performance.

In a demonstration study by Sommer and Olsen (1980), a typical small classroom was converted into what the researcher called a "soft

classroom." Rows of chairs were replaced with cushioned benches around the walls, carpets were added, lighting was made softer, and colorful mobiles were hung. Students reacted enthusiastically with such comments as "It's dynamite!" or "I'm really impressed!" Comparisons of student behavior in the soft classroom and other classrooms on campus suggested that student participation in class discussion was two or three times greater in the more attractive room.

A more carefully controlled study of classroom environments was conducted by Wollin and Montage (1981). They selected two identical classrooms located side by side in the psychology building. The control classroom, which they called the "sterile classroom," had white walls, a gray carpet, and rows of plastic desks. The experimental classroom, which they called the "friendly classroom," was redecorated with the help of a design consultant. Several walls were painted bright colors, art posters were hung on the walls, large plants were added to the room, and colorful Chinese kites were hung from the ceiling. In addition to traditional desks, a part of the room was outfitted with area rugs, color-coordinated cushions, and wooded cubes to provide nontraditional seating.

The researchers investigated how these two different environments affected performance in actual college classes. Two professors teaching introductory psychology agreed to participate in

Many solutions to today's environmental problems require that people change their daily behavior (Stern, 1992). The slogan "reduce, reuse, recycle" highlights the benefits of consuming fewer resources, reusing products as long as possible, and recycling materials such as glass and aluminum. Many of the social psychological principles presented throughout this book are being used successfully to help people conserve natural resources.

When the University of California at Santa Cruz wanted undergraduates to conserve water by taking shorter showers, they posted signs in the men's shower rooms urging bathers to "(1) wet down, (2) turn water off, (3) soap up, (4) rinse off." But only 6 percent of students complied with the posted request. Psychologist Elliot Aronson (1990) used conformity pressure to improve matters dramatically. He had a research assistant wait in the shower room, poised to take a shower, until a student entered the room. Then the confederate showered, carefully following the instructions on the sign.

Nearly half of students who encountered this energy-conscious confederate followed the recommended procedures. When there were two water-saving confederates, compliance by students increased to 67 percent. The confederates provided models of energy-saving behavior and created a social norm about appropriate shower-room behavior. Under these conditions, most bathers conformed to the energy-saving group standard.

In another study, Aronson and Marti Gonzales (1990) worked with the Pacific Gas and Electric Company to improve their energy conservation program for homeowners. In the program, an expert visited homes to make suggestions about ways to save energy by insulating attics, weather-stripping drafty windows and doors, and so on. Alas, only 20 percent of homeowners who received this expert advice actually followed through with the suggested repairs. Aronson and Gonzalez proposed several ways to improve the program.

First, based on findings from social cognition research, homeowners should be given vivid, concrete, and personal information. For example, the staff expert might say:

> You know, if you were to add up all the cracks around and under these doors here, you'd have the equivalent of a hole the size of a basketball. . . . Think for a moment about all the heat that would escape from a hole that size. That's why I recommend you install weather-stripping. (p. 320)

Second, homeowners were asked to make a public commitment, so they would feel cognitive dissonance if they did not make repairs as promised. An expert might ask (p. 320), "When do you think you'll have the weather-stripping completed? . . . I'll give you a call around then, just to see how it's coming along."

Using these and other research-based principles, over 60 percent of homeowners were persuaded to follow through with energy saving home improvements. In sum, social psychological principles have proved to be handy tools in efforts to protect the physical environment.

These second graders spend many hours each day at school. How might the design of this classroom affect their school experience?

the study although they were not informed of the purpose of the research. When school began, each class was randomly assigned to one of the two rooms. Halfway through the term, the classes switched rooms, so that students in both classes spent half the term in the control room and half in the "friendly" room. Students were not told they were being studied; the switch in rooms was explained as occurring because the original room was needed for videotaping.

The most striking finding from this study was that students performed significantly better on regular course exams when they were in the friendly rather than the sterile classroom. It thus appears that the physical environment can affect the learning that occurs, at least as measured by scores on tests. In addition, students were asked to evaluate their instructor halfway through the term and again at the end of the term. The instructors were rated significantly more positively during the time the class met in the attractive classroom. In the experimental room, instructors were evaluated as more knowledgeable, more interesting, and better organized than they were in the control room. So our evaluations of other people are at least partly influenced by the physical setting in which we interact with them.

Dormitory Design

College dormitories are generally built according to two different designs. One type has single or double rooms located along a long corridor, with social areas and bathrooms shared by all corridor residents. A second type has suites of rooms consisting of several bedrooms located around a common living room, usually with the residents of just these bedrooms sharing bathroom facilities. The amount of space available to each resident is approximately the same for both designs. Yet the two designs seem to have different effects on the residents.

A series of studies compared corridor and suite arrangements (Baum, Aiello, & Calesnick, 1978; Baum & Valins, 1977). The research indicates that students who live in suite-type dormitories are more sociable and friendlier. At first glance, this seems obvious. Clearly, if you share a living room with, say, nine other people (five bedrooms with two people each), you will get to know these nine other students. In a sense, you have a "family" living situation. If you share a room with only one person, it takes greater effort to get to know other people on the floor.

As we noted in Chapter 9 on interpersonal attraction, proximity is one of the major factors in liking and friendship. The suite arrangement puts more people in close proximity and, therefore, should lead to more friendships. Thus far, this follows directly from our knowledge of the effects of proximity and certainly would be expected. The striking aspect of the work by Baum and Valin is that these sociability differences seem to carry over into the world outside the dormitory. When the students are observed in the psychology laboratory, the suite residents are friendlier than the corridor residents. For example, in one study a student arrived at the laboratory and was shown into a room in which another student (actually a confederate) was sitting. There were several chairs in the room, and the question was how close to the other student the subject would sit. Suite residents tended to sit closer than corridor residents and to initiate more conversations.

One problem with this research is that students are not always randomly assigned to rooms. Perhaps more sociable people request assignment to suites. Another problem is that suites are sometimes newer than corridor dorms, and the two types of housing are sometimes located on different parts of the campus. To overcome these problems, Baum and Davis (1980) conducted an intervention experiment. They obtained permission to assign first-year women students randomly to living conditions. To control the environment further, the researchers devised the architectural intervention shown in Figure 16-3.

Baum and Davis selected two identical long-corridor floors in the same building, each housing about 40 students. On the intervention floors, they converted several bedrooms in the middle of the corridor into lounges and installed doors to divide the corridor into two smaller units, each housing about 20 students. As a further comparison, they studied a "short" corridor in another building that also housed about 20 students. In all settings, students had about the same amount of physical space, and the density was relatively high. The researchers gave questionnaires to dorm residents at the beginning of the school year and at several times during the year. They made systematic

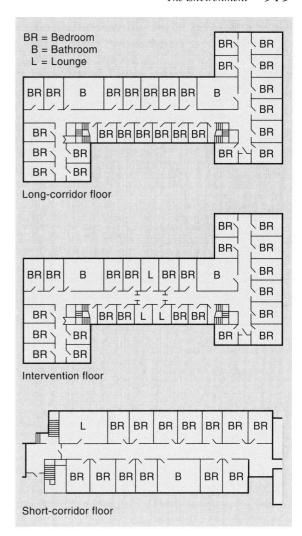

Figure 16-3 Floor plans of the dormitory floors. The intervention floor was originally identical to the long-corridor floor, but was remodeled to form two short corridors separated by doors and lounges. The short-corridor floor was in another building. (*Source:* Adapted from Baum & Davis, 1980, p. 475.)

observations of social interaction in the dorm and of behavior in a laboratory situation.

The results of the experiment were consistent with earlier findings. After living in the dorm for several weeks, residents on the short corridors reported feeling less crowded, having fewer problems regulating social contacts in the dorm, and having a greater sense of control over life in the dorm than did students in the long corridor. Short-corridor residents also reported that they were more successful in making friends in the dorm, and they were observed to have more social interactions in lounges and corridors. In the laboratory, students who had been randomly assigned to short corridors showed greater friendliness toward a research confederate and expected to have more control over the experiment than did long-corridor residents. These results provide strong evidence that an architectural design feature—in this case the size of the residential living group—can significantly affect feelings and social interactions.

Two main factors appear to be at work in these dormitory settings. First, smaller residential units (suites and short corridors) are more conducive to group formation and friendship than are larger units. Since it is usually more pleasant to interact with friends than with strangers, dorm designs that encourage friendships are experienced as more positive.

Second, smaller residential units increase students' sense of personal control over the environment. In long-corridor dorms, students are constantly required to meet and interact with many others on the floor. When they walk to the bathroom or common lounge areas, they necessarily share the corridor and facilities with many others, most of whom are not friends and with whom they might prefer not to interact. Thus, they are overloaded with social contacts and have difficulty avoiding them. In contrast, those who live in suites or short corridors have a self-contained living unit they share only with people they get to know quite well. They, therefore, have much more control over their social interactions, which presumably increases satisfaction with their residence and their general sense of control over their lives.

High-Rise and Low-Rise Housing

Although students are naturally concerned about dormitory design, a much more serious problem for our society is how high-rise housing affects people. Since the 1950s, vast numbers of high-rise buildings have been constructed for our rapidly expanding population. Some of these buildings are

No particular type of housing, whether high-rise or low-rise, new buildings or old buildings, single-family or multiple resident is inherently good or bad. A key factor is the ability of residents to select the type of housing they prefer. These photos contrast two older neighborhoods in Brooklyn, New York—one an elegant street of well-preserved homes and the other a run-down old building sprayed with graffiti.

huge—30 or 40 stories, with hundreds or even thousands of individual apartments; others are smaller. But all contrast sharply with the private homes or four-story apartment houses characteristic of previous housing. It has become a matter of great social importance to determine whether high-rise housing provides a good living environment.

THE FAILURES: PRUITT-IGOE. Some high-rise buildings have been major failures. They have gotten run down, the halls have been defaced, the apartments have been allowed to deteriorate, crime and vandalism have made the buildings unsafe, and people have moved out whenever they could. The most dramatic example of this kind of failure is the Pruitt-Igoe project built in the 1950s in St. Louis. Designed by a leading architect, the complex had 33 high-rise buildings with 2800 modern apartments. Built with public funds for low- and middle-income families, the "showcase" project soon became a disaster.

Located in the midst of an urban slum, the project never attracted middle-income families who could afford to live in better neighborhoods, and so rental revenues were less than anticipated. Teenage gangs invaded the halls and elevators to rob and terrorize residents. Walls were covered with graffiti, and physical conditions worsened as needed maintenance and repairs were not made. Tenants who could find other housing moved out. Ultimately, conditions deteriorated to such a point that the buildings were condemned and torn down. The multimillion-dollar housing project was a total loss.

PSYCHOLOGICAL EFFECTS. On the one hand, we know that most high-rise buildings, both public and private, have been successful at least to the extent that people continue to live in them and function reasonably well. In cities such as Toronto, San Francisco, and Boston, high-rise apartments and condominiums in fashionable neighborhoods are considered very desirable. The central question addressed by environmental psychologists is whether high-rise and low-rise buildings have different psychological effects on residents, and in particular, whether high-rise housing is typically harmful.

In general, research does not find major differences between the health or general well-being of those who live in high-rise versus low-rise housing. A few studies have found that high-rise residents are less happy with their social relations, more concerned about safety, and feel more crowded (Holahan & Wilcox, 1978; McCarthy & Saegert, 1978). But other studies have found the opposite: High-rise residents reported feeling more content with their buildings and more satisfied with their social relations (Friedman, 1979; Michelson, 1977). Overall, few consistent differences have been found.

In understanding these results, it is important to keep in mind that the experience of high-rise living can vary considerably. Living in the penthouse of a beautiful high-security apartment building is quite different from living at the top of a poorly maintained public housing project in a rundown area. Further, it is likely that high-rise housing (or, for that matter, any kind of housing) may not be suitable for everyone. Although research has not produced consistent differences between high- and low-rise housing, there is no question that some people prefer one or the other.

Parents with young children often complain that high-rise housing presents great difficulties in supervising their children (Michelson, 1970). A parent who lives on the twentieth floor cannot watch a child in the playground at street level. Many parents are reluctant to let their young children ride elevators alone, so that even if they can play on the street, it is inconvenient to get them there. Perhaps because of this, residents of high-rise housing are often less satisfied with their housing than are people who live in their own homes. None of these differences is large or related to any noticeable differences in health or general satisfaction, but the differences do exist. In other words, people complain more about high-rise housing, even though research has not shown any actual negative effects on well-being.

As with the dormitory design studies, research on high-rise housing faces enormous difficulty in making valid comparisons of the residents of the various kinds of buildings. People are not randomly assigned to housing in our society, so that residents of different buildings almost always differ in potentially important ways. In cities like New York, which has many high-rise apartments, upper-, middle-, and working-class families all live in high-rise buildings. Many New Yorkers who can afford to live anywhere choose to live in a high-rise building in the center of the city. In other words, high-rise buildings are not only for low-income families. But middle-class and upper-class families do generally have a choice, whereas poorer families often are forced to live in a high-rise because it is the only housing available. This lack of choice may itself cause problems, and it should, therefore, probably be a matter of public policy to provide as much choice in housing as posible.

KEY TERMS

built environment	personal space	territorial behaviors
crowding	proxemics	territorial markers
environmental psychology	social density	territory

SUMMARY

1. Environmental psychology considers how the physical environment affects people's behavior and well-being. Major topics in environmental psychology include how humans use space, crowding, noise, and the design of buildings.

2. Proxemics is a general term for the study of how people use space. Personal space refers to the physical space immediately around a person that the person treats as an extension of the self. The distance we prefer to stand from other people depends on our ethnic or cultural background, our gender, and our relation to the other people. Hall has distinguished four basic zones for interpersonal interaction: intimate, personal, social, and public distance.

3. A territory is an area controlled by a person or group. Altman has distinguished primary, secondary, and public territories. People use various markers to identify and lay claim to their territory. Our reaction to someone who enters our territory depends on how we interpret the act—as friendly, rude, hostile, and so on.

4. Crowding is the subjective experience of feeling cramped and not having enough space. In contrast, social density refers to the objective number of people in a given area. According to the sensory overload theory of crowding, high social density creates an unpleasantly high level of stimulation.

Another view is that high density may cause people to experience a distressing loss of personal control. A final perspective is that we feel crowded when we attribute our physiological arousal to the presence of too many people.

5. Research shows that high residential density does not always have negative consequences. Harmful effects are minimized when residents have a cooperative attitude, when individuals perceive some degree of control over the environment, and when living in cramped quarters is temporary.

6. Noise affects us less than we might think. If noise is not so loud that it causes physical damage, people usually adapt to short exposure to loud noise and perform most tasks at their normal level. Only complex tasks seem to be impaired by short-term loud noise. Prolonged exposure to loud noise, however, can have negative effects on hearing and intellectual performance.

7. Architectural design can influence people's behavior. College students who live in suite-type dormitories and in small living units are more sociable and friendlier than those who live on long corridors with many rooms side-by-side. Smaller residential units may make it easier to form friendships and may also increase a sense of personal control. However, high-rise housing is not necessarily worse than low-rise housing.

SUGGESTED READINGS

Cohen, S., Evans, G. W., Stokols, D. S., & Krantz, D. S. (1986). *Behavior, health and environmental stress.* New York: Plenum. Considers the impact of environmental stress on human behavior and well-being.

Fisher, J. D., Bell, P. A., & Baum, A. (Eds.) (1990). *Environmental psychology* (3rd ed.). New York: Holt, Rinehart & Winston. A comprehensive survey of the field of environmental psychology.

Hall, E. T. (1966). *The hidden dimension.* New York: Doubleday. A fascinating classic analysis of personal space in social life.

Sommer, R. (1969). *Personal space: The behavioral basis for design.* Englewood Cliffs, NJ: Prentice-Hall. A classic and highly readable discussion of the topic.

Stern, P. C. (1992). Psychological dimensions of global environmental change. *Annual Review of Psychology, 43,* 269–302. A recent review that explores how people affect the global environment.

Stokols, D., & Altman, I. (Eds.) (1987). *Handbook of environmental psychology.* New York: Wiley. This two-volume collection of chapters by leading experts provides a professional-level overview of current research and theory in the field.

17
Politics

FOCUS OF THIS CHAPTER

Political Socialization
Public Opinion and Voting
Mass Media
A New Look at the Media
International Conflict

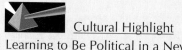
Cultural Highlight
Learning to Be Political in a New
Culture

Research Closeup
Attitudes Toward Abortion

In 1961, during the earliest days of John F. Kennedy's presidency, his administration engineered a disastrous and ill-conceived invasion of Cuba in an effort to overthrow the Communist regime of Fidel Castro. Soon thereafter, the Soviet Union began to place nuclear missiles in Cuba. In 1962 the United States discovered the presence of these missiles, and Kennedy ordered a naval blockade of Cuba, demanding their removal. This confrontation sent the world into a crisis, since neither Kennedy nor the Soviet leader, Khrushchev, seemed willing to back down. American preparations to destroy the missiles accelerated, as did the Soviet and Cuban preparations to make them ready. A week of escalating tensions seemed to bring the two superpowers ever closer to an exchange of nuclear arms that could destroy much of human civilization. Finally, a private deal was struck which allowed the Soviets to remove the missiles in exchange for American concessions elsewhere in the world.

The world has never come closer to nuclear annihilation. Both Kennedy and Khrushchev were looking over their shoulders at their own publics: An important election was just weeks away in the United States; the Russian leader was in constant danger of being overthrown. And much depended on the two leaders themselves: on their emotions (Was it too humiliating to back down?), on their own goals (How important was victory over the enemy compared to the avoidance of nuclear holocaust?), and on the perceptions they had of each other (Did the other want peace or victory at all costs? Could he be reasoned with?). Moreover, each leader spent long hours each day deliberating with groups of advisors. What role was played by the dynamics of those groups?

Of course, Kennedy and Khrushchev did not remain heads of state forever. So a critical question to ask is how do such leaders come into power, and how are they replaced? In the United States the answer would seem to be fairly simple: Presidents are elected by the voters, so we must look at the determinants of voting behavior. President Kennedy was a Democrat, as was his successor, Lyndon B. Johnson. But since then, Republicans have been more successful than Democrats. Why do such changes occur? Do voters make reasoned and informed decisions based on fundamental issues, such as national defense, a balanced budget, and the environment? Or do they just respond to superficial political commercials on television?

Such questions are the stuff of political psychology. They have resulted in basic research on political socialization, public opinion and voting behavior, the impact of the media, and international conflict. These are the topics we discuss in this chapter.

POLITICAL SOCIALIZATION

Our political lives begin in childhood just as do many other aspects of our lives. Fundamental political attitudes, like basic social and moral values, racial attitudes, and other crucial predispositions, seem to be acquired prior to adulthood (Hyman, 1959). This suggests a close look at pre-adult **political socialization.**

Pre-adult Socialization

Attitudes are assumed to be learned in the same way as any other disposition, through the basic processes of association, reinforcement, and imitation, as indicated in Chapter 6. This means that parents may have a great deal of influence. For example, the central variable in the ordinary citizen's voting decision is **party identification,** a standing preference for one political party or the other. The classic analysis of American voting behavior, *The American Voter* (Campbell, Converse, Miller, & Stokes, 1960), found that party identification was by far the single most important determinant of the vote, that most people perceived themselves as not having changed their party preference for many years, and that most perceived their parents' preferences as closely resembling their own. As a result, this analysis concluded that party identification was typically developed before adulthood and significantly influenced by one's family.

Party identification is a good starting point for examining the political socialization process. One major national survey of high school seniors showed that they strongly tended to favor the political party of their parents; only about 10 percent favored the opposite party (Jennings & Niemi, 1974). This is shown in Table 17-1. The same survey revealed that in the last election, 83 percent of the high school students favored the same presidential candidate as their parents had.

However, parent–offspring agreement was much lower in many other respects. For example, when the high school students were asked a series of questions about how much "the people in government" can be trusted, as many students disagreed with their parents as agreed with them. Why do parents sometimes have a major impact on their children's attitudes, and sometimes not?

Surprisingly, adolescents' relationships with their parents have relatively little to do with political agreement or disagreement with them. Adolescents who were angry at their parents were about as likely to agree with them as those who felt warmly toward Mom and Dad (Jennings & Niemi, 1974). More important is the clarity and frequency of the communication of parents' attitudes to their offspring. And this varies greatly. Parents communicate clearly and repeatedly their presidential preference in the heat of an election campaign; 92 percent of the students in the study were able to report accurately which candidate their parents favored. But on other issues, the students were strikingly inaccurate; indeed, it often appeared they were simply guessing about their parents' orientations. For example, they were quite inaccurate about their parents' levels of interest in politics (Niemi, 1974).

This has two implications. First, some parents influence their children's political attitudes more than others. Those who are most influential are the ones who themselves are most politicized—those who read the political news most often and who participate in politics in the widest variety of ways (Beck & Jennings, 1991). Second, parents influence their children's attitudes more in some regards than others, having the most influence on concrete questions like party identification, religious denomination, or prejudices against minority groups, and the least on more diffuse issues where communica-

TABLE 17-1
Relationship Between Party Preferences of Parents and Their Adolescent Offspring

High School Seniors (*N* = 1852)

Parent	Democratic	Independent	Republican		Total
Democratic	66.0%	26.7%	7.3%	=	100.0%
Independent	29.2	53.6	17.2	=	100.0
Republican	12.7	36.3	50.9	=	99.9
Total	43.0	35.7	21.3	=	100.0%

Source: Adapted from Jennings & Niemi (1974).

tion is likely to be fuzzy, such as religious philosophy or political cynicism. And parents have more influence on issues that come up repeatedly, like partisan elections or race relations, and the least on those that come up only once in a long while, like attitudes toward Argentina or the metric system (Sears, 1983). For the same reasons, peer influence is stronger than parental influence on things adolescents are more likely to discuss with each other, such as drugs and music.

Do the effects of parental influence last, or do they disappear after the child leaves home? The same study afforded a good test of lasting influence, because these high school seniors were reinterviewed at ages 25 and 34. Parental influence on offspring party identification was at its peak when the offspring were adolescents, though it continued to be significant even into their thirties. As parental influence waned, the offspring's attitudes about the major issues of the day became more important. Indeed, by age 34, such issues as the Vietnam War were playing as important a role as were parental attitudes (Niemi & Jennings, 1991). So our parents' attitudes continue to influence us well into adulthood, though gradually sharing the stage with our own independent responses to the political issues of the day.

Persistence of Early Socialization

This raises the question of the **persistence** of such early-socialized predispositions across the life span. Do early-socialized political attitudes tend to persist throughout our lives or are we always open to influence? Basic attitudes such as party identification and racial attitudes do persist to an impressive degree (Converse & Markus, 1979; Jennings & Markus, 1984). If they change at all, it tends to be during early adulthood, when these attitudes have usually not hardened yet, and especially when the dominant political complexion of the individual's social environment has changed. For example, young adults' party identifications did change in response to major political events such as the Vietnam War or racial conflict (Markus, 1979).

One particularly interesting case of potential change, therefore, occurs when young people are exposed to new ideas at college. Students who have spent most of their years living in their parents' homes and surrounded by childhood friends can, at college, be introduced to new kinds of people with many new and different beliefs. Not surprisingly, this exposure can have a profound effect.

A classic demonstration of such change was provided by Theodore Newcomb's (1943) study of alumnae of Bennington College. This small, exclusive women's college in Vermont first opened, with a very liberal faculty, in the early 1930s. Most of the students came from affluent, conservative families; indeed, among the parents, Republicans outnumbered Democrats by more than two to one. And as we would expect from our earlier discussion, before they came to college, these students had adopted much the same views as their parents. Yet many of the students became much more liberal as they progressed through school. These attitude changes were most common among students who identified most with Bennington and who had the closest social relationships with other students and faculty. For these students, Bennington served as an important reference group, and its dominant liberal norms brought about substantial attitude change. By the time they graduated, a large number of the once-conservative students had defected to the Democratic party (only 60 percent of the Republican mothers wound up with Republican daughters), while the offspring of liberal parents tended not to change (93 percent of the Democratic mothers wound up with Democratic daughters) (Alwin, Cohen, & Newcomb, 1991).

What happened to the students' attitudes after they left school? Did their new-found liberalism persist or did they regress to their parents' conservatism? In fact, 20 years later their political views had remained remarkably stable. Those who left college as liberals were still liberals, and the conservatives were still conservatives. A later study done nearly 50 years after they graduated found that their political preferences were "unbelievably stable" over those many decades (Alwin et al., 1991, p. 154).

The critical factor determining this persistence was the social environment the women entered after college, particularly their husbands and friends. Liberal women had generally married liberal husbands and had liberal close friends: About 85 percent voted for the same presidential candidate as their husbands in the 1940, 1960, and 1980 elections, and only a little over 10 percent reported that their best friend had a different party preference from their own. The Bennington alumnae's own political preferences were almost perfectly stable for the nearly 50 years after graduation if they had husbands and friends who agreed with them. The occasional regressions could be attributed to the fact that some liberal women had married husbands in occupations such as banking or corporation law, and so had moved into a politically conservative world. They were much more likely to have switched their political preferences if their husbands or close friends dissented from them.

Of course, it is a rare college that shows the political homogeneity of the small, exclusive, isolated, and highly liberal Bennington campus. The most important conclusion of the Bennington study is that mere exposure to information is not sufficient to change basic political attitudes. Intense, interpersonal contact such as that in the Bennington experience is necessary and, indeed, may be necessary for years afterward if the change is to be maintained. And such contact is most likely to produce change if it occurs relatively early in life.

So what can we say more generally about how political attitudes change over the life span? Three general models might be contrasted

(Sears, 1989): (1) The *persistence* model suggests that preadult attitudes remain more or less the same through our lifetime (or perhaps even strengthen with time). (2) The *impressionable years* hypothesis suggests that people are unusually susceptible to influence in late adolescence and early adulthood, as we leave the parental home and begin to establish our own identities, but thereafter our attitudes stabilize and do not change much further. (3) The *lifelong openness* model views attitudes as always open to influence.

A few longitudinal studies have followed individuals' political attitudes over many years. They tend to find that core political preferences, such as party identification and political ideology, change very little after early adulthood. This was true of the Bennington alumnae, as we have seen. These two political attitudes were also highly stable over the life span in a large sample of Californians (Sears & Funk, 1990). The average age of the respondents was 29 in 1940, and 66 in 1977. Over this long period of time, there was some drift toward the Republican party, but most people stuck with their original preference, as shown in Table 17-2. Similar levels of stability emerge from studies of nationally representative samples followed over shorter periods (Green & Palmquist, 1990; Krosnick, 1991).

In all these studies, young adults changed much more often than did older people. For example, in the latter studies, adults aged 18–25 showed substantial attitude change, but those aged 34 and over showed almost none (Alwin et al., 1991; Jennings & Markus, 1984; Sears, 1983;

TABLE 17-2
Stability of Party Identification, 1940–1977

1940	1977			
	Democrat (%)	Independent (%)	Republican (%)	Total
Democrat	62.2	6.7	31.1	36.0
Independent	28.6	17.5	54.0	13.8
Republican	10.5	7.4	82.1	50.2
Total	31.6	8.6	60.0	100.0

Source: Sears & Funk (1990, Table 9). Based on 456 cases.

also see Sears & Funk, 1990). So it would seem that the "impressionable years" hypothesis is most accurate: While people are in their twenties, their political preferences can undergo a good bit of change one way or the other, but thereafter, they tend to be quite stable.

It turns out that young adults are more likely to immigrate to a new country than are older people. As a result, an interesting implication of the "impressionable years" hypothesis is that young adults are the most likely to be influenced by the new political culture they join. The CULTURAL HIGHLIGHT discusses the political preferences of new Asian and Latino immigrants to the United States.

PUBLIC OPINION AND VOTING

A second major focus in political psychology has been on public opinion and voting behavior. The main method for studying these topics has been public opinion surveys. Are these reliable? We often hear that they are not, and indeed read about conflicting and fast-changing results during election campaigns. But it turns out that much of the disagreement and volatility is due to the fact that many voters do not arrive at firm decisions until relatively late. In fact, polls taken close to Election Day generally prove to be quite accurate. As shown in Table 17-3, in 1992 the major polls came very close, slightly overestimating the Clinton vote, and underestimating Perot support.

An influential early analysis of voter deci-sion-making was *The People's Choice* (Lazarsfeld, Berelson, & Gaudet, 1948), a careful study of the 1940 campaign. It explained voting behavior as stemming from individuals' membership in social groups with clear political norms. Catholics, the working class, and city dwellers were more likely to vote Democratic, while Protestants, the middle class, and those living in rural areas were more likely to vote Republican. These differences were later explained as resulting from direct interpersonal influence: Parents passed their partisan preferences on to children, and husbands and wives and coworkers influenced each other, making sure that each other did not stray from the "right" vote for their social category (Berelson, Lazarsfeld, & McPhee, 1954). The dominant causal factors were groups and social influence.

Party Identification

Later studies produced a theory of voting behavior that focused on individual decision-making (rather than social influence), published in the important book, *The American Voter* (Campbell et al., 1960). It had two dominant features. First, it argued that voters are minimally informed and largely nonideological. In the absence of much information about the candidates and issues, and without strong ideological moorings, how do voters decide? Primarily by applying their own party identification, a "standing decision" to favor one side rather than the other. By a simple process of **cognitive**

TABLE 17-3
Accuracy of Final Polls Done for Major News Organizations in 1992

	Date	Clinton (%)	Bush (%)	Perot (%)	Number of Cases
Actual Outcome	3 Nov	43	38	19	101,133,038
Polls					
Gallup–USA–CNN	1–2 Nov	46	39	15	1589
NBC News/Wall St Jrnl	1 Nov	46	38	16	1008
CBS News/NY Times	31 Oct–2 Nov	46	38	16	1731
ABC News	31 Oct–1 Nov	45	38	16	908

Note: In these polls, 4 percent of respondents, on the average, did not express a preference; they have been dropped from the analysis.
Source: Adapted from Ladd (1992, p. 11).

CULTURAL HIGHLIGHT
Learning to Be Political in a New Culture

The 1970s and 1980s witnessed a tremendous new wave of immigration to the United States, especially from Latin America and Asia. The acquisition of political preferences by immigrants in their new culture provides an interesting test case of the persistence of early political socialization.

Did these immigrants become Democrats, as had those arriving a century earlier from Ireland, Italy, Poland, Hungary, Russia, and other European nations? Did they retain distinctive traces of their own national backgrounds?

There are three general hypotheses:

1. The "melting pot" hypothesis would suggest that immigrants arrive with the traditional attitudes and values of their own culture, but gradually assimiliate the attitudes of the dominant society. Their Initial experience of discrimination and economic inequality might lead them to join the Democratic party. But as their own economic well-being increased, they might move toward the Republican party, as have the European ethnic groups.
2. Immigrants might well import old loyalties and antagonisms from their original countries. For example, refugees from Communism, who came to the United States from Cuba, Vietnam, Korea, and Taiwan, might have arrived with stronger anti-Communist sentiments than, say, those from Mexico or the Philippines, where Communism was not a major issue. If so, they might

have been attracted by the vigorous anti-Communism of the Republican party (Cain et al., 1991). Similarly, an "emergent ethnicity" perspective would suggest that Latinos from such different countries as Cuba and Mexico might generate distinctive and separate ethnic groups, competing for political clout (de la Garza et al., 1992).

3. Alternatively, a "politicized ethnics" hypothesis suggests that immigrants rebuffed by discrimination reject core American values, instead developing a strong ethnic identity (Falcon et al., 1992). This could even be "panethnic," supporting all immigrants.

Two major recent studies have provided data on these hypotheses: an in-depth study of Latino and Asian immigrants in California by Bruce Cain and his colleagues (1991), and a national study of Latinos by Rodolfo de la Garza and his colleagues (e.g., 1992).

Consistent with the "melting pot" hypothesis, both studies revealed Latinos to be a strongly Democratic group overall; for example, in 1988, Dukakis won about two-thirds of the Latino vote, despite losing the election (DeSipio & de la Garza, 1992). And this reflected an early and stable choice of party: less than 2 percent of the Latino Democrats had ever been Republicans (DeSipio & de la Garza, 1992).

Do immigrants, like other Americans, become more Republican as they become more affluent? As would be expected, among Latinos, low income and

unionized workers tended to be more Democratic than the more affluent (Cain et al., 1991). And the few Latino Republicans more often had a history of being ex-Democrats than vice versa, suggesting that economic success may indeed erode Democratic support among minorities.

The immigrants did seem to have "imported" some of their earlier anti-Communist sympathies, since the Republicans won majorities among those fleeing Cuba, Korea, Taiwan, Hong Kong, and Southeast Asia, whereas the Democrats led Republicans by 40 percent among Mexican Americans and by 52 percent among Puerto Ricans (Cain et al., 1991; DeSipio & de la Garza, 1992). The Republican edge among refugees from Cuba and Asia was especially large among those immigrating relatively early, when Communism was the biggest threat (for example, right after the Vietnam war). So there is evidence that adaptation to the American political culture is colored by orientations imported from abroad.

Is there evidence of an identification with a "pan-ethnic" Latino group rather than the broader culture? Not really. Latinos support just as many restrictions as Anglos do on additional immigration to the United States from Latin America. And the more fully "Americanized" Latinos—those who are born in the United States and mainly speak English—are especially restrictive. So there is no evidence that they feel closer to immigrants as a whole than to American culture in general (de la Garza et al., 1992).

consistency (as outlined in Chapter 6), party identification determines the voter's attitudes toward the candidates and issues of the current election campaign. For example, in 1992 lifelong Republicans tended to evaluate George Bush favorably and Bill Clinton unfavorably, and approve of Bush's opposition to tax increases or abortion. These attitudes toward the candidates and issues of the campaign, shaped by a stable and powerful party identification, prove to predict the individual's vote quite accurately.

In the years since it was published, *The American Voter* has been challenged from a number of perspectives. The major criticism contends that the key factors are current political and economic realities rather than long-standing psychological dispositions such as party identification. The underlying question is one that runs through the political psychological approach: Are voters uninformed, irrational, and operating from long-standing preferences adopted many years earlier? Or are they informed, sensible, and rational, adjusting their attitudes when external reality changes?

Revisionists argue that voters do not just habitually and unthinkingly vote for the same party year after year, but make sensible judgments each election year about the past performance of the current president, and then vote to support or oppose his party accordingly. And poor performance by one's own party when in power can weaken one's party identification (e.g., Fiorina, 1981). Similarly, the revisionists suggest that in congressional elections, a key factor is the incumbents' real service to their constituents, such as trying to help constituents with problems with Social Security or other federal bureaucracies. Some members of Congress are quite visible and effective in dealing with their constituents' problems with the federal government, while others are not, and the effective ones are more likely to get re-elected than are the ineffective ones (Mann & Wolfinger, 1980). Moreover, an individual's party identifications can shift in response to other on-going political issues: Vietnam and busing (in the early 1970s), economic recessions, and controversial candidates such as Jesse Jackson (Franklin, 1984; Luskin, McIver, & Carmines, 1989; Sears, Citrin, & Kosterman, 1987).

One reason for the stability of party identification is continuing affection for past leaders of one's own party. Many Democrats still remember the Kennedy administration with great affection, so invoking its symbols (such as with this official Bachrach portrait) often reinforces their party loyalty.

At least on a short-term basis, the cumulative impact of many such small changes in individual party identification can shift the overall balance of party support toward the party of the president when things are going well (MacKuen, Erikson, & Stimson, 1989; Weisberg & Smith, 1991). The overall party balance can also be shifted a little by such campaign events as controversial primaries, scandals, and the "bandwagon" of a looming victor (Allsop & Weisberg, 1988). Major long-term changes are much less common, though there is consensus on at least one: the major shift of Southern white voters to the Republican party, whose roots lie in Southern opposition to the civil rights movement in the late 1950s (Miller, 1991).

So, overall, the emphasis among researchers has probably shifted toward modifying the view that party identification is acquired in permanent form in early adolescence. As we have seen, there is evidence that early adulthood is a formative period with lasting effects. Thereafter, party identification still tends to be very stable; few voters change very much once they are mature adults. Moreover, individual vote decisions are just as consistent with party identification as they were in the earliest days of voting research; indeed, consistency was at a high point in 1988 (Miller, 1992). However, there is now greater appreciation for how people adjust their preferences (even if only modestly) later in life to accommodate changed realities.

Economic Voting

Another major area of contention concerns the role of current economic realities. Kramer (1971) observed that the outcomes of elections were strongly correlated with the health of the general economy. One researcher estimates that a growth of 1 percent in per capita personal income over the year prior to a presidential election adds about 2 percent to the vote of the incumbent (Markus, 1992). Hence, the president's political party tends to lose ground when the economy is weak, and does well when the economy is strong.

This finding would seem on the surface to indicate that voters were voting their pocketbooks: When they are doing well financially, they support the party in power, and when they are doing poorly, they throw the rascals out. If so, this would support a **self-interest** hypothesis. But such economic voting could be explained another way. Even voters who are doing well financially may vote against the president's party when the national economy is doing poorly. That is, people may vote on the basis of what is good for the nation as a whole rather than on the basis of what is good for them personally. This is the **sociotropic** hypothesis.

Considerable careful research has been done to test these alternative hypotheses. In general, sociotropic voting is much more common than self-interested, pocketbook voting (Kinder & Kiewiet, 1979). There is a small but statistically significant amount of pocketbook voting in presidential elections, but none at all in congressional elections (Kiewiet, 1983; Markus, 1992). The clear finding is that voters' sociotropic judgments of the economy are more powerful than self-interested judgments about their personal

financial situations, in Europe as well as in the United States (Lewis-Beck, 1988). This mirrors the finding that material self-interest often plays a surprisingly minor role in racial and ethnic prejudices, as discussed in Chapter 7.

Why is self-interested voting comparatively rare? One answer often given is that the personal effects of government policies on individuals are not large enough, direct enough, or clear enough to the individual to influence their votes (Green, 1988; Sears & Funk, 1991). A second answer is that voters compartmentalize their personal experiences from their knowledge of the society as a whole. So personal experiences affect voters' judgments only about the seriousness of their own economic problems, while exposure to the media is more important for judgments about the economy as a whole (for example, estimates of the national unemployment rate). The twain do not meet (Mutz, 1992). A third answer is that voters attribute changes in their personal financial well-being to their own personal situations, abilities, and efforts, and not to the government or the president. If we lose our job, we blame the boss, an inept firm that is losing business, or perhaps our lack of skill or lazy work habits. We usually do not blame the president. This is consistent with our observation in Chapter 4 that Americans are biased toward internal attributions for their own situation, the so-called "ethic of self-reliance."

On the other hand, people are likely to attribute responsibility for the nation's economy as a whole to the president. Many blamed George Bush for the recession of 1992, and it cost him many votes. People tend, then, to be influenced by conditions for which the president is plausibly responsible—the state of the general economy—but not by conditions for which he is likely not to be responsible—the voter's own pocketbook (Feldman, 1982). One consequence is that the health of the economy affects congressional voting more in years with a presidential contest than in off-year elections, when there is none (Erikson, 1990). Why the difference? In presidential years, a good economy helps the president, and a bad economy hurts him, and some of that effect rubs off on those running in the president's party for Congress (a "presidential coattails" effect). In off-years, no presidential coattails exist, and voters tend to respond more to local issues.

Consistency and Ideology

Another question that has drawn much attention is the degree of consistent, abstract thinking in public opinion. This, too, raised the fundamental question of whether the general public thinks politically in an informed, sensible, coherent, and sophisticated manner, or uses such simple cues as a candidate's political party without greater thought. Early research suggested that relatively few voters think about politics in terms of a broad, abstract political **ideology** such as liberalism or conservatism (Campbell et al., 1960). Similarly, voters often are not consistent across issues; strong environmentalists are not necessarily likely to favor government aid for child care, even though both are liberal positions (Converse, 1964). And most people want to reduce taxes, but at the same time want to maintain or even expand such government programs as spending on the public schools (Sears & Citrin, 1985). People are often similarly inconsistent on issues of civil liberties: Almost everyone believes in the general principle of free speech for all, but many would not extend free speech to the Communist party (Sullivan, Pierson, & Marcus, 1982). And, as we saw in Chapter 7, there is much inconsistency in the realm of race and ethnicity: Most people endorse general principles of equality, such as the principle of racially integrated schools, but oppose the main mechanisms designed to bring it about, such as busing (Sears & Allen, 1984).

This view of the public as inconsistent and illogical has been extensively challenged by scholars who believe that citizens respond in a rational way to political realities. They argue that the public thinks ideologically only when political elites offer genuinely different ideological alternatives, as they generally do not (Nie et al., 1979); that freedom of speech for groups such as Communists is denied only when the groups are perceived as being dangerous, such as at the height of the Cold War in the early 1950s (Sullivan et al., 1982); that the white public supports integration but not such obviously ineffective policies as busing (Roth, 1990); and that most people support tax cuts to reduce waste in government rather than wanting cuts in essential government services. But no matter whether one interprets these inconsistencies as rational or irrational, there is general agreement that they exist.

Such inconsistencies also suggested a low level of ideological thinking in the mass public; people are not likely to have broad-ranging abstract ideologies if they are not consistent across issues. But there is some evidence that ideology has become increasingly important in partisan politics. Younger voters, within the North and South alike, in recent years seem increasingly to be choosing a party based on ideological affinity—the liberal voters becoming Democrats, and the conservatives, Republicans (Carmines & Stanley, 1992; Miller, 1991). As a result, the younger generation of Democrats and Republicans are more polarized on the issues than earlier generations of partisans, with the Democrats much more liberal than Republicans on such issues as abortion, minority rights, and cutting defense spending (Miller, 1992).

Group Conflict

The early voting studies emphasized social and political groups as key determinants of political behavior, while later studies emphasized individual choice. Today there is renewed interest in groups in politics, focusing especially on racial and gender conflict. As we saw in Chapter 7, racial attitudes clearly play an important role in determining policy preferences on issues such as busing and affirmative action; evaluations of black political candidates; and welfare, tax, and government spending reductions. There is disagreement about whether these racial attitudes mainly date from preadult socialization, are a realistic response to the threats posed by blacks to whites' superior position on our society, or result from the "group-serving" attributions people have about the causes of minorities' disadvantages in jobs, income, housing, and education (see Bobo, 1988a; Kluegel & Smith, 1986; Sears, 1988). But there is no disagreement that racial attitudes are politically important.

THE GENDER GAP. The women's movement and the many postwar changes in women's roles in society have prompted renewed attention to gender conflict in politics. Indeed, gender differences in political attitudes have become increasingly prominent. Women are now consistently more Democratic and liberal than men, more favorable to social services, and, especially, more unfavorable to the use of war and military force in foreign affairs. These differences are usually described as the **gender gap** (Shapiro & Mahajan, 1986; Frankovic, 1982; Mueller, 1991). This finding extends beyond the United States; for example, Danish women were more hesitant about membership in NATO and the European Community than were Danish men (Togeby, 1992).

The gender gap is considerably larger today than it was 30 years ago. Why has it grown? The major hypothesis links it to changes in women's social roles that have influenced their **group consciousness.** Women today are more likely to

be working, highly educated, unmarried, and free of care-taking for small children. This change of focus from the family to the workplace has the potential for increasing sensitivity to discrimination against women, increasing support for women's issues, such as equal pay, affirmative action, abortion, the Equal Rights Amendment, and increasing political liberalism in general (Klein, 1984; Gurin, 1985).

Consistent with this hypothesis, young, single, well-educated working women support "a women's perspective" that focuses on programs that help children, the elderly, and other disadvantaged people, and greater opposition to war and other manifestations of political force, more than do women in more traditional social roles (older, married, less-educated homemakers). Similarly, Conover (1988) found that women who viewed themselves as "feminists" were indeed more liberal than either men or nonfeminist women in these respects.

But whether the "gender gap" in political attitudes is due to group consciousness and heightened feminism is less clear. First of all, women's overall sense of group consciousness seems to be too weak to explain these political effects (Gurin, 1985). Moreover, the circumstances of women's private lives seem to have rather little spillover into their political attitudes (Sapiro, 1983; Sears & Huddy, 1990). Nor are women, in general, and women in these more modern social roles, in particular, much more favorable to programs targeted for women than are men or more traditional women. Political candidates' stands on such programs have about the same effects on men's votes as on women's votes (Mansbridge, 1985). It turns out that men who approve of feminism also share these same liberal political views; that is, feminist men are just as different from nonfeminists (men or women) as feminist women are (Sears & Huddy, 1990). Indeed, the gender gap exists both among feminists and nonfeminists (Cook & Wilcox, 1991). Both of these effects are shown in Table 17-4.

Evidence from the recent past suggests that the gender gap is not principally due to increased group consciousness among women generated by changes in their social roles.

The women's movement, like many other popular social movements, attracts much of its participation and visibility from mass marches and meetings focused on key issues. Opposition to restrictive abortion legislation has helped mobilize much support for the women's movement and for NOW, one of its key organizations.

TABLE 17-4
Support for Aid to the Disadvantaged (Food Stamps, Medicare) as a Function of Gender and Feminism

	Feminists	Nonfeminists
Men	Medium	Low
Women	High	Medium

Source: Adapted from Cook & Wilcox (1991).

Rather, the best evidence is that it is mostly due to women's long-standing greater aversion to the use of force, whether in war, building a strong military, capital punishment, or harsh responses to crime (Mansbridge, 1985; Smith, 1984). And other variables altogether may be responsible for divisions of opinion on issues conventionally associated with women, as discussed in the RESEARCH CLOSEUP on attitudes toward abortion.

THE SEXUALITY GAP.   A related case concerns gays and lesbians. Both began to "come out of the closet" in the late 1970s, and then developed a highly active political movement, partly in response to the tragic AIDS epidemic. Is there evidence of widespread group consciousness among gay and lesbian voters that might produce a "sexuality gap" analogous to the gender gap? And are gays and lesbians, therefore, part of a broader liberal coalition with other minority groups?

The exit polls done after the 1990 congressional elections found that about 1 percent of the voters identified themselves as gays or lesbians, a group that was predominantly young, urban, and well-educated (Hertzog, 1992). They were indeed more liberal politically than were straight voters and more likely to vote for Democratic candidates. But even in this group, the gender gap emerges. Lesbians (but not gay men) were more likely than straight voters to describe themselves as "strong feminists." And gay men were much more likely than lesbians to favor deployment of troops in the Persian Gulf. In further analyses, the greater liberalism of gay and lesbian voters than straight voters turned out to explain the other attitudinal differences between them. So there is evidence for a distinctively liberal political culture in this group, which could give rise to group consciousness. But the gender gap involving opposition to political violence transcends even sexual orientation; women, whatever their sexual persuasion, dislike it more than men.

MASS MEDIA

Another major area of research focuses on the role of the media in politics. Everyone is familiar with seeing the president speak on television, and watching the news at night. We live in a mass media era, in which people are said to spend more time with television than they do with one another. Sometimes it seems that nothing of any importance occurs in politics that is not due to television. But as we discovered in the chapter on aggression when we examined the effects of media violence on real-life behavior, the media may not dominate people's lives as much as this statement would imply.

Three Eras

Research on the effects of the mass media in politics has gone through three phases. The first began in the 1920s and 1930s when radio became widely available throughout the Western world, and talking movies, with accompanying newsreels, became a source of mass entertainment. For the first time, charismatic political leaders such as Hitler, Mussolini,

RESEARCH CLOSEUP

Attitudes Toward Abortion

One of the most difficult political controversies in America today is abortion. The pro-choice advocates believe that women should control their own reproductive activities, and so should have the right to choose whether or not to have an abortion. The pro-life activists believe that abortion is the murder of an unborn child, and so a crime. The Supreme Court's 1973 decision, *Roe v. Wade,* gave women the constitutional right to an abortion, but did not end the political controversy; if anything it intensified it. Today there is great pressure within the Supreme Court to reverse that decision. The Democratic party presidential candidates have in recent years strongly supported the pro-choice position, while the Republican party candidates have strongly opposed it, placing the issue squarely in the middle of partisan politics.

In general, public opinion about abortion has been remarkably constant since the *Roe v. Wade* decision. Almost everyone (over 90 percent) supports a woman's right to an abortion if the pregnancy endangers her health; almost as many (about 85 percent) support that right if the fetus has a possible birth defect or if the pregnancy resulted from rape. The public is split about evenly on the more controversial

questions of whether or not a woman should be allowed to choose abortion if her family is too poor to afford more children or if for any reason the family wants no more children.

What determines which side of this controversy people come down on? In general it seems not to be due to self-interest. Women and men do not differ, on balance, even though it is women's bodies that are at issue. And gay men and lesbians, for whom pregnancy is not an issue, are more than twice as likely as straight voters to support legalized abortion. Rather, the most central determinant seems to be religiosity, with evangelical Protestants and Catholics being the most opposed to abortion, and the unreligious being most pro-choice (Hertzog, 1992; Sears & Huddy, 1990; Blauwkamp, Fastnow, & Kellstedt, 1992; Welch & Leege, 1992).

Perhaps the most influential analysis of this is Kristin Luker's (1984). She argues that the pro-choice and pro-life activists have two quite different world views, going far beyond the issue of abortion. For traditional Christians (whether Protestant or Catholic), religion is part of a general sense of what is natural in human life. God and nature have intended sexual relations

for procreation rather than recreation, and women to bear and rear children, and to be the core of family life in the home while men work. Humans should not interfere with the natural processes of life and death. In short, abortion (as well as birth control and euthanasia) is immoral because it is contrary to the natural way of life that God has laid down. For the pro-choice activists, rationality supersedes these natural laws. Sex is for intimacy between individuals and for pleasure; family planning is critical; pragmatism, not morality, should be the basis for attitudes toward abortion.

A recent test of this hypothesis contrasted the attitudes of the most extreme pro-choice and the most extreme pro-life ordinary citizens (Blauwkamp et al., 1992). A sampling of the results is shown in the table below.

Not surprisingly, then, the *Roe v. Wade* decision, rather than converting the pro-life advocates to a pro-abortion position, had the effect of polarizing the public around the issue. For example, after the decision, devout Catholics who were aware of the decision became more opposed to discretionary abortion, while less devout Catholics became more favorable to it (Franklin & Kosaki, 1989).

Attitude	Pro-choice	Pro-life
Women should not work outside the home.	28%	63%
Premarital sex is always wrong.	8	62
Divorce should be harder to obtain.	37	78
Euthanasia should be allowed for people with incurable diseases.	88	34
The Bible is God's word and all it says is true.	13	55
It is important to believe in God without doubt.	34	76
People should pray several times a day.	12	43

Churchill, and Franklin Roosevelt could reach huge masses of people not merely through the printed word but through radio and movie newsreels. They seemed to have an almost magical power to sway ordinary people. Though social scientists conducted little empirical analysis, they assumed that this propaganda was extremely persuasive. Why? Because, they assumed, the audience was captive, attentive, and gullible (Institute for Propaganda Analysis, 1939).

These speculations highlighted the need for more systematic tests of media impact. A second phase, therefore, consisted of systematic empirical research on the impact of the mass media, using the new method of public opinion polling. The most influential early study, that of the 1940 presidential campaign (Lazarsfeld et al., 1948), reported four main findings. First, relatively few voters changed their preferences throughout the whole campaign. Second, those changes that did occur were not closely linked to mass media exposure, contrary to the fears of the earlier analysts. Rather, people ultimately voted in line with their own social background. True, many voters had been undecided and subsequently made up their minds, but even these people decided according to their predispositions. Third, each candidate's campaign communications mainly reached people who had already supported him anyway. That is, voters tended to expose themselves to the side they already preferred, a phenomenon called *selective exposure*. Finally, interpersonal contacts with friends, coworkers, and family members, rather than media propaganda, tended to be responsible for the attitude changes that did occur. The major conclusion was that the voting decision was "a social experience," and that the media reinforced prior predispositions rather than converting people from one side to the other. A good deal of other research in the 1940s and 1950s yielded similar findings, described generally as the **minimal effects model** (see Klapper, 1960).

The last two decades have ushered in still a third era, one of renewed respect for the power of the media in politics. Many believe that television in particular has powerful persuasive effects, rendering the pre-television minimal

Saddam Hussein is a modern version of the seemingly all-powerful foreign dictator who is perceived, rightly or wrongly, as commanding vast public support in his nation because of his clever manipulation of the mass media.

effects model outdated. Several kinds of evidence have been given to support this changed perspective. There is the seeming devotion of the American public to television; supposedly, the average adult spends as much time watching television as working. There are important changes in the political uses of television. Presidents have increasingly been able to reach vast audiences through "command performances" on prime-time television. "Media experts" have become increasingly prominent in producing television commercials for political campaigns. Political "spin-doctors" are hired by candidates to help put a positive "spin" on events, so that the media interprets their candidate favorably. In this new media world, selective exposure should be no obstacle because brief political commercials are sneaked into the middle of entertainment programs, television news covers all sides of a campaign, televised debates present all candidates to large audiences, and television personalities like Larry King and Phil Donahue bring candidates into their entertainment programs. And, finally, the predispositional factors central to earlier models of voting behavior, such as party identification, social class, region, and religion, are said to have declining impact on voting behavior, leaving voters freer to be influenced by what they see and hear on television.

Let us then take a closer look at the contemporary role of the media, first assessing the overall impact of the media in politics, and then looking at some areas in which the media play their most substantial role.

Limited Effects

In general, the mass media are not as successful in producing massive changes in attitudes as this "new look" suggests. Many apparent cases of mass persuasion turn out, on close study, to have produced remarkably little real change.

Among the big media events in recent years have been televised debates between the major presidential candidates. For example, the 1980 Carter–Reagan debate, held a week before election day and often regarded as a major influence in Reagan's last-minute victorious surge, brought only 7 percent of Carter's previous supporters to Reagan's side, according to a CBS News poll done immediately after the debate. In a close race such changes were important, but they cannot be said to have been massive.

Research has also examined the effects of regular media programming on political attitudes. Some television series have dealt explicitly with problems of racism and prejudice, and have been enormously popular. The television series "Roots," depicting the history of African Americans from preslavery life in Africa to the present, played to record-breaking audiences in 1976. However, exposure to the series had no significant effect on whites' perceptions of the hardships of slavery or on racial egalitarianism. Viewers' reactions to the series were most strongly determined by their preexisting racial attitudes (Hur & Robinson, 1978; Ball-Rokeach et al., 1981). Similarly, reactions to Archie Bunker, the bigoted working-class white man who was the lead character in the series "All in the Family," were strongly determined by the

viewer's prior level of racial prejudice (Brigham & Giesbrech, 1976). In both cases, reinforcement of prior predispositions, rather than attitude change, seemed to be the major effect. Why are the media generally so ineffective in producing major changes of political attitudes? That is, what are the major obstacles they face in political life?

LOW LEVELS OF EXPOSURE. People in the business of affecting public attitudes know that their most critical and difficult problem is reaching the people they want to influence. For example, television news is often thought to be highly influential because so many people watch it. But do they? One typical study found that on an average weeknight, only 23 percent of the adult population watched one of the nightly national network news programs. Most adults (53 percent) never watched even one such program in a two-week span (J. Robinson, 1971). Another study showed that even these relatively few watchers seem not to have been watching very carefully. People who had watched an evening network news show could recall, later on in the evening, only an average of 6 percent of the stories it covered (Neuman, 1976).

Major political events, like presidential debates, would seem to be exceptions. For example, 80 million people were said to have watched at least one of the four debates in the presidential campaign of 1976. But only a minority watched more than one debate, and only about a quarter of the public watched even one debate all the way through (Sears & Chaffee, 1979). Most viewers consider a situation comedy, a football game, or a good movie more interesting than a political speech. Thus, in politics and public affairs, the percentage of the potential audience reached by any message is quite small. And given relatively poor attention among the minority who are reached by it, massive attitude change would seem to be unlikely.

How can we reconcile these statistics with the many claims of vast television audiences? For many years television ratings were largely based on whether the family TV set was on or off. But this obviously does not tell us whether anyone is watching. Indeed, movies taken of operating television sets in living rooms show that about 20 percent of the time no one in the room is watching, and another 20 percent of the time there is no one in the room at all! And even during the 60 percent of the time when an operating television set is being watched, the viewers are often doing something else as well. One study listed a vast variety of distracting activities being carried out at the same time, such as pacing, ironing, playing Monopoly, talking on the telephone, wrestling, conversing, or undressing (see Comstock et al., 1978).

More recently a "peoplemeter" system was introduced which required each individual to press a button when tuning in or out. This eliminates the hard-working but viewer-less television sets. But it involves much more work for the viewer, and as a result relatively few people agree to do it. This system also overestimates diligent attention to any given show, because it is insensitive to rapid-fire changes between channels (Milavsky, 1992). So it is likely that such rating systems also tend to overestimate attentiveness to television programs.

RESISTANCE. Even a communicator who has been successful in getting the message to the target is a long way from changing the target's opinion. For example, both Democrats and Republicans watched the Reagan–Carter TV debate in 1980, but they differed enormously in their evaluations of the opponents. The overwhelming journalistic consensus was that Reagan had "won" the debate. Yet, as you can see in Table 17-5, only 10 percent of pro-Carter

As is often the case, hard-working political speakers appearing on an equally hard-working television set are all but ignored by "viewers" who are much more interested in their own social lives.

viewers thought Reagan had won. New information seems to be incorporated into existing attitudes without changing them very much. This seems to be a typical response to most such mass communications. Why is this so? The communications that draw a large audience usually happen also to encounter strong, highly committed attitudes in a great many people. The result is that people use a variety of modes of resolution other than attitude change to restore cognitive consistency.

All the modes of resolution discussed in Chapter 6 are relevant here. For one thing, people are likely to reject outright arguments that are discrepant from their own previous attitudes. Many of the pro-Carter viewers felt that

TABLE 17-5
Voters' Judgments of Who Won the 1980 Carter–Reagan Debate

Predebate Preference	Who Won?			
	Carter	No Choice	Reagan	Total
Carter	69%	21%	10%	100%
Anderson	31	28	41	100
Undecided	27	43	30	100
Reagan	5	13	82	100

Note: Data from a nationwide CBS News/New *York Times* telephone survey of Americans of voting age.
Source: Adapted from CBS News release, October 29, 1980.

the debate had reaffirmed their initial judgment and that they did not need to think about it further. Source derogation also takes place. Many of the pro-Carter voters thought that Reagan was poorly informed and too old and that Carter had a better grasp of the complexities of the presidency, so they rejected Reagan. Perceptual distortions follow the same pattern. Voters distort the positions on issues taken by candidates to make them more consistent with their own preferences. Many of the pro-Carter voters saw Reagan as a war-hungry hawk, perceiving him as likely to get us into World War III, disregarding his desire to achieve "peace through strength." Similarly, they perceived Carter as promoting peace, disregarding his increasingly confrontive stance toward Iran and the USSR. The result of using all these modes of resolution is that people can expose themselves to discrepant information in the media and not show any real attitude change.

A NEW LOOK AT THE MEDIA

It seems to be true that the political media do not create vast attitude changes most of the time. But, as indicated, researchers have increasingly gone beyond such simple demonstrations of modest impact to look closely at media events that do break through these barriers and generate considerable influence.

A good example is the "rally round the flag effect." Often presidential job approval rises after some international crisis that reflects poorly on both the nation and the president. For example, when a secret U-2 spy plane was shot down over the Soviet Union, leading Soviet Premier Khrushchev to cancel a summit conference, approval for President Eisenhower increased. President Kennedy's approval also increased after the disastrous invasion of the Bay of Pigs, in Cuba, and the near-disastrous Cuban Missile Crisis.

Originally, scholars believed this increased approval resulted from the arousal of patriotism: When the nation has been embarrassed, we rush to the president's support. But more recently Brody (1991) has argued that public response depends to a great extent on the response of opposition political leaders, as conveyed through the media. If leaders of both parties support the president, the public will as well. But if a number of prominent political leaders oppose the president's action, the public will respond in terms of whether things have gone well or badly, approving the president's successes and disapproving his failures. In the three cases just mentioned, nearly all political leaders supported the president. The same occurred when the American hostages were taken prisoner in Teheran in 1979, and when President Reagan ordered the invasion of Grenada, in 1983; in both cases public approval of the president increased. However, when the Iran-Contra scandal broke, in 1986, Democrats were critical of President Reagan and his administration, and his support dropped substantially, with one-third of his previous supporters disapproving his overall job performance (Brody, 1991).

What, then, are the conditions in which the mass media can have such dramatic effects on public opinion?

Massive Exposure

Truly massive public exposure to political events can produce major effects. For example, the three television networks covered the events immediately following the shooting of President John F. Kennedy virtually nonstop for four days. They covered the confusion at the hospital where the dying president was taken; the swearing-in of his successor, Lyndon B. Johnson; the murder of Lee Harvey Oswald, the alleged assassin; the services; the cortege to Arlington Cemetery; the burial there; several processions through the streets of Washington; and countless retrospectives and interviews with prominent people. The networks devoted, on the average, almost 70 hours to these events (Rubin, 1967). The average American adult watched 34 hours of this coverage.

The emotional and attitudinal effects of this massive exposure were extraordinary. According to a survey completed the week after Kennedy's death (Sheatsley & Feldman, 1965), 53 percent said they had cried, and 30 percent said they had felt more upset than most people (and only 8 percent, less). Only 19 percent of the public said they had carried on "pretty much as usual" (Sheatsley & Feldman, 1965). The attitudinal effects were no less impressive. Before the assassination, Kennedy had not been thought of as a particularly exceptional president. He had barely won election, was rated by the public as doing no better a job than most presidents, and was judged by historians to be only a little above average among American presidents. Yet in the post-assassination survey, half the population called Kennedy one of the best two or three presidents in history, and only 2 percent called him "somewhat below average." It is impossible to separate the effects of the assassination itself from those of its television coverage in producing these changes. But it is widely agreed that the television coverage was instrumental in making the event among the most memorable in American history.

Another dramatic series of events concerned the Watergate scandal. At the height of his political fortunes, immediately after a smashing reelection victory in 1972, President Richard M. Nixon slowly but surely was revealed as having participated in covering up a burglary of Democratic party headquarters carried out by some of his campaign workers. Most of his top aides were sooner or later implicated in the scandal and were imprisoned, and Nixon himself ultimately became the first American president to resign in disgrace. The events came to a head when a tape recording of Nixon's private conversations was made public, revealing his complicity in the cover-up. Massive media coverage of it produced, in a period of just three days, an increase of 15 percent in those desiring Nixon's impeachment and forceful removal from office (Laing & Stevenson, 1976). This major change in public attitude forced the president to resign.

In general, presidential debates are among the best-watched regular features of the political landscape. In 1992, over 100 million viewers were said to have tuned in to one or more of the debates between Bill Clinton, George Bush, and Ross Perot. Yet as we saw earlier, many people watch debates superficially, and most people see their own preferred candidate as the winner.

The dominant effect of presidential debates upon individual viewers is reinforcement of their prior preferences. Here, in 1992, all three candidates were attractive and well-informed, and the usual result obtained. But the presence of the third-party candidate Ross Perot did add a new element, making preferences unusually volatile through the campaign.

So the most common effect of a presidential debate is simply to reinforce earlier preferences.

In some sense this is not very surprising. Usually opposing debaters are highly skilled politicians, and can barrage the public with esoteric facts and acronyms and obscure references. It should be hard for the average person to see a clear advantage for one side or the other. Yet as Table 17-5 shows, there usually is some tilt to one side or the other. In 1980, Ronald Reagan received a slight edge, based on the fact that his partisans rarely considered Carter the winner, and the uncommitteds tended to favor Reagan over Carter. How does this happen?

It turns out that the media's judgment of the debate "winner" is very important in producing this tilt. For example, in the second 1988 presidential debate, Michael Dukakis was asked how he would respond if his wife were sexually assaulted. The media consensus was that he responded too mechanically and unemotionally, as was typical of his campaign style, and they declared George Bush the debate "winner." Viewers who were questioned immediately after the debate saw Bush as the winner by 44 to

TABLE 17-6
Who Won the Second 1988 Presidential Debate?

	Immediate Post-test			Two-Week Recall		
	Democrats	Independents	Republicans	Democrats	Independents	Republicans
Bush	8%	19%	75%	26%	54%	86%
Neither	40	43	16	19	21	10
Dukakis	52	38	9	55	25	4
Total	100%	100%	100%	100%	100%	100%

Source: Adapted from Lanoue (1991, p. 85).

30 percent. But those who responded four days later, after the media verdict had time to come in, saw him as the winner by a much larger margin, 52 to 8 percent (Lanoue, 1991). And, as is shown in Table 17-6, by two weeks later Bush was seen as the overwhelming winner by both Republicans and Independents, and even by many Democrats.

A number of studies in different countries have now shown that the main persuasive effect of these debates (that is, aside from reinforcing earlier preferences) is created by these judgments of "who won." And the biggest persuasive effect of these media verdicts occurs among the less informed, who probably have paid less attention to the debate itself and are probably more vulnerable to change because they are not initially so committed to one side or the other (Lanoue, 1992; Schrott, 1990).

These instances of major media impact rank among the relatively few political events that have attracted very high levels of media exposure in the general public. So part of the key to overcoming the obstacles to change is massive exposure.

Long-term Exposure

Most studies of media impact deal with relatively brief or short-term mass communications—single programs on TV or newspaper endorsements in a particular campaign. But many important changes of attitude may result from exposure to the media over long periods of time. The long Cold War surely solidified nega-tive attitudes toward the Soviet Union. The liberalized treatment of sexuality on television and in the movies that began in the 1960s has contributed to much more liberal attitudes toward sex in the general public.

One careful study of long-term persuasive effects by the mass media investigated 80 different instances in which public opinion polls repeated exactly the same item over a period of several months (Page & Shapiro, 1992). In half the cases, public opinion had changed significantly in the interim. The authors then analyzed the content of television news to see what might have produced those changes. The major finding was that public opinion on these many issues was stable over time; not much change occurred. This is not surprising given what we have been discussing. But the authors did find a significant effect of news coverage, above and beyond that. In particular, they found that substantial changes were induced by news commentaries, such as those by anchor persons, reporters in the field, or special commentators. They also found that "experts" or research reports had significant effects as well. And presidents who were popular at the time also were persuasive, as in the case of Ronald Reagan's denunciations of the Soviet Union early in his first term.

In short, it may be that significant persuasive effects by the media require repeated pounding over a considerable period of time, rather than a one-shot magic bullet. Indeed, the operating principle of campaign media consultants, such as, in 1992, Bill Clinton's advisor James Carville or George Bush's advisor James Baker, is to select a few simple themes and hammer away at them repeatedly day after day, rather than trying to deal with all the nation's problems one at a time.

Weak Attitudes

Not all attitudes are emotionally laden and deeply held. The media may have a major persuasive impact when members of the audience are not especially committed to their attitudes. Similarly, attitudes toward relatively new and unfamiliar attitude objects, such as Ross Perot or the "ethnic cleansing" of Bosnia by Serbian forces or a new toxic waste problem may depend on media coverage. For the same reason, the media may be more decisive in primary and nonpartisan elections than in general elections, because these elections involve fewer standing predispositions. Voters may like the campaign commercials of one candidate only a little bit better than those of the other, but if they are both Republicans, at least that slight difference will not be overwhelmed by party identification.

Conveying Information

The media also have some success in providing information. Children learn a great deal from television programs ranging from "Sesame Street" to weather forecasts (Comstock et al., 1978). And in politics, presidential debates increase voters' familiarity with the candidates' positions on campaign issues (Sears & Chaffee, 1979).

One of the earliest demonstrations of this information gain from mass communications came from wartime research by Hovland, Lumsdaine, and Sheffield (1949). The Army commissioned them to evaluate the effectiveness of orientation films shown to draftees and volunteers. These films were intended to explain the reasons for World War II, to make new soldiers enthusiastic about the war effort and more eager to fight.

The researchers did not find much evidence of the hoped-for attitude change. Attitudes toward our allies the British or toward our ene-

Media coverage of campaigns tends to emphasize campaign stops such as this, without as much attention to the issues being debated. California senatorial candidate Dianne Feinstein (ultimately victorious), like most candidates for sub-presidential office, seeks the publicity that a presidential campaign attracts.

mies the Germans and the Japanese were largely unaffected. But viewing the films did markedly increase levels of information about the war. For example, the films clearly communicated factual details about the air war over Britain, such as the relative sizes of the German and British air forces, the focusing of German bombings on ports and ships, and the fact that the Germans would have physically invaded England except for the resistance of the British air force.

Nevertheless, it would be a mistake to exaggerate the amount of information conveyed by television news. We already mentioned Neuman's (1976) study indicating that viewers could recall only 6 percent of the stories on the national news earlier that evening. People do not usually pay close attention to television news. Also, TV news tends to emphasize the more entertaining features of the day's events. For example, when it comes to elections, TV news emphasizes the campaign as a competitive contest—who is winning, polls, size of campaign audiences, advertising strategies, fund-raising strategies, delegate counts, who made the latest mistake, and pictures of motorcades or people in funny hats. Complex policy positions normally do not receive detailed media coverage. One-third of all the television news stories on the 1988 primaries referred to the candidates' poll standings (Ansolabahere, Behr, & Iyenger, 1991). So regular viewers of TV news often know little more about candidates' policies than do nonviewers (Patterson & McClure, 1976).

537

Agenda Setting

In recent years, much attention has been paid to the media's role in **agenda setting.** Issues given a great deal of media coverage tend to become regarded as the most important problems facing the nation. Political leaders then tend to be evaluated in terms of their ability to solve those problems. In this sense the media are said to set the agenda for political discussion: They influence not *what* the public thinks, but what the public thinks *about*.

One important early study showed that the public's sense of priorities (as reflected in the Gallup poll question, "What is the most important problem facing the nation?") was determined by the volume of news coverage given various issues. Thus, media coverage of the Vietnam War, the ghetto riots, assassinations, and campus unrest of the 1960s, and of Watergate in the 1970s, made these issues the number one problems of the day. Interestingly enough, the public's priorities bore more relationship to the volume of media coverage than to such indicators of "reality" as the number of troops actually involved in Vietnam, the real crime rate, and so on (Funkhouser, 1973).

Such studies might only reflect a decision by the media to cover the problems already worrying the public; that is, the public's priorities may dictate media coverage, rather than vice versa. That is no doubt part of the story. But a number of careful experiments have indicated that greater television news coverage induces higher issue salience regardless of the viewer's previous priorities. In one, adults viewed television newscasts in which the amount of coverage given particular issues was varied experimentally. This manipulation significantly influenced the perceived importance of these issues, even on a questionnaire given 24 hours later (Iyengar & Kinder, 1987).

One implication of the agenda-setting argument is that media attention can determine which attitude viewers will bring to bear on their political choices. To illustrate this, another experiment showed that manipulating issue salience influenced the basis for the respondents' evaluations of the president. Respondents tended to base their approval of the president's overall performance on his handling of the particular issue made salient in the experiment. For example, when energy shortages were most intensively covered, viewers tended to evaluate the president's overall performance primarily in terms of how well they felt he was handling the energy problem (Iyenger & Kinder, 1987).

In a real-world application of this finding, Krosnick and Kinder (1990) addressed the sharp drop in Ronald Reagan's approval ratings after the Iran-Contra scandal became public, in November 1986. They showed that attitudes about American intervention in Nicaragua had become more influential in the public's evaluations of Reagan. Presumably, media coverage of Iran-Contra made it more salient, and so he tended to be appraised more in terms of voters' attitudes about that issue. These studies indicate that under the right circumstances television news can have an agenda-setting effect. Similarly, the economic recession was highly salient when George Bush ran for reelection in 1992, so he tended to be judged in terms of voters' assessments of the economy. But if the elec-

The Iran-Contra scandal in 1986 was a major blow to the Reagan administration. Ollie North, here being sworn in for congressional testimony, sought to overcome its negative implications by presenting himself as a patriotic military officer.

tion had occurred a year earlier, he might have been judged in terms of the much more successful Persian Gulf war.

Finally, differences between types of issues seem to affect the ability of the media to agenda-set. The media seem most influential for "rapid onset" issues, such as the sudden breaking of the Iran-Contra scandal, the outbreaks of wars, ghetto riots, or the toppling of Communist regimes in East Europe. They seem less powerful for long-term or slowly evolving issues, such as the environment or poverty (Ansolabahere et al., 1991).

Framing

The implication of the agenda-setting argument is that the salience of an issue is crucial to its political impact. But it also implies that the **framing** of any given issue can also be important. A classic example concerns the public's attitudes toward American military intervention in Korea in the early 1950s. The public strongly supported intervention, often by as much as two-to-one, when they were asked, "Do you think the United States was right or wrong in sending American troops to stop the Communist invasion of South Korea?" But when they were asked, "Do you think we did the right thing in getting into the fighting in Korea last summer or should we have stayed out?" the public was at best evenly divided, and after the first year of that conflict, mostly opposed to intervention (Mueller, 1973). Apparently framing the issue to make "the Communist invasion" salient stimulated much more public support for military action. Similarly, during the mid-1980s, support for American funding of the Contra rebels in Nicaragua was greatly enhanced when it was explicitly stated that soldiers other than Americans would be doing the fighting (Lockerbie & Borrelli, 1990). On the domestic front, framing government aid to the disadvantaged as "assistance to the poor" yields more than twice the public support as framing it as "welfare," even though the terms refer to much the same programs (Smith, 1987).

Stereotypes about black welfare mothers—unemployed, unmarried, with several children from several fathers—are among the most politically powerful in American society. Every candidate loves to run against them, even though welfare in fact does not represent a terribly large drain on tax revenues.

Another important distinction is between *episodic* and *thematic* framing of issues. Episodic news stories depict public issues in terms of concrete instances, usually focusing on a specific individual and often using pictures of that person. A good example would be a story on the general problem of homelessness, but focusing especially on the plight of a specific homeless person (Iyengar, 1991). In contrast, thematic frames place issues in more general or abstract contexts, often having reporters ("talking heads") discussing general conditions. Not surprisingly, television news tends to be dominated by episodic framing, both because of severe time constraints and because most viewers find it more interesting.

The interesting consequence is that episodic framing tends to produce individualistic (or dispositional) attributions of responsibility for events, whereas thematic framing tends to produce societal attributions. For example, episodic coverage of black poverty tends to lead viewers to hold individuals responsible for racial inequality, especially poor black people and black adult single mothers. Thematic coverage of the general issue of racial discrimination, much of it emanating from general studies and reports coming from the federal government, has the opposite effect, of increasing its attribution to societal conditions rather than to prejudiced individuals (Iyengar, 1991).

Media Bias

Media attention to a particular issue, or a particular framing of an issue, seems to increase its salience and therefore its political power. One implication is that any systematic biases in the focus of media attention should also be able to bias what the voters think about, and therefore what issues are most important in their choices.

Careful studies of presidential campaigns (e.g., Patterson, 1980) have found that television and the newspapers are not especially biased toward one side or the other. But they focus most intensively on "the horserace," as indicated earlier. Women candidates in particular are disadvantaged by this: They receive less overall coverage than do their male opponents, and more of it focuses on their "viability" (how likely they are to win or lose), with some tendency to consider them less likely to win (Kahn & Goldenberg, 1991). This is not a trivial bias, since voters give more support to the specific candidate they think more likely to win—the so-called "bandwagon effect" (Bartels, 1988). Indeed, the publicity given to "the year of the woman" in 1992 came about precisely because for once many women seemed likely to win.

Another media bias is toward a focus on the character of potential leaders rather than on the issues. In 1988, the media began by concentrating heavily on George Bush's reputation as a "wimp," and later on Michael Dukakis' supposed lack of emotion. In 1992, the media focused intensively on Bill Clinton's supposedly deceptive responses to questions about his family life and draft status while in school, and on Ross Perot's supposed paranoiac tendencies. In general, as we saw in our discussion of attribution theory (Chapter 4), dispositional attributions are greatest when the individual is particularly

unusual, and therefore salient, in his or her context. So this media focus on character seems to be most intense when the candidate comes from an unusual background; in 1984, Jesse Jackson, as the only major black candidate, attracted much more character coverage than did the other Democratic candidates (Ansolabahere et al., 1991).

The media, therefore, do not often seem to produce major political attitude changes except when exposure is massive or long term. They are more likely to have significant effects in providing information, or influencing which issues are salient or how they are framed. But even in these cases we should not overestimate the magnitude of effects. As with media violence, it is much easier to document effects in the laboratory than in real life.

INTERNATIONAL CONFLICT

Another major influence on political psychology has been international conflict. During the 1950s and 1960s, the Cold War inspired much psychological work on international conflict, just as today much work is focused on international tensions in and around the Middle East and Eastern Europe. Specific crises have also been a focus of attention, such as the Cuban Missile Crisis or the negotiations at Munich in 1938 that led to Hitler's takeover of parts of Czechoslovakia.

In Chapter 7, we discussed a number of theories about the origins of intergroup conflict. Social learning theories look to children's socialization of prejudices toward outgroups. The frustration–aggression theory suggests that when one group frustrates another, the other will respond aggressively. Social identity theory suggests that people will have higher self-esteem if they identify with a group that is superior to its rivals, so they work for better outcomes for their own group. Realistic group conflict theory suggests that antagonisms between groups arise from real conflicts over scarce resources; the same two nations cannot both inhabit the same rich oil fields that lie between their capitals.

Presumably all these factors are at work in producing international conflicts. A comprehensive psychological analysis of such conflicts should consider many factors, including mutual perceptions of contending parties, attitudes toward each party (such as nationalism and out-group antagonisms), economics, social roles, organizational behavior and group dynamics within decision-making groups, and bargaining and negotiation (e.g., Stagner, 1967). We can cover only a small portion of this terrain here.

Images of the Enemy

A convenient starting point is the images that contending adversaries hold about themselves and each other. These can focus on nations, political leaders, or populaces. For example, we might be interested in the important question during the Cold War of whether or not American decision makers viewed the Soviet government as fundamentally hostile to the United States. Similarly, we might be interested in the images that officials in the U.S. State Department had of the images that Soviet decision makers had, in turn, of American leaders' intentions.

The first priority for psychologists has been to identify patterns of misperception. In particular, people seem to delight in having a foreign enemy, and so they develop passionately held **enemy images.** Cognitive consistency theories (see Chapter 6) predict that perceptions will be biased toward consistency with basic attitudes. So when people have a strong commitment to viewing another nation as the enemy, many of their other perceptions fall into line. For example, during the Cold War, American decision makers tended to perceive the Soviet Union as expansionist, ruthless, heartless, atheistic, and deceitful. Soviet leaders were thought to support peaceful solutions to conflict only when faced with superior power. In general, enemies are perceived as having bad intentions, poor morals, and bad traits (Finlay, Holsti, & Fagan, 1967). A strongly felt enemy image will produce such biases as believing in "the diabolical enemy," "the moral self," and "the virile self" (White, 1970).

Group-serving attributions emerge as well. Images of the enemy lead to positive attribu-

tions for the actions taken by one's own nation and negative attributions for those taken by the enemy. Burn and Oskamp (1989) asked adults in California to provide explanations for similar actions taken by the Soviet Union and by the United States. They found that actions taken by the Soviet Union received much more negative attributions: For example, the Soviet invasion of Afghanistan was given a negative attribution by 57 percent, whereas the U.S. invasion of Grenada by only 27 percent (and the air attack on Libya by only 12 percent). Usually our own nation's military actions are seen as defensive, whereas the enemy's military actions represent aggressive desires for power (Silverstein & Flamenbaum, 1989).

The same is true of a nation's positive actions: If our nation does it, we explain it positively, but not if the enemy does it. In one study, a newspaper story described the heroic action of an icebreaker in cracking an escape route through the arctic ice that allowed 1000 trapped whales to escape. When it was described as a U.S. boat, the American subjects explained the action in altruistic terms (e.g., "to save the whales"). When it was described as a Soviet boat, it was explained as being self-serving (e.g., "to generate favorable publicity"). In general, the United States was evaluated as acting on a more moral basis than was the USSR (Sande, Goethals, Ferrari, & Worth, 1989).

The cognitive consistency idea would lead us to expect that images of the enemy would be systematically related to other attitudes the individual holds. For example, Hurwitz and Peffley (1990) found that negative images of the Soviet Union were related to patriotism, to moral traditionalism, and to Christian fundamentalism. This web of consistent attitudes makes images of the enemy surprisingly hard to change, even when rapidly changing events ought to change them. Peffley and Hurwitz (1992) found that from 1987 to 1988, a period of great change in USSR–U.S. relations (including initiatives to cut nuclear arms by both Reagan and Gorbachev; summit meetings and signed agreements; and great popularity for Gorbachev within the United States), the best predictor of images of the USSR in 1988 was still the individual's attitude in 1987.

Boris Yeltsin, like Gorbachev before him, was enormously popular among Americans for his support of democratic principles and his desire to end the Cold War peacefully.

Nevertheless, change does occur sometimes. Yatani and Bramel (1989) have traced Americans' attitudes toward the Soviet Union over the period of the Cold War (from 1953 to 1988) and found substantial drops in negativity from 1953 to 1974, from 90 to 50 percent unfavorable. Then tensions rose again, so that by 1984 again 90 percent were unfavorable. Americans then softened once more, so that by 1988 only 70 percent were unfavorable. The best predictors of individuals' changes, as one might expect, were evaluations of Soviet behavior during that period (Peffley & Hurwitz, 1992). And changes toward more positive images of the USSR were associated with increased support for friendly policies (regarding issues such as defense spending, Star Wars, or the nuclear freeze).

Another implication of the cognitive consistency idea is that images of the enemy should be symmetrical: The **mirror image** suggests that we will explain our own country's actions favorably, and the enemy's negatively, even when the actions are very similar (Bronfenbrenner, 1961). We believe that our enemy is aggressive and immoral, and they believe the same thing about us. So, if Americans perceived the Soviets as the enemy and the United States as moral and honest, it would not be surprising if the Soviets had a very similar black-and-white portrait of the United States in mind. Each side believes it has peaceful intentions and is afraid of the other side; the other side is perceived as aggressive

and threatening, so one's own militarism is justified as self-defense.

Another illusion has been described as the *blacktop illusion:* the tendency to see the enemy's government as evil, but the people of that country as being basically good (White, 1970). To test this, Burn and Oskamp (1989) asked Californians to rate the Soviet and U.S. people and government on a series of adjectives, such as "friendly" or "peace-loving" or "bad." They found that in general the United States was rated more favorably than the USSR, but that the people of the USSR were rated more favorably than their government. This is shown in Figure 17-1.

Figure 17-1   American students' evaluations of citizens and governments of the USA and the USSR. (*Source:* Adapted from Burn & Oskamp, 1989, p. 80.)

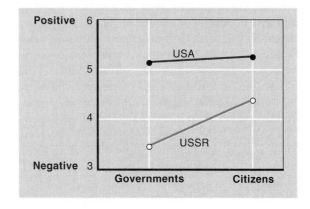

In short, as Finlay and colleagues (1967, p. 7) indicated, "It seems that we have always needed enemies and scapegoats; if they have not been readily available, we have created them." They serve a variety of functions for leaders and followers alike, sometimes justifying actions that might otherwise be improper or illegal, and at other times as a means for diverting attention from other pressing and more difficult problems. And, as social identity theory would predict, they provide a means by which we can inflate our own worth and values.

Belief Systems

A central tenet of social cognition theories in psychology (see Chapter 3) is that information processing tends to be "theory driven" rather than "data driven." We used the term *schema* to describe these theories in that earlier chapter. This leads us to consider the schemas, or belief systems, that decision makers have about international conflicts.

Two quite different belief systems are the "deterrence" and "spiral" models of international relations (Jervis, 1976). The deterrence model holds that a powerful nation must be firm in its resolve and not give potential aggressors concessions; indeed, it must be willing to go to war to defend its interests. Firmness can check aggression. The idea is that if you give aggressors an inch, they will take a mile, as in the case of British Prime Minister Neville Chamberlain's capitulation to Adolf Hitler in Munich in 1938. The spiral model, instead, holds that other nations are likely to develop aggressive intentions sooner or later, so to protect one's security it is necessary at all times to be the aggressor. This viewpoint, not surprisingly, tends to bias the perceiver toward seeing danger everywhere.

An especially important notion is that of a leader's **operational code** (Leites, 1951; George, 1969), that is, a leader's beliefs about the nature of politics and political conflict, historical developments, and strategy and tactics. This too is an example of a schema. Leites suggests that the operational codes of the Bolshevik leaders who led the Russian Revolution, and led the Soviet Union for many years, were quite different from those of contemporary American leaders. The Bolsheviks were willing to engage in high-risk activities as long as subsequent events could be controlled, so that the sequence could be aborted in the event of failure; American leaders, with their sensitivity to public opinion and concern about the next election, abhorred the idea of public failure, and thus poorly understood Soviet leadership.

One particularly interesting set of theories held by decision makers involve the "lessons" they have "learned from history" (Jervis, 1976). For example, Franklin Roosevelt, who was Secretary of the Navy at the end of World War I, was much impressed by Woodrow Wilson's failure to bring the United States into an international peace-keeping organization, and so at the end of World War II was willing to make important concessions to the Soviet Union to ensure that all nations joined the United Nations. On the other hand, John F. Kennedy, whose father was ambassador to Great Britain when the British government was appeasing Hitler at Munich, later in life was resolutely opposed to making concessions to the Soviet Union. Each had "learned from history" during his formative years, but quite different lessons!

One danger is that too often those lessons are learned early in life in a particular historical context, and applied much later on when that original context may be irrelevant or misleading. The complaint that military leaders are always "fighting the last war" reflects this sometimes dated quality of the lessons of history. On the other hand, there is the familiar cliche that "those who are ignorant of history are condemned to repeat it." Another danger, as with cognitive biases in general, is that the "lessons of history" give too much weight to firsthand or vivid experiences, or to efforts that were successful even if for accidental reasons (Jervis, 1976).

Belief systems should produce more rational decisions if they are well informed and well integrated. The notion of **integrative complexity** has been used to describe such belief systems. It is composed of two dimensions: *differentiation* (the number of aspects of the problem perceived by the leader) and *integration* (perceiving the various parts of the problem as related to each other). A leader is likely to be thought more sensible if he or she takes into account many factors in thinking about enemy military intentions, such as the enemy's economic resources, real national interests, fear of invasion, and ideological desires for world domination. Similarly, a leader is likely to be regarded as more rational if his or her perceptions of enemy intentions are integrated with knowledge about what kinds of military forces the enemy has, the enemy's economic resources, the relevant geography, and so on.

The integrative complexity of decision makers' belief systems depends in part on the situation. For example, one hypothesis is that in revolutionary phases, leadership requires single-minded devotion to the cause, simple messages around which followers can unite, and simple goals that can be the basis of swift and concerted action. As a result, the writings of Washington, Lenin, and Mao Tse-Tung were rather low in integrative complexity during the revolutionary phases of their careers. On the other hand, after a revolution has succeeded, the enemy has been defeated, and the revolutionaries take power, they must administer the country in all its complexities. At that point they need to be more aware of complexity, qualify their assertions, and so on. Indeed, the integrative complexity of such revolutionaries' rhetoric increased substantially after they took power. And it increased more for those who were successful—like Lenin—than for those who were unsuccessful—like his failed rival Trotsky (Suedfeld & Rank, 1976).

Another hypothesis is that international crises are more likely to be solved without use of force when decision makers are using integratively complex thinking. In such highly complex situations, integrated thinking is required to discuss and evaluate all possible alternatives. For example, the integrative complexity of messages exchanged by American and Soviet leaders prior to the outbreak of the Korean conflict in 1950 was quite low. But during the Cuban Missile Crisis, which was resolved without

bloodshed, both sides exhibited much more complex thinking (Suedfeld & Tetlock, 1977).

A central question motivating much of this research is whether foreign policy decision makers are making rational or irrational decisions. A formal definition of rationality would surely not fit most of the cases we have discussed. Many biases and errors intrude, just as we would have expected from our discussions of decision making in earlier chapters. Yet a more modest definition of rationality may come closer. Simon (1985) has offered the notion of *bounded rationality* that suggests practical decision makers are pretty rational within their limits: They do not have all the information, they do not have all the time necessary to evaluate the information they have, they take various cognitive shortcuts, they choose alternatives that are "good enough" rather than "perfect," and they are subject to a wide variety of irrational pressures. But they are often as rational as can be expected under the circumstances.

Conflict Resolution

Conflict often arises from **competitive interdependence,** as we saw in Chapter 7 on prejudice. When two groups are in a relationship in which what one group gets depends in part on what the other gets, they compete for the resources, and conflict is produced (Sherif et al., 1961). Yet when there are realistic conflicts between nations, it is not necessarily the case that competition benefits anyone, even the winner. Rather, there often are cooperative solutions that would benefit both more. To be sure, the big winners in World War II, the United States and the Soviet Union, benefited more than did the losers, Germany and Japan. But it was at terrible cost to all concerned, in terms of civilian and military dead and wounded, and devastated cities and economies. Over twenty million people died in the Soviet Union alone during that war. There might have been cooperative solutions that would have benefited everyone more. Competitive interdependence between nations often has both competitive and cooperative solutions. The two parties can fight it out, with one winning and one losing. Or, sometimes they fight it out, and both lose, as would be the case in a nuclear exchange. Or, sometimes they cooperate, such that neither gains as much as they might by winning, but both profit in the long run.

Reward structures that are mixtures of cooperation and competition are often described in terms of the **prisoner's dilemma game** (see Chapter 11). This is the situation in which one prisoner cannot talk to his pal. The jailer offers a deal: Either prisoner can get off if he confesses and implicates the other prisoner. If neither confesses, they both get short jail terms. But if they both confess, they both get long terms. So the prisoner can cooperate with his partner in crime and keep mum and get a short jail term. Or he can compete and confess, in which case he may get off altogether or he may be in jail for the maximum term. International conflicts have much of this same character. By cooperating with other nations with whom we have conflicts, we may at least get something. By going to war, we may win, though usually painfully, or everyone may lose big.

How can international conflicts best be resolved? Deutsch (1973) has offered what he describes as a "crude law of social relations": cooperative behavior breeds cooperation in return, and competition inspires competition from others. In an interaction with another group or individual, the person who makes the first move can set the tone of the interaction. In the prisoner's dilemma game, if one person takes a cooperative stance initially, sacrificing the chance for a really big gain for the possibility that both players will win small gains, it is more likely that the other person will also cooperate. If the first person chooses a response that is likely to hurt the other person grievously, that is likely to be reciprocated as well.

TIT FOR TAT AND GRIT. The interesting aspect of the prisoner's dilemma game is that the most effective strategy for earning points for one's own side, over the long term, may be Deutsch's principle. This is called the **"tit-for-tat" strategy.** It starts the interaction with a cooperative response. Thereafter, each time the opponent responds cooperatively, the player cooperates. But if the opponent chooses a competitive response, the player retaliates. Axelrod (1984) held an electronic tournament that came up with exactly this outcome. He invited 14 experts in game theory to program optimal strategies for playing the game. Then he played each of them against the others, and against a computer program that generated random responses, in games of 200 trials each. He found that the tit-for-tat strategy consistently produced the best outcomes for the individual. To win, then, Axelrod concluded the best player should not start a fight (that is, should always initiate cooperation, or respond cooperatively to the opponent's cooperative stance), should not hold grudges (that is, if the opponent switches to cooperation after a period of competition, the player should not vindictively continue to compete), and should not allow himself or herself to be taken advantage of (that is, should retaliate if the opponent switches to a competitive stance).

The implication is that a peaceful gesture is usually helpful unless the opponent has been consistently hostile. This idea has been applied to international relations in the form of a strategy called **GRIT** (graduated reciprocation in tension reduction). This was proposed by Charles Osgood (1962) at a time of extreme tension over nuclear weapons between the United States and the Soviet Union. It proposed that one side make small concessions on its own to reduce tensions between the two superpowers, as a way of seducing the other side into making reciprocal concessions. It assumed that the tit-for-tat strategy would occur, but that it needed to be triggered by some unilateral gesture of tension reduction.

Osgood advocated that the United States gradually reduce armaments unilaterally, but without jeopardizing our own security either in terms of the potential for nuclear retaliation or in conventional arms. Our own reductions should be graduated depending on the opponent's response: If the Soviet Union makes small cuts, so should we; if they make large cuts, so should we. Our tension-reducing acts need to be clear-cut and verifiable, and public, and include an explicit invitation for the opponent to reciprocate. And they should take place over a wide range of geographical regions and dimensions of conflict—diplomatic, military, educational, and whatever.

Several examples of the GRIT strategy seemed to have occurred during the Cold War. In the mid-1950s, Khrushchev appears to have used it in trying to defuse tension around the status of Austria, which was occupied by both Soviet and U.S. forces. A resulting treaty neutralized that country (Larson, 1986). Not long after the world came to the brink of nuclear war in the Cuban Missile Crisis, President Kennedy announced a unilateral initiative: the ending of nuclear tests in the atmosphere. Several minor mutual diplomatic concessions followed, and then agreements to put in a "hot line" between the two national leaders to help avoid accidental nuclear war, to direct air traffic between Moscow and New York, to sell surplus wheat to the Russians, and other tension-reducing moves. Shortly before President Kennedy was assassinated later that year, tensions seemed to resume again, perhaps because the president began to look forward to his campaign for reelection and did not wish to appear "soft" toward the Soviet Union. But this period represents an interesting experiment in international negotiation (Etzioni, 1967).

Third-Party Mediation. Another approach to international conflict involves the good works of some third party who serves as a mediator. A most successful example was President Jimmy Carter's mediation of conflicts between Israel, as represented by Prime Minister Begin, and Egypt, represented by President Sadat. He succeeded in isolating the two leaders at the presidential retreat at Camp David, and then engaged in "shuttle diplomacy," personally shuttling back and forth between the two leaders. Finally, he obtained a historic agreement between the two warring nations, one that resulted in mutual diplomatic recognition, a peace treaty, and the return of the captured Sinai Peninsula to Egypt.

Later efforts have been made by a wide variety of social scientists to play a similar mediating role to create understanding between hostile parties. One has been the effort by Kelman and Cohen (1986) to reduce tensions between Palestinians and Israelis. The basic idea is that the participants need to analyze not only their own perspectives but those of their adversaries and to recognize the shared nature of the problem. While there have been no extensive evaluations of this approach, it is a promising one and has the value of keeping communication open between groups that frequently seem to prefer to go to war with each other.

Crisis Management

How do political leaders deal with international (or even domestic) crises? When John F. Kennedy and his advisors attempted to deal with the missiles in Cuba, what determined whether they would be successful or not? Clearly they could have triggered a major war, but they did not. On the other hand, they might have defused the crisis without risking war, and they did not. What makes leaders more or less successful in dealing with such crises?

One factor inherent in international crises is psychological stress. Such stress can have a number of negative effects, such as reducing the complexity of information processing, and it can lead to defensive avoidance and wishful thinking. Janis and Mann's (1977) conflict theory of decision-making centers on emotion-laden decisional conflicts, the various patterns of coping behavior common in such conflicts, the antecedents of such coping patterns, and their various consequences for decisional rationality. Janis and Mann offer various techniques for coping constructively with stress, primarily relying on vigilance. Decision makers need to inform themselves adequately beforehand about the decision, but particularly about the emotions likely to accompany the decision and its aftermath, and come to grips with them.

Finally, most foreign policy decisions are made with extensive small-group deliberation, so it is perhaps not surprising that one of the most influential efforts by a political psychologist involves **groupthink.** As discussed in Chapter 11, groupthink occurs when a group of people working together form a highly cohesive, tight group with high morale. Subtly they begin to reject people who don't agree with the group, reject differing ideas, and take on an illusion of invulnerability. They then begin to exhibit many symptoms of poor decision-making, such as incompletely surveying alternative possibilities, failure to examine the risks of the preferred choice, and selective biases in evaluating information.

As we indicated earlier, Janis (1982) applied this theory to numerous cases of foreign policy decision-making. He suggested that the American government's lack of response to information concerning a forthcoming Japanese attack on Pearl Harbor came about through groupthink, an unwillingness to take seriously information that would threaten the foundations of their current policies. He also suggests that groupthink helped to foster all the illusions that led to the disastrous American invasion of Castro's Cuba at the Bay of Pigs in 1961.

On the other hand, there are things that can be done to prevent or minimize groupthink. As we indicated earlier, the leader can encourage each member to air objections and be critical of the group's consensus. Outside experts can be called in to challenge the group's decision. Devil's advocates or subcommittees can be formed within the group to come up with any plausible alternative. Indeed, Janis suggests that the Kennedy administration's handling of the Cuban Missile Crisis exhibited some of these desirable features. The president even arranged to be absent at some key meetings so that the others would not be so concerned with pleasing him by agreeing with whatever he said.

CONCLUSIONS

The psychological approach to politics is distinctive in two respects. First, it tends to be a comprehensive approach: The political psychologist tries to take into account any and all forces on human behavior. Second, the political psychologist emphasizes distinctively psychological factors such as stress, cognitive consistency, cognitive biases, and group influence. These factors tend to emphasize irrational influences on the individual's behavior. A rival point of view, in many respects, is the economic approach, which views people as more narrowly motivated by the rational pursuit of material interests. As with many other topics discussed in this book, this contrast of perspectives provides a creative tension that in the long run helps to illuminate the many complex aspects of the human species.

KEY TERMS

agenda-setting	group consciousness	party identification
cognitive consistency	groupthink	persistence
competitive interdependence	ideology	political socialization
enemy image	integrative complexity	prisoner's dilemma game
framing	minimal effects model	self-interest
gender gap	mirror image	sociotropic
GRIT	operational code	tit-for-tat strategy

SUMMARY

1. Basic political attitudes are often acquired before adulthood. They are vulnerable to change in early adulthood, but are quite persistent thereafter. Party identification is influenced to some extent by one's parents, although not as exclusively as once thought.

2. The dominant theory of voting behavior views a longstanding party identification, acquired early in life, as the major influence on the vote. Voters are thought to be generally ill informed and nonideological, and to have rather weak attitudes on issues.

3. This dominant theory has been challenged in recent years by the view that voters do respond in a moderately informed manner to the realities of life, in terms of their economic situations, issue differences between candidates, presidential performance, and constituency service. Ideology plays a more central role than it once did.

4. Intergroup conflict is receiving much current attention, especially racial and gender conflict. The "gender gap" is becoming an important political reality.

5. In the 1930s the mass media were thought to be awesomely powerful new weapons, and in the 1940s and 1950s to have minimal effects. Today there is renewed respect for their role. Nevertheless, far-ranging attitude changes are rarely produced by the media.

6. Major obstacles include lack of exposure to discrepant information and the resistance to change of highly committed attitudes.

7. The media can produce major changes in political attitudes on those rare occasions when there is massive exposure to politics. The media can also be effective through repeated exposure over long time periods, changing low-commitment attitudes, providing information, in agenda setting, and in framing issues.

8. A number of common misperceptions in international relations have been identified, including the need to identify an enemy, the mirror images that contending powers have of each other, and the tendency to overuse the "lessons of history."

9. Elite decision-making in international relations is also subject to bias due to the stress and emotionality inevitably associated with it, and to the group dynamics of decision-making elites.

SUGGESTED READINGS

Alwin, D. F., Cohen, R. L., & Newcomb, T. M. (1991). *Political attitudes over the life span: The Bennington women after fifty years.* Madison: University of Wisconsin Press. The report of a fifty-year followup of the classic Newcomb study of Bennington alumnae, along with careful reanalysis of the original results.

Ansolabahere, S., Behr, R., & Iyengar, S. (1991). Mass media and elections: An overview. *American Politics Quarterly, 19,* 109–139. A brief review of some of the more interesting recent developments in research on campaign media.

Campbell, A., Converse, P. E., Miller, W. E., & Stokes, D. E. (1960). *The American voter.* New York: Wiley. The most influential empirical study of voting behavior.

Janis, I. L. (1982). *Victims of groupthink* (2nd ed.). Boston: Houghton Mifflin. A series of case studies analyzing foreign policy "fiascoes" (and some successes) as a result of "groupthink." Includes chapters on Pearl Harbor, the Bay of Pigs, and Watergate.

Jervis, R. (1976). *Perception and misperception in international politics.* Princeton, NJ: Princeton University Press. The best application of social cognition theory and research to government decision makers' perceptions of international relations; many fascinating case studies.

Kinder, D. R., & Sears, D. O. (1985). Public opinion and political action. In G. Lindzey and E. Aronson (Eds.), *Handbook of social psychology* (3rd ed., Vol. 2). New York: Random House. A comprehensive account of research on public opinion concerning politics in the United States. Relates that research to the social psychological principles discussed in this chapter.

Lau, R. R., & Sears, D. O. (1986). *Political cognition: The 29th Annual Carnegie Symposium on Cognition.* Hillsdale, NJ: Erlbaum. A collection of papers that apply social cognition research and theory to politics. The schema concept appears most often.

McGuire, W. I. (1986). The myth of massive media impact:

Savagings and salvagings. In G. Comstock (Ed.), *Public Communication and Behavior* (Vol. 1). Orlando, FL: Academic Press. A thorough but surprisingly brief review of the empirical evidence on the 12 principal areas of hypothesized media impact: "The demonstrated impacts are surprisingly slight."

Political Psychology. A quarterly journal that publishes a wide variety of research, ranging from psychobiography and peace research to voting behavior.

Sears, D. O., & Funk, C. F. (1991). The role of self-interest in social and political attitudes. In M. P. Zanna, *Advances in Experimental Social Psychology* (Vol. 24, pp. 1–91). Orlando: Academic Press. The most comprehensive review of the research showing limitations on the role of self-interest in public opinion.

Shapiro, R. Y., & Mahajan, H. (1986). Gender differences in policy preferences: A summary of trends from the 1960s to the 1980s. *Public Opinion Quarterly, 50,* 42–61. The best brief summary of the historical origins of the gender gap.

White, R. K. (Ed.) (1986). *Psychology and the prevention of nuclear war.* New York: New York University Press. A broad collection of the best of psychologists' thinking about international conflict in the nuclear era.

Glossary

Actor-observer bias The tendency for observers to overestimate the importance of the actor's dispositions, and for the actor to overestimate the importance of the situation in explaining the actor's behavior.

Additive principle In impression formation, the idea that information about a person or attitude is processed in terms of its evaluative implications, and then added together to form an overall impression. Sometimes contrasted with the *averaging principle*.

Affective component That part of an *attitude* consisting of a person's emotional feelings associated with beliefs about an attitude object; consists mainly of the evaluation of the object (like–dislike, pro–con).

Affiliation The basic human tendency to seek the company of other people.

Agenda-setting The process in which mass communications focus public attention on certain issues, and therefore determine which issues the public is concerned about. If the media focus intensively on inflation, the public becomes concerned with inflation; if they focus on the Middle East, so will the public.

Aggression Any action intended to hurt another person.

Aggression anxiety Anxiety about expressing overt aggression, usually with respect to a particular target.

Altruism An act performed voluntarily to help another person when there is no expectation of receiving a reward in any form. See also *prosocial behavior*.

Ambivalent racism A new form of racism that combines conflicting pro-minority and anti-minority elements, such as egalitarian values and stereotypes that minorities do not work hard enough.

Androgyny People who believe they possess both traditionally feminine and masculine characteristics. An androgynous person's self-concept includes both masculine, or instrumental, qualities (e.g., being independent and strong) and feminine, or expressive, qualities (e.g., being nurturant and gentle).

Anger Aggressive feelings.

Antisocial aggression Aggressive acts such as murder that violate commonly accepted social norms.

Archival research The analysis of data already collected for another purpose, such as census data or legal records of births, deaths, and marriages.

Association A link in memory between different stimuli that occur together in time and place. Through pairing, reactions to one stimulus become associated with the other. This is one of the basic processes by which learning occurs.

Associationistic model of impression formation The viewpoint that people organize their impressions of other people in terms of their beliefs about how traits go together.

Assumed similarity effect In intergroup relations, the tendency for members of an ingroup to assume that fellow members share their attitudes and values.

Attachment The emotional bonds that form between people in a close relationship. During infancy, attachment is seen when a child responds positively to one special person, wants to be with that person, seeks the person out when frightened, etc.

Attitude Enduring response disposition with an *affective component*, a *behavioral component* and a *cognitive component*. We develop and hold attitudes toward persons, objects, and ideas.

Attitude-discrepant behavior Acts inconsistent with a person's attitudes. When an individual behaves in a way inconsistent with a belief, *cognitive dissonance* is produced and there is a tendency for the attitude to change. See *cognitive dissonance theory*.

Attribution The process by which people use information to make inferences about the causes of behavior or attitudes.

550

Attribution theory The principles that determine how attributions are made and what effects these causal attributions have.

Averaging principle In impression formation, the idea that information about a person or attitude is processed in terms of its evaluative implications, and then averaged together to form an overall attitude. Sometimes contrasted with the *additive principle*.

Aversive racism Attitudes toward members of a racial group that combine both egalitarian social values and negative emotions, resulting in avoidance of that racial group. For example, whites may value equality but have negative feelings toward blacks, and so avoid blacks.

Balance theory Heider proposed that we strive to maintain consistency among our sentiment and unit relations. We are motivated to like people we are connected to by physical proximity or other links, to like people we agree with, and to dislike those we disagree with.

Behavioral component That part of an *attitude* consisting of the person's tendencies to act toward the attitude object. A child's attitude toward a pet cat may include the tendencies to pet and cuddle the animal.

Behavioral intention The conscious intention to carry out a specific act.

Behavioral self-blame Blaming one's own actions for a victimization that has befallen the self.

Behaviorism The influential analysis of learning associated with Watson, Pavlov, and Skinner. It investigates only overt behavior, not subjective states such as thoughts or feelings. Behaviorism identifies association and reinforcement as the key determinants of learning.

Biopsychosocial model The view that a person's state of health is jointly determined by biological factors (such as exposure to a virus), psychological factors (such as stress), and social factors (such as degree of social support).

Body language Information transmitted about attitudes, emotions, and so on by nonverbal bodily movements and features, such as posture, stance, or touch.

Brainstorming A technique for coming up with new and creative solutions for problems. Members of a group discuss a problem and generate as many different solutions as they can, withholding criticism until all possibilities have been presented.

Breakpoints The starting or ending points of a behavioral act, as perceived by an observer.

Broad-spectrum cognitive-behavioral therapy The use of a broad array of cognitive-behavioral intervention techniques to modify an individual's behavior.

Built environment Buildings, roads, shopping centers, and other structures built by humans.

Bystander effect When other people are present, it is less likely that any one person will offer help to a stranger in distress. The diffusion of responsibility created by the presence of other people is one explanation for the bystander effect.

Case history information Information about a particular person or event. This kind of information often has a more persuasive impact on people's judgments than objectively better but less vivid statistical information.

Categorization The process by which we perceive people or other stimuli in groups or categories rather than perceiving each individual in isolation from the others.

Catharsis Freud's idea that by expressing *aggression*, a person's aggressive drive can be reduced.

Causal attribution See *attribution*

Central traits A trait is central to the extent that it is associated with many of the stimulus person's other characteristics. Traits such as being warm or cold are considered central because they are important in determining overall impressions.

Characterological self-blame Blaming one's enduring traits or personality for a victimization that has befallen the self.

Close relationship A personal relationship involving much interdependence. Partners in close relationships usually interact frequently, have a strong influence on each other, and engage in a variety of activities together.

Cognitive component That part of an *attitude* consisting of the person's beliefs, knowledge, and facts about the attitude object.

Cognitive consistency Tendency for people to seek consistency among their attitudes; regarded as a major determinant of attitude formation and change.

Cognitive dissonance theory Theory developed by Festinger according to which inconsistency (*dissonance*) between two cognitive elements produces pressure to make these elements consonant. It has been applied to a wide range of phenomena, including decision making, attitude-discrepant behavior, and interpersonal attraction.

Cognitive miser The view that people have limited information-processing capabilities, and therefore adopt various cognitive shortcuts. For example, we cannot perceive all stimuli in our perceptual field at once, so we focus on the most salient ones.

Cognitive response theory The theory that attitude change following receipt of communication depends on the cognitive responses it evokes. If the change produces negative thoughts, it will be rejected; if it evokes positive thoughts, it will be accepted. *Counterarguing* is a crucial mechanism for resisting persuasion, according to this theory.

Cohesiveness In group dynamics, the forces, both positive and negative, that cause members to remain in a group. Cohesiveness is a characteristic of a group as a whole, and results from the degree of *commitment* of each individual to the group.

Commitment to an attitude The perception that one's decision cannot be changed or revoked; a key determinant of cognitive dissonance.

Commitment to a relationship All the forces that act to keep a person in a relationship or group. Positive forces include interpersonal attraction and satisfaction with a relationship; negative forces include such barriers to ending a relationship as the lack of alternatives or having made large investments in the relationship.

Communication networks In some groups, there are constraints on the channels of communication available to members. Four types of communication networks are the circle, chain, wheel, and Y-pattern.

Companionate love A somewhat practical type of love that emphasizes trust, caring, and tolerance of the partner's flaws. Companionate love may develop slowly in a relationship as partners become more interdependent. Sometimes contrasted with *passionate love*.

Comparison level A standard we use to evaluate the quality of our social relationships. Our comparison level refers to the level of outcomes (benefits and costs) we expect or believe we deserve based on our past experience in relationships.

Comparison level for alternatives A standard we use to evaluate the quality of our social relationships. Our comparison level for alternatives refers to evaluating one particular relationship against other relationships that are currently available to us.

Competitive interdependence Situation in which the outcomes of two people or groups depend on each other, so that the rewards one gets reduce the rewards the other gets. Wars, athletic contests, or business competition are examples.

Compliance Performance of an act at another's request.

Confirmatory hypothesis testing Selectively extracting from others information that preferentially confirms a hypothesis, instead of gathering information evenhandedly that both favors and opposes the hypothesis.

Conformity Voluntary performance of an act because others also do it. Conformity often results from a person's desire to be right (informational influence) and/or desire to be liked (normative influence).

Conjunction error An error that occurs when people believe that the likelihood of several events co-occurring is higher (because the events seem to go together) than the likelihood of any of the individual events.

Contact theory The theory that prejudice against a social group can be reduced by appropriate kinds of contact with individual members of that group.

Contingency model of leadership effectiveness Fiedler's model distinguishing between task-oriented and relationship-oriented leaders. When the group situation is either highly favorable or highly unfavorable to control by the leader, task-oriented leaders are more effective. In intermediate situations where the leader has moderate control, relationship-oriented leaders are more successful.

Contrast In the study of attitude change, the tendency to perceive a communicator's position as being farther away from the individual's own position than it actually is.

Coping The process of managing internal or environmental demands that are appraised as taxing or exceeding one's resources. Coping may involve active problem-solving efforts and/or efforts at emotional control.

Correlational research Passively measuring two variables and determining whether or not they are associated with each other. Studies relating smoking to lung cancer are correlational: They measure the amount of smoking each person has done and whether or not the person gets lung cancer in order to determine if the two factors are related. The major problem with correlational designs is determining whether or not a correlation reflects a cause-and-effect relationship.

Counterarguing In attitude change, one mechanism for resisting influence by discrepant communications: The individual considers and actively rebuts the arguments made by the communicator.

Covariation Judgments of covariation involve determining how strongly two things are related such as the time of day and frequency of crime, or the ingestion of caffeine and alertness. When social perceivers expect two things to go together, they tend to overestimate the actual degree of covariation.

Credibility In attitude change, a communicator's credibility depends on his or her perceived expertise about the topic and how much he or she is trusted by the individual receiving the communication.

Crowding The subjective experience of feeling cramped or not having enough space.

Cultural stereotype Societal-level images of members of a social group such as those found in art, literature, religious teachings, and the mass media. For example, TV commercials may portray women as worried consumers and men as knowledgeable experts. See also *Personal stereotype*.

Cybernetic theory of self-regulation The process by which people compare their behavior to a standard, decide that it either matches the standard or not, and continue adjusting and comparing until the standard is met or abandoned. Self-awareness is argued to be a precondition for this type of self-regulation.

Date rape (or acquaintance rape) Forced sexual activity that occurs between two people who are at least mildly acquainted and who may be dating.

Debriefing An essential feature of ethical research, in which after the subjects' participation is over, the purposes and procedures of the research study are explained to the subjects, their questions are answered, and the scientific value of the research is discussed.

Decision-making theories According to decision-making theories, people calculate the costs and benefits of various actions, and select the best alternative in a fairly logical way. Two specific examples of this perspective are *expectancy-value theory* and *incentive theory*.

Dehumanization Taking away the personhood or human qualities of another person or group through one's actions or the ways one thinks about the person or group. Dehumanizing another person is thought to facilitate *aggression* against that person.

Deindividuation Loss of a sense of personal identity and responsibility which can lead people to do things they would normally not do when alone. Anonymity is a key factor in deindividuation.

Demand characteristics Aspects of a study that make subjects more aware of their participation in research and thus bias their behavior. For example, subjects may try to avoid negative evaluations from the experimenter or try to cooperate with the experimenter to verify the hypothesis.

Dependent variable In an experiment, the responses to the *independent variable* being manipulated or measured.

Desensitization When over-exposure to material that normally evokes strong emotions, such as violence or sexuality, makes the individual insensitive to it.

Diffusion of responsibility The presence of other people can make each individual feel less responsible for events that occur or for solving problems. This can decrease the likelihood that a person will take action, for instance to help a stranger in distress.

Dimensional view of impression formation The view that people's perceptions of others rely on a small number of underlying person-relevant dimensions, such as sociability and intellect.

Discounting principle In making *attributions*, the tendency to reduce reliance on one particular cause to the extent that other plausible causes exist. If, for example, a judge gives the death penalty to a criminal, we might conclude that she was generally a tough judge, but we would be less likely to do so if we also discovered that the law required the death penalty for this particular crime.

Discrepancy In the study of attitude change, the distance between the communicator's and the target's position on the issue discussed in the communication. A communicator may argue that tuition should be doubled; that position will be highly discrepant to a student who believes it should not change, but only moderately discrepant to a student who thinks a modest increase is reasonable.

Discrimination The behavioral component of group antagonism. People discriminate against the disliked group by refusing its members access to desired jobs, educational opportunities, country clubs, restaurants, places of entertainment, and so on.

Disinhibition General loosening of control over anger when it has once been released under socially approved conditions; that is, once a person has committed a socially approved aggressive act, he or she has fewer inhibitions about aggression under other conditions.

Displaced aggression The expression of *aggression* against a target other than the source of attack or frustration, usually a safer target.

Dispositional attribution Perceiving the cause of a person's action as being in his or her own dispositions, such as personality, ability, or attitudes.

Dispositional optimism A generalized expectation, held by some people and not others, that good outcomes will occur in one's life.

Dissonance The state of aversive arousal that results when a person holds simultaneously two beliefs that conflict with or contradict each other. See also *cognitive dissonance theory*.

Distraction Stimulus that draws attention away from a persuasive message. It sometimes increases attitude change by making it harder for people to defend a position against the arguments in the message.

Door-in-the-face technique A technique for gaining compliance with a request by first asking for a much larger request. After the larger request is refused, the person is more likely to agree to the second, smaller request.

Downward social comparison The comparison of one's traits or abilities with someone who is worse off than the self.

Ego-involvement The subjective linking of an attitude to strong ego needs, thereby making the attitude more emotionally laden and more resistant to change.

Elaboration-likelihood model A theory of persuasion and attitude change in which the key variable is the amount of careful thought given to the arguments (elaboration likelihood). With more careful processing, attitude change will depend more on the real strength of the arguments and less on peripheral cues.

Empathy Feelings of sympathy and caring for others—in particular, sharing vicariously or indirectly in the suffering of other people. Strong feelings of empathy can motivate a person to help someone in need.

Enemy image Strongly felt perceptions that a national enemy is evil and intends aggression against one's own country.

Environmental psychology A branch of psychology that studies the relationship between the physical environment and human behavior and well-being.

Equity The principle that two people who make equal contributions to a task should receive equal rewards.

Equity theory An offshoot of *social exchange theory* that focuses on fairness in relationships. A relationship is equitable when the ratio of a person's profits to contributions is the same for everyone. The theory postulates that when individuals perceive inequity, both underbenefited and overbenefited partners feel distress and take steps to restore equity.

Ethnic identity The part of an individual's self-knowledge that concerns his or her membership in a particular ethnic group, together with the value and emotional significance attached to that membership.

Ethnocentrism The belief that the ingroup is the center of the social world and superior to outgroups.

Evaluation The most important basic dimension underlying impression formation and attitudes; the goodness or badness of another person, object, or concept. See also *affective component*.

Evaluation apprehension A person's concern for how others evaluate him or her; often a concern for looking good in public.

Exchange theory See *social exchange theory*.

Exemplar An example of a category that embodies the significant attributes of the category or the ideal of that category. For example, a robin is an exemplar of the category "bird."

Expectancy-value theory This theory states that decisions are based on the combination of two factors: (1) the value of the various possible outcomes of the decision and (2) the likelihood or probability that each outcome will actually occur.

Expectation states theory According to this theory, a person's status in a group may be affected by such diffuse status characteristics as age, ethnicity, or wealth.

Experiment Type of research in which the researcher randomly assigns people to two or more conditions, varies in a controlled manner the treatment each condition is given, and then measures the effects on the subjects' responses. Though experiments are often difficult to arrange, they have the advantage of yielding clear information about cause and effect. Any differences between groups in the outcome of the experiment must be due to the variables that were experimentally manipulated.

Experimenter bias Biases introduced into the results of a study, usually in the direction of falsely confirming the hypothesis, through unintentional actions of the researcher.

External attributions Attributions of causality for a person's behavior or attitudes to factors external to the individual, such as the situation, other people, or luck.

External validity Extent to which the results of a study are generalizable to other populations and settings.

False consensus Bias in perceptions of others such that one exaggerates how common one's own opinions or behaviors are.

False uniqueness Bias in perceptions of others such that one exaggerates how uniquely good one's own abilities are.

Field experiment Study in which variables are systematically manipulated and measured in real-life, nonlaboratory settings.

Figure-ground principle In social perception, the basic principle that attention is drawn to stimuli that stand out against a background. Figural stimuli are those that stand out; the background is called the ground. This principle has generated much of the research on *salience* in the area of social perception.

Foot-in-the-door technique A technique for gaining compliance with a request by first getting the person to comply with a smaller request. After agreeing to a smaller request, the person is more likely to comply with the larger request.

Forewarning In attitude change, informing recipients of the position to be taken in a persuasive communication, or that the communicator is intending to persuade them, prior to the receipt of the communication.

Framing How the media describe a particular issue. For example, affirmative action can be framed as reverse discrimination against whites, or as helping to ensure equality for minorities.

Frustration The blocking or thwarting of goal-directed behavior. A child is frustrated when a parent refuses to let the child color the bathroom wallpaper with crayons or smear ice cream on the dining room table.

Frustration-aggression hypothesis In its strongest form, this hypothesis asserts that frustration always creates feelings of aggression, and that aggression is always caused by frustration.

Fundamental attribution error The tendency for observers to overestimate the causal importance of a person's dispositions and to underestimate the importance of the situation when they explain the person's actions.

Gender gap Differences between women and men in their attitudes on political and social issues.

Gender identity The self-knowledge that one is male or female. Gender identity is acquired early in life.

Gender self-concept The degree to which a person perceives that he or she possesses traditionally masculine or feminine characteristics. See also *androgyny*.

Gender stereotype Beliefs about the typical personal attributes of males and females. According to traditional gender stereotypes, women are believed to have expressive or communal qualities, such as being nurturing and gentle. Men are believed to have instrumental or agentic qualities such as being independent, assertive, and competent. See also *androgyny*.

Gender typing The process of labeling things, activities and people as "masculine" or "feminine." For example, many people consider dolls, ruffles, and housecleaning to be feminine.

Gestalt The theory that people form coherent and meaningful perceptions based on the entire perceptual field, so that the whole is different from the sum of its parts.

GRIT Graduated reciprocation in tension reduction; a complex formula for de-escalating conflict between two superpowers, initiated by small unilateral concessions by one side.

Group A social aggregate in which members are interdependent (have mutual influence on each other) and have at least the potential for mutual interaction.

Group consciousness Strong identification with the ingroup plus the feeling that the ingroup is being treated unfairly. Group consciousness is theorized to motivate political action that will further group aims.

Group identification The individual's affective attachment to a reference group.

Group norms See *social norms*.

Group-serving biases Members of an ingroup tend to hold favorable attributions for the performance of members of the ingroup (internal attributions for success, external for failures), and unfavorable attributions for performance by members of the outgroup.

Group polarization When a group discusses an issue, people often come to support more extreme positions than they did initially. This sometimes leads to a *risky shift*, and sometimes to a cautious shift, depending on the initial views of group members.

Groupthink The impairment in decision making and sound judgment that can occur in highly cohesive groups. Group members ignore contradictory information, ostracize dissentors, and unify around their decision even if it is irrational.

Halo effect A liked person is assumed to have good qualities of many kinds, whether or not the observer has any information about those qualities.

Hardiness A personality variable consisting of a sense of commitment, a positive response to challenge, and an internal sense of control that seems to help people cope effectively with stress.

Health behavior An action undertaken by a person who is healthy to enhance or maintain good health.

Health belief An attitude about a particular health practice that influences the willingness to adopt that practice; may include beliefs about personal susceptibility, the efficacy of the health practice, or the severity of the health risk among others.

Heuristic A shortcut for problem solving that reduces complex or ambiguous information to more simple judgmental operations.

Ideal self The representation of attributes one would like to have or possess.

Ideology An abstract, general belief system that encompasses consistent attitudes toward many different issues. Liberalism and conservatism are the most common ideologies in Western industrial countries.

Illusion of control A bias whereby we perceive ourselves as being able to control our lives and the events around us more than is the case in fact.

Illusory correlation The belief that two things are related to each other because prior expectations dictate that they ought to go together, when in fact those things bear little or no relationship to each other.

Imitation See *modeling*.

Implicit personality theory The ordinary person's theory about which personality traits go with other traits, such as "weak" going with "cowardly," or "calm" going with "decisive."

Incentive theory This theory views decision making as a process of weighing the pros (positive incentives) and cons (negative incentives) of various possible alternatives and then adopting the best one.

Independent self The sense of one's self as bounded, unitary, and separate from the social context.

Independent variable The variable in a study that is interpreted as the cause of changes in the *dependent variable*. The independent variable may be systematically manipulated by the researcher in an experiment, or passively measured in a correlational study.

Informed consent The requirement that research subjects must freely choose to participate after being informed about the study, the procedures that will be used, and the costs and benefits of the research.

Ingratiation Flattering or doing favors for another person in order to get that person to like you.

Ingroup The group to which an individual belongs; membership in it forms part of his or her social identity. See also *outgroup*.

Ingroup favoritism effect The tendency to give more favorable evaluations and greater rewards to members of one's ingroup than to members of outgroups.

Inoculation In attitude change, McGuire's notion that people become more resistant to the effects of persuasive communications when they have been exposed to weak counterarguments.

Integrative complexity An index of the complexity of a person's thinking about a particular issue, based on the number of dimensions taken into consideration and the complexity of connections among them

Interdependence The condition in which two or more people have some degree of mutual influence on each other's feelings, thoughts, or behaviors.

Interdependent self The sense of self as flexible, variable, and connected to the social context.

Internal attributions Attributions of causality to factors internal to the individual, such as the person's attitudes, personality, ability, emotions, or effort.

Internal validity The extent to which cause and effect conclusions can validly be drawn from the research.

Jealousy Occurs when a person perceives a real or potential attraction between his or her partner and a rival. Jealousy is a reaction to a perceived threat by a rival to the continuity or quality of a valued relationship. Feelings of anger, anxiety, and depression are common.

Just world The belief that people get what they deserve. If good things happen to people, it is because they have worked hard, been honest, or been foresighted; if bad things happen to them, it is because they were lazy, careless, stupid, or dishonest. One consequence of this belief is that victims are blamed for their misfortunes, even if in reality they are not to blame.

Learning theory The central idea in learning theory is that a person's behavior is determined by prior learning. Current behavior is shaped by past experience. In any given situation, a person learns certain behaviors which, over time, may become habits. When presented with the same situation, the person tends to behave in the same habitual way.

Legitimate authority In many situations, social norms permit those in authority to make requests. Illustrations of legitimate authority include the government's right to ask citizens to pay taxes; parents' right to ask their children to wash the dinner dishes; and an employer's right to assign duties to an employee.

Locus of control The tendency to explain events in terms of one's own behavior versus forces in the environment. Those favoring explanations centering on the self are said to have an internal locus of control; those favoring explanations centering on environmental factors are termed external in locus of control.

Logical error The tendency to impute attributes to people that are consistent with what we already know about them. For example, upon learning that a man is kind, we might also regard him as generous and sociable.

Loneliness The psychological discomfort we feel when our social relations lack some essential feature. This deficit may be quantitative (too few relationships) or qualitative (unsatisfying relationships).

Low-ball technique A technique for gaining compliance in which the influencer obtains a commitment from the person before revealing hidden costs of the request.

Matching principle In dating and marriage, people tend to select partners who are similar to themselves in attitudes, values, ethnic background, religion, social class, education, and many other personal characteristics.

Mere exposure effect Simply being exposed frequently to a person or object tends to increase our liking for that person or object. Repeated exposure most often enhances liking when our initial reaction to the person is neutral or positive, when no

conflict of interests exists, and when the repetition is not so great that it causes satiation.

Message learning The theory that attitude change depends on the individual's learning the content of the communication.

Meta-analysis A quantitative approach to summarizing and synthesizing the results of many empirical studies on a topic, such as sex differences in aggression. Statistics are used to estimate the overall size of the "effect" or sex difference, and also to test for the consistency (homogeneity) of a finding across studies.

Middle-range theories Theories that attempt to account for major categories of behavior, but do not attempt to cover all human behavior in general. A middle-range theory might try to explain attitude change, attribution, or aggression, but not all three at once.

Minimal effects model The theory that mass communications mainly reinforce the recipient's prior attitudes rather than create widespread attitude change.

Minimal intergroup situation The basic research situation used to test social identity theory: People are arbitrarily classified into groups (e.g., the red and the blue teams), and then allowed to allocate rewards to each other.

Minimal risk The idea that the risk anticipated in any research project must be no greater than the risk encountered in daily life.

Minority influence Influence that members of a minority have over the larger majority in a group.

Mirror image The images held by members of two conflicting nations such that each group feels that their own nation is peace-loving and that the other nation is hostile and threatening.

Misattribution Assigning the cause of a particular behavior or emotional state to a stimulus other than the actual cause, such as thinking a lecture is exciting when actually you are excited by having drunk ten cups of coffee.

Modeling People often learn behaviors and social attitudes simply by observing the attitudes and behaviors of other people, known technically as models. Modeling occurs when a person not only observes but actually copies the behavior of a model. Observational learning can occur without any external reinforcement. However, whether or not a person actually performs or models a behavior learned through observation will be influenced by the consequences the action has for the person. Modeling is also known as *imitation*.

Modes of resolution   In attitude change, the various alternative ways in which a target of a discrepant communication can reduce inconsistency, such as attitude change, source derogation, or misperception.

Mood-congruent memory   The tendency for people to remember material whose valence fits their current mood state. For example, a person in a good mood is more likely to remember positive material.

Naive psychology   The ordinary person's informal theories about what determines human behavior.

Negativity effect   Tendency for impressions to be influenced more by negative traits than by positive traits. Hence positive impressions are more vulnerable to change than negative impressions.

Nonverbal leakage   The communication of true emotions through nonverbal channels even when the person's verbal communications tries to cover them up.

Norm   See *social norms*.

Norm of reciprocity   The social norm that we should reward those who reward us. For example, if someone helps us, we feel obligated to help them in return.

Norm of social justice   Human groups develop norms about fairness and the just distribution of resources. Norms of social justice, such as equity, may encourage *prosocial behavior*.

Norm of social responsibility   A social norm dictating that we should help others who depend on us. This may contribute to *prosocial behavior*.

Observational learning   Learning by watching what others do and doing the same; also applies to forming attitudes by modeling those of others such as parents or teachers.

Old-fashioned racism   Old-fashioned stereotypes of white racial superiority and segregationist attitudes.

Operational code   A political leader's beliefs about the nature and history of politics, and the best political strategies.

Operational definition   The specific procedure or operation that is used to measure or manipulate a variable in a research study.

Ought self   The representation of attributes one believes one should possess, based on one's obligations and responsibilities or the expectations of others.

Outgroup   Any group other than the *ingroup.*

Outgroup homogeneity effect   Perception that members of the outgroup are more similar to each other than members of the ingroup are to each other.

Overjustification   Giving people rewards for performing a task can undermine their intrinsic interest in the task, presumably because they attribute their liking for the task to the reward rather than to their own intrinsic interest in the task.

Paralanguage   Information conveyed by variations in speech other than actual words and syntax, such as pitch, loudness, hesitations, and so on.

Party identification   A person's underlying, stable preference for one political party over its rivals.

Passionate love   The emotionally charged type of love that sometimes characterizes the early stages of romantic relationships. Sometimes contrasted with *companionate love.*

Peripheral cues   Aspects of the communication situation that are irrelevant to the content of the message, but which can influence attitude change when the individual is not engaged in systematic processing (e.g., nice music, long or beautifully written messages).

Persistence   As used in political psychology, persistence refers to the long-time stability of socio-political attitudes throughout a person's lifespan.

Person perception   Process of forming impressions of others, making judgments about their personalities, and adopting hypotheses about the kind of persons they are.

Personal distress   An individual's reactions to the suffering of others, including horror, shock, helplessness, or concern. Since personal distress focuses on the self, it can motivate people to ignore or avoid the suffering of others, rather than to offer assistance.

Personal entitlement   What a person believes that he or she deserves from a job or relationship.

Personal space   The physical space immediately around their bodies that people treat as though it were a part of themselves. Hall has suggested four basic zones for interpersonal interaction: intimate, personal, social, and public.

Personal stereotype   An individual's own beliefs about the attributes of members of a particular group. Personal stereotypes may be similar to or different from *cultural stereotypes.*

Pessimistic explanatory style   The tendency to explain negative events that befall the self in terms of internal, stable and global qualities of the self.

Phantom-other technique A laboratory technique to study interpersonal attraction in which one person is provided information about another person (who, in reality, doesn't exist).

Political socialization The process by which young people acquire political attitudes; it often (but not always) occurs in the preadult years and with parental influence.

Positive illusions Mildly but falsely positive self-enhancing perceptions of one's personal qualities.

Positivity bias General tendency to express positive evaluations of people more often then negative evaluations. Also called the "leniency effect" or "person positivity bias."

Possible selves Schemas that people hold concerning what they may become in the future.

Power See *social power*.

Prejudice The affective component of group antagonisms; disliking a group or members of a group.

Primacy The tendency to use an initial impression to organize and interpret subsequent information.

Priming effect The tendency for recently used or thought about material to influence the interpretation of subsequent information.

Principle of least interest According to social exchange theory, the balance of power in a relationship is affected by the relative dependency of the two partners. According to the principle of least interest, the partner who is less interested (less dependent) will tend to have greater power.

Prisoner's dilemma game A laboratory game widely used in studies of competition and cooperation. It poses the fundamental dilemma of whether to compete (with the hope of gaining large rewards at the expense of the other person) or to cooperate (with the hope of receiving lesser personal rewards but greater joint rewards.)

Private self-consciousness A chronic tendency to focus on the private self. Privately self-conscious people try to figure themselves out, think about themselves a lot and are attentive to their inner feelings.

Prosocial aggression Aggressive acts that support commonly accepted social norms, such as a soldier shooting an enemy sniper during combat.

Prosocial behavior An act that helps or is intended to help others, regardless of the helper's motives. Prosocial behavior is a broader category than *altruism*.

Prototype A *schema* defined by the specific features of a particular type of person, such as librarian or snob.

Proxemics The term used by Hall to describe the study of how people use space.

Psychoanalytic theory Theory of human behavior based originally on Freud's work. It emphasizes instincts, unconscious motivation, and the ego defenses people construct to protect themselves against their own irrational drives.

Psychodynamic theories Theories that analyze attitudes and behavior as resulting from deep motivational tensions and conflicts. *Psychoanalytic theory* is the best known of these.

Psychological control The belief that one can exert personal control over events, independent of whether or not that control actually exists or is ever exercised.

Public self-consciousness A chronic tendency to be concerned with how one appears to others. Publicly self-conscious people are concerned with what others think of them, the way they look, and how they appear to others. Contrasts with *private self-consciousness*.

Punishment The application of an aversive stimulus that reduces the likelihood that the preceding response will occur.

Random assignment Placement of subjects into experimental conditions in a manner which guarantees that assignment is made entirely by chance, such as by using a random numbers table. This is an essential characteristic of an experiment.

Random sample A group of people participating in a study who are selected from the broad population by a random process, and who therefore are representative of that broad population.

Rape Forced sexual activity without one partner's consent.

Rational model of inference A model assuming a logical, correct way to put information together to reach a judgment.

Reactance Brehm's concept that people attempt to maintain their freedom of action. When this freedom is threatened, people do whatever they can to restore it, for instance, by refusing to comply with a request.

Realistic group conflict The theory that antagonism between groups arises from real conflicts of interest and the frustrations those conflicts produce. For example, two groups in conflict over the fishing rights in a certain area may develop prejudices and act aggressively toward each other as a result.

Reasoned action model A model predicting an individual's overt behavior from conscious behavioral intentions, which in turn are based on calculations about the effects of his or her behavior and others' evaluations of it.

Reference group A group to which a person belongs or uses as a basis of comparison. The group serves as a standard for the person's own behavior and attitudes. Group norms can act as a persuasive force leading to attitude change, or can prevent change by supporting the individual's position when it is attacked.

Reflected appraisal Perceptions of how others perceive and evaluated us.

Reinforcement The process by which a person or animal learns to perform a particular response by being rewarded when it is performed.

Relapse prevention Procedures incorporated into health behavior change programs that train people to identify situations that may lead them to return to prior faulty health habits; usually involves training in coping skills for use in high-risk-for-relapse situations.

Related-attributes similarity Similarity with another person, not on a target attribute, but on attributes related to that target attribute, such as background or preparation.

Relative deprivation Feelings of personal or social discontent that arise from the belief that persons or groups are doing worse than others, or worse than they did in the past

Replication Because any single study is flawed, a hallmark of good research is replication. In its simplest form, replication means that we are able to reproduce the findings of others researchers if we recreate their methods. It is also important to conduct conceptual replications, in which different research procedures are used to explore the same conceptual relationship.

Reverse-causality problem The problem that arises in correlational research when the presumed cause might in fact be the actual effect. Children who watch a lot of television do less well in school than children who watch little television. But is their television viewing causing their poor grades? Or does their poor school performance cause them to escape from schoolwork by watching TV?

Risky shift After taking part in a group discussion of an issue, people are sometimes willing to support riskier decisions that they were before the group discussion. This is part of a more general process of *group polarization*, which can lead either to riskier or more cautious decisions, depending on the initial views of group members.

Role See *social role*.

Salience The quality that makes a particular stimulus stand out and be noticed. Bright, noisy, colorful, unusual, and novel stimuli are usually the most salient.

Sanctioned aggression Aggression that is permissible (though not necessarily encouraged) according to the norms of the individual's social groups.

Schema An organized system or structure of cognitions about some stimulus or type of stimulus, such as a person, personality type, group, role, or event.

Self-affirmation People cope with specific threats to their self-worth by reaffirming unrelated aspects of themselves.

Self-awareness The state of experiencing one's self as an object of one's own attention.

Self-centered bias Taking more than one's share of responsibility for a jointly produced outcome.

Self-complexity The number of dimensions that people use to think about themselves. Some people think about themselves in many ways, whereas other people think of themselves in one or two main ways.

Self-concept The collection of beliefs we hold about ourselves.

Self-disclosure A special type of conversation in which we share intimate information or feelings about the self with another person. Self-disclosure can be descriptive (revelations describe things about ourselves) or evaluative (emphasis is given to our personal assessment of people and situations).

Self-discrepancy A discrepancy between how we perceive ourselves to be and how we would ideally like to be or believe others think we should be.

Self-efficacy Specific expectations that we hold about our abilities to accomplish certain tasks.

Self-enhancement The need to hold a positive view of the self and to protect one's self from negative feedback.

Self-esteem The value a person places on himself or herself.

Self-evaluation maintenance model Tesser's analysis of when people react to the success of others with pride (basking in reflected glory) versus discontent (suffering by comparison). A key factor is whether or not the performance of the other is relevant to our self-concept.

Self-fulfilling prophecy The tendency for people's expectations to influence their attitudes and behavior. Prejudice can serve as a self-fulfilling prophecy by influencing how the prejudiced person acts toward the other, which may in turn influence the target to act in a way that confirms the first person's prejudices.

Self-handicapping Engaging in actions that produce insurmountable obstacles to success, so the inevitable failure can later be attributed to the obstacle rather than one's own lack of ability.

Self-interest The hypothesis that attitudes or behavior are motivated by what is best for the individual's short-term material well-being.

Self-monitoring In the study of self-presentation, self-monitoring refers to the tendency to emphasize impression management to a great extent. Snyder et al. have developed a paper-and-pencil test to assess this personality disposition. On the Self-Monitoring Scale, high scorers are especially sensitive to situational cues about appropriate behavior.

In health psychology, self-monitoring refers to observing and recording a target behavior (such as smoking) to highlight its frequency and the factors with which it co-occurs.

Self-perception theory The idea that people infer their attitudes from their overt behavior and from their perceptions of the external situation, rather than from their own internal states.

Self-presentation Deliberate efforts to act in ways that create a particular impression of the self, often a favorable impression.

Self-promotion Conveying positive information about one's self to others through one's actions or by saying positive things about one's self.

Self-reference effect The improved memory of others' characteristics that results from perceivers linking them to their own characteristics.

Self-regulation The ways people control and direct their own actions.

Self-schema A cognitive structure that represents how one thinks about one's self in a particular domain and how one organizes one's experience in that domain.

Self-serving attributional bias The tendency for people to see their positive behaviors as internally caused and their negative behaviors (such as failures) as caused by external circumstances.

Self-verification The process of seeking out and interpreting situations to confirm one's self-conceptions and avoiding or resisting situations and feedback that differ from existing self-conceptions.

Sexism Prejudice (negative attitudes) and discrimination (biased behavior) based on a person's gender.

Sexual harassment Unwelcome sexual advances, requests for sexual favors, and other verbal or physical conduct of a sexual nature that are connected to employment or create an intimidating, hostile, or offensive work environment.

Shift of meaning Tendency for the connotations of a trait to change when placed in a different context. This is the explanation for context effects by cognitive theories of impression formation.

Shock-competition technique Experimental procedure in which subjects compete in a reaction time game, and the winner shocks the loser.

Shock-learning technique Experimental procedure in which a naive subject is a "teacher" and is supposed to shock the "learner" (who is a confederate) when the learner makes an error.

Situation attribution Perceiving the cause of a person's action as lying in situational forces acting upon the person, such as social influence or economic incentives.

Sleeper effect Delayed attitude changes that are not apparent immediately after exposure to the communication.

Social cognition The study of how people form inferences and make judgments from social information.

Social comparison The act of evaluating one's abilities, opinions, or emotions with respect to another person or persons.

Social comparison theory Festinger proposed that people have a drive to evaluate themselves. In the absence of objective nonsocial criteria, people evaluate themselves by comparison with other people. In an uncertain or ambiguous situation, people may want to affiliate with others in order to make social comparisons.

Social compensation Occurs when an individual expends great effort in a collective setting in order to compensate for others in the group who are believed to be performing inadequately.

Social density The objective number of people in a given space, such as the number of people sharing a dorm room or the number of people living per square mile in a major city.

Social dilemma A situation in which the most rewarding short-term choice for an individual will ultimately lead to negative outcomes for all concerned. Social dilemmas pit the short-term interests of the individual against the long-term interests of the group (including the individual).

Social exchange theory   An analysis of interpersonal interaction in terms of the costs and benefits each person gives and receives. Because people in a relationship or group are interdependent (that is, the outcomes one person receives depend on what others do, and vice versa), individuals must coordinate their behavior to maximize their joint benefits.

Social facilitation   The tendency for people (and other kinds of animals) to perform better on simple, well-learned tasks when others are present than when they are alone.

Social identity   In the study of the self, that part of an individual's self-concept which derives from his or her membership in a social group or groups, together with the value and emotional significance attached to that membership.

Social identity theory   A theory that people spontaneously categorize the social world into ingroups and outgroups, and develop higher self-esteem if their ingroups have more status than the outgroups.

Social impact theory   According to Latané, the influence (either positive or negative) of an audience on a target individual depends on three factors: the number of observers, the strength of the audience (e.g., their importance), and the immediacy of the audience in time or space.

Social inhibition   Occurs when the presence of other people impairs or inhibits an individual's performance.

Social interaction   Occurs when two or more people influence each other—verbally, physically, or emotionally. Talking to a therapist, debating with classmates, angrily arguing with a friend, and bumping into a person in an elevator are examples.

Socialization   The process by which a person acquires the rules, standards, and values of his or her family, group, and culture.

Social leadership   Refers to activities designed to promote group harmony and *cohesiveness*. The social leader focuses on the social and emotional aspects of interaction in order to keep a group running smoothly and happily. Sometimes contrasted with *task leadership*.

Social learning theory   A modern offshoot of behaviorism that places primary emphasis on how people learn social behaviors from one another,

especially through social reinforcement and *modeling*.

Social loafing   Individuals sometimes work less hard as members of a group than they would if they worked alone. Individuals may feel that their own efforts will be less recognizable in a group, which leads to a diffusion of responsibility and diminished effort by individuals.

Social norms   Rules and expectations about what members of a social group should do or be like. These standards determine whether an individual's specific actions, attitudes, or beliefs are approved or disapproved by the individual's social group. Also called "group norms."

Social penetration   Altman and Taylor's theory about the process by which people gradually attain closeness and intimacy in a relationship. The theory emphasizes that as a relationship develops, self-disclosure increases in both breadth (range of topics) and depth (intimacy).

Social power   This refers to one person's ability to influence deliberately the behavior, thoughts or feelings of another person.

Social psychology   The scientific study of how the thoughts, feelings, and behaviors of individuals are influenced by other people.

Social role   A set of social norms (rules and understandings) about how a person in a particular social position (such as mother or professor) is expected to behave. Roles define the rights and responsibilities of members of couples, groups, and other social units.

Social status   A person's rank or privilege in a group, based on such characteristics as position in a business, age, or gender.

Social support   An interpersonal exchange characterized by emotional concern, instrumental aid, the provision of information to another, or help in self-appraisal. Social support is believed to buffer people against the adverse effects of stress and may promote physical health as well.

Sociobiology   A field in biology that uses evolutionary theory to explain the social behavior of humans and other animals.

Sociotropic   The idea that political behavior is motivated by perceptions of what is best for the collectivity (the nation, the society), rather than by what is best for the self.

Source derogation   In persuasive communication situations, reducing inconsistency by derogating the source of a discrepant communication rather than changing one's attitudes.

Statistical information In social cognition, this refers to information based on a number of individuals or events, such as averages or totals. Such information tends to be less persuasive and to have less impact on judgments than inferior but more vivid *case history information.*

Stereotype Beliefs about the typical characteristics of members of a group or social category. In the study of prejudice, this is the cognitive component of group antagonism.

Stress A process of appraising environmental events as harmful, threatening, or challenging and of responding to that appraisal with physiological, emotional, cognitive, and behavioral changes. Stress occurs when people perceive that their personal resources may not be sufficient to meet the demands of the environment.

Stressful life event An event in a person's life that requires him or her to make changes; negative, ambiguous and uncontrollable events as most likely to be perceived as stressful; believed to contribute to the likelihood of illness.

Subcategorization Breaking down large categories of people such as women or the elderly into subcategories such as homemakers, professional women, or grandmothers.

Supportive defense In attitude change, positive arguments for an individual's own position, provided in advance of a persuasive attack to help protect that attitude.

Symbolic racism Antagonism toward a racial group based on symbols and values rather than self-interest. For example, opposition to policies promoting equality for African Americans may be based both in antagonism toward blacks and in support for traditional social values.

Systematic processing Careful scrutiny of the arguments in a persuasive communication. Gives argument strength more weight, induces counterarguing, and makes attitude change more enduring. Minimizes the role of peripheral cues.

Task leadership Activities designed to accomplish the goals of a group and to get the work of the group done successfully. The task leader directs and organizes the group in carrying out a specific task. Sometimes contrasted with *social leadership.*

Territorial behavior Actions designed to stake out or mark a territory and to claim ownership.

Territorial markers Objects and nonverbal gestures that people use to mark and personalize their territories. For example, a person may stake out a seat in the library using a sweater, sunglasses, and notebook.

Territory An area controlled by a specific individual or group. Altman has distinguished among primary, secondary, and public territories.

That's-not-all technique A technique for gaining compliance in which the influencer first offers one deal and then, while the person is considering this possibility, improves the offer.

Third-variable problem A problem with interpreting correlational research. When two variables are correlated with each other, is one the cause of the other? Or is some third variable the cause of both?

Tit-for-tat strategy In the *prisoner's dilemma game,* tit-for-tat is the optimal strategy. The player should start by cooperating, and then do whatever the opposing player did the round before.

Transfer of affect Changing attitude A by transferring to it the affect one already has toward object B.

Transsexuals Persons whose psychological gender identity differs from their biological sex, for example, persons who are anatomically male but believe that they are really female trapped in a male body.

Type A behavior A behavioral and emotional style of coping with stress, marked by hostility and an aggressive struggle to achieve more and more in less time, often in competition with others. This method of coping with stress is a risk factor for coronary heart disease.

Typicality effect The tendency to behave in ways more consistent with one's prejudices about an outgroup toward an outgroup member who is seen as most typical of that group. For example, a homophobic person might be more hostile toward a gay man perceived as stereotypically effeminate than toward a gay man perceived as masculine.

Typological view of impression formation The viewpoint that people's impressions of others are organized according to particular types of people, such as extraverts or introverts.

Upward social comparison The comparison of one's traits or abilities with someone who is better off than the self.

Working self-concept Those aspects of the self-concept that are salient in a particular situational context and that guide an individual's thoughts, emotions, and actions in that context.

References

Abel, E. L. (1977). The relationship between cannabis and violence: A review. *Psychological Bulletin, 84,* 193–211.

Abel, G. G., Rouleau, J.-L., & Coyne, B. J. (1987). Behavioral medicine strategies in medical patients. In A. Stoudemire & B. S. Fogel (Eds.), *Principles of medical psychiatry* (pp. 329–345). Orlando, FL: Grune & Stratton.

Abelson, R. P. (1976). Script processing in attitude formation and decison making. In J. S. Carroll & J. W. Payne (Eds.). *Cognition and social behavior* (pp. 33–46). Hillsdale, NJ: Erlbaum.

Abelson, R. P., Aronson, E., McGuire, W. J., Newcomb, T. M., Rosenberg, M. J., & Tannenbaum, P. H. (Eds.). (1968). *Theories of cognitive consistency: A sourcebook.* Chicago: Rand McNally.

Aboud, R. (1988). *Children and prejudice.* New York: Basil Blackwell.

Abrams, D., Wetherell, M., Cochrane, S., Hogg, M. A., & Turner, J. C. (1990). Knowing what to think by knowing who you are: Self-categorization and the nature of norm formation, conformity, and group polarization. *British Journal of Social Psychology, 29,* 97–119.

Abramson, L. Y., Seligman, M. E. P., & Teasdale, J. D. (1978). Learned helplessness in humans: Critique and reformulation. *Journal of Abnormal Psychology, 87,* 49–74.

Abramson, P. E., Goldberg, P. A., Greenberg, J. H., & Abramson, U. M. (1977). The talking platypus phenomenon: Competency ratings as a function of sex and professional status. *Psychology of Women Quarterly, 2,* 114–124.

Adams, F. M., & Osgood, C. E. (1973). A cross-cultural study of the affective meanings of color. *Journal of Cross-Cultural Psychology, 4,* 135–156.

Adorno, T. W., Frenkel-Brunswik, E., Levinson, D. J., & Sanford, R. N. (1950). *The authoritarian personality.* New York: Harper & Row.

Agar, A. H. (1981). Ethnography as an interdisciplinary campground. In J. H. Harvey (Ed.), *Cognition, social behavior and the environment.* Hillsdale, NJ: Erlbaum.

Ageton, S. S. (1983). *Sexual assault among adolescents.* Lexington, MA: Lexington Books.

Ahammer, I. M., & Murray, J. P. (1979). Kindness in the kindergarten: The relative influence of role playing and prosocial television in facilitating altruism. *International Journal of Behavioral Development, 2,* 133–157.

Ahmed, S. M. S. (1979). Helping behavior as predicted by diffusion of responsibility, exchange theory, and traditional sex norms. *Journal of Social Psychology, 109,* 153–154.

Aiello, J. (1987). Human spatial behavior. In D. Stokols & I. Altman (Eds.), *Handbook of environmental psychology.* New York: Wiley.

Aiello, J. R., & Cooper, R. E. (1972). The use of personal space as a function of social affect. *Proceedings of the 80th Annual Convention of the American Psychology Association, 7,* 207–208.

Aiello, J. R., & Jones, S. E. (1971). Field study of the proxemic behavior of young school children in three subcultural groups. *Journal of Personality and Social Psychology, 19,* 351–356.

Ainsworth, M. D. S., Blehar, M. C., Waters, E., & Wall, S. (1978). *Patterns of attachment: A psychological study of the strange situation.* Hillsdale, NJ: Erlbaum.

Ajzen, I. (1985). From intentions to actions: A theory of planned action. In J. Kuhl & J. Beckman (Eds.), *Action control: From cognition to behavior* (pp. 11–39). New York: Springer.

Ajzen, I., & Fishbein, M. (1977). Attitude-behavior relations: A theoretical analysis and review of empirical research. *Psychological Bulletin, 84,* 888–918.

Ajzen, I., & Fishbein, M. (1980). *Understanding attitudes and predicting social behavior.* Englewood Cliffs, NJ: Prentice-Hall.

Ajzen, I., & Madden, T. J. (1986). Prediction of goal-directed behavior: Attitudes, intentions, and perceived behavioral control. *Journal of Experimental Social Psychology, 22,* 453–474.

Albright, L., Kenny, D. A., & Malloy, T. E. (1988). Consensus in personality judgments at zero acquaintance. *Journal of Personality and Social Psychology, 55,* 387–395.

Alder, C. (1985). An exploration of self-reported sexually aggressive behavior. *Crime and Delinquency, 31,* 306–331.

Allen, R. B., & Ebbesen, E. B. (1981). Cognitive processes in person perception: Retrieval of personality trait and behavioral information. *Journal of Experimental Social Psychology, 17,* 119–141.

Allen, V. L., & Levine, J. M. (1971). Social support and conformity: The role of independent assessment of reality. *Journal of Experimental Social Psychology, 7,* 48–58.

Allen, V. L., & Wilder, D. A. (1975). Categorization, belief similarity, and intergroup discrimination. *Journal of Personality and Social Psychology, 32,* 971–977.

Allen, V. L., & Wilder, D. A. (1979). Group categorization and attribution of belief similarity. *Small Group Behavior, 10,* 73–80.

Alley, T. R. (Ed.). (1988). *Social and applied aspects of perceiving faces.* Hillsdale, NJ: Erlbaum.

Allgeier, E. R., & Byrne, D. (1973). Attraction toward the opposite sex as a determinant of physical proximity. *Journal of Social Psychology, 90,* 213–219.

Allgood-Merten, B., & Stockard, J. (1991). Sex role identity and self-esteem: A comparison of children and adolescents. *Sex Roles, 25,* 129–139.

Allport, F. H. (1920). The influence of the group upon association and thought. *Journal of Experimental Psychology, 3,* 159–182.

Allport, F. H. (1924). *Social psychology*. Boston: Riverside Editions, Houghton Mifflin.

Allport, G. W. (1954). *The nature of prejudice.* Garden City, NY: Doubleday.

Allred, K. D., & Smith, T. W. (1989). The hardy personality: Cognitive and physiological responses to evaluative threat. *Journal of Personality and Social Psychology, 56,* 257–266.

Allsop, E., & Weisberg, H. F. (1988). Measuring change in party identification in an election campaign. *American Journal of Political Science, 32,* 996–1017.

Altemeyer, B. (1988). *Enemies of freedom: Understanding right-wing authoritarianism.* San Francisco: Jossey-Bass.

Altman, I. (1975). *The environment and social behavior.* Monterey, CA: Brooks/Cole.

Altman, I., & Haythorn, W. W. (1965). Interpersonal exchange in isolation. *Sociometry, 23,* 411–426.

Altman, I., Nelson, P. A., & Lett, E. E. (1972). The ecology of home environments. *Catalog of Selected Documents in Psychology.* Washington, D.C.: American Psychological Association.

Altman, I., & Taylor, D. A. (1973). *Social penetration: The development of interpersonal relationships.* New York: Holt, Rinehart and Winston.

Altman, I., Vinsel, A., & Brown, B. (1981). Dialectic conceptions in social psychology: An application to social penetration and privacy regulation. In L. Berkowitz (Ed.), *Advances in experimental social psychology* (Vol 14 pp. 76–100). New York: Academic Press.

Alwin, D. F., Cohen, R. L., & Newcomb, T. M. (1991). *Political attitudes over the life span: The Bennington women after fifty years.* Madison: University of Wisconsin Press.

Alwitt, L. F., & Mitchell, A. A. (Eds.). (1985). *Psychological processes and advertising effects: Theory, research, and application.* Hillsdale, NJ: Erlbaum.

Amabile, T. M., Hennessey, B. A., & Grossman, B. S. (1986). Social influences on creativity: The effects of contracted-for reward. *Journal of Personality and Social Psychology, 50,* 14–23.

Amato, P. R. (1983). Helping behavior in urban and rural environments: Field studies based on a taxonomic organization of helping episodes. *Journal of Personality and Social Psychology, 45*(3), 571–586.

Amato, P. R. (1990). Personality and social network involvement as predictors of helping behavior in everyday life. *Social Psychology Quarterly, 53,* 31–43.

American Cancer Society. (1989). *Cancer facts and figures—1989.* Atlanta, GA: American Cancer Society.

American Heart Association. (1984). *Heartfacts, 1984.* Dallas, TX: American Heart Association.

Amirkhan, J. H. (1990). A factor analytically derived measure of coping: The coping strategy indicator. *Journal of Personality and Social Psychology, 59,* 1066–1074.

Andersen, S. M. (1990). The inevitability of future suffering: The role of depressive predictive certainty in depression. *Social Cognition, 8,* 203–228.

Andersen, S. M., & Klatzky, R. L. (1987). Traits and social stereotypes: Levels of categorization in person perception. *Journal of Personality and Social Psychology, 53,* 235–246.

Andersen, S. M., Klatzky, R. L., & Murray, J. (1990). Traits and social stereotypes: Efficiency differences in social information processing. *Journal of Personality and Social Psychology, 59,* 192–201.

Anderson, C. A. (1991). How people think about causes: Examination of the typical phenomenal organization of attributions for success and failure. *Social Cognition, 9,* 295–329.

Anderson, C. A., & Godfrey, S. S. (1987). Thoughts about actions: The effects of specificity and availability on imagined behavioral scripts on expectations about oneself and others. *Social Cognition, 5,* 238–258.

Anderson, C. A., Jennings, D. L., & Arnoult, L. H. (1988). The validity and utility of the attributional style construct at a moderate level of specificity. *Journal of Personality and Social Psychology, 55,* 979–990.

Anderson, C. A., & Riger, A. L. (1991). A controllability attributional model of problems in living: Dimensional and situational interactions in the prediction of depression and loneliness. *Social Cognition, 9,* 149–181.

Anderson, C. A., & Sedikides, C. (1991). Thinking about people: Contributions of a typological alternative to associanistic and dimensional models of person perception. *Journal of Personality and Social Psychology, 60,* 203–217.

Anderson, N. H. (1959). Test of a model for opinion change. *Journal of Abnormal and Social Psychology, 59,* 371–381.

Anderson, N. H. (1965). Averaging vs. adding as a stimulus-combination rule in impression formation. *Journal of Experimental Psychology, 70,* 394–400.

Anderson, N. H. (1966). Component ratings in impression formation. *Psychonomic Science, 6,* 279–280.

Anderson, N. H. (1968a). A simple model for information integration. In R. P. Abelson et al. (Eds.), *Theories of cognitive consistency: A sourcebook* (pp. 731–743). Chicago: Rand McNally.

Anderson, N. H. (1968b). Likableness ratings of 555 personality-trait words. *Journal of Social Psychology, 9,* 272–279.

Ansolabahere, S., Behr, R., & Iyengar, S. (1991). Mass media and elections: An overview. *American Politics Quarterly, 19,* 109–139.

Anthony, T., Cooper, C., & Mullen, B. (1992). Cross-racial facial identification: A social cognitive integration. *Personality and Social Psychology Bulletin, 18,* 296–301.

Apple, W., & Hecht, K. (1982). Speaking emotionally: The relation between verbal and vocal communication of affect. *Journal of Personality and Social Psychology, 42,* 864–875.

Apple, W., Streeter, L. A., & Krauss, R. M. (1979). Effects of pitch and speech rate on personal attributions. *Journal of Personality and Social Psychology, 37,* 715–727.

Apostle, R. A., Glock, C. Y., Piazza, T., & Suelzle, M. (1983). *The anatomy of racial attitudes.* Berkeley: University of California Press.

Arkin, R. M., & Baumgardner, A. H. (1985). Self-handicapping. In J. H. Harvey & G. Weary (Eds.), *Basic issues in attribution theory and research* (pp. 169–202). New York: Academic Press.

Armstrong, E. A. (1965). *Bird display and behavior: An introduction to the study of bird psychology,* 2nd ed. New York: Dover.

Arndt, W. B., Jr., Foehl, J. C., & Good, F. E. (1985). Specific sexual fantasy themes: A multidimensional study. *Journal of Personality and Social Psychology, 48,* 472–480.

Aron, A. (1988). The matching hypothesis reconsidered again: Comment of Kalick and Hamilton. *Journal of Personality and Social Psychology, 54,* 441–446.

Aron, A., Aron, E. N., & Smollan, D. (1992). Inclusion of other in the self scale and the structure of interpersonal closeness. *Journal of Personality and Social Psychology, 63,* 596–612.

Aronson, E. (1990). Applying social psychology to desegregation and energy conservation. *Personality and Social Psychology Bulletin, 16,* 118–132.

Aronson, E., Brewer, M., & Carlsmith, J. M. (1985). Experimentation in social psychology. In G. Lindzey & E. Aronson (Eds.), *The handbook of social psychology,* 3rd ed. (Vol. 1, pp. 441–486). New York: Random House.

Aronson, E., & Gonzalez, A. (1988). Desegregation, jigsaw, and the Mexican-American experience. In P. A. Katz & D. A. Taylor (Eds.), *Eliminating racism: Profiles in controversy* (pp. 301–314). New York: Plenum Press.

Aronson, E., & Gonzalez, M. H. (1990). Alternative social influence processes applied to energy conservation. In J. Edwards, R. S. Tindale, L. Heath, & E. J. Posavac (Eds.), *Social influence processes and prevention* (pp. 301–326). New York: Plenum Press.

Aronson, E., & Linder, D. (1965). Gain and loss of esteem as determinants of interpersonal attractiveness. *Journal of Experimental Social Psychology, 1,* 156–171.

Aronson, E., Stephan, C., Sikes, J., Blaney, N., & Snapp, M. (1978). *The jigsaw classroom.* Beverly Hills, CA: Sage.

Aronson, E., Willerman, B., & Floyd, J. (1966). The effect of a pratfall on increasing interpersonal attractiveness. *Psychonomic Science, 4,* 227–228.

Asch, A. (1988). Disability: Its place in the psychology curriculum. In P. A. Bronstein & K. Quina (Eds.), *Teaching a psychology of people: Resources for gender and sociocultural awareness* (pp. 156–167). Washington, DC: American Psychological Association.

Asch, S. E. (1946). Forming impressions of personality. *Journal of Abnormal and Social Psychology, 41,* 258–290.

Asch, S. (1955). Opinions and social pressure. *Scientific American, 19,* 31–35.

Ashmore, R. D., & Del Boca, F. (1976). Psychological approaches to understanding intergroup conflict. In P. A. Katz (Ed.), *Towards the elimination of racism* (pp. 73–124). Elmsford, NY: Pergamon Press.

Ashmore, R. D., Del Boca, F. K., & Wohlers, A. J. (1986). Gender stereotypes. In R. D. Ashmore & F. K. Del Boca (Eds.), *The social psychology of female-male relations* (pp. 69–119). New York: Academic Press.

Ashton, N. L. Shaw, M. E., & Worsham, A. P. (1980). Affective reactions to interpersonal distances by friends and strangers. *Bulletin of the Psychonomic Society, 15,* 306–308.

Aspinwall, L. G., Kemeny, M. E., Taylor, S. E., Schneider, S. G., & Dudley, J. P. (1991). Psychosocial predictors of gay men's AIDS risk-reduction behavior. *Health Psychology, 10,* 432–444.

Atkeson, B. M., Calhoun, K. S., Resick, P. A., & Ellis, E. M. (1982). Victims of rape: Repeated assessment of depressive symptoms. *Journal of Consulting and Clinical Psychology, 50,* 96–102.

Atkin, C. (1979). Research evidence on mass mediated health communication campaigns. In D. Nimmo (Ed.), *Communication yearbook 3.* New Brunswick, NJ: Transaction Books.

Attorney General's Commission on Pornography. (1986). *Final Report.* Washington, DC: U.S. Department of Justice.

Attridge, M., Creed, M., Berscheid, E., & Simpson, J. A. (1992). *Predicting the stability of romantic relationships from individual versus couple data.* Unpublished manuscript, University of Minnesota.

Austin, W. (1980). Friendship and fairness: Effects of type of relationship and task performance on choice distribution rules. *Personality and Social Psychology Bulletin, 6,* 402–408.

Averill, J. R. (1983). Studies on anger and aggression: Implications for theories of emotion. *American Psychologist, 38,* 1145–1160.

Averill, J. R., & Boothroyd, P. (1977). On falling in love in conformance with the romantic ideal. *Motivation and Emotion, 1*(3), 235–247.

Axelrod, R. (1984). *The Evolution of Cooperation.* New York: Basic Books.

Babad, E., Bernieri, F., & Rosenthal, R. (1989). Nonverbal communication and leakage in the behavior of biased and unbiased teachers. *Journal of Personality and Social Psychology, 56,* 89–94.

Baldwin, J. A., Brown, R., & Rackley, R. (1990). Some socio-behavioral correlates of African self-consciousness in African-American college students. *The Journal of Black Psychology, 17,* 1–17.

Baldwin, M. W., Carrell, S. E., & Lopez, D. F. (1990). Priming relationship schemas: My advisor and the Pope are watching me from the back of my mind. *Journal of Experimental Social Psychology, 26,* 435–454.

Bales, R. F. (1970). *Personality and interpersonal behavior.* New York: Holt, Rinehart and Winston.

Ball-Rokeach, S. J., Grube, J. W., & Rokeach, M. (1981). Roots: The next generation—Who watched and with what effect? *Public Opinion Quarterly, 45,* 58–68.

Bandura, A. (1973). *Aggression: A social learning analysis.* Englewood Cliffs, NJ: Prentice-Hall.

Bandura, A. (1977). *Social learning theory.* Englewood cliffs, NJ: Prentice-Hall.

Bandura, A (1986). *Social foundations of thought and action: A social cognitive theory.* Englewood Cliffs, NJ: Prentice-Hall.

Bandura, A., Cioffi, D., Taylor, C. B., & Brouillard, M. E. (1988). Perceived self-efficacy in coping with cognitive stressors and opioid activation. *Journal of Personality and Social Psychology, 55,* 479–488.

Bandura, A., Ross, D., & Ross, S.A. (1961). Transmission of aggression through imitation of aggressive models. *Journal of Abnormal and Social Psychology, 63,* 575–582.

Bandura, A., Ross, D., & Ross, S. A. (1963). Imitation of film-mediated aggressive models. *Journal of Abnormal and Social Psychology, 66,* 3–11.

Barbaree, H. E., & Marshall, W. L. (1991). The role of male sexual arousal in rape: Six models. *Journal of Consulting and Clinical Psychology, 59,* 621–630.

Bargh, J. A. (1984). Automatic and conscious processing of social information. In R. S. Wyer & T. K. Srull (Eds.), *Handbook of social cognition* (Vol. 3, pp. 1–43). Hillsdale, NJ: Erlbaum.

Barker, R. G., Dembo, T., & Lewin, K. (1941). Frustration and regression: An experiment with young children. *University of Iowa Studies in Child Welfare, 18*(1).

Barnett, P. A., & Gotlib, I. H. (1988). Psychosocial functioning and depression: Distinguishing among antecedents, concomitants, and consequences. *Psychological Bulletin, 104,* 97–126.

Barnett, R. C., Davidson, H., & Marshall, N. L. (1991). Physical symptoms and the interplay of work and family roles. *Health Psychology, 10,* 94–101.

Barnett, R. C., Marshall, N. L., & Singer, J. D. (1992). Job experiences over time, multiple roles, and women's mental health: A longitudinal study. *Journal of Personality and Social Psychology, 62*, 634–644.

Barnlund, D. C. (1989). *Communicative styles of Japanese and Americans*. Belmont, CA: Wadsworth Publishing.

Baron, R. A. (1971a). Magnitude of victim's pain cues and level of prior anger arousal as determinants of adult aggressive behavior. *Journal of Personality and Social Psychology, 17*, 236–243.

Baron, R. A. (1971b). Aggression as a function of magnitude of victim's pain cues, level of prior anger arousal, and aggressor-victim similarity. *Journal of Personality and Social Psychology, 18*, 48–54.

Baron, R. A. (1974). Aggression as a function of victim's pain cues, level of prior anger arousal, and exposure to an aggressive model. *Journal of Personality and Social Psychology, 29*, 117–124.

Baron, R. A. (1977). *Human aggression*. New York: Plenum Press.

Baron, R. M., & Rodin, J. (1978). Perceived control and crowding stress: Processes mediating the impact of spatial and social density. In A. Baum & Y. Epstein (Eds.), *Human response to crowding*. Hillsdale, NJ: Erlbaum.

Baron, R. M., Mandel, D. G., Adams, C. A., & Griffen, L. M. (1976). Effects of social density in university residential environments. *Journal of Personality and Social Psychology, 34*, 434–446.

Baron, R. S. (1986). Distraction-conflict theory: Progress and problems. In L. Berkowitz (Ed.), *Advances in experimental social psychology* (Vol. 20). New York: Academic Press.

Baron, R. S., Burgess, M. L., & Kao, C. F. (1991). Detecting and labeling prejudice: Do female perpetrators go undetected? *Personality and Social Psychology Bulletin, 17*, 115–123.

Baron, R. S., Cutrona, C. E., Hicklin, D., Russell, D. W., & Lubaroff, D. M. (1990). Social support and immune function among spouses of cancer patients. *Journal of Personality and Social Psychology, 59*, 344–352.

Bartels, L. M. (1988). *Presidential primaries and the dynamics of public choice*. Princeton: Princeton University Press.

Bass, B. M. (1985). *Leadership and performance beyond expectations*. New York: Free Press.

Bassili, J. N., & Provencal, A. (1988). Perceiving minorities: A factor-analytic approach. *Personality and Social Psychology Bulletin, 14*, 5–15.

Bassili, J. N., & Racine, J. P. (1990). On the process relationship between person and situation judgments in attribution. *Journal of Personality and Social Psychology, 59*, 881–890.

Batson, C. D., Cochran, P. J., Biederman, M. F., Blosser, J. L., Ryan, M. J., & Vogt, B. (1978). Failure to help when in a hurry: Callousness or conflict? *Personality and Social Psychology Bulletin, 4*(1), 97–101.

Batson, C. D., Dyck, J. L., Brandt, J. R., Batson, J. G., Powell, A. L., McMaster, M. R., & Griffit, C. (1988). Five studies testing two new egoistic alternatives to the empathy-altruism hypothesis. *Journal of Personality and Social Psychology, 55*(1), 52–77.

Batson, C. D., & Oleson, K. C. (1991). Current status of the empathy-altruism hypothesis. In M. S. Clark (Ed.), *Prosocial behavior* (pp. 62–85). Newbury Park, CA; Sage.

Baum, A. (1990). Stress, intrusive imagery, and chronic distress. *Health Psychology, 9*, 653–675.

Baum, A., Aiello, J. R., & Calesnick, L. E. (1978). Crowding and personal control: Social density and the development of learned helplessness. *Journal of Personality and Social Psychology, 36*, 1000–1011.

Baum, A., & Davis, G. E. (1980). Reducing the stress of high-density living: An architectural intervention. *Journal of Personality and Social Psychology, 38*(3), 471–481.

Baum, A., & Paulus, P. (1987). Crowding. In D. Stokols & I. Altman (Eds.), *Handbook of environmental psychology*. New York: Wiley.

Baum, A., & Valins, S. (1977). *Architecture and social behavior: Psychological studies of social density*. Hillsdale, NJ: Erlbaum.

Baum, J. G., Clark, H. B., & Sandler, J. (1991). Preventing relapse in obesity through posttreatment maintenance systems: Comparing the relative efficacy of two levels of therapist support. *Journal of Behavioral Medicine, 14*, 287–302.

Baumeister, R. F. (1982). A self-presentational view of social phenomena. *Psychological Bulletin, 91*, 3–26.

Baumeister, R. F. (1986). *Identity: Cultural change and the struggle for self*. New York: Oxford University Press.

Baumeister, R. F. (1988). Anxiety and deconstruction: On escaping the self. In J. M. Olson & M. P. Zanna (Eds.), *Self-inference processes: The Ontario Symposium* (Vol. 6). Hillsdale, NJ: Erlbaum.

Baumeister, R. F. (1990). Anxiety and deconstruction: On escaping the self. In J. M. Olson & M. P. Zanna (Eds.), *Self-inference processes: The Ontario Symposium* (Vol. 6, pp. 259–291). Hillsdale, NJ: Erlbaum.

Baumeister, R. F., Chesner, S. P., Senders, P. S., & Tice, D. M. (1988). Who's in charge here: Group leaders do lend help in emergencies. *Personality and Social Psychology Bulletin, 14*, 17–22.

Baumeister, R. F., Hutton, D. G., & Tice, D. M. (1989). Cognitive processes during deliberate self-presentation: How self-presenters alter and misinterpret the behavior of their interaction partners. *Journal of Experimental Social Psychology, 25*, 59–78.

Baumeister, R. F., & Scher, S. J. (1988). Self-defeating behavior patterns among normal individuals: Review and analysis of common self-destructive tendencies. *Psychological Bulletin, 104*, 3–22.

Baumeister, R. F., & Steinhilber, A. (1984). Paradoxical effects of supportive audiences on performance under pressure: The home field disadvantage in sports championships. *Journal of Personality and Social Psychology, 47*(1), 85–93.

Baumgardner, A. H. (1990). To know oneself is to like oneself: Self-certainty and self-affect. *Journal of Personality and Social Psychology, 58*, 1062–1072.

Baumrind, D. (1964). Some thoughts on the ethics of research: After reading Milgram's "Behavioral study of obedience." *American Psychologist, 19*, 421–423.

Bavelas, J. B., Black, A., Lemery, C. R., & Mullett, J. (1986). "I show how you feel": Motor mimicry as a communicative act. *Journal of Personality and Social Psychology, 50*, 322–329.

Baxter, T. L. & Goldberg, L. R. (1988). Perceived behavioral consistency underlying trait attributions to oneself and another: An extension of the actor-observer effect. *Personality and Social Psychology Bulletin, 13*, 437–447.

Beaman, A. L., Barnes, P. J., Klentz, B., & McQuirk, B. (1978). Increasing helping rates through information dissemination: Teaching pays. *Personality and Social Psychology Bulletin, 4*(3), 406–411.

Bechtold, A., Naccarato, M. E., & Zanna, M. P. (1986). *Need for structure and the prejudice-discrimination link.* Paper presented at the annual meetings of the Canadian Psychological Association, Toronto, Ontario.

Beck, L., McCauley, C., Segal, M., & Hershey, L. (1988). Individual differences in prototypicality judgments about trait categories. *Journal of Personality and Social Psychology, 55,* 286–292.

Beck, P. A., & Jennings, M. K. (1991). Family traditions, political periods, and the development of partisan orientation. *Journal of Politics, 53,* 742–763.

Becker, F. D. (1973). Study of spatial markers. *Journal of Personality and Social Psychology, 26*(3), 439–445.

Bellezza, F. S. (1984). The self as a mnemonic device: The role of internal cues. *Journal of Personality and Social Psychology, 47,* 506–516.

Belloc, N. D., & Breslow, L. (1972). Relationship of physical health status and family practices. *Preventive Medicine, 1,* 409–421.

Bem, D. J. (1967). Self-perception: An alternative interpretation of cognitive dissonance phenomena. *Psychological Review, 74,* 183–200.

Bem, D. J. (1972). Self-perception theory. In L. Berkowitz (Ed.), *Advances in experimental social psychology* (Vol. 6, pp. 1–62). New York: Academic Press.

Bem, S. L. (1974). The measurement of psychological androgyny. *Journal of Consulting and Clinical Psychology, 42,* 155–162.

Bem, S. L. (1975). Sex role adaptability: One consequence of psychological androgyny. *Journal of Personality and Social Psychology, 31,* 634–643.

Bem, S. L. (1985). Androgyny and gender schema theory: A conceptual and empirical integration. In T. B. Sonderegger (Ed.), *Nebraska Symposium on Motivation: Psychology and gender* (pp. 179–226). Lincoln: University of Nebraska Press.

Bem, S. L., Martyna, W., & Watson, C. (1976). Sex typing and androgyny: Further explorations of the expressive domain. *Journal of Personality and Social Psychology, 43,* 1016–1023.

Bensley, L. S., & Wu, R. (1991). The role of psychological reactance in drinking following alcohol prevention messages. *Journal of Applied Social Psychology, 21,* 1111–1124.

Benson, H., Greenwood, M. M., & Klemchuck, H. (1975). The relaxation response: Psychophysiological aspects and clinical applications. *International Journal of Psychiatry in Medicine, 6,* 87–98.

Benson, P. L., Karabenick, S. A., & Lerner, R. M. (1976). Pretty pleases: The effects of physical attractiveness, race, and sex on receiving help. *Journal of Experimental Social Psychology, 12,* 409–415.

Berelson, B. R., Lazarsfeld, P. F., & McPhee, W. N. (1954). *Voting: A study of opinion formation in a presidential campaign.* Chicago: University of Chicago Press.

Bergen, D. J., & Williams, J. E. (1991). Sex stereotypes in the United States revisited: 1972–1988. *Sex Roles, 24,* 413–423.

Berger, J., Webster, M., Ridgeway, C., & Rosenholtz, S. J. (1986). Status cues, expectations, and behavior. In E. J. Lawler (Ed.), *Advances in group processes* (Vol 3, pp. 1–22). Greenwich, CT: JAI Press.

Berglas, S., & Jones, E. E. (1978). Drug choice as a self-handi-

capping strategy in response to noncontingent success. *Journal of Personality and Social Psychology, 36,* 405–417.

Berkman, L. F., & Syme, S. L. (1979). Social networks, host resistance, and mortality: A nine-year follow-up study of Alameda County residents. *American Journal of Epidemiology, 109,* 186–204.

Berkowitz, L. (1972). Social norms, feelings, and other factors affecting helping and altruism. In L. Berkowitz, (Ed.), *Advances in experimental social psychology* (Vol. 6). New York: Academic Press.

Berkowitz, L. (1974). Some determinants of impulsive aggression: The role of mediated associations with reinforcements for aggression. *Psychological Review, 81,* 165–176.

Berkowitz, L. (1983). Aversively stimulated aggression: Some parallels and differences in research with animals and humans. *American Psychologist, 38,* 1135–1144.

Berkowitz, L. (1984). Some effects of thoughts on anti- and prosocial influences of media events: A cognitive-neoassociation analysis. *Psychological Bulletin, 95,* 410–427.

Berkowitz, L. (Ed.). (1988). *Advances in experimental social psychology: Social psychological studies of the self: Perspectives and programs* (Vol. 21). New York: Academic Press.

Bernard, J. (1972). *The future of marriage.* New York: Bantam.

Bernard, L. C. (1980). Multivariate analysis of new sex role formulations and personality. *Journal of Personality and Social Psychology, 38,* 323–336.

Bernstein, M., & Crosby, F. (1980). An experimental examination of relative deprivation theory. *Journal of Experimental Social Psychology, 16,* 442–456.

Berry, D. S. (1990). Taking people at face value: Evidence for the kernel of truth hypothesis. *Social Cognition, 8,* 343–361.

Berry, D. S. (1991). Accuracy in social perception: Contributions of facial and vocal information. *Journal of Personality and Social Psychology, 61,* 298–307.

Berry, D. S. & Zebrowitz, L. A. (1988a). What's in a face? Facial maturity and the attribution of legal responsibility. *Personality and Social Psychology Bulletin, 14,* 23–33.

Berry, D. S. & Zebrowitz, L. A. (1988b). The impact of age-related craniofacial changes in social perception. In T. R. Alley (Ed.), *Social and applied aspects of perceiving faces* (pp. 63–87). Hillsdale, NJ: Erlbaum.

Berry, J. W. (1967). Independence and conformity in subsistence-level societies. *Journal of Personality and Social Psychology, 7,* 415–418.

Berry, J. W., Kalin, R., & Taylor, D. M. (1977). *Multiculturalism and ethnic attitudes in Canada.* Ottawa: Minister of Supply and Services.

Berry, J. W., Poortinga, Y. H., Segall, M. H., & Dasen, P. R. (1992). *Cross-cultural psychology: Research and applications.* New York: Cambridge University Press.

Berscheid, E. (1983). Emotion. In H. H. Kelley et al. *Close relationships* (pp. 110–168). New York: W. H. Freeman.

Berscheid, E. (1992). A glance back at a quarter century of social psychology. *Journal of Personality and Social Psychology, 63,* 525–533.

Berscheid, E., Graziano, W., Monson, T., & Dermer, M. (1976). Outcome dependency: Attention, attribution, and attraction. *Journal of Personality and Social Psychology, 34,* 978–989.

Berscheid, E., & Walster, E. (1967). When does a harm-doer compensate a victim? *Journal of Personality and Social Psychology, 6,* 435–441.

Berscheid, E., & Walster, E. (1978). *Interpersonal attraction,* 2nd ed. Reading, MA: Addison-Wesley.

Berscheid, E., Snyder, M., & Omoto, A. M. (1989). Issues in studying close relationships: Conceptualizing and measuring closeness. In C. Hendrick (Ed.), *Close relationships* (pp. 63–91). Newbury Park, CA: Sage Publications.

Beville, H. M., Jr. (1985). *Audience ratings: Radio, television, and cable.* Hillsdale, NJ: Erlbaum.

Bickman, L., & Kamzan, M. (1973). The effect of race and need on helping. *Journal of Social Psychology, 89,* 37–77.

Biernat, M. (1991a). Gender stereotypes and the relationship between masculinity and femininity: A developmental analysis. *Journal of Personality and Social Psychology, 61,* 351–365.

Biernat, M. (1991b). A multicomponent, developmental analysis of sex typing. *Sex Roles, 24,* 567–586.

Biglan, A., Metzler, C. W., Wirt, R., Ary, D., Noell, J., Ochs, L., French, C., & Hood, D. (1990). Social and behavioral factors associated with high-risk sexual behavior among adolescents. *Journal of Behavioral Medicine, 13,* 245–262.

Billings, A. C., & Moos, R. H. (1984). Coping, stress, and social resources among adults with unipolar depression. *Journal of Personality and Social Psychology, 46,* 877–891.

Bird, C. E., & Fremont, A. M. (1991). Gender, time use, and health. *Journal of Health and Social Behavior, 32,* 114–129.

Birdwhistell, R. I. (1970). *Kinetics and context: Essays on body motion communications.* Philadelphia: University of Pennsylvania Press.

Birt, C. M., & Dion, K. L. (1987). Relative deprivation theory and responses to discrimination in a gay male and lesbian sample. *British Journal of Social Psychology, 26,* 139–145.

Bishop, G. D. (1990). Understanding the understanding of illness: Lay disease representations. In J. A. Skelton & R. T. Croyle (Eds.), *Mental representation in health and illness.* New York: Springer-Verlag.

Blanchard, R., & Steiner, B. W. (Eds.). (1990). *Clinical management of gender identity disorders in children and adults.* Washington, DC: American Psychiatric Press.

Blanck, P. D., Bellack, A. S., Rosnow, R. L., Rotheram-Borus, M. J., & Schooler, N. R. (1992). Scientific rewards and conflicts of ethical choices in human subjects research. *American Psychologist, 47,* 959–965.

Blaney, P. H. (1986). Affect and memory: A review. *Psychological Bulletin, 99,* 229–246.

Blass, T. (1991). Understanding behavior in the Milgram obedience experiment: The role of personality, situations, and their interactions. *Journal of Personality and Social Psychology, 60,* 398–413.

Blau, P. M. (1964). *Exchange and power in social life.* New York: Wiley.

Blauwkamp, J. M., Fastnow, C. L., & Kellstedt, L. A. (1992). Religion and abortion attitudes: An update and extension of the Luker thesis. Presented at the Annual Meeting of the American Political Science Association, Chicago.

Blumenthal, J. A., & Emery, C. F. (1988). Rehabilitation of patients following myocardial infarction. *Journal of Consulting and Clinical Psychology, 56,* 374–381.

Blumenthal, M. D., Kahn, R. L., Andrews, F. M., & Head, K. B. (1972). *Justifying violence: Attitudes of American men.* Ann Arbor, MI: Institute for Social Research.

Blumstein, P., & Schwartz, P. (1983). *American couples: Money, work, sex.* New York: Pocket Books.

Boal, K. B., & Bryson, J. M. (1988). Charismatic leadership: A phenomenological and structural approach. In J. G. Hunt, B. R. Baliga, H. P. Dachler, & C. A. Schriesheim (Eds.), *Emerging leadership vistas* (pp. 11–28). Lexington, MA: Lexington Books.

Bobo, L. (1988a). Group conflict, prejudice, and the paradox of contemporary racial attitudes. In P. A. Katz & D. A. Taylor (Eds.), *Eliminating racism: Profiles in controversy* (pp. 85–114). New York: Plenum.

Bobo, L. (1988b). Attitudes toward the black political movement: Trends, meaning, and effects on racial policy preferences. *Social Psychology Quarterly, 51,* 287–302.

Bobo, L. (1989). Worlds apart: Blacks, whites, and explanations of racial equality. Paper presented at the meetings of the Midwest Political Science Association, Chicago.

Bobo, L. (1991). Social responsibility, individualism, and redistributive policies. *Sociological Forum, 6,* 71–92.

Bobo, L. & Kluegel, J. R. (1991). Modern American prejudice: Stereotypes, social distance, and perceptions of discrimination toward blacks, Hispanics, and Asians. Paper presented at annual meeting of the American Sociological Association, Cincinnati.

Bochner, S., & Insko, C. A. (1966). Communicator discrepancy, source credibility, and opinion change. *Journal of Personality and Social Psychology, 4,* 614–621.

Boer, C. de. (1977). The polls: Women at work. *Public Opinion Quarterly, 41,* 268–277.

Bohner, G., Bless, H., Schwarz, N., & Strack, F. (1988). What triggers causal attributions? The impact of valence and subjective probability. *European Journal of Social Psychology, 18,* 335–345.

Bolger, N., DeLongis, A., Kessler, R. C., & Schilling, E. A. (1989). Effects of daily stress on negative mood. *Journal of Personality and Social Psychology, 57,* 808–818.

Bond, C. R., Jr., & Brockett, D. R. (1987). A social context-personality index theory of memory acquaintances. *Journal of Personality and Social Psychology, 52,* 1110–1121.

Bond, C. R., Jr., & Sedikides, C. (1988). The recapitulation hypothesis in person retrieval. *Journal of Experimental Social Psychology, 24,* 195–221.

Bond, M. H. (1983). A proposal for cross-cultural studies of attribution. In M. Hewstone (Ed.), *Attribution theory: Social and functional extensions.* Oxford, England: Basil Blackwell.

Bons, P. M., & Fiedler, F. E. (1976). Changes in organizational leadership and the behavior of relationship- and task-motivated leaders. *Administrative Science Quarterly, 21,* 433–472.

Bontempo, R., Lobel, S., & Triandis, H. (1990). Compliance and value internalization in Brazil and the U. S. *Journal of Cross-Cultural Psychology, 21,* 201–213.

Booth, A. (1976). *Urban crowding and its consequences.* New York: Praeger.

Borden, R. J. (1980). Audience influence. In P. B. Paulus (Ed.), *Psychology of group influence* (pp. 99–132). Hillsdale, NJ: Erlbaum.

Borgida, E., Conner, C., & Manteufel, L. (1992). Understanding living kidney donation: A behavioral decision-making perspective. In S. Spacapan & S. Oskamp (Eds.), *Helping and being helped in the real world* (pp. 183–211). Newbury Park, CA: Sage.

Borgida, E. & DeBono, K. G. (1989). Social hypothesis-testing and the role of expertise. *Personality and Social Psychology Bulletin, 15,* 212–221.

Borgida, E., & Howard-Pitney, B. (1983). Personal involvement and the robustness of perceptual salience effects. *Journal of Personality and Social Psychology, 45,* 560–570.

Borkenau, P., & Liebler, A. (1992). Trait inferences: Sources of validity at zero acquaintance. *Journal of Personality and Social Psychology, 62*, 645–657.

Bornstein, R. F. (1989). Exposure and affect: Overview and meta-analysis of research, 1968-1987. *Psychological Bulletin, 106*, 265–289.

Bornstein, R. F., Kale, A. R., & Cornell, K. R. (1990). Boredom as a limiting condition on the mere exposure effect. *Journal of Personality and Social Psychology, 58*, 791–800.

Boucher, J., & Osgood, E. E. (1969). The Pollyanna hypothesis. *Journal of Verbal Learning and Verbal Behavior, 8*, 1–8.

Bower, G. H., & Gilligan, S. G. (1979). Remembering information related to one's self. *Journal of Research in Personality, 13*, 420–432.

Bowlby, J. (1969). *Attachment and loss:* Vol. 1. Attachment. New York: Basic Books.

Bowlby, J. (1988). *A secure base: Parent-child attachment and healthy human development.* New York: Basic Books.

Boyd, B., & Wandersman, A. (1991). Predicting undergraduate condom use with the Fishbein and Ajzen and the Triandis attitude-behavior models: Implications for public health interventions. *Journal of Applied Social Psychology, 21*, 1810–1830.

Bradburn, N. (1969). *The structure of psychological well-being.* Chicago: Aldine, 1969.

Bradbury, T. N., & Fincham, F. D. (1988). Individual difference variables in close relationships: A contextual model of marriage as an integrative framework. *Journal of Personality and Social Psychology, 54*, 713–721.

Bradbury, T. N., & Fincham, F. D. (1990). Attributions in marriage: Review and critique. *Psychological Bulletin, 107*, 3–33.

Bradbury, T. N., & Finchma, F. D. (1992). Attributions and behavior in marital interaction. *Journal of Personality and Social Psychology, 63*, 613–628.

Bradley, G. W. (1978). Self-serving biases in the attribution process: A reexamination of the fact or fiction question. *Journal of Personality and Social Psychology, 36*, 56 71.

Braiker, H. B., & Kelley, H. H. (1979). Conflict in the development of close relationships. In R. L. Burgess & T. L. Huston (Ed.), *Social exchange in developing relationships.* New York: Academic Press.

Brehm, J. W. (1956). Post-decision changes in desirability of alternatives. *Journal of Abnormal and Social Psychology, 52*, 384–389.

Brehm, J. W. (1966). *A theory of psychological reactance.* New York: Academic Press.

Brehm, S. S. (1992). *Intimate relationships*, 2nd ed. New York: McGraw-Hill.

Brehm, S. S., & Brehm, J. W. (1981). *Psychological reactance: A theory of freedom and control.* New York: Academic Press.

Bretl, D. J., & Cantor, J. (1988). The portrayal of men and women in U.S. television commercials: A recent content analysis and trends over 15 years. *Sex Roles, 18*, 595–609.

Brewer, M. B. (1979). In-group bias in the minimal intergroup situation: A cognitive-motivational analysis. *Psychological Bulletin, 86*, 307–324.

Brewer, M. B. (1986). The role of ethnocentrism in intergroup conflict. In S. Worchel & W. G. Austin (Eds.), *Psychology of intergroup relations* (pp. 88–102). Chicago: Nelson-Hall.

Brewer, M. B. (1988). A dual process model of impression formation. In T. K. Srull & R. S. Wyer, Jr. (Eds.), *Advances in social cognition* (Vol. 1, pp. 1–36). Hillsdale, NJ: Erlbaum.

Brewer, M. B. (1991). The social self: On being the same and different at the same time. *Personality and Social Psychology Bulletin, 17*, 475–482.

Brewer, M. B., Dull, V., & Lui, L. (1981). Perceptions of the elderly: Stereotypes as prototypes. *Journal of Personality and Social Psychology, 41*(4), 656–670.

Brewer, M. B., & Kramer, R. M. (1986). Choice behavior in social dilemmas: Effects of social identity, group size, and decision framing. *Journal of Personality and Social Psychology, 50*, 543–549.

Brewer, M. B., & Miller, N. (1984). Beyond the contact hypothesis: Theoretical perspectives on desegregation. In N. Miller & M. B. Brewer (Eds.), *Groups in contact: The psychology of desegregation* (pp. 281–302). New York: Academic Press.

Briar, S. (1966). Welfare from below: Recipients' view of the public welfare system. In J. Brock (Ed.), *The law of the poor.* San Francisco: Chandler.

Briggs, J. L. (1970). *Never in anger: Portrait of an Eskimo family.* Cambridge, MA: Harvard University Press.

Briggs, S. R., & Creek, J. M. (1988). On the nature of self-monitoring: Problems with assessment; problems with validity. *Journal of Personality and Social Psychology, 54*, 663–678.

Brigham, J. C. & Giesbrecht, L. W. (1976). All in the family: Racial attitudes. *Journal of Communication, 26*, 75–84.

Broadbent, D. E. (1957). Effects of noise on behavior. In C. M. Harris (Ed.), *Handbook of noise control.* New York: McGraw-Hill.

Brockner, J., DeWitt, R. L., Grover, S., & Reed T. (1990). When it is especially important to explain why: Factors affecting the relationship between managers' explanations of a layoff and survivors' reactions to the layoff. *Journal of Experimental Social Psychology, 26*, 389–407.

Brody, R. A. (1991). *Assessing the president: The media, elite opinion, and public support* Stanford: Stanford University Press.

Bronfenbrenner, U. (1961). The minor image in Soviet-American relations. *Journal of Social Issues, 18*, 45–56.

Brown, B. B. (1987). Territoriality. In D. Stokols & I. Altman, (Eds.), *Handbook of environmental psychology.* New York: Wiley.

Brown, J. D. (1986). Evaluations of self and others: Self-enhancement biases in social judgments. *Social Cognition, 4*, 353–376.

Brown, J. D. (1990). Evaluating one's abilities: Shortcuts and stumbling blocks on the road to self-knowledge. *Journal of Experimental Social Psychology, 26*, 149–167.

Brown, J. D., & Gallagher, F. M. (1992). Coming to terms with failure: Private self-enhancement and public self-effacement. *Journal of Experimental Social Psychology, 28*, 3–22.

Brown, J. D., & McGill, K. L. (1989). The cost of good fortune: When positive life events produce negative health consequences. *Journal of Personality and Social Psychology, 57*, 1103–1110.

Brown, J. D., & Smart, S. A. (1991). The self and social conduct: Linking self-representations to prosocial behavior. *Journal of Personality and Social Psychology, 60*, 368–375.

Brown, P., Keenan, J. M., & Potts, G. R. (1986). The self-reference effect with imagery encoding. *Journal of Personality and Social Psychology, 51*, 897–906.

Brown, R. (1974). Further comment on the risky shift. *American Psychologist, 29*, 468–470.

Brown, R. (1988). *Group processes: Dynamics with and between groups.* New York: Basil Blackwell.

Brownell, A. (1982). Obesity: Understanding and treating a serious, prevalent and refractory disorder. *Journal of Consulting and Clinical Psychology, 50*, 820–840.

Brownell, K. D., Marlatt, G. A., Lichtenstein, E., & Wilson, G. T. (1986). Understanding and preventing relapse. *American Psychologist, 41*, 765–782.

Brownell, K. D., Stunkard, A. J., & McKeon, P. E. (1985). Weight reduction at the work site: A promise partially fulfilled. *American Journal of Psychiatry, 142*, 47–52.

Brownlow, S. & Zebrowitz, L. A. (1990). Facial appearance, gender, and credibility in television commercials. *Journal of Nonverbal Behavior, 14*, 51–60.

Brownmiller, S. (1975). *Against our will: Men, women, and rape.* New York: Bantam.

Bryan, J. H., & Test, N. A. (1967). Models and helping: Naturalistic studies in aiding behavior. *Journal of Personality and Social Psychology, 6*, 400–407.

Buck, R. (1984). *The communication of emotions.* New York: Guilford.

Bulman, R. J., & Wortman, C. B. (1977). Attributions of blame and coping in the "real world": Severe accident victims react to their lot. *Journal of Personality and Social Psychology, 35*, 351–363.

Bureau of the Census (1992, March). *1990 Census of population and housing: Summary population and housing characteristics.* U.S. Department of Commerce.

Burger, J. M. (1986). Increasing compliance by improving the deal: The that's-not-all technique. *Journal of Personality and Social Psychology, 51*, 277–283.

Burger, J. M., & Petty, R. E. (1981). The low-ball compliance technique: Task or person commitment? *Journal of Personality and Social Psychology, 40*, 492–500.

Burgess, R. L., & Huston, T. L. (Eds.). (1979). *Social exchange in developing relationships.* New York: Academic Press.

Burgoon, J. K. (1991). Relational message interpretations of touch, conversational distance, and posture. *Journal of Nonverbal Behavior, 15*(4), 233–259.

Burgoon, J. K., Parrott, R., Le Poire, B. A., Kelley, D. L., Walther, J. B., & Perry, D. (1989). Maintaining and restoring privacy through communication in different types of relationships. *Journal of Social and Personal Relationships, 6*, 131–158.

Burish, T. C., & Bradley, L. A. (1983). *Coping with chronic disease: Research and applications.* New York: Academic Press.

Burn, S. M., & Oskamp, S. (1989). Ingroup biases and the U.S.-Soviet conflict. *Journal of Social Issues, 45*, 73–89.

Burnkrant, R. E., & Howard, D. J. (1984). Effects of the use of introductory rhetorical questions versus statements on information processing. *Journal of Personality and Social Psychology, 47*, 1218–1230.

Burnstein, E., & Vinokur, A. (1975). What a person thinks upon learning he has chosen differently from others: Nice evidence for the persuasive-arguments explanation of choice shifts. *Journal of Experimental and Social Psychology, 11*, 412–426.

Burt, M. R. (1980). Cultural myths and supports for rape. *Journal of Personality and Social Psychology, 38*, 217–230.

Bushman, B. J. & Geen, R. G. (1990). Role of cognitive-emotional mediators and individual differences in the effects of media violence on aggression. *Journal of Personality and Social Psychology, 58*, 156–163.

Buss, A. H. (1961). *The psychology of aggression.* New York: Wiley.

Butterworth, G. (1992). Origins of self-perception in infancy. *Psychological Inquiry, 3*, 103–111.

Buunk, B. P., Collins, R. L., Taylor, S. E., Van Yperen, N., & Dakof, G. A. (1990). The affective consequences of social comparison: Either direction has its ups and downs. *Journal of Personality and Social Psychology, 59*, 1238–1249.

Buunk, B. P., Van Yperen, N. W., Taylor, S. E., & Collins, R. L. (1991). The drive upward revisited: Upward affiliation as a response to marital stress. *European Journal of Social Psychology, 21*, 529–546.

Bylsma, W. H., & Major, B. (1992). Two routes to eliminating gender differences in personal entitlement: Social comparison and performance evaluations. *Psychology of Women Quarterly, 16*, 193–200.

Byrne, D. (1971). *The attraction paradigm.* New York: Academic Press.

Byrne, D., Clore, G. L., & Smeaton, G. (1986). The attraction hypothesis: Do similar attitudes affect anything? *Journal of Personality and Social Psychology, 51*(6), 1167–1170.

Cacioppo, J. T., Marshall-Goodell, B. S., Tassinary, L. G., & Petty, R. E. (1992). Rudimentary determinants of attitudes: Classical conditioning is more effective when prior knowledge about the attitude stimulus is low than high. *Journal of Experimental Social Psychology, 28*, 207–233.

Cacioppo, J. T., Martzke, J. S., Petty, R. E., & Tassinary, L. G. (1988). Specific forms of facial EMG response index emotions during an interview: From Darwin to the continuous flow hypothesis of affect-laden information processing. *Journal of Personality and Social Psychology, 54*, 592–604.

Cacioppo, J. T., Petty, R. E., Losch, M. E., & Kim, H. S. (1986). Electromyographic activity over facial muscle regions can differentiate the valence and intensity of affective reactions. *Journal of Personality and Social Psychology, 50*, 260–268.

Cain, B. E., Kiewiet, D. R., & Uhlaner, C. J. (1991). The acquisition of partisanship by Latinos and Asian Americans. *American Journal of Political Science, 35*, 390–422.

Caldwell, M. A., & Peplau, L. A. (1982). Sex differences in same-sex friendship. *Sex Roles, 8*(7), 721–732.

Campbell, A., Converse, P. E., Miller, W. E., & Stokes, D. E. (1960). *The American voter.* New York: Wiley.

Campbell, D. T. (1975). On the conflicts between biological and social evolution and between psychology and moral tradition. *American Psychologist, 30*(12), 1103–1126.

Campbell, D. T., & Stanley, J. C. (1963). *Experimental and quasi-experimental designs for research.* Chicago: Rand McNally.

Campbell, J. D. (1986). Similarity and uniqueness: The effects of attribute type, relevance, and individual differences in self-esteem and depression. *Journal of Personality and Social Psychology, 50*, 281–294.

Campbell, J. D. (1990). Self-esteem and clarity of the self-concept. *Journal of Personality and Social Psychology, 59*, 538–549.

Campbell, J. D., & Fairey, P. J. (1989). Informational and normative routes to conformity: The effect of faction size as a function of norm extremity and attention to the stimulus. *Journal of Personality and Social Psychology, 57*, 457–468.

Campbell, J. D., Tesser, A., & Fairey, P. J. (1986). Conformity and attention to the stimulus: Some temporal and contextual dynamics. *Journal of Personality and Social Psychology, 51*(2), 315–324.

Cantor, N., & Mischel, W. (1979). Prototypes in person perception. In L. Berkowitz (Ed.), *Advances in experimental social psychology* (Vol. 12, pp. 4–52). New York: Academic Press.

Cantrambone, R., & Markus, H. (1987). The role of self-schemas in going beyond the information given. *Social Cognition, 5*, 349–368.

Caporael, L. R., & Brewer, M. B. (Eds.). (1991). Issues in evolutionary psychology. *Journal of Social Issues, 47*(whole number 3).

Carballo-Dieguez, A. (1989). Hispanic culture, gay male culture, and AIDS: Counseling implications. *Journal of Counseling and Development, 68*, 26–30.

Carli, L. L., Ganley, R., & Pierce-Otay, A. (1991). Similarity and satisfaction in roommate relationships. *Personality and Social Psychology Bulletin*, 419–426.

Carlo, G., Eisenberg, N., Troyer, D., Switzer, G., & Speer, A. L. (1991). The altruistic personality: In what contexts is it apparent? *Journal of Personality and Social Psychology, 61*, 450–458.

Carlson, M., Marcus-Newhall, A., & Miller, N. (1989). Evidence for a general construct of aggression. *Personality and Social Psychology Bulletin, 15*, 377–389.

Carlson, M., & Miller, N. (1987). Explanation of the relation between negative mood and helping. *Psychological Bulletin, 102*(1), 91–108.

Carlson, M., Charlin, V., & Miller, N. (1988). Positive mood and helping behavior: A test of six hypotheses. *Journal of Personality and Social Psychology, 55*(2), 211–229.

Carlston, D. E., & Shovar, N. (1983). Effects of performance attributions on others' perceptions of the attribution. *Journal of Personality and Social Psychology, 44*, 515–525.

Carmines, E. G., & Stanley, H. W. (1992). The transformation of the New Deal party system: Social groups, political ideology, and changing partisanship among Northern whites, 1972–1988. *Political Behavior, 14*, 213–237.

Carpenter, S. L. (1988). Self-relevance and goal-directed processing in the recall and weighting of information about others. *Journal of Experimental Social Psychology, 24*, 310–322.

Carter, D. B. (1987). The roles of peers in sex role socialization. In D. B. Carter (Ed.), *Current conceptions of sex roles and sex typing: Theory and research* (pp. 101–121). New York: Praeger.

Carver, C. S., & Scheier, M. F. (1981). *Attention and self-regulation: A control theory approach to human behavior.* New York: Springer.

Carver, C. S., Scheier, M. F., & Weintraub, J. K. (1989). Assessing coping strategies: A theoretically based approach. *Journal of Personality and Social Psychology, 56*, 267–283.

Cash, T. F., Gillen, B., & Burns, D. S. (1977). Sexism and "beautyism" in personnel consultant decision making. *Journal of Applied Psychology, 62*, 301–310.

Casselden, P. A., & Hampson, S. E. (1990). Forming impressions from incongruent traits. *Journal of Personality and Social Psychology, 59*, 353–362.

Cataldo, M. F., Green, L. W., Herd, J. A., Parkinson, R. S., & Goldbeck, W. B. (1986). Preventive medicine and the corporate environment: Challenge to behavioral medicine. In M. F. Cataldo & T. J. Coates (Eds.), *Health and industry: A behavioral medicine perspective* (pp. 399–419). New York: Wiley.

Catania, J. A., Coates, T. J., Stall, R., Bye, L., Kegeles, S. M., Capell, F., Henne, J., McKusick, L., Morin, S., Turner, H., & Pollack, L. (1991). Changes in condom use among homosexual men in San Francisco. *Health Psychology, 10*, 190–199.

Cate, R. M., & Lloyd, S. A. (1992). *Courtship.* Newbury Park, CA: Sage.

Cate, R. M., Lloyd, S. A., & Long, E. (1988). The role of rewards and fairness in developing premarital relationships. *Journal of Marriage and the Family, 50*, 443–452.

Cater, D., & Strickland, D. (1975). *TV violence and the child.* New York: Russell Sage.

Cervone, D., & Peake, P. K. (1986). Anchoring, efficacy, and action: The influence of judgmental heuristics on self-efficacy judgments and behavior. *Journal of Personality and Social Psychology, 50*, 492–501.

Chafetz, M. E. (1970). No patient deserves to be patronized. *Medical Insight, 2*, 68–75.

Chaiken, S. (1980). Heuristic versus systematic information processing and the use of source versus message cues in persuasion. *Journal of Personality and Social Psychology, 39*, 752–766.

Chaiken, S., & Stangor, C. (1987). Attitudes and attitude change. In M. R. Rosenzweig & L. W. Porter (Eds.), *Annual review of psychology, 38*, 575–630.

Chaikin, A. L., & Derlega, V. J. (1974). Liking for the norm-breaker in self-disclosure. *Journal of Personality, 42*, 117–129.

Chaikin, A. L., Gillen, H. B., Derlega, V., Heinen, J., & Wilson, M. (1978). Students' reactions to teachers' physical attractiveness and nonverbal behavior: Two exploratory studies. *Psychology in the Schools, 15*, 588–595.

Champion, V. L. (1990). Breast self-examination in women 35 and older: A prospective study. *Journal of Behavioral Medicine, 13*, 523–538.

Chaney, E. F., O'Leary, M. R., & Marlatt, G. A. (1978). Skill training with alcoholics. *Journal of Consulting and Clinical Psychology, 46*, 1092–1104.

Chapman, L. J., & Chapman, J. P. (1967). Genesis of popular but erroneous diagnostic observations. *Journal of Abnormal Psychology, 72*, 193–204.

Chavira, V., & Phinney, J. S. (1991). Adolescents' ethnic identity, self-esteem, and strategies for dealing with ethnicity and minority status. *Hispanic Journal of Behavioral Sciences, 13*, 226–227.

Chen, H., Yates, B. T., & McGinnies, E. (1988). Effects of involvement on observers' estimates of consensus, distinctiveness, and consistency. *Personality and Social Psychology Bulletin, 14*, 468–478.

Chen, S. C. (1937). Social modification of the activity of ants in nest-building. *Physiological Zoology, 10*, 420–436.

Cheng, P. W., & Novick, L. R. (1990). A probabilistic contrast model of causal induction. *Journal of Personality and Social Psychology, 58*, 545–567.

Chesney, M. A., Eagleston, J. R., & Rosenman, R. H. (1981). Type A behavior: Assessment and intervention. In C. K. Prokop & L. A. Bradley (Eds.), *Medical psychology: Contributions to behavioral medicine* (pp. 20–34). New York: Academic Press.

Christie, R., & Jahoda, M. (Eds.). (1954). *Studies in the scope* and method of "the authoritarian personality": Continuities in social research. Glencoe, IL: The Free Press.

Cialdini, R. B. (1985). *Influence: Science and practice.* Glenview, IL: Scott, Foresman.

Cialdini, R. B. (1988). *Influence: Science and practice,* 2nd ed. Glenview, IL: Scott, Foresman.

Cialdini, R. B., Borden, R. J., Thorne, A., Walker, M. R., Freeman, S., & Sloan, L. R. (1976). Basking in reflected glory: Three (football) field studies. *Journal of Personality and Social Psychology, 34,* 366–375.

Cialdini, R. B., Cacioppo, J. T., Bassett, R., & Miller, J. A. (1978). Low-ball procedure for producing compliance: Commitment then cost. *Journal of Personality and Social Psychology, 36,* 463–476.

Cialdini, R. B., & De Nicholas, M. E. (1989). Self-presentation by association. *Journal of Personality and Social Psychology, 57,* 626–631.

Cialdini, R. B., Schaller, M., Houlihan, D., Arps, K., Fultz, J., & Beaman, A. (1987). Empathy-based helping: Is it selflessly or selfishly motivated? *Journal of Personality and Social Psychology, 52*(4), 749–758.

Cialdini, R. B., Vincent, J. E., Lewis, S. K., Catalan, J., Wheeler, D., & Darby, B. L. (1975). Reciprocal concessions procedure for inducing compliance: The door-in-the-face technique. *Journal of Personality and Social Psychology, 31,* 206–215.

Citrin, J., Reingold, B., & Green, D. P. (1990). American identity and the politics of ethnic change. *Journal of Politics, 52,* 1124–1154.

Citrin, J., Reingold, B., Walters, E., & Green, D. P. (1990). The "Offical English" movement and the symbolic politics of language in the United States. *Western Political Quarterly, 43,* 535–559.

Clark, M. S. (Ed.). (1991). *Prosocial behavior.* Newbury Park, CA: Sage Publications.

Clark, M. S., Milberg, S., & Erber, R. (1984). Effects of arousal on judgments of others' emotions. *Journal of Personality and Social Psychology, 46,* 551–560.

Clark, M. S., & Mills, J. (1979). Interpersonal attraction in exchange and communal relationships. *Journal of Personality and Social Psychology, 37,* 12–24.

Clark, M. S., Mills, J., & Powell, M. C. (1986). Keeping track of needs in communal and exchange relationships. *Journal of Personality and Social Psychology, 51*(2), 333–338.

Clark, M. S., & Taraban, C. (1991). Reactions to and willingness to express emotion in communal and exchange relationships. *Journal of Experimental Social Psychology, 27,* 324–336.

Clark, R. D. (1990). Minority influence: The role of argument refutation of the majority position and social support for the minority position. *European Journal of Social Psychology, 20,* 489–497.

Clark, R. D., & Word, L. E. (1972). Why don't bystanders help? Because of ambiguity? *Journal of Personality and Social Psychology, 24,* 392–400.

Clark, R. D., & Word, L. E. (1974). Where is the apathetic bystander? Situational characteristics of the emergency. *Journal of Personality and Social Psychology, 29,* 279–287.

Clary, E. G., & Orenstein, L. (1991). The amount and effectiveness of help: The relationship of motives and abilities to helping behavior. *Personality and Social Psychology Bulletin, 17,* 58–64.

Clary, E. G., & Snyder, M. (1991). A functional analysis of altruism and prosocial behavior: The case of volunteerism.

In M. S. Clark (Ed.), *Prosocial behavior* (pp. 119–147). Newbury Park, CA: Sage Publications.

Clifford, M. M., & Walster, E. (1973). Research note: The effects of physical attractiveness on teacher expectations. *Sociology of Education, 46,* 248–258.

Clore, G. L., Bray, R. B., Itkin, S. M., & Murphy, P. (1978). Interracial attitudes and behavior at a summer camp. *Journal of Personality and Social Psychology, 36,* 107–116.

Cochran, S. D., & Hammen, C. L. (1985). Perceptions of stressful life events and depression: A test of attributional models. *Journal of Personality and Social Psychology, 48,* 1562–1571.

Cochran, S. D., & Mays, V. M. (1990). AIDS-related sexual behavior and disclosure: Is it safe if you ask? *New England Journal of Medicine, 322,* 774–775.

Cody, R., & Lee, C. (1990). Behaviors, beliefs, and intentions in skin cancer prevention. *Journal of Behavioral Medicine, 13,* 373–390.

Cohen, C. E. (1981). Person categories and social perception: Testing some boundaries of the processing effects of prior knowledge. *Journal of Personality and Social Psychology, 40,* 441–452.

Cohen, S., Evans, G. W., Krantz, D. S., Stokols, D., & Kelly, S. (1981). Aircraft noise and children: Longitudinal and cross-sectional evidence on adaptation to noise and the effectiveness of noise abatement. *Journal of Personality and Social Psychology, 40,* 331–345.

Cohen, S., Glass, D. C., & Singer, J. E. (1973). Apartment noise, auditory discrimination, and reading ability in children. *Journal of Experimental Social Psychology, 9,* 407–422.

Cohen, S., & Hoberman, H. M. (1983). Positive events and social supports as buffers of life change stress. *Journal of Applied Social Psychology, 13,* 99–125.

Cohen, S., & Lezak, A. (1977). Noise and attentiveness to social cues. *Environment and Behavior, 9,* 559–572.

Cohen, S., & Weinstein, N. (1981). Nonauditory effects of noise on behavior and health. *Journal of Social Issues, 37*(1) 36–70.

Cohen, S., & Wills, T. A. (1985). Stress, social support, and the buffering hypothesis. *Psychological Bulletin, 98,* 310–357.

Cole, P. (1974). Morbidity in the U.S. In C. L. Erhardt, & J. Berlin (Eds.), *Mortality and morbidity in the U.S.* (pp. 65–104). Cambridge, MA: Harvard University Press.

Coleman, J. F., Blake, R. R., & Mouton, J. S. (1958). Task difficulty and conformity pressures. *Journal of Abnormal and Social Psychology, 57,* 120–122.

Collins, B. E., & Aspinwall, L. G. (1989, May). *Impression management in negotiation for safer sex.* Paper presented for symposium on Negotiating Safer Sex: Personal and Interpersonal Issues, at the Second Iowa Conference on Personal Relationships, Iowa City, IA.

Collins, N. L., & Read, S. J. (1990). Adult attachment, working models, and relationship quality in dating couples. *Journal of Personality and Social Psychology, 58,* 644–663.

Collins, R. L., Taylor, S. E., & Skokan, L. A. (1990). A better world or a shattered vision? Changes in perspectives following victimization. *Social Cognition, 8,* 263–285.

Coltrane, S., & Ishii-Kuntz, M. (1992). Men's housework: A life course perspective. *Journal of Marriage and the Family, 54,* 43–57.

Commission on Obscenity and Pornography. (1970). *Report*

of the commission on obscenity and pornography. New York: Bantam.

Comstock, G. (1982). Violence in television content: An overview. In D. Pearl, L. Bouthilet, & J. Lazar (Eds.), *Television and behavior: Ten years of scientific progress and implications for the Eighties*. Vol. II: *Technical reviews*. Rockville, MD: National Institute of Mental Health.

Comstock, G., Chaffee, S., Katzman, N., McCombs, M., & Roberts, D. (1978). *Television and human behavior*. New York: Columbia University Press.

Condry, J., & Condry, S. (1976). Sex differences: A study in the eye of the beholder. *Child Development, 47*, 812–819.

Connelly, M. (1989, Sept. 15). Truck driver honored for heroism in fire. *Los Angeles Times*, Part II, pp. 8, 12.

Conover, P. J. (1988). Feminists and the gender gap. *Journal of Politics, 50*, 985–1010.

Converse, P. E. (1964). The nature of belief systems in mass publics. In D. E. Apter (Ed.), *Ideology and discontent* (pp. 206–261). New York: Free Press.

Converse, P. E., & Markus, G. B. (1979). Plus ça change . . . : The new CPS election study panel. *American Political Science Review, 73*, 32-49.

Cooley, C. H. (1902). *Human nature and the social order*. New York: Scribners.

Cook, E. A., & Wilcox, C. (1991). Feminism and the gender gap: A second look. *Journal of Politics, 53*, 1111–1122.

Cook, S. W. (1984). Cooperative interaction in multi-ethnic contexts. In N. Miller & M. Brewer (Eds.), *Groups in contact: The psychology of desegregation* (pp. 156–186). New York: Academic Press.

Cook, S. W. (1988). The 1954 social science statement and school desegregation: A reply to Gerard. In P. A. Katz & D. A. Taylor (Eds.), *Eliminating racism: Profiles in controversy* (pp. 237–256). New York: Plenum.

Cook, S. W., & Pelfrey, M. (1985). Reactions to being helped in cooperating interracial groups: A context effect. *Journal of Personality and Social Psychology, 49*(5), 1231–1245.

Cooper, J., & Fazio, R. H. (1984). A new look at dissonance theory. In L. Berkowitz (Ed.), *Advances in experimental social psychology* (Vol. 17, pp. 229–265). New York: Academic Press.

Coovert, M. D., & Reeder, G. D. (1990). Negativity effects in impression formation: The role of unit formation and schematic expectations. *Journal of Personality and Social Psychology, 26*, 49–62.

Cousins, S. D. (1989). Culture and self-perception in Japan and the United States. *Journal of Personality and Social Psychology, 56*, 124–131.

Cox, D. J., Tisdelle, D. A., & Culbert, J. P. (1988). Increasing adherence to behavioral homework assignments. *Journal of Behavioral Medicine, 11*, 519–522.

Cox, M. J., Owen, M. T., Henderson, V. K., & Margand, N. A. (1992). Prediction of infant-father and infant-mother attachment. *Developmental Psychology, 28*, 474–483.

Coyne, J. C., & Smith, D. A. F. (1991). Couples coping with a myocardial infarction: A contextual perspective on wives' distress. *Journal of Personality and Social Psychology, 61*, 404–412.

Craig, K. D., & Patrick, C. J. (1985). Facial expression during induced pain. *Journal of Personality and Social Psychology, 48*, 1080–1091.

Craig, R. S. (1992). The effect of television day part and gen-der portrayals in television commercials: A content analysis. *Sex Roles, 26*, 197–211.

Craik, F. I. M., & Tulving, E. (1975). Depth of processing and the retention of words in episodic memory. *Journal of Experimental Psychology: General, 194*, 268–294.

Crary, W. G. (1966). Reactions to incongruent self-experiences. *Journal of Consulting Psychology, 30*, 246–252.

Crittenden, K. S., & Lamug, C. B. (1988). Causal attribution and depression: A friendly refinement based on Philippine data. *Journal of Cross-Cultural Psychology, 19*, 216–231.

Crocker, J. (1981). Judgment of covariation by social perceivers. *Psychological Bulletin, 90*, 272–292.

Crocker, J., Hannah, D. B., & Weber, R. (1983). Person memory and causal attributions. *Journal of Personality and Social Psychology, 44*, 55–66.

Crocker, J., & Luhtanen, R. (1990). Collective self-esteem and ingroup bias. *Journal of Personality and Social Psychology, 58*, 60–67.

Crocker, J., Thompson, L. L., McGraw, K. M., & Ingerman, C. (1987). Downward comparison, prejudice, and evaluations of others: Effects of self-esteem and threat. *Journal of Personality and Social Psychology, 52*, 907–916.

Crocker, J., Voelkl, K., Testa, M., & Major, B. (1991). Social stigma: The affective consequences of attributional ambiguity. *Journal of Personality and Social Psychology, 60*, 218–228.

Crosby, F. J. (1982). *Relative deprivation and working women*. New York: Oxford University Press.

Crosby, F. J. (1991). *Juggling*. New York: Free Press.

Cummings, K. M., Jette, A. M., & Rosenstock, I. M. (1978). Construct validation of the health belief model. *Health Education Monographs, 6*, 394–405.

Cunningham, M. R. (1979). Weather, mood, and helping behavior: Quasi-experiments with the sunshine Samaritan. *Journal of Personality and Social Psychology, 37*(11), 1947–1956.

Cunningham, M. R., Shaffer, D. R., Barbee, A. P., Wolff, P. L., & Kelley, D. J. (1990). Separate processes in the relation of elation and depression to helping: Social versus personal concerns. *Journal of Experimental Social Psychology, 26*, 13–33.

Current Population Reports (1989, January). *Projections of the population of the United States by age, sex, and race, 1988 to 2080*. Bureau of the Census, Series P-25, No. 1018.

Curtis, R. C., & Miller, K. (1986). Believing another likes and dislikes you: Behaviors making the beliefs come true. *Journal of Personality and Social Psychology, 51*, 284–290.

Dabbs, J. M., Jr., & Leventhal, H. (1986). Effects of varying the recommendations in a fear-arousing communication. *Journal of Personality and Social Psychology, 4*, 525–531.

Dakof, G. A., & Taylor, S. E. (1990). Victims' perceptions of social support: What is helpful from whom? *Journal of Personality and Social Psychology, 58*, 80–89.

Darley, J. M., & Batson, C. D. (1973). "From Jerusalem to Jericho": A study of situational and dispositional variables in helping behavior. *Journal of Personality and Social Psychology, 27*, 100–108.

Darley, J. M., & Fazio, R. H. (1980). Expectancy confirmation processes arising in the social interaction sequence. *American Psychologist, 35*, 867–881.

Darley, J. M., Fleming, J. H., Hilton, J. L., & Swann, W. B., Jr. (1988). Dispelling negative expectancies: The impact of interaction goals and target characteristics on the expectancy confirmation process. *Journal of Experimental Social Psychology, 24,* 19–36.

Darley, J. M., & Latané, B. (1968). Bystander intervention in emergencies: Diffusion of responsibility: *Journal of Personality and Social Psychology, 8,* 377–383.

Darwin, C. (1871). *The descent of man.* London: Murray.

Davidson, A. R., & Jaccard, J. J. (1979). Variables that moderate the attitude-behavior relation: Results of a longitudinal survey. *Journal of Personality and Social Psychology, 37,* 1364–1376.

Davis, J. H. (1989). Psychology and the law: The last 15 years. *Journal of Applied Social Psychology, 19,* 199–230.

Davis, K. E., & Kirkpatrick, L. A. (in press). Attachment style, gender and relationship stability: A longitudinal analysis. *Journal of Personality and Social Psychology.*

Davis, M. S. (1968). Variation in patients' compliance with doctor's advice: An empirical analysis of patterns of communication. *American Journal of Public Health, 58,* 274–288.

Dawes, R., Faust, D., & Meehl, P. E. (1989). Clinical versus actuarial judgment. *Science, 243,* 1668–1674.

Deaux, K. (1976). *The behavior of women and men.* Monterey, CA: Brooks/Cole.

Deaux, K., & Emswiller, T. (1974). Explanations of successful performance on sex-linked tasks: What is skill for the male is luck for the female. *Journal of Personality and Social Psychology, 29,* 80–85.

Deaux, K., & Lewis, L. (1984). Structure of gender stereotypes: Interrelationships among components and gender label. *Journal of Personality and Social Psychology, 46,* 991–1004.

Deaux, K., & Major, B. (1987). Putting gender into context: An interactive model of gender-related behavior. *Psychological Review, 94,* 369–389.

Deaux, K., & Ullman, J. C. (1983). *Women of steel.* New York: Praeger.

Deci, E. L., & Ryan, R. M. (1985). *Intrinsic motivation and self-determination in human behavior.* New York: Plenum.

DeFour, D. C., & Hirsch, B. J. (1990). The adaptation of black graduate students: A social network approach. *American Journal of Community Psychology, 18,* 487–503.

DeJarnett, S., & Raven, B. (1981). The balance, bases, and modes of interpersonal power in black couples. *The Journal of Black Psychology, 7(2),* 367–374.

de la Garza, R. O., Falcon, A., Garcia, F. C., & Garcia, J. A. (1992). Ethnicity and attitudes toward immigration policy. The case of Mexicans, Puerto Ricans and Cubans in the United States. Paper presented at the Annual Meeting of the American Political Science Association, Chicago.

Dembroski, T. M., & Costa, P. T., Jr. (1987). Coronary prone behavior: Components of the Type A pattern and hostility. *Journal of Personality, 55,* 211–235.

Dengerink, H. A., Schnedler, R. W., & Covey, M. K. (1978). Role of avoidance in aggressive responses to attack and no attack. *Journal of Personality and Social Psychology, 36,* 1044–1053.

Department of Health and Human Services. (1981). *Alcohol and health.* Rockville, MD: Secretary of Health and Human Services, National Institute of Alcohol Abuse and Alcoholism.

DePaulo, B. M. (1990). *Nonverbal behavior and self-presentation.* Manuscript submitted for publication.

DePaulo, B. M. (1992). Nonverbal behavior and self-presentation. *Psychological Bulletin, 111,* 203–243.

DePaulo, B. M., & Kirkendol, S. E. (1989). Motivational impairment effect in the communication of deception. In J. C. Yuille (Ed.), *Credibility assessment* (pp. 51–70). Brussels: Kluwer.

DePaulo, B. M., Kirkendol, S. E., Tang, J., & O'Brien, T. (1988). The motivational impairment effect in the communication of deception: Replications and extensions. *Journal of Nonverbal Behavior, 12,* 177–202.

DePaulo, B. M., LeMay, C. S., & Epstein, J. (1991). Effects of importance of success and expectations for success on effectiveness of deceiving. *Personality and Social Psychology Bulletin, 1,* 14–24.

DePaulo, B. M., Rosenthal, R., Eisenstat, R. A., Rogers, P. L., & Finkelstein, S. (1978). Decoding discrepant nonverbal cues. *Journal of Personality and Social Psychology, 36,* 313–323.

DePaulo, B. M., Rosenthal, R., Green, C. R., & Rosenkrantz, J. (1982). Diagnosing deceptive and mixed messages from verbal and nonverbal cues. *Journal of Personality and Social Psychology, 18,* 433–446.

DePaulo, B. M., Stone, J. I., & Lassiter, G. D. (1985a). Deceiving and detecting deceit. In B. R. Schlenker (Ed.), *The self and social life* (pp. 323–370). New York: McGraw-Hill.

DePaulo, B. M., Stone, J. I., & Lassiter, G. D. (1985b). Telling ingratiating lies: Effects of target sex and target attractiveness on verbal and nonverbal deceptive success. *Journal of Personality and Social Psychology, 48,* 1191–1203.

Derlega, V. J. (1984). Self-disclosure and intimate relationships. In V. J. Derlega (Ed.), *Communication, intimacy, and close relationships* (pp. 1–10). New York: Academic Press.

Derlega, V. J., & Chaikin, A. L. (1975). *Sharing intimacy: What we reveal to others and why.* Englewood Cliffs, NJ: Prentice-Hall.

Derlega, V. J., Durham, B., Gockel, B., & Sholis, D. (1981). Sex differences in self-disclosure: Effects of topic content, friendship, and partner's sex. *Sex Roles, 7(4),* 433–447.

Derlega, V. J., & Grzelak, A. L. (1979). Appropriate self-disclosure. In G. J. Chelune (Ed.), *Self-disclosure: Origins, patterns, and implications of openness in interpersonal relationships.* San Francisco: Jossey-Bass.

DeSipio, L., & de la Garza, R. O. (1992). Will Latino numbers equal political clout? Core voters, swing voters, and the potential vote. Paper presented at the Annual Meeting of the American Political Science Association, Chicago.

Deutsch, R. M., & Lamberti, D. M. (1986). Does social approval increase helping? *Personality and Social Psychology Bulletin, 12(2),* 149–157.

Deutsch, M. (1973). *The Resolution of Conflict: Constructive and Destructive Processes.* New Haven, CT: Yale University Press.

Deutsch, M. (1985). *Distributive justice: A social psychological perspective.* New Haven, CT: Yale University Press.

Deutsch, M., & Collins, M. E. (1951). *Interracial housing: A psychological evaluation of a social experiment.* Minneapolis: University of Minnesota Press.

Deutsch, M., & Krauss, R. M. (1960). The effect of threat on interpersonal bargaining. *Journal of Abnormal and Social Psychology, 61,* 181–189.

Devine, P. G. (1989). Stereotypes and prejudice: Their automatic and controlled components. *Journal of Personality and Social Psychology, 56,* 5–18.

Devine, P. G., & Baker, S. M. (1991). Measurement of racial stereotype subtyping. *Personality and Social Psychology Bulletin, 17,* 44–50.

Devine, P. G., Hirt, E. R., & Gehrke, E. M. (1990). Diagnostic and confirmation strategies in trait hypothesis testing. *Journal of Personality and Social Psychology, 58*, 952–963.

Devine, P. G., Monteith, M. J., Zuwerink, J. R., & Elliot, A. J. (1991). Prejudice with and without compunction. *Journal of Personality and Social Psychology, 60*, 817–830.

Devine, P. G., Sedikides, C., & Fuhrman, R. W. (1989). Goals in social information processing: The case of anticipated information. *Journal of Personality and Social Psychology, 56*, 680–690.

Diehl, M., & Stroebe, W. (1991). Productivity loss in idea-generating groups: Tracking down the blocking effect. *Journal of Personality and Social Psychology, 61*, 392–403.

Diener, F. (1980). Deindividuation: The absence of self-awareness and self-regulation in group members. In P. B. Paulus (Ed.), *Psychology of group influence*. Hillsdale, NJ: Erlbaum.

Diener, F., Fraser, S. C., Beaman, A. L., & Kelem, Z. R. T. (1976). Effects of deindividuation variables on stealing among Halloween trick-or-treaters. *Journal of Personality and Social Psychology, 33*, 178–183.

Dillard, J. P., Hunter, J. E., & Burgoon, M. (1984). Sequential-request persuasvie strategies: Meta-analysis of foot-in-the-door and door-in-the-face. *Human Communication Research, 10*, 461–488.

DiMatteo, M. R., & DiNicola, D. D. (1982). *Achieving patient compliance: The psychology of the medical practitioner's role* (pp. 55–84). New York: Pergamon.

DiMatteo, M. R., Friedman, H. S., & Taranta, A. (1979). Sensitivity to bodily nonverbal communications as a factor in practitioner-patient rapport. *Journal of Nonverbal Behavior, 4*, 18–26.

DiMatteo, M. R., Hays, R. D., & Prince, L. M. (1986). Relationship of physicians' nonverbal communication skill to patient satisfaction, appointment noncompliance, and physician workload. *Health Psychology, 5*, 581–594.

Dimitrovsky, L., Singer, J., & Yinon, Y. (1989). Masculine and feminine traits: Their relation to suitedness for and success in training for traditionally masculine and feminine army functions. *Journal of Personality and Social Psychology, 57*, 839–847.

Dindia, K., & Allen, M. (1992). Sex differences in self-disclosure: A meta-analysis. *Psychological Bulletin, 112*, 106–124.

DiNicola, D. D., & DiMatteo, M. R. (1984). Practitioners, patients, and compliance with medical regimens: A social psychological perspective. In A. Baum, S. E. Taylor, & J. E. Singer (Eds.), *Handbook of psychology and health* (Vol. 4, pp. 55–84). Hillsdale, NJ: Erlbaum.

Dion, K. L., & Dion, K. K. (1973). Correlates of romantic love. *Journal of Consulting and Clinical Psychology, 41*, 51–56.

Dodge, K. (1986). A social information processing model of social competence in children. In M. Perlmutter (Ed.), *The Minnesota symposium on child psychology (Vol. 18): Cognitive perspectives on children's social and behavioral development* (pp. 77–126). Hillsdale, NJ: Erlbaum.

Dodge, K., & Coie, J. (1987). Social information processing factors in reactive and proactive aggression in children's peer groups. *Journal of Personality and Social Psychology, 53*, 1146–1158.

Dodge, K. A., & Tomlin, A. M. (1987). Utilization of self-schemas as a mechanism of interpretational bias in aggressive children. *Social Cognition, 5*, 280–300.

Doherty, D., & Schlenker, B. R. (1991). Self-consciousness and strategic self-presentation. *Journal of Personality, 59*, 1-18.

Dolgin, K. G., Meyer, L., & Schwartz, J. (1991). Effects of gender, target's gender, topic, and self-esteem on disclosure to best and midling friends. *Sex Roles, 25*, 311–329.

Dollard, J., Doob, L., Miller, N. E., Mowrer, O. H., & Sears, R. (1939). *Frustration and aggression*. New Haven, CT: Yale University Press.

Dona, G. (1991). Acculturation and ethnic identity of Central American refugees in Canada. *Hispanic Journal of Behavioral Sciences, 13*, 230–231.

Donat, P. L. N., & D'Emilio, J. (1992). A feminist redefinition of rape and sexual assault: Historical foundations and change. *Journal of Social Issues, 48*, 9–22.

Donnerstein, E. (1983). Erotica and human aggression. In R. Geen & E. Donnerstein (Eds.), *Aggression: Theoretical and empirical reviews* (pp. 127–154). New York: Academic Press.

Donnerstein, E., & Barrett, G. (1978). Effects of erotic stimuli on male aggression toward females. *Journal of Personality and Social Psychology, 36*, 180–188.

Donnerstein, E., & Berkowitz, L. (1981). Victim reactions in aggressive erotic films as a factor in violence against women. *Journal of Personality and Social Psychology, 41*, 710–724.

Donnerstein, E., & Wilson, D. W. (1976). Effects of noise and perceived control on ongoing and subsequent aggressive behavior. *Journal of Personality and Social Psychology, 34*, 774–781.

Dornbush, S. M., Hastorf, A. H., Richardson, S. A., Muzzy, R. E., & Vreeland, R. S. (1965). The perceiver and the perceived: Their relative influence on the categories of interpersonal cognition. *Journal of Personality and Social Psychology, 1*, 434–440.

Douthitt, R. A. (1989). The division of labor within the home: Have gender roles changed? *Sex Roles, 20*, 693–704.

Dovidio, J. F. (1984). Helping behavior and altruism: An empirical and conceptual overview. In L. Berkowitz (Ed.), *Advances in experimental social psychology* (Vol. 17, pp. 361–427). New York: Academic Press.

Dovidio, J. F., & Gaertner, S. L. (Eds.). (1986). *Prejudice, Discrimination, and Racism*. New York: Academic Press.

Dovidio, J. F., Piliavin, J. A., Gaertner, S. L., Schroeder, D. A., & Clark, R. D., III. (1991). The arousal: Cost-reward model and the process of intervention: A review of the evidence. In M. S. Clark (Ed.), *Prosocial behavior* (pp. 86–117). Newbury Park, CA: Sage Publications.

Downey, G., Silver, R. C., & Wortman, C. B. (1990). Reconsidering the attribution-adjustment relation following a major negative event: Coping with the loss of a child. *Journal of Personality and Social Psychology, 59*, 925–940.

Doyle, J. (1989). *The male experience*, 2nd ed. Dubuque, IA: W. C. Brown.

Drigotas, S. M., & Rusbult, C. E. (1992). Should I stay or should I go? A dependence model of breakups. *Journal of Personality and Social Psychology, 62*, 62–87.

Dube, E. F. (1982). Literacy, cultural familiarity, and "intelligence" as determinants of story recall. In U. Neisser (Ed.), *Memory observed: Remembering in natural contexts* (pp. 274–292). San Francisco: W. H. Freeman.

Dunn, D. S., & Wilson, T. D. (1990). When the stakes are high: A limit to the illusion-of-control effect. *Social Cognition, 8*, 305–323.

Dunning, D., Griffin, D. W., Milojkovic, J. D., & Ross, L.

(1990). The overconfidence effect in social prediction. *Journal of Personality and Social Psychology, 58,* 568–581.

Durkin, K. (1987). Sex roles and the mass media. In D. J. Hargreaves, & A. M. Colley (Eds.), *The psychology of sex roles* (pp. 201–214). New York: Hemisphere.

Duval, S., & Wicklund, R. A. (1972). *A theory of objective self-awareness.* New York: Academic Press.

Dweck, D. S. (1975). The role of expectations and attributions in the alleviation of learned helplessness. *Journal of Personality and Social Psychology, 31,* 674–685.

Dweck, C. S., & Licht, B. G. (1980). Learned helplessness and intellectual achievement. In M. E. P. Seligman & J. Garber (Eds.), *Human helplessness: Theory and applications* (pp. 197–222). New York: Academic Press.

Eagly, A. H. (1978). Sex differences in influenceability. *Psychological Bulletin, 85,* 86–116.

Eagly, A. H. (1983). Gender and social influence: A social psychological analysis. *American Psychologist, 38*(9), 971–981.

Eagly, A. H. (1987). *Sex differences in social behavior: A social-role interpretation.* Hillsdale, NJ: Erlbaum.

Eagly, A. H., Ashmore, R. D., Makhijani, M. G., & Longo, L. C. (1991). What is beautiful is good, but . . . : A meta-analytic review of research on the physical attractiveness stereotype. *Psychological Bulletin, 110,* 109–128.

Eagly, A. H., & Crowley, M. (1986). Gender and helping behavior: A meta-analytic review of the social psychological literature. *Psychological Bulletin, 100*(3), 283–308.

Eagly, A. H., & Johnson, B. T. (1990). Gender and leadership style: A meta-analysis. *Psychological Bulletin, 108,* 233–256.

Eagly, A. H., & Karau, S. J. (1991). Gender and the emergence of leaders: A meta-analysis. *Journal of Personality and Social Psychology, 60,* 685–710.

Eagly, A. H., Makhijani, M. G., & Klonsky, B. G. (1992). Gender and the evaluation of leaders: A meta-analysis. *Psychological Bulletin, 111,* 3–22.

Eagly, A. H., & Steffen, V. J. (1986). Gender and aggressive behavior: A meta-analytic review of the social psychological literature. *Psychological Bulletin, 100*(3), 309–330.

Eagly, A. H., & Wood, W. (1982). Inferred sex differences in status as a determinant of gender stereotypes about social influence. *Journal of Personality and Social Psychology, 43,* 915–928.

Eagly, A. H., & Wood, W. (1985). Gender and influenceability: Stereotype versus behavior. In V. E. O'Leary, R. K. Unger, & B. S. Wallston (Eds.), *Women, gender, and social psychology.* Hillsdale, NJ: Erlbaum.

Eagly, A. H., & Wood, W. (1991). Explaining sex differences in social behavior: A meta-analytic perspective. *Personality and Social Psychology Bulletin, 17,* 306–315.

Edwards, W. (1954). The theory of decision-making. *Psychological Bulletin, 51,* 380–417.

Einhorn, H. J., & Hogarth, R. M. (1981). Behavioral decision theory: Processes of judgment and choice. *Annual Review of Psychology, 32,* 53–88.

Eisen, S. V. (1979). Actor–observer differences in information inference and causal attribution. *Journal of Personality and Social Psychology, 37,* 261–272.

Eisenberg, N. (1991). Meta–analytic contributions to the literature on prosocial behavior. *Personality and Social Psychology Bulletin, 17,* 273–282.

Eisenberg, N., & Fabes, R. A. (1990). Empathy: Conceptualization, measurement, and relation to prosocial behavior. *Motivation and Emotion, 14,* 131–149.

Eisenberg, N., & Miller, P. A. (1987). The relation of empathy to prosocial and related behaviors. *Psychological Bulletin, 10*(1), 91–119.

Ekman, P. (1972). Universals and cultural differences in facial expressions of emotion. In J. K. Cole (Ed.), *Nebraska symposium on motivation, 1971* (pp. 207–283). Lincoln: University of Nebraska Press.

Ekman, P. (1982). *Emotion in the human face* (2nd ed.) Cambridge: Cambridge University Press.

Ekman, P., & Friesen, W. V. (1971). Constants across cultures in the face and emotion. *Journal of Personality and Social Psychology, 17,* 124–129.

Ekman, P., & Friesen, W. V. (1974). Detecting deception from the body or face. *Journal of Personality and Social Psychology, 29,* 288–298.

Ekman, P., Friesen, W. V., & O'Sullivan, M. (1988). Smiles when lying. *Journal of Personality and Social Psychology, 54,* 414–420.

Ekman, P., Friesen, W. V., & Scherer, K. (1976). Body movements and voice pitch in deceptive interaction. *semiotica, 16,* 23–27.

Ekman, P., Sorenson, E. R., & Friesen, W. V. (1969). Pancultural elements in facial displays of emotion. *Science, 164,* 86–88.

Elliott, T. R., Witty, T. E., Herrick, S., & Hoffman, J. T. (1991). Negotiating reality after physical loss: Hope, depression, and disability. *Journal of Personality and Social Psychology, 61,* 608–613.

Ellis, E. M., Atkeson, B. M., & Calhoun, K. S. (1981). An assessment of long–term reactions to rape. *Journal of Abnormal Psychology, 90,* 263–266.

Ellis, R. J. (1988). Self–monitoring and leadership emergence in groups. *Personality and Social Psychology Bulletin, 14,* 681–693.

Ellis, S. J., & Noyes, K. H. (1990). *By the people: A history of Americans as volunteers, revised ed.* San Francisco: Jossey-Bass.

Ellsworth, P. C., & Carlsmith, J. M. (1973). Eye contact and gaze aversion in an aggressive encounter. *Journal of Personality and Social Psychology, 28,* 280–292.

Ellsworth, P. C., Friedman, H. S., Perlick, D., & Hoyt, M. E. (1978). Some effects of gaze on subjects motivated to seek or to avoid social comparison. *Journal of Personality and Social Psychology, 14,* 69–87.

Ember, C. R. (1973). Feminine task assignment and the social behavior of boys. *Ethos, 1,* 424–439.

Emswiller, T., Deaux, K., & Willits, J. E. (1971). Similarity, sex, and requests for small favors. *Journal of Applied Social Psychology, 1*(3), 284–291.

Engel, G. L. (1971). Sudden and rapid death during psychological stress. *Annals of Internal Medicine, 74,* 771–782.

English, E. H., Baker, T. B. (1983). Relaxation training and cardiovascular response to experimental stressors. *Health Psychology, 2,* 239–259.

Erber, R. (1991). Affective and semantic priming: Effects of mood on category accessibility and inference. *Journal of Experimental Social Psychology, 27,* 480–498.

Erber, R., & Fiske, S. T. (1984). Outcome dependency and attention to inconsistent information. *Journal of Personality and Social Psychology, 47,* 709–726.

Erdley, C. A., & D'Agostino, P. R. (1988). Cognitive and

affective components of automatic priming effects. *Journal of Personality and Social Psychology, 54*, 741–747.

Erikson, R. S. (1990). Economic conditions and the congressional vote: A review of the macrolevel evidence. *American Journal of Political Science, 34*, 373–399.

Eron, L. D. (1987). The development of aggressive behavior from the perspective of a developing behaviorism. *American Psychologist, 42*, 435–442.

Eron, L. D., Huesmann, L. R., Lefkowitz, M. M., & Walder, L. O. (1972). Does television violence cause aggression? *American Psychologist, 27*, 253–263.

Esser, J. K., & Komorita, S. S. (1975). Reciprocity and concession making in bargaining. *Journal of Personality and Social Psychology, 31*, 864–872.

Esses, V. M. (1989). Mood as a moderator of acceptance of interpersonal feedback. *Journal of Personality and Social Psychology, 57*, 769–781.

Etaugh, C., & Liss, M. B. (1992). Home, school, and playroom: Training grounds for adult gender roles. *Sex Roles, 26*, 129–147.

Etzioni, A. (1967). The Kennedy experiment. *Western Political Quarterly, 20*, 361–380.

Evans, G. W., & Cohen, S. (1987). Environmental stress. In D. Stokols & I. Altman (Eds.), *Handbook of environmental psychology*. New York: Wiley.

Evans, G. W., Kliewer, W., & Martin, J. (1991). The role of the physical environment in the health and well–being of children. In H. E. Schroeder (Ed.), *New directions in health psychology assessment* (pp. 127–157). New York: Hemisphere.

Falcon, A., de la Garza, R. O., Garcia, F. C., & Garcia, J. A. (1992). Ethnicity and American political values: A comparison of Puerto Ricans and Anglos. Paper presented at the Annual Meeting of the American Political Science Association, Chicago.

Farrenkopf, T. (1974). *Man–environment interaction: An academic department moves into a new building*. Unpublished doctoral dissertation, University of Massachusetts.

Fauconnet, P. (1928). *La responsabilité*. Paris: Alcan.

Fazio, R. H. (1981). On the self–perception explanation of the overjustification effect: The role of the salience of initial attitude. *Journal of Experimental Social Psychology, 17*, 417–426.

Fazio, R. H. (1987). Self–perception theory: A current perspective. In M. P. Zanna, J. M. Olson, & C. P. Herman (Eds.), *Social influence: The Ontario Symposium* (Vol. 5). Hillsdale, NJ: Erlbaum.

Fazio, R. H., Effrein, E. A., & Falender, V. J. (1981). Self–perceptions following social interaction. *Journal of Personality and Social Psychology, 41*, 232–242.

Fazio, R. H., Sanbonmatsu, D. M., Powell, M. C., & Kardes, F. R. (1986). On the automatic activation of attitudes. *Journal of Personality and Social Psychology, 50*, 229–238.

Feather, N. T., & Simon, J. G. (1975). Reactions to male and female success and failure in sex–linked occupations: Impressions of personality, causal attributions, and perceived likelihood of different consequences. *Journal of Personality and Social Psychology, 31*(1), 20–31.

Fein, S., Hilton, J. L., & Miller, D. T. (1990). Suspicion of ulterior motivation and the correspondence bias. *Journal of Personality and Social Psychology, 58*, 753–764.

Feingold, A. (1988). Matching for attractiveness in romantic partners and same–sex friends: A meta–analysis and theoretical critique. *Psychological Bulletin, 104*, 226–235.

Feingold, A. (1990). Gender differences in effects of physical attractiveness on romantic attraction: A comparison across five research paradigms. *Journal of Personality and Social Psychology, 59*, 981–993.

Feingold, A. (1992). Good–looking people are not what we think. *Psychological Bulletin, 111*, 304–341.

Feldman, R. E. (1968). Response to compatriot and foreigner who seek assistance. *Journal of Personality and Social Psychology, 10*(3), 202–214.

Feldman, R. S., & Rimé, B. (Eds.). (1991). *Fundamentals of nonverbal behavior*. New York: Cambridge University Press.

Feldman, S. (1982). Economic self–interest and political behavior. *American Journal of Political Science, 26*, 446–466.

Feldman–Summers, S., Gordon, P. E., & Meagher, J. R. (1989). The impact of rape on sexual satisfaction. *Journal of Abnormal Psychology, 88*, 101–105.

Feletti, G., Firman, D., & Sanson–Fisher, R. (1986). Patient satisfaction with primary–care consultations. *Journal of Behavioral Medicine, 9*, 389–399.

Felson, R. B., & Reed, M. D. (1986). Reference groups and self–appraisals of academic ability and performance. *Social Psychology Quarterly, 49*, 103–109.

Felton, B. J., Revenson, T. A., & Hinrichsen, G. A. (1984). Stress and coping in the explanation of psychological adjustment among chronically ill adults. *Social Science and Medicine, 18*, 889–898.

Fenigstein, A., Scheier, M. F., & Buss, A. H. (1975). Public and private self–consciousness: Assessment and theory. *Journal of Consulting and Clinical Psychology, 43*, 522–527.

Feshbach, S. (1955). The drive–reducing function of fantasy behavior. *Journal of Abnormal and Social Psychology, 50*, 3–12.

Feshbach, S. (1961). The stimulating versus cathartic effects of a vicarious aggressive activity. *Journal of Abnormal and Social Psychology, 63*, 381–385.

Feshbach, S. (1970). Aggression. In P. Mussen (Ed.), *Carmichael's Manual of Child Psychology* (Vol. 2). New York: Wiley.

Feshbach, S., & Singer, R. D. (1971). *Television and aggression*. San Francisco: Jossey–Bass.

Festinger, L. (1954). A theory of social comparison processes. *Human Relations, 7*, 117–140.

Festinger, L. (1957). *A theory of cognitive dissonance*. Evanston, IL: Row, Peterson.

Festinger, L., & Carlsmith, J. M. (1959). Cognitive consequences of forced compliance. *Journal of Abnormal and Social Psychology, 58*, 203–210.

Festinger, L., Pepitone, A., & Newcomb, T. (1952). Some consequences of deindividuation in a group. *Journal of Abnormal and Social Psychology, 47*, 383–389.

Festinger, L., Schachter, S., & Back, K. (1950). *Social pressures in informal groups: A study of human factors in housing*. Stanford University Press.

Fiedler, F. E. (1978). Recent developments in research on the contingency model. In L. Berkowitz (Ed.), *Group processes* (pp. 209–225). New York: Academic Press.

Fiedler, F. E. (1981). Leadership effectiveness. *American Behavioral Scientist, 24*(5), 619–632.

Fiedler, K. (1991). The tricky nature of skewed frequency tables: An information loss account of distinctiveness–based illusory correlations. *Journal of Personality and Social Psychology, 60*, 24–36.

Fillingim, R. B., & Fine, M. A. (1986). The effects of internal versus external information processing on symptom perception in an exercise setting. *Health Psychology, 5,* 115–123.

Fincham, F. D., & Bradbury, T. N. (1991). Marital conflict: Towards a more complete integration of research and treatment. In J. P. Vincent (Ed.), *Advances in family intervention, assessment and theory,* Vol. 5, pp. 1–24. London: Jessica Kingsley Publishers.

Fincham, F. D., & Bradbury, T. N. (in press). Marital satisfaction, depression, and attributions: A longitudinal analysis. *Journal of Personality and Social Psychology.*

Finkelman, J. M., & Glass, D. C. (1970). Reappraisal of the relationship between noise and human performance by means of a subsidiary task measure. *Journal of Applied Psychology, 54,* 211–213.

Finlay, D. J., Holsti, O. R., & Fagen, R. R. (1967). *Enemies in politics.* Chicago: Rand McNally.

Fiorina, M. P. (1981). *Retrospective voting in American national elections.* New Haven, CT: Yale University Press.

Fischer, W. F. (1963). Sharing in pre-school children as a function of amount and type of reinforcement. *Genetic Psychology Monographs, 68,* 215–245.

Fishbein, M. (1980). A theory of reasoned action: Some applications and implications. In M. M. Page (Ed.), *1979 Nebraska Symposium on motivation.* Lincoln: University of Nebraska Press.

Fisher, A. (1991). Sociobiology: A new synthesis comes of age. *Mosaic, 22,* 2–17.

Fisher, J. D., Nadler, A., & Whitcher–Alagna, S. (1982). Recipient reactions to aid. *Psychological Bulletin, 91,* 33–54.

Fiske, A. P., Haslam, N., & Fiske, S. T. (1991). Confusing one person with another: What errors reveal about the elementary forms of social relations. *Journal of Personality and Social Psychology, 60,* 656–674.

Fiske, S. T. (1980). Attention and weight in person perception: The impact of negative and extreme behavior. *Journal of Personality and Social Psychology, 38,* 889–906.

Fiske, S. T. (1982). Schema–triggered affect: Applications to social perception. In M. S. Clark & S. T. Fiske (Eds.), *Affect and cognition: The 17th annual Carnegie Symposium on Cognition* (pp. 55–78). Hillsdale, NJ: Erlbaum.

Fiske, S. T. (1993). Social cognition and perception. In M. R. Rosenzweig & L. W. Porter (Eds.), *Annual review of psychology* (Vol. 44, pp. 2–23).

Fiske, S. T., Bersoff, D. N., Borgida, E., Deaux, K., & Heilman, M. E. (1991). Social science research on trial: Use of sex stereotyping research in Price Waterhouse v. Hopkins. *American Psychologist, 46,* 1049–1060.

Fiske, S. T., Neuberg, S. L. (1990). A continuum of impression formation, from category-based to individuating processes: Influences of information and motivation of attention and interpretation. In M. P. Zanna (Eds.), *Advances in experimental social psychology* (Vol. 23, pp. 1–73). New York: Academic Press.

Fiske, S. T., Neuberg, S. L., Beattie, A. E., & Milberg, S. J. (1987). Category-based and attribute–based reactions to others: Some informational conditions of stereotyping and individuating processes. *Journal of Experimental Social Psychology, 23,* 399–427.

Fiske, S. T., & Taylor, S. (1984). *Social cognition.* Reading, MA: Addison-Wesley.

Fiske, S. T., & Taylor, S. E. (1991). *Social cognition,* 2nd ed. New York: McGraw–Hill.

Fiske, S. T., & Von Hendy, H. M. (1992). Personality feedback and situational norms can control stereotyping processes. *Journal of Personality and Social Psychology, 62,* 577–596.

Fleming, J., & Darley, J. M. (1989). Perceiving choice and constraint: The effects of contextual and behavioral cues on attitude attribution. *Journal of Personality and Social Psychology, 56,* 27–40.

Fletcher, G. J. O., & Ward, C. (1988). Attribution theory and processes: Cross-cultural perspective. In M. H. Bond (Ed.), *The cross-cultural challenge to social psychology* (pp. 230–244). Newbury Park, CA: Sage Publications.

Flett, G. L., Pliner, P., & Blankstein, K. R. (1989). Depression and components of attributional complexity. *Journal of Personality and Social Psychology, 56,* 757–764.

Flink, C., Boggiano, A. K., & Barrett, M. (1990). Controlling teaching strategies: Undermining children's self-determination and performance. *Journal of Personality and Social Psychology, 59,* 916–924.

Flink, C., & Park, B. (1991). Increasing consensus in trait judgments through outcome dependency. *Journal of Experimental Social Psychology, 27,* 453–467.

Flowers, M. L. (1977). A laboratory test of some implications of Janis's groupthink hypothesis. *Journal of Personality and Social Psychology, 35,* 888–896.

Foa, U. G. (1971). Interpersonal and economic resources. *Science, 71,* 345–351.

Foa, U. G., & Foa, E. B. (1974). *Societal structures of the mind.* Springfield, IL: Charles C. Thomas.

Folkes, V. S. (1982). Forming relationships and the matching hypothesis. *Personality and Social Psychology Bulletin, 8*(4), 631–636.

Folkes, V. S., & Sears, D. O. (1977). Does everybody like a liker? *Journal of Experimental Social Psychology, 13,* 505–519.

Folkman, S., & Lazarus, R. S. (1980). An analysis of coping in a middle–aged community sample. *Journal of Health and Social Behavior, 21,* 219–239.

Fong, G. T., Krantz, D. H., & Nisbett, R. E. (1986). The effects of statistical training on thinking about everyday problems. *Cognitive Psychology, 18,* 253–292.

Forsterling, F. (1989). Models of covariation and attribution: How do they relate to the analogy of analysis of variance? *Journal of Personality and Social Psychology, 57,* 615–625.

Forsyth, D. R. (1990). *Group dynamics,* 2nd ed. Pacific Grove, CA: Brooks/Cole.

Fossett, M. A., & Kiecolt, K. J. (1991). A methodological review of the sex ratio: Alternatives for comparative research. *Journal of Marriage and the Family, 53*(4), 941–957.

Frank, F. D., & Drucker, J. (1977). The influence of evaluatee's sex on evaluation of a response on a managerial selection instrument. *Sex Roles, 3,* 59–64.

Frank, M. G., & Gilovich, T. (1988). The dark side of self– and social perception: Black uniforms and aggression in professional sports. *Journal of Personality and Social Psychology, 54,* 74–85.

Frank, M. G., & Gilovich, T. (1989). Effect of memory perspective on retrospective causal attributions. *Journal of Personality and Social Psychology, 57,* 399–403.

Franke, R., & Leary, M. R. (1991). Disclosure of sexual orientation by lesbians and gay men: A comparison of private and public processes. *Journal of Social and Clinical Psychology, 10,* 262–269.

Franklin, C. H. (1984). Issue preferences, socialization, and the evolution of party identification. *American Journal of Political Science, 28,* 459–478.

Franklin, C. H., & Kosaki, L. C. (1989). Republican schoolmaster: The U. S. Supreme Court, public opinion, and abortion. *American Political Science Review, 83,* 751–772.

Frankovic, K. A. (1982). Sex and politics—new alignments, old issues. *PS, 15,* 439–448.

Fraser, C., Gouge, C., & Billig, M. (1971). Risky shifts, cautious shifts, and group polarization. *European Journal of Social Psychology, 1,* 7–30.

Frazier, P. A. (1990). Victim attributions and post-rape trauma. *Journal of Personality and Social Psychology, 59,* 298–304.

Freedman, J. L. (1984). Effect of television violence on aggressiveness. *Psychological Bulletin, 96,* 227–246.

Freedman, J. L. (1986). Television violence and aggression: A rejoinder. *Psychological Bulletin, 100,* 372–378.

Freedman, J. L., Cunningham, J. A., & Krismer, K. (1992). Inferred values and the reverse-incentive effect in induced compliance. *Journal of Personality and Social Psychology, 62,* 357–368.

Freedman, J. L., & Fraser, S. C. (1966). Compliance without pressure: The foot-in-the-door technique. *Journal of Personality and Social Psychology, 4,* 195–202.

French, D. C., & Stright, A. L. (1991). Emergent leadership in children's small groups. *Small Group Research, 22,* 187–199.

French, J., & Raven, B. (1959). The bases of social power. In D. Cartwright, (Ed.), *Studies in social power* (pp. 150–167). Ann Arbor, MI: Institute for Social Research.

Fried, R., & Berkowitz, L. (1979). Music hath charms . . . and can influence helplessness. *Journal of Applied Social Psychology, 9,* 199–208.

Friedman, H., & Zebrowitz, L. A. (1992). The contribution of typical sex differences in facial maturity to sex role stereotypes. *Personality and Social Psychology Bulletin, 18,* 430–438.

Friedman, H. S., Riggio, R. E., & Casella, D. F. (1988). Nonverbal skill, personal charisma, and initial attraction. *Personality and Social Psychology Bulletin, 14,* 203–211.

Friedman, H. S., & Booth-Kewley, S. (1987). The "disease-prone" personality: A meta–analytic view of the construct. *American Psychologist, 42,* 539–555.

Friedman, H. S., & Miller-Herringer, T. (1990). *The nonverbal display of emotion: Effects of expressiveness, self-monitoring, and personality.* Manuscript submitted for publication.

Friedman, M., & Rosenman, R. H. (1974). *Type A behavior and your heart.* New York: Knopf.

Friedrich, L. K., & Stein, A. H. (1973). Aggressive and prosocial television programs and the natural behavior of preschool children. *Monographs of the Society for Research in Child Development, 38*(4, Serial No. 151).

Friedrich–Cofer, L., & Huston, A. C. (1986). Television violence and aggression: The debate continues. *Psychological Bulletin, 100,* 364–371.

Frieze, I. H. (1983). Investigating the causes and consequences of marital rape. *Signs: Journal of Women in Culture and Society, 8,* 532–553.

Froming, W. J., & Carver, C. S. (1981). Divergent influences of private and public self-consciousness in a compliance paradigm. *Journal of Research in Psychology, 15,* 159–171.

Funder, D. C. (1987). Errors and mistakes: Evaluating the accuracy of social judgment. *Psychological Bulletin, 101,* 75–90.

Funkhouser, G. R. (1973). The issues of the sixties: An exploratory study in the dynamics of public opinion. *Public Opinion Quarterly, 37,* 62–75.

Gabrenya, W. K., Wang, Y., & Latané, B. (1985). Social loafing on an optimizing task: Cross-cultural differences among Chinese and Americans. *Journal of Cross–Cultural Psychology, 16,* 223–242.

Gabrielcik, A., & Fazio, R. H. (1984). Priming and frequency estimation: A strict test of the availability heuristic. *Personality and Social Psychology Bulletin, 10,* 85–89.

Gaertner, S. L., Mann, J., Murrell, A., & Dovidio, J. F. (1989). Reducing intergroup bias: The benefits of recategorization. *Journal of Personality and Social Psychology, 57,* 239–249.

Gal, R., & Lazarus, R. S. (1975). The role of activity in anticipating and confronting stressful situations. *Journal of Human Stress, 1,* 4–20.

Gangestad, S. W., Simpson, J. A., DiGeronimo, K., & Bisk, M. (1992). Differential accuracy in person perception across traits: Examination of a functional hypothesis. *Journal of Personality and Social Psychology, 62,* 688–698.

Gannon, L., Luchetta, T., Rhodes, K., Pardie, L., & Segrist, D. (1992). Sex bias in psychological research. Progress or complacency? *American Psychologist, 47,* 389–396.

Garnets, L., & Pleck, J. (1979). Sex role identity, androgyny, and sex role transcendence: A sex role strain analysis. *Psychology of Women Quarterly, 3,* 270–283.

Gartner, R. (1990). The victims of homicide: A temporal and cross–national comparison. *American Sociological Review, 55.*

Garza, R. T., & Santos, S. J. (1991). Ingroup/outgroup balance and interdependent interethnic behavior. *Journal of Experimental Social Psychology, 27,* 124–137.

Gavanski, I., & Roskos–Ewoldsen, D. R. (1991). Representativeness and cojoint probability. *Journal of Personality and Social Psychology, 61,* 181–194.

Geen, R. G. (1991). Social motivation. *Annual Review of Psychology, 42,* 377–399.

Geen, R. G., & O'Neal, E. C. (1969). Activation of cue-eliciting aggression by general arousal. *Journal of Personality and Social Psychology, 11,* 289–292.

Geen, R. G., & Pigg, R. (1970). Acquisition of an aggressive response and its generalization to verbal behavior. *Journal of Personality and Social Psychology, 15,* 165–170.

Geen, R. G., & Quanty, M. B. (1977). The catharsis of aggression: An evaluation of a hypothesis. In L. Berkowitz (Ed.), *Advances in experimental social psychology* (Vol. 10, pp. 2–39). New York: Academic Press.

Geertz, C. (1974). From the native's point of view: On the nature of anthropological understanding. In K. Basso & H. Selby (Eds.), *Meaning in anthropology* (pp. 221–237). Albuquerque: University of New Mexico Press.

Geiselman, R. E., Haight, N. A., & Kimata, L. G. (1984). Context effects on the perceived physical attractiveness of faces. *Journal of Personality and Social Psychology, 20,* 409–424.

George, A. L., (1969). The "operational code": A neglected approach to the study of political leaders and decision making. *International Studies Quarterly, 13,* 190–222.

George, D. M. (1992). *An attribution–empathy–efficacy model of helping behavior.* Unpublished doctoral dissertation, University of California, Los Angeles.

George, J. M. (1991). State or trait: Effects of positive mood on prosocial behaviors at work. *Journal of Applied Psychology, 76,* 299–307.

Gerard, H. B. (1988). School desegregation: The social science role. In P. A. Katz & D. A. Taylor (Eds.), *Eliminating racism: Profiles in controversy* (pp. 225–236). New York: Plenum.

Gergen, K. J., Ellsworth, P., Maslach, C., & Seipel, M. (1975). Obligation, donor resources, and reactions to aid in three cultures. *Journal of Personality and Social Psychology, 31,* 390–400.

Gettys, L. D., & Cann, A. (1981). Children's perceptions of occupational sex stereotypes. *Sex Roles, 7,* 301–308.

Gibson, J. L., & Duch, R. M. (1992). Anti–Semitic attitudes of the mass public: Estimates and explanations based on a survey of the Moscow Oblast. *Public Opinion Quarterly, 56,* 1–28.

Gielen, A. C., Eriksen, M. P., Daltroy, L. H., & Rost, K. (1984). Factors associated with the use of child restraint devices. *Health Education Quarterly, 11,* 195–206.

Gilbert, D. T., & Jones, E. E. (1986). Perceiver-induced constraint: Interpretations of self-generated reality. *Journal of Personality and Social Psychology, 50,* 269–280.

Gilbert, D. T., & Krull, D. S. (1988). Seeing less and knowing more: The benefits of perceptual ignorance. *Journal of Personality and Social Psychology, 54,* 193–202.

Gilbert, D. T., Krull, D. S., & Pelham, B. W. (1988). Of thoughts unspoken: Social inference and the self-regulation of behavior. *Journal of Personality and Social Psychology, 55,* 685–694.

Gilbert, D. T., McNulty, S. E., Giuliano, T. A., & Benson, J. E. (1992). Blurry words and fuzzy deeds: The attribution of obscure behavior. *Journal of Personality and Social Psychology, 62,* 18–25.

Gilbert, D. T., Pelham, B. W., & Krull, D. S. (1988). On cognitive busyness: When person perceivers meet persons perceived. *Journal of Personality and Social Psychology, 54,* 733–739.

Gilovich, T. (1987). Secondhand information and social judgment. *Journal of Experimental Social Psychology, 23,* 59–74.

Gilovich, T. (1990). Differential construal and the false consensus effect. *Journal of Experimental Social Psychology, 59,* 623–634.

Glamser, F. D. (1990). Contest location, player misconduct, and race: A case of English soccer. *Journal of Sport Behavior, 13*(1), 41–49.

Glass, D. C. (1977). *Behavior patterns, stress, and coronary disease.* Hillsdale, NJ: Erlbaum.

Glass, D. C., & Singer, J. E. (1972). *Urban stress.* New York: Academic Press.

Gleicher, F., & Petty, R. E. (1992). Expectations of reassurance influence the nature of fear-stimulated attitude change. *Journal of Experimental Social Psychology, 28,* 86–100.

Glick, P., DeMorest, J. A., & Hotze, C. A. (1988). Self-monitoring and beliefs about partner compatibility in romantic relationships. *Personality and Social Psychology Bulletin, 14,* 485–494.

Glick, P., Zion, C., & Nelson, C. (1988). What mediates sex discrimination in hiring decisions? *Journal of Personality and Social Psychology, 55,* 178–186.

Godwin, D. D. (1991). Spouses' time allocation to household work: A review and critique. *Lifestyles: Family and Economic Issues, 12,* 253–294.

Goethals, G., & Klos, D. S. (Eds.). (1970). *Experiencing youth: First–person accounts.* Boston: Little, Brown.

Goethals, G. R., & Darley, J. M. (1987). Social comparison theory: Self-evaluation and group life. In B. Mullen & G. R. Goethals (Eds.), *Theories of Group Behavior* (pp. 21–48). New York: Springer–Verlag.

Goffman, E. (1952). On cooling the mark out: Some aspects of adaptation to failure. *Psychiatry, 15,* 451–463.

Goffman, E. (1959). *The presentation of self in everyday life.* Garden City, NY: Doubleday.

Gold, E. (1986). Long-term effects of sexual victimization in childhood: An attributional approach. *Journal of Consulting and Clinical Psychology, 54,* 471–475.

Goldberg, P. (1968). Are women prejudiced against women? *TransAction, 5,* 28–30.

Golden, J. S., & Johnston, G. D. (1970). Problems of distortion in doctor-patient communications. *Psychiatry in Medicine, 1,* 127–149.

Goldstein, A. (1990). Desert culture shock: For the U.S. troops, an Arab primer. *Washington Post, August 23,* D1, D2.

Goldstein, J. H., Davis, R. W., & Herman, D. (1975). Escalation of aggression: Experimental studies. *Journal of Personality and Social Psychology, 31,* 162–170.

Goodchilds, J., Zellman, G., Johnson, P., & Giarusso, R. (1988). Adolescents and their perceptions of sexual interactions. In A. W. Burgess (Ed.), *Rape and sexual assault* (Vol. 2, pp. 245–270). New York: Garland.

Goodenow, C., Reisine, S. T., & Grady, K. E. (1990). Quality of social support and associated social and psychological functioning in women with rheumatoid arthritis. *Health Psychology, 9,* 266–284.

Goranson, R. E., & Berkowitz, L. (1966). Reciprocity and responsibility reactions to prior help. *Journal of Personality and Social Psychology, 3,* 227–232.

Gottman, J. M. (1979). *Marital interaction: Experimental investigations.* New York: Academic Press.

Gottman, J. M., & Krokoff, L. J. (1989). Marital interaction and satisfaction: A longitudinal view. *Journal of Consulting and Clinical Psychology, 57,* 47–52.

Gottman, J. M., Markman, H. J., & Notarius, C. I. (1977). The topography of marital conflict: A sequential analysis of verbal and nonverbal behavior. *Journal of Marriage and the Family, 39,* 461–478.

Gouldner, A. W. (1960). The norm of reciprocity: A preliminary statement. *American Sociological Review, 25,* 161–179.

Graham, S. (1992). "Most of the subjects were white and middle class": Trends in published research on African Americans in selected APA journals, 1970–1989. *American Psychologist, 47,* 629–639.

Graham, S., & Barker, G. P. (1990). The down side of help: An attributional-developmental analysis of helping behavior as a low-ability cue. *Journal of Educational Psychology, 82,* 7–14.

Graham, S., Hudley, C., & Williams, E. (1992). An attributional approach to aggression in African-American children. *Developmental Psychology, 28,* 731–740.

Graham, S., & Weiner, B. (1991). Testing judgments about attribution-emotion-action linkages: A lifespan approach. *Social Cognition, 9,* 254–276.

Granberg, D. (1987). Candidate preference, membership group, and estimates of voting behavior. *Social Cognition, 5,* 323–335.

Gray, C., Russell, P., & Blockley, S. (1991). The effects upon helping behaviour of wearing pro-gay identification. *British Journal of Social Psychology, 30,* 171–178.

Graziano, W. G., Moore, J. S., & Collins, J. E., II. (1988). Social cognition as segmentation of the stream of behavior. *Developmental Psychology, 24,* 61–72.

Green, D. P., & Palmquist, B. (1990). Of artifacts and partisan instability. *American Journal of Political Science, 34,* 872–902.

Green, D. P., & Palmquist, B. (1992). How stable is party identification? Paper presented at the Annual Meeting of the American Political Science Association, Chicago.

Green, R., & Fleming, D. T. (1990). Transsexual surgery follow-up: Status in the 1990s. *Annual Review of Sex Research, 1,* 163–174.

Green, S. K., Buchanan, D. R., & Heuer, S. K. (1984). Winners, losers, and choosers: A field investigation of dating initiation. *Personality and Social Psychology Bulletin, 10,* 502–511.

Greenberg, J., & Cohen, R. L. (Eds.). (1982). *Equity and justice in social behavior.* New York: Academic Press.

Greenberg, J., & Pyszczynski, T. (1986). Persistent high self-focus after failure and low self-focus after success: The depressive self-focusing style. *Journal of Personality and Social Psychology, 50,* 1039–1044.

Greenberg, M. S., & Frisch, D. M. (1972). Effects of intentionality on willingness to reciprocate a favor. *Journal of Experimental Social Psychology, 8,* 99–111.

Greenwald, A. G. (1980). The totalitarian ego: Fabrication and revision of personal history. *American Psychologist, 35,* 603–618.

Greenwald, A. G., & Banaji, M. R. (1989). The self as a memory system: Powerful, but ordinary. *Journal of Personality and Social Psychology, 57,* 41–54.

Greenwell, J., & Dengerink, H. A. (1973). The role of perceived versus actual attack in human physical aggression. *Journal of Personality and Social Psychology, 26,* 66–71.

Greer, S. (1974). Psychological aspects: Delay in the treatment of breast cancer. *Proceedings of the Royal Society of Medicine, 64,* 470–473.

Gregory, W. L., Cialdini, R. B., & Carpenter, K. M. (1982). Self–relevant scenarios as mediators of likelihood estimates and compliance: Does imagining make it so? *Journal of Personality and Social Psychology, 43,* 89–99.

Gross, A. E., & Latané, J. G. (1974). Receiving help, reciprocation, and interpersonal attraction. *Journal of Applied Social Psychology, 4*(3), 210–223.

Gross, A. E., Wallston, B. S., & Piliavin, I. M. (1979). Reactance, attribution, equity, and the help recipient. *Journal of Applied Social Psychology, 9*(4), 297–313.

Gruder, C. L., Romer, D., & Korth, B. (1978). Dependency and fault as determinants of helping. *Journal of Experimental Social Psychology, 14,* 227–235.

Guerin, B. (1986). Mere presence effects in humans: A review. *Journal of Experimental Social Psychology, 22,* 38–77.

Gupta, G. R. (1992). Love, arranged marriage, and the Indian social structure. In J. J. Macionis & N. V. Benokraitis (Eds.), *Seeing ourselves: Classic, contemporary and cross–cultural readings in sociology,* (pp. 262–270). Englewood Cliffs, NJ: Prentice–Hall.

Gurin, P. (1985). Women's gender consciousness. *Public Opinion Quarterly, 49,* 142–163.

Guttentag, M., & Secord, P. F. (1983). *Too many women: The sex ratio question.* Beverly Hills, CA: Sage Publications.

Hacker, H. M. (1981). Blabbermouths and clams: Sex differences in self-disclosure in same-sex and cross-sex friendship dyads. *Psychology of Women Quarterly, 5*(3), 385–401.

Haglund, K. (1992). Violence research is due for attention. *Journal of NIH Research, 4.*

Hall, E. T. (1966). *The hidden dimension.* New York: Doubleday.

Hall, E. T. (1973). *The silent language.* Garden City, NY: Doubleday.

Hall, J. A. (1978). Gender effects in decoding nonverbal cues. *Psychological Bulletin, 85*(4), 845–857.

Hall, J. A. (1984). *Nonverbal sex differences: Communication accuracy and expressive style.* Baltimore: Johns Hopkins University Press.

Hall, K. R. L. (1960). Social vigilance behavior of the chacuma baboon (*Papio ursinus*). *Behavior, 16*(3), 261–294.

Hallinan, M. T. (1992). Determinants of students' friendship choices. *Advances in Group Processes, 9,* 163–183.

Hamill, R., Wilson, T. D., & Nisbett, R. E. (1980). Insensitivity to sample bias: Generalizing from atypical cases. *Journal of Personality and Social Psychology, 39,* 578–589.

Hamilton, D. L. (1981). Cognitive representations of persons. In E. T. Higgins, C. P. Herman, & M. P. Zanna (Eds.), *Social cognition: The Ontario symposium* (Vol. 1, pp. 135–159).

Hamilton, D. L. (1989). Understanding impression formation: What has memory research contributed? In P. R. Solomon, G. R. Goethals, C. M. Kelley, & B. R. Stephens (Eds.), *Memory: Interdisciplinary approaches* (pp. 221–242). New York: Springer–Verlag.

Hamilton, D. L., & Gifford, R. K. (1976). Illusory correlation in interpersonal perception: A cognitive basis of stereotypic judgments. *Journal of Experimental Social Psychology, 12,* 392–407.

Hamilton, D. L., & Trolier, T. K. (1986). Stereotypes and stereotyping: An overview of the cognitive approach. In J. F. Dovidio & S. L. Gaertner (Eds.), *Prejudice, discrimination, and racism* (pp. 127–164). New York: Academic Press.

Hamilton, D. L., & Zanna, M. P. (1972). Differential weighting of favorable and unfavorable attributions in impressions of personality. *Journal of Experimental Research in Personality, 6,* 204–212.

Hamilton, V. L. (1978). Obedience and responsibility: A jury simulation. *Journal of Personality and Social Psychology, 36,* 126–146.

Hampson, S. E., Glasgow, R. E., & Toobert, D. J. (1990). Personal models of diabetes and their relations to self–care activities. *Health Psychology, 9,* 632–646.

Hanna, W. J., & Rogovsky, B. (1986). Women and disability: Stigma and "the third factor." Unpublished manuscript, Department of Family and Community Development, University of Maryland, College Park, described in A. Asch & M. Fine (Eds.), *Women with disabilities,* p. 15. Philadelphia: Temple University Press, p. 15.

Hansen, G. L. (1985). Perceived threats and marital jealousy. *Social Psychology Quarterly, 48*(3), 262–268.

Harackiewicz, J. M., Sansone, C., & Manderlink, G. (1985). Competence, achievement orientation, and intrinsic motivation: A process analysis. *Journal of Personality and Social Psychology, 48,* 493–508.

Harbridge, J., & Furnham, A. (1991). Lay theories of rape. *Counselling Psychology Quarterly, 4,* 3–25.

Harburg, E., Erfurt, J. C., Havenstein, L. S., Chape, C., Schull, W. J., & Shork, M. A. (1973). Socio-ecological stress, suppressed hostility, skin color, and black-white male blood pressure: Detroit. *Psychosomatic Medicine, 35,* 276–296.

Hare–Mustin, R. T., & Marecek, J. (1988). The meaning of difference: Gender theory, postmodernism, and psychology. *American Psychologist, 43,* 455–464.

Harkins, S. G. (1987). Social loafing and social facilitation. *Journal of Experimental Social Psychology, 23,* 1–18.

Harkins, S. G., & Szymanski, K. (1989). Social loafing and group evaluation. *Journal of Personality and Social Psychology, 56,* 934–941.

Harkness, A. R., DeBono, K. G., & Borgida, E. (1985). Personal involvement and strategies for making contingency judgments: A stake in the dating game makes a difference. *Journal of Personality and Social Psychology, 49,* 22–32.

Harris, M. J., Milich, R., Johnston, E. M., & Hoover, D. W. (1990). Effects of expectancies on children's social interactions. *Journal of Experimental Social Psychology, 26,* 1–12.

Harris, P. R. (1980). *Promoting health—preventing disease: Objectives for the nation.* Washington, D.C.: U.S. Government Printing Office.

Hartmann, D. P. (1969). Influence of symbolically modeled instrumental aggression and pain cues on aggressive behavior. *Journal of Personality and Social Psychology, 11,* 280–288.

Hass, R. G., Katz, I., Rizzo, N., Bailey, J., & Eisenstadt, D. (1991). Cross–racial appraisal as related to attitude ambivalence and cognitive complexity. *Personality and Social Psychology Bulletin, 17,* 83–92.

Hastie, R. (1984). Causes and effects of causal attribution. *Journal of Personality and Social Psychology, 46,* 44–56.

Hastie, R., & Kumar, P. A. (1979). Person memory: Personality traits as organizing principles in memory for behavior. *Journal of Personality and Social Psychology, 37,* 25–38.

Hastie, R., Park, B., & Weber, R. (1984). Social memory. In R. S. Wyer & T. K. Srull (Eds.), *Handbook of social cognition* (Vol. 1, pp. 151–212). Hillsdale, NJ: Erlbaum.

Hastorf, A., & Isen, A. M. (1982). *Cognitive social psychology.* New York: Elsevier–North Holland.

Hau, K–T., & Salili, F. (1991). Structure and semantic differential placement of specific causes: Academic causal attributions by Chinese students in Hong Kong. *International Journal of Psychology, 26,* 175–193.

Hauenstein, M. S., Schiller, M. R., & Hurley, R. S. (1987). Motivational techniques of dieticians counseling individuals with Type II diabetes. *Journal of the American Dietetic Association, 87,* 37–42.

Hatfield, E., & Rapson, R. L. (1987). Passionate love: New directions in research. In W. H. Jones & D. Perlman (Eds.), *Advances in personal relationships* (Vol. 1, pp. 109–139). Greenwich, CT: JAI Press.

Hatfield, E., & Sprecher, S. (1986). Measuring passionate love in intimate relations. *Journal of Adolescence, 9,* 383–410.

Hatfield, E., Brinton, C., & Cornelius, J. (1989). Passionate love and anxiety in young adolescents. *Motivation and Emotion, 13,* 271–289.

Hawkes, G. R., & Taylor, M. (1975). Power structure in Mexican and Mexican-American farm labor families. *Journal of Marriage and the Family, 37,* 807–811.

Haynes, S. G., Feinleib, M., & Kannel, W. B. (1980). The relationship of psychosocial factors to coronary heart disease in the Framingham Study, III: Eight-year incidence of coronary heart disease. *American Journal of Epidemiology, 111,* 37–58.

Hazan, C., & Hutt, M. J. (1991). *From parents to peers: Transitions in attachment.* Unpublished manuscript, Department of Human Development, Cornell University.

Hazan, C., & Shaver, P. (1987). Romantic love conceptualized as an attachment process. *Journal of Personality and Social Psychology, 52,* 511–524.

Hazan, C., & Shaver, P. R. (in press). Attachment as an organizational framework for research on close relationships. *Psychological Inquiry.*

Heath, L., Acklin, M., & Wiley, K. (1991). Cognitive heuristics and AIDS risk assessment among physicians. *Journal of Applied Social Psychology, 21,* 1859–1867.

Heaton, T. B., & Albrecht, S. L. (1991). Stable unhappy marriages. *Journal of Marriage and the Family, 53,* 747–758.

Heckhausen, H., & Strang, H. (1988). Efficiency under record performance demands: Exertion control—An individual difference variable? *Journal of Personality and Social Psychology, 55,* 489–498.

Hedge, A., & Yousif, Y. H. (1992). Effects of urban size, urgency, and cost of helpfulness: A cross-cultural comparison between the United Kingdom and the Sudan. *Journal of Cross–Cultural Psychology, 23,* 107–115.

Heider, F. (1958). *The psychology of interpersonal relations.* New York: Wiley.

Hendrick, C., & Hendrick, S. (1989). Research on love: Does it measure up? *Journal of Personality and Social Psychology, 56,* 784–794.

Hendrick, S. S., & Hendrick, C. (1992). *Romantic love.* Newbury Park, CA: Sage Publications.

Hennigan, K. M., Heath, L., Wharton, J. D., Del Rosario, M. L., Cook, T. D., & Calder, B. J. (1982). Impact of the introduction of television on crime in the United States: Empirical findings and theoretical implications. *Journal of Personality and Social Psychology, 42,* 461–477.

Hepworth, J. T., & West, S. G. (1988). Lynchings and the economy: A time-series reanalysis of Hovland & Sears (1940). *Journal of Personality and Social Psychology, 55,* 239–247.

Hern, W. M. (1991). Proxemics: The application of theory to conflict arising from antiabortion demonstrations. *Population and Environment: A Journal of Interdisciplinary Studies, 12*(4), 379–388.

Hertzog, M. W. (1992). Is there a sexuality gap? A comparative analysis of gay men, lesbians and heterosexuals in the 1990 national and state exit polls. Presented at the Annual Meeting of the American Political Science Association, Chicago.

Hewstone, M. (1989). *Causal attribution: From cognitive processes to cognitive beliefs.* Oxford, England: Basil Blackwell.

Hewstone, M., & Islam, M. R. (1992). Intergroup attributions and affective consequences in majority and minority groups. Paper presented at joint meeting of the European Association of Experimental Social Psychology and the Society for Experimental Social Psychology, Leuven, Belgium.

Hewstone, M., & Jaspars, J. (1982). Intergroup relations and attribution processes. In H. Tajfel (Ed.), *Social identity and intergroup relations* (pp. 99–133). Cambridge: Cambridge University Press.

Higgins, E. T. (1989). Continuities and discontinuities in self–regulatory and self-evaluative processes: A developmental theory relating self and affect. *Journal of Personality, 57,* 407–444.

Higgins, E. T., & Bargh, J. A. (1987). Social cognition and social perception. *Annual Review of Psychology, 38,* 369–425.

Higgins, E. T., Klein, R., & Strauman, T. (1985). Self-concept discrepancy theory: A psychological model for distinguishing among different aspects of depression and anxiety. *Social Cognition, 3,* 51–76.

Higgins, E. T., Rholes, W. S., & Jones, C. R. (1977). Category accessibility and impression formation. *Journal of Experimental Social Psychology, 13,* 141–154.

Higgins, E. T., Ruble, D. N., & Hartup, W. W. (1983). *Social cognition and social development.* Cambridge: Cambridge University Press.

Hill, C. T., Rubin, Z., & Peplau, L. A. (1976). Breakups before marriage: The end of 103 affairs. *Journal of Social Issues, 32*(1), 147–168.

Hill, T., Smith, N. D., & Hoffman, H. (1988). Short note: Self–image bias and the perception of other persons' skills. *European Journal of Social Psychology, 18,* 293–298.

Hirt, E., & Kimble, C. E. (1981, May). *The home-field advantage in sports: Differences and correlates.* Paper presented at the annual meeting of the Midwestern Psychological Association, Detroit.

Hirt, E. R. (1990). Do I see only what I expect? Evidence for an expectancy-guided retrieval model. *Journal of Personality and Social Psychology, 58,* 937–951.

Hochbaum, G. (1958). *Public participation in medical screening programs* (DHEW Publication No. 572, Public Health Service). Washington, D.C.: U.S. Government Printing Office.

Hochschild, J. L., & Herk, M. (1989). "Yes, but . . .": Principles and caveats in American racial attitudes. In J. Chapman (Ed.), *NOMOS: Majorities and minorities: Political and philosophical perspectives.* New York: New York University Press.

Hodges, B. H. (1974). Effect of valence on relative weighting in impression formation. *Journal of Personality and Social Psychology, 30,* 378–381.

Hoffman, C., Mischel, W., & Baer, J. S. (1984). Language and person cognition: Effects of communicative set on trait attribution. *Journal of Personality and Social Psychology, 46,* 1029–1043.

Hoffman, M. L. (1981). Is altruism part of human nature? *Journal of Personality and Social Psychology, 40*(1), 121–137.

Hogg, M. A., & Abrams, D. (1990). *Social identifications: A social psychology of intergroup relations and group processes.* New York: Routledge.

Hogg, M. A., & Turner, J. C. (1987). Social identity and conformity: A theory of referent information influence. In W. Doise & S. Moscovici (Eds.), *Current issues in European social psychology* (Vol. 2, pp. 139–182). New York: Cambridge University Press.

Holahan, C. J., & Moss, R. H. (1987). Risk, resistance, and psychological distress: A longitudinal analysis with adults and children. *Journal of Abnormal Psychology, 96,* 3–13.

Holahan, C. J., & Wilcox, B. L. (1978). Residential satisfaction and friendship formation in high- and low-rise student housing: An interactional analysis. *Journal of Educational Psychology, 70,* 237–241.

Holland, D., & Skinner, D. (1987). Prestige and intimacy: The cultural models behind Americans' talk about gender types. In D. Holland & N. Quinn (Eds.), *Cultural models in language and thought* (pp. 78–111). New York: Cambridge University Press.

Hollander, E. P. (1985). Leadership and power. In G. Lindzey & E. Aronson (Eds.), *Handbook of social psychology,* 3rd ed. (Vol. 2, pp. 485–538). New York: Random House.

Holmes, T. H., & Rahe, R. H. (1967). The social readjustment rating scale. *Journal of Psychosomatic Research, 11,* 213–218.

Holtgraves, T., & Srull, T. K. (1989). The effects of positive self-descriptions on impressions: General principles and individual differences. *Personality and Social Psychology Bulletin, 15,* 452–462.

Holtz, R., and Miller, N. (1985). Assumed similarity and opinion certainty. *Journal of Personality and Social Psychology, 48,* 890–898.

Holtzworth–Munroe, A., & Jacobson, N. S. (1985). Causal attributions of married couples: When do they search for causes? What do they conclude when they do? *Journal of Personality and Social Psychology, 48,* 1398–1412.

Holyoak, K. J., & Gordon, P. C. (1983). Social reference points. *Journal of Personality and Social Psychology, 5,* 881–887.

Hook, J. G., & Cook, T. D. (1979). Equity theory and the cognitive ability of children. *Psychological Bulletin, 86,* 429–445.

Hornstein, H. A., Fisch, E., & Holmes, M. (1968). Influence of a model's feeling about his behavior and his relevance as a comparison other than observers' helping behavior. *Journal of Personality and Social Psychology, 10,* 222–226.

House, J. S., Landis, K. R., & Umberson, D. (1988). Social relationships and health. *Science, 241,* 540–545.

Houston, B. K., & Kelly, K. E. (1989). Hostility in employed women: Relations to work and marital experiences, social support, stress, and anger expression. *Personality and Social Psychology Bulletin, 15,* 175–182.

Hovland, C. I. (1959). Reconciling conflicting results derived from experimental and survey studies of attitude change. *American Psychologist, 14,* 8–17.

Hovland, C. I., Janis, I. L., & Kelley, H. H. (1953). *Communication and persuasion.* New Haven, CT: Yale University Press.

Hovland, C. I., & Sears, R. R. (1940). Minor studies of aggression: Correlation of lynchings with economic indices. *Journal of Psychology, 9,* 301–310.

Howard, D. J. (1990). Rhetorical question effects on message processing and persuasion: The role of information availability and the elicitation of judgment. *Journal of Experimental Social Psychology, 26,* 217–239.

Howard, J. A. (1984). Societal influences on attribution: Blaming some victims more than others. *Journal of Personality and Social Psychology, 47,* 494–505.

Howard, J., & Rothbart, M. (1980). Social categorization and memory for in-group and out-group behavior. *Journal of Personality and Social Psychology, 38,* 301–310.

Hsu, F. L. K. (1981). *Americans and Chinese: Passages to difference* (3rd ed.). Honolulu: University Press of Hawaii.

Huang, L. C., & Harris, M. B. (1973). Conformity in Chinese and Americans: A field experiment. *Journal of Cross-Cultural Psychology, 4,* 427–434.

Hubler, S., & Silverstein, S. (1992, December 29). Women's

pay in state lags 31% behind men's. *Los Angeles Times,* A1, 18, 19.

Hudley, C., & Graham, S. (1992). *An attributional intervention to reduce peer directed aggression among African-American boys.* Manuscript submitted for publication.

Huesmann, L. R. (1982). Television violence and aggressive behavior. In D. Pearl, L. Bouthilet, & J. Lazar (Eds.), *Television and behavior: Ten years of scientific progress and implications for the eighties:* Vol. II: *Technical reviews.* Rockville, MD: National Institute of Mental Health.

Huesmann, L. R. (1986). Cross-national communalities in the learning of aggression from media violence. In L. R. Huesmann & L. D. Eron (Eds.), *Television and the aggressive child: A cross-national comparison* (pp. 239–257). Hillsdale, NJ: Erlbaum.

Huesmann, L. R. (1988). An information processing model for the development of aggression. *Aggressive Behavior, 14,* 13–24.

Huesmann, L. R., Eron, L., Lefkowitz, M. M., & Walder, L. O. (1984). The stability of aggression over time and generation. *Developmental Psychology, 20,* 1120–1134.

Huesmann, L. R., & Miller, L. S. (in press). Long-term effects of repeated exposure to media violence in childhood. To appear in G. Comstock (Ed.), *Public communication and behavior* (Vol. 3). Orlando, FL: Academic Press.

Hui, C. H. (1990). Work attitudes, leadership styles, and managerial behaviors in different cultures. In R. W. Brislin (Ed.), *Applied cross-cultural psychology* (pp. 186–208). Newbury Park, CA: Sage Publications.

Hull, J. G., & Bond, C. F., Jr. (1986). Social and behavioral consequences of alcohol consumption and expectancy: A meta–analysis. *Psychological Bulletin, 99,* 347–360.

Hull, J. G., & Mendolia, M. (1991). Modeling the relations of attributional style, expectancies, and depression. *Journal of Personality and Social Psychology, 61,* 85–97.

Hummert, M. L., Crockett, W. H., & Kemper, S. (1990). Processing mechanisms underlying use of the balance schema. *Journal of Personality and Social Psychology, 58,* 5–21.

Hunt, M. M. (1959). *The natural history of love.* New York: Knopf.

Hur, K. K., & Robinson, J. P. (1978). The social impact of "Roots." *Journalism Quarterly, 55,* 19–24.

Hurwitz, J., & Peffley, M. (1990). Public images of the Soviet Union: The impact on foreign policy attitudes. *Journal of Politics, 52,* 3–28.

Huston, T. L. (1983). Power. In H. H. Kelley et al., *Close relationships* (pp. 169–219). New York: W. H. Freeman.

Huston, T. L., Ruggiero, M., Conner, R., & Geis, G. (1981). Bystander intervention into crime: A study based on naturally–occurring episodes. *Social Psychology Quarterly, 44*(1), 14–23.

Hyde, J. S. (1986). Gender differences in aggression. In J. S. Hyde & M. C. Linn (Eds.), *The psychology of gender: Advances through meta-analysis* (pp. 51–66). Baltimore: Johns Hopkins University Press.

Hyde, J. S. (1991). *Half the human experience: The psychology of women,* 4th ed. Lexington, MA: D. C. Heath.

Hyde, J. S., & Linn, M. C. (1986). *The psychology of gender: Advances through meta–analysis.* Baltimore: Johns Hopkins University Press.

Hyman, J. (1959). *Political socialization.* Glencoe, IL: Free Press.

Immigration and Naturalization Service. (1989, August).

1988 Statistical yearbook of the immigration and naturalization service. U. S. Department of Justice. PB89–193932.

Institute for Propaganda Analysis. (1939). *The fine art of propaganda: A study of Father Coughlin's speeches.* New York: Harcourt Brace.

Insko, C. A., Smith, R. H., Alicke, M. D., Wade, J., & Taylor, S. (1985). Conformity and group size: The concern with being right and the concern with being liked. *Personality and Social Psychology Bulletin, 11*(1), 41–50.

Isen, A. M. (1970). Success, failure, attention, and reaction to others: The warm glow of success. *Journal of Personality and Social Psychology, 15,* 294–301.

Isen, A. M. (1984). Toward understanding the role of affect in cognition. In R. S. Wyer, Jr., & T. K. Srull (Eds.), *Handbook of social cognition* (Vol. 3, pp. 179–236). Hillsdale, NJ: Erlbaum.

Isen, A. M. (1987). *Advances in experimental social psychology* (Vol. 20, pp. 203–253). New York: Academic Press.

Isen, A. M., & Levin, P. F. (1972). Effects of feeling good on helping: Cookies and kindness. *Journal of Personality and Social Psychology, 21,* 384–388.

Isen, A. M., Clark, M., & Schwartz, M. F. (1976). Duration of the effect of good mood on helping: Footprints on the sands of time. *Journal of Personality and Social Psychology, 34,* 385–393.

Isen, A. M., Nygren, T. E., & Ashby, F. G. (1988). Influence of positive affect on the subjective utility of gains and losses: It is just not worth the risk. *Journal of Personality and Social Psychology, 55,* 710–717.

Isen, A. M., & Simmonds, S. F. (1978). The effect of feeling good on a helping task that is incompatible with good mood. *Social Psychology Quarterly, 41,* 346–349.

Isenberg, D. J. (1986). Group polarization: A critical review and meta–analysis. *Journal of Personality and Social Psychology, 50*(6), 1141–1151.

Iyengar, S. (1991). *Is anyone responsible? How television frames political issues.* Chicago: University of Chicago Press.

Iyengar, S., & Kinder, D. R. (1987). *News that matters: Television and American opinion.* Chicago, IL: University of Chicago Press.

Izard, C. E. (1971). *The face of emotion.* New York: Appleton–Century–Crofts.

Jackman, M. R., & Crane, M. (1986). "Some of my best friends are black . . .": Interracial friendship and whites' racial attitudes. *Public Opinion Quarterly, 50,* 459–486.

Jackman, M. R., & Muha, M. J. (1984). Education and intergroup attitudes: Moral enlightenment, superficial democratic commitment, or ideological refinement? *American Sociological Review, 49,* 751–769.

Jackson, J. M. (1987). Social impact theory: A social forces model of influence. In B. Mullen & G. R. Goethals (Eds.), *Theories of group behavior* (pp. 111–124). New York: Springer-Verlag.

Jackson, J. M., & Williams, K. D. (1985). Social loafing on difficult tasks: Working collectively can improve performance. *Journal of Personality and Social Psychology, 49*(4), 937–942.

Jackson, L. A. (1992). *Physical appearance and gender: Sociobiological and sociocultural perspectives.* Albany: State University of New York Press.

Janis, I. L. (1982). *Groupthink: Psychological studies of policy decisions and fiascoes,* 2nd ed. Boston: Houghton Mifflin.

Janis, I. L. (1983). Improving adherence to medical recommendations: Prescriptive hypotheses derived from recent research in social psychology. In A. Baum, S. E. Taylor, & J. Singer (Eds.), *Handbook of Psychology and health* (Vol. 4, pp. 113–148). Hillsdale, NJ: Erlbaum.

Janis, I. L., & Mann, L. (1977). *Decision making*. New York: Free Press.

Janoff–Bulman, R. (1979). Characterological versus behavioral self-blame: Inquiries into depression and rape. *Journal of Personality and Social Psychology, 37,* 1798–1809.

Jellison, J. M., & Green, J. (1981). A self-presentation approach to the fundamental attribution error: The norm of internality. *Journal of Personality and Social Psychology, 40,* 643–649.

Jemmott, J. B., Ashby, K. L., & Lindenfeld, K. (1989). Romantic commitment and the perceived availability of opposite–sex persons: On loving the one you're with. *Journal of Applied Social Psychology, 19,* 1198–1211.

Jemmott, J. B. III, Croyle, R. T., & Ditto, P. H. (1988). Commonsense epidemiology: Self–based judgments from laypersons and physicians. *Health Psychology, 7,* 55–73.

Jemmott, J. B. III, & Locke, S. E. (1984). Psychosocial factors, immunologic mediation, and human susceptibility to infectious diseases: How much do we know? *Psychological Bulletin, 95,* 78–108.

Jenkins, C. D., Zyzanski, S. J., & Roseman, R. H. (1979). *Jenkins Activity Survey*. Cleveland, OH: Psychological Corp.

Jenkins, M. J., & Dambrot, F. H. (1987). The attribution of date rape: Observer's attitudes and sexual experiences and the dating situation. *Journal of Applied Social Psychology, 17,* 875–895.

Jennings, J., Gies, F. L., & Brown, V. (1980). Influence of television commercials on women's self-confidence and independent judgment. *Journal of Personality and Social Psychology, 38*(2), 203–210.

Jennings, M. K., & Markus, G. B. (1984). Partisan orientations over the long haul: Results from the three-wave political socialization panel study. *American Political Science Review, 78,* 1000–1018.

Jennings, M. K., & Niemi, R. G. (1974). *The political character of adolescence*. Princeton, NJ: Princeton University Press.

Jensen, I., & Gutek, B. (1982). Attributions and assignment of responsibility in sexual harassment. *Journal of Social Issues, 38,* 121–136.

Jervis, R. (1976). *Perception and misperception in international politics*. Princeton, NJ: Princeton University Press.

Jessor, T. (1988). Personal interest, group conflict, and symbolic group affect: Explanations for whites' opposition to racial equality. Unpublished doctoral dissertation, Department of Psychology, University of California, Los Angeles.

John, R. (1988). The Native American family. In C. H. Mindel, R. W. Habenstein, & R. Wright (Eds.), *Ethnic families in America* (3rd ed.), (pp. 325–363). New York: Elsevier.

Johnson, R. D., & Downing, L. L. (1979). Deindividuation and valence of cues: Effects of prosocial and antisocial behavior. *Journal of Personality and Social Psychology, 37,* 1532–1538.

Johnson, T. E., and Rule, B. G. (1986). Mitigating circumstance information, censure, and aggression. *Journal of Personality and Social Psychology, 50,* 537–542.

Johnston, L., & Hewstone, M. (1992). Cognitive models of stereotype change: 3. Subtyping and the perceived typi-

cality of disconfirming group members. *Journal of Experimental Social Psychology, 28,* 360–386.

Jones, D. M., & Broadbent, D. E. (1987). Noise. In G. Salvendy (Ed.), *Handbook of human factors* (pp. 623–649). New York: John Wiley and Sons.

Jones, E. E. (1979). The rocky road from acts to dispositions. *American Psychologist, 34,* 107–117.

Jones, E. E., & Berglas, S. (1978). Control of attributions about the self through self–handicapping strategies: The appeal of alcohol and the role of underachievement. *Personality and Social Psychology Bulletin, 4,* 200–206.

Jones, E. E., Davis, K. E., & Gergen, K. J. (1961). Role-playing variations and their informational value for person perception. *Journal of Abnormal and Social Psychology, 63,* 302–310.

Jones, E. E., & Harris, V. A. (1967). The attribution of attitudes. *Journal of Experimental Social Psychology, 3,* 1–24.

Jones, E. E., Kanouse, D. E., Kelley, H. H., Nisbett, R. E., Valins, S., & Weiner, B. (1972). *Attribution: Perceiving the causes of behavior*. Morristown, NJ: General Learning Press.

Jones, E. E., & McGillis, D. (1976). Correspondent inferences and the attribution cube: A comparative reappraisal. In J. H. Harvey, W. J. Ickes, & R. F. Kidd (Eds.), *New Directions in attribution research* (Vol. 1, pp. 389–420). Hillsdale, NJ: Erlbaum.

Jones, E. E., & Nisbett, R. E. (1972). The actor and the observer: Divergent perceptions of the causes of behavior. In E. E. Jones et al. (Eds.), *Attribution: Perceiving the causes of behavior* (pp. 79–94). Morristown, NJ: General Learning Press.

Jones, E. E., & Pittman, T. (1982). Toward a general theory of strategic self-presentation. In J. Suls (Ed.), *Psychological perspectives on the self* (Vol. 1, pp. 231–262). Hillsdale, NJ: Erlbaum.

Jones, E. E., Wood, G. C., & Quattrone, G. A. (1981). Perceived variability of personal characteristics in in-groups and out-groups: The role of knowledge and evaluation. *Personality and Social Psychology Bulletin, 7,* 523–528.

Jose, P. E., & McCarthy, W. J. (1988). Perceived agentic and communal behavior in mixed–sex interactions. *Personality and Social Psychology Bulletin, 14,* 57–67.

Judd, C. M., Drake, R. A., Downing, J. W., & Krosnick, J. A. (1991). Some dynamic properties of attitude structures: Context–induced response facilitation and polarization. *Journal of Personality and Social Psychology, 60,* 193–202.

Judd, C. M., & Johnson, J. T. (1981). Attitudes, polarization, and diagnosticity: Exploring the effect of affect. *Journal of Personality and Social Psychology, 41,* 26–36.

Judd, C. M., & Park, B. (1988). Out-group homogeneity: Judgments of variability at the individual and group levels. *Journal of Personality and Social Psychology, 54,* 778–788.

Judd, C. M., Ryan, C. S., & Park, B. (1991). Accuracy in the judgment of in-group and out-group variability. *Journal of Personality and Social Psychology, 61,* 366–379.

Jussin, L. (1989). Teacher expectations: Self-fulfilling prophecies, perceptual biases, and accuracy. *Journal of Personality and Social Psychology, 57,* 469–480.

Kagan, S. (1977). Social motives and behaviors of Mexican-American and Anglo-American children. In J. L. Martinez (Ed.), *Chicano psychology* (pp. 45–86). New York: Academic Press.

Kagan, S., & Knight, G. P. (1979). Cooperation-competition and self-esteem. *Journal of Cross-Cultural Psychology, 10,* 457–467.

Kagan, S. (1984). Interpreting Chicano cooperativeness: Methodological and theoretical considerations. In J. L. Martinez & R. H. Mendoza (Eds.), *Chicano psychology* (2nd ed.), (pp. 289–333). New York: Academic Press.

Kagan, S., & Knight, G. P. (1979). Cooperation-competition and self-esteem: A case of cultural relativism. *Journal of Cross-Cultural Psychology, 10,* 457–467.

Kagan, S., & Madsen, M. C. (1971). Cooperation and competition of Mexican, Mexican-American, and Anglo-American children of two ages under four instructional sets. *Developmental Psychology, 5,* 32–39.

Kahn, K. F., & Goldenberg, E. N. (1991). Women candidates in the news: An examination of gender differences in U.S. Senate campaign coverage. *Public Opinion Quarterly, 55,* 180–199.

Kahneman, D., & Miller, D. T. (1986). Norm theory: Comparing reality to its alternatives. *Psychological Review, 93,* 136–153.

Kahneman, D., Slovic, P., & Tversky, A. (1982). *Judgment under uncertainty: Heuristics and biases.* Cambridge: Cambridge University Press.

Kahneman, D., & Tversky, A. (1982). The simulation heuristic. In D. Kahneman, P. Slovic, & A. Tversky (Eds.), *Judgment under uncertainty: Heuristics and biases* (pp. 201–209). New York: Cambridge University Press.

Kalick, S. M., & Hamilton, T. E. (1988). Closer look at a matching simulation: Reply to Aron. *Journal of Personality and Social Psychology, 54,* 447–451.

Kameda, T., Stasson, M. F., Davis, J. H., Parks, C. D., & Zimmerman, S. K. (1992). Social dilemmas, subgroups, and motivation loss in task-oriented groups: In search of an "optimal" team size in division of work. *Social Psychology Quarterly, 55,* 47–56.

Kammeyer, K. C. W., Ritzer, G., & Yetman, N. R. (1992). *Sociology: Experiencing changing societies* (5th ed.). Boston: Allyn & Bacon.

Kandel, D. (1978). Similarity in real-life adolescent friendship pairs. *Journal of Personality and Social Psychology, 36,* 306–312.

Kanekar, S., Shaherwalla, A., Franco, B., Kunju, T., & Pinto, A. J. (1991). The acquaintance predicament of a rape victim. *Journal of Applied Social Psychology, 21,* 1524–1544.

Kanin, E. J., Davidson, K. R., & Scheck, S. R. (1970). A research note on male-female differentials in the experience of heterosexual love. *Journal of Sex Research, 6,* 64–72.

Kanner, A. D., Coyne, J. C., Schaeffer, C., & Lazarus, R. S. (1981). Comparison of two modes of stress measurement: Daily hassles and uplifts versus major life events. *Journal of Behavioral Medicine, 4,* 1–39.

Kaplan, K. J., Firestone, I. J., Degnore, R., & Morre, M. (1974). Gradients of attraction as a function of disclosure probe intimacy and setting formality: On distinguishing attitude oscillation from attitude change—Study one. *Journal of Personality and Social Psychology, 30,* 638–646.

Kaplan, R. M., Anderson, J. P., & Wingard, D. L. (1991). Gender differences in health-related quality of life. *Health Psychology, 10,* 86–93.

Karabenick, S. A., & Knapp, J. R. (1988). Effects of computer privacy on help-seeking. *Journal of Applied Social Psychology, 18*(6), 461–472.

Karlin, R. A., Epstein, Y. M., & Aiello, J. R. (1978). Strategies for the investigation of crowding. In A. Esser & B. Greenbie (Eds.), *Design for community and privacy.* New York: Plenum.

Kassin, S. M., & Lepper, M. R. (1984). Oversufficient and insufficient justification effects: Cognitive and behavioral development. *Advances in Motivation and Achievement, 3,* 73–106.

Katz, D., & Braly, K. W. (1933). Racial stereotypes of 100 college students. *Journal of Abnormal and Social Psychology, 28,* 280–290.

Katz, I., & Hass, R. G. (1988). Racial ambivalence and American value conflict: Correlational and prime studies of dual cognitive structures. *Journal of Personality and Social Psychology, 55,* 893–905.

Katz, I., Wackenhut, J., & Hass, R. G. (1986). Racial ambivalence, value duality, and behavior. In J. F. Dovidio & S. L. Gaertner (Eds.), *Prejudice, discrimination, and racism* (pp. 35–60). New York: Academic Press.

Kaufert, J. M., Rabkin, S. W., Syrotuik, J., Boyko, E., & Shane, F. (1986). Health beliefs as predictors of success of alternate modalities of smoking cessation: Results of a controlled trial. *Journal of Behavioral Medicine, 9,* 475–489.

Kaufman, M. R. (1970). Practicing good manners and compassion. *Medical insight, 2,* 56–61.

Keating, C. F., Mazur, A., Segall, M. H., Cysneiros, P. G., DiVale, W. T., Kilbride, J. E., Komin, S., Leahy, P., Thurman, B., & Wirsing, R. (1981). Culture and the perception of social dominance from facial expression. *Journal of Personality and Social Psychology, 40,* 601–614.

Keenan, J. M., Golding, J. M., & Brown, P. (1992). Factors controlling the advantage of self–reference over other-reference. *Social Cognition, 10,* 79–94.

Kelley, H. H. (1950). The warm-cold variable in first impressions of persons. *Journal of Personality, 18,* 431–439.

Kelley, H. H. (1967). Attribution theory in social psychology. In D. Levine (Ed.), *Nebraska Symposium on Motivation* (pp. 192–238). Lincoln: University of Nebraska Press.

Kelley, H. H. (1972). Attribution in social interaction. In E. E. Jones et al. (Eds.), *Attribution: Perceiving the causes of behavior* (pp. 1–26). Morristown, NJ: General Learning Press.

Kelley, H. H. (1979). *Personal relationships: Their structures and processes.* Hillsdale, NJ: Erlbaum.

Kelley, H. H. (1983). Love and commitment. In H. H. Kelley et al., *Close relationships* (pp. 265–314). New York: W. H. Freeman.

Kelley, H. H., Berscheid, E., Christensen, A., Harvey, J. H., Huston, T. L., Levinger, G., McClintock, E., Peplau, L. A., & Peterson, D. R. (1983). *Close relationships.* New York: W. H. Freeman.

Kelley, H. H., & Thibaut, J. W. (1978). *Interpersonal relations: A theory of interdependence.* New York: Wiley-Interscience.

Kelly, J. R., & McGrath, J. E. (1985). Effect of time limits and task types on task performance and interaction of four–person groups. *Journal of Personality and Social Psychology, 49,* 395–407.

Kelman, H. C., & Cohen, S. P. (1986). Resolution of international conflict: An interactional approach. In S. Worchel & W. G. Austin (Eds.), *Psychology of intergroup relations* (pp. 323–342). Chicago: Nelson-Hall Publishers.

Kelman, H. C., & Hamilton, V. L. (1989). *Crimes of obedience: Toward a social psychology of authority and responsibility.* New Haven, CT: Yale University Press.

Kenrick, D. T., & Johnson, G. A. (1979). Interpersonal attraction in aversive environments: A problem for the classical conditioning paradigm? *Journal of Personality and Social Psychology, 37,* 572–579.

Kenrick, D. T., McCreath, H. E., Govern, J., King, R., & Bordin, J. (1990). Person–environment intersections: Everyday settings and common trait dimensions. *Journal of Personality and Social Psychology, 58,* 685–698.

Kephart, W. (1967). Some correlates of romantic love. *Journal of Marriage and the Family, 29,* 470–479.

Kernis, M. H. (1984). Need for uniqueness, self-schemas, and thought as moderators of the false–consensus effect. *Journal of Experimental Social Psychology, 20,* 350–362.

Kernis, M. H., Brockner, J., & Frankel, B. S. (1989). Self-esteem and reactions to failure: The mediating role of overgeneralization. *Journal of Personality and Social Psychology, 57,* 707–714.

Kernis, M. H., & Grannemann, B. D. (1990). Excuses in the making: A test and extension of Darley and Goethals' attributional model. *Journal of Experimental Social Psychology, 26,* 337– 349.

Kernis, M. H., & Wheeler, L. (1981). Beautiful friends and ugly strangers: Radiation and contrast effects in perception of same-sex pairs. *Personality and Social Psychology Bulletin, 7,* 617–620.

Kessler, R. C., & McLeod, J. D. (1985). Social support and mental health in community samples. In S. Cohen & S. L. Syme (Eds.), *Social support and health* (pp. 219–240). Orlando, FL: Academic Press.

Kilpatrick, D. G., Resick, P. A., & Veronen, L. J. (1981). Effects of a rape experience. *Journal of Social Issues, 37,* 105–122.

Kim, M. P., & Rosenberg, S. (1980). Comparison of two structural models of implicit personality theory. *Journal of Personality and Social Psychology, 38,* 375–389.

Kimball, M. M. (1986). Television and sex-role attitudes. In T. M. Williams (Ed.), *The impact of television: A natural experiment in three communities* (pp. 265–301). Orlando, FL: Academic Press.

Kinder, D. R., & Kiewiet, D. R. (1979). Economic discontent and political behavior: The role of personal grievances and collective economic judgments in congressional voting. *American Journal of Political Science, 23,* 495–527.

Kinder, D. R., & Sears, D. O. (1981). Prejudice and politics: Symbolic racism versus racial threats to the good life. *Journal of Personality and Social Psychology, 40,* 414–431.

Kinder, D. R., & Sears, D. O. (1985). Public opinion and political action. In G. Lindzey & E. Aronson (Eds.), *Handbook of social psychology,* 3rd ed. (Vol. 2, pp. 659–741). Reading, MA: Addison–Wesley.

King, C. E., & Christensen, A. (1983). The relationship events scale: A Guttman scale of progress in courtship. *Journal of Marriage and the Family, 45,* 671–678.

Kipnis, D. (1984). The use of power in organizations and in interpersonal settings. In S. Oskamp (Ed.), *Applied social psychology annual 5* (pp. 179–210). Beverly Hills, CA: Sage Publications.

Kirscht, J. P., & Dillehay, R. C. (1967). *Dimensions of authoritarianism.* Lexington: University of Kentucky Press.

Kirscht, J. P., & Rosenstock, I. M. (1979). Patients' problems in following recommendations of health experts. In G. C. Stone, F. Cohen, & E. Adler (Eds.), *Health psychology—A handbook* (pp. 189–216). San Francisco: Jossey–Bass.

Kitano, H. H. L. (1988). The Japanese American family. In C. H. Mindel, R. W. Habenstein, & R. Wright (Eds.), *Ethnic families in America,* 3rd ed. (pp. 258–275). New York: Elsevier.

Kitayama, S. (1992). Some thoughts on the cognitive-psycho-dynamic self from a cultural perspective. *Psychological Inquiry, 3,* 41–43.

Kitayama, S., Markus, H., Tummala, P., Kurokawa, M., & Kato, K. (1990). *Culture and self-cognition.* Unpublished manuscript.

Klapper, J. T. (1960). *The effects of mass communications.* Glencoe, IL: Free Press.

Klayman, J., & Ha, Y.-W. (1987). Confirmation, disconfirmation, and information in hypothesis testing. *Psychological Review, 94,* 211–228.

Klein, E. (1984). *Gender politics: From consciousness to mass politics.* Cambridge, MA: Harvard University Press.

Klein, S. B., & Loftus, J. (1990). Rethinking the role of organization in person memory: An independent trace storage model. *Journal of Personality and Social Psychology, 59,* 400–410.

Klein, S. B., Loftus, J., & Burton, H. A. (1989). Two self-reference effects: The importance of distinguishing between self-descriptiveness judgments and autobiographical retrieval in self-referent encoding. *Journal of Personality and Social Psychology, 56,* 853–865.

Klein, W. M., & Kunda, Z. (1992). Motivated person perception: Constructing justifications for desired beliefs. *Journal of Experimental Social Psychology, 28,* 145–168.

Klinnert, M. D. (1981, April). *Infants' use of others' facial expressions for regulating their own behavior.* Paper presented at the annual meeting of the Society for Research in Child Development, Boston.

Kluegel, J. R. (1990). Trends in whites' explanations of the black-white gap in socioeconomic status, 1977–1989. *American Sociological Review, 55,* 512–525.

Kluegel, J. R., & Bobo, L. (1993). Dimensions of whites' beliefs about the black-white socioeconomic gap. In P. Sniderman, P. Tetlock, & E. Carmines (Eds.), *Race and politics in American society.* Stanford, CA: Stanford University Press.

Kluegel, J. R., & Smith, E. R. (1983). Affirmative action attitudes: Effects of self-interest, racial affect, and stratification beliefs on whites' views. *Social Forces, 61,* 797–824.

Kluegel, J. R., & Smith, E. R. (1986). *Beliefs about inequality.* Hawthorne, NY: Aldine.

Knight, G. P., & Chao, C. (1991). Cooperative, competitive, and individualistic social values among 8- to 12-year-old siblings, friends, and acquaintances. *Personality and Social Psychology Bulletin, 17,* 201–211.

Knight, G. P., & Kagan, S. (1977). Acculturation of prosocial and competitive behaviors among second- and third-generation Mexican-American children. *Journal of Cross-Cultural Psychology, 8,* 273–284.

Kobasa, S. C. (1979). Stressful life events and health: An inquiry into hardiness. *Journal of Personality and Social Psychology, 37,* 1–11.

Kohlberg, L. (1966). A cognitive-developmental analysis of children's sex-role concepts and attitudes. In E. E. Maccoby (Ed.), *The development of sex differences.* Stanford, CA: Stanford University Press.

Kohn, P. M., Lafreniere, K., & Gurevich, M. (1991). Hassles, health, and personality. *Journal of Personality and Social Psychology, 61,* 478–482.

Koltun, A., & Stone, G. A. (1986). Past and current trends in patient noncompliance research: Focus on diseases, regimens-programs, and provider-disciplines. *Journal of Compliance in Health Care, 1,* 21–32.

Komarita, S. S., Parks, C. D., & Hulbert, L. G. (1992). Reciprocity and the induction of cooperation in social dilemmas. *Journal of Personality and Social Psychology, 62,* 607–617.

Konecni, V. J., & Doob, A. N. (1972). Catharsis through displacement of aggression. *Journal of Personality and Social Psychology, 23,* 379–387.

Konecni, V. J., & Ebbesen, E. B. (1976). Disinhibition versus the cathartic effect: Artifact and substance. *Journal of Personality and Social Psychology, 34,* 352–365.

Konecni, V. J., Libuser, L., Morton, H., & Ebbeson, E. B. (1975). Effects of a violation of personal space on escape and helping responses. *Journal of Personality and Social Psychology, 11,* 288–299.

Korte, C. (1971). Effects of individual responsibility and group communication on help-giving in an emergency. *Human Relations, 24,* 149–159.

Korte, C., & Grant, R. (1980). Traffic noise, environmental awareness, and pedestrian behavior. *Environment and Behavior, 12,* 996–1003.

Koss, M. P., & Oros, C. J. (1982). Sexual Experiences Survey: A research instrument investigating sexual aggression and victimization. *Journal of Consulting and Clinical Psychology, 50,* 455–457.

Kovel, J. (1970). *White racism: A psychohistory.* New York: Pantheon.

Kowalski, R. M., & Leary, M. R. (1990). Strategic self-presentation and the avoidance of aversive events: Antecedents and consequences of self-enhancement and self–depreciation. *Journal of Experimental Social Psychology, 26,* 322–336.

Krahe, B. (1991). Social psychological issues in the study of rape. In W. Stroebe & M. Hewstone (Eds.), *European review of social psychology* (Vol. 2, pp. 279–309). London: John Wiley.

Kramer, G. H. (1971). Short-term fluctuations in U.S. voting behavior, 1896–1964. *American Political Science Review, 65,* 131–143.

Krantz, D. S., & Deckel, A. W. (1983). Coping with coronary heart disease and stroke. In T. G. Burish & L. A. Bradley (Eds.), *Coping with chronic disease: Research and applications* (pp. 85–107). New York: Academic Press.

Krause, L. E., & Stoddard, S. (1989). *Chartbook on disabilities in the United States. An InfoUse Report.* Washington, DC: U.S. National Institute of Disability and Rehabilitation.

Krauss, R. M., Apple, W., Morency, N., Wenzel, C., & Winton, W. (1981). Verbal, vocal, and visible factors in judgments of another's affect. *Journal of Personality and Social Psychology, 40,* 312–320.

Krauss, R. M., Geller, V., & Olson, C. (1976, September). *Modalities and cues in the detection of deception.* Paper presented at the annual meeting of the American Psychological Association.

Krauss, R. M., Morrel-Samuels, P., & Colasante, C. (1991). Do conversational hand gestures communicate? *Journal of Personality and Social Psychology, 61,* 743–754.

Kraut, R. E. (1978). Verbal and nonverbal cues in the perception of lying. *Journal of Personality and Social Psychology, 36,* 380–391.

Kravitz, D. A., & Martin, B. (1986). Ringlemann rediscovered: The original article. *Journal of Personality and Social Psychology, 50*(5), 936–941.

Krebs, D. L., & Miller, D. T. (1985). Altruism and aggression. In G. Lindzey & E. Aronson (Eds.), *Handbook of social psychology,* 3rd ed. (Vol. 2, pp. 1–71). New York: Random House.

Krosnick, J. A. (1991). The stability of political preferences: Comparisons of symbolic and nonsymbolic attitudes. *American Journal of Political Science, 35,* 547–576.

Kruglanski, A. W., & Mayseless, O. (1988). Contextual effects in hypothesis testing: The role of competing alternatives and epistemic motivations. *Social Cognition, 6,* 1–20.

Kuhlman, D. M., & Wimberley, D. L. (1976). Expectations of choice behavior held by cooperators, competitors, and individualists across four classes of experimental game. *Journal of Personality and Social Psychology, 34,* 69–81.

Kuiper, N. A., & Derry, P. A. (1982). Depressed and nondepressed content self-reference in mild depression. *Journal of Personality, 50,* 67–79.

Kuiper, N. A., & MacDonald, M. R. (1982). Self and other perception in mild depressives. *Social Cognition, 1,* 233–239.

Kuiper, N. A., Olinger, L. J., MacDonald, M. R., & Shaw, B. F. (1985). Self-schema processing of depressed and nondepressed content: The effects of vulnerability to depression. *Social Cognition, 3,* 77–93.

Kuiper, N. A., & Rogers, T. B. (1979). Encoding of personal information: Self-other differences. *Journal of Personality and Social Psychology, 37,* 499–514.

Kulik, J. A., & Mahler, H. I. M. (1989). Stress and affiliation in a hospital setting: Preoperative roommate preferences. *Personality and Social Psychology Bulletin, 15,* 183–193.

Kunda, Z. (1987). Motivated inference: Self-serving generation and evaluation of causal theories. *Journal of Personality and Social Psychology, 53,* 636–647.

Kurdek, L. A. (1992). Relationship stability and relationship satisfaction in cohabiting gay and lesbian couples: A prospective longitudinal test of the contextual and interdependence models. *Journal of Social and Personal Relationships, 9,* 125–142.

Lacroix, J. M., Martin, B., Avendano, M., & Goldstein, R. (1991). Symptom schemata in chronic respiratory patients. *Health Psychology, 10,* 268–273.

Ladd, E. C. (1992). The polls in 1992: A Roper review. *The Public Perspective, 4,* 11.

Laerum, E., Johnsen, N., Smith, P., & Larsen, S. (1987). Can myocardial infarction induce positive changes in family relationships? *Family Practice, 4,* 302–305.

Laing, R. D., & Stevenson, R. (1976). Public opinion trends in the last days of the Nixon administration. *Journalism Quarterly, 53,* 294–302.

Lambert, W. E., & Klineberg, O. (1967). *Children's views of foreign peoples.* New York: Appleton-Century-Crofts.

Landman, J. (1988). Regret and elation following action and inaction: Affective responses to positive versus negative outcomes. *Personality and Social Psychology Bulletin, 13,* 524–536.

Langer, E. J. (1975). The illusion of control. *Journal of Personality and Social Psychology, 32,* 311–328.

Langer, E. J., Blank, A., & Chanowitz, B. (1978). The mindlessness of ostensibly thoughtful action. *Journal of Personality and Social Psychology, 36,* 635–642.

Langer, E. J., & Rodin, J. (1976). The effects of choice and enhanced personal responsibility for the aged: A field experiment in an institutional setting. *Journal of Personality and Social Psychology, 34,* 191–198.

Lanoue, D. J. (1991). The "turning point": Viewers' reactions to the second 1988 presidential debate. *American Politics Quarterly, 19,* 80–95.

Lanoue, D. J. (1992). One that made a difference: Cognitive consistency, political knowledge, and the 1980 presidential debate. *Public Opinion Quarterly, 56,* 168–184.

La Piere, R. T. (1934). Attitudes vs. actions. *Social Forces, 13,* 230–237.

Larsen, R. J. (1992). Neuroticism and selective encoding and recall of symptoms: Evidence from a combined concurrent–retrospective study. *Journal of Personality and Social Psychology, 62,* 480–488.

Larson, D. (1986). Crisis prevention and the Austrian State Treaty. *International Organization,* (Winter), 27–60.

Larson, R., Csikszentmihalyi, M., & Graef, R. (1982). Time alone in daily experience: Loneliness or renewal? In L. A. Peplau & D. Perlman (Eds.), *Loneliness: A sourcebook of current theory, research and therapy* (pp. 40–53). New York: Wiley–Interscience.

Lassiter, G. D. (1986). Effect of superfluous deterrence on the perception of others. *Journal of Experimental Social Psychology, 22,* 163–175.

Lasswell, M., & Lobsenz, N. M. (1980). *Styles of loving.* New York: Ballantine.

Latané, B. (1981). The psychology of social impact. *American Psychologist, 36,* 343–356.

Latané, B., & Darley, J. M. (1970). *The unresponsive bystander: Why doesn't he help?* New York: Appleton-Century-Crofts.

Latané, B., & Wolf, S. (1981). The social impact of majorities and minorities. *Psychological Review, 88,* 438–453.

Latané, B., Williams, K., & Harkins, S. (1979). Many hands make light the work: The causes and consequences of social loafing. *Journal of Personality and Social Psychology, 37,* 822–832.

Lau, R. R. (1982). Negativity in political perception. *Political Behavior, 4,* 358–378.

Lau, R. R. (1985). Two explanations for negativity effects in political behavior. *American Journal of Political Science, 29,* 119–138.

Lau, R. R., and Russell, D. (1980). Attributions in the sports pages. *Journal of Personality and Social Psychology, 39,* 29–38.

Lau, R. R., Bernard, T. M., & Hartman, K. A. (1989). Further explorations of common-sense representations of common illness. *Health Psychology, 8,* 195–219.

Lau, R. R., Kane, R., Berry, S., Ware, J., & Roy, D. (1980). Channeling health: A review of the televised health campaigns. *Health Education Quarterly, 7,* 56–89.

Laughlin, P. R., & Adamopoulos, J. (1980). Social combination processes and individual learning for six-person cooperative groups on an intellective task. *Journal of Personality and Social Psychology, 38,* 941–947.

Lazarsfeld, P. F., Berelson, B., & Gaudet, H. (1948). *The people's choice,* 2nd ed. New York: Columbia University Press.

Lazarus, A. A. (1971). *Behavior therapy and beyond.* New York: McGraw-Hill.

Lazarus, R. S. (1966). *Psychological stress and the coping process.* New York: McGraw-Hill.

Lazarus, R. S., & Folkman, S. (1984). *Stress, appraisal, and coping.* New York: Springer-Verlag.

Lazarus, R. S., & Launier, R. (1978). Stress–related transactions between person and environment. In L. A. Pervin & M. Lewis (Eds.), *Internal and external determinants of behavior* (pp. 287–327). New York: Plenum.

Le Bon, G. (1896). *The crowd: A study of the popular mina.* London: Ernest Benn.

Leary, M. R., Rogers, P. A., Canfield, R. W., & Coe, C. (1986). Boredom in interpersonal encounters: Antecedents and social implications. *Journal of Personality and Social Psychology, 51*(5), 968–975.

Leary, M. R., & Shepperd, J. A. (1986). Behavioral self-handicaps versus self–reported handicaps: A conceptual note. *Journal of Personality and Social Psychology, 51,* 1265–1268.

Leary, W. E. (1990, January 25). Risk of hearing loss is growing, panel says. *New York Times,* p. B11.

Leavitt, H. J. (1951). Some effects of certain communication patterns on group performance. *Journal of Abnormal and Social Psychology, 46,* 38–50.

Lee, H.-C.-B. (1991). The attitudes toward rape victims scale: Reliability and validity in a Chinese context. *Sex Roles, 24,* 599–603.

Lee, J. A. (1973). *The colors of love.* New York: Bantam.

Leigh, H., & Reiser, M. F. (1986). Comparison of theoretically oriented and patient-oriented behavioral science courses. *Journal of Medical Education, 61,* 169–174.

Leites, N. (1951). *The operational code of the politburo.* New York: McGraw–Hill.

Lemyre, L., & Smith, P. M. (1985). Intergroup discrimination and self-esteem in the minimal group paradigm. *Journal of Personality and Social Psychology, 49,* 660–670.

Lenney, E. (1977). Women's self-confidence in achievement settings. *Psychological Bulletin, 84,* 1–13.

Leonard, K. E. (1989). The impact of explicit aggressive and implicit nonaggressive cues on aggression in intoxicated and sober males. *Personality and Social Psychology Bulletin, 15,* 390–400.

Lepper, M., Greene, D., & Nisbett, R. (1973). Undermining children's interest with extrinsic rewards. A test of the "overjustification hypothesis." *Journal of Personality and Social Psychology, 28,* 129–137.

Lerner, M. J. (1965). The effect of responsibility and choice on a partner's attractiveness following failure. *Journal of Personality, 33,* 178–187.

Lerner, M. J. (1970). The desire for justice and reactions to victims. In J. McCauley & L. Berkowitz (Eds.), *Altruism and helping behavior.* New York: Academic Press.

Lerner, M. J. (1980). *The belief in a just world: A fundamental delusion.* New York: Plenum.

Leventhal, H., & Cleary, P. D. (1980). The smoking problem: A review of the research and theory in behavioral risk modification. *Psychological Bulletin, 88,* 370–405.

Leventhal, H., & Nerenz, D. R. (1982). A model for stress research and some implications for the control of stress disorders. In D. Meichenbaum & M. Jaremko (Eds.), *Stress prevention and management: A cognitive behavioral approach.* New York: Plenum.

Leventhal, H., Nerenz, D., & Strauss, A. (1980). Self-regulation and the mechanisms for symptom appraisal. In D. Mechanic (Ed.), *Psychosocial epidemiology.* New York: Watson.

Levett, A., & Kuhn, L. (1991). Attitudes towards rape and rapists: A white, English-speaking South African student sample. *South African Journal of Psychology, 21,* 32–37.

Le Vine, R. A., & Campbell, D. T. (1972). *Ethnocentrism:*

Theories of conflict, ethnic attitudes, and group behavior. New York: Wiley.

Levine, J. M., & Moreland, R. L. (1990). Progress in small group research. *Annual Review of Psychology, 41,* 585–634.

Levine, R. V. (1988). The pace of life across cultures. In J. E. McGrath (Ed.), *The social psychology of time: New perspectives* (pp. 39–60). Newbury Park, CA: Sage.

Levine, R. V. (1990). The pace of life. *American Scientist, 78,* 450–459.

Levinger, G., & Snoek, J. G. (1972). *Attraction in relationship: A new look at interpersonal attraction.* Morristown, NJ: General Learning Press.

Levinson, R. M. (1975). Sex discrimination and employment practices: An experiment with unconventional job inquiries. *Social Problems, 22,* 533–543.

Levy-Bruhl, L. (1925). *How natives think.* New York: Alfred A. Knopf.

Lewin–Epstein, N. (1991). Determinants of regular source of health care in black, Mexican, Puerto Rican, and non-Hispanic white populations. *Medical Care, 29,* 543–557.

Lewinsohn, P. M., Mischel, W., Chaplin, W., & Barton, R. (1980). Social competence and depression: The role of illusory self–perceptions. *Journal of Abnormal Psychology, 89,* 203–212.

Lewis–Beck, M. S. (1988). *Economics and elections: The major Western democracies.* Ann Arbor: University of Michigan Press.

Ley, D., & Cybriwsky, R. (1974). Urban grafitti as territorial markers. *Annals of the Association of American Geographers, 64,* 491–505.

Leyens, J. P., Camino, L., Parke, R. D., & Berkowitz, L. (1975). Effects of movie violence on aggression in a field setting as a function of group dominance and cohesion. *Journal of Personality and Social Psychology, 32,* 346–360.

Liberman, A., & Chaiken, S. (1991). Value conflict and thought-induced attitude change. *Journal of Experimental Social Psychology, 27,* 203–216.

Lichtenstein, M., & Srull, T. K. (1987). Processing objectives as a determinant of the relationship between recall and judgment. *Journal of Experimental Social Psychology, 23,* 93–118.

Lichter, D. T., McLaughlin, D. K., Kephart, G., & Landry, D. J. (1992). Race and the retreat from marriage: A shortage of marriageable men? *American Sociological Review, 57,* 781–799.

Liebrand, W. B. G., & van Run, G. J. (1985). The effects of social motives on behavior in social dilemmas in two cultures. *Journal of Experimental Social Psychology, 21,* 86–102.

Liebrand, W. G., Wilke, H. A., & Messick, D. M. (Eds.). (1992). *Social psychological approach to social dilemmas.* Tarrytown, NY: Pergamon Press.

Lin, Y. C. (1992). *The construction of the sense of intimacy from everyday social interaction.* Unpublished doctoral dissertation, University of Rochester.

Linder, D. E., Cooper, J., & Jones, E. E. (1967). Decision freedom as a determinant of the role of incentive magnitude in attitude change. *Journal of Personality and Social Psychology, 6,* 245–254.

Lindman, R., Jarvinen, P., & Vidjeskog, J. (1987). Verbal interactions of aggressively and non-aggressively predisposed males in a drinking situation. *Aggressive Behavior, 13,* 187–196.

Linville, P. W. (1982). The complexity-extremity effect and age–based stereotyping. *Journal of Personality and Social Psychology, 42,* 193–211.

Linville, P. W. (1985). Self-complexity and affective extremity: Don't put all your eggs in one cognitive basket. *Social Cognition, 3,* 94–120.

Linville, P. W., Fisher, G. W., & Salovey, P. (1989). Perceived distributions of the characteristics of in-group and out-group members: Empirical evidence and a computer simulation. *Journal of Personality and Social Psychology, 52,* 165–188.

Linville, P. W., & Jones, E. E. (1980). Polarized appraisals of outgroup members. *Journal of Personality and Social Psychology, 38,* 689–703.

Linville, P. W., Salovey, P., & Fisher, G. W. (1986). Stereotyping and perceived distributions of social characteristics: An application to ingroup-outgroup perception. In J. F. Dovidio & S. L. Gaertner (Eds.), *Prejudice, discrimination, and racism* (pp. 165–208). New York: Academic Press.

Linz, D., Donnerstein, E., & Penrod, S. (1984). The effects of multiple exposures to filmed violence against women. *Journal of Communication, 34,* 130–147.

Linz, D. G., Donnerstein, E., & Penrod, S. (1988). Effects of long-term exposure to violent and sexually degrading depictions of women. *Journal of Personality and Social Psychology, 55,* 758–768.

Linz, D., Wilson, B. J., & Donnerstein, E. (1992). Sexual violence in the mass media: Legal solutions, warnings, and mitigation through education. *Journal of Social Issues, 48,* 145–172.

Lipscomb, D. M. (1982). Killing your ears with the sound of music. *Science year.* Chicago: World Book.

Lipset, S. M. (1963). *The first new nation: The United States in historical and comparative perspective.* New York: Basic Books.

Lisak, D., & Roth, S. (1988). Motivational factors in non-incarcerated sexually aggressive men. *Journal of Personality and Social Psychology, 55,* 795–802.

Little, K. B. (1968). Cultural variations in social schemata. *Journal of Personality and Social Psychology, 10,* 1–7.

Littlefield, C. H., Rodin, G. M., Murray, M. A., & Craven, J. L. (1990). Influence of functional impairment and social support on depressive symptoms in persons with diabetes. *Health Psychology, 9,* 737–749.

Littlepage, G. E. (1991). Effects of group size and task characteristics on group performance: A test of Steiner's model. *Personality and Social Psychology Bulletin, 17,* 449–456.

Lockerbie, B., & Borrelli, S. A. (1990). Question wording and public support for Contra aid, 1983–1986. *Public Opinion Quarterly, 54,* 195–208.

Locksley, A., Borgida, E., Brekke, N., & Hepburn, C. (1980). Sex stereotypes and social judgment. *Journal of Personality and Social Psychology, 39*(5), 821–831.

Lord, C. G. (1980). Schemas and images as memory aids: Two modes of processing social information. *Journal of Personality and Social Psychology, 38,* 257–269.

Lord, C. G., Desforges, D. M., Ramsey, S. L., Trezza, G. R., & Lepper, M. R. (1991). Typicality effects in attitude-behavior consistency: Effects of category discrimination and category knowledge. *Journal of Experimental Social Psychology, 27,* 550–575.

Lord, C. G., Lepper, M. R., & Mackie, D. (1984). Attitude prototypes as determinants of attitude-behavior consistency. *Journal of Personality and Social Psychology, 46,* 1254–1266.

Lord, C. G., Lepper, M. R., & Preston, E. (1984). Considering the opposite: A corrective strategy for social judgment. *Journal of Personality and Social Psychology, 47,* 1231–1243.

Lorge, I. (1936). Prestige, suggestion, and attitudes. *Journal of Social Psychology, 7,* 386–402.

Losch, M. E., & Cacioppo, J. T. (1990). Cognitive dissonance may enhance sympathetic tonus, but attitudes are changed to reduce negative affect rather than arousal. *Journal of Experimental Social Psychology, 26,* 289–304.

Loscocco, K. A., & Spitze, G. (1990). Working conditions, social support, and the well-being of female and male factory workers. *Journal of Health and Social Behavior, 31,* 313–327.

Losh-Hesselbart, S. (1987). Development of gender roles. In M. B. Sussman & S. K. Steinmetz (Eds.), *Handbook of marriage and the family* (pp. 535–563). New York: Plenum.

Lovibond, S. H., Birrell, P. C., & Langeluddecke, P. (1986). Changing coronary heart disease risk-factor status: The effects of three behavioral programs. *Journal of Behavioral Medicine, 9,* 415–437.

Ludwig, D., Franco, J. N., & Malloy, T. E. (1986). Effects of reciprocity and self-monitoring on self-disclosure with a new acquaintance. *Journal of Personality and Social Psychology, 50,* 1077–1082.

Luhtanen, R., & Crocker, J. (1992). A collective self-esteem scale: Self-evaluation of one's social identity. *Personality and Social Psychology Bulletin, 18,* 302–318.

Lukas, J. A. (June 9, 1968). Edward Kennedy pays tribute to brother in crowded cathedral. *The New York Times,* pp. 1, 53– 54.

Luker, K. (1984). *Abortion and the politics of motherhood.* Berkeley: University of California Press.

Lurigio, A. J., & Carroll, J. S. (1985). Probation officers' schemata of offenders: Content, development, and impact on treatment decisions. *Journal of Personality and Social Psychology, 48,* 1112–1126.

Luskin, R. C., McIver, J. P., & Carmines, E. G. (1989). Issues and the transmission of partisanship. *American Journal of Political Science, 33,* 440–458.

Lynch, J. G., Jr., & Ofir, C. (1989). Effects of cue consistency and value on base-rate utilization. *Journal of Personality and Social Psychology, 56,* 170–181.

Lydon, J. E., Jamieson, D. W., & Zanna, M. P. (1988). Interpersonal similarity and the social and intellectual dimensions of first impressions. *Social Cognition, 6,* 269–286.

Lyons, R. F. (1991). The effects of acquired illness and disability on friendships. In W. H. Jones & D. Perlman (Eds.), *Advances in personal relationships: A research annual,* Vol. 3, pp. 233–277. London: Jessica Kingsley Publishers.

Lytton, H., & Romney, D. M. (1991). Parents' differential socialization of boys and girls: A meta-analysis. *Psychological Bulletin, 109,* 267–296.

Maass, A., & Clark, R. D. (1984). Hidden impact of minorities: Fifteen years of minority influence research. *Psychological Bulletin, 95,* 428–450.

Maass, A., Clark, R. K., & Haberkorn, G. (1982). The effects of differential ascribed category membership and norms on minority influence. *European Journal of Social Psychology, 12,* 89–104.

Maass, A., & Volpato, C. (1989). Gender differences in self-

serving attributions about sexual experience. *Journal of Applied Social Psychology, 19,* 517–542.

Maccoby, E. E. (1990a). Gender and relationships: A developmental account. *American Psychologist, 45,* 513–520.

Maccoby, E. E. (1990b). Interview in the *American Psychological Society Observer,* July, pp. 4–6.

Maccoby, E. E. (1991). Gender segregation in the workplace: Continuities and discontinuities from childhood to adulthood. In M. Frankenhaeuser, U. Lundberg, & M. Chesney (Eds.), *Women, work, and health* (pp. 3–16). New York: Plenum.

MacDonald, W. S., & Oden, C. W. (1973). Effects of extreme crowding on the performance of five married couples during twelve weeks of intensive training. *Proceedings of 81st Annual Convention of the American Psychological Association, 8,* 209–210.

Mace, D., & Mace, V. (1960). *Marriage east and west.* New York: Doubleday.

Mack, D. E. (1971). Where the black matriarchy theorists went wrong. *Psychology Today, 4,* 24, 86–87.

Mackie, D. M. (1986). Social identification effects in group polarization. *Journal of Personality and Social Psychology, 50*(4), 720–728.

Mackie, D. M., & Worth, L. T. (1989). Differential recall of subcategory information about in-group and out-group members. *Personality and Social Psychology Bulletin, 15,* 401–413.

Mackie, D. M., Worth, L. I., & Asuncion, A. G. (1990). Processing of persuasive in-group messages. *Journal of Personality and Social Psychology, 58,* 812–822.

MacKuen, M. B., Erikson, R. S., & Stimson, J. A. (1989). Macropartisanship. *American Political Science Review, 83,* 1125–1142.

Madden, T. J., Ellen, P. S., & Ajzen, I. (1992). A comparison of the theory of planned behavior and the theory of reasoned action. *Personality and Social Psychology Bulletin, 18,* 3–9.

Madsen, M. C. (1971). Developmental and cross-cultural differences in the cooperative and competitive behavior of young children. *Journal of Cross-Cultural Psychology, 2,* 365–371.

Maheswaran, D., & Chaiken, S. (1991). Promoting systematic processing in low-motivation settings: Effect of incongruent information on processing and judgment. *Journal of Personality and Social Psychology, 61,* 13–25.

Major, B. (1987). Gender, justice, and the psychology of entitlement. In P. Shaver & C. Hendrick (Eds.), *Review of Personality and Social Psychology, 7,* 124–146.

Major, B. (1989). Gender differences in comparisons and entitlement: Implications for comparable worth. *Journal of Social Issues, 45*(4), 99–115.

Major, B., Cozzarelli, C., Testa, M., & McFarlin, D. B. (1988). Self-verification versus expectancy confirmation in social interaction: The impact of self–focus. *Personality and Social Psychology Bulletin, 14,* 346–359.

Major, B., McFarlin, D. B., & Gagnon, D. (1984). Overworked and underpaid: On the nature of gender differences in personal entitlement. *Journal of Personality and Social Psychology, 47,* 1399–1412.

Malamuth, N. M. (1981). Rape proclivity among males. *Journal of Social Issues, 37,* 138–156.

Malamuth, N. M., & Briere, J. (1986). Sexual violence in the media: Indirect effects on aggression against women. *Journal of Social Issues, 42,* 75–92.

Malamuth, N. M., & Ceniti, J. (1986). Repeated exposure to violent and nonviolent pornography: Likelihood of raping ratings and laboratory aggression against women. *Aggressive Behavior, 12,* 129–137.

Malamuth, N. M., & Check, J. V. P. (1981). The effects of mass media exposure on acceptance of violence against women: A field experiment. *Journal of Research in Personality, 15,* 436–446.

Malamuth, N. M., Check, J. V. P., & Briere, J. (1986). Sexual arousal in response to aggression: Ideological, aggressive, and sexual correlates. *Journal of Personality and Social Psychology, 50,* 330–340.

Malamuth, N. M., & Donnerstein, E. (Eds.). (1984). *Pornography and sexual aggression.* New York: Academic Press.

Malamuth, N. M., Sockloskie, R. J., Koss, M. P., & Tanaka, J. S. (1991). Characteristics of aggressors against women: Testing a model using a national sample of college students. *Journal of Consulting and Clinical Psychology, 59,* 670–681.

Malatesta, C. Z., & Haviland, J. M. (1982). Learning display rules: The socialization of emotion expression in infancy. *Child Development, 53,* 991–1003.

Malloy, T. E., & Albright, L. (1990). Interpersonal perception in a social contest. *Journal of Personality and Social Psychology, 58,* 419–428.

Mann, T. E., & Wolfinger, R. E. (1980). Candidates and parties in congressional elections. *The American Political Science Review, 74,* 617–632.

Manne, S. L., & Zautra, A. J. (1989). Spouse criticism and support: Their association with coping and psychological adjustment among women with rheumatoid arthritis. *Journal of Personality and Social Psychology, 56,* 608–617.

Mansbridge, J. J. (1985). Myth and reality: The ERA and the gender gap in the 1980 election. *Public Opinion Quarterly, 49,* 164–178.

Marin, B. V., Marin, G., Perez–Stable, E. J., Otero-Sabogal, R., & Sabogal, F. (1990). Cultural differences in attitudes toward smoking: Developing messages using the theory of reasoned action. *Journal of Applied Social Psychology, 20,* 478–493.

Marin, B. V., & Marin, G. (1990). Effects of acculturation on knowledge of AIDS and HIV among Hispanics. *Hispanic Journal of Behavioral Sciences, 12,* 110–121.

Marin, G., Marin, B. V., Otero-Sabogal, R., Sabogal, F., & Perez-Stable, E. J. (1989). The role of acculturation in the attitudes, norms, and expectancies of Hispanic smokers. *Journal of Cross–Cultural Psychology, 20,* 399–415.

Marin, G., & Triandis, H. C. (1985). Allocentrism as an important characteristic of the behavior of Latin Americans and Hispanics. In R. Diaz-Guerrero (Ed.), *Cross-cultural and national studies in social psychology* (pp. 69–80). Amsterdam: North–Holland.

Marks, G. (1984). Thinking one's abilities are unique and one's opinions are common. *Personality and Social Psychology Bulletin, 10,* 203–208.

Marks, G., & Miller, N. (1987). Ten years of research on the false–consensus effect: An empirical and theoretical review. *Psychological Bulletin, 102,* 72–90.

Markstrom-Adams, C. (1989). Androgyny and its relation to adolescent psychosocial well-being: A review of the literature. *Sex Roles, 21,* 325–340.

Markus, G. B. (1979). The political environment and the dynamics of public attitudes: A panel study. *American Journal of Political Science, 23,* 338–359.

Markus, G. B. (1992). The impact of personal and national economic conditions on presidential voting, 1956–1988. *American Journal of Political Science, 36,* 829–834.

Markus, H. (1977). Self-schemata and processing information about the self. *Journal of Personality and Social Psychology, 35,* 63–78.

Markus, H. R., & Kitayama, S. (1991). Culture and the self: Implications for cognition, emotion, and motivation. *Psychological Review, 98,* 224–253.

Markus, H., & Nurius, P. (1986). Possible selves. *American Psychologist, 41,* 954–969.

Markus, H., & Ruvolo, A. (1989). Possible selves: Personalized representations of goals. In L. A. Pervin (Ed.), *Goal concepts in personality and social psychology* (pp. 211–242). Hillsdale, NJ: Erlbaum.

Markus, H., & Smith, J. (1981). The influence of self-schemata on the perception of others. In N. Cantor & J. Kihlstrom (Eds.), *Personality, cognition, and social interaction* (pp. 233–262). Hillsdale, NJ: Erlbaum.

Markus, H., Smith, J., & Moreland, R. L. (1985). Role of the self–concept in the perception of others. *Journal of Personality and Social Psychology, 49,* 1494–1512.

Markus, H., & Wurf, E. (1987). The dynamic self-concept: A social psychological perspective. *Annual Review of Psychology, 38,* 299–337.

Markus, H., & Zajonc, R. B. (1986). The cognitive perspective in social psychology. In G. Lindzey & E. Aronson (Eds.), *Handbook of social psychology,* 3rd ed. (Vol. 1, pp. 137–230). New York: Random House.

Marlatt, G. A., & George, W. H. (1988). Relapse prevention and the maintenance of optimal health. In S. Shumaker, E. Schron, & J. L. Ockene (Eds.), *The adoption and maintenance of behaviors for optimal health.* New York: Springer.

Marlatt, G. A., & Gordon, J. R. (1985). *Relapse prevention: Maintenance strategies in addictive behavior change.* New York: Guilford.

Martin, B. A. (1989). Gender differences in salary expectations when current salary information is provided. *Psychology of Women Quarterly, 13,* 87–96.

Martin, C. L. (1987). A ratio measure of sex stereotyping. *Journal of Personality and Social Psychology, 52,* 489–499.

Maruyama, G., Fraser, S. C., & Miller, N. (1982). Personal responsibility and altruism in children. *Journal of Personality and Social Psychology, 42*(4), 658–664.

Maslach, C., Santee, R. T., and Wade, C. (1987). Individuation, gender role, and dissent: Personality mediators of situational forces. *Journal of Personality and Social Psychology, 53,* 1088–1093.

Maslach, C., Stapp, J., & Santee, R. T. (1985). Individuation: Conceptual analysis and assessment. *Journal of Personality and Social Psychology, 49,* 729–738.

Matarazzo, J. D. (1980). Behavioral health and behavioral medicine: Frontiers for a new health psychology. *American Psychologist, 35,* 807–817.

Matarazzo, J. D. (1983). Behavioral health: A 1990 challenge for the health science professions. In J. D. Matarazzo, N. E. Miller, S. M. Weiss, J. A. Herd, & S. M. Weiss (Eds.), *Behavioral health: A handbook of health enhancement and disease prevention* (pp. 3–40). New York: Wiley.

Mathes, E. W., Adams, H. E., & Davies, R. M. (1985). Jealousy: Loss of relationship rewards, loss of self-esteem, depression, anxiety and anger. *Journal of Personality and Social Psychology, 48,* 1552–1561.

Matheson, K., Holmes, J. G., & Kristiansen, C. M. (1991). Observational goals and the integration of trait perceptions and behavior: Behavioral prediction versus impression formation. *Journal of Experimental Social Psychology, 27,* 138–160.

Mathews, K. E., & Canon, L. K. (1975). Environmental noise level as a determinant of helping behavior. *Journal of Personality and Social Psychology, 32*(4), 571–577.

Matlin, M., & Stang, D. (1978). *The Pollyanna principle: Selectivity in language, memory, and thought.* Cambridge, MA: Schenkman.

Matsuda, N. (1985). Strong, quasi-, and weak conformity among Japanese in the modified Asch procedure. *Journal of Cross-Cultural Psychology, 61,* 83–97.

Matsumoto, D. (1992). American-Japanese cultural differences in the recognition of universal facial expressions. *Journal of Cross–Cultural Psychology, 23,* 72–84.

Matthews, K. A. (1988). Coronary heart disease and Type A behavior: Update on and alternative to the Booth-Kewley and Friedman (1987) quantitative review. *Psychological Bulletin, 104,* 373–380.

May, J. L., & Hamilton, P. A. (1980). Effects of musically evoked affect on women's interpersonal attraction toward and perceptual judgments of physical attractiveness of men. *Motivation and Emotion, 4,* 217–228.

Mayer, J. D., Gayle, M., Meehan, M. E., & Haarman, A-K. (1990). Toward better specification of the mood-congruency effect in recall. *Journal of Experimental Social Psychology, 26,* 465–480.

Mayer, J. D., & Salovey, P. (1988). Personality moderates the interaction of mood and cognition. In K. Fiedler & J. Forgas (Eds.), *Affect, cognition, and social behavior* (pp. 87–99). Toronto, Canada: Hogrefe.

Mays, V. M., & Cochran, S. D. (in press). Ethnic and gender differences in beliefs about sex partner questioning to reduce HIV risk. *Journal of Adolescent Research.*

McArthur, L. A. (1972). The how and what of why: Some determinants and consequences of causal attribution. *Journal of Personality and Social Psychology, 22,* 171–193.

McArthur, L. Z. (1981). What grabs you? The role of attention in impression formation and causal attribution. In E. T. Higgins, C. P. Herman, & M. P. Zanna (Eds.), *Social cognition: The Ontario symposium* (Vol. 1, pp. 201–246). Hillsdale, NJ: Erlbaum.

McArthur, L. Z., & Baron, R. (1983). Toward an ecological theory of social perception. *Psychological Review, 90,* 215–238.

McArthur, L. Z., & Post, D. L. (1977). Figural emphasis and person perception. *Journal of Personality and Social Psychology, 13,* 520–535.

McArthur, L. Z., & Resko, B. G. (1975). The portrayal of men and women in American TV commercials. *Journal of Social Psychology, 97,* 209–220.

McCabe, V. (1988). Facial proportions, perceived age, and caregiving. In T. R. Alley (Ed.), *Social and applied aspects of perceiving faces* (pp. 89–95). Hillsdale, NJ: Erlbaum.

McCain, G., Cox, V. C., & Paulus, P. B. (1980). *The effect of prison crowding on inmate behavior.* Washington, DC: National Institute of Justice.

McCarthy, D., & Saegert, S. (1978). Residential density, social overload, and social withdrawal. *Human Ecology, 6,* 253–272.

McCaul, K. D., Veltum, L. G., Boyechko, V., & Crawford, J. J.

(1990). Understanding attributions of victim blame for rape: Sex, violence, and foreseeability. *Journal of Applied Social Psychology, 20,* 1–26.

McClelland, D. C. (1976). *The achieving society.* New York: Irvington.

McCleod, J. D., & Kessler, R. C. (1990). Socioeconomic status differences in vulnerability to undesirable life events. *Journal of Health and Social Behavior, 31,* 162–172.

McClintock, C. G., & Liebrand, W. B. G. (1988). Role of interdependence structure, individual value orientation, and another's strategy in social decision making: A transformational analysis. *Journal of Personality and Social Psychology, 55,* 396–409.

McConahay, J. B. (1982). Self-interest versus racial attitudes as correlates of anti-busing attitudes in Louisville: Is it the buses or the blacks? *Journal of Politics, 44,* 692–720.

McConahay, J. B. (1986). Modern racism, ambivalence, and the modern racism scale. In J. F. Dovidio & S. L. Gaertner (Eds.), *Prejudice, discrimination, and racism* (pp. 91–126). New York: Academic Press.

McConahay, J. B., Hardee, B. B., & Batts, V. (1981). Has racism declined in America? It depends upon who is asking and what is asked. *Journal of Conflict Resolution, 25,* 563–579.

McConahay, J. B., & Hough, J. C., Jr. (1976). Symbolic racism. *Journal of Social Issues, 32,* 23–45.

McCrae, R. R., & Costa, P. T., Jr. (1987). Validation of the five-factor model of personality across instruments and observers. *Journal of Personality and Social Psychology, 52,* 81–90.

McDonald, J. (1990). Some situational determinants of hypothesis-testing strategies. *Journal of Experimental Social Psychology, 26,* 255–274.

McFarland, C., Ross, M., & DeCourville, N. (1989). Women's theories of menstruation and biases in recall of menstrual symptoms. *Journal of Personality and Social Psychology, 57,* 522–531.

McFarland, C., Ross, M., & Giltrow, M. (1992). Biased recollections in older adults: The role of implicit theories of aging. *Journal of Personality and Social Psychology, 62,* 837–850.

McFarlane, A. H., Norman, G. R., Streiner, D. L., Roy, R., & Scott, D. J. (1980). A longitudinal study of the influence of the psychosocial environment on health status: A preliminary report. *Journal of Health and Social Behavior, 21,* 124–133.

McGonagle, K. A., Kessler, R. C., & Schilling, E. A. (1992). The frequency and determinants of marital disagreements in a community sample. *Journal of Personal and Social Relationships, 9,* 507–524.

McGrath, J. E. (1984). *Groups: Interaction and performance.* Englewood Cliffs, NJ: Prentice-Hall.

McGuire, W. J. (1969). The nature of attitudes and attitude change. In G. Lindzey & E. Aronson (Eds.), *The handbook of social psychology,* 2nd ed. (Vol. 3, pp. 136–314). Reading, MA: Addison–Wesley.

McGuire, W. J., & McGuire, C. V. (1982). Significant others in self-space. In J. Suls (Ed.), *Psychological perspectives on the self* (Vol. 1, pp. 71–96). Hillsdale, NJ: Erlbaum.

McGuire, W. J., & Padawer-Singer, A. (1976). Trait salience in the spontaneous self-concept. *Journal of Personality and Social Psychology, 33*(6), 743–754.

McKinney, K., & Maroules, N. (1991). Sexual harassment. In

E. Grauerholz & M. A. Koralewski (Eds.), *Sexual coercion* (pp. 29–44). Lexington, MA: Lexington Books.

McMillan, J. R., Clifton, A. K., McGrath, D., & Gale, W. S. (1977). Women's language: Uncertainty or interpersonal sensitivity and emotionality? *Sex Roles, 3*(6), 545–559.

Medvene, L. (1992). Self-help groups, peer helping, and social comparison. In S. Spacapan & S. Oskamp (Eds.), *Helping and being helped: Naturalistic studies* (pp. 49–81). Newbury Park, CA: Sage.

Meehl, P. E. (1954). *Clinical versus statistical prediction: A theoretical analysis and review of the literature.* Minneapolis: University of Minnesota Press.

Mehlman, R. C., & Snyder, C. R. (1985). Excuse theory: A test of the self–protective role of attributions. *Journal of Personality and Social Psychology, 49,* 994–1001.

Mehrabian, A. (1972). *Nonverbal communication.* Chicago: Aldine–Atherton.

Meichenbaum, D. H., & Jaremko, M. E. (Eds.). (1983). *Stress reduction and prevention.* New York: Plenum.

Merei, F. (1949). Group leadership and institutionalization. *Human Relations, 2,* 23–29.

Messick, D., & Brewer, M. B. (1983). Solving social dilemmas: A review. In L. Wheeler & P. Shaver (Eds.), *Review of personality and social psychology* (Vol. 4, pp. 11–44). Beverly Hills: Sage Publications.

Meyer, A. J., Nash, J. D., McAlister, A. L., Maccoby, N., & Farquhar, J. W. (1980). Skills in training in cardiovascular health education campaign. *Journal of Consulting and Clinical Psychology, 48,* 129–142.

Meyer, C. B., & Taylor, S. E. (1986). Adjustment to rape. *Journal of Personality and Social Psychology, 50,* 1226–1234.

Meyer, D., Leventhal, H., & Gutmann, M. (1985). Common–sense models of illness: The example of hypertension. *Health Psychology, 4,* 115–135.

Meyer, J. P., & Mulherin, A. (1980). From attribution to helping: An analysis of the mediating effects of affect and expectancy. *Journal of Personality and Social Psychology, 39*(2), 201–210.

Meyerowitz, B. E. (1980). Psychosocial correlates of breast cancer and its treatments. *Psychological Bulletin, 87,* 108–131.

Michaels, J. W., Bloommel, J. M., Brocato, R. M., Linkous, R. A., & Rowe, J. S. (1982). Social facilitation and inhibition in a natural setting. *Replications in Social Psychology, 2,* 21–24.

Michelson, W. (1970). *Man and his urban environment: A sociological approach.* Reading, MA: Addison-Wesley.

Michelson, W. (1977). *Environmental choice, human behavior, and residential satisfaction.* New York: Oxford University Press.

Midlarsky, E., Bryan, J. H., & Brickman, P. (1973). Aversive approval: Interactive effects of modeling and reinforcement on altruistic behavior. *Child Development, 44,* 321–328.

Mikulincer, M., & Nachshon, O. (1991). Attachment styles and patterns of self-disclosure. *Journal of Personality and Social Psychology, 61,* 321–331.

Milavsky, J. R. (1992). Review: How good is the A. C. Nielsen People-Meter system? A review of the report by the Committee on Nationwide Television Audience Measurement. *Public Opinion Quarterly, 56,* 102–115.

Milavsky, J. R., Kessler, R., Stipp, H., & Rubens, W. S. (1982). Television and aggression: Results of a panel study. In D. Pearl, L. Bouthilet, & J. Lazar (Eds.), *Television and behavior: Ten years of scientific progress and implications for the Eighties.* Vol. II: *Technical reviews.* Rockville, MD: National Institute of Mental Health.

Milgram, S. (1963). Behavioral study of obedience. *Journal of Abnormal and Social Psychology, 67,* 371–378.

Milgram, S. (1964). Issues in the study of obedience: A reply to Baumrind. *American Psychologist, 19,* 848–852.

Milgram, S. (1965). Some conditions of obedience and disobedience to authority. *Human Relations, 18,* 57–75.

Milgram, S. (1970). The experience of living in cities. *Science, 167,* 1461–1468.

Milgram, S. (1974). *Obedience to authority: An experimental view.* New York: Harper & Row.

Milgram, S., Bickman, L., & Berkowitz, L. (1969). Note on the drawing power of crowds of different size. *Journal of Personality and Social Psychology, 13,* 79–82.

Milgram, S., & Shotland, R. L. (1973). *Television and antisocial behavior: Field experiments.* New York: Academic Press.

Millar, M. G., & Tesser, A. (1989). The effects of affective-cognitive consistency and thought on the attitude-behavior relation. *Journal of Experimental Social Psychology, 25,* 189–202.

Miller, A. G. (1976). Constraint and target effects in the attribution of attitudes. *Journal of Experimental Social Psychology, 12,* 325–339.

Miller, A. G. (1986). *The obedience experiments: A case study of controversy in social science.* New York: Praeger.

Miller, A. G., Jones, E. E., & Hinkle, S. (1981). A robust attribution error in the personality domain. *Journal of Experimental Social Psychology, 17,* 587–600.

Miller, C. E. (1989). The social psychological effects of group decision rules. In P. B. Paulus (Ed.), *Psychology of group influence,* 2nd ed. (pp. 327–356). Hillsdale, NJ: Erlbaum.

Miller, C. T., & Felicio, D. M. (1990). Person-positivity bias: Are individuals liked better than groups? *Journal of Experimental Social Psychology, 26,* 408–420.

Miller, D. T., & Ross, M. (1975). Self–serving biases in the attribution of causality: Fact or fiction? *Psychological Bulletin, 82,* 213–225.

Miller, D. T., & Turnbull, W. (1986). Expectancies and interpersonal processes. *Annual Review of Psychology, 37,* 233–256.

Miller, J. G. (1984). Culture and the development of everyday social explanation. *Journal of Personality and Social Psychology, 46,* 961–978.

Miller, J. G., Bersoff, D. G., & Harwood, R. L. (1990). Perceptions of social responsibilities in India and in the United States: Moral imperatives or personal decisions? *Journal of Personality and Social Psychology, 58,* 33–47.

Miller, J. G., & Luthar, S. (1989). Issues of interpersonal responsibility and accountability: A comparison of Indians' and Americans' moral judgments. *Social Cognition, 3,* 237–261.

Miller, L. C. (1990). Intimacy and liking: Mutual influence and the role of unique relationships. *Journal of Personality and Social Psychology, 59,* 50–60.

Miller, L. C., & Kenny, D. A. (1986). Reciprocity of self-disclosure at the individual and dyadic levels: A social relations analysis. *Journal of Personality and Social Psychology, 50,* 713–719.

Miller, N., & Brewer, M. B. (1986). Categorization effects on ingroup and outgroup perception. In J. F. Dovidio & S. L. Gaertner (Eds.), *Prejudice, discrimination, and racism* (pp. 209–230). Orlando, FL: Academic Press.

Miller, N., & Cooper, H. M. (Eds.). (1991). Special Issue: Meta–analysis in personality and social psychology. *Personality and Social Psychology Bulletin,* (entire number 3).

Miller, S. M. (1979). Controllability and human stress: Method, evidence, and theory. *Behavior Research and Therapy, 17,* 287–304.

Miller, S. M., & Mangan, C. E. (1983). Interacting effects of information and copying style in adapting to gynecologic stress: Should the doctor tell all? *Journal of Personality and Social Psychology, 45,* 223–236.

Miller, W. E. (1991). Party identification, realignment, and party voting: Back to the basics. *American Political Science Review, 85,* 557–568.

Miller, W. E. (1992). Generational changes and party identification. *Political Behavior, 14,* 333–352.

Mills, J., & Clark, M. S. (1982). Exchange and communal relationships. In L. Wheeler (Ed.), *Review of personality and social psychology,* (pp. 121–144). Beverly Hills: Sage.

Mills, J., Clark, M. S., & Mehta, P. (1992). *Effects of communal relationship strength upon the perception of altruism and selfishness.* Unpublished manuscript, Department of Psychology, University of Maryland, College Park.

Mills, R. S. L., & Grusec, J. E. (1989). Cognitive, affective, and behavioral consequences of praising altruism. *Merrill-Palmer Quarterly, 35*(3), 299–326.

Mischel, W. (1979). On the interface of cognition and personality: Beyond the person-situation debate. *American Psychologist, 34,* 740–754.

Misumi, J. (1985). *The behavioral science of leadership: An interdisciplinary Japanese research program.* Ann Arbor, MI: University of Michigan Press.

Mita, T. H., Dermer, M., & Knight, J. (1977). Reversed facial images and the mere-exposure hypothesis. *Journal of Personality and Social Psychology, 35,* 597–601.

Mitchell, R. E. (1971). Some social implications of high-density housing. *American Sociological Review, 36,* 18–29.

Mizokawa, D. T., & Ryckman, D. B. (1990). Attributions of academic success and failure: A comparison of six Asian-American ethnic groups. *Journal of Cross-Cultural Psychology, 21,* 434–451.

Mogielnicki, R. P., Neslin, S., Dulac, J., Balestra, D., Gillie, E., & Corson, J. (1986). Tailored media can enhance the success of smoking cessation clinics. *Journal of Behavioral Medicine, 9,* 141–161.

Molm, L. D. (1985). Relative effects of individual dependencies: Further tests of the relation between power imbalance and power use. *Social Forces, 63*(3), 810–837.

Molm, L. D. (1988). The structure and use of power: A comparison of reward and punishment power. *Social Psychology Quarterly, 51,* 108–122.

Monson, T. C., & Snyder, M. (1977). Actors, observers, and the attribution process: Toward a reconceptualization. *Journal of Experimental Social Psychology, 13,* 89–111.

Montgomery, B. M. (1988). Quality communication in personal relationships. In S. W. Duck (Ed.), *Handbook of personal relationships* (pp. 343–359). Chichester, England: Wiley.

Moorhead, G., Ference, R., & Neck, C. P. (1991). Group decision fiascoes continue: Space shuttle Challenger and a revised groupthink framework. *Human Relations, 44,* 539–550.

Morawski, J. G. (1987). The troubled quest for masculinity, femininity, and androgyny. In P. Shaver & C. Hendrick, (Eds.), *Sex and gender* (pp. 44–69). Newbury Park, CA: Sage.

Moreland, R. L., & Beach, S. R. (1992). Exposure effects in the classroom: The development of affinity among students. *Journal of Experimental Social Psychology, 28,* 255–276.

Moretti, M. M., & Higgins, E. T. (1990). Relating self-discrepancy to self-esteem: The contribution of discrepancy beyond actual–self ratings. *Journal of Experimental Social Psychology, 26,* 108–123.

Moriarty, T. (1975). Crime, commitment, and the responsive bystander. Two field experiments. *Journal of Personality and Social Psychology, 31,* 370–376.

Morris, W. N., & Miller, R. S. (1975). The effects of consensus–breaking and consensus-preempting partners on reduction in conformity. *Journal of Experimental Social Psychology, 11,* 215–223.

Morse, J. M., & Morse, R. M. (1988). Cultural variation in the inference of pain. *Journal of Cross-Cultural Psychology, 19,* 232–242.

Morse, S., & Gergen, K. J. (1970). Social comparison, self-consistency, and the concept of self. *Journal of Personality and Social Psychology, 16,* 148–156.

Morton, T. L. (1978). Intimacy and reciprocity of exchange: A comparison of spouses and strangers. *Journal of Personality and Social Psychology, 36,* 72–81.

Moscovici, S. (1985). Social influence and conformity. In G. Lindzey & E. Aronson (Eds.), *Handbook of social psychology,* 3rd ed. (Vol. 2, pp. 347–412). New York: Random House.

Moscovici, S., Lage, E., & Naffrechoux, M. (1969). Influence of a consistent minority on the responses of a majority in a color perception task. *Sociometry, 32,* 365–379.

Moscovici, S., Mugny, G., & Van Avermaet, E. (Eds.). (1985). *Perspectives on minority influence.* New York: Cambridge University Press.

Moser, D. V. (1992). Does memory affect judgment? Self–generated versus recall memory measures. *Journal of Personality and Social Psychology, 62,* 555–563.

Moss, M. K., & Page, R. A. (1972). Reinforcement and helping behavior. *Journal of Applied Social Psychology, 2,* 360–371.

Muehlenhard, C. L. (1988). Misinterpreted dating behaviors and the risk of date rape. *Journal of Social and Clinical Psychology, 6,* 20–37.

Muehlenhard, C. L., & MacNaughton, J. S. (1988). Women's beliefs about women who "lead men on." *Journal of Social and Clinical Psychology, 7,* 65–79.

Mueller, C. (1991). The gender gap and women's political influence. *The Annals of the American Academy of Political and Social Science, 515,* 23–37.

Mueller, J. E. (1973). *War, presidents, and public opinion.* New York: Wiley.

Mullen, B. (1985). Strength and immediacy of sources: A meta-analytic evaluation of the forgotten elements of social impact theory. *Journal of Personality and Social Psychology, 48,* 1458–1466.

Mullen, B. (1991). Group composition, salience, and cognitive representations: The phenomenology of being in a group. *Journal of Experimental Social Psychology, 27,* 297–323.

Mullen, B., Atkins, J. L., Champion, D. S., Edwards, C., Hardy, D., Story, J. E., & Vanderklok, M. (1985). The false consensus effect: A meta–analysis of 115 hypothesis tests. *Journal of Experimental Social Psychology, 21,* 262–283.

Mullen, B., & Hu, L. (1988). Social projection as a function of cognitive mechanisms: Two meta–analytic integrations. *British Journal of Social Psychology, 27*, 333–356.

Mullen, B., Johnson, C., & Salas, E. (1991). Productivity loss in brainstorming groups: A meta-analytic integration. *Basic and Applied Social Psychology, 12*, 3–23.

Mullen, B., & Riordan, C. A. (1988). Self–serving attributions for performance in naturalistic settings: A meta–analytic review. *Journal of Applied Social Psychology, 18*, 3–22.

Murray, N., Sujan, H., Hirt, E. R., & Sujan, M. (1990). The influence of mood on categorization: A cognitive flexibility interpretation. *Journal of Personality and Social Psychology, 59*, 411–425.

Mutchler, J. E., & Burr, J. A. (1991). Racial differences in health and health care service utilization in later life: The effect of socioeconomic status. *Journal of Health and Social Behavior, 32*, 342–356.

Mutz, D. C. (1992). Mass media and the depoliticization of personal experience. *American Journal of Political Science, 36*, 483–508.

Myers, A. M., & Gonda, G. (1982). Utility of the masculinity-femininity construct: Comparison of traditional and androgyny approaches. *Journal of Personality and Social Psychology, 43*(3), 514–523.

Myers, J. K., Lindenthal, J. J., & Pepper, M. P. (1972). Life events and mental status: A longitudinal study. *Journal of Health and Social Behavior, 13*, 398–406.

Myrdal, G. (1944). *An American dilemma.* New York: Harper and Row.

Nadler, A. (1991). Help-seeking behavior: Psychological costs and instrumental benefits. In M. S. Clark (Ed.), *Prosocial behavior* (pp. 290–311). Newbury Park, CA: Sage.

Nakamura, M., Buck, R., & Kenny, D. A. (1990). Relative contributions of expressive behavior and contextual information to the judgment of the emotional state of another. *Journal of Personality and Social Psychology, 59*, 1032–1039.

Nasby, W. (1989). Private self-consciousness, self-awareness, and the reliability of self-reports. *Journal of Personality and Social Psychology, 56*, 950–957.

National Institute of Mental Health. (1982). Television and behavior: Ten years of scientific progress and implications for the eighties. Vol. I: *Summary report.* Rockville, MD: National Institute of Mental Health.

National Victim Center. (1992). *Rape in America: A report to the nation.* Arlington, VA: National Victim Center.

Navarro, V. (1990). Race or class versus race and class: Mortality differentials in the United States. *The Lancet, November 17th.*

Nemeth, C. J. (1992). Minority dissent as a stimulant to group performance. In S. Worchel, W. Wood, & J. A. Simpson (Eds.), *Group process and productivity* (pp. 95–111). Newbury Park, CA: Sage Publications.

Nemeth, C., & Chiles, C. (1988). Modelling courage: The role of dissent in fostering independence. *European Journal of Social Psychology, 18*, 275–280.

Nemeth, C., & Kwan, J. (1987). Minority influence, divergent thinking, and detection of correct solutions. *Journal of Applied Social Psychology, 17*, 788–799.

Nemeth, C., Mosier, K., & Chiles, C. (1992). When convergent thought improves performance: Majority versus minority influence. *Personality and Social Psychology Bulletin, 18*, 139–144.

Nerenz, D. R., & Leventhal, H. (1983). Self-regulation theory in chronic illness. In T. G. Burish & L. A. Bradley (Eds.), *Coping with chronic disease: Research and applications* (pp. 13–35). New York: Academic Press.

Neuberg, S. L. (1989). The goal of forming accurate impressions during social interactions: Attenuating the impact of negative expectancies. *Journal of Personality and Social Psychology, 56*, 374–386.

Neuman, W. R. (1976). Patterns of recall among television news viewers. *Public Opinion Quarterly*, 115–123.

Newcomb, T. M. (1943). *Personality and social change.* New York: Dryden Press.

Newcomb, T. M. (1961). *The acquaintance process.* New York: Holt.

Newtson, D. (1976). Foundations of attribution: The perception of ongoing behavior. In J. H. Harvey, W. J. Ickes, & R. F. Kidd (Eds.), *New directions in attribution research* (Vol. 1, pp. 223–248). Hillsdale, NJ: Erlbaum.

Newtson, D., Engquist, G., & Bois, J. (1977). The objective basis of behavior units. *Journal of Personality and Social Psychology, 35*, 847–862.

Newtson, D., Hairfield, J., Bloomingdale, J., & Cutino, S. (1987). The structure of action and interaction. *Social Cognition, 5*, 191–237.

Nickerson, S., Mayo, C., & Smith, A. (1986). Racism in the courtroom. In J. F. Dovidio & S. L. Gaertner (Eds.), *Prejudice, discrimination, and racism* (pp. 255–278). Orlando, FL: Academic Press.

Nie, N. H., Verba, S., & Petrocik, J. R. (1979). *The changing American voter,* enlarged ed. Cambridge, MA: Harvard University Press.

Niemi, R. G. (1974). *How family members perceive each other.* New Haven, CT: Yale University Press.

Niemi, R. G., & Jennings, M. K. (1991). Issues and inheritance in the formation of party identification. *American Journal of Political Science, 35*, 970–988.

Nieva, V., & Gutek, B. (1981). *Women and work: A psychological perspective.* New York: Praeger.

Nisbett, R. E., Caputo, C., Legant, P., & Maracek, J. (1973). Behavior as seen by the actor and as seen by the observer. *Journal of Personality and Social Psychology, 27*, 154–164.

Nisbett, R. E., Fong, G. T., Lehman, D. R., & Chang, P. W. (1987). Teaching reasoning. *Science, 238*, 625–631.

Nisbett, R. E., Krantz, D. H., Jepson, C., & Fong, G. T. (1982). Improving inductive inference. In D. Kahneman, P. Slovic, & A. Tversky (Eds.), *Judgment under uncertainty: Heuristics and biases* (pp. 445–462). New York: Cambridge University Press.

Nisbett, R. E., & Kunda, Z. (1985). Perception of social distribution. *Journal of Personality and Social Psychology, 48*, 297–311.

Nisbett, R. E., & Ross, L. (1980). *Human inference: Strategies and shortcomings of social judgment.* Englewood Cliffs, NJ: Prentice–Hall.

Nisbett, R. E., & Schachter, S. (1966). Cognitive manipulation of pain. *Journal of Experimental Social Psychology, 2*, 227–236.

Nisbett, R. E., & Wilson, T. D. (1977). Telling more than we can know: Verbal reports on mental processes. *Psychological Review, 84*, 231–259.

NORC (1991). Racial stereotypes widely embraced by whites. Press release, Chicago.

Novak, D. W., & Lerner, M. J. (1968). Rejection as a consequence of perceived similarity. *Journal of Personality and Social Psychology, 9,* 147–152.

Nowak, A., Szamrej, J., & Latané, B. (1990). From private attitude to public opinion: A dynamic theory of social comparison. *Psychological Review, 97,* 362–376.

Ohbuchi, K., Kameda, M., & Agarie, N. (1989). Apology as aggression control: Its role in mediating appraisal of and response to harm. *Journal of Personality and Social Psychology, 56,* 219–227.

Okie, S. (1991). Study links cancer, poverty. *Washington Post, April 17th.*

Oliner, S. P., & Oliner, P. M. (1988). *The altruistic personality: Rescuers of Jews in Nazi Europe.* New York: Free Press.

Olmstead, R. E., Guy, S. M., O'Malley, P. M., & Bentler, P. M. (1991). Longitudinal assessment of the relationship between self-esteem, fatalism, loneliness, and substance abuse. *Journal of Social Behavior and Personality, 6(4),* 749–770.

Olsen, L. (1988). *Crossing the schoolhouse border: Immigrant students and the California Public Schools.* San Francisco: California Tomorrow (Fort Mason, Building B, San Francisco, CA 94123).

Olson, J. M. (1988). Misattribution, preparatory information, and speech anxiety. *Journal of Personality and Social Psychology, 54,* 758–767.

Olson, J. M. (1992). Self–perception of humor: Evidence for discounting and augmentation effects. *Journal of Personality and Social Psychology, 62,* 369–377.

Olson, J. M., & Ross, M. (1988). False feedback about placebo effectiveness: Consequences for the misattribution of speech anxiety. *Journal of Experimental Social Psychology, 24,* 275– 291.

Olweus, D. (1979). Stability of aggressive reaction patterns in males: A review. *Psychological Bulletin, 86,* 852–875.

Orbell, J. M., van de Kragt, A. J. C., & Dawes, R. M. (1988). Explaining discussion–induced cooperation. *Journal of Personality and Social Psychology, 54,* 811–819.

Orvis, B. R., Kelly, H. H., & Butler, D. (1976). Attributional conflict in young couples. In J. H. Harvey, W. Ickes, & R. F. Kidd (Eds.), *New directions in attribution research.* (Vol. 1, pp. 353–386). Hillsdale, NJ: Erlbaum.

Osborn, A. F. (1957). *Applied imagination.* New York: Scribners.

Osbourne, R. E., & Gilbert, D. T. (1992). The preoccupational hazards of social life. *Journal of Personality and Social Psychology, 62,* 219–228.

Osgood, C. E. (1962). *An alternative to war or surrender.* Urbana, IL: University of Illinois Press.

Osgood, C. E. (1977). Objective cross-national indicators of subjective culture. In Y. H. Poortinga (Ed.), *Basic problems in cross-cultural psychology.* Amsterdam: Swets & Zeitlinger.

Osgood, C. E., May, W. H., & Miron, M. S. (1975). *Cross-cultural universals of affective meaning.* Urbana: University of Illinois Press.

Osgood, C. E., Suci, G. J., & Tannenbaum, P. H. (1957). *The measurement of meaning.* Urbana: University of Illinois Press.

Ouchi, W. G. (1981). *Theory Z: How American business can meet the Japanese challenge.* New York: Avon Books.

Page, B. I., & Shapiro, R. Y. (1992). *The rational public: Fifty years of trends in Americans' policy preferences.* Chicago: University of Chicago Press.

Park, B. (1986). A method for studying the development of impressions of real people. *Journal of Personality and Social Psychology, 51,* 907–917.

Park, B., & Flink, C. (1989). A social relations analysis of agreement in liking judgments. *Journal of Personality and Social Psychology, 56,* 506–518.

Park, B., & Hahn, S. (1988). Sex-role identity and the perception of others. *Social Cognition, 6,* 61–87.

Park, B., & Judd, C. M. (1989). Agreement on initial impressions: Differences due to perceivers, trait dimensions, and target behaviors. *Journal of Personality and Social Psychology, 56,* 493–505.

Park, B., & Judd, C. M. (1990). Measures and models of perceived group variability. *Journal of Personality and Social Psychology, 59,* 173–191.

Park, B., & Rothbart, M. (1982). Perception of out-group homogeneity and levels of social categorization: Memory for the subordinate attributes of in-group and out-group members. *Journal of Personality and Social Psychology, 42,* 1051–1068.

Park, C., Cohen, L. H., & Herb, L. (1990). Intrinsic religiousness and religious coping as life stress moderators for Catholics versus Protestants. *Journal of Personality and Social Psychology, 59,* 562–574.

Parke, R. D., Berkowitz, L., Leyens, J. P., West, S. G., & Sebastian, R. J. (1977). Some effects of violent and nonviolent movies on the behavior of juvenile delinquents. In L. Berkowitz (Ed.), *Advances in experimental social psychology* (Vol. 10, pp. 1136–1173). New York: Academic Press.

Parker, S. D., Brewer, M. B., & Spencer, J. R. (1980). Natural disaster, perceived control, and attributions to fate. *Personality and Social Psychology Bulletin, 6,* 454–459.

Parkinson, B. (1985). Emotional effects of false autonomic feedback. *Psychological Bulletin, 98,* 471–494.

Parlee, M. B. (1979, October). The friendship bond. *Psychology Today,* pp. 43–54, 113.

Parrott, W. G., Sabini, J., & Silver, M. (1988). The roles of self-esteem and social interaction in embarrassment. *Personality and Social Psychology Bulletin, 14,* 191–202.

Patterson, M. L., & Sechrest, L. B. (1970). Interpersonal distance and impression formation. *Journal of Personality, 38,* 161–166.

Patterson, T. E. (1980). *The mass media election: How Americans choose their president.* New York: Praeger.

Patterson, T. E., & McClure, R. D. (1976). *The unseeing eye.* New York: Putnam.

Paulus, P. B., Dzindolet, M. T., Poletes, G., & Camacho, L. M. (1993). Perception of performance in group brainstorming: The illusion of group productivity. *Personality and Social Psychology Bulletin, 19,* 78–89.

Paunonen, S. V. (1989). Consensus in personality judgments: Moderating effects of target–rater acquaintanceship and behavior observability. *Journal of Personality and Social Psychology, 56,* 823–833.

Paunonen, S. V. (1991). On the accuracy of ratings of personality by strangers. *Journal of Personality and Social Psychology, 61,* 471–477.

Pavelchak, M. A. (1989). Piecemeal and category-based evaluation: An idiographic analysis. *Journal of Personality and Social Psychology, 56,* 354–363.

Pazy, A. (1992). Sex-linked bias in promotion decisions: The role of candidate's career relevance and respondent's prior experience. *Psychology of Women Quarterly, 16,* 209–228.

Pearlin, L. I., & Schooler, C. (1978). The structure of coping. *Journal of Health and Social Behavior, 19,* 2–21.

Pederson, L. L. (1982). Compliance with physician advice to

quit smoking: A review of the literature. *Preventive Medicine, 11,* 71–84.

Peffley, M., & Hurwitz, J. (1992). International events and foreign policy beliefs: Public response to changing Soviet-U.S. relations. *American Journal of Political Science, 36,* 431–461.

Pennebaker, J. W. (1983). Accuracy of symptom perception. In A. Baum, S. E. Taylor, & J. Singer (Eds.), *Handbook of psychology and health* (Vol. 4, pp. 189–217). Hillsdale, NJ: Erlbaum.

Pennebaker, J. W., & Beall, S. (1986). Confronting a traumatic event: Toward an understanding of inhibition and disease. *Journal of Abnormal Psychology, 95,* 274–281.

Pennebaker, J. W., Colder, M., & Sharp, L. K. (1990). Accelerating the coping process. *Journal of Personality and Social Psychology, 58,* 528–537.

Pennebaker, J. W., & Lightner, J. M. (1980). Competition of internal and external information in an exercise setting. *Journal of Personality and Social Psychology, 39,* 165–174.

Pennebaker, J. W., Kiecolt–Glaser, J., & Glaser, R. (1988). Disclosure of traumas and immune function: Health implications for psychotherapy. *Journal of Consulting and Clinical Psychology, 56,* 239–245.

Pepitone, A., & Triandis, H. C. (1988). On the universality of social psychological theories. *Journal of Cross–Cultural Psychology, 18,* 471–498.

Peplau, L. A. (1984). Power in dating relationships. In J. Freeman (Ed.), *Women: A feminist perspective,* 3rd ed. Palo Alto, CA: Mayfield.

Peplau, L. A., & Campbell, S. M. (1989). The balance of power in dating and marriage. In J. Freeman (Ed.), *Women: A feminist perspective,* 4th ed. (pp. 121–137). Mountain View, CA: Mayfield.

Peplau, L. A., & Perlman, D. (1982). *Loneliness: A sourcebook of current theory, research and therapy.* New York: Wiley–Interscience.

Perdue, C. W., & Gurtman, M. B. (1990). Evidence for the automaticity of ageism. *Journal of Experimental Social Psychology, 26,* 199–216.

Perlman, D. (1990). *Age differences in loneliness: A meta-analysis.* Paper presented at the annual meeting of the American Psychological Association. Boston, August.

Perry, D. G., Perry, L. C., & Weiss, R. J. (1989). Sex differences in the consequences that children anticipate for aggression. *Developmental Psychology, 25,* 312–319.

Pervin, L. A. (Ed.). (1992a). *Psychological Inquiry, 3*(1) whole issue.

Pervin, L. A. (Ed.). (1992b). *Psychological Inquiry, 3*(2) whole issue.

Pessin, J. (1933). The comparative effects of social and mechanical stimulation on memorizing. *American Journal of Psychology, 45,* 263–270.

Peterson, C., & Seligman, M. E. P. (1984). Causal explanations as a risk factor for depression: Theory and evidence. *Psychological Review, 91,* 347–374.

Peterson, C., Seligman, M. E. P., & Vaillant, G. E. (1988). Pessimistic explanatory style is a risk factor for physical illness: A thirty-five-year longitudinal study. *Journal of Personality and Social Psychology, 55,* 23–27.

Peterson, D. R. (1983). Conflict. In H. H. Kelley et al., *Close relationships* (pp. 360–396). New York: Freeman.

Peterson, R. R., & Gerson, K. (1992). Determinants of responsibility for child care arrangements among dual-earner couples. *Journal of Marriage and the Family, 54,* 527–536.

Pettigrew, T. F. (1985). New black-white patterns: How best to conceptualize them? In R. H. Turner & J. F. Short, Jr. (Eds.), *Annual Review of Sociology, 11,* 329–346.

Pettigrew, T. F. (1988). Integration and pluralism. In P. A. Katz & D. A. Taylor (Eds.), *Eliminating racism: Profiles in controversy* (pp. 19–30). New York: Plenum.

Petty, R. E., & Cacioppo, J. T. (1981). *Attitudes and persuasion: Classic and contemporary approaches.* Dubuque, IA: Brown.

Petty, R. E., & Cacioppo, J. T. (1990). Involvement and persuasion: Tradition versus integration. *Psychological Bulletin, 107,* 367–374.

Petty, R. E., & Cacioppo, J. T. (1986). *Communication and persuasion: Central and peripheral routes to attitude change.* New York: Springer-Verlag.

Phares, E. J., Wilson, K. G., & Klyver, N. W. (1971). Internal-external control and attribution of blame under neutral and distractive conditions. *Journal of Personality and Social Psychology, 18,* 285–288.

Phinney, J. S. (1990). Ethnic identity in adolescents and adults: Review of research. *Psychological Bulletin, 108,* 499–514.

Phinney, J. S. (1991). Ethnic identity and self-esteem: A review and integration. *Hispanic Journal of Behavioral Sciences, 13,* 193–208.

Piliavin, I. M., Piliavin, J. A., & Rodin, J. (1975). Costs, diffusion, and the stigmatized victim. *Journal of Personality and Social Psychology, 32*(3), 429–438.

Piliavin, I. M., Rodin, J., & Piliavin, J. A. (1969). Good Samaritanism: An underground phenomenon? *Journal of Personality and Social Psychology, 13*(4), 289–299.

Piliavin, J. A., & Callero, P. L. (1991). *Giving blood: The development of an altruistic identity.* Baltimore, MD: The Johns Hopkins University Press.

Piliavin, J. A., & Charng, H. (1990). Altruism: A review of recent theory and research. *Annual Review of Sociology, 16,* 27–65.

Pilisuk, M., Boylan, R., & Acredolo, C. (1987). Social support, life stress, and subsequent medical care utilization. *Health Psychology, 6,* 273–288.

Plous, S. (1989). Thinking the unthinkable: The effects of anchoring on likelihood estimates of nuclear war. *Journal of Applied Social Psychology, 19,* 67–91.

Pratkanis, A. R., Greenwald, A. G., Leippe, M. R., & Baumgardner, M. H. (1988). In search of reliable persuasion effects. III: The sleeper effect is dead. Long live the sleeper effect. *Journal of Personality and Social Psychology, 54,* 203–218.

Pratto, F., & John, O. P. (1991). Automatic vigilance: The attention–grabbing power of negative social information. *Journal of Personality and Social Psychology, 61,* 380–391.

Prentice-Dunn, S., & Spivey, C. B. (1986). Extreme deindividuation in the laboratory. *Personality and Social Psychology Bulletin, 12,* 206–215.

Prentky, R. A., & Knight, R. A. (1991). Identifying critical dimensions for discriminating among rapists. *Journal of Consulting and Clinical Psychology, 59,* 643–661.

Price, V., & Hsu, M. (1992). Public opinion about AIDS policies: The role of misinformation and attitudes toward homosexuals. *Public Opinion Quarterly, 56,* 29–52.

Pryor, J. B., Reeder, G. D., & McManus, J. A. (1991). Fear and loathing in the workplace: Reactions to AIDS-infected co-workers. *Personality and Social Psychology Bulletin, 17,* 133–139.

Pyszczynski, T. A., & Greenberg, J. (1981). Role of disconfirmed expectancies in the instigation of attributional processing. *Journal of Personality and Social Psychology, 40,* 31–38.

Pyszczynski, T., Hamilton, J. C., Herring, F. H., & Greenberg, J. (1989). Depression, self-focused attention, and the negative memory bias. *Journal of Personality and Social Psychology, 57,* 351–357.

Quinley, H. E., & Glock, C. Y. (1979). *Anti-semitism in America.* New York: Free Press.

Rahe, R. H., Mahan, J. L., & Arthur, R. J. (1970). Prediction of near–future health change from subjects' preceding life changes. *Journal of Psychomatic Research, 14,* 401–406.

Rands, M., & Levinger, G. (1979). Implicit theories of relationship: An intergenerational study. *Journal of Personality and Social Psychology, 37,* 649–661.

Rapoport, R. B., Stone, W. J., & Abramowitz, A. I. (1990). Sex and the caucus participant: The gender gap and presidential nominations. *American Journal of Political Science, 34,* 725–740.

Raven, B. H. (1992). A power/interaction model of interpersonal influence: French and Raven thirty years later. *Journal of Social Behavior and Personality, 7,* 217–244.

Raven, B. H., & Rubin, J. Z. (1983). *Social psychology,* 2nd ed. New York: Wiley.

Read, S. J. (1987). Similarity and causality in the use of social analogies. *Journal of Experimental Social Psychology, 23,* 189–207.

Read, S. J., & Cesa, I. L. (1991). This reminds me of times when . . .: Expectation failures in reminding and explanation. *Journal of Experimental Social Psychology, 27,* 1–25.

Reed, G. M. (1989). Stress, coping, and psychological adaptation in a sample of gay and bisexual men with AIDS. Unpublished doctoral dissertation, University of California, Los Angeles.

Reeder, G. D., Fletcher, G. J. O., & Furman, K. (1989). The role of observers' expectations in attitude attribution. *Journal of Experimental Social Psychology, 25,* 168–188.

Reeder, G. D., McCormick, C. B., & Esselman, E. D. (1987). Self-referent processing and recall of prose. *Journal of Educational Psychology, 79,* 243–248.

Regan, D. T. (1968). *The effects of a favor and liking on compliance.* Unpublished doctoral dissertation, Stanford University.

Regan, D. T., & Totten, J. (1975). Empathy and attribution: Turning observers into actors. *Journal of Personality and Social Psychology, 32,* 850–856.

Reid, J. (1973). *The best little boy in the world.* New York: Ballantine.

Reis, H. T. (1992). *The interpersonal context of emotions: Gender differences in intimacy and related behaviors.* Rochester, NY: University of Rochester. Unpublished manuscript.

Reis, J., & Herz, E. J. (1989). An examination of young adolescents' knowledge of and attitude toward sexuality according to perceived contraceptive responsibility. *Journal of Applied Social Psychology, 19,* 231–250.

Reis, H. T., & Jackson, L. A. (1981). Sex differences in reward allocation: Subjects, partners, and tasks. *Journal of Personality and Social Psychology, 40,* 465–478.

Reis, H. T., Senchak, M., & Solomon, B. (1985). Sex differences in the intimacy of social interaction: Further examination of potential explanations. *Journal of Personality and Social Psychology, 48,* 1204–1217.

Reis, H. T., & Shaver, P. (1988). Intimacy as an interpersonal process. In S. W. Duck (Ed.), *Handbook of personal relationships* (pp. 367–389). New York: Wiley.

Reis, H. T., & Wheeler, L. (1991). Studying social interaction with the Rochester Interaction Record. In M. P. Zanna (Ed.), *Advances in experimental social psychology, Vol. 24,* pp. 269–318. New York: Academic Press.

Rhodewalt, F., & Marcroft, M. (1988). Type A behavior and diabetic control: Implications of psychological reactance for health outcomes. *Journal of Applied Social Psychology, 18,* 139–159.

Rhodewalt, F., Morf, C., Hazlett, S., & Fairfield, M. (1991). Self–handicapping: The role of discounting and augmentation in the preservation of self-esteem. *Journal of Personality and Social Psychology, 61,* 122–131.

Rhodewalt, F., & Strube, M. J. (1985). A self-attribution-reactance model of recovery from injury in Type A individuals. *Journal of Applied Social Psychology, 15,* 330–344.

Rhodewalt, F., & Zone, J. B. (1989). Appraisal of life change, depression, and illness in hardy and nonhardy women. *Journal of Personality and Social Psychology, 56,* 81–88.

Richmond, V. P., McCroskey, J. C., & Payne, S. K. (1991). *Nonverbal behavior in interpersonal relations,* 2nd ed. Englewood Cliffs, NJ: Prentice Hall.

Richmond, V. P., & McCroskey, J. C. (Eds.). (1992). *Power in the classroom: Communication, control, and concern.* Hillsdale, NJ: Erlbaum.

Richmond, V. P., McCroskey, J. C., & Payne, S. K. (1991a). Space. *Nonverbal behavior in interpersonal relations,* 2nd ed. (pp. 117–138). Englewood Cliffs, NJ: Prentice Hall.

Richmond, V. P., McCroskey, J. C., & Payne, S. K. (1991b). Environment. *Nonverbal behavior in interpersonal relations,* 2nd ed. (pp. 155–175). Englewood Cliffs, NJ: Prentice Hall.

Richmond, V. P., McCroskey, J. C., & Payne, S. K. (1991c). Intercultural relationships. *Nonverbal behavior in interpersonal relations,* 2nd ed. (pp. 291–310). Englewood Cliffs, NJ: Prentice Hall.

Richmond, V. P., & Roach, K. D. (1992). Power in the classroom: Seminal studies. In V. P. Richmond & J. C. McCroskey (Eds.), *Power in the classroom: Communication, control, and concern* (pp. 47–65). Hillsdale, NJ: Erlbaum.

Ridgeway, C. L. (1983). *The dynamics of small groups.* New York: St. Martin's Press.

Ridley-Johnson, R., Surdy, T., & O'Laughlin, E. (1991). Parent survey on television violence viewing: Fear, aggression, and sex differences. *Journal of Applied Developmental Psychology, 12,* 63–71.

Risman, B. J. (1987). Intimate relationships from a microstructural perspective: Men who mother. *Gender and Society, 1,* 6–32.

Robinson, C. C., & Morris, J. T. (1986). The gender-stereotyped nature of Christmas toys received by 36-, 48-, and 60-month-old children. *Sex Roles, 15*(1/2), 21–32.

Robinson, J., & McArthur, L. Z. (1982). Impact of salient vocal qualities on causal attribution for a speaker's behavior. *Journal of Personality and Social Psychology, 43,* 236–247.

Rodin, J., & Janis, I. L. (1979). The social power of healthcare practitioners as agents of change. *Journal of Social Issues, 35,* 60–81.

Rodin, J., & Langer, E. J. (1977). Long-term effects of a control-relevant intervention with the institutionalized aged. *Journal of Personality and Social Psychology, 35,* 897–902.

Rodin, J., & Salovey, P. (1989). Health psychology. *Annual Review of Psychology, 10,* 533–579.

Rogers, R. W. (1984). Changing health-related attitudes and behavior: The role of preventive health psychology. In

J. H. Harvey, J. E. Maddux, R. P. McGlynn, & C. D. Stoltenberg (Eds.), *Social perception in clinical and counseling psychology* (Vol. 2, pp. 91–112). Lubbock: Texas Tech University Press.

Rogers, T. B., Kuiper, N. A., & Kirker, W. S. (1977). Self-reference and the encoding of personal information. *Journal of Personality and Social Psychology, 35*, 677–688.

Rose, S., & Frieze, I. H. (1989). Young singles' scripts for a first date. *Gender & Society, 3*, 258–268.

Rosen, B., & Jerdee, T. H. (1978). Perceived sex differences in managerially relevant characteristics. *Sex Roles, 4*, 837– 843.

Rosenbaum, M. E. (1986). The repulsion hypothesis: On the nondevelopment of relationships. *Journal of Personality and Social Psychology, 51*, 1156–1166.

Rosenbaum, R. M. (1972). *A dimensional analysis of the perceived causes of success and failure.* Unpublished doctoral dissertation, University of California, Los Angeles.

Rosenberg, M. (1965). *Society and the adolescent self-image.* Princeton, NJ: Princeton University Press.

Rosenberg, M. (1979). *Conceiving the self.* New York: Basic Books.

Rosenberg, S. (1976). New approaches to the analysis of personal constructs in personal perception. In A. W. Lanfield (Ed.), *Nebraska symposium on motivation* (pp. 179–242). Lincoln: University of Nebraska Press.

Rosenberg, S., Nelson, C., & Vivekananthan, P. S. (1968). A multidimensional approach to the structure of personality impressions. *Journal of Personality and Social Psychology, 9*, 283–294.

Rosenkrantz, P., Vogel, S., Bee, H., Broverman, I., & Broverman, D. M. (1968). Sex-role stereotypes and self–concepts in college students. *Journal of Consulting and Clinical Psychology, 32*, 287–295.

Rosenman, R. (1978). The interview method of assessment of the coronary–prone behavior pattern. In T. Dembroski, S. Weiss, J. Shields, S. Haynes, & M. Feinleib (Eds.), *Coronary–prone behavior* (pp. 55–70). New York: Springer–Verlag.

Rosenstock, I. M. (1966). Why people use health services. *Milbank Memorial Fund Quarterly, 44,* 94ff.

Rosenthal, E. (1990). Health problems of inner city poor reach crisis point. *New York Times, December 24th.*

Rosenthal, R. (1986). Media violence, antisocial behavior, and the social consequences of small effects. *Journal of Social Issues, 42*, 141–154.

Roskies, E. (1980). Considerations in developing a treatment program for the coronary–prone (Type A) behavior pattern. In P. O. Davidson & S. M. Davidson (Eds.), *Behavior medicine: Changing health lifestyles* (pp. 38–69). New York: Brunner/Mazel.

Roskos-Edoldsen, D. R., & Fazio, R. H. (1992). The accessibility of source likability as a determinant of persuasion. *Personality and Social Psychology Bulletin, 18*, 19–25.

Ross, A. S. (1971). Effect of increased responsibility on bystander intervention: The presence of children. *Journal of Personality and Social Psychology, 19*, 306–310.

Ross, L. (1977). The intuitive psychologist and his shortcomings: Distortions in the attribution process. In L. Berkowitz (Ed.), *Advances in experimental social psychology* (Vol. 10, pp. 174–221). New York: Academic Press.

Ross, L., Greene, D., & House, P. (1977). The "false consensus effect": An egocentric bias in social perception and attribution processes. *Journal of Experimental Social Psychology, 13*, 279–301.

Ross, M. (1975). Salience of reward and intrinsic motivation. *Journal of Personality and Social Psychology, 32*, 245–254.

Ross, M., & Fletcher, G. J. O. (1985). Attribution and social perception. In G. Lindzey & E. Aronson (Eds.), *Handbook of social psychology.* New York: Random House.

Ross, M., & Sicoly, F. (1979). Egocentric biases in availability and attribution. *Journal of Personality and Social Psychology, 37*, 322–336.

Rotenberg, K. J., & Cranwell, F. R. (1989). Self-concept in American Indian and white children. *Journal of Cross-Cultural Psychology, 20*, 39–53.

Roth, B. M. (1990). Social psychology's "racism." *The Public Interest, 98*, 28–36.

Rothbart, M. (1976). Achieving racial equality: An analysis of resistance to social reform. In P. A. Katz (Ed.), *Towards the elimination of racism* (pp. 341–375). Elmsford, NY: Pergamon.

Rothbart, M. (1992). Stability and change in stereotypic beliefs. Paper presented at joint meeting of the European Association of Experimental Social Psychology and the Society for Experimental Social Psychology, Leuven.

Rothbart, M., & Lewis, S. (1988). Inferring category attributes from exemplar attributes: Geometric shapes and social categories. *Journal of Personality and Social Psychology, 55*, 861–872.

Rothbaum, F., Weisz, J. R., & Snyder, S. S. (1982). Changing the world and changing the self: A two-process model of perceived control. *Journal of Personality and Social Psychology, 42*, 5–37.

Rotter, J. B. (1966). Generalized expectancies for internal versus external control of reinforcement. *Psychological Monographs, 80* (1, Whole No. 609).

Ruback, R. B. (1987). Deserted (and nondeserted) aisles: Territorial intrusion can produce persistence, not flight. *Social Psychology Quarterly, 50*(3), 270–276.

Ruback, R. B., & Innes, C. A. (1988). The relevance and irrelevance of psychological research: The example of prison crowding. *American Psychologist, 43*(9), 683–693.

Ruback, R. B., & Pandey, J. (1991). Crowding, perceived control, and relative power: An analysis of households in India. *Journal of Applied Social Psychology, 21*, 315–344.

Ruback, R. B., Pape, K. D., & Doriot, P. (1989). Waiting for a phone: Intrusion on callers leads to territorial defense. *Social Psychology Quarterly, 52*(3), 232–241.

Rubin, L. (1976). *Worlds of pain.* New York: Basic Books.

Rubin, Z. (1970). Measurement of romantic love. *Journal of Personality and Social Psychology, 16*, 265–273.

Rubin, Z. (1973). *Liking and loving: An invitation to social psychology.* New York: Holt, Rinehart and Winston.

Rubin, Z. (1980). *Children's friendships.* Cambridge, MA: Harvard University Press.

Rubin, Z., Hill, C. T., Peplau, L. A., & Dunkel-Schetter, C. (1980). Self-disclosure in dating couples: Sex roles and the ethic of openness. *Journal of Marriage and the Family, 42*, 305–317.

Ruble, D. N., & Stangor, C. (1986). Stalking the elusive schema: Insights from developmental and social-psychological analyses of gender schemas. *Social Cognition, 4*, 227–261.

Runciman, W. G. (1966). *Relative deprivation and social justice.* Berkeley: University of California Press.

Rusbult, C. E. (1980). Commitment and satisfaction in romantic associations: A test of the investment model. *Journal of Experimental Social Psychology, 16*, 172–186.

Rusbult, C. E. (1983). A longitudinal test of the investment model: The development (and deterioration) of satisfaction and commitment in heterosexual involvements. *Journal of Personality and Social Psychology, 45,* 101–117.

Rusbult, C. E. (1987). Responses to dissatisfaction in close relationships: The exit-voice-loyalty-neglect model. In D. Perlman & S. Duck (Eds.), *Intimate relationships: Development, dynamics, and deterioration* (pp. 209–237). Beverly Hills, CA: Sage Publications.

Rusbult, C. E., Farrell, D., Rogers, G., & Mainous, A. G. (1988). Impact of exchange variables on exit, voice, loyalty, and neglect: An integrative model of responses to declining job satisfaction. *Academy of Management Journal, 31,* 599–627.

Rusbult, C. E., Verette, J., Whitney, G. A., Slovik, L. F., & Lipkus, I. (1991). Accommodation processes in close relationships: Theory and preliminary empirical evidence. *Journal of Personality and Social Psychology, 60,* 53–78.

Rusbult, C. E., Zembrodt, I. M., & Gunn, L. K. (1982). Exit, voice, loyalty, and neglect: Responses to dissatisfaction in romantic involvements. *Journal of Personality and Social Psychology, 43,* 1230–1242.

Rush, M. C., & Russell, J. E. A. (1988). Leader prototypes and prototype–contingent consensus in leader behavior descriptions. *Journal of Experimental Social Psychology, 24,* 88–104.

Rushton, J. P., & Campbell, A. C. (1977). Modeling, vicarious reinforcement and extraversion on blood donating in adults: Immediate and long–term effects. *European Journal of Social Psychology, 7,* 297–306.

Rushton, J. P., & Teachman, G. (1978). The effects of positive reinforcement, attributions, and punishment on model-induced altruism in children. *Personality and Social Psychology Bulletin, 4,* 322–325.

Russell, J. A., & Bullock, M. (1985). Multidimensional scaling of emotional facial expressions: Similarity from pre-schoolers to adults. *Journal of Personality and Social Psychology, 48,* 1290– 1298.

Ruvolo, A. P., & Markus, H. R. (1992). Possible selves and performance: The power of self-relevant imagery. *Social Cognition, 10,* 95–124.

Ryan, K. M. (1988). Rape and seduction scripts. *Psychology of Women Quarterly, 12,* 237–245.

Ryan, W. (1971). *Blaming the victim.* New York: Vintage.

Saal, F. E., Johnson, C. B., & Weber, N. (1989). Friendly or sexy? It may depend on whom you ask. *Psychology of Women Quarterly, 12,* 263–276.

Saegert, S., & Winkel, G. H. (1990). Environmental psychology. *Annual Review of Psychology, 41,* 441–477.

Safer, M. A., Tharps, Q. J., Jackson, T. C., & Leventhal, H. (1979). Determinants of three stages of delay in seeking care at a medical care clinic. *Medical Care, 17,* 11–29.

Sagar, H., & Schofield, J. W. (1980). Racial and behavioral cues in black and white children's perceptions of ambiguously aggressive acts. *Journal of Personality and Social Psychology, 39,* 590–598.

Salancik, G. R., & Conway, M. (1975). Attitude inferences from salient and relevant cognitive content about behavior. *Journal of Personality and Social Psychology, 32,* 829–840.

Salovey, P. (Ed.). (1991). *The psychology of jealousy and envy.* New York: Guilford Press.

Salovey, P. (1992). Mood–induced self-focused attention. *Journal of Personality and Social Psychology, 62,* 699–707.

Salovey, P., & Birnbaum, D. (1989). Influence of mood on health-relevant cognitions. *Journal of Personality and Social Psychology, 57,* 539–551.

Salovey, P., Mayer, J. D., & Rosenhan, D. L. (1991). Mood and helping: Mood as a motivator of helping and helping as a regulator of mood. In M. S. Clark (Ed.), *Prosocial behavior* (pp. 215–237). Newbury Park, CA: Sage.

Salovey, P., & Rodin, J. (1991). Provoking jealousy and envy: Domain relevance and self-esteem threat. *Journal of Social and Clinical Psychology, 10,* 395–413.

Sampson, E. E. (1977). Psychology and the American ideal. *Journal of Personality and Social Psychology, 35,* 767–782.

Sanbonmatsu, D. M., & Fazio, R. H. (1990). The role of attitudes in memory-based decision making. *Journal of Personality and Social Psychology, 59,* 614–622.

Sande, G. N., Ellard, J. H., & Ross, M. (1986). Effect of arbitrarily assigned status labels on self-perceptions and social perceptions: The mere position effect. *Journal of Personality and Social Psychology, 50,* 684–689.

Sande, G. N., Goethals, G. R., Ferrari, L., & Worth, L. T. (1989). Value-guided attributions: Maintaining the moral self-image and the diabolical enemy-image. *Journal of Social Issues, 45,* 91–118.

Sande, G. N., Goethals, G. R., & Radloff, C. E. (1988). Perceiving one's own traits and others': The multifaceted self. *Journal of Personality and Social Psychology, 54,* 13–20.

Sanna, L. J., & Shotland, R. L. (1990). Valence of anticipated evaluation and social facilitation. *Journal of Experimental Social Psychology, 26,* 82–92.

Sansone, C., Sachau, D. A., & Weir, C. (1989). Effects of instruction on intrinsic interest: The importance of context. *Journal of Personality and Social Psychology, 57,* 819–829.

Sapiro, V. (1983). *The political integration of women.* Urbana: University of Illinois Press.

Sarason, I. G., Johnson, J. H., & Siegel, J. M. (1978). Assessing the impact of life changes: Development of the Life Experience Survey. *Journal of Consulting and Clinical Psychology, 46,* 932 946.

Sarnoff, I., & Zimbardo, P. G. (1961). Anxiety, fear and social affiliation. *Journal of Abnormal and Social Psychology, 62,* 356–363.

Satow, K. L. (1975). Social approval and helping. *Journal of Experimental Social Psychology, 11,* 501–509.

Savage, D. G. (1992, June 25). Prayers banned at school ceremonies. *Los Angeles Times,* pp. A1, A12.

Scanzoni, L. D., & Scanzoni, J. (1981). *Men, women and change,* 2nd ed. New York: McGraw-Hill.

Scarpaci, J. L. (1988). Help-seeking behavior, use, and satisfaction among frequent primary care users in Santiago de Chile. *Journal of Health and Social Behavior, 29,* 199–213.

Schachter, S. (1959). *The psychology of affiliation.* Stanford, CA: Stanford University Press.

Schachter, S. (1964). The interaction of cognitive and physiological determinants of emotional state. In L. Berkowitz (Ed.), *Advances in experimental social psychology* (pp. 49–80). New York: Academic Press.

Schachter, S., & Singer, J. E. (1962). Cognitive, social, and physiological determinants of emotional state. *Psychological Review, 69,* 379–399.

Schain, W. S. (1976). Psychological issues in counseling mastectomy patients. *Counseling Psychologist, 6,* 45–49.

Schaller, M. (1992). In-group favoritism and statistical reasoning in social inference: Implications for formation and maintenance of group stereotypes. *Journal of Personality and Social Psychology, 63,* 61–74.

Schaller, M., & Cialdini, R. B. (1988). The economics of empathic helping: Support for a mood management motive. *Journal of Experimental Social Psychology, 24,* 163–181.

Schaller, M., & Maass, A. (1989). Illusory correlation and social categorization: Toward an integration of motivational and cognitive factors in stereotype formation. *Journal of Personality and Social Psychology, 56,* 709–721.

Schaufeli, W. B. (1988). Perceiving the causes of employment: An evaluation of the causal dimensions in a real-life situation. *Journal of Personality and Social Psychology, 54,* 347–356.

Scheier, M. F., & Carver, C. S. (1980). Private and public self–attention, resistance to change, and dissonance reduction. *Journal of Personality and Social Psychology, 39,* 390–405.

Scheier, M. F., & Carver, C. S. (1983). Two sides of the self: One for you and one for me. In J. Suls & A. G. Greenwald (Eds.), *Psychological perspectives on the self* (Vol. 2, pp. 123–158).

Scheier, M. F., Matthews, K. A., Owens, J. F., Magovern, G. J., Sr., Lefebvre, R. C., Abbott, R. A., & Carver, C. S. (1989). Dispositional optimism and recovery from coronary artery bypass surgery: The beneficial effects on physical and psychological well-being. *Journal of Personality and Social Psychology, 57,* 1024–1040.

Schlenker, B. R. (1980). *Impression management: The self-concept, social identity, and interpersonal relations.* Monterey, CA: Brooks/Cole.

Schlenker, B. R., & Trudeau, J. V. (1990). Impact of self-presentations on private self-beliefs: Effects of prior self-beliefs and misattribution. *Journal of Personality and Social Psychology, 58,* 22–32.

Schlenker, B. R., & Weigold, M. F. (1990). Self-consciousness and self-presentation: Being autonomous versus appearing autonomous. *Journal of Personality and Social Psychology, 59,* 820–828.

Schmidt, F. L. (1992). What do data really mean? Research findings, meta-analysis, and cumulative knowledge in psychology. *American Psychologist, 47,* 1173–1181.

Schmidt, G., & Weiner, B. (1988). An attribution-affect-action theory of behavior: Replications of judgments of help-giving. *Personality and Social Psychology Bulletin, 14,* 610–621.

Schmitt, D. R., & Marwell, G. (1972). Withdrawal and reward reallocation as responses to inequity. *Journal of Experimental Social Psychology, 8,* 207–221.

Schneider, D. J., Hastorf, A. H., & Ellsworth, P. C. (1979). *Person perception* (2nd ed.). Reading, MA: Addison-Wesley.

Schoen, R., & Wooldredge, J. (1989). Marriage choices in North Carolina and Virginia, 1969–71 and 1979–81. *Journal of Marriage and the Family, 51,* 465–481.

Schofield, J. (1978). School desegregation and intergroup relations. In D. Bar-Tal & L. Saxe (Eds.), *Social psychology of education: Theory and research.* New York: Wiley.

Schopler, J., & Stockdale, J. E. (1977). An interference analysis of crowding. *Journal of Environmental Psychology and Nonverbal Behavior, 1,* 81–88.

Schrott, P. R. (1990). Electoral consequences of "winning" televised campaign debates. *Public Opinion Quarterly, 54,* 567–585.

Schul, Y., & Burnstein, E. (1990). Judging the typicality of an instance: Should the category be accessed first? *Journal of Personality and Social Psychology, 58,* 964–974.

Schult, D. G., & Schneider, L. J. (1991). The role of sexual provocativeness, rape history, and observer gender in perceptions of blame in sexual assault. *Journal of Interpersonal Violence, 6,* 94–101.

Schuman, H., Steeh, C., & Bobo, L. (1985). *Racial attitudes in America: Trends and interpretation.* Cambridge, MA: Harvard University Press.

Schuster, B., Forsterling, F., & Weiner, B. (1989). Perceiving the causes of success and failure: A cross-cultural examination of attributional concepts. *Journal of Cross-Cultural Psychology, 20,* 191–213.

Schwartz, B., & Barsky, S. (1977). The home advantage. *Social Forces, 55,* 641–661.

Schwartz, G. S., Kane, T. R., Joseph, J. M., & Tedeschi, J. T. (1978). The effects of post-transgression remorse on perceived aggression, attribution of intent, and level of punishment. *Journal of Social and Clinical Psychology, 17,* 293–297.

Schwartz, S. H. (1990). Individualism-collectivism: Critique and proposed refinements. *Journal of Cross-Cultural Psychology, 21,* 139–157.

Schwartz, S. H., & Gottlieb, A. (1980). Bystander anonymity and reactions to emergencies. *Journal of Personality and Social Psychology, 39,* 418–430.

Schwarz, N., Bless, H., & Bohner, G. (1991). Mood and persuasion: Affective states influence the processing of persuasive communications. *Advances in Experimental Social Psychology, 24,* 161–199.

Schwarz, N., Bless, H., Strack, F., Klumpp, G., Rittenauer-Schatka, H., & Simons, A. (1991). Ease of retrieval of information: Another look at the availability heuristic. *Journal of Personality and Social Psychology, 61,* 195–202.

Scott, J. E., & Cuvelier, S. J. (1987). Violence in *Playboy* magazine: A longitudinal analysis. *Archives of Sexual Behavior, 16,* 279–288.

Scully, D., & Marolla, J. (1984). Convicted rapists' vocabulary of motive excuses and justifications. *Social Problems, 31,* 530–544.

Searcy, E., & Eisenberg, N. (1992). Defensiveness in response to aid from a sibling. *Journal of Personality and Social Psychology, 62,* 422–433.

Sears, D. O. (1982). *Positivity bias in evaluation of public figures.* Paper presented at the annual meetings of the American Political Science Association, Denver, CO.

Sears, D. O. (1983). The persistence of early political predispositions: The roles of attitude object and life stage. In L. Wheeler & P. Shaver (Eds.), *Review of Personality and Social Psychology* (Vol. 4, pp. 79–116). Beverly Hills: Sage.

Sears, D. O. (1983). The person-positivity bias. *Journal of Personality and Social Psychology, 44,* 233–250.

Sears, D. O. (1986). College sophomores in the laboratory: Influences of a narrow database on social psychology's view of human nature. *Journal of Personality and Social Psychology, 51,* 515–530.

Sears, D. O. (1988). Symbolic racism. In P. Katz & D. Taylor (Eds.), *Eliminating racism: Profiles in controversy* (pp. 53–84). New York: Plenum.

Sears, D. O. (1989). Whither political socialization research? The question of persistence. In O. Ichilov (Ed.), *Political socialization, citizenship education, and democracy* (pp. 69–97). New York: Teachers College Press.

Sears, D. O., & Allen, H. M., Jr. (1984). The trajectory of local desegregation controversies and whites' opposition to busing. In N. Miller & M. Brewer (Eds.), *Groups in contact: The psychology of desegregation* (pp. 123–151). New York: Academic Press.

Sears, D. O., & Chaffee, S. H. (1979). Uses and effects of the 1976 debates: An overview of empirical studies. In S. Kraus (Ed.), *The great debates, 1976: Ford vs. Carter* (pp. 223–261). Bloomington: Indiana University Press.

Sears, D. O., & Citrin, J. (1985). *Tax revolt: Something for nothing in California,* enlarged ed. Cambridge, MA: Harvard University Press.

Sears, D. O., Citrin, J., & Kosterman, R. (1987). Jesse Jackson and the Southern white electorate in 1984. In L. W. Moreland, R. P. Steed, & T. A. Baker (Eds.), *Blacks in Southern politics* (pp. 209–225). New York: Praeger.

Sears, D. O., & Funk, C. L. (1990). The persistence and crystallization of political attitudes over the life-span: The Terman Gifted Children Panel. Presented at the Annual Meeting of the American Sociological Association, Washington, D.C.

Sears, D. O., & Huddy, L. (1990). On the origins of political disunity among women. In L. A. Tilly & P. Gurin (Eds.), *Women, politics, and change* (pp. 249–277). New York: Russell Sage.

Sears, D. O., & Huddy, L. (1993). The symbolic politics of opposition to bilingual education. In J. Simpson & S. Worchel (Eds.), *Conflict between people and peoples.* Chicago: Nelson–Hall.

Sears, D. O., & Kinder, D. R. (1985). Whites' opposition to busing: On conceptualizing and operationalizing group conflict. *Journal of Personality and Social Psychology, 48,* 1141–1147.

Sears, D. O., & Kosterman, R. (1991). Is it really racism? The origins and dynamics of symbolic racism. Paper presented at the annual meeting of the Midwest Political Science Association, Chicago.

Sears, D. O., & McConahay, J. B. (1973). *The politics of violence: The new urban blacks and the Watts riot.* Boston: Houghton Mifflin. Reprinted by University Press of America, 1981.

Sears, D. O., & Whitney, R. E. (1973). Political persuasion. In I. deS. Pool, W. Schramm, F. W. Frey, N. Maccoby, & E. B. Parker (Eds.), *Handbook of communication* (pp. 253–289). Chicago: Rand McNally.

Sears, R. R., Maccoby, E., & Levin, H. (1957). *Patterns of child rearing.* Evanston, IL: Row, Peterson.

Sears, R. R., Whiting, J. W. M., Nowlis, V., & Sears, P. S. (1953). Some child-rearing antecedents of aggression and dependency in young children. *Genetic Psychological Monographs, 47,* 135–236.

Sedikides, C. (1990). Effects of fortuitously activated constructs versus activated communication goals on person impressions. *Journal of Personality and Social Psychology, 58,* 397–408.

Sedikides, C., & Jackson, J. M. (1990). Social impact theory: A field test of source strength, source immediacy and number of targets. *Basic and Applied Social Psychology, 11*(3), 273–281.

Segal, M. W. (1974). Alphabet and attraction: An unobtrusive measure of the effect of propinquity in a field setting. *Journal of Personality and Social Psychology, 30,* 654–657.

Seligman, C., Bush, M., & Kirsch, K. (1975). Relationship between compliance in the foot-in-the-door paradigm and size of first request. *Journal of Personality and Social Psychology, 33,* 517–520.

Selye, H. (1956). *The stress of life.* New York: McGraw-Hill.

Selye, H. (1976). *Stress in health and disease.* Woburn, MA: Butterworth.

Semin, G. R. (1980). A gloss on attribution theory. *British Journal of Social and Clinical Psychology, 19,* 291–300.

Shakin, M., Shakin, D., & Sternglanz, S. H. (1985). Infant clothing: Sex labeling for strangers. *Sex Roles, 12,* 955–964.

Shaver, P., & Klinnert, M. D. (1982). Schachter's theories of affiliation and emotion: Implications of developmental research. In L. Wheeler (Ed.), *Review of personality and social psychology* (Vol. 3). Beverly Hills, CA: Sage Publications.

Shaver, P., & Rubenstein, C. (1980). Childhood attachment experience and adult loneliness. In L. Wheeler (Ed.), *Review of personality and social psychology* (Vol. 1, pp. 42–73). Beverly Hills, CA: Sage Publications.

Shaver, P. R., & Hazan, C. (forthcoming). Adult romantic attachment: Theory and evidence. In D. Perlman & W. Jones (Eds.), *Advances in personal relationships,* Vol. 4.

Shaw, M. E. (1981). *Group dynamics: The psychology of small group behavior,* 3rd ed. New York: McGraw-Hill.

Sheatsley, P. B., & Feldman, J. J. (1965). A national survey of public reactions and behavior. In B. S. Greenberg & E. B. Parker (Eds.), *The Kennedy assassination and the American public* (pp. 149–177). Stanford, CA: Stanford University Press.

Shelton, J. L., & Levy, R. L. (1981). *Behavioral assignments and treatment compliance: A handbook of clinical strategies.* Champaign, IL: Research Press.

Sheppard, J. A., & Arkin, R. M. (1989). Determinants of self-handicapping: Task importance and the effects of preexisting handicaps on self-generated handicaps. *Personality and Social Psychology Bulletin, 15,* 101–112.

Sheppard, J. A., & Wright, R. A. (1989). Individual contributions to a collective effort: An incentive analysis. *Personality and Social Psychology Bulletin, 15,* 141–149.

Sherbourne, C. D., & Hays, R. D. (1990). Marital status, social support, and health transitions in chronic disease patients. *Journal of Health and Social Behavior, 31,* 328–343.

Sherif, M. (1935). An experimental study of stereotypes. *Journal of Abnormal and Social Psychology, 29,* 371–375.

Sherif, M., & Cantril, H. (1947). *The psychology of ego-involvements.* New York: Wiley.

Sherif, M., Harvey, O. J., White, B. J., Hood, W. R., & Sherif, C. W. (1961). *Intergroup conflict and cooperation: The robber's cave experiment.* Norman: University of Oklahoma Press.

Sherman, S. J., Judd, C. M., & Park, B. (1989). Social cognition. *Annual Review of Psychology, 40,* 281–336.

Sherman, S. J., Presson, C. C., Chassin, L., Corty, E., & Olshavsky, R. (1983). The false consensus effect in estimates of smoking prevalence: Underlying mechanisms. *Personality and Social Psychology Bulletin, 9,* 197–208.

Sherrod, D. R. (1974). Crowding, perceived control and behavioral aftereffects. *Journal of Applied Social Psychology, 4,* 171–186.

Sherrod, D. R., & Downs, R. (1974). Environmental determinants of altruism: The effects of stimulus overload and perceived control on helping. *Journal of Experimental Social Psychology, 10,* 468–479.

Shikani, K. (1978). Effects of self-esteem on attribution of success-failure. *Japanese Journal of Experimental Social Psychology, 18,* 47–55.

Shinar, E. H. (1975). Sexual stereotypes of occupations. *Journal of Vocational Behavior, 7,* 99–110.

Shoda, Y., Mischel, M., & Wright, J. C. (1989). Intuitive interactionism in person perception: Effects of situation-behavior relations on dispositional judgments. *Journal of Personality and Social Psychology, 56,* 41–53.

Shotland, R. L., & Craig, J. (1988). Can men and women differentiate between friendly and sexually interested behavior? *Social Psychology Quarterly, 51,* 66–73.

Shotland, R. L., & Huston, T. L. (1979). Emergencies: What are they and do they influence bystanders to intervene? *Journal of Personality and Social Psychology, 37*(10), 1822–1834.

Shotland, R. L., & Straw, M. K. (1976). Bystander response to an assault: When a man attacks a woman. *Journal of Personality and Social Psychology, 34,* 990–999.

Showers, C. (1992). Compartmentalization of positive and negative self-knowledge: Keeping bad apples out of the bunch. *Journal of Personality and Social Psychology, 62,* 1036–1049.

Shumaker, S. A., & Hill, D. R. (1991). Gender differences in social support and physical health. *Health Psychology, 10,* 102–111.

Shweder, R. A., & Bourne, E. J. (1984). Does the concept of the person vary cross-culturally? In R. A. Shweder & R. A. LeVine (Eds.), *Culture theory: Essays on mind, self, and emotion* (pp. 158–199). Cambridge, England: Cambridge University Press.

Sidanius, J. (1993). The psychology of group conflict and the dynamics of oppression: A social dominance perspective. In W. J. McGuire & S. Iyengar (Eds.), *Current approaches to political psychology.* Durham, NC: Duke University Press.

Siebenaler, J. B., & Caldwell, D. K. (1956). Cooperation among adult dolphins. *Journal of Mammology, 37,* 126–128.

Siegel, D., Grady, D., Browner, W. S., & Hulley, S. B. (1988). Risk factors modifications after myocardial infarction. *Annals of Internal Medicine, 109,* 213–218.

Signorielli, N., & Lears, M. (1992). Children, television, and conceptions about chores: Attitudes and behaviors. *Sex Roles, 27,* 157–170.

Silverman, F. H., & Klees, J. (1989). Adolescents' attitudes toward peers who wear visible hearing aids. *Journal of Communication Disorders, 22,* 147–150.

Silverman, I. (1964). Self–esteem and differential responsiveness to success and failure. *Journal of Abnormal and Social Psychology, 69,* 115–119.

Silverstein, B., & Flamenbaum, C. (1989). Biases in the perception and cognition of the actions of enemies. *Journal of Social Issues, 45,* 51–72.

Simon, R. W., Eder, D., & Evans, C. (1992). The development of feeling norms underlying romantic love among adolescent females. *Social Psychology Quarterly, 55,* 29–46.

Simon, H. A. (1985). Human nature in politics: The dialogue of psychology with political science. *American Political Science Review, 79,* 293–304.

Simpson, J. A. (1990). Influence of attachment styles on romantic relationships. *Journal of Personality and Social Psychology, 59,* 971–980.

Simpson, J. A., Campbell, B., & Berscheid, E. (1986). The association between romantic love and marriage:

Kephart (1967) twice revisited. *Personality and Social Psychology Bulletin, 12,* 363–372.

Simpson, J. A., Gangestad, S. W., & Lerma, M. (1990). Perception of physical attractiveness: Mechanisms involved in the maintenance of romantic relationships. *Journal of Personality and Social Psychology, 59,* 1192–1201.

Simpson, J. A., Rholes, W. S., & Nelligan, J. S. (1992). Support seeking and support giving within couples in an anxiety-provoking situation: The role of attachment styles. *Journal of Personality and Social Psychology, 62,* 434–446.

Singer, E., Rogers, T. F., & Corcoran, M. (1987). The polls—a report: AIDS. *Public Opinion Quarterly, 51,* 580–595.

Sistrunk, F., & McDavid, J. W. (1971). Sex variable in conformity behavior. *Journal of Personality and Social Psychology, 17,* 200–207.

Six, B., & Eckes, T. (1991). A closer look at the complex structure of gender stereotypes. *Sex Roles, 24,* 57–71.

Skolnick, A. S. (1987). The intimate environment: Exploring marriage and the family. Boston: Little, Brown & Co.

Skolnick, P. (1977). Helping as a function of time of day, location, and sex of victim. *Journal of Social Psychology, 102,* 61–62.

Skov, R. B., & Sherman, S. J. (1986). Information-gathering processes: Diagnosticity, hypothesis-confirmatory strategies, and perceived hypothesis confirmation. *Journal of Experimental Social Psychology, 22,* 93–121.

Skrypnek, B. J., & Snyder, M. (1982). On the self-perpetuating nature of stereotypes about women and men. *Journal of Experimental Social Psychology, 18,* 277–291.

Slivken, K. E., & Buss, A. H. (1984). Misattribution and speech anxiety. *Journal of Personality and Social Psychology, 47,* 396–402.

Slochower, J., Wein, L., White, J., Firstenberg, S., & DiGuilio, J. (1980). Severe physical handicaps and helping behavior. *Journal of Social Psychology, 112,* 313–314.

Slovic, P., Fischhoff, B., & Lichtenstein, S. (1977). Behavioral decision theory. In M. R. Rosenzweig & L. W. Porter (Eds.), *Annual review of psychology* (Vol. 28, pp. 1–39). Palo Alto, CA: Annual Reviews.

Slusher, M. P., & Anderson, C. A. (1987). When reality monitoring fails: The role of imagination in stereotype maintenance. *Journal of Personality and Social Psychology, 52,* 653–662.

Smeaton, G., Byrne, D. (1987). The effects of R-rated violence and erotica, individual differences, and victim characteristics on acquaintance rape proclivity. *Journal of Research in Personality, 21,* 171–184.

Smith, E. E., & Medin, D. L. (1981). *Categories and concepts.* Cambridge, MA: Harvard University Press.

Smith, E. R. (1991). Illusory correlation in a simulated exemplar–based memory. *Journal of Personality and Social Psychology, 27,* 107–123.

Smith, E. R., & Lerner, M. (1986). Development of automatism of social judgments. *Journal of Personality and Social Psychology, 50,* 246–259.

Smith, L. (1992, October 30). Not only fun, but p. c. too. *Los Angeles Times,* E1, 8.

Smith, M. D., & Hand, C. (1987). The pornographic/aggression linkage: results from a field study. *Deviant Behavior, 8,* 389–399.

Smith, R. E. (1989). Effects of coping skills training on generalized self–efficacy and locus of control. *Journal of Personality and Social Psychology, 56,* 228–233.

Smith, S. H., Whitehead, G. J., III, & Sussman, N. M. (1990). The positivity bias in attributions: Two cross-cultural investigations. *Journal of Cross-Cultural Psychology, 21,* 283–301.

Smith, S. S., & Richardson, D. (1983). Amelioration of deception and harm in psychological research: The important role of debriefing. *Journal of Personality and Social Psychology, 44,* 1075–1082.

Smith, T. W. (1984). The polls: Gender and attitudes toward violence. *Public Opinion Quarterly, 48,* 384–396.

Smith, T. W. (1987). That which we call welfare by any other name would smell sweeter. *Public Opinion Quarterly, 51,* 75–83.

Smith, T. W. (1991). Ethnic images. GSS Topical Report No. 19. Chicago: National Opinion Research Center.

Smith, T. W. (1992). Changing racial labels: From colored to Negro to black to African American. GSS Topical Report No. 22. Chicago: National Opinion Research Center.

Smith, T. W., & Brown, P. C. (1991). Cynical hostility, attempts to exert social control, and cardiovascular reactivity in married couples. *Journal of Behavioral Medicine, 14,* 581–592.

Sniderman, P. M., & Brody, R. A. (1977). Coping: The ethic of self–reliance. *American Journal of Political Science, 21,* 501–522.

Snodgrass, S. E. (1992). Further effects of role versus gender on interpersonal sensitivity. *Journal of Personality and Social Psychology, 62,* 154–158.

Snow Country. (1991). Name that snow. *Snow Country, 4,* 32.

Snyder, C. R., & Fromkin, H. L. (1980). *Uniqueness: The human pursuit of difference.* New York: Plenum.

Snyder, C. R., & Higgins, R. L. (1988). Excuses: Their effective role in the negotiation of reality. *Psychological Bulletin, 104,* 23–35.

Snyder, C. R., Lassegard, M. A., & Ford, C. E. (1986). Distancing after group success and failure: Basking in reflected glory and cutting off reflected failure. *Journal of Personality and Social Psychology, 51(2),* 382–388.

Snyder, M. (1987). *Public appearances/private realities: The psychology of self-monitoring.* New York: Freeman.

Snyder, M., Berscheid, E., & Glick, R. P. (1985). Focusing on the exterior and the interior: Two investigations of the initiation of personal relationships. *Journal of Personality and Social Psychology, 48(6),* 1427–1439.

Snyder, M., & Gangestad, S. (1981). Hypothesis-testing processes. In J. H. Harvey, W. Ickes, & R. F. Kidd (Eds.), *New directions in attribution research* (Vol. 3, pp. 171–198). Hillsdale, NJ: Erlbaum.

Snyder, M., & Gangestad, S. (1986). On the nature of self-monitoring: Matters of assessment, matters of validity. *Journal of Personality and Social Psychology, 51,* 125–139.

Snyder, M., & Omoto, A. M. (1992a). Who helps and why? The psychology of AIDS volunteerism. In S. Spacapan & S. Oskamp (Eds.), *Helping and being helped in the real world* (pp. 213–239). Newbury Park, CA: Sage.

Snyder, M., & Omoto, A. M. (1992b). Volunteerism and society's response to the HIV epidemic. *Current Directions in Psychological Science, 1,* 113–116.

Snyder, M., & Swann, W. B., Jr. (1978). Hypothesis-testing processes in social interaction. *Journal of Personality and Social Psychology, 36,* 1202–1212.

Snyder, M., Tanke, E. D., & Berscheid, E. (1977). Social perception and interpersonal behavior: On the self-fulfilling

nature of social stereotypes. *Journal of Personality and Social Psychology, 35,* 656–666.

Sommer, R. (1969). *Personal space: The behavioral basis of design.* Englewood Cliffs, NJ: Prentice-Hall.

Sommer, R., & Olsen, H. (1980). The soft classroom. *Environment and Behavior, 12(1),* 3–16.

Sorenson, S. B., & White, J. W. (1992). Adult sexual assault: Overview of research. *Journal of Social Issues, 48,* 1–8.

Sorrentino, R. M., & Roney, C. J. R. (1986). Uncertainty, orientation, achievement-related motivation, and task diagnosticity as determinants of task performance. *Social Cognition, 4,* 420–436.

South, S. J., & Lloyd, K. M. (1992). Marriage opportunities and family formation: Further implications of imbalanced sex ratios. *Journal of Marriage and the Family, 54(2),* 440–451.

Spence, J. T. (1991). Do the BSRI and PAQ measure the same or different concepts? *Psychology of Women Quarterly, 15,* 141–165.

Spence, J. T., & Helmreich, R. L. (1978). *Masculinity and femininity: The psychological dimensions, correlates, and antecedents.* Austin: University of Texas Press.

Spencer, M. B., & Markstrom–Adams, C. (1990). Identity processes among racial and ethnic minority children in America. *Child Development, 61,* 290–310.

Spradley, J. P., & Phillips, M. (1972). Culture and stress: A quantitative analysis. *American Anthropologist, 74,* 518–529.

Sprafkin, J. N., Liebert, R. M., & Poulos, R. W. (1975). Effects of prosocial televised example on children's helping. *Journal of Experimental Child Psychology, 20,* 119–126.

Sprecher, S. (1992). How men and women expect to feel and behave in response to inequity in close relationships. *Social Psychology Quarterly, 55,* 57–69.

Sprecher, S., Aron, A., Hatfield, E., Cortese, A., Potapova, E., & Levitskaya, A. (1992, July). *Love: American style, Russian style, and Japanese style.* Paper presented at the sixth International Conference on Personal Relationships, Orono, Maine.

Srull, T. K., & Wyer, R. S., Jr. (1979). The role of category accessibility in the interpretation of information about persons: Some determinants and implications. *Journal of Personality and Social Psychology, 37,* 1660–1672.

Stagner, R. (1967). *Psychological aspects of international conflict.* Belmont, CA: Brooks/Cole Publishing Co.

Stangor, C. (1990). Arousal, accessibility of trait constructs, and person perception. *Journal of Experimental Social Psychology, 26,* 305–321.

Stangor, C., & Ruble, D. N. (1987). Development of gender role knowledge and gender constancy. In L. S. Liben & M. L. Signorella (Eds.), *Children's gender schemata,* pp. 5–22. San Francisco: Jossey-Bass.

Stangor, C., Sullivan, L. A., & Ford, T. E. (1991). Affective and cognitive determinants of prejudice. *Social Cognition, 9,* 359–380.

Stanley, S. M., & Markman, H. J. (1992). Assessing commitment in personal relationships. *Journal of Marriage and the Family, 54,* 595–608.

Staples, R., & Mirande, A. (1980). Racial and cultural variation among American families: A decennial review of the literature on minority families. *Journal of Marriage and the Family, 42,* 887–903.

Stasser, G., & Titus, W. (1985). Pooling of unshared information in group decision making: Biased information sampling during discussion. *Journal of Personality and Social Psychology, 48,* 1467–1478.

Statistical Abstract of the United States (1991). Washington, DC: U. S. Department of Commerce.

Steblay, N. M. (1987). Helping behavior in rural and urban environments: A meta-analysis. *Psychological Bulletin, 102,* 346–356.

Steele, C. M. (1988). The psychology of self-affirmation: Sustaining the integrity of the self. In L. Berkowitz (Ed.), *Advances in experimental psychology* (Vol. 21, pp. 261–302). New York: Academic Press.

Steele, C. M., & Southwick, L. (1985). Alcohol and social behavior. I: The psychology of drunken excess. *Journal of Personality and Social Psychology, 48,* 18–34.

Steele, D. V., Gotmann, M., Leventhal, H., & Easterling, D. (1983). Symptoms and attributions as determinants of health behavior. Unpublished manuscript, University of Wisconsin, Madison.

Stein, J. A., Fox, S. A., & Murata, P. J. (1991). The influence of ethnicity, socioeconomic status, and psychological barriers on use of mammography. *Journal of Health and Social Behavior, 32,* 101–113.

Stein, J. A., Newcomb, M. D., & Bentler, P. M. (1992). The effect of agency and communality on self-esteem: Gender differences in longitudinal data. *Sex Roles, 26,* 465–483.

Steiner, I. D. (1972). *Group process and productivity.* New York: Academic Press.

Stephan, F. F., & Mishler, E. G. (1952). The distribution of participation in small groups. *American Sociological Review, 17,* 598–608.

Stephan, W. G. (1985). Intergroup relations. In G. Lindzey and E. Aronson (Eds.), *Handbook of social psychology,* 3rd ed. (Vol. 2, pp. 599–658). New York: Random House.

Stern, P. C. (1992). Psychological dimensions of global environmental change. *Annual Review of Psychology, 43,* 269–302.

Sternberg, R. J., Conway, B. E., Ketron, J. L., & Bernstein, M. (1981). People's conceptions of intelligence. *Journal of Personality and Social Psychology, 41,* 37–55.

Stevens, G., Owens, D., & Schaefer, E. C. (1990). Education and attractiveness in marriage choices. *Social Psychology Quarterly, 53,* 62–70.

Stiff, J. B., Miller, G. R., Sleight, C., Mongeau, P., Garlick, R., & Rogan, R. (1989). Explanations for visual cue primacy in judgments of honesty and deceit. *Journal of Personality and Social Psychology, 56,* 555–564.

Stipek, D., Weiner, B., & Li, K. (1989). Testing some attribution–emotion relations in the People's Republic of China. *Journal of Personality and Social Psychology, 56,* 109–116.

Stipp, H., & Kerr, D. (1989). Determinants of public opinion about AIDS. *Public Opinion Quarterly, 53,* 98–106.

Stokols, D., & Altman, I. (Eds.). (1987). *Handbook of environmental psychology.* New York: Wiley.

Stone, A. A., Greenberg, M. A., Kennedy-Moore, E., & Newman, M. G. (1991). Self-report, situation-specific coping questionnaires: What are they measuring? *Journal of Personality and Social Psychology, 61,* 648–658.

Stoner, J. A. F. (1961). *A comparison of individual and group decisions involving risk.* Unpublished masters thesis. Cambridge, MA: Massachusetts Institute of Technology.

Storms, M. D. (1973). Videotape and the attribution process: Reversing actors' and observers' points of view. *Journal of Personality and Social Psychology, 27,* 165–175.

Stouffer, S. A., Suchman, E. A., DeVinney, L. C., Star, S. A.,

& Williams, R. M., Jr. (1949). *The American soldier: Adjustment during army life.* New York: Wiley.

Stover, R. G., & Hope, C. A. (1993). *Marriage, family, and intimate relations.* New York: Harcourt Brace Jovanovich.

Strack, S., Blaney, P. H., & Gschneidinger, R. J. (1985). Pessimistic self-preoccupation, performance deficits, and depression. *Journal of Personality and Social Psychology, 49,* 1076–1085.

Straus, M. A., & Gelles, R. J. (1986). Societal change and change in family violence from 1975 to 1985 as revealed by two national surveys. *Journal of Marriage and the Family, 48,* 465–479.

Straus, M. A., Gelles, R. J., & Steinmetz, S. K. (1981). *Behind closed doors: Violence in the American family.* Garden City, NY: Doubleday/Anchor.

Strayer, F. F., Wareing, S., & Rushton, J. P. (1979). Social constraints on naturally occurring preschool altruism. *Ethology and Sociobiology, 1,* 3–11.

Struch, N., & Schwartz, S. H. (1989). Intergroup aggression: Its predictors and distinctness from in-group bias. *Journal of Personality and Social Psychology, 56,* 364–373.

Suedfeld, P., & Rank, D. (1976). Revolutionary leaders: Long-term success as a function of changes in conceptual complexity. *Journal of Personality and Social Psychology, 34,* 169–178.

Suedfeld, P., & Tetlock, P. E. (1977). Integrative complexity of communications in international crises. *Journal of Conflict Resolution, 21,* 169–184.

Sullivan, J. L., Piereson, J., & Marcus, G. E. (1982). *Political tolerance and American democracy.* Chicago: University of Chicago Press.

Suls, J., & Fletcher, B. (1985). The relative efficacy of avoidant and nonavoidant coping strategies: A meta-analysis. *Health Psychology, 4,* 249–288.

Suls, J., & Mullen, B. (1981). Life change in psychological distress: The role of perceived control and desirability. *Journal of Applied Social Psychology, 11,* 379–389.

Sundstrom, E., & Sundstrom, M. G. (1977). Personal space invasions: What happens when the invader asks permission? *Environmental Psychology and Nonverbal Behavior, 2,* 76–82.

Surgeon General's Scientific Advisory Committee. (1972). *Television and growing up: The impact of televised violence: Report to the Surgeon General.* U. S. Public Health Service, Dept. of Health, Education, and Welfare Publication N. HSM 72–9090. Rockville, MD: National Institute of Mental Health.

Surra, C. A. (1990). Research and theory on mate selection and premarital relationships in the 1980s. *Journal of Marriage and the Family, 52,* 844–865.

Surra, C. A., & Longstreth, M. (1990). Similarity of outcomes, interdependence, and conflict in dating relationships. *Journal of Personality and Social Psychology, 59,* 501–516.

Sussman, N. M., & Rosenfeld, H. M. (1982). Influence of culture, language, and sex on conversational distance. *Journal of Personality and Social Psychology, 42,* 66–74.

Swann, W. B., Jr. (1983). Self–verification: Bringing social reality into harmony with the self. In J. Suls & A. G. Greenwald (Eds.), *Social psychology perspectives* (Vol. 2, pp. 33–66). Hillsdale, NJ: Erlbaum.

Swann, W. B., Jr. (1984). Quest for accuracy in person perception: A matter of pragmatics. *Psychological Review, 91,* 457–477.

Swann, W. B., Jr., & Ely, R. J. (1984). A battle of wills: Self-verification versus behavioral confirmation. *Journal of Personality and Social Psychology, 46,* 1287–1302.

Swann, W. B., Jr., Giulano, T., & Wegner, D. M. (1982). Where leading questions can lead: The power of conjecture in social interaction. *Journal of Personality and Social Psychology, 42,* 1025–1035.

Swann, W. B., Jr., & Hill, C. A. (1982). When our identities are mistaken: Reaffirming self-conceptions through social interaction. *Journal of Personality and Social Psychology, 43,* 59–66.

Swann, W. B., Jr., & Pelham, B. W. (1990). *Embracing the bitter truth: Positivity and authenticity in social relationships.* Unpublished manuscript, University of Texas, Austin.

Swann, W. B., Jr., & Read, S. J. (1981a). Acquiring self-knowledge: The search for feedback that fits. *Journal of Personality and Social Psychology, 41,* 1119–1128.

Swann, W. B., Jr., & Read, S. J. (1981b). Self-verification processes: How we sustain our self-conceptions. *Journal of Experimental Social Psychology, 17,* 351–370.

Swann, W. B., Jr., Stein-Seroussi, A., & Giesler, R. B. (1992). Why people self-verify. *Journal of Personality and Social Psychology, 62,* 392–401.

Swann, W. B., Jr., & Stephenson, B. (1981). Curiosity and control: On the determinants of the search for social knowledge. *Journal of Personality and Social Psychology, 40,* 635–642.

Sweeney, P. D., Anderson, K., & Bailey, S. (1986). Attributional style in depression: A meta-analytic review. *Journal of Personality and Social Psychology, 50,* 974–991.

Swenson, C. H. (1972). The behavior of love. In H. A. Otto (Ed.), *Love today* (pp. 86–101). New York: Dell.

Swim, J., Borgida, E., Maruyama, G., & Myers, D. G. (1989). Joan McKay versus John McKay: Do gender stereotypes bias evaluations? *Psychological Bulletin, 105,* 409–429.

Symons, D. (1979). *The evolution of human sexuality.* New York: Oxford University Press.

Tajfel, H. (1969). Cognitive aspects of prejudice. *Journal of Social Issues, 25,* 79–97.

Tajfel, H. (1981). *Human groups and social categories.* Cambridge, England: Cambridge University Press.

Tajfel, H. (Ed.). (1982). *Social identity and intergroup relations.* Cambridge, England: Cambridge University Press.

Tajfel, H., Billig, M. G., Bundy, R. P., & Flament, C. (1971). Social categorization and intergroup behavior. *European Journal of Social Psychology, 1,* 149–178.

Tajfel, H., & Turner, J. C. (1986). The social identity theory of intergroup behavior. In S. Worchel & W. G. Austin (Eds.), *Psychology of Intergroup Relations,* 2nd ed. (pp. 7–24). Chicago: Nelson-Hall.

t'Hart, P. (1990). *Groupthink in government: A study of small groups and policy failure.* Rockland, MA: Swets & Zeitlinger.

t'Hart, P. (1991). Irving L. Janis' victims of groupthink. *Political Psychology, 12,* 247–279.

Takata, T. (1987). Self-deprecative tendencies in self-evaluation through social comparison. *Japanese Journal of Experimental Social Psychology, 27,* 27–36.

Tanford, S., & Penrod, S. (1984). Social influence model: A formal integration of research on majority and minority influence processes. *Psychological Bulletin, 95,* 189–225.

Taylor, D. A., & Katz, P. A. (1988). Conclusion. In P. A. Katz & D. A. Taylor (Eds.), *Eliminating racism: Profiles in controversy* (pp. 359–369). New York: Plenum.

Taylor, D. W., Berry, P. C., & Block, C. H. (1958). Does group participation when using brainstorming facilitate or inhibit creative thinking? *Administrative Science Quarterly, 2,* 23–47.

Taylor, J., & Riess, M. (1989). "Self-serving" attributions to valenced causal factors: A field experiment. *Personality and Social Psychology Bulletin, 15,* 337–348.

Taylor, S. E. (1975). On inferring one's attitudes from one's behavior: Some delimiting conditions. *Journal of Personality and Social Psychology, 31,* 126–131.

Taylor, S. E. (1979). Hospital patient behavior: Reactance, helplessness, or control? *Journal of Social Issues, 35,* 156–184.

Taylor, S. E. (1981a). The interface of cognitive and social psychology. In J. H. Harvey (Ed.), *Cognition, social behavior, and the environment* (pp. 189–212). Hillsdale, NJ: Erlbaum.

Taylor, S. E. (1981b). A categorization approach to stereotyping. In D. L. Hamilton (Ed.), *Cognitive processes in stereotyping and intergroup behavior* (pp. 83–114). Hillsdale, NJ: Erlbaum.

Taylor, S. E. (1981c). The impact of health institutions on recipients of services. In A. Johnson, O. Grusky, & B. Raven (Eds.), *Contemporary health services: A social science perspective* (pp. 103–137). Boston: Auburn House.

Taylor, S. E. (1982). Social cognition and health. *Personality and Social Psychology Bulletin, 8,* 549–562.

Taylor, S. E. (1983). Adjustment to threatening events: A theory of cognitive adaptation. *American Psychologist, 38,* 1161–1173.

Taylor, S. E. (1990). Health psychology: The science and the field. *American Psychologist, 45,* 40–50.

Taylor, S. E. (1991a). Asymmetrical effects of positive and negative events: The mobilization-minimization hypothesis. *Psychological Bulletin, 110,* 67–85.

Taylor, S. E. (1991b). *Health psychology* (2nd ed.). New York: Random House.

Taylor, S. E., & Aspinwall, L. G. (1990). Psychological aspects of chronic illness. In G. R. VandenBos & P. T. Costa, Jr. (Eds.), *Psychological aspects of serious illness* (pp. 3–60). Washington, DC: American Psychological Association.

Taylor, S. E., & Brown, J. D. (1988). Illusion and well-being: A social psychological perspective on mental health. *Psychological Bulletin, 103,* 193–210.

Taylor, S. E., & Clark, L. F. (1986). Does information improve adjustment to noxious events? In M. J. Saks & L. Saxe (Eds.), *Advances in applied social psychology* (Vol. 3, pp. 1–28). Hillsdale, NJ: Erlbaum.

Taylor, S. E., & Crocker, J. (1981). Schematic bases of social information processing. In E. T. Higgins, C. P. Herman, & M. P. Zanna (Eds.), *Social cognition: The Ontario symposium* (Vol. 1, pp. 89–134). Hillsdale, NJ: Erlbaum.

Taylor, S. E., Crocker, J., Fiske, S. T., Sprinzen, M., & Winkler, J. D. (1979). The generalizability of salience effects. *Journal of Personality and Social Psychology, 37,* 357–368.

Taylor, S. E., & Fiske, S. T. (1975). Point of view and perceptions of causality. *Journal of Personality and Social Psychology, 32,* 439–445.

Taylor, S. E., & Fiske, S. T. (1978). Salience, attention, and attribution: Top of the head phenomena. In L. Berkowitz (Ed.), *Advances in experimental social psychology* (Vol. 11, pp. 249–288). New York: Academic Press.

Taylor, S. E., Fiske, S. T., Close, M., Anderson, C., & Ruderman, A. (1977). *Solo status as a psychological variable:*

The power of being distinctive. Unpublished manuscript, Harvard University, Cambridge, MA.

Taylor, S. E., Fiske, S. T., Eticoff, N. C., & Ruderman, A. J. (1978). Categorical and contextual bases of person memory. *Journal of Personality and Social Psychology, 36,* 778–793.

Taylor, S. E., Helgeson, V. S., Reed, G. M., & Skokan, L. A. (1991). Self–generated feelings of control and adjustment to physical illness. *Journal of Social Issues, 47,* 91–109.

Taylor, S. E., Kemeny, M. E., Aspinwall, L. G., Schneider, S. G., Rodriguez, R., & Herbert, M. (in press). Optimism, coping, psychological distress, and high-risk sexual behavior among men at risk for AIDS. *Journal of Personality and Social Psychology.*

Taylor, S. E., & Koivumaki, J. H. (1976). The perception of self and others: Acquaintanceship, affect, and actor-observer differences. *Journal of Personality and Social Psychology, 33,* 403–408.

Taylor, S. E., Lichtman, R. R., & Wood, J. V. (1984). Attributions, beliefs about control, and adjustment to breast cancer. *Journal of Personality and Social Psychology, 46,* 489–502.

Taylor, S. E., & Lobel, M. (1989). Social comparison activity under threat: Downward evaluation and upward contacts. *Psychological Review, 96,* 569–575.

Taylor, S. E., & Thompson, S. C. (1982). Stalking the elusive "vividness" effect. *Psychological Review, 89,* 155–181.

Taylor, S. P., & Gammon, C. B. (1975). Effects of type and dose of alcohol on human physical aggression. *Journal of Personality and Social Psychology, 32,* 169–175.

Taylor, S. P., Gammon, C. B., & Capasso, D. R. (1976). Aggression as a function of the interaction of alcohol and threat. *Journal of Personality and Social Psychology, 34,* 938–941.

Taylor, S. P., Schmutte, G. T., Leonard, K. E., & Cranston, J. W. (1979). The effects of alcohol and extreme provocation on the use of a highly noxious electrical shock. *Motivation and Emotion, 3,* 73–81.

Taylor, S. P., & Sears, J. D. (1988). The effects of alcohol and persuasive social pressure on human physical aggression. *Aggressive Behavior, 14,* 237–243.

Taynor, J., & Deaux, K. (1973). When women are more deserving than men: Equity, attribution and perceived sex difference. *Journal of Personality and Social Psychology, 28,* 360–367.

Taynor, J., & Deaux, K. (1975). Equity and perceived sex differences: Role of behavior as defined by the task, the mode and the action. *Journal of Personality and Social Psychology, 32,* 381–390.

Tedesco, L. A., Keffer, M. A., & Fleck-Kandath, C. (1991). Self-efficacy, reasoned action, and oral health behavior reports: A social cognitive approach to compliance. *Journal of Behavioral Medicine, 14,* 341–356.

Tedin, K. L. (1974). The influence of parents on the political attitudes of adolescents. *American Political Science Review, 68,* 1579–1592.

Tenenbaum, G., & Furst, D. M. (1986). Consistency of attributional responses by individuals and groups differing in gender, perceived ability and expectations for success. *British Journal of Social Psychology, 25,* 315–321.

Tesser, A. (1988). Toward a self–evaluation maintenance model of social behavior. In L. Berkowitz (Ed.), *Advances in experimental social psychology,* (Vol. 21, pp. 181–227). New York: Academic Press.

Tesser, A., & Collins, J. E. (1988). Emotion in social reflection and comparison situations: Intuitive, systematic, and exploratory approaches. *Journal of Personality and Social Psychology, 55,* 695–709.

Tesser, A., & Conlee, M. C. (1975). Some effects of time and thought on attitude polarization. *Journal of Personality and Social Psychology, 31,* 262–270.

Tesser, A., & Paulhus, D. (1983). The definition of self: Private and public self-evaluation maintenance strategies. *Journal of Personality and Social Psychology, 44,* 672–682.

Tesser, A., Pilkington, C. J., & McIntosh, W. D. (1989). Self-evaluation maintenance and the mediational role of emotion: The perception of friends and strangers. *Journal of Personality and Social Psychology, 57,* 442–456.

Tessler, R. C., & Schwartz, S. H. (1972). Help-seeking, self-esteem, and achievement motivation: An attributional analysis. *Journal of Personality and Social Psychology, 27,* 318–326.

Tetlock, P. E. (1983). Policymakers' images of international conflict. *Journal of Social Issues, 39,* 67–86.

Tetlock, P. E. (1985). Accountability: A social check on the fundamental attribution error. *Social Psychology Quarterly, 48,* 227–236.

Tetlock, P. E., & Boettger, R. (1989). Accountability: A social magnifier of the dilution effect. *Journal of Personality and Social Psychology, 57,* 388–398.

Tetlock, P. E., Peterson, R. S., McGuire, C., Chang, S., & Feld, P. (1992). Assessing political group dynamics: A test of the groupthink model. *Journal of Personality and Social Psychology, 63,* 403–425.

Tetlock, P. E., Skitka, L., & Boettger, R. (1989). Social and cognitive strategies for coping with accountability, conformity, complexity and bolstering. *Journal of Personality and Social Psychology, 57,* 632–640.

Thibaut, J. W., & Kelley, H. H. (1959). *The social psychology of groups.* New York: Wiley.

Thibodeau, R. (1989). From racism to tokenism: The changing face of blacks in *New Yorker* cartoons. *Public Opinion Quarterly, 53,* 482–494.

Thompson, S. C. (1981). Will it hurt less if I can control it? A complex answer to a simple question. *Psychological Bulletin, 90,* 89–101.

Thompson, S. C., & Kelley, H. H. (1981). Judgments of responsibility for activities in close relationships. *Journal of Personality and Social Psychology, 41,* 469–477.

Thompson, V. L. S. (1990). Factors affecting the level of African American identification. *The Journal of Black Psychology, 17,* 19–35.

Thompson, V. L. S. (1991). Perceptions of race and race relations which affect African American identification. *Journal of Applied Social Psychology, 21,* 1502–1516.

Thompson, W. C., Cowan, C. L., & Rosenhan, D. L. (1980). Focus of attention mediates the impact of negative affect on altruism. *Journal of Personality and Social Psychology, 38,* 291–300.

Thoreson, C. E., & Mahoney, M. J. (1974). *Behavioral self-control.* New York: Holt.

Thornton, B., Ryckman, R. M., Kirchner, G., Jacobs, J., Kaczor, L., & Kuehnel, R. H. (1988). Reaction to self–attributed victim responsibility: A comparative analysis of rape crisis counselors and lay observers. *Journal of Applied Social Psychology, 18,* 409–422.

Tice, D. M. (1991). Esteem protection or enhancement? Self–

handicapping motives and attributions differ by trait self–esteem. *Journal of Personality and Social Psychology, 60,* 711–725.

Tilker, H. A. (1970). Socially responsible behavior as a function of observer responsibility and victim feedback. *Journal of Personality and Social Psychology, 14,* 95–100.

Tillman, W. S., & Carver, C. S. (1980). Actors' and observers' attributions for success and failure: A comparative test of predictions from Kelley's cube, self-serving bias, and positivity bias formulations. *Journal of Experimental Social Psychology, 16,* 18–32.

Ting–Toomey, S. (1991). Intimacy expression in three cultures: France, Japan, and the United States. *International Journal of Intercultural Relations, 15,* 29–46.

Togeby, L. (1992). The gender gap in foreign policy attitudes: Why are women more liberal than men? Paper presented at the annual meeting of the American Political Science Association, Chicago.

Toi, M., & Batson, C. D. (1982). More evidence that empathy is a source of altruistic motivation. *Journal of Personality and Social Psychology, 43,* 281–292.

Toobert, D. J., & Glasgow, R. E. (1991). Problem solving and diabetes self-care. *Journal of Behavioral Medicine, 14,* 71–86.

Top, T. J. (1991). Sex bias in the evaluation of performance in the scientific, artistic, and literary professions: A review. *Sex Roles, 24,* 73–106.

Toris, C., & DePaulo, B. M. (1984). Effects of actual deception and suspiciousness of deception on interpersonal perceptions. *Journal of Personality and Social Psychology, 47,* 1063–1073.

Trafimow, D., Triandis, H. C., & Goto, S. G. (1991). Some tests of the distinction between the private self and the collective self. *Journal of Personality and Social Psychology, 60,* 649–655.

Triandis, H. C. (1989). The self and social behavior in differing cultural contexts. *Psychological Review, 96,* 506–520.

Triandis, H. C. (1990). Cross-cultural studies of individualism and collectivism. In J. Berman (Ed.), *Nebraska Symposium on Motivation, 1989* (pp. 41–122). Lincoln: University of Nebraska Press.

Triandis, H. C., Bontempo, R., Villareal, M. J., Asai, M., & Lucca, N. (1988). Individualism and collectivism: Cross-cultural perspectives on self-ingroup relationships. *Journal of Personality and Social Psychology, 54,* 323–338.

Triandis, H. C., McCusker, C., & Hui, C. H. (1990). Multimethod probes of individualism and collectivism. *Journal of Personality and Social Psychology, 59,* 1006–1020.

Trimble, J. E. (1988). Stereotypical images, American Indians, and prejudice. In P. A. Katz & D. A. Taylor (Eds.), *Eliminating racism: Profiles in controversy* (pp. 181–202). New York: Plenum.

Triplett, N. (1898). The dynamogenic factors in pacemaking and competition. *American Journal of Psychology, 9,* 507–533.

Trivers, R. L. (1971). The evolution of reciprocal altruism. *Quarterly Review of Biology, 46,* 35–57.

Trope, Y. (1975). Seeking information about one's own ability as a determinant of choice among tasks. *Journal of Personality and Social Psychology, 32,* 1004–1013.

Trope, Y. (1979). Uncertainty–reducing properties of achievement tasks. *Journal of Personality and Social Psychology, 37,* 1505–1518.

Trope, Y. (1980). Self–assessment, self-enhancement, and taste preference. *Journal of Experimental Social Psychology, 16,* 116–129.

Trope, Y. (1983). Self–assessment in achievement behavior. In J. M. Suls & A. G. Carver (Eds.), *Psychological perspectives on the self* (Vol. 2, pp. 93–122). Hillsdale, NJ: Erlbaum.

Trope, Y. (1986). Identification and inferential processes in dispositional attribution. *Psychological Review, 93,* 239–257.

Trope, Y., & Bassok, M. (1982). Confirmatory and diagnosing strategies in social information gathering. *Journal of Personality and Social Psychology, 43,* 22–34.

Trope, Y., & Mackie, D. M. (1987). Sensitivity to alternatives in social hypothesis–testing. *Journal of Experimental Social Psychology, 23,* 445–459.

Trost, M. R., Maass, A., & Kenrick, D. T. (1992). Minority influence: Personal relevance biases cognitive processes and reverses private acceptance. *Journal of Experimental Social Psychology, 28,* 234–254.

Trzebinski, J., & Richards, K. (1986). The role of goal categories in person impression. *Journal of Experimental Social Psychology, 22,* 216–227.

Tucker, M. B. (1986). Sex ratio imbalance among Los Angeles Afro-Americans. *ISSR Working Papers in the Social Sciences, 24*(4). Los Angeles: Institute for Social Science Research, University of California.

Tucker, M. B., & Mitchell-Kernan (1990). New trends in black American interracial marriage: The social structural context. *Journal of Marriage and the Family, 52,* 209–218.

Turk, D. C., & Kerns, R. D. (1985). *Health, illness, and families: A life–span perspective.* New York: Wiley.

Turk, D. C., & Meichenbaum, D. (1989). Adherence to self-care regimens: The patient's perspective. In R. H. Rozensky, J. J. Sweet, & S. M. Tovian (Eds.), *Handbook of clinical psychology in medical settings.* New York: Plenum.

Turk, D. C., Rudy, T. E., & Salovey, P. (1986). Implicit models of illness. *Journal of Behavioral Medicine, 9,* 453–474.

Turner, R. H. (1962). Role-taking: Process versus conformity. In A. H. Rose (Ed.), *Human behavior and social processes: An interactionist approach.* Boston: Houghton Mifflin.

Tversky, A., & Kahneman, D. (1973). Availability: A heuristic for judging frequency and probability. *Cognitive Psychology, 5,* 207–232.

Tversky, A., & Kahneman, D. (1974). Judgment under uncertainty: Heuristics and biases. *Science, 185,* 1124–1131.

Tyler, T. R., & Devintz, V. (1981). Self-serving bias in the attribution of responsibility: Cognitive versus motivational explanations. *Journal of Experimental Social Psychology, 17,* 408–416.

Tyler, T. R., & Sears, D. O. (1977). Coming to like obnoxious people when we must live with them. *Journal of Personality and Social Psychology, 35,* 200–211.

Ugwuegbu, D. C. E. (1979). Racial and evidential factors in juror attribution of legal responsibility. *Journal of Experimental Social Psychology, 15,* 133–146.

Unger, R., & Crawford, M. (1992). *Women and gender: A feminist psychology.* New York: McGraw-Hill.

U.S. Bureau of the Census (1990). *Statistical abstract of the United States, 1990.* Washington, DC: Government Printing Office.

U.S. Merit Systems Protection Board. (1981). *Sexual harassment in the Federal workplace: Is it a problem?* Washington, DC: Office of Merit Systems Review and Studies.

Uzark, K. C., Becker, M. H., Dielman, T. W., & Rocchini, A. P. (1987). Psychosocial predictors of compliance with a weight control intervention for obese children and adolescents. *Journal of Compliance in Health Care, 2,* 167–178.

Valins, S. (1966). Cognitive effects of false heart-rate feedback. *Journal of Personality and Social Psychology, 4,* 400–408.

Vallacher, R. R., & Wegner, D. M. (1987). What do people think they're doing? Action identification and human behavior. *Psychological Review, 94,* 3–15.

Vallacher, R. R., & Wegner, D. M. (1989). Levels of personal agency: Individual variation in action identification. *Journal of Personality and Social Psychology, 57,* 660–671.

Vallacher, R. R., Wegner, D. M., & Frederick, J. (1987). The presentation of self through action identification. *Social Cognition, 5,* 301–322.

Vallacher, R. R., Wegner, D. M., & Somoza, M. P. (1989). That's easy for you to say: Action identification and speech fluency. *Journal of Personality and Social Psychology, 56,* 199–208.

Vallone, R. P., Griffin, D. W., Lin, S., & Ross, L. (1990). Overconfident prediction of future actions and outcomes by self and others. *Journal of Personality and Social Psychology, 58,* 582–592.

Valois, P., Desharnis, R., & Godin, G. (1988). A comparison of the Fishbein and Ajzen and the Triandis attitudinal models for the prediction of exercise intention and behavior. *Journal of Behavioral Medicine, 11,* 459–472.

Van der Velde, F., & Van der Pligt, J. (1991). AIDS-related health behavior: Coping, protection motivation, and previous behavior. *Journal of Behavioral Medicine, 14,* 429–452.

Van Heck, G. L., & Dijkstra, P. (1985). The scope and generality of self-other asymmetry in person perception. *European Journal of Social Psychology, 15,* 125–145.

Van Yperen, N. W., & Buunk, B. P. (1990). A longitudinal study of equity and satisfaction in intimate relationships. *European Journal of Social Psychology, 20,* 287–309.

Van Yperen, N. W., & Buunk, B. P. (1991). Sex-role attitudes, social comparison, and satisfaction with relationships. *Social Psychology Quarterly, 54,* 169–180.

Vanneman, R. D., & Pettigrew, T. F. (1972). Race and relative deprivation in the urban United States. *Race, 13,* 461–486.

Vinsel, A., Brown, B. B., Altman, I., & Foss, C. (1980). Privacy regulation, territorial displays, and effective individual functioning. *Journal of Personality and Social Psychology, 39*(6), 1104–1115.

Viemero, V., & Paajanen, S. (1992). The role of fantasies and dreams in the TV viewing-aggression relationship. *Aggressive Behavior, 18,* 109–116.

Vitaliano, P. P., DeWolfe, D. J., Maiuro, R. D., Russo, J., & Katon, W. (1990). Appraised changeability of a stress as a modifier of the relationship between coping and depression: A test of the hypothesis of fit. *Journal of Personality and Social Psychology, 59,* 582–592.

Von Baeyer, C. L., Sherk, D. L., & Zanna, M. P. (1981). Impression management in the job interview: When the female applicant meets the male (chauvinist) interviewer. *Personality and Social Psychology Bulletin, 7*(1), 45–52.

Vogel, D. A., Lake, M. A., Evans, S., & Karraker, K. H. (1991). Children's and adults' sex-stereotyped perceptions of infants. *Sex Roles, 24,* 605–616.

Volpato, C., Maass, A., Mucchi-Faina, A., & Vitti, E. (1990). Minority influence and social categorization. *European Journal of Social Psychology, 20,* 119–132.

Wagner, H. L., MacDonald, C. J., & Manstead, A. S. R. (1986). Communication of individual emotions by spontaneous facial expressions. *Journal of Personality and Social Psychology, 50,* 737–743.

Walker, I., & Mann, L. (1987). Unemployment, relative deprivation, and social protest. *Personality and Social Psychology Bulletin, 13,* 275–283.

Wall, J. A., Jr. (1977). Operantly conditioning a negotiator's concession making. *Journal of Experimental Social Psychology, 13,* 431–440.

Wallbott, H. H., & Scherer, K. R. (1986). Cues and channels in emotion recognition. *Journal of Personality and Social Psychology, 51,* 690–699.

Waller, W. (1938). *The family: A dynamic interpretation.* New York: Dryden Press.

Wallerstein, J. S., & Kelly, J. B. (1975). The effects of parental divorce: Experiences of the preschool child. *Journal of the American Academy of Child Psychiatry, 14,* 600–616.

Wallston, B. S., Alagna, S. W., DeVellis, B. McE., & DeVellis, R. F. (1983). Social support and physical health. *Health Psychology, 2,* 367–391.

Walsh, R. P., Swenson, L. C., Ingham, M., & Testa, C. (1992, April). *Constructing materials that attract dates in a video dating service.* Paper presented at the annual meeting of the Western Psychological Association, Portland, Oregon.

Walster, E., Aronson, E., & Abrahams, D. (1966). On increasing the persuasiveness of a low-prestige communicator. *Journal of Experimental Social Psychology, 2,* 325–343.

Walster, E., & Walster, G. W. (1963). Effects of expecting to be liked on choice of associates. *Journal of Abnormal and Social Psychology, 67,* 402–404.

Walster, E., Walster, G. W., & Berscheid, E. (1978). *Equity: Theory and research.* Boston: Allyn & Bacon.

Walster, E., Walster, G. W., & Traupmann, J. (1978). Equity and premarital sex. *Journal of Personality and Social Psychology, 36,* 82–92.

Walster, E., Aronson, E., Abrahams, D., & Rottman, L. (1966). Importance of physical attractiveness in dating behavior. *Journal of Personality and Social Psychology, 4,* 508–516.

Waltz, M. (1986). Marital context and post-infarction quality of life: Is it social support or something more? *Social Science and Medicine, 22,* 791–805.

Ware, J. E., Jr., Davies-Avery, A., & Steward, A. L. (1978). The measurement and meaning of patient satisfaction: A review of the literature. *The Health and Medical Care Services Review, 1,* 1–15.

Warner, M. G., & Fineman, H. (1988, September 26). Bush's media wizard: A down-and-dirty street fighter reshapes the veep. *Newsweek,* 19–20.

Watanabe, T. (1992, October 27). "Doll wars" challenge female ideal. *Los Angeles Times,* H2.

Waterman, A. S., & Archer, S. L. (1990). A life-span perspective on identity formation: Developments in form, function, and process. In P. B. Baltes, D. L. Featherman, & R. M. Lerner (Eds.), *Life-span development and behavior* (Vol. 10, pp. 29–57). Hillsdale, NJ: Erlbaum.

Watkins, M. (1978, January 9). Why N.B.A. teams succeed at home. *The New York Times,* p. C–23.

Watson, D. (1982). The actor and the observer: How are their perceptions of causality different? *Psychological Bulletin, 92,* 682–700.

Watson, D. (1989). Strangers' ratings of the five robust personality factors: Evidence of a surprising convergence with self-report. *Journal of Personality and Social Psychology, 57,* 120–128.

Watson, D., & Pennebaker, J. W. (1989). Health complaints, stress, and distress: Exploring the central role of negative affectivity. *Psychological Review, 96,* 234–254.

Wattenberg, M. P. (1984). *The decline of American political parties, 1952–1980.* Cambridge, MA: Harvard University Press.

Weary, G., Jordon, J. S., & Hill, M. G. (1985). The attributional norm of internality and depressive sensitivity to social information. *Journal of Personality and Social Psychology, 49,* 1283–1293.

Webb, B., Worchel, S., Riechers, L., & Wayne, W. (1986). The influence of categorization on perceptions of crowding. *Personality and Social Psychology Bulletin, 12*(4), 539–546.

Weber, S. J., & Cook, T. D. (1972). Subject effects in laboratory research: An examination of subject roles, demand characteristics, and valid inferences. *Psychological Bulletin, 77,* 273–295.

Weber, R., & Crocker, J. (1983). Cognitive process in the revision of stereotypic beliefs. *Journal of Personality and Social Psychology, 45,* 961–977.

Wegner, D. M., & Crano, W. D. (1975). Racial factors in helping behavior: An unobtrusive field experiment. *Journal of Personality and Social Psychology, 32,* 901–905.

Wegner, D. M., Vallacher, R. R., Kiersted, G. W., & Dizadji, D. (1986). Action identification in the emergence of social behavior. *Social Cognition, 4,* 18–38.

Weigel, R. H., Loomis, J. W., & Soja, M. J. (1980). Race relations on prime time television. *Journal of Personality and Social Psychology, 39,* 884–893.

Weiner, B. (1979). A theory of motivation for some classroom experience. *Journal of Educational Psychology, 71,* 3–25.

Weiner, B. (1980). A cognitive (attribution)-emotion-action model of motivated behavior: An analysis of judgments of help-giving. *Journal of Personality and Social Psychology, 39,* 186–200.

Weiner, B. (1982). The emotional consequences of causal attributions. In M. S. Clark & S. T. Fiske (Eds.), *Affect and cognition: The 17th annual Carnegie Symposium on Cognition* (pp. 185–210). Hillsdale, NJ: Erlbaum.

Weiner, B. (1986). *An attributional theory of motivation and emotion.* New York: Springer–Verlag.

Weiner, B. (1990). On perceiving the other as responsible. *Nebraska Symposium on Motivation, 38,* 165–198.

Weiner, B., Amirkhan, J., Folkes, V. S., & Verette, J. A. (1987). An attributional analysis of excuse giving: Studies of a naive theory of emotion. *Journal of Personality and Social Psychology, 52,* 316–324.

Weiner, B., Perry, R. P., & Magnusson, J. (1988). An attributional analysis of reactions to stigmas. *Journal of Personality and Social Psychology, 55,* 738–748.

Weiner, B., Russell, D., & Lerman, D. (1979). The cognition-emotion process in achievement-related contexts. *Journal of Personality and Social Psychology, 37,* 1211–1220.

Weisberg, H. F., & Smith, C. E., Jr. (1991). The influence of the economy on party identification in the Reagan years. *Journal of Politics, 53,* 1077–1092.

Weiss, R. L., & Heyman, R. E. (1990). Observation of marital interaction. In F. D. Fincham & T. N. Bradbury (Eds.), *The psychology of marriage: Basic issues and applications.* (pp. 87– 117). New York: Guilford Press.

Weiss, R. S. (1973). *Loneliness: The experience of emotional and social isolation.* Cambridge, MA: MIT Press.

Weiss, R. S. (1974). The provisions of social relationships. In Z. Rubin (Ed.), *Doing unto others.* Englewood Cliffs, NJ: Prentice–Hall.

Welch, M. R., & Leege, D. C. (1992). Abortion attitudes and the potential for political mobilization among American Catholics: Symbolic politics, boundary maintenance, and the power of a galvanizing issue. Paper presented at the annual meeting of the American Political Science Association, Chicago.

Weldon, E., & Gargano, G. M. (1988). *Personality and Social Psychology Bulletin, 14,* 159–171.

Wells, G. L., & Gavanski, I. (1989). Mental stimulation of causality. *Journal of Personality and Social Psychology, 56,* 161–169.

Wells, G. L., Taylor, B. R., & Turtle, J. W. (1987). The undoing of scenarios. *Journal of Personality and Social Psychology, 53,* 421–430.

Wells, W. D. (1973). *Television and aggression: Replication of an experimental field study.* Unpublished manuscript, Graduate School of Business, University of Chicago.

Werner, C. M., Brown, B. B., & Damron, G. (1981). Territorial marking in a game arcade. *Journal of Personality and Social Psychology, 41*(6), 1094–1104.

Westen, D. (1988). Transference and information processing. *Clinical Psychology Review, 8,* 161–179.

Wetzel, C. G., & Walton, M. D. (1985). Developing biased social judgments: The false-consensus effect. *Journal of Personality and Social Psychology, 49,* 1352–1359.

Wheeler, L., Reis, H. T., & Bond, M. H. (1989). Collectivism-individualism in everyday social life: The Middle Kingdom and the melting pot. *Journal of Personality and Social Psychology, 57,* 79–86.

White, G. L. (1976). *The social psychology of romantic jealousy.* Doctoral dissertation, University of California, Los Angeles, University of Microfilms No. 77–7700.

White, G. L., & Mullen, P. E. (1989). *Jealousy: Theory, research, and clinical strategies.* New York: Guilford Press.

White, J. W., & Sorenson, S. B. (1992). A sociocultural view of sexual assault: From discrepancy to diversity. *Journal of Social Issues, 48,* 187–195.

White, P. A. (1991). Ambiguity in the internal/external distinction in causal attribution. *Journal of Experimental Social Psychology, 27,* 259–270.

White, R. K. (1970). *Nobody wanted war: Misperception in Vietnam and other wars.* Garden City, NY: Doubleday.

Whitley, B. E. (1983). Sex role orientation and self-esteem: A critical meta-analytic review. *Journal of Personality and Social Psychology, 44,* 765–778.

Whitley, B. E. (1988). Masculinity, femininity, and self-esteem: A multitrait–multimethod analysis. *Sex Roles, 18,* 419–431.

Whitley, B. E., Jr. (1990). The relationship of heterosexuals' attributions for the causes of homosexuality to attitudes toward lesbians and gay men. *Personality and Social Psychology Bulletin, 16,* 369–377.

Whitney, K., Sagrestano, L. M., & Maslach, C. (1992). *The behavioral expression of individuation through creativity, leadership, and nonverbal expressiveness.* Unpublished manuscript, University of California, Berkeley.

Whyte, W. H., Jr. (1956). *The organization man.* New York: Simon & Schuster.

Wicklund, R. A., & Frey, D. (1980). Self-awareness theory: When the self makes a difference. In D. M. Wegner & R. R. Vallacher (Eds.), *The self in social psychology* (pp. 31–54). New York: Oxford University Press.

Wicklund, R. A., & Gollwitzer, P. M. (1982). *Symbolic self-completion.* Hillsdale, NJ: Erlbaum.

Wiebe, D. J., & McCallum, D. M. (1986). Health practices and hardiness as mediators in the stress-illness relationship. *Health Psychology, 5,* 425–438.

Wiesenthal, D. L., Endler, N. S., Coward, T. R., & Edwards, J. (1976). Reversibility of relative competence as a determinant of conformity across different perceptual tasks. *Representative Research in Social Psychology, 7,* 319–342.

Wilder, D. A. (1977). Perception of groups, size of opposition, and social influence. *Journal of Experimental Social Psychology, 13,* 253–258.

Wilder, D. A. (1990). Some determinants of the persuasive power of in-groups and out-groups: Organization of information and attribution of independence. *Journal of Personality and Social Psychology, 59,* 1202–1213.

Wilder, D. A., & Shapiro. P. (1991). Facilitation of outgroup stereotypes by enhanced ingroup identity. *Journal of Experimental Social Psychology, 27,* 431–452.

Williams, J. E., & Best, D. L. (1990a). *Measuring sex stereotypes: A multinational study,* rev. ed. Newbury Park, CA: Sage.

Williams, J. E., & Best, D. L. (1990b). *Sex and psyche: Gender and self viewed cross-culturally.* Newbury Park, CA: Sage.

Williams, K. D., & Karau, S. J. (1991). Social loafing and social compensation: The effects of expectations of co–worker performance. *Journal of Personality and Social Psychology, 61,* 570–581.

Williamson, G. M., & Clark, M. S. (1969). Providing help and desired relationship type as determinants of changes in moods and self-evaluations. *Journal of Personality and Social Psychology, 56*(5), 722–734.

Williamson, G. M., & Clark, M. S. (1992). Impact of desired relationship type on affective reactions to choosing and being required to help. *Personality and Social Psychology Bulletin, 18,* 10–18.

Williamson, J. B. (1974). The stigma of public dependency: A comparison of alternative forms of public aid to the poor. *Social Problems, 22,* 213–238.

Wills, T. A. (1981). Downward comparison principles in social psychology. *Psychological Bulletin, 90,* 245–271.

Wills, T. A. (1991). Social support and interpersonal relationships. In M. S. Clark (Ed.), *Prosocial behavior: Review of Personality and Social Psychology,* 12, pp. 265–289 (Vol.). Newbury Park, CA: Sage.

Wills, T. A. (1992). The helping process in the context of personal relationships. In S. Spacapan & S. Oskamp (Eds.), *Helping and being helped in the real world* (pp. 17–48). Newbury Park, CA: Sage.

Wilson, E. O. (1971). *The insect societies.* Cambridge, MA: Harvard University Press.

Wilson, E. O. (1975). *Sociobiology, the new synthesis.* Cambridge, MA: Harvard University Press.

Wilson, L., & Rogers, R. W. (1975). The fire this time: Effects of race of target, insult, and potential retaliation on black aggression. *Journal of Personality and Social Psychology, 32,* 857–864.

Winkler, J., & Taylor, S. E. (1979). Preference, expectations, and attributional bias: Two field studies. *Journal of Applied Social Psychology, 2,* 183–197.

Winter, D. G. (1988). The power motive in women—and men. *Journal of Personality and Social Psychology, 54,* 510–519.

Winter, L., & Uleman, J. S. (1984). When are social judg-

ments made? Evidence for the spontaneousness of trait inferences. *Journal of Personality and Social Psychology, 47,* 237–252.

Winter, L., Uleman, J. S., & Cunniff, C. (1985). How automatic are social judgments? *Journal of Personality and Social Psychology, 49,* 904–917.

Wispé, L. G., & Freshley, H. B. (1971). Race, sex, and sympathetic helping behavior: The broken bag caper. *Journal of Personality and Social Psychology, 17,* 59–65.

Wolf, S. (1987). Majority and minority influence: A social impact analysis. In M. P. Zanna, J. M. Olson, & C. P. Herman (Eds.), *Social influence: The Ontario Symposium,* (Vol. 3, pp. 207–235). Hillsdale, NJ: Erlbaum.

Wollin, D. D., & Montagne, M. (1981). College classroom environment. *Environment and Behavior, 13*(6), 707–716.

Wong, P. T. P., & Weiner, B. (1981). When people ask "why" questions, and the heuristics of attributional search. *Journal of Personality and Social Psychology, 40,* 650–663.

Wood, J. V. (1989). Theory and research concerning social comparisons of personal attributes. *Psychological Bulletin, 106,* 231–248.

Wood, J. V., Saltzberg, J. A., & Goldsamt, L. A. (1990). Does affect induce self-focused attention? *Journal of Personality and Social Psychology, 58,* 899–908.

Wood, J. V., Saltzberg, J. A., Neale, J. M., Stone, A. A., & Rachmiel, T. B. (1990). Self-focused attention, coping responses, and distressed mood in everyday life. *Journal of Personality and Social Psychology, 58,* 1027–1036.

Wood, R., & Bandura, A. (1989). Impact of conceptions of ability on self-regulatory mechanisms and complex decision making. *Journal of Personality and Social Psychology, 56,* 407–415.

Wood, W., & Kallgren, C. A. (1988). Communicator attributes and persuasion: Recipients' access to attitude-relevant information in memory. *Personality and Social Psychology Bulletin, 14,* 172–182.

Woodworth, R. D. (1938). *Experimental psychology.* New York: Holt.

Worchel, S. (1984). The darker side of helping: The social dynamics of helping and cooperation. In E. Staub et al. (Eds.), *Developing and maintenance of prosocial behavior: International perspective on positive morality.* New York: Plenum.

Worchel, S., & Teddie, C. (1976). The experience of crowding: A two-factor theory. *Journal of Personality and Social Psychology, 34,* 30–40.

Worchel, S., & Yohai, S. (1979). The role of attribution in the experience of crowding. *Journal of Personality and Social Psychology, 15,* 91–104.

Worth, L. T., & Mackie, D. M. (1987). The cognitive mediation of positive affect in persuasion. *Social Cognition, 5,* 76–94.

Wortman, C. B. (1975). Some determinants of perceived control. *Journal of Personality and Social Psychology, 31,* 282–294.

Wortman, C. B., & Dunkel-Schetter, C. (1979). Interpersonal relationships and cancer: A theoretical analysis. *Journal of Social Issues, 35,* 120–155.

Wright, E. F., Luus, C. A. E., & Christie, S. D. (1990). Does group discussion facilitate the use of consensus information in making causal attributions? *Journal of Personality and Social Psychology, 59,* 261–269.

Wright, J. C., & Dawson, V. L. (1988). Person perception and the bounded rationality of social judgment. *Journal of Personality and Social Psychology, 55,* 780–794.

Wu, C., & Shaffer, D. (1987). Susceptibility to persuasive appeals as a function of source credibility and prior experience with the attitude object. *Journal of Personality and Social Psychology, 52,* 677–688.

Wuensch, K. L., Castellow, W. A., & Moore, C. H. (1991). Effects of defendant attractiveness and type of crime on juridic judgment. *Journal of Social Behavior and Personality, 6,* 713–724.

Wurf, E., & Markus, H. (1983, August). *Cognitive consequences of the negative self.* Paper presented at the annual meetings of the American Psychological Association, Anaheim, CA.

Wurtele, S. K., & Maddux, J. E. (1987). Relative contributions of protection motivation theory components in predicting exercise intentions and behavior. *Health Psychology, 6,* 453–466.

Wyer, R. S., Jr. (1974). Changes in meaning and halo effects in personality impression formation. *Journal of Personality and Social Psychology, 29,* 829–835.

Wyer, R. S., Jr., & Srull, T. K. (1980). The processing of social stimulus information: A conceptual integration. In R. Hastie et al. (Eds.), *Personal memory: The cognitive basis of social perception* (pp. 227–300). Hillsdale, NJ: Erlbaum.

Wyer, R. S., Jr., & Srull, T. K. (1981). Category accessibility: Some theoretical and empirical issues concerning the processing of social stimulus information. In E. T. Higgins, C. P. Herman, & M. P. Zanna (Eds.), *Social cognition: The Ontario symposium* (Vol. 1, pp. 161–198). Hillsdale, NJ: Erlbaum.

Wyer, R. S., Jr., & Srull, T. K. (1986). Human cognition in its social context. *Psychological Review, 93,* 322–359.

Wyer, R. S., Jr., Srull, T. K., & Gordon, S. (1984). The effects of predicting a person's behavior on subsequent trait judgments. *Journal of Experimental Social Psychology, 20,* 29–46.

Wyer, R. S., Jr., Srull, T. K., Gordon, S., & Hartwick, J. (1982). Effects of processing objectives on the recall of prose material. *Journal of Personality and Social Psychology, 43,* 674–688.

Xiaghe, X., & Whyte, M. K. (1990). Love matches and arranged marriages: A Chinese replication. *Journal of Marriage and the Family, 52,* 709–722.

Yammarino, F. J., & Bass, B. M. (1990). Transformational leadership and multiple levels of analysis. *Human Relations, 43*(10), 975-995.

Yatani, C., & Bramel, D. (1989). Trends and patterns in Americans' attitudes toward the Soviet Union. *Journal of Social Issues, 45,* 13–32.

Yee, D. K., & Eccles, J. S. (1988). Parent perceptions and attributions for children's math achievement. *Sex Roles, 19,* 317–333.

Yelsma, P., & Athappilly, K. (1988). Marital satisfaction and communication practices: Comparisons among Indian and American couples. *Journal of Comparative Family Studies, 19,* 37–54.

Yzerbyt, V. Y., & Leyens, J.-P. (1991). Requesting information to form an impression: The influence of valence and confirmatory status. *Journal of Experimental Social Psychology, 27,* 337–356.

Zahn–Waxler, C., Radke-Yarrow, M., Wagner, E., & Chapman, M. (1992). Development of concern for others. *Developmental Psychology, 28,* 126–136.

Zajonc, R. B. (1965). Social facilitation. *Science, 149,* 269–274.

Zajonc, R. B. (1968). Attitudinal effects of mere exposure. *Journal of Personality and Social Psychology* (Monograph Suppl., Pt. 2), 1–29.

Zajonc, R. B., & Markus, H. (1984). Affect and cognition: The hard interface. In C. E. Izard, J. Kagan, & R. B. Zajonc (Eds.), *Emotions, cognition, and behavior* (pp. 73–102). Cambridge: Cambridge University Press.

Zajonc, R. B., Pietromonaco, P., & Bargh, J. (1982). Independence and interaction of affect and cognition. In M. S. Clark & S. T. Fiske (Eds.), *Affect and cognition: The 17th annual Carnegie symposium on cognition* (pp. 211–228). Hillsdale, NJ: Erlbaum.

Zanna, M. P., & Fazio, R. H. (1982). The attitude-behavior relation: Moving toward a third generation of research. In M. P. Zanna, E. T. Higgins, & C. P. Herman, *Consistency in Social Behavior: The Ontario Symposium* (Vol. 2, pp. 283–301). Hillsdale, NJ: Erlbaum.

Zanna, M. P., & Hamilton, D. L. (1977). Further evidence for meaning change in impression formation. *Journal of Experimental Social Psychology, 13,* 224–238.

Zborowski, M. (1952). Cultural components in responses to pain. *Journal of Social Issues, 8,* 16–30.

Zebrowitz, L. A. (1990). *Social perception.* Pacific Grove, CA: Brooks/Cole.

Zebrowitz, L. A., & Montepare, J. M. (1992). Impressions of babyfaced individuals across the life span. *Developmental Psychology, 28,* 1143–1152.

Zebrowitz, L. A., Tenenbaum, D. R., & Goldstein, L. H. (1991). The impact of job applicants' facial maturity, sex, and academic achievement on hiring recommendations. *Journal of Applied Social Psychology, 21,* 525–548.

Zeichner, A., & Pihl, R. O. (1979). Effects of alcohol and behavior contingencies on human aggression. *Journal of Abnormal Psychology, 88,* 153–160.

Zeprun, J. G. (1990). Sexual assault victims faced with legal bias. *Boston Globe* (January 22), 10.

Zillmann, D. (1988). Cognition-excitation interdependencies in aggressive behavior. *Aggressive Behavior, 14,* 51–64.

Zillmann, D., & Bryant, J. (1974). Effect of residual excitation on the emotional response to provocation and delayed aggressive behavior. *Journal of Personality and Social Psychology, 30,* 782–791.

Zimbardo, P. G. (1970). The human choice: Individuation, reason and order versus deindividuation, impulse and chaos. In N. J. Arnold & D. Levine (Eds.), *Nebraska symposium on motivation, 1969.* Lincoln: University of Nebraska Press.

Zimmerman, D. H., & West, C. (1975). Sex roles, interruptions and silences in conversation. In B. Thorne & N. Henley (Eds.), *Language and sex: Difference and dominance* (pp. 105–129). Rowley, MA: Newbury House.

Zuckerman, M., Amidon, M. D., Bishop, S. E., & Pomerantz, S. D. (1982). Face and tone of voice in the communication of deception. *Journal of Personality and Social Psychology, 43,* 347–357.

Zuckerman, M., DePaulo, B. M., & Rosenthal, R. (1981). Verbal and nonverbal communication of deception. In L. Berkowitz (Ed.), *Advances in experimental social psychology* (Vol. 14, pp. 2–60). New York: Academic Press.

Zuckerman, M., Larrance, D. T., Spiegel, N. H., & Klorman, R. (1981). Controlling nonverbal displays: Facial expressions and tone of voice. *Journal of Experimental Social Psychology, 17,* 506–524.

Zuroff, D. C. (1989). Judgments of frequency of social stimuli: How schematic is person memory? *Journal of Personality and Social Psychology, 56,* 890–898.

PHOTO CREDITS

Author Index

Subject Index